Understanding Human Behavior and the Social Environment

SIXTH EDITION

Charles Zastrow
University of Wisconsin–Whitewater

Karen K. Kirst-Ashman
University of Wisconsin–Whitewater

THOMSON

BROOKS/COLE

Australia · Canada · Mexico · Singapore · Spain
United Kingdom · United States

THOMSON

BROOKS/COLE

Executive Editor: Lisa Gebo

Assistant Editor: Alma Dea Micheleana

Editorial Assistant: Sheila Walsh

Technology Project Manager: Barry Connolly

Marketing Manager: Caroline Concilla

Marketing Assistant: Mary Ho

Advertising Project Manager: Tammi Strang

Project Manager, Editorial Production: Matt Ballantyne

Print/Media Buyer: Doreen Suruki

Permissions Editor: Joohee Lee

Production Service: G&S Typesetters, Inc.

Text Designer: Patrick Devine Design

Photo Researcher: Sue C. Howard

Copy Editor: Barry Lenner

Illustrator: G&S Typesetters, Inc.

Cover Designer: Bill Stanton

Cover Image: Courtesy of PhotoDisc

Part and Chapter Opening Image: Getty/The Image Bank/Hans Wolf

Perspective Image: Getty/The Image Bank/Peter DeLory

Highlight Image: Getty/The Image Bank/Hans Wolf

Spotlight on Diversity Image: Getty/Taxi/Chip Simons

Compositor: G&S Typesetters, Inc.

Text and Cover Printer: Quebecor World, Taunton

For more information about our products, contact us at:

Thomson Learning Academic Resource Center

1-800-423-0563

For permission to use material from this text, contact us by:

Phone: 1-800-730-2214

Fax: 1-800-730-2215

Web: http://www.thomsonrights.com

Brooks/Cole—Thomson Learning

10 Davis Drive

Belmont, CA 94002

USA

Asia
Thomson Learning
5 Shenton Way #01-01
UIC Building
Singapore 068808

Australia/New Zealand
Thomson Learning
102 Dodds Street
Southbank, Victoria 3006
Australia

Canada
Nelson
1120 Birchmount Road
Toronto, Ontario M1K 5G4
Canada

Europe/Middle East/Africa
Thomson Learning
High Holborn House
50/51 Bedford Row
London WC1R 4LR
United Kingdom

Latin America
Thomson Learning
Seneca, 53
Colonia Polanco
11560 Mexico D.F.
Mexico

Spain/Portugal
Paraninfo
Calle/Magallanes, 25
28015 Madrid, Spain

Library of Congress Control Number: 2003101368

Student Edition: ISBN 0-534-60831-0

Instructor's Edition: ISBN 0-534-60832-9

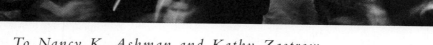

To Nancy K. Ashman and Kathy Zastrow

Charles Zastrow, MSSW and PhD, is a professor in the Social Work Department, University of Wisconsin−Whitewater. He has worked as a practitioner in a variety of public and private social welfare agencies and has chaired 13 social work accreditation site visit teams for the Council on Social Work Education (CSWE). He recently was a two-term member of the Accreditation Commission of CSWE. He is a member of the National Association of Social Workers, the Council on Social Work Education, and the NASW Register of Clinical Social Workers. He is certified as an independent clinical social worker in Wisconsin. In addition to this text, Dr. Zastrow has written four other textbooks: *Introduction to Social Work and Social Welfare* (7th ed.); *The Practice of Social Work* (7th ed.); *Social Work with Groups* (5th ed.); and *Social Problems: Issues and Solutions* (5th ed.). He is also the author of *You Are What You Think: A Guide to Self-Realization.*

Karen K. Kirst-Ashman, MSSW, PhD, and a licensed independent clinical social worker, is a professor in the Social Work Department, University of Wisconsin−Whitewater. She has worked as a practitioner and administrator in child welfare and mental health agencies. She has been a member of the board of directors for the Council on Social Work Education in addition to being an accreditation site visitor and a member of NASW. She serves as a consulting editor for the *Journal of Social Work Education, Affilia,* and *Arête.* She received the University of Wisconsin−Whitewater's Excellence in Teaching Award in 1986. Other books she has authored or coauthored include: *Introduction to Social Work and Social Welfare: Critical Thinking Perspectives; Human Behavior, Communities, Organizations, Groups, and the Macro Social Environment: An Empowerment Approach; Understanding Generalist Practice* (3rd ed.); *Generalist Practice with Organizations and Communities* (2nd ed.); and *The Macro Skills Workbook* (2nd ed.).

Table of Contents

Part One
Infancy and Childhood

Chapter 2

Biological Systems and Their Impacts on Infancy and Childhood   47

Chapter 9

Gender Roles and Sexism   327

Part Three
Middle Adulthood

Chapter 10

Biological Systems and Their Impacts on Middle Adulthood   359

Part Four

Later Adulthood

Chapter 14

**Biological Systems and Their Impacts on
Later Adulthood   509**

Chapter 15

Psychological Systems and Their Impacts on Later Adulthood   535

Chapter 16

Social Systems and Their Impacts on Later Adulthood   560

An 18-year-old man, who sees no reason to live anymore, threatens to kill himself. A couple suddenly separate after 23 years of marriage. A young family plagued by unemployment is evicted from their apartment, and moves into a tent. A demonstration is staged because a local factory refuses to hire African American workers. Why do people do what they do? The main focus of this text is on assessment—that is, this text presents material to help readers understand the underlying reasons why people act the way they do, and to help them evaluate the strengths and deficits in their biological, psychological, and social development. A variety of theories and research about human growth and development are presented. The theories cover both the internal and external variables that influence human behavior.

This text is especially written for undergraduate and graduate courses in human behavior and the social environment (HBSE). The Council on Social Work Education (CSWE), the national accrediting body, provides the following guidelines for HBSE content in its Educational Policy and Accreditation Standards (EPAS):

> *Social work education programs provide content on the reciprocal relationships between human behavior and social environments. Content includes empirically based theories and knowledge that focus on the interactions between and among individuals, groups, societies, and economic systems. It includes theories and knowledge of biological, sociological, cultural, psychological, and spiritual development across the life span; the range of social systems in which people live (individual, family, group, organizational, and community); and the ways in which social systems promote or deter people in maintaining or achieving health and well-being.[1]*

EPAS also require that content on the following be incorporated throughout the curriculum: values and ethics, diversity, populations-at-risk, and social and economic justice.

For a number of years, social work programs have struggled to develop an HBSE curriculum that covers the extensive content mandated in EPAS for HBSE. This text is designed to facilitate the coverage of such content. The text has the following thrusts:

- It uses a systems model, titled the "Systems Impact Model" (described in Chapter 1), that incorporates some ecological concepts. This model allows the authors to present a vast array of theories and research to explain and describe human development and behavior. It focuses on individual functioning within systems of various sizes (including families, groups, organizations, and communities).

- It presents substantial information on human diversity and populations-at-risk, including material on groups distinguished by age, class, color, disabilities, ethnicity, family structure, gender, marital status, natural origin, race, religion, sex, and sexual orientation.

- It uses a life-span approach that allows for a description of human growth and development from conception through adulthood.

- It identifies biological, psychological, and sociological systems that influence development for each age group.[2] Interactions among these systems are discussed in some depth. For many of the biopsychosocial theories described, content about values and ethical issues is included.

- It presents material on strategies that promote social and economic justice.

- It describes normal developmental tasks and milestones for each age group.

- It describes the impact of social and economic forces on individuals, social systems, and societies.

- It presents material on the attainment and maintenance of optimal mental and physical health and well-being. It also describes the ways in which systems promote or deter health and well-being.

- It presents material, using a four-faceted approach, to evaluate theory, and describes how diverse theories can be applied to client situations.

A major thrust of this text is to present the material in a readable fashion. Numerous case examples, photographs, and illustrations are used in presenting provocative and controversial issues about human behavior. As

---

[1]Council on Social Work Education, *Educational Policy and Accreditation Standards* (Alexandria, VA: Council on Social Work Education, 2001).

[2]In some cases the biological, psychological, and sociological variables overlap. For example, a midlife crisis often involves a combination of biological, psychological, and sociological variables. Therefore, the authors may, rather arbitrarily, cover some material under one heading (for example, biological aspects) when a strong case can be made that it should be covered under some other heading (that is, psychological aspects or sociological aspects).

much as possible, jargon-free language is used so that the reader can readily grasp theory.

New in this edition are the following: a response to the required content on HBSE as specified in the Educational Policy and Accreditation Standards; the use of contingency theories as a newer approach to organizational theory; international perspectives on abortion policy; a new definition of "giftedness" and new material on intelligence testing; diverse perspectives on the family life cycle; data on cultural context and parenting style; educational programming that responds to cultural values; data on child physical abuse versus discipline in diverse cultural contexts; a discussion of psychological maltreatment; new content on the differential death rates of white women and women of color; professional approaches to counseling suicidal people; cross-cultural perspectives on gender role development; cultural differences in the incidence of sexual assault; a discussion of transgender people as a dimension of diversity; cultural scripts as a determinant of sexual behavior; information on ecstasy (a recreational drug); the treatment approach to drug abuse in the Netherlands; updated information on Alzheimer's; cross-cultural research on centenarians; material on great-grandparenthood; the cultural and historical context of death and bereavement; a discussion of NASW's standards for culturally competent practices in social work; ethnic-group identities for minority adolescents; guidelines for leading multiracial groups; AIDS in Africa; and a description of Temporary Assistance to Needy Families (TANF).

Accompanying the text is a WebTutor Student Manual that has been designed to enhance students' ability to comprehend and assimilate course content. Use of the Student Manual also minimizes the need for supplementary handouts. In the Student Manual, all of the chapters are outlined to assist in note-taking during lectures and while reading the text. Additionally, a variety of classroom exercises, role-playing, and issues for discussion are included for each chapter. The authors have found that student involvement, through the use of such experiential exercises and classroom discussion, greatly improves both the students' understanding of content and their ability to relate content to social work practice.

The text is composed of 16 chapters. In those instances where the text is used for a one-semester course, the authors have found that it is useful to divide the text into four components for the purpose of administering examinations. Each component focuses on one of the four specified phases of the life span. These phases are: infancy and childhood (Chapters 2 through 4); adolescence and young adulthood (Chapters 6 through 8); middle adult-hood (Chapters 10 through 12); and later adulthood (Chapters 14 through 16). A fourth chapter, chosen from the remaining chapters, may be added to each component. The remaining four chapters are: Chapter 1, "Theoretical Perspectives on Human Behavior and the Social Environment"; Chapter 5, "Ethnocentrism and Racism"; Chapter 9, "Gender Roles and Sexism"; and Chapter 13, "Sexual Orientation."

In those programs that use the text for more than one semester (for example, those programs that spend one semester on each half of the life span), the four life-span phases can be broken down even further in a fashion similar to that mentioned above.

The authors have been asked how so much material can be covered in this one volume. When told the topic of the text, a friend (who happens to be an accountant) asked, "Human behavior? Well, isn't that everything?" Our response must be that, yes, it involves everything about people that social workers need to know. We have found that we must make choices regarding what content is most important to cover. Those programs that allow more time for HBSE can address the significant issues and topics examined in the text much more thoroughly. We ourselves have found that requiring prerequisite courses in biology, psychology, and sociology has allowed us to spend more time focusing on issues critical for social workers in practice.

Our overall intent is to provide a dynamic, interesting, and relevant social work perspective on human behavior and the social environment. We strive to enhance students' understanding of social work values, develop their ability to empathize with people in situations different from their own, and help them focus on the need for changes in the impinging environment and sometimes in the client. We hope students will be able to relate these values and this knowledge to how social workers make assessments in real practice situations. We endeavor to portray social work as the fascinating, useful field that it is.

Acknowledgments

We wish to express our heartfelt appreciation to the following people for helping to conceptualize various chapters and for assisting in a number of ways with the writing: Nick Ashman, David Cohen, Patricia Danielson, Tim Larson, Phil McCullough, Kathy Moretz, Steve Noll, and David Runyon. We also want to express our indebtedness to Lisa Gebo, and the other staff members at Brooks/Cole Publishing Co.

Mezzo and Macro Systems Content

Social workers intervene in the following systems: micro (individuals), mezzo (families and small groups), and macro (communities and organizations). Micro content is covered in every chapter in this text.

Mezzo systems (families and small groups)

Chapter 1
Theoretical Perspectives on Human Behavior and the Social Environment
• Micro, mezzo, and macro systems
• Interactions between micro systems and mezzo systems

Chapter 2
Biological Systems and Their Impacts on Infancy and Childhood
• Infertility
• Causes of infertility
• Psychological reactions to infertility
• Treatment of infertility
• Alternatives available to the infertile couple
• A feminist perspective on infertility counseling

Chapter 4
Social Systems and Their Impacts on Infancy and Childhood
• The family environment
• Membership in family groups: Variations in family structure
• Positive family functioning
• Effects of social forces and policies on family systems: Helpful or hurtful?
• The dynamics of family systems
• The family life cycle
• The application of systems theory principles to families
• The importance of parental attention
• Impacts of common life events on children
• Membership in family systems
• Membership in sibling subsystems
• Ethnic and cultural differences in families
• Child abuse and neglect
• Incidence and demographics of child abuse and neglect
• Physical child abuse
• Child neglect
• Sexual abuse
• Suggestions for talking to children victimized by sexual abuse

Chapter 5
Ethnocentrism and Racism
• Ethnic groups and ethnocentrism
• Greater interaction between minority groups and the majority group
• Learning the culture of the group

Chapter 6
Biological Systems and Their Impacts on Adolescence and Young Adulthood
• Teenage fathers
• Macro systems treatment of sex education

Chapter 7
Psychological Systems and Their Impacts on Adolescence and Young Adulthood
• Community responses to suicide: Prevention and crisis intervention

Chapter 8
Social Systems and Their Impacts on Adolescence and Young Adulthood
• Interaction in families: Effective communication between parents and children
• Ethnic group identity for minority adolescents
• Interaction in family systems: Choosing a personal lifestyle
• Marriage
• Theories about why people choose each other as mates
• Predictive factors leading to marital happiness/unhappiness
• Guidelines for building and maintaining a happy marriage
• Cohabitation
• Parenthood
• Parental gender preferences
• Childless couples

Chapter 9
Gender Roles and Sexism
• Battered women
• The battering cycle

Chapter 10
Biological Systems and Their Impacts on Middle Adulthood
• Sex in marriage
• Extramarital sexual relationships
• Sex following divorce

Chapter 11
Psychological Systems and Their Impacts on Middle Adulthood
• Mezzo system interactions: Nonverbal communication
• Interaction in family systems: A theoretical approach to drug abuse
• Application of theory to client situations: Treatment for the chemically dependant person and his or her family

Chapter 12
Social Systems and Their Impacts on Middle Adulthood
• Family mezzo system problems
• Empty-shell marriages
• Divorce
• Facts above divorce
• The effects of a divorce on children depend on what happens after the divorce
• Single-parent families
• Temporary Assistance to Needy Families (TANF)
• Blended families
• Mothers working outside the home
• The "sandwich" generation
• Assessing and intervening in family systems
• Family norms
• Family system assessment: The ecomap
• Family system assessment: The genogram
• Family problems and social work roles

Chapter 13
Sexual Orientation
• Lesbian and gay parents

Chapter 15
Psychological Systems and Their Impacts on Later Adulthood
• Marriage
• Death of spouse
• Remarriage
• Family system relationships
• Grandparenthood
• Great-grandparenthood

Chapter 16
Social Systems and Their Impacts on Later Adulthood
• Elder abuse

Mezzo and Macro Systems Content, continued

Macro systems (communities and organizations)

Chapter 1
Theoretical Perspectives on Human Behavior and the Social Environment
- Macro, mezzo, and macro systems
- The social environment
- Interactions between micro systems and macro systems
- The impact of social forces
- The relationship between organizational macro systems and client systems
- The relationship between the community macro system and the client system
- The relationship between organizational and community macro systems
- Institutional values macro system
- The effects of institutional values and organizational macro systems on clients
- The impacts of organizations
- What are organizations?
- Organizational theories
- Viewing organizations from a system perspective
- The exceptional problems of social service organizations
- Communities and human behavior
- Theoretical perspectives on communities
- Models of community
- Characteristics of three models of community change
- Hispanic women, community development, and social action

Chapter 2
Biological Systems and Their Impacts on Infancy and Childhood
- The impact of macro system policies on practice and access to abortion services
- The effects of macro systems on infertility

Chapter 3
Psychological Systems and Their Impacts on Infancy and Childhood
- Macro system responses to cognitive disabilities
- The Americans with Disabilities Act: A macro system addresses a population-at-risk
- Macro system responses to learning disabilities

Chapter 4
Social Systems and Their Impacts on Infancy and Childhood
- Effects of social forces and policies on family systems: Helpful or hurtful?
- A macro system response (to child maltreatment): Child Protective Services

- A macro system response (to child maltreatment): Involvement of the courts
- Prevention of sexual abuse: The need for a macro system response

Chapter 5
Ethnocentrism and Racism
- Aspects of social and economic forces: Prejudice, discrimination, and oppression
- Institutional values and racism: Discrimination in systems
- Discrimination and oppression in organizational macro systems
- Discrimination and oppression in community macro systems
- Impacts of social and economic forces: The effects and costs of discrimination and oppression
- Strategies to promote social and economic justice
- Mass media appeals: Striving to change institutional values
- Greater interaction between minority groups and the majority group
- Civil rights laws: Changing the legal macro system
- Activism
- School busing: A community initiative
- Affirmative action: A macro system response
- Confronting racist remarks and actions
- Minority-owned businesses
- Confronting community problems: Inner cities
- Grassroots organizations: Implementing change in community macro systems

Chapter 8
Social Systems and Their Impacts on Adolescence and Young Adulthood
- Macro system problems: Crime and delinquency
- Macro system problems: Delinquent gangs

Chapter 9
Gender Roles and Sexism
- Economic inequality
- Sexual harassment; strengthening the definition: A macro system response
- Community responses to battered women: Their alternatives
- Strategies for empowering women and achieving sexual equality

Chapter 10
Biological Systems and Their Impacts on Middle Adulthood
- Impacts of social and economic forces: AIDS discrimination and oppression
- Macro system responses to AIDS

Chapter 12
Social Systems and Their Impacts on Middle Adulthood
- Macro social system theories
- The functionalist perspective
- The conflict perspective
- The interactionist perspective
- Poverty: Impacts of social and economic forces
- Application of functionalism to poverty
- Application of interactionist theory to poverty
- Social work with organizations
- Analyzing a human services organization
- The autocratic model
- The custodial model
- The scientific management model
- The human relations model
- Theory X and Theory Y
- The collegial model
- Management by objectives
- Total quality management
- Summary comments about models of organizational behavior

Chapter 13
Sexual Orientation
- Discrimination and the impacts of homophobia
- Gay and lesbian pride and a sense of community
- The impacts of social and economic forces: Legal issues
- Community responses: Violence against lesbian and gay people

Chapter 16
Social Systems and Their Impacts on Later Adulthood
- Current services: Macro system responses
- Older Americans Act of 1965
- Old Age, Survivors, Disability and Health Insurance (OASDHI)
- Supplemental Security Income (SSI)
- Medicare
- Mediaid
- Food stamps
- Adult protective services
- Additional programs
- Nursing homes
- Community options program: Providing alternatives to nursing home placement
- The elderly are a powerful political force
- Changing a macro system: Finding a social role for the elderly

Human Diversity Content

Appreciation of diversity is a major theme in social work education. This text infuses diversity throughout the book in every chapter. An innovation in this edition is to emphasize some of this content in "Spotlights on Diversity." The following material summarizes the diversity content that is covered. Because this book assumes a chronological approach to the life span, it is assumed that some dimensions of diversity are intrinsically covered, including those related to clients' age, gender, and family structure (See "Mezzo Systems" for content on families). Many of the content areas cited below are included as "Spotlights on Diversity."

Chapter 1
Theoretical Perspectives on Human Behavior and the Social Environment
- Diversity, oppression, and populations-at-risk
- Hispanic women, community development, and social action

Chapter 2
Biological Systems and Their Impacts on Infancy and Childhood
- International perspectives on abortion policy
- Effects of abortion on women and men
- A feminist perspective on abortion counseling

Chapter 3
Psychological Systems and Their Impacts on Infancy and Childhood
- Sensitivity to diversity when examining psychological theories
- Feminist theories
- A cross-cultural perspective on self-esteem
- Cultural biases and IQ tests
- The Americans with Disabilities Act: A macro system addresses a population-at-risk
- Understanding people with disabilities
- People with developmental disabilities as a population-at-risk

Chapter 4
Social Systems and Their Impacts on Infancy and Childhood
- Membership in family groups: Variations in family structure
- Membership in family systems
- Membership in sibling subsystems
- Diverse perspectives on the family life cycle
- Cultural context and parenting style
- Ethnic and cultural differences in families
- Educational programming that responds to cultural values
- Diverse cultural contexts for discipline and abuse of children

Chapter 5
Ethnocentrism and Racism
(Although the entire chapter addresses diversity in terms of class, color, culture, ethnicity, national origins, and populations-at-risk, the following content is of special significance.)

- Ethnic groups and ethnocentrism
- Race and racism
- Violence against minorities in the United States
- Aspects of social and economic forces: prejudice, discrimination, and oppression
- Racial and ethnic stereotypes
- Racial and ethnic discrimination is the problem of whites
- White privilege
- Race is a social concept
- Institutional values and racism: Discrimination in systems
- Discrimination and oppression in organizational macro systems
- Discrimination and oppression in community macro systems
- Sources of prejudice and discrimination
- Is racial discrimination based on criminal thinking?
- Impacts of social and economic forces: The effects and costs of discrimination and oppression
- The effects of discrimination on human growth and development
- History and culture of African Americans
- Effects of discrimination on development of self-concept
- The Africentric perspective and worldview
- Kwanzaa
- Strategies to promote social and economic justice
- Civil rights laws: Changing the legal macro system
- Rosa Parks's act of courage sparked the civil rights movement
- Affirmative action: A macro system response
- Confronting racist remarks and actions
- Minority-owned businesses
- Grassroots organizations: Implementing change in community macro systems
- Social work practice with racial and ethnic groups
- Ethnic-sensitive practice
- Empowerment
- Strengths perspective
- Culturally competent practice

- The future of American race and ethnic relations
- A dream of the end of racism

Chapter 6
Biological Systems and Their Impacts on Adolescence and Young Adulthood
- Differential death rates for white women and women of color
- Racial and other differences in adolescent sexual activity
- Empowerment through sex education for Native Americans

Chapter 7
Psychological Systems and Their Impacts on Adolescence and Young Adulthood
- Race, culture, ethnicity, and identity development
- Lesbian and gay adolescents
- Moral development and women: Gilligan's approach
- Critical thinking: Evaluation through spiritual development
- Fowler's theory of faith development
- Spirituality and social work practice
- Suicide and adolescent Hispanic females

Chapter 8
Social Systems and Their Impacts on Adolescence and Young Adulthood
- Ethnic group identity for minority adolescents
- The RAP framework for leading multiracial groups

Chapter 9
Gender Roles and Sexism
(Although the entire chapter addresses diversity in terms of gender, the following content is of special significance.)
- Cross-cultural perspectives on gender role development
- Gender/racial comparison of median weekly earnings
- Cultural differences in the incidence of violence against women
- Strategies for combating sexism and achieving sexual equality

Chapter 10
Biological Systems and Their Impacts on Middle Adulthood
- The double standard of aging
- Cultural differences in women's experience of menopause

Human Diversity Content, *continued*

- People living with AIDS: A population-at-risk
- AIDS in Africa

Chapter 11
Psychological Systems and Their Impacts on Middle Adulthood
- Application of Levinson's theories to women: An evaluation
- Cultural scripts are a determinant of sexual behavior
- A treatment model from another culture: The Dutch approach

Chapter 12
Social Systems and Their Impacts on Middle Adulthood
- Poverty: Impacts of social and economic forces
- The rich and the poor
- Personal income disparities are astounding
- Who are the poor?
- Poverty perpetuates poverty
- What causes poverty?
- The culture of poverty: Evaluation of theory and its application to client situations
- Poverty is functional
- Application of functionalism to poverty

- Application of conflict theory to poverty
- Application of interactionist theory to poverty
- Temporary Assistance to Needy Families (TANF)

Chapter 13
Sexual Orientation
(Although the entire chapter addresses diversity in terms of gender, the following content is of special significance.)
- Transsexual and transgender people
- Discrimination and the impacts of homophobia
- Gay and lesbian pride an a sense of community
- Ethnicity and sexual orientation
- Social work with lesbian and gay people: Promoting optimal well-being

Chapter 14
Biological Systems and Their Impacts on Later Adulthood
- Internationally noted individuals document age need not be a barrier to being productive
- Longevity: Cross-cultural research on centenarians

Chapter 15
Psychological Systems and Their Impacts on Later Adulthood
(Although the entire chapter addresses diversity in terms of the elderly, the following content is of special significance.)
- Low status and ageism
- Triple jeopardy: Being female, African American and old
- Spirituality and religion
- The cultural-historical context of death and bereavement

Chapter 16
Social Systems and Their Impacts on Later Adulthood
(Although the entire chapter addresses diversity in terms of the elderly, the following content is of special significance.)
- The elderly: A population-at-risk
- High status for the elderly in China, Japan, and other countries
- Cultural differences in seeking health care: The case of elderly Mexican Americans

CHAPTER 1

Theoretical Perspectives on Human Behavior and the Social Environment

A midwestern farm family goes bankrupt after losing federal financial support and protection. The family is forced to pack up all of its belongings, leave its home state, and move to Florida, where they can afford only a canvas tent in which to live.

A 2½-year-old baby girl has not yet begun to take her first steps or to say more than the words "mama" and "dada." She is an only child. Her parents worry that she seems to be lagging behind other children her age and they wonder if something is wrong.

Two teenagers feel they are deeply in love. They struggle with many issues. Should they "make love"? Should they use some method of birth control? What if pregnancy should occur? Should they get married?

A 75-year-old widower finds his health failing. He has trouble reading and is beginning to stumble frequently. He has lived alone in his modest home since his wife died twelve years ago. His two adult children are pressuring him to sell his house and move into a nursing home. He likes both his home and his independence. What should he do?

Each of these vignettes reflects a real-life situation involving individuals, each with unique qualities, addressing issues related to their current stage of life. In each situation people are raising questions, facing crises, or making decisions. The basic task of social work is to "help people meet their needs and carry out their responsibilities" throughout their life spans (Siporin, 1975, p. 3). In other words, social workers help people enhance their own functioning. Yet, in order to help people do this, social workers must first understand the processes of human behavior. Only then can they apply techniques and skills to help clients make decisions and solve problems.

A PERSPECTIVE

The goals of this text are to explore the dynamics of human behavior and prepare a foundation of knowledge upon which to build practice skills. Social workers assist people in making decisions and in solving their problems. One of the primary steps in the helping process is assessment. Assessment involves evaluation of some human condition or situation. It also involves making decisions about what aspects of the behavior or situation need to be changed.

Social work emphasizes a focus that stretches far beyond that of the individual. Assessment in social work addresses all aspects of clients' situations. Social workers concentrate on understanding the many aspects of any particular client problem. A social worker assesses both the individual client's behavior and all the social systems in which the client is involved. These systems include families, work groups and environments, social agencies, organizations, neighborhoods, communities, and even local, state, and national government.

In many cases something external to the client may be causing the problem. The client's family may not be functioning well. There may be difficulties beyond the client's control in his or her workplace. Existing social service organizations may not be providing what clients need. Resources may be too difficult to obtain, inadequate, or even nonexistent. Organizational policies or laws affecting the client may be unfair. Thus, assessment in social work targets clients' relationships with individuals, groups, organizations, and communities. Deciding what to do about any specific problem may directly involve any of these systems.

This chapter will:

▶ Discuss the importance of foundation knowledge within the purpose and process of social work.

▶ Explain the significance of foundation knowledge for assessment.

▶ Describe systems theories and their relevance for social work.

▶ Formulate a model for viewing, assessing, and understanding human behavior that concentrates on the interactions of micro, mezzo, and macro systems.

▶ Define organizations as macro systems and explain their involvement with clients.

▶ Discuss communities as macro systems, examine their impacts on human behavior, and introduce three models of community practice.

▶ Describe the major roles assumed by social workers as they practice within the context of micro, mezzo, and macro systems.

🍃 Foundation Knowledge and the Purpose of Social Work

In order to recognize the significance of foundation knowledge, the purpose and process of social work need to be understood. Social work may be viewed as having three major thrusts (Baer & Federico, 1978, p. 68). First, social workers can help people solve their problems and cope with their situations. Second, social workers can work with systems, such as social agencies, organizations, communities, and government bureaucracies, so that people can have better access to the resources and services they need. Third, social workers can "link people with systems" (Baer & Federico, 1978, p. 68), so that clients themselves have access to resources and opportunities. Much of social work, then, involves social functioning.

People interact with other people, with organizations (such as social service agencies), and with small groups (such as families and colleagues in the workplace). Social work targets not only how individuals behave, but also how these other systems and people affect each other.

An example is a family of five in which both parents work at low-paying jobs in order to make a marginal living. The father works at a small, nonunionized leather-processing plant. The mother works as a waitress at a short-order diner. Suddenly, the father is laid off. For a short time the family survives on unemployment compensation. When that runs out, they face a serious financial crisis. Despite a great effort, the father is unable to find another job. In desperation, the family applies for public assistance. Due to some unidentified error in the lengthy application process, the payments are delayed for two months.

Meanwhile, the family is forced to eat poorly and is unable to pay rent and utility bills. The phone is disconnected, the electricity is turned off, and the landlord threatens to evict them. Reacting to the externally imposed stress, the parents begin to fight verbally and physically. The children complain because they are hungry. This intensifies the parents' sense of defeat and disillusionment. As a result of stress and frustration, the parents hit the children to keep them quiet.

Although this example has not been presented in detail, it illustrates that people are integrally involved with other systems in their environment. A social worker reviewing this case might assess how the family and other systems in the environment have had an impact on each other. First, the father's life is seriously affected by his place of employment, the leather factory, when he is laid off. He then seeks unemployment compensation, which affects that system by dipping into its funds. When those benefits cease, the family then affects the public assistance system by drawing on its funds. The public assistance system, in turn, impacts the family by delaying their payments. The resulting frustration affects all family members, as the parents are unable to cope with their stress. The entire situation can be viewed as a series of dynamic interactions between people and their environment.

Social workers today are *generalists*. A generalist practitioner is one who uses a wide range of knowledge and skills to help people with an extensive array of problems and issues. These include anything from "individualized personal issues" to "very broad problems that affect whole

communities" (Kirst-Ashman & Hull, 2002, p. 4). Social workers must be able to view a problem situation from multiple perspectives in the context of the entire social environment. This sets the stage for numerous intervention approaches.

✿ Foundation Knowledge and the Process of Social Work: The Importance of Assessment

Social work practice usually involves several basic steps. First, the problem or situation is scrutinized and understood. In other words, an *assessment* of the problematic situation is made. Second, a specific *plan* of action is developed in which goals are carefully selected and clearly specified. Third, the actual *intervention* or *implementation* of the plan occurs; this is the "doing" part of the process. It may involve providing counseling to an individual, or it may entail working with a large organization to change its policies to better accommodate its clients' needs. Fourth, progress toward solving the problem is subject to *evaluation*. To what extent have the goals established with the client been met? Fifth, the social work process calls for a *termination* of the intervention. This includes ending the process and summarizing what has been accomplished (Kirst-Ashman & Hull, 1999).

Accurate assessment is a critically important step in the social work process (Hepworth, Rooney, & Larsen, 1997; Sheafor, Horejsi, & Horejsi, 1997; Richmond, 1917). Information about the problem or situation needs to be gathered, analyzed, and interpreted. Regardless of the specific type of situation, careful thought is necessary in order to make effective decisions about how to proceed. Assessment also involves basic knowledge and assumptions about human behavior. Social workers need to have a foundation of information and understanding about human behavior so that they can help clients identify and select alternatives.

For example, a social worker who is trying to help a potentially suicidal adolescent needs certain types of information. The worker needs to know some of the reasons why people commit suicide so that he or she knows what questions to ask, how to react to and treat the person, and what alternatives and supports to pursue.

Additionally, the worker must be able to identify what resources are readily available to suicidal adolescents. How can the crises be addressed immediately, simply to keep them alive? What supportive resources are available to keep them from suicidal thoughts in the future? Where can a social worker refer them to get help?

Working with clients whose racial and ethnic backgrounds differ from the worker's own provides another example of the importance of foundation knowledge. The worker needs to have at least general information about clients' cultural values and the potentially differential treatment they have experienced (for example, racial discrimination). Only then can the worker empathize with a particular client's situation and help the client identify realistic alternatives.

Bartlett (1970) calls for a common base of social work practice. This base involves common values such as the belief that each individual has the right to make decisions about what to do in his or her own life. This base also involves common skills. For example, social workers need to know how to conduct an interview and how to help people identify and evaluate their various alternatives. Finally, social workers need a common base of knowledge. They must have access to certain types of information in order to plan effective interventions. They must be educated in the basic knowledge of human behavior before any skills can be applied.

This textbook focuses on how people act within the context of their environments. People are dramatically affected by the other people, groups, and organizations around them. A young child may be devastated by a sharp scolding from a parent. The presence or absence of friends and social supports within office work environments may determine whether employees love or hate their jobs. Which candidates are elected to Congress may affect the taxes an individual is required to pay, the types of freedom a person can enjoy, and the absolute quality of life itself.

This text aims to clarify some of the reasons why people behave the way they do. It will present basic concepts in human development and examine normal developmental life events. It will do so within the context of the communities and environments in which people live. It will also concentrate on the impacts that organizations, policies, and communities have on individuals.

◟ Impacts of Systems in the Environment

Because the environment is so important in the analysis and understanding of human behavior, we start by defining this conceptual perspective. Social work focuses on the interactions between individuals and various systems in the environment. Such a conceptual perspective provides social workers with a symbolic representation or picture of how to view the world.

Systems theories make up a broad category of such symbolic representations. They involve concepts that emphasize interactions and relationships among various systems, including individuals, families, groups, organizations, or communities. Systems theories provide a broad approach to understanding the world and can be applied to a multitude of settings. This text assumes a systems theories approach that also incorporates some basic concepts from the ecological perspective (which will be discussed in the next section). Merging systems theories with an ecological perspective is sometimes referred to as *ecosystems theory* (Beckett & Johnson, 1995; Kirst-Ashman, 2000). In such a perspective, people are thought of as being involved in constant interaction with various systems in the environment. These include family, friends, work, social service, government, employment, religion, goods and services, and educational systems. Systems theories portray people as dynamically involved with each system. Social work practice is directed at improving the interactions between clients and systems.

Understanding Key Concepts in Systems Theories

A number of terms are important to an understanding of systems theories and their relationship to social work practice. These include *system, boundaries, subsystem, homeostasis, role, relationship, input, output, feedback, interface, differentiation, entropy, negative entropy,* and *equifinality.*

A *system* is a set of elements that are orderly and interrelated to make a functional whole. A large nation, a public social services department, and a newly married couple are all examples of systems. We will refer primarily to social systems, that is, those systems that are composed of people and affect people.

Boundaries are the repeatedly occurring patterns of behavior that characterize the relationships within a system and give that system a particular identity. Chess and Norlin (1991) explain: "The boundary defines the subject system. In so doing, it also defines the appropriate roles that will be enacted by those comprising the system, for example, student, professor, secretary, or department chair. Like our skin, one purpose of a boundary is to protect the system so that its function is not adversely affected by external influences" (p. 18).

A boundary may exist between parents and their children. Parents maintain family leadership and provide support and nurturance to their children. A boundary may also exist between the protective service workers in a large county social service agency and those who work in financial assistance. These are orderly and interrelated groups set apart by specified boundaries in terms of their designated job responsibilities and the clients they serve. Yet, each group is part of the larger social services agency.

A *subsystem* is a secondary or subordinate system. It may be thought of as a smaller system within a large system. Obvious examples of subsystems are the parental and sibling subsystems within a family. The group of protective services workers in the large social services agency forms one subsystem and the financial assistance workers another. These subsystems are set apart by designated boundaries, yet still are part of the larger, total system.

Homeostasis is the tendency for a system to maintain a relatively stable, constant state of balance. If something disturbs the balance, the system will readjust itself and regain stability. A homeostatic family system is one that is functioning in such a way that it can continue to function and stay together. A homeostatic social services agency is one that works to maintain its ongoing existence. However, neither the family nor the agency is necessarily functioning as well or as effectively as possible. Homeostasis merely means maintaining the status quo. Sometimes that status quo can be ineffective, inefficient, or seriously problematic.

A *role* is "a culturally determined pattern of behavior expected of an individual in a specified social relationship" (Norlin & Chess, 1997, p. 56). Each individual involved in a system assumes a role within that system. For instance, a person in the role of social worker is expected to behave in certain "professional" ways as defined by the profession's code of ethics. Each of us probably fulfills numerous roles because we are involved in multiple systems. The social worker may also assume the roles of spouse and parent within the family system. Additionally, that person may assume the role of executive director within the National Association of Social Workers' state chapter, the role of little league coach, and that of Sunday school teacher.

A *relationship* is "the mutual emotional exchange; dynamic interaction; and affective, cognitive, and behavioral connection" between two or more persons or systems (Barker, 1999, p. 407). For example, a social worker may have a professional relationship with a client. They communicate and interact in order to meet the client's needs. Relationships may exist between systems of any size. A client may have a relationship with an agency; one agency may have a relationship with another agency.

Input involves the energy, information, or communication flow received from other systems. A parent may receive input from a child's grade school principal, noting that the child is doing poorly in physical education. A public agency may receive input from the state in the form of funding.

Output, on the other hand, is what happens to input after it has been processed by some system. For instance, output for a social services agency for people who are substance abusers might be 150 hours of individual counseling, 40 hours of group counseling, 30 hours of family counseling, 10 hours of drug-education sessions at local schools, and 50 hours of liaison work with other agencies involved with clients.

Note that the term *output* is qualitatively different from *outcome,* a term frequently used in social work education. Output is a more general term for the result of a process. Outcomes are specified variables that are measured for the purpose of evaluation. For example, outcomes for the

© Tom McCarthy/Photri

This family illustrates the concept of homeostasis. Despite its members' individual preoccupations, the family stays together and functions effectively.

social services agency mentioned above might include clients' decreased use of addictive substances, enhanced communication among family members receiving treatment, and decreased use of drugs and alcohol by students receiving drug education. Output is what is done, which may or may not have value. Outcomes measure positive effects of a system's process.

An issue that this text will continue to address is the importance of evaluating whether a system's inputs are worth the outputs. Is an agency, for example, achieving the outcomes it hopes to? Is the agency using its resources efficiently and effectively? Or can those resources be put to a better use by providing some other type of service (output)?

If clients receiving treatment from the substance abuse counseling agency described previously continue to abuse drugs and alcohol at the same rate, to what extent is the treatment effective? Since treatment is expensive, is the agency's input worth its output? Is the agency achieving its outcomes? If the agency typically sees little progress at the end of treatment for clients, we have to question the agency's usefulness. Should the agency's treatment process be changed to achieve better outcomes? Or, should the agency be shut down totally so that resources (input) could be better invested in some other agency or treatment system?

Feedback is a special form of input. It involves a system receiving information about its own performance. As a result of *negative feedback,* the system can choose to correct any deviations or mistakes and return to a more homeostatic state. For example, a supervisor may tell a social work supervisee that he or she is filling out an important agency form incorrectly. This allows the worker the opportunity to correct his or her behavior and complete the form appropriately.

Positive feedback is also valuable. This involves a system receiving information about what it is doing correctly in order to maintain itself and thrive. Getting a 97 percent on a history exam provides a sixth grader with the information that she has mastered most of the material. An agency that receives a specific federal grant has gotten the feedback that it has developed a plan worthy of such funding.

An *interface* is the point where two systems (including individuals, families, groups, organizations, or communities) come into contact with each other or communicate. For example, one interface is the written contract established between a field instructor in an adoptions agency and a student intern placed under his or her supervision. At the beginning of the semester, they discuss plans and goals for the semester. What tasks will the student be given and what levels of performance are expected? With

the help of the student's field liaison (that is, the student's university professor), a written contract is established that clarifies these expectations. Contracts generally involve written, oral, or implied agreements between persons concerning their goals, procedures, techniques, time frames, and reciprocal responsibilities during some time period in their relationship.

At his midterm evaluation, the student receives a grade of D. Although he is devastated, he still has half a semester to improve. Focusing on the interface between the field instructor and field intern (in this case, the contract they established at the beginning of the semester) provides direction concerning what to do about the problem of poor performance in his internship. By reviewing the terms specified in the contract, the instructor and student, with the liaison's help, can elaborate upon problems and expectations. Where did the student go wrong? Which of the student's expectations did the field instructor fail to fulfill? They can then establish a new contract concerning the student's performance for the remainder of the semester.

It is still up to the student to "make or break" his field experience. However, the interface (contract) provides a clearly designated means of approaching the problem. Having the field instructor and field liaison vaguely tell the student that he needs "to improve his performance" would probably accomplish little. Rather, identifying and using the interface in the form of the student-instructor contract provides a specific means for attacking the problem.

Interfaces are not limited to those between individual systems. Interfaces can characterize interactions among virtually any size system. For example, there is an interface between the adoptions agency providing the student placement and the university social work program that places the student intern. This interface involves the specified agreements concerning each of these two larger systems' respective responsibilities and expectations.

Differentiation is a system's tendency to move from a more simplified to a more complex existence. Relationships, situations, and interactions tend to get more complex over time. For example, in the life of any particular family, each day adds new experiences. New information is gathered, and new options are explored. The family's life becomes more complex. And, as a social services agency continues over time, it may develop more detailed policies and programs.

Entropy is the tendency of a system to progress toward disorganization, depletion, and death. Nothing lasts forever. People age and eventually die. Young families get older, and children leave to start their own families. As time passes, older agencies and systems are eventually replaced by new ones.

Negative entropy is the process of a system toward growth and development. In effect, it is the opposite of entropy. Individuals develop physically, intellectually, and emotionally as they grow. Social service agencies grow and develop new programs and clientele.

Equifinality refers to the fact that there are many different means to the same end. It is important not to get locked into only one way of thinking. In any situation, there are alternatives. Some may be better than others, but nonetheless, there are alternatives. For instance, as a social worker you may get needed resources for a family from a variety of sources. These may include financial assistance, housing allowances, food stamps, grants, or private charities. You may have to choose among the alternatives available from a variety of agencies.

Highlight 1.1 demonstrates the application of the key concepts to systems theories in a case example of physical child abuse.

The Ecological Perspective: Important Concepts

This text assumes an approach that integrates both systems theories and ecological concepts. We have indicated that such merging is sometimes called *ecosystems theory* (Beckett & Johnson, 1995; Kirst-Ashman, 2000). One definition of ecosystems theory is "systems theory used to describe and analyze people and other living systems and their transactions" (Beckett & Johnson, 1995, p. 1391). There is some disagreement about how systems and ecological pespectives fit together. The reason is that some of the terms that are used in both systems theories and the ecological perspective (for example, *input*) have slightly different definitions.

At various times, each perspective has been described as a theory, a model, or a theoretical underpinning. A *theory* is a coherent group of principles, concepts, and ideas organized to explain some observable occurrence or trend. A *model* on the other hand, is a description or representation to help *visualize* a process or thing that exists. Models are guides for how to view and assess situations. *Theoretical underpinnings* are the theoretical foundations for any particular way of thinking.

Though systems and ecological terms may overlap, they still can help guide our way of thinking. How should we view and analyze the world around us? What aspects are important to assess when figuring out how to solve a problem? Both systems theories and the ecological perspective provide useful means for social workers to view

the world. Together they focus on systems within the environment and describe how these systems interact with and affect people.

In essence, the ecological model might be considered an offshoot or interpretation of systems theories. An ecological approach provides a more specific view of the world within a social work perspective. The ecological perspective tends to place greater emphasis on individuals and individual family systems. Systems theories, on the other hand, assume a broader perspective. They can be used to describe the dynamics in a social service agency or the functioning of a human family.

Either perspective can serve the purpose of conceptualizing human behavior. Each provides a framework or a way of analyzing a situation to understand more clearly why people behave the way they do. Because the ecological perspective is a subset of systems theory, we periodically use some of the terms derived from it throughout the text. The following are some of the major terms employed in the ecological perspective.

Social Environment. The *social environment* involves the conditions, circumstances, and human interactions that encompass human beings. Individuals must have effective interactions with this environment in order to survive and thrive. The social environment includes the actual physical setting that the society or culture provides. This involves the type of home a person lives in, the type of work a person does, the amount of money that is available, and the laws and social rules people live by. The social environment also includes the individuals, groups, organizations, and systems with which a person comes into contact, including family, friends, work groups, and governments. Social institutions such as health care, housing, social welfare, and educational systems are yet other aspects of this social environment.

Transactions. People communicate and interact with others in their environments. These interactions are referred to as *transactions*. Transactions are active and dynamic, because, something is communicated or exchanged. They may be positive or negative. An example of a positive transaction is the revelation that the one you dearly love also loves you in return. Another positive transaction is the receipt of a paycheck after two weeks of work. An example of a negative transaction is being fired from a job that you've had for fifteen years. Another example of a negative transaction is an irritable neighbor complaining to the police about your dog barking all night long.

Highlight 1.1

Case Example of Physical Child Abuse

The Presenting Problem

As she was baking Christmas cookies, Mrs. Green overheard Mr. Horney in the next apartment screaming at his son, Jimmy. Mrs. Green became very disturbed. Jimmy, who was only 6, was crying. Next, Mrs. Green heard sharp cracks that sounded like a whip or a belt. This was not the first time; however, she hated to interfere in her neighbor's business. She recalled that last summer she had noticed strange looking bruises on Jimmy's arms and legs, as well as on those of his 4-year-old sister, Sherry. She just couldn't stand it any more. She finally picked up the phone and reported what she knew to the public Social Services Department. She asked that the Horneys not be told who had called to report the situation. She was assured that the report would remain confidential. State law protects persons who report suspected child abuse or neglect by ensuring their anonymity if they wish.

The Investigation

Ms. Samantha Chin was the Protective Services Worker assigned to the case. She visited the Horney home the day after Mrs. Green made the report. Both Mr. and Mrs. Horney were home. Ms. Chin explained to them that she had come to investigate potential child abuse.

She then proceeded to assess the functioning of the family *system*. Mr. and Mrs. Horney formed a parental *subsystem* within that system. Ms. Chin solicited *input* from that subsystem.

Harry Horney was 38 years old. He was a tall, slightly overweight, balding man dressed in an old blue shirt and coveralls. He spoke in a gruff voice, but expressed a strong desire to cooperate. He also had a faint odor of beer on his breath.

Marion Horney was a pale, thin, soft-spoken woman of 32. Mrs. Horney looked directly at the worker, shook her head in a determined manner, and stated that she was eager to cooperate. However, she often deferred to Mr. Horney when spoken to or asked a question.

Ms. Chin asked to examine the children. Together, the children formed a sibling *subsystem* within the larger family *system*. She found slash-like bruises on their arms and legs. When Mr. Horney was asked how the children got these bruises, he replied that they continually made noise when he was trying to watch the football game on television or sleep. He stated that they had to learn discipline in order to survive in life. He just strapped them a little now and then to teach them a lesson. It was no different from his treatment at the hands of his own father. He also stated that his neighbors could just keep their noses out of the way he wanted to raise his kids. This comment reflected how the family itself was a *subsystem* of the larger *community system* and did not escape notice.

Ms. Chin replied that the state's intent was to protect the children from abuse or neglect. The *interface* between the state and the family was Ms. Chin's contact. She explained that citizens were encouraged to make a report even if the abuse or neglect was only suspected. Ms. Chin added that the anonymity of people who made reports was protected by state law.

When asked how she felt about discipline, Mrs. Horney said she agreed with her husband regarding how he chose to punish the children. Mr. Horney was the main disciplinarian, and Mrs. Horney felt all he was doing was teaching the children a lesson or two in order to maintain control and respect.

The Children

Jimmy was an exceptionally nonresponsive child of relatively small stature for his age. When he was asked a question, he tended to avoid eye contact and mumbled only one-word answers. When his father asked him to enter or leave the room, he did so immediately and quietly. His mother mentioned that he was having some problems with reading in school.

Sherry, on the other hand, was an extremely eager and aggressive child. When asked to do something, she initially ignored the request and continued her own activities. She refused to comply until her parent raised his or her voice. At that point she would look up and very slowly do what she was told, often requiring several proddings. At other times, Sherry would aggressively pull at her parents' clothing, trying to get their attention. She would also scream at them loudly and ask for things such as food, even though this interrupted their ongoing conversation.

Parental History and Current Status

In order to do an accurate assessment, Ms. Chin asked the Horneys various questions about themselves, their histories, and their relationship with each other. Mr. Horney came from a family of ten. His father drank a lot and frequently used a belt to discipline his children. He remembered being very poor and having to work most of his life. At age 16 he dropped out of high school because he was able to get a job in a steel mill.

Mrs. Horney came from a broken family; her father had left when she was 3. This reflected a state of *entropy* or disorganization. She had two older brothers who, she felt, often teased and tormented her. She described her mother as being a quiet, disinterested woman who rarely stated her own opinions and liked to keep to herself. The family had always been on welfare. Mrs. Horney dropped out of high school to marry Mr. Horney when she was 17. At that time Mr. Horney was 23 and had already held six different jobs since he had started working at the steel mill seven years before.

The Horneys' marriage had not been an easy one. It was marked by poverty, frequent unemployment, and frequent moves. Mr. Horney had been laid off 19 months ago from his last assembly-line job at a local tractor factory. He stated that he was "very disgusted" that the family had to rely on welfare. Despite his frequent job changes, he had always been able to make it on his own without any assistance. Yet this time he had just about given up getting another job. He stated that he didn't like to talk to Mrs. Horney very much about his problems because it made him feel weak and incompetent. He didn't really have any "buddies" he liked to talk to or do things with either. All he seemed to be doing lately was watching television, sleeping, and drinking beer. He was even starting to watch the daytime soap operas.

Mrs. Horney was resigned to her fate. She did pretty much what her husband told her to do. She told Ms. Chin that she never did have much confidence in herself. She said that she and Mr. Horney were never really able to talk much.

The Horneys had been living in their current apartment for the past six months. However, as usual, they were finding it hard to keep up with the rent and thought they'd have to move soon. The family's *output* was surpassing its *input*. This deficit could affect the family's *homeostasis*, or stability, and ability to function effectively. Moving so often made it hard to get involved and make friends in any neighborhood. Mrs. Horney said she'd always been a lonely person.

The Assessment of Human Behavior

Factors that must be considered in the assessment of a child-abuse case include physical and behavioral indicators, and certain aspects of social functioning that tend to characterize abusive families. Before Ms. Chin could plan an appropriate and effective intervention, she needed to understand the dynamics of the behavior involved in this family situation. Additionally, she needed to know what resources or *input* were available to help the family.

Physical Indicators of Abuse Although definitions vary depending on medical, social, and legal emphases, simply put, physical child abuse is "non-accidental injury inflicted by a caregiver" (Crosson-Tower, 2002, p. 92). Physical indicators of abuse include bruises and welts, burns, lacerations and abrasions, skeletal injuries, head injuries, and internal injuries (Crosson-Tower, 2002; Kemp, 1998; Rycus, Hughes, & Garrison, 1989).

Often it is difficult to determine whether a child's injury is the result of abuse or a simple accident. For instance, a black eye may indeed have been caused by being hit by a baseball instead of a parent's fist. However, certain factors suggest child abuse. These include an inconsistent medical history, injuries that do not seem to coincide with developmental ability (for example, it is not logical that an 18-month-old girl broke her leg when running and falling when she is not yet old enough to walk well), and odd patterns of injuries (for example, a series of small circular burns from a cigarette or a series of bruises healed to various degrees).

In Jimmy's and Sherry's case, slashlike bruises were apparent on their arms and legs. Upon further investigation, the worker established that these did result from disciplinary beatings by the children's family. Cases of discipline often involve a discretionary decision on the part of the worker. The issue concerns parental rights to discipline versus children's rights and well-being. The worker must assess the situation and determine whether abuse is involved.

Behavioral Indicators of Abuse Ms. Chin needed to know not only what types of physical indicators are involved in child abuse but also the behavioral indicators of abused chil-

dren. These types of behaviors differ from "normal" behavior. She needed to know the parameters of normal behavior in order to distinguish it from the abnormal behavior typically displayed by abused children.

Abused children are often overly compliant and passive (Crosson-Tower, 2002; Kolko, 2002). If a child acts overly eager to obey and/or is exceptionally quiet and still, this may be a reaction to abuse. Such children may be seeking to avoid further abuse by maintaining a low profile and avoiding notice by the abuser. Jimmy manifested some of these behaviors. He was afraid of being disciplined and so maintained as innocuous a profile as possible. This was a logical approach for him to take in order to avoid being hurt.

Sherry, on the other hand, assumed an aggressive, attention-getting approach; another behavior pattern frequently displayed by abused children (Crosson-Tower, 2002; Kolko, 2002). She frequently refused to comply with her parents' instructions until they raised their voices, and often demanded additional prodding. She also tried to get their attention by pulling at them and screaming requests at them. This approach is also typical of certain abused children. Since Sherry was not getting the attention she needed through other means, she was acting aggressively to get it, even though such behavior was inappropriate. Ms. Chin needed to be knowledgeable about the normal attention needs of a 4-year-old in order to understand the dynamics of this behavior.

One other symptom typical of abused children is a lag in development (Kemp, 1998; Kolko, 2002; LeVine & Sallee, 1999). Jimmy was small for his age and was having difficulty in school. Ms. Chin needed to be aware of the normal parameters of development for a 6-year-old in order to be alert to developmental lags. She also needed to know that such lags were potential indicators of abuse.

Family Social Functioning Not only the children but also the parents must be assessed. A worker must understand the influence of both personal and environmental factors on the behavior of the parents. Only then can these factors be targeted for intervention and the abusive behaviors be changed.

Personal parental factors that are related to abuse include unfulfilled needs for nurturance and dependence, isolation, and lack of nurturing child-rearing practices (Crosson-Tower, 2002; Kemp, 1998). Ms. Chin discovered in her interview that both parents were isolated and alone. They had no one to turn to for emotional support. There was no place where they could appropriately and harmlessly vent their frustrations. Nor had either parent learned appropriate child-rearing practices in their families of origin. Mr. Horney had learned excessive discipline—to be strict and punitive. Mrs. Horney had learned compliance and passivity—to be helpless and to believe she could have no effect on others, no matter what she did.

Environmental factors are equally important in the assessment of this case. Specific factors related to abuse often include lack of support systems, marital problems, and life crises (Crosson-Tower, 2002; Kemp, 1998). Life can become more difficult and complicated. *Differentiation*, in a negative sense, can occur.

Highlight 1.1

Case Example of Physical Child Abuse (continued)

Neither parent had been able to develop an adequate support system. Due to frequent moves, they had not been able to develop *relationships* with neighbors or others in the community *systems* of which they were part. Nor could they turn to each other for emotional support. They had never learned how to communicate effectively within a marital relationship. Finally, they were plagued by the serious life crises of poverty and unemployment. All of these things contributed to the abusive situation.

Making Connections with Available Resources

Ms. Chin considered several treatment directions. *Equifinality* is reflected in the range of options available. Of course, resource availability in the client's community system is critically important. If resources had not been available, Ms. Chin may have faced quite a dilemma. Should she work to help get appropriate resources developed? If so, what kind? How should she proceed? This would involve focusing on aspects of the larger social systems in which her clients lived.

However, the Horneys' community had a number of resource input possibilities. A Parents Anonymous group and various social groups were available to decrease the Horneys' social isolation. (Parents Anonymous is a self-help organization, similar to Alcoholics Anonymous, for parents who have abused or neglected their children.) Individual and marital counseling were available to improve the Horneys' personal self-images and to enhance marital communication. A visiting homemaker could encourage Mrs. Horney to more assertively undertake her homemaking and child-rearing tasks. She could also provide personal support. Parent Effectiveness Training could be used to teach the Horneys parenting skills and alternatives to harsh discipline. Finally, Mr. Horney could be encouraged to get reinvolved in a job search. An employment specialist at the agency could help him define and pursue alternative employment possibilities. The intent was to help the Horneys achieve *negative entropy.*

Ms. Chin discussed these alternatives with the Horneys. In essence, she provided them with *input* and *feedback.* Together they determined which were possible and realistic. They then decided which should be pursued first. Mr. Horney admitted that he could use some help in finding a job, which he stated was his highest priority. He agreed to contact the agency job specialist to help him reinstitute his job search. Mrs. Horney liked the idea of having a visiting homemaker. She felt that this would help her get her work done, and it would also give her someone to talk to. Both agreed to attend a Parents Anonymous group on a trial basis. They were not interested in pursuing marriage counseling or Parent Effectiveness Training now, but would keep it in mind for the future.

Commentary

Situations involving physical child abuse comprise only one category among many in which social workers collect information, assess the situation, and make recommendations for intervention. These situations include unwanted pregnancy, drug and alcohol abuse, potential suicide, AIDS, poverty, cognitive disability, domestic violence, racial discrimination, and grief over illness or death. For any of these situations, social workers need a base of knowledge to understand what pressures are having impacts upon their clients. They need to know what kinds of information are important and what kinds of questions to ask. Finally, workers need to assess the environmental context in which clients face their problems in order to help clients get needed services. The intent of this text is to provide the foundation for this knowledge base. (Child abuse, neglect, and sexual abuse will be discussed much more extensively in a later chapter.)

Energy. *Energy* is the natural power of active involvement between people and their environments. Energy can take the form of input or output. Input is the form of energy coming into a person's life and adding to that life. For example, an elderly person whose health is failing may need input in the form of substantial physical assistance and emotional support in order to continue performing the daily tasks necessary to stay alive. Another example of input is a teacher giving a student feedback on a term paper.

Output, on the other hand, is a form of energy going out of a person's life or taking something away from it. For instance, parents may expend tremendous amounts of energy in taking care of their young children. So may a person who volunteers time and effort to work on the campaign of a politician he or she supports.

Interface. The *interface* in the ecological perspective is similar to that in systems theory. It is the exact point at which the interaction between an individual and the environment takes place. During an assessment, the interface must be clearly in focus in order to target the appropriate interactions for change. For example, a couple entering marriage counseling initially state that their problem concerns disagreements about how to raise their children. Upon further exploration, however, the real problem is discovered, namely, their inability to communicate feelings to each other. The actual problem, the inability to communicate, is the interface where one individual impacts the other. If the interface is inaccurately targeted, much time and useless energy can be wasted before getting at the real problem.

The ecological perspective, however, differs from systems theories in its tendency to emphasize interfaces concerning individuals and small groups such as families. It is more difficult to apply the ecological perspective's conception of interfaces to those involving only larger systems such as systems communities and organizations.

Adaptation. *Adaptation* refers to the capacity to adjust to surrounding environmental conditions. It implies change. A person must change or adapt to new conditions and circumstances in order to continue functioning effectively. Social workers frequently help people in their process of adaptation to a new marriage partner, a new job, or a new neighborhood. Adaptation usually requires energy in the form of effort. Social workers often help direct people's energies so that they are most productive.

Not only are people affected by their environments, but environments are also affected by people in their process of adaptation. People change their environments in order to adapt successfully. For instance, a person might find it hard to survive a winter in Montana in the "natural" environment without shelter. Therefore, those who live in Montana manipulate their environment by clearing land and by constructing heated buildings. They change their environment in order to survive in it. Therefore, adaptation is often a two-way process involving both the individual and the environment.

Coping. *Coping* is a form of adaptation that implies a struggle to overcome problems. Although adaptation may involve responses to new conditions that are either positive or negative, coping refers to the way people deal with the negative experiences they encounter. For example, a person might have to cope with the sudden death of a parent, a primary family wage earner losing a job, gangs that are vandalizing the community, or vital public assistance payments that are significantly decreased.

At least five types of coping skills are important for people to develop (Barker, 1999). First, people need to solicit and obtain the types of information they need to function well. For instance, an elderly person who becomes sick needs to know how to obtain Medicare benefits. Second, people need coping skills concerning thinking about and planning for the future. For example, a person who loses a job needs to develop a plan for finding another one. Third, coping skills involve controlling emotions. For example, a minor disagreement with a spouse should not

result in a major battle involving screaming, scratching, and punching. Fourth, people need coping skills to control their needs for immediate gratification. For instance, a family needs to budget its income so that there is food on the table at the end of the week, instead of spending money on a new television set. Finally, coping skills involve identifying alternative ways of approaching a problematic situation and evaluating the pros and cons of each alternative.

Social workers are frequently called upon to help clients develop coping skills. A major theme in the helping process involves working with clients to evaluate alternatives and choose the one that's best for them. Evaluating alternatives will be addressed again later in this chapter.

Interdependence. The final ecological concept is that of *interdependence,* which is the mutual reliance of each person upon every other person. An individual is interdependent or reliant upon other individuals and groups of individuals in the social environment.

A person cannot exist without other people. The businessperson needs the farmer to produce food. He or she also needs customers to purchase goods. The farmer needs the businessperson to provide money to buy seed, tools, and other essentials. The farmer becomes the customer for the businessperson. People, especially in a highly industrialized society, are interdependent; they need each other in order to survive.

People's Involvement with Multiple Systems

The interactions between people and the various systems within their environment have tremendous impact upon human behavior. The model proposed in this text emphasizes several aspects of this interaction. Ecosystems theory provides us with the basis for understanding our assessment model.

We have established that people are constantly and dynamically involved in interactions with their social environment. Social work assessment tries to answer the question, "What is it in any particular situation that causes a problem to continue despite the client's expressed wish to change it?" An ecosystems approach provides a perspective for assessing many aspects of a situation. Clients are affected by and in constant dynamic interactions with other systems in their social environments. These include families, groups, organizations, institutions, and communities.

Figure 1.1 Human Behavior Involves Multiple Systems

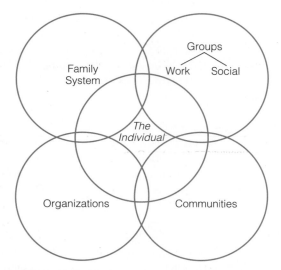

Each individual is involved in multiple systems consisting of families, groups, organizations, and communities.

Figure 1.1 portrays the dynamic interactions of clients with other systems in the social environment.

Micro, Mezzo, and Macro Systems

A system is a set of elements that are interrelated to make a functional whole. For our purposes, we will distinguish three basic types of systems throughout this text: micro, mezzo, and macro systems. *Micro system* refers to an individual. In a broad sense, a person is a type of system that entails biological, psychological, and social systems. All of these systems interact. A micro orientation to social work practice involves focusing on an individual's needs, problems, and strengths. It also stresses how that individual might address issues, generate solutions, and make the best, most effective choices possible. Micro practice, then, involves working with an individual and enhancing that person's functioning.

Mezzo system refers to any small group, including family, work groups, and other social groups. Sometimes for assessment purposes it is difficult to clearly differentiate between issues involving a micro system (individual) and a mezzo system (small group) with which the individual is involved. This is because individuals are so integrally involved in interactions with others close to them. In many cases, we will make an arbitrary distinction between an issue concerning a micro system and one concerning a mezzo system.

Macro system refers to systems larger than small groups. A macro orientation involves focusing on the social, po-

litical, and economic conditions and policies that affect people's overall access to resources and quality of life. Macro practice in social work, then, involves striving to improve the social and economic context in which people live.

The Social Environment

Figure 1.2 illustrates how all systems function within the social environment. We have already established that the social environment involves the conditions, circumstances, and human interactions that encompass human beings. We have also emphasized that people depend upon effective interactions with this environment in order to survive and thrive. Therefore, all problems should be assessed within the social environment's context. This entails focusing on micro, mezzo, and macro system interactions.

Interactions Between Micro Systems and Mezzo Systems

Individual micro systems interact with various other mezzo systems in the social environment as illustrated in Figure 1.2. For the purposes of the diagram, only one circle is used to portray the numerous potential mezzo systems with which an individual micro system may be involved. The double pointed arrow between the circles representing micro and mezzo systems emphasizes the dynamic two-way interactions between these two types of systems.

For instance, a 16-year-old individual family member can affect her entire family by running away to San Francisco and roaming the streets there. The same individual may be strongly affected by her entire family group. Her family may become "fed up" with her behavior and ignore her existence, much to her surprise and dismay.

Interactions Between Micro Systems and Macro Systems

Individual micro systems are also continuously and seriously affected by the macro systems with which they interact within the social environment. Four major types of macro systems impact individual clients: *culture, communities, institutions,* and *organizations*. All four are intertwined.

Culture is the configuration of shared attitudes, values, goals, spiritual beliefs, social expectations, arts, technology, and behaviors that characterize a broader society in which people live. A *community* is "a number of people who have something in common with one another that connects them in some way and that distinguishes them

Figure 1.2 Multiple Interacting Systems in the Social Environment

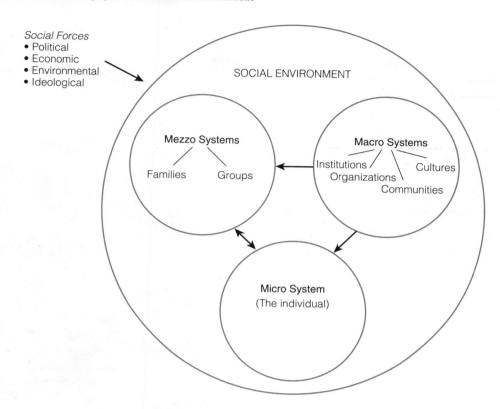

from others." The common feature might be a neighborhood where people live, an activity people share such as jobs, or other connections like "ethnic identification" (Homan, 1999, p. 8).

An *institution* is "a fundamental custom or behavior pattern of a culture, such as marriage, justice, welfare, and religion"; it may also be "an organization established for some public purpose and the physical facility in which its work occurs, such as a prison" (Barker, 1999, p. 244). *Organizations* are structured groups of people who come together to work toward some mutual goal and perform established work activities that are divided among various units. Organizations have a clearly defined membership in terms of knowing who is in and who is out (Daft, 2001; Hellriegel, Slocum, & Woodman, 2001).

We have emphasized the importance of clients' interactions with the many systems engulfing them. It is easy for practitioners, especially those who are new to the field, to focus on micro and mezzo systems. Assuming a "clinical" approach targets trying to change individuals within the context of small groups and families.

We have also emphasized that a unique and vital aspect of social work is assessing the effects of macro systems on individual client systems. Kettner, Daley and Nichols (1985) suggest that two broad theoretical perspectives most clearly underlie practice with large systems; these are organizational theory and community theory.

Organizational theory includes specific attempts to understand how organizations function, what improves or impairs the ability of an organization to accomplish its mission, and what motivates people to work toward organizational goals. Some approaches to organizational theory have focused on management or leadership style; others have dealt with structural issues such as organizational hierarchy, planning, staffing patterns, and budgeting. Groups considered as organizations include virtually every structure with staff, policies, and procedures whose purpose is to continue operation in order to attain certain goals. For example, schools, public social welfare departments, and an agency operating four group homes for adults with cognitive disabilities are all types of organizations.

The second theoretical framework, *community theory,* has two primary components. They are the nature of communities and social work practice within communities.

Warren (1978) has conceptualized communities from multiple perspectives. For example, you may think of a community as having specific geographical boundaries like those of a city. Or, you can conceive of communities as groups with shared interests and beliefs. An example is the professional social work community. On the other hand, the community may be seen as a target for change, either as the problem or as the context within which change occurs (Netting, Kettner, & McMurtry, 2001). Both these perspectives have advantages. Both make it easier to assess problems, decide among several possible interventions, and evaluate possible outcomes. Both community and organizational theories will be discussed more thoroughly later on.

The Impact of Social Forces

The final aspect of Figure 1.2 to keep in mind is the impact of social forces upon the social environment. There are at least four social forces that effect changes in the social environment: *political, economic, environmental,* and *ideological forces.*

Political forces are the current governmental structure, laws to which people are subject, and the overall distribution of power among the populace. *Economic forces* include the resources that are available, how they are distributed, and how they are spent. *Environmental forces* concern the status of the physical environment in view of exploding populations and incessant industrialization. Finally, *ideological forces* involve the values and beliefs to which people in the social environment adhere.

The turbulent interaction of these forces and their effects on each other are striking. For example, take the national health care crisis. Political forces determine the governmental structure concerning what services must be provided to whom. The same forces govern the regulation of health care services and insurance for that health care. Economic forces involve who pays for these services. Should health services be paid for by private insurance companies with premiums paid by employers and employees? Or, should working people pay their own premiums directly? What about the significant unemployment rate and high proportion of women and children without health insurance? Should the federal government pay for everyone's health care? If so, where will it get the money? If large amounts of money are spent on health care, which resources will be left over to care for and clean up the environment? What is more important— an expansive health care system or a livable environment? Or can we have both?

Ideologically, decisions must be made about how the political system should function, how money should be spent, and what aspects of life should receive high

Political and economic forces in the global international environment affect the North American economies. Here picketers advocate for citizens to support their own economy by purchasing American-made goods, instead of those manufactured elsewhere.

priority. With limited resources, should these resources be spent on cleaning up cancer-causing toxic wastes or on heart transplants? In view of limited resources, who should receive help—an elderly man rapidly losing his mental capacities through Alzheimer's disease, a premature crack-addicted baby with a 50 percent chance of surviving with multiple health problems, or a person who has been diagnosed HIV positive who needs thousands of dollars a year for medication and treatments to survive?

The Relationships among Biological, Psychological, and Social Systems

We have established a context for assessing human behavior as one involving multiple interactions with mezzo and macro systems within the social environment. Additionally, there are biological, psychological, and social events that occur normally over an individual's life span and constantly interact with each other. For example, individuals normally master various biological, psychological, and social tasks at predictable periods in their development. We will consider these three themes (biological, psychological, and social) as separate interacting systems that have momentous impacts on the individual client system.

Figure 1.3 illustrates the dynamic interactions among the biological, psychological, and social systems within any one micro system. Double pointed arrows represent this ongoing involvement among these three systems. The individual system functions by interacting with the many other mezzo systems and macro systems within the social environment. These systems are portrayed by increasingly larger circles enveloping the circle depicting the individual, the micro system.

Two aspects of this interaction among the three systems are critical for social workers to understand. First, social workers need to know what the normal milestones are for each of these areas. Only then can they distinguish

the normal from the abnormal in order to decide who is in need of intervention. Second, social workers must understand how each of these systems affects what occurs in the other systems. It's helpful to view the interactions of the systems from a chronological perspective.

Normal Developmental Milestones. Normal developmental milestones include those significant biological, psychological, emotional, intellectual, and social points of development that normally occur in a person's life span. This category focuses on the individual as a distinct entity. It provides a perspective on what can be considered normal. Topics include motor development, personality development, motivation, social development, and learning.

For example, consider a baby's normal motor development. By age three, most children begin to jump and hop on one foot, climb stairs by alternating feet on each stair, and dress and undress themselves to some extent (Lefrancois, 1999, p. 189). Or, consider the normal developmental occurrences for the elderly. Older persons tend to have important changes in their sleeping patterns,

Figure 1.3 The Relationships among Biological, Psychological, and Social Systems

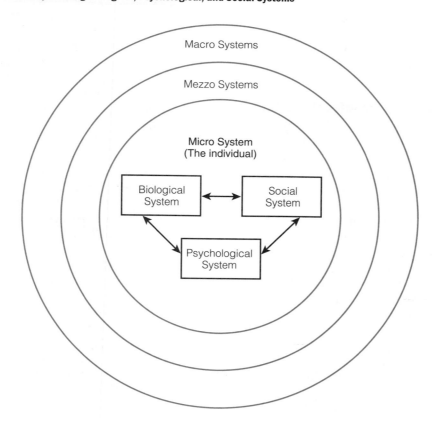

such as taking longer to fall asleep and typically sleeping for shorter time periods at night (Bootzin et al., 1996; Kail & Cavanaugh, 2000).

In order to distinguish between what is normal and what is pathological, one must have a clear understanding of normal developmental milestones at any age. The term "normal" is used here to refer to levels of functioning that are considered appropriate for a particular age level. Social work practitioners must be able to distinguish between situations that merit intervention and those that do not. Much time and effort can be wasted on trying to solve "problems" that are really not problems at all. For instance, it is needless to worry about a baby who is not walking at the age of twelve months. However, it may merit investigation if that baby is still not beginning to walk by the age of twenty-four months. Likewise, consider the elderly person with sleeping problems. It may be senseless to worry about a tendency to sleep lightly when that is simply a normal sign of age. Social workers may help people adjust their expectations so that they are more reasonable. People can be helped to stop worrying about what is really the normal state of things. On the other hand, sleeping problems at the age of fifty may merit further exploration. At this earlier point in life, such problems may be caused by stress or some physiological problem.

Normal developmental milestones provide a baseline for assessing human behavior. The extent of the problem or abnormality can be assessed only to the extent that it deviates from what is normal or typical.

Bio-Psycho-Social Systems Affect Each Other

Social workers should not focus on a problem involved in only one system (that is, biological, psychological, or social) and ignore how other systems are affected. Figure 1.3 connects the three systems with double pointed arrows to emphasize that they affect each other.

Consider a depressed adolescent. Although his psychological state, or depression, may be the presenting problem, problems related to other systems may also be evident. His psychological depression may cause him to withdraw from others and become isolated. Thus, his social interaction may be drastically affected. He may stop eating and/or exercising, which would have a significant impact on his biological system.

Another example involves an alcohol-addicted adult. Her drinking affects her biological, psychological, and social systems. Biologically, she loses weight and has frequent physical problems such as severe hangover headaches. Her physical health affects her psychological health in that she frequently becomes disgusted with herself. Her

psychological condition affects her interactions with those close to her, and they begin to avoid her. Hence, her social system is affected. Social isolation, in turn, enhances her psychological desire to drink and escape, and her physical condition continues to deteriorate.

Note that social workers assess the functioning of various bio-psycho-social systems within the context of professional values and ethics. Highlight 1.2 reflects on the importance of this perspective and elaborates with some examples.

A Chronological Perspective. For a coherent approach to changes that take place during a person's life span, this text will assume a chronological perspective. Each of the three systems (biological, psychological, and social) will be examined within this framework. Starting with conception and ending with death, human behavior will be explored within the context of the different phases or age periods in a person's life. These periods include infancy and childhood, adolescence and young adulthood, middle adulthood, and later adulthood.

Throughout these life periods, people tend to experience common life events. There is a greater tendency for certain types of occurrences to happen at certain times of life. For example, adolescence is a time when people establish an identity. Adolescents strive for independence and search for a place to fit into social peer groups. Sometimes adolescence is even more stressful. It may be marked by running away from home or by delinquency.

Marriage and having children are characteristic events of early and middle adulthood. Sometimes people face unplanned pregnancy and single parenthood during this time of life. Some people must deal with divorce. Life events in later adulthood include retirement and readjustments to married life when children leave home. Although many elderly people remain deeply involved in family and community life, disengagement theory predicts that others will become increasingly isolated and detached from society (Cumming & Henry, 1961; Dacey & Travers, 2002). Additionally, many elderly people must cope with increasingly more serious health problems and illnesses.

These experiences or life events—identity crises, marriage and children, retirement, and detachment—all tend to happen during certain periods of life. Each of these common events will be addressed within the context of the time of life when it characteristically occurs. The variety of experiences that may be considered "typical" is great. However, there are certain life events that social workers are frequently called upon to help people cope with. We will arbitrarily select and focus on some of these experiences based on their relevance to practice.

Highlight 1.2

Application of Values and Ethics to Bio-Psycho-Social System Assessments

Social workers assess problems and attempt to understand human behavior within the context of social work values and ethics. The National Association of Social Workers' (NASW) Code of Ethics (1996) focuses on six areas involving how a worker should behave in a professional role. These include ethical responsibilities: (1) *to clients;* (2) *to colleagues;* (3) *in practice settings;* (4) *as professionals;* (5) *to the social work profession;* and (6) *to the broader society.*

Social workers should always keep in mind their clients' rights and well-being. To the best of their ability, social workers should strive to abide by professional ethical principles, respect the rights and needs of others, and make decisions about right and wrong consistent with their professional ethics. This sounds simple.

But consider the following scenarios, all occurring within the context of social work assessment.

Scenario 1: You are a social worker at a shelter for runaways, assessing an unmarried, pregnant 15-year-old who has been living "on the streets." She is in her seventh month of pregnancy. She is addicted to cocaine, which she has been using throughout the pregnancy (prenatal influences will be discussed in Chapter 2). She has been informed of the potential side effects of her cocaine use upon the fetus, which are likely to result in an infant who will require more attention than that given to infants born to nonaddicted mothers. She adamantly states she will keep the baby and figure out what to do with her addiction after it's born. You have serious concerns for the infant's well-being. You personally feel that the young woman should place the baby for adoption or at least in foster care until she can solve her own problems. What is the ethical thing to do?

Scenario 2: You are a hospital social worker assessing a client with AIDS. (AIDS is covered in detail in Chapter 10.) He tells you that he has had unprotected intercourse with dozens of women since he received his positive HIV diagnosis. He has shared his diagnosis with none of these women. He boldly states that he is incredibly angry that he has the disease and plans to continue having intercourse with as many women as he can. You feel that it is both unethical and hazardous to his sex partners for him not to tell them about their potential exposure to the disease. Clients are supposed to be able to make choices about their own behavior. You are supposed to keep the interactions between you and your client confidential. But what about the unsuspecting victims of your client's choices? What is the ethical thing to do?

Scenario 3: You are an Adult Protective Services social worker. Your job is to make assessments and pursue interventions to make certain that vulnerable older adults with limited ability to take care of their basic needs get "the support and assistance they require" (Austin, 1995, p. 89). You are assessing an elderly woman in her own home. Her physical and intellectual health is deteriorating. The woman lives alone in a run-down apartment in a poor section of town. She has no close family. She insists that she wants to remain in her home. Your agency supervisor has told you that elderly people deemed unable to take care of themselves must be placed in a nursing home facility. However, you also know that the only nursing home facilities available to poor elderly people in the area are run-down, understaffed, and offer a minimal quality of life. Ethically, your client has the right to make her own decisions. However, you fear that she may fall and remain helpless, turn the gas stove on and forget to light the flame, or have some other accident. What is the ethical thing to do?*

Each of these situations portrays an ethical dilemma. Dilemmas involve problematic situations for which possible solutions are imperfect and unsatisfactory. In other words, your ethical guidelines conflict with each other. There is no one perfect answer that can possibly abide by all of the ethical principles in the professional code. You are "stuck" with deciding what to do. Many such dilemmas are encountered in social work practice.

Three basic suggestions guide your procedure. They are made within the context of assessing human behavior in order to lay the groundwork for determining what intervention to pursue:

1. Put your theoretical and factual knowledge base about human behavior to work. (This text intends to provide you with such a base.)

2. Identify your own values concerning the issues and then distinguish between your values and professional ethics.

3. Weigh the pros and cons of each alternative available to you and your client, and then proceed with the alternative you determine is the most positive.

There are no perfect answers. Following is an example of how these suggestions may be applied to scenario 1.

In scenario 1 (the pregnant, unmarried, 15-year-old cocaine addict), first gather the knowledge you need. You need to know the effects of cocaine on prenatal development (described in Chapter 2), the dynamics of drug addiction (discussed in Chapter 11), and the needs of newborn infants in general (addressed in Chapters 2, 3, and 4). Such information can give you clues regarding what types of information you need to know in order to plan interventions.

The second step is to recognize clearly your own personal values and biases. You should not impose your values upon your client. Strive to make decisions that coincide as much as possible with professional ethics.

Finally, identify the alternatives available to you, weigh the pros and cons of each, and make the decision you consider to be the most ethical. Knowledge of human behavior in the areas cited above can lead you to the questions you need to ask in order to make an effective,

Highlight 1.2

Application of Values and Ethics to Bio-Psycho-Social System Assessments (continued)

ethical decision along with your client. Questions in scenario 1 might include:

- What are the client's drug-using behaviors?
- What are the potential effects on the child?
- How motivated is the client to enter a drug treatment program?
- What resources for drug treatment and other supportive services for unmarried teen mothers are available?

- If not available, can needed services be initiated and developed?
- What resources can you turn to in order to maximize the child's well-being?

You can address the dilemmas posed in scenarios 2 and 3 in a similar manner. What theoretical and factual knowledge do you have about human behavior that can be applied to your understanding of the situation? What personal values and biases do you hold concerning the client and the client's situation? What alternatives are available to you and your client, what are the pros and cons of each? Answers to these questions will guide you to the alternative that is the most ethical to pursue.

Diversity, Oppression, and Populations-at-Risk

Social workers must be aware of human differences and the effects they have on human behavior. Any time a person can be identified as belonging to a group that differs in some respect from the majority of others in society, that person is subject to the effects of that diversity, including discrimination. Variables that may place people at special risk of discrimination include those related to "clients' age, class, color, culture, disability, ethnicity, family structure, gender, marital status, national origin, race, religion, sex, and sexual orientation" (Council on Social Work Education, 2001, 3.3).

Membership in groups other than the young, white, male heterosexual mainstream can place people at increased risk of discrimination and oppression. Discrimination concerns "the prejudgment and negative treatment of people based on identifiable characteristics such as race, gender, religion, or ethnicity" (Barker, 1999, p. 132). Oppression involves putting extreme limitations and constraints on the members of an identified group "in a cruel and unjust manner" (Nichols, 1999, p. 927). Picture a woman in an all-male business establishment. Think of a 62-year-old person applying for a sales job in a department store where everyone else is under 40. Or, consider an African American person applying for membership in an all-white country club.

Membership in any group provides a certain set of environmental circumstances. A Chicano adolescent from a Mexican American inner-city neighborhood has a different social environment from that of an upper-middle-class adolescent of European descent living in the well-to-do suburbs of the same city.

Group Membership and Values. Sensitivity to group differences is critical in understanding any individual's behavior. This is important from two perspectives. First, the values or orientation of a particular group will affect how an individual behaves. For instance, an individual with a sexual orientation for the same gender may very well choose to participate in social activities with others of the same orientation. The individual might tend to avoid bars and nightclubs where heterosexual singles meet and might join activities or social clubs aimed at helping people with a sexual orientation toward the same gender meet each other.

The Macro System Perspective on Group Differences. There is a second important perspective concerning sensitivity to group differences. The first perspective focused on how the group member feels and chooses to act. The second perspective directs attention to how other people and groups in the social environment view the (diverse) group in question. The diverse group may be the object of *prejudgments* (predetermined assumptions made without assessing facts) and *stereotypes* (standardized views, about people who belong to some group, that do not take into account individual qualities and differences). Each group member has a tendency to lose his or her individual identity and assume the group identity in the eyes of others in the environment. To these outsiders, the characteristics of the group become the characteristics of the individual, whether the individual actually has them or not.

For example, consider a young, single, African American mother of three young children who is receiving public aid. She applies for a service job behind the counter of a local delicatessen. The deli is run by a lower-middle-class white family that holds many of the larger society's traditional values. These values include the ideas that the head of the household must be a man and that women should stay home and take care of the children. The owner of the deli, a man and head of the family, interviews the young woman and makes several assumptions.

The first assumption is that the woman has no business not being married. The second is that she should be staying at home with her children. The third assumption is that the woman, because of her color, is probably lazy and undependable anyway. He uses the excuse that she has no experience in this particular job and refuses to hire her. This young woman has run up against serious difficulties in her job search. In addition, she may have problems getting adequate day care for her young children. Taken together, all these difficulties may prevent her from finding a job and getting off public aid.

In assessing behavior one must be aware of limitations imposed by the environment. Otherwise, impossible alternatives might be pursued. In practice, a social worker who does not understand these things might continue to pressure the young woman in the example to go out and get a job. Since she was already trying and failing, this additional pressure might make her turn against the social worker and the social service system. She might just give up.

Awareness of how prejudgments and stereotypes affect people is important because it involves professional values, one of the foundation blocks of social work. Reamer (1995) articulates basic social work values and emphasizes the importance of adherence to them. These values include "individual worth and dignity, . . . client self-determination, . . . commitment to social change and social justice, . . . client empowerment, equal opportunity, nondiscrimination, [and] respect for diversity" (p. 894). Spotlight 1.1, including Figure 1.4, describes the position of diverse groups in the social environment.

Spotlight on Diversity 1.1 Social Work Values and Sensitivity to Diverse Populations

Sensitivity to human diversity is very important in social work practice. Therefore, this orientation is given a central role in the assessment of human behavior. Figure 1.4 portrays the two perspectives on human diversity.

The larger circle depicts the values and attitudes of the majority of people in the social environment. The smaller circle, which intersects and goes a bit beyond the edge of the larger circle, represents the values and attitudes of some group. This may be any group that is different in some way from the majority. This difference may be an ethnic diversity, a racial diversity, or a diversity of sexual orientation.

The diverse group circle extends beyond the larger circle of the entire social environment. This represents the values and attitudes held by the group that are not held by others in the environment. The small central circle represents the sum total of stereotypes and prejudgments held by people in the social environment. The fact that the diverse group circle intersects the stereotype circle reflects the prejudgments held about that particular diverse group.

The diverse group circle also intersects the other general section of the social environment circle. The diverse group is still part of the total social environment. This intersection reflects the values and attitudes held in common with others in the social environment.

The two perspectives focused on here are reflected by the two shaded areas. The first is the perspective held by the diverse group that is different from the perspective of others in the environment. The second is the overlap of the diverse group and the stereotyped attitudes held in the social environment. This represents the prejudices to which the diverse group is subjected.

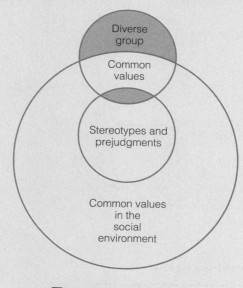

Figure 1.4 Value Diagram: Diverse Groups in the Social Environment

Diverse group

Common values

Stereotypes and prejudgments

Common values in the social environment

☐ Unique values held by the diverse group

☐ Stereotypes and prejudgments about the diverse group that are held by other segments in the social environment

🌿 The Systems Impact Model

The systems impact model (SIM) proposes that social work practitioners work not only with clients to solve clients' problems but also with the many other major systems with which the client is involved. SIM proposes that a primary pursuit of social work goes far beyond counseling individual clients at the micro level or working with small groups at the mezzo level. Rather, SIM emphasizes that social workers must often work within the existing institutional and organizational structure on their clients' behalf. Often, the target must be to change or improve how services are delivered and resources distributed. Targets of change may also involve improving conditions and services within a community.

Figure 1.5 illustrates the systems impact model. Circles represent the various systems involved. For instance, the three large circles above the client system depict major macro systems that strongly impact the client system. Arrows illustrate inputs or impacts. The arrows' directions indicate which system is the sender and which the receiver. Double pointed arrows indicate some degree of mutual input.

The Client System

First of all, note that the client system[1] is in the center of the model. This client system may be an individual, a family, or a small group struggling to cope with some serious problem. The client system may also be a community desperately battling to stay economically viable. Or, it may be an agency unable to get the resources it needs to survive and prosper.

This text focuses on individuals as they mature over their life span and as members of other systems, including families, peer and work groups, organizations, and communities (CSWE, 2001). It emphasizes people's relationships and interactions with larger macro systems. Most generalist social workers will have individuals, families, and small groups as their primary client systems. For these reasons, the following discussion will refer to the individual, family, or small group as the *client system*. Clients will be viewed within the context of larger macro systems such as organizations and communities.

The Relationship Between Organizational Macro Systems and Client Systems

Figure 1.5 shows how organizational systems can affect client systems, depicted by the arrow leading from the organizational systems circle to the client system circle. For our purposes, organizations will include those structures that process and distribute resources to client systems. Examples are county social service departments, residential treatment centers for teenagers with serious behavioral problems, private adoption agencies, Planned Parenthood clinics, and shelters for homeless people. All use their allocated resources to provide services that meet their clients' needs. (Organizations will be discussed more thoroughly later in this chapter and in Chapter 12.)

Because clients have no formal working role within organizations, they have little direct impact on most organizational systems, especially those providing resources to them. However, clients can pursue agency change (for example, to improve service provision) by using tactics like joining other clients with similar concerns and pressuring agency administrators for change, contacting the media about problems, or approaching policy-makers and

Figure 1.5 The Systems Impact Model

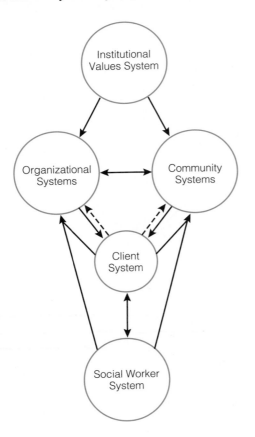

1. The concept of *client system* was initiated by A. Pincus and A. Minahan in *Social Work Practice: Model and Method* (Itasca, IL: Peacock, 1973).

politicians with recommendations. Nonetheless, clients generally have relatively little power to generate change compared to those in decision-making positions. Therefore, a dashed arrow leads from the client system to the organizational system, implying lesser influence.

The Relationship Between the Community Macro System and the Client System

The circle to the right of the organizational systems circle in Figure 1.5 represents the community macro system. We have described a community as a group of people who have something in common with each other that links them and differentiates them from others who are not part of the community.

Communities provide people with necessary input via resources, jobs, and social support systems. However, problems evident in communities can have devastating effects on community residents' ability to function in a healthy way. For instance, the increasingly poor financial condition of urban inner cities results in crime and delinquency, drug problems, environmental pollution, neglect of the elderly, child abuse, and unemployment.

Community systems have significant impacts on individuals, including clients. Hence, Figure 1.5 shows a solid arrow leading from the community to the client. By definition, clients are units or subsystems within the larger community. As integral parts of this larger macro system, clients also can develop avenues to affect their community. The dashed arrow leading from the client circle to

the community circle indicates that clients have less power on the much larger community system.

The Relationship Between Organizational and Community Macro Systems

In Figure 1.5 the double pointed arrow connecting the organizational system circle and the community system circle shows that these two types of macro systems affect and interact with each other. Organizational systems providing services have distinctive effects on the resources made available to community residents. Likewise, the problems and needs evident in a community influence the nature and distribution of services. For example, effective agencies do not provide services the community doesn't need.

Institutional Values Macro System

The upper circle in Figure 1.5 portrays the institutional values system. We will define this system as involving the strong, historically rooted values and beliefs governing the distribution of resources. For example, a strong institutional value is that children should not be physically damaged by adults, including their parents. Hence, we have protective service agencies and departments that exist to prevent and stop such abuse. Another example of a strong institutional value is the punishment of convicted criminals. Thus, we have a major federal and state prison system. Another example of a strongly rooted institutional

An electric chair: Death as punishment for murder is a widely debated institutionalized value in this country.

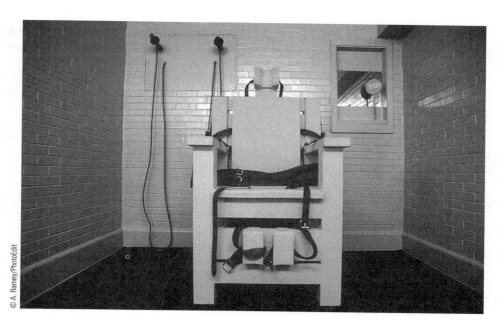

value is that all citizens have the right to publicly provided education. Therefore, public schools are available to everyone in the nation. Taken collectively, these institutional values become an institutional values system.

Many institutional values are in a state of flux or confusion. This happens when large factions of people in the social environment have strongly divergent opinions. For instance, many states are debating whether to institute the death penalty for those who commit murder. Most states do not have a death penalty, reflecting the institutional value that civilized nations do not kill their citizens regardless of their crimes. However, states that adopt the death penalty hold the institutionalized value that death is a fair consequence for murder.

Another example of an institutionalized value being debated is the controversial antiabortion versus prochoice issue. People have extremely strong opinions concerning abortion.

Institutional values affect the structure, function, and composition of communities. For instance, one nationally held institutional value is that all citizens have the right to a free education. However, another institutional value is that each locality should finance its public schools through local taxes. Therefore, the quality of education can vary drastically from the rich suburbs to the poor inner city.

In Figure 1.5, note that the arrows connecting the institutional values systems and the organizational and community systems are directed only one way. This indicates that institutional value systems usually have tremendous impacts on organizational and community systems. However, the latter have little reciprocal impact.

This is not to imply that institutional values cannot be changed. Rather, it reflects that there is no clearly established means of doing so. In a practical manner, SIM emphasizes relationships among client, social worker, and macro systems and more clearly identifies the potential means for change.

The Effects of Institutional Values and Organizational Macro Systems on Clients

Both organizational systems and institutional values systems have impacts on clients. They dictate what resources and services clients deserve or need. If organizational systems and institutional values work against a resource, then that resource will not be provided. For example, it is often very difficult for single mothers receiving public assistance to find affordable and adequate day care for their children while they participate in job training programs or look for jobs. Providing these mothers with good day care has not been an institutional value. This does not

mean that mothers do not need this resource or that they should not have it. It simply means that this particular resource has not been considered valuable enough to be offered by the institutional powers-that-be.

The Social Worker System

We now come to the most critical aspect of the model, namely, how you as a social work practitioner fit in. As a worker you will probably have direct dealings with micro and mezzo systems. You may be in the position of coordinating numerous resources on behalf of your client systems. You also, however, need to be constantly aware of the impacts macro systems have on your clients.

Figure 1.5 illustrates both the social worker system's relationships with the client system and with macro systems. Client and social worker systems have reciprocal interactions, shown by the two-way arrow. They communicate and work together to solve the client's problems and meet the client's needs.

Figure 1.5 also depicts how you as the social worker may work with a client system in changing macro systems, including organizations and communities, to get what clients need. The collaborative effort between client and social worker systems is emphasized by the combined arrows leading from both of these to the organizational and community systems circles. Clients certainly can and have initiated and implemented macro system changes to gain rights and improve services by themselves. However, the perspective employed here stresses how social workers can use their skills and expertise to work with clients in pursuit of this process.

The Social Worker and Organizational Systems: Promotion of Social and Economic Justice. Concerning organizational systems, two issues are relevant. First, the organizational system in need of change may be your own organization or it may be another macro system involved with the client. The methods you use to seek change probably will differ significantly in each case.

Second, you probably will be employed by an organization. Therefore, you must be aware of its policies and restrictions. You will have to make decisions regarding the extent to which you must comply with these policies in order to perform and keep your job. You may well find yourself in the position of "bucking the system," that is, confronting it and seeking some kind of change.

The Social Worker and Community Systems: Promotion of Social and Economic Justice. When you as a social worker assess a client's involvement with the community system, you may determine that there is a need for improvement or change. For instance, you may act as a catalyst for community development. Therefore, you might work to improve linkages among community residents so that they can work together more effectively; connect people with existing resources; and develop new resources, or expand already existing ones, to meet residents' emerging needs (Homan, 1999).

The intent here is not to teach practice skills but to make you aware of the types of skills you will need in practice. The first step in the planned change or problem-solving process is to teach you how to assess the environmental impacts on any client system. Because of macro systems' potent effects on clients, examining the macro aspects of a situation is vitally important.

The Impacts of Organizations

Organizations represent one category of macro systems that have major impacts on human behavior. Our focus is on organizations that provide social services. Social services include the work that social work practitioners and other helping professionals perform for: improving people's physical and mental health, promoting self-determination and independence, fortifying family bonds, enhancing quality of life, and seeking the effective functioning of individuals, families, groups, and communities. One type of social services organization frequently referred to in the social work field is the *social agency.* This is an organization providing social services overseen by a board of directors and usually staffed by various personnel including social workers, members of other professions, paraprofessionals, and clerical staff (Barker, 1999). The terms "social services," "human services," and sometimes "social welfare" are often used interchangeably when referring to organizations, agencies, and agency personnel.

Organizations are particularly important to you for two reasons. First, most likely you will be employed by one. Your organization's policies, goals, and restrictions will directly affect what work you can and cannot do with clients. The second reason for their significance is that often the organization, not the client, may be the source of the problem. (We will discuss this later in greater depth.) Therefore, you will need to evaluate for yourself how well your own organization is functioning in order to do your work effectively.

To assess the effectiveness of any organization, you need to understand some basic organizational concepts. Here we will define the concept of organization, discuss a few of the primary organizational theories, and explain how organizations provide or fail to provide services and resources to clients.

What Are Organizations?

Since organizations are systems, all of the systems concepts discussed earlier apply to them. Organizations are in constant interaction with other systems in the environment. Some systems provide organizations with resources (for example, public funds, fees, or grants). Other systems are their clients who receive their services and output resources.

Organizations are "(1) social entities that (2) are goal directed, (3) are designed as deliberately structured and coordinated activity systems, and (4) are linked to the external environment" (Daft, 2001, p. 12). Four elements stand out in this definition.

First, organizations are *social entities.* That is, organizations are made up of people, with all their strengths and failings. Organizations dictate how people should behave and what responsibilities employees must assume as they do their jobs. Individuals bring to their jobs their own values and personalities affecting how they behave in the organizational environment.

Second, organizations are *goal-directed.* They exist for some specified purpose. An organization specializing in stock brokering exists to help clients develop financial packages that make money. Social service organizations exist to provide services and resources to help people with designated needs. An organization must clearly define its goals so that workers can evaluate the extent to which it achieves these goals.

The third key concept in the definition is that organizations are *deliberately structured and coordinated activity systems.* Activity systems are clusters of work activities performed by designated units within an organization. Such systems are guided by the practical application of knowledge to achieve desired ends. Organizations coordinate the functioning of various activity systems to enhance efficiency in attaining desired goals. They have structures that include policies for how the organization should be run, hierarchies of how personnel are supervised and by whom, and different units working in various ways to help the organization function.

A homeless shelter in a large city is an example of an activity system. Staff include intake workers, care supervisors, vocational counselors, social workers, administrative staff, and support staff. They work together to provide short-term emergency shelter for people in need and transitional help toward independence. People receive food, shelter, showers, and clothing on an emergency basis; transitional services aim "to help people reintegrate into the community" by providing "life-skills training classes, housing search assistance, and counseling" (Johnson, 1995, p. 1342). The shelter has an established policy manual concerning staff and client procedures to keep things running smoothly. There is a clear delineation regarding various staffpersons' responsibilities and who reports to whom in the supervisory hierarchy.

The forth concept inherent in the definition of organizations is *linkage to the external environment*. Thus, an organization is in constant interaction with other systems in the social environment, including individuals, groups, other organizations, and communities. Agencies providing social services interact dynamically with clients, funding sources, legislative and regulatory agencies, politicians, community leaders, and other social service agencies.

Organizational Theories

In order to work within organizations, to evaluate them, and sometimes to change them, it is helpful to understand the major theories regarding their operation. Such a perspective is also useful in determining the kinds of organizational structures that are most effective in specific client situations.

Organizational theories have been borrowed from the business and management fields. Businesses and social service organizations have many things in common. Both need resources (money) to operate. Both produce products via some kind of process. A business might manufacture the product lawn mowers; a social services organization might produce the product improved family functioning.

Many organizational theories contradict each other. This is probably because there is such a vast range of organizational structures, functions, and goals. Here we will briefly introduce five theoretical perspectives regarding how organizations should be run. These include classical scientific management theories, human relations theories, structuralist models, systems theories (Sarri, 1987, pp. 30–32), and contingency theories (Daft, 2001). Chapter 12 explores a broader range of theories in much greater detail.

Classical Scientific Management Theories. Classical scientific management theories emphasize that a formal structure and rigid organizational network of employees is most important in having an organization run well and achieve its goals (Holland & Petchers, 1987; Sarri, 1987). Each employee holds a clearly defined job and is told exactly how that job should be accomplished. These

theories call for minimal independent functioning on the part of employees (Netting, Kettner, & McMurtry, 1993). Supervisors closely monitor employees' work. Efficiency is important. How people feel about their jobs is insignificant. Nor do employees have input regarding how organizational goals can best be reached.

Traditional bureaucracies demonstrate the application of classical scientific management theories. Bureaucracies emphasize highly specialized units that perform clearly specified job tasks, minimal ability on the part of employees to make independent judgments and decisions, and numerous specific rules to maintain control. The Social Security Administration, an urban county's department of social services, and the Pentagon are examples.

Human Relations Theories. Human relations theories emphasize "the role of the informal, psychosocial components of organizational functioning" (Holland & Petchers, 1987, p. 206). In this view, satisfied, happy employees will be the most productive. Important concepts include "employee morale and productivity; . . . satisfaction, motivation, and leadership; and . . . the dynamics of small-group behavior" (Sarri, 1987, p. 31). Organizational leaders strive to enhance their workers' morale.

The immediate work group (mezzo system) is critical. Employees are encouraged to work cooperatively and participate in group decision making. Employers encourage employee input concerning organizational policies and practices.

Structuralist Models. Structuralist models emphasize "both structure and process" in viewing organization (Sarri, 1987, p. 31). Such models focus on both the rational structure of an organization and the more irrational, imperfect behavior of the people involved in that structure. Employee satisfaction is not considered as important; however, employees' productivity is. Therefore, there is an emphasis on decision making. Decisions are made carefully, and all variables are taken into consideration in order to optimize worker productivity.

Systems Theories. Systems theories involve the systems concepts we have already discussed. A systems approach "construes the organization as a social system with interrelated parts, or subsystems, functioning in interaction and equilibrium with one another. It thinks of the organization as an adaptive whole rather than as a structure that is solely rational-legal" (Holland & Petchers, 1987, p. 207). In some ways, systems theories "attempt to synthesize structuralist and human relations perspectives" (Sarri, 1987, p. 32). Systems theories generally take other theories into account to reach a more flexible, comprehensive means of viewing organizations.

Systems theories emphasize the interactions of the various subsystems involved. They also stress the importance of the environment and the impacts of other systems on the organization. Irrational interactions are expected rather than ignored. Systems theories emphasize constant assessment and adjustment.

Contingency Theories. A recent trend in organizational theory development involves contingency theories. Daft (2001) explains:

> ***Contingency*** *means that one thing depends on other things, and for organizations to be effective, there must be a "goodness of fit" between their structure and the conditions in their external environment. What works in one setting may not work in another setting. There is not one best way. Contingency theory means "it depends." [An approach may work or it may not, depending on the unique organizational conditions.] . . . Today almost all organizations operate in highly uncertain environments. Thus, we are involved in a significant period of transition, in which the dominant paradigm of organization theory and design is changing as dramatically as it was changed with the dawning of the Industrial Revolution.* (p. 24)

Evaluation of Theory: Which Organizational Theory Is Best? No one really knows which organizational theory is best. As time passes, these theoretical perspectives rise and fall in popularity. It is beyond the scope of this text to explore organizational theory other than to provide a foundation to help you understand human behavior within the context of macro systems.

Because of its flexibility and the complexities of working with real clients, this text will view organizations primarily from a systems perspective. We've already established that systems theory fits well with social work. However, occasionally, other theories (or ways of perceiving the world) are useful. For instance, classical scientific management theories and structuralist models provide interesting views of bureaucracy.

Here we will describe some common problems encountered by practitioners working within organizations. The concept of goal displacement and its implications for social workers will be discussed.

❦ Viewing Organizations from a Systems Perspective

As social workers, we want to serve our clients as best we can. We want the social service organizations in which we work to be as effective as they can be. We also want other organizations with which our clients have transactions to be as effective as possible. We need to maintain constant awareness of how well social service organizations are serving clients. Therefore, we continuously need to assess to what extent each organization is attaining its goals.

Social service organizations can be compared to other organizations, such as businesses, in a variety of ways. Social service organizations take input (which at its most primitive level is financial), process this input through service provision, and produce some output (namely, results for clients). Figure 1.6 illustrates this process and compares it to that of a business organization. As an example, we will compare social service organizations to a make-believe

Figure 1.6 **Pretendo and FUBAR: Similar Processes of Businesses and Social Service Organizations**

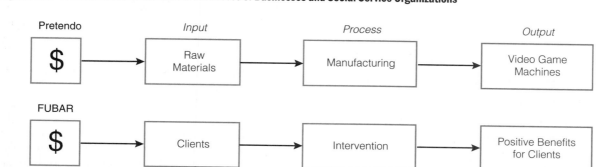

business, involved in manufacturing video games, that we'll call Pretendo. We will call our social services organization Financial Urban Base of Area Resources (FUBAR).

Resource Input

Figure 1.6 shows that both FUBAR and Pretendo begin with inputs. Pretendo uses its financial resources to purchase materials such as metals, wires, and plastic to prepare for the production process. Pretendo gets its funds from sources such as stockholder investments and prior profits from selling Pretendo equipment.

FUBAR, on the other hand, applies its financial resources to clients. Social service organizations differ strikingly from manufacturing-business organizations in that their "raw material" is clients (Holland & Petchers, 1987). FUBAR receives its resources from public tax moneys and a variety of private sources (such as donations, fees, and grants). It then applies these financial resources to some type of helping process.

Process

Both Pretendo and FUBAR process their "raw material." Pretendo sends theirs through a manufacturing production process in which materials are gradually reshaped, blended, and recombined to produce the desired product, Pretendo video games.

FUBAR, on the other hand, uses a completely different process on its "raw material." Instead of a manufacturing process, it provides some type of intervention. This intervention can involve counseling, financial assistance, or any other type of service provision possible in social service organizations.

Output

Both Pretendo and FUBAR produce output (that is, some finished product) at the end of their processes. Pretendo produces new video games ready to be marketed. FUBAR applies its process (intervention) to produce some positive effects on and for clients. Such effects may include improved family relationships, mental health, or financial status.

The Exceptional Problems of Social Service Organizations

A number of problems that do not affect private business plague social service organizations. Most are based on the fact that working with people is infinitely more complicated than working with materials.

As populations continue to expand worldwide, resources continue to shrink. The shrinking of resources means that funding becomes more difficult to obtain. It also means that competition becomes more intense. The result is that organizations producing higher quality products at lower costs requiring less input will be more likely to survive than those that are less effective and efficient. Pretendo will thrive if it produces high quality video games at competitive prices. Likewise, FUBAR will be likely to thrive if it can show that its outcomes on clients are positive and valuable.

Before you as a practitioner can begin to assess the effectiveness of organizations for your clients, you need to understand some of the problems afflicting these organizations. Organizational problems are almost never easy to address and change. Organizational problems include uncertainties in the environment, vague processes, vague goals, and goal displacement.

The Shifting Environment. The environment in which social service organizations strive to exist is constantly in flux. Social forces impact other macro organizations and influence political policies, which, in turn, modify the availability of funding. Thus, Holland & Petchers (1987, p. 208) explain:

> Financial support from public and private sources must be sought, maintained, and protected while community expectations and priorities shift from one problem or need to another. Legal requirements and policies regulating operations undergo modification. Service technologies evolve in new directions, not always in consonance with consumer or public preferences.

Social forces jar social service organizations unpredictably and severely. To survive and effectively meet their goals of helping clients, these organizations must be keenly aware of external influences and their effects. Organizations must be able to react quickly to changing needs and demands.

Vagueness of Process. Interventions performed by a variety of individual practitioners and other staff are difficult to measure and monitor. They are unlike manufacturing machines that punch out slabs of metal which can be measured. Raw materials are predictably uniform. Effectiveness can be evaluated in terms of a machine's accuracy and efficiency (that is, how fast the machine can punch out slabs). Work routines are predictable, repetitive, and relatively easy to monitor and control.

Professional staff in social services organizations vary widely. Clients vary even more. Therefore, social service organizations have multiple, immeasurable, human factors involved in the intervention process. Because people vary drastically more than inanimate materials such as metal slabs, practitioners who work with people must have much more flexibility than metal slab punchers. Workers in organizations need to have some degree of discretion, or ability to make decisions, in working with their clients. This, in turn, makes the monitoring of the intervention process even more difficult.

Vagueness of Goals. Accountability is critically important to social work practitioners today. *Accountability* is a practitioner's responsibility to clients, community, and agency for ethical and effective practice. Individual practitioners and whole agencies are called upon to prove that their performance is productive and valuable. A way to do this is to define specific, measurable goals and monitor the extent to which they are achieved.

Superficially, this sounds simple. However, how can a practitioner prove that a client has been helped? For instance, if you are teaching child management techniques to physically abusive parents, how do you know when you've been successful? When they can pass a written test quizzing them on the specific techniques? Or, when they strike their children only on the hands and rump instead of on the head? Or when they hit their children only once each day instead of a dozen times? Human behavior is difficult to define and measure.

Evaluating the outcomes of an entire organization or even of a program, including goals, effectiveness, and efficiency, is much more difficult than evaluating the outcomes of micro or mezzo interventions. This is due to the increased number of variables involved. In order to evaluate program outcomes, Holland and Petchers (1987) emphasize that, first, "service content must also be made clear, with uniform definitions describing program activities." They continue, "For consequences to be attributed to an activity, it is necessary to state exactly what a client has received from a given treatment or service and to determine whether that content has remained consistent over the course of the intervention" (p. 213). This is not an easy task.

The Pros and Cons of Centralized versus Decentralized Organizations. Organizations can be placed on a continuum to show their degree of centralization. At one end are extremely centralized organizations, run according to classical scientific management theories. Their lines of authority are clearly established, and there is a strict hierarchy of authority. Workers have little discretion. Responsibilities are defined and implemented from above; feedback from below is unwanted.

An example of centralization might be a probation and parole department. Clients for any particular officer in any unit tend to have very similar characteristics. Procedures and treatment plans are relatively uniform in approach. Clients and officers must abide by clearly defined rules and regulations, and officers have little discretion.

On the opposite side of the centralization continuum are extremely decentralized organizations. These organizations contrast sharply with centralized organizations in terms of flexibility. Decentralized organizations provide and encourage greater worker discretion. They often have a wide variety of clients with vastly different problems, issues, and backgrounds. Workers in such organizations need discretion to make plans for viable solutions. For example, a community crisis intervention organization might be extremely decentralized. Clients coming in for help might have problems ranging from depression to illness to job loss to executive-level stress. Workers need a broad range of discretion to address a wide variety of problems.

Goal Displacement

A major problem encountered by workers in organizations involves goal displacement. *Goal displacement* was originally defined as "substitution of a legitimate goal with another goal which the organization was not developed to address, for which resources were not allocated, and which it is not known to serve" (Etzioni, 1964, p. 10). Holland and Petchers (1987) interpret this meaning by stating that "goal displacement often occurs when the means to a goal becomes the goal itself. In recent years, goal displacement has become a serious concern in human service organizations" (p. 208). Goal displacement occurs when an organization continues to function but no longer achieves its goals. A typical scenario in social service organizations occurs when following the organization's rules becomes more important than providing services to clients.

An Example of Goal Displacement. A large county Department of Social Services (previously referred to as the "public welfare department") comes to mind. It is located in the shell of an old department store, with high ceilings and myriad worker cubicles, somewhat resembling a beehive. All outside windows have been sealed with bricks because the administration determined that the building had "heating and ventilation problems." No one really knows what that means. However, everyone in the building knows that the building's interior is isolated from the outside world.

When you enter the main door of the building, it is difficult to figure out where to go for which services even if you are a professional social worker. You probably have to stand in line for fifteen to twenty minutes simply to get the information you need to figure out where to go.

When you finally find the waiting area for the services you need, you have to stand in line again for another twenty minutes or so to get the forms you need to fill out in order to get the services. You then take the twenty pages of complicated forms to fill out and find a seat. The chairs are made of hard plastic. It takes approximately an hour to fill out the forms—assuming you can read English well. You probably do not understand some of the questions, so you leave the spaces blank. You then take the forms up to the desk where they are placed in a pile. You must wait your turn in order to see an intake worker (someone who begins the process to provide services). You may wait two to three hours.

Finally, your name is called and you are instructed to go to cubicle 57 to see Ms. Simpson. You enter the cubicle and find Ms. Simpson sitting at her desk reading your forms. You begin a discussion with her concerning the additional information she needs in order to process your application for services. It seems, she indicates, that a number of critical elements of information are missing. Look at those blanks. She then tells you that you need to get the critical information before you can continue the application process. The critical information is somewhere at home. Well, that's all right, she says. Just go home, get it, and start this whole process over again tomorrow. At least you know where the waiting room is now.

In this example, the organization is supposed to provide services to people in need. However, the complicated process, commonly called "red tape," is more important to organization workers than whether or not clients get needed services.

People's access to resources has a major impact on the options available to them and, in effect, how they behave. Poverty and lack of resources are at the root of many of your clients' problems. Therefore, it is crucial to understand how organizations affect resource provision. Such a background can enable you to identify ways to make changes in systems so that your clients are better served.

For instance, consider the example concerning the county social services department. As a worker in that agency, there are several things you might try to change. You might work with other workers and the administration to shorten the tedious forms. You might also explore ways to get information out to community residents regarding the documentation and information they must bring when applying for services. Simple things like putting up clearly visible signs instructing people where to go when they first enter the building might be helpful. Even advocating for comfortable waiting room chairs would be useful. A wide range of social work roles to make positive change will be discussed later in this chapter and throughout the text.

Systems Theory, Organization, and Goal Displacement. We have established that it is helpful to view social service organizations in ways similar to those used for business and industry. In industry, resources or *inputs* are *processed* by the organizational system that turns out some product or *output*. Essentially the same thing happens in social service organizations. They take resources (input) and, in response to social forces and institutionalized values, apply some process (procedures for providing services) to produce output (actual service provision or some other benefits for clients).

When goal displacement occurs, however, the emphasis is often placed on the *process* rather than the *product*. People in organizational systems begin to think of the rigid process of providing services as the product. The process rather than effective provision of services then becomes the organization's product. Such goal displacement is illustrated in Figure 1.7.

Communities and Human Behavior

We have established that organizational macro systems have major effects on clients. We have also indicated that community macro systems become extremely significant when we try to understand human behavior. Thus, the concept of community is very significant for social workers. We have defined *community* as a group of people who have something in common with each other that links them and distinguishes them from others who are not part of the community. This definition is tremendously broad in terms of whom and what a community can include. Does a community include all the people living on one city block? Or is the community a group of people with common issues, problems, and concerns? For example, there is the social work community and the community of people with physical disabilities. Does the word *community* connote a certain ethnic, cultural, or racial group? How large or small should a community be? Can the United States be considered a community?

Because of the wide range of possible meanings, we will focus here on three major concepts inherent in our

Figure 1.7 The Process of Goal Displacement

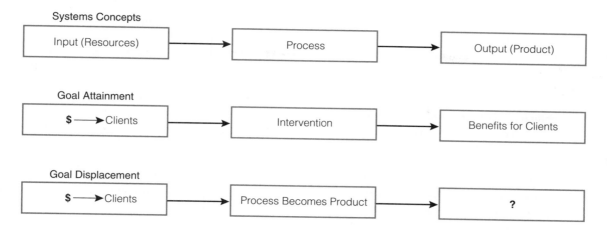

broad definition. First, we have a designated group of people, and we could thus establish a list of the individuals involved in a particular community. Second, this group has something in common. Such commonality may include values, resources, services, interests, or location. Third, because of the community's commonality, individuals interact in some way or have the potential to do so.

From a social work perspective these concepts are very important. A community can be organized so that its citizens can work together and solve their mutual problems, or improve their overall quality of life. Social workers can use their macro practice skills to mobilize citizens within communities in order to accomplish the goals they define for themselves.

Theoretical Perspectives on Communities

Communities vary widely. Think of a mammoth twenty-story, urban, public housing project. In contrast, consider suburban neighborhoods that require each home to be built on a minimum of four acres of land at a minimum cost of $500,000. Now contemplate neighborhoods in New York City where thousands of people work, buy groceries, eat, sleep, and play within a few city blocks of each other. Finally, consider rural farm communities where individual farmers keep livestock and harvest thousands of bushels of grain.

Despite these broad contrasts, we can use a variety of theoretical perspectives to examine communities and gain greater understanding of how they work. Here we will focus on geographically based communities and view them in four ways. These theoretical perspectives include structural, sociopsychological, human ecology, and social

systems (Fellin, 2001a, 2001b; Martinez-Brawley, 1995; Rothman, 1987).

Structural Perspective. Structure refers to how individuals fit into the organized whole. The structural perspective emphasizes how people are linked to their overriding governmental structure through communities. Three dimensions of communities are emphasized.

First, communities are *political entities,* "organized as a province, a city, a township, a neighborhood, and so on" (Martinez-Brawley, 1995, p. 539). Local governments exert control over their citizens, state or provincial governments over local, and national over all units below. As political entities, communities "carry out many political and social functions and mediate between the state as a central power and the individual" (Martinez-Brawley, 1995, p. 539).

The second dimension related to the political is *power.* As just stated, the structural perspective focuses on how larger units exert power and control over their smaller units or subsystems. The structural perspective on communities implies "an uneven distribution of influence, economic resources, status, or decision-making prerogatives within the community" (Rothman, 1987, p. 309). As communities are subsystems of larger governmental units having greater amounts of power in varying degrees, so citizens as subsystems of communities have unequal power. Wealthier citizens who are bank presidents, business CEOs (chief executive officers), or physicians likely wield greater power and influence over what happens in a community than do poor, unemployed citizens. Similarly, elected officials have greater power than citizens not holding office.

The third dimension inherent in the structural approach involves *geographical organization* of communities. Is the population concentrated in some areas, or more evenly distributed throughout? Where are business and residential areas located? How are streets and highways plotted? What are the boundaries that distinguish one community from another?

Sociopsychological Perspective. A sociopsychological perspective of a community involves how its members feel about themselves and interact with one another (Martinez-Brawley, 1995). People's feelings about their relationship to and with their community are paramount. To what extent do residents feel that they are part of their community? Do they interact frequently with neighbors, or do they feel isolated and alone? Do they feel that they fit in? Do they suffer racial or other discrimination, enhancing alienation from the community? How safe do they feel? Do they perceive themselves as victims of discrimination, crimes, and violence, or do they consider themselves productive members of a community who are in control of their environment?

An example comes to mind that can be viewed from a sociopsychological perspective. Fabian, age 42, lived in a modest home on Main Street in Butterbrickle, a small midwestern village at the edge of a large city. He had cerebral palsy, a disability resulting from damage to the brain at birth and manifested by muscular incoordination and speech disturbances. As his mobility was seriously restricted, he had made his home readily accessible for his wheelchair. He was a bright, personable, assertive individual who comfortably felt an integral part of his community. From a sociopsychological perspective, he experienced "significance and security . . . enhanced by familiarity with the environment, a sense of being known . . . and the affection and support of friends and neighbors" (Martinez-Brawley, 1995, p. 540).

Fabian's disability, limited mobility, and special bathroom needs made it difficult for him to find employment, especially in tiny Butterbrickle. Thus, he was dependent on his SSI (Supplemental Security Income) payments, which were adequate to meet his monthly house payments and basic living expenses but left little for recreation or amenities. He loved to putter in his small garden and became quite an effective gardener. Each summer neighbors praised the beauty, color, and lushness of his flowers. Suddenly, Fabian came up with an idea: What about turning his hobby into a profitable business? Why not sell his flowers and significantly enhance his meager income? "Fabian's Fabulous Flowers" became a reality as he put up a sign and arranged plank shelves on sawhorses in his front yard, covering them with dozens of potted plants. Many customers responded to the dazzling display, and Fabian found himself making a small supplemental income.

However, his immediate neighbors were enraged that Fabian had turned a residential plot into commercial property that devalued the worth of their own properties and intensified parking congestion. Instead of applauding his flowers, neighbors demanded Fabian stop his commercial enterprise immediately. He refused. As a result, the neighbors complained to the village administrator that this "continuous yard sale" violated zoning regulations. The administrator subsequently contacted Fabian and told him to terminate his business unless he received a special permit.

Fabian decided to advocate for himself, submitted the necessary information to the village board of appeals for such a permit, and requested the required hearing. All neighbors were notified and attended the event. After many questions and much fiery debate, the board ultimately decided to grant Fabian his special permit. One of their considerations in making this decision was Fabian's difficulty in finding work elsewhere because of his special physical needs.

Fabian's neighbors remained irate, stopped speaking to him, and ignored his existence. He had increased his economic status and enhanced his independence. However, from a sociopsychological perspective, his social acceptance and standing in his immediate community was strikingly diminished. He no longer felt part of the "we" along with his community neighbors.

Human Ecology Perspective. A human ecology perspective of a community "focuses on the relationship of populations to their environment, especially in regard to spacial organization—that is, how people and services are distributed. Emphasis is placed on the 'division of labor' within a community—types of occupational groups, and how a structure of occupational stratification emerges through an interdependence within and between communities" (Fellin, 2001b, p. 119). The ecological approach considers how the environment affects human development, interaction, and quality of life.

This view emphasizes both how population is distributed within a geographical area and how individuals interact with others in their social environment. Part of this interaction involves access to resources. In any community, some population groups inevitably will have greater access than others. We discussed some ecological concepts earlier in the chapter. Additional ecological concepts that apply to community macro systems include *competition, segregation,* and *integration* (Fellin, 2001b, p. 119).

Competition concerns how community members vie for "the use of land . . . [and] seek an 'advantage of place' for commercial, industrial, institutional, and residential purposes" (Fellin, 2001b, p. 119). Each community has only so much space and so many resources available. People therefore compete to attain their share, or at least enough to survive. As we know, huge inequities exist in terms of individuals' resources. Some may be rich and powerful, while others are bereft and homeless.

Segregation is the detachment or isolation of some group having certain common characteristics (such as race, ethnicity, or religion) through social pressure, restrictive laws, or personal choice. *Integration,* on the other hand, refers to the process of bringing together and blending a range of groups (including people of different races and ethnic backgrounds) into a unified, functional whole.

Such ecological concepts as competition, segregation, and integration can help you as a social worker analyze a community in terms of its fairness and supportiveness to all of its members. Fellin (2001b) explains that "membership in these groups affects the quality of life of people in positive and negative ways. People benefit or suffer as a result of their social positions within communities, through differential life chances, employment opportunities, access to social and material resources, and social relationships" (p. 121).

Viewing communities from a human ecology perspective helps you to focus on the inequities and problems faced by people who have less resources (in effect, less energy) than others in the community. It provides a useful assessment mechanism for understanding why people act as they do within the context of the larger community macro system. An example concerns the life circumstances and reactions of people brought up in two families from diverse backgrounds within the same metropolitan community. Fred and Ed were brothers, both in their 30s. They grew up in the rural outskirts of the Milwaukee area. Both benefited from a good school system, a middle-class upbringing with adequate financial support, and a college education. Both worked full time and could afford to purchase a home, make house and car payments on time, and even put a little away in savings.

Ed was married to Ursula, 23, who had a younger brother Doug, 19. Ursula and Doug grew up in a single-parent home in a poor urban neighborhood on the south side of Milwaukee. Resources were scarce. Their schools, having access to few resources, were unable to provide them with the academic skills necessary to pursue a college education successfully. Doug dropped out of high

school as soon as he could at the age of 16. Ursula finished high school. Both worked at fast-food establishments earning minimum wage. Ursula's economic state improved considerably when she married Ed. Doug lived in a one-room apartment where he shared a bathroom with eight other men who lived on the same floor.

In their early years, Fred and Ed were separated from Ursula and Doug by social class. *Social class* "refers to inequalities among people measured in such terms as socioeconomic status and life-style" (Fellin, 2001b, p. 121). In turn, indicators of social class usually include job type, educational level, amount of income, and typical manner of living. After her marriage, Ursula was integrated into a higher social class.

A family gathering at Fred's brought Ed, Ursula, Doug, and an array of other relatives and in-laws together. This event became the interface where the individuals met. After several hours of eating and drinking, Doug began to reveal his anger. He raged about how he never had the chances that Fred and Ed had, and how he never would. Ed and Ursula tried to calm Doug down. Nothing seemed to work. Finally, Doug pounded on the hood of Fred's 1999 red Camaro, cursing and swearing. Then he stomped over to his decrepit '91 Dodge Omni and drove off before his concerned sister and brother-in-law could stop him.

The point of this story is that access to resources within a community can have profound impacts on human behavior. Communities and people's status within them are critically significant to their quality of life. Some might think that Doug should have tried to improve his position in life. How difficult would it be for Doug to achieve the lifestyle enjoyed by Fred and Ed? How likely was it that Doug could attain a quality of life similar to that of his brother-in-law?

As a postscript to this story, Doug developed a drinking problem. He eventually got into a violent fight with another man at a bar who shot him in the kneecap. Doug consequently had a permanent partial disability that seriously curtailed his potential to maintain most employment available at minimum wage. Fred had the dents in his car repaired for about $1,500, of which he had to pay the $500 deductible on his collision insurance. Ed and Ursula thereafter maintained only minimal contact with Doug, fearing his violent eruptions.

As a social worker, you have the responsibility to examine the community macro environment in which your clients reside. Certainly, you are concerned about how specific clients function as individuals. However, the effects of the environment in which they live cannot be ignored. Assessment of human behavior within the community context is necessary to propose solutions that address the larger issues affecting a broad range of clients. A subsequent section will explain some specific goals you as a practitioner may develop within community environments.

Social Systems Perspective. The social systems perspective emphasizes analyzing how the various social subsystems within the community interact with each other. It helps you view clients in the context of the larger community system. Homan (1999) comments on how systems theory applies to communities:

> *Each organism—a city, a neighborhood, an individual—is a system that requires ongoing input in the form of nutrients and other energy. The system takes in energy to grow, produce, and sustain life and to maintain its equilibrium. As the system processes the input it receives, this energy is converted to productive output, which is expressed in activity (such as work), in seeking new input [such as financial investments, business development, or home building and renovation], or in discarding used input as waste. (pp. 28–29)*

A strength of the systems perspective on communities is the emphasis on interconnections. Primary social units or subsystems within communities include "formal organizations, such as businesses, governmental units, churches, schools, health care organizations, and social welfare agencies" in addition to informal subsystems such as families and social groups (Fellin, 1995a, p. 32). The dynamic interaction between clients and other community subsystems is an important focus of social work assessment. Each subsystem is integrally involved with other subsystems in the community. Family members work in organizations and businesses, attend school, socialize with friends, work out at health clubs, receive health and dental care, and pursue myriad activities within their community. Homan (1999) reflects:

> *In healthy communities members are able to meet their needs sufficiently well that energy can be directed beyond matters of basic survival to those of personal and community development. Healthy communities provide ways for members not only to survive but to grow; not only to receive but to contribute. (p. 30)*

For social workers, the community context can be the focus of attention. How does the community affect the client? Is the client receiving the resources (input) she needs for optimum health and well-being? Is affordable housing adequate to meet client's needs? Are jobs available that correspond with client's skills? Is the community growing and thriving, or is it shriveling and dying? Are

adequate resources available in the forms of social services and health care? Answers to these questions can provide clues about what you can do to help clients. Working with community subsystems to provide needed services and advocating for resources when services are inadequate are fundamental dimensions of social work.

Highlight 1.3 summarizes the three models discussed below.

Models of Community

A variety of approaches have been developed for community practitioners to bring about community change. Rothman (2001) has categorized them into three models: *locality development, social planning,* and *social action.* These models are "ideal types." Actual approaches to community change have tendencies or emphases that categorize them in one of the three models; yet most approaches also have components characteristic of one or both of the other models. Advocates of the social planning model, for example, may at times use community change techniques (such as wide discussion and participation by a variety of groups) that are characteristic of the other two models. At this point we will not attempt to deal with the mixed forms, but for analytical purposes will instead view the three models as "pure" forms.

Locality Development Model. The locality development model (also called community development) asserts that community change can best be brought about through broad participation of a wide spectrum of people at the local community level. The model seeks to involve a broad cross-section of people (including the disadvantaged and the power structure) in identifying and solving their problems. Some themes emphasized in this model are democratic procedures, a consensus approach, voluntary cooperation, development of indigenous leadership, and self-help.

The roles of the community practitioner in this approach include: enabler, catalyst, coordinator, and teacher of problem-solving skills and ethical values. The approach assumes that conflicts that arise between various interest groups can be creatively and constructively handled. It encourages people to express their differences but assumes people will put aside their self-interests in order to further the interests of their community. The basic theme of this approach is, "Together we can figure out what to do and then do it." The approach seeks to use discussion and communication between different factions to reach consensus about the problems to focus on and the strategies to resolve these problems. A few examples of locality

Highlight 1.3

Characteristics of Three Models of Community Change

Characteristic	Locality Development	Social Planning	Social Action
1. Goals	Self-help; improve community living; emphasis on process goals.	Use problem-solving approach to resolve community problems; emphasis on task goals.	Shift power relationships and resources to an oppressed group; create basic institutional change, emphasize task and process goals.
2. Assumptions concerning community	Everyone wants community living to improve and is willing to contribute to that improvement.	Social problems in the community can be resolved through the efforts of planning experts.	The community has a power structure and one or more oppressed groups, so social injustice is a major problem.
3. Basic change strategy	Broad cross-section of people involved in identifying and solving problems.	Experts using fact-gathering and problem-solving approach.	Members of oppressed groups organize to take action against the power structure—i.e., the enemy.
4. Characteristic change tactics and techniques	Consensus: communication among community groups and interests; group discussion.	Consensus or conflict.	Conflict or contest: confrontation, direct action, negotiation.
5. Practitioner roles	Catalyst; facilitator; coordinator; teacher of problem-solving skills.	Expert planner, fact gatherer; analyst; program developer; and implementer.	Activist; advocate agitator; broker; negotiator; partisan.
6. Views of power structure	Members of power structure are collaborators in a common venture.	Power structure is employers and sponsors.	Power structure is external target of action, oppressors to be coerced or overturned.
7. Views of client population	Citizens.	Consumers.	Victims.
8. Views of client role	Participant in a problem-solving process.	Consumer or recipient.	Employer or constituent.

development efforts include neighborhood work programs conducted by community-based agencies; Volunteers in Service to America; village-level work in some overseas community development programs, including the Peace Corps; and a variety of activities performed by self-help groups. A case example of the locality development model is the following.

Robert McKearn, a social worker for a juvenile probation department, noticed that an increasing number of school-age children were being referred to his office by the police department, school system, and parents from a small city of 11,000 people in the county served by his agency. The charges included status offenses (such as truancy from school) and delinquent offenses (such as shoplifting and burglary). Mr. McKearn noted that most of these children were from single-parent families.

Mr. McKearn contacted the community mental health center, the self-help organization Parents Without Partners, the pupil services department of the public school system, the county social services department, some members of the clergy, and the community mental health center in the area. Nearly everyone he contacted saw an emerging need to better serve children in single-parent families. The pupil services department mentioned that such children were performing less well academically in school and tended to display more serious disciplinary problems.

Mr. McKearn arranged a meeting of representatives from the groups and organizations that were contacted.

At the initial meeting a number of concerns were expressed about the problematic behaviors being displayed by children who had single parents. The school system considered these children to be "at risk" for higher rates of truancy, dropping out of school, delinquent activities, suicide, emotional problems, and unwanted pregnancies. Although a number of problems were identified, no one at this initial meeting was able to suggest a viable strategy to better serve single parents and their children. The community was undergoing an economic recession; therefore, funds were unavailable for an expensive new program.

Three more meetings were held. At the first two a number of suggestions for providing services were discussed, but all were viewed as either too expensive or impractical. At the fourth meeting of the group, a single parent representing Parents Without Partners mentioned that she was aware that Big Brothers and Big Sisters programs in some communities were of substantial benefit to children who were raised in single-parent families. This idea seemed to energize the group. Suggestions began to "piggy back." The group, however, determined that funds were unavailable to hire staff to run a Big Brothers and Big Sisters program. However, Rhona Quinn, a social worker in the pupil services department, noted that she was willing to identify at-risk younger children in single-parent families and that she would be willing to supervise qualified volunteers in a "Big Buddy" program.

Mr. McKearn mentioned that he was currently supervising a student in an undergraduate field placement for an accredited social work program from a college in a nearby community. He noted that perhaps arrangements could be made for undergraduate social work students to be "big buddies" for their required volunteer experience. Rhona Quinn said she would approve of the suggestion if she could have the freedom to screen interested applicants for "big buddies." Arrangements were made over the next two months for social work students to be "big buddies" for at-risk younger children from single-parent families. After a two-year experimental period, the school system found the program sufficiently successful that it assigned Ms. Quinn half-time to supervise the program, which included selecting at-risk children, screening volunteer applicants, matching children with "big buddies," monitoring the progress of each matched pair, and conducting follow-up to ascertain the outcome of each pairing.

In summary, locality development focuses on communities helping themselves. It stresses participation by as many community residents a possible who work together to solve problems and achieve mutually beneficial goals. Social workers tend to serve as catalysts, facilitators, coordinators, and teachers of problem-solving skills.

Social Planning Model. The second model, the social planning approach, emphasizes a technical process of problem solving. The approach assumes that community change in a complex industrial environment requires highly trained and skilled planners who can guide complex change processes. The role of the expert is stressed in this approach. The expert or planner is generally employed by a segment of the power structure, such as area planning agency, city or county planning department, mental health center, United Way board, or Community Welfare Council. There is a tendency for the planner to serve the interests of the power structure that employs him or her. Building community capacity or facilitating radical social change is generally not an emphasis in this approach.

The planner's roles in this approach include gathering facts, analyzing data, and serving as program designer, implementer, and facilitator. Community participation may vary from little to substantial, depending on the community's attitudes toward the problems being addressed. For example, an effort to design and obtain funding for a community center for the elderly may or may not result in substantial involvement by interested community groups, depending on the politics surrounding such a center. Much of the focus of the social planning approach is on identifying needs and on arranging and delivering goods and services to people who need them. The change focus of this approach is, "Let's get the facts and take the next rational steps." A case example of the social planning model is the following.

The mayor and city council of a medium-sized midwestern city became increasingly concerned about the deterioration of community living that was occurring in the northeast area of the city. The mayor and city council passed a resolution directing the City Planning Department to develop an approach to combat a variety of social ills (including rising rates of crime, racial conflict, and a lack of recreational resources for children and adults) in this section of the city. The planning department assigned Jose Cruz (an MSW social worker with eleven years of social planning experience) to develop a proposal to improve the community.

Mr. Cruz first contacted and introduced himself to community leaders in this neighborhood: city aldermen, county board supervisors, members of the clergy, administrators of community service agencies, and business leaders. He then arranged and led five focus groups in this neighborhood with these community leaders. (Focus groups provide one method for gathering data. They typically include six to twelve members who meet to discuss and brainstorm about an issue and are usually led by a moderator who keeps the group on task.) Mr. Cruz's first focal topic was, "What do you see as the major problems in this community?" Common responses were a deteriorating community, high rates of crime, lack of community resources, racial conflict, and lack of a sense of community among the residents. Mr. Cruz also led several focus groups of citizens in the community who were invited to the meetings by members of the clergy in the neighborhood. Responses of the citizens were similar to those identified by community leaders.

Once the major concerns were identified, Mr. Cruz invited those who attended the first focus groups to attend one of a second set of focus groups. At these he asked, "Given the fact that this neighborhood is experiencing high rates of crime, racial conflict, single-parent families, lack of recreational resources for children and adults, and a lack of community pride, what can we do to combat these problems?" A number of focus group members suggested building a neighborhood center in a neighborhood park to provide a variety of cultural, recreational, social, and educational programs.

Mr. Cruz then urged interested community leaders and citizens to form a Neighborhood Center Planning Committee. Thirty-three community residents agreed to be on this committee. Mr. Cruz worked with the committee to prepare an architectural design for the Center. This committee, with Mr. Cruz's assistance, then prepared a budget to build and operate the Center, with funding from a variety of sources—federal funding, city funding, neighborhood fundraising, and a contribution from the United Way. Mr. Cruz and the Neighborhood Center Planning Committee then presented the proposal to the City Planning Department, which rapidly approved it. The proposal was then presented to the mayor and the city council, who deliberated about it for fourteen months but eventually approved it. Groundbreaking for the Center will soon begin.

In summary, social planning involves the use of experts to assist communities in solving problems. Such experts gather facts and apply skills to propose and implement solutions that benefit community residents. Social work roles in social planning include expert planner, fact gatherer, program developer, and implementor.

Social Action Model. The third model, the social action approach, assumes there is a disadvantaged (often oppressed) segment of the population that needs to be organized, perhaps in alliance with others, in order to pressure the power structure for increased resources or for treatment more in accordance with democracy or social justice. Social action approaches at times seek basic changes in major institutions or seek changes in basic policies of formal organizations. Such approaches often seek redistribution of power and resources. Whereas locality developers envision a unified community, social action advocates see the power structure as the opposition—the target of action. Perhaps the best-known social activist was Saul Alinsky (1972) who ad-

vised, "Pick the target, freeze it, personalize it, and polarize it" (p. 130).

The roles of the community practitioner is this approach include advocate, agitator, activist, partisan, broker, and negotiator. Tactics used in social action projects include protests, boycotts, confrontation, and negotiation. The change strategy is one of "Let's organize to overpower our oppressor" (Alinsky, 1969, p. 72). The client population is viewed as being "victims" of the oppressive power structure. Examples of the social action approach include boycotts during the civil rights movement during the 1960s, strikes by unions, protests by antiabortion groups, and protests by African American and Native American groups.

The social action model is not widely used by social workers at present. Many workers find that being involved in social action activities may lead their employing agencies to penalize them with unpleasant work assignments, low merit increases, and denial of promotions. Many agencies will accept minor and moderate changes in their service delivery systems but are threatened by the prospect of radical changes that are often advocated by the social action approach.

Saul Alinsky (1972, pp. 145–146) provides the following example of a creative social action effort:

> I was lecturing at a college run by a very conservative, almost fundamentalist Protestant denomination. Afterward some of the students came to my motel to talk to me. Their problem was that they couldn't have any fun on campus. They weren't permitted to dance or smoke or have a can of beer. I had been talking about the strategy of effecting change in a society and they wanted to know what tactics they could use to change their situation. I reminded them that a tactic is doing what you can with what you've got. "Now, what have you got?" I asked. "What do they permit you to do?" "Practically nothing," they said, "except—you know—we can chew gum." I said, "Fine. Gum becomes the weapon. You get 200 or 300 students to get two packs of gum each, which is quite a wad. Then you have them drop it on the campus walks. This will cause absolute chaos. Why, with 500 wads of gum I could paralyze Chicago, stop all the traffic in the Loop." They looked at me as though I was some kind of nut. But about two weeks later I got an ecstatic letter saying. "It worked! It worked! Now we can do just about anything so long as we don't chew gum."

Spotlight 1.2 focuses on the efforts of Hispanic women in community development and social action.

In summary, social action involves pressuring the power structure to provide resources or improve the treatment of oppressed populations who are victims. In the

Spotlight on Diversity 1.2		Hispanic Women, Community Development, and Social Action

Historically, Hispanic people have frequently been involved in community development and social action (Weil & Gamble, 1995). For example, consider La Raza Unida, a "political movement and party, comprising mostly Chicano people and others of Spanish-speaking heritage, that advocates for policies and candidates favorable to the needs of Hispanic people" (Barker, 1999, p. 269; Green, 1999). A range of Hispanic organizations have worked to improve political, economic, and social conditions in numerous development and action projects (Weil & Gamble, 1995).

A Brief Note about Terms
It is important to clarify some of the terms used when referring to Hispanic people. To begin with, Longres (1995) reflects upon the term *Hispanic:* "Hispanics have in common a historical connection with Spain and the Spanish language, but this connection is filtered through the proud heritage of separate heterogeneous nations. It is only as people from these groups have become part of the United States that the need has arisen for a general term to describe them; as such we may be witnessing the emergence of a new ethnic group unique to the United States" (p. 1214).

However, the correct term to use when referring to people of Spanish origin is debatable (Longres, 1995). The terms *Hispanic* and *Latino* are often considered to be interchangeable (Barker, 1999; Longres, 1995). Castex (1994) suggests that the term *Hispanic/Latino* be used (p. 288). The U.S. government defines *Hispanic* people as "Spanish-origin," "Spanish-speaking," or "Spanish-surnamed" (Longres, 1995, p. 1214). It is important to note that the term *Hispanic* often describes a variety of groups originating in very different places. These include people from Mexico, who are often referred to as "Mexican American" or "Chicano." Spanish-speaking people from Puerto Rico often prefer to be known as "Puerto Rican," "Newyorican," "Boricua," or "Borinqueno." People from Cuba, Nicaragua, El Salvador, Peru, and Chile are other groups who might be included under the Hispanic umbrella.

An example of the complexity of this issue comes to mind: A social worker who identified herself as Hispanic was actively involved in advocacy on behalf of Hispanic people in general and poor women in particular. She was interested in joining an organization that advocated for the rights of Hispanics, called "The Chicano Initiative" (CI). Originally from Argentina, she expressed serious concern regarding her membership in a Chicano organization because she was not of Mexican descent. Members of the organization, however, valued her interest, input, and efforts. They indicated that their intent was to involve a broad-based membership of people who originated from countries with a Spanish heritage. The members welcomed all people, regardless of their origins, who were interested in CI's cause. The social worker joined the organization and became quite a "gangbuster" in getting things done.

As a social worker you need to keep in mind both ethnic status issues and individual needs (Castex, 1994, p. 290). With what ethnic group does your client identify? How might you address your client within the parameters of his or her culture, being sensitive to individual differences? What might you learn from your client about his or her ethnic heritage and cultural expectations of you?

Hispanic Women's Accomplishments in Communities
Lazzari, Ford, and Haughey (1996) studied "the contributions of twenty-one Hispanic women who were identified as being active in the community" (p. 197). The women used a variety of terms to describe themselves, including Chicana, Hispanic, Latina, Spanish American, Mexicana, Mexican, Mestiza, and Peruvian. They ranged in age from the 20s to the 50s. Nineteen were bilingual, and the remaining two spoke only English but expressed a desire to learn Spanish. All were either employed in, or served as volunteers for, social service agencies. Services focused on a wide range of fields including "education; health care; local government and law enforcement; county social services; grassroots community organizations; and services for senior citizens, people with disabilities, and people who abuse substances" (p. 199).

The study's participants felt strongly about actually being able to make a difference in the communities they served. They felt they made strides in combating social "oppression (racism, sexism, and discrimination)" and enhancing "the appreciation of diversity" (for example,

---

pursuit of social justice, the power structure is viewed as the adversary so conflict, confrontation, and direct action is often used. Social workers pursuing social action often serve as advocates, activists, agitators, brokers, and negotiators.

❧ Social Worker System Roles

Understanding the roles used in practice helps set the stage for skill acquisition. Roles are the expected behaviors and professional functions considered important for social workers. They help tie knowledge to practice.

The following sections describe some of the roles workers use at various levels of practice. Some roles are more useful in a macro system context; others relate primarily to micro or mezzo systems. Many can be applied at all three levels of generalist practice. Keep in mind that for any particular intervention, a worker may assume a number of roles, often at the same time. Generalist practitioners need to be flexible and capable of working with multiple systems.

Roles especially useful for macro system intervention include: *enabler, mediator, broker, integrator/coordinator, manager, educator, analyst/evaluator, facilitator, initiator, negotiator,*

identifying the fact that certain diverse groups had insufficient access both to resources and to important decision-making roles in government and social agencies) (p. 200).

Hispanic women in the study identified four major factors that nurtured and upheld them during their community work. The first factor was *"seeing the need."* As one participant stated: "I see a big, big need. . . . I see a lot of kids that are really losing who they are, and so [there is] all this turmoil and then hate. It just seems to me [that] they're going through so many more struggles than I did. . . . I guess that [is what] keeps me really involved" (p. 201).

A second factor that supported the women's community endeavors was *"feeling personal satisfaction"* (p. 210). A study participant stated: "I think [of] the changes that I've seen . . . people are more open, discrimination is not as bad . . . . What a different life my two grandchildren are having in school. . . . So, I see those changes, and that makes me happy" (p. 201).

The third factor assisting in the community change process involved *obtaining help and support from other people.* It was important to receive support from a number of sources including family, friends, and other women who believed in their efforts.

The fourth supportive factor involved a cluster of *personal beliefs and characteristics* that participants felt helped them in accomplishing their goals. Such beliefs included: having a powerful feeling of responsibility and accountability for people's well-being; living in and being part of the community; and "being a part of religion, faith, and spirituality" (p. 202).

In effect, these women serve as positive role models working toward community development and change. This is so not only for Hispanic workers and volunteers but for social work practitioners in general. The women studied demonstrated it is possible to undertake a wide variety of social work roles in macro practice, including advocate, enabler, manager, educator, facilitator, and mediator.

© David Bacon

Dolores Huerta, vice president and founder of the United Farm Workers, talks to union members in Delano, California. She is one of many prominent Hispanic women activists.

and *advocate* (Kahn, 1995; Yessian & Broskowski, 1983). Figures 1.8 through 1.18 illustrate these roles. Circles represent worker, client, and macro systems. Lines and arrows depict how systems relate to each other. Macro systems are usually organizations or communities. Client systems can be individuals, families, small groups, communities, or organizations.

Enabler

In the enabler role, a worker helps a client cope with various stresses ranging from crisis situations like divorce or job loss to community issues such as inadequate housing or day care. Skills used in the enabler role include "conveying hope, reducing resistance and ambivalence, recognizing and managing feelings, identifying and supporting personal strengths and social assets," breaking down problems into more manageable parts, emphasizing goals, and identifying ways to attain them (Barker, 1999, p. 154). Enablers are helpers. Practitioners can function in the role of enabler for micro, mezzo, or macro systems.

Figure 1.8 illustrates the enabler role. The arrows pointing from the worker to the client system circles portray the social worker's support. The desired result is that

Figure 1.8 **The Enabler Role**

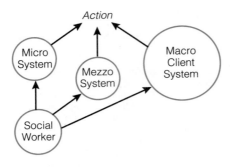

Figure 1.9 **The Mediator Role**

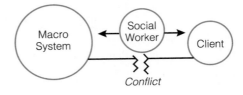

Figure 1.10 **The Integrator/Coordinator Role**

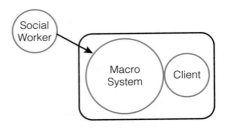

the client system will be better able to pursue some course of action.

This definition of the term "enabler" is very different from the definition of "enabler" as used in the area of chemical dependency. There the term refers to a family member or friend who helps the substance abuser to continue to use and abuse the drug of his or her choice.

Mediator

The mediator role involves resolving arguments or conflicts among micro, mezzo, or macro systems. At the macro level, the mediator helps various factions (subsystems) within a community, or a community and some other system, work out their differences. At the micro and mezzo levels, mediation is becoming increasingly important in resolving divorce and child custody cases.

The mediator role may involve improving communication among dissident individuals or groups and helping those involved come to a compromise. A mediator remains neutral and does not side with either party in the dispute. Mediators make sure they understand the positions of both parties. They may help to clarify positions, recognize miscommunication about differences, and help those involved present their cases clearly.

Figure 1.9 illustrates the mediator role. The central worker circle shows that a mediator maintains a neutral stance between the involved parties, taking no one's side. The broken line beneath the social worker circle portrays the broken lines of communication and, in this case, the macro system's and the client's inability to settle differences.

Integrator/Coordinator

Integration is the process of bringing together various parts to form a unified whole. Coordination involves bring components together in some kind of organized

manner. A generalist social worker can function as an integrator/coordinator "in many ways, ranging from . . . advocacy and identification of coordination opportunities, to provision of technical assistance, to direct involvement in the development and implementation of service linkages" (Yessian & Broskowski, 1983, p. 184).

In Figure 1.10, the box enclosing the macro and client systems represents the coordinated interaction between those two systems. The arrow pointing from the social worker to the box depicts the worker's active involvement in coordinating all the systems involved.

Manager

Management in social work involves having some level of administrative responsibility for a social agency or other unit in order to accomplish the following: establish organizational goals; administer social service programs; improve agency effectiveness and efficiency; obtain financial resources; solicit community support; and coordinate the work of agency staff. Management tasks include planning programs, getting and distributing resources, developing and establishing organizational structures and processes, evaluating programs, and implementing program changes when needed (Patti, 1983). Figure 1.11 portrays the social worker as a manager within the larger agency macro system. In this case, the macro system employs the worker to supervise staff who also work for that system.

Figure 1.11 **The Manager Role**

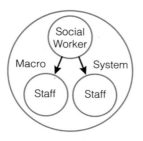

Figure 1.12 **The Educator Role**

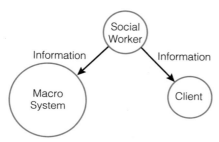

Figure 1.13 **The Analyst/Evaluator Role**

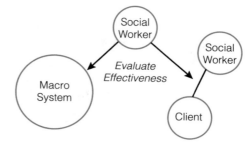

Figure 1.14 **The Broker Role**

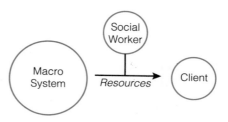

Educator

The educator role involves giving information and teaching skills to client and other systems. To be an effective educator, the worker must first be knowledgeable. Additionally, the worker must be a good communicator so that information is conveyed clearly and is understood by the client or macro system. Figure 1.12 illustrates the educator role.

Analyst/Evaluator

Social workers with a broad knowledge base of how various systems function can analyze or evaluate how well programs and systems work. They can also evaluate the effectiveness of their own interventions. Arrows in Figure 1.13 lead from the social worker to the macro system and the connected social worker and client. They indicate that a worker can evaluate the effectiveness of intervention with respect to a worker's treatment of an individual client or the work of an entire agency.

Broker

A broker helps link clients (individuals, groups, organizations, or communities) with community resources and services. A broker may help a client obtain emergency food or housing, legal aid, or other needed resources. A broker also helps put "various segments of the community" in touch with one another "to enhance their mutual interests" (Barker, 1999, p. 55). In micro and mezzo systems, the role of broker requires that the worker be familiar with community services, have general knowledge about eligibility requirements, and be sensitive to client needs.

In Figure 1.14, the line from the social worker to the arrow portrays a worker's role as broker. It illustrates the worker's active involvement in obtaining resources for the client. The arrow points from the macro system, which provides resources, to the client system, which receives them.

Facilitator

A facilitator is "one who serves as a leader for some group experience" (Barker, 1999, p. 165). The group may be a family therapy group, a task group, a sensitivity group, an educational group, a self-help group, or a group with some other focus. The facilitator role may also apply to macro practice. In this context, a facilitator assumes "the responsibility to expedite the change effort by bringing together people and lines of communication, channeling their activities and resources, and providing them with access to expertise" (p. 165).

Figure 1.15 **The Facilitator Role**

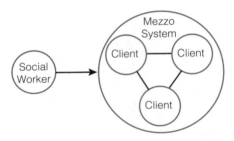

Figure 1.16 **The Initiator Role**

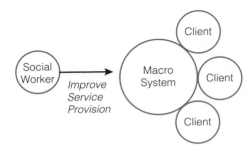

In Figure 1.15, the arrow pointing from the worker to the mezzo system depicts the worker's leadership as facilitator with respect to the group system. Client system circles portray group members or subsystems within the mezzo system. Lines connecting the client systems represent group interaction and communication.

Initiator

The initiator is the person or persons who call attention to an issue (Kettner, Daley, & Nichols, 1985). The issue may be a problem existing in the community, a need, or simply a situation that can be improved. It is important to recognize that a problem does not have to exist before the initiator steps in. Often, preventing problems or enhancing existing services are satisfactory reasons for a change effort. A social worker may recognize that a policy is creating problems for particular clients and bring this to the supervisor's attention. A client may identify ways that service could be improved. In each case, the person is playing the role of initiator. Usually, this role must be followed up by other kinds of work, because pointing out existing or potential problems doesn't guarantee that they will be solved.

Figure 1.17 **The Negotiator Role**

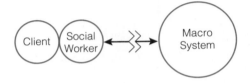

In Figure 1.16, the arrow from the worker to the macro system portrays a worker initiating a new idea regarding how the macro system could improve its service provision to clients. The smaller client system circles interface with the larger macro system circle to represent the importance and intensity of clients' involvement with macro systems.

Negotiator

A negotiator represents an organization, a group, or an individual that is trying to gain something from another group or system. Somewhat like mediation, negotiation involves finding a middle ground that all sides can live with and achieving consensus whenever possible. Unlike mediators, who play a neutral role, negotiators clearly ally themselves with one of the sides involved. Figure 1.17 portrays the client and worker systems joined together on one side of the conflict and the macro system on the other.

Advocate

Advocacy involves "the act of directly representing, defending, intervening, supporting, or recommending a course of action on behalf of one or more individuals, groups, or communities, with the goal of securing or retaining social justice" (Mickelson, 1995, p. 95). The advocate role involves stepping forward and speaking on the behalf of the client system. This may be especially appropriate when a client system has little power to get what it needs. Advocacy often involves expending more effort than is absolutely necessary to accomplish the job. It also may entail taking risks, especially when advocating on behalf of a client who faces a larger, more powerful system.

The advocate role is one of the most important roles a generalist social worker can assume, despite its potential difficulties. It is often undertaken when the client system is in desperate need of help. In Figure 1.18, the arrow leading from the worker to the macro system is thick.

Figure 1.18 The Advocate Role

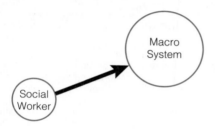

This represents the significant amount of energy it often takes to impact larger, more powerful systems.

❦ Assessment, Problem Solving, and Social Work: The Underlying Theme

Assessment involves analyzing situations in terms of interactions among client systems and other systems within the social environment. This is the initial step in helping people solve their problems and improve their lives. In practice, social workers help initiate effective change where problems are identified. Regardless of the particular role assumed, an underlying theme involves identifying alternative actions and helping client systems choose which alternative to take.

There are always reasons why people behave the way they do. The elements involved include interactions with other systems, stage of normal development, and aspects of human diversity. However, there are always other alternatives. A primary task of social work is to help people define the other alternatives available to them. Often people have tunnel vision. Because of stress or habit or lack of experience, people fail to realize that other alternatives exist. Not only do alternatives need to be defined, but they also must be evaluated. The positive and negative consequences of each alternative need to be clearly stated and weighed. Figure 1.19 illustrates the process of evaluating alternatives. The client system might be micro, mezzo, or macro, illustrated by the three circles. A line leads from the circles to the evaluation process. An individual, a group, or a large organization may have to make decisions regarding how to proceed.

Much of generalist social work practice is probably done with individual clients and small groups. Thus,

Figure 1.19 Social Workers Help Client Systems Evaluate Alternatives

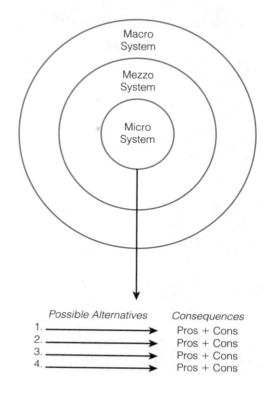

Highlight 1.4, "Case Example: Unplanned Pregnancy," shows how an individual client might be helped to identify the various alternatives available, evaluate the consequences of each, and finally select a course of action.

❦ Summary

Foundation knowledge is essential to understanding the purpose and process of social work. This knowledge is necessary for the assessment of human behavior prior to acquiring practice skills. Multiple systems are involved in human behavior; the context of practice can be perceived as interacting micro, mezzo, and macro systems. Several types of interactions include: those between micro and mezzo systems; those between micro and macro systems; the impacts of social forces; relationships among biological, psychological, and social systems that affect individuals as micro systems; and the effects on systems of diversity, oppression, and populations-at-risk.

Highlight 1.4

Case Example: Unplanned Pregnancy

Mona, 16, is a high school sophomore who just found out that she is two months pregnant. The father is Fred, a 17-year-old high school junior.

Mona and Fred have been going steady for two years. They think they love each other. Mona is a vivacious, outgoing cheerleader, and Fred is a muscular, handsome quarterback on the school football team. They are both involved in school activities and have never thought very much about the future.

Mona hasn't told Fred about being pregnant. She's very confused about what to do. She doesn't know how he'll react. Mona hasn't told her parents either. They're very religious, and Mona is afraid that they'll be terribly disappointed in her. She doesn't know what to do.

Mona finally gets up enough courage to talk to the school social worker, Ms. Peterson. Ms. Peterson is a warm, empathetic individual who encourages Mona to talk about her situation. Mona shares her shock and dismay over her situation. She had simply avoided thinking about birth control or possible pregnancy. It had been easier not to worry about it and take her chances.

With Ms. Peterson's encouragement, Mona considers her alternatives. One alternative would be to have an abortion. The positive consequence of that would be a relatively fast termination of the problem and its implications. The negative consequences would include the cost, any difficulty she might encounter in setting up an appointment, and any physical discomfort the procedure would cause. The most serious negative consequence for Mona would be the guilt she says she would feel. She believes that abortion is morally wrong.

A second alternative would be to keep the baby and raise it herself. The positive consequence would be the fact that she would accept responsibility for the child she had conceived. The negative consequences would be the financial, social, and educational difficulties she would have to face in order to support and care for her child.

A third alternative would be to keep the child and marry Fred. Mona feels that this is a rather vague alternative. She doesn't know if Fred would want to get married. Although the positive consequence would be a two-parent, "normal" home for the baby, Mona doesn't feel that either she or Fred is ready for the responsibilities of marriage.

A fourth alternative would be to have the baby and give it up for adoption. The positive consequences would be that her baby would live and have a home. The negative consequences would be that she would have to face the social consequences of being a pregnant high school sophomore and all of the accompanying gossip. The other major negative consequence would be the pain and regret she would experience when she gave up her baby.

Ms. Peterson should not, nor does she want to, make Mona's decision for her. It is up to Mona to weigh the positive and negative consequences of each alternative and make a decision. However, Ms. Peterson helps Mona think through her situation and her various alternatives.

Mona finally decides to have the baby and give it up for adoption. After weighing each positive and negative consequence within her own personal value system, she decides that this is the best route for her to take. She knows she will have to talk to Fred and to her parents first, but feels that at least she has defined her own perspective.

The systems impact model (SIM) emphasizes how organizations and communities affect client systems. Organizations can be viewed from a systems perspective. Models of community practice include locality develop-ment, social planning, and social action. Social workers assume a wide range of roles in practice when undertaking assessment and problem solving.

InfoTrac College Edition Keywords

| child abuse | diversity | goal displacement | oppression | population-at-risk | problem solving | social planning model |

On the Internet

National Clearinghouse on Child Abuse Neglect and Information

http://www.calib.com/nccanch/

The clearinghouse is a national resource for professionals and others seeking information on child abuse and neglect, and on child welfare.

National Association of Social Workers (NASW)

www.naswdc.org

The National Association of Social Workers (NASW) works to enhance the professional growth and development of its members, to create and maintain professional standards, and to advance sound social policies.

World Wide Web Resources for Social Work

http://www.nyu.edu/socialwork/wwwrsw/

This site was created to facilitate social workers' access to information available on the WWW. The mission of this site has always been to help social workers throughout the world obtain the WWW–based information they need.

Council on Social Work Education

http://www.cswe.org/

CSWE works to ensure the preparation of competent social work professionals by providing national leadership and a forum for collective action. The main responsibility of CSWE is therefore to promote and maintain the high quality of social work education.

Infancy and Childhood

Chapter 2
Biological Systems and Their
Impacts on Infancy and Childhood

Chapter 3
Psychological Systems and Their
Impacts on Infancy and Childhood

Chapter 4
Social Systems and Their
Impacts on Infancy and Childhood

Biological Systems and Their Impacts on Infancy and Childhood

Juanita lovingly watched her 1-year-old Enrico as he lay in his crib playing with his toes. Enrico was a first child, and Juanita was very proud of him. She was bothered, however, by the fact that he could not sit up by himself. Living next door was a baby about Enrico's age, whose name was Teresa. Not only could she sit up by herself, but she could stand alone and was even starting to crawl. Juanita thought that it was odd that the two children could be so different and have such different personalities. That must be the reason, she thought. Enrico was just an easygoing child. Perhaps he was also a bit stubborn. Juanita decided that she wouldn't worry about it. In a few weeks Enrico would probably start to sit up.

Knowledge of normal human development is critical in order to understand and monitor the progress of children as they grow. In the example, Enrico was indeed showing some developmental lags. He was in need of an evaluation to determine his physical and psychological status so that he might receive help.

A PERSPECTIVE

The attainment of normal developmental milestones has a direct impact on the client. Biological, psychological, and social development systems operate together to affect behavior. This chapter will explore some of the major aspects of infancy and childhood that social workers must understand in order to provide information to clients and make appropriate assessments of client behavior.

This chapter will:

▶ Describe the dynamics of human reproduction including conception, diagnosis of pregnancy, fetal development, prenatal influences and assessment, problem pregnancies, and the actual birth process.

▶ Explain normal developmental milestones as children progress through infancy and childhood.

▶ Explore abortion and infertility, two critical decision-making situations and life events that concern the decision to have children.

❧ The Dynamics of Human Reproduction

Chuck and Christine had mixed emotions about the pregnancy. It had been an accident. They were both in their mid-30s and already had a vivacious 4-year-old daughter named Hope. Although Hope had been a joy to both of them, she had also placed serious restrictions on their lifestyle. They were looking forward to her beginning school. Christine had begun to work part-time and was planning to go to full-time as soon as Hope turned 5.

Now all that had changed. To complicate the matter, Chuck, a university professor, had just received an exciting job offer in Hong Kong—the opportunity of a lifetime. They had always dreamed of spending time overseas.

The unexpected pregnancy provided Chuck and Christine with quite a jolt. Should they terminate the pregnancy and go on with their lives in exotic Hong Kong? Should they have the baby overseas? Questions concerning foreign prenatal care, health conditions, and health facilities flooded their thoughts. Would it be safer to remain in the states and turn down this golden opportunity? Christine was 35. Her reproductive clock was ticking away. Soon risk factors concerning having a healthy, normal baby would begin to skyrocket. This might be their last chance to have a second child. Chuck and Christine did some serious soul searching and fact searching in order to arrive at their decision.

Yes, they would have the baby. Once the decision had been made, they were filled with relief and joy. They also decided to take the job in Hong Kong. They would use the knowledge they had about prenatal care, birth, and infancy to maximize the chance of having a healthy, normal baby. They concluded that this baby was a blessing who would improve, not impair, the quality of their lives.

The decision to have children is a serious one. Ideally, a couple should examine all alternatives. Children can be wonderful. Family life can involve pleasurable activities, pride, and fullness to life. On the other hand, children can cause stress. They demand attention, time, and effort and can be expensive to care for. Information about conception, pregnancy, birth, and childrearing can only help people make better, more effective decisions.

Conception

Sperm meets egg; a child is conceived. But in actuality, it is not quite that simple. Many couples who strongly desire to have children have difficulty conceiving. Many others whose last desire is to conceive do so with ease. Some amount of chance is involved. Generally speaking, a woman has approximately a 25 percent chance of getting pregnant after one month of unprotected intercourse, a 63 percent chance after six months, and an 80 percent chance after one year (Masters, Johnson, & Kolodny, 1995).

Conception refers to the act of becoming pregnant. Sperm need to be deposited in the vagina near the time of ovulation. *Ovulation* involves the ovary's release of a mature egg into the body cavity near the end of one of the fallopian tubes. A woman is born with approximately 400,000 immature eggs, about half of which still remain alive at puberty. Usually the two ovaries alternate releasing an egg on a monthly basis. Fingerlike projections called *fimbriae* at the end of the fallopian tube draw the egg into the tube. From there the egg is gently moved along inside the tube by tiny hairlike extensions called *cilia*. Fertilization actually occurs in the third of the fallopian tube nearest the ovary.

If a sperm has gotten that far, conception may occur. After *ejaculation*, or the discharge of semen by the penis, the sperm travels up into the uterus and through the fallopian tube to meet the egg. Sperm are equipped with a tail that can lash back and forth, propelling them forward. The typical ejaculate, an amount of approximately one teaspoon full, usually contains between 100 million and 600 million sperm (Strong, DeVault, Sayad, & Yarber, 2002). Unlike females who are born with a finite number of eggs, males continually produce new sperm. Fertilization is, therefore, quite competitive. It is also hazardous. The majority of these sperm don't get very far. Many spill out of the vagina, drawn by gravity. Others are killed by the acidity of the vagina. Still others swim up the wrong fallopian tube. Perhaps only 100 to 200 finally reach the egg (Byer, Shainberg, & Galliano, 2002). The journey to the egg takes approximately 2 hours. By the time a sperm reaches the egg, it has swum a distance 3,000 times its own length; an equivalent swim for a human being would be more than 3 miles (Hyde & DeLamater, 2000).

Although sperm may survive in a woman's body from 48 to 72 hours, "many are killed by the acidic environment of the vagina" (Byer et al., 2002). Therefore, sexual intercourse should occur not more than 3 days before ovulation or one day after for fertilization to take place. The egg itself is capable of being fertilized for 12 to 24 hours after ovulation.

The actual fertilization process involves a cluster of sperm secreting an enzyme and depositing it on the egg. This enzyme helps to dissolve a gelatinous layer surrounding the egg and allows for the penetration of a sperm. The egg also takes an active part in the fertilization process. The egg selects and embraces one specific sperm with tiny projections extended from its surface. It then rejects other sperm by producing a brief electrical charge on its surface. This is followed by the production of a hard coating of protein which makes it difficult for the other sperm to penetrate.

Fertilization occurs during the exact moment when the egg and sperm combine. Eggs that are not fertilized by sperm simply disintegrate. The genetic material in the egg and sperm combine to form a single cell called a *zygote*. Eggs contain an X chromosome. Sperm may contain either an X or a Y chromosome. Eggs fertilized by a sperm with an X chromosome will result in a female; those fertilized by sperm with a Y chromosome will result in a male.

The single-celled zygote begins its cell division process approximately 30 hours after fertilization. The cell divides to form two cells, then four, then eight, and so on. After 4 to 7 days, the new mass of cells, called *blastocyst,* attaches itself to the lining of the uterus. If attachment does not occur, the newly formed blastocyst is simply expelled.

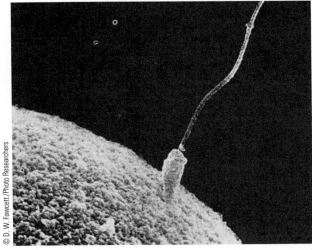

Fertilization occurs when egg and sperm combine. By the time this human sperm has reached the egg, it will have swum a distance 3,000 times its own length.

© D. W. Fawcett/Photo Researchers

From the point of attachment until 8 weeks of gestation, the *conceptus,* or product of conception, is called an *embryo.* From 8 weeks until birth, it is referred to as a *fetus. Gestation* refers to the time passing during a pregnancy from conception to birth.

Diagnosis of Pregnancy

Pregnancy can be diagnosed by using laboratory tests, by observing the mother's physical symptoms, or by performing a physical examination. Many women first become aware of the pregnancy when they miss a menstrual period. However, women also can miss periods as a result of stress, illness, or worry about possible pregnancy. Some pregnant women will even continue to menstruate for a month or even more. Therefore, lab tests are often needed to confirm a pregnancy. Such lab tests are 98 to 99 percent accurate (Hyde & DeLamater, 2000), and can be performed at a Planned Parenthood agency, a medical clinic, or a physician's office.

Most pregnancy tests work by detecting human chorionic gonadotropin (HCG) in a woman's urine or blood. HCG is a hormone secreted by the placenta. Highly accurate tests can detect HCG in a blood sample within a week after conception and in urine as early as the first day of a missed menstrual period (Allgeier & Allgeier, 2000).

The use of home pregnancy tests has become very common (these are often referred to as early pregnancy tests, or EPTs). Like some laboratory tests, they measure HCG levels in urine. They are very convenient, relatively inexpensive, and can be used as early as the first day after a menstrual period was supposed to start. Results can be obtained as early as 20 minutes after beginning the test. Despite claims by manufacturers that results are highly accurate, they can result in "both false positive and false negative results"; therefore, "they should always be confirmed by a health-care practitioner" (Crooks & Baur, 2002, p. 338).

Despite the supposition that EPTs are highly accurate, there is room for error. If instructions are not followed perfectly, results can be faulty. For instance, exposure to sunlight, accidental vibrations, using an unclean container to collect urine, or examining results too early or too late all can end in an erroneous diagnosis. False negatives (that is, showing that a woman is not pregnant when she really is) are more common than false positives (that is, showing that a woman is pregnant when she really is not). Regardless, it is suggested that a woman confirm the results either by waiting a week and administering another EPT or by having a laboratory diagnosis performed. Early knowledge of pregnancy is important either to begin early health care or to make a decision about terminating a pregnancy.

Fetal Development during Pregnancy

An average human pregnancy lasts 266 days. It is most easily conceptualized in terms of trimesters, or three periods of 3 months each. Each trimester is characterized by certain aspects of fetal development.

The First Trimester. The first trimester is sometimes considered the most critical. Due to the embryo's rapid differentiation and development of tissue, the embryo is exceptionally vulnerable to the mother's intake of noxious substances and to aspects of the mother's health.

By the end of the first month, a primitive heart and digestive system have developed. The basic initiation of a brain and nervous system are also apparent. Small buds that eventually become arms and legs are appearing. In general, development starts with the brain and continues down throughout the body. For example, the feet are the last to develop. In the first month, the embryo bears little resemblance to a baby because its organs have just begun to differentiate.

The embryo begins to resemble human form more closely during the second month. Internal organs become more complex. Facial features including eyes, nose, and mouth begin to become identifiable. The 2-month-old embryo is approximately an inch long and weighs about two-thirds of an ounce.

The third month involves the formation of arms, hands, legs, and feet. Fingernails, hair follicles, and eyelids

develop. All the basic organs have appeared, although they are still underdeveloped. By the end of the third month bones begin to replace what had been cartilage. Fetal movement is frequently detected at this time.

During the first trimester, the mother experiences various symptoms. This is primarily due to the tremendous increase in the amount of hormones her body is producing. Symptoms frequently include tiredness, breast enlargement and tenderness, frequent urination, and food cravings. Some women experience nausea, referred to as morning sickness.

It might be noted that these symptoms resemble those often cited by women when first taking birth control pills. This is due to the fact that the pill, by introducing hormones or artificial hormones that resemble those of pregnancy, tricks the body into thinking it is pregnant. In this way it stops the body from ovulating at all. The pill as a form of birth control is discussed more thoroughly in Chapter 6.

The Second Trimester. Fetal development continues during the second trimester. Toes and fingers separate. Skin, fingerprints, hair, and eyes develop. A fairly regular heartbeat emerges. The fetus begins to sleep and wake at regular times. Its thumb may be inserted into its mouth.

For the mother, most of the unappealing symptoms occurring during the first trimester subside. She is more likely to feel the fetus's vigorous movement. Her abdomen expands significantly. Some women suffer edema, or water retention, which results in swollen hands, face, ankles, or feet.

The Third Trimester. The third trimester involves the completed development of the fetus. Fatty tissue forms underneath the skin, filling out the fetus's human form. Internal organs complete their development and become ready to function. The brain and nervous system become completely developed.

An important concept that is especially relevant during the sixth and seventh months of gestation is that of *viability*. This refers to the ability of the fetus to survive on its own if separated from its mother. Although a fetus reaches viability near the end of the second trimester, "only a minority of babies born at the end of the second trimester who weigh under 2 pounds will survive—even with intense medical efforts" (Rathus, Nevid, & Fichner-Rathus, 2002, p. 346).

The viability issue becomes especially critical when referring to abortion. The question focuses on the ethics involved in aborting a fetus that, with external medical help, would be able to survive. This issue indicates the importance of obtaining an abortion early in the pregnancy when that is the chosen course of action.

For the mother, the third trimester may be a time of some discomfort. The uterus expands, and the mother's abdomen becomes large and heavy. The additional weight frequently stresses muscles and skeleton, often resulting in backaches or muscle cramps. The size of the uterus may exert pressure on other organs, causing discomfort.

In the past, pregnant women were afraid of gaining too much weight. A pregnant woman should gain from 25 to 35 pounds during her pregnancy (Lefrancois, 1999). Too little weight gain creates more risks than too much weight gain. Women who stay within the recommended weight gain limitations have significantly fewer stillbirths, low birth weight babies, and late miscarriages. Some of the added weight can be attributed to the baby itself, amniotic fluid, and the placenta. Other normal weight increases include those of the uterus, blood, and breasts as part of the body's natural adaptation to pregnancy.

Prenatal Influences

Numerous factors can influence the health and development of the fetus. These include the mother-to-be's nutrition, drugs and medication, alcohol consumption, smoking habits, age, and a number of other factors.

Nutrition. A pregnant woman is indeed eating for two. Not only does the amount of food need to increase, but also the quality of food needs careful monitoring and attention. Pregnant women need approximately 300 calories a day more than normal to provide adequate nourishment for themselves and the growing fetus (Carroll & Wolpe, 1996). Poor nutrition results in premature birth and low birth weight (Kail & Cavanaugh, 2000). A poor diet can also affect the development of the central nervous system of the fetus and leave the newborn vulnerable to disease (Guttmacher & Kaiser, 1986; Kail & Cavanaugh, 2000; Shaw et al., 1995).

It is especially important for pregnant women to get enough protein, folic acid (a B vitamin), iron, calcium, and other vitamins (Hyde & DeLamater, 2000; Papalia, Olds, & Feldman, 2001). Hyde and DeLamater (2000) explain: "Protein is important for building new tissues. Folic acid is also important for growth; symptoms of folic acid deficiency are anemia and fatigue. A pregnant woman needs much more iron than usual, because the fetus draws off iron for itself from the blood that circulates to the placenta. Muscle cramps, nerve pains, uterine ligament pains, sleeplessness, and irritability may all be symptoms of a calcium deficiency" (p. 157).

Drugs and Medication. Because the effects of many drugs on the fetus are unclear, pregnant women are cautioned to be wary of drug use. Drugs may enter the bloodstream of the fetus after passing across the placenta. Drugs and medication should be taken only after consultation with a physician. The effects of such drugs usually depend on the amount taken and the gestation stage during which they were taken. This is especially true for the first trimester when the embryo is very vulnerable.

Teratogens are substances, including drugs, that cause malformations in the fetus. Certain drugs can cause malformations of certain body parts or organs. The so-called thalidomide babies of the early 1960s are a tragic example of the potential effects of drugs. Thalidomide, a type of tranquilizer, was found to produce either flipperlike appendages in place of arms or legs, or no arms or legs at all.

A variety of prescription drugs have been found to produce teratogenic effects. For instance, long-term use of antibiotics has been established as being harmful to the fetus (Hyde & DeLamater, 2000). One type of antibiotic, tetracycline, has been linked to stained teeth and deformed bone structures. Other antibiotics can cause deafness. The drug isoretinoin (Accutane), used to treat severe cases of acne, has been linked to several other serious birth defects involving the brain, skull, face, thymus, and heart (Lammer et al., 1985; Masters et al., 1995; Papalia et al., 2001). Generally speaking, women should avoid taking drugs or medications during pregnancy and while breast-feeding unless such medication is absolutely necessary.

Even nonprescription, over-the-counter drugs such as aspirin or caffeine should be consumed with caution (Lefrancois, 1999; Masters et al., 1995). Ordinary aspirin, for example, has been found to cause bleeding in both the infant and the mother (Friedman & Polifka, 1996; Lefrancois, 1999; Stockman, 1990). Such bleeding could have adverse effects in the event that the infant is born prematurely or is below normal birth weight.

The research is mixed regarding caffeine's effects on fetal development. Some research revealed that drinking greater amounts of coffee, such as 3 or more cups a day, contributed to low birth weight and possibly to prematurity; other research found no such relationship when the mother stopped ingesting caffeine early in the pregnancy (Newman & Newman, 1999). While some research found a relationship between caffeine consumption and miscarriage (Infante-Rivard et al., 1993), other research found no such relationship (Friedman & Polifka, 1996). Thus, it appears that the verdict is not yet in concerning the effects of caffeine. An expectant mother's safest bet is to be cautious.

Drug addiction can result in numerous problems. Such drugs include barbiturates, heroin, and amphetamines. Potential problems include low birth weight, premature birth, convulsions, and depressed breathing (Masters et al., 1995). Newborns of drug addicts tend to be addicted themselves. These infants actually suffer withdrawal symptoms during their first few days of life. Cocaine use during pregnancy can result in infants being sluggish, unresponsive, or irritable, making it difficult for them to relate normally to caregivers (Papalia et al., 2001). Other effects include muscle tremors; sleeping, feeding, and elimination problems; developmental delays; and cognitive processing problems (Lefrancois, 1999; Santrock, 2002b).

Alcohol. Alcohol consumption during pregnancy can have grave effects on a fetus. The condition is termed *fetal alcohol syndrome* (FAS). Babies of women who were heavy drinkers during pregnancy have "unusual facial characteristics [including widely spaced eyes, short nose, and thin upper lip], small head and body size, congenital heart defects, defective joints, poor mental capabilities, and abnormal behavior patterns" (Kail & Cavanaugh, 2000; Strong & DeVault, 1997, p. 405). Effects stretch into childhood and include "a short attention span, restlessness, irritability, hyperactivity, learning disabilities, and motor impairments." Symptoms continuing into childhood and adulthood can include delayed growth, intellectual deficits (including mental retardation), and behavioral problems (Byer et al., 2002; Papalia et al., 2001; Strong et al., 2002). The severity of defects increase with the amount of alcohol consumed during pregnancy (Byer et al., 2002). However, there is evidence that even more moderate alcohol consumption such as one or 2 drinks a day can harm the fetus (Byer et al., 2002; Lefrancois, 1999; Santrock, 2002b). *Fetal alcohol effects* (FAE) is a condition that manifests relatively less severe (yet still significant) problems, presumably resulting from lower levels of alcohol consumption during pregnancy.

Smoking. Numerous studies associate smoking with "lower birth weights, shortened pregnancies, higher rates of spontaneous abortions, more frequent complications of pregnancy and labor, and higher rates of perinatal mortality (death of the fetus or newborn near the time of the birth)" (Masters et al., 1995, p. 111; Santrock, 2002a). Even secondhand smoke is thought to pose a danger to a fetus (Lefrancois, 1999). Some research found a relationship between a mother's smoking during pregnancy and a child's having behavioral and emotional problems when the child reaches school age (Papalia et al., 2001; Santrock, 2002b).

Age. The pregnant woman's age may affect both the woman and the child. Women "between ages 16 and 35 tend to provide a better uterine environment for the developing fetus and to give birth with fewer complications than do women under 16 or over 35" (Newman & Newman, 1999, p. 120). For example, although a woman at age 25 has a 1-in-2,000 chance of giving birth to a baby with Down syndrome,[1] the likelihood increases to about 1 in 100 when she reaches 40 and 1 in 10 at 50 (Santrock, 2002a). It is thought that a contributing factor to Down syndrome is deterioration of the female's egg or the male's sperm as people age (Kail & Cavanaugh, 2000; Newman & Newman, 1999). A number of other syndromes associated with neurological problems, congenital heart defects, and retarded growth are also more likely to occur in babies of older women (Dill & McGillivray, 1992; Lefrancois, 1999). Women aged 35 and over account for almost 11 percent of all births in the United States (U.S. Census Bureau, 2000).

Teen mothers account for almost 13 percent of all U.S. births (U.S. Census Bureau, 2000). They are more likely to experience miscarriages, premature births, and stillbirths than other mothers (Lefrancois, 1999), and their children are more likely to have a low birth weight and neurological problems (Santrock, 2002b).

Other Factors. Other factors have been found to affect prenatal and postnatal development. For example, lower income level and socioeconomic class can pose health risks to the prenatal child and the mother (Newman & Newman, 1999). Illness during pregnancy may damage the developing fetus. Rubella (German measles) can cause physical or mental disabilities in the fetus if a woman contracts it during the first 3 months of pregnancy (Strong et al., 2002). Prevention of rubella is possible by vaccination. However, this should not be done during a pregnancy because of negative effects on the fetus.

Transmission of acquired immune deficiency syndrome (AIDS) has received major attention in recent years. Contraction of the disease may occur when the mother's blood intermingles with that of the fetus in the uterus or during birth. It is estimated that 15 to 30 percent (with a range of 13 to 40 percent) of infants born to

---

1. Down syndrome is a congenital condition resulting from a chromosomal abnormality. It is characterized by cognitive disability and other physical features including thick folds in the corners of the eyes, making them appear slanted; short stature; a wide, short skull; broad hands with short fingers; and wide spaces between the first and second toes (Kauffman, 1994; Webster's, 1995). People with the most common type of Down syndrome, trisomy 21, have an extra chromosome.

HIV-positive mothers will contract the disease (Hatcher et al., 1998). HIV or human immunodeficiency virus is a retrovirus that attacks a person's immune system, often resulting in AIDS. HIV-positive infants once had a negative prognosis. However, beginning the use of AZT (a drug used to treat people infected with HIV) and antibiotics shortly after birth allows about one-third of the HIV-infected infants to reach age 8, 10, or even older ("AIDS Kids Beat Odds Against Survival," 1994). Women can decrease the likelihood of infecting their babies with HIV if they take AZT during pregnancy and then give birth by Caesarean section (a surgical procedure described later in the chapter) (American Association of Sex Educators, Counselors, and Therapists [AASECT], March 1999; Strong et al., 2002). Chapter 10 addresses the issue of AIDS more thoroughly.

Prenatal Assessment

Tests are available to determine if a developing fetus has any of a variety of defects. These include *ultrasonography, amniocentesis, chorionic villi sampling,* and *maternal blood tests.*

Ultrasonography, (also known as ultrasound), the most common method of fetal diagnosis, involves using high frequency sound waves to produce the image of the fetus on a television-like screen (Kail & Cavanaugh, 2000; Strong et al., 2002). This test can be performed as early as the fourth or fifth week of pregnancy and can determine the fetus's gender, position in the uterus, and gross physical abnormalities.

Amniocentesis involves the insertion of a needle through the abdominal wall and into the uterus to obtain amniotic fluid for determination of fetal gender or chromosomal abnormalities. The amniotic fluid contains fetal cells that can be analyzed for a variety of birth defects including Down syndrome, muscular dystrophy,[2] and spina bifida.[3] The gender of the fetus can also be determined. Amniocentesis is recommended for women who have had a baby with a birth defect, who may be a genetic carrier of such a defect, and who are over age 35 (Hyde, 2000; Strong et al., 2002). A disadvantage of amniocentesis is that the test cannot be performed until the twelfth to sixteenth weeks of pregnancy. Two to three weeks are required to complete the testing (Kail & Cavanaugh, 2000; Strong & DeVault, 1997). Testing during the fifteenth or sixteenth week tends to be more accurate. However, earlier testing

is useful; if a serious problem is discovered, the people involved have more time to decide whether or not to terminate a pregnancy. Another disadvantage to amniocentesis is that there is a 0.5 to 2 percent risk of fetal death, depending on how early the test is performed; earlier testing increases this likelihood (Strong & DeVault, 1997; Strong et al., 2002).

Chorionic villi sampling (CVS) is another method of diagnosing defects in a developing fetus. It involves the insertion of a thin plastic tube through the vagina or a needle through the abdomen into the uterus. A sample of the chorionic villi ("tiny threadlike protrusions on the chorion membrane that surrounds the fetus") is taken for analysis of potential genetic irregularities (Masters et al., 1995, p. 128). Research suggests that CVS is as accurate as amniocentesis (Hyde & DeLamater, 2000). There are two major advantages of CVS. First, it can be performed by the eighth or ninth week of pregnancy, and second, results can be obtained within 24 hours (Kail & Cavanaugh, 2000). Couples may have a different perspective on whether to abort or keep a defective fetus at this early stage of the pregnancy. A disadvantage of CVS is a slightly higher risk of fetal death than with amniocentesis (Hyde & DeLamater, 2000; Masters et al., 1995). Additionally, some questions have been raised regarding possible limb deformities resulting from CVS (Carroll & Wolpe, 1996). Further research is needed to address these concerns.

Maternal blood tests done between the fifteenth and twentieth weeks of gestation detect a variety of conditions. For instance, the amount of a substance called alpha-feto protein (AFP) can be measured. High levels of AFP forewarn about abnormalities of the brain and spinal cord. Testing AFP levels can also detect Down syndrome (Haddow et al., 1992). Ultrasonography, amniocentesis, or both can then be used to verify the presence of such congenital conditions.

Access to Prenatal Care: Obstacles in the Macro Environment

An ongoing theme in this book is how people function within the context of their environments. Prenatal care is considered vital "because it provides social workers and other health professionals with opportunities to identify pregnant women who are at risk of premature or low-weight births, and to deliver the medical, nutritional, educational, or psychosocial interventions that can promote positive pregnancy outcomes" (Perloff & Jeffee, 1999, p. 117). Early prenatal care is especially significant because of the developing fetus's vulnerability. It is important not to assume that all women's access to such care is equal.

---

2. Muscular dystrophy is a group of hereditary diseases characterized by progressive wasting of muscles.

3. Spina bifida is a condition in which the spinal column has not fused shut and, consequently, some nerves remain exposed.

Cook, Selig, Wedge, and Gohn-Baube (1999) investigated women's perceptions of barriers to using prenatal care. The sample consisted of 115 low-income women hospitalized in a large urban hospital's postpartum unit. Low-income women were targeted "because the barriers experienced by this population can be formidable with the daily stresses of survival overshadowing the perceived need for prenatal care" (Cook et al., 1999, p. 131). The most difficult obstacles cited included "feeling embarrassed about one's pregnancy, hearing bad things about the prenatal clinic, not wanting family or friends to know about the pregnancy, disliking the kind of care received at the clinic, lacking trust in the health care system, being affected by the personal problems of family or friends, and lack of evening or weekend clinic hours" (p. 133). The most severe barrier was lack of evening or weekend clinic hours. Obstacles often cited included environmental aspects of the prenatal clinics such as overly long waiting periods, crowded conditions, and inconvenient hours.

Perloff and Jaffee (1999) investigated information about prenatal care on 265,360 birth certificates for all children born in New York City within a 2-year period. They found that "both living in a distressed neighborhood and living in a neighborhood with few office-based primary care physicians significantly increased the likelihood of beginning prenatal care late" (p. 122).

These studies highlight the importance of a supportive, accessible environment to promote optimum health and well-being. There are several implications for social work practice (Cook et al., 1999; Perloff & Jaffee, 1999). First, workers can help women navigate a complex health care system, making certain they have ready access to available insurance and Medicaid payments. Second, practitioners can advocate with clinics to improve their internal environments. Providing child care, magazines, comfortable furniture, and refreshments can significantly improve the clinic experience. Third, workers can assist pregnant women "in gaining access to clinic resources (for example, appointments, laboratory tests, and educational seminars) through regular, ongoing contact with clients" (Cook et al., 1999, p. 136). Fourth, practitioners can "develop innovative service delivery models" including screening women during their initial visit to identify those at greatest risk, mailing or calling reminders of clinic appointments, and participating in community outreach. The latter might entail conducting door-to-door case finding of pregnant women to expedite early initiation of prenatal care. This could involve sharing information about risks posed without care, benefits of care, and the availability of services.

Problem Pregnancies

In addition to factors that can affect virtually any pregnancy, other problems can develop under certain circumstances. These problems include ectopic pregnancies, toxemia, and Rh incompatibility. Spontaneous abortions also happen periodically.

Ectopic Pregnancy. When a fertilized egg begins to develop somewhere other than in the uterus, it is called an *ectopic pregnancy* or *tubal pregnancy*. In most cases, the egg becomes implanted in the fallopian tube. Much more rarely, the egg is implanted outside of the uterus somewhere in the abdomen.

Ectopic pregnancies most often occur due to a blockage in the fallopian tube caused by anatomical irregularities, scar tissue, or tumors (Masters et al., 1995). The current rate of ectopic pregnancy has increased dramatically from what it was 20 years ago (Hyde & DeLamater, 2000; Kelly, 2001). This may be attributed partially to increasing rates of sexually transmitted diseases that result in infection and subsequent scar tissue (Carroll & Wolpe, 1996; Hyde & DeLamater, 2000).

Ectopic pregnancies in the fallopian tubes may "spontaneously abort and be released into the abdominal cavity, or the embryo and placenta may continue to expand, stretching the tube until it ruptures" (Hyde & DeLamater, 2000, p. 170). In the latter case, surgical removal is necessary to save the mother's life. One other approach involves injection of the drug methotrexate (originally developed for cancer treatment) on an outpatient basis (Carson & Buster, 1993). The drug causes the body to absorb the fetus before any rupture occurs.

Toxemia. *Toxemia* or *pregnancy-induced hypertension* is "a condition of a mother involving high blood pressure, edema [abnormal accumulation of fluid and resultant swelling of various body cavities], protein in the urine, and convulsions during the latter half of pregnancy" (Carroll & Wolpe, 1996, p. 777). It has also been referred to as eclampsia. Kidney malfunctioning results in a type of blood poisoning. In extreme instances it can cause coma and even death. Between 6 and 7 percent of women experience during pregnancy (Carroll & Wolpe, 1996). Toxemia's cause is unknown.

Rh Incompatibility. *Rh incompatibility* occurs when the mother has Rh− blood and the fetus Rh+. This can happen only when the father's blood is Rh+. Because most people have Rh+ blood, the condition is fairly rare. The mother's blood forms antibodies in defense against the fetus's incompatible blood. Problems are less likely to occur in the first pregnancy than in later ones, because antibodies have not yet had the chance to form. The consequence to an affected fetus can be cognitive disability,[4] anemia, or death.

Fortunately, Rh incompatibility can be dealt with successfully. The mother is injected with a serum, RhoGam, that prevents the development of future Rh− sensitivity. This must be administered within 72 hours after the first child's birth or after a first abortion. In those cases where Rh sensitivity already exists, the newborn infant or even the fetus within the uterus can be given a blood transfusion.

Spontaneous Abortion. A *spontaneous abortion* or *miscarriage* is the termination of a pregnancy due to natural causes before the fetus is capable of surviving on its own. Ten to 20 percent of all known pregnancies result in spontaneous abortion (Crooks & Baur, 2002). The vast majority of miscarriages occur within the first trimester. The woman may not even be aware of the pregnancy. Thus, a spontaneous abortion often occurs without the pregnant woman's knowledge. Sometimes it is perceived as an extremely heavy menstrual period.

Most frequently, spontaneous abortions occur as a result of a defective fetus or some physical problem of the expectant mother. Maternal problems may include a uterus that is "too small, too weak, or abnormally shaped, . . . maternal stress, nutritional deficiencies, excessive vitamin A, drug exposure, or pelvic infection" (Carroll & Wolpe, 1996, p. 392).

The Birth Process

Labor involves "rhythmic, regular contractions of the uterus that result in delivery of the child, the placenta, and membranes" (Masters et al., 1995, p. 114). Toward the end of the pregnancy, hormonal production by the placenta decreases. *Prostaglandins* are chemical substances that appear to stimulate the uterine muscles thereby causing contractions. Additionally, *oxytocin,* a substance released by the pituitary gland late in pregnancy, apparently causes the powerful uterine contractions late in the birth process that are necessary to expel or push out the fetus.

Before labor, several clues appear that are especially important. First, there is usually a small bloody discharge

of mucus. This is actually the expulsion of the plug of mucus that remained in the cervical opening throughout the pregnancy in order to prevent germs from entering the uterus. Second, the bag of water that acts as a cushion to protect the fetus is "released in varying amounts from a trickle to a gush" (Allgeier & Allgeier, 2000, p. 209).

The third major indication of beginning labor is the uterine contractions. These contractions have a clearly defined rhythm. Initially, they may be 10 to 20 minutes apart and last 40 to 60 seconds each. As labor progresses, they increase in frequency, intensity, and duration as the body prepares to ease the fetus out during the birth process.

Sometimes women experience what is termed *false labor,* which involves contractions called *Braxton-Hicks contractions.* However, unlike in true labor, they occur very irregularly and frequently far apart. Additionally, there is no hardening of the abdominal muscles in preparation for the birth. These contractions can be confusing and cause a mother a false alarm.

Stages of Labor. The birth process itself involves three stages. Initially during the first stage of labor, the cervix is dilated or opened in preparation for the baby to pass through it. Contractions begin between 10 to 20 minutes apart in the early first stage and build to 2 to 4 minutes apart. Contractions continue to build in intensity and duration, often causing substantial pain to the mother. The water bag releases its contents toward the end of this stage. The first stage, the longest stage of labor, averages somewhere between 12 to 15 hours for the first pregnancy and 8 hours for later babies.

The second stage of labor marks the time when the baby is actually born. This stage begins when contractions are about 2 to 3 minutes apart and last for about 60 to 70 seconds each. The cervix is completely dilated and the baby begins to move through the vagina. The head usually emerges first. However, depending on the baby's position, some other body part may appear first. The average length of this stage is 80 minutes in first pregnancies and 30 minutes in later ones (Masters et al., 1995, p. 116).

During the second stage, the mother typically feels the urge to "bear down." This pushing, if done properly, may serve to facilitate the baby's movement out of the uterus and vagina. Each contraction also helps to move the baby farther along.

Sometimes an episiotomy is performed during this stage. An *episiotomy* involves making a small incision in the skin just behind the vagina. Its purpose is to relieve pressure on the strained tissues and help to provide a

---

4. Note that here we use the term *cognitive disability* to refer to the condition formerly referred to as *mental retardation.* This is a condition in which a person has intellectual functioning that is significantly below average and has accompanying deficits in adaptive functioning, both of which occur before age 18. The term *cognitive disability* portrays a less negative concept than mental retardation.

Figure 2.1 Forms of Birth Presentation

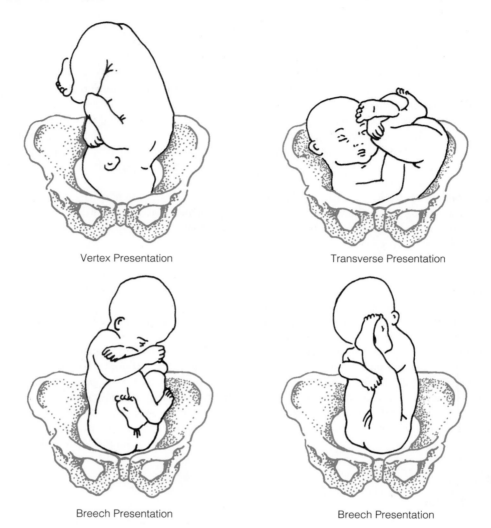

Vertex Presentation

Transverse Presentation

Breech Presentation

Breech Presentation

larger opening through which the baby can emerge. One reason physicians give for performing an episiotomy is that "if it is not done, the baby's head may rip" the tissue around the vagina; "a neat incision is easier to repair than a ragged tear" (Hyde & DeLamater, 2000, p. 161). However, many women question the necessity of having an episiotomy in view of the pain and discomfort it causes (including itching while it heals).

After the baby completely emerges, the umbilical cord, which still attaches the baby to its mother, is clamped and severed about 3 inches from the baby's body. Because there are no nerve endings in the cord, this does not hurt. The small section of cord remaining on the infant gradually dries up and simply falls off.

The third stage of labor involves delivery of the *afterbirth*. The placenta and other fetal material making up the afterbirth detaches itself from the uterine walls and is expelled, often with the help of a few contractions. Finally, the episiotomy, if performed, is stitched up.

Birth Positions. Approximately 95 percent of babies are born with their heads emerging first. Referred to as a *vertex presentation,* this is considered the normal birth position and most often requires no assistance with instruments. Various birth positions are illustrated in Figure 2.1.

Most other babies are born in a *breech presentation.* Here the buttocks and feet appear first and the head last as the baby is born. This type of birth may merit more careful

Chapter 2 Biological Systems and Their Impacts on Infancy and Chi...

58

attention. However, usually it can be detected ahead of time and a satisfactory delivery can be made.

A small proportion of babies are born with a *transverse presentation.* Here the baby lies crossways in the uterus. During birth, a hand or arm usually emerges first in the vagina. Such positions merit special attention. Either the baby must be turned during labor so that a normal birth can be accomplished or a caesarean section must be performed.

A *caesarean section,* or *C section,* is a surgical procedure in which the baby is removed by making an incision in the abdomen through the uterus. Caesarean sections account for almost 21 percent of all births in the United States (U.S. Bureau of the Census, 1998). Caesarean sections are necessary when the baby is in a difficult prenatal position, when the baby's head is too large to maneuver out of the uterus and vagina, when fetal distress is detected, or when the labor has been extremely long and exhausting. Today it is usually safe with only minimal risks to the mother or infant. The mother's recovery, however, will be longer because the incisions must heal.

Natural Childbirth. In natural childbirth, the emphasis is on education for the parents, especially the mother. The intent is to maximize her understanding of the process and to minimize her fear of the unknown. Natural childbirth also emphasizes relaxation techniques. Mothers are encouraged to tune in to their normal body processes and learn to consciously relax when under stress. They are taught to breathe correctly and to facilitate the birth process by bearing down in an appropriate manner. The Lamaze method is currently popular in the United States.

Many women prefer natural childbirth because it allows them to experience and enjoy the birth to the greatest extent possible. When done correctly, pain is minimized. Anesthetics are usually avoided so that maximum feeling can be attained. It allows the mother to remain conscious throughout the birth process.

Newborn Assessment. Birth is a traumatic process that is experienced more easily by some newborns, often referred to as *neonates,* and with more difficulty by others. Evaluation scales have been developed to assess an infant's condition at birth. The sooner such problems can be attended to, the greater the chance of having the infant be normal and healthy. Two such scales are the Apgar and Brazelton.

In 1953 Virginia Apgar developed a scale that assesses the infant's heart rate, breathing, muscle tone, reflex response, and skin color (Apgar, 1958). Each of these five variables is given a score of 0 to 2. Evaluation of these

signs usually occurs twice—at 1 minute and at 5 after birth. A maximum score of 10 is possible. S 7 through 10 indicate a normal, healthy infant. Sc 4 through 6 suggest that some caution be taken an the infant be carefully observed. Scores of 4 or below warn that problems are apparent. In these cases, the infant needs immediate emergency care.

A second scale used to assess the health of a newborn infant is the Brazelton Neonatal Behavioral Assessment Scale (1973). Whereas the Apgar scale addresses the gross or basic condition of an infant immediately after birth, the Brazelton assesses the functioning of the central nervous system and behavioral responses of a newborn. This scale focuses on finer distinctions of behavior such as the infant's rooting and sucking reflexes and the ability to respond to various types of external stimuli. The scale is usually first administered 2 to 3 days after birth and then again about 9 to 10 days after birth. Extremely low scores can indicate brain damage (Santrock, 2002b).

Birth Defects. *Birth defects* refer to any kind of disfigurement or abnormality present at birth. Birth defects are much more likely to characterize fetuses that are miscarried. *Miscarriage* provides a means for the body to prevent seriously impaired or abnormal births. The specific types of birth defects are probably infinite; however, some tend to occur with greater frequency.

Down syndrome is a disorder involving an extra chromosome that results in various degrees of cognitive disability. Accompanying physical characteristics include a broad, short skull; widely spaced eyes with an extra fold of skin over the eyelids; a round, flattened face; a flattened nose; a protruding tongue; shortened limbs; and defective heart, eyes, and ears (Barker, 1999; Papalia et al., 2001; Santrock, 2002a). We've already noted that a woman's chances of bearing a child with Down syndrome increase significantly with her age.

Spina bifida is a condition in which the spinal column has not fused shut and consequently some nerves remain exposed. Surgery immediately after birth closes the spinal column. Muscle weakness or paralysis and difficulties with bladder and bowel control often accompany this condition. Frequently occurring along with spina bifida is *hydrocephalus,* in which an abnormal amount of spinal fluid accumulates in the skull, possibly resulting in skull enlargement and brain atrophy. Spina bifida occurs in 1 out of 1,000 births.

Low Birth Weight and Preterm Infants. Low birth weight and preterm status (prematurity) pose grave problems for newborns. Low birth weight is defined as

5½ pounds or less. Approximately 7.6 percent of babies born in the United States (or 1 out of 13) have low birth weights (Papalia et al., 2001). Babies born in the thirty-sixth week of gestation (the period of time between conception and birth) or earlier are called *preterm* or *premature.* The normal period of gestation is 38 to 42 weeks. About 10 percent of all births are preterm (Lefrancois, 1999).

Some low birth weight infants are also born preterm. They weigh less because they haven't had the necessary time to develop. Others born after a full gestation period suffer low birth weight for other reasons, such as poor prenatal nutrition resulting in delayed fetal development. Both low birth weight and preterm status place infants at high risk for a range of problems.

In the past, low birth weight infants often died. Today, most infants weighing at least 3.3 pounds survive when they receive appropriate intensive care. However, the less infants weigh, the greater the likelihood is that they will die or suffer negative consequences including developmental delays and inferior intellectual performance. (Lefrancois, 1999; Newman & Newman, 1999; Papalia et al., 2001).

Risk factors contributing to low birth weights fall into four major categories: demographic variables (such as age, race, education); medical factors occurring before the pregnancy (such as earlier miscarriages); medical factors occurring during the pregnancy (such as abnormally low maternal weight gain); and "prenatal behavioral and environmental factors" (such as use of alcohol or drugs) (Papalia et al., 1998, p. 91).

Premature babies may suffer negative consequences related to low birth weight. They are also more likely to experience "lower intelligence, a higher incidence of cerebral palsy,[5] and general developmental retardation" than babies born after a normal gestation period (Lefrancois, 1999, p. 118). Of course, such consequences depend on how premature the infants are and the extent to which their physiological systems have suffered any harm. A shortened period of gestation does not necessarily cause permanent damage to a newborn. Santrock (2002a) explains: "The neurological development of a short-gestation infant continues after birth on approximately the same timetable as if the infant still were in the womb. For example, consider an infant born after a gestation period of thirty weeks (Koenigsberger, 2000). At 38 weeks, approximately 2 months after birth, this infant shows the

same level of brain development as a 38-week fetus who is yet to be born" (p. 111).

The specific reason for prematurity is unknown (Creasy, 1990). However, factors such as smoking, maternal age, drug intake, poverty, poor nutrition, and certain illnesses (such as gonorrhea) during pregnancy are related to prematurity (Donders et al., 1993; Lefrancois, 1999).

Social work roles that are used to help pregnant women bear healthy infants might include that of broker to help women get the resources they need. These resources include access to good nutrition and prenatal care. If such resources are unavailable, especially to poor women, social workers might need to advocate on the women's behalf. Funding sources and services might need to be developed.

Treatment for low birth weight babies includes immediate medical attention to meet their special needs and provision of educational and counseling support. Group counseling for parents and weekly home visits to teach parents how to care for their children, play with them, and provide stimulation to develop cognitive, verbal, and social skills also appear to be helpful (Infant Health and Development Program, 1990).

Other Factors at Birth Affecting the Neonate. Two other conditions that have serious effects on an infant at birth are *phenylketonuria* (PKU) and *anoxia.* PKU is a genetic condition whereby an infant is unable to metabolize milk properly. It is caused by a malfunctioning of the liver so that any foods containing protein cannot be properly assimilated. Instead, substances remain and build up in the blood. These substances eventually damage the brain and result in cognitive disability. Approximately 1 child in every 10,000 to 20,000 live births is affected by this condition (Santrock, 2002a).

Fortunately, PKU can be detected early by a simple blood test given to the baby before leaving the hospital. On detection, a special diet that prevents the accumulation of harmful substances in the bloodstream can be administered. Cognitive disability is then prevented. Eventually, some children suffering from PKU can resume a normal diet.

The other critical condition that affects some children at birth is *anoxia.* Anoxia refers to the deprivation or absence of oxygen during birth. Oxygen deprivation can result in brain damage or even death. Anoxia can cause cerebral palsy, a condition characterized by various degrees of muscular incoordination, speech disturbances, and/or perceptual and cognitive difficulties. The Apgar rating soon after birth is helpful in identifying problems often related to anoxia.

---

5. Cerebral palsy is "a disability resulting from damage to the brain before, during, or shortly after birth and outwardly manifested by muscular incoordination and speech disturbances" (Webster's, 1995, p. 187).

🌿 Early Functioning of the Neonate

The average full-term newborn weighs about 7½ pounds and is approximately 20 inches long (so most weigh between 5½ and 10 pounds, and measure between 18 and 22 inches long). Girls tend to weigh a bit less and are shorter than boys. Many parents may be surprised at the sight of their newborn who does not resemble the cute, pudgy, smiling, gurgling baby typically shown in television commercials. Rather, the baby is probably tiny and wrinkled with a disproportionate body and squinting eyes. Newborns need time to adjust to the shock of being born. Meanwhile, they continue to achieve various milestones in development. They gain more and more control over their muscles and are increasingly better able to think and respond.

First, newborn babies generally spend much time sleeping, although the time spent decreases as the baby grows older. Second, babies tend to respond in very generalized ways. They cannot make clear distinctions among various types of stimuli; nor can they control their reactions in a precise manner. Any type of stimulation tends to produce a generalized flurry of movement throughout the entire body.

Several reflexes that characterize newborns should be present in normal neonates. First, there is the *sucking response*. This obviously facilitates babies' ability to take in food. Related to this is a second basic reflex, rooting.

Normal babies will automatically move their heads and begin a sucking motion with their mouths whenever touched even lightly on the lips or cheeks beside the lips. The *rooting reflex* refers to this automatic movement toward a stimulus.

A third important reflex is *Moro's reflex,* or *startle response*. Whenever infants hear a sudden loud noise, they will automatically react by extending their arms and legs, spreading their fingers, and throwing their heads back. The purpose of this reflex is unknown, and it seems to disappear after a few months of life.

Three additional reflexes are the walking reflex, the grasping reflex, and the Babinski reflex. The *walking reflex* involves infants' natural tendency to lift a leg when held in an upright position with feet barely touching a surface. In a way, it resembles the beginning motions involved in walking. The *grasping reflex* refers to a newborn's tendency to grasp and hold objects such as sticks or fingers when placed in the palms of their hands. Finally, the *Babinski reflex* involves the stretching, fanning movement of the toes whenever the infant is stroked on the bottom of his or her feet.

🌿 Developmental Milestones

As infants grow and develop, their growth follows certain patterns and principles. At each stage of development, people are physically and mentally capable of performing

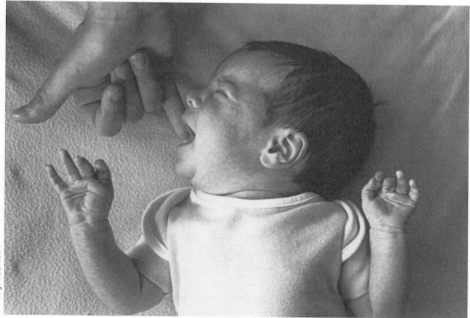

A newborn baby demonstrates the rooting reflex. A normal baby will automatically begin a sucking motion when touched on the lips or cheeks.

certain types of tasks. *Human development* is the continuous process of growth and change, involving physical, mental, emotional, and social characteristics, that occurs over a life span. Human development is predictable in that the same basic changes occur sequentially for everyone. However, enough variation exists to produce individuals with unique attributes and experiences.

Four major concepts are involved in understanding the process of human development: (1) growth as a continuous, orderly process; (2) specific characteristics of different age levels; (3) the importance of individual differences; and (4) the effects of both heredity and the social environment.

Growth as a Continuous, Orderly Process

People progress through a continuous, orderly sequence of growth and change as they pass from one age level to another. This has various implications. For one thing, growth is continuous and progressive. People are continually changing as they get older. For another thing, the process is relatively predictable and follows a distinct order. For example, an infant must learn how to stand up before learning how to run. All people tend to follow the same order in terms of their development. For instance, all babies must learn how to formulate verbal sounds before learning how to speak in complete sentences.

Several subprinciples relate to the idea that development is an orderly process (Papalia et al., 1998). One is that growth always follows a pattern from simpler and more basic to more involved and complex. Simple tasks must be mastered before more complicated ones can be undertaken.

Another subprinciple is that aspects of development progress from being more general to being more specific. Things become increasingly more differentiated. For example, infants initially begin to distinguish between human faces and other objects such as balloons. This is a general developmental response. Later they begin to recognize not only the human face, but also the specific faces of their parents. Eventually, as they grow older they can recognize the faces of Uncle Horace, Mr. Schmidt the grocer, and their best friend Joey. Their recognition ability has progressed from being very basic to being very specific.

Two other subprinciples involve cephalocaudal development and proximodistal development. *Cephalocaudal development* refers to development from the head to the toes. Infants begin to learn how to use the parts of their upper body such as the head and arms before their legs. *Proximodistal development* refers to the tendency to develop aspects of the body trunk first and then later master

manipulation of the body extremities (first the arms and then the hands).

Specific Characteristics of Different Age Levels

A second basic developmental principle is that each age period tends to have specific characteristics. During each stage of life, from infancy throughout adulthood, "normal" people are generally capable of performing certain tasks. Capabilities tend to be similar for all people within any particular age category. Developmental guidelines provide a very general means for determining whether an individual is progressing and developing normally.

Individual Differences

The third basic principle of development emphasizes the fact that people have individual differences. Although people tend to develop certain capacities in a specified order, the ages at which particular individuals master certain skills may show a wide variation. Some people may progress through certain stages faster. Others will take more time to master the same physical and mental skills. Variation may occur in the same individual from one stage to the next. The specific developmental tasks and skills that characterize each particular age level may be considered an average of what is usually accomplished during that level. Any average may reflect a wide variation. People may still be very "normal" if they fall at one of the extremes that make up the average.

The Nature-Nurture Controversy

A fourth principle involved in understanding human development is that both heredity and the surrounding environment affect development. Individual differences, to some extent, may be influenced by environmental factors. People are endowed with some innate ability and potential. In addition, the impinging environment acts to shape, enhance, or limit that ability.

For example, take a baby who is born with the potential to grow and develop into a normal adult, both physically and intellectually. Nature provides the individual baby with some prospective potential. However, if the baby happened to be living in Ethiopia or Somalia during the African famine, the environment or nature may have had drastic effects on the baby's development. Serious lack of nourishment limits the baby's eventual physical and mental potential.

Due to the complicated composition of human beings, the exact relationship between hereditary potential and environmental effects is unclear. It is impossible to quantify how much the environment affects development compared to how much development is affected by heredity. This is often referred to as the *nature-nurture controversy*. Theorists assume stands at both extremes. Some state that nature's heredity is the most important. Others hypothesize that the environment imposes the crucial influence.

You might consider that each individual has a potential that is to some extent determined by inheritance. However, this potential is tremendously maximized or minimized by what happens to people in their own environments.

Former president Ronald Reagan maintained only a C average in college. Yet he was able to attain the most powerful position in the country. It is difficult to determine how much of his success was due to innate ability and how much to situations and opportunities he encountered in his environment.

Our approach is that a person develops as the result of a multitude of factors including those that are inherited and those that are environmental.

Relevance to Social Work

Knowledge of human development and developmental milestones can be directly applied to social work practice. Assessment is a basic fact of intervention throughout the life span. In order to assess human needs and human behavior accurately, the social worker must know what is considered normal or appropriate. He or she must decide when intervention is necessary and when it is not. Comparing observed behavior with what is considered "normal" behavior provides a guideline for these decisions.

This book will address issues in human development throughout the life span. A basic understanding of every age level is important for generalist practice. However, an understanding of the normal developmental milestones for young children is especially critical. Early assessment of potential developmental lags or problems allows for maximum alleviation or prevention of future difficulties. For example, early diagnosis of a speech problem will cue parents and teachers to provide special remedial help for a child. The child will then have a better chance to make progress and possibly even catch up with peers.

Profiles of Normal Development

Research has established indicators of normality such as when children typically can say their first word, run adeptly, or throw a ball overhand. Children progress through an organized sequence of behavior patterns as they mature. Highlight 2.1, titled "Developmental Milestones for Children from Ages 4 Months to 11 Years," describes this progression.

We emphasize that individuals vary greatly in their attainment of specific developmental milestones. The developmental milestones provide a general baseline for assessment and subsequent intervention decisions. If a child is assessed as being grossly behind in terms of achieving normal developmental milestones, then immediate intervention may be needed. On the other hand, if a child is only mildly behind his or her normal developmental profile, then no more than close observation may be appropriate. In the event that the child continues to fall further behind, help can be sought and provided.

ᘛ Significant Issues and Life Events

Two significant issues will be discussed that relate to the decision of whether or not to have children. They have been selected because of the great number of people they impact and because they often pose a serious crisis for the people involved. The issues are abortion and infertility.

ᘛ The Abortion Controversy: Impacts of Social and Economic Forces

Many unique circumstances are involved in any unplanned pregnancy. Individuals must evaluate for themselves the potential consequences of each alternative and assess the positive and negative consequences of each.

A basic decision involved in unplanned pregnancy is whether to have the baby. If the decision is made to have the baby, and the mother is unmarried, a subset of alternatives must be evaluated from that point. One option is to marry the father (or to establish some other ongoing relationship with him). A second alternative is for the mother to keep the baby and live as a single parent. Recently the media have given increasing attention to fathers who seek custody. Perhaps, joint custody is a viable option. Or, the mother's parents (the child's grandparents) or other relatives either could keep the baby or assist in its care. Still another option is to have the baby and place it for adoption.

Each choice involves both positive and negative consequences. States may allow abortion as a legal alternative.

Highlight 2.1

Developmental Milestones for Children from Ages 4 Months to 11 Years

These milestones reflect only an average indication of typical accomplishments. Children need not follow this profile exactly to the letter. Normal human development provides for much individual variation. Parents do not have to be concerned if their child cannot yet stand alone at 13 months instead of the average 12 months. However, serious lags in development or those that continue to increase in severity should be attended to. This list can act as a screening guide to determine if a child might need more extensive evaluation.

Each age profile is divided into five assessment categories. They include motor or physical behavior, play activities, adaptive behavior that involves taking care of self, social responses, and language development. All five topics are addressed together at each developmental age level in order to provide a more complete assessment profile.

Age 4 Months

Motor: 4-month-old infants typically can balance their heads at a 90-degree angle. They can also lift their heads and chests when placed on their stomachs in a prone position. They begin to discover themselves. They frequently watch their hands, keep their fingers busy, and place objects in their mouths.

Adaptive: Infants are able to recognize their bottles. The sight of a bottle often stimulates bodily activity. Sometimes teething begins this early, although the average age is closer to 6 or 7 months.

Social: These infants are able to recognize their mothers and other familiar faces. They imitate smiles and often respond to familiar people by reaching, smiling, laughing, or squirming.

Language: The 4-month-old will turn his/her head when a sound is heard. Verbalizations include gurgling, babbling, and cooing.

Age 8 Months

Motor: 8-month-old babies are able to sit alone without being supported. They usually are able to assist themselves into a standing position by pulling themselves up on a chair or crib. They can reach for an object and pick it up with all their fingers and a thumb. Crawling efforts have begun. These babies can usually begin creeping on all fours, displaying greater strength in one leg than the other.

Play: The baby is capable of banging two toys together. Many can also pass an object from one hand to the other. These babies can imitate arm movements such as splashing in a tub, shaking a rattle, or crumpling paper.

Adaptive: Babies of this age can feed themselves pieces of toast or crackers. They will be able to munch instead of being limited to sucking.

Social: Babies of this age can begin imitating facial expressions and gestures. They can play "pat-a-cake," "peekaboo," and wave "bye-bye."

Language: Babbling becomes frequent and complex. Most babies will be able to attempt copying the verbal sounds they hear. Many can say a few words or sounds such as "mama" or "dada." However, they don't yet understand the meaning of words.

Age 1 Year

Motor: By age 1 year, most babies can crawl well, which makes them highly mobile. Although they usually require support to walk, they can stand alone without holding on to anything. They eagerly reach out into their environments and explore things. They can open drawers, undo latches, and pull on electrical cords.

Play: 1-year-olds like to examine toys and objects both visually and by touching them. They typically like to handle objects by feeling them, poking them, and turning them around in their hands. Objects are frequently dropped and picked up again one time after another. Babies this age like to put objects in and out of containers. Favorite toys include large balls, bottles, bright dangling toys, clothespins, and large blocks.

Adaptive: Because of their mobility, 1-year-olds need careful supervision. Because of their interest in exploration, falling down stairs, sticking forks in electric sockets, and eating dead insects are constant possibilities. Parents need to scrutinize their homes and make them as safe as possible.

Babies are able to drink from a cup. They can also run their spoon across their plate and place the spoon in their mouths. They can feed themselves with their fingers. They begin to cooperate while being dressed by holding still or by extending an arm or a leg to facilitate putting the clothes on. Regularity of both bowel and bladder control begins.

Social: 1-year-olds are becoming more aware of the reactions of those around them. They often vary their behavior in response to these reactions. They enjoy having an audience. For example, they will tend to repeat behaviors that are laughed at. They will also seek attention by squealing or making noises.

Language: By 1 year, babies begin to pay careful attention to the sounds they hear. They can understand simple commands. For instance, on request they often can hand you the appropriate toy. They begin to express choices about the type of food they will accept or about whether it is time to go to bed or not. They are imitating sounds more frequently and can meaningfully use a few other words in addition to "mama" and "dada."

Age 18 Months

Motor: By 18 months, a baby can walk. Although these children are beginning to run, their movements are still awkward and result in frequent falls. Walking up stairs can be accomplished by a caregiver holding the baby's hand. These babies can often descend stairs by themselves but only by crawling down backwards or by sliding down by sitting first on one step and then another. They are also able to push large objects and pull toys.

Play: Babies of this age like to scribble with crayons and build with blocks. However, it is difficult for them to place even three or four blocks on top of each other. These children like to move toys and other objects from one place to another. Dolls or stuffed animals frequently are carried about as regular companions. These toys are also often shown affection such as hugging. By 18 months, babies begin to imitate some of the simple things that adults do such as turning pages of a book.

Adaptive: Ability to feed themselves is much improved by age 18 months. These babies can hold their own glasses to drink from, usually using both hands. They are able to use a spoon sufficiently to feed themselves.

By this age, children can cooperate in dressing. They can unfasten zippers by themselves and remove their own socks or hats. Some regularity has also been established in toilet training. These babies often can indicate to their parents when they are wet and sometimes wake up at night in order to be changed.

Social: Children function at the solitary level of play. It is normal for them to be aware of other children and even enjoy having them around, however, they don't play with other children.

Language: Children's vocabularies consist of more than three but less than fifty words. These words usually refer to people, objects, or activities with which they are familiar. They frequently chatter using meaningless sounds as if they were really talking like adults. They can understand language to some extent. For instance, children will often be able to respond to directives or questions such as "Give Mommy a kiss," or "Would you like a cookie?"

Age 2 Years

Motor: By age 2, children can walk and run quite well. They also can often master balancing briefly on one foot and throwing a ball in an overhead manner. They can use the stairs themselves by taking one step at a time and by placing both feet on each step. They are also capable of turning pages of a book and stringing large beads.

Play: 2-year-olds are very interested in exploring their world. They like to play with small objects such as toy animals and can stack up to six or seven blocks. They like to play with and push large objects such as wagons and walkers. They also enjoy exploring the texture and form of materials such as sand, water, and clay. Adults' daily activities such as cooking, carpentry, or cleaning are frequently imitated. Two-year-olds also enjoy looking at books and can name common pictures.

Adaptive: 2-year-olds begin to be capable of listening to and following directions. They can assist in dressing rather than merely cooperating. For example, they may at least try to button their clothes, although they are unlikely to be successful. They attempt washing

their hands. A small glass can be held and used with one hand.

They use spoons to feed themselves fairly well. Two-year-olds have usually attained daytime bowel and bladder control with only occasional accidents. Nighttime control is improving but still not complete.

Social: These children play alongside each other, but not with each other in a cooperative fashion. They are becoming more and more aware of the feelings and reactions of adults. They begin to seek adult approval for correct behavior. They also begin to show their emotions in the forms of affection, guilt, or pity. They tend to have mastered the concept of saying "No," and use it frequently.

Language: 2-year-olds can usually put two or three words together to express an idea. For instance, they might say, "Daddy gone," or "Want milk." Their vocabulary usually includes more than fifty words. Over the next few months, new vocabulary will steadily increase into hundreds of words. They can identify common facial features such as eyes, ears, nose, and so on. Simple directions and requests are usually understood. Although 2-year-olds cannot yet carry on conversations with other people, they frequently talk to themselves or to their toys. It's common to hear them ask "What's this?" in their eagerness to learn the names of things. They also like to listen to simple stories, especially those with which they are very familiar.

Age 3 Years

Motor: At age 3, children can walk well and also run at a steady gait. They can stop quickly and turn corners without falling. They can go up and down stairs using alternating feet. They can begin to ride a tricycle. Three-year-olds participate in a lot of physically active activities such as swinging, climbing, and sliding.

Play: By age 3, children begin to develop their imagination. They use books creatively such as making them into fences or streets. They like to push toys such as trains or cars in make-believe activities. When given the opportunity and interesting toys and materials, they can initiate their own play activities. They also like to imitate the activities of others, especially those of adults. They can cut with scissors and can make some controlled markings with crayons.

Adaptive: 3-year-olds can actively help in dressing. They can put on simple items of clothing such as pants or a sweater, although their clothes may turn out backwards or inside out. They begin to try buttoning and unbuttoning their own clothes. They eat well by using a spoon and have little spilling. They also begin to use a fork. They can get their own glass of water from a faucet and pour liquid from a small pitcher. They can wash their hands and face by themselves with minor help. By age 3, children can use the toilet by themselves, although they frequently ask someone to go with them. They need only minor help with wiping. Accidents are rare, usually happening only occasionally at night.

Social: 3-year-olds tend to pay close attention to the adults around them and are eager to please. They attempt to follow directions and are responsive to

Highlight 2.1

Developmental Milestones for Children from Ages 4 Months to 11 Years (continued)

approval or disapproval. They also can be reasoned with at this age. By age 3, children begin to develop their capacity to relate to and communicate with others. They show an interest in the family and in family activities. Their play is still focused on the parallel level where their interest is concentrated primarily on their own activities. However, they are beginning to notice what other children are doing. Some cooperation is initiated in the form of taking turns or verbally settling arguments.

Language: 3-year-olds can use sentences that are longer and more complex. Plurals, personal pronouns such as "I," and prepositions such as "above" or "on" are used appropriately. Children are able to express their feelings and ideas fairly well. They are capable of relating a story. They listen fairly well and are very interested in longer, more complicated stories than they were at an earlier age. They also have mastered a substantial amount of information including their last name, their gender, and a few rhymes.

Age 4 Years

Motor: 4-year-olds tend to be very active physically. They enjoy running, skipping, jumping, and performing stunts. They are capable of racing up and down stairs. Their balance is very good, and they can carry a glass of liquid without spilling it.

Play: By age 4, children have become increasingly more creative and imaginative. They like to construct things out of clay, sand, or blocks. They enjoy using costumes and other pretend materials. They can play cooperatively with other children. Simple figures can be drawn, although they are frequently inaccurate and without much detail. Four-year-olds can also cut or trace along a line fairly accurately.

Adaptive: 4-year-olds tend to be very assertive. They usually can dress themselves. They've mastered the use of buttons and zippers. They can put on and lace their own shoes, although they cannot yet tie them. They can wash their hands without supervision. By age 4, children demand less attention while eating with their family. They can serve themselves food and eat by themselves using both spoon and fork. They

can even assist in setting the table. Four-year-olds can use the bathroom by themselves, although they still alert adults of this and sometimes need assistance in wiping. They usually can sleep through the night without having any accidents.

Social: 4-year-olds are less docile than 3-year-olds. They are less likely to conform, in addition to being less responsive to the pleasure or displeasure of adults. Four-year-olds are in the process of separating from their parents and begin to prefer the company of other children over adults. They are often social and talkative. They are very interested in the world around them and frequently ask "what," "why," and "how" questions.

Language: The aggressiveness manifested by 4-year-olds also appears in their language. They frequently brag and boast about themselves. Name calling is common. Their vocabulary has experienced tremendous growth; however, they have a tendency to misuse words and some difficulty with proper grammar. Four-year-olds talk a lot and like to carry on long conversations with others. Their speech is usually very understandable with only a few remnants of earlier, more infantile speech remaining. Their growing imagination also affects their speech. They like to tell stories and frequently mix facts with make-believe.

Age 5 Years

Motor: 5-year-olds are quieter and less active than 4-year-olds. Their activities tend to be more complicated and more directed toward achieving some goal. For example, they are more adept at climbing and at riding a tricycle. They can also use roller skates, jump rope, skip, and succeed at other such complex activities. Their ability to concentrate is also increased. The pictures they draw, although simple, are finally recognizable. Dominance of the left or right hand becomes well established.

Play: Games and play activities have become both more elaborate and competitive. Games include hide-and-seek, tag, and hopscotch. Team playing begins. Five-year-olds enjoy pretend games of a more elaborate nature. They like to build houses and forts with blocks and to participate in more dramatic play such as playing house or being a space invader. Singing songs, dancing, and playing records are usually very enjoyable.

Abortion is defined as "the termination of a pregnancy before the fetus can survive outside the uterus" (Masters et al., 1995, p. 178). Thus, social workers may find themselves in the position of helping their clients explore abortion as one possibility open to them. Highlight 2.2 provides a case example of how a young woman struggled with her dilemma.

The concept of abortion inevitably elicits strong feelings and emotions in people. These feelings can be very positive or negative. People who take stands against abortion often do so on moral and ethical grounds. A common theme is that each "unborn child" has "the right to life." On the opposite pole are those who feel strongly in favor of abortion. They feel that women

Adaptive: 5-year-olds can dress and undress themselves quite well. Assistance is necessary only for adjusting more complicated fasteners and tying shoes. These children can feed themselves and attend to their own toilet needs. They can even visit the neighborhood by themselves, needing help only in crossing streets.

Social: By age 5, children have usually learned to co-operate with others in activities and enjoy group activities. They acknowledge the rights of others and are better able to respond to adult supervision. They have become aware of rules and are interested in conforming to them. Five-year-olds also tend to enjoy family activities such as outings and trips.

Language: Language continues to develop and become more complex. Vocabulary continues to increase. Sentence structure becomes more complicated and more accurate. Five-year-olds are very interested in what words mean. They like to look at books and have people read to them. They have begun learning how to count and can recognize colors. Attempts at drawing numbers and letters are begun, although fine motor coordination is not yet well enough developed for great accuracy.

Ages 6 to 8 Years

Motor: Children ages 6 to 8 years are physically independent. They can run, jump, and balance well. They continue to participate in a variety of activities to help refine their coordination and motor skills. They often enjoy unusual and challenging activities, such as walking on fences, which help to develop such skills.

Play: These children participate in much active play such as kickball. They like activities such as gymnastics and enjoy trying to perform physical stunts. They also begin to develop intense interest in simple games such as marbles or tiddlywinks and collecting items. Playing with dolls is at its height. Acting out dramatizations becomes very important, and these children love to pretend they are animals, horseback riders, or jet pilots.

Adaptive: Much more self-sufficient and independent, these children can dress themselves, go to bed alone, and get up by themselves during the night to go to the bathroom. They can begin to be trusted with an allowance. They are able to go to school or to friends' homes alone. In general, they become increasingly more interested in and understanding of various social situations.

Social: In view of their increasing social skills, they consider playing skills within their peer group increasingly important. They become more and more adept at social skills. Their lives begin to focus around the school and activities with friends. They are becoming more sensitive to reactions of those around them, especially those of their parents. There is some tendency to react negatively when subjected to pressure or criticism. For instance, they may sulk.

Language: The use of language continues to become more refined and sophisticated. Good pronunciation and grammar are developed according to that which they've been exposed to. They are learning how to put their feelings and thoughts into words to express themselves more clearly. They begin to understand more abstract words and forms of language. For example, they may begin to understand some puns and jokes. They also begin to develop reading, writing, and numerical skills.

Ages 9 to 11 Years

Motor: Children continue to refine and develop their coordination and motor skills. They experience a gradual, steady gain in body measurements and proportion. Manual dexterity, posture, strength, and balance improve. This period of late childhood is transitional to the major changes experienced during adolescence.

Play: This period frequently becomes the finale of the games and play of childhood. If it has not already occurred, boys and girls separate into their respective same-gender groups.

Adaptive: Children become more and more aware of themselves and the world around them. They experience a gradual change from identifying primarily with adults to formulating their own self identity. They become more independent. This is a period of both physical and mental growth. These children push themselves into experiencing new things and new activities. They learn to focus on detail and accomplish increasingly difficult intellectual and academic tasks.

Social: The focus of attention shifts from a family orientation to a peer orientation. They continue developing social competence. Friends become very important.

Language: A tremendous increase in vocabulary occurs. These children become adept at the use of words. They can answer questions with more depth of insight. They understand more abstract concepts and use words more precisely. They are also better able to understand and examine verbal and mathematical relationships.

have "the right to choice" over their own bodies and lives.

The issue concerning unplanned and, in this context, unwanted pregnancy provides an excellent example of how institutional values affect the options available to clients. In June 1992, the Supreme Court ruled that states could have extensive power in restricting abortions, al-though they could not outlaw all abortions. If abortions are illegal or unavailable to specific groups in the population, then women's choices about what to do are much more limited.

The abortion issue illustrates how clients function within the contexts of their mezzo and macro environments. For example, perhaps a woman's parents are

Highlight 2.2

Case Example: Single and Pregnant

Roseanne was 21 years old and 2 months pregnant. She was a junior at a large midwestern state university, majoring in social work. Hank, the father, was a 26-year-old divorcé she met in one of her classes. He already had a 4-year-old son named Ronnie.

Roseanne was filled with ambivalent feelings. She had always pictured herself as being a mother someday. However, not now. She felt she loved Hank but had many reservations about how he felt in return. She'd been seeing him once or twice a week for the past few months. Hank didn't really take her out much, and she suspected that he was also dating other women. He had even asked her to babysit for Ronnie while he went out with someone else.

That was another thing—Ronnie. She felt Ronnie hated her. He would snarl whenever she came over and make nasty, cutting remarks. Maybe he was jealous that his father was giving Roseanne attention.

The pregnancy was an accident. She simply didn't think anything would happen. She knew better now that it was too late. Hank had never made any commitment to her. In some ways she felt he was a creep, but at least he was honest. The fact was that he just didn't love her.

The problem was, What should she do? A college education was important to her and to her parents. Money had always been a big issue. Her parents helped her as much as they could, but they also had other children in college. Roseanne worked odd, inconvenient hours at a fast-food restaurant for a while. She also worked as a cook several nights a week at a diner.

What if she kept the baby? She was fairly certain Hank didn't want to marry her. Even if he did, she didn't think she'd want to be stuck with him for the rest of her life.

How could she possibly manage on her own with a baby? She shared a two-bedroom apartment with three other female students. How could she take care of a baby with no money and no place to go? She felt dropping out of school would ruin her life. The idea of "going on welfare" instead of working in welfare was terrifying. On the other hand, the idea of an abortion scared her. She had heard so many people say that it was "murder."

Roseanne made her decision, but it certainly was not an easy one. She carefully addressed and considered the religious and moral issues involved in terminating a pregnancy. She decided that she would have to face the responsibility and the guilt. In determining that having a baby at this time would be disastrous for both herself and for a new life, she decided to have an abortion.

Fourteen years have passed. Roseanne is now 35. She is no longer in social work although she finished her degree. She does have a good job as a court reporter. This job suits her well. She's been married to Tom for 3 years. Although they have their ups and downs, she is happy in her marriage. They love each other very much and enjoy their time together.

Roseanne thinks about her abortion once in a while. Although she is using no method of birth control, she has not yet gotten pregnant. Possibly, she never will. Tom is 43. He had been married once before and has an adult child from that marriage. He does not feel it is a necessity for them to have children.

Roseanne is ambivalent. She is addressing the possibility of not having children and is looking at the consequences of that alternative. She puts it well by saying that sometimes she mourns the loss of her unborn child. Yet, in view of her present level of satisfaction and Tom's hesitation about having children, she feels that her life thus far has worked out for the best.

---

unwilling to help her with a newborn or the child's father shuns involvement. In both these instances some of the woman's potential mezzo system options have already been eliminated.

Options are also affected by macro environments. If abortion is illegal, then social agencies are unable to provide them. Another possibility is that states can legally allow abortions only under extremely limited circumstances. For instance, they may be allowed only if the conception is the product of incest or rape, or if the pregnancy and birth seriously endanger the pregnant woman's life.

Even if states allow abortions, the community in which a pregnant woman lives can pose serious restrictions on her options. For instance, a community renowned for having a strong and well-organized anti-abortion movement may be supportive of actions (including legal actions) to curtail abortion services. Abortion clinics can be picketed, patients harassed, and clinic staff personally threatened. Such strong community feelings can force clinics to close.

Additionally, the abortion issue provides an excellent opportunity to distinguish between personal and professional values. Each of us probably has an opinion about abortion. Some of us most likely have very strong opinions either one way or the other. In practice, our personal opinions really don't matter. However, our professional approach does. As professionals it is our responsibility to help clients come to their own decisions. Our job is to assist clients in assessing their own feelings and values, in identifying available alternatives, and in evaluating as objectively as possible the consequences of each alternative.

The National Association of Social Workers (NASW) has established a policy statement on its position on abortion. Policy is a clearly stated or implicit procedure, plan, rule, or stance concerning some issue that serves to

A confrontation at an abortion demonstration. The abortion issue is one of the most controversial in this country.

© Stephanie Maze/CORBIS

guide decision making and behavior. The statement reads: "The social work profession's position concerning abortion, family planning, and other reproductive health services is based on the principle of self-determination. . . . Every individual (within the context of his or her value system) must be free to participate or not participate in abortion, family planning, and other reproductive services." (NASW, 1997, pp. 113–114). The statement continues: "The profession supports . . . [t]he provision of reproductive health services including abortion services that are legal, safe, and free from duress for both patients and providers." Even more specifically, NASW

- "supports a woman's right to seek and obtain a medically safe abortion under dignified circumstances;
- opposes government restrictions on access to reproductive health services, including abortion services, or on financing for them in health insurance and foreign aid programs;
- opposes any special conditions and requirements, such as mandatory counseling or waiting periods, attached to the receipt of any type of reproductive health care."

Five aspects of abortion are discussed here. First, the current impacts of legal and political macro systems are described. Second, the abortion process itself and the types of abortion available are explained. Third, some of the psychological effects of abortion are briefly examined. Fourth, the arguments for and against abortion are

compared and assessed. Fifth, a variety of social work roles with respect to the abortion issue are described.

The Impacts of Macro System Policies on Practice and Access to Services

We have established that institutional values affect laws. In many cases, laws can be considered a reflection of institutional values. Laws, in turn, regulate policy regarding how people can make decisions and choose to act. Government and agency policies specify and regulate what services organizations can provide to women within communities. Subsequently, whether services are available or not controls the choices available to most pregnant women.

The abortion debate focuses on two opposing perspectives, antiabortion and pro-choice. Carroll and Wolpe (1996) describe the antiabortion stance as the belief "that human life, and therefore personhood, begins at conception, and so an embryo, at any stage of development, is a person. Therefore, . . . aborting a fetus is murder, and . . . the government should make all abortions illegal" (p. 434).

Pro-choice advocates, on the other hand, focus on a woman's right to choose whether to have an abortion. They believe that a woman has the right to control what happens to her own body and to "care for her life, her happiness, her well-being (and in some cases the well-being of her present and future family and children)" (Ruth, 1998, p. 249).

Over the past three decades the political controversy over abortion has been raging. In 1973 the U.S. Supreme

Spotlight on Diversity 2.1 — International Perspectives on Abortion Policy

The following are brief summaries of policies concerning abortion that have been adopted by countries around the world. Obviously, huge variations exist:

BRAZIL: Estimates are that 30 percent of all pregnancies end in abortion, which is illegal (Byer et al., 2002).

EGYPT: Abortion is illegal unless the woman's life is in danger; however, abortions are performed surreptitiously in private Cairo clinics (Kelly, 2001).

FRANCE: The national health care system pays for abortions in government-approved clinics for any reason up to the tenth week of pregnancy. Single minors must obtain parental consent (Kelly, 2001). Women are required to wait one week, receive counseling concerning abortion alternatives, and be provided with contraceptive information (Byer et al., 2002).

GREAT BRITAIN: Women seeking abortions must be authorized by two physicians; abortion was legalized in 1967 and is no longer a major political dispute (Kelly, 2001).

IRELAND: Although abortion is illegal in Ireland, "thousands of women go to other countries each year for the procedure" (Kelly, 2001, p. 335).

JAPAN: Abortions are usually legal up to 22 weeks of gestation, but can be performed after that if the mother's life is in danger; the husband's or partner's consent is usually necessary (Kelly, 2001).

LATIN AMERICA: Abortion is illegal in all countries but Barbados and Cuba; there is current debate about legalizing it elsewhere (Byer et al., 2002; Kelly, 2001).

LATVIA: Abortion is the primary form of birth control; there is some evidence that abortion is more common than live births (Byer et al., 2002).

POLAND: Since 1992, when the government deemed abortions illegal, self-induced abortions have become rampant (Byer et al., 2002; Kelly, 2001).

RUSSIA: Abortions are legal and used to terminate about two-thirds of pregnancies; typically, Russian women will have a number of abortions over their lifetimes (Kelly, 2001).

TURKEY: Any woman can have an abortion up to the tenth week of gestation; significant numbers of pregnancies result in abortion (Byer et al., 2001).

Court decision known as *Roe* v. *Wade* overruled state laws that prohibited or restricted a woman's right to obtain an abortion during the first 3 months of pregnancy. States were allowed to impose restrictions in the second trimester only when such restrictions related directly to the mother's health. Finally, during the third trimester states could restrict abortions or even forbid them excluding those necessary to preserve a woman's life and health. Women, in essence, won the right to "privacy," or, in other words, "the right to be left alone" (Hartman, 1991, p. 267). This, of course, is a pro-choice stance.

It appears that the courts have gotten increasingly more conservative concerning abortion. In 1992 the Supreme Court ruled that states had the right to restrict abortions as they saw fit, except that they could not outlaw *all* abortions. Additionally, the Court has put restrictions of increasing severity into place. In *Harris* v. *McRae* (1980) the Court confirmed that both Congress and individual states could legally refuse to pay for abortions. This significantly impacted poor women.

In *Webster* v. *Reproductive Health Services* (1989), the Supreme Court upheld a restrictive Missouri law. This law "prohibits performing abortions in public hospitals unless the mother's life is in danger; forbids the spending of state funds for counseling women about abortion; and requires doctors to add an expensive layer of testing before performing abortions after twenty weeks if they feel it will help them determine whether a fetus would be viable outside the womb" (Wermiel & McQueen, 1989, p. 1).

Since this decision, many states have passed bills imposing restrictions on abortions. For example, as of this writing, 43 states require minors to notify, or obtain permission from, an adult—usually a parent—before obtaining an abortion; additionally, 22 states "have mandatory waiting periods that prohibit a woman from obtaining an abortion until a specified period of time after receiving a state-mandated lecture or materials" (National Abortion and Reproductive Rights Action League [NARAL], 2002).

The abortion debate continues. New decisions are made daily at the state and federal levels. However, a number of issues remain in the forefront when assessing the impacts on clients' rights and on their ability to function. Several have surfaced in recent years and will probably continue to characterize the abortion debate. We will discuss a number of them here: limiting financial support, limiting access to services, consideration of the mother's condition, consideration of fetal condition, violence against abortion clinics, and fetal tissue research. Spotlight 2.1 portrays an international perspective on abortion policy.

Limiting Financial Support. One clear trend since 1973 has been the antiabortion faction's pressure to limit public financial support for abortion. For example, federal funding can be withheld from agencies providing counseling for pregnant women and women seeking birth control methods. Congress provides funding to thousands of clinics that serve millions of low-income women through Title X of the Public Health Service Act enacted in 1970. Thus, limiting public funding would have the greatest impact on poor women who cannot afford expensive private care.

Planned Parenthood organizations throughout the country are an example of agencies that would be affected if public funding were withheld. Planned Parenthood's philosophy is that women have the right to control their own bodies. This includes the right to accurate information about available options. Planned Parenthood espouses the concept of family planning: "making deliberate and voluntary decisions about reproduction . . . [including] the number and timing of pregnancies after considering economic circumstances, life goals, the nature of the reproductive process, and contraception methods" (Barker, 1999, p. 168). Planned Parenthood clinics present abortion as a viable alternative that women can choose.

Hartman (1991) questions the antiabortion or pro-life stance. She asks why those supporting "life" and the restriction of resources for abortion don't also support "life" for the child and family before and after the birth. She states:

> the right to life, if it truly begins at conception, should not end at the moment of birth. . . . Although the rights of the unborn have been defended, social and health programs needed to enhance the lives of infants and children have been decimated. If we really care so much about life, about children, how can we allow one in five to live in poverty? How can we tolerate being nineteenth among the nations in infant mortality? If we believe in the fetus's right to life, why have funds been cut for prenatal care? If we want to protect children, we must make social and economic supports available to their parents. (p. 468)

Limiting Access to Services. Any court rulings that impose limitations on decision making make getting an abortion more difficult. Escalating costs make access to abortion more difficult for poor women. Additionally, such tactics as not allowing abortions to be performed in public hospitals (to which poor women have primary access) significantly inhibit their ability to choose abortion.

Another way of limiting access is to require an arbitrary waiting period after a woman has made her decision (for example, 24 hours) before she can have an abortion. The decision to abort can be very painful for many reasons, and a waiting period can result in significant stress. Still another way of limiting access to services involves requiring young women to notify or get permission from their parents before having an abortion. Fear of confronting parents may cause many young women to delay making the decision to have an abortion.

One other means of limiting access to abortion involves requiring extensive testing for fetal viability, a fetus's ability to survive independently outside of the womb. Antiabortion factions have suggested that a number of complex and expensive tests be required before second trimester abortions can be performed. Cost, in this case, would inhibit access.

Condition of the Woman. Some people support the idea that abortion is acceptable under some specific conditions. One involves the mother's health. Should an abortion be performed if carrying the fetus to full-term will kill the mother? Whose life is more important, that of the mother or that of the fetus?

Should a woman impregnated during rape or incest be forced to carry the fetus to term? Is it fair to force a woman who has suffered the horror of a sexual assault to live with that assault's results, an unwanted child, for the rest of her life?

Fetal Condition. The condition of the fetus illustrates another circumstance where some consider abortion acceptable. If the fetus is severely damaged or defective, should the mother be forced to carry it to term? A subsidiary question relates to that posed earlier by Hartman (1991). If a woman is forced to carry and bear a child, why isn't similar force or support used to provide her with resources to care for herself and the child before and after birth? To what extent would a mother being forced to bear a child with severe disabilities also be forced to provide the huge resources necessary for maintaining such a child?

Violence Against Clinics. The abortion controversy has been fraught with violence. Dr. Barnett Slepian, a New York "obstetrician and gynecologist who refused to stop performing abortions despite constant harassment, became the third doctor and seventh person killed since 1993 by anti-abortion extremists" (AASECT, January 1999a, p. 14). Shortly after the murder, the owner of a Web site called "The Nuremberg Files" reportedly "marked a line through Slepian's name on his roster of abortion providers. . . . [This man] compares doctors who perform abortions to Nazi war criminals, and says he seeks to record their crimes so that they can be prosecuted in the future." Visitors to the site will find information about abortion providers, including pictures, driver's license numbers and addresses" (AASECT, January 1999, p. 14). The National Abortion Federation indicates that there have been more than 1,700 attacks on abortion providers since 1977 (AASECT, January 1999a).

Bombings and arson also characterize violence against clinics; the peak year for bombings was 1984 when eleven took place and for arson 1992 when twenty-one fires were set (Whitman, 1998). New federal legislation passed in 1994, "which created penalties for obstructing, intimidating, or interfering with women seeking abortions, helped slash the number of clinic blockades from 210 in 1989 to twenty-five" in 1997 (Whitman, 1999, p. 22).

Although some types of antiabortion violence have decreased over time, the threat of occurrence remains scary for patients and clinic staff. "Disruptive tactics like picketing, hate mail, and bomb threats" continue to reach record highs (Whitman, 1999, p. 22). Indeed, the number of abortion providers has shown "a sharp and ongoing drop" since 1982 (Whitman, 1999, p. 20).

As the 1994 legislation reflects, there in ongoing potential for policy changes concerning violence against clinics and harassment of patients and personnel.

Abortion clinics and pro-choice groups stress that they are functioning legally and need protection from harassment and violence. Antiabortion supporters, on the other hand, pursue activities, sometimes extreme, to inhibit and stop abortions from being performed. To the extent that violence against clinics and harassment of clinic staff and patients continue, women's access to legal abortions may be significantly curtailed. For whatever reason, the number of U.S. abortions performed has reached its record low since 1978 according to the Centers for Disease Control and Prevention[6] (Griffin, 2000).

Fetal Tissue Research. A recent controversial issue related to abortion involves the use of fetal tissue (stem cells) for scientific health research and treatment. Stem cells are "cells extracted from embryos created for fertility treatments but not used to produce children" (Lacayo, 2001, p. 17). McCammon and her associates (1998) explain that "fetal tissue is uniquely suitable for medical research in that it is 'nonspecific,' meaning it can develop into any kind of tissue (such as muscle or organ) if it is transplanted into humans" (p. 204). Fetal cells, in contrast to mature adult cells, "keep growing rapidly after being transplanted" and have a "talent for secreting a cocktail of chemicals that help restore and replace damaged tissue" (Watson, 1994, p. 50). Additionally, they are less likely "to be rejected by the recipient's immune system than tissues transplanted from other adults" (Kelly, 2001, p. 335).

Researchers have used fetal tissue to develop vaccines including those for polio and rubella (McCammon et al., 1998). The first fetal cell transplant for Parkinson's disease[7] was performed in 1988 when cells were implanted into a patient's brain (McCammon et al., 1998). Other possibilities include transplants for treating Alzheimer's disease, spinal cord damage, epilepsy, and various neuromuscular disorders (Kelly, 2001; Lacayo, 2001). Still other research has focused on the possibility of correcting at least 155 genetic disorders in fetuses; "while still developing in the womb, fetuses with certain genetic disorders can receive transplants from nondefective fetal tissue and subsequently develop into normal, healthy infants" (McCammon et al., 1998, p. 204).

The debate regarding whether federal funding should be channeled for fetal tissue research has been seething for more than a decade. "Religious conservatives argue that using those stem cells means deriving benefit from the destruction of human embryos—fertilized eggs in the early stages of development—in their eyes no less a crime than abortion" (Lacayo, 2001, p. 17).

In 2001 President George W. Bush established a widely reported compromise concerning this debate. He determined that federal funding would only be provided for research on the existing 65 stem cell lines that have already been "harvested" or prepared for use. No new ones would be eligible for funding.

This issue raises still other questions concerning human embryonic tissue: "Is an embryo growing in a Petri dish the same as one growing in a womb? Is it O.K. to experiment on it if it's going to be destroyed anyway?" (Gibbs & Duffy, 2001, p. 12). Is the protection of unused fetal tissue more important than the possibility that its use

---

6. The Centers for Disease Control and Prevention (CDCP) is an Atlanta-based national health organization, under the auspices of the U.S. Department of Health and Human Services, that coordinates efforts to prevent the spread of disease. Efforts include conducting research, analyzing data, and distributing information about disease and its incidence.

7. Parkinson's disease is a progressive disease of the nervous system, usually occurring later in life, that is characterized by muscular weakness, tremors, and a shuffling gait.

in research could improve and save the lives of numerous people? Would pregnant women be encouraged to seek abortions if they thought fetal tissue could benefit medical research? Would people and organizations start buying and selling fetal tissue for profit?

We have just scratched the surface of some of the debates currently raging. Social workers need to understand the issues and the context in which opposing views are raised in order to help clients make difficult decisions. The abortion issue with its potent pro-choice and anti-abortion factions in the political arena illustrates the impact that macro systems can have on individual lives. The extent to which national policies limit the availability of abortion services relates directly to service accessibility. Organizations in the macro environment must have the sanction of the national and state macro systems in order to provide women with free choice.

The next section describes the incidence of abortion, common abortion procedures, and the pros and cons of abortion. Finally, various social work roles concerning the issue are discussed.

Incidence of Abortion

The Centers for Disease Control and Prevention cites the following facts concerning the incidence of abortion (Griffin, 2000):

- In 1997, 1,184,758 abortions were performed in the United States.
- This figure reflects a 3 percent decrease from the 1,221,585 abortions performed in 1996.
- However, the rate of abortion remained stable since 1995 in that 20 abortions were performed for every 1,000 women aged 15 to 44.

According to Ginsberg (1995), "about 40 percent of teen pregnancies end in abortion. . . . Although white women have about 65 percent of all abortions, the non-white abortion rate is more than twice that of the white rate. Hispanic women are 60 percent more likely to have abortions than non-Hispanic women.

"Women who claim no religious affiliation are four times as likely to have abortions as are religious women" (Wagner, 1996, p. 8). More specifically, "Roman Catholic women are 30 percent more likely to have abortions than Protestant women; Jewish women are less likely to have them" (Ginsberg, 1995, p. 239); and "eighteen percent of abortion patients describe themselves as born-again or evangelical Christians" (Wagner, 1996, p. 8).

Methods of Abortion

Several different procedures are used to perform abortions. The major variable that determines the procedure is how far the pregnancy has progressed. Methods used during the first trimester include vacuum aspiration and abortion-inducing drugs such as RU 486 or methotrexate. Second trimester procedures include dilation and evacuation, and induction of labor.

Vacuum Aspiration. Vacuum aspiration (also referred to as vacuum curettage or vacuum suction), by far the most common abortion technique, is performed in over 90 percent of all abortions (Rathus et al., 2002). It is a relatively simple procedure performed during the first trimester of pregnancy usually under local anesthesia.

The procedure involves first dilating the cervix (that is, widening the opening into the uterus) by inserting a series of metal rods with increasing diameters. Then, a small tube is inserted into the vagina and then through the cervix into the uterus. The tube is connected to a suction machine that vacuums out the fetal tissue from the uterus. The physician may then use a scoop-like instrument called a curette to scrape out any remaining tissue.

Sometimes, a stick of seaweed called laminaria is inserted into the cervix to cause dilation and decrease the risk of lacerating or tearing the cervix. Most dilation occurs within about 6 hours. Synthetic dilators have also been developed that appear to work even better than laminaria (Cates & Ellertson, 1998).

Vacuum aspiration can be performed up to 12 weeks into the pregnancy (Kelly, 2001; Rathus et al., 2002). The entire procedure takes about 10 minutes (Crooks & Baur, 2002). It can be performed on an outpatient basis with local anesthesia in a physician's office, a clinic, or a hospital. Most clinics require patients to remain in the recovery room for approximately an hour afterward to make certain there is no hemorrhaging or allergic reactions to the anesthetic used (Masters et al., 1995).

Complications of vacuum aspiration occur very rarely; they include "hemorrhage, [uterine] perforation, and infection" (Allgeier & Allgeier, 2000, p. 258). Research has established that no negative effects occur with respect to "subsequent fertility, subsequent pregnancy outcomes, or the risk of subsequent ectopic (tubal) pregnancy" (Masters et al., 1995).

Abortion-Inducing Drugs. Mifepristone, or RU 486 the name given during initial testing), is a drug that prevents the uterine lining from getting the hormones it needs to continue supporting the fertilized egg, which then dies. Most effective during the first 7 weeks of pregnancy, the process involves several steps (Strong et al., 2002). First, a woman sees a physician to verify the pregnancy. Second, mifepristone is administered. Two days later, she is given misopristol (a type of hormone), which causes uterine contractions that result in expulsion of the fetal material. Finally, she makes a follow-up visit to the physician after about 12 days to make certain the procedure worked. Side effects may include nausea, vomiting, headaches, fatigue, and abdominal pain. It is estimated that this procedure effectively terminates the pregnancy in about 95 percent of cases.

Advantages of RU 486 include: being able to perform the procedure early in the pregnancy; low incidence of side effects; no need for surgery or anesthesia; and little risk of infection or perforation of the uterus. A disadvantage is the potential bleeding and discomfort occurring between administration of the drugs and expulsion of fetal material—a process that may take days instead of minutes.

Mifepristone, approved for distribution in the United States in 2000, has caused considerable debate, despite the fact that it has been used for over a decade in various other countries including France, Great Britain, and China. Antiabortion proponents worry it may make abortions too readily available. On the other hand, it has also shown "promise for treating breast cancer, endometriosis, . . . Cushing's disease,[8] forms of leukemia, malaria, advanced anemia, other cancers, and perhaps AIDS" (Allgeier & Allgeier, 2000, p. 256).

Dilation and Evacuation. Second trimester abortions are more complicated and involve greater risks. An abortion method that can be used during the fourth and fifth months of pregnancy is dilation and evacuation (D & E). This method resembles vacuum aspiration in that fetal material is initially suctioned out of the uterus and then usually scraped out with a curette. However, because a D & E is performed later in pregnancy, a greater amount of fetal material must be removed. General anesthesia instead of local is often used (Allgeier & Allgeier, 1995). Potential complications include those associated with vacuum aspiration and those resulting from general anesthesia.

Inducing Labor. During the second trimester miscarriages can be induced by using three main agents, hypertonic saline, hypertonic urea, and prostaglandin E2.

8. Cushing's disease is a condition characterized by obesity and muscular weakness due to excess corticosteroids produced by the adrenal or pituitary glands.

However, these substances are used in only 1 percent of all abortions in the United States. D & E procedures can be performed more quickly, are safer, and cost less (Cates & Ellertson, 1998).

Labor can be induced by injecting hypertonic saline through the abdomen into the amniotic sac through a fine tube (Cates & Ellertson, 1998; Hyde & DeLamater, 2000). Some of the amniotic fluid is first removed through the tube and then replaced with saline solution. Labor and expulsion of the fetus result. Hypertonic urea can be injected in a similar manner with similar results. Prostaglandin E2 is available as a suppository that is inserted into the vagina to induce labor. These three methods have disadvantages: they take hours of time; they cause the patient emotional and physical distress; they are more hazardous than other methods; and they are more expensive than the other abortion methods discussed earlier.

The Importance of Context and Timing

The risk of dying from an abortion is between 0.4 and 1 in 100,000 (McCammon et al., 1998). Problems are less likely to occur when the pregnancy is early, the woman is healthy, the woman is not ambivalent about having the procedure, and follow-up care is readily available (Cates & Ellertson, 1998). "Women are ten times more likely to die from childbirth than from abortion" (McCammon et al., 1998, p. 210). In contrast, there are almost 20 maternal deaths per 100,000 pregnancies resulting in birth.

Denney and Quadagno (1992) comment on the risks associated with abortion: "Abortion-related health risks are greatly reduced if the pregnancy is terminated as early as possible, if the patient is healthy, if the clinician is skilled and uses sterile technique, and if the woman is confident in her decision to have the abortion. . . . The most common problems include infection, retained products of conception in the uterus, continuing pregnancy, cervical or uterine trauma, and bleeding" (p. 250). Spotlight 2.2 explores the long-term effects of abortion on women and men.

Arguments For and Against Abortion

Numerous arguments have been advanced for and against permitting abortions. Many of these views are related to how facts are interpreted and presented. Following is a sampling of arguments in favor of abortion rights:

- Permitting women to obtain an abortion corresponds with the principle of self-determination and allows women to have greater freedom of choice concerning their own bodies and lives.

Spotlight on Diversity 2.2   Effects of Abortion on Women and Men

We have established that vacuum aspiration during the first trimester has little, if any, effect on a woman's subsequent physical condition or pregnancies. If researchers discover any negative effects in the future, they will likely involve specific abortion techniques, such as the way dilation is induced, the method of curettage employed to remove fetal material, and the fetus's age. When abortions are performed during the first trimester and vacuum aspiration is used, there is "little effect on subsequent fertility or on the risk of spontaneous abortions, premature delivery, and low birthweight babies (Cates & Ellertson, 1998, p. 696; Haffner, 1995). There also appears to be little danger associated with the use of RU 486 with prostaglandins (Hyde & DeLamater, 2000; Masters et al., 1995). The latter's long-term safety is being determined by ongoing testing.

Substantial research has determined that most women experience no serious psychological effects after having an abortion (Adler et al., 1992; Allgeier & Allgeier, 2000; Cates & Ellertson, 1998; Kelly, 1998; Russo & Dabul, 1997). In actuality, serious psychological distress is far less prevalent than the occurrence of postpartum depression in women who carry their pregnancies to term (Adler & Tschann, 1993). Adler (1989) testified before a congressional committee and summarized existing information about long-term effects. It was concluded "that severe negative reactions to legal abortions are rare, that the greatest distress is experienced before the abortion,

and that the predominant post-abortion emotions are positive" (Lott, 1994, p. 206).

Terminating a pregnancy is often a difficult and complex decision. Lott (1994) describes the plight of women considering abortion: "For most women in this country abortion is a last resort. Religious, moral, and medical considerations enter in, so do fear for one's health and safety and for one's future ability to have children. Issues must also be resolved relating to a woman's relationship with the man who participated in the conception" (p. 205).

However, women's negative feelings are not necessarily of long duration, especially if counseling is sought to help deal with these issues (Masters et al., 1995).

Men and Abortion
A frequently ignored psychological aspect of abortion is the male's reaction to the process. Many men experience a sense of "powerlessness" and feelings of "residual guilt, sadness, and remorse" (Strong et al., 2002, pp. 364–365). A man may feel ambivalence about the pregnancy and the abortion similar to that felt by his pregnant partner (Byer et al., 2002). Many clinics now provide counseling for male partners of women seeking abortion (Strong et al., 2002). Both partners should receive the counseling they need to make difficult decisions. Women whose partners support and help them through an abortion experience less trauma and respond more positively after it is over (Adler et al., 1990).

- If abortions were prohibited, women would seek illegal abortions as they did in the past. No law has ever stopped abortion and no law ever will. Performed in a medical clinic or hospital, an abortion is relatively safe; but performed under unsanitary conditions, perhaps by an inexperienced or unskilled abortionist, the operation is extremely dangerous and may even imperil the woman's life.

- If abortions were prohibited, some women would attempt to self-induce abortions. Such attempts can be life-threatening. Women have tried such techniques as severe exercise, hot baths, and pelvic and intestinal irritants, and have even attempted to lacerate the uterus with such sharp objects as nail files and knives.

- No contraceptive method is perfectly reliable. All have failure rates and disadvantages. Contraceptive information and services are not readily available and accessible to all women, particularly teenagers, the poor, and rural women.

- Abortions are necessary in many countries with soaring birth rates. Contraceptives may be in-

adequate, unavailable, or beyond what people can afford. Abortion appears to be a necessary population-control technique to preserve the quality of life. (In some countries the number of abortions is approaching the number of live births.)

Opponents of abortion argue:

- The right of a fertilized egg to life is basic and should in no way be infringed.

- A woman who chooses to have an abortion is selfish. She prefers her own pleasure over the life of her unborn child.

- In a society where contraceptives are so readily available, there should be no unwanted pregnancies and therefore no need for abortion.

- Abortion is immoral and against certain religious beliefs. For example, Pope John Paul II condemns abortion as a sign of the "encroaching 'culture of death' that threatens human dignity and freedom" (Woodward, 1995, p. 56).

- People supporting abortion are antifamily. People should take responsibility for their behavior, cease nonmarital sexual intercourse, and bear children within a family context.

A professional social worker must be aware of arguments on both sides of the issue. Only then can he or she assist a client in making the decision that the client determines is right for her.

Social Worker Roles and Abortion

Social workers can assume a variety of roles when helping women with unwanted pregnancies. Among them are enabler, educator, broker, and advocate. First, as *enablers,* social workers can help women make decisions about what they will do. This involves helping clients identify alternatives and evaluate the pros and cons of each. Chilman (1987) reflects upon how social workers can counsel women concerning abortion:

> *The ultimate decision . . . should be made chiefly by the pregnant woman herself, preferably in consultation with the baby's father and family members. To make the decision that is best for the couple and their child, the pregnant woman— ideally, with the expectant father—needs to view each option in the context of the couple's present skills, resources, values, goals, emotions, important interpersonal relationships, and future plans. The counselor's role is to support and shape a realistic selection of the most feasible pregnancy resolution alternative. (p. 6)*

A second role social workers can assume is that of *educator.* This involves providing the pregnant woman with accurate information about the abortion process, adoption, fetal development, and options available to her. The educator role may also entail providing birth control information to avoid subsequent unwanted pregnancies.

A third social work role involves being a *broker.* Regardless of her final decision, a pregnant woman will need to acquaint herself with the appropriate resources. These include abortion clinics, prenatal health counseling, and adoption services. A social worker can inform her of available resources, explain them, and help her obtain them.

Finally, a social worker can function as an *advocate* for a pregnant woman. A woman might want an abortion, yet live in a state that severely restricts getting them; if she is poor, her access to an abortion is even further restricted. A worker can advocate on this woman's behalf to improve her access to abortion or to financial support for abortion services. Another form of advocacy would be to work to change the laws and policies that inhibit women

from getting the services they need. If a woman decides against an abortion, a social worker can advocate for the resources and services the woman needs to support herself and her pregnancy.

Highlight 2.3 illustrates how social workers can use an ethical principles framework to resolve abortion-related dilemmas.

✥ Infertility

Ralph and Carol, both age 28, had been married for 5 years. Ralph was a drill press operator at a large bathroom fixture plant. Carol was a waitress at a Mexican restaurant. They both liked their jobs well enough. They were earning an adequate enough income to purchase a small three-bedroom home and to enjoy some pleasurable amenities such as going out to dinner occasionally, taking annual camping vacations, and having cable television.

However, they felt something was wrong. Although Carol had stopped taking birth control pills more than 3 years before, she had still not gotten pregnant. She had read in some recent issue of *Cosmopolitan* that women over age 35 had a much greater chance of having a child with mental retardation or birth defects. Although she still had a few years, she was concerned. She and Ralph had always wanted to have as large a family as they could afford. This meant that they had better get going.

The couple really didn't talk much about the issue. Neither one wanted to imply that something might be wrong with the other one. The idea that one or both might be infertile was not appealing. It was almost easier to ignore the issue and hope that it would resolve itself in a pregnancy. After all, they did still have a few years.

Infertility is "the inability or diminished ability to produce children" (Byer et al., 2002). Although many people assume that they will automatically be able to conceive if they don't use birth control, this is obviously not always the case.

Couples who are unable to conceive after one year of regular sexual intercourse face the possibility of infertility. At this point, it is usually recommended that potential physical problems in one or both members of the couple be explored. The number of infertile couples is significant. It is estimated that about 10 to 15 percent of couples are infertile (Santrock, 2002a; G.K. Stewart, 1998a). However, this is an aggregate statistic that does not take into account the effects of age or a wide range of other conditions. Therefore, the 10 to 15 percent summary figure is probably not useful to individual couples seeking

Highlight 2.3

Abortion-related Ethical Dilemmas in Practice

Picture yourself as a professional social worker in practice. What happens when your own personal values seriously conflict with those expressed by your client? A basic professional value clearly specified in the National Association of Social Workers (NASW) Code of Ethics is the right of clients to make their own decisions.

By definition, an ethical dilemma involves conflicting principles. When two or more ethical principles oppose each other, it is impossible to make a "correct" decision that satisfies both or all principles involved. There is no perfect solution. For example, if a 15-year-old client tells you that he plans to murder his mother, you are caught in an ethical dilemma. It is impossible to maintain confidentiality with your client (a basic social work professional value) and yet do all you can to protect his mother from harm.

A wide range of situations involving abortion can place workers in situations involving ethical dilemmas. Loewenberg and Dolgoff (1996) have formulated a hierarchy of ethical principles to provide a guide for making difficult decisions. They suggest which principle should have priority over the other when two ethical principles conflict. The hierarchy can be helpful in working through difficult situations.

The hierarchy involves the following (pp. 62–64):

- *Principle 1: "Protection of life"* is of utmost importance. This might include provision of adequate food, shelter, clothing, or health care. It might concern acting in response to a person's suicide threat or threat of physically harming another. This principle applies not only to clients but also to others whose survival is imperiled.

- *Principle 2:* After protection of life, social workers should strive to *nurture equality and address inequality.* "Equal persons have the right to be treated equally and non-equal persons have the right to be treated differently if the inequality is relevant to the issue in question" (p. 63). On the one hand, groups should be treated equally and have equal access to resources. On the other hand, groups who are oppressed or hold lesser status should be treated specially so that their rights are not violated. For example, consider a child abuse situation. Because the child does not hold an "equal" position with that of an abusive parent, "the principles of confidentiality and autonomy with respect to the abusing adult are of a lower rank order than the obligation to protect the child even when it is not a question of life and death" (p. 63).

- *Principle 3:* Social workers should make practice decisions that *"foster a person's autonomy, independence, and freedom."* Persons should be allowed to make their own choices about their lives. However, this should not be at the expense of their own or someone else's life as Principle 1 prescribes. Maintaining autonomy should not be

pursued if equality supported by Principle 2 would be sacrificed.

- *Principle 4:* Social workers should pursue an option that results in the *"least harm"* to those involved in the decision and its results.

- *Principle 5:* Social workers should make practice decisions that promote a *"better quality of life for all people."* People's overall well-being is important. This involves not only the well-being of an individual or family, but also that of entire communities.

- *Principle 6:* Social workers should *respect people's privacy and maintain confidentiality.* However, this principle is superseded when people's quality of life is endangered.

- *Principle 7:* Practice decisions should allow workers to *be honest and disclose all available information.* Workers should be able to provide any information that they deem necessary in any particular situation. However, the "truth" should not be told for its own sake when it violates a client's confidentiality, which is championed by Principle 6.

Following are illustrations of ethical dilemmas concerning abortion that a worker might face in practice. The first illustration provides an example of how Loewenberg and Dolgoff's hierarchy of ethical principles might be applied. The rest furnish scenarios for you to work out yourself. Remember, there are no easy nor "perfect" answers.

Illustration A

A 16-year-old young woman was raped by a middle-aged man as she walked home from school one night and became pregnant. Both she and her parents are horrified and plagued with worry. They come to you for help. The girl desperately wants an abortion.

Application of Ethical Principles for Illustration A

Consider Principle 1, the need to protect life. If you personally adopt an antiabortion stance and feel that abortion is murder, what do you do? A professional social worker's personal values must be acknowledged yet put aside in professional situations. The young woman and her parents want her to have the abortion.

We then look at Principle 2, which calls for the nurturance of equality and the combating of inequality. According to this principle, people should be treated equally. In this case they should have equal access to services. A neighboring state, its border only 25 miles away, allows abortions for all women who want them within the first trimester. Is this fair? Is this ethical? Should you help the young woman and her parents seek an abortion in a state that has different rules? Or, should you work actively in your own state to advocate for change so that abortion would be a legal alternative for clients such as this?

Now consider Principle 3, which stresses people's right to autonomy, independence, and freedom. The young woman has the right to make her own decision.

Highlight 2.3

Abortion-related Ethical Dilemmas in Practice (continued)

Your state might legally allow abortions to all women seeking them, or it might restrict them to only those women who have been raped or sexually abused. Or, your state might ban all abortions unless the life of the mother is critically endangered.

If an abortion is legal in your state for a young woman like this, you as a worker can help her get one. She has made her decision. It is her legal right. However, if your state does not allow her to have a legal abortion, you are confronted with another dilemma.

Principle 4 refers to choosing options that result in the least harm to those involved. Principle 5 reflects the importance of maintaining an optimum quality of life. If this young woman is prevented from having an abortion, will her future be harmed? In what ways might she lose control over her life? How will her short-term and long-term quality of life be affected?

This discussion simply raises questions and issues. Each case is unique. Circumstances and attitudes vary widely. It is a professional social worker's ethical responsibility to resolve dilemmas and help clients solve problems to the best of that worker's ability. Each client should be helped to identify alternatives, evaluate the pros and cons of each, and come to a final decision. There are no absolute answers or perfect solutions.

Consider the following cases. How would you apply the hierarchy of ethical principles for each?

Illustration B

A 45-year-old woman becomes pregnant. She already has seven children and numerous grandchildren. Her personal physician refused to prescribe birth control pills for her because of her age and other health reasons. Nor did he discuss other forms of birth control with her or offer her the alternative of sterilization. Physically, it would be hazardous for her to have any more children. She comes to you, distraught and crying. She doesn't know what to do.

Illustration C

A 32-year-old woman with a developmental disability becomes pregnant. She has a severe cognitive disability and is unable to take care of herself independently. She has a history of numerous sexual encounters. Her genetic background indicates that she would probably have a child with developmental disability. It is clear that she would be unable to care for any child herself.

Illustration D

A 19-year-old college student is 6 weeks pregnant. She has been going with her boyfriend for 7 months. For the past 3 months they have been seeing only each other but do not consider themselves "serious" as yet. She had been using the diaphragm and contraceptive cream, but they failed to protect her. She doesn't want a baby right now. However, she feels terribly guilty about getting pregnant.

Illustration E

A married 24-year-old woman is pregnant. She already has one child with a genetic defect. She and her husband have been through genetic evaluation and counseling at a local university. The conclusion is that because both parents have a history of significant genetic problems, the chances for a normal child are extremely small. The couple was deciding upon a sterilization procedure when she became pregnant.

Illustration F

A married 28-year-old medical technician has been unaware of being pregnant until now, the seventh week of gestation. Throughout her entire pregnancy she has been exposed to dangerous X-ray radiation. The possibility that her fetus has been damaged from the radiation is very high. She and her husband want children at some time, but they dread the thought of having a baby with a serious impairment.

Illustration G

Four months ago a married man of 42 had a vasectomy. His 41-year-old wife just found out that she is 5 weeks pregnant. Some sperm apparently had still been present in his semen. The couple already have three children in their teens. They do not want more.

Illustration H

A 14-year-old girl is pregnant. It happened one night when she was out drinking. She had never really considered using birth control. She's shocked that she's pregnant and is having difficulty thinking about the future.

---

infertility counseling. Many other factors should be considered. For example, consider the statement that older women experience increased infertility. Although this is generally true, recent research has found significant differences depending on the specific age. Kalb (2001) remarks: "Among healthy couples in their mid-20s who are not using birth control—at a time when most American women have babies—about one in four will get pregnant each month. By 30, fertility rates begin to slowly decline. But the greatest risk, say doctors, is pushing childbearing to the late 30s and 40s, when the chance of conception drops by 5 to 10 percent a year" (p. 45).

Gibbs (2002) indicates: "According to the Centers for Disease Control, once a woman celebrates her 42nd birthday, the chances of her having a baby using her own eggs, even with advanced medical help, are less than 10%. At age 40, half of her eggs are chromosomally abnormal; by 42, that figure is 90%" (p. 51).

Additionally, other factors, such as medical history and frequency of intercourse, may interact with a woman's age and contribute to infertility. Some women at age 40 can conceive while others in their early 20s find it impossible to do so.

Causes of Infertility

Of all infertility cases, males are responsible for approximately 40 percent; and females, for about 40 percent; both contribute in about 10 percent of cases, and reasons are unknown in the remaining 10 percent (McAnulty & Burnette, 2001). The following sections explore some of the major causes of infertility in both men and women.

Female Infertility. The most common cause of infertility in women involves blocked fallopian tubes (Lefrancois, 1999; Strong et al., 2002). *Pelvic inflammatory disease* (PID) is an infection of the female reproductive tract (especially the fallopian tubes) that can cause inflammation and scar tissue that blocks tubes. It often results from sexually transmitted diseases (STDs) such as gonorrhea and chlamydia (both described in Chapter 6). Tumors or various congenital abnormalities can also cause blocked tubes.

Another major cause of infertility for women is failure to ovulate (Hyde & DeLamater, 2000). Many possible causes exist for not ovulating, including chronic illnesses, ovarian or hormonal abnormalities, vitamin deficiency or malnutrition, and occasionally emotional stress. Whether ovulation has occurred can be detected by monitoring a woman's daily morning temperature. Basal body temperature charts can be used for this purpose. A woman may experience a slight dip in body temperature on the day before ovulation. Immediately after ovulation, the body temperature rises slightly (0.2 to 0.6 degrees Fahrenheit) and maintains this higher level for 10 to 16 days. No temperature rise at all is one indication that a woman is not ovulating. Ovulation can also be determined by examining hormonal levels or scrapings of the uteral lining.

A more accurate means of detecting ovulation than basal body temperature charts are urine tests that can be done by individuals themselves in their own homes. These tests operate on a similar principle to home pregnancy tests, monitoring the levels of luteinizing hormone (LH) in the urine.

Numerous other conditions can contribute to infertility. Abnormally thick mucus on the cervix, sometimes referred to as "hostile mucus," acts as a barrier, preventing sperm from entering the uterus. *Endometriosis*—the growth of tissue resembling that of the uterine lining outside the uterus—which often results in severe pain, can cause infertility (Strong et al., 2002). Smoking may increase a woman's chance of infertility (Bolumar, 1996; Crooks & Baur, 2002; Curtis et al., 1997; Strong et al., 2002). Being below normal weight is sometimes related

to irregular ovulatory cycles, which can, in turn, be related to infertility (Byer et al., 2002; Frish, 1988). Being overweight is also associated with infertility; obese women have some tendency to ovulate less frequently (Byer et al., 2002; Shoupe, 1991).

Exposure to toxic substances, such as contaminated water, food, or air, as well as the ingestion of some drugs can lead to infertility. For example, regular use of barbiturates or narcotics may decrease the frequency of ovulation and affect its regularity. Smoking and heavy alcohol use are related to lower rates of conception and increased likelihood of spontaneous abortion. Certain types of surgery involving a woman's reproductive system may result in adhesions that obstruct conception. Exposure to radiation in occupational or therapeutic settings can affect fertility; damage is related to the amount of exposure and the parts of the body exposed.

Male Infertility. The most common causes of male infertility are low sperm counts and decreased sperm motility (sperm's ability to maneuver quickly and vigorously) (Kelly, 2001; Strong et al., 2002). Numerous conditions can affect sperm count. Environmental toxins, declining health conditions, medical problems, shifting sexual practices, and increased stress levels have all been blamed as contributors (AASECT, March 1995; Allgeier & Allgeier, 2000).

Other factors leading to low sperm count include damaged veins in the scrotum or testes, resulting in an increased amount of accumulated blood. The subsequent rise in temperature impairs sperm production. Certain infections such as mumps when acquired in adulthood can cause inflammation or swelling of the testes. Oftentimes, the tiny tubes that produce and store sperm may be crushed, resulting in a decrease or cessation of sperm manufacture.

Undescended testes can result in infertility (Masters et al., 1995). Allgeier and Allgeier (1995) explain that "during prenatal development, the testes are positioned high in the abdominal cavity, but by birth, the testes have normally descended from the abdomen to the scrotum. In about 2 percent of males, however, one or both of the testes remain inside the abdominal cavity and must be brought down surgically" (p. 467). Prepuberty surgery usually results in normal fertility, but a postpuberty operation for this condition often leads to infertility.

Various types of drugs, including alcohol, cigarettes, narcotics, and marijuana, are associated with increased infertility in men (Masters et al., 1995; G.K. Stewart, 1998a; Strong et al., 2002). Cocaine use also has been found to affect male infertility (Bracken et al., 1990; Santrock, 2002a). Large amounts of cocaine interfere with luteinizing hormone release which, in turn, directly affects testosterone levels. Testosterone is necessary for manufacturing sperm, and decreased testosterone levels may lead to decreased sperm production. Cocaine use also causes arteries to constrict. Reduced blood flow to the testes may contribute to the inhibition of sperm production.

Couple-Related Causes of Infertility. Sometimes, infertility results from a mixture of conditions and behavior shared by a couple. It may involve timing and frequency of intercourse or specific coital techniques used (G.K. Stewart, 1998a). Occasionally, infertility is a consequence of antibodies produced by a woman that attack the man's sperm (Allgeier & Allgeier, 1995; Byer et al. 2002). This makes the sperm cluster together instead of individually seeking to fertilize an egg.

Psychological Reactions to Infertility

Some people experience serious reactions to infertility. They may show signs of depression, guilt, deprivation, frustration, or anger as they pursue infertility counseling. They may feel that their lives are out of their control. In many ways feelings resemble those of grieving and include denial, anger, bargaining, depression, and, finally, acceptance (Kübler-Ross, 1969; Hatcher et al., 1994).

Especially for those who really desire to have children, infertility can be associated with failure. This is compounded by the fact that even the most intimate partners often don't feel comfortable talking about their sexuality, let alone the fact that something may be wrong with it. Some men associate their potency with their ability to father children. Traditionally, women have placed great importance on their roles as wife and mother. Hopefully, with the greater flexibility of women's roles today, the technological advances aimed at improving fertility, and the new options available to infertile couples, the negative psychological reactions to infertility will be minimized.

Treatment of Infertility

Treatment for infertility depends, of course, on the specific problem involved and its seriousness. It is not necessarily an easy or effective process. It can also be very expensive. Spotlight 2.3 reflects one woman's difficult experience with infertility treatment and describes a feminist perspective on infertility counseling.

Microsurgery has been used to correct blocked fallopian tubes and varicose veins in the scrotum and testes. For women who have abnormally thick cervical mucus, artificial insemination by the male partner, described below, presents an alternative.

For women who have problems ovulating, drugs such as Chlomid or Pergonal might be prescribed to stimulate ovulation (Byer et al., 2002; Rosenfeld, 2000). Note, however, that questions have been raised in a study published in the *New England Journal of Medicine;* researchers cite an "'unacceptable' risk of pregnancy with three or more fetuses" and the dangers associated with multiple births, when using "injectable hormones that stimulate ovaries to release eggs" (Vajjhala, 2000).

Unfortunately, the treatment for male infertility is much less advanced, except for the use of microsurgery for some conditions, as mentioned earlier.

Alternatives Available to the Infertile Couple

The first thing to be done in the case of suspected infertility is to bring the matter out into the open. People need to talk about their ideas and feelings. Only then can the various alternatives be identified and a plan of action determined.

After at least 1 year of trying to conceive, both partners should pursue a medical evaluation to help determine if anything is physically wrong. The couple's sexual practices concerning pregnancy should also be discussed to make certain that they have accurate and specific information.

Adoption. Adoption is the legal act of taking in a child born to other parents and formally making that child a full member of the family. To provide a home and family for a child who has none is a viable and beneficial option for infertile couples.

Currently there is an emphasis on encouraging parents to adopt children with special needs, that is, children who require "special efforts" for adoptive placement (Downs et al., 1996, p. 345). Factors involved in "special needs" may include "ethnic background, age, membership in a minority or sibling group, or the presence of factors such as medical conditions or physical, mental, or emotional handicaps that make it reasonable to conclude that the child cannot be placed with adoptive parents without providing adoption assistance or medical assistance" (Barth, 1995, p. 50).

Artificial Insemination. Artificial insemination or intrauterine insemination is "the introduction of sperm in the reproductive tract through means other than sexual intercourse" (Rathus et al., 2002, p. 334). This method can be used when the woman is fertile. Sixty to 75 percent of women become pregnant after using artificial insemination (Kelly, 2001).

Human sperm can be frozen, thawed, and used to impregnate for long periods of time. (The length of time

Spotlight on Diversity 2.3

A Feminist Perspective on Infertility Counseling

An infertile woman tells her story:

Oh, sure, I've had infertility counseling. I still have a bill for $24,456 that the infertility clinic says my husband, Kenny, and I are responsible for paying. Our health maintenance organization (HMO) was supposed to pay for it, but they just stopped after paying half the expenses. Now we're getting bills along with nasty, threatening letters from the clinic. I never did get pregnant. I guess I'm not going to have any kids. That's the bottom line.

When we first went to the clinic, they all were so optimistic and smiled all the time. Of course, we couldn't go to the first clinic we tried. They wouldn't accept HMO insurance payments; they wanted regular private insurance to pick up the tab. Anyway, the waiting room at our clinic is full of happy, smiling baby pictures. The atmosphere was all so positive. I must've asked the staff there a hundred times what their success rate was. I must've gotten the answer back a hundred times that they don't know because it's different every time. Well, of course, it's different every time. You either get pregnant or you don't. I didn't, so my success rate must be zero.

So they tell you that first you have to have a laparoscopy, an endometrial biopsy, and a hysterosalpingogram. I won't bother telling you what they all are except that they're supposed to check out if I'm physically normal. They're complicated, they're time consuming, and they're expensive. That's only a few of the things you have to have done, and of course, you have to get examined every time you go in. Kenny, of course, had to have all his tests, too. He loved that. One of them involved either bringing his semen "specimen" into the clinic in a cute little jar within an hour of getting it—you know what I mean. Or else, he could do it and give it there. That was only shades of things to come.

In the end, they couldn't find anything wrong with either of us. Oh, great. We've been married for 12 years, I'm 34 years old, and they couldn't find anything wrong. Can you believe it? Time's gone so fast and we always thought that there'd be plenty of time for children and that it would just happen at some point. Well, it didn't. We knew my biological clock was ticking, so we thought we'd better be more aggressive about getting me pregnant.

So back to my story about the clinic. The first optimistic phase of treatment involves what they call an Ovu-stick kit. This is a slick $150 a month for the kit alone. Every month you go in on day 5 of your menstrual cycle. Okay, that's just the start. Then you have an ultrasound and they check you out to see if your follicles are developing or something like that. Then if the old follicles are okay, you go in again on day 10 to have them checked again. So, then on day 10 you start your Ovu-stick kit. You test your urine sample every day with one of the sticks that comes with the kit. When the stick "has any color change," then you're supposed to ovulate within 24 hours. Well, I swear in 8 months, my stick never did change color right. I kept asking them, "How much color change?" They kept answering "any color change" and around we'd go. Never once did I hit the old ovulation on the head, so to speak. We'd have intercourse as instructed either that night or the next morning, headache

or not, and then I'd run into the clinic to see if it worked. Nope. We were always either too early for ovulation or too late. They always liked to have you pop in at the clinic around 9 in the morning, too. Now I'm a homemaker who does not work outside the home. What in heaven's name would I have done if I was holding down a job?

Meanwhile, by the way, I of course was taking my temperature every day and charting it because you're supposed to notice a change when you ovulate. Well, some people's temperatures may change, but mine didn't. I couldn't get that sucker to vary more than two-tenths of a degree. Tough luck for me. That's frustration.

So they decided that doing "it," that is, having regular old intercourse by ourselves, wasn't cutting it and we needed to try the next step. That's artificial insemination. This was Kenny's favorite part. Remember, I always had to figure out if it was time for the big O (that is, ovulation) first. Then for 3 days in a row, Kenny was supposed to have his little specimen bottle filled with semen. Kenny leaves for work every day at about 6:30 A.M. He just loved getting his specimen on demand every day for three days in a row. Of course, as I've already mentioned, he could pop into the clinic at about 9:00 A.M. when it was convenient for them and get his little specimen to give them right there. Of course, he'd have to take 3 half sick-days off from work every month to do it. His boss would love that. So, poor old Kenny, who reminded me frequently that he was no "spring chicken" anymore and this whole thing made him feel like a "stud bull," could never do more than 2 days in a row no matter how hard he tried.

I of course was the one who ended up taking the bottle in, getting injected with it, and lying on the table for a half hour in a humiliating wait to have it "take." That, by the way, cost $350 each time, plus there was an injection fee. If you happened to ovulate, or in my case thought I might, on a weekend, my local clinic was closed. Then I had to drive way down into the city to go to another much busier clinic with a much longer waiting line.

I haven't even mentioned the hormones, worth $3,700 altogether, that they gave me during the process to make me ovulate more regularly. All that did was make me gain 8 pounds.

And then there were the comments. I'd talk to my sister every other day or so and every other day or so like a clock, she'd ask me, "Are you pregnant yet?" What's an appropriate answer? My mother-in-law had her own approach to the matter. Her song went, "Oh, don't worry, just keep trying. You'll get pregnant yet." Please! But the best part of the comments were from Kenny's brother, Steve. He thought it was cute to talk about Kenny's virility quotient as -2 on a scale from 1 to 10. Cute, very cute.

So we stopped. As they say, we had had it. If I sound like I'm angry and cynical, you bet I am. When our insurance stopped paying halfway through my treatment, the people at the clinic stopped smiling. As I popped in one day with my little bottle of Kenny's specimen, they abruptly said that they're sorry, but unless I sign this paper right this very minute which says that I will be responsible for the payments if the insurance doesn't

Spotlight on Diversity 2.3   *(continued)*

come through, the treatment was finished right now. To say I was under duress is an understatement. So I signed in desperation.

How do I feel? I feel manipulated and used. There were other methods they could've used. But they wanted us to jump through the hoops first. They knew that we were an older couple. They knew that time was an issue for us. They knew that we were desperate. They could've gone to some of the other, possibly more effective methods earlier. But then it wouldn't have cost as much, would it? What about freezing some of Kenny's semen, so he wouldn't have to go through what to him was such a humiliating ordeal on a regular basis? Why couldn't they have helped us work around our established habits so that their complicated, demanding instructions would've been more "do-able" for us?

So we are kidless, and that's okay. Now I tell my sister and my mother-in-law and Kenny's brother point-blankly, "No, we're not going to have children." I am resolved and am trying to turn to other things in life.

My final thought is not earth shattering and probably not very new. Infertility counseling is only for the very, very rich.

This is the story of an infertile woman. She candidly expressed her feelings, her frustrations, and finally the resolution of her infertility crisis.

Solomon (1988) suggests a feminist approach to counseling women who discover themselves to be infertile. The medical establishment tends to view infertility as a medical problem that needs to be solved, as dysfunctional equipment that needs to be fixed. Social attitudes tend to support this medical view. In many ways, Solomon continues, society views infertile women similarly to women who have been raped. First, most people in society aren't aware of the immense impact the crisis of infertility, as does rape, has on a woman. Second, people tend to look down on infertile women, as they do rape victims. Third, infertile women experience feelings such as shock, denial, and anger as do people confronted with any serious loss. Fourth, people in the general population tend to assign stereotypes to infertile women. For instance, many think when a woman is infertile, she becomes "desperate," that "she loses all personal control,"

and that she can't possibly live a well-rounded, worthwhile life without bearing children (Pfeffer, 1985). Fifth, infertility poses a major life crisis for a woman, as does rape. People in crisis are generally more vulnerable, more suggestible, and more easily manipulated than they are during more normal times.

Solomon proposes a two-pronged approach to infertility treatment. First, women must be dealt with on a "personal level" (Solomon, 1988, p. 47). Women who are experiencing the crisis of infertility should be treated as people with other crises are treated. A woman needs to be encouraged to identify and express her feelings, even when they hurt, come to accept her situation, and eventually make decisions about how she wants to proceed. Too frequently, infertile women are told what to do by medical professionals and are led to follow extensive, expensive, complicated, time-consuming procedures that may have little chance of success. It should be acknowledged that the infertile woman is more vulnerable and more likely to respond to medical direction than when she is not experiencing a crisis. Instead, the infertile woman may need specific information about the options available to her, the risks, the amounts of effort required to pursue treatment, and help in evaluating which alternative is to her individual best advantage. Each woman needs to evaluate if she really wants to put forth the amount of effort needed. Infertile women need to be empowered to make their own choices.

The second level involved in the feminist treatment of infertility addresses the more general social attitudes about infertility and expectations about what infertile women should do. Infertile women are stigmatized. They are viewed by society as having something wrong with them, as being incomplete. These attitudes need to be changed. The positive qualities of any life choice need to be emphasized. Women need to recognize their value as an individual human being, not as a failure or success because of their ability or lack of ability to bear children. People as citizens, advocates, and social workers can form pressure groups to encourage more extensive research into the causes and treatment of infertility and to alter the traditional manner in which fertility treatment is done. Women need to be and feel empowered, and to have their choices maximized.

that sperm can be frozen has not been determined; it is generally acknowledged that 5 years would be safe with close to 100 percent assurance.)

A sperm bank collects and maintains sperm for private citizens for a fee depending on length of time. The sperm is usually withdrawn at some later date to impregnate (with a physician's assistance) a woman.

The sperm used in artificial insemination may be the husband's (called AIH). It is possible to pool several ejaculations from a man with a low sperm count and to inject

them simultaneously into the vaginal canal of his spouse, thus vastly increasing the chance of pregnancy. AIH may also be used for family planning purposes—for example, a man might deposit his sperm in the bank, then receive a vasectomy, and then later withdraw the sperm to have children. High-risk jobs might prompt a man to make a deposit in case of death or sterility.

A second type of artificial insemination, called AID, uses sperm from someone other than the husband. AID has been used for several decades to circumvent male infertility and also when it is known that the husband is a carrier of a genetic disease (for example, a condition such as hemophilia). In recent years an increasing number of single women are requesting the services of a sperm bank. A woman requests the general genetic characteristics she wants from the father, and the sperm bank then tries to match the request from the information known about their donors. Donors are paid for their sperm and remain anonymous.

A third type of artificial insemination has received considerable publicity. Some married couples, in which the wife is infertile, may contract with another woman to be artificially inseminated with the husband's sperm. Under the terms of the contract this surrogate mother is paid and expected to give the infant to the married couple shortly after birth.

A number of ethical and legal questions have been raised about artificial insemination. Many religious leaders claim that God did not mean for people to reproduce this way. In the case of AID, certain psychological stresses are placed on husbands and on marriages, as the procedure emphasizes the husband's infertility and involves having a baby that he has not fathered. On a broader dimension, artificial insemination raises such questions as, What are the purposes of marriage and of sex? What will happen to male/female relationships if we do not even have to see each other to reproduce?

There are other possible legal implications. What happens if the sperm at a bank is not paid for? Would it become the property of the bank? Could it be auctioned off? If a woman was artificially inseminated by a donor and the child was later found to have genetic defects, could the parents bring suit against the physician, the donor, or the bank? Does the child have a right to know who his or her biological father is? What about frozen sperm used to inseminate a woman after the donor's death? Could such children be considered the donor's heirs?

In September 1993, a California Supreme Court judge ruled that it was legal for William E. Kane, a Los Angeles lawyer, "to will fifteen vials of his frozen sperm to his lover before he committed suicide" (AASECT, October 1993, p. 9). Kane's children from a prior marriage "argued that state law proscribed [forbid as unlawful] preservation of sperm for artificial insemination after a donor's death and that any children conceived would cause them emotional and financial distress" (p. 9). Subsequent questions concerned the rights of Kane's lover and any children she might have to inherit part of Kane's estate.

A similar case involves Nancy Hart who impregnated herself using her eggs and her husband Ed's stored sperm 3 months after he died from cancer (AASECT, February.

1995a). She did this at her late husband's urging that a child be his last gift to her. Hart's problem involved the state of Louisiana's refusal to pay Social Security survivor's benefit to her child. Normally, the state would pay $700 per month to any child of a deceased person who had contributed to Social Security through taxes. Because the state refused to acknowledge Ed Hart as the child's father, the child would receive no benefits.

In Vitro Fertilization. In vitro fertilization (IVF) is a process in which eggs are removed from a woman's body, fertilized with sperm in a laboratory, and then implanted in the woman's uterus. The procedure is often referred to as "test-tube babies." However, this phrase is inaccurate because "these babies are not born in a test tube"; rather, the eggs are placed in a laboratory petri dish where sperm are added and conception occurs (Carroll & Wolpe, 1996, p. 372). Thereafter, the fertilized egg is transferred to the woman's uterus. Before egg removal, the woman is given fertility drugs to encourage multiple egg production. The process was developed to help women whose fallopian tubes are damaged, blocked, or even absent and the normal process of fertilization is difficult or impossible. It is also useful for women with severe endometriosis (Masters et al., 1995).

The first successful IVF procedure took place in Oldham, England, in 1978. Baby Louise, weighing 5 pounds, 12 ounces, was born to her parents Lesley and John Brown. The world was stunned by such a feat. The physicians who developed the technique, Patrick Steptoe and Robert Edwards, had attempted the process more than thirty times before they achieved this first success. Today, approximately 60,000 procedures are performed in the United States each year with an average birthrate of about 25 percent (Gibbs, 2002). Each IVF attempt costs about $8,000, and several attempts are usually necessary to achieve success (Strong et al., 2002). IVF continues today to be the most uncomplicated and most commonly used technique in reproductive technology (Kelly, 2001; Strong et al., 2002).

As with artificial insemination, the ethical issues, legal complications, and other potential problems with IVF are numerous. For example, a Dutch woman underwent IVF after trying to conceive unsuccessfully for 5 years (AASECT, August 1995). The process was successful; twins were born—one black and one white. The University Hospital at Itrecht deemed "the mix-up 'a deeply regrettable mistake,' and took responsibility for accidentally fertilizing the woman's eggs with sperm from a man from Aruba, as well as that of her husband" (AASECT, August 1995).

Another problematic incident involved a Providence, Rhode Island, hospital that lost the embryos of two women prior to implantation during the in vitro fertilization process (AASECT, November 1995). One couple stated that three embryos had been lost before implantation. Another couple claimed that six embryos were lost during freezing. Often, when in vitro fertilization has occurred in the laboratory, some of the embryos are implanted in the woman's uterus and others are frozen in preparation for future implantation. In response to the two lawsuits filed, the hospital's head of gynecology said that "the embryos probably perished during routine procedures, which he described as a common occurrence" (p. 6).

Other issues are the high costs and the relatively poor success rates involved for many couples. Although fertilization rates in laboratory dishes can be quite high, the actual birthrate is much lower due to complications. Women with special risk factors, such as being older or having had recurrent miscarriages, are much more likely to experience failure. Couples should not be misled by false or unclear advertising. For example, clinics may advertise success rates of 25 to 50 percent. However, these figures may refer to the number of pregnancies initially achieved. The percentage of those coming to term are actually much lower. The Federal Trade Commission has filed charges against clinics for such distorted advertising. In reality, success rates vary dramatically from clinic to clinic (Begley, 1995). Additionally, success is less likely with each subsequent procedure.

Gamete Intrafallopian Transfer (GIFT). In gamete intrafallopian transfer (GIFT), a doctor places collected eggs and sperm directly into a fallopian tube. Resulting embryos can then drift into the uterus. GIFT differs from IVF only in where fertilization takes place. In IVF, fertilization occurs in a petri dish, and in GIFT, fertilization occurs in the fallopian tube. All other aspects of the two processes are alike. GIFT can be performed only in those cases where the fallopian tubes are clear and healthy. It may be used successfully with women who have endometriosis or when no specific cause for infertility has been identified. GIFT is not useful for women with blocked fallopian tubes, a common cause of female infertility. The success rate is approximately 28 percent (Kelly, 2001).

Zygote Intrafallopian Transfer (ZIFT). Zygote intrafallopian transfer (ZIFT) is similar to GIFT. In the ZIFT procedure, eggs and sperm are first combined in a laboratory dish. The fertilized egg is then immediately transferred to the fallopian tube. An advantage of this technique is that fertilization is known to have taken place (whereas GIFT couples can only hope that it will take place). The success rate is approximately 24 percent (Kelly, 2001).

Direct Sperm Injection. Direct sperm injection, or intracytoplasmic sperm injection (ICSI), is a relatively new technique. A physician, using a microscopic pipette (a narrow tube into which fluid is drawn by suction), "injects a single sperm from a man's ejaculate into an egg" (Begley, 1995, p. 41). The resulting zygote is subsequently placed in the uterus. The first successful birth in the United States using direct sperm injection occurred late in 1993. The procedure has a success rate of 24 percent (Kelly, 2001; Strong et al., 2002). Direct sperm injection is especially useful for men who have "low sperm counts or large numbers of abnormal sperm" (Strong et al., 1999, p. 377).

Surrogate Motherhood. Thousands of married couples who want children but who are unable to reproduce because the woman is infertile have turned to surrogate motherhood. A surrogate can give birth to a baby conceived by artificial insemination using the sperm of the husband. Or, a woman can function as a surrogate without using her own genetic material. For example, any egg fertilized using the GIFT or ZIFT process may be transferred to the surrogate mother's fallopian tube. A surrogate is paid from $10,000 to more than $25,000 (Strong et al., 2002). On birth, the surrogate mother terminates her parental rights, and the child is legally adopted by the donor(s) of the egg and/or sperm. Highlight 2.4 discusses a range of ethical dilemmas concerning surrogate motherhood.

Acceptance of Childlessness. For some infertile couples, accepting childlessness may be the most viable option. Each alternative has both positive and negative consequences that need to be evaluated. The positive aspects of childlessness need to be identified and appreciated. Increasing numbers of people are choosing to remain childless for various reasons. Not having children allows the time and energy that children would otherwise demand to be devoted to other activities and accomplishments. These include work, career, and recreational activities. A couple might also have more time to spend with each other and invest in their relationship as a couple. Children are expensive and time consuming.

On the one hand, children can provide great joy and fulfillment. On the other hand, they also can cause problems, stress, and strain. Infertile couples (as well as fertile couples) may benefit from evaluating both sides of the issue. There are aspects that can be identified and appreciated when pursuing either alternative.

Highlight 2.4

Ethical Dilemmas Concerning Surrogate Motherhood

Couples using the services of a surrogate mother are generally delighted with this medical technique and believe it to be a highly desirable solution to their personal difficulty. However, other groups assert that surrogate motherhood raises a number of moral, legal, and personal issues.

A number of theologians and religious leaders firmly believe God intended conception to occur only among married couples through sexual intercourse. These religious leaders view surrogate motherhood as ethically wrong. Some religious leaders also assert that it is morally despicable for a surrogate mother to accept a fee. They maintain procreation is a blessing from God and should not be commercialized. Also criticized is the use of a human being as a commodity that can be purchased by people with enough money.

Surrogate motherhood also raises complicated legal questions, which have considerable social consequences. For example, surrogate mothers usually sign a nonbinding contract stipulating the mother will give up the child for adoption at birth. What if the surrogate mother changes her mind shortly before birth and decides to keep the baby? These legal questions are still being debated.

Consider the widely publicized "Baby M" case that focused public attention on the surrogate motherhood issue. In 1986, Mary Beth Whitehead of Brick Township, New Jersey, changed her mind about giving up the baby born to her as a surrogate. This was despite the fact that she had contracted with William and Elizabeth Stern to give up to them the child fathered by William Stern's sperm through artificial insemination. Upon the infant girl's birth, Whitehead found that she was too emotionally attached to the child to give her up willingly. After a controversial trial, which received national attention, the courts upheld the contract and gave custody of the baby to the Sterns. This was the first judicial ruling on a disputed surrogate contract in this nation. The judge ruled the contract was valid because just as men have a constitutional right to sell their sperm, women can decide what to do with their wombs (Budiansky, 1988). A higher court later overturned the decision not to permit visitation partially because it was Whitehead's egg that Stern's sperm had fertilized (Kelly, 1994).

Court decisions may vary from one area or case to another, however. In 1993, the California Supreme Court denied all rights to a surrogate mother who had borne a child produced by the contracting couple's own egg and sperm. The court determined that because the surrogate had no genetic relationship with the child, she was bound to comply with the contract. Various states have initiated legislation concerning surrogacy. However, the specific conditions and issues involved in regulation or prohibition are still being debated.

Many surrogate mothers are married and already have children. A number of issues are apt to arise. How does the husband of a surrogate mother feel about his wife being pregnant by another man's sperm? How does such a married couple explain to their children that their half-brother or half-sister will be given up for adoption to another family? How does such a married couple explain their situation to relatives, neighbors, and the surrounding community? If the child is born with severe mental or physical handicaps, who will care for the child and pay for the expenses? Will it be the surrogate mother and her husband, the contracting adoptive couple, or society?

One case highlighting the surrogacy issue's complexity occurred in 1991 when a South Dakota woman became pregnant with her own grandchildren (Nass, 1991). Arlette Schweitzer, a 42-year-old librarian, already had two grown children of her own, Christa, 22, and Curtis, 26. When Christa was 14, she found out she had no uterus. Even at that age, her mother indicated, Christa was devastated. In a visit to the Mayo Clinic 2 years later, Arlette got the idea of lending Christa her uterus. In February 1991, eggs were taken from Christa's normal ovaries, fertilized in a laboratory with her husband Kevin's sperm, and implanted in Arlette's womb. Shortly thereafter, Christa found out Arlette was pregnant with her own twin daughters, who were born in due course.

Many feminists believe that surrogate motherhood is just another means of exploiting women. Ince (1989) investigated the process and procedures by which a woman became a surrogate mother. After visiting an agency as a potential surrogate, she raised many serious questions. Some involved the adequacy of the screening process. For instance, because she was "obviously bright," no intelligence testing was performed (p. 276). Additionally, she found the other medical and psychological tests extremely lacking.

Ince also raised numerous questions about the legal protections the surrogate could expect. For example, if the contracting adoptive parents decide to breach the contract, it is the surrogate, not the company, who must sue the couple for her contracted fees. Ince states, "The company holds all of the funds, makes the profit, and attempts to take a minimum of the financial/legal risks" (p. 282). One of the clauses in the contract stated that upon the physician's recommendation, the surrogate would have to undergo amniocentesis. In the event of an abnormality, the surrogate must get an abortion at the adoptive couple's request. Ince noted that the lawyer who was present while the contract was being discussed was very concerned about the abortion clause. His point was that there might be difficulties forcing the surrogate to have an abortion when the surrogate could get her full fee even if the infant was born abnormal. Nor was the surrogate protected by anonymity. The biological father would know her city of residence and would have access to a variety of personal documents including her name from the child's birth certificate, and her own medical and psychological records.

Finally, Ince noted the distant manner in which the spouse of the biological father is treated. She is referred to only rarely as "wife of the father" or "the potential stepmother," and has no clearly defined participation or place in the entire process (p. 282). Ince summarizes the profits of women serving as surrogates:

Highlight 2.4

Abortion-related Ethical Dilemmas in Practice (continued)

It is a myth that women are easily making large sums of money as surrogates. The director of this program acknowledges that the woman who goes through a lengthy insemination process may end up being paid less than one dollar per hour for her participation. To earn this sum, she is completely "on-call" for the company. She may be required to undergo invasive diagnostic procedures, forfeit her job, and perhaps undergo minor surgery with its attendant morbidity and mortality risks. Of course, should there be a miscarriage or failure to conceive, the surrogate receives no compensation at all. (p. 281)

Many look upon women who serve as surrogates with disdain. They are considered to be reproductive prostitutes who sell themselves and their offspring for cash. Ince suggests that even when the surrogate's contributions to humanity and to helping others are being emphasized, the surrogate still sounds like "a happy hooker with a heart of gold" (p. 284).

A final consideration regarding surrogacy is the much overlooked well-being of the children themselves. Can or should they be considered property? Should their best interests instead of those of their procreators be taken into account? At some point in their lives, should they be told that they have a surrogate mother somewhere? How will this affect their own psychological well-being? In summary, surrogate motherhood is a very complicated issue.

The Effects of Macro Systems on Infertility

Unlike abortion issues, which are fairly well crystallized and articulated, the issues and institutional values concerning infertility and reproductive technologies are only now being discovered and defined. Abortion has been available for a long time. However, modern technology has allowed for sophisticated means of artificial fertilization to be undertaken for less than two decades. Additionally, new developments are rapidly advancing.

A major issue is that most fertility enhancement techniques are expensive. They may be available, but not to poor people and the uninsured. Organizations within the community will provide services only if they are paid. Is this fair or appropriate? Should infertile wealthy people be allowed to enjoy such advances when infertile poor people are not? Should these expensive advances be pursued at all in view of the world's exploding population? Vital philosophical and ethical issues are involved here. Once again, there are no easy answers.

Social Work Roles and Infertility

Social workers may assume a number of roles when helping people address infertility: enabler, mediator, educator, broker, analyst/evaluator, and advocate. Social workers can *enable* people in making their decisions concerning the options available to infertile people. In cases in which the members of a couple disagree for some reason, a social worker can assume a *mediator* role to help them come to some compromise or mutually satisfactory decision. The social worker as *educator* can inform clients about options and procedures with specific and accurate data. The *broker* role is used to connect clients with the specific resources and infertility procedures they need.

The role of *analyst/evaluator* might be used to evaluate the effectiveness of treatment generally provided by an organization. For instance, if effectiveness rates at a particular fertility clinic are 5 percent or less, a social worker might help to evaluate the reasons for this. He or she might make it known to the agency, clients, and community environment that the clinic needs to improve its effectiveness. As an *advocate*, a social worker might need to speak on behalf of clients if they are being denied services if the process for receiving infertility treatment is overly cumbersome or expensive.

✿ Summary

Human reproduction is a complex process. Prenatal influences that affect the fetus include the mother's nutrition, drugs and medication, alcohol usage, smoking habits, age, and other factors such as specific illnesses (for example, rubella or AIDS) during pregnancy. Methods of prenatal assessment include ultrasound, amniocentesis, chorionic villi sampling, and maternal blood tests. Conditions that cause problem pregnancies are ectopic pregnancies, toxemia, and Rh incompatibility. Spontaneous abortions also occur periodically. Stages in the birth process include initial contractions and dilation of the cervix, the actual birth, and afterbirth. Birth positions include the most common vertex position, breech presentations, and transverse presentations. Birth defects include Down syndrome and spina bifida. Other factors affecting development include low birth weight, prematurity, PKU, and anoxia.

There are many developmental milestones as children grow older. Typical motor, play, adaptive, social, and language profiles for children at various age levels provide guidelines for assessment, although individual variations must be appreciated.

Significant issues related to human reproduction are abortion and infertility.

Macro system policies and the battle between prochoice and antiabortion forces affect service delivery. Controversial issues include limiting financial support, restricting access to services, addressing the pregnant woman's condition, assessing fetal condition, violence against clinics, and fetal tissue research.

Fewer abortions are being performed in the United States now than in the past, although the rate of abortion remains stable. Methods of abortion include vacuum aspiration, abortion-inducing drugs, dilation and evacuation, and inducing labor. Women who have had abortions generally experience no serious long-term psychological effects, although the decision to terminate a pregnancy is often a difficult and complex one. Men may also experience psychological distress following an abortion, a fact that is often ignored.

Proponents and opponents of abortion have developed arguments in support of their respective stances. Many women face serious ethical dilemmas with respect to unwanted pregnancy. Professional social workers have an obligation to assist pregnant clients in evaluating the various alternatives open to them so that they can make their own decisions.

Ten to fifteen percent of all U.S. couples are infertile. The most common cause in women is blocked fallopian tubes. Other causes include failure to ovulate, being overweight or underweight, abnormally thick cervical mucus, endometriosis, smoking, and exposure to toxic substances. Most male infertility is caused by a low sperm count and decreased sperm motility, although other reasons include physical damage to the reproductive tract, undescended testes, and use of certain drugs. Sometimes infertility results from a mixture of conditions shared by a couple.

People may suffer serious psychological reactions to infertility. Treatment of infertility includes drugs and microsurgery. A feminist approach to treating infertile women emphasizes dealing with the issue on a personal level and enhancing empowerment. Other alternatives available to infertile couples involve adoption, artificial insemination, in vitro fertilization, gamete intrafallopian transfer, zygote intrafallopian transfer, direct sperm injection, surrogate motherhood, and acceptance of childlessness. An ethical issue is the cost of treatment that limits access to those who are not wealthy. Social workers may assume many roles in helping people choose alternatives.

InfoTrac College Edition Keywords

abortion	conception	infertility	problem pregnancies
birth defects	developmental milestones	prenatal assessment	

On the Internet

Child Care Bureau

http://www.acf.dhhs.gov/programs/ccb/

The Child Care Bureau is dedicated to enhancing the quality, affordability, and availability of child care for all families. The Child Care Bureau administers federal funds to states, territories, and tribes to assist low-income families in accessing quality child care for children when the parents work or participate in education or training.

Head Start and Early Head Start

http://www2.acf.dhhs.gov/programs/hsb/index.htm?/

Head Start and Early Head Start are comprehensive child-development programs that serve children from birth to age 5, pregnant women, and their families. They are child-focused programs and have the overall goal of helping young children in low-income families prepare for school.

National Abortion and Reproductive Rights Action League

http://www.naral.org/index.html

For over thirty years, NARAL has been the political arm of the pro-choice movement and a strong advocate of reproductive freedom and choice. NARAL's mission is to protect and preserve the right to choose while promoting policies and programs that improve women's health and make abortion less necessary.

The Ultimate Pro-Life Resource List

http://www.prolifeinfo.org/

The Ultimate Pro-Life Resource List strongly opposes abortion-related violence.

CHAPTER 3

Psychological Systems and Their Impacts on Infancy and Childhood

"Hey, Barry, wha'd ya get on that spelling test?"

"I got an 87. How about you?"

"Aw, I got a 79. If I get a C in spelling, my ma will kill me."

"Yeah, Susie got a 100 again. She always ruins it for the rest of us by getting straight A's. I'm so sick of Ms. Butcherblock comparing us to her."

"I hear Billy flunked again. He's never going to make it into fifth grade."

"Yeah, Bill's an okay guy, but he sure isn't very smart."

"Only 10 more minutes to recess. I'm gettin' out there first and get the best ball."

"Wanna bet? I'll race ya!"

Psychology is defined as the science of mind and behavior. Human psychological development involves personality, cognition, emotion, and self-concept. Each child develops into a unique entity with individual strengths and weaknesses. However, at the same time some principles and processes apply to the psychological development of all people. Likewise, virtually everyone is subject to similar psychological feelings and reactions that affect their behavior.

This example portrays two schoolboys discussing their current academic careers. Numerous psychological concepts and variables are impacting even this simple interaction. The boys are addressing their own and their peers' ability to learn and achieve. Learning is easier for some children and more difficult for others. Personality characteristics also come into play. Some children are more dominant and aggressive. Others are more passive. Some young people are more motivated to achieve and win. Others are less interested and enthusiastic. Finally, some children feel good about themselves, and others have poor self-concepts.

A PERSPECTIVE

Psychological variables interact with biological and social factors to affect an individual's situation and behavior. In systems terminology we refer to each cluster of variables (that is, psychological, biological, or social) as a separate system. Each system influences the potential courses of action available to a person at any point in time. This chapter will focus on some of the psychological concepts that critically impact children as they grow up. There are four major thrusts. The first presents a perspective on how personalities develop. The second provides a basic understanding of how children think and learn. The third focuses on emotion; and the fourth, on self-concept.

This chapter will:

▶ Summarize prominent psychological theories concerning personality development, including psychodynamic, neo-Freudian psychoanalytic, behavioral, phenomenological, and feminist theories.

▶ Suggest a procedure for evaluating theory and discuss some concepts useful in enhancing sensitivity to human diversity when doing so.

▶ Examine Piaget's theory of cognitive development.

▶ Describe the concept of emotion.

▶ Discuss self-concept and self-esteem and emphasize the importance of a cross-cultural perspective.

▶ Examine the concepts of intelligence and intelligence testing, emphasizing the potential cultural and other biases involved.

▶ Explore cognitive disabilities (mental retardation), learning disabilities, attention-deficit hyperactivity disorder, and their effects on children, and current macro system responses.

Theories of Psychological Development

How many times have you heard someone make statements such as the following: "She has a great personality" or, "He has a personality like a wet dishrag." *Personality* is the complex cluster of mental, emotional, and behavioral characteristics that distinguish a person as an individual. The term may encompass a wide array of characteristics that describe a person. For instance, a person may be described as aggressive, dominant, brilliant, or outgoing. Another individual may be characterized by such terms as slow, passive, mousy, or boring. Because personality can include such varying dimensions of personal characteristics, explaining its development can be difficult.

The following section reviews a number of psychological theories that aim to provide a framework for explaining why individual personalities develop as they do. Many more psychological theories exist. Theories addressed in this text were chosen because of their historical significance, widespread use, and relevance to social work assessment and practice. They include psychodynamic theory, neo-Freudian psychoanalytic theory, phenomenological, and feminist theories. Behavioral theory is mentioned only briefly here; Chapter 4 covers it extensively within the context of its application to effective parenting. Chapter 7 addresses other psychological theories in depth, including those of Erickson and Kohlberg, and applies them to adolescence and young adulthood.

Psychodynamic Theory

Sigmund Freud is perhaps the best known of all personality theorists. The following section discusses psychodynamic theory in some detail because of its historical significance. Arlow (1995) explains: "Originating as a method for treating psychoneurotic disorders, psychoanalysis has come to serve as the foundation for a general theory of psychology. Knowledge derived from the treatment of individual patients has led to insights into art, religion, social organization, child development, and education" (p. 15).

Freud's conception of the mind was two-dimensional, as is indicated in Figure 3.1. One dimension of the mind consisted of the "conscious," the "preconscious," and the "unconscious." Freud thought that the mind was composed of thoughts (ideas), feelings, instincts, drives, conflicts, and motives. Most of these elements in the mind were thought to be located in the unconscious or preconscious. Elements in the preconscious area had a fair chance to become conscious, whereas elements in the unconscious were unlikely to arise to a person's conscious mind. The small conscious cap at the top of this diagram indicates Freud's theory that a person was aware of only a fraction of the total thoughts, drives, conflicts, motives, and feelings in the mind.

The repressed area was a barrier under which disturbing material (primarily thoughts and feelings) had been placed by the defense mechanism of repression. *Repression* is a process in which unacceptable desires, memories, and thoughts are excluded from consciousness by sending the material into the unconscious under the repressed barrier. Freud thought that once material has been repressed, it has energy and acts as an unconscious irritant, producing unwanted emotions and bizarre behavior, such as anger, nightmares, hallucinations, and enuresis.

The Id, Superego, and Ego. The second dimension of the mind was composed of the id, superego, and ego. Each of these parts is interrelated and impacts the functioning of each other.

The *id* is the primitive psychic force hidden in the unconscious. It represents the basic needs and drives on which other personality factors are built. The id involves all of the basic instincts that people need to survive. These include hunger, thirst, sex, and self-preservation. The id is governed by the pleasure principle; that is, the instincts within the id seek to be expressed regardless of the consequences. Freud believed that these basic drives or instincts involved in the id provide the main energy source for personality development. When the id is deprived of

Figure 3.1 Freud's Conception of the Mind

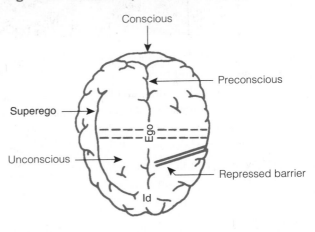

one of its needs, the resulting tension motivates a person to relieve the discomfort and satisfy the need. The id's relationship with the ego allows a person to rationally determine a means to fulfill the need.

The *ego* is the rational component of the mind. It begins to develop, through experience, shortly after birth. The ego controls a person's thinking and acts as the coordinator of personality. Operating according to the reality principle, the ego evaluates consequences and determines courses of action in a rational manner. The id indicates to a person what is needed or wanted. The ego then helps the person figure out how to get it.

The third component of this dimension of the mind is the *superego* or conscience. Normally developing between the ages of 3 and 5, it consists of the traditional values and mores of society that are interpreted to a child by the parents. The superego's main function is to determine whether something is right or wrong. When an instinctual demand strives for expression that the superego disapproves of, the superego sends a signal of anxiety as a warning to the ego to prevent the expression of the instinct. The emotion of guilt is said to originate from the superego. Without the superego to provide a sense of right and wrong, a person would be completely selfish. That is, a person would use ego to rationally determine a means of getting what the id wanted, regardless of the consequences on other people.

An example of how the id, ego, and superego might function together is provided in the case of a 9-year-old girl looking at compact disks in her favorite store. Although the girl adores Nasal Thrusters and Sleek Spit (a group hitting the top of the charts), she had only $.67 to her name. Her id, functioning by the pleasure principle,

Highlight 3.1

Definitions of Common Defense Mechanisms Postulated by Psychoanalytic Theory

Compensation: making up for a real or fancied achievement or superiority. A common example is an effort to achieve success in one field after failure in another.

Repression: mechanism through which unacceptable desires, feelings, memories, and thoughts are excluded from consciousness by being sent down deep into the unconscious.

Sublimation: mechanism whereby consciously unacceptable instinctual demands are channeled into acceptable forms for gratification. For example, aggression can be converted into athletic activity.

Denial: mechanism through which a person escapes psychic pain associated with reality by unconsciously rejecting reality. For example, a mother may persistently deny that her child has died.

Identification: mechanism through which a person takes on the attitudes, behavior, or personal attributes of another person whom he had idealized (parent, relative, popular hero, etc.).

Reaction Formation: development of socially acceptable behavior or attitudes that are the opposite of one's repressed unconscious impulses. Reaction formation is apparent in individuals who turn anal impulses into scrupulous cleanliness.

Regression: mechanism that involves a person falling back to an earlier phase of development in which he or she felt secure. Some adults when ill, for example, will act more childish and demanding, with the unconscious goal of having others around them give them more care and attention.

Projection: mechanism through which a person unconsciously attributes his or her own unacceptable ideas or impulses to another. For example, a person who has an urge to hurt others may feel that others are trying to hurt him.

Rationalization: mechanism by which an individual, faced with frustration or with criticism of his actions, finds justification for them by disguising from himself (as he hopes to disguise from others) his true motivations. Often this is accomplished by a series of excuses that are believed by the person. For example, a student who fails an exam may blame it on poor teaching or having long work hours, rather than consciously acknowledging the real reasons, for instance, that she had "partied hardy" the night before.

---

urges her to get that newly released CD. Her ego reasons that she could slip the CD under her jacket and race out of the store as fast as she can manage. Her ego also encourages her to look to see if anyone, especially those "nosey" clerks, are anywhere around. She's just about to do it when her superego propels itself into action. Clearly reminding her that stealing is wrong, it raises questions such as what would her parents think about her if she were to get caught. They would be terribly disappointed. Maybe she would even be kicked out of Girl Scouts. As a result, the girl gave the CD one last lingering look, sighed, and started on her way home. Her ego had already begun to work on how much lawn-mowing she would have to do to earn the money needed to purchase the CD.

Psychosexual Development. Freud came to realize that many people had sexual conflicts, and he made sexuality a focus of his theories. The term used for the energy of the id's biological instincts was *libido*. This energy was primarily conceived as being sexual energy. Freud thought sexuality included physical love, affectionate impulses, self-love, love for parents and children, and friendship associations.

Freud further conceptualized that people in their development of personality progressed through five consecutive phases. During any one of the earlier phases, conflicts or disturbances could arise that, if not resolved, could fixate that person in some ways at that particular level of development. According to Freud, the term *fixated* meant that a person's personality development was largely, though not completely, halted at a particular stage. In order to develop optimal mental health, an individual would either have to resolve these crises and/or use one of several defense mechanisms. A *defense mechanism* involves any unconscious attempt to adjust to conditions that are painful. These conditions may include anxiety, frustration, or guilt. Defense mechanisms are measures through which a person preserves his self-esteem and softens the blow of failure, deprivation, or guilt. Some of these mechanisms are positive and helpful. Others only help to avoid positive resolution of conflict. Definitions of common defense mechanisms postulated by Freud are given in Highlight 3.1, "Definitions of Common Defense Mechanisms Postulated by Psychoanalytic Theory."

Freud's phases of psychosocial and personality development include the oral, anal, phallic, latency, and genital stages.

Oral Stage. This phase extends from birth to approximately 18 months. It is called oral because the primary activities of a child are centered around feeding and the organs (mouth, lips, and tongue) associated with that function. Feeding is considered to be an important area of conflict, and a child's attention is focused on receiving and taking. People fixated at this stage were thought to have severe personality disorders, such as schizophrenia or psychotic depression.

Anal Stage. Between the ages of 18 months and 3 years, a child's activities are mainly focused on giving and withholding, primarily connected with retaining and passing feces. Bowel training is an important area of conflict. People fixated at this stage have such character traits as messiness, stubbornness, rebelliousness; or they may have a reaction formation and have such opposite traits as being meticulously clean and excessively punctual.

Phallic Stage. From ages 3 through 5, the child's attention shifts to the genitals. Prominent activities are pleasurable sensations from genital stimulation, showing off one's body, and looking at the bodies of others. Also, a child's personality becomes more complex during this stage. Although self-centered, the child wants to love and be loved and seeks to be admired. Character traits that are apt to develop from fixation at this stage are pride, promiscuity, and self-hatred.

Boys and girls experience separate complexes during this stage. Boys encounter an *Oedipus complex.* This is the dilemma faced by every son at this age when he falls sexually in love with his mother. At the same time he is antagonistic toward his father, whom he views as a rival for her affections. As the intensity of both these relationships mount, the son increasingly suffers from *castration anxiety;* that is, he fears his father is going to discover his "affair" with his mother and remove his genitals. Successful resolution of the Oedipus complex occurs through defense mechanisms. A typical resolution is for the son to first repress his feelings of love for his mother and his hostile feelings toward his father. Next, the son has a reaction formation in which he stops viewing his father negatively, and turns this around and has positive feelings toward his father. The final step is for the son to identify with his father, and thereby seek to take on the attitudes, values, and behavior patterns of his father.

Girls, on the other hand, undergo an *Electra complex* during this phallic state. Freud believed girls fall sexually in love with their father at this age. Meanwhile, they also view their mother with antagonism. Because of these relationships, girls also suffer from castration anxiety, but the nature of this anxiety is different from that of boys.

Castration anxiety in a girl results from the awareness that she lacks a penis. She then concludes she was castrated in infancy and blames her mother for this. Freud went on to theorize that because girls believe they have been castrated they come to regard themselves as inferior to boys (i.e., they have penis envy). Therefore, they perceive that their role in life is to be submissive and supportive of males. Freud did not identify the precise processes for resolution of the Electra complex in girls.

Latency Stage. This stage usually begins at the time when the Oedipus/Electra complexes are resolved and ends with puberty. The sexual instinct is relatively unaroused during this stage. The child can now be socialized and become involved in the education process and in learning skills.

Genital Stage. This stage, which occurs from puberty to death, involves mature sexuality. The person reaching this stage is fully able to love and to work. Again, we see Freud's emphasis on the *work ethic,* the idea that hard work is a very important part of life, in addition to being necessary to attaining one's life goals. This ethic was highly valued in Freud's time. Freud theorized that personality development was largely completed by the end of puberty, with few changes hypothesized.

Psychopathological Development. Freud theorized that disturbances can arise from several sources. One source was traumatic experiences that a person's ego is not able to directly cope with and thereby strives to resolve using such defense mechanisms as repression. Breuer and Freud (1895) provide an example of a woman named Anna O. who developed a psychosomatic paralysis of her right arm. Anna O. was sitting by her father's bedside (her father was gravely ill) when she dozed off and had a nightmare that a big black snake was attacking her father. She awoke terrified and hastily repressed her thoughts and feelings about this nightmare for fear of alarming her father. During the time she was asleep, her right arm was resting over the back of a chair and became "numb." Freud theorized that the energy connected with the repressed material then took over physiological control of her arm, and a psychological paralysis resulted.

In addition to unresolved traumatic events, Freud thought that internal unconscious processes could also cause disturbances. There was a range of possible sources. An unresolved Electra or Oedipus complex could lead to a malformed superego and thus lead a person to have a variety of sexual problems—such as frigidity, promiscuity, sexual dysfunctions, excessive sexual fantasies, and nightmares with sexual content. Unresolved internal conflicts (e.g., an unconscious liking and hatred of one's parents) may be another source that causes such behavioral problems as hostile and aggressive behavior and such emotional problems as temper tantrums. Fixations at early stages of development were another source that largely prevented development at later stages and led the person to display such undesirable personality traits as messiness or stubbornness.

As indicated earlier, the main source of anxiety was thought to be sexual frustrations. Freud thought that anxiety would arise when a sexual instinct sought expression but was blocked by the ego. If the instinct was not then diverted through defense mechanisms, the energy connected with sexual instincts was transformed into anxiety.

Obsessions (a recurring thought such as a song repeatedly on your mind) and *compulsions* (such as an urge to step on every crack of a sidewalk) were thought to be mechanisms through which a person was working off energy connected with disturbing unconscious material.

Unconscious processes were thought to be the causes for all types of mental disorders. These unconscious processes were almost always connected with traumatic experiences, particularly those in childhood.

Critical Thinking: Evaluation of Psychodynamic Theory

Critical thinking is the ability to use intellectual and "affective processes which evaluate statements, arguments, and experiences by judging the validity and/or worth of those statements, arguments, and experiences" (Lindsay, 1995, p. 20). In other words, critical thinking entails the ability to evaluate carefully the validity of an assumption and even of a so-called fact. Critical thinking can be used concerning almost any issue, condition, statement, or theory, including psychodynamic theory.

Freud was virtually the first to focus on the impact of the family on human development. He was also one of the earliest, most positive proponents of good mental health. However, he was a product of the past century, and many of his ideas are subject to serious contemporary criticisms.

First, research does not support either the existence of his theoretical constructs or the effectiveness of his therapeutic method. Part of this lack may be due to the abstract nature of his concepts. It is very difficult, if not impossible, to pinpoint the location and exact nature of the superego.

The second criticism involves the lack of clarity in many of his ideas. For instance, although Freud asserts that the resolution of a boy's Oedipus complex results in the formation of the superego, he never clarifies how this

occurs. Nor does he ever clearly explain the means by which girls might resolve the Electra complex.

The Electra complex leads us to a third criticism of Freud's theories. Women never really attain either an equal or a positive status within the theory. Essentially, women are left in the disadvantaged position of feeling perpetual grief at not having a penis, suffering eternal inferiority with respect to men, and being doomed to the everlasting limbo of inability to resolve their Electra complexes.

Neo-Freudian Psychoanalytic Developments

Since Freud's time, many have modified and expanded on his theories and ideas. These theorists, often referred to as neo-Freudians, or ego psychologists, include Carl Jung, Erich Fromm, Alfred Adler, and Harry Stack Sullivan, among others. In general, they are more concerned with the ego and the surrounding social environment than the role of instincts, libido, and psychosexual stages, which were central to Freud's perspective.

Carl Jung, who lived from 1875 to 1961, was a Swiss psychologist originally associated with Freud. He later developed his own approach to psychology, called *analytic psychology*. Jung thought of the mind as more than merely a summation of an individual's past experiences. He proposed the idea of an inherited "collective unconscious." Each person's individual experiences somehow melded into this collective unconscious, which was part of all people. He theorized that this gave people a sense of their goals and directions for the future. Jung stressed that people have a religious, mystical component in their unconscious. Jung was fascinated with people's dreams and the interpretation of their meaning. He also minimized the role that sexuality plays in emotional disorders.

Erich Fromm came to the United States from Germany in 1934. Whereas Freud had a primarily biological orientation in his analysis of human behavior, Fromm had a social orientation. In other words, he hypothesized that people are best understood within a social context. He focused on how people interact with others. Individual character traits then evolve from these social interactions with others. Fromm used psychoanalysis as a tool for understanding various social and historical processes and the behavior of political leaders.

Alfred Adler was also associated with Freud in his earlier years. After breaking with Freud in 1911 because of his basic rejection of Freud's libidinal theory, he went on to develop what he called "individual psychology" that emphasized social interaction. Adler saw people as creative, responsible individuals who guide their own growth and development through interactions with others in their social environment (Beckett & Johnson, 1995; Mosak, 1995). Adler theorized that each person's unique striving process or lifestyle "is sometimes self-defeating because of inferiority feelings. The individual with 'psycho-pathology' is discouraged rather than sick, and the thera-peutic task is to encourage the person to activate his or her social interest and to develop a new lifestyle through relationship, analysis, and action methods" (Mosak, 1995, p. 51). This social interest, an inborn trait, guides each person's behavior and stresses cooperation with others.

Of all the neo-Freudians, Harry Stack Sullivan, an American psychiatrist who lived from 1892 to 1949, made perhaps some of the most radical deviations from Freudian theory. He abandoned many of the basic Freudian concepts and terms. Like Adler, Sullivan em-phasized that each individual personality developed on the basis of interpersonal relationships. He proposed that people generally have two basic needs, one for security and one for satisfaction. Whenever a conflict arose be-tween these two needs, the result was some form of emo-tional disturbance. He emphasized that to improve inter-action, communication problems must be overcome. Sullivan placed "greater emphasis upon developmental child psychology" than did Adler and proposed six devel-opmental stages ranging from infancy to late adolescence (Mosak, 1995, p. 55).

Neo-Freudians have had a great impact on the way we think about ourselves and on the ways in which we view psychotherapy. However, they have not produced hypo-theses that are specific enough to be tested scientifically. In addition, most of these theorists were psychotherapists and writers focusing on philosophical interest rather than scientists who conducted rigorous research. Therefore, their major usefulness may involve providing ideas and ways to think about human behavior rather than con-tributing to the scientific foundation of psychology.

Behavioral Theories

Behavioral or *learning theories* differ from many other per-sonality theories in one basic way. Instead of focusing on internal motivations, needs, and perceptions, they focus on specific observable behaviors.

Behavioral theories state that people learn or acquire their behaviors. This learning process follows certain ba-sic principles. For example, behavior can be increased or strengthened by receiving positive reinforcement.

Behavioral theories encompass a vast array of different perspectives and applications. However, they all focus on behavior and how it is learned. More recently, greater attention has been given to the complex nature of social

situations and how people react in them (Kazdin, 2001). This involves people's perceptions about different situa-tions and their ability to distinguish between one and an-other. More credit is given to people's ability to think, discriminate, and make choices. This perspective in be-havioral theory is frequently called *social learning* or *social behavioral theory.* Behavior is seen as occurring within a so-cial context. Chapter 4 discusses social learning theory in depth and applies it to effective parenting. Therefore, it is addressed only briefly here.

Phenomenological Theories: Carl Rogers

Phenomenological or *self theories* of personality focus on "the way the world appears" to particular individuals and how they attach meanings to their "experiences and feelings" (Raskin & Rogers, 1995, p. 140). A person is viewed as having various experiences and developing a personality as a result of these subjective experiences, rather than as be-ing born with a specified personality framework. It also asserts that there are no predetermined patterns of per-sonality development. Rather, phenomenological or the-ories recognize a wider range of options or possibilities for personality development, depending on the individual's life experiences. Uniqueness of the individual personality is emphasized. Each individual has a configuration of per-sonal experiences that will produce a personality unlike any others. This is a relatively positive theoretical approach in that it focuses on growth and self-actualization.

One of the most well-known self theorists, Carl Rogers, is the founder of client-centered (more recently termed person-centered) therapy, which is based on his self theory.[1] One of Rogers's basic concepts in self theory is the concept of *self*. Self is equivalent to *self-concept*. Rogers defines these terms as the "organized, consistent, concep-tual gestalt composed of perceptions of the characteristics of the 'I' or 'me' and the perceptions of the relationships of the 'I' or 'me' to others and to various aspects of life, to-gether with the values attached to these perceptions" (Rogers, 1959, p. 200). A person is the product of his or her own experience and how she or he perceives these expe-riences. Life, therefore, provides a host of opportunities to grow and thrive.

Rogers maintains that there is a natural tendency to-ward *self-actualization,* that is, a tendency for every person to develop capacities in ways that serve to maintain or enhance the person (Rogers, 1959). People are naturally

---

1. This material on client-centered therapy is adapted from Charles Zastrow, *The Practice of Social Work,* 3rd ed., 1989, pp. 357–360. Used with permission of Wadsworth Pub. Co., Belmont, CA.

Highlight 3.2

Rogers's Other Key Concepts

The following are definitions of some of Rogers's other key concepts.

Ideal self: the self-concept that one would like to possess; what one would like to be.

Incongruence between self and experience: a discrepancy that exists between one's self-concept and what one experiences. Example: An individual may perceive herself as outgoing, attractive, and sociable, but when together with others may generally feel ignored. When such a discrepancy exists, a person will feel tension, internal confusion, and anxiety.

Psychological maladjustment: exists when a person denies or distorts significant experiences. A psychologically maladjusted person is one who has an incongruence between self and experience.

Congruence, congruence of self and experience: one's concept of self is consistent with what one experiences.

Need for positive regard: need to be valued and held in esteem by others.

Need for self-regard: need to value oneself.

Conditions of worth: conditions of worth result from taking on those values of others that are inconsistent with one's self-actualization motive. A person has conditions of worth when she feels her worth as a person is judged conditionally upon certain behaviors. She will avoid those behaviors that she feels valued low on. The result is that some behaviors are regarded positively, which are not actually experienced as satisfying, while other behaviors are regarded negatively, which are not actually experienced as unsatisfying.

---

motivated toward becoming fulfilled through new experiences.

In contrast to Freud, who viewed the basic nature of humans as being "evil" (having immoral, asocial instincts), Rogers views the basic nature of humans as being inherently good. Rogers believes further that if a person remains relatively free of influence attempts from others, the self-actualization motive will lead to a sociable, cooperative, creative, and self-directed person. Highlight 3.2 defines several other key concepts inherent in self-theory.

The driving force in personality development is seen by client-centered theorists as the "self-actualization motive," which seeks to optimally develop a person's capacities. As an infant grows, the infant's "self-concept" begins to be formed. The development of the self-concept is highly dependent on the individual's *perceptions* of his experiences. The person's perceptions of experiences are influenced by the "need for positive regard" (to be valued by others). The need for positive regard is seen as a universal need in every person (Rogers, 1959). Out of the variety of experiences of frustration or satisfaction of the need for positive regard, the person develops a "sense of self-regard," that is, a learned sense of self that is based on the perception of the regard he has received from others.

Emotional and behavior problems develop when the child *introjects* (takes on) those values of others that are consistent with his self-actualizing motive. Introjecting values inconsistent with one's self-actualizing motive results in "conditions of worth." For example, a child may introject values from his or her parents that sex is dirty or that

dancing is bad. Rogers adds that a child is apt to be influenced by others because of the need for positive regard.

When a person has conditions of worth, the result is that some behaviors are regarded positively (e.g., avoiding all sexual activity) by the person, which are not internally experienced as unsatisfying. Meador and Rogers (1979) then state:

> *What happens to the actualizing tendency as conditions of worth develop in the self-regard system? The actualizing tendency remains the basic motivation for the individual. However, a conflict develops between his organismic needs and his self-regard needs, now containing conditions of worth. The individual, in effect, is faced with the choice between acting in accord with his organismic sense or censoring the organismic urging and acting in accord with the condition of worth he had learned. (p. 144)*

Such conditions of worth lead to an "incongruence between self and experience." For example, a person may feel morally righteous and view himself or herself as being a value setter for refusing to dance or date, but yet experience that peers relate to him or her as being a prude with archaic values. When a discrepancy exists between one's self-concept and one's experiences, one will feel tension, anxiety, and internal confusion.

A person responds to this "incongruence" in a variety of ways. One way is to use various defense mechanisms. A person may *deny* that experiences are in conflict with his or her self-concept. Or the person may *distort* or *rationalize* the experiences so that they are perceived as being consistent with his or her self-concept. If a person is unable to reduce the inconsistency through such defense mechanisms, the person is forced to directly face the fact that incongruences exist between self and experiences, which will lead the person to feel unwanted emotions (such as anxiety, tension, depression, guilt, or shame).

Feminist Theories

Feminist theories are based on the concept of feminism and the basic themes involved in that definition. Feminism is the "doctrine advocating social, political, and economic rights for women equal to those of men" and the "movement for the attainment of such rights" (Nichols, 1999, p. 483). They are included here with other theories of personality development because they provide a context for women's development and experience throughout the life span.

Hyde (1996) remarks on the development of feminist theories:

> The feminist perspective was created by no single person. Instead, numerous writers have contributed their ideas. This is quite consistent with the desire of feminists to avoid power hierarchies and not to have a single person become the authority. But it also means that the feminist perspective . . . has been drawn from many sources. (p. 62)

Because of the multiple origins and ongoing nature inherent in their development, we refer to feminist *theories* instead of feminist theory. At least nine principles underlie these approaches.

First, feminist theories emphasize the *"elimination of false dichotomies"* (Van Den Bergh & Cooper, 1986, p. 4). That is, people should critically evaluate the way thought and behavioral expectations are structured within the culture. Western culture emphasizes separating people, things, and events into mutually exclusive categories. For example, people are classified as either *male* or *female* on the basis of biology. These categories are "viewed as mutually exclusive entities that should be manifest for one gender but not the other. Distinctions between the sexes, rather than commonalities, are emphasized" (Van Den Bergh & Cooper, 1986, p. 4). A traditional Western view stresses "the division between male and female behavioral traits such as the woman being the social and emotional caretaker and the man assuming the instrumental [that is, working, decision-making, maintaining strength] role,"—rather, a feminist perspective emphasizes "attending to a balance between autonomy and relationship competence for both genders" (Land, 1995, p. 10).

A second principle underlying feminist theories *"rethinking knowledge"* (Hunter College Women's Studies Collective, 1995, p. 63). In some ways, this is related to the first principle because they both involve how people think and view the world. Rethinking knowledge involves critically evaluating not only *how* you think about something, but also *what* you think about. It involves which ideas and thoughts are considered to reflect "facts" and which are thought to have value. The Hunter College Women's Studies Collective (1995) explains:

> Not only have topics of interest to women, but of less interest to men, such as rape, the sexual abuse of children, employment patterns among women, or the histories of women's lives, been simply left out of traditional disciplines, but the very concepts and assumptions with which inquiry has proceeded have reflected a male rather than a universal point of view. (p. 63)

A third dimension characterizing feminist theories is the recognition that differences exist in male and female experiences throughout their life spans (Land, 1995). One aspect of this dimension is the feminist focus on the impacts of gender role socialization. A gender role is the "cluster of socially defined expectations that people of one gender are expected to fulfill" (Hyde & DeLamater, 2000, p. 672). Socialization is the developmental process of teaching members of a culture the appropriate and expected pattern of values and behavior. Hyde (1996) elaborates:

> From their earliest years, children are socialized to conform to these roles. . . . Essentially, gender roles tell children that there are certain things they may not do, whether telling a girl that she cannot be a physicist or a boy that he cannot be a nurse. Because gender roles shut off individual potential and aspirations, feminists believe that we would be better off without such roles or at least they need to be radically revised. (p. 64)

Gilligan's (1982) work on the moral development of women, described in Chapter 7, provides a good example of work focusing on gender-related differences in life experience. Her proposed sequence of levels and transitions differ significantly from the traditional stages of moral development proposed by Kohlberg (1963, 1968, 1969, 1981), the latter relating primarily to the experience of men.

A fourth principle inherent in feminist theories is the *end of patriarchy,* the doctrine maintaining that men hold positions of power and authority, head families, and provide the basis for tracing descent in family lineage (Bricker-Jenkins & Hooyman, 1986; Bricker-Jenkins & Lockett, 1995, p. 2531). Simply stated, feminist theories refute the concepts of male dominance, female submission, and gender discrimination. The traditional view of power is analogous to that of money in that there is some finite amount over which some people have control and others do not (Van Den Bergh & Cooper, 1986). Such views focus on using power to dominate and control others who should be dependent and subservient. (Chapter 9 discusses some of the issues involved in greater depth.) Rather, a feminist perspective stresses that power should be reconceptualized and viewed as "infinite, a widely distributed energy of influence, strength, effectiveness, and responsibility" (Van Den Bergh & Cooper, 1986, pp. 5–6). This view assumes that power is limitless and should be nurtured in each individual.

The fifth feminist principle, closely related to that of ending patriarchy, is that of *empowerment* (Bricker-Jenkins & Hooyman, 1986; Bricker-Jenkins & Lockett, 1995; Land, 1995; Suarez, Lewis, & Clark, 1995), earlier defined as "a process of increasing personal, interpersonal, or political power so that individuals can take action to improve their life situations" (Gutierrez, 1999, p. 149). A feminist perspective emphasizes the need to empower women, enhance their potential for self determination, and expand opportunities. Means of empowerment include assertiveness training, enhancing self-esteem, improving communication and problem-solving skills, and learning conflict resolution and negotiating skills (Van Den Bergh & Cooper, 1986).

A sixth concept underlying feminist theories is that of *"valuing process equally with product"* (Bricker-Jenkins & Hooyman, 1986; Suarez et al., 1995; Van Den Bergh & Cooper, 1986, p. 6). It is not only important *what* you get done, but *how* you get it done. A traditional patriarchal approach stresses the importance of the end result. For example, the fact that a male chief executive officer of a large oil company has amassed amazing wealth is considered significant. The traditional view would not consider how he had hoarded his wealth (by ruthlessly stepping on competitors, breaking environmental regulations, and consistently making decisions in his own, not the employees' nor the public's, best interests) would not be considered as significant. Feminist theories focus on decision making based on equality and participation by all. The concept of "having power over" others is irrelevant. Thus, feminist theories focus on aspects of process such as making certain all participants have the chance to speak and be heard, adhering to principles of ethical behavior, working toward agreement or consensus, and considering personal issues as important.

A seventh underlying principle in feminist theories is the idea that *"the personal is political"* (Bricker-Jenkins & Hooyman, 1986; Bricker-Jenkins & Lockett, 1995 p. 2531; Van Den Bergh & Cooper, 1986, p. 9). Personal experience is integrally intertwined with the social and political environment. Sexism, "the individual attitudes and institutional arrangements that discriminate against people, usually women and girls, because of sex role

stereotyping and generalizations," is the result of the social and political structure (Barker, 1999, p. 437). It does not simply involve problems experienced by isolated individuals.

Another implication of this principle is that the political environment can be changed and improved by personal actions. In this way personal experience can be used to alter the political environment that, in turn, can improve the personal experience. For example, individual women can collectively campaign for a candidate who supports women's issues, thus applying their personal actions to the political arena. As a result, the candidate gets elected and seeks to improve her supporters' work environments and access to resources, a political result that affects women's personal lives.

An eighth feminist principle involves *unity and diversity;* related concepts are "sisterhood" and "solidarity" (Bricker-Jenkins & Lockett, 1995, p. 2531; Bricker-Jenkins & Hooyman, 1986). Women working together can achieve a better quality of life for all. In order to remain unified, women must appreciate each other's differences. Diversity is viewed as a source of strength.

A ninth dimension inherent in feminist theories is *consciousness raising,* the development of "critical awareness of the cultural and political factors that shape identity, personal and social realities, and relationships" and of one's position and opinions with respect to these issues (Bricker-Jenkins & Lockett, 1995, p. 2533). In order to support and act on the preceding principles, people must be aware of them. Consciousness raising involves ongoing thought, communication, learning, and mutual support. Women must progress through the phases of learning about themselves, becoming aware of the environmental elements affecting their lives, evaluating the quality of their environment, and proposing changes where needed.

We have reviewed a number of psychological theories about human behavior that can help us better understand how people function. A subsequent section examines how theories are relevant to social work practice and Highlight 3.3 proposes an approach for evaluating theory. Spotlight 3.1 stresses the importance of being sensitive to diversity when evaluating theories.

Critical Thinking About the Relevance of Theory to Social Work

Chapter 1 defines the word *theory* as a coherent group of principles, concepts, and ideas organized to explain some observable occurrence or trend. In effect, theory provides a way for people to view the world. It helps them to sort out and make sense of what they see. Likewise, it aids

Highlight 3.3

Critical Thinking and Evaluation of Theory

The Evaluation of Theory

There are many ways to evaluate theory. This is partly because theories can concern virtually anything from the best method of planting a garden to whether intelligent extraterrestrials exist. Four major approaches for evaluating theory are provided here. The approaches are applied to various theories throughout the text and are not necessarily presented in order of importance. Different theories may require different orders and emphases in terms of how they can best be evaluated.

1. *Evaluate the theory's application to client situations.* In what ways is the theory relevant to social work? In what ways does the theory provide a means to help us think about our clients and how to help them? For example, a theory about the mating patterns of gorillas would probably be very difficult to apply to any practice situation. However, a theory that hypothesizes how interpersonal attraction occurs between people might help you to work with an extremely shy, lonely young adult with serious interpersonal problems.

2. *Evaluate the research supporting the theory.* Research often involves singular, obscure, or puzzling findings. Such findings may be vague and may or may not be true. For example, the sample of people studied in a particular research project may have been extremely small. Thus, results may have been due primarily to chance. Or, the sample may not have resembled the entire population very well. Therefore, the results should be applied only

to the sample studied and not to anything or anybody else. (Consider this a commercial for why you need to take a research course!) On the one hand, it's important to be cautious about assuming that any research study establishes a *fact*. On the other hand, when more and more studies continue to support each other, a fact (or, as close as we can come to a fact) may begin to develop.

A student once complained to me about her textbook. She said that the author confused her by presenting "facts"— in reality, research findings—that were contradictory. She said she hated such contradictions and wanted the author to tell her what was or was not a fact. My response to her was that I didn't think the world was like that. It cannot be so clearly divided, even though it sometimes seems that it would be more convenient that way. Facts are the closest estimation to the truth we can come to based on the limited information we have. For example, people believed that the world was flat until somebody discovered that it was round. They believed that the northern lights were reflections of sunlight off the polar ice cap until someone discovered that they are really the effect of solar radiation on the earth's ionosphere.

Research can help to establish whether theories portray facts or not. In other words, research can help determine how accurate and useful any particular theory is. We need theories to guide our thinking and our work.

However, there are at least two problems with evaluating research in support of a theory. First, you might not have access to all, most, or any of the relevant research. Research findings (which often are interpreted as facts)

---

them in understanding how and why things are the way they are and work the way they do. Different theories provide us with different explanations.

For instance, consider the differences between systems theory and the medical model when trying to explain the reasons for human behavior. From the 1920s to the 1960s, social work programs used a *medical model* approach to human behavior. The medical model approach was developed by Sigmund Freud. This theoretical approach views clients as "patients." The task of the social worker providing services is to first diagnose the causes of a patient's problems and then provide treatment. The patient's problems are viewed as being inside the patient.

With respect to emotional and behavioral problems, the medical model conceptualizes such problems as "mental illnesses." People with such problems are then given medical labels such as *schizophrenic, psychotic, manic-depressive,* or *insane.* Adherents of the medical approach believe the disturbed person's mind is affected by some

generally unknown, internal condition, thought to be due to a variety of possible causative factors inside the person. These include genetic endowment, metabolic disorders, infectious diseases, internal conflicts, unconscious uses of defense mechanisms, and traumatic early experiences that cause emotional fixations and prevent future psychological growth.

In the 1960s, social work began questioning the usefulness of the medical model. Environmental factors were shown to be at least as important in causing a client's problems as internal factors. Also, research was demonstration that psychoanalysis was probably ineffective in treating clients' problems (Stuart, 1970). Social work shifted at least some of its emphasis to a reform approach. A reform approach seeks to change *systems* to benefit clients. The anti-poverty programs, such as Head Start and the Job Corps, are examples of efforts to change systems to benefit clients.

In the past two decades social work has increasingly focused on using a systems approach to viewing clients

can be found in thousands of journals. Second, there may be no research specifically directed at finding the specific facts you need to help you verify a theory in your own mind.

3. *Evaluate the extent to which the theory coincides with social work values and ethics.* Does the theory involve an underlying assumption that coincides with the mission of social work? According to the National Association of Social Workers' (NASW) Code of Ethics, "the primary mission of the social work profession is to enhance human well-being and help meet the basic human needs of all people, with particular attention to the needs and empowerment of people who are vulnerable, oppressed, and living in poverty" (NASW Code of Ethics, Preamble, 1996).

One example of how a theory can support or contradict professional ethics involves the ethical standard that social workers must be "sensitive to cultural and ethnic diversity and strive to end discrimination, oppression, poverty, and other forms of social injustice" (NASW Code of Ethics, Preamble, 1996). Consider a theory that one group of people is by nature more intelligent than another group. This theory obviously conflicts with professional values. Therefore, it should not be used or supported by social workers.

Another example is the theory that women are too emotional, flighty, and lacking in intellectual capability to vote or hold a political office. This theory was espoused by the powerful majority of men who held public office until 1920, when women finally won the right to vote after a long, drawn-out battle for this right. This theory, too, stands in direct opposition to professional values and ethics.

Another section discusses the importance of being sensitive to human diversity when examining psychological theories. It also introduces several concepts that are useful in that process.

4. *Evaluate the existence and validity of other comparable theories.* Are there other theories that adhere better to the first three evaluation criteria? If so, which theory or theories should be chosen to guide our assessments and practice?

The medical model and systems theory were compared earlier. The social work profession now subscribes to systems theory, which provides a better perspective for respecting peoples' dignity and rights and for targeting the macro environment in order to effect change, reduce oppression, and improve social conditions.

Sometimes two or more theories will have basic similarities. Recall the discussion concerning the differences between systems theory and the ecological model in Chapter 1. Both approaches provide frameworks for how to analyze the world and what to emphasize. Many of the concepts they employ are similar or identical. It was concluded that the ecological model is an offshoot of systems theory. This text assumes a systems theory perspective, yet adopts some ecological concepts. For instance, the term *system* is used in both. Both *social environment* and *coping* are ecological terms. Thus, many times it may be determined that a combination of theories provides the best framework for viewing the world within a social work context. Each social worker needs to determine the theoretical framework or combination of frameworks best suited for his or her practice context.

At other times no theory will be perfectly applicable. Perhaps you will decide that only one or two concepts make any sense to you in terms of working with clients. The quest for the perfect theory resembles the pursuit of the perfect fact. It's very difficult to achieve perfection. Thus, when evaluating theories, be flexible. Decide which concepts in any particular theory have the most relevance to you and your work with clients.

and the world surround them. This approach integrates both treatment and reform by emphasizing the dysfunctional transactions between people and their physical and social environments. Human beings are viewed as being in constant interaction with other micro, mezzo, and macro systems within their social environment.

Social workers started to explore both causes and solutions in the environment encompassing any individual client instead of blaming the client. For instance, consider a person who is unemployed and poverty stricken. A social worker assuming a systems perspective would assess the client system-in-situation. This worker would assess not only the problems and abilities of the client but would also appraise the client's interactions with the multiple systems impacting her or him. What services are available to help the person develop needed job skills? What housing is available in the meantime? What aspects of the macro systems in the environment are contributing to the high unemployment and poverty rates? What

services need to be developed in order to respond to these needs?

In contrast, the medical model might orient a worker to try to cure or "fix" the individual by providing counseling to help her or him develop a better attitude toward finding a job. There would be an underlying assumption that it was the individual micro system that was somehow at fault.

Thus, theory helps us as social workers decide how to go about helping people. The medical model versus systems theory is only one example. Throughout this text, a broad range of theories will be presented concerning various aspects of human development and behavior. Evaluation of their relevance will often be provided. You, as a future social worker, will be expected to learn how to evaluate theories for yourselves in order to apply them to your practice situations. Highlight 3.3 provides some suggestions for how to do this. Spotlight 3.1 stresses the importance of being sensitive to diversity when evaluating theories.

Spotlight on Diversity 3.1

Being Sensitive to Diversity When Examining Psychological Theories

Psychological theories of development often focus on pre-scribed stages through which people progress throughout their lives. Such theories are also oriented to expectations about what is normal and what is abnormal during each stage. An issue facing us as we evaluate psychological theories is the rigidity with which some attempt to structure human development. In reality, people experience different worlds as they progress through their lives and time. Their experiences are altered by their "race, ethnicity, social class, and gender socialization" (Devore & Schlesinger, 1999, p. 64). A woman will experience life differently than a man because of variables related to being a woman. An American of Asian background will encounter different treatment and issues than an American of Northern European origins moving through the same time. Thus, it is critically important to be sensitive to the vast differences people can experience because of their membership in certain groups or other characteristics.

For more than 30 years, social work has been moving to view clients and the world from a less rigid, more open-minded perspective that is sensitive to diversity and individual differences. The field has worked "to encompass new perspectives on women's development and roles and the unique experiences, characteristics, strengths, and coping strategies of African Americans, Latinos, Asians, and other people of color and of other oppressed groups such as gay men and lesbians," in addition to incorporating principles such as empowerment (Goldstein, 1995). We have established that *empowerment* is "a process of increasing personal, interpersonal, or political power so that individuals can take action to improve their life situations" (Gutierrez, 1990, p. 149). It is up to us as social workers to be sensitive to people's varying perspectives and needs. We must not make value judgments based on rigid assumptions about how people are *supposed* to behave. Rather, we must maintain flexibility thinking about human behavior and nurture our appreciation of differences.

Germain (1991) maintains that it is important to view "transitions, life events, and other life issues as outcomes of person(s): environment processes rather than as separate segments of life confined to predetermined ages and stages of experience" (p. 149). Devore and Schlesinger (1999) reflect on how various transitional points are experienced differently depending on an individual's life context (variables affecting a person's life such as race, ethnicity, class, gender, sexual orientation, and disability). They divide the life course into seven transitional points—entry, childhood, adolescence, emerging adulthood, adulthood, later adulthood, and old age (pp. 68–69). Persons with divergent characteristics and backgrounds can experience these transitional points in distinctly different ways.

For example, during the childhood transitional period, children's psychological profiles are shaped by the ideas of their parents and of other people around them. On the one hand, "Japanese mothers [tend to] assume young children to be independent by nature, with a need to be drawn into dependence. Infants are indulged as they mature; persuasion and reasoning are used to assure compliance to the mother's edict. By school age, children

know what is expected. Because of their mother's sacrifice on their behalf, they must succeed. Their failure would be their mother's failure as well" (Devore & Schlesinger, 1996, p. 85). On the other hand, some Italian parents engender a cultural expectation that child rearing requires "continual vigilance, given the belief in the fallibility of human nature, particularly evident in children. Many feel that there is a potential for evil and that parents must prevent its expression in neglect of family, disrespect, or sexual misbehavior by females" (p. 85). Thus, people's psychological profiles and resultant behavior are shaped by expectations and treatment during the childhood portion of their life course.

Other examples of life course differences involves the adolescent transitional period. Children raised in different cultural environments with different experiences and treatment view their developing life and gender roles in very diverse ways. A female Puerto Rican adolescent learns her expected role by closely observing her mother and caring for the family's children; however, there often is no mention of sex (Devore & Schlesinger, 1996). Adolescent African Americans in urban areas, on the other hand, often receive very different messages that diverge for young men and women. Young women may learn that having babies "despite social immaturity is essential to becoming a woman" (p. 88). Young African-American men, in contrast, may receive the message that "manhood . . . must be attained before one can be an effective father" (p. 88).

The transitional period of emerging adulthood provides more examples of diverse life course experiences (Devore & Schlesinger, 1996). Young people experience this as a time of decision making about marrying or remaining single and pursuing a work or career path. In the United States, white youth who attended suburban high schools with strong support systems and high performance demands may find attending college a viable path, especially with parental or other support. However, Native Americans who attended Bureau of Indian Affairs boarding schools that required only seventh- or eighth-grade achievement by the end of high school may find themselves being denied such "access to the mainstream" (p. 92). Their experience and treatment may lead to disappointment and despair.

The important point here is the need for sensitivity to diversity when evaluating human behavior, regardless of which theory you apply.

Other concepts are also helpful when examining and evaluating psychological theories and their application to diverse populations. They include the dual perspective and the worldview, spirituality, and strengths perspectives (Beckett & Johnson, 1995; Leashore, 1995; Saleeby, 2002).

The Dual Perspective

When observing and appreciating people's diverse backgrounds and psychological orientations, a *dual perspective* can provide insight, especially about people who belong to groups outside of the majority population. In this perspective, "all people adapt to and interact with two environments: (1) the family and community . . . labeled the *nurturing environment,* and (2) the larger environment of white people, the *sustaining environment.* The sustaining environment contains social systems such as employment that provide for survival needs. The nurturing environment offers expressive features such as belonging" (Beckett & Johnson, 1995, p. 1392).

Most Euro-Americans experience these two environments melded together to support them and provide them with consistency. However, many other ethnic and racial groups experience a much poorer fit between the two. Any particular group may have a strong nurturing environment in family, friends, and even a neighborhood that provides emotional strength. However, the larger sustaining environment may not be at all supportive or consistent with the more intimate nurturing environment. To the extent that the sustaining environment provides a group with inadequate educational preparation and confronts its members with prejudice, discrimination, and less than equal treatment, they are unable to function as well as their Euro-American counterparts in that environment. The greater the incongruence between the sustaining and the nurturing environments, the more difficulty people will have. This lack of fit is an important focus for social workers.

Norton (1993) conducted an ongoing long-term study of children from their second day after birth to age 9. She studied how differential socialization in their nurturing environment caused them to experience different perceptions of how time is structures. *Socialization* is "the process by which individuals become competent, participating members of a society, that is, the process by which adults prepare children for competent adulthood in their own social group" (p. 83).

Thirty-seven women and their children were studied. They were selected because they were considered at high risk of having a poor fit with the sustaining environment. Variables thought related to a poor fit included living with older family members, having an educational level not extending beyond high school when their babies were born, and living in urban areas where average income and housing value were below median levels while "housing density, transience, vacant housing, crime, and neonatal mortality" levels were above the median (p. 85). Data collection involved videotaping the interaction and communication between mothers and children at regular intervals.

A primary variable studied was the children's grasp of seriation: "the ordering of events in a temporal sequence before they can develop an understanding of the past, present, and future" (p. 86). A test specifically measuring children's acquisition of the seriation concept was administered. This variable was chosen because "understanding physical time is particularly critical in a modern, highly technological society such as the United States, in which much of the organization of economic and social behavior depends on a commonly understood location of events and procedures in time and in which a highly developed sense of self is necessary to operate in a complex world where norms change rapidly" (pp. 86–87). Many of the children studied lived in homes where families observed "little or no routine," because mothers did not work outside the home and "did not have anyplace to go" (p. 87). Therefore, these mothers had little reason to plan or pay close attention to how they and their children spent their time. However, some of the mothers studied talked significantly more about time to their children than others, such as mentioning birthdays and designated time periods. Additionally, they participated in activities with their children that required the structuring and sequencing of time.

Results indicated that a significant relationship existed between children's ability to grasp the seriation concept and the number of statements about time mothers made to their children. Time statements include, for example, mentioning minutes, hours, and days as they relate to how much time one has now, has left, or will have in relation to some aspect of life. Norton postulates that because the major language used in the United States is based on the time concept, children exposed to this concept more thoroughly in their early youth will be better prepared to adjust to a school environment where the concept of time is very important. If children's nurturing environment at home is incongruent with the sustaining environment in the outside world, the children will have difficulties in later life. The dual perspective encourages us to acknowledge and understand such incongruities so that we can develop solutions.

© Chip Henderson/Getty Images

The African American worldview is characterized by a strong achievement-and-work orientation.

Worldview

A second concept helpful for appreciating diversity when applying psychological theory to behavior is the worldview perspective. *Worldview* concerns "one's perceptions of oneself in relation to other people, objects, institutions, and nature. It relates to one's view of the world and one's role and place in it" (Leashore, 1995, p. 112). Adopting a worldview involves looking beyond the narrow boundaries of our daily existence. It means developing an openness and awareness of life in other neighborhoods, counties, states, and countries. It also requires developing an appreciation of differences instead of fear and aversion. It encourages us to allow new perceptions of the world to penetrate our consciousness instead of clinging doggedly to what we already know. There are many other ways to live than the way we are accustomed to. Leashore provides an example: "The worldviews of African-Americans are shaped by unique and important experiences, such as racism and discrimination, and involve, in varying degrees, traditional attributes of the African-American family and community life, such as strong ties to immediate, extended family, and . . . [other] kin; a strong religious orientation; a strong achievement orientation; a strong work orientation; and egalitarian role sharing" (p. 112).

Spirituality

A third concept important in understanding human diversity and psychological development is *spirituality,* "the views and behaviors that express a sense of relatedness to something greater than the self; spirituality connotes transcendence or a level of awareness that exceeds ordinary physical and spatial boundaries" (Beckett & Johnson, 1995, p. 1393). The spiritual domain is an important means by which many people organize their view of the world. The spiritual dimension is part of their reality. Therefore, it must be considered when you assess human behavior from a psychological perspective even though you may have very different beliefs concerning spirituality than you clients or your colleagues.

Spiritual beliefs can provide people with hope, support, and guidance as they progress through life. Spirituality, including Fowler's (1981) seven stages of faith, will be discussed further in Chapter 7. Chapter 15 explores spirituality and some of the major religions.

The Strengths Perspective

The strengths perspective is a fourth concept that is useful in increasing sensitivity to human diversity. It focuses social workers' attention on "the strengths, abilities, and positive qualities people have instead of on pathology, which emphasizes problems, defects, and inabilities" (Leashore, 1995, p. 113). Saleeby (1992) explains: "Social work, like so many other helping professions, has constructed much of its theory and practice around the supposition that clients become clients because they have deficits, problems, pathologies, and diseases; that they are, in some critical way, flawed or weak. This orientation is rooted in a past where certainties and conceptions about the moral defects of the poor, the despised, and the deviant" were the primary focus of attention (p. 3).

The strengths perspective shifts our focus as social workers to the positive aspects of human behavior. This includes people's "talents, abilities, capacities, skills, resources, and aspirations" (Weick et al., 1989, p. 352). Such a positive approach helps us to become more open-minded, understanding, and appreciative of individual differences when applying psychological theories.

🌿 Cognitive Development: Piaget

Specific theories concerning how people develop their capacities to think and understand have also been developed. *Cognition* involves the ability to take in information, process it, store it, and finally retrieve and use it. In other words, cognition involves the ability to learn and to think. The most noted of the cognitive theorists is probably Jean Piaget. Piaget (1952) proposed that people go through various stages in learning how to think as they develop from infancy into adulthood. His theory, which concerns the stages through which people must progress in order to develop their cognitive or thinking ability, was derived from careful observations of his own children's growth and development.

Piaget postulates that virtually all people learn how to think in the same way. That is, as people develop they all go through various stages of how they think. In infancy and early childhood, thinking is very basic and concrete. As children grow, thinking progresses and becomes more complex and abstract. Each stage of cognitive development is characterized by certain principles or ways in which an individual thinks.

The following example does an exceptionally good job of illustrating how these changes occur. In his studies, Piaget would show children of various ages two glass containers filled with a liquid. The containers were identical in size and shape, and held an equal amount of liquid (see Figure 3.2). Children inevitably would agree that each container held the same amount of liquid. Piaget then would take the liquid from one of the containers and pour in into another taller, narrower glass container. Interestingly enough, he found that children under age 6 would frequently say that the taller glass held more even though the amount of liquid in each was identical. Children approximately aged 6 or older, however, would state that

Figure 3.2 Conservation

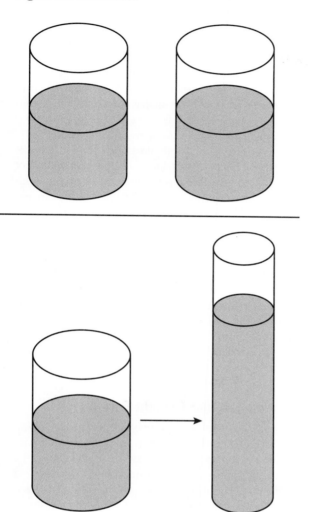

Children under age 6 would say that the taller glass holds more, even though the amount of liquid in each is identical.

despite the different shapes, both containers held the same amount of liquid. Later, it was established that the results of this experiment were the same for children of various backgrounds and nationalities.

This example demonstrated how children in different cognitive stages thought about or conceptualized the problem. Younger children tended to rely directly on their visual perceptions in order to make a decision about which glass held more or less liquid. Older children, however, were able to do more logical thinking about the problem. They thought about how liquid could take various forms and how the same amount could look different depending on its container. The older children illustrated a higher, more abstract level of cognitive development. This particular concept involving the idea that a substance can be changed in one way (e.g., shape) while remaining the same in another (e.g., amount) is called *conservation*.

These ways of thinking about and organizing ideas and concepts depending on one's level of cognitive development are called *schema*. A person perceives the world at an increasingly more abstract level during each stage. In other words, different aspects of the environment are emphasized depending on a person's cognitive level of development.

Piaget hypothesizes that all people go through the cognitive stages in the same order. An individual progresses through them in a continuous manner. In other words, a child does not wake up one morning and suddenly state, "Aha, I'm now in the preoperational stage of development!" Rather, children gradually progress through each stage with smooth and continual transitions from one stage to the next. Each stage acts as a foundation or prerequisite for the next. Three other concepts that are also important are adaptation, assimilation, and accommodation.

Adaptation refers to the capacity to adjust to surrounding environmental conditions. It involves the process of changing in order to fit in and survive in the surrounding environment. Piaget would say that adaptation is composed of two processes, assimilation and accommodation.

Assimilation refers to the taking in of new information and the resulting integration into the schema or structure of thought. In other words, when a person is exposed to a new situation, event, or piece of information, not only is the information received and thought about at a conscious level, but it is also integrated into a way of thinking. The information is stored in a way so that it may be used later in problem-solving situations.

For example, go back to the situation where young children observe and judge the quantities of liquid in glass containers. Younger children, those under age 6, assimilate information at a level using only their observations. Items and substances are only as they appear before their eyes. These children could not think of items as changing, as being somewhere else, or as being in a different context. They could not yet assimilate such information using higher, more logical levels of thought where some qualities of a substance could change while others remain the same. Children of age 6 or older can think about substances or items that are not immediately before their eyes. They can think about other different circumstances and situations.

Accommodation refers to the process by which children change their perceptions and actions in order to think using higher, more abstract levels of cognition. Children assimilate (take in) new information and eventually accommodate it. That is, they build on the schema they already have and use new, more complex ways of thinking. Children aged 6 or older have accommodated the information about the liquid-filled glass containers. Furthermore, they can think about changes in substance in a more abstract way. They can think of the liquid, not only as being held in a container of a specific shape and size, but also as it may be held in other containers of other shapes and sizes.

Piaget describes four major stages of cognitive development: the sensorimotor period, the preoperational thought period, the period of concrete operations, and the period of formal operations. Each stage will be described below.

The Sensorimotor Period

The sensorimotor period extends from birth to approximately 2 years of age. During this period, a child progresses from simple thoughtless reflex reactions to a basic understanding of the environment. Three major accomplishments are made during the sensorimotor period. First, children learn that they have various senses through which they can receive information. Additionally, they begin to understand that they can receive different kinds of sensory information about the same object in the environment.

For example, initially an infant may see and hear her parents squabbling over who will take the new Buick with air conditioning on a 99 degree summer day and who will take the old Ford Escort with no air conditioning. Even though she will hear and see them squabbling, she will not be able to associate the two types of sensory information as referring to the same aspect of her environment, namely her parents. By the end of the sensorimotor period, she will understand that she can both hear and see her parents at the same time. She will perceive their interaction from both modes of sensory input.

A second major accomplishment during the sensorimotor period is the exhibition of *goal-directed behavior.* Instead of displaying simple responses randomly, the child will purposefully put together several behaviors in order to accomplish a simple goal. For example, a child will reach for a piece of a wooden puzzle in order to attempt placement into its appropriate slot. The child will plan to put the puzzle together. However, because a child's thinking during the sensorimotor period is still very concrete, the ability to plan very far ahead is extremely limited.

The third major accomplishment during the sensorimotor period is the understanding that objects are permanent. This is the idea that objects continue to exist even when they are out of sight and out of hearing range. The concept of *object permanence* is the most important schema acquired during the sensorimotor period. Initially, children immediately forget about objects as soon as they no longer can perceive them. By age 2, children are generally able to think about the image of something that they can't see or hear, and can solve a simple problem in relationship to that image. Children begin to use *representation,* that is, the visual imagining of an image in their minds, which allows them to begin solving problems.

For example, take 2-year-old Ricky who is very attached to his "blanky," an ancient, ragged, yellow blanket that he loves dearly. Ricky is in the midst of playing with his action garage toy set with his "blanky" placed snugly next to him. Ricky's mother casually walks into the room, gently picks up the "blanky," and walks down the hallway to the bedroom. Instead of forgetting about the "blanky" as soon as it's out of sight, Ricky immediately gets up and starts actively seeking out his "blanky," calling for it relentlessly. Even though he can't presently see it and he doesn't know exactly where his mother put it, Ricky is able to think of the "blanky" and begin a quest in search of it. Furthermore, he is able to run around the house and look for it in various nooks and crannies, thinking about where it might be.

The Preoperational Thought Period

Piaget's second stage of cognitive development, the *preoperational thought period,* extends from approximately ages 2 to 7. Some overlap from one stage to another should be expected. A child's thinking continues to progress to a more abstract, logical level. Although children are still tied to their physical and perceptual experiences, their ability to remember things and to solve problems continues to grow.

During the preoperational stage, children begin to use symbolic representations for things in their environment. Children are no longer bound to actual concrete perception. They can think in terms of symbols or mental representations of objects or circumstances.

Words provide an excellent example of symbolic representation. Children may symbolize an object or situation with words and then reflect on the object or situation later by using the words. In other words, language can be used for thought even when objects and situations are not present.

Barriers to the Development of Logical Thinking. Despite children's progress toward more abstract thinking, three major obstacles to logical thinking exist during the preoperational period: egocentrism, centration, and irreversibility.

Egocentrism. In egocentrism, a child is unable to see things from anybody else's point of view. The child is aware only of himself or herself, and the needs and perspectives of others don't exist.

Piaget illustrated this concept by showing a child a doll in a three-dimensional scene. With the child remaining in the same position, the doll could be moved around the scene so that the child could observe it from different perspectives. The child would then be shown various pictures and asked what the scene would look like from the doll's perspective or point of view. Piaget found that the child would often choose the wrong picture. The child would continue to view the scene from his or her own perspective. It was difficult if not impossible for the child to imagine that the doll's perspective or point of view could be any different from the child's own.

Centration. Centration refers to a child's tendency to concentrate on only one detail of an object or situation and ignore all other aspects.

To illustrate centration, refer back to the example in which a child is asked to evaluate the amounts of liquid in two glasses. The child would observe the same amount of liquid being poured into two different shaped containers. One container was short and squat, and the other, tall and thin. When asked which container held more liquid, the child would frequently answer that the tall, thin container did. In this situation, the child was focusing on the concept of height instead of width. She was unable to focus on both height and width at the same time. Only one aspect of the situation was used to solve the problem. This is a good example of how centration inhibits more mature, logical thought.

Irreversibility. Irreversibility refers to a child's ability to follow and think something through in one direction without being able to imagine the relationship in reverse. For example, 4-year-old Gary might be asked, "Who are your cousins?" Gary might then reply, "Sherrie, Donna, Lorrie, and Tanya." If Gary is then asked who is Sherrie's cousin, he will probably say he doesn't know. Gary is able to think through a situation in one direction, but is unable to reverse his train of thought. He knows that Sherrie is his cousin. However, he is unable to see the reverse of that relationship, namely that he is also Sherrie's cousin.

Developing Cognitive Ability. Despite barriers to the development of logical thought, several concepts illustrate ways in which children progress in their ability to think. Major changes concerning these concepts are made between the onset of the preoperational thought period and the culmination of adult logical thinking. Children gradually improve their perceptions and grasp of these concepts.

Classification. Classification refers to a child's ability to sort items into various categories according to certain characteristics. The characteristics might include shape, color, texture, or size. Children gradually develop the ability to distinguish differences between objects and categorize them to reflect these differences.

For example, 2½-year-old Karen is given a bag of red, blue, and green "creepy crawlers." In this case the creepy crawlers consist of soft, plastic lizards, all of which are the same size and shape. When asked to put all the red lizards together in a heap, Karen is unable to do so. She cannot yet discriminate between the colors in order to categorize or classify the lizards according to their color. However, when Karen is given the same task at age 7, she is easily able to put the red, blue, and green lizards in their respective heaps. She has acquired the concept of classification.

Seriation. Seriation refers to a child's ability to arrange objects in order according to certain characteristics. These characteristics might include size, weight, volume, or length.

For example, a child is given a number of soda straws cut to various lengths. The child's ability to arrange such objects from shortest to longest improves as the child's cognitive ability develops. By age 4 or 5, a child is usually able to select both the longest and the shortest straws. However, the child still has difficulty discriminating among the middle lengths. By age 5 or 6 the child will probably be able to order the straws one by one from shortest to longest. However, this would probably be done with much concentration and some degree of difficulty. By age 7, the task of ordering the straws would probably be much easier.

The ability to apply seriation to various characteristics develops at different ages depending on the specific characteristic. For example, children are usually unable to order a series of objects according to weight until age 9. Seriation according to volume is typically not possible until approximately age 12.

Conservation. Conservation refers to a child's ability to grasp the idea that while one aspect of a substance (e.g., quantity or weight) remains the same, another aspect of that same substance (e.g, shape or position) can be changed.

For example, 4-year-old Bart is given two wads of "silly putty" of exactly equal volume. One wad is then rolled into a ball and the other is patted into the shape of a pancake. When asked which wad has a greater among of material in it, Bart is likely to say that the pancake does. Even though Bart initially saw that the two wads were exactly equal, he focused on only the one dimension of area. In terms of area alone, the pancake appeared to Bart as if it had more substance. However, by the time Bart reached age 6 or 7, he would probably be able to state that both wads had equal substance. He would know that matter can take different forms and still have the same amount of material.

As with seriation, children achieve the ability to understand conservation at different ages depending on the characteristic to be conserved (Papalia et al., 1998). For example, whereas conservation of substance is typically attained by age 6 or 7, the concept of conservation of weight is usually not achieved until age 9 or 10. Conservation of volume is usually not mastered until age 11 or 12.

The Period of Concrete Operations

The period of *concrete operations* extends from approximately age 7 to 11 or 12 years. During this stage, a child develops the ability to think logically on a concrete level. In other words, a child has mastered the major impediments to logical thinking that were evident during earlier stages of cognitive development.

The child now develops the capacity to see things from other people's points of view. Understanding and empathy are substantially increased during this period.

More complex thinking is developed. Situations and events can be viewed and examined in terms of many variables. The child gradually becomes less limited by centration. A child is no longer limited to solving a problem in terms of only one variable; rather, a number of variables can be taken into account. In the glass example, the child would begin to think in terms of height, volume, substance, and shape all at the same time.

A child also develops the ability to conceptualize in terms of reversibility during this period. Relationships begin to be understood from various perspectives. Returning to an example presented earlier, Gary would now understand that not only was Sherrie his cousin, but also that he was her cousin.

The concepts of classification, seriation, and conservation would also be mastered. During the period of concrete operations a child gains much flexibility in thinking about situations and events. Events are appraised from many different points of view.

Additionally, children develop their use of symbols to represent events in the real world. Their ability to understand math and to express themselves through language greatly improves. Correspondingly, their memories become sharper.

Despite the great gains in cognitive development made during the stage of concrete operations, a child is still somewhat limited. Although events are viewed from many perspectives, these perspectives are still tied to concrete issues. Children think about things they can see, hear, smell, or touch. Their focus is on thinking about *things* instead of *ideas*. Children must enter the final stage of cognitive development, the period of formal operations, before they can fully develop their cognitive capability.

The Period of Formal Operations

The final stage of cognitive development is the period of *formal operations*. This period, beginning at approximately age 11 or 12 and extending to approximately age 16, characterizes cognitive development during adolescence. Technically, this chapter addresses childhood and not adolescence. However, for the purposes of continuity, Piaget's fourth period of cognitive development will be discussed here.

Abstract thought reaches its culmination during the period of formal operations. Children become capable of taking numerous variables into consideration and creatively formulating abstract hypotheses about how things work or about why things are the way they are. Instead of being limited to thought about how things are, children begin to think about how things could be. They begin to analyze why things aren't always as they should be.

For example, Meredy, age 10, is still limited by the more concrete type of thinking that characterizes the period of concrete operations. She is aware that a nuclear bomb was dropped on Hiroshima near the close of World War II. When asked about why this happened, she might say that the United States had to defend its own territory and this was a means of bringing the war to an end. She can conceptualize the situation and analyze it in terms of some variables. In this case the variables might include the fact that the United States was at war and had to take actions to win that war. Her ability to think through the situation might extend no further than that. When asked the same question at age 15, Meredy might have quite a different answer. She might talk about what a difficult decision such a step must have been in view of the tremendous cost in human life. She might describe the incident as one of various tactical strategies that might have been taken. She also might elaborate on the political impacts caused by the event. In other words, Meredy's ability to consider numerous variables from many perspectives would improve drastically during the period of formal operations.

Three major developments characterize adolescent thought. First, the adolescent is able to identify numerous variables that affect a situation—an event can be viewed from many perspectives. Second, the adolescent can analyze the effects of one variable on another, that is, can hypothesize about relationships and think about changing conditions. Third, an adolescent is capable of *hypothetical-deductive* reasoning. In other words, an adolescent can systematically and logically evaluate many possible relationships in order to arrive at a conclusion. Various possibilities can be scrutinized in a conditional "if-then" fashion. For instance, the adolescent might begin thinking in terms of: if certain variables exist, then certain consequences will follow.

Critical Thinking: Evaluation of Piaget's Theory

Some criticisms of Piaget's theory have been expressed, which both address his general approach and raise questions about specific concepts. One general criticism is that the vast majority of his suppositions are based on his observations of his own children instead of on scientific studies conducted under laboratory conditions. Questions have been raised about the manner in which he observed and interviewed his children, the language he used to obtain information from them, and personal biases that may have emerged. His findings were primarily based on only three subjects, his own children, instead of on a variety of subjects from different backgrounds.

A second general criticism involves the fact that Piaget focuses on the "average" child. Questions can be raised regarding who the "average child" really is. Cultural, socioeconomic, and ethnic differences were not taken into account.

Consideration of only limited dimensions of human development poses yet a third general criticism. Little is said of personality or emotional growth except in specific instances where they relate directly to cognitive development. The effects of social interaction are virtually ignored. Piaget concentrates on how children see and think of objects instead of the people closest to them.

The idea that cognitive growth through these stages stops at adolescence is a fourth general criticism. Riegel (1973) suggests adding a fifth stage as people move into and through adulthood. In this stage, there would be "no clear plateaus—no levels of cognitive accomplishment clearly evident in the ability to solve a new class of problems. Instead, there is a renewed realization that development occurs on different levels, that it is replete with contradictions," and that different levels of behavior are entirely appropriate (Lefrancois, 1996, p. 402).

However, some research suggests that progression even to the period of formal operations does not occur for all people (Newman & Newman, 1999). Tremendous variation exists among individuals. Only one in three young adolescents thinks at the formal operations level (Santrock, 1999).

Piaget (1972) has offered several possible explanations for such findings. First, an individual's social environment may influence cognitive development. Persons from deprived environments many not be offered the same types of stimulation and support necessary to achieve such high levels of cognition. Second, individual differences might have to be taken into account. Some persons might not have the necessary ability to attain the levels of thought that characterize the formal operations period. Finally, even if a person develops a capacity for formal operational thought, this capacity may not be versatile in its application to all problems. In other words, some individuals might be unable to use formal operations with some problems or in some situations.

Questions have also been raised regarding the meaning and appropriate age level attributed to some of Piaget's specific concepts. He appears to have erred by underestimating children's abilities concerning various conceptual achievements. Some research replicates Piaget's in terms of principle. However, by simplifying the language used to communicate with children and by using words and concepts with which they are familiar, the children's performance tends to improve. In other words, sometimes when children can relate better to the experiment, they better understand what is expected from them and thus can perform better.

For example, consider research that involves object permanence, the concept that objects continue to exist even when they're out of sight. According to Piaget, children don't attain this skill until nearing age 2, at the end of the sensorimotor period. However, Baillargeon (1987) cleverly adapted his experimental procedure to eliminate the need for infants to have a higher level of muscular coordination than is developmentally possible at their age in order to respond appropriately. He found that by 4½ months, and some by age 3½ months, babies indicated that they were aware of object permanence.

Piaget's examination of egocentricity has also received some criticism. Egocentrism involves the concept that a child is unable to see things from anyone else's perspective but his own.

The idea that children in this age group are so self-centered may be overly harsh. Many parents may think of incidences where their young children appeared to show genuine empathic ability. For example, 4-year-old Johnnie approaches his father after finding a robin's egg that fell from the nest. He states, "Daddy, poor birdie. She lost her baby."

Additionally, there is some evidence that children are not quite as egocentric as Piaget initially proclaimed and that their thinking is much more complex (Dacey & Travers, 2002; Dunn, Brown, Slomkowski et al., 1991; Lefrancois, 1999; Papalia et al., 2001). A child's ability to empathize with others depends somewhat on the circumstances and the issues involved. For example, children living in families that encourage discussion of feelings are more adept in recognizing other people's emotions.

Piaget initially investigated egocentricity by having children observe three fabricated "mountains" of unequal heights placed on a table. Children were able to walk around the table and look at the mountains from various perspectives. They were then asked to sit in a chair at the table. A doll was placed in a chair on the opposite side of the table. The children were then shown a variety of photographs of the "mountains," which illustrated how they looked from a number of perspectives. Piaget asked the children to select the picture that best showed how the mountains looked from where the doll sat. Children in the preoperational stage would choose the picture that best showed the mountains from where they themselves sat, not from where the doll sat. Piaget concluded, then, that the children had not yet worked through the barrier of egocentrism because they couldn't comprehend the view of the mountains from the doll's perspective.

When a variation of the mountain task was used, the results were quite different (Hughes, 1975; Papalia et al., 2001). Instead of "mountains," a child was seated in front of a square table with dividers on the top to divide it into four equal sectors. The researcher placed a doll in one of the sectors and a police officer figure in another sector. The child was then asked if she thought the police officer could see the doll from where he stood. The task was then complicated by placing another police officer figure somewhere on the table. The researcher then asked the child to place the doll somewhere on the table where she thought neither police officer could see her. Of thirty children aged 3½ to 5 years, 90 percent responded correctly. Most of these young children could clearly see the situation from another's perspective. These results differ significantly from Piaget's. Perhaps children had trouble understanding the concept of fake "mountains" on a table, with which they were unfamiliar. On the other hand, perhaps children could better relate to and understand the concepts of police officers and dolls, both of which were familiar to them.

These and other studies point to the fact that the cognitive development of children is a very complicated process, perhaps much more so than Piaget could guess. It's interesting to note that a major thrust of these more recent studies is to emphasize what young children *can* do rather than what they *cannot* do.

Regardless of the various criticisms, Piaget must be given great credit. Decades ago, he provided us with a foundation for thinking about cognitive development and has tremendously influenced research in this area. Additionally, he set the stage for establishing appropriate expectations regarding what types of things children at various age levels can realistically accomplish.

🌿 Emotional Development

The concepts of *personality* and *cognition* are complex and abstract. No single, clear definition is available for either. Nor is the relationship between them explicitly defined. It is not clear exactly how thinking affects personality or how personality affects thinking. The tremendous amount of variation from one individual to another, and even one individual's varying reactions from one particular situation to another, makes it even more difficult to comprehend these concepts.

Emotions are also involved in a person's development. They complicate the profile of an individual's personality even further. For our purposes, *emotion* will be defined as the complex combination of feelings and moods that involves subtle psychological reactions and is expressed by displaying characteristic patterns of behavior. For example, a 4-year-old boy's goldfish might be found floating belly-up one morning. On hearing the unhappy news, the boy might become upset. His heart might start beating faster, and his breathing might accelerate. Finally, he might run to his room and start to cry. In this case, the boy experienced an emotion. His body responded as he became upset. Finally, the behavior of crying clearly displayed his emotional state.

Infants' Emotions

Bridges (1932), a very early researcher of infants' emotions, claimed that infants initially showed only one basic emotion, namely excitement. Watson (1919), another early researcher, felt that infants were capable of three basic emotions: love, rage, and fear. Each of these emotions, according to Watson was emitted as a reflex reaction to a specific stimulus. For example, an infant would experience love if stroked softly and spoken gently to by a parent, rage if physically restrained, and fear if suddenly startled by an unexpected loud noise.

However, more recent research indicates that infants can experience a much wider range of emotion within the first few months of life. This research has focused on the interpretation of infants' facial expressions to determine the emotions they're feeling (Izard & Malatesta, 1987). Observers participating in the experiment believed that emotions including joy, interest or general excitement, sadness, fear, and to a lesser extent, disgust, surprise, and anger could be recognized.

Immediately upon birth, infants can express general interest, disgust, and distress. Other emotions including surprise, anger, and sadness occur approximately during the third to fourth month of life. Fear is displayed during months 5 through 7. Emotions that reflect *self-awareness* tend to develop later, some not until they begin their second year. Self-awareness is the realization that one is a unique entity distinctly separate from the surrounding environment and is involved in interaction with people and things in that environment. Such emotions include shyness, jealousy, pride, and shame.

Crying. One means by which babies can clearly display their emotions is through crying (Berk, 1999; Pinyerd, 1994). Wolff (1969) analyzed tape recordings of crying babies and distinguished four basic types of crying. First, there is the rhythmic hunger cry. This tends to be the most frequent cry used both when a child is hungry and also after a child has been displaying some other type of crying for a period of time. A second type of crying is the anger cry. This is a loud cry where the baby forces a large column of air through the vocal cords. Third is the cry of pain. This type of crying is characterized by an initial loud wail with no preceding sniffling or moaning. The cry may be followed by the baby holding its breath for a long period. The fourth type of crying is the cry of frustration. This begins with two or three long cries; the baby does not hold its breath when crying in this manner. Crying that is extreme, incessant, or of an odd quality more likely reflects some physiological problem (Pinyerd, 1994).

As babies grow older, "parents respond to more subtle cues in the cry—not just intensity, but whimpering and calling sounds—to detect anxiety in their infant" (Berk, 1999, p. 157). Little evidence exists that mothers or females are naturally more capable of responding more nurturantly to infants' crying than fathers or other males (Rosenblith, 1992; Santrock, 1999).

Smiling and Laughing. Babies can also express themselves emotionally through smiling and laughing. Infants smiling at their parents and their parents smiling back provides a major means for fostering the primary relationship between children and parents.

Gewirtz (1965) proposed that babies progress through three phases of smiling. *Reflex smiling* is the first phase. Almost immediately after birth, infants can be observed smiling. At one time this was thought to be related to gastrointestinal gas. However, research indicated that it occurs automatically as a function of central nervous system development and frequently just before a baby falls asleep (Papalia et al., 2001). When an infant displays a reflex smile, only muscles in the lower part of the face, not the forehead or eyes, are involved.

The second phase involves *social smiling*. During this phase, infants smile in response to someone they see or hear. Their attention is being more directed toward other people. Many infants display social smiling by their fourth week (Lefrancois, 1999).

The final phase is the *selective social* phase in which children smile in reaction to people and sounds they recognize. This phase begins by about 3½ months (Lefrancois, 1999). The smiling process reflects infants' gradual orientation toward other people and social relationships.

© Tamara Reynolds/Getty Images

Fortunately for infants, most parents are exceptionally responsive to the cries of their children.

Laughing begins at about the fourth month. The older they get, the more frequently babies laugh and the more they find to laugh at. It is thought that to some extent laughter presents a means of releasing tension in situations that might otherwise be frightening or unpredictable (Lefrancois, 1999; Papalia et al., 2001).

Infants and Temperament

It's difficult to refer to personality with respect to infants. Personality implies a complex mixture of attitudes, expressions, and behaviors that develop over time and characterize a specific individual. Infants don't yet have enough breadth or ability for expression to portray the complexity inherent in personality. Rather, psychologists tend to refer to an infant's temperament instead of personality. *Temperament* is each individual's distinguishing mental and emotional nature that results in a characteristic pattern of responses to people and situations.

A classic study of infant temperament and its implications for later life was undertaken by Thomas, Chess, and Birch (1968, 1970), beginning in 1956. Referred to as the New York Longitudinal Study (NYLS), this research investigated 85 families with a total of 141 children. All families had highly educated members with professional backgrounds. The researchers identified nine components of temperament. These included: type and amount of physical activity; predictability of daily routines, such as eating or sleeping; the extent to which a person approaches or withdraws from new situations; how adaptable a person is to change in the environment; the intensity of stimulation needed to elicit a response; how energetically or intensively a person responds; overall disposition ranging from "crabby" to cheerful; how readily a person can be distracted from ongoing activities; and the amount of attention a person can devote to an activity in spite of obstacles.

On the basis of these components, Thomas and his associates (1968, 1970) found that children generally fall into one of three categories. *Easy* children are those whose lives have a relatively predictable, rhythmic pattern. They are generally cheerful and easy to get along with. They accept change well and are interested in new situations. The second category of child temperament includes *difficult* children. These are children who are frequently irritable, have much irregularity in their daily pattern of activities, and have much difficulty adapting to new situations. They also tend to have intense reactions when confronted with something unfamiliar. Finally, there are the *slow-to-warm-up* children. They tend to have a generally low level off activity, a mild temperament, and

moderate reactions to new situations and experiences. They tend to withdraw from the unfamiliar, at least initially, and are slow to make changes in themselves.

As with most things in life, many children do not fit neatly into one category of temperament or another. Many children show a combination of difficult and easy characteristics, yet still fall clearly within the realm of what is considered normal (Thomas & Chess, 1984). For instance, a child may have an extremely irregular sleeping schedule, yet reach out and adapt quickly to new, unfamiliar people. Another child may be cheerful and easygoing most of the time, but stubborn and difficult to live with on some occasions. The research points to some general tendencies. However, each infant, child, and adult is a unique person.

Note that temperament may be viewed in a number of other ways. Clinical observations often are too extensive, time-consuming, and troublesome to be practical. Thus, research is frequently based on parental observation. Increasingly, research points to the involvement of a genetic predisposition in some dimensions of temperament such as level of activity, emotional make-up, and sociability (Braungart et al., 1992; Buss & Plomin, 1986). Certain aspects of temperament such as sociability and level of activity maintain a moderate level of stability from early infancy to toddlerhood (Bates, 1987). However, the relationship between temperament in infancy and in later life is still unclear (Newman & Newman, 1999). Oberklaid and his associates (1993) studied later preschool behavior of children whose mothers described them as "difficult" as infants. They found that only 17.5 percent of these children actually manifested later behavioral problems. This only slightly exceeded the 14 percent of children displaying problems in the entire group. In fact, gender (being male) and lower socioeconomic status were better predictors of preschool behavior problems than maternal labeling.

An infant's temperament does not necessarily lock the child into a predetermined personality profile; environment significantly affects behavior (Kagen, 1992). Factors such as positive nurturing, family interaction, and parental satisfaction are related to infants who are considered easier to care for (Wilson, Hall, & White, 1994). Perhaps a more adequate perspective concerning temperament is that each of us is born with a general predisposition to a certain type of temperament. As life proceeds, we react to various situations and make changes in how we display or manifest our temperament.

A major variable related to overall adjustment may be the "goodness" or "poorness" of fit between the individual and the impinging social environment (Thomas &

Chess, 1984). To a great extent, this is related to expectations. For instance, consider parents who expect to have a dynamic, motivated child who is eager for new experiences. If they discover that they have a mild-mannered, hesitant, slow-to-warm-up child, they may be very disappointed. They may even place inordinate pressure on the child to be very different than the child naturally is. On the other hand, consider parents who sustain a family climate where moods are intense, daily routines are irregular, and changes are assimilated slowly. A difficult child's fit in such a family may be good. The family many not view the child as difficult at all, but rather as normal.

This material on temperament can have practical applications. It's important for parents to recognize the fact that their child does have a temperament of his or her own that may be very different from their own temperaments. Then they can consciously make adjustments in their own behavior and expectations to help that child along. For instance, a slow-to-warm-up child can be given more time to adjust to new situations, and parents of a difficult child who has trouble organizing the day in a predictable manner can help by providing structure. They can help the child learn how to formulate plans and carry them out.

✿ Self-Concept and Self-Esteem

All individuals form impressions about who they think they are. It's almost as if each person develops a unique theory regarding who exactly she feels she is. This personal impression is referred to as the *self-concept*. The idea of self-concept was introduced earlier in a discussion of Carl Rogers's self theory. A related idea is that of self-esteem. *Self-esteem* refers to a person's judgment of his or her own value. Although self-concept may include more aspects about the self than just value, many times the two terms are used interchangeably.

Self-concept is an important theme throughout mental health literature. Improving one's self-concept is often seen as a therapeutic goal for people with adjustment problems. One's self-concept is important throughout life. In order to continue working, living, striving, and positively interacting with others, one must have a positive self-concept. In other words, one must feel good enough about oneself to continue living and being productive. This is just as true for children as it is for adults. Highlight 3.4 demonstrates the effects of positive and negative self-concepts in children.

The self-concept is an abstract idea. It is difficult to explain exactly what it involves. However, it is still an important factor in a person's ability to function. People of virtually any age need to feel good about themselves in order to be confident and enjoy life's experiences.

Theoreticians have emphasized the social significance of the self-concept and have labeled it "the meeting ground of the individual and society" (Markus & Nurius, 1984, p. 147). Middle childhood is the period when children are confronted with social expectations and demands. They become aware of the importance of the social setting and begin evaluating how they fit in.

Highlight 3.4

The Effects of Positive and Negative Self-Concepts

Two 5-year-old girls, one with a good self-concept and the other with a relatively poor self-concept, illustrate the enormous effects of one's self-concept. Julie, who has a positive perception of self, is fairly confident in new situations. When she enters kindergarten, she assertively introduces herself to her peers and eagerly makes new friends. She frequently becomes a leader in their games. She often volunteers to answer her teacher's questions. Her teacher considers her happy and well adjusted.

In contrast, Mary has a relatively poor self-concept. She does not think very highly of herself or her abilities. On her first day of kindergarten, she usually stays by herself or lingers on the fringes of activities. She speaks little to others out of fear that they might criticize her. She really wants to be liked but is worried that there is nothing to like about her. Thus, it is easier for her to remain quiet and unobtrusive. For example, one day the teacher brings out pieces of colored clay for the children to play with. Being so quiet and afraid, Mary does not rush up to her teacher to get hers even though playing with clay is one of her favorite pastimes. Rather, she waits until everyone else has their clay and is returning to their seats.

By the time Mary is close to the teacher, all the clay has been handed out. Instead of clay her teacher gives her a coloring book and some crayons. Mary takes them passively and begins to color a big yellow duck. All the while she is crying silently to herself. She is very disappointed that she did not get any clay. She also is hoping no one will notice that she is different from everyone else. Mary has a poor self-concept. She is afraid of others and what they might think. She does not have much self-esteem.

One way of exploring the issue of self-esteem or self-worth stems from Harter's work (1987, 1988, 1990, 1993, 1998). (For the purposes of our discussion the terms *self-esteem* and *self-worth* will be used interchangeably.) Harter postulates that children develop a sense of *global self-worth,* an overall view of how positively they feel about themselves, in two ways. First, self-worth is based on how competent children perceive themselves to be. Second, self-esteem depends on the amount of social support they receive from those around them. By age 4, children demonstrate that they have developed a sense of self-esteem, although they are unable to describe this sense in words until about age 8 (Papalia et al., 1998).

In exploring self-worth, Harter asked elementary school children how competent and confident they felt about five different areas of their lives. The first, scholastic competence, involved how well children felt they performed in doing schoolwork. The second area concerned athletic competence, the children's perception of their sports prowess. Third, children were asked about their social competence, that is, how well-accepted and popular they felt they were. The fourth area of competence concerned behavioral conduct, or how the children felt others viewed their behavior. The fifth area was physical appearance, how attractive they felt they appeared to others and how they felt about their specific physical characteristics (such as height, weight, hair, or facial attractiveness). In addition to these five areas, Harter asked questions directed at the children's overall sense of global self-worth.

Harter's research resulted in at least three major findings. First, the most significant variable contributing to self-esteem was how much positive regard children felt from people around them. The most important people were parents and classmates, followed by friends and teachers. It is interesting that these children rated classmates above friends in terms of importance. Perhaps they felt more social pressure and experienced more painful criticism from peers they were not close to. It is also interesting that children at all grade levels rated their parents highly in importance. This contradicts the idea that as children grow up, their peers become more significant to them and their parents lose ground.

A second research finding was the ranking of the five areas. For both younger children (grades three through five) and older children (grades six through eight), physical appearance was the most important and behavioral conduct was the least important.

A third significant result involved the relationship between self-worth and affect (emotional mood). Children who felt a more positive global self-worth tended to be happier. They also were more likely to involve themselves in activities, trust in their own beliefs, express a high level of self-confidence, and handle criticism better. Those children who had a poorer sense of global self-worth were less happy, sad, and even depressed. They tended to hold themselves back from activities and be watchers rather than doers. They also were more likely to criticize themselves and to experience frustration more easily.

Some research indicates that the most significant variable contributing to self-esteem is how much positive regard children feel from people around them. Here children hugging each other and demonstrating mutual positive regard serve to enhance their self-esteem.

Spotlight on Diversity 3.2 — A Cross-Cultural Perspective on Self-Esteem

Social workers must be sensitive to cultural differences in how children develop self-esteem. Such sensitivity greatly enhances one's ability to understand interpersonal dynamics in a range of settings and to work effectively for people of diverse backgrounds. Children acquire distinctly different expectations depending on their cultural environment.

Rotheram-Borus and Phinney (1990) explored self-esteem and social expectations in groups of African American and Mexican American children. They showed 213 third and sixth graders videotapes depicting common daily social interactions. They asked the children to share their thoughts about what they saw. At least three significant findings emerged. First, the Mexican American children were more oriented to working in groups under supervision than were the African American children. In terms of enhancing self-esteem, we might deduce that a group-oriented learning environment would be beneficial for Mexican American children. It might increase their comfort level, their sense of competence, and their positive feelings about themselves. The African American children, on the other hand, might benefit more from individualized activity.

A second finding was that the African American children were more likely to participate in active movement and were more verbally and emotionally demonstrative than the Mexican American children. Perhaps providing an environment that emphasizes and reinforces action-oriented activities might promote African American children's feelings of competence and, hence, enhance their feeling of self-worth. A learning environment that is less activity-oriented might promote self-esteem for Mexican American children.

A third finding of the study indicated that both African American and Mexican American children were responsive and relatively submissive to people in authority. The Mexican American children were more likely to express bad feelings in response to scenarios involving authority

figures, whereas African American children were more apologetic. Possible implications involve improved communication with these populations of children. Being sensitive to how children tend to respond and paying attention to their needs and perspectives can provide insight regarding how to communicate and work with them. Awareness of diverse dynamics and interaction patterns can only enhance understanding.

Lamarine (1987) studied self-esteem and attitudes about health in Native American fourth-through-sixth graders. One finding was that the older the children were, the weaker the relationship was between self-esteem and having good health attitudes. An implication of this finding is that younger children might be more effective targets for changing health attitudes in order to enhance self-esteem. Perhaps if they adopt improved attitudes toward maintaining good health along with the socially desirable behavior that relates to good health, they would feel better about themselves and experience an improved global self-worth. Pueblo and Navajo children demonstrated the strongest relationship between self-esteem and health attitudes, whereas Apache children exhibited no correlation.

Pang and her associates (1985) examined a range of research on how Asian American and Pacific American children viewed themselves physically and racially. The researchers found that, generally speaking, these children had more negative self-concepts than Anglo children. An ensuing study included third-generation (Sansei) and fourth-generation (Yonsei) Japanese American children. The research compared these children's perceptions with those of Anglo-American children. The Japanese American children received lower scores on all the measures of physical self-concept. This research points to a need for increased sensitivity to the physical self-concepts of Japanese American children. Emphasizing their many positive physical attributes might be helpful in bolstering that dimension of their self-esteem.

The implications of this study are that it is important to enhance children's self-esteem, especially those children with exceptionally low levels. In fact, most programs aimed at helping parents develop effective child management skills stress the significance of developing children's self-esteem (Silvestri, Dantonio, & Eason, 1994).

Spotlight 3.2 explores a cross-cultural perspective on self-esteem.

❧ Significant Issues and Life Events

Several issues and life events that can impact children have been chosen for discussion. Their selection is based on the importance of the effects they have on children and on the

probability that social workers will encounter these issues in practice. The issues include intelligence testing along with its potential problems, and cultural biases, cognitive disabilities (mental retardation), learning disabilities, and attention–deficit hyperactivity disorder. Content focuses on both characteristics and treatment.

Intelligence and Intelligence Testing

Intelligence may be defined as the ability to understand, to learn, and to deal with new, unknown situations. Beyond this general definition, little is known about the origins of intelligence. Attempts to refine and clarify the definition have ranged from primitive measurement of head size, referred to as *phrenology,* to the listing of specific mental abilities that are supposed to be involved in intelligence (e.g., the ability to perceive spatial relationships, perceptual speed, memory, word fluency, reasoning, numerical ability, and verbal ability) (Thurstone, 1938).

Cattell's Fluid and Crystallized Intelligence.

Cattell (1971) identifies two different types of intelligence, fluid and crystallized. *Fluid intelligence* involves an individual's natural aptitude for solving highly conceptual problems, and other problems; remembering facts; attending to the task at hand; and calculating numerical figures. This type of intelligence is innate and, therefore, theoretically not subject to change over the life span. Such native aspects of intelligence include the ability to perform abstract computations and memory capabilities. *Crystallized intelligence,* on the other hand, involves intellectual abilities that emphasize verbal communication and involve the ability to learn from others in the social environment through education and interaction. For instance, a person can learn a language or increase vocabulary. And a person can acquire new information and benefit from what has been learned through experience.

It would logically follow then that while fluid intelligence would remain relatively constant throughout the life span, crystallized intelligence has the potential to increase.

Sternberg's Triarchic Theory of Intelligence.

Sternberg (1984, 1985, 1986, 1987, 1990, 1996, 2000a, b) has proposed a triarchic theory of human intelligence that emphasizes the context in which behavior occurs. He believes that three major components are involved in intelligence. These components are integrally related to a person's adaptive behavior, that is, what is relevant in the individual person's environment. For example, Bill Klumpe's business was to install septic tanks around small towns and rural farmlands in southeastern Wisconsin. Septic tanks were necessary because public sewers were unavailable throughout the area. Bill's reading skills were so poor that he had barely passed the written test to get his driver's license. The advent of calculators was a blessing to him because he was not adept at adding and subtracting numbers when figuring out what his customers owed him.

However, Bill was the best septic tank installer people around the area had ever seen. He had learned the business as a teenager and now, in his 50s, he knew just about everything about septic tanks. He could look at a piece of schedule 40 PVC piping and know immediately if it was the right size for the proper drainage capacity. His gaskets were perfect, and his pipe couplings never leaked. His buddies at the bowling alley tavern sometimes would tease him, "You don't have a brain in your head, but you sure can dig!" Sternberg would say that what Bill had was

intelligence. He had the capability to use his mind extremely well in those areas that were most significant to him.

Thus, Sternberg's model emphasizes the relevance of what people think about. The three specific components of intelligence are the componential, experiential, and contextual elements. The *componential* element involves how people think about, process, and analyze information to solve problems and evaluate their results. People who have high levels of componential intelligence also score highly on intelligence tests and are good at debate and formulating arguments.

The second component of intelligence, according to Sternberg, is the *experiential* element. This involves a person's actual doing of a task. It is the insightful, perceptive facet of intellect that enables an individual to put together information in new and creative ways. For example, Einstein conceptualized a theory of relativity. Part of this has to do with being able to master some tasks so that they become almost automatic. The mind then can devote greater attention to solving new parts of a problem or to working on new and better ways of accomplishing a task.

For example, Ruth, a medical transcriber at a large suburban hospital, types all the technical medical reports that physicians dictate on tape so that the information becomes part of each patient's permanent medical record. Over her many years of experience, she has identified a large body of technical medical words that are used repeatedly. In order to save time and make herself more efficient, she has developed a coding system that uses symbols or abbreviations to represent technical words and has encoded these into her word-processing software. For instance, when she types the letters *cd,* the computer interprets the letters to mean *cephalopelvic disproportion,* which the processor automatically prints. This system allows Ruth to concentrate more closely on the new, unknown, or most difficult terminology.

Sternberg's third component of intelligence is the *contextual* element. This involves the practical aspect of how people actually adapt to their environment. Within an individual's personal situation, it involves what knowledge is learned and how that knowledge can best be put to use in a practical sense.

To illustrate these three components, consider three undergraduate social work students, Jackie, Danielle, and Sara. Jackie had gotten almost straight A's in high school. In college she was a "whiz" at taking both multiple-choice and true-or-false exams. However, she did not do nearly as well on essay exams, especially when they involved applications to problem situations in practice (for example, how a social worker would intervene in a family where alcohol abuse was involved). She also had a terrible time when she entered her first social work practice course where she had to learn and apply interviewing skills in role plays. Eventually, she switched her major to sociology. She felt she could best apply her interest in working with people if she went on to graduate school in sociology and eventually did social research.

Danielle, on the other hand, did extremely well on essay exams but not as well on the objective multiple-choice and true-or-false tests. She got A's in the social work practice courses, which involved articulating how she would help people solve problems in the field. Her instructors praised her for her creativity and ideas. When she got into her field internship, she performed relatively well. She was able to apply her knowledge and skills to practice situations. She had some difficulty, however, working with clients who came from socioeconomic and ethnic backgrounds radically different than hers. Her final grade in field was an A−.

Sara barely got her college application accepted. She was in the lowest 25 percent of her high school graduating class, which meant she had to begin college on probation. She barely squeaked by each semester with the minimal cumulative grade point necessary. She also managed to attain the required grade point necessary to get into her advanced social work courses and continue on in the major. However, when she finally got into her field placement, her social work supervisor raved about what an excellent student she was. Sara was able to take on difficult cases early in the semester and required relatively little supervision. Sara's personal manner was such that she established relationships quickly with clients. She was able to make clear applications of the practice skills she had learned in her courses. It almost seemed like working with people as a social worker came naturally to her. She seemed to have a natural sense of what to do in situations that were completely foreign to her. She received an A in fieldwork, which contrasted with her C+ cumulative grade. The agency later enthusiastically hired her.

Each of these three individuals is strong in one component in Sternberg's model of intelligence. Jackie was strong in the componential aspect of intelligence. She could conceptualize extremely well at abstract levels and clearly remember facts and details. Danielle's strength lay in the experiential component of intelligence. She was creative and insightful. She could take recommendations for what to do in a specific situation and clearly apply them. Sara excelled in the contextual aspect of intelligence. She could adapt virtually to any situation and solve problems in a very practical sense.

In real life, people can be strong in any or all of these components. They have an intellectual mixture of strengths and weaknesses.

Intelligence Testing. We have established that there is no absolute, clear, specific definition of intelligence. It is at this point that it's important to distinguish between intelligence and the intelligence quotient, commonly referred to as IQ. Many mistakenly assume that an IQ represents the absolute quantity of intelligence that a person possesses. This is not true. An IQ really stands for how well an individual might perform on a specific intelligence test in relation to how well others perform on the same test. The IQ, then, involves two basic facets. One is the score that a person attains on a certain type of test. The second is the person's relative standing within the peer group.

An IQ score is the best thing available to attempt measuring whatever intelligence is. Such a statement may not inspire confidence in the value of one's IQ. However, perhaps it should elicit caution. IQ scores can be used to determine grade school placement, admission to special programs, and encouragement or lack thereof to attend college. A person who is aware of having a low IQ score may establish lower expectations. These lower expectations may act as a barrier to what actually could be achieved. She might become the victim of a self-fulfilling prophecy, that is, what she expects is what she gets.

This could have been the case, for example, for a returning college student who was the mother of three children. She was also receiving social insurance benefits because of a permanent disability. Her vocational counselor had told her that her IQ was not nearly high enough for success in college. He suggested that she stay home and enjoy her moderate financial benefits. Although his statements discouraged her, she had the courage and stamina to enroll with a full course load at a well-respected state university. Her final grade report after her first semester indicated that she had achieved a perfect 4.0 average. She immediately returned to her vocational counselor and requested financial assistance for a microcomputer to assist her in her course work. He responded by mumbling in an embarrassed manner that that might be a good idea.

Intelligence testing is done in both group and individual formats. Many school systems use group testing because it is less time-consuming and cheaper. Individual tests, however, tend to be more precise and useful in targeting specific areas of need. Frequently used tests including the Stanford-Binet Test and the Wechsler Intelligence Scale are described.

The Stanford-Binet IQ Test. One of the most common intelligence tests is the Stanford-Binet (Terman, 1960). First used in 1905, it has continued to be refined. Schools frequently use the Stanford-Binet to determine program and grade placement and potential academic success.

Scores on the Stanford-Binet can be obtained in four areas which include short-term memory, quantitative reasoning, verbal reasoning, and abstract/visual reasoning. Additionally, a composite score reflects the individual's IQ. The average IQ is about 100; a little more than two-thirds of all people score between 85 and 115.

In the past the Stanford-Binet was criticized because of its heavy emphasis on verbal ability. Children whose verbal ability is not strong for some reason may not have had their actual intellectual ability adequately reflected. However, a new edition was published with the intent of diminishing that bias and other biases.

Changes in the new edition include focusing less on verbal ability and more on other avenues of reasoning. For example, a child might be asked to define several words, such as *banana* or *pencil,* as part of the verbal assessment, and then be asked to draw a course through a maze to test other aspects of thinking ability (Santrock, 2002b). The test is also designed to be more evenly responsive to a broad range of groups differing significantly in geographic location, ethnicity, and gender. Newly designed norms take into account socioeconomic level and the existence of disabilitating conditions.

The Wechsler Tests. Two variations of the Wechsler Tests are the Wechsler Intelligence Scale for Children—Third Edition (WISC-III) and the Wechsler Adult Intelligence Scale—Third Edition (WAIS-III). The Wechsler Tests provide a single overall IQ score; and also a separate *verbal* score (related to the use and understanding of language), and a *performance* score (related to problem solving and thinking in ways that do not use language, such as completing pictures). This makes it easier to pinpoint specific deficits and potential problems. For example, if a child performs significantly better on the performance segments than on the verbal ones, this may provide a clue that a learning disability, or some other perceptual deficit, is present.

Below are the WAIS-III classifications and their respective scores:

- very superior—130 and above
- superior—120–129
- bright normal—110–119
- average—90–109
- dull normal—80–89
- borderline—70–79
- mentally retarded—below 70

For these classifications, 50 percent of people score within the normal range; 16.1 percent score in both the bright normal and dull normal ranges; 6.7 percent, in both the superior and borderline ranges; and only 2.2 percent, in both the very superior and mentally retarded ranges.

Targeting Special Needs. Perhaps one of the most beneficial uses of IQ tests is in targeting special needs. For example, IQ is one of the measures used to identify gifted people. One of the many definitions for *giftedness* includes the following five dimensions:

1. *Excellence,* i.e., excelling in the performance of some behavior(s) or function(s), above what peers can generally achieve.

2. *Rarity,* i.e., exhibiting qualities or functions that few people have.

3. *Demonstrability,* i.e., validating that the qualities or functions exist by demonstrating them to others (In other words, just because people *say* they're really gifted, it doesn't mean they really are; they must *do* something to prove it).

4. *Productivity,* i.e., demonstrating qualities or functions that result in something being produced or happening as a result.

5. *Value,* i.e., having qualities or functions that others value and respect (Hallahan & Kauffman, 2000, p. 475; Sternberg & Zhang, 1995).

Once identified, gifted people can then be nurtured to develop their gift or talent.

In the past, IQ was often the only means used to identify gifted people. However, as the definition of giftedness implies, it is now one of a range of measures used. Areas of giftedness might include *analytic* (the ability to carefully analyze a problem or issue, dissect it, and understand it—a quality measured by traditional intelligence tests); *synthetic* (the ability to be insightful, creative, perceptive, and imaginative—qualities often manifested by people excelling in the arts and sciences); and *practical* (the ability to function exceptionally well in daily life experiences and situations—a quality often demonstrated by people with flourishing careers) (Hallahan & Kauffman, 2000, pp. 473–474; Sternberg, 1997). A range of 3–5 percent of the U.S. school population is identified as gifted, although the numbers vary radically, depending on the definition of giftedness used.

IQ tests also can be used as an indicator for people who fall below the "normal" range of intelligence so that they might receive the special help they need. A later section will address this in depth.

Spotlight on Diversity 3.3		Cultural Biases and IQ Tests

It is critical to be vigilant concerning the potential for cultural biases in IQ tests. White middle- and upper-class children historically have had an unfair advantage over nonwhite children on these tests. Similarly, urban children have had advantages over rural children, and middle-class children over lower-class children in general. Biases can involve the use of words, concepts, and contexts that are more familiar to some children than to others.

For example, Kail and Cavanaugh (2000, p. 214) discuss the question, "A conductor is to an orchestra as a teacher is to what?" They pose the possible answers as "book," "school," "class," or "eraser." Children who have been exposed to the concept of "orchestra," perhaps having attended a concert, are more likely to provide the correct answer than children who have little or no idea what orchestras or conductors are.

What is considered significant by members of a culture can influence how children respond to questions posed by IQ tests. For example, the Western approach to labeling living things involves clustering them together under biological classifications (Papalia & Olds, 1995). Thus, a Western person might organize the white-rumped sandpiper and the Bohemian waxwing under the general category of *birds*. Birds in general might then be organized along with mammals, fish, and reptiles under the umbrella term of *animals*. The Kpelle people of Liberia in Africa think very differently, however. To them it would be more logical and, hence, more intelligent to cluster concepts together on the basis of function (Papalia & Olds, 1995). A Kpelle person might associate the word *animal* with the word *eat,* the word *knife* with the word *meat,* or the word *rake* with the word *leaf.*

Other examples involve the Iatmul people of Papua, New Guinea, and the people of the Caroline Islands (Santrock, 2002b). The Iatmuls consider intelligence to be the ability to remember the various names of 10,000 to 20,000 clans. The Caroline Islanders see intelligence as the ability to navigate well by observing and interpreting the stars.

Even testing situations and children's comfort level in them can affect IQ test results. Specific variables include the test-takers' relationship with the test-giver, their ability to sit quietly and respond to instructions, and their understanding of the dynamics involved in taking tests successfully, such as going through the entire test first, answering the questions they know, pacing themselves, and then returning to the more difficult items so that they are able to complete most of the test (Ceci, 1991).

Experience in school has also been found to influence IQ test performance (Lefrancois, 1999). Ceci (1991) discovered a positive relationship between the grade level attained in school and IQ, in addition to a correlation between school absences and decreased IQ. Other research revealed consequential differences in IQ between Peruvian children in school and those who were not in school (Stevenson et al., 1991).

Much attention has been paid to *cultural fairness* in IQ tests. Culture-fair IQ tests try to include test items and terms that are familiar to children from as many cultural and socioeconomic backgrounds as possible. However, because a totally "culture-free" test (that is, one with no culturally biased content at all) is impossible to achieve, it is important to remain sensitive to fairness and strive to make tests as "culture-fair" as possible.

Kail and Cavanaugh (1996) reflect on the overall value of IQ tests:

Most intelligence tests predict success in a school environment that often encompasses middle-class values. Tests do so for African-American and Hispanic-American students as well as for European-American students. Regardless of their racial or ethnic group, children with low test scores are usually not destined for success in school. . . . Outside of school, test scores are almost meaningless; intelligence tests measure "school smarts," not "street smarts." Consequently, when one group has higher average scores than another, this means that one group has more of the specific skills that are critical for success in the middle-school environment, not that they have more of some pervasive general-purpose ability called intelligence. (p. 198)

Other Potential Problems with IQ Scores. The use of IQ tests alone to categorize people is problematic for several reasons. One is cultural bias, discussed in Spotlight 3.3. Another is that the definition of IQ is arbitrary. At its most basic level, an IQ score reflects how well people perform on an IQ test. It does not provide a reliable indication of competence in the real world.

Another problem with IQ tests is that placing IQ labels on people may become self-fulfilling prophecies. An individual with a low IQ score may stop trying to reach his or her true potential. A person labeled with a high IQ may develop an inappropriately superior, even arrogant attitude. We all probably know people like this.

Another potential problem with IQ scores is that they do not take into account motivation. A person with a lower IQ score who works hard and is motivated to achieve may attain much higher levels of achievement and success than a person with a higher IQ who is not motivated to use it. Simply having the ability does not necessarily mean that it will be put to use.

Many aspects of an individual's personality, ability to interact socially, and adapt to society are not directly related to IQ. In effect, IQ is only one facet of an individual. People have numerous other strengths and weaknesses that make up their unique personalities. Each person is an individual whose worth and dignity merit appreciation.

Spotlight on Diversity 3.4

What Are People with Cognitive Disabilities Like?

There are huge differences in the capabilities of people who have cognitive disabilities, depending on their strengths and level of functioning. Therefore, it is important to maintain a strengths perspective and consider each person as an individual with his or her own special abilities and potential. Compared to people who have "normal" IQs, people with cognitive disabilities tend to experience deficits in seven basic areas. These include *attention, memory, self-regulation, language development, academic achievement, social development,* and *motivation* (Hallahan & Kauffman, 2000, pp. 137–138). It is important to remember that not all cognitively disabled people have deficits in all areas.

This discussion on problems associated with cognitive disabilities is negatively oriented. It focuses on people's deficits instead of their strengths. However, you need to understand where people with cognitive disabilities are likely to experience problems in order to emphasize and enhance their strengths in those and other areas.

People with cognitive disabilities may have trouble paying *attention* to ongoing activities and events as carefully as other people do. They may be easily distracted or pay attention to things other than what they are supposed to attend to.

Research has established that people with cognitive disabilities experience difficulty with *memory,* the second problem area. They may be weaker in their ability to remember things recently told to them or experienced by them. Complex ideas are more difficult for them to retain than simpler concepts.

Self-regulation, a third problematic area, is a person's ability to organize thinking and plan ahead. People with cognitive disabilities may have less ability to organize their thoughts. For instance, when students take essay exams, they may use these acronyms (words formed from the initial letter or letters of each of the successive parts of some complex term or succession of steps) to help them remember a series of steps or ideas.

Language development is the fourth area of difficulty that is evident in almost all people with cognitive disabilities (Warren & Abbeduto, 1992). They usually take longer to master language skills. They will probably require more time to understand ideas and concepts. They may display speech and pronunciation problems. It follows that with the difficulties described so far, people with cognitive disabilities will lag behind their peers in *academic achievement,* the fifth major problematic area.

Poor *social development* is a sixth area of potential difficulty. This may be due to low levels of self-esteem and poor self-concepts. It may be due to having more difficulty learning how to respond appropriately in social situations. It also may result in more disruptive behavior than their peers. If children with cognitive disabilities have difficulties in learning, especially in academic settings, disruptive behavior may be a way for them to get attention or amuse themselves.

The seventh area of possible difficulty is *motivation.* People with cognitive disabilities generally do poorly in school compared with their peers and may develop a long history of defeat and failure. If they think that they will fail no matter how hard they try, they may not try to succeed at all.

We have established that people with cognitive disabilities are often placed in categories called mild, moderate, severe, and profound (APA, 2000). The following

People Who Have Cognitive Disabilities: A Population-at-Risk

Mental retardation, or *cognitive disability,* is a condition characterized by intellectual functioning that is significantly below average and accompanying deficits in adaptive functioning, both of which occurred before age 18 (American Psychiatric Association [APA], 2000). Here we will refer to people with mental retardation as people with *cognitive disabilities.* Note two important points: First, the term cognitive disability has a less negative connotation than that of mental retardation. Second, it is important to refer to people with cognitive disabilities as *people* before referring to any disability they might have. For example, referring to them as *mentally* or *cognitively challenged people* tends to emphasize the disability because the disability is stated first. Our intent is simply to respect their right to equality and dignity.

Individuals with cognitive disabilities, to some degree, are unable intellectually to grasp concepts and function as well and as quickly as their peers. It is estimated that between 2.5 and 3 percent of people have cognitive disabilities; however, if people's level of adaptive functioning is also considered, the number is probably closer to 1 percent (DeWeaver, 1995). The following sections will elaborate on the definition of cognitive disability, the significance of support systems, and what people who have cognitive disabilities are like (See Spotlight 3.4.)

Defining Cognitive Disability. There are three major parts in the definition of cognitive disability (referred to as mental retardation) in the *Diagnostic and Statistical Manual-IV* (DSM-IV-TR) (2000) published by the American Psychiatric Association (APA). First, a person must score significantly below average in general intellectual functioning on IQ tests. This usually means achieving a score of 70 or below, although this figure can vary 5 points above or below depending on the test used and personal characteristics of the person being tested (APA, 1994). Second, a person must have deficits in adaptive functioning; that is, the person is unable to function well enough to be

profiles of each category are based on descriptions in *DSM-IV-TR*. The intent is to provide you with some general ideas about the types of support people may need.

Eighty-five percent of people with cognitive disabilities fall within the *mild* category. In the past, these people were referred to as "educable" in that they often achieve academic skills up to a sixth-grade level. As preschoolers, people with mild disabilities often develop social and communication skills, demonstrate minimal sensory or motor impairment, and generally fit in fairly well with their peers. In fact, the great majority of people with cognitive disabilities are very similar to everybody else except that they are a bit slower in learning and don't progress quite as far as others in the "normal" population. Their limitations usually become more evident as they advance in school. As adults, "they usually achieve social and vocational skills adequate for minimum self-support, but may need supervision, guidance, and assistance, especially when under unusual social or economic stress" (p. 43). With appropriate supports, people with mild disabilities "can usually live successfully in the community, either independently or in supervised settings" (p. 43).

People with *moderate* disabilities account for about 10 percent of people with cognitive disabilities. In the past, the term "trainable" was often used when referring to these people. This is not a useful term because it implies that these people cannot be "educated," only "trained." People with moderate disabilities develop communication skills in childhood and can progress educationally up to the second grade level. They "profit from vocational training and, with moderate supervision, can attend to their personal care" (p. 43). Often, they can learn to get around by themselves to everyday destinations they're used to. As adults, most are capable of

working in "unskilled or semiskilled work under supervision in sheltered workshops or in the general workforce" (p. 43). They can function well in their communities, usually living in a supervised environment.

People with *severe* cognitive disabilities make up 3 to 4 percent of all people with cognitive disabilities. In early childhood they develop little, if any, speech. As childhood progresses, they can develop some speech capability and skills to take personal care of themselves. They usually have difficulty acquiring reading or counting skills but can sometimes learn "sight reading of some 'survival' words" (p. 43). As adults, they can learn to execute very basic tasks with careful supervision. Most learn to fit well in their communities. They usually live with their families or in some other closely supervised, structured setting.

People with *profound* cognitive disabilities account for 1 to 2 percent of all people with cognitive disabilities. Most have "an identified neurological condition that accounts" for their cognitive disabilities (p. 43). Almost all demonstrate substantial sensory and motor difficulties. When provided with careful supervision, high degrees of structure in their living environment, and "an individualized relationship with a caregiver," they can make maximum progress. "Motor development and self-care and communication skills may improve if appropriate training is provided" (p. 43). Some people with profound cognitive disabilities can master very basic tasks in carefully supervised and controlled living environments.

People with cognitive disabilities have strengths and weaknesses just like the rest of us. Each is a unique individual. Most people with cognitive disabilities are pretty much like everybody else, but they have less intellectual potential. They have similar feelings, joys, and needs. And they have rights.

---

totally independent, responsible enough to take care of his or her physical needs, and/or socially responsible for his or her own behavior and interaction with others. The third important part of the definition is that disability must manifest itself during the period from birth to age 18.

Traditionally, four categories of cognitive disability have been recognized; these categories place significant emphasis on IQ scores (APA, 2000). (A later section will describe each category more thoroughly.) The categories are:

Mild	IQ of 50–55 to approximately 70
Moderate	IQ of 35–40 to 50–55
Severe	IQ of 20–25 to 35–40
Profound	IQ below 20 or 25

The ranges in each category reflect both the varying results that can be attained on different IQ tests, the 5 percent measurement error in taking the tests, and the importance of taking adaptive functioning into account (APA, 2000). For example, a person scoring 40 on an IQ

test but suffering from serious deficits in adaptive ability might be placed in the "Severe" category. On the other hand, another person scoring 40 who has many adaptive strengths might be placed in the "Moderate" category.

The *DSM-IV-TR* is the primary diagnostic tool used in the United States for mental and emotional disorders. Both the APA and the American Association of Mental Retardation (AAMR) stress the use of ten adaptive skill areas when evaluating an individual's ability to function independently. These domains are *communication, self-care, home living, social/interpersonal skills, use of community resources, self-direction, functional academic skills, work, lesiure, health, and safety* (APA, 2000, p. 41). Highlighting adaptive ability and achievement in this way allows the individual to be evaluated as a unique functioning entity. Older definitions of cognitive disability placed greater importance on IQ alone—which does not necessarily provide an accurate picture of someone's ability to function and make decisions on a daily basis. The varying capabilities of individuals with cognitive disabilities receives further attention in Spotlight 3.4.

The Significance of Support Systems. In addition to highlighting adaptive skill areas, the AAMR stresses the importance of evaluating "the patterns of support systems and their required intensities (intermittent, limited, extensive, and pervasive)" in addition to considering IQ and adaptive skill acquisition (DeWeaver, 1995, p. 713). *Intermittent support* is the occasional provision of support whenever it is needed. People needing only intermittent support function fairly well by themselves; they need help from family, friends, or service-providing agencies only sporadically. This usually occurs when they are experiencing periods of stress or major life transitions (such as a health crisis or job loss). *Limited support* is intensive help or training provided for a limited time to teach specific skills, such as job skills, or to assist in major life transitions such as moving from one's parental home. *Extensive support* is long-term, continuous support that usually occurs daily and affects major areas of life both at home and at work. Finally, *pervasive support* is continuous, consistent, and concentrated. People need pervasive support for on-going survival.

This conceptualization of support systems fits well with the systems impact model (SIM) described in Chapter 1. SIM views people as being integrally involved with the micro, mezzo, and macro systems around them. People who have cognitive disabilities require some degree of support. This support systems perspective helps us to view them positively as individuals integrally involved with other systems in the social environment.

The support systems perspective also coincides well with social work values in at least four ways (DeWeaver, 1995). First, instead of labeling people as having mild, moderate, severe, or profound cognitive disabilities, it stresses people's ability to function and achieve for themselves with various levels of support from others. It looks at what people can do with some help, rather than what they cannot do. Second, it moderates the emphasis historically placed on "the medical aspects of disabilities and puts them in the proper perspective as only one area of concern" (p. 713). Medical labels are not necessarily useful when determining what you can do to help people. For example, labeling a person as having severe cognitive disability or mental retardation is not as useful as saying that this person requires extensive support. Third, the support systems perspective shifts the primary assessment focus from IQ to adaptive skills. Fourth, because of its focus on individual strengths, it "provides for cultural and linguistic diversity in the assessment process" (p. 713). Those involved in assessment are not limited to examining one or two variables. Rather, they are encouraged to explore virtually any aspect of the individual's environment.

Macro System Responses to Cognitive Disabilities. The programs available for people with cognitive disabilities depend on policies that dictate where public funds should and will be spent. Once again, we see how policy (such as federal and state law) affects social work practice. Policies provide the rules for how organizations can spend money and what services they can provide. Social workers must do their jobs within the context of the organizations they work for.

Services for people who have cognitive disabilities or some other developmental disability[2] are paid for primarily by federal and state programs. Fully 95 percent of the federal money designated to help people with development disabilities is administered through programs under the U.S. Department of Health and Human Services. The rest is administered through the Department of Education.

Here we address two issues involved in developing programs and providing services for people with cognitive disabilities: deinstitutionalization and community-based services. The important thing to remember throughout our discussion is that intelligence, although an important variable in terms of daily living and ability, is only one of many factors affecting people's lives. Limited intelligence may reduce some of the alternatives available to an individual. However, other alternatives are available to that person to construct a rich, satisfying, and fulfilling life. A basic task of the social worker might be to help that person identify alternatives and weigh the various consequences of each.

Deinstitutionalization. *Deinstitutionalization* is the process of relocating people who need a significant level of care (e.g., people with cognitive disabilities, physical disabilities, or mental illness) from a structured institutional residence to a typical community setting. An assumption is that supportive community-based services and resources will take the institution's place in meeting people's needs.

---

2. A *developmental disability* is one of a number of conditions, including cognitive disabilities, that produce "functional impairment as a result of disease, genetic disorder, or impaired growth pattern before adulthood" (Barker, 1999, p. 126). Other developmental disabilities include learning disabilities, autism, cerebral palsy, orthopedic problems, hearing problems, and epilepsy.

These boys with cognitive disabilities receive awards at the University of North Carolina Special Olympics.

© Billy E. Barnes/PhotoEdit

Deinstitutionalization is supported by a number of rationales (Segal, 1987). First, the oppression caused by institutional living has been extensively documented. Second, costs of institutionalizing people are high. Third, social research continues to document that total institutionalization is frequently ineffective. Fourth, institutional values have increasingly emphasized the civil rights of all citizens, including people with cognitive disabilities; institutionalization severely inhibits civil rights. Fifth, newer policies have been and are being developed to provide aid to people in ways other than placing them in large residential facilities.

Historically, most federal money has been spent on maintaining people with cognitive disabilities in institutional settings. Worse, most of these institutions were actually intended for housing people who had mental illnesses (Segal, 1987). Current legislation, however, supports deinstitutionalization and the development of alternative services. Spotlight 3.5 elaborates on this.

Concerns about deinstitutionalization have focused on "inappropriate discharges, too many discharges, and community services being overrun with the demands of these clients" (DeWeaver, 1995, p. 717). If deinstitutionalization is to work effectively, community, state, and national macro systems must invest enough resources to provide adequate levels of support for people with varying needs.

Community-Based Services. The Accreditation Council for Services for the Mentally Retarded and other Developmentally Disabled Persons supports the philosophy of enhancing "the development and well-being of individuals with developmental disabilities while maximizing their achievement of self-determination and autonomy" (McDonald-Wikler, 1987, p. 430). Thus, if part of this thrust is to move people with cognitive disabilities out of institutions, it follows that they need to be moved somewhere in the community.

The subsequent question is, "Where?" Places may include housing in "smaller community-based facilities, foster homes, board and care homes, and some large group homes" (Segal, 1987, p. 379). Such settings should be structured to maximize clients' autonomy. McDonald-Wikler (1987) summarizes what many states have done to develop family support programs. Numerous state legislatures

> had either passed formal family support legislation or are plotting such programs in order to secure the maintenance of the . . . person [with developmental disabilities] in the family home, thereby avoiding the emotional and financial cost of placing the person in an alternative living environment. Support is typically provided through cash subsidies or vouchers given directly to the family for the purchase of individually relevant support services. Services commonly include respite care, transportation, and counseling. (p. 430)

An important concept related to community-based services is *normalization*. This means arranging the environmental context for people with cognitive disabilities so that it is as "normal" as possible. The lives of people who have cognitive disabilities should be as similar to those of people in the "normal," overall population as they can be.

Spotlight on Diversity 3.5

The Americans with Disabilities Act: A Macro System Addresses a Population-at-Risk

The intent of the Americans with Disabilities Act (ADA), enacted in mid-1990 and fully implemented in mid-1994, was "to provide America's 49 million . . . people [who have physical or mental disabilities] with access to public areas and workplaces" and "to puncture the stifling isolation of . . . people [with disabilities] and draw them into the mainstream of public life" (Smolowe, July 1995). It aimed to help people with disabilities who "are statistically the poorest, least educated, and largest minority population in America" to enjoy more normalized work and community lives (Kopels, 1995, p. 337; U.S. House of Representatives, 1990). The ADA includes under its umbrella people who have cognitive disabilities, other developmental disabilities, and physical disabilities. It "defines people with disabilities as those who (a) have a physical or mental impairment that substantially limits one or more major life activities, (b) have a record of such an impairment, or (c) are *regarded* as having such an impairment" (Kopels, 1995, p. 339).

The ADA is one attempt by a national macro system to improve the lives of a population-at-risk and provide them with greater social and economic justice (Kopels, 1995). The ADA consists of five major provisions. Title I forbids job and employment discrimination of people with disabilities. This includes discrimination concerning "job application procedures, hiring, advancement, compensation, job training, and other conditions and privileges of employment *simply because they have disabilities*" (p. 399; emphasis added). Title II forbids public facilities, organizations, and transportation providers to discriminate against people with disabilities. Title III "prohibits discrimination in public accommodations and services operated by private entities" (p. 338). Title IV requires that state and national telecommunication relay services accommodate people with hearing impairments and allow them communications access. Title V includes a number of miscellaneous provisions relating to more specific aspects of service provision and access.

The law requires "universal access to public buildings, transit systems, and communications networks" (Smolowe, July 1995, p. 54). Significant gains have been made in terms of curb ramps, wide bathroom stalls, and public vehicles with lifts for wheelchairs for persons with physical disabilities.

However, employers and public agencies must make only "reasonable accommodation." In reality, they are not compelled to provide such access or encouragement if the ensuing costs would result in "undue hardship," often in the form of excessive financial burdens. Because of the vagueness in terminology and lack of specification regarding how changes must be implemented, gains have been limited (Smolowe, July 1995). What do the words *reasonable accommodation, undue hardship,* and *excessive financial burdens* mean? What kind of accommodation is reasonable? How much money is excessive? How can discrimination against capable people with cognitive or other developmental disabilities be prohibited and enforced?

In fact, the hiring rate of people with disabilities by large corporations has increased only a tiny amount over the past 10 years, and the percent of people with disabilities hired by small businesses has decreased from 54 to 48 percent. This is true despite the fact that office modification costs to increase accessibility appear to be relatively meager. One survey of corporate executives, about four-fifths of whom had altered their office space, indicated that it cost only about $223 per person with a disability to do so. A legislative representative for the National Federation of Independent Business reflected on the hiring decrease by small businesses, "They're fearful if it doesn't work out, they can't fire them [people with disabilities]" (Smolowe, July 1995, p. 55).

Less than one-third of people with disabilities are employed, which is about the same proportion it was in 1990 before the ADA passed (Smolowe, July 1995; Shapiro, 2000). Therefore, the battle for equal access and opportunity for people with disabilities has not been won. Much of the public attention to the act has focused on people with physical disabilities, many of whom require wheelchairs for transportation. Where do people with cognitive and other developmental disabilities fit in? Kopels (1995) states that the ADA "will be successful only to the extent that these individuals [with disabilities] and those who advocate on their behalf learn about the ADA and use it as a means to ensure employment opportunities" (p. 345). Mackelprang and Salsgiver (1996) call for the social work profession to ally itself with the movement to enhance access for people with physical or mental disabilities; they encourage social workers to "become more involved in disability advocacy work in agencies with activist philosophies" and to work with the disability movement to "better empower oppressed and devalued groups, and understand the needs of people with disabilities" (p. 134).

Social Work Roles. Social workers can perform many roles when working with people who have cognitive or other developmental disabilities. Social workers can function as *enablers,* helping people with cognitive disabilities and their families make decisions and solve problems. Social workers can be *brokers,* linking clients to the resources (for example, transportation, job placements, or group homes) they need in order to go about their daily lives. *Educator* is another major role. People who have cognitive disabilities may need information about employment, interpersonal relationships, and even personal hygiene. Social workers can also function as *coordinators* who oversee a range of supportive services clients need.

| Spotlight on Diversity 3.6 | People with Developmental Disabilities: Population-at-Risk |

Cognitive disabilities and learning disabilities are among a number of *developmental disabilities*. These are conditions that produce "functional impairment as a result of disease, genetic disorder, or impaired growth pattern before adulthood" (Barker, 1999, p. 126). People with developmental disabilities are at risk of being oppressed, discriminated against, ignored, ridiculed, and denied equal rights.

All developmental disabilities have five aspects in common (McDonald-Wikler, 1987, p. 422). First, they all result from some specific mental and/or physical problem. Second, they appear before age 22. Third, the conditions are permanent. Fourth, they result in "substantial functional limitations" that occur in at least three areas of daily life (such as the ability to communicate with others, take care of oneself on a daily basis, or live independently). Fifth, developmental disabilities demonstrate the need for lifelong supplementary help and services.

Cognitive disabilities and learning disabilities are discussed in this chapter. The remaining disabilities, which include autism, cerebral palsy, orthopedic problems, hearing problems, and epilepsy, are described here.

Autism is a condition characterized by intense inner directedness. Autistic persons pay little or no attention to what occurs in the world outside themselves. Their behavior is often bizarre. Problems include: inability to participate in normal communication with other people; indulgence in repetitive, self-stimulating movements of extremities; severe sensory distortions (such as feeling pain when being slightly touched); and lack of normal emotional reactions to others, including attachment.

Cerebral palsy is a disability involving problems in muscular control and coordination resulting from damage to the brain's muscle control centers before or during birth. Muscle movements are very stiff and difficult, jerky, or unbalanced. Depending on the extent of damage, "lack of balance, tremors, spasms, seizures, difficulty in walking, poor speech, poor control of face muscles, problems in seeing and hearing, and mental retardation" can result (McDonald-Wikler, 1987, p. 424).

Orthopedic problems are "physical conditions that interfere with the functioning of the bones, muscles, or joints" (McDonald-Wikler, 1987, p. 424). To be classed as developmental disabilities, they must be present from birth and affect at least three areas of basic life functioning. Examples include congenital malformations of the spine, bone deformities, and missing extremities such as arms or toes.

Hearing problems range from mild hearing losses to total deafness. They are considered developmental disabilities because of their impact on speech development and the ability to communicate.

Epilepsy (commonly referred to as *seizure disorders*) consists of various disorders marked by disturbed electrical rhythms of the central nervous system and manifested in convulsive attacks. Symptoms range from periods of unconsciousness resembling daydreaming to violent convulsions.

Concurrent disabilities are also common (DeWeaver, 1995). For example, a person with cognitive disabilities might also have a hearing impairment and a malformed spine.

Social workers can also fulfill roles within the macro system context. They can assume administrative functions as *general managers* within agencies providing services to clients and their families. In this capacity they can *evaluate* the effectiveness of the services provided. Are clients getting what they really need? Is service provision as efficient as possible? Finally, social workers can serve as *initiators, negotiators,* and *advocates.* In communities and states where needed services are not readily available or are nonexistent, practitioners can work with organizational, community, and government macro systems to change policies so that clients can have access to what they need.

People with Learning Disabilities: A Population-at-Risk

A *learning disability* is "a disorder in one or more of the basic psychological processes involved in understanding or using language . . . which may manifest itself in an imperfect ability to listen, think, speak, read, write, spell, or do

mathematical calculations" (McDonald-Wikler, 1987, p. 425). A learning disability is different from either cognitive disability or emotional disturbance. Rather, learning disabilities entail a breakdown in processing information. Difficulties involve either absorbing information in the first place or subsequently using this information to communicate. Both cognitive disabilities and learning disabilities are considered *developmental disabilities*. Spotlight 3.6 explains more about developmental disabilities.

This definition of learning disabilities is vague. The reason is that it encompasses a broad range of more specific types of learning difficulties. Four basic factors appear to characterize learning disabilities in general. First, there are distinct *discrepancies* between a child's expected performance according to his or her IQ test results and actual performance. A child who has cognitive disabilities, on the other hand, will tend to function poorly across the board.

A second characteristic of learning disabilities is that some central nervous system dysfunction results in a problem in *psychological processing*. In the past it was thought that learning disabilities might be caused by some form of brain damage. However, little evidence of any tissue damage in children with learning disabilities has been found (Hallahan & Kauffman, 2000). Therefore, current thought emphasizes brain *dysfunction* or abnormal operation in the processing of thoughts.

A third characteristic of learning disabilities is that the child's deficits will come together to form a convergence or *focus* in how information is processed. Therefore, problems in information processing tend to be concentrated in one of the abilities needed to develop competence in language or math. The condition then is frequently manifested "in disorders of listening, thinking, talking, reading, writing, spelling, or arithmetic" (Lefrancois, 1999, p. 269).

A fourth characteristic of learning disabilities involves *nonacceptance of other causes* to explain the problem. There is no clearly identifiable reason why the deficient areas exist. For instance, the disability is not due to the fact that a child's eyes are not functioning properly or that the child has cognitive disabilities.

Children with learning disabilities currently make up 4 to 5 percent of school children ages 6 to 17 and more than half of all students identified as needing placement in special education classes (Hallahan & Kauffman, 2000).

Learning Disabilities Involve Problems in Processing. A number of possible processing problems that interfere with an individual's ability to use language and reasoning result in a learning disability. One involves the inability to grasp the meanings of words or how words relate to each other in terms of grammatical position.

A second processing problem related to language acquisition and usage concerns auditory processing difficulties. Some children have trouble paying attention to what is being said; the problem concerns being able to focus on the sounds most important in conveying meaning. Other children have trouble discriminating between one sound and another. For example, instead of hearing the word "bed," a child may hear the word "dead." The result is confusion for the child and difficulty in understanding and following instructions. Still other children have trouble recalling what has been said in the correct sequence. This also makes it difficult to follow instructions correctly. They cannot understand the proper order in which they are supposed to do things. These children have special difficulties in remembering content in a series format (for example, months of the year).

A third processing problem concerning language is demonstrated by children who have trouble saying what they mean or would like to say. Sometimes this involves problems with grammar. Other children may have difficulty remembering the words they want to say. Still others have trouble telling a story so that it makes sense or describing an event or situation so that the listener can understand it.

Learning disabilities can also be involved in visual perception problems in which children have difficulty in seeing things as they really are. Some children have problems understanding spatial relationships. They might see items or symbols reversed. They might also judge distances between one item and another inaccurately.

Still another processing problem demonstrated in some children with learning disabilities concerns memory and recall. Such children find it difficult to remember accurately what they have seen or heard. They commonly misspell words and forget where they placed objects.

What Causes Learning Disabilities? The specific causes of learning disabilities of most children are unknown. Potential causes tend to fall into two categories: organic and biological (such as neurological damage from disease, prenatal deprivation of some kind, or malnutrition); and genetic (hereditary) (Hallahan & Kauffman, 2000). More extensive research concerning these possibilities is necessary to establish causes. The broad range of behaviors clustered under the title "learning disabilities" and their frequently vague descriptions make it difficult to pinpoint causal relationships.

It is often difficult to identify learning disabilities because the children in question function normally in other areas. The first clue is usually a problem in academic work. Other symptoms include a lack of attentiveness in classes; thoughtless, impulsive, overly active behavior; frequent mood shifts; difficulties in remembering symbols; lack of motor coordination in writing or play activities; apparent problems in speaking or listening; and other difficulties in completing academic work. These difficulties are often vague enough to raise questions about a child's emotional health, family life, motivation to achieve, or intellectual level. Once a learning disability is suspected, assessment may involve standardized tests, such as achievement tests, as well as a range of other evaluative approaches, administered by teachers, that focus on individual work and progress.

Attention-Deficit Hyperactivity Disorder. We have established that not enough is known about the nervous system to physically pinpoint where and why the nerve cells in the brain are not working properly. However, one

Highlight 3.5

The Effects of a Learning Disability

Stevie was 16. He couldn't read or add numbers. As a matter of fact, he felt he couldn't do anything right. Other people seemed to think he was dumb. He even had to go to a special school. He didn't feel dumb, though. He couldn't read, but he understood things. He could even find his way around his hometown of Milwaukee without being able to read one street sign.

His parents and his brothers and sisters had given up on trying to help him read. He knew they were tired of trying. But he never did anything right. Then they'd get mad, and he'd get mad right back. He'd go out and break some windows and shoplift. That's why he had to go to a special school. People there weren't retarded. They had what teachers and staff called "behavior problems."

One time his teachers almost taught him to write his name. He must've practiced it a thousand times. After a couple of months he almost got it right. But he just forgot it again. He liked the staff at school. Sometimes they let him do jobs like washing the chalkboards or taking messages to the cook. He liked having responsibility. Nobody ever trusted him with jobs at home.

Stevie didn't like to think about the future. The world looked pretty dim for someone who couldn't read or write.

---

condition in particular has been labeled, studied, and given much public attention. *Attention-deficit hyperactivity disorder (ADHD)* is a syndrome of learning and behavioral problems beginning in childhood that is characterized by a persistent pattern of inattention, excessive physical movement, and impulsivity that appear in at least two settings (including home, school, work, or social contexts). Although some consider ADHD as a "subtype of learning disability" (Santrock, 1999, p. 272), it is also a psychiatric diagnosis (APA, 2000). It is estimated that 3 to 7 percent of all school children have ADHD (APA, 2000).

This definition has several dimensions. First, a child manifests a pattern of ADHD symptoms before the age of 7, although the pattern may not be identified until much later. A second dimension of ADHD is that it occurs in multiple settings, not just in one context or with one person. It involves uncontrollable behavior that is not necessarily related to a particular context. Finally, three primary clusters of behavior characterize ADHD. The first is *inattention*. Behavioral symptoms include messy work, carelessly handled tasks, frequent preoccupation, easy distractibility, aversion to tasks that require attention and greater mental exertion, serious problems in organizing tasks and activities, and difficulties attending to ongoing conversations. The second cluster of behaviors concerns *excessive physical movement* that is difficult to control (hyperactivity). This involves almost constant action, squirming or being unable to sit down at all, demonstrating great difficulty in attending to quiet activities, and talking nonstop. The third batch of behaviors falls under the umbrella of *impulsivity*. This is characterized by extreme impatience, having great difficulty in waiting for one's turn, and making frequent interruptions and intrusions.

Effects of Learning Disabilities on Children. Learning disabilities may psychologically affect children in several ways (APA, 2000; Eaton, Lippmann, & Riley, 1980; Hallahan & Kauffman, 2000; Silver, 1992). They include fear of failure, withdrawal, helplessness, and low self-esteem reactions. Highlight 3.5 provides one case example of psychological effects.

Children with learning disabilities often become experts in failure. Through no fault of their own, they are unable to learn or do things the way other children can. Some children may fail in school or in sports so frequently that they no longer will attempt new things. They begin to assume that no matter what they do, they will just fail anyway. This *fear of failure reaction* often results in almost the complete avoidance of new experiences. Because the child refuses to take any new risks, potential progress is halted.

Other children take the fear of failure reaction a step further. Not only do they avoid new experiences, but they withdraw into themselves. This is called *withdrawal reaction*. People and activities seem to have caused them only failure and humiliation in the past. The safest alternative then is to withdraw into themselves. To a limited extent, this may be a healthy means of coping. However, in extreme cases children may isolate themselves and become totally preoccupied with their own thoughts.

The *helpless reaction* is another means of responding to a learning disability. Children may use the fact that they cannot do some things in order to get out of doing other things they are capable of doing. The vague and complicated nature of learning disabilities does not help this situation. For example, a mother may ask her daughter to do her homework. The daughter responds, "Gee, Mom,

I don't know how." The daughter's learning disability involves reading. Her homework is an arithmetic assignment which she has no more difficulty completing than her peers. However, because of her learning disability, the daughter is perceived as being helpless in her mother's eyes. As a result, the mother does not make the daughter do her homework.

Another possible reaction of a child with learning disabilities is that of *low self-esteem*. These children are likely to see other children do things they cannot. Perhaps others make critical comments to them. Teachers and parents may show at least some impatience and frustration at the children's inability to understand or perform in the areas affected by their learning disabilities. These children are likely to internalize their failures. The result may be that they feel inferior to others, and they may develop low self-esteem.

What are the long-term effects of learning disabilities? Some people with learning disabilities may continue to experience problems in work and social adjustment as adults (APA, 2000; Kail & Cavanaugh, 2000). However, how people with learning disabilities are treated and accepted is critical in terms of their satisfaction and achievement as adults.

Various factors appear to be related to the successful life transition of people with learning disabilities including persistence in not giving up, setting and working toward goals, realistically acknowledging weaknesses, getting strong social support from people around them, and receiving ongoing educational help to continue adjusting to disabilities. (Gerber, Ginsberg, & Reiff, 1992; Hallahan & Kauffman, 2000; Kavale, 1988; Murphy, 1992; Reiff & Gerber, 1992; Reiff, Gerber, & Ginsberg, 1997; Spekman, Goldberg, & Herman, 1992).

Treatment for Learning Disabilities. There are at last two dimensions to treatment for learning disabilities. One concerns the educational environment and planning. The second involves parents' and others' treatment of a person with learning disabilities in the home and other social settings.

Educational treatment for children with learning disabilities focuses on designing an individualized special education program for the child to emphasize strengths and minimize weaknesses. For a child with a visual perceptual disorder, emphasis might be placed on providing material that the child can hear rather than see. For example, instead of reading an assignment in a textbook, a tape recording of the assignment might be made available. Other means of tailoring a special education program

include breaking down tasks into smaller, more workable units so that children will more likely understand the process and achieve success.

Within the educational context, there are at least three major approaches to individualized instruction (Hallahan & Kauffman, 2000). The first is a *multisensory approach*. This involves presenting material to the child using as many senses as possible. For example, a young boy with a learning disability who is trying to master addition skills might first be to told verbally how to accomplish the task. Then he might be shown on the board or by using cue cards how the addition procedure is performed. He might also be encouraged to carry out the addition task by using actual objects, enhancing his learning through his sense of touch.

The second common approach is *cognitive training*. This approach focuses on procedures to teach children with learning disabilities how to change their patterns of thinking. One cognitive training technique is self-instruction. Here, the idea is to develop the child's ability to attend to a task by breaking it up into a series of steps, modeling the task for the child, and then carefully supervising until he or she learns the process. For example, a five-step procedure for learning how to solve math word problems entails "saying the problem out loud, looking for important words and circling them, drawing pictures to help explain what was happening, writing the math sentence, and writing the answer" (p. 181).

A third approach is *direct instruction*. This method, usually used to improve math and reading skills, emphasizes drilling and practicing. Teachers instruct small groups of children with clearly specified lessons and provide them with immediate feedback, correcting wrong answers and praising right ones.

Additional techniques are suggested to help children who have ADHD (Hallahan & Kauffman, 1994). One is to provide a highly structured classroom environment with minimal distracting stimuli. For example, the room might be soundproof and students might work in enclosed cubicles devoid of distractions. The teacher encourages the students to focus only on the structured task at hand.

Behavior modification offers techniques that are helpful for children with ADHD (Silver, 1992; Wodrich, 1994). Chapter 4 discusses behavior modification techniques with respect to effective parenting. For ADHD children, behavior modification focuses on specifying and reinforcing good behavior and decreasing poor behavior by monitoring and structuring each behavior's consequences.

Various medications, such as Ritalin, are also used to treat ADHD. However, there are some concerns regarding the possibility of side effects such as growth retardation (although this is largely unsubstantiated), appetite loss, or difficulties sleeping, in addition to the possibility of overmedication (Hancock, 1996; Silver, 1992).

Outside the educational arena, children with learning disabilities need help within their family and other social settings. Some of the suggestions for helping children in educational settings also apply to many social contexts. For example, use of behavior modification techniques can help children change their behavior so that it is more socially appropriate. Also important in both educational and social environments is development of a positive self-concept. First, the positive things that children do should be emphasized. Problems are easy to see, but good behaviors and accomplishments often go unnoticed. Second, children should feel loved, not for their behavior, but, rather, for who they are. Third, confidence can be developed in children by giving them responsibility for things they are capable of accomplishing. Success at tasks helps them to develop faith in themselves. Third, comparisons to others and what they accomplish should be avoided. The child's own accomplishments should be the focus of attention. Fourth, structure in the form of clear guidelines for behavior is helpful. If the child knows what is acceptable and what is not, he or she is less likely to make mistakes. The child will also probably respond to the fact that someone cares enough to put forth the effort to provide structure.

Other forms of treatment are also used to enhance social functioning in families with a child who has learning disabilities (Silver, 1992). Educating both the child with a learning disability and those around that person can help all involved understand what the disability entails and modify their expectations accordingly. Individual and family counseling can improve communication and increase family members' understanding of how others view the disability. It can also help them develop problem-solving strategies to improve a child's behavior and cope with interpersonal irritations.

Macro System Responses to Learning Disabilities.
Major legislation has positively affected educational programming for learning disabled people in the past few decades (McDonald-Wikler, 1987). The 1975 Education for All Handicapped Children Act (P.L. 94–142) mandated that all states provide educational opportunities for all children regardless of level of ability or disability. In accordance with this law, school systems have responded with the concept of *inclusion*. Through inclusion, students with disabilities are assimilated into regular classrooms with same-age peers, but also receive the special attention and help they need to maximize their performance. Children with learning disabilities and children with cognitive disabilities and other developmental disabilities are thus guaranteed the right to an education. States and communities are no longer able to ignore or reject children with learning disabilities. Excuses such as high costs or lack of existing facilities are no longer acceptable. This illustrates how legislation forces state, community, and organizational macro systems to respond to a social need.

Social Work Roles.
Social work roles with respect to clients with learning disabilities are similar to those used with clients who have cognitive disabilities. Social workers function as brokers to help link clients with resources. Practitioners function as advocates to effect positive change in macro systems that are not responsive to clients' needs.

❧ Summary

Major theories of personality development include psychodynamic, neo-Freudian psychoanalytic, behavioral, and phenomenological theories. Freud's psychoanalytic theory, the predominant psychodynamic theory, emphasizes concepts including the id, superego, ego, libido, fixation, defense mechanisms, Oedipus complex, and Electra complex. His proposed stages of psychosexual development include oral, anal, phallic, latency and genital. Criticisms of psychoanalytic theory include lack of supportive research, poor clarity of ideas, and failure to address adequately the status of women.

The neo-Freudian psychoanalytic theorists include Carl Jung, Erich Fromm, Alfred Adler, and Harry Stack Sullivan. Respective theoretical emphases include analytic psychology for Jung, a social context for Fromm, individual psychology for Adler, and individual personality development based on interpersonal relationships for Sullivan.

Behavioral theory is one of the most useful theories of human behavior and is discussed more thoroughly in Chapter 4. The self theory of Carl Rogers is a phenomenological approach, and emphasizes the ideas of self-concept, self-actualization, ideal self, incongruence between self and experience, the need for positive regard, and conditions of worth, among others.

Feminist theories are based on the concept of feminism and reflect a range of theories. Major underlying principles include: the elimination of false dichotomies; rethinking knowledge; differences in male and female experiences throughout their life spans; the end of patriarchy; empowerment, valuing process equally with product; the personal is political; unity and diversity; and consciousness raising.

The means of evaluating theories' relevance to social work involves evaluating the following: the theory's application to client situations; the research supporting the theory; the extent to which the theory coincides with social work values and ethics; and the existence and validity of other comparable theories. It is important to be sensitive to diversity when examining psychological theories. Important concepts are the dual perspective, worldview, spirituality, and the strengths perspective.

Piaget's theory of cognitive development involves the following stages: (1) the sensorimotor period; (2) the preoperational thought period; (3) the period of concrete operations; and (4) the period of formal operations. Important concepts include conversation, schema, adaptation, assimilation, accommodation, object permanence, representation, egocentrism, centration, irreversibility, classification, seriation, and conversation. Criticisms of Piaget's theory include: the fact that observations were based on his own children; a focus on the "average child"; consideration of limited dimensions of human development; and the premise that cognitive growth stops at adolescence.

People begin displaying their emotions and temperament in infancy. Early behaviors include crying, smiling, and laughing. A major variable related to overall adjustment may be the "goodness" or "poorness" of fit between the individual and the impinging environment.

It is important to enhance children's self-esteem, especially those children with exceptionally low levels. Social workers must be sensitive to cultural differences in how children develop self-esteem.

Intelligence is the ability to understand, learn, and deal with new, unknown situations. Cattell identifies two types of intelligence, fluid and crystallized. Sternberg's triarchic theory of intelligence emphasizes componential, experiential, and contextual elements. Intelligence tests include the Stanford-Binet IQ Test and the Wechsler Intelligence Scale Tests. Giftedness involves analytic, synthetic, and practical abilities. It is critical to be vigilant concerning the potential for cultural biases and other potential problems in IQ tests.

Cognitive disability is a condition characterized by intellectual functioning that is significantly below average and accompanying deficits in adaptive functioning, both of which occur before age 18. Support systems are important for people with cognitive disabilities. Problem areas for people with cognitive disabilities include attention, memory, self-regulation, language development, academic achievement, social development, and motivation. Macro system responses to cognitive disabilities include deinstitutionalization, community-based services, and the Americans with Disabilities Act.

Learning disabilities involve discrepancies between a child's performance according to IQ testing and his or her actual performance, problems in psychological processing, a focus in how information is processed, and nonacceptance of other causes. Specific causes of learning disabilities are unknown. Learning disabilities may psychologically affect children in several ways including fear of failure, withdrawal, helpless, and low self-esteem reactions. Treatment approaches include a multisensory approach, cognitive training, and direct instruction.

Both cognitive disabilities and learning disabilities are under the umbrella of developmental disabilities, along with a number of other conditions. Attention-deficit hyperactivity disorder is a syndrome of learning and behavioral problems beginning in childhood that is characterized by a persistent pattern of inattention, excessive physical movement, and impulsivity that appear in at least two settings.

InfoTrac College Edition Keywords

behavioral theories	cognitive disabilities	feminist theories	learning disabilities	psychoanalytic theory
cognitive development	emotional development	intelligence testing	phenomenological theories	

On the Internet

American Association on Mental Retardation

http://www.aamr.org/

AAMR promotes progressive policies, sound research, effective practices, and universal human rights for people with intellectual disabilties.

Eunice Kennedy Shriver Center

http:/www.umassmed.edu/shriver/

The center promotes the understanding of the neurological, cognitive, and behavioral development associated with developmental disabilities, emphasizing mental retardation.

Learning Disabilities Association of America

http://www.ldanatl.org/

LDA (formerly ACLD, the Associatin for Children and Adults with Learning Disabilities) was formed in 1964 by a group of concerned parents on behalf of children with learning disabilities. LDA is the only national organization devoted to defining and findind solutions for the broad spectrum of learning disabilities.

CHAPTER 4

Social Systems and Their Impacts on Infancy and Childhood

"My dad could punch out your dad, I bet!," Jimmy yelled at Harry, the neighborhood bully. Harry had just bopped Jimmy in the nose. Jimmy, who was small for his age, felt hurt. So he resorted to name calling as he edged away from his aggressor. Since his own house was a full two blocks away, Jimmy had to do some fast thinking about how to get there without every-body thinking he was chicken. The worst thing was that Harry was also a pretty fast runner.

To Jimmy's surprise and delight, Harry was apparently losing interest in this particular quarry. Somebody called out from the next block and was trying to interest Harry, a good fullback, in a game of football.

Scowling, Harry shouted back to Jimmy, "Oh, get out of here, you punky fry. Your dad sucks eggs!" He then darted down the block and into the sunset.

That last remark did not make much sense, although Harry's intent was to be as nasty as possible (intellect was not his strong suit). The important thing, however, was that Harry was running in the other direction. Any of the other guys who happened to witness this incident might just think that it was Harry who was running scared. Nonetheless, Jimmy thought it best not to reply, just in case Harry decided to change his mind.

"Whew!," thought Jimmy. "That was a close one." He was usually pretty good at staying far out of Harry's way. This meeting was purely an accident. He was on his way home from a friend's house after working on a class project. That was another story. Their project in-volved growing bean plants under different lighting conditions. The bean plants that were supposed to be growing good beans weren't. Jimmy secretly suspected that his partner was eating the beans.

Jimmy had better things to do now at any rate. He had to finish his homework. His parents had promised to buy him a new stereo boom box if he maintained at least a

B+ average for the whole year. Harry would probably flunk this year anyhow. He was big, but he was also pretty stupid.

Jimmy hightailed it down the street. He imagined hearing the tones of Ear Discharge, his favorite rock group. The horrible Harry affair was soon forgotten.

A PERSPECTIVE

The attainment of primary social developmental milestones and the significant life events that tend to accompany them have tremendous impacts on the developing individual and that individual's transactions with the environment. Family and peer group mezzo systems are dynamically involved in children's growth, development, and behavior. Social interaction in childhood provides the foundation for building an adult social personality. Children and their families do not function in a vacuum. Macro systems within the environment, including communities, government units, and agencies, can provide necessary resources to help families address issues and solve problems typically experienced by children. Impinging macro systems within the social environment can either help or hinder family members to fulfill their potential.

This chapter will:

► Explain the concept of socialization.
► Explore the family environment, variations in family structures, the impacts of social forces on family systems, diverse perspectives on the family life cycle, and the dynamics of family systems.
► Apply systems theory principles to families.
► Describe the basic concepts of learning theory and how such principles as positive reinforcement, punishment, and time-out from reinforcement can be applied to effective parenting.
► Examine some common life events that affect children, including membership in sibling subsystems, gender role socialization, ethnic and cultural differences in families, play with peers, television, and the school environment.
► Explore the dynamics and effects of physical abuse, neglect, emotional maltreatment, and sexual abuse on children.

❧ Socialization

Socialization is the process whereby children acquire knowledge about the language, values, etiquette, rules, behaviors, social expectations, and all the subtle, complex bits of information necessary to get along and thrive in a particular society.

Although socialization continues throughout life, most of it occurs in childhood. Children need to learn how to interact with other people. They must learn which behaviors are considered acceptable and which are not. For example, children need to learn that they must abide by the directives of their parents, at least most of the time. They must learn how to communicate to others what they need in terms of food and comfort. On the other hand, they also need to learn what behaviors are not considered appropriate. They need to learn that breaking windows and spitting in the eyes of other people when they don't get their way will not be tolerated.

Because children start with knowing nothing about their society, the most awesome socialization occurs during childhood. This is when the fundamental building blocks of their consequent attitudes, beliefs, and behaviors are established.

🌿 The Family Environment

Because children's lives are centered initially within their families, the family environment becomes the primary agent of socialization. The family environment involves the circumstances and social climate within families. Because each family is made up of different individuals in a different setting, each family environment is unique. The environments can differ in many ways. For example, one obvious difference is socioeconomic level. Some families live in luxurious twenty-four-room estates, own a Mercedes and an SUV in addition to the family minivan, and can afford to have shrimp cocktail for an appetizer whenever they choose. Other families subsist in two-room shacks, struggle with payments on their used 1996 Chevy, and have to eat macaroni made with artificial processed cheese four times a week.

This section addresses several aspects of the family environment. They include variations in family structures, positive family functioning, impacts of social forces and policies on family systems, and the application of systems theory principles to families.

Membership in Family Groups: Variations in Family Structure

Families in the United States today are no longer characterized by two first-time married parents who live blissfully together with their 2.5 children. The traditional "nuclear family" included parents married one time, with one or more children. Today, only about 35 percent of all families include married parents with their own children, and this figure includes parents who have been married to someone else before (U.S. Census Bureau, 2001).

Today's families are more likely to conform to a varied medley of structures and configurations. *Family structure* is "the nuclear family as well as those non-traditional alternatives to nuclear family which are adopted by persons in

committed relationships and the people they consider to be 'family'" (Commission of the Council on Social Work Education, 2002). Scrutinizing this definition shows how flexible the notion of family has become.

A family is a *primary group*. This entails "people who are intimate and have frequent face-to-face contact with one another, have norms [that is, expectations regarding how members in the group should behave] in common, and share mutually enduring and extensive influences" (Barker, 1999, p. 376). Thus, family members as members of a primary group have significant influence on each other. The second concept in the definition of family involves "obligations for each other," which means mutual commitment and responsibility for other family members. The third concept in the definition is "common residences." That is, to some extent, family members live together.

Families, then, may consist of intact two-parent families with or without children, single-parent families, blended families, stepfamilies, or any other configuration that fits our definition. Some of these terms are defined as follows:

A *single-parent family* is a family household where one parent resides with the children but without the other parent. It should be noted that 76 percent of single-parent families are headed by women (U.S. Census Bureau, 2001).

Stepfamilies are primary groups where one parent resides, or both parents reside, with children from prior marriages or unions. Members may include stepmothers, stepfathers, and any children either may have from prior marriages. Stepfamilies may also include children born to the currently married couple. Stepfamilies have become extremely common in view of the fact that about half of all marriages end in divorce. Stepfamilies may also become very complex when one or both spouses were married more than once and/or have children from a variety of relationships.

A *blended family* is any nontraditional configuration of people who live together, are committed to each other, and perform functions traditionally assumed by families. Such relationships may not involve biological or legal linkages. The important thing is that such groups *function* as families.

This discussion is extremely relevant to social workers. It is critically important that you be sensitive to the various configurations families may take. Open-mindedness is essential when assessing the strengths of any family group. Workers should not make assumptions about how families *should* be, but should work with the family group that *is*. New evolving issues for social workers to address include: life differences for various cultural and socioeconomic groups; the increasing "number of adults . . . choosing not to marry or, like gays and lesbians, [who] are prevented from marrying"; the poor who find marriage "almost impossible to afford"; growing numbers of adults delaying childbearing or choosing not to have children; and the soaring prevalence of divorce, remarriage, and stepfamily integration (Carter & McGoldrick, 1999, p. xv). (Family configurations are discussed more thoroughly in Chapter 12.)

Positive Family Functioning

In view of the vast range of family configurations, it is extremely difficult to define a "healthy" family. However, at least two concepts are important when assessing the effectiveness of a family. These include how well *family functions* are undertaken and how well family members *communicate* with each other.

Family functions include a wide range of caregiving functions including nurturing and socializing children, providing material and emotional support, and assuming general responsibility for the well-being of all members. Children must be nurtured and taught. All family members need adequate resources to thrive. Additionally, family members should be able to call on each other for help when necessary.

Good communication is the second characteristic of "healthy" families. Communication and autonomy are closely related concepts. Good communication involves clear expression of personal ideas and feelings even when they differ from those of other family members. On the other hand, good communication also involves being sensitive to the needs and feelings of other family members. Good communication promotes compromise so that the most important needs of all involved are met. In families that foster autonomy, boundaries for roles and relationships are clearly established. All family members are held responsible for their own behavior. Under these conditions, family members much less frequently feel the need to tell others what to do or "push each other around." (Family communication is discussed more thoroughly in Chapter 12.)

Negotiation is also clearly related to good communication and good relationships. When faced with decisions or crises, healthy families involve all family members, so as to come to solutions for the mutual good. Conflicts are settled through rational discussion and compromise instead of open hostility and conflict. If one family member feels strongly about an issue, healthy families work to accommodate his or her views in a satisfactory way. Both unhealthy and healthy families suffer conflict and disagreements, but a healthy family deals with conflict much more rationally and effectively.

Families can be compared and evaluated on many other dimensions and variables. The specific variables are not as important as the concept that children are socialized according to the makeup of their individual family environments. The family teaches children what types of transactions are considered appropriate. They learn how

Negotiation is a healthy response to family decisions or crises. It should involve all family members.

to form relationships, handle power, maintain personal boundaries, communicate with others, and feel that they are an important subset of the whole family system.

Effects of Social Forces and Policies on Family Systems: Helpful or Hurtful?

We have established that families provide an immediate, intimate social environment for children as they develop. However, families do not exist in a vacuum. They are in constant interaction with numerous other systems permeating the macro social environment. Families can provide caregiving and nurturance only to the extent that other macro systems in the environment provide support. These macro systems, which include communities and organizations, are in turn directly impacted by the social forces driving daily life.

Social forces include the political, economic, environmental, and ideological. They are abstract and difficult to define, and they are almost inseparably entangled with each other. Yet, they form the foundation resources that families need.

For example, unemployment may soar because of an economic slump. Political decisions such as increasing business taxes may have sparked the slump. Ideologically, the general public may feel that in "a free country" of rugged individualists, it is each person's responsibility to find and succeed in work. The public may not support political decisions to subsidize workers by providing long-term unemployment benefits or developing programs for job retraining. At the same time, legislators concerned about the increasing unemployment rate and their reelection may hesitate to impose increasing restrictions on business and industry such as more stringent (and more costly) pollution control regulations. Thus, the physical environment suffers.

This example, of course, is overly simplistic. Volumes have been written on each aspect of the political, economic, environmental, and ideological aspects of the social environment. However, the point is that it is impossible to comprehend a family's situation without assessing that family within the context of the macro social environment. The resources available to a family are directly affected by the ensuing social forces. For example, economic downturns and unemployment may leave a parent jobless and poverty-stricken. That parent will then be less able to provide the food, shelter, health care, and other necessities for a family environment in which children can flourish.

Likewise, the resources available to agencies and communities for dispersal to clients depend on the legislative and organizational policies resulting from social forces. For instance, U.S. society is structured so that all citizens have the right to receive a high school education. This idea is based in ideology that, in turn, is reflected by legislative and administrative policy that regulates how that education is provided.

Public day care, on the other hand, is not provided to working parents on a universal basis. Day care involves an agency or a program that provides supervision and care for children while parents or guardians are at work or otherwise unavailable. There are many historical ideological reasons for this lack. For one, traditional thought is that a woman's place is in the home and that she should be the primary caretaker of the children (Spakes, 1992). However, today over 60 percent of women work outside of the home, most out of economic necessity (U.S. Census Bureau, 2001). For women with children under age 6, 70.5 percent of single mothers, almost 63 percent of married mothers, and almost 77 percent of mothers who are widowed, divorced, or separated, work outside of the home (U.S. Census Bureau, 2001). Monumental evidence suggests that although most women in heterosexual relationships work, they still continue to carry the overwhelming responsibility both for child care and other household tasks (Freeman, 1995; Lott, 1994; Renzetti and Curran, 1995; Ruth, 1998; Sapiro, 1999). Additionally, although most people marry, about one-half of all marriages end in divorce (Berk, 1999; Coleman & Cressey, 1999). We have already noted that over three-quarters of all single-parent families are headed by women (U.S. Census Bureau, 2001). (Many of these issues will be discussed more thoroughly in Chapter 9.)

In summary, a number of facts point to the need for adequate day care to serve the nation's children. First, most women work outside of the home from economic necessity. Second, it remains women's additional burden to be primary homemakers. Third, many women have no mate to help in child-care responsibilities.

Yet, day-care facilities are inadequate to meet the nation's needs (Newman & Newman, 1999). Parents often struggle to find adequate, affordable, and accessible day care for their children. Many day-care centers refuse to accept small infants because of the difficulty in their care. Furthermore, numerous children in the United States are provided day care in private homes, unregulated by public standards.

Why doesn't the government require that facilities be developed to meet the day-care need? There is no clear answer. Cost may be one possibility. Low priority may be another. As a student social worker, what do you think? Is the need real? How critical is it, especially for women? As you take courses in social policy and practice techniques, will you be motivated to seek out answers for how to solve this problem and others like it?

The Dynamics of Family Systems

In order to understand family functioning, it's helpful to view the family within a system's perspective. Systems theory applies to a multitude of situations, ranging from the internal mechanisms of a computer to the bureaucratic functioning of a large public welfare department to the interpersonal relationships within a family. Regardless of the situation, understanding systems theory concepts helps you to understand dynamic relationships among people. Systems theory helps to conceptualize how a family works. Basic systems theory concepts were introduced in Chapter 1. Highlight 4.1 reviews those concepts and shows how they can be applied to family systems.

Systems theory also helps us understand how a family system is intertwined with many other systems. Each

Highlight 4.1

The Application of Systems Theory Principles to Families

A number of the basic systems theory concepts introduced in Chapter 1 will be briefly redefined here and then applied to examples of family situations.

Systems

A *system* is a set of elements that form an orderly, interrelated, and functional whole. Several aspects of this definition are important. The idea that a system is a "set of elements" means that a system can be composed of any type of things as long as these things have some relationship to each other. Things may be people, or they may be mathematical symbols. Regardless, the set of elements must be orderly. In other words, the elements must be arranged in some order or pattern that is not simply random. The set of elements must also be interrelated. They must have some kind of mutual relationship or connection with each other. Additionally, the set of elements must be functional. Together they must be able to perform some regular task, activity, or function and fulfill some purpose. Finally, the set of elements must form a whole.

Families are systems. Any particular family is composed of a number of individuals, the elements making up the system. Each individual has a unique relationship with the other individuals in the family. Spouses normally have a special physical and emotional relationship with each other. In a family with seven children, the two oldest sisters may have a special relationship with each other that is unlike their relationship with any of the other siblings. Regardless of what the relationships are, together the family members function as a family system. These relationships, however, are not always positive and beneficial. Sometimes, a relationship is negative or even hostile. For example, a 3-year-old daughter may be fiercely jealous of and resentful toward her newborn brother.

Homeostasis

Homeostasis refers to the tendency for a system to maintain a relatively stable, constant state of equilibrium or balance. A homeostatic family system functions effectively. The family system is maintaining itself and may even be thriving. However, a homeostatic family system is not necessarily a perfect family. Mother may still become terribly annoyed at father for never wanting to go out dancing. Ten-year-old Bobby may still be maintaining a D average in English. Nonetheless, the family is able to continue its daily existence, and the family system itself is not threatened.

Homeostasis is exceptionally important in determining whether outside therapeutic intervention is necessary. Absolute perfection is usually unrealistic. However, if the family's existence is threatened, the system may be in danger of breaking apart. In these instances, the family system no longer has homeostasis.

For instance, an 89-year-old maternal grandmother no longer can care for herself. She has been living alone since the death of her husband 20 years ago. Her eyesight is failing, and her rheumatoid arthritis puts her in constant pain. She remains fairly alert, however, with only some minor forgetfulness. Mother refuses to place grandmother in a nursing home. She feels responsible for her mother because she is the only child, and she would like to "pay back" all the care she received as a child.

Father, however, hates the idea of having his mother-in-law move in. Grandmother, he feels, has always tried to intervene in his marriage. He feels that she takes sides with his wife and constantly tells him what to do. He also feels she talks incessantly and is so hard of hearing that she listens to old Lawrence Welk reruns loud enough to deafen him, even as he works down in the basement.

Father relents, and grandmother moves in. Mother and father start quarreling more and more over grandmother. Soon they seem to be quarreling over everything. Mother has to quit her job because grandmother requires more care and attention than she expected. The family had just purchased a new home with high mortgage payments. Without mother's salary, money becomes scarce for food, clothing, and other necessities. Mother and father fight over the financial situation; each blames the other for buying the expensive new home to begin with. The children's grades in school start dropping, and they begin to display some behavior problems. Father threatens to leave if

The Application of Systems Theory Principles to Families (continued)

things don't improve. The family system's homeostasis is threatened. At this point, intervention might take the form of family counseling to help the family clearly identify their problems, voice their opinions, and come to some mutually agreed upon resolutions. Couple's counseling might be involved to improve the communication between mother and father. Social services might be needed to help the family and grandmother decide what her best care alternative might be, including consideration of placement in a nursing home. In order for the family to survive, homeostasis must be restored and maintained.

Subsystems

A *subsystem* is a secondary or subordinate system—a system within a system. The most obvious examples of this are the parental and sibling subsystems. Other more subtle subsystems may also exist depending on the boundaries established within the family system. A

mother might have a daughter to whom she feels especially close. These two might form a subsystem within a family system, apart from other family members. Sometimes subsystems exist because of more negative circumstances within family systems. A subsystem might exist within a family with an alcoholic father. Here the mother and children might form a subsystem in coalition against the father.

Boundaries

Boundaries are repeatedly occurring patterns of behavior that characterize the relationships within a system and give that system a particular identity. In a family system, boundaries determine who are members of that particular family system and who are not. Parents and children are within the boundaries of the family system. Close friends of the family are not.

Boundaries may also delineate subsystems within a system. For instance, boundaries separate the spouse subsystem within a family from the sibling subsystem. Each subsystem has its own specified membership. Either a family member is within the boundaries of that subsystem or he is not.

Input

Input can be defined as the energy, information, or communication flow received from other systems. Families are not isolated, self-sufficient units. Each family system is constantly interacting with its environment and with other systems. For example, one type of input into a family system is the money received for the parents' work outside of the home. Another type of input involves the communication and supportive social interaction family members receive from friends, neighbors, and relatives. Schools also provide input in the form of education for children and progress reports concerning that education.

Output

Output is the energy, information, or communication emitted from a system to the environment or to other systems. Work, whether it be in a job situation, a school setting, or in the home, can be considered output. Financial output is another form. This is necessary for the purchase of food, clothing, shelter, and the other necessities of life.

An important thing to consider about output is its relationship to input. If a family system's output exceeds its input, family homeostasis may be threatened. In other words, if more energy is leaving a family system than is coming in, tensions may result and functioning may be impaired. For example, in a multiproblem family troubled by poverty, illness, lack of education, isolation, loneliness, and delinquency, tremendous amounts of effort and energy may be expended simply to stay alive. At the same time, little help and support may be coming in. The result would be severely restricted family functioning and lack of homeostasis.

Feedback

Feedback is a system's receipt of information from an outside source about its own performance or behavior. Feedback can be given to an entire family system, a

A subsystem may be subtle—a mother might feel especially close to one child.

© Myrleen Cate

subsystem (such as a marital pair), or an individual within the family system.

Feedback can be information obtained from outside the system. For example, a family therapist can provide a family with information about how it is functioning. Feedback can also be given from one individual or subsystem within the family system to another. For example, the sibling subsystem might communicate to the alcoholic mother that they are suffering from the consequences of her alcoholic behavior. Finally, a system, subsystem, or individual within a system can give feedback to those outside of the family system. For instance, a family might contact their landlord and give him feedback that their kitchen sink is backing up. They might also add that he won't see another rent check until it's fixed.

Feedback can be either positive or negative. Positive feedback involves information about what a system is doing right in order to maintain itself and thrive. Positive feedback can provide specific information so that members in a family system are aware of the positive aspects of their functioning. For example, a mother works outside her home as a computer programmer. During her job performance evaluation, her supervisor may tell her that she has maintained the highest accuracy record in the entire department. This indicates to her that her conscientiousness in this respect is valued and should be continued.

Negative feedback can also be valuable. Negative feedback involves providing information about problems within the system. As a result of negative feedback, the system can choose to correct any deviations or mistakes and return to a more homeostatic state. For example, the mother mentioned earlier who works as a computer programmer can receive negative feedback during the same job evaluation. Her supervisor indicates that she tends to fall behind on her weekly written reports. Although she feels the reports are extraordinarily dull and tedious to complete, her supervisor's feedback gives her the information she needs to perform her job better.

Perhaps the most relevant example for social workers concerning feedback is its application in a family treatment setting. When a family comes in for help about a particular problem, feedback can raise their awareness about their functioning. It can help them correct areas where they are making mistakes. It can also encourage them to continue positive interactions. For example, if every time a husband and wife discuss housework responsibilities they yell at each other about what the other does not do, a social worker can give them feedback that their yelling is accomplishing nothing. Constructive suggestions might then be given about how the couple could better resolve their differences over who takes out the garbage, who makes the breakfast orange juice, and who separates the colors from the whites in the laundry.

Positive feedback might also be given. The husband and wife may not be aware that when asked a question about their feelings for each other or about how they like to raise their children, they are very supportive of each other. They immediately look to each other to check out the other's feelings. They smile at each other and encourage the other's opinions. Giving them specific positive feedback about these interactions by describing their behaviors to them may be helpful. Such feedback may encourage them to continue these positive interactions. It may also suggest to them that they could apply similar positive means to resolving other differences.

Entropy

Entropy is the natural tendency of a system to progress toward disorganization, depletion, and in essence, death. The idea is that nothing lasts forever. People age and eventually die. Young families get older, and children leave to start their own families. Family systems are constantly in the process of change; conditions change.

Homeostasis itself is dynamic in that it involves constant change and adjustment. Families are never frozen in time. Family members are constantly changing and responding to new situations and challenges.

Negative Entropy

Negative entropy is the process of a system moving toward growth and development. In effect, it is the opposite of entropy. Goals in family treatment often involve striving to make conditions and interactions better than they were before. A relationship between quarreling spouses can improve. Physical abuse of a child can be stopped. Negative entropy must be kept in mind when helping family systems grow and develop to their full potential.

Equifinality

Equifinality refers to the fact that there are many different means to the same end. It is important not to get locked into only one way of thinking, because in any particular situation, there are alternatives. Some may be better than others, but there are alternatives. It's easy to get trapped into tunnel vision in which no other options are apparent. Frequently, family systems need help in defining and evaluating the options available to them.

Consider, for instance, a family in which the father abruptly loses his job. Instead of wallowing in remorse, other alternatives might be pursued. The family might consider relocating where a similar position might be available. The mother, who previously had not worked outside of the home, might look into the possibility of finding a job herself, to help the family's financial situation. Moving to less expensive housing might be considered. Finally, the father might look into other types of work, at least temporarily. There are always alternatives. The important thing is to recognize and consider them.

Differentiation

Differentiation is a system's tendency to move from a more simplified to a more complex existence. In other words, relationships, situations, and interactions tend to get more complex over time instead of more simplified.

For example, two people might fall in love, marry, and begin to establish their lives together. They have three children, and each parent works full time in order to save enough for a modest home of their own. As time goes on, marital problems and disputes develop as their lives grow more complicated with children and responsibilities. Their initial simple life becomes clouded with children's illnesses, car payments, job stresses, and other mundane occurrences. Systems theory provides a framework for viewing this couple's relationship. It provides for the acknowledgment of an increasing complexity. From a helping perspective, the basic fact of the couple's affection and commitment to each other may need to be identified and emphasized.

member of a family is affected by what happens to any of the other members. Each member and the family as a whole are also affected by the many other systems in the family's environment. For instance, if Johnny flunks algebra, the family works with the school system to help him make improvements. The entire family might have to cancel their summer vacation because Johnny has to attend summer school. The school system directly impacts the family system.

A second example concerns Shirl, Johnny's mother and the family's primary breadwinner. She works as an engineering supervisor for Bob Bear, a corporation based in Racine, Wisconsin, that makes various sized tractors. New World International, an immense conglomerate corporation, owns Bob Bear. What if New World International decides to close down the Bob Bear plant in Racine because of inadequate profits and decides to move the large plant to Bonetraill, North Dakota? Bonetraill is a far cry from small, but urban Racine. One possibility for the family is to move two states away to a totally different environment because Shirl has been offered a comparable position in Bonetraill. Lennie, Johnny's father, is a journalist for the local paper. In the event of a move, he would have to find a new job. The whole family would have to leave their neighborhood and friends. Another alternative is for Shirl to seek a new job in the Racine area. However, the economy there is depressed, and she would have difficulty finding a position with a salary anywhere near the one she is currently earning. Thus, the family system is seriously affected by the larger Bob Bear system, and the Bob Bear system by the even larger New World International system.

Another important reason can be given for understanding systems theory as it relates to families. Intervention in families with problems is a major concern of social work. *Family therapy* is intervention by a social worker or other family therapist with members of a family to improve communication and interaction among members and to pursue other changes and goals they wish to pursue. Family therapy is based on the idea that the family is a system. In finding solutions to problems within a family, the target of intervention is the family system.

Whether a particular problem is initially defined as an individual member's or as the entire family's, a family therapist views this problem as one involving the entire family system. The entire family should be the focus of treatment. In family therapy, the specific relationships between various family members in the family system need to be closely observed. Family interaction is discussed more thoroughly in Chapter 12.

The Family Life Cycle

One other aspect of the family needs to be examined. This text assumes a chronological framework. People functioning within their environments are not stagnant; they change. And just as people change, so do families. Families have life cycles of their own.

Several decades ago, the family life cycle and the types of experiences family members had during specified phases of the cycle were much more predictable than today. This is no longer the case. There is no "typical" cycle.

The traditional family life cycle was conceptualized as having six major phases (Carter & McGoldrick, 1980). Each phase focused on some emotional transition in terms of intimate relationships with other people and on changes of personal status. Stages included:

1. separating an unattached young adult from his or her family of origin;
2. marrying and establishing an identity as part of a couple, versus as an individual;
3. having and raising young children;
4. dealing with adolescent children striving for independence, and refocusing on the couple relationship as adolescents gain that independence;
5. sending children forth into their own new relationships, addressing midlife crises, and coping with the growing disabilities of aging parents;
6. adjusting to aging and addressing the inevitability of one's own death.

Carter and McGoldrick (1999) propose a new way of thinking about families that greatly expands the traditional family life-cycle perspective. Families progress through phases, but not in such a neat, predictable manner. Yes, the happenings described above can and do occur, but not necessarily in that order or at all. Rather, each family experiences a complex existence where it, as a system and as a collection of individuals, is subject to living in an environmental context involving "race, ethnicity, class, gender, sexual orientation, religion, age, family status" and "disability" (p. 21). Spotlight 4.1 explores diverse perspectives on the family life cycle.

Within the context of the family system's life cycle, we will now turn our attention back to the social development of young children. We will focus on how children become integrated into their family system and on how they learn to behave (or misbehave). Learning theory provides a relevant, conceptual base for understanding

Spotlight on Diversity 4.1   Diverse Perspectives on the Family Life Cycle

Hines and her colleagues (1999) maintain that ethnic identity and culture are intimately involved with a family's experience in each stage of every family's life cycle. They note further, however, that the "consciousness of ethnic identity varies greatly within groups and from one group to another" (p. 69). People experience *acculturation*, "an ethnic person's adoption of the dominant culture in which he or she is immersed. There are several degrees of acculturation; a person can maintain his or her own traditional cultural beliefs, values, and customs from the country of origin to a greater or lesser extent" (Lum, 2000, p. 201).

The following examples portray how cultural values and membership in various diverse groups affect family relationships and interaction during each phase of the traditional family life cycle.

Stage 1: Separating from One's Family of Origin

Separating from one's family of origin may have both positive and negative dimensions. Fulmer (1999) describes this period, usually ranging from about ages 18 to 21, as one focused on learning how to work, concentrating on self-development, viewing the world from a naive and idealistic perspective, and seeking perfect love. It is a time characterized by seeking new and exciting experiences, and also by maintaining some kind of connection with one's roots.

This period may pose additional challenges for gay men or lesbians. Fulmer (1999) explains:

Gay young adults face an extra readjustment in their relationships with their families or origin if they are coming out [identifying themselves as being gay and sharing this information with others] to them for the first time. They often report having felt like outsiders to their families for some time. It may be a relief from such estrangement to be more authentic and open. Unfortunately, however, they often confront denial, anger, criticism, or rejection from at least some family members. While their families may mellow with time, this can be a period of feeling cut off from one's family or origin with a deep loss of continuity and support. (p. 225)

Fulmer (1999) continues, regarding common situations experienced by lesbians:

Young lesbians also do not usually come out until young adulthood. They tend to bond earlier into stable couples than gay men do. Because their identity is then partially expressed as a member of a partnership, they want to present themselves as couples to their families (just as married heterosexuals do). Their appearing as a couple makes their homosexuality much more difficult for their families to deny, however. They may wish to visit or attend family rituals with their partners, forcing themselves, their partners, and their families to decide how "out" they want to be. If the partner isn't welcome, the young adult has a hard choice, as does the family. (p. 226)

Stage 2: Marrying and Establishing an Identity As a Couple

To varying degrees, marriage generally can require adjustment, compromise, and struggle. Even small issues like how to arrange cereal boxes on the shelf, make spaghetti, or take out the garbage can require communication and cooperation.

Consider people who have another national origin and who enter the United States as a newly married couple. *National origin*, another dimension of diversity, involves the country of origin of individuals, their parents, or their ancestors. According to Ahearn (1995), people coming here might have any of the following statuses:

- *Displaced people* are those people who have been uprooted within their own country. . . .

- *Refugees* are people who have crossed national boundaries in search of refuge. . . . [They include] people who flee to another country out of a fear of persecution because of religion, political affiliation, race, nationality, or membership in a particular group.

- *Immigrants* are those individuals who have been granted legal permanent residence in a country not their own.

- *Migrants* are those people, usually workers, who have temporary permission to live in a country, but plan to return to their country of origin.

- *Illegal aliens* are people who migrate illegally to another country. (p. 771)

Newly married people who come here must deal not only with the usual adjustments involved in marrying or living together, but also with the additional stress of acculturation and new status. Hernandez and McGoldrick (1999) explain:

New immigrant couples are confronted with the challenges of their migration-related transformations as they negotiate differences in world view, beliefs, religion, class, and cultural background. Often the level of adaptation varies between the partners and causes serious conflicts. The lack of social supports forces partners to become more dependent on each other, a situation that fosters isolation and overwhelms each of the partners. Racial and ethnic prejudice can seriously compound a couple's conflict. (pp. 174–175)

Nimmagadda and Balgopal (2000) comment on immigrants who arrive here first and then face the possibility of marriage:

Because the Asian tradition of marriage is based on the philosophy of "marry first and then fall in love," arranged marriage versus love marriage is a source of conflict for many Asian Americans. Parents still hold considerable influence over the selection of mates for their children, but increasingly their sons and daughters are gaining more control over whom they marry . . .

Probably one of the main fears of South Asian immigrants is the issue of "outmarriage"—that is, their children marrying a person outside their ethnic community. Among Asian Indians, Segal (1997) writes, this fear is twofold—first, because the parents fear that their children will lose their cultural heritage; and second, because of the belief that most American marriages end in divorce. For nearly all Asians, dating is a cause of conflict between parents and children, because in most Asian communities, dating is often equated with sexual activity, which is unacceptable before marriage. Thus, the recent immigrants do not tolerate dating, which is further complicated if their children go out with individuals of other ethnicities, especially non-Asians. (p. 43)

Stage 3: Having and Raising Young Children

Cultural values significantly affect how children are socialized, what values they acquire, and what behaviors they learn. Gardiner, Mutter, and Kosmitzki (1998) explain that "one cannot view the socialization of certain behaviors independently from the cultural context. Cultures define the basic values and ideals as well as the agents who teach the values and the settings in which they are taught" (p. 148).

Kerig, Alyoshina, and Volovich (1993) studied the gender-role socialization of children in Russia and came to some conclusions concerning how this process resulted in subsequent characteristics and behavior. Gardiner and his colleagues (1998) explain:

In Russian society, children are surrounded by female caretakers (mothers, teachers, doctors, day-care workers), whereas men are relatively little involved in family and household matters. This situation provides a young girl with a large number of female role models in different familial and professional roles. She is presented with an image of women that is versatile and active, and she has the opportunity to practice behavior appropriate for her gender, following that of her mother or other female role models. As a consequence, she is socialized into a very active and dominant role. This socialization pattern is continued in adolescence and adulthood.

Russian society expects women to be as involved in the work force as are men, and also to take over most of the housework. This dual identity reinforces the image of the woman as active and dominant. However, the Russian stereotype expects women to be passive and obedient; active, masculine behaviors are viewed as highly undesirable. This apparent contradiction between stereotype and social norm provides a dilemma for Russian women unless they are very flexible in their behavior and can adjust to the demands of different situations. At home and at work, they need to be able to be active and energetic, but in their social interactions with men, they need to be feminine (i.e., passive and weak) . . .

Russian boys, on the other hand, have few opportunities to practice active, dominant behavior. They are surrounded by female authority figures and caretakers involved in female activities. At the same time, Russian culture strongly disapproves of aggressiveness and emphasizes cooperation and caring. As a result of these social constraints, a young boy frequently withdraws and responds with passivity, which represents highly unmasculine behavior. Understandably, a young boy experiences a certain amount of confusion trying to

define his gender identity in a context in which he is not able to observe or practice masculine behavior. Only later in adolescence do many young men compensate for their lack of masculine behavior by becoming involved in motorcycle gangs or even engaging in antisocial activities such as vandalism, substance abuse, and physical and sexual abuse of women. (pp. 146–147)

Stage 4: Dealing with Adolescent Children

In the United States, adolescence can be a difficult period. Adolescents strive to establish their own identities, which often results in conflict with parents. Parents often struggle to maintain control while adolescents vehemently resist it. Ethnic diversity and cultural values can add to the complexity of these scenarios.

Garcia-Preto (1998) describes the cultural dilemmas and difficulties that young Latinas[1] and their families face as these young women enter adolescence and young adulthood:

Most Latina mothers "go into high gear to guard their daughters' virginity, especially as they reach adolescence. It is as if we hear a call to respond to an ancient cultural myth about women and virginity that [e]nsures women safe futures in the hands of honorable men, but only if they are virgins. This myth emanates from the double standard about gender roles in patriarchal societies (such as those in Latin America and the Caribbean), which limits the sexual freedom of women and gives men authority over them. . . . Although the double standard also applies to a lesser extent in the United States, women in U.S. society tend to experience greater sexual freedom than Latinas do in their countries of origin. . . .

In the United States, adolescent girls are given freedom to go out with girlfriends, sleep at their houses, talk with boys, and go on dates without chaperones. In contrast, Latinas tend to be supervised more closely when they go out with friends; dating doesn't take place until much later; and it is not unusual for chaperones to be present on dates. The emphasis is on protecting a girl's virginity and keeping her reputation unmarred. The responsibility for this task is given primarily to mothers. The extent to which Latino families living in this country hold on to these values depends on the length of time they have lived here, their level of education and social status, and the place where they settle. The greater the cultural gap between families and the new culture, the more likely it is for conflicts to erupt between mothers and daughters during adolescence around the issue of virginity, since children tend to adapt faster than parents to a new culture. (pp. 333–334)

How can these disputes and dilemmas be resolved? Garcia-Preto (1998) provides several suggestions. First, mothers and daughters can work on "[c]hoosing what to keep from their old culture and what to take from the new culture" (p. 335). Second, they can focus on each other's strengths, such as their genuine caring for each other and

---

1. *Latina* is the feminine form of *Latino* in Spanish.

their concern for each other's well-being. Third, they can seek to understand each other's feelings and their respective points of view. Fourth, they can address what options are available and what compromises are possible.

Stage 5: Addressing Midlife Crises

Almost 22 percent of African American families live below the poverty line, compared to 7.3 percent of white families (U.S. Census Bureau, 2001). Hines (1999) describes some of the midlife issues faced by African American families:

> Families in later life are likely to consist of a child generation, a young adult parent generation, a middle-aged grandparent generation, and one or even two elderly great-grandparent generations. In contrast to middle-class families, this phase of the life cycle does not signify retirement or a lessening of daily responsibilities for poor African Americans. Many continue working to make ends meet in spite of poor health. Even when they do retire, it is unlikely they will have "empty nests." Instead, they are likely to be active members of expanding households and family systems, frequently providing care to grandchildren, adult children, and other elderly kin. Although women in this stage are likely to be in bad health and have extremely low incomes, it is they who are most likely to provide stability for children when the system is threatened with dissolution because parents cannot fulfill their roles. (p. 338)

Increasing numbers of African American grandparents are assuming responsibility for their grandchildren (Cox, 2002; Dhooper & Moore, 2001; Okazawa-Rey, 1998). Primary reasons include crack cocaine or alcohol addiction, incarceration for drug- or alcohol-related crimes, mental illness, and unwillingness to surrender custody of grandchildren to public foster care (Cox, 2002; Okazawa-Rey, 1998). "Surrogate parenting has been a pattern for African American grandparents in U.S. society" (Cox, 2002, p. 46).

These grandparents experience undue pressures when assuming such responsibility and are "prone to an increased incidence or exacerbation of depression and insomnia, hypertension, back and stomach problems, . . . as well as increased use of alcohol and cigarettes. . . . In addition, grandparents tend to ignore their problems and associated stresses to meet the needs of their grandchildren" (Cox, 2002, p. 46).

Cox (2002) calls for *empowerment practice* on their behalf and explains:

"The immediate goals of empowerment practice are to help clients achieve a sense of personal power, become more aware of connections between individual and community problems, develop helping skills, and work collaboratively toward social change" (p. 46, citing Gutierrez, GlenMaye, & DeLois, 1995).

Cox calls for providing grandparents with information on a range of relevant topics and teaching them various skills to empower them. The recommended curriculum includes the following content: "(1) introduction to empowerment; (2) importance of self-esteem; (3) communicating with grandchildren; (4) dealing with loss and grief; (5) helping grandchildren deal with loss; (6) dealing with behavior problems; (7) talking to grandchildren about sex, HIV/AIDS, and drugs; (8) legal and entitlement issues; (9) developing advocacy skills; (10) negotiating systems; [and] (11) making presentations" so that they might share their knowledge with others (p. 47).

Stage 6: Adjusting to Aging and Dealing with Eventual Death

Depending on your cultural background, there are numerous ways of viewing and dealing with old age and death. For example, Dhooper and Moore (2001) maintain:

> Native American[2] elderly, those aged 65 and above, are more traditional in their philosophy and values and have a deeper understanding of racism and oppression against Native people as a result of having a longer history of experience with these forces. Some of them were children when in 1901 the BIA [Bureau of Indian Affairs] sanctioned field agents to alter Native customs. "Forbidden were the wearing of long hair by males, face painting of both sexes, and wearing Indian dress" (Hirschfelder & Kreipe de Montano, 1993, p. 22). . . . The elderly have been the vanguards of their culture and have passed down their traditions and cultural beliefs throughout the generations. Through the elderly "traditional values are sustained. . . . The ancient languages are spoken and taught, traditional ceremonies are observed and baskets are woven" (Hall, 1997, p. 755). As such they are held in high regard by their people and are treated respectfully. "Generally Native American traditional values consist of sharing, cooperation and a deep respect for elders." (Garrett, 1999, p. 87) (p. 191)

Similarly, various cultures view and deal with death very differently. Simon (1996) describes how the Lebanese deal with it:

> Lebanese families are generally very expressive in their response to death, even after several generations of living in the United States. Extreme displays of emotion are common, and it is not unusual for older family members to ask the deceased to get up and perform a favored deed one last time (i.e., to dubkee, a Lebanese dance, or cook a favored meal). After the deceased is unable to respond to the request, the grief of the family is amplified and followed by wailing and crying. For immigrant Lebanese several decades ago, it was not uncommon to jump into the grave at the cemetery if a child had preceded a parent in death. In recent times Lebanese American reactions to death are less dramatic but still highly emotional and demonstrative. Calmness at wakes is perceived as a lack of love for the deceased, and emotional outbursts are perceived as respect for the deceased. Because of the strong bonds and emotional attachments of Lebanese families, wakes and funerals are highly charged experiences. (p. 374)

Almeida (1996) describes the Hindu perception and treatment of death:

> Death is a particularly potent symbolic event among Hindus, given their beliefs about karma [destiny]. . . . As

---

2. "Note that *American Indian* and *Native American* are both accepted terms for referring to indigenous peoples of North America, although *Native American* is a broader designation because the U.S. government includes Hawaiians and Samoans in this category. There are close to 450 Native groups" (American Psychological Association, 2001, p. 68).

Spotlight on Diversity 4.1 *(continued)*

with weddings, traditional rituals associated with death and mourning are likely to be modified when Indians live in the United States. Mourning cycles vary, but . . . customs include a 10- to 12-day mourning ritual . . . in addition to requiring extensive absence from work. In keeping with Indian sex-role traditions, widows are expected to perform many rituals of sacrifice glorifying the family, whereas widowers and other family members are not required to observe such rites. (p. 408)

Mindell (2001) explains Jewish families' view and handling of death:

Judaism, regardless of denomination—Reform, Conservative, or Orthodox—has the overriding values of honoring the dead and comforting the mourners. Burial is usually within twenty-four hours after the death and the funeral service begins with the cutting of a garment or a black ribbon attached to the mourners, the immediate family of the deceased. This ritual is a visual representation of the individual being separated—cut away—from the loved one. The period of mourning at home after the burial lasts for one week. This ritual is called Shiva, the Hebrew word for seven.

Friends, family, and neighbors visit the mourners in the home during Shiva, which provides the opportunity to share stories about the deceased, how his or her life touched others, and provide the bereaved a supportive environment to also share memories and to grieve. The first thirty days, referred to as Sheloshim, the Hebrew word for thirty, after the funeral is a time when the family might attend morning and evening services. Mourning ends after the first year, the Yahzeit, the family lights a special twenty-four-hour memorial candle. Mourning is seen as a process that has stages and takes time. Rituals enable the living to remember the dead.

The religious customs that are practiced during the continuum of an individual's life allow one to cope with difficult happenings, experiences, and emotions, in a supportive, emotional "home" as she or he struggles to make sense out of events that seem to have no meaning. The manner in which the struggle is done, the emotions expressed, and how the community supports its members reflect the religious and cultural history of the group and help to define the identity of the members of the group. (pp. 200–201)

---

how socialization and learning occur. Thus, substantial emphasis will be placed on understanding the theoretical basis for learning theory and its applications to practical parenting.

Learning Theory

"Mom! I want a candy bar! You promised! I want one right now! Mom!," Four-year-old Huey screamed as loudly as he possibly could. He and his mother were standing in the checkout line at the local supermarket. An elderly woman was checking out in front of them. Two other women and a man were waiting in line behind them.

Huey's mother saw everybody looking at her and her young son. Huey simply would not stop screaming. She tried to "shush" him. She scolded him in as much of a whisper as she could muster. She threatened that he would never see the inside of a McDonald's again. Absolutely nothing would work. Huey just kept on screaming.

Finally, in total exasperation, his mother grabbed the nearest candy bar off the shelf, ripped off the wrapper, and literally stuck the thing into Huey's mouth. A peaceful silence came over the grocery store. All witnessing the

event breathed a sigh of relief. Huey stood there with a happy smile on his sticky face. One might almost say he was gloating.

The family environment has already been established as the primary agent of children's socialization. It provides the critical social environment in which children learn. The next logical question to address concerns how children learn. The social and emotional development of children is frequently a focus of social work intervention. Children sometimes create behavior problems. They become difficult for parents and other supervising adults to manage. When they enter school, these management problems often continue. Teachers and administration find some children difficult to control. Frequently, as children get older, problems escalate.

Children can learn how to be affectionate, considerate, fun-loving, and responsible. But they can also learn how to be selfish, spoiled, and inconsiderate. This latter state is not good for parents and other supervising adults, nor for the children themselves. Children need to cooperate with others. They need to know how to get along in social settings in order to become emotionally mature, well-adjusted adults. Learning theory concepts are useful for recognizing why anyone, child or adult, behaves the way he or she does. However, the concepts are especially helpful when addressing the issue of behavior management.

Critical Thinking: Evaluation of Theory

In order to change behavior, it first must be understood. *Learning theory* is a theoretical orientation that conceptualizes the social environment in terms of behavior, its preceding events, and its subsequent consequences. It poses that behavior can be learned and, therefore, maladaptive behavior can be unlearned. Learning theory provides a framework for understanding how behavior develops. We will focus on learning theory for several reasons. First, it emphasizes the social functioning of persons within their environments (Harrison, 1995). The total person in dynamic interaction with all aspects of the environment is the focus of attention. This is in contrast to many other theoretical approaches that focus primarily on the individual's personality or isolated history.

Second, learning theory emphasizes the importance of assessing observable behaviors. It also stresses the use of behaviorally specific terms in defining behaviors. This helps to make any particular behavior more clearly understandable.

Finally, learning theory provides a positive approach. The underlying idea is that behaviors develop through learning them, and, therefore undesirable behaviors can be unlearned. This allows for positive behavioral changes. Instead of individuals being perceived as victims of their personal histories and personality defects, they are seen as dynamic living beings capable of change.

Behavior modification is a therapeutic application of learning theory principles. Much evidence supports the effectiveness of behavioral techniques for a wide variety of human problems and learning situations (Kazdin, 2001; Sundel & Sundel, 1999).

Respondent Conditioning

Respondent conditioning refers to the emission of behavior in response to a specific stimulus. It is also referred to as *classical* or *Pavlovian conditioning*. A particular stimulus elicits a particular response. The stimulus can be a word, a sight, or a sound.

For example, Martha, who has been on a strict diet for a week, stops by to visit her friend Evelyn. Evelyn is in the process of preparing a lobster dinner. She is also baking a German chocolate cake for dessert. Martha begins salivating at the thought of such appetizing food. Martha's response, salivation, occurs as a result of the stimulus, witnessing Evelyn's preparation of the wonderful, albeit fattening, food. Figure 4.1 portrays this relationship.

Much respondent behavior is unlearned; that is, a response is naturally emitted after exposure to a stimulus. This stimulus is called an *unconditioned stimulus*.

Figure 4.1 A Stimulus-Response Relationship

Lobster and German chocolate cake (*Unconditioned stimulus*) → Martha's salivation (*Response*)

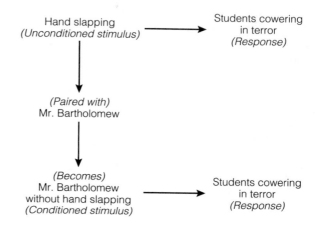

Figure 4.2 Respondent Conditioning

Hand slapping (*Unconditioned stimulus*) → Students cowering in terror (*Response*)

(*Paired with*) Mr. Bartholomew

(*Becomes*) Mr. Bartholomew without hand slapping (*Conditioned stimulus*) → Students cowering in terror (*Response*)

Respondent conditioning occurs when a person learns to respond to a new stimulus that does not naturally elicit a response. This new stimulus is called a *conditioned stimulus*. In order to accomplish this, the new stimulus is paired with the stimulus that elicited the response naturally. The person then learns to associate the new stimulus with a particular response even though it had nothing to do with that response originally.

For example, Mr. Bartholomew, a third-grade teacher, slaps students very hard on the hand when they talk out of turn. As a result of this stimulus, the slapping, students fear Mr. Bartholomew. By associating Mr. Bartholomew with getting a slap on the hand, the students eventually learned to fear Mr. Bartholomew even when he wasn't slapping them. Mr. Bartholomew himself had been paired with the hand slapping until he elicited the same response that the slapping did. Figure 4.2 helps to illustrate this relationship.

Some behavioral techniques used by social workers involve the principles of respondent conditioning. *Systematic desensitization* is an example. This technique can be applied when a person is subject to extreme fear or anxiety over something, for example, snakes, enclosed places, or school. Systematic desensitization usually has two major thrusts. First, the client is exposed very gradually to the thing he fears. Second, while the client is being exposed to the fearful item or event, he is also taught an incompatible response. The incompatible response must be something that cannot occur at the same time as the anxiety and fear. A good example of an incompatible response is progressive relaxation.

For example, the client learns how to control his body and relax. At the same time the standard procedure is that he is exposed to the feared item or event in increasing amounts or degrees. A person who fears rats might first be shown a picture of a rat in the distance while, at the same time, using his newly acquired relaxation skills. Anxiety and fear cannot occur at the same time that the individual is in a relaxed state. They are incompatible responses.

The individual might then be shown an 8-by-10 inch photo of a rat. Once again, the individual would use relaxation techniques to prevent anxiety from occurring. The client would be exposed to rats in a more and more direct manner until the client could actually hold a laboratory rat in his hand. The client would gradually learn to use the incompatible relaxation technique to quell any anxiety that rats might once have elicited.

A variety of techniques based on respondent conditioning have also been used to treat enuresis, or bedwetting, overeating, cigarette smoking, alcohol consumption, and sexual deviations (Kazdin, 2001; O'Leary & Wilson, 1987; Sundel & Sundel, 1999). However, they are not nearly as many nor are they as common as those behavioral techniques based on operant conditioning discussed in a later section.

Modeling

The second type of learning is called modeling. *Modeling refers to the learning of behavior by observing another individual engaging in that behavior.* In order to learn from a model, an individual does not necessarily have to participate in the behavior. An individual needs only watch how a model performs the behavior. For obvious reasons, modeling is also called observational learning. A behavior can be learned simply by observing its occurrence.

Modeling is important within the context of practical parenting. Parents can model appropriate behavior for their children. For example, a father might act as a model for his son concerning how to play baseball. The father can teach his son how to throw and catch a ball by doing it himself. The child can learn by watching his father.

In social work intervention, modeling can be used to model appropriate treatment of children so that parents may observe. For example, 5-year-old Larry, who frequently has behavior problems, may pick up a pencil that the social worker accidentally dropped and return it to the social worker. The social worker may then model

for the parent how the child can be positively reinforced for his good behavior. The social worker may say, "Thank you for picking up my pencil for me, Larry. That was very helpful of you."

Another example of modeling within a social work practice context is role playing. For example, a social worker might ask a parent who has trouble controlling her son to role play that son and mimic his behavior. She is instructed to act the way she thinks her son would act. The social worker may then model for the parent some appropriate, effective things to say to the son when the son behaves in that way. Such modeling provides the opportunity for the parent to learn new ways of responding to her son.

Modeling can also teach children inappropriate and ineffective behavior. For example, consider a mother who strikes other family members whenever she gets the least bit irritated with them. She is likely to act as a model for that type of behavior. Her children may learn that striking others is the way to express their anger.

Some classic research studied the effects of positive and negative consequences on modeling (Bandura, 1965). Children were shown a film of an adult hitting and kicking a large doll, obviously modeling aggressive behavior. Afterward, the children were divided into three groups. Each group then observed the model experiencing different respective consequences. One group of children viewed the model being punished for the aggressive behavior. Another group of children saw the model being rewarded for the same behavior. A third group of children saw the model being ignored. The children were then placed in situations where they could display aggression. Children who saw the model receive a reward for aggressive behavior and those who saw him experience no consequences clearly displayed more aggressive behavior than those children who saw the model punished. It was ascertained that all the children had learned the aggressive behavior; when they were told they would receive a reward for being aggressive, they all could indeed be aggressive. The conclusion is that modeling behavior can be affected both by consequences to the model and to the observer.

Other conditions can also affect the effectiveness of modeling or the degree to which modeling works. These include: "the similarity of the model to the observer; the prestige, status, and expertise of the model; and the number of models observed. As a general rule, imitation of a model by an observer is greater when the model is similar to the observer, more prestigious, and higher in status and expertise than the observer and when several models perform the same behavior" (Kazdin, 2001, pp. 24–25; Sundel & Sundel, 1999).

Modeling has been used in a variety of clinical settings including the control of fear and the development of social skills. Usually, it's used in conjunction with other behavioral techniques.

Operant Conditioning

Operant conditioning is one of the dominant types of learning focused on in the United States. It allows for the easiest and most practical understanding of behavior. Many treatment applications are based on the principles of operant conditioning.

Operant conditioning is "a type of learning in which behaviors are influenced primarily by the consequences that follow them" (Kazdin, 2001, p. 458). New behaviors can be shaped, weak behaviors can be strengthened, strong behaviors can be maintained, and undesirable behaviors can be weakened and eliminated. The emphasis lies on the consequences of behavior. What follows a particular behavior affects how frequently that behavior will occur again, as illustrated in Highlight 4.2.

The ABCs of Behavior

One way of conceptualizing operant behavior is to divide it into its primary parts. These include antecedents, behaviors, and consequences. Another way of referring to them is the ABCs of behavior.

Antecedents are the events occurring immediately before the behavior itself. These events set the stage for the behavior to occur. For instance, some individuals state that they are able to quit smoking cigarettes except when they are socializing in a bar or nightclub. The bar conditions act as a stimulus for smoking behavior, whereas other environments do not. In other words, the bar setting acts as an antecedent for smoking behavior.

Behavior is "any observable and measurable response or act. . . . Behavior is occasionally broadly defined to include cognitions, psychophysiological reactions, and feelings, which may not be directly observable but are defined in terms that can be measured by means of various assessment strategies" (Kazdin, 2001, p. 450). The important phrase here is that behavior is "defined in terms that can be measured." Therefore, even thoughts and feelings can be changed as long as words can be found to clearly describe what they are. For instance, specific messages that people send to themselves can be altered as long as these messages can be clearly defined and measured. A person who frequently tells herself, "I am so fat," can have that message changed to, "I am a worthwhile person." Each time she tells herself this message, it can be noted and, therefore, the overall frequency measured.

Most behavior involved in operant conditioning is observable. Even thoughts and feelings frequently occur with accompanying behaviors. For example, Ieasha is a 6-year-old child who has been clinically diagnosed as depressed. Any thoughts she has about being depressed are not noticeable. However, she makes frequent statements about what a bad girl she is, how her parents don't like her, and what it would be like to die. These statements can be observed and noted. Such statements might be used as indicators for childhood depression.

Highlight 4.2

Consequences and Recurring Behavior

The Johnsons hired their neighbor, nine-year-old Eric, to mow their lawn once a week during the summer. Eric, not being sophisticated in the ways of money management, failed to discuss how much he would be paid per hour. Eric slaved away for 4 hours one Saturday afternoon when he would rather have been playing baseball.

When Eric had finished, Mr. Johnson came out, complimented Eric on what a fine job he had done, and gave him $4.50 for his trouble. Unfortunately $4.50 worked out to be $1.125 per hour. Mr. Johnson thought this was more than adequate. Mr. Johnson himself had been paid only a grand total of $.50 for doing a similar job when he was a boy. Eric, however, felt this was more than chintzy on Mr. Johnson's part. He knew $4.50 would barely cover a few brief video games down at Video Heaven. It would not nearly begin to finance the new baseball glove he wanted.

The consequences for Eric's lawn-mowing behavior were not positive. He did not receive his expected $12. Thus, Eric never mowed Mr. Johnson's lawn again. Instead he turned to other more generous and benevolent neighbors to upgrade his financial future. He also learned to make salary one of his first items on his business agenda. If Mr. Johnson had given him his expected rate of $3 an hour, Eric would have been a dependable and industrious worker for him throughout the summer. In other words, more favorable consequences for Eric would have encouraged his lawn-mowing behavior. He would have been conditioned to mow Mr. Johnson's lawn. As it turned out, Mr. Johnson was doomed to mowing his own lawn for the remainder of the summer.

Ieasha's statements can also be measured; that is, the types of statements she makes and how often she makes them can be counted and evaluated. She might make a statement concerning what a bad girl she is twelve times per day, about how her parents dislike her five times per day, and about her own death sixteen times per day. When her depression begins to subside, these types of verbal statements may decrease in frequency and severity. For example, Ieasha may only make derogatory remarks about herself four times per day instead of twelve. She may say only once each day that her parents dislike her. Statements about death may disappear altogether.

In addition to verbal behavior, physical behavior or actions may also be observed and measured. Besides making statements that indicate she's depressed, Ieasha may spend much of her time sitting in a corner, sucking her thumb, and gazing off into space. The exact amount of time she spends displaying these specific behaviors may be observed and measured. For example, Ieasha initially may spend 5 hours each day sitting in a corner. When depression begins to wane, she may spend only half an hour in the corner.

The final component as a basis for operant conditioning involves the consequences of the behavior. A consequence may be either something that is given or something that is withdrawn or delayed. In other words, something happens as a direct result of a particular behavior. Consequences are best described in terms of reinforcement and punishment.

Reinforcement

Reinforcement refers to a procedure or consequence that increases the frequency of the behavior immediately preceding it. If the behavior is already occurring at a high frequency level, then reinforcement maintains the behavior's frequency. A behavior occurs under certain antecedent conditions. If the consequences of the behavior serve to make that behavior occur more often or be maintained at its current high rate, then those consequences are considered reinforcing. Reinforcers strengthen behavior and make them more likely to occur in the future (Sundel & Sundel, 1999).

Positive Reinforcement. Reinforcement can be either positive or negative. *Positive reinforcement* refers to positive events or consequences that follow a behavior and strengthen it. In other words, something is added to a situation and encourages a particular behavior. For example, 8-year-old Herbie receives a weekly allowance of $12 if he straightens up his room and throws all of his dirty laundry down the clothes chute. Receiving his allowance serves to strengthen, or positively reinforce, Herbie's cleaning behavior.

Negative Reinforcement. *Negative reinforcement* is the removal of a negative event or consequence that serves to increase the frequency of a particular behavior. There are two important aspects of this definition. First, something must be removed from the situation. Second, the frequency of a particular behavior is increased. In this manner positive and negative reinforcement resemble each other. Both function as reinforcement that, by definition, serves to increase or maintain the frequency of a behavior.

A good example of negative reinforcement is a seat belt buzzer in a new car. The car door is opened and a loud and annoying buzzer is activated. It will not stop until the driver's seat belt is fastened. Conceptually, the buzzer functions as a negative reinforcer because it increases the frequency of buckling seat belts. The buzzer is also negative or aversive. It increases seat belt buckling behavior because people are motivated to stop (remove) it.

Another example of negative reinforcement is Orlando, a college sophomore trying to study in his dorm room one Thursday night. His next-door neighbor, Gavin, has decided that Thursday nights are much better for partying than for studying. Gavin, therefore, decides to invite a bunch of his friends over to participate in some illegal substance. Gavin cranks up his CD player to the highest vibration level it can tolerate.

Orlando tries to ignore this nuisance and continues trying to study until he can't stand it anymore. In a state of fury, he stomps up to the wall between the rooms, smashes his fist on it several times, and screams, "Shut the #$@*$%& up in there!!!"

On the other side of the wall, Gavin says to his buddies, "That guy is such a dweeb. If I don't turn it down, he'll probably 'narc' on me to the hall director. Let's go somewhere else." He turns off his CD player and leaves with his friends.

Evaluating this scenario with learning theory leads to several conclusions. First, Orlando's screaming behavior served as negative reinforcement for Gavin's turning off his CD player and leaving the room. Orlando's screaming was aversive to Gavin. In order to terminate it, Gavin turned off his music and left. Moreover, from then on, Gavin made it a point to turn off his CD player whenever Orlando was around and leave his room when he wanted to party. Thus, Orlando's (aversive) screaming reinforced (increased the frequency of) Gavin's turning off his CD player and leaving his room when he wanted to party.

Looking at his situation from another perspective, Gavin's room-leaving behavior served as positive reinforcement for Orlando's screaming behavior. Orlando was positively reinforced for screaming because he got what he wanted, namely, peace and quiet. Orlando became much more likely to scream at Gavin in the future (that is, Orlando was reinforced), because he immediately received something positive as a result of his behavior.

Although at first glance this may appear obvious and simplistic, it is easy to become confused about the type of reinforcement that is occurring. In any particular situation, both positive and negative reinforcement may be taking place at the same time. Consider, for instance, the example given initially to illustrate learning theory. It involved 4-year-old Huey and his mother at the supermarket. Huey yelled for a candy bar. His mother finally gave in and thrust one into his mouth. His crying immediately stopped. Both positive and negative reinforcement were occurring in this example. Mother's giving Huey the candy bar served as a positive reinforcer. Huey received something positive that he valued. At the same time he learned that he could get exactly what he wanted from his mother by screaming in the supermarket. Giving him the candy bar positively reinforced his bad behavior. That type of behavior would be, therefore, more likely to occur in the future.

At the same time, negative reinforcement was occurring in this situation. Mother's giving-in behavior was encouraged or strengthened. She learned that she could stop Huey's obnoxious yelling by giving him what he wanted, namely, a candy bar. Huey's yelling, therefore, acted as negative reinforcement. It increased his mother's "giving-in" behavior by motivating her to stop or to escape from his yelling.

Punishment

Punishment and negative reinforcement are frequently mistaken for each other. Perhaps this is because they both concern something negative or aversive. However, they represent two distinctly different concepts.

Punishment is the presentation of an aversive event or the removal of a positive reinforcer, which results in the decrease in frequency of a particular behavior. Two aspects of this definition are important. First, the result of punishment is the decrease in a behavior's frequency. This is in direct opposition to negative reinforcement, which increases a behavior's frequency.

Second, punishment can be administered in two different ways. One way involves presenting a negative or aversive event immediately after a behavior occurs.

Negative events may include spankings, scoldings, electric shocks, additional demands on time, or embarrassing criticisms. For example, 10-year-old Susie hadn't studied for her social studies exam. Her parents had already complained about the last report card. She just hadn't given the test much thought until Ms. McGuilicutte was handing out the test papers. Susie looked over her test paper and gasped. Nothing looked even vaguely familiar. She was sitting next to Janet, whom she considered the class genius. She figured that just a few brief glances at Janet's paper wouldn't hurt anybody. However, Susie was wrong. Ms. McGuilicutte immediately noticed Susie's wandering attention. Ms. McGuilicutte swooped down on Susie and confiscated her test paper. In front of the entire class Susie was told that cheating resulted not only in an F grade, but also in 2 weeks of detentions after school. Susie was mortified. She vowed to herself that she would never cheat again.

Susie received extremely aversive consequences as the result of her cheating behavior. The consequences included not only a failing test grade and 2 weeks of detentions, but also humiliation in front of her peers. Her cheating behavior decreased in frequency to zero.

The second way in which punishment can be administered is by withdrawing a positive reinforcer. Once again, the result may be a decrease in the frequency of a particular behavior. For example, 7-year-old Robbie thought it was funny to belch at the table during dinner. Several times his parents asked him to stop belching. Each time Robbie was quiet for about a minute and then started belching again. Finally, his mother stated firmly that such belching was considered rude behavior and that, as punishment, Robbie would not receive the banana split she had planned for his dessert. Robbie whined and pleaded, but his mother refused to give it to him. Robbie loved desserts, and banana splits were his favorite. Robbie never belched at the table again, at least not purposefully. Removal of the positive reinforcer, namely the banana split, had served as punishment. The punishment resulted in an abrupt decrease in belching behavior.

It should be emphasized that the term punishment as it is used in learning theory does not necessarily mean physical punishment. For some of us, the word may bring to mind pictures of parents putting children over their knees and spanking them. Punishment does not have to be physical. Verbal reprimands such as a mother saying how disappointed she is that she caught her daughter "making out" with her boyfriend in the family room can also serve as punishment. The reprimand functions as a punishment if the behavior decreases. Likewise, withdrawal of a valued activity, such as not allowing a child to go to a popular movie, can be a punishment if it acts to decrease or stop some negative behavior.

Extinction

Extinction is the process whereby reinforcement for a behavior stops, resulting in the eventual decrease in frequency and possible eradication of that behavior. Reinforcement simply stops; nothing is actively taken away. Note that extinction and punishment are two separate concepts. As Kazdin (2001) notes, "In extinction, *a consequence that was previously provided no longer follows the response.* An event or stimulus (money, noise) is neither taken away nor presented. In punishment, some aversive event follows a response (a reprimand) or some positive event (money) is taken away" (p. 58). In everyday life, extinction often takes the form of ignoring a behavior that was previously reinforced with attention.

An example of extinction concerns the reduction of tantrum behaviors in a 21-month-old child. When put to bed, the child screams until his parents return to the room to comfort him. This provides positive reinforcement for the child's behavior. The parents are instructed to put the child to bed, leave the room, and ignore his screaming. The first night, the child screams for 45 minutes. However, the next night when the parents leave the room, no screaming occurs. Eventually, withdrawing the positive reinforcer of attention results in the total elimination of the child's tantrums. Ignoring, therefore, can be used as an effective means of extinction.

Extinction occurs with many other reinforcers in various daily situations. For example, if putting a quarter in a coffee machine results in nothing but a gush of clear, hot water without the cup, use of that coffee machine will probably be extinguished. Likewise, say you're having difficulty in your biology lab course. You don't understand what the professor is saying during lectures and you're not sure what he wants from you on exams (you've already received a D+ grade on two of them). Three times you try to see your professor during his office hours and each time he is not there. Eventually, you stop trying to see him, despite your frustration. Your behavior involved in seeing him to get help has been extinguished.

One other aspect of extinction is important to note. Frequently, when reinforcement initially is stopped, a brief increase in the frequency or intensity of the behavior may occur. This is referred to as an *extinction burst.* For example, consider again tantrums in a small child. When the reinforcement of attention is withdrawn, the child's behavior might escalate temporarily. If the child in the past had always received positive reinforcement through attention for his behavior, it might be very confusing suddenly to receive no attention for that very same behavior. The child may try exceptionally hard to get the attention to which he was accustomed. The intensity of the undesirable behavior can seriously strain the patience and tolerance of parents. However, eventually the child will learn that the tantrums are not reinforced and are, therefore, simply not worth the effort. Thus, the tantrum behavior is extinguished.

The relationships between extinction, punishment, positive reinforcement, and negative reinforcement are summarized in Figure 4.3.

Figure 4.3 Positive Reinforcement, Negative Reinforcement, Punishment, and Extinction

Here the differences between positive reinforcement, negative reinforcement, punishment, and extinction are summarized. Important differences involve what happens and what results with each behavioral approach.

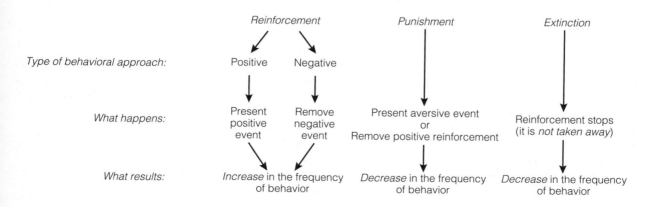

Applications of Learning Theory to Practice

As children become socialized, they learn and assimilate various behaviors. Because learning is a complicated process, the behaviors they sometimes learn are not those that their parents would prefer. Behavior management is a major issue for many parents.

Parents have various alternative ways of responding to a child's behavior. At any point an individual can take alternative plans of action. For each alternative there are consequences. The critical task is to evaluate each alternative and select the one with the most advantageous results. Learning theory concepts provide parents with a means of understanding the alternatives open to them and of predicting the potential consequences of each alternative. It can help them gain control over their children's behavior.

An example of parental alternatives in response to behavior is provided by Danny, age 4. At the dinner table, Danny nonchalantly and without warning says an unmentionable four-letter word. Danny's parents are shocked. At this point, they can respond in several different ways. They can ignore the fact that Danny said the word. Without being given undue attention, saying the word may be stopped. A second alternative is to tell Danny calmly that the word is not considered a very nice word. They might add that some people use it when they're angry and that other people don't really like to hear it. They might also ask him to not use the word anymore. A third alternative is for the parents to display their horror and disbelief, scream at Danny never to say that word again, and send him up to bed without being allowed to finish his supper.

When this incident actually occurred, the parents opted to respond as described in the third alternative. Poor Danny really didn't understand what the word meant. He had just heard it on the playground that afternoon. He was amazed at the response of his parents and at the attention he received. His mother reported that for the following 2 years, he continued to repeat that unmentionable four-letter word virtually everywhere. He said it to the dentist, to the grocer, to the police officer, and even to his grandmother. His mother reported that after a while she would have been willing to pay Danny to stop using that word, if such a strategy would have worked.

In Danny's situation, his parents' attention became a strong positive reinforcer. Perhaps if they had stopped and thought in terms of learning theory principles, they could have gained immediate control of the situation and never thought another thing of it.

The Use of Positive Reinforcement

Positive reinforcement is based on the very fundamental idea that behavior is governed by its consequences. If the consequences of a particular behavior are positive or appealing, then the individual will tend to behave that way. In other words, the frequency of that behavior will be increased.

Positive reinforcement provides a valuable means of behavioral control. It has been established as an appropriate technique for achieving positive behavioral changes in numerous situations (Kazdin, 2001; Sundel & Sundel, 1999). The use of positive reinforcement helps to reduce the risk that clients begin associating the negative effects of punishment, for example, with the therapist, resulting in an aversion to therapy. Positive reinforcement also can teach an individual exactly how to improve his or her behavior.

Various aspects of positive reinforcement will be discussed here. First, we'll examine the types of reinforcers available. The differences between positive reinforcement and the use of rewards will be explained. Finally, we'll offer suggestions for maximizing the effectiveness of positive reinforcement.

Types of Positive Reinforcers

Reinforcers can be separated into two major categories, primary and secondary. *Primary* or *unconditioned reinforcers* are rewarding in themselves, without any association with other reinforcers. They include objects and activities that people naturally find valuable. Food, water, candy, and sex are examples of primary reinforcers. Individuals respond positively to them naturally, without having to learn their value.

Secondary reinforcers, on the other hand, have values that are learned through association with other reinforcers. The key idea is that they must be learned. Alone they have no intrinsic value. Money perhaps is the most easily understood example. A thousand dollar bill in itself is nothing but a small piece of high quality paper with printed symbols on it. However, it is associated with things of value. It can be used to purchase actual items ranging from diamonds to pistachio nuts. Money is valuable only because it is associated with other concrete primary reinforcers.

The concepts of primary and secondary reinforcers can readily be applied to treatment situations. For example, a child with a developmental disability may not initially value verbal praise. He may not yet have learned to associate verbal praise with his actual behavior. A social worker may be working with the child concerning his ability to dress himself. Initially, saying, "That's good," may mean nothing to the child. However, saying, "That's good," while at the same time giving the child a small chocolate star, may eventually give the verbal praise some meaning. The child learns to associate verbal praise with the positive value of the candy. Eventually, the praise itself becomes reinforcing to the child, even without the candy. This technique involves pairing a primary reinforcer, the chocolate star, with a secondary reinforcer, verbal praise. The secondary reinforcer becomes valuable to the child through its initial association with the candy.

Secondary Reinforcers

Four major types of secondary reinforcers will be addressed here. They include material reinforcers and nonfood consumables, activities, social reinforcers, and tokens (Fischer & Gochros, 1975; Kazdin, 1994).

Material Reinforcers and Nonfood Consumables.
Material reinforcers are specific objects or substances that can be used as rewards to increase specific behaviors. Eight-year-old Herbie received an allowance for cleaning his room. Herbie's cleaning behavior was strengthened or reinforced by receiving an allowance.

Money might be considered an object (a specific, tangible thing) that reinforces a behavior. Other objects that might have been used as tangible reinforcers for Herbie include records and toys. Each of these items would have acquired their value through learning. Therefore, they would be considered secondary reinforcers.

Food has already been established as a primary reinforcer along with a number of other things that are naturally reinforcing; learning is not involved. In addition, people can learn to value some nonfood consumables. Examples include cigarettes, gum, and chewing tobacco. Although these are not naturally desired, a taste for them can be acquired. Because they are material substances, they will be included in this category of secondary reinforcers.

Activities. Activities make up the second category of secondary reinforcers. *Activities* are tangible events whose value has been learned. Positively reinforcing activities for children might include watching television, playing with friends, staying up late at night, being read to, going shopping, or visiting the stock car races.

For example, 12-year-old Gina hates doing her homework at night. However, she loves going to the movies on Saturdays. Her parents positively reinforce her for doing

an hour's worth of homework 5 nights per week by giving her money to go to the movies on Saturday. Going to the movies is an activity that serves as positive reinforcement for Gina's doing her homework.

Premack (1965) recognized that people have hierarchies of preferred behavior. In other words, any individual when given a choice will choose one behavior over another behavior. For instance, if given a choice, an individual might prefer to plant flowers in the garden over doing the laundry. The *Premack Principle* states that "the opportunity to engage in a high-probability behavior (a preferred behavior) as a consequence for a low-probability behavior (a less-preferred behavior)" will "increase the low-probability behavior," but never vice versa (Miltenberger, 2001, p. 70). Thus, more-preferred activities can be used to reinforce less-preferred activities. Consider the person who prefers garden work over laundry. Allowing him to plant the garden after he completes the laundry will serve to reinforce the laundry-related behavior. He will be more likely to do the laundry if he knows he can plant the garden afterwards.

We've established that fun, exciting activities can serve as secondary reinforcers if they are indeed valued and enjoyed by the person involved. The *Premack Principle* implies that activities needn't be special or extremely valued but simply preferred in order to act as a secondary reinforcer. The garden work might not be something the same individual would choose if a weekend in Las Vegas were also given as an option. However, he still would choose the garden over the laundry. Therefore, the garden could be used as a secondary reinforcer for the laundry. Following the same line of thinking, a trip to Las Vegas could be used as a secondary reinforcer to working in the garden or to doing the laundry.

One of the implicit assumptions here is that each individual will have a different hierarchy of preferred activities. For example, on camping trips, Nick prefers the following specific activities in this order, from most preferred to least preferred: reading *Peterson's 4-Wheel & Off-Road* magazine; cooking the food; doing the dishes; reading science fiction, especially space horror stories. Karen, on the other hand, prefers the specified camping activities in this order: reading science fiction, especially space horror stories; doing the dishes; cooking the food; reading *Peterson's 4-Wheel & Off-Road* magazine ("Winch Wisdom," the title of the leading article, doesn't excite her at all). For Karen, reading science fiction would function as a secondary reinforcer for any of the other three activities. She would be more likely to do any of them if she could read science fiction afterwards. For Nick, however, the science fiction would not serve to reinforce any of the other activities, whereas reading *Peterson's 4-Wheel & Off-Road* magazine would.

Social Reinforcers. Material reinforcers and activities are not the only things that people learn to value. Various aspects of social interaction can also be considered valuable. *Social reinforcers* include words and gestures used to indicate caring and concern toward another person. These can be communicated in one of two ways, either by giving verbal or physical praise. Verbal praise involves words or phrases that indicate approval or appreciation of someone's specific behavior, such as, "Good job," "You did that very well," or, "That's terrific!"

Effective verbal praise is directed at a specific behavior or activity. The person receiving the praise should be clearly aware of what the praise concerns. For instance, 8-year-old Linda did the dishes without being asked for the 2 days her mother was out of town attending a professional conference. Her mother, on her return home, stated, "Thank you very much for helping out and doing the dishes. I understand you did them without even being told. I really appreciate your help." Linda's mother made it very clear exactly what Linda did that was appreciated. When such praise acts to strengthen Linda's dishwashing behavior in the future, it is positive reinforcement. If Linda's mother instead had stated to Linda, "You're a very good girl," it may not have been clear to Linda exactly why she was good. The positive regard communicated by such a statement, of course, is valuable in itself. However, Linda may have understood her mother to mean that she was good because she didn't cry when her mother left or because she stayed up only one-half hour past her bedtime. Linda may not have understood that her mother appreciated her washing dishes, and thus may never have done so without being told again.

The second type of social reinforcement is physical praise. Physical praise involves communicating appreciation or praise through physical gestures or body posture. This may simply involve a smile or a nod of the head. Hugging, clapping, or even winking can also indicate praise.

Consider, for example, how a smile might acquire significance. An infant may not initially value her mother's smile. However, the infant may soon learn to associate the smile with comfort, warmth, and food. Eventually, the smile itself becomes reinforcing. It is a secondary reinforcer. The infant learns to value it. The smile is valued not because it is of value itself, but because the infant has learned to associate it with things of value.

The effects of social reinforcement are illustrated by Beverly, age 5, who had acquired a role in the kinder-garten play. Her part involved playing a duck whose job it was to waddle back and forth across the stage. Beverly was extremely nervous about her part because she was an exceptionally shy child. She even had to get a new yellow dress and wear red boots to help characterize her role. She had been practicing her waddling for days before the play. Finally, the critical night arrived. It was almost time to initiate her waddle and dare to venture out on the stage. At the last minute, she almost backed down and started crying. However, she looked out into the audience and saw her parents in the second row, looking directly at her. They were both smiling proudly and nodding their heads. With such encouragement, she waddled across that stage like no one had ever waddled before. Her parents' obvious approval and encouragement had served to positively reinforce her acting and waddling behavior. After this experience, she was much more likely to volunteer and participate in activities that required performing before an audience.

Tokens. Tokens provide the fourth category of secondary reinforcers. *Token reinforcers* are designated symbolic objects reflecting specific units of value that an individual can exchange for some other commodity that he or she wants. Tokens can include poker chips, artificial coins, points, checkmarks, or gold stars. In and of themselves, they mean nothing. However, they can be associated with something of value and eventually be exchanged for that item or activity.

A practical application of tokens is the use of a token economy in child management. For example, a bicycle might serve as a strong positive reinforcer for a particular child. However, it is absurd to give the child a bicycle every time the child cleans his or her room. Rather, a system can be designed in which a child can earn tokens. The child can be told that if she earns a certain number of tokens, she can exchange them for a bicycle. Tokens become a secondary reinforcer. A large sum of tokens can be used to acquire a bicycle, the item of real value.

Reinforcers versus Rewards

A distinction must be made between reinforcers and rewards. A reward is not necessarily a positive reinforcer. A reward is something that is given in return for a service or a particular achievement. It may or may not increase the frequency of a particular behavior. A soldier might receive a medal of honor at the end of a war for shooting down 27 enemy planes. This is a reward. This reward does not, however, increase the frequency of this individual's shooting down more planes during his civilian life.

Reinforcers, by definition, increase the frequency of a behavior. Receiving an A on an exam is a positive reinforcer for studying behavior if it serves to increase the frequency of a particular student's studying in preparation for exams. However, the student may not value the grade very much. The A may not serve to motivate him to increase or maintain studying behavior. The student becomes bored with studying and receives C and D grades on the next two exams. In this case, the A grade might be considered a reward for performance on one exam. However, the grade is not a positive reinforcer because it neither maintained nor increased the frequency of his studying.

By definition, something serves as reinforcer only if it increases behavior. A positive reinforcer needs to be valued by an individual for it to be effective. Not all items, activities, and social interactions are reinforcing to all people. A roller-coaster ride at Disney World may be positively reinforcing for a third grader whose dream it is to visit Disney World. However, that same ride may not be at all reinforcing to the third grader's father who tends to become ill on roller coasters.

Suggestions for Using Positive Reinforcement

Four suggestions to enhance the use of positive reinforcement involve the quality, the immediacy, and the frequency of positive reinforcement, and the use of small steps for shaping behavior.

Quality of Positive Reinforcement. In order to be considered reinforcement, an item or event must actually increase the frequency of some behavior. We've already established that what is reinforcing for one person may not be reinforcing for another.

A more subtle issue, however, involves the varying degrees of reinforcement value of any particular reinforcer. A particular positive reinforcer might be more reinforcing in one form than in another.

A high school senior working as a part-time janitor at a small local inner tube factory provides an example. The young man, Dave, is working to save for a down payment on his own car. The idea of owning a car is very reinforcing to him. Because of the tremendous costs involved in purchasing a car, Dave had decided to be satisfied with almost anything that he could reasonably afford. However, when he found a 1998 tomato red Mustang with black racing trim for sale down the block, his working behavior sharply increased. He asked if he could double his working hours. To Dave, the Mustang served as a much stronger positive reinforcer than an older, beat-up station wagon.

Immediacy of Positive Reinforcement. Positive reinforcement has a greater effect on behavior if it is administered immediately or shortly after the behavior occurs (Miltenberger, 2001; Sundel & Sundel, 1999). It's important that the behavior and the positive reinforcement occur very close to each other in time. Positive reinforcement loses its effect if it is delayed too long. For example, a 5-year-old boy brushes his teeth without being told one morning. Praising him for this behavior immediately after he's finished or even while he's brushing will have a much greater effect on whether he brushes his teeth again on his own than if he's praised when he gets into bed at night. By bedtime, it becomes more difficult for him to associate the praise with the specific teeth-brushing behavior.

Frequency of Positive Reinforcement. The most effective way to increase a particular behavior is to reinforce it every time it occurs. This is referred to as *continuous reinforcement*. For example, Kaitlyn, age 12, is supposed to do her math homework every night. If Kaitlyn's teacher collects the assignments every morning and gives Kaitlyn credit for doing them, Kaitlyn is likely to complete her homework every night. However, if Kaitlyn's teacher collects only the Thursday night homework, Kaitlyn is less likely to do her homework every night.

Continuous reinforcement is the most effective in establishing a particular behavior. However, if the positive reinforcement stops for some reason, the behavior is likely to extinguish rapidly. For example, Kaitlyn's teacher collects her homework every morning for 2 months. Suddenly, the teacher decides that it's no longer necessary to collect the homework. As a result, there is a fairly strong likelihood that Kaitlyn will stop doing her homework if she no longer gets credit for it.

An alternative to continuous reinforcement is *intermittent reinforcement*. In this, a behavior is not reinforced every time it is performed, but is reinforced only occasionally. In the real world, continuous reinforcement is difficult to administer. It is difficult to be with a person every minute of the day in order to observe that person's behavior. Sometimes intermittent reinforcement is a viable alternative.

Intermittent reinforcement is not as powerful in initially establishing a behavior. It may take longer to establish the behavior. The behavior may not occur as regularly as it would under the conditions of continuous reinforcement. For example, Kaitlyn might not do her homework every night because of the chance it wouldn't be collected the next day.

However, intermittent reinforcement is less subject to extinction. That is, suppose Kaitlyn's teacher had only occasionally collected her homework. Suddenly, she no longer collects the homework. Kaitlyn would be more likely to continue doing the homework after an intermittent schedule of reinforcement than after a continuous schedule. When she was accustomed to intermittent reinforcement, Kaitlyn would be more likely to continue doing her homework on the chance that it might be collected again. If homework collection stops abruptly after continuously being collected, Kaitlyn would probably think that her teacher no longer liked to collect it. As a result, Kaitlyn would probably stop doing her homework.

Each type of intermittent reinforcement dictates a different procedure for how frequently or in what order reinforcement should be administered. These various procedures are referred to as *schedules of reinforcement*.

Shaping Behavior. Sometimes the behavior that's supposed to be positively reinforced never occurs. It is impossible to reinforce a behavior that isn't there. In such cases, a technique called *shaping* can be used. Shaping refers to the reinforcement of successive approximations, that is, small steps of progress, made toward the final desired behavior.

For example, 7-year-old Ralph is terrified of the water. His mother thinks that it would be valuable for him to learn to swim. However, swimming behavior cannot be reinforced because Ralph simply refuses to enter a swimming pool. In this case, it might be useful to break down the specific behavior into smaller, more manageable pieces of behavior. For instance, swimming might be broken down into the following smaller segments of behavior: going to the beach and playing far away from the water, playing several feet away from the water, playing while sitting in an inch of water, wading, entering the water waist deep, moving arms around in the water, briefly dunking head beneath the water, and finally starting to practice beginning swimming strokes. At each step, Ralph could be positively reinforced with praise, attention, or toys for participating in that step. Eventually, his behavior could be shaped so that he would participate in behavior resembling swimming. Specific swimming techniques could then be initiated and reinforced.

The Use of Punishment

Punishment is frequently and often unwillingly chosen as the first alternative in controlling children's behavior. Often punishment is used in the name of discipline. Punishment involves either the application of an aversive consequence or the removal of a positive reinforcer. In either case the result is a decrease in the frequency of a behavior.

Potential Negative Consequences. Before using punishment as a means of behavioral management, it's important to consider the potential negative consequences involved. Five of them will be mentioned here (Kazdin, 2001; Miltenberger, 2001; Sundel & Sundel, 1999). First, punishment tends to elicit a negative emotional response. The child may come to dislike the learning situation. For example, if a child is punished for spelling some words wrong in a composition, the child may no longer want to write at all. The child may also have a negative reaction toward the person administering the punishment.

For example, a young woman in junior high school was walking through the crowded halls from study hall to her next class. The gruff varsity football coach grabbed her by the shoulder and shouted, "Act like a lady!" She had no idea what he was referring to. However, from that time on, she avoided both crowded hallways and that football coach whenever she could. She had developed an intense dislike for the man.

This example also illustrates the second possible negative side effect of punishment, namely avoidance of either the punishing person or the punitive situation. In homes where physical punishment is used freely and regularly, children may try to stay away from the home as much as possible. Lying may provide another effective means of avoiding punitive situations. (Children sometimes learn to lie because parents set the price for honesty too high.)

The third possible negative effect of punishment is that it can teach children to be aggressive. Another way of saying this is that a punishing agent models aggressive behavior. Children can learn that the way to deal with frustration or with not getting their own way is to hit or scream. This can carry over to their interactions with peers, siblings, or adults. An example is an adolescent who was diagnosed as "emotionally disturbed." When he was a small child, physical punishment was used frequently in the home. By the time he reached age 16 and had grown to be 6 feet, 3 inches tall, a different problem became apparent in the home. The boy began to physically assault his mother whenever they had disagreements. He had learned to be aggressive.

The fourth potential problem with using punishment, specifically physical punishment, is the possibility of physically harming the child. A parent may lose control or not be aware of his or her real strength. Without initial intent, physical damage may result.

Finally, there is a fifth reason for questioning the use of punishment. Punishment teaches people what they should

The use of positive reinforcement, combined with a serious talk about behavior, is usually more effective than punishment in establishing positive behavioral change.

© David Harry Stewart./Getty Images

not do but gives them no indication as to what they *should* do. Scolding a child for being impolite when visiting Aunt Edna does not help the child know how she could have treated Aunt Edna more appropriately.

In summary, all five of these considerations involve losing control of the consequences of punishment. The outcome of punishment is unpredictable, and therefore it should be used with extreme care.

The Nature of Punishment. Punishment has several characteristics (Kazdin, 2001; Miltenberger, 2001). First, a decrease in the frequency of a behavior usually occurs relatively soon after the punishment is presented. If the behavior doesn't decrease almost immediately after the supposed punishment starts, there is a good possibility it never will. The implication is not to continue punishment if it doesn't work almost immediately.

For example, 1-year-old Tyrone was crawling happily on his mother's kitchen floor when he accidentally discovered the electric socket. His mother, who was watching him out of the corner of her eye, ran over to him, slapped his hand, and raised her voice in a loud, "No!" He looked at her and returned his attention immediately to the socket. This occurred four times after which his mother slapped him even harder. He then started crying, and she removed him to another room. In this incident, scolding and hitting was not effective. Tyrone's mother's attention appeared to positively reinforce Tyrone's playing with the electric socket. Scolding and hitting was not

effective even after several attempts. It was not likely that it would ever work. Calmly diverting Tyrone's attention might have been a more effective approach to controlling Tyrone's behavior.

Another characteristic of punishment is that its effects, although often immediate, frequently do not last very long. Relatively soon after receiving punishment, a person has the tendency to revert to the old behavior. For example, a driver may receive a speeding ticket for driving 87 mph on a 55 mph expressway. For a while he takes care to drive within the speed limit. However, he soon finds it too restrictive and time consuming to drive so slowly. His speeds gradually creep up to the old levels of 85 to 90 mph.

A third characteristic of punishment is that its effects are frequently limited to the conditions where the punishment occurred. In other words, punishment tends to work only in the specific situation in which it occurred or only with the person who administered the punishment. For example, Trudy, age 7, likes to spit at people as they pass by her on the sidewalk. Her mother spanks her when she sees this behavior. Therefore, Trudy never spits in front of her mother. However, when her mother is in the house or at the grocery store, or when Trudy is at the babysitter's, she continues to spit at passers-by. The babysitter spanked her twice, but it didn't change Trudy's behavior. Spanking functioned as punishment for Trudy only when her mother was present and only when her mother administered it.

The Effectiveness of Punishment. Miltenberger (2001) comments that "[a]uthority figures such as governments, police, churches, or parents impose punishment to inhibit inappropriate behavior—that is, to keep people from breaking laws or rules. Punishment may involve prison time, the electric chair, fines, the threat of going to hell, spanking, or scolding. However, the everyday meaning of punishment is very different from the technical definition of punishment used in behavior modification" (pp. 103–104).

Sundel and Sundel (1999) reflect:

> *Despite the disadvantages of punishment and the stringent requirements for ensuring its effectiveness, punishment is still commonly used as a behavioral control technique. One reason for this is that punishment usually works immediately to suppress undesired behavior. Therefore, the short-term consequences are reinforcing for the individual who administers the punishment. For example, Mel spanked his daughter Terri when she complained about eating her vegetables. Terri stopped complaining; thus, her father was reinforced for spanking her. (p. 123)*

This everyday scenario focuses on the immediate, short-term effects of punishment, not really on long-term effects or consequences other than the immediate cessation of the targeted behavior. Kazdin (2001) discusses the use of punishment as a means of behavior modification:

> *There has been extensive debate within the profession regarding the use of aversive events. . . . Many of the discussions have focused on self-injurious (e.g., head banging, face slapping) and aggressive behavior (e.g., fighting). Behaviors that are dangerous warrant immediate attention and require complete elimination if at all possible. Early in the development of behavior modification, electric shock was used (brief, mild, and delivered on few occasions) and was shown to be effective in eliminating self-injurious behavior. This was significant because in a number of instances, the behavior was long-standing and had not responded to other treatments. Over the past several years, significant advances have been made in devising alternative procedures to reduce and eliminate dangerous behaviors. (p. 415)*

In summary, punishment may be effective when used to curb extremely self-destructive or aggressive behavior in cases in which other treatment approaches have failed. The process concerning the problematic behavior's dynamics should be carefully assessed to determine the appropriateness and potential effectiveness of punishment. Serious thought should go into the method of punishment to be used. It should be the least severe possible to be effective. The well-being of the person experiencing the behavioral program should always be of paramount importance. Finally, the potential side effects of punishment, mentioned earlier, should be cautiously considered.

Suggestions for Using Punishment. When the decision is made to use punishment, follow three suggestions for maximizing its effectiveness (Kazdin, 2001; Miltenberger, 2001; Sundel & Sundel, 1999). First, intervention should occur early; that is, punishment should be administered as soon as possible after the behavior that is to be punished occurs.

For example, 10-year-old Santiago had been stealing compact disks for about 6 months. One afternoon he decided to shoplift a CD from Kmart. Although he made it out to the parking lot, his friend, Maynard, was not so lucky. A huge male clerk grabbed Maynard by the wrist as he was hoisting a CD under his T-shirt. Santiago, although feeling very bad that his friend got caught, also felt relieved that he did not.

Two weeks later Santiago's father received a phone call from the police. Apparently under duress and with the promise of a lesser punishment, Maynard had relented and given the police Santiago's name. Santiago's punishment was being grounded for the next month. Being grounded involved reporting in by 8:00 P.M. every night including weekends. Although Santiago was not particularly happy about his situation, he was more unhappy about being caught than about stealing a CD. He interpreted his punishment to mean, "Don't get caught." The punishment had virtually no effect on his CD-stealing behavior. He continued to steal CDs, but did so with exceptional care. In this situation, because the punishment was not administered soon after the stealing behavior occurred, it had little effect.

A second suggestion for using punishment is to administer the punishing consequences every time the behavior occurs. In Santiago's situation, he was punished only one time. Many other times his stealing behavior was positively reinforced by his getting and enjoying the CDs he wanted. Receiving a punishment every time a behavior occurs helps to strengthen the idea that the consequence of that particular behavior is unappealing.

The third suggestion concerning the use of punishment is the most important. At the same time that punishment is used, a complementary program should be used to reinforce other more appropriate behaviors. Punishment has been found to be most effective when an individual is being reinforced for adapting more appropriate behaviors at the same time. For example, a therapeutic goal for a child with profound cognitive disabilities was to walk instead of crawl (O'Brien, Azriu, & Bugle, 1974).

Punishment for crawling involved restraining him from movement for 5 seconds. However, this did not really serve as punishment because the child's crawling behavior didn't decrease. Nor did his walking behavior increase. Eventually, a new approach was tried. While the child was being restrained from crawling, he was also encouraged or positively reinforced for moving his body. This included being helped to walk. As a result, his walking behavior increased and his crawling behavior decreased. In this case, punishment was effective when the child was reinforced for a more appropriate behavior at the same time. It has been found that the negative side effects of punishment, such as resentment toward the punitive person, aggressive behavior, and avoidance of the punitive situation, are not nearly as great when reinforcement for alternative appropriate behaviors is used (Carey & Bucher, 1986).

Additionally, Patterson (1975) makes a fourth suggestion for using punishment: to remain calm while administering it. Excessive attention directed at a particular behavior may serve as a positive reinforcer for that behavior rather than a punishment. For example, 18-month-old Petey discovered a book of matches lying on the coffee table. He immediately sat down and started to play with them. His mother saw him, ran over to him, and spanked him. She also took away the matches. Because both of Petey's parents smoked, it was fairly likely that Petey would find more matchbooks lying around the house. In fact, he found some the next day. His mother responded in a similar manner. Petey learned that he could get attention from his mother by playing with matches. As a result, he loved to find matches and play with them. Although his mother's attention was negative, it was forceful enough to serve as positive reinforcement. Petey continued to play with matches every chance he got.

🌿 Additional Issues

In addition to the focus on positive reinforcement and punishment, three additional issues merit attention here. They concern common elements encountered in practice. The additional issues include accidental training, the use of behaviorally specific terminology, measuring improvement, and the importance of parental attention.

Accidental Training

Thus far, the discussion has emphasized planned behavioral change. However, many times reinforcement and punishment affect behavior without conscious planning.

Behavior can be increased or decreased without intention. When attempting to understand the dynamics of behavior, it's important to understand that accidental training does occur.

Negative attention is frequently an effective means of providing accidental training. Attention, even in the form of yelling, can function as positive reinforcement. Even though it is supposed to be negative, the social reinforcement value can be so strong that the behavior will be strengthened instead of weakened. For example, if mother yells at Freddie for picking her favorite peonies, then Freddie may learn that picking those peonies will make his mother yell. If Freddie continues to pick the peonies and his mother continues to yell at him for it, the yelling has served to reinforce his peony-picking behavior. Highlight 4.3 provides another example of accidental training.

Behaviorally Specific Terminology

A major advantage of conceptualizing behavior in terms of learning theory is the emphasis on *specificity*. A behavior must be clearly and concisely defined. A clear description of behavior allows for all involved in the behavioral management of a child to understand exactly what behavior, including problem behavior, involves.

For example, Bertha, age 9, was described by her teachers as too passive. It is difficult to know what is meant by "too passive." The word *passive* is relatively abstract. The image of a passive Bertha is quite vague. However, if Bertha's passivism is defined in terms of her behavior, as it would be with a learning theory conceptualization, the image of Bertha becomes more distinct. Bertha's passivism might be described behaviorally in the following way:

Bertha sits quietly by herself during classes and recesses at school. She avoids social contact with peers during recess by walking to the far side of the playground away from the other children. She does not volunteer information during class. When asked a question, she typically shrugs her shoulders as if she does not know the answer. She then avoids eye contact and looks down toward the ground. She is consistently standing last in lines for lunch, for recess, or for returning to school. When other children push her out of their way, she allows herself to be pushed without comment.

Learning theory mandates clear behavioral descriptions in order to conceptualize any particular behavior. The antecedents, the behavior itself, and the consequences of the behavior must be clearly defined in order to make

Highlight 4.3

Accidental Training

Tommy was an only child. His parents, who were in their late 30s, had tried to have children for years without success. When Tommy came along, they were overjoyed. Both parents thought almost everything Tommy did was "simply darling." One time, when Tommy was 3 years old, he approached some dinner guests and asked for money. He had learned that money bought ice cream, and so on. Two things occurred. First, his parents thought it was cute, so they laughed. Then they appropriately told him that asking for money was not a good thing to do. But they maintained happy, smiling faces all the while. Tommy thus received massive social reinforcement in the form of praise and attention for his begging behavior. Second, Tommy did receive one dollar and fifty cents, which he later spent for mocha-fudge ice cream. The guests were not quite as entertained by Tommy's behavior as

his parents were. But, they felt he was a cute kid and gave him money to avoid embarrassment in front of his parents.

The next time Tommy's parents had guests, Tommy did the same thing. He came out for display, said hello, and then asked them if he could have some money. He received a similar reaction. As time went on, Tommy consistently continued his begging behavior in front of guests. His parents became less entertained as the years passed. They discovered that an 8-year-old Tommy coming out and asking guests for money was no longer as cute as a 3-year-old doing the same thing. However, by the time Tommy was 8, they were having a terrible time trying to decrease or extinguish his begging behavior. For an extended period of time, Tommy had accidentally been trained to beg. Such extensive accidental training had become very difficult to extinguish.

---

changes in the behavior. The behavioral description of Bertha provides a much clearer picture than merely labeling Bertha as being "too passive."

Measuring Improvement

Observation of behavior becomes much easier when it has been specifically described. Subsequently, improvements in behavior become more clearly discernable. For example, it might be difficult to establish if Bertha is becoming less passive. However, it is much easier to determine the number of times Bertha assertively raises her hand to answer a question in class.

Behavior must be observable in order to measure if it has improved. In other words, it must be very clear when the behavior occurs and when it does not. In Bertha's situation, the frequency of hand-raising in class has been targeted as a behavior that involves passivism. If Bertha never raises her hand to answer a question, she will be considered passive. If she raises her hand frequently, on the other hand, she will not be considered passive.

For the sake of this illustration, hand-raising is used as a means to measure passivism. Clearly stated behaviors can be counted. For example, in Bertha's case, each time she raises her hand above shoulder level after her teacher has asked the class a question could count as one hand-raising behavior. In an actual situation, Bertha's other behaviors could also be used. These might include behaviors such as the amount of time she spends talking to peers or the number of times she answers her teacher's questions. Her

improvement might be measured by using a summation of a variety of measures.

The first step, then, is targeting a behavior to change. The next step is determining how severe the problem is in the first place. This must be known in order to tell when improvements have been made. In Bertha's case, the hand-raising must be counted and a baseline established. A *baseline* refers to the frequency with which behavior occurs before behavior modification begins. After a baseline is established, it is easy to determine when a change in the frequency of the behavior has occurred. The change is the difference between how frequently that behavior occurred at the baseline and how frequently the behavior occurs after the behavior modification program has begun.

For example, during the first month of school, Bertha raises her hand to answer a question zero times per school day. However, by the seventh month of school, she raises her hand to answer a question an average of six times per day. If one of the means of measuring passivism is the number of times Bertha raises her hand in class, then Bertha can easily be described as less passive during the seventh month of school than during the first.

The final point concerning behavioral specificity involves how the behaviors are counted in the first place—who keeps track of the frequency of the behavior and how this is done. Behavior checklists and charts can be developed for this purpose. A behavior checklist simply allows for a place to make note of when a behavior occurs. For example, a two-dimensional chart might have

Table 4.1	Behavior Chart: Number of Times Bertha Raises Her Hand				
	Mon.	**Tues.**	**Wed.**	**Thurs.**	**Fri.**
8:00–9:00 A.M.	0	0	0	0	0
10:00–11:00 A.M.	0	0	0	0	0
11:00 A.M.–12:00 P.M.	0	0	0	0	0
12:00–1:00 P.M.	0	0	0	0	1
1:00–2:00 P.M.	0	1	1	0	1
2:00–3:00 P.M.	0	0	1	3	3

each day of the week listed on the horizontal axis. Each day might be broken down into individual hours on the vertical axis on the left-hand side. Table 4.1 illustrates how this might be applied to Bertha's situation.

Whenever Bertha would raise her hand in class, her teacher would make a note of it on her behavior checklist. The total number of times could be counted. It could thus be clearly established if an improvement occurred.

We have not addressed the specific types of treatment that could be used in Bertha's situation to decrease her passivism. A treatment program could be established in various ways. For example, positive reinforcement could be administered whenever she raises her hand. This could be in the form of verbal praise, a piece of candy, or a token that could be applied to something she really wanted.

The Importance of Parental Attention

One of the criticisms of the application of learning theory has been that it is a rigid and somewhat cold dissection of human behavior. Warmth, caring, and human concern are not readily evident. This certainly does not have to be the case. The importance of parents communicating with their children and genuinely showing spontaneous concern for them should not be overlooked. Learning theory provides a framework for analyzing and gaining control over behavior. Other important aspects of human relationships can occur concurrently with programs based on learning theory.

For example, Gordon (1975) emphasizes the importance of active listening in his suggestions for effective parenting. A parent and a child often have different ways of saying things. Each has a different perspective. Active listening encourages a parent to stop for a moment and consciously examine what the child is saying. The idea is for the parent to look at the issue from the child's perspective. This may not be clear from the particular words the child has spoken. The parent then is urged to reflect these feelings back to the child. The end result of a parent taking the time to understand a child should be an enhancement of the warmth and caring between them.

Charlene and her mother provide an example of active listening. Charlene, age 7, comes home after school, crying. She says to her mother, "Betty invited everybody but me to her birthday party." Instead of passing it off as a simple childhood disappointment, Charlene's mother stops for a moment and thinks about what this incident might mean to Charlene. She replies to Charlene, "You really feel left out and bad about this, don't you?" Charlene comes into her mother's arms and replies, "I sure do, Mom." In this instance, her mother simply reflected to Charlene her empathy and concern. As a result, Charlene felt that her mother really understood. Warmth and feeling was apparent in their interchange.

Although this interaction is not structured within learning theory terms, it certainly illustrates the basic components of warmth and empathy necessary in the parent-child relationship. Feelings and communication are ongoing, dynamic parts of that relationship. They occur simultaneously along with the ongoing management of children's behavior.

❧ A Specific Treatment Situation: Time-Out from Reinforcement

Extensive volumes have been written concerning the various aspects of learning theory and its applications. Specific concepts have already been discussed. We have selected a specific treatment situation has been selected to illustrate the application of these concepts using specific techniques. It focuses on concepts frequently used by social work practitioners. The treatment situation presented here involves the use of a time-out from reinforcement procedure.

The term *time-out* refers to a time-out from reinforcement. In this procedure, previous reinforcement is withdrawn, with the intended result being a decrease in the frequency of a particular behavior. It is a form of extinction. Instead of applying some aversive consequences such as a spanking after a behavior occurs, a child is simply removed from the reinforcing circumstances. If a child gets no attention or positive reinforcement for a behavior, that behavior will eventually diminish.

For example, 4-year-old Vernite loves to play with her Legos. However, Vernite has difficulty sharing them with other children. When another child picks up one of the pieces, Vernite will typically run over to that child, pinch him, take the toy, and place it in a pile with the rest of her own Legos. As a result, other children don't like Vernite very much.

The goal here might be to decrease Vernite's selfish behavior. Selfish behavior is defined as the series of behaviors involved in pinching and taking toys away from other children. A time-out from reinforcement procedure can be used in order to control Vernite's selfish behavior. Whenever Vernite pinches another child or takes a Lego away from that child, her mother immediately picks her up and puts her in a corner behind a screen for 3 minutes. At the end of that time, her mother picks Vernite up again and puts her back in the play situation. What happens from Vernite's perspective is that the positively reinforcing situation filled with fun, Legos, and other children is removed. (In actuality, of course, it is Vernite who is removed.) Without receiving the reinforcement of having the toys for herself, Vernite's selfish behavior should eventually disappear. She should learn that such behavior is inappropriate, and, in effect, not worth its consequences. Vernite's selfish behavior should eventually be extinguished.

Improving Effectiveness

Several aspects of time-outs tend to improve their effectiveness. The following are suggestions for using time-outs:

1. A time-out should be applied immediately after the targeted behavior occurs in order for it to be effective.

2. Time-outs should be applied consistently. A time-out should occur as a consequence every time the targeted behavior occurs.

3. Time-outs should extend from several seconds to several minutes (usually a maximum of 10). Such short periods of time have been shown to be effective (Kazdin, 2001; Sundel & Sundel, 1999). Longer periods of time do not increase the effectiveness of the time-out (Kazdin, 2001). The relationship between the targeted behavior and the time-out

becomes too distant. An extended time-out of an hour, for instance, may also take on some of the potential negative consequences of a more severe form of punishment such as resentment toward the person administering the time-out.

4. The time-out should take place in a very boring place. An ideal time-out should provide absolutely no positive reinforcement. This might be a chair facing a corner or another room devoid of stimulating objects and pictures. If the time-out location is exciting or stimulating, it might serve to positively reinforce a negative target behavior rather than to extinguish it.

5. The person, frequently a parent, who is administering the time-out should be careful not to give the child positive reinforcement in the form of attention while the time-out is taking place. A parent might simply state to the child, "Time-out." The child should then be removed to the time-out location with as little show of emotion as possible. No debate should take place.

6. A child should be told ahead of time exactly which behaviors will result in a time-out. The length of the time-out should also be specified. The intent is to help the child understand exactly what he or she is doing wrong and what the resulting consequences will be.

7. If the child refuses to go to the time-out location, he or she may have to be physically taken there. This should be done with as little show of emotion as possible. The child should be gently restrained from all activity until the time-out can begin.

8. The most important thing to remember about using the time-out procedure is that positive reinforcement should be used to reinforce more appropriate replacement behaviors for the same situation. Appropriate behavior should be praised as soon as it occurs after the time-out has taken place. For example, when Vernite is returned to the play scene, she should be praised for playing with her own toys and not taking them away from other children. Her mother might simply say, "Look how well you're playing and sharing now, Vernite. Good girl."

A simple anecdote taking place in a local supermarket illustrates the ingenuity and creativity with which a time-out might be used. A mother was shopping with her 2-year-old sitting in a shopping cart. Suddenly for no apparent reason the child began to scream. Much to the surprise of onlooking shoppers, the mother calmly removed her raincoat and placed it over the child's head for 20 seconds. People who are unfamiliar with the time-out technique may have thought she was trying to suffocate the child. However, she performed the procedure calmly and gently. When she removed the raincoat, there sat a peaceful and quiet child. The mother had no further problems with screaming behavior in the supermarket that day. What this mother did was to remove the child from all positive reinforcement for a brief period of time. The child learned that screaming led to no positive consequences. Thus the screaming stopped.

"Grounding"

One other thing should be noted regarding the use of time-outs. Frequently, parents use grounding or sending children to their rooms to curb children's behavior. Although superficially these techniques might resemble time-outs, they don't seem to be very effective. Perhaps too many positive reinforcers are available in a child's room. Oftentimes this form of time-out is administered long after the actual behavior occurs. The actual time of restriction is certainly longer than the recommended time period of a maximum of several minutes.

🌿 Impacts of Common Life Events on Children

Some basic aspects of family functioning have already been examined. These included a conceptualization of family systems and an examination of learning theory applied to parenting situations. Several other social aspects of childhood merit attention. Common events or situations involving the family that frequently impact the lives of children are discussed here. These include membership in sibling subsystems and gender role socialization. Ethnic and cultural differences in families, the social aspects of play with peers, the influence of television, and the school environment are also examined. The incidence and dynamics of physical abuse, neglect, emotional maltreatment, and sexual abuse of children are explored. Finally, treatment of child abuse and neglect are explained.

Membership in Family Systems

We have established that the family environment is of crucial importance to a child. Even though as children grow they become more and more involved with their peers, the family itself remains very important (Carter & McGoldrick, 1999). A good family environment provides nurturance, support, guidance, and a safe, secure place to which children can turn.

Baumrind (1971, 1991a, b, 1993, 1996) conducted an interesting series of studies to evaluate how parents actually go about their business of parenting. Three basic styles of parenting emerged. First, *permissive* parenting encourages children to be independent and to make their own decisions. Permissive parents are very nondirective and avoid trying to control their children. The second parenting style is *authoritarian*. Parents adopting this style have definite ideas about how children should behave. These parents do not hesitate to make rules and tell their children what to do. They emphasize control and conformity. The third parenting style is *authoritative*. Parents using this style are neither permissive nor authoritarian, but somewhere in the middle. On the one hand, they provide control and consistent support. On the other hand, they involve their children in decision making and encourage the development of independence.

Which parenting style is the most effective? There is some evidence that an authoritative—not authoritarian—approach to parenting is preferable in terms of children's resulting adjustment and social status among their peers (Bronstein et al., 1993; Dekovic & Janssens, 1992). Dacey and Travers (2002) describe this style: "Authoritative parents are high on control (they have definite standards for their children), high on clarity of communication (the children clearly understand what is expected of them), high in maturity demands (they want their children to behave in a way appropriate for their age), and high in nurturance (a warm, loving relationship exists between parents and children)" (p. 187).

There is a potential problem with the conclusion that an authoritative style is best: it may not clearly reflect the values and effective child-rearing practices evident in other cultures. Spotlight 4.2 addresses the importance of cultural context in the assessment of the effectiveness of parenting style. Spotlight 4.3 explores ethnic and cultural differences in families.

A variety of other issues involving children and families will be discussed in Chapter 12. These include single-parent families, families of divorce, blended families, mothers working outside of the home, family communication, family interaction, and common problems facing families.

Membership in Sibling Subsystems

Siblings compose a child's most intimate and immediate peer group. Brothers and sisters will impact the development and behavior of a child. Siblings learn how

Spotlight on Diversity 4.2

Cultural Context and Parenting Style

Various ethnic groups have markedly different parenting styles that don't fit neatly into the permissive/authoritarian/authoritative classification system. Specific variations involve how parents perceive and demonstrate caring and control. For example, Chinese-American parents are generally viewed as more demanding concerning control of their children's behavior (Berk, 1999; Papalia et al., 2001). For one thing, "most Chinese parents strictly control their children's aggressive behavior" and demand "that their children display no aggressive behavior under any circumstances" (Ou & McAdoo, 1999, p. 255). The Baumrind system emphasizes control as characterizing an authoritarian parenting style. Berk (1999) notes, however, that "control in Chinese families does not have the same meaning as authoritarian child rearing [does] in Western culture. Instead, it reflects the Confucian belief in self-discipline, respect for elders, and socially desirable behavior, taught by parents who are deeply concerned and involved in the lives of their children" (p. 398). Chinese tradition emphasizes that a "child, no matter how old, should remain emotionally and financially attached to the parents," and there are "strong indications of a lack of independence training in child rearing" (Lin & Liu, 1999, p.238). The Chinese view control of children as a means to teach "obedience and cooperation," the "values most emphasized"; "[f]requent receiving and giving of help between generations is seen by Chinese as an indication of family solidarity. Most children are expected to turn their earnings over to their parents to be used for general family needs" (p. 238).

So what Western eyes might view as an authoritarian trait is really a demonstration of warmth, support, and caring from the Chinese perspective. These latter values more closely characterize authoritative parents in Baumrind's classification system, but "without the emphasis on the American values of individuality, choice, and freedom" (Papalia et al., 2001, p. 301).

Berk (1999) considers parenting styles and expectations evident in other cultures: "In Hispanic and Asian Pacific Island families, firm insistence on respect for parental authority, particularly that of the father, is paired with unusually high maternal warmth. As in Chinese families, this combination reflects parental commitment rather than authoritarianism. It is believed to promote compliance, identification with parents and close relatives, and strong feelings of family loyalty" (p. 398).

Despite huge variation, there is some evidence that African-American mothers, especially young, single women with less education, tend to maintain a strict upper hand in controlling children's behavior (Berk, 1999; Papalia et al., 2001). But Berk (1999) comments that "[s]trict demands for compliance, however, make sense under certain conditions. When parents have few social supports and live in dangerous neighborhoods, forceful discipline may be necessary to protect children from becoming victims of crime or involved in antisocial activities" (p. 399).

In summary, it is important to recognize the cultural context of child rearing, parental expectations, and social responsibilities before stating unilaterally that one parenting style is "best."

Spotlight on Diversity 4.3

Ethnic and Cultural Differences in Families: Empowerment through Appreciation of Strengths

The father's role in the family, availability and nature of support systems, and perspectives on disciplining children vary greatly among cultures (Santrock, 1999). Despite these variations, research on 186 cultures throughout the world revealed a pattern of successful parenting (Santrock, 1999; Whiting & Edwards, 1988). The variables that emerged are *consistency* in the form of supportive control and genuine *caring* for children.

When assessing the dynamics of families from various cultures, three factors are important. First, cultural variations involving expectations and values reflect each culture. Second, people of different cultures living in the United States and Canada experience varying degrees of assimilation into the majority culture simply by living there. Third, people not having a white European origin frequently experience discrimination and oppression because of their differences.

Two other perspectives are helpful when thinking about multicultural diversity in families: cultural pluralism and internal variations or subgroups within a culture. In conceptualizing a multicultural nation, it is helpful to think in terms of *cultural pluralism* instead of a melting pot. A melting pot implies that all people blend together into one uniform whole. Cheese fondue comes to mind, where the cheese and other ingredients blend together in one bubbling mass. This is not really the case with a multicultural society. Rather, people from different cultures come together, and each cultural group retains its own rich spirit and customs. This is cultural pluralism. One of those huge lollipops made up of multi-colored swirls comes to mind. It is one mammoth piece of candy, yet it is made up of distinct swirls of brilliant blue, red, yellow, orange, pink, and green color blending together to various degrees.

Spotlight on Diversity 4.3   *(continued)*

Still another perspective useful in understanding cultural diversity involves respecting and appreciating the differences within large groups. For example, among Native Americans, there are over 450 specific groups (American Psychological Association, 2001).

The following section will discuss some of the values, beliefs, and perspectives assumed by several cultural groups in American society. They include Hispanics, Native Americans, and Asian Americans.

Hispanic Families

Chapter 1 established that the terms *Hispanic* and *Latino* have generally been used to refer to people originating in countries where Spanish is spoken. However, we also noted that the terms in reality refer to people originating in a number of places. No one term is acceptable to all the groups of Spanish-speaking people. Hispanic groups in the United States include people who categorize themselves as Mexican American (66 percent); Central and South American (14.5 percent); Puerto Rican (9 percent); Cuban American (almost 4 percent); and "other Hispanic" (almost 6.5 percent) (U.S. Census Bureau, 2001, p. 43). However, for any particular family, Goldenberg and Goldenberg (1998) caution: "Socioeconomic, regional, and demographic characteristics vary among Hispanic American groups, making cultural generalizations risky. Within groups, the counselor needs to be alert to the client's generation level, acculturation level, languages spoken, educational background, socioeconomic status, rural or urban residence, adherence to cultural values, and religiosity/spirituality" (p. 307).

Keeping in mind that specific variations exist within the many subgroups, we will discuss some cultural themes important to Hispanic families in general. These include the significance of a common language, the importance of family relationships including extended family, and the traditional strictness of gender roles.

The first theme important in understanding the environment for children growing up in Hispanic families is the significance of a *common language*. Everyday communication among Hispanic people is frequently in English (e.g., 63 percent for Mexican Americans, 50 percent for Puerto Ricans, and 31 percent for Cuban Americans), but the uniting symbolic importance of the Spanish language should not be disregarded (Longres, 1995). So many cultural activities and aspects of pride are associated with Spanish. Consider the cultural events and holidays (for example, Cinco de Mayo for Mexican Americans, which celebrates the glorious day a small Mexican army defeated a French army battalion), history and traditions, and "Spanish posters, and foods associated with Spanish-speaking homelands" that are so meaningful in daily cultural life (Longres, 1995, p. 1215).

A second theme involves the importance of both nuclear and extended *family relationships* (Longres, 1995). Hispanic people generally place great value on maintaining the original two-parent family and its intensive involvement with the extended family. Commitment to the extended family group and upholding responsibilities to family members are emphasized. This is generally true for Mexican American, Puerto Rican, and Cuban American families (Chilman, 1993). It is also important to be aware of the community support systems often available to Hispanic families. These include *botanicas, bodegas, clubs sociales, como familial, compadrazo,* and faith healers. Chilman (1993) explains: "*Botanicas* are shops that sell herbs as well as records and novels in Spanish. *Bodegas* are grocery stores, but they also serve as information centers for the Hispanic community, providing such information as where folk healers can be found. [Mexican, Puerto Rican, and Cuban Hispanic cultures espouse folk healers who help people deal with physical, emotional, and spiritual difficulties.] *Club sociales* provide recreation as well as links to community resources, including employment and housing." There also are "special friends who furnish reciprocal support called *como familial*" . . . and "the ritual kinship of *compadrazo,*" . . . people who "participate in baptisms, first communions, confirmations, and marriages, and often serve as parent substitutes" (p. 160).

A third theme often characterizing Hispanic families is the *strict division of gender roles* (Chilman, 1993; Dhooper & Moore, 2001; Longres, 1995). This division may vary from one Hispanic group to another and from one family to another depending, for one thing, on the degree of assimilation into the "mainstream" culture. For example, recent evidence suggests that women working outside of the home results in greater egalitarian values and behaviors. However, Longres (1995) reports that "Latinos traditionally espouse patriarchal, heterosexual, and authoritarian norms. Traditionally, male and female roles were strictly divided and positive value was given to responsible male authority and female devotion to home, children, and husband" (p. 1216). Children are supposed to treat their elders with great respect, obey their father's directives, and demonstrate devotion to their mother. Once again, the extent of a family's assimilation can affect how individual members uphold the values mentioned. For example, clinicians have observed that conflicts between Puerto Rican youth and their parents, especially immigrants, are common as children "seek to become completely 'Americanized' in our highly individualistic, competitive society" (Chilman, 1993, p. 149).

Native-American Families

We have stressed that there are hundreds of Native-American groups with hundreds of dialects. Sensitivity to differences among tribes and appreciation of these differences is vital to effective social work practice. However, as with Hispanic people, several themes characterize many Native American groups. These include the importance of extended family, individualism, harmony with nature, the concept of time, and spirituality.

As with Hispanic people, family ties, including those with *extended family,* are very important (Ho, 1987; Paniagua, 1994). Extended family members include parents, children, cousins, aunts, uncles, and grandparents; additionally, other people can become family members with all the related involvement by becoming the namesake for a child. The importance of self is secondary to that of the family and of the tribe. Children receive supervision and instruction both from their parents and from relatives of several generations; thus, biological parents have "greater opportunity to engage in more fun-oriented activities with their children" and often are able to establish relationships with their children that are "less pressured and more egalitarian than that of the dominant culture" (Ho, 1987, p. 76).

A second significant concept in Native American culture involves the emphasis on *individualism* (Dhooper & Moore, 2001). Although Native American life emphasizes collective work and common goals, it also stresses having respect for each individual and that individual's right to have opinions (Paniagua, 1994). Therefore, Native American "children are rarely told directly what to do and are often encouraged to make their own decisions" (p. 79). Fathers or older male adults in a family do not control families. Rather, they administer or organize the family so that it may arrive at a decision regarding how to proceed.

A third theme that characterizes Native American culture is that of *harmony with nature*. Ho (1987) explains: Native Americans "hold nature as extremely important for they realize that they are but one part of a greater whole. There are many rituals and ceremonies among the tribes that express both their reverence for nature's forces and their observance of the balance that must be maintained between them and all other living and nonliving things" (p. 71).

A fourth theme of Native American life, related to harmony with nature, is the *concept of time* (Ho, 1987; Paniagua, 1994). Time is considered an aspect of nature. Time flows along with life and therefore should not control or dictate how you live. Hence, other aspects of life including interactions with other people become more important than punctuality.

The fifth theme reflecting the perspective of many Native Americans is that of *spirituality* (Dhooper & Moore, 2001; Ho, 1987). Spirituality, involving both tribal religion and Christianity, plays a critical role in the lives of many Native Americans. Although religious beliefs vary from one tribe to another, according to Ho (1987) "religion is incorporated into their being from the time of conception, when many tribes perform rites and rituals to ensure the delivery of a healthy baby, to the death ceremonies, where great care is taken to promote the return of the person's spirit to the life after this one" (p. 73).

Asian American Families

People who are typically considered Asian Americans are composed of three basic groups that, in turn, consist of numerous subgroups. These are Asian Americans (Japanese, Chinese, Filipinos, Asian Indians, and Koreans), Pacific Islanders (Hawaiians, Samoans, and Guamanians), and Southeast Asians (Vietnamese, Cambodians, and Laotians) (Paniagua, 1994). Obviously, there is great variation among these groups, despite the fact that they are clustered under the umbrella term Asian

Americans. Here we discuss four themes that tend to characterize many Asian American families: the significance of family, interdependence, investment made in children, and patriarchal hierarchy.

Like Hispanic people and Native Americans, Asian Americans tend to consider the *family as the primary unit* and individual family members as secondary in importance (Balgopal, 1995; Goldenberg & Goldenberg, 1994). Phillips (1996) describes a key concept: "The welfare and the integrity of the family are of great importance. The individual is expected to submerge or to repress emotions, desires, behaviors, and individual goals to further the welfare of family and maintain its reputation. The individual is obligated to save face, so as to not bring shame onto the family. Therefore, there is incentive to keep problems within the family so that the family will not 'lose face'" (p. 1).

A second theme, related to the significance of the family, involves *interdependence* (Balgopal, 1995; Philips, 1996). For example, Chinese culture emphasizes "kinship from birth to death, and it is expected that the family will serve as a major resource in providing stability, a sense of self-esteem, and satisfaction" (Goldenberg & Goldenberg, 1994, p. 254). Such respect and responsibility for the family are expected even when family members move to another country and rarely see the rest of the family again. An expectation that children will care for elderly parents is also important (Balgopal, 1995; Green, 1999).

A third theme characterizing many Asian American families involves the high priority on *investment made in children*. (Goldenberg & Goldenberg, 1994; Green, 1999; Wong, 1988). Parents often allow young children much greater freedom in developmental tasks than is considered appropriate in the "mainstream" culture. For example, parents might delay toilet training until the children themselves demand it, and older children up to age 10 or 11 are often allowed to sleep with parents (Berg & Jaya, 1993). Asian American parents might be more indulgent generally than their white counterparts. However, they also tend to have high expectations regarding the children's behavior and tend to impose stricter discipline when misbehavior occurs (Goldenberg & Goldenberg, 1994; Green, 1994; 1995; Ho, 1987).

A fourth theme involves *patriarchal hierarchy* (Balgopal, 1995; Goldenberg & Goldenberg, 1994; Green, 1999; Ho, 1987). Balgopal (1995) explains: "Asian families are generally patriarchal, and in traditional Asian families, age, sex, and generational status determine the roles that members play. The father is the head of the family, and his authority is unquestioned; he is the main disciplinarian and is usually less approachable and more distant than the mother, who is the nurturer and caretaker" (p. 234).

A Note on Difference

Our discussion concerning cultural themes of values and behaviors is general and brief. Actual practices may vary dramatically from one ethnic group to another and from one family to another. The point here is to enhance your sensitivity to and appreciation of potential cultural differences so that you may better understand and serve your clients.

to play with each other. They act as models for each other. They also learn how to fight with each other.

The Coming of a New Baby. Picture a 3½-year-old child waiting patiently for her mother to come home from the hospital with her new baby sister. When Mom arrives, imagine her surprise when she sees her beloved mother holding a blanket that looks like it has a tiny doll in it. Her mother is smiling and cooing down at the "doll." The little girl thinks to herself, "That must be my baby sister." She feels surprise, wonderment, happiness, and worry all at once, but is unable to articulate these feelings. Her general impression of the whole new situation is, "Now what?"

The coming of a new baby changes a child's family environment. Children's reactions to the change in circumstances vary dramatically. Some may withdraw into themselves and regress to more babylike behavior. Others may show open hostility toward the new baby and suggest giving it back. One 3-year-old boy was found holding a safety pin near his new infant brother, contemplating poking him in the eye. Still other children happily and proudly accept the family's new addition and enjoy holding and playing with him or her.

Because of the complexity of the issue and the lack of clear-cut research, it is difficult to propose how to make the transition as easy as possible. Dr. Benjamin Spock (Spock, 1976; Spock & Rothenberg, 1985), the famous pediatrician who gave several generations of parents advice about how to raise their children, provided some logical suggestions. First, children should be told in advance about all the changes they are to experience. Changes might include sharing a bedroom or having the new baby use their old high chair. Preparing them in this way is supposed to minimize surprises. Not knowing what's going to happen is scary for children. Second, Spock suggested continuing to talk to older children and emphasizing how much they are loved and valued. Finally, children should be encouraged to express their feelings, including the negative ones, so that parents can allay their children's fears and address problems as they occur.

Sibling Interaction. More than 80 percent of children in the United States have at least one brother or sister (Berk, 1999; Santrock, 2002b). Sibling interaction involves a multitude of behaviors and feelings. Siblings fight with each other but they also play with each other, work together, and show affection such as hugging each other (Cicirelli, 1994). Siblings appear to get along better when neither sibling has an exceptionally volatile temperament

(Brody, Stoneman, & McCoy, 1994). Sibling relationships also tend to be more positive in families where the parents' relationship is positive, warm, and congenial (Volling & Belsky, 1992).

The Effects of Birth Order, Family Size, and Family Spacing. It is difficult to establish definite facts concerning birth order and development because so many factors are involved (e.g., parenting style, cultural expectations, socioeconomic status, number of persons residing in the family). Some research indicates that parents have higher expectations for their first-born children's achievements (Furman, 1995) and tend to give them more attention (Santrock, 2002b). Parents apparently learn from experience and become more comfortable and less demanding with later-born children (Kail & Cavanaugh, 2000). First-born children tend to score higher on achievement tests, go to college, and be cited more frequently in *Who's Who;* they are also more likely to conform to parental requests and be more self-controlled (Kail & Cavanaugh, 2000; Santrock, 2002b). An only child appears to surpass a child with siblings in several areas, including intelligence, academic achievement, and social adjustment (Falbo & Polit, 1986).

Gender Role Socialization

Infants are treated differently by virtue of their gender from the moment that they are born (Strong et al., 2002; Hyde & DeLamater, 2000). There is almost immediate segregation by pink or blue clothing. Based on gender, parents tend to hold girls more gently and play with boys more roughly (Strong et al., 2002). A basic question remains unresolved. To what extent are males and females inherently different and in what ways?

This question relates to the nature-nurture argument regarding why people become the people they do. Supporters of the nature idea argue that people are innately programmed with inborn, genetic, or natural predispositions. According to the nurture perspective, people are the product of their environment. That is, people are affected by what happens to them from the day they're born; they learn from their environment and are shaped by it. Each side of the debate has evidence and research to support its perspective. Probably the answer lies somewhere in the middle. People are probably born with certain potentials and predispositions that are then shaped, strengthened, or suppressed by their environments. Gender roles will be discussed again later in this chapter, in regard to gender differences in play, and more extensively in Chapter 9.

❧ The Social Environment: Peers, Television, and School

The family does not provide the only means of socialization for children. They are also exposed to other children as they play and to other adults, especially in the school setting. The transactions children have with their peers and with adults in school directly affect both the children's behavior and their social development. Children learn how to relate to others socially. They learn what types of social behaviors others expect from them. They also are influenced by the amount of time they spend watching television. Issues to be addressed here include the social aspects of play, the influence of television, and the role of the school. The impact of each will be related to the social development of children.

The Social Aspects of Play with Peers

Luther, who is 8, screamed at the top of his lungs, "Red light, green light, hope to see the ghosts tonight!" He spun around and peered through the darkness. He was playing his favorite game, and he was "it." That meant that he counted to 20 and then had to find the others and tag them. The first one tagged had to be "it" the next time.

"Where were those other kids anyway?" he said silently to himself. Randy usually hides in the garbage can. He thinks that that makes him smell so unappealing that no one will look for him there. Siggy, on the other hand, likes to hide in the bushes by the drainage ditch. However, a lot of mosquitos were likely to consume anybody brave enough to venture over in that direction.

Horace was always an enigma. Luther never knew exactly where he was likely to hide. Once he had managed to squeeze into old Charlie's dog house. Charlie was a miniature mongrel.

On serious consideration of which route to take, Luther decided that the garbage can was his fastest and easiest bet. Just as Luther could've sworn that he heard Randy sneeze inside of the garbage can, he heard his mother's call. "Luther, you get in here this minute. I told you four times that you have to be home by 8:30 on weeknights. Come in right now, do you hear!"

"Aw, rats," mumbled Luther. Just when he started to have some fun, he always had to quit and go home. Along came the other guys. See, he was right. Randy was in the garbage can and, sure enough, Siggy popped out from behind the bushes by the drainage ditch. As usual, he was scratching. Randy's mother was really going to give it to him when he got home. He did smell awfully

bad. Horace appeared suddenly out of nowhere. He wasn't about to waste a good secret hiding place for nothing.

All four boys dragged themselves home. They walked as slowly as they could and procrastinated appropriately. Another hard summer's day of play was done, but they were already thinking about tomorrow.

Children's play serves several purposes. It encourages children to use their muscles and develop physically. It allows them to fantasize and think creatively. Finally, play enables children to learn how to relate to peers. Play provides a format for learning how to communicate, compete, and share. It functions as a major avenue of socialization.

Garvey (1977) defines play as activity that involves the following five qualities: First, play must be something that is done purely for enjoyment and not for a reward or because it is considered appropriate. Second, play has no purpose other than to be an end in itself. Third, people who play choose to do it. No one can force a person to play. Fourth, play involves active participation in an activity. Either mentally or physically the individual must be involved. Pure observation does not qualify as play. Fifth, play enhances socialization and creativity. Play provides a context in which to learn interaction, physical, and mental skills.

Play and Interaction.   There are at least two basic ways of looking at how children play. These include social play and fantasy play. *Social play* involves the extent to which children interact with other children as they play. *Fantasy play* involves what children think about and how they imagine their pretend games as they play.

Social Play.   Parten (1932) conceptualized a model for how children progress in their development of social play. Her research, which was done in the 1920s, focused on children aged 2 to 5. Observations of the children in action led to the proposition that there are actually six different levels of play. Theoretically, children progress through the following levels as they get older:

1. *Unoccupied behavior:* Unoccupied behavior involves little or no activity. A child might be sitting or standing quietly. Frequently, the child's attention is focused on observing something going on around him.

2. *Onlooker play:* A child involved in onlooker play is simply observing the playing behavior of other children. The child is mentally involved in what the

other children are doing. However, the child is not physically participating in the play. Onlooker play differs from solitary play in that the child's attention is focused on the play of peers, instead of on simply anything that might be happening around him or her.

3. *Solitary play:* Solitary play involves the child playing independently. No attention is given to other children or what they might be doing.

4. *Parallel play:* A child involved in parallel play is playing independently but is playing in a similar manner or with similar toys as other children in the immediate vicinity. The child is playing essentially the same way as the other children, although no interaction occurs.

5. *Associative play:* Here children play together. There is some interaction but the interaction is not organized. For example, children may share toys or activities and talk with each other. However, their play is very individualized. Each child plays independently from the others and focuses on individual activities.

6. *Cooperative play:* Cooperative play involves organized interaction. Children play with each other in order to attain a similar goal, make something together, or dramatize a situation together. Attention is focused on the group activity. Cooperation is necessary. Children clearly feel that they are a part of the group.

Parten proposed that different age levels are characterized by different types of play. Two-year-old children tend to play by themselves. By age 3, parallel play begins to be evident. Associative play is engaged in by more and more children as they reach the age of 4. By age 5, most children participate in cooperative play.

Questions have been raised about the validity of Parten's levels of play (Papalia et al., 2001). For one thing, in what ways is solitary play really less mature than play occurring in groups? Much of children's solitary play is thoughtful, educational, and creative by nature, helping them to develop more advanced cognitive thinking. Where do such solitary activities such as drawing or building with blocks and Legos fit into Parten's conception of normal play development?

Parents need to be aware of the normal developmental aspects of play at different age levels. Expectations of parents and other caregivers need to be realistic. Children should be encouraged to play with other children in ways appropriate to their age level. Yet, children should not be pushed into activities that are beyond them. Children who are isolated in their play activities at an age when they need to be more outgoing may need encouragement in that direction. Parents and other caregivers can help children develop their play and interactional skills.

Gender Differences in Play. Two gender-related differences in behavior appear early in life (Hyde & DeLamater, 2000; Lips, 1995; Lott 1994). One is a difference in aggressive behavior with respect to play. Boys behave more aggressively than girls. The other early behavioral difference is in toy preference. By age 3 or 4 girls begin choosing to play with dolls and participate in housekeeping play. Boys are oriented toward more masculine toys such as trucks and guns. The reasons for these differences are not clear. Perhaps children play with the toys they are given and encouraged to play with. Girls' rooms are filled with dolls and items devised for playing house. Boys' rooms display various action-oriented toys such as cars, trucks, guns, and sports equipment.

For example, when Aunt Karen took 3-year-old Andrea, her niece and the "apple of her eye," to Kmart one day to buy her a toy, Andrea headed straight for the "girls' toys," not the "boys' toys." When Aunt Karen suggested Andrea look at some *fun* trucks and cars (Aunt Karen knew that it was good for girls to become oriented to cars and trucks, both because they'll have to use real ones someday and because such play aids in the development of spatial perception skills), Andrea screwed up her nose and said "NO! Those are boys' toys!" It was interesting because in real life, Andrea's mother was the person who did most of the mechanical fixing and all of the outdoor work at their 4-acre home. The impact of the media, especially television, and Andrea's observation of other people must have been very great.

Another reason for the differences in toy preference may be that children, who become conscious of gender by age 2½ (Masters et al., 1995), learn early how they should be playing. They watch television and observe Mommy and Daddy; they learn that girls and boys should like to do different things.

Lott (1987) suggests that there are at least three logical reasons why girls' behavior is less aggressive than that of boys. They all seem to relate to and reinforce each other. First, girls have fewer chances to "practice" aggressive behavior such as fighting, breaking, or hurting things. Second, girls' aggressive behavior is less likely to be encouraged by adults than the aggressive behavior of boys.

For instance, Aunt Karen had an opportunity to observe 3-year-old Andrea in the company of her male and female nursery school peers. They were on a field trip to a local pumpkin farm with the idea of picking some small pumpkins. All of the boys in Andrea's group were kicking, screaming, punching, bumping, running, and making "BRRRRRRRR" and "GRRRRRRRR" sounds. Several of the mothers calmly observed, smiled, and made proud comments like, "Isn't he a *real* boy." Meanwhile the girls stood silently on the sidelines watching the boys have "fun." When one girl tried to get involved, her mother said, "Oh, no, Chrissy, you might get hurt. Those boys are so rough."

A third reason why girls are less aggressive, according to Lott, is that girls are less likely to "experience success" at being aggressive than are boys. Boys are encouraged by adults to be more practiced at aggression than girls. Girls, on the other hand, are reinforced for being gentler and more "ladylike."

The Peer Group and Popularity. The *peer group* is made up of a child's equals. It can have an increasing impact on children as they get older, more independent, and more experienced. On a positive note, the peer group provides an arena for children to learn about themselves, build their self-concepts, and learn how to interact with others. On a negative note, the peer group can place pressure on children to do things they would never consider doing on their own.

Some children get along fabulously with peers; others are avoided, isolated, and withdrawn. What makes a child popular? (For that matter, what makes an adult popular?) Researchers have studied popular and unpopular children and concluded that popular children tend to display certain characteristics (Newcomb, Bukowski & Pattee, 1993; Papalia et al., 2001). They tend to be friendly with others and interact easily. They are neither too aggressive nor too passive. They tend to be trustworthy and able to supply emotional responsiveness and support to peers. They usually are bright and creative, yet don't act superior or arrogant.

On the other hand, children who are unpopular tend to be characterized by opposite traits. They are socially immature. They tend either to be too pushy and demanding, or very shy and withdrawn. They might not be the brightest children around nor the most attractive. They may not have the listening skills and the ability to empathize with others that popular children seem to have. Such children tend to find friends with similar types of social problems (Hartup, 1989).

A common technique for examining children's interaction is referred to as *sociometry*. This involves asking children questions about their relationships and feelings toward other people. The relationships can be illustrated on a diagram called a *sociogram*. Children in a group might be asked questions such as which three peers they like the best, which three they like the least, who they most admire, who would they like to sit next to, or who are they most afraid of. Each child can be represented by a circle. Arrows can then be drawn to the people they indicate in answer to each question.

Sociograms are shown in Figure 4.4. A sociogram can be created to illustrate the results of each question asked.

Figure 4.4   Sociograms of a Special Education Class

Sociogram A

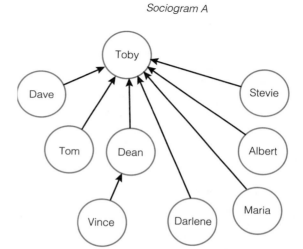

Students were asked whom they felt was the strongest leader in the group. Arrows reflect their feelings. Toby clearly has that status.

Sociogram B

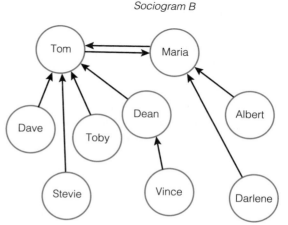

Here students were asked which person they liked the most in the group. Tom and Maria appear to be the most popular.

Our example plots out two questions. The first reflects students' feelings about who they thought was the strongest leader in the group. The second illustrates which peer they most liked in the group.

Sociogram A clearly illustrates that Toby is thought to be the strongest leader in the group. He is bright, energetic, and very "street smart." However, Sociogram B clearly illustrates that he is not the most popular or best liked in the group. Both Tom and Maria shine there. They both are more mature than the other group members. They are assertive and fairly self-confident, yet don't impose their will on the others. They are among the brightest in the group. Toby, on the other hand, is more feared than respected. The others admire his apparent sophistication, yet don't trust him. He doesn't let anyone get close to him emotionally or physically. He keeps his distance.

Vince's opinions differ radically from those of other group members. Vince stays by himself most of the time. He loves to wander off whenever he can. He sees Dean as being both a strong and likeable leader. Dean is a very active, verbal person who is always in the center of activity. He has some trouble controlling his behavior and tends to provoke the other students. Perhaps Vince admires Dean's involvement.

These two sociograms are examples of how insights into a group's interaction can be obtained and visually pictured. Although they only begin to portray some of the complexities of the group's interaction, they do provide some interesting clues.

We've been speaking of children as being popular or unpopular. It is as if on a popularity scale from 1 to 10, each child is either a very unpopular 1 or a very popular 10. In real life, of course, most people lie somewhere in between. They may have some of the characteristics of "the popular person," but not others.

It appears that social skills provide a primary basis for popularity. It follows, then, that because skills in general can be learned, social skills can be learned and popularity increased. Bierman and Furman (1984) studied fifth and sixth graders who had difficulty relating to peers. Children who were both trained in interpersonal skills (e.g., how to start conversations, use empathy, ask relevant questions) and allowed to practice skills with peers were liked significantly more by peers both immediately after practice sessions and 6 weeks later. Children without training, and those who received training but weren't given the opportunity to practice what they had learned, showed no such increased popularity. The implication here is that both training and practice can improve social skills and provide one viable alternative for young people

who are depressed, lacking in self-esteem, isolated, or suicidal.

The Influence of Television

Because television has become such a common aspect of a child's environment, it merits a few comments here. Children "spend at least twice as much time watching TV than they do in school" (Dacey & Travers, 2002, p. 260). If continued at that rate, a high school graduate would have spent a full 2 years watching television for 24 hours a day (Kail & Cavenaugh, 2000). Of course, this is only an average. Some children watch more television than others. For example, children from lower-income families watch more television than their counterparts in families with higher economic status (Huston & Wright, 1998).

A major question raised about the impact of television is whether TV teaches children to be violent and aggressive. Research indicates that television does influence and increase children's violent behavior (Berk, 1999; Mifflin, 1999a, 1999b; National Institute of Mental Health [NIMH], 1982; Newman & Newman, 1999). Consider that children watch between 10,000 and 15,000 violent acts on television annually, over a quarter of which involve using guns; additionally, 61 percent of all shows include violence, with children's programs portraying the most violent content (Strasburger & Donnerstein, 1999). Other findings reveal how more than 70 percent of characters demonstrating violence on television display no regret or guilt over what they had done; over half of the violent acts avoid any portrayal of a victim's suffering; and over 40 percent of violent acts are committed by good-looking, admired characters (the *National Television Violence Study*—NTVS, 1996).

Three processes may operate to increase children's aggression in response to TV violence (Newman & Newman, 1999). First, children may model the violent behavior they see. If Rambo and other famous movie and TV characters can do it, why can't they? Second, violence is arousing, so children are more likely to lose control and become more violent. TV violence can serve as a stimulus to trigger increased emotionality and aggression. Third, regular exposure to TV violence can influence a child's value system and beliefs about how the world really is. Children who see a lot of violence may take it for granted that violence happens everywhere much of the time. How many times might a child watch a young man get "blown away" in vivid blood-red color before that image becomes commonplace in that child's mind?

Other research establishes a relationship between the amount of violent television viewed in childhood and the amount of aggressiveness manifested by participants as adults (Huesmann & Miller, 1994; Kail & Cavanaugh, 2000). In other words, children who watched more violent television may actually display more violent behavior themselves when they grow up. However, a causal relationship cannot be established here (Mifflin, 1999a). For example, maybe these children were more predisposed to violence to begin with.

Children's cartoons are among the most "violent fare" television offers, "followed by toy commercials" (Levine, 1994; Mediasope, 1996). Picture such cartoons as *Teenage Mutant Ninja Turtles, Spider Man, Secret Files of the Spy Dogs, Woody Woodpecker, Donald Duck Presents,* and the *Roadrunner.* How many times has the coyote been blown up with a stick of dynamite given him by the roadrunner? Or Donald Duck smashed by a baseball bat or pushed off a steep cliff? When you really think about it, the implications of this amount of violence depicted are scary.

Other concerns have also surfaced concerning unsuitable messages television conveys to children. For example, more and more people have expressed serious apprehension about the increasing amount and explicitness of sex on television (Lacayo, 1995b; Silver, 1995). Former Senator Bob Dole (R-Kans.) "accused the powers behind American movies, music, and television of flooding the country with 'nightmares of depravity'" and warned that "the more extreme products of pop culture threaten to undermine American kids" (Lacayo, 1995b, pp. 25–26).

Public concern also focuses on television's portraying an accurate picture of the world in terms of ethnic and other diversity. For example, although African Americans make up 10–15 percent of television characters (relfecting their approximate proportion in the U.S. population), Native Americans, Hispanics, and Asian Americans are rarely portrayed (Huston & Wright, 1998).

Additionally, women are grossly underrepresented, portraying only about one-third of television characters; worst yet, when they are represented, they are often depicted as being "passive and emotional," most are unemployed, and "those who have jobs are often in stereotypical female careers such as teachers or secretaries" (Huston & Wright, 1998; Kail & Cavanaugh, 2000, p. 263). Elderly people are also primarily overlooked, as only 5 percent of television personalities are 60 or older (Kail & Cavanaugh, 2000).

There is another side to television, however. According to Newman and Newman (1999), "Many programs, some developed for children and others intended for a broader viewing audience, convey positive ethical messages about the value of family life, the need to work hard and sacrifice in order to achieve important goals, the value of friendship, the importance of loyalty and commitment in relationships, and many other cultural values" (p. 242). There was *Mr. Rogers' Neighborhood,* where "it's a beautiful day in the neighborhood" every single day, which was found to have positive effects on children's social behavior (Huston & Wright, 1998). There's also *Sesame Street,* which emphasizes the development of reading and arithmetic skills in addition to imparting such values as consideration for others' feelings.

Television affects children. Following the April 1999 massacre by two teens of 12 high school students and a teacher at Columbine High School in Littleton, Colorado, then president Clinton made three pleas to the media (Harris, 1999). First, "he urged movie studios to stop showing guns in ads and previews that children can see" (p. A3). Second, "he asked theaters and video stores to more rigorously enforce rules barring unchaperoned children under age 17 from viewing R-rated movies" (p. A3). Third, "he called for re-evaluating the ratings system, 'especially the PG rating,' to decide whether the ratings are 'allowing too much gratuitous violence' in movies approved for children" (p. A3).

The American Academy of Pediatrics (1986) suggests that parents scrutinize their children's viewing behavior by observing how their children act after watching TV and by watching the programs themselves. Limits should be set regarding what is appropriate and what is not. When violence does occur, parents should talk to children about it. Parents can emphasize that violence is a bad way to solve problems and that there are better, nonviolent ways available. The American Academy of Pediatrics also suggests that "children under 2 years old should not watch television, older children should not have television sets in their bedrooms, and pediatricians should have parents fill out a 'media history' on office visits" (Mifflin, 1999b, p. A1).

The School Environment

School provides a major arena for socialization, where children are taught social customs, rules, and communication skills. Schools can influence children's dreams and aspirations about future careers. Schools help to mold the ways in which children think. Specific issues related to the school environment will be discussed here. They include the teacher's impact, freedom in the classroom, and the effects of social class and race.

The Teacher's Impact. Students frequently perform at the level of their teachers' expectations. This is sometimes

enhance comprehension of topics being addressed (Papalia, et al., 2001).

The Classroom Environment. A number of facets in the classroom environment, including class size and classroom setting, affect children's ability to learn. One study found that fourth- and fifth-grade students in smaller classes of 13 to 17 made greater strides in achievement than students in larger classes (Mosteller, 1995). Other evidence indicates that this is even more important for the earlier grades, when children need more help and direction (Blatchford & Mortimore, 1994). If this makes sense and sounds good, why are most classes significantly larger? The answer, of course, is money. The smaller the class size, the more teachers, and the more money for salaries, a school requires.

Another facet of the classroom environment involves providing a traditional or a more open setting for learning. The *traditional* approach involves students who passively sit at their desks while they are being taught by a teacher. The goal is knowledge acquisition. An *open* classroom, on the other hand, encourages more active learning on the students' behalf, where they actively participate in problem-solving processes, receive more individual attention, and learn together in small groups.

There is some evidence that the achievement of older students who are educated in traditional classrooms slightly exceeds that of students learning in open classrooms (Berk, 1999). However, open settings have other benefits, such as encouraging critical thinking, enhancing self-reliance, developing communication skills with other students, and getting more enjoyment out of the school experience (Berk, 1999; Walberg, 1986). Spotlight 4.4 discusses how an educational program was developed to emphasize cultural strengths and meet the educational needs of Hawaiian students.

Race, Ethnicity, and Schools. Gaps exist between the educational attainment of whites and some other ethnic groups including African Americans and Hispanics. Although the educational breach between African Americans and whites has significantly decreased, some differences continue (Leashore, 1995). Specifically, 78.5 percent of African Americans as compared to almost 85 percent of whites aged 25 or over completed 4 years of high school; similarly, 16.5 percent of African Americans compared to over 26 percent of whites age 25 or over completed 4 years of college or more (U.S. Census Bureau, 2001). However, problems do exist. Leashore (1995) explains: "African American children and youths are more likely than are whites to drop out of school.

Children watch many hours of television every week. During this time they witness many acts of violence on the screen. Most research indicates that television can increase violent behavior in children.

referred to as a *self-fulfilling prophecy*—i.e., that students will perform to the level of expectation placed upon them. Higher expectations, therefore, can result in greater achievement.

There is some indication that low achievers are even more responsive to higher teacher expectations than are higher achievers (Madom, Jussim, & Eccles, 1997). Teachers should avoid categorizing students as poor performers, but, rather, should encourage them to work to the best of their ability. The following traits are among those characterizing the most effective teachers:

- having organized, efficient classroom and time-management skills;

- having faith in their students' ability to learn and achieve;

- providing students with a range of different learning experiences (e.g., discussion, problem solving, practice, peer tutoring, small-group work) to

Spotlight on Diversity 4.4

Educational Programming That Responds to Cultural Values

The Kamehameha Early Education Program (KEEP) was developed to focus on the cultural values of Native Hawaiians and to enhance students' learning processes (KEEP, 2002; Tinzmann et al., 1990). Phenice (1999) describes some aspects of Hawaiian culture:

Cooperating, not only within the family but also with others in the ethnic community as well as in society is an expectation inculcated in children at a very young age. Values such as harmony with nature and humanity are fundamental in their cognitive expressions. When there is a conflict with another, there is a saying, ho oponopono, which means to have a frank discussion to set matters right in order to restore a good relationship with the other, whether within the family or within the community. This process includes praying together, respecting all viewpoints, and forgiving. Historically strength as a group came from cooperating and not competing with one another. (p. 115)

Western thought and values emphasize individualism, competition, and winning. Children take achievement tests where they are ranked in competition with each other. A grade of C is considered average, whereas a grade of A is exceptional. Traditional classrooms emphasize individual accomplishments and success. Winners of sports and other competitive events are admired as heroes. Anything that involves winners, of course, also includes losers, who are looked down upon and often considered inferior.

KEEP is built on the principle of collaborative classroom work that complies well with Hawaiian cultural values. Classrooms are broken down, not into individuals, but small groups of students who work together to assess issues, develop projects, and solve problems. All participants' input is valued and encouraged as groups focus on sharing the knowledge of individual members. Teachers encourage student input into activities by providing options students can choose. For example, a teacher might address the topic of Hawaiian geography. Student groups then might be allowed to determine how they will study this topic—by developing maps and charts, creating a videotape, or writing a paper on the subject. Another example of teacher/student collaboration involves a teacher assigning the topic of "garbage" to student groups and asking them to develop their own goals for a project (Tinzmann, et al., 1990). "In one group, a student wanted to find out if garbage is a problem, another wanted to know what happens to garbage, a third wanted to know what is being done to solve the problem of garbage. The fourth member could not think of a goal, but agreed that the first three were important and adopted them" (p. 5).

Another process used by KEEP teachers is the use of *talk story,* a manner of speaking that is common in Hawaiian communities, where a group of individuals all contribute to the reiteration or creation of a story by contributing small pieces (KEEP, 2000). Together, the small student groups compose the final result.

Research suggests KEEP is effective in enhancing learning. Children of color performed better on achievement tests than their peers who attended schools using traditional classroom settings (Berk, 1999; Papalia, et al., 2001). Programs using KEEP principles, and adopting learning approaches to incorporate respective cultural values, have also been developed elsewhere, such as the Navajo reservation in Arizona.

Those who remain in school tend to earn lower grades, score below the average on standardized tests, and are more likely to be suspended or expelled" (p. 108).

Many Hispanics also tend to lag somewhat behind their non–Hispanic white counterparts in educational attainment. Only about 57 percent of Hispanics age 25 or over complete 4 years of high school or more and 10.6 percent complete 4 years of college or more (U.S. Census Bureau, 2001). This contrasts starkly with the 83 and 25 percent, respectively, of whites attaining the same educational status.

A number of reasons may account for the discrepancies in educational attainment between whites, African Americans, and Hispanics. Some educators have attributed this phenomenon to external factors such as lower socioeconomic status (Duncan & Brooks-Gunn, 2000). Both African Americans and Hispanics are more likely to have lower socioeconomic status than whites. Are schools in poorer neighborhoods receiving necessary resources to provide students with a good education? Other reasons for the discrepancy in educational attainment may involve internal variables, such as a social atmosphere, that discourage students and obstructs their performance. Also, textbooks and instructional materials may not adequately reflect relevant cultural values and ethnicity. For example, to what extent are African American and Hispanic history, literature, and values emphasized? Are teachers' and educational administrators' expectation levels for their students of different cultures too low? Do teachers have biases about the capabilities of students in particular ethnic groups?

Ongoing research is needed to establish what is really happening in school environments. Perhaps greater resources are necessary to update materials and enhance the multicultural learning atmosphere. Other targets of change may include teacher attitudes and skills. Teachers may require special training to meet the special needs of people from various cultural backgrounds.

Here an angry mother holds her son's hand and grips his face tightly with her other hand. Angry outbursts and loss of emotional control on the part of parents can result in child abuse.

🌿 Child Maltreatment

Ralphie, age 8, came to school one day with his arm in a gigantic cast. His teacher asked him what had happened. He said he fell down the steps and broke it. He didn't seem to want to talk about it much more. When pressed about why the cast had to be so large, he replied, "Oh, that's 'cause I busted it in a couple of places." The teacher thought to herself how strange it was that he suffered such a severe injury from a simple fall. Eight-year-olds are usually so resilient.

Angel, age 4, didn't want to sit down when one of her caregivers at the day-care center asked her to. It was almost as if she was in pain. The caretaker called the center's nurse to examine Angel. The nurse found a doughnut-shaped burn on her buttocks. When asked how it happened, Angel said she didn't remember. The nurse thought to herself how strange this situation was.

As the Kirby Vacuum salesman left the porch of the last house he visited, he wondered to himself how people could possible live that way. There were three filthy, un-kempt small children eating Fruit Loops and glued to a blaring television set. He chastised himself for his poor judgment. That family certainly didn't look like it could afford a dust cloth, let alone a Kirby. He couldn't believe the woman's comments as he was leaving the home. There was a small puppy who leisurely urinated on the porch before his and the woman's very eyes. She looked at the salesman, making no effort to clean up the mess, and said, "Well, at least he didn't do it inside the house." She then turned around and walked back into the house.

Tony thought Alicia, one of his classmates at school, was just beautiful, albeit a little shy. They were both 14. He finally mustered up the courage to go over, talk to her, and ask her if she would like to go to the school dance next Friday night. She shrunk back from him as if she were terrified and said, in a whisper, that she couldn't possibly go. She added apologetically that her mother worked Friday nights and her "Daddy" always took her to the movies. That struck Tony as odd. However, he wasn't up to fighting with parents. Alicia was cute, but she wasn't the only girl around.

Each of the vignettes illustrates children who are being maltreated. Children can be abused or neglected in a number of ways. The umbrella term that includes all of them is child "maltreatment" (Kadushin & Martin, 1988, p. 226). *Maltreatment* includes physical abuse; being given inadequate care and nourishment; deprivation of adequate medical care; insufficient encouragement to attend school consistently; exploitation by being forced to work too hard or too long; "exposure to unwholesome or demoralizing circumstances"; sexual abuse; and emotional abuse and neglect (p. 226). Definitions used by legal and social service agencies vary from locality to locality and state to state. However, most definitions include the above eight aspects of maltreatment.

Many entire books have been written about each form of maltreatment. It is beyond the scope of this book to address them all in great depth. Usually, however, all can be clustered under two headings, child abuse (which includes both physical and sexual abuse) and child neglect. Child maltreatment is a critical issue for social workers to understand. They need to be aware of the clues that maltreatment is occurring. They also need to understand the dynamics of how child victims and their abusers behave in order to assess a situation and make treatment plans. Here we will discuss the incidence and demographics of child maltreatment; the definitions of physical abuse, neglect, emotional maltreatment, and sexual abuse; the characteristics of victims and abusers; and some basic treatment approaches.

Incidence of Child Maltreatment

The actual number of child-abuse and neglect cases is difficult to determine. Definitions for who can and who can't be included in specific categories vary. How cases are reported and data gathered also vary dramatically. One thing is certain: the chances are that any reported figures reflect a small percent of actual cases. Indications are that vast numbers of cases remain unreported.

Nearly 2.9 million cases of child maltreatment were reported in one year (Downs et al., 1996). Of these, 52 percent were neglect, 24 percent were physical abuse, 12 percent were sexual abuse, 6 percent were psychological maltreatment, and the remainder reflect cases that don't fit well into other categories (Videka-Sherman & Mancini, 2001).

Physical Child Abuse

Physical abuse can be defined very generally as "nonaccidental injury inflicted on a child" usually by a caregiver, other adults, or, sometimes, an older child (Crosson-Tower, 2001, p. 196). Some definitions focus on whether the alleged abuser's purpose is to intentionally harm the child. Other definitions ignore the intent and instead emphasize the potential or actual harm done to the child. However, there often is a very fine line between physical abuse and parental discipline. Historically, parents have had the right to bring up their children as they see fit. This has included administering punishment to curb behavior when they thought it was necessary. Consider a father who beats his 13-year-old daughter on the buttocks with a belt because her math grade dropped over the course of a year from an A- to a C. Is that his right or is that child abuse?

Spotlight 4.5 raises some questions concerning what is considered appropriate parental discipline and what is considered abuse in diverse cultural contexts.

Characteristics of Physically Abused Victims. Both physical indicators and behavioral indicators provide clues that a child is being physically abused. Physical indicators can be broken down into six basic categories.

1. *Bruises*. Bruises on any infant should be suspect. Infants are not yet mobile. Therefore, it's not likely that they can bruise themselves. Bruises in unusual places or forming unusual patterns may be indicators of physical abuse. Bruises that take a recognizable shape such as a hand mark or a belt mark should be noted. Finally, bruises that display a variety of colors may portray abuse. This may be an indication that a series of bruises have been received over time. On lighter skinned people, bruises usually progress from an initial bright red to blue to blackish-purple within the first day; they become shaded with a dark green color after about 6 days and finally turn pale green or yellow after 5 to 10 days.

2. *Lacerations*. Cuts, scrapes, or scratches, especially if they occur frequently or their origin is poorly explained may indicate physical abuse. Lacerations on the face and genitalia should be noted. Bite marks also may indicate abuse.

3. *Fractures*. Bone fractures and other skeletal injuries may indicate abuse. Strangely twisted fractures and multiple fractures are especially telltale signs. Infants' fractures may be the result of abuse. Additional indicators are joint dislocations and injuries where the periosteum, the thin membrane covering the bone, is detached.

4. *Burns*. Burns, especially ones that take odd forms or are in patterns, may indicate abuse. Children have been burned by cigarettes and ropes (from being tied up and confined). Burns that occur on inaccessible portions of the body such as the stomach,

---

Spotlight on Diversity 4.5

Diverse Cultural Contexts: Discipline or Abuse?

Crosson-Tower (2001) reflects on some of the issues concerning the cultural context of abuse versus parental discipline:

> Some cultures have customs or practices that child protection [agencies] would consider abusive. For example, some Vietnamese families, in a ritual called cao gio, rub their children with a coin heated to the point that it leaves burn marks. It is an intentional act, but designed, in that culture, to cure a variety of ills. Do the good intentions of the parents therefore exempt this practice from being considered abuse? Similarly, the use of corporal punishment is sanctioned in many Hispanic cultures, but is seen as abusive in this culture when it becomes excessive. Some child protection advocates adopt the "when in Rome do as the Romans do" attitude that says that minorities must abide by the laws of the culture in which they now reside. One Puerto Rican social worker, working in a predominantly Hispanic section of New York City, vehemently disagreed.
>
> "Yes, there are laws," he said, "but those laws were made by anglos. It is fair to deprive new immigrants of everything including their customs? Maybe the laws should be changed?"
>
> The reality is that, if a child is reported as being harmed for whatever reason, a child protection agency will usually investigate. If the reason is one of culture, this will be considered. (p. 196)

genitals, or soles of the feet are clues to abuse. Patterned burns may indicate that the child has been burned with some hot utensil. Saclike burns result when a hand or foot has been submerged into a hot liquid. A donut-shaped burn will occur on the buttocks if a child has been immersed in very hot water. The central unburned area results from where the child's skin touched the bottom of the receptacle holding the water.

5. *Head injuries.* Head injuries that can indicate abuse include skull fractures, loss of hair due to vigorous pulling, and subdural hematomas (that is, blood collected beneath the outer covering of the brain after strenuous shaking or hitting has occurred). Black eyes should be suspect. Retinas may detach or hemorrhage if a child is shaken vigorously.

6. *Internal injuries.* Children have received injuries to their spleen, kidneys, and intestines due to hitting and kicking. The vena cava, the large vein by which blood is brought from the lower extremities to the heart, may be ruptured. Peritonitis, where the lining of the abdominal cavity becomes inflamed, can be another indicator of abuse.

Some of the major questions to ask yourself if you think a child may have been physically abused include the following:

- Does this child get hurt too often for someone his or her age?

- Does the child have multiple injuries?

- Do the injuries occur in patterns, assume recognizable shapes, or look like some of the injuries described earlier?

- Are the injuries such that they don't seem possible for a child at that stage of development?

- Do the explanations given for the injuries make sense?

If something doesn't seem right to you, something may be wrong. If a little voice in the back of your mind is saying, "Oh-oh, that certainly is odd," pay attention. It might be a clue to abuse.

In addition to physical indicators, behavioral indicators provide a second major dimension of clues to physical abuse. A physically abused child tends to exhibit behavioral extremes. Virtually all children may display these extreme behaviors at one time or another. However, the frequency and severity of these behaviors in abused children are clearly notable. At least three categories, plus a variety of specific behavioral indicators, have been established. (Beeler et al., 1990; Crosson-Tower, 2001, 2002; Kolko, 2002; LeVine & Sallee, 1999):

1. Extremely passive, accommodating, submissive behaviors aimed at preserving a low profile and avoiding potential conflict with parents that might lead to abuse. Abused children can be exceptionally calm and docile. They have learned this behavior in order to avoid any possible conflict with the abusive parents. If they are invisible, the parent may not be provoked. Many times abused children will even avoid playing because it draws too much attention to themselves. This behavioral pattern is sometimes called hypervigilance.

2. Notably aggressive behaviors and marked overt hostility toward others, caused by rage and frustration at not getting needs met. Other physically abused children assume an opposite approach to the overly passive manner identified earlier. These children are so desperately in need of attention that they will try almost anything to get it. Even if they can provoke only negative attention from their parents, their aggressive behavior is reinforced.

3. Developmental lags. Because abused children are forced to direct their attention and energy to coping with their abusive situation, they will frequently show developmental delays. These may appear in the form of language delays, poorly developed social skills for their age level, or lags in motor development.

Characteristics of Abusers. The dynamics behind child physical abuse are complex and varied. However, the general characteristics of it tend to fall within six major domains (Crosson-Tower, 2001, 2002; Kolko, 2002; LeVine & Sallee, 1999; Miller-Perrin & Perrin, 1999). Although no one person may have all the problems mentioned, a person will likely experience some.

Need for Personal Support and Nurturance. A basic quality characterizing abusers is low self-esteem. Their emotional needs often remain unfulfilled from their own childhoods. Because their own needs were not met, they are unable to meet the needs of their children. They often invite rejection and hostility because they have little confidence in their own abilities. They don't know how to reach out for support. On the one hand, they often feel they are undeserving. On the other hand, they still have desperate needs for human support. Many perpetrators were themselves abused as children. Note however, that "most abused children do not become abusive parents" (Kolko, 2002, p. 26; Widom, 1989). Some research indicates that only 30 percent of people who were abused as children become abusive later themselves (Kaufman & Zigler, 1987).

Social Isolation. Perpetrators' own self-confidence may be low. They feel that no one will like them, so they isolate themselves. They reject attention, even though they really need others for emotional support. They fear rejection, so they don't try to reach out to others. As a result, when normal everyday stresses build up, they have no one to help them cope.

Communication and Relationship Difficulties. Relationships that abusers do have with family, a significant other, and others are often stormy. Communication may be difficult, hostile, and ineffective. Low self-esteem can also affect the relationship with a partner or a significant other. Abusers may not know how to get their needs met. They may allow their disappointments and anger to build up because they don't know how to express these feelings more appropriately to others. They may feel isolated and alone even within a marriage or partnership. Children may become easy targets for parents who can't communicate with each other. Children may provide a conduit for the expression of violence and anger that are really directed at a spouse or a significant other.

Poor Parenting Skills. Many abusive people don't know how to raise their children in a nurturant family environment. Their own family of origin's environment may have been hostile and abusive. They may never have observed nurturant behavior on the part of their own parents and caregivers. They couldn't learn what they weren't taught.

Additionally, their expectations for what constitutes inappropriate behavior at the various development levels may be lacking. For instance, their demands on the child for behavioral submission and even perfection may be very inappropriate. Parenting behavior may be inconsistent, hostile, or lacking in positive interaction.

Poor General Coping Skills. Perpetrators may be unable to cope with stress, lashing out at their children instead. They may lack anger-management skills. In addition to not knowing how to meet their own emotional needs, they may not have learned to separate their feelings and emotions from their behavior. Therefore, if they get mad, they don't talk about it; they hit.

Another unlearned skill involves the appropriate delineation of responsibility. There is a tendency to blame others for their mistakes. For example, it's the child's fault that he got hit and broke his arm, because he was naughty.

They may also lack decision-making or problem-solving skills. Abusers tend to have little confidence in their own ability, and so have little faith in their own judgment. They have difficulty articulating and evaluating the pros and cons of their alternatives, and are indecisive.

One other skill abusers often fail to master is how to delay their own gratification. The situation here and now becomes all-important. If a child misbehaves, a kick will take care of it immediately. If their stress level is too high, they need immediate relief. They focus on the moment and have trouble looking at what the consequences of their behavior will be in the future.

Extreme External Stress and Life Crises. Child abuse is related to lower socioeconomic status. Poverty causes stress. The abuser, who may lack coping strategies anyway, may feel isolated and incompetent. Additional life crises like losing a job, illness, a marital or family relationship dispute, or even a child's behavior problem, may push people over the brink so that they cannot cope. They may take out their stress on the easiest, most available targets—their children.

Child Neglect

Because neglect involves the absence of resources instead of the presence of something that is negative, it is difficult to define. Every social environment is different. When does a family environment cease being adequate and instead display neglect?

Wolock and Horowitz (1984, p. 15) define child neglect as "the failure of the child's parent or caretaker, who has the material resources to do so, to provide minimally adequate care in the areas of health, nutrition, shelter, education, supervision, affection or attention." Two of the most frequent aspects of neglect involve "deprivation of necessities" and "inadequate supervision" (Kadushin & Martin, 1988, p. 230). Whereas child abuse involves harming a child through actions, child neglect causes a child harm by *not* doing what's necessary. Neglect occurs when children are not given what they need to survive and thrive. This includes the need for supervision. Children need someone to direct them, care for them, support their daily activities, and give them emotional support.

We've already discerned that many times neglect is related to poverty. Many neglectful parents haven't the resources to take care of themselves or their children. For instance, one woman who was charged with child neglect described her living conditions to a judge. She lived in a small, third-floor flat without hot water. She said, "It is an awful place to live. The wallpaper is in strips, the floor board is cracked. The baby is always getting splinters in his hands. The bathroom is on the floor above and two other families use it. The kitchen is on the first floor. I share it with another woman. I have no place to keep food. We buy for one meal at a time" (Hancock, 1963, p. 5).

A young social worker recounts a visit to a family suspected of child neglect:

It was my first visit to the Peterson's home, or should I say second floor flat. The house was in a very poor area in the inner city of Milwaukee. I was supposed to do an initial family assessment. Both parents and three small children were there. The house was filthy. Dirty laundry was heaped in piles on the living room floor. The walls were smeared with grease. Wads of dust rolled along the floor; if they had been at my apartment, I would've called them dinosaur dust bunnies.

The flat was small. The only furniture I could see included two double beds in the tiny living room, and a cheap, old dinette and appliances in the kitchen. The family asked me to sit at the old kitchen table. The chairs were black; I had to restrain myself from wiping one off with a Kleenex before I sat down. But I didn't want to offend my clients. I was clearly aware of my middle-class bias already. None of the children were wearing shoes, which might not be too unusual for summer. However, black dirt streaked all of the children's white arms, legs, feet, hands, and faces. Their hair was dirty and snarled.

As we talked, the parents asked me if I'd like a cup of coffee. The coffee maker in front of me was filthy as was the cup they gave me. It matched the dirty dishes heaped high in the sink. Again, not wanting to offend my clients, I gratefully accepted the coffee. As we talked, I accepted the second cup of coffee and then a third. That was my mistake. Suddenly it occurred to me I desperately needed to use the bathroom. I wondered where it was. I asked if I could, and Mr. Peterson said, "Sure, just a minute." He stood up from the table, picked up a door that had been leaning against the wall around the corner, pointed to a literally open door out of my direct view around the refrigerator. Mortified as I was, I stepped into the bathroom. He laid the door in place (there were no hinges) and said he'd hold it until I was finished. Well, what else was there to do at that point? After I finished, I meekly said, "I'm through," at which point he picked up the door and put it back in its place leaning against the wall. We continued with the interview. One thing is for sure; my coffee drinking behavior on home visits will never be the same!

Characteristics of Neglected Children. Each of us has infinite needs. To define and categorize all that we need to maintain physical and emotional health would be an awesome task. This is why neglect is often difficult to define for any specific family situation. Nonetheless, we will present eight general indicators of child neglect here (Crosson-Tower, 2002; Zuravin & Taylor, 1987). They provide at least a basis for assessment of situations in which neglect may be involved. As with the characteristics of physically abused children, it should be noted that not all of these characteristics apply to all neglected children. However, any one of them might be an indicator of neglect.

1. *Physical health care.* Illnesses are not attended to, and proper dental care is not maintained.

2. *Mental health care.* Children's mental health problems are either ignored or left unattended.

3. *Supervision.* Children often or almost always are left alone without adequate supervision. Very young children or even infants may be left unattended. Another common situation is when very young children are left in the supervision of other children who themselves are too young to assume such responsibility. A third common situation occurs when unsupervised children get involved in activities in which they may harm themselves. For example, we periodically read in the newspaper that a young, unsupervised child plays with matches, starts a fire, and burns down the house or apartment building and usually dies in the fire. A fourth example involves children who don't receive adequate supervision to get them to school on time, or at all.

4. *Substitute child care.* The most blatant form of neglect is abandonment, when parents leave children alone and unattended. A related scenario involves parents who fail to return when they're supposed to, thereby leaving designated care providers in the lurch, not knowing what to do with the children.

5. *Housing hazards.* Housing may have inadequate heat, ventilation, or safety features. Dangerous substances such as drugs or weapons may be left in children's easy reach. Electrical fixtures may not be up to code and therefore may be dangerous.

6. *Household sanitation.* Food may be spoiled. The home may be filled with garbage or excrement. Plumbing might not work or be backed up.

7. *Personal hygiene.* Children's clothing may be ripped, filthy, and threadbare. Their hair might be

unkempt and dirty. They themselves might be un-bathed and odorous.

8. *Nutrition.* Children who frequently complain that they're hungry and searching for food may be victims of neglect. Children receiving food that provides them with inadequate nutrition may be neglected. Significant delays in development resulting from malnutrition may also be a clue to neglect.

Two pronounced physical conditions that can result from extreme neglect are nonorganic failure-to-thrive syndrome and psychosocial dwarfism (Tower, 2002). *Nonorganic failure to thrive syndrome* occurs in infancy. It is characterized by infants who are below the fifth percentile in weight, and sometimes in height (Faller et al., 1981). This means that 95 percent of all other infants that age weigh more. Additionally, the infant must have had normal health at one time. Lags in psychomotor development are also apparent.

Psychosocial dwarfism (PSD) can affect children age 18 months to 16 years. In these children, "emotional deprivation promotes abnormally low growth. PSD children are also below the fifth percentile in weight and height, exhibit retarded skeletal maturation, and a variety of behavioral problems" (Tower, 2002, p. 73). Additionally, they tend to have speech difficulties and problems in their social interactions.

Characteristics of Neglectful Parents. Crosson-Tower (2001) explains: "Parents who neglect were often neglected themselves as children. For them, it is a learned way of life. Their childhoods have produced in them—nothing but anger and indifference. Their adult lives are dedicated to meeting the needs that were not met for them as they were growing up" (p. 203).

Polansky and his colleagues (1975, 1991) studied mothers who neglected their children and divided them into five types:

1. The indifferent, lethargic mother is best described as numb. She has little or no emotional response and has little energy to do anything.

2. The impulsive, irresponsible mother treats her children inconsistently and often inattentively. She has poor impulse control and lacks coping strategies.

3. The depressed mother is reacting to life's unhappy circumstances by giving up. Unlike the indifferent mother, she experiences extreme emotion by being depressed and miserable.

4. Mothers with mental retardation neglect children because of their intellectual inabilities and a lack of the adequate support they need to help them assume their responsibilities. Note that not all women with mental retardation neglect their children.

5. Mothers with serious mental illness, such as psychosis, are unable to function due to bizarre thought processes, delusions, or extreme anxiety.

Emotional Maltreatment

Emotional or psychological maltreatment includes both emotional abuse and emotional neglect. *Emotional abuse,* like other abuse, is more aggressively active and negative. It is "belittling, humiliating, rejecting, undermining a child's self-esteem, and generally not [conducive to] creating a positive atmosphere for a child" (Cohen, 1992, p. 175). *Emotional neglect,* like other forms of neglect, involves passively failing to meet children's needs. It is the "passive or passive/aggressive inattention to the child's emotional needs, nurturing, or emotional well-being" (Brassard, Germaine, & Hart, 1987, p. 267). Parents may deprive an infant of needed holding and attention or may simply ignore children who are in desperate need of emotional involvement. Both emotional neglect and abuse focus on interfering with a child's psychological development and well-being.

There are five basic categories of behavior involved in emotional maltreatment (Garbarino, Guttmann, & Seeley, 1986; Winton & Mara, 2001, pp. 90–91):

1. *Rejection* includes "abandoning the child, failing to acknowledge the child, scapegoating the child [i.e., placing unjustified blame on a child for some behavior or problem or criticizing a child unfairly], and verbally humiliating the child." A parent might emphasize how stupid a child is in front of her friends or neighbors.

2. *Isolation* includes "keeping the child away from a variety of appropriate relationships." It might involve not allowing a child to play normally with peers or seeing other close family members. It might also involve locking a child in a closet for days, months, or years.

3. *Terrorizing* involves "threatening and scaring the child." A parent might threaten to kill a child's beloved pet Chihuahua if he doesn't do the dishes. Or a caregiver might hold a child outside a second-story window and threaten to drop her if she doesn't start "acting her age."

4. *Ignoring* involves failing to respond to a child or simply pretending that the child isn't there. Parents watching television might ignore children's pleas for help with homework or requests for food, thereby forcing children to take care of themselves.

5. *Corrupting* includes "encouraging or supporting illegal or deviant behaviors." A caregiver might force a child to shoplift or drink beer.

Characteristics of Emotionally Maltreated Children. Extensive research reveals that a multitude of problems in adulthood are related to psychological maltreatment during childhood. These include low self-esteem, anxiety, depression, a negative view of life, increased suicide potential, emotional instability, difficulties with impulse control, substance abuse, eating disorders, relationship difficulties, violence, criminal behavior, school problems, and poor performance on intelligence and achievement tests (Hart et al., 2002).

Characteristics of Perpetrators. Like other parents and caregivers who abuse or neglect, those who psychologically maltreat their children usually suffer serious emotional problems or deficits themselves. They may find themselves in a marriage or a partnership that is disappointing or bland, and may seek easy targets (namely, children) for venting their anger and frustration (Covitz, 1986). Like other people who maltreat children, perpetrators may lack coping skills to deal with their problems and emotional issues. Their own emotional needs may not have been met in childhood. Their own parents may have lacked nurturing skills and, thus, failed to teach perpetrators how to be good parents. They may also be dealing with personal problems such as mental illness (O'Hagan, 1993) or alcoholism (Morrow, 1987).

A Macro System Response: Child Protective Services

An abused or neglected child is usually referred to a *child protective services (CPS)* unit. Liederman (1995) describes the function of such units: "CPS agencies investigate reports of child abuse and neglect, assess the degree of harm and the ongoing risk of harm to the child, determine whether the child can remain safely in the home or should be placed in the custody of the state, and work closely with the family or juvenile court regarding appropriate plans for the child's safety and well-being" (p. 425).

CPS workers are usually employed by state or county public agencies whose designated task it is to protect children from harm. During the intervention process, CPS staff work with the courts to declare that children require protection and to determine appropriate safe placement for them. Additionally, CPS workers help families establish treatment plans to address and remedy problems. In the event that problems cannot be resolved, CPS workers try to develop alternative long-term or permanent placement of the children.

Treatment of Physical Abuse, Neglect, and Emotional Maltreatment: Social Work Role

Treatment of physical abuse, neglect, and psychological maltreatment follows the same sequential steps used in other areas of social work intervention. These include receipt of the initial referral, gathering of information about the case through a social study, assessment of the situation, case planning including goal-setting, provision of treatment, evaluation of the effects of treatment, and termination of the case (Kadushin & Martin, 1988). Assessment focuses on many of the dynamics of the case that we've already discussed. A number of variables have been found to affect a worker's decision that a case merits agency intervention (Kadushin & Martin, 1988; Meddin, 1985; Rosen, 1981; Sheafor, Horejsi, & Horejsi, 2000). These include:

1. Clearly visible proof of abuse or environmental characteristics that obviously endanger a child.

2. The degree of the child's helplessness and vulnerability (for example, a physically disabled child or an infant are extremely vulnerable).

3. Self-destructive behavior on the part of the child.

4. A long history of severe abuse.

5. Abusers who show no or little regret for their child's abuse and have difficulty accepting responsibility.

6. Abusers who openly reject the child or blame the child for the problem.

7. Serious emotional disturbances on the part of parents.

8. Lack of cooperation on the part of the parents.

9. Families who are exposed to numerous and severe psychological and social pressures.

10. Isolation of the family and lack of social support systems.

General treatment goals include stopping the maltreatment and strengthening the family enough to keep it together and, hopefully, have it thrive. "Now the predominant belief is that the biological family is the least restrictive environment and the best place for a child to develop if safety and nurturing can be assured" (Mather & Lager, 2000, p. 132). Specific treatment modalities may include family therapy, involvement in support groups (e.g., Parents Anonymous), couple's counseling, or individual counseling, depending on the family's and the individual family members' needs.

Parents may need to learn how to identify their feelings and express them appropriately. They may need to learn how to communicate their needs to others and, in two-parent homes, to each other. They may need to build their self-concepts. They may also need to master effective child management techniques in order to gain control and avoid abusive situations. They may need to be taught how to provide a nurturant family environment for their children and improve their parent-child relationships.

Many times outside resources are helpful. Day care for children can provide some respite for parents and time for themselves. Homemaker service provides training for household management and makes available to them an individual to give support and nurturance. Parental aides can work in homes, form relationships with parents, and model both how to nurture children and effective child management techniques.

Physically abused children also need treatment including medical services for physical damage. Children suffering from developmental delays may need special therapy or remedial help. Exposure to appropriate adult role models through day care is often used. Organizations such as Big Brothers and Big Sisters provide another means of support.

Individual or group counseling may be needed for the maltreated child. Tower (2002) mentions three major categories of victims' needs that should be addressed. These categories relate directly to the characteristics of maltreated children that we've discussed. The first need involves improving the victim's relationships with other people, including both peers and adults. Their old behavior patterns most likely involved either defensive withdrawal or inappropriate aggression. New, more effective social interaction techniques need to be established. The second need involves helping victims learn how to express their feelings. Some maltreated children withhold and suppress their feelings to avoid confrontations; other abused children have never learned how to control their aggressive impulses. The third need concerns the maltreated child's self-concept. For the many reasons we've discussed, maltreated children have a poor opinion of themselves and have little confidence in their own abilities.

A Macro System Response: Involvement of the Courts

Courts become involved in maltreatment cases when "parents abandon their children, severely injure or kill them, place them in imminent danger, sexually abuse them, or fail to cooperate with the protective services agency" (Tower, 2002, p. 282). This is a very difficult and scary process for both the family and victim. Juvenile court procedures vary from state to state. However, most involve three processes, namely the petition, the adjudication, and the disposition.

The *petition* involves a written complaint being submitted to the court that the alleged abuse or neglect has occurred. *Adjudication* involves a hearing where the alleged abuse or neglect is proven or discounted. Both parents and victim are represented by separate legal counsel. The *disposition* involves a hearing where the court determines what is to be done with the child. This is a separate hearing from the adjudication, where it is determined whether the abuse or neglect actually happened. The court process is complex and often lengthy. A large number of variations including additional investigations and settlements are possible.[3] Protective service workers and other social workers are frequently called upon to provide input to aid in the court's decision. Such input often is very influential and can have direct impact on what happens to a child.

Sexual Abuse

Sexual abuse is "any sexual activity with a child where consent is not or cannot be given. . . . This includes sexual contact that is accomplished by force or threat of force, regardless of the age of the participants, and all sexual contact between an adult and a child, regardless of whether there is deception or the child understands the sexual nature of the activity. Sexual contact between an older and a younger child also can be abusive if there is a significant disparity in age, development, or size, rendering the younger child incapable of giving informed consent. The sexually abusive acts may include sexual penetration, sexual touching, or noncontact sexual acts such as exposure or voyeurism" (the act of gaining sexual gratification from watching people who are naked or en-

---

3. For additional information on court involvement, see Tower (2002) for an excellent description of the process.

gaging in sexual activies) (Berliner & Elliott, 2002, p. 55). *Incest,* a special form of sexual abuse, involves "sexual activities between a child and a relative, defined fairly broadly as a parent, stepparent, parent's live-in partner or lover, foster parent, sibling, cousin, uncle, aunt, or grandparent" (McAnulty & Burnette, 2001, p. 410). "Sexual activities" can include a wide variety of sexual behaviors including "pornographic photography, sexual gestures, parental exposure of genitalia, fondling, petting, fellatio, cunnilingus, intercourse, and any and all varieties of sexual contact" (Mayer, 1983, p. 4).

Although all states forbid sexual abuse (Myers, 1998), specific statutes, definitions, and punishments vary widely. Concerning incidence of sexual abuse, it is estimated that at least 20–25 percent of women and 5–15 percent of men have been victims of sexual abuse (Berliner & Elliott, 2002; Finkelhor, 1994). Many experts feel that cases of sexual abuse are vastly underreported (Berliner & Elliott, 2002; Widom & Morris, 1997; Williams, 1994).

The Dynamics of Child Sexual Abuse. A major myth involved in child sexual abuse is that children should be warned about strangers. They're told that they should not get into cars when strangers offer them lollipops and they should not talk to strange men who are hiding behind park bushes. The reality is that children are in much greater danger from people who are close to them, from people whom they trust.

Children are easy victims for sexual abuse. Because of the anxiety most people harbor about sexuality in general, children have little information about sex. They have limited life experience upon which to base judgments. Thus, they can easily be misled and tricked. They are small compared to adults and are easily intimidated. Adults, in some ways, are godlike to children. Adults tell them what to do, when to go to bed, when they can cross the street, and if they can go to McDonald's. Children are oriented toward obeying adults and most likely want to please them, especially those adults who control their access to being loved, having food and shelter, and feeling safe.

The "vast majority of offenders are male, although boys are more likely than girls to be abused by women (20 percent vs. 5 percent) . . . , and 40 percent of the reported cases of day care sexual abuse involve female offenders" (Berliner & Elliott, 2002, pp. 56–57). Sixty percent of sexual abuse occurs within the family (Tower, 2002). This does not mean that the remaining 40 percent is perpetrated by strangers. Rather, much extrafamilial abuse is done by others who are close to the family and trusted by the child. Only 5–15 percent of sexual abuse is committed by strangers (Berliner and Elliott, 2002). When sexual abuse is perpetrated by someone outside the family, that person is usually called a *pedophile* (someone who prefers children for sexual gratification). Because of its prevalence, we focus on incest in the following discussion.

Progression of the incestuous relationship is usually gradual. It may even appear innocent enough at first. For instance, the adult might appear nude or undress before a child. It then progresses to greater and greater intimacy. Carnes (1983) suggests that there are five phases of sexual abuse. First comes the *engagement* phase. Here the perpetrator will experiment with the child to see how close he can get and how the child will react. The second phase is the *sexual interaction* phase. Sexual activity in various degrees of intimacy occurs during this phase. Often the longer this phase lasts, the more intimate the abuser becomes with the victim. The third phase is one of *secrecy.* Sexual activity has already occurred so the abuser will use some manipulations to hold the victim ensnared in the abuse. For instance, the perpetrator might say, "Don't you tell your mommy; she won't like you anymore," or, "This is our special secret because I love you so very much," or "If you tell anybody, I'll punish you." Threats and guilt are used to maintain the secret. The fourth phase is the *disclosure.* For one reason or another, the victim reveals that abuse has occurred. It may be physically initiated if the child contracts a sexually transmitted disease or is damaged in some way. It may be the result of an accident if the sexual activity was observed or someone noted and reported the child's indicative behavior. It may be that the victim feels she must tell someone because she can't stand it anymore. The fifth and final phase is *post-disclosure.* This is a time of high anxiety for both victim and family. Feelings may include denial on the part of the perpetrator, guilt and insecurity on the part of the victim, and anger on the part of other family members.

The following factors increase the risk of sexual abuse (Berliner & Elliott, 2002; Crosson-Tower, 2002; McAnulty & Burnett, 2001).

Child risk factors include:

- Being a girl.
- Being at an age slightly before puberty.
- Having a disability—children with disabilities are more vulnerable and less able to defend themselves.

Family risk factors are:

- Absence of a biological parent from the home—stepfather or a mother's boyfriend may be present.

- Family conflict and communication problems—when communication is poor, roles may become blurred. For example, when husband and wife or partners are in conflict, the male partner may turn to a female child to fulfill his needs.

- Family isolation—because secrecy is necessary for abuse to occur, a family may intensify its isolation even more.

- Having a mother who is not readily available to children (e.g., being ill or employed outside the home)—if communication is poor between mothers and daughters, it becomes even more difficult for daughters to turn to their mothers for help.

Consider the unknown proportion of mothers that do not know that the incest is occurring. The marriage is conflictual. Communication is lacking between the woman and her husband and the woman and her daughter. She may see things that are strange, but she works hard to deny them. She has a lot to lose if the incest is brought out into the open. She may feel resentment toward a daughter who has taken her husband and lover away from her. She may feel shame that this taboo is occurring within her own family. She may feel guilt for being such a failure to her husband that he had to turn to another. She may desperately fear having her family ripped apart. It is a very difficult situation for a mother in the incest triangle. She is not the abuser. Yet no alternatives are available to her that offer her a happy solution.

In some ways the mother in the incestuous triangle is also a victim. She has been raised in a patriarchal society where she has been taught to be dependent, unassertive, and passive. She has also been taught that she is supposed to be the caretaker of the emotional well-being of her family. She has not been given the skills needed to aggressively fight for herself and her daughter in this desperate situation.

Characteristics of Sexual Abuse Victims. Children who are sexually abused may display a variety of physical, psychological, and behavioral indicators. Physical indicators may include a variety of physical problems that are sexually related such as sexually transmitted diseases, problems with the throat or mouth, difficulties with urination, penile or vaginal discharge, or bruises in the genital area. Pregnancy is also an indicator.

Psychological indicators include low self-esteem, emotional disturbance, anger, fear, anxiety, and depression, sometimes to the point of becoming suicidal (Berliner &

Elliott, 2002; McAnulty & Burnette, 2001). Behavioral indicators include withdrawing from others and experiencing difficulties in peer interaction. Although depression and aggressive behavior can characterize victims of either gender, girls are more likely to experience depression and boys are more likely to act out aggressively (Finkelhor, 1990). Often, victims of either gender engage in excessive sexual activity and inappropriate sexual behavior (Friedrich et al., 2001).

Behavior related to sex that strikes you as being odd may also be an indicator. This refers once again to your "gut reaction" that something's wrong. For example, a child may know sexual terms or display sexual gestures that strike you as being inappropriate for her age level. A child may touch herself or others inappropriately in a sexual manner. A child may express desperate fears about being touched, undressing and taking showers in gym class, or of being alone with a certain gender or with certain people.

Specific things that children say may strike you as being odd and may be indicative of sexual abuse. For instance, a child may say: "Daddy and I have a secret"; "My babysitter wears red underwear"; or "I don't like going to Aunt Shirley's house. She diddles me."

Long-Term Effects of Sexual Abuse. We emphasize that, although there is significant research that indicates that sexual abuse victims can suffer long-term results, this is a very complex issue. Abuse can vary in intensity, duration, and extent of trauma to the survivor. Long-term effects vary dramatically from one person to another. Receiving treatment can also help survivors deal with issues and effects.

Research has established that survivors, as compared with people who have not been sexually abused, are more likely to experience emotional problems such as depression, fear of relationships, interpersonal problems, sexual dysfunctions, and symptoms of posttraumatic stress (Berliner & Elliott, 2002). *Posttraumatic stress disorder* is a condition where a person continues to reexperience an excessively traumatic event like a bloody battle experience or a sexual assault. Symptoms include extreme anxiety; nightmares; an inability to sleep or stay awake; an inability to concentrate; and explosive, angry emotional outbursts.

Note that because of the tremendous disparity in how sexual abuse affects individuals, no specific variables are consistently linked to long-term problems (Miller-Perrin & Perrin, 1999). A significant number of survivors fail to develop serious problems in adulthood (Finkelhor, 1990).

Perhaps as many as one-third of survivors report having no problems, and many who do have problems indicate that they get better as time passes (Kendall-Tackett, Williams, & Finkelhor, 1993; Rind, Tromovitch, & Bauserman, 1998).

Research has established that the following 5 variables increase the risk of more serious problems in adulthood for survivors of sexual abuse (Berliner & Elliott, 2002; Crosson-Tower, 2002; Finkelhor, 1990; Luster & Small, 1997; McAnulty & Burnette, 2001; Rind & Tromovitch, 1997):

1. *Closer relationship to the perpetrator.* Sexual abuse by a family member, or by another person the victim feels close to and trusts, is related to deeper trauma in adulthood.

2. *Duration of the abuse.* The longer the abuse continued, the greater the likelihood of long-term negative effects. However, even a single incident can cause severe trauma if extremely violent or sadistic behavior (the infliction of pain on the survivor for the offender's sexual gratification) occurred (Beitchman et al., 1992).

3. *Use of force and the intensity of abuse.* Using force or causing pain tends to result in more devastating effects. The occurrence of penal penetration is also related to greater trauma.

4. *Absence of parental and other support.* When a victim first reveals the abuse, lack of support from those close to her potentially results in greater long-term problems. If others criticize or blame her, she may suffer significant psychological distress. The victim may even decide to hide into adulthood what she may perceive as her "dirty secret." See Highlight 4.4 for suggestions about how to talk and positively relate to victims of sexual abuse.

5. *Inability of the survivor to cope.* Some individuals have a personality structure that naturally allows them to

---

Highlight 4.4

Suggestions for Talking to Children Victimized by Sexual Assault

- Always believe the child. It takes courage to talk about such difficult things, and it's easy to turn the child off.

- Be warm and empathic. Encourage the child to talk freely to you. Reflecting the child's feelings back is useful.

- Don't react with shock or disgust no matter what the child tells you. That only communicates to the child that he or she is the one to blame.

- Encourage the child to share all feelings with you, including the negative ones. Even getting the angry feelings out helps the child overcome the feelings of victimization. Give the child the chance to ventilate his or her feelings so he or she can deal with them.

- *Listen* to the child. Don't disagree or argue. Interrupt only when you have to in order to understand what the child is saying.

- Talk to the child in a private place. The child may feel much more comfortable if others aren't around to hear.

- Tell the child that he or she is not the only child who has had this experience. Other children have, too.

- Allow the child to express feelings of guilt. Emphasize to the child that it was *not* his or her fault. The adult abuser is the one who has a problem and needs help.

- Talk in language that the child can understand. Give accurate information when it's needed. Let the child repeat things back to you to make certain he or she understands.

- Tell the child that you are very glad he or she told you about the incident(s). Emphasize that it was the *right* thing to do.

- Ask if the child would like to ask you any questions, and be sure to answer them honestly.

- Do not treat the child any differently after he or she has told you. This only communicates that you think he or she is to blame or did the wrong thing.

- If the child asks you to keep the abuse secret, answer honestly. Tell the child that you only want to help, that secrets that hurt people aren't good to keep, and that the secrets need to be brought out into the open in order to help the person who abused him or her.

- Finally, depending on your situation, don't let the issue drop. If you are the social worker involved, pursue the problem. Otherwise, tell the parents and/or the appropriate authorities so that the child can get help.

cope more effectively with crises and stress. Human personality is a complicated concept.

Treatment of Sexual Abuse: Social Work Role. Because of its prevalence, we will focus on treatment of the incestuous family. Treatment usually progresses through three phases (Tower, 2002, pp. 318–320). The first is the *disclosure-panic* phase. Strong feelings characterize this period of crisis. Family members display much anger and denial. The victim is often frightened about what will happen and eager to blame herself. The second phase is the *assessment-awareness* phase. During this phase, the family acknowledges that the abuse has occurred and struggles to deal with its consequences. Family members learn about themselves and the dynamics involved in their family interaction. The social worker works to redefine and realign the boundaries of subsystems within the family. This phase tends to be characterized by conflicting feelings. On the one hand, they are angry that the abuse has occurred and eager to blame each other. On the other hand, they are struggling to realign their relationships and express the feelings of love they have for each other. The third phase is the *restructure* phase. Here the family regains emotional health. Boundaries are clearly established and family members learn how to function within them. Communication is greatly enhanced and members can use it to work out their differences. Parents take responsibility for their behavior, and the victim feels much better about herself.

Treatment has several major objectives (Kadushin & Martin, 1988). The first is to have the abuser accept responsibility for his behavior. The second is for the victim to acknowledge that the abuse was not her fault, that she can forgive other family members, and that she feels more confident in her ability to say "no" in potentially abusive situations. A third is to have the mother improve her own self-esteem, her feeling of significance and control within the family, and her ability to protect her children from abuse. A fourth objective is to develop communication among all family members, especially the marital subsystem, in order to maintain the appropriate subsystem boundaries.

Treatment themes for all family members include enhancement of self-concept and self-confidence, improved communication of feelings and ideas, and definition and maintenance of appropriate boundaries between the various subsystems. Several specific goals are important for the victim (Mayer, 1983). First, she needs to learn how to identify, express, and share her feelings, even when they are negative and frightening. Second, she needs to develop her assertiveness skills. She needs to

develop confidence that her own needs are important and that both her needs and the needs of others should be addressed in her relationships with others. Many times group treatment is also helpful for her to achieve these goals.

Prevention of Sexual Abuse: The Need for a Macro System Response. The ideal way of dealing with sexual abuse is to prevent it from happening at all. Information and education are the keys to prevention. Parents need both education about how to raise children and knowledge that in the event they are in crisis resources are available to help. Parenting education could be made a required part of all high school curricula. Special programs could be made readily available in the community to help parents with these issues.

Educating Children about Sexual Abuse. Children need to be educated about sexual abuse. There are three basic preventative approaches. First, children should be taught that their bodies are their own and that they have private places where nobody can force them to be touched. What comes to mind are the parents who tell their 4-year-old son to go up to each relative at the culmination of an extended family event and "give them a kiss." The child obviously finds this distasteful. He frowns, looks down at his shoes, and hides behind his mother. He knows that old Aunt Hilda gives really slobbery, wet ones. And, she hugs him like The Crusher in a wrestling match, too. He hates the very thought of it, even though his aunt is a kind person who loves him.

Children should have the right to say no if they don't want to have such intimacy. Parents and teachers can help children determine what are "good touches" and what are "bad touches." They can also help children develop the confidence to say "no" to adults in uncomfortable situations involving touching them in ways they don't like.

A second preventative measure for children is to learn correct sexual terminology right from the beginning. It's easy for parents, especially if they're uncomfortable with sexual terminology themselves, to sugar-coat words and refer to "ding-dongs" and "bumps." One 3-year-old girl came out into the midst of a family gathering and told her mother, "My pooderpie hurts." She had her hand placed over her clothes on her genital area. Her mother, with a look of terror, desperation, and embarrassment, jumped up and dashed off with her to the bathroom. Apparently, the little girl had to urinate and didn't identify the feeling as such. A few months later, the same 3-year-old was chattering on about some topic that was desperately important to a 3-year-old, pointed to her buttocks, and interjected something about her pooderpie again. My reaction was, "Yikes, the pooderpie has moved. Where will it go next?"

The point is that if this little girl would tell someone that a person touched her pooderpie, that someone might respond, "Oh, that's nice." Whomever she tells would have no idea what she was talking about. Inaccurate, childish terminology does not equip children with the communication skills they need if they encounter a sexually abusive situation. Children need to be able to specify what people are doing or have tried to do to them. Only then can their caregivers adequately protect them.

This leads to our third preventative suggestion. Lines of communication between caregivers and children should be encouraged and kept open. Children need to be able to feel that they can share things with parents, including the things that bother them. In the event that children are placed in a potentially abusive situation, they need to be encouraged and to be able to "tell someone."

◖ Summary

Socialization refers to the process through which individuals learn proper ways of acting in a culture. Wide variations exist in family structures. Social forces and macro systems can affect families both positively and negatively. Systems theory concepts can be readily applied to family systems. Family life cycles often involve environmental variables such as culture, ethnicity, and sexual orientation.

Learning theory provides an exceptionally useful means of conceptualizing and understanding human behavior. It is a theoretical orientation that emphasizes behavior, its preceding event, and its subsequent consequences. Major approaches within learning theory include respondent conditioning, which focuses on stimuli and responses; modeling, which is based on observation; and operant conditioning, which emphasizes regulating the consequences of behavior. Major terms in operant conditioning are positive and negative reinforcement, punishment, and extinction.

Applications of learning theory to practice include the use of positive reinforcement, punishment, and time-out from reinforcement. When using positive reinforcement, quality, immediacy, and frequency is important. When using punishment, it's important to attend to potential negative consequences and use punishment only selectively. Other significant issues in the application of learning theory include accidental training, using behaviorally specific terminology, measuring improvement, and the importance of parental attention.

As members of family systems, children are affected by sibling subsystems and gender role socialization. The father's role in the family, availability and nature of support systems, and perspectives on disciplining children vary greatly among cultures. Two important dimensions concerning family diversity are cultural pluralism and internal variations, or subgroups, within a culture. Themes in understanding Hispanic and Latino families include the significance of a common language, the importance of family relationships, and the strict division of gender roles. Concepts especially relevant to Native American families are the importance of extended family, emphasis on individualism, the significance of harmony with nature, treatment of time, and spirituality. Themes that characterize Asian American families include the importance of family as the primary unit, interdependence among family members, investment in children, and patriarchal hierarchy.

Play is a significant aspect of children's interaction and development. Children tend to progress through developmental levels of play. Gender differences exist in terms of aggression and toy preference. Peer groups and popularity are very important to children. Children spend enormous amounts of time watching television, resulting in concerns about the portrayal of violence, sexually explicit situations, an unrealistic depiction of the world, and the underrepresentation of women. The school environment also provides a major arena for socialization.

Large numbers of children are physically abused, neglected, emotionally maltreated, or sexually abused. Indications of physical abuse include bruises, lacerations, fractures, burns, head injuries, internal injuries, extremely passive or aggressive behavior, role reversals with parents, and lags in development. Child neglect is often characterized by lack of adequate physical or mental health care, supervision, and basic housing conditions including sanitation, personal hygiene, and nutrition, as well as substitute child care. Emotional maltreatment involves active abuse such as belittling, rejecting, or terrorizing, in addition to ignoring and failing to meet emotional needs. Child protective services and the courts reflect macro system responses to child maltreatment. Sexual abuse often occurs in a gradual process by someone a child knows and trusts. Physical and behavioral indicators of abuse may be evident. Treatment for sexual abuse involves emphasizing that the abuser is responsible, enhancing family members' self-esteem, and improving family communication. Prevention through education is recommended.

InfoTrac College Edition Keywords

child abuse   empowering families   school environment   socialization
child neglect   family life cycle   sexual abuse

On the Internet

Australia Family Resources

http://www.happyfamiliesdownunder.com.au/

Their goal is for happy families down under to become the one-stop place where families of any background can easily access a vast array of information to meet their special needs.

International Child Abuse Network

http://www.yesican.org/

Mission statement: Working worldwide to break the cycle of child abuse.

Parenting Today's Teen

http://parentingteens.about.com/

Information, insight, and support are provided for parents of teens.

Zero to Three

http://www.zerotothree.org/

Zero to Three's mission is to promote the healthy development of our nation's infants and toddlers by supporting and strengthening families, communities, and those who work on their behalf.

CHAPTER 5

Ethnocentrism and Racism

Abraham Lincoln has the reputation of being the key person in ending slavery in our country. Yet, it appears that Lincoln held racist beliefs, as indicated in the following excerpt from a speech he delivered in 1858:

> *I will say, then, that I am not, nor ever have been in favor of bringing about in any way the social and political equality of the white and black races; that I am not, nor ever have been, in favor of making voters or jurors of Negroes, nor of qualifying them to hold office, nor to inter-marry with white people . . . and inasmuch as they cannot so live, while they do remain together there must be the position of superior and inferior, and I as much as any other man am in favor of having the superior position assigned to the white race.*

Such a statement needs to be viewed in its historical context. Our country was more racist years ago than it is today. Lincoln, who was in the vanguard of moving for greater equality for African Americans, was also socialized by his culture to have racist attitudes. (The impact of culture on individuals was discussed in Chapter 1.)

A PERSPECTIVE

Nearly every time we turn on the evening news on television, we see ethnic and racial conflict—riots, beatings, murders, and civil wars. In recent years we have seen clashes resulting in bloodshed in areas ranging from Northern Ireland to Iraq, from Bosnia to Israel, and from the United States to South America. Practically every nation with more than one ethnic group has had to deal with ethnic conflict. The oppression and exploitation of one ethnic group by another is particularly ironic in democratic nations, considering these societies claim to cherish freedom, equality, and justice. In reality, the dominant group in all societies that controls the political and economic institutions rarely agrees to share equally its power and wealth with other ethnic groups. Ethnocentrism and racism are factors that can adversely affect the growth and development of minority group members.

This chapter will:

▶ Define and describe ethnic groups, ethnocentrism, racial groups, racism, prejudice, discrimination, oppression, and institutional discrimination.
▶ Outline the sources of prejudice and discrimination.
▶ Summarize the effects and costs of discrimination and oppression and describe effects of discrimination on human growth and development.
▶ Suggest strategies to promote social and economic justice.
▶ Outline some guidelines for social work practice with racial and ethnic groups.
▶ Forecast the pattern of race and ethnic relations in the United States in the future.

🌿 Ethnic Groups and Ethnocentrism

An ethnic group has a sense of togetherness, a conviction that its members form a special group, and a sense of common identity or peoplehood. Barker (1999) defines an *ethnic group* as "a distinct group of people who share a common language, set of customs, history, culture, race, religion, or origin" (p. 159).

Practically every ethnic group has a strong feeling of *ethnocentrism,* "an orientation or set of beliefs that holds one's own culture, ethnic or racial group, or nation is superior to others" (Barker, 1999, p. 160). Ethnocentrism leads members of ethnic groups to view their culture

Navajo Indians creating a traditional sand painting in Hogan, Arizona. Members of ethnic groups share a feeling of common identity.

© Paul Chesley/Getty Images

Spotlight on Diversity 5.1

Violence Against Minorities in the United States

Minorities have been subjected to extensive violence by whites in our society. (It has been a two-way street because a number of whites have been subjected to violence by nonwhites.)

During the second half of the nineteenth century, frequent massacres of Chinese mining and railroad workers occurred in the West. During one railroad strike in 1885, white workers stormed a Chinese community in Rock Springs, Wyoming, murdered 16 persons, and burned all the homes to the ground. No one was arrested. In 1871 a white mob raided the Chinese community in Los Angeles, killing 19 persons and hanging 15 to serve as a warning to survivors (Pinkney, 1972).

Pinkney (1972) comments on the treatment of African American slaves by their white owners:

Few adult slaves escaped some form of sadism at the hands of slaveholders. A female slaveholder was widely known to punish her slaves by beating them on the face. Another burned her slave girl on the neck with hot tongs. A drunken slaveholder dismembered his slave and threw him piece by piece into a fire. Another planter dragged his slave from bed and inflicted a thousand lashes on him. (p. 73)

Slaveowners often used a whip, made of cowskin or rawhide, to control their slaves. An elaborate punishment system was developed, linking the number of lashes to the seriousness of the offenses with which slaves were charged.

Shortly before the Civil War, roving bands of whites commonly descended on African American communities and terrorized and beat the inhabitants. Slaves sometimes struck back and killed their slaveowners or other whites. It has been estimated that during Reconstruction, more than 5,000 African Americans were killed in the South by white vigilante groups (Pinkney, 1972).

Following the Civil War, lynching of African Americans increased and continued into the 1950s. African Americans were lynched for such minor offenses as peeping into a window, attempting to vote, using offensive remarks, seeking employment in a restaurant, getting into a dispute with a white person, and expressing sympathy for another African American who had already been lynched. Arrests for lynching African Americans were rare. Lynch mobs included not only men, but sometimes also women and children. Some lynchings were publicly announced and the public was invited to participate. The public often appeared to enjoy the activities and urged the active lynchers on to greater brutality.

Race riots between whites and African Americans have also been common since the Civil War. During the summer of 1919, for example, 26 major race riots occurred, the most serious of which was in Chicago. In this riot, which lasted from July 27 to August 2, 38 persons were killed, 537 were injured, and more than 1,000 were left homeless (Waskow, 1967).

Native Americans have been subjected to kidnapping, massacre, conquest and forced assimilation, and

---

as superior, as the one that other cultures should adopt. Ethnocentrism also leads to prejudice against foreigners, who may be viewed as barbarians, uncultured people, or savages.

Feelings of ethnic superiority within a nation are usually accompanied by the belief that political and economic domination by one's own group is natural, is morally right, is in the best interest of the nation, and perhaps also is God's will. Ethnocentrism has been a factor leading to some of the worst atrocities in history, such as the American colonists' nearly successful attempt to exterminate Native Americans and Adolf Hitler's mass executions of more than 6 million European Jews, and millions more gypsies, people with disabilities, and other minority group members.

In interactions between nations, ethnocentric beliefs sometimes lead to wars and serve as justifications for foreign conquests. At practically any point in the last several centuries at least a few wars have occurred between nations in which one society has been seeking to force its culture on another or to eradicate another culture. For example, Israel has been involved in bitter struggles with Arab countries in the Middle East for more than 4 decades over

territory ownership. Bosnians, Serbs, Croats, and others are fighting for domination in what was once Yugoslavia.

Spotlight 5.1 details some of the violence against minorities that has taken place in U.S. history.

Race and Racism

Although a racial group is often also an ethnic group, the two groups are not necessarily the same. A *race* is believed to have a common set of physical characteristics. But the members of a racial group may or may not share the sense of togetherness or identity that holds an ethnic group together. A group that is both a racial group and an ethnic group is Japanese Americans, who have some common physical characteristics and also have a sense of peoplehood (Coleman & Cressey, 1984). On the other hand, white Americans and white Russians are of the same race, but they hardly have a sense of togetherness. In addition, some ethnic groups are composed of a variety of races. For example, a religious group (such as Roman Catholic) is sometimes considered an ethnic group and is composed of members from diverse racial groups.

murder. Some tribes were completely exterminated. The treatment of Native Americans by whites in North American stands as one of the most revolting series of acts of violence in history.

The extermination of Native Americans began with the early Pilgrims. They were the first to establish a policy to massacre and exterminate Native Americans in this country. In 1636 the Massachusetts Bay Puritans sent a force to massacre the Pequot, a division of the Mohegan tribe. The dwellings were burned, and 600 inhabitants were slaughtered (Pinkney, 1972).

In 1642 the governor of New Netherlands began offering bounties for Native American scalps. A year later this same governor ordered the massacre of the Wappinger tribe. Pinkney (1972) describes the massacre:

During the massacre infants were taken from their mother's breast, cut in pieces and thrown into a fire or into the river. Some children who were still alive were also thrown into the river, and when their parents attempted to save them they drowned along with their children. When the massacre was over, the members of the murder party were congratulated by the grateful governor. (p. 96)

A major motive for this violence was that the European settlers were land-hungry. The deliberate massacre and extermination of Native Americans continued from the 1660s throughout most of the 1800s. The whites frequently made and broke treaties with Native Americans during these years—and ended up taking most of their land and sharply reducing their population. For example,

in a forced march on foot covering several states, an estimated 4,000 Cherokees died from cold and exhaustion in 1838 (Pinkney, 1972). During these years Native Americans were considered savage beasts. Many whites felt, "The only good Indian is a dead one," and they exterminated Native Americans because it was felt they impeded economic progress.

Today, racial clashes between minority group members still occur, but on a smaller scale on the street and in some of our schools. Recent years have seen a resurgence of the Ku Klux Klan, the American Nazi Party, and other white power groups such as "skinheads." Demonstrations by these organizations have led to several bloody clashes between supporters and those opposed to these racist groups.

Throughout U.S. history there have also been incidents of police brutality by white officers against members of minority groups. For example, police brutality received national attention in 1991 when an African American motorist, Rodney King, was stopped after a lengthy car chase and beaten by four club-wielding white police officers in Los Angeles. The beatings were videotaped by a bystander. Mr. King received more than 50 blows from clubs and sustained 11 fractures in his skull, a broken ankle, and a number of other injuries. In April 1992, a jury (with no African American members) found the police officers "not guilty" on charges of using excessive force. The reaction of African Americans and others in Los Angeles has been described as the worst civil unrest in more than a century—nearly 60 people were killed and over $800 million in damage occurred from rioting, looting, and destruction over a period of 3 days.

In contrast to ethnocentrism, racism is more likely to be based on physical differences than on cultural differences. *Racism* is "stereotyping and generalizing about people, usually negatively, because of their race; commonly a basis of discrimination against members of racial minority groups" (Barker, 1999, p. 397). Similar to ethnocentric ideologies, most racist ideologists assert that members of other racial groups are inferior. Some white Americans in this country have gone to extreme and morally reprehensible limits to seek to attain greater control and power over other racial groups.

☙ Aspects of Social and Economic Forces: Prejudice, Discrimination, and Oppression

Barker (1999) defines prejudice as: "An opinion about an individual, group, or phenomenon that is developed without proof or systematic evidence. This prejudgment may be favorable but is more often unfavorable and may become institutionalized in the form of a society's laws or

customs" (p. 373). *Prejudice,* in regard to race and ethnic relations, is making negative prejudgments. Prejudiced people apply racial stereotypes to all or nearly all members of a group according to preconceived notions of what they believe the group to be like and how they think the group will behave. Racial prejudice results from the belief that people who have different skin color and other physical characteristics also have innate differences in behaviors, values, intellectual functioning, and attitudes.

The word *discrimination* has two very different meanings. It has the positive meaning "the process of distinguishing between two objects, ideas, situations or stimuli" (Barker, 1999, p. 133). However, in group relations, it is "the prejudgment and negative treatment of people based on identifiable characteristics such as race, gender, religion, or ethnicity" (Barker, 1999, p. 133). Racial or ethnic discrimination involves denying to members of minority groups equal access to opportunities, residential housing areas, membership in religious and social organizations, involvement in political activities, access to community services, and so on.

Prejudice is a combination of stereotyped beliefs and negative attitudes, so that prejudiced individuals *think about people* in a predetermined, usually negative, categorical way. *Discrimination* involves physical actions, unequal *treatment of people* because they belong to a category. Discriminatory behavior often derives from prejudiced attitudes. Merton (1949), however, noted that prejudice and discrimination can occur independently of each other. Merton (1949) described four different types of people in terms of prejudice:

1. *The unprejudiced nondiscriminator,* in both belief and practice, upholds American ideals of freedom and equality. This person is not prejudiced against other groups and, on principle, will not discriminate against them.

2. *The unprejudiced discriminator* is not personally prejudiced but may sometimes, reluctantly, discriminate against other groups because it seems socially or financially convenient to do so.

3. *The prejudiced nondiscriminator* feels hostile toward other groups but recognizes that law and social pressures are opposed to overt discrimination. Reluctantly, this person does not translate prejudice into action.

4. *The prejudiced discriminator* does not believe in the values of freedom and equality and consistently discriminates against other groups in both word and deed.

An example of an unprejudiced discriminator is the unprejudiced owner of a condominium complex in an all-white middle-class suburb who refuses to sell a condominium to an African American family because of fear (founded or unfounded) that the sale would reduce the sale value of the remaining units. An example of a prejudiced nondiscriminator is a personnel director of a fire department who believes Mexican Americans are unreliable and poor firefighters yet complies with affirmative action efforts to hire and train Mexican American firefighters.

It is very difficult to keep personal prejudices from eventually leading to some form of discrimination. Strong laws and firm informal social norms are necessary to break the relationships between prejudice and discrimination.

Discrimination is of two types. *De jure discrimination* is legal discrimination. The so-called Jim Crow laws in the South (enacted shortly after the Civil War ended) gave force of law to many discriminatory practices against African Americans, including denial of the right to trial, prohibition against voting, and prohibition against interracial marriage. Today, in the United States, there is no de jure racial discrimination because such laws have been declared unconstitutional.

De facto discrimination refers to discrimination that actually exists, whether legal or not. Most acts of de facto discrimination abide by powerful informal norms that are discriminatory. Cummings (1977) gives an example of this type of discrimination and urges victims to confront assertively such discrimination:

Scene: department store. Incident: several people are waiting their turn at a counter. The person next to be served is a black woman; however, the clerk waits on several white customers who arrived later. The black woman finally demands service, after several polite gestures to call the clerk's attention to her. The clerk proceeds to wait on her after stating, "I did not see you." The clerk is very discourteous to the black customer, and the lack of courtesy is apparent, because the black customer had the opportunity to observe treatment of the other customers. De facto discrimination is most frustrating . . .; [after all, say some] the customer was served. Most people would rather just forget the whole incident, but it is important to challenge the practice even though it will possibly put you through more agony. One of the best ways to deal with this type of discrimination is to report it to the manager of the business. If it is at all possible, it is important to involve the clerk in the discussion. (p. 200)

Barker (1999) defines oppression as: "the social act of placing severe restrictions on a group or institution. Typically, a government or political organization that is in power places these restrictions formally or covertly on oppressed groups so that they may be exploited and less able to compete with other social groups" (p. 339). *Oppression* is the unjust or cruel exercise of authority or power. Members of minority groups in our society are frequently victimized by oppression from segments of the white power structure. Oppression and discrimination are closely related because all acts of oppression are also acts of discrimination.

Racial and Ethnic Stereotypes

Barker (1999) defines stereotypes as "preconceived and relatively fixed ideas about an individual, group, or social status. These ideas are usually based on superficial characteristics or overgeneralizations of traits observed in some members of the group" (p. 465). Racial and ethnic *stereotypes* involve attributing a fixed and usually inaccurate or unfavorable conception to a racial or ethnic group. Stereotypes are closely related to the way we think, because we seek to perceive and understand things in categories. We need categories to group things that are similar in order to study them and to communicate about them. We have stereotypes about many categories, including mothers, fathers, teenagers, communists, Republicans, school teachers, farmers, construction workers, miners, politicians, Mormons, and Italians. These stereotypes may contain some useful and accurate information about a member in any category. Yet, each member of any category will have many characteristics that are not suggested by the stereotypes, and is apt to have some characteristics that run counter to some of the stereotypes.

Racial stereotypes involve differentiating people in terms of color or other physical characteristics. For example, historically there was the erroneous stereotype that Native Americans become easily intoxicated and irrational when using alcohol. This belief was then translated into laws that prohibited Native Americans from buying and consuming alcohol. A more recent stereotype is that African Americans have a natural ability to play basketball and certain other sports. While at first glance, such a stereotype appears complimentary to African Americans, it has broader, negative implications. The danger is that, if people believe the stereotype, they may also feel that other abilities and capacities (such as intelligence, morals, and work productivity) are also determined by race. In other words, believing this positive stereotype increases the probability that people will also believe negative stereotypes.

❦ Racial and Ethnic Discrimination Is the Problem of Whites

From its earliest days, our society has singled out certain minorities to treat unequally. Barker (1999) defines a *minority* as "a group, or a member of a group, of people of a distinct racial, religious, ethnic, or political identity that is smaller or less powerful than the community's controlling group" (p. 304).

Myrdal (1944) pointed out that minority problems are actually majority problems. The white majority determines the place of nonwhites and other ethnic groups in our society. The status of different minority groups varies in our society because whites apply different stereotypes to various groups. For example, African Americans are viewed and treated differently from Japanese Americans. Johnson (1973) noted, "Minority relationships become recognized by the majority as a social problem when the members of the majority disagree as to whether the subjugation of the minority is socially desirable or in the ultimate interest of the majority" (p. 344). Concern about discrimination and segregation has also received

increasing national attention because of a rising level of aspiration among minority groups who demand (sometimes militantly) equal opportunities and equal rights.

Our country was supposedly founded on the principle of human equality. The Declaration of Independence and the Constitution assert equality, justice, and liberty for all. Yet, in practice, our society has always discriminated against minorities.

The groups of people who have been singled out for unequal treatment in our society have changed somewhat over the years. In the late 1800s and early 1900s, people of Irish, Italian, and Polish descent were discriminated against, but that discrimination has been substantially reduced. In the nineteenth century, Americans of Chinese descent were severely discriminated against. However, this also has been declining for many decades.

White Privilege

An underexposed part of racism in America is that white people (and white men in particular) have privileges that other Americans do not have. Below is a list of some of these privileges (McIntosh, 1988):

- White people can go shopping alone and be pretty well assured that they will not be followed or harassed.

- White people have no problem finding housing to rent or purchase in an area they can afford and want to live in.

- White people can feel assured that their children will be given curricular materials in school that testify to the existence of their race.

- White people can go into any supermarket and find the staple foods that fit with their cultural traditions.

- When white people use checks, credit cards, or cash, they can be sure that their skin color is not being taken into account when their financial reliability is questioned.

- White people are never asked to speak for all white people.

- White people can go into a hairdresser's shop and find someone who can cut their hair.

- White people can be sure that their neighbors in nice and affordable neighborhoods will be neutral or pleasant to them.

- White people can assume that police officers will provide protection and assistance.

- White people can be sure that their race will not count against them if they need legal or medical help.

❧ Race Is a Social Concept

Ashley Montague (1964) considered the concept of race to be one of the most dangerous and tragic myths in our society. Race is erroneously believed by many to be a biological classification of people. Yet, surprisingly to some, there are no clearly delineating characteristics of any race. Throughout history, the genes of different societies and racial groups have occasionally been intermingled. No racial group has any unique or distinctive genes. In addition, biological differentiations of racial groups have gradually been diluted through various sociocultural factors. These factors include changes in preferences of desirable characteristics in mates, effects of different diets on those who reproduce, and such variables as wars and diseases in selecting those who will live to reproduce (Johnson, 1973).

In spite of definitional problems, it is necessary to use racial categories in the social sciences. Race has important (though not necessarily consistent) social meanings for people. In order to have a basis for racial classifications, social scientists have used a social, rather than a biological, definition. A social definition is based on the way in which members of a society classify each other by physical characteristics. For example, a frequently used social definition of an African American is anyone who either displays overt African American physical characteristics or is known to have an African American ancestor (Schaefer, 2002).

A social definitional approach to classifying races sometimes results in different societies using different definitions of *race*. For example, in the United States anyone who is known to have an African American ancestor is considered to be African American; in Brazil, anyone known to have a white ancestor is considered to be white (Schaefer, 2002).

Race, according to Montague (1964), becomes a dangerous myth when people assume that physical traits are linked with mental traits and cultural achievements. Every few years, it seems, some noted scientist stirs the country by making this erroneous assumption. For example, Herrnstein and Murray (1994) assert that whites, on the average, are more intelligent, because IQ tests show that whites average scores of 10 to 15 points higher than African Americans. Herrnstein and Murray's findings have been sharply criticized by other authorities as falsely assuming that IQ is largely genetically determined (Lefrancois, 1996). These authorities contend that IQ is substantially influenced by environmental factors, and it is likely that the average achievement of African Americans, if given similar opportunities to realize their potentialities, would be the same as whites. Also, it has been charged

that IQ tests are racially slanted. The tests ask the kinds of questions that whites are more familiar with and thereby more apt to answer correctly.

Johnson (1973) summarizes the need for an impartial, objective view of the capacity of different racial groups to achieve:

> *Race bigots contend that, the cultural achievements of different races being so obviously unlike, it follows that their genetic capacities for achievements must be just as different. Nobody can discover the cultural capacities of any population or race . . . until there is equality of opportunities to demonstrate the capacities. (p. 50)*

Most scientists, both physical and social, now believe that in biological inheritance all races are alike in everything that really makes any difference (such as problem-solving capacities, altruistic tendencies, and communication capacities). With the exception of several very small, inbred, isolated, primitive tribes, all racial groups appear to show a wide distribution of every kind of ability. All important race differences that have been noted in personality, behavior, and achievement (e.g., high school graduation rates) appear to be primarily due to environmental factors.

❧ Institutional Values and Racism: Discrimination in Systems

In the last 4 decades, institutional racism has become recognized as a major problem. *Institutional racism* refers to discriminatory acts and policies against a racial group that pervade the major macro systems of society, including the legal, political, economic, and educational systems. Some of these discriminatory acts and policies are illegal, whereas others are not. Barker (1999) defines institutional racism as "those policies, practices, or procedures embedded in bureaucratic structures that systematically lead to unequal outcomes for people of color" (p. 244). Institutional racism can best be understood by a systems perspective on discrimination. (For more information on how institutional values and systems affect people, see the Systems Impact Model in Chapter 1.)

Institutional values form the foundation for macro system policies. These policies are enacted in organizations and communities. Here we refer to institutional racism as a prevailing orientation demonstrated in policies and procedures throughout our entire culture. It is an all-encompassing term that envelopes institutional values, communities, and organizational macro systems.

In contrast to institutional racism is *individual racism,* which Barker (1999) defines as "the negative attitudes one person has about all members of a racial or ethnic group, often resulting in overt acts such as name-calling, social exclusion, or violence" (p. 239). Carmichael and Hamilton (1967) make the following distinction between individual racism and institutional racism:

> *When white terrorists bomb a black church and kill five black children, that is an act of individual racism, widely deplored by most segments of society. But when in the same city . . . five hundred black babies die each year because of the lack of proper food, shelter, and medical facilities, and thousands more are destroyed and maimed physically, emotionally, and intellectually because of conditions of poverty and discrimination in the black community, that is a function of institutional racism. (p. 4)*

Discrimination and Oppression in Organizational Macro Systems

Institutional discrimination is "prejudicial treatment in organizations based on official policies, overt behaviors, or behaviors that may be covert but approved by those with power" (Barker, 1999, p. 244). Discrimination is built, often unwittingly, into the very structure and form of our society. It is demonstrated by how organizational macro systems treat clients. The following examples reflect how agencies can engage in institutional discrimination: A family counseling agency with branch offices assigns less-skilled counselors and provides lower-quality services in an office located in a minority neighborhood. A human services agency encourages white applicants to request funds for special needs (e.g., clothing) or to use certain services (e.g., day-care and homemaker services with the costs charged to the agency), while nonwhite clients are not informed or are less enthusiastically informed of such services. A human services agency takes longer to process the requests of members of minority groups for funds and services. A police department discriminates against nonwhite staff in work assignments, hiring practices, promotion practices, and pay increases. A probation and parole agency tends to ignore minor violations of the rules for parole of white clients but seeks to return to prison nonwhite parolees having minor violations of those rules. A mental health agency tends to assign psychotic labels to nonwhite clients, but assigns labels indicating less serious disorders to white clients. White staff at a family counseling center are encouraged by their white executive board to provide intensive services to clients with whom they have a good relationship (often white clients). On the other hand, they are told to give less attention to those clients "they aren't hitting it off well with" (these clients may be disproportionately nonwhite).

Whether these differences in treatment are undertaken consciously or not, they nevertheless represent institutional discrimination.

Discrimination and Oppression in Community Macro Systems

Institutional racism also pervades community life. It is a contributing factor to the following: The unemployment rate for nonwhites has consistently been over twice that for whites. The infant mortality rate for nonwhites is nearly twice as high as for whites. The life expectancy age for nonwhites is several years less than for whites. The average number of years of educational achievement for nonwhites is considerably less than for whites (Kornblum & Julian, 2001).

Many examples of institutional racism are found in the educational macro system. Schools in white neighborhoods generally have better facilities and more highly trained teachers than those in minority neighborhoods. Minority families are, on the average, less able to provide the hidden costs of free education (higher property taxes, transportation, class trips, clothing, and supplies), and, therefore, their children become less involved in the educational process. History texts in the past concentrated on achievements of white people and gave scant attention to minorities. Henry (1967) wrote in the 1960s about the effects of such history on Native American children:

> *What is the effect upon the student, when he learns that one race, and one alone, is the most, the best, the greatest; when he learns that Indians were mere parts of the landscape and wilderness which had to be cleared out, to make way for the great "movement" of white population across the land; and when he learns that Indians were killed and forcibly removed from their ancient homelands to make way for adventurers (usually called "pioneering goldminers"), for land grabbers (usually called "settlers"), and for illegal squatters on Indian-owned land (usually called "frontiersmen")? What is the effect upon the young Indian child himself, who is also a student in the school system, when he is told that Columbus discovered America, that Coronado "brought civilization" to the Indian people, and that the Spanish missionaries provided havens of refuge for the Indians? Is it reasonable to assume that the student, of whatever race, will not discover at some time in his life that Indians discovered America thousands of years before Columbus set out upon his voyage; that Coronado brought death and destruction to the native*

peoples; and that the Spanish missionaries, in all too many cases, forcibly dragged Indians to the missions? (p. 22)

Since the 1960s and the civil rights movement, the true story of minorities and their experiences are being better told.

Our criminal justice macro system also has elements of institutional racism. Our justice system is supposed to be fair and nondiscriminatory. The very name of the system, *justice,* implies fairness and quality. Yet, in practice, racism is evident. Although African Americans compose only about 12 percent of the population, they make up about 50 percent of the prison population (U.S. Census Bureau, 2001). (There is considerable debate as to what extent this is due to racism as opposed to differential crime rates by race.) The average prison sentence for murder and kidnapping is longer for African Americans than for whites. Nearly half of those sentenced to death are African American (U.S. Census Bureau, 2001). Police departments and district attorney's offices are more likely to enforce vigorously the kinds of laws broken by lower-income groups and minority groups than by middle- and upper-class white groups. Poor people are substantially less likely to be able to post bail. As a result, they are forced to remain in jail until their trial, which often takes months or sometimes more than a year. Unable to afford a well-financed defense (including the prices charged by the most successful criminal defense teams), they are more likely to be found guilty.

❦ Sources of Prejudice and Discrimination

No single theory provides a complete picture of why racial and ethnic discrimination occurs. By being exposed to a variety of theories, social workers should at least be better sensitized to the nature and sources of discrimination. The sources of discrimination come from inside and outside a person.

Projection

Projection is a psychological defense mechanism in which one attributes to others characteristics that one is unwilling to recognize in oneself. Many people have personal traits they dislike in themselves. They desire to get rid of such traits, but this is not always possible. Such people may project some of these traits onto others (often to some other group in society), thus displacing the negative feelings they would otherwise direct at themselves. In the

process, they then condemn those onto whom they have projected the traits.

For example, a minority group may serve as a projection of a prejudiced person's fears and lusts. People who view African Americans as lazy or preoccupied with sex may be projecting onto African Americans their own internal concerns about their industriousness or their sexual fantasies. While some whites view African Americans as promiscuous, historically it has generally been white men who forced African American women (particularly slaves) into sexual encounters. It appears many white males felt guilty about these sexual desires and adventures and dealt with their guilt by projecting their own lusts and sexual conduct onto African Americans.

Frustration-Aggression

Another psychological need satisfied by discrimination is the release of tension and frustration. All of us at times become frustrated when we are unable to achieve or obtain something we desire. Sometimes we strike back at the source of frustration, but many times direct retaliation is not possible. For example, we are reluctant to tell our employers what we think of them when we feel we are being treated unfairly because we fear repercussions.

Some frustrated people displace their anger and aggression onto a *scapegoat*. The scapegoat may be a particular person or it may be a group of people. Similar to people who take out their job frustrations at home on their spouses or family pets, some prejudiced people vent their frustrations on minority groups. (The term *scapegoat* derives from an ancient Hebrew ritual in which the goat was symbolically laden with the sins of the entire community and then chased into the wilderness. It "escaped," hence the term scapegoat. The term was gradually broadened to apply to anyone who bears the blame for others.)

Countering Insecurity and Inferiority

Still another psychological need that may be satisfied through discrimination is the desire to counter feelings of insecurity or inferiority. Some insecure people seek to feel better about themselves by putting down another group. They then can tell themselves that they are better than these people.

Authoritarianism

A classic work on the causes of prejudice is *The Authoritarian Personality* by Adorno, Frenkel-Brunswik, Devinson, and Sanford (1950). Shortly after World War II, these researchers studied the psychological causes of the development of European fascism and concluded that a distinct type of personality was associated with prejudice and intolerance. The *authoritarian personality* is inflexible and rigid and has a low tolerance for uncertainty. This type of personality has a great respect for authority figures and quickly submits to their will. Such a person highly values conventional behavior and feels threatened by unconventional behavior of others. In order to reduce this threat, such a personality labels unconventional people as being immature, inferior, or degenerate and thereby avoids any need to question his or her own beliefs and values. The authoritarian personality views members of minority groups as being unconventional, degrades them, and tends to express authoritarianism through prejudice and discrimination.

History

Historical explanations can also be given for prejudice. Kornblum and Julian (2001) note that the groups now viewed by white prejudiced persons as being second class are groups that have been either conquered, enslaved, or admitted into our society on a subordinate basis. For example, African Americans were imported as slaves during our colonial period and stripped of human dignity. Native Americans were conquered, and their culture was viewed as inferior. Mexican Americans were allowed to enter this country primarily to do seasonal, low-paid farm work.

Competition and Exploitation

Our society is highly competitive and materialistic. Individuals and groups compete daily with one another to acquire more of the available goods. These attempts to secure economic goods usually result in a struggle for resources and power. In our society, once whites achieved dominance, they then used (and still are using) their power to exploit nonwhites through cheap labor—for example, as sweatshop factory laborers, migrant farm hands, maids, janitors, and bellhops.

Members of the dominant group know they are treating the subordinate group as inferior and unequal. To justify such discrimination, they develop an ideology (set of beliefs) that their group is superior, and therefore that it is right and proper that they have more rights, goods, and so on. Sometimes they assert that God selected their group to be dominant. Furthermore, they assign inferior traits to the subordinate group and conclude that the minority needs and deserves less because it is biologically inferior. Throughout history in most societies, the dominant group (which has greater power and wealth) has sought to maintain the status quo by keeping those who have the least in an inferior position.

Socialization Patterns

Prejudice is also a learned phenomenon and is transmitted from generation to generation through socialization processes. Our culture has stereotypes of what different minority group members "ought to be" and the ways minority group members "ought to behave" in relationships with members of the majority group. These stereotypes provide norms against which a child learns to judge persons, things, and ideas. Prejudice, to some extent, is developed through the same processes by which we learn to be religious or patriotic, to appreciate and enjoy art, or to develop our value system. Prejudice, at least in certain segments in our society, is thus a facet of the normative system of our culture.

Belief in the One True Religion

Some people are raised to believe that their religion is the one true religion—and that they will go to heaven, while everyone who believes in a different religion is a heathen who will be eternally damned. A person with such a belief system comes to the conclusion that he or she is one of "God's chosen few." Feeling superior to others often leads a person to devalue "heathens," and then to treat them in an inferior way. The influence of belief in the "one true religion" has led to an extensive number of wars between societies, each of which thought its religion was superior. Such societies thought they were justified in spreading their chosen religion through any possible means, including by physical force.

An excellent question to ponder is, "If a social worker believes his or her religion is the one true religion, can that social worker fully accept clients who are members of some other religious faith?" The belief in the one true religion may be one of the most crucial determinants in developing an attitudinal system of racial prejudice.

Evaluation of Discrimination Theories

No single theory explains all causes of prejudices because prejudices have many origins. Taken together, however, they identify a number of causative factors. All theories assert that the causative factors of prejudice are in the personality and experiences of the person holding the prejudice, and not in the character of the group against whom the prejudice is directed.

A novel experiment documenting that prejudice does not stem from contact with the people toward whom prejudice is directed was conducted by Eugene Hartley (1946). Hartley gave his subjects a list of prejudiced responses to Jews and African Americans and

Is Racial Discrimination Based on Criminal Thinking?

Why do people discriminate on the basis of racial differences? Why do these people believe that it is proper to do so? One way of analyzing the problem of racial discrimination is to look at the thought processes that lead to racism. Benjamin's (1991) theory that racism is "a process of justification for the domination, exploitation, and control of one racial group by another" supports the idea that specific thought processes are involved. One such set of thoughts that has been used to justify racism provides the basis for *Social Darwinism,* the belief that the "superior race" must dominate all other races in order to ensure survival.

Benjamin's definition links the thought processes behind racism to the widely accepted theories of *criminal thinking,* theories that note that certain thinking patterns are attributed to the criminal personality that differ significantly from the thought processes of noncriminals—and that are used by the criminal to justify criminal activities (Ellis, 1957; Freyhan, 1955; Keniston, 1965; Yochelson & Samenow, 1976). If we accept the American ideals of human dignity, freedom, and justice for all, then the idea that one group should dominate, exploit, and control another group is maladaptive. Thus, we can theorize that the thinking patterns that enable the racist to justify these coercive acts must be flawed. Not only do such patterns constitute "errors" in thinking from the "perspective of responsibility" (Yochelson & Samenow, 1976, p. 251), they also are used to strip others of their personal dignity and freedom, and they cause these victims to receive unequal treatment.

An Overview of Criminal Thinking

The concept of criminal thinking (Yochelson & Samenow, 1976) derives from the theory of rational therapy "self-talk" developed by Albert Ellis (1957). It refers to the idea that certain irrational beliefs are held by persons who commit crimes, which allow them to tell themselves that their behavior is acceptable. For example, an accountant who embezzles from her employer may rationalize her crime by telling herself that she deserves the money because she has been underpaid by her employer for the last 7 years; or that it is a temporary loan that she expects to replace once she has become financially stable again; or that the employer is so wealthy the small amount she is taking will never be missed.

Treatment programs to rehabilitate juvenile delinquents, sex offenders, domestic abuse perpetrators, and others who make excuses for their maladaptive behaviors use various terms for this type of rationalization. For the purposes of this discussion they can be thought to be synonymous: errors in thinking, criminal thinking, faulty thinking, and deviant thinking. During a decade of study of the criminal personality, Dr. Samuel Yochelson defined and conceptualized a number of errors in thinking that he found to be common among the criminal population (Yochelson & Samenow, 1976). Yochelson's definitions and later variations (Bays & Freeman-Longo, 1989) are paraphrased and summarized below.

Power Thrust: The criminal inflates low self-esteem by viewing himself or herself as an all-powerful, unique individual whose needs must come first and who can force others to meet those needs. The criminal rejects legitimate authority.

Ownership: An extreme form of control over others based on the criminal's attitude that his or her rights are unlimited; allows criminal to disregard all personal and social boundaries.

Failure to Consider Injury to Others: The criminal minimizes or denies injuring victims by an immediate criminal act or its far-reaching effects on the victims and others in society in order to maintain his or her self-image.

Lack of Empathy: The criminal can maintain feelings of uniqueness only by refusing to consider the experiences or feelings of others.

Good Person Self-Image: The criminal has a distorted view of self as a good person who can do no wrong and may offer examples of "goodness" as evidence.

Closed Channel Thinking: The secretiveness, closed-mind, and self-righteous attitude of the criminal do not allow for an open channel of communication or for being receptive to other points of view. Criminals acknowledge the faults of others but are not self-critical.

Victim Stance: The criminal avoids taking responsibility for behavior by blaming others and by viewing himself or herself as a victim of others; often includes blaming the victim.

Disregard for Responsible Performance: The criminal's energy and motivation are directed toward self-serving goals rather than socially responsible activities. The criminal avoids and disregards personal obligations in order to maintain a power position.

Lack of a Time Perspective: Refers to several aberrations in time concepts, including the failure to make positive changes based on past experiences and the tendency to live for the moment (instant gratification) rather than anticipate future benefits or outcomes.

Fear of Fear: Fear reactions are not used as a guide to responsible living, but are taken as threats to the criminal's self-esteem. Criminals often have irrational fears.

Lack of Trust: Trust of others is seen as a weakness and interferes with the criminal's need for power and control.

Thinking Errors Common to Racist Beliefs

In the following discussion of racist thinking, the term *racist* will not be limited to bigots and white supremists who hold extreme beliefs. The term will include everyone whose beliefs and thoughts contain elements of racial or ethnic prejudice and/or who have supported racial or ethnic discrimination to any degree. We will use the set of "thinking errors" that were just described as the standard by which we can test our theory of the racist's flawed, or criminal, thinking.

Three of these thinking errors account for many of the severest forms of domination, exploitation, and control of minority populations. They are the power thrust, ownership, and a failure to consider injury to others. Everything we know about racial discrimination allows us to acknowledge that it is based on a *power thrust*—control of one person over others and a resulting sense of power or triumph (Yochelson & Samenow, 1976). Slaveholding is ownership by definition, and it is human control carried to the extreme. White ownership of black populations did not end with emancipation; white society's sustained attitude of control over African Americans continued well into the 1960s. Yochelson and Samenow (1976) referred to the criminal's view of people as "pawns or checkers waiting for me to deal with them as I wish" (p. 381), and this aptly describes the real-life effect of institutional discrimination—especially as it is experienced by people of color in the lower socioeconomic levels. Whenever people of color are forced to suffer (by comparison to their white counterparts) from lower grades of service, fewer opportunities for advancement, higher rates of infant mortality, longer periods of incarceration, and fewer options for neighborhoods in which they may live, then a racist society has met the criteria for the type of criminal thinking referred to as *failure to consider injury to others*.

Oppression of people of color continues to occur because of two additional errors in thinking on the part of the racist: a lack of empathy and a distorted self-image. If we believe that others are inferior to us, it reduces our motivation to empathically consider how they might feel or otherwise be affected by unequal treatment. Racists, like criminals, put considerable effort into building a good person self-image. The good person self-image was held by slave owners who asserted that they treated their slaves well. This self-image is reclaimed by white society every time it adopts a benevolent social policy, such as affirmative action. We would all like to view ourselves as good people. In fact, social work counselors are taught specific skills that allow them to help individuals strengthen their sense of self-worth. The error in thinking occurs when individuals hold this belief on the basis of a few good deeds and do not acknowledge their other destructive behaviors.

Is the white racist guilty of closed channel thinking? We don't have to belong to a white supremacist group to be self-righteous and closed-minded. Many of us are guilty of not being particularly "open" in either our thinking or our communication with others, particularly when we feel that our viewpoint is justified. Anyone who has tried to reason with a bigoted relative or colleague is aware of the impossibility of finding a receptive listener. Closed channel thinkers tend to overgeneralize and to see the world in absolute terms; good and bad, right and wrong, black and white.

Racists also justify their narrow ethnocentric viewpoint by adopting a victim stance. This can be done by assuming an attitude of being victimized by "heavy tax burdens that force us to support people who are taking advantage of us—and who are undeserving." Racists blame the politicians and government for making people of color dependent on social welfare programs. They blame the victim by classifying people of color as lazy, illiterate, and irresponsible; and they point to high rates of school failure, unemployment, illegitimate births, and crime in the inner cities to support this characterization. Society has created a no-win situation for oppressed people of color, because many whites also believe themselves to be victimized by people of color who compete for their jobs, their educational scholarships, and their tax dollars to upgrade housing and public services in the inner cities. The victim perspective is all-encompassing and self-serving. It is used by the racist to justify discrimination and promotes a disregard for responsible performance. After all, if we can convince ourselves that people of color are already taking advantage of a too-benevolent society, then there is no need to support social welfare programs or to make any effort toward improving their opportunities for success.

Racists demonstrate a lack of time perspective in their failure, or refusal, to consider the long-term benefits of providing all people with equal opportunities to be successful, contributing members of society. Again, this is a self-serving attitude that places the present needs of a few above the future outcomes of many. Prejudice, racism, and racial discrimination are based on a fear of fear. In this case, there is an irrational fear that equality, shared power, integrated living, and racial blending (intermarriage) somehow threaten the worth and well-being of white society. A lack of trust, which is implicit in all areas of racism, fosters the desire of many in the dominant mainstream society to retain their power position.

From these comparisons, it appears that racist thinking shares many common elements with criminal thinking. In addition, it seems likely that racist thinking is not limited to the "prejudiced discriminators" (Merton, 1949) who openly embrace white supremacy. It is employed as well by those of us who fall into the less obvious categories of "prejudiced nondiscriminators" and "unprejudiced discriminators" (Merton, 1949). In many regions of the United States a pervasive atmosphere of distrust fed by irrational fears has fostered a racist mentality among the general population. The same errors in thinking that are attributed to the criminal personality are used to justify the domination, exploitation, and control of people of color by the mainstream white society.

Source: Patricia Danielson, social worker, Jefferson County Human Services Dept., Jefferson, WI.

to three groups that did not even exist: Wallonians, Pireneans, and Danireans. Prejudiced responses included such statements as, "All Wallonians living here should be expelled." The respondents were asked to state their agreement or disagreement with these prejudiced statements. The experiment showed that most of those who were prejudiced against Jews and African Americans were also prejudiced against people whom they had never met or heard about.

Closely related to the theories about the sources of racial and ethnic prejudice and discrimination is the conceptualization that compares racist thinking to criminal thinking. Spotlight 5.2 explores the question, "Is racial discrimination based on criminal thinking?"

❧ Impacts of Social and Economic Forces: The Effects and Costs of Discrimination and Oppression

Racial discrimination is a barrier in our competitive society to obtaining the necessary resources to lead a contented and comfortable life. Being discriminated against due to race makes it more difficult to obtain adequate housing, financial resources, a quality education, employment, adequate health care and other services, equal justice in civil and criminal cases, and so on.

Discrimination also has heavy psychological costs. All of us have to develop a sense of identity—who we are and how we fit into a complex, swiftly changing world. Ideally, it is important that we form a positive self-concept and strive to obtain worthy goals. Yet, according to Cooley's (1902) "looking-glass self," our idea of who we are and what we are is largely determined by the way others relate to us. When members of a minority group are treated by the majority group as if they are inferior, second-class citizens, it is substantially more difficult for such members to develop a positive identity. Thus, people who are the objects of discrimination encounter barriers to developing their full potential as human beings.

Young children of groups who are the victims of discrimination are likely to develop low self-esteem at an early age. African American children who have been subjected to discrimination even display a preference for white dolls and white playmates over black (Schaefer, 2002).

Pinderhughes (1982) has noted that the history of oppression of African Americans, combined with racism and exclusion, have produced a "victim system."

> *A victim system is a circular feedback process that exhibits properties such as stability, predictability, and identity that are common to all systems. This particular system threatens self-esteem and reinforces problematic responses in communities, families, and individuals. The feedback works as follows: Barriers to opportunity and education limit the chance for achievement, employment, and attainment of skills. This limitation can, in turn, lead to poverty or stress in relationships, which interferes with adequate performance of family roles. Strains in family roles cause problems in individual growth and development and limit the opportunities of families to meet their own needs or to organize to improve their communities. Communities limited in resources (jobs, education, housing, etc.) are unable to support families properly and the community all too often becomes an active disorganizing influence, a breeder of crime and other pathology, and a cause of even more powerlessness. (p. 109)*

Discrimination also has high costs for the majority group. It impairs intergroup cooperation and communication. Discrimination also is a factor in contributing to social problems among minorities—for example, high crime rates, emotional problems, alcoholism, drug abuse—all of which have cost billions of dollars in social programs. It has been argued that discrimination is a barrier to collective action (e.g., unionization) among whites and nonwhites (particularly people in the lower income classes) and, therefore, is a factor in perpetuating low-paying jobs and poverty. Less affluent whites who could benefit from collective action are hurt.

The effects of discrimination are even reflected in life expectancy. The life expectancy of nonwhites is 6 years less than that of whites in the United States (U.S. Census Bureau, 2001). The fact is that nonwhites tend to die earlier than whites because they receive inferior health care, food, and shelter.

Finally, discrimination in the United States undermines some of our nation's political goals. Many other nations view us as hypocritical when we advocate human rights and equality. In order to make an effective argument for human rights on a worldwide scale, we must first put our own house in order by eliminating racial and ethnic discrimination. Few Americans realize the extent to which racial discrimination damages our international reputation. Nonwhite foreign diplomats to America often complain about being victims of discrimination because they are mistaken for being members of American minority groups. With most of the nations of the world being nonwhite, our racist practices severely damage our influence and prestige.

❧ The Effects of Discrimination on Human Growth and Development

The effects of discrimination will be illustrated by examining the research conducted on African Americans, the largest racial minority group, composing about 12 percent of the population in the United States. We begin by examining some background material on the history and culture of African Americans in our society.

History and Culture of African Americans

The United States has always been a racist country. Although our country's founders talked about freedom, dignity, equality, and human rights, our economy before the Civil War depended heavily on slavery.

Many slaves came from cultures that had well-developed art forms, political systems, family patterns, religious beliefs, and economic systems. However, their home culture was not European, and, therefore, slave owners viewed their cultural patterns as being of no consequence. They prohibited slaves from practicing and developing their art, language, religion, and family life. For want of practice, their former culture soon died in America.

The life of a slave was harsh. Slaves were viewed not as human beings but as chattel to be bought and sold. Long, hard days were spent working in the fields, with the profits of their labor going to their white owners. Whippings, mutilations, and hangings were commonly accepted control practices. The impetus to enslave African Americans was not simply racism because many whites believed that it was to their economic advantage to have a cheap supply of labor. Cotton growing, in particular, was thought to require a large labor force that was also cheap and docile. Marriages among slaves were not recognized by the law, and slaves were often sold with little regard to effects on marital and family ties. Throughout the slavery period and even after it, African Americans were discouraged from demonstrating intelligence, initiative, or ambition. For a period of time, it was illegal to teach African Americans to read or write.

Some authorities (Henderson & Kim, 1980) have noted that opposition to the spread of slavery preceding the Civil War was primarily due to the Northern fears of competition from slave labor and the rapidly increasing migration of African Americans to the North and West, rather than to moral concern for human rights and equality. Few whites at the time understood or believed in the principle of racial equality—not even Abraham Lincoln, who believed that African Americans were inferior to whites.

Following the Civil War, the federal government failed to develop a comprehensive program of economic and educational aid to African Americans. As a result, most African Americans returned to being economically dependent on the same planters in the South who had held them in bondage. Within a few years, laws were passed in the Southern states prohibiting interracial marriages and requiring racial segregation in schools and public places.

A rigid caste system in the South hardened into a system of oppression known as Jim Crow laws. The system prescribed how African Americans were supposed to act in the presence of whites, asserted white supremacy, embraced racial segregation, and denied political and legal rights to African Americans. African Americans who opposed Jim Crow laws were subjected to burnings, beatings, and lynchings. Jim Crow laws were used to teach African Americans to view themselves as inferior and to be servile and passive in interactions with whites.

World War II opened up new employment opportunities for African Americans. A large migration of African Americans from the South began. Greater mobility afforded by wartime conditions led to upheavals in the traditional caste system. Many African Americans served in the armed forces during this war, fought and died for their country, and yet their country maintained segregated facilities. Awareness of disparity between the ideal and reality led many people to try to improve race relations, not only for domestic justice and peace, but to answer criticism from abroad. With each gain in race relations, more African Americans were encouraged to press for their rights.

A major turning point in African American history was the U.S. Supreme Court decision in *Brown* v. *Board of Education* in 1954, which ruled that racial segregation in public schools was unconstitutional. Since 1954, a number of organized efforts have been made by both African Americans and certain segments of the white population to secure equal rights and opportunities for African Americans. Attempts to change deeply entrenched racist attitudes and practices have produced much turmoil: the burning of many inner cities in the late 1960s, the assassination of Martin Luther King Jr., and clashes between African American militant groups and the police. There have also been significant advances. Wide-ranging civil rights legislation protecting rights in areas such as housing, voting, employment, and use of public transportation and facilities has been passed. During the riots in 1968 the National Advisory Commission on Civil Disorders (Gelman, 1988) warned that our society was careening "toward two societies, one black, one white—separate and unequal" (p. 19).

America today is not the bitterly segregated society that the riot commission envisioned. African Americans and whites now more often work together, and lunch together—yet few really count the other as friends.

Four out of five African Americans now live in metropolitan areas, more than half of them in the central cities (U.S. Census Bureau, 2001). U.S. cities are still largely segregated, with African Americans primarily living in separate neighborhoods. In recent years, the main thrust of the civil rights movement among African Americans has been economic equality. The economic gap between African Americans and whites continues to be immense. African American families are three times as likely as white families to fall below the poverty line (U.S. Census Bureau, 2001). Since the early 1950s, the African American unemployment rate has been approximately twice that for whites. Unemployment is an especially severe problem for African American teenagers, whose rate of unemployment is substantially higher than for white youth and has run as high as 50 percent (U.S. Census Bureau, 2001).

We, as a nation, have come a long way since the U.S. Supreme Court's decision in 1954. But we still have a long way to go before we eliminate African American poverty and oppression. Living conditions in African American ghettos remain as bleak as they were when our inner cities erupted in the late 1960s.

Two developments have characterized the socioeconomic circumstances of African Americans in recent years. A middle class has emerged that is better educated, better paid, and better housed than any group of African Americans that has gone before it. However, as middle-class African Americans move to better neighborhoods, they leave behind those who are living in poverty. The group that has been left behind generates a disproportionate share of the social pathology that is associated with the inner city—including high rates of crime, unemployment, drug abuse, school dropouts, births outside of marriage, and families receiving public assistance.

More than half of all African American children are being raised in single-parent families (U.S. Census Bureau, 2001). However, many of the children living in single-parent families are living in family structures composed of some variation of the extended family. Many single-parent families move in with relatives during adversity, including economic adversity. In addition, African American families of all levels rely on relatives to care for their children while they work.

Schaefer (2002) summarizes five strengths identified by the National Urban League that allow African American families to function effectively in a racist society:

1. *Strong kinship bonds.* Blacks are more likely than whites to care for children and the elderly in an extended family network.

2. *A strong work orientation.* Poor blacks are more likely to be working, and poor black families often include more than one wage earner.

3. *Adaptability of family roles.* In two-parent families, the egalitarian pattern of decision making is the most common. The self-reliance of black women who are the primary wage earners best illustrates this adaptability.

4. *A high achievement orientation.* Working-class blacks indicate a greater desire for their children to attend college than working-class whites. Even a majority of low-income African Americans desire to attend college.

5. *A strong religious orientation.* Black churches since the time of slavery have been the source of many significant grassroots organizations.

While it is a reality that many African American families are headed by single mothers, it would be a serious error to view such family structures as inherently pathological. A single parent with good parenting skills, along with a supportive extended family, can lead to healthy family functions.

Subcultures of African Americans have vocabularies and communication styles that differ from the dominant white culture. Young children raised in these subcultures often have difficulty understanding the English language spoken in schools. African American dialects appear to be the result of a creolized form of English that was at one time spoken on Southern plantations (Dillard, 1972). (*Creolized* refers to a language based on two or more languages that serves as the native language of its speaker.) Present-day African American English is a combination of the linguistic remnants of its Southern plantation past and a reflection of the current African American sociocultural situation. As such, it is a dialect in its own right and should not be perceived as just a distortion of standard English. Most adult African Americans are at least bilingual, being fluent in an African American dialect and in standard English.

Religious organizations that are predominantly African American have tended not only to have a spiritual mission, but also to have been highly active in social action efforts to combat racial discrimination. Many prominent African American leaders, such as Martin Luther King Jr. and Jesse Jackson, have been members of the clergy. African American churches have served to develop leadership skills and as social welfare organizations to meet basic needs, such as clothing, food, and shelter. African American churches are support systems for troubled individuals and families.

Many African Americans have had the historical experience of being subjected to negative evaluations by school systems, social welfare agencies, health-care institutions, and the justice system. Because of their past experiences, African Americans are likely to view such institutions with apprehension. Schools, for example, have erroneously perceived African Americans as being less capable of developing cognitive skills. Such perceptions about school failure are often a self-fulfilling prophecy. If African American children are expected to fail in school systems, teachers are likely to put forth less effort in challenging them to learn, and African American children may then put forth less effort to learn, resulting in a lower level of achievement.

Some of the attitudes and behaviors exhibited by African Americans who seek services from white social agencies are often labeled resistant. However, the attitudes and behaviors and better be viewed as attempts at coping with powerlessness and racism. For example, if there are delays in provision of services, African Americans may convey apathy or disparage the agency because they interpret the delay as being due to racism; they then respond in ways they have learned in the past to handle discrimination.

Effects of Discrimination on Development of Self-Concept

The term *self-concept* refers to the positive and negative thoughts and feelings that one has toward one's self. It is often used interchangeably with such terms as self-image, sense of self, self-esteem, and identity. A positive self-concept is a key element in school achievement, in positive social interactions with others, and in emotional, social, and intellectual growth (Santrock, 1999).

Solomon (1983) notes that if African American adults accept society's label of inferiority, they are likely to convey such thoughts and feelings to their children. The children are likely not only to develop a negative self-concept but also to put less effort into developing cognitive skills and school achievement. Because of low self-esteem and underdeveloped cognitive skills they are less likely to develop interpersonal and technical skills, which then results in having difficulties in social interactions and to being restricted in adulthood to low-paying, low-skill jobs. The vicious circle is then completed when such difficulties confirm and reinforce feelings of inferiority and of negative value, feelings that are then passed on to their children.

A number of studies have been conducted on the extent to which discrimination adversely affects self-concept development in African American children. Very significantly, these studies indicate that the African American child's conceptualization of self does not necessarily have to be impaired by racism. Concludes Powell (1983):

> *Afro-Americans have survived a harsh system of slavery, repression, and racism. Although there have been casualties, there have been many more survivors, achievers, and victors. The cultural heritage of coping with adversity and overcoming has been passed on from generation to generation, laced with stories of those with remarkable courage and fortitude. (p. 73)*

Given the pervasiveness of racism and discrimination in our society, why is it that many African American children overcome this obstacle in self-concept development and develop a fairly positive sense of self-esteem?

The reason appears to involve the fact that every person is embedded simultaneously in at least two systems: one is the larger society and the other is one's immediate social and physical environment. The latter environment includes family members, other relatives, peers, friends, and neighbors. One's immediate environment appears to be the predominant system in shaping one's self-concept. It appears that the child who is loved, accepted, and supported in his immediate environment comes to love and respect himself as someone worthy of love.

African American children, as they grow older, learn of the larger society's devaluation. Practically all African American children are aware by age 7 or 8 of the social devaluation placed on their racial group (Schaefer, 2002). But the awareness of this devaluation does not necessarily extend to the African American child's self-evaluation. The sense of self developed in the immediate environment acts as a buffer against the potential devaluation by the larger society.

Certainly, racism has the potential for adverse effects on self-esteem development of African American children. In spite of racism in our economic, political, and social structures, African American families have not only survived but have interacted with their children in ways that foster the development of a positive identity. Celebrations, such as Kwanzaa (see Spotlight 5.3), are ways of promoting pride for African Americans in their racial identity.

The Africentric Perspective and Worldview

African American culture has numerous components: elements from traditional African culture; elements from slavery, reconstruction, and subsequent exposure to racism and discrimination; and elements from "mainstream" white culture. An emerging perspective is the *Africentric perspective* (Devore & Schlesinger, 1996), which acknowledges African culture and expressions of African beliefs, values, institutions, and behaviors. It recognizes that African Americans have retained, to some degree, a number of elements of African life and values.

The Africentric perspective asserts that the use of Eurocentric theories of human behavior to explain the behavior and ethos of African Americans is often inappropriate. Eurocentric theories of human behavior were developed in European and Anglo-American cultures. Eurocentric theorists have historically vilified people of African descent and other people of color. Such theorists have explicitly or implicitly claimed that people of African descent were pathological or inferior in their social, personality, or moral development (Schiele, 1996). The

Spotlight on Diversity 5.3 | Kwanzaa

Kwanzaa means "first fruits of the harvest" in Swahili. Kwanzaa is a 7-day festival observed by some African Americans in late December and early January. It is not a substitute for Christmas, and it is a nonreligious celebration. Many people who celebrate Kwanzaa also celebrate Christmas. Inspired by a traditional African harvest festival, it was originated in 1966 by M. Ron Karenga, a Los Angeles–based activist, to increase awareness of the African heritage and encourage the following seven qualities which are stated in Swahili and English:

Umoja (unity). African Americans strive for unity within family, community, and the world as a whole.

Kujichagulia (self-determination). African Americans define themselves and have the determination not to accept or internalize negative definitions.

Ujima (collective work and responsibility). African Americans live, work, and are responsible for harmonizing personal wants and needs with the collective wants and needs of the race.

Ujamaa (cooperative economics). African Americans become their own economic bosses through owning and supporting African American businesses.

Nia (purpose). African Americans contribute distinct gifts to the world, and they propose to develop those gifts and talents.

Kuumba (creativity). African Americans are creative, and all that they touch is made more beautiful through the contact.

Imani (faith). African Americans remain alive, giving, and compassionate people because of their faith that, though African Americans suffer in their todays, they will succeed in their tomorrows.

Kwanzaa is a time to rededicate efforts to putting these principles into daily practice. Each day during the festival in the homes of many celebrants, a family member discusses one of the principles. The festival seeks to unite and empower African Americans in joyous testimony that they are a distinct people with a specific culture and perspective. Celebrants light a candle each night of their festival. On the last day, family members tend to exchange small gifts—generally gifts that have cultural significance.

A mother helps her child light the candles at the beginning of the festival of Kwanzaa.

© Meryl Levin

origins of this denigration can be found in the slave trade, as slave traders and owners were pressed to justify the enslavement of Africans. The fallout of Eurocentric theories is the portrayal of the culture of people of African descent as having contributed little of value to world development and human history.

The Africentric perspective seeks to dispel the negative distortions about people of African ancestry by legitimizing and disseminating a *worldview* that goes back thousands of years and that exists in the hearts and minds of many people of African descent today. Worldview involves one's perceptions of oneself in relation to other people, objects, institutions, and nature. The worldviews of African Americans are shaped by unique and important experiences, such as racism and discrimination, an African heritage, traditional attributes of the African American family and community life, and a strong religious orientation.

The Africentric perspective also seeks to promote a worldview that will facilitate human and societal transformation toward moral, spiritual, and humanistic ends. It also seeks to persuade people of different cultural and ethnic groups that they share a mutual interest in this regard. The Africentric perspective rejects the idea that the individual can be understood separately from others in his or her social group. It emphasizes a collective identity that encourages sharing, cooperation, and social responsibility.

The Africentric perspective also emphasizes the importance of spirituality, which includes moral development and attaining meaning and identity in life. It views the major sources of human problems in the United States as being oppression and alienation. Oppression and alienation are generated not only by prejudice and discrimination, but also by a worldview that teaches people to see themselves primarily as material, physical beings seeking immediate pleasure. It is further asserted that this worldview discourages spiritual and moral development.

The Africentric perspective has been used to provide explanations of the origins of specific social problems. For example, violent crimes by youths are thought to be a result of the limited options and choices they have to advance themselves economically. Youths seek a life of street crime as a logical means to cope with, and protest against, a society that practices pervasive employment discrimination. These youths mentally calculate that they can make more money from street crime than from attending college or starting a legitimate business. Turning to a life of crime is also thought more likely to occur in a society with a worldview that deemphasizes spiritual and moral development.

The Africentric perspective values a more holistic, spiritual, and optimistic view of human beings. It supports the "strengths perspective" and "empowerment" concepts of social work practice, which are described later in this chapter.

❧ Strategies to Promote Social and Economic Justice

A wide range of strategies have been developed to reduce racial and ethnic discrimination and oppression. These strategies include the following: mass media appeals, strategies to increase interaction among racial and ethnic groups, civil rights laws, activism, school busing,

affirmative action programs, confrontation of racist and ethnic remarks and actions, minority-owned businesses, confrontation of the problems in inner cities, and grass-roots organizations. Because racism is a more serious problem in our society than ethnocentrism, most of the strategies against discrimination primarily focus on curtailing racial discrimination and oppression.

Mass Media Appeals: Striving to Change Institutional Values

The mass media are able to reach large numbers of people simultaneously. By expanding public awareness of the existence of discrimination and its consequences, the media may strengthen control over racial and ethnic extremists. But newspapers, radio, and television have limitations in changing prejudiced attitudes and behaviors; they are primarily providers of information and seldom have a lasting effect in changing deep-seated prejudices through propaganda. Highly prejudiced persons are often unaware of their own prejudices. Even if they are aware of their prejudices, they generally ignore mass media appeals as irrelevant to them or dismiss the appeals as propaganda.

However, the media probably have had a significant impact in reducing discrimination through showing nonwhites and whites harmoniously working together in commercials, on news teams, and on TV shows. These settings provide at least one avenue for changing institutional values rooted in racism and discrimination.

Greater Interaction Between Minority Groups and the Majority Group

Increased contact between minority groups and the majority group is not in itself sufficient to alleviate prejudice. In fact, increased contact may, in some instances, highlight the differences between groups and increase suspicions and fear. Prejudice is likely to be increased when contacts are tension laden or involuntary (Schaefer, 2002). Prejudice is likely to subside when individuals are placed in situations in which they share characteristics in nonracial and nonethnic matters—for example, as co-workers, fellow soldiers, or classmates. Equal-status contacts, rather than inferior-superior status contact, are also more apt to reduce prejudices (Schaefer, 2002).

Civil Rights Laws: Changing the Legal Macro System

In the past 40 years, equal rights have been legislated in areas of employment, voting, housing, public accommodation, and education. A key question is, "How effective are laws in changing prejudice?"

Proponents of civil rights legislation make certain assumptions. The first is that new laws will reduce discriminatory behavioral patterns. The laws define what was once normal behavior (discrimination) as now being deviant behavior. Through time, it is expected that attitudes will change and become more consistent with the forced nondiscriminatory behavior patterns.

A second assumption is that the laws will be used. Civil rights laws were enacted after the Civil War but were seldom enforced and gradually were eroded. It is also unfortunately true that some officials will find ways of evading the intent of the law by eliminating only the extreme, overt symbols of discrimination, without changing other practices. Thus, the enactment of a law is only the first step in the process of changing prejudiced attitudes and practices. However, as Martin Luther King Jr. noted, "The law may not make a man love me, but it can restrain him from lynching me, and I think that's pretty important."

Activism

The strategy of activism attempts to change the structure of race relations through direct confrontations of discrimination and segregation policies. Activism has three types of politics: the politics of creative disorder, the politics of disorder, and the politics of escape.

The *politics of creative disorder* operates on the edge of the dominant social system and includes school boycotts, rent strikes, job blockades, sit-ins (for example, at businesses that are alleged to discriminate), public marches, and product boycotts. This type of activism is based on the concept of nonviolent resistance. A dramatic illustration of nonviolent resistance began on December 1, 1955, in Montgomery, Alabama, when Rosa Parks refused to give up her seat on a bus to a white person. Spotlight 5.4 describes Rosa Parks's act of courage.

The *politics of disorder* reflects alienation from the dominant culture and disillusionment with the political system. Those being discriminated against resort to mob uprisings, riots, and other forms of violence.

In 1969, the National Commission on Causes and Prevention of Violence reported that 200 riots had occurred in the previous 5 years when inner cities erupted (Sullivan et al., 1980). In 1992, there was a devastating riot in the inner city of Los Angeles following the "not guilty" verdict by a jury to charges that four white police officers used excessive force in arresting Rodney King, an African American. The focus of most of these riots has been minority group aggression against white-owned property. In 2001 rioting occurred in Cincinnati after an African American had been shot and killed by a white police officer.

The *politics of escape* engages in rhetoric about minority victimization. But, because the focus is not on solutions, the rhetoric has not been productive, except perhaps for providing an emotional release.

Spotlight on Diversity 5.4	Rosa Parks's Act of Courage Sparked the Civil Rights Movement

On December 1, 1955, Rosa Parks was in a hurry. She had a lot of things to do. When the bus came to the boarding area where she was standing in Montgomery, Alabama, she got on without paying attention to the driver. She rode the bus often and was aware of Montgomery's segregated seating laws, which required blacks to sit at the back of the bus.

In those days in the South, black people were expected to board the front of the bus, pay their fare, then get off and walk outside the bus to reboard on the back. But Rosa Parks noted the back was already crowded, standing room only, with black passengers even standing on the back steps of the bus. It was apparent to Rosa that it would be all but impossible to reboard at the back. Besides, bus drivers sometimes drove off and left black passengers behind, even after accepting their fares. Rosa Parks spontaneously decided to take her chances. She paid her fare in the front of the bus, then walked down the aisle, and took a seat toward the back of the bus that was still in the area reserved for whites. At the second stop after boarding, a white man got on and had to stand.

The bus driver saw the white man standing, and ordered Rosa Parks to move to the back. She refused, thinking, "I want to be treated like a human being." Two police officers were called and they arrested Rosa. She was taken to city hall, booked, fingerprinted, jailed, and fined. Her arrest and subsequent appeal all the way to the U.S. Supreme Court, were the catalyst for a year-long boycott of the city buses by blacks, who composed 70 percent of the bus riders. The boycott inspired Martin Luther King Jr. to become involved. The boycott ended when the Supreme Court declared Montgomery's segregated seating laws unconstitutional. Rosa Parks's unplanned defiance of the segregated seating law sparked the civil rights movement. This movement not only has promoted social and economic justice for African Americans, but also has served to inspire other groups to organize to advocate for their civil rights. These groups include other racial and ethnic groups, women, the elderly, persons with a disability, and gays and lesbians.

The principal value of social protest seems to be the stimulation of public awareness of certain problems. The civil rights protests in the 1960s made practically all Americans aware of the discrimination to which non-white groups were being subjected. With this awareness, at least some of the discrimination has ceased, and race relations have improved. Continued protest beyond a certain (although indeterminate) point, however, appears to have little additional value (Sullivan et al., 1980).

School Busing: A Community Initiative

Housing patterns in many large metropolitan centers have led to de facto segregation; that is, African Americans and certain other nonwhite groups live in one area, while whites live in another. This segregation has affected educational opportunities for nonwhites. Nonwhite areas have fewer financial resources, and, as a result, the educational quality is often substantially lower than in white areas. In the past 3 decades courts in a number of metropolitan areas have ordered that a certain proportion of nonwhites must be bused to schools in white areas, and that a certain proportion of whites must be bused to schools in nonwhite areas. The objectives are twofold: to provide equal educational opportunities and to reduce racial prejudice through interaction.

In some areas, school busing has become accepted and appears to be meeting the stated objectives. In other areas, however, the approach is highly controversial and has exacerbated racial tensions. Busing in these areas is claimed (1) to be highly expensive; (2) to destroy the concept of the "neighborhood school," whereby the facility serves as the recreation, social, and educational center of the community; and (3) to result in lower-quality education. A number of parents in these areas feel so strongly about busing that they are sending their children to private schools. In addition, some have argued that busing increases "white flight" from neighborhoods where busing has been ordered. As a result, in some communities, busing programs that once carried black students to white schools now simply move them from one black neighborhood to a school system that predominately has black students (Eddings, 1997).

Busing may also intensify racial tensions. For example, in Boston in 1975, a federal judge ordered school busing in order to counter housing segregation patterns. The Irish and Polish residents of South Boston (who saw themselves as oppressed ethnic minorities) violently opposed the busing, and racial tensions intensified for several years. Sociologists also voice concern that school busing in an atmosphere of hostility may reduce the quality of education and increase racial prejudices and tensions.

Three decades of school busing have failed to deliver all the benefits its boosters hoped for and its critics demanded. Scores of studies generally agree that white students do not suffer academically from school integration via busing (Eddings, 1997). Integration via busing appears to improve the academic performance of African American students, but mainly in the primary grades, not in junior high or high school (Eddings, 1997).

There have been other benefits of integration via busing. African Americans who attended elementary and high schools with whites are substantially more likely to attend white-majority colleges, get jobs in desegregated workplaces that offer higher pay, and have white friends as adults. Also, African American students who go to integrated suburban schools rather than segregated city ones are less likely to drop out of high school, get in trouble with the police, drop out of college, or bear a child before age 18, and they are more likely to have white friends and live in integrated neighborhoods. Whites also benefit from attending school with African American students because they learn more about diversity and tend to more thoroughly confront their racial stereotypes (Tye, 1992).

Are the benefits of school busing worth the costs? This is a very complex issue, and as yet there is no definitive answer. The financial costs of busing children from one school district to another are high. Many authorities in both white and nonwhite neighborhoods are now increasingly arguing it would be better to use the money currently spent on busing to improve school facilities. Critics assert that busing for integration purposes almost always becomes a major obstacle for parental involvement in the school system, due to the long distances created between the location of the schools and the residences of the parents. Extensive parental involvement is associated with higher quality educational achievement of students; parental involvement leads to teachers, parents, and school administrators working together to improve school facilities and to develop innovative programs to instruct students (Coleman & Kerbo, 2002).

Surveys indicate a majority of Americans (including a large number of African Americans) oppose busing for integration purposes (Eddings, 1997). The main reason for the growing opposition to busing is that it often has not raised educational achievements of students of color (Eddings, 1997). As a result, it is unlikely there will be a resurgence of political support for expanding efforts to promote busing for integration purposes.

School busing to achieve integration was vigorously pursued by the court system and the Justice Department in the 1970s. In 1981 the Reagan administration stated it would be much less active in advocating busing as a vehicle to achieve integration. Three presidential administrations (George Bush, Bill Clinton, and George W. Bush) have also been fairly inactive in promoting school busing. In the past decade there has been less emphasis in many communities on using busing to achieve integration. In 1991 the U.S. Supreme Court ruled that busing to achieve integration, when ordered, need not be continued indefinitely. The ruling allows communities to end court-ordered busing by convincing a judge they have done everything reasonable to eliminate discrimination against African Americans.

Affirmative Action: A Macro System Response

Affirmative action programs require that employers demonstrate that they are actively employing minority applicants. Employers can no longer defend themselves by claiming that a decision not to hire a minority group member was based on some criterion other than ethnic group membership. If the percentage of minority group members in their employ is significantly lower than the percentage in the workforce, employers must accept a goal for minority employment and set up timetables stating when these goals are likely to be met.

Affirmative action programs provide for preferential hiring and admission requirements (e.g., admission to medical schools) for minority applicants. Affirmative action programs cover all minority groups including women. These programs also require that employers make active efforts to locate and recruit qualified minority applicants and, in certain circumstances, have hard quotas under which specific numbers of minority members must be accepted to fill vacant positions. For example, a university with a high proportion of white male faculty may be required to fill half of its faculty vacancies with women and other minority groups. Affirmative action programs require that employers must demonstrate according to a checklist of positive measures that they are not guilty of discrimination.

A major dilemma with affirmative action programs is that preferential hiring and quota programs involve *reverse discrimination,* in which qualified majority-group members are sometimes arbitrarily excluded. A number of lawsuits have been filed over the years in which complainants have alleged they have been victimized by reverse discrimination. The best-known case to date has been that of Alan Bakke, who was initially denied admission to the medical school at the University of California at Davis in

1973. He alleged reverse discrimination because he had higher grades and higher scores on the Medical College Admissions Tests than several minority applicants who were admitted under the university's minorities quota policy. In 1978, his claim was upheld by the U.S. Supreme Court in a precedent-setting decision (Sindler, 1978). The court ruled that strict racial quotas were unconstitutional, but did not rule out that race might be used as one among many criteria in making admissions decisions.

Supporters of affirmative action programs note that the majority group expressed little concern about discrimination when its members were the beneficiaries instead of the victims of discrimination. They also assert there is no other way to make up rapidly for past discrimination against minorities—many of whom may presently score slightly lower on qualification tests because they have not had the opportunities and the quality of training that the majority group members have had.

With affirmative action programs, some minority group members are given preferential treatment, which results in some whites being discriminated against. But minority group members still face more employment discrimination than whites do.

Affirmative action programs raise delicate and complex questions about achieving equality through giving preferences in hiring and admissions to minorities. Yet, no other means has been found to end subtle discrimination in hiring and admissions.

Admission to educational programs and well-paying jobs are crucial elements in working toward integration. The history of immigrant groups who have made it (such as the Irish, Japanese, and Italians) suggests equality will be achieved only when minority group members gain middle- and upper-class status. Once such status is achieved, the minority group members become an economic and political force to be reckoned with. The dominant groups are pressured into modifying their norms, values, and stereotypes. For this reason, a number of authorities have noted that the elimination of economic discrimination is a prerequisite for achieving equality and harmonious race relations (Kornblum & Julian, 1998). Achieving educational equality between races is also crucial because lower educational attainments lead to less prestigious jobs, lower incomes, lower-living standards, and the perpetuation of racial inequalities from one generation to the next.

Critics of affirmative action asssert that it is a highly politicized and painful remedy that has stigmatized many of those it was meant to help. Affirmative action is now perceived by many in our society as a system of preferences for the unqualified. Critics further assert that while affirmative action may have been necessary 30 years ago to make sure that minority candidates received fair treatment to counter the social barriers to hiring and admission that stemmed from centuries of unequal treatment, such programs are no longer needed. They assert that it is wrong to discriminate against white males for the sole purpose of making up for an injustice that somebody's great-grandfather may have done to somebody else's great-grandfather. They assert that it is wrong for the daughter of a wealthy African American couple, for example, to be given preference in employment over the son of a homeless alcoholic who happens to be white.

In 1996 voters in the state of California passed Proposition 209, which explicitly rejects the idea that women and other minority group members could get special consideration when applying for jobs, government contracts, or university admission. This affirmative action ban became law in California in August 1997. In addition, a number of lawsuits have been filed objecting to reverse discrimination. If the courts rule in favor of those filing the lawsuits, the power of affirmative action programs will be sharply reduced. In November 1997 the U.S. Supreme Court rejected a challenge to the California law that ended racial and gender preferences in that state. This Supreme Court action clears the way for other states and cities to ban affirmative action.

Supporters of affirmative action believe that if we abandon affirmative action, we return to the old-boy network. They assert that affirmative action has helped a number of women and people of color to attain a good education and higher paying positions, and thereby to remove themselves from the ranks of the poor. They assert that in a society in which racist and sexist attitudes remain, it is necessary to have affirmative action in order to give women and people of color a fair opportunity at attaining a quality education and well-paying jobs.

Is there a middle ground for the future of affirmative action? Zuckerman (1995) recommends:

> The vast majority of Americans would probably accept a return to the original notion of affirmative action—an aggressive outreach to minorities to make sure they have a fair shot. They would probably see a social benefit in accepting that racial justice might be relevant in a tiebreaker case, or might even confer a slight advantage. The goal must be a return to policies based on evenhandedness for individuals rather than for groups. Then employers can concentrate on whether a minority applicant is the right person for the job rather than being moved by whether the applicant looks litigious. All employees could take it for granted that they had a fair shot. (p. 112)

© Rick Gerharter

In the mid-1990s, the future of affirmative action became a hotly debated national issue. Here, in a San Francisco rally, students protest a University of California regents' decision to end affirmative action.

Confronting Racist Remarks and Actions

Racist jokes and sarcastic remarks help shape and perpetuate stereotypes and prejudices. Whites and nonwhites need to tactfully but assertively indicate they do not view such remarks as being humorous or appropriate. It is also important that people tactfully and assertively point out the inappropriateness of racist actions by others. Such confrontations make explicit that subtle racist remarks and actions are discriminatory and harmful, which has a consciousness raising effect. Gradually, it is expected that such confrontations will reduce racial prejudices and actions.

Noted nineteenth-century author, lecturer, and abolitionist Frederick Douglass stated:

> Power concedes nothing without a demand—it never did, and it never will. Find out just what people will submit to, and you've found out the exact amount of injustice and wrong which will be imposed upon them. This will continue until they resist, either with words, blows, or both. The limits of

tyrants are prescribed by the endurance of those whom they oppress. (quoted in Cummings, 1977, p. 201)

Minority-Owned Businesses

Many people aspire to run their own business. Running a business is particularly attractive to many members of minority groups. It means an opportunity to increase one's income and wealth. It is also a way to avoid some of the racial and ethnic discrimination that occurs in the work world, such as the "glass ceilings" that block the promotion of qualified minority workers in corporations.

Since the 1970s, federal, state, and local governments have attempted to assist minority-owned businesses in a variety of ways. Programs have provided low-interest loans to minority-owned businesses. There are set-aside programs that stipulate that government contracts must be awarded to a minimum proportion, usually 10 to 30 percent, of minority-owned businesses. Some large urban areas have created enterprise zones, which encourages employment and investment in blighted neighborhoods through the use of tax breaks. Minority-owned businesses have slowly been increasing in numbers. Yet only a small fraction of the total number of people classified as being a member of a minority group have benefited from government support of minority-owned businesses (Schaefer, 1996).

Confronting Community Problems: Inner Cities

It is difficult to find the right adjectives to describe the dismal living conditions in inner cities. The following apply: decaying, inhuman, dreadful, distasteful, shocking, and degrading. Inner cities are primarily inhabited by the poor, the elderly, and members of minority groups, particularly African Americans and Hispanics. Many inner cities have an ethnic concentration, such as African American, Mexican American, Cuban, or Puerto Rican.

Inner cities have high rates of crime, illiteracy, births out of marriage, single-parent households, mental illness, suicide, drug and alcohol abuse, unemployment, infant mortality, rape, aggravated assault, and delinquency. High proportions of the residents are on welfare. Many city services are inferior in inner cities. Schools are inferior, streets are narrow and often filled with pot holes. Police and fire protection services are inadequate to meet the needs of the neighborhoods.

The housing is crowded and decaying, and much of it is substandard. Heat in winter is often inadequate. Many units lack adequate plumbing. Broken windows, peeling paint, and doors hanging off their hinges are common. Minority group members inhabit much of this substandard housing because most cannot afford an alternative, and because discrimination makes it difficult to relocate—even for those whose incomes would enable them to move.

One of the factors that is leading to the decline of inner cities is the sharp decline of blue-collar jobs in our society. Many blue-collar jobs are unskilled or semi-skilled jobs that require less training and education than white-collar and service jobs. The employable in inner cities have in the past largely held blue-collar jobs. For a neighborhood to resist deterioration, a minimal economic base must be maintained. As blue-collar jobs decline, and the quality of municipal services (such as transportation and public schools) deteriorates, faith in community revitalization fades.

Decaying inner cities are a national disgrace. Our country is the richest and most powerful in the world, yet we have been unable to improve living conditions for the poor in our inner cities.

Our country has tried a variety of approaches to improve inner-city living conditions. Programs and services provided include work training, job placement, financial assistance through public welfare, low-interest mortgages to start businesses, Head Start, drug and alcohol treatment, crime prevention, housing, rehabilitation, day-care services, health-care services, and public health services.

One of the most comprehensive undertakings to assist inner cities was the Model Cities Program, which was part of the War on Poverty in the 1960s. Several inner cities were targeted for this massive intervention. The program involved tearing down dilapidated housing and constructing comfortable living quarters. Salvageable buildings were renovated. In addition, these Model City projects had a variety of programs that provided job training and placement, health-care services, social services, and educational opportunities. The results were depressing. The communities have again deteriorated. Living conditions are as bleak, or bleaker, than at the start of the Model City interventions (Kornblum & Julian, 2001).

To date, all programs that have been tried have had, at best, only short-term success. No other conclusion can be made. Inner cities continue to have abysmal living conditions. The federal government, in the past two decades, appears to have given up trying to improve living conditions, as federal programs for inner cities have either been eliminated or sharply cut back.

In 1996 federal legislation was enacted that dismantled the AFDC program, and created the Temporary Assistance to Needy Families (TANF) program. This legislation is having a significant impact in inner cities. The entire concept of poor families being entitled to basic human and health services as a basic right is shifting back to the assumption that charity and a paying job can respond more cheaply to local social problems than public services can. The legislation calls for the following: (a) Each state sets its own rules and amounts for financial assistance. The federal government provides block grants to states to assist in financing the programs that are developed; (b) recipients of financial benefits receive no more than 2 years of assistance without working, and there is a 5-year life-time limit of benefits for adults. The impact of TANF on poor people in inner cities is not yet fully known.

Our society, for better or worse, is a materialistic one. The two main legitimate ways to get material goods are by getting a good education and by obtaining a job that pays a living wage. It appears that many inner-city residents believe that prospects are bleak for getting a good education (when only inferior schools exist in their areas) or a living-wage job (when they have few marketable job skills). Many turn to illegitimate ways to get material goods (shoplifting, drug trafficking, robbery, and con games). Many have also turned to immediate gratifications (including sex and drug highs). Their value system includes being dependent on the government through welfare for a substandard lifestyle.

Our society has tried a variety of programs in the past to combat the problems faced by inner-city residents. All past programs have largely failed to improve our inner cities. At the present time our federal government has a laissez-faire approach, and conditions are deteriorating in many of our inner cities. Are there workable alternatives? One alternative is the development and support of grassroots organizations.

Grassroots Organizations: Implementing Change in Community Macro Systems

The efforts of some grassroots organizations at times have positive, long-lasting effects. *Grassroots organizations* are composed of community residents who work together to improve their community. It may be that lasting changes can be made in a neighborhood only when the residents themselves are inspired, in some way, to improve their own community. The following description is an illustration of a successful grassroots effort in Cochran Gardens, St. Louis, Missouri (Boyte, 1989).

Cochran Gardens, a low-income housing project, was typical of many deteriorating housing projects in large urban areas. It was characterized by rubbish, graffiti, broken windows, frequent shootings, crime, drug trafficking, and angry and fearful people.

Bertha Gilkey grew up in this housing project. At a young age, Gilkey believed the neighborhood could improve if residents worked together. As a teenager she attended tenant meetings in a neighborhood church. When she was 20 years old, she was elected to chair this tenants' association.

Gilkey and her group started with small projects. They asked tenants what they really wanted that was realistic to achieve. There was a consensus that the housing project needed a usable laundromat, because previous laundromats had all been vandalized and the only working one in the project had no locks; in fact the entry door had been stolen. Bertha and her group requested and received a door from the city housing authority. The organization then held a fundraiser for a lock and another fundraiser for paint. After the organization painted the laundromat, residents were pleased to have an attractive working laundromat, which increased their interest in joining and supporting the tenants' association. The association then organized to paint the hallways of the housing project, floor by floor. Everyone who lived on a floor was responsible for being involved in painting the hallway floor. Gilkey (quoted in Boyte, 1989) states:

> Kids who lived on the floor that hadn't been painted would come and look at the painted hallways and then go back and hassle their parents. The elderly who couldn't paint prepared lunch so they could feel like they were a part of it too. (p. 3)

The organization continued to initiate and successfully complete new projects to spruce up the neighborhood. Each success inspired more and more residents to take pride in their neighborhood and to work toward making improvements. While improving the physical appearance of the housing project, Gilkey and the tenants' organization also reintroduced a conduct code for the project. A committee formulated rules of behavior and elected monitors on each floor. The rules included no loud disruptions, no throwing garbage out the windows, and no fights. Slowly residents got the message, and living conditions improved, one small step at a time. The building was renamed Dr. Martin Luther King Jr. Building. (Symbols are important in community development efforts.) The organization also held a party and a celebration for each successfully completed project.

Another focus of Gilkey's efforts was to reach out to children and adolescents. The positives were highlighted. The young people wrote papers in school on "What I Like about Living Here." In art class they built a cardboard model of the housing project that included the buildings, streets, and playground. Such efforts were designed to build the self-esteem of the young people, and to instill a sense of pride in their community.

Today, Cochran Gardens is a public housing project with flower-lined paths, trees, and grass—a beautiful and clean neighborhood filled with trusting people who have a sense of pride in their community. The high-rises have been completely renovated. There is a community center, tennis courts, playgrounds, and town-house apartments to reduce density in the complex. Cochran Gardens is managed by the tenants. The association (now named Tenant Management Council) has ventured into owning and operating certain businesses: a catering service, day-care centers, health clinics, and a vocational training program (Gilkey, 2001).

The Cochran success has been based on the principles of self-help, empowerment, responsibility, and dignity. Gilkey (quoted in Boyte, 1989) states:

> *This goes against the grain, doesn't it? Poor people are to be managed. What we've done is cut through all the bullshit and said it doesn't take all that. People with degrees and credentials got us in this mess. All it takes is some basic skills. . . . If we can do it in public housing, it can happen anywhere. (p. 5)*

Such successes suggest it is desirable for our federal, state, and city governments to seek to improve innercity conditions by encouraging and supporting (including financially) grassroots efforts.

An ongoing rehabilitation program conducted by a resident grassroots organization has contributed to the success of Cochran Gardens, a low-income housing project in St. Louis, Missouri.

🌿 Social Work Practice with Racial and Ethnic Groups

Social workers and other helping persons have many of the prejudices, stereotypes, and misperceptions of the general society. There is a danger that a social worker will use her or his own cultural, social, or economic values in assessing and providing services to clients.

The problematic nature of cross-cultural social work does not preclude its effectiveness. While many white practitioners can establish productive working relationships with minority clients, others cannot. In other instances, minority practitioners are sometimes effective and sometimes not with others of the same race or ethnic group.

Ethnic-Sensitive Practice

Traditionally, professional social work practice has used the medical model for the delivery of services. The medical model is a deficit model that focuses on identifying problems or deficits within a person. The medical model largely ignores environmental factors that impact the person-in-situation. A major shortcoming of a deficit model is that it focuses on the deficits of a person or a group while ignoring strengths and resources. (When one emphasizes only the shortcomings of a person, that person's self-esteem is apt to be severely affected negatively; that person may define himself or herself in terms of shortcomings and, in the process, overlook strengths and resources.)

A better model is ethnic-sensitive practice, which seeks to incorporate understanding of diverse ethnic, cultural, and minority groups into the theories and principles that guide social work practice (Devore & Schlesinger, 1996). Ethnic-sensitive practice is based on the view that practice must be attuned to the values and dispositions related to clients' ethnic group membership and social-class position. Ethnic-sensitive practice requires that social workers have an in-depth understanding of the effects of oppression on racial and ethnic groups.

Another important segment of the conceptual framework is the concept of the "dual perspective" mentioned in Chapter 3 (Beckett & Johnson, 1995; Norton, 1978). This concept is derived from the view that all people are a part of two systems: (1) the dominant or sustaining system (the society that one lives in), which is the source of power and economic resources; and (2) the nurturing system, composed of the physical and social environment of family and community. The dual perspective concept asserts that the adverse consequences of an oppressive society on the self-concept of a person of color or of any minority group can be partially offset by the nurturing system.

Ethnic-sensitive practice requires that social workers have a special obligation to be aware of and to seek to redress the oppression experienced by ethnic groups. Ethnic-sensitive practice assumes that each ethnic group's members have a history that has a bearing on the members' perceptions of current problems. For example, the individual and collective history of many African Americans leads to the expectation that family resources will be available in times of trouble (Devore & Schlesinger, 1996). Ethnic-sensitive practice, however, assumes that the present is most important. For example, many Mexican American and Puerto Rican women currently feel tension as they attempt to move beyond traditionally defined gender roles into the mainstream as students and paid employees (Devore & Schlesinger, 1996).

Ethnic-sensitive practice introduces no new practice principles or approaches. Instead, it urges the adaptation of prevailing therapies, social work principles, and skills to take account of ethnic reality. Regardless of which practice approach is used, Three concepts and perspectives that are emphasized are empowerment, the strengths perspective, and culturally competent practice.

❧ Empowerment

Empowerment has been defined as "the process of helping individuals, families, groups, and communities increase their personal, interpersonal, socioeconomic, and political strength and influence toward improving their circumstances" (Barker, 1999, p. 153). In working with an ethnic or racial group, empowerment counters the negative image of the group (which has been established through a long history of discrimination), with a positive value or image and an emphasis on the ability of each

group member to influence the conditions of his or her life. Empowerment counters hopelessness and powerlessness with the belief that each person is able to address problems competently, beginning with a positive view of the self. Empowerment counters oppression and poverty by helping members of ethnic groups increase their ability to make and implement basic life decisions.

❧ Strengths Perspective

The strengths perspective is closely related to empowerment. The *strengths perspective* seeks to identify, use, build, and reinforce the strengths that people have, in contrast to the pathological perspective, which focuses on their deficiencies (see Chapter 3). It emphasizes people's abilities, interests, aspirations, resources, beliefs, and accomplishments. For example, strengths of African Americans in the United States include the following: There are more than 100 predominantly African American colleges and universities; fraternal and women's organizations; and social, political and professional organizations. Many of the schools, businesses, churches, and organizations that are predominantly African American have developed social service programs—such as family support services, mentoring programs, food and shelter services, transportation services, and educational and scholarship programs. Through individual and organized efforts, self-help approaches and mutual aid traditions continue among African Americans. African Americans tend to have strong ties to immediate, extended family. They tend to have a strong religious orientation, a strong work and achievement orientation, and egalitarian role sharing (Billingsley, 1993).

Culturally Competent Practice

By the middle of the twenty-first century, projections indicate that nearly half of the population of the United States will be composed of people of color (Dhooper & Moore, 2001). Increasingly, social workers will be dealing with people who are more diverse, politically more active, and more aware of their rights. It is, therefore, incumbent for social workers to become increasingly culturally competent. In order to become culturally competent, a social worker needs to: (1) become aware of culture and its pervasive influence; (2) learn about her or his own culture; (3) recognize her or his own ethnocentricity; (4) learn about other cultures; (5) acquire cultural knowledge about the clients she or he is working with;

and (6) adapt social work skills and intervention approaches to the needs and styles of the cultures of these clients (Dhooper & Moore, 2001).

In 2001, The National Association of Social Workers (2001) approved the following ten standards for cultural competence in social work practice:

Standard 1. *Ethics and Values*—Social workers shall function in accordance with the values, ethics, and standards of the profession, recognizing how personal and professional values may conflict with or accommodate the needs of diverse clients.

Standard 2. *Self-Awareness*—Social workers shall seek to develop an understanding of their own personal cultural values and beliefs as one way of appreciating the importance of multicultural identities in the lives of people.

Standard 3. *Cross-Cultural Knowledge*—Social workers shall have and continue to develop specialized knowledge and understanding about the history, traditions, values, family systems, and artistic expressions of major client groups that they serve.

Standard 4. *Cross-Cultural Skills*—Social workers shall use appropriate methodological approaches, skills, and techniques that reflect the workers' understanding of the role of culture in the helping process.

Standard 5. *Service Delivery*—Social workers shall be knowledgeable about and skillful in the use of services available in the community and broader society and be able to make appropriate referrals for their diverse clients.

Standard 6. *Empowerment and Advocacy*—Social workers shall be aware of the effect of social policies and programs on diverse client populations, advocating for and with clients whenever appropriate.

Standard 7. *Diverse Workforce*—Social workers shall support and advocate for recruitment, admissions and hiring, and retention efforts in social work programs and agencies that ensure diversity within the profession.

Standard 8. *Professional Education*—Social workers shall advocate for and participate in educational and training programs that help advance cultural competence within the profession.

Standard 9. *Language Diversity*—Social workers shall seek to provide or advocate for the provision of information, referrals, and services in the language appropriate to the client, which may include use of interpreters.

Standard 10. *Cross-Cultural Leadership*—Social workers shall be able to communicate information about diverse client groups to other professionals.[*]

Learning the Culture of the Group. In working with a diverse culture the following questions are crucial: How are the members likely to view someone from a different culture? What kinds of communications and actions are likely to lead to the development of a relationship? How do members view asking for help from a social agency? If the agency is viewed as being part of the dominant white society that has devalued this group in the past, how are the members likely to view the social agency? What are the values of the group? When the members of this group need help, who are they most likely to turn to—relatives, friends, neighbors, churches, social agencies, the school system, or the local government? What are culturally acceptable ways of providing help to people in need?

As a corollary of becoming accepted by clients of diverse racial or ethnic groups, the social worker must live his or her personal life in a manner that will not offend important values and mores of those groups.

There are an *immense* number of different racial and ethnic groups in our society. It is beyond the scope of this chapter to describe the unique characteristics of these diverse groups. Instead, a few characteristics of some minority groups will be summarized to illustrate the importance of learning about the minority group of a client. For example, when working with Native Americans it is considered rude—an attempt to intimidate, in fact—to maintain direct eye contact (Hull, 1995).

Chicano men, as contrasted to Anglo men, have been described as exhibiting greater pride in their maleness (Schaefer, 2002). *Machismo*—a strong sense of masculine pride—is highly valued among Chicano men and is displayed by males to express dominance and superiority. *Machismo* is demonstrated differently by different people. Some may seek to be irresistible to women and to have a number of sexual partners. Some resort to weapons or fighting. Some interpret *machismo* to mean pride in one's manhood, honor, and ability to provide for one's family. Others boast of their achievements, even those that never occurred. Recent writers have noted that the feminist movement, urbanization, upward mobility, and acculturation are contributing to the decline of *machismo*

(Shaefer, 1996). Chicanos also tend to be more "familistic" than Anglos. *Familism* is the belief that the family takes precedence over the individual. Schaefer (1996) notes:

> *Familism is generally regarded as good . . . as an extended family provides greater emotional strength at times of family crisis. The many significant aspects of familism include: (1) the importance of the* compadrazo *(godparent-godchild relationship); (2) the benefits of financial dependency on kin; (3) the availability of relatives as a source of advice; and (4) active involvement of the elderly within the family. (pp. 294–295)*

On the negative side, familism may discourage youth from pursuing opportunities that will take them away from the family. It should be noted that differences between Chicanos and Anglos with regard to *machismo* and familism are ones of degree, not of kind.

Hull (1995) suggests that natural support systems are a useful resource in providing assistance to Chicanos. These support systems include extended family, folk healers, religious institutions, and merchant and social clubs. The extended family includes the family of origin, nuclear family members, other relatives, godparents, and those considered to be like family. Folk healers are prominent in Chicano communities. Some use treatments that blend natural healing methods with religious or spiritual beliefs. Religious institutions (especially the Roman Catholic church) provide such services as pastoral counseling, emergency money, job-locating and housing assistance, and some specialized programs, such as drug-abuse treatment and prevention. Merchant and social clubs can provide such items as native foods, herbs, referral to other resources, credit and information, prayer books, recreation, and the services of healers. The reluctance of Chicano clients to seek help from a social welfare agency can be reduced by use of these natural support systems. Outreach can be done through churches and community groups. If a social welfare agency gains a reputation of utilizing such natural support systems in the intervention process, Chicanos will have greater trust in the agency and be much more apt to seek help. Utilizing such natural support systems also increases the effectiveness of the intervention process.

Religious organizations that are predominantly African American usually have a social and spiritual mission. They are apt to be highly active in efforts to combat racial discrimination. Many prominent African American leaders, such as the late Martin Luther King Jr. and Jesse Jackson, have been members of the clergy. African American churches have served to develop leadership skills. They have also served as social welfare organizations to meet such basic needs as food, clothing, and shelter. African American churches are natural support systems that workers need to utilize to serve troubled African American individuals and families.

Self-Awareness of Values, Prejudices, and Stereotypes. Because social workers live in a society in which racial and ethnic prejudices abound, they also have prejudices and stereotypes. Think about these questions: In the past year, have you listened to some racial or ethnic jokes? Did you laugh? If you did laugh, do you think your laughter, in a small way, was perpetuating some racial or ethnic stereotypes? Have you told in the past year some racial or ethnic jokes? If yes, was the content derogatory? By telling such jokes, are you demonstrating some of your prejudices and stereotypes? By telling such jokes, are you not, in some way, reinforcing some of the harmful stereotypes and prejudices that exist in our society?

Racial and ethnic prejudices can be demonstrated by the following exercise:

Assume you are single; place a check mark beside the following ethnic and racial groups that you would be hesitant or reluctant to marry a member of:

___Iranian	___White American
___Chinese	___Egyptian
___Japanese	___Irish
___Samoan	___Cuban
___Filipino	___Puerto Rican
___African American	___German
___Native American	___Vietnamese
___Italian	___French
___Mexican	___Russian

If you have checked some of these (and most people check several), analyze your thoughts as to why you would be hesitant to marry those you have checked. There is a fair chance that such an analysis will help you identify some of your prejudices.

A helping professional needs to be aware of his or her racial and ethnic stereotypes and prejudices in order to remain objective in working with clients. When working with a client of a group that you have negative perceptions about, you should continually be asking the following questions: Am I individualizing this person as a unique person with worth, or am I making the mistake of viewing this person in terms of my prejudices and stereotypes? Am I working up to my full capacities with this individual? Or am I seeking to cut corners by probing less deeply, by not fully informing this person of the services he or she is eligible for, or by wanting to end the interview before fully exploring all the client's problems and fully exploring all possible alternatives? When we have negative stereotypes about someone, there is a strong likelihood that we will discriminate against that person when we are providing services. Being aware of our stereotypes is the first step in preventing such discrimination.

Application of Theory to Practice: Techniques of Intervention. The third area is for the social worker to learn which intervention approaches are likely to be effective, and which are likely to be ineffective with the ethnic or racial group he or she is working with. Several guidelines will be presented for illustrative purposes.

Social workers should seek to use their own patterns of communication and avoid the temptation to adopt the client's accent, vocabulary, or speech (Hull, 1995). The worker who seeks to speak like the client is apt to make mistakes in enunciations, and thereby come across as a phony, or may offend the client if the client interprets the worker's communication to be mimicry.

A social worker with an urban background who has a job in a small rural community needs to live his personal life in a way that is consistent with community values and standards. A worker who gains a reputation as being a violator of community norms will not be effective in a small community. Neither the power structure nor a majority of clients are likely to give such a worker credibility. A worker in a small community needs to identify community values in areas such as the following: religious beliefs and patterns of expression, dating and marriage patterns, values toward domestic and wild animals (for example, opposing deer hunting in many communities may run counter to strong local values), drug usage, political beliefs and values, and sexual mores. Once such values are identified, the social worker needs to seek to achieve a balance between the kind of lifestyle he wants and the kind of lifestyle the community expects he will live.

Hull (1995) recommends using all of the formalities in initial meetings with adult clients of diverse racial and ethnic groups. Such usage should include the formal title (Mr., Miss, Mrs., Ms.), the client's proper full name, greeting with a handshake, and the other courtesies usually extended. In initial contacts workers should also usually show their agency identification and state reasons for the meeting.

Agencies and social workers should establish working hours that coincide with the needs of the groups being served. Doing so may mean having evening and weekend hours to avoid forcing clients, already with financial difficulties, to lose time from their jobs.

In the area of group services to racially diverse clients, Hull (1995) recommends that membership be selected in such a manner that no one race vastly outnumbers the others. Sometimes it is necessary to educate clients about the processes of individual or group counseling. Using words common to general conversation is much better than using technical and sophisticated jargon that clients are not likely to comprehend.

In working with adult clients who are not fluent in the English language, it is generally a mistake to use bilingual children of the clients as interpreters (Hull, 1995). Having children as interpreters is embarrassing to the parents because it places them in a position of being partially dependent on their children and erroneously suggests the parents are deficient in learning essential communication mechanisms. In addition, children often lack an adult's knowledge, which reduces their value as interpreters. Also, in using interpreters the worker should direct his conversation to the client and not to the interpreter. Talking to the interpreter diverts attention from the client and places the client in the position of bystander rather than the central figure in the relationship.

Native Americans place a high value on the principle of self-determination (Hull, 1995). This sometimes provides a perplexing dilemma for a social worker who wonders "How can I help if I can't intervene?" Native Americans will request intervention only infrequently, and the white worker needs to have patience and wait for the request. How long this will take varies. During the waiting period the non–Native American worker should be available and may offer assistance as long as there is no hint of coercion. Once help is accepted, the worker will be tested. If the client believes the worker has been helpful, the word will spread, and the worker is likely to have more requests for help. If the client concludes the worker is lacking in helpful capacities, this assessment will also spread, and the worker will have an even more difficult task in being sought out by potential clients.

In establishing rapport with African American, Hispanic, Native American, or clients of other groups who have suffered from racial oppression, a peer relationship should be sought in which there is mutual respect and mutual sharing of information. A white superiority type of relationship should be rejected totally because it is likely to be interpreted by racially diverse clients as being offensive—which in fact it is.

Social Work Roles for Countering Discrimination

Social workers have an obligation to work vigorously to end racial discrimination as well as other forms of discrimination. The major professional social work organizations have, over the years, taken strong positions aimed at ending racial discrimination. The National Association of Social Workers, for example, has lobbied for the passage of civil rights legislation. The Code of Ethics of NASW (1996) has the following explicit statement about discrimination:

> Social workers should act to prevent and eliminate domination of, exploitation of, and discrimination against any person, group, or class on the basis of race, ethnicity, national origin, color, sex, sexual orientation, age, marital status, political belief, religion, or mental or physical disability. (p. 24)

The Council on Social Work Education (CSWE), in its Educational Policy and Accreditation Standards (EPAS) (2001), requires, in baccalaureate and master's programs in social work, that content on racism be included in the social work curriculum. EPAS also require that accredited programs must also provide considerable content on populations-at-risk, on diversity, and on the promotion of social and economic justice. Professional social work education is committed to preparing social work students to understand and appreciate cultural and social diversity. Students are taught to understand the dynamics and consequences of oppression, and they learn to use intervention strategies to combat social injustice, oppression, and their effects. There is an Association of Black Social Workers, which has been very active in combating racial prejudice and discrimination.

In working to end racial and other forms of discrimination, social workers can take on a variety of roles. They can be *advocates* for equal treatment for those who are being oppressed or discriminated against. They can be *analysts* of societal conditions that result in institutional racism and then be *advocates* for the development of programs to counter such racism. They can be *initiators* of action by seeking to inform social service systems and the political systems of social injustices and then advocating for changes in policies and programs. At times, they can fulfill an *educator* role by giving information on options to counter oppression and by conveying information on how to organize and advocate for change. If several organizations are working somewhat independently to counter related forms of discrimination and oppression, social workers can serve as *integrators/coordinators* by seeking to have these organizations form a coalition in which they work together in some organized manner to effect change. At times, social workers may, in the role of *counselor,* work with oppressed individuals and small groups to problem-solve personal concerns related to being victimized by oppression and discrimination. Social workers may also be *brokers* by linking oppressed client systems with needed resources.

❦ The Future of U.S. Race and Ethnic Relations

It is clear that minorities such as African Americans, Hispanics, Asian Americans, and Native Americans will assertively, and sometimes aggressively, pursue a variety of strategies to change racist prejudices and actions. Counteractions by certain segments of the white dominant group are also likely to occur. (Even in the social sciences, every action elicits a reaction.) For example, in recent years, memberships in organizations that advocate white supremacy, such as the Ku Klux Klan have increased.

Minorities have been given hope of achieving equality of opportunity and justice. Their hope has been kindled, and they will no longer submit to a subordinate status. Struggles to achieve racial equality will continue.

What will be the pattern of race relations in the future? Gordon (1961) outlined three possible patterns of intergroup relations: Anglo-conformity, melting pot, and cultural pluralism:

> Anglo-conformity *assumes the desirability of maintaining modified English institutions, language, and culture as the dominant standard in American life. In practice, "assimilation" in America has always meant Anglo-conformity, and the groups that have been most readily assimilated have been those that are ethnically and culturally most similar to the Anglo-Saxon group [early British colonists].*
>
> The melting pot *is, strictly speaking, a rather different concept, which views the future American society not as a modified England but rather as a totally new blend, both culturally and biologically, of all the various groups that inhabit the United States. In practice, the melting pot has been of only limited significance in the American experience.*
>
> Cultural pluralism *implies a series of coexisting groups, each preserving its own tradition and culture but each loyal to an overarching American nation. Although the cultural enclaves of some immigrant groups, such as the Germans, have declined in importance in the past, many other groups, such as the Italians, have retained a strong sense of ethnic identity and have resisted both Anglo-conformity and inclusion in the melting pot. (pp. 363–365)*

Members of some European ethnic groups such as the British, French, and Dutch formed the dominant culture of the United States. Other European ethnic groups such as the Irish, Italians, Polish, Germans, Scandinavians, Greeks, and Hungarians are now nearly fully assimilated and integrated.

Cultural pluralism appears to be the form that race and ethnic relations are presently taking. Renewed interest on the part of a number of ethnic European Americans in expressing their pride in their own customs, religions, and

Spotlight on Diversity 5.5

A Dream of the End of Racism

In 1963, Martin Luther King Jr. delivered a speech in which he stated a hope and a goal that racism will one day be ended. An excerpt from that speech follows:

I say to you today, my friends, that is spite of the difficulties and frustrations of the moment, I still have a dream. It is a dream deeply rooted in the American dream. I have a dream that one day this nation will rise up and live out the true meaning of its creed: "We hold these truths to be self-evident: that all men are created equal." I have a dream that one day on the red hills of Georgia the sons of former slaves and the sons of former slaveowners will be able to sit down together at the table of brotherhood. . . . I have a dream that my four children will one day live in a nation where they will not be judged by the color of their skin but by the content of their character. . . . This is our hope. This is the faith with which I return to the South. With this faith we will

be able to hew out of the mountain of despair a stone of hope. With this faith we will be able to transform the jangling discords of our nation into a beautiful symphony of brotherhood. With this faith we will be able to work together, to pray together, to struggle together, to go to jail together, to stand up for freedom together, knowing that we will be free one day. . . . Let freedom ring from Lookout Mountain of Tennessee! Let freedom ring from every hill and every molehill of Mississippi. From every mountainside, let freedom ring. When we let freedom ring, when we let it ring from every village and every hamlet, from every state and every city, we will be able to speed up that day when all of God's children, black men and white men, Jews and Gentiles, Protestants and Catholics, will be able to join hands and sing in the words of the old Negro spiritual, "Free at last! free at last! thank God Almighty, we are free at last!"

linguistic and cultural traditions is evident. Slogans on buttons and signs say "Kiss me, I'm Italian," "Irish Power," and "Polish and Proud." African Americans, Native Americans, Hispanics, and Asian Americans are demanding entry into mainstream America but are not demanding assimilation. They want coexistence in a pluralistic society while seeking to preserve their own traditions and cultures. They are finding a source of identity and pride in their own cultural backgrounds and histories.

Some progress has been made toward ending discrimination since the *Brown* v. *Board of Education* decision in 1954. Yet equal opportunity for all people in America, as expressed in Martin Luther King's famous 1963 speech (see Spotlight 5.5), is still only a dream.

❧ Summary

Our country has always been racist and ethnocentric. Discrimination and oppression continue to have tragic consequences for those who are victims. In our country's history, racial discrimination has had violent and tragic consequences for many nonwhite groups. Individuals who are targets of ethnic or racial discrimination are excluded from certain types of employment, educational and recreational opportunities, certain residential housing areas, membership in certain social and religious organizations,

certain political activities, access to some community services, and so on. Discrimination is also a serious obstacle to developing a positive self-concept, and has heavy psychological and financial costs. Internationally, the racism and ethnocentrism that are widely known to occur in this country severely damage our credibility in promoting human rights.

Theories of the sources of discrimination include: projection, frustration–aggression, countering insecurity and inferiority, the authoritarian personality, historical explanations, competition and exploitation, and socialization processes, and the belief in only one true religion.

There are numerous racial and ethnic groups in our society, each with its unique culture, language, history, and special needs. This uniqueness needs to be understood and appreciated if we are to achieve progress toward ethnic and racial equality.

Strategies against discrimination include mass media appeals, increased interaction between minority groups and the majority group, civil rights legislation, protests and activism, affirmative action, school busing, minority-owned businesses, confronting racist and ethnic remarks and actions, confronting problems in inner cities, and grassroots organizations. Three possible patterns of intergroup ethnic and race relations in the future are Anglo-conformity, melting pot, and cultural pluralism. Cultural pluralism is the form that race and ethnic relations are presently taking, and may well take in the future.

InfoTrac College Edition Keywords

Afrocentrism
Anglo conformity

cultural pluralism
ethnic-sensitive practice

ethnocentrism
projection

violence against minorities
white privilege

On the Internet

Africentric Personal Development

http://www.apdsinc.org/programs.htm

The Africentric Personal Development Shop, Inc., offers a variety of clinical services as well as a continuum of personal, family, and community development programs.

CSWE EPAS

http://www.cswe.org/accreditation/EPAS/EPAS_star.htm

The Council on Social Work Education's (CSWE) Educational Policy and Accreditation Standards (EPAS) promote academic excellence in baccalaureate and master's social work education. The EPAS specify the curricular content and educational context to prepare students for professional social work practice. The EPAS set forth basic requirements for these purposes. Beyond these basic requirements of EPAS, individual programs focus on areas relevant to their institutional and program mission, goals, and objectives.

National Association for Chicana and Chicano Studies

http://clnet.ucr.edu/research/NACCS/mission.htm

Its goals are: to advance the interest and needs of the Chicana and Chicano community; to advance research in Chicana and Chicano Studies; to advance the professional interest and needs of Chicanas and Chicanos in the academy.

Native Elder Health Care

http://www.uchsc.edu/ai/nehcrc/

The Native Elder Health Care Resource Center (NEHCRC), initially funded by the Administration on Aging for a four-year period beginning on February 1, 1994, is a national resource center for older American Indians, Alaska Natives, and Native Hawaiians, with special emphasis on culturally competent health care.

CHAPTER 6

Biological Systems and Their Impacts on Adolescence and Young Adulthood

Roger sat in study hall gazing out of the window. He had an intense, pained expression on his face. Roger was 15 years old, and not one thing was going right for him. His arms were too long for the rest of his body. He felt like he couldn't walk from the desk to the door without tripping at least once. Homecoming was coming up soon, and his face suddenly looked like a pepperoni pizza. Amanda, the light of his life, wouldn't even acknowledge his existence. To top it all off, even if he managed to get Amanda to go to homecoming with him, he'd still either have to scrounge up another, older couple to drive or else have his father drive them to the dance. How humiliating. Roger continued to gaze out of the study hall window. The primary theme in his thoughts was, "Life is hard."

Change and adjustment characterize adolescence and young adulthood. Roger is not unique. Like other people his age, he is trying to cope with drastic physical changes, increasing sexual awareness, desires to fit in with the peer group, and the desperate need to develop a personal identity.

We have established that the attainment of developmental milestones is directly related to human behavior. We have also established that within any individual (micro system), the biological, psychological, and social systems mutually affect each other. Together, they interact and significantly impact growth, development, and ultimately well-being.

Biological development and maturation affect both how adolescents perceive themselves and how they behave. Rapid and uneven physical growth may cause awkwardness. Awkwardness may result in feeling self-conscious and consequently uncomfortable in social interactions. As we will point out, for example, some psychological behavioral differences exist between males who develop earlier and later than those who develop at an average rate.

219

Biological development often affects the transactions between individuals and their immediate social environments. For instance, when adolescents begin to attain physical and sexual maturity, sexual relationships may begin to develop. Likewise, new and different alternatives become available to adolescents and young adults as they mature. For example, alternatives concerning sexuality may range from no sexual activity to avid and frequent sexual relations. These new alternatives merit evaluation in terms of their positive and negative consequences. Decisions need to be made about such critical issues as whether to have sexual relations or not, which, if any, methods of birth control to use, and whether or not to enter into marriage.

A PERSPECTIVE

Chapters 6, 7, and 8 address, respectively, the biological, psychological, and social-environmental aspects of adolescence and young adulthood. The goal is to provide a framework for a better understanding of this difficult, yet exciting, time of life.

This chapter will:

▶ Explore some of the major physical changes that occur during adolescence and puberty.

▶ Describe the adolescent growth spurt, the secular trend, and both primary and secondary sex characteristics.

▶ Appraise some of the psychological reactions related directing to physical changes.

▶ Recognize the contributions of physical development, health status, and other factors to health during young adulthood.

▶ Explore some of the issues and life crises, including sexual activity, unplanned pregnancy, teenage fatherhood, motivation for pregnancy, sex education (especially in the age of AIDS), sexually transmitted diseases, and methods of contraception, that tend to affect adolescents.

❦ Adolescence

Adolescence is the time of life between childhood and adulthood. The word is derived from the Latin verb *adolescere,* which means "to grow into maturity." There is no precise point in time when adolescence begins or ends. Adolescence should be differentiated from puberty, which is more specific. *Adolescence* might be considered a cultural concept that refers to a general time during life. *Puberty,* on the other hand, is a physical concept that refers to the specific time during which people mature sexually and become capable of reproduction.

Some societies have specific rites of passage or events to mark the transition from childhood into adulthood. For example, among the Mangaia of the South Pacific (Hyde & DeLamater, 2000; Marshall, 1980), when a boy reached the age of 12 or 13 years, he participated in a ceremony where a superincision was made on his penis. The cut was made along the entire length of the top of the penis. After the extremely painful ceremony was completed, the boy ran out into the ocean or a stream to ease the pain, and typically exclaimed, "Now I am really a man."

Our society has no such distinct entry point into adulthood. Although we might breathe a sigh of relief at not having such a painful custom, we're still left with the problem of the vague transitional period we call adolescence. There are no clear-cut guidelines for how adolescents are supposed to behave. On the one hand, they are children, but on the other hand, they are adults.

Some occurrences tend to contribute to becoming an adult. These include getting a driver's license, graduating from high school, graduating from college, and perhaps getting married. However, not all individuals do these things. Some young people drop out of high school, and many high school graduates don't go on to college. A substantial number of young people choose not to marry or to marry much later in life. Even people who do go through these rites do so with varying levels of maturity and ability to handle responsibility. At any rate, becoming an adult still remains a confusing concept.

The gradual, but major, physical changes do not help to clarify the issue. Adolescents must strive to cope with drastic changes in size and form, in addition to waves of new hormones sweeping through their bodies. Resulting emotions are often unexpected and difficult to control. Within this perspective of change and adjustment, we will look more closely at specific physical changes and at the effects of these changes on the developing personality. Much of the data on biological growth are based on the classic research by Tanner (1964, 1967, 1968, 1970, 1971, 1990).

Puberty

Puberty is the period when a person becomes physically mature and able to reproduce. It is marked by the sudden enlargement of the reproductive organs and sexual genitalia and the development of secondary sex characteristics.

Girls begin the changes of puberty sometime between 8 and 13 years of age. Boys generally start about 2 years later than girls. Girls reach their full adult height by about 17 years of age; and boys, by about 21 years of age.

The 2-year age difference in beginning puberty causes more than its share of problems for adolescents. Girls tend to become interested in boys before boys begin noticing girls. One dating option for girls involves older boys of the middle or late teens. This can serve to substantially raise parental anxiety. An option for boys is to date girls who tower over them.

There is a wide age span for both boys and girls when puberty begins. Although in general there is a 2-year

difference, substantial individual differences also must be taken into account. In other words, one boy may begin puberty 4 years earlier than another.

Acting as a catalyst for all of these changes is an increase in the production of hormones. *Hormones* are chemical substances secreted by the endocrine glands. Among other things, they stimulate growth of sexual organs and characteristics. Each hormone targets specific areas and stimulates growth. For example, testosterone directly affects growth of the penis, facial skin, areas in the brain, and even cartilage in the shoulder joints. In women the uterus and vagina respond to the female hormones of estrogen and progesterone.

There is some evidence that hormonal production during adolescence is associated with increased aggression in boys and both increased aggression and depression in girls (Brooks-Gunn, 1988). However, the relationship between hormones and emotions is not a simple one. Social forces in adolescence are formidable. As we will see in later chapters, peer influence and approval are critically important. For instance, adolescents tend to become sexually active not only when their hormone production escalates but when their friends start to be sexually active (Brooks-Gunn, 1988). An individual's biological subsystem is intertwined with both the psychological and the social subsystems.

The Growth Spurt

The initial entrance into puberty is typically characterized by a sharp increase in height. During this spurt, boys and girls typically grow between 2 and 5 inches. Before the growth spurt, boys tend to be 2 percent taller than girls. However, because girls start the spurt earlier, they tend to be taller, to weigh more, and to be stronger than boys during ages 11 to 13. By the time both sexes have completed the spurt, boys once again are larger than girls.

The adolescent growth spurt affects virtually the entire body including most aspects of the skeletal and muscular structure. However, boys and girls grow differently during this period. Boys' shoulders get relatively wider, and their legs and forearms relatively longer than those of girls. Girls, on the other hand, grow wider in the pelvic area and hips. This is to enhance childbearing capability. Girls also tend to develop a layer of fat over the abdomen, hips, and buttocks during puberty. This eventually will give a young woman a more shapely, rounded physique. However, the initial chubby appearance can cause the adolescent a substantial amount of emotional stress. Crash and starvation diets can create a physical health hazard during this period.

Adolescents tend to have unequal and disproportionate growth. Most adolescents have some features that look disproportionate. The head, hands, and feet reach adult size and form first, followed by the legs and arms. Finally, the body's trunk reaches its full size. A typical result of this unequal growth is motor awkwardness and clumsiness. Until the growth of bones and muscles stabilizes, and the brain adjusts to an essentially new body, awkward bursts of motion and misjudgments of muscular control will result.

The Secular Trend

People generally grow taller and bigger than they did a century ago. They also reach sexual maturity and their adult height faster than in the past. This tendency toward increasing size and earlier achievement of sexual maturity is referred to as the *secular trend*.

The trend apparently has occurred on a worldwide basis, especially in industrialized nations such as those of Western Europe and Japan. It has not been as evident in less developed countries (Martorell, Mendoza, & Castillo, 1988). This suggests that an increased standard of living along with better health care and nutrition is related to the trend.

This secular trend seems to have reached its peak and stopped. A 14-year-old boy of today is approximately 5 inches taller than a boy of the same age in 1880.

Primary and Secondary Sex Characteristics

A major manifestation of puberty is the development of primary and secondary sex characteristics. *Primary sex characteristics* are those directly related to the sex organs and reproduction. The key is that they have a direct role in reproduction. For females these include development of the uterus, vagina, and ovaries. The uterus is an organ about the size of a fist and is shaped like an upside-down pear. It provides an environment where a fetus can develop. The vagina is the barrel-shaped organ into which a penis is inserted during intercourse and through which a baby passes when it is born. The ovaries are the major sex glands in a female, which both manufacture sex hormones and produce eggs that are ready for fertilization.

For males primary sex characteristics include growth of the penis and development of the prostate gland and the testes. The penis is the male sexual organ through which urine passes out of the body as waste and through which semen passes during orgasm. The prostate gland, which is located below the bladder, is responsible for most of the ejaculate or whitish alkaline substance that makes up semen, which carries the sperm. The testes are the male

sex glands that both manufacture sex hormones and produce sperm.

Secondary sex characteristics include those traits that distinguish the sexes from each other, but play no direct role in reproduction. These include menstruation, hair growth, development of breasts, voice changes, skin changes, and nocturnal emissions.

Proof of Puberty. The most notable indication that a female has achieved the climax of puberty is her first *menstruation,* also called *menarche.* Menstruation is the monthly discharge of blood and tissue debris from the uterus when fertilization has not taken place. This initially occurs when a girl's height spurt has slowed down. The average age is 12.8 to 13.2 years. Usually, the first periods do not include ovulation, or release of a ripened egg by the ovaries. Therefore, a young girl is usually unable to conceive until 12 to 18 months after her first period.

A wide variation in the age of occurrence for first menstruation is found from one female to another. A Peruvian girl of age 5 is the youngest mother ever recorded to have a healthy baby. This occurred in 1939. The baby was born by caesarean section. At the time, physicians found that she was mature sexually, and that she apparently had begun menstruation at the age of one month. The youngest parents known are an 8-year-old mother and 9-year-old father. This Chinese couple had a son in 1910 (Hyde, 1982).

It is somewhat more difficult to establish that a boy has entered the full throes of puberty. One of the more reliable signs is the presence of live sperm in the urine. Both semen, which contains sperm, and urine travel through the penis via a tube called the *urethra.* Sometimes sperm remain in the urethra after ejaculating and are later transported out of the penis by urine.

Hair Growth. Hair begins to grow in the pubic area during puberty. After a period of months and sometimes years, this hair changes in texture. It becomes curlier, coarser and darker. About 2 years after the appearance of pubic hair, axillary hair begins to grow on the armpits. However, the growth of axillary hair varies so much from one person to another that in some people axillary hair growth appears before the appearance of pubic hair. Boys' facial hair also begins to grow on the upper lip and gradually spreads to the chin and cheeks. Chest hair appears relatively late in adolescence.

Development of Breasts. Breast development is usually one of the first signs of sexual maturity in girls. The nipples and areola, the darkened areas surrounding the nipples, enlarge. Breasts initially tend to be cone-shaped and eventually assume a more rounded appearance.

Some women in our culture tend to be preoccupied with breast size and feel that breasts come in one of two sizes—too small or too large. However, all breasts are functionally equipped with 15 to 20 clusters of mammary or milk-producing glands. Each gland has an individual opening to the nipple or tip of the breast into which the milk ducts open. The glands themselves are surrounded by various amounts of fatty and fibrous tissue. The nipples are also richly supplied with sensitive nerve endings, which are important in erotic stimulation. There is no indication that breast size is related to a woman's ability to experience pleasurable sensation (Masters et al., 1995).

Some adolescent boys also undergo temporary breast development. Although this may cause some anxiety concerning their masculinity, this enlargement is not abnormal. Hyde and DeLamater (2000) indicate that this occurs in approximately 80 percent of boys in puberty. The probable cause is small amounts of female sex hormones produced by the testes. The condition usually disappears within about a year.

Voice Changes. Boys undergo a noticeable lowering in the tone of their voices which usually occurs fairly late in puberty. The process involves a significant enlargement of the larynx or Adam's apple and a doubling in the length of the vocal cords. Many times it takes 2 years or more for boys to gain control over their new voices.

Girls also experience a slight voice change during adolescence, although it's not nearly as extreme as the change undergone in boys. Girls' voices achieve a less high-pitched, more mature tone due to a slight growth of the larynx.

Skin Changes. Adolescence brings about increased activity of the sebaceous glands, which manufacture oils for the skin. Skin pores also become coarser and increase in size during adolescence. The result is frequently a rapid production of blackheads and pimples, commonly referred to as acne, on the face and sometimes on the back. Unfortunately, a poor complexion is considered unappealing in many cultures (Hyde & DeLamater, 2000). Acne adds to the stress of adolescence. It tends to make young people feel even more self-conscious about their bodies and physical appearance.

Nocturnal Emissions. Approximately 80 percent of all males have nocturnal emissions at one time or another (Ortiz, 1989). A nocturnal emission is the ejaculation or emission of semen while a person is asleep. The highest frequency of approximately once a month tends to occur during the late teens. The number then tapers off during the 20s, and finally stops after age 30.

Nocturnal emissions are a natural means of relieving sexual tension. Often, but not always, they are accompanied by sexual dreams. It's important that adolescents understand that this is a normal occurrence and that there's nothing physically or mentally wrong with them.

Some evidence indicates that females also have orgasms during sleep. However, these apparently don't occur as frequently or as early as males's nocturnal emissions. Almost 40 percent of women experience a nocturnal orgasm by the age of 45 (Ortiz, 1989). Only 8 percent reported having orgasms during sleep more frequently than five times per year.

Psychological Reactions to Physical Changes

One thing that marks adolescence is self-criticism. Physical imperfections are sought out, emphasized, and dwelled on. It may be a large lump on a nose. Or it may be an awesome derriere. Or it may even be a dreadful terror of braces locking unromantically during a goodnight kiss. Adolescents seek to conform to their peers. Any aspect that remains imperfect or too noticeable becomes the object of criticism. Perhaps it's because the age is filled with change and mandatory adjustment to that change that adolescents strive to conform. Perhaps before an individual personality can develop, a person needs some predictability and security.

A substantial amount of research focuses on adolescents' perceptions of themselves. Special areas of intense interest include body image, self-concept, weight level, weight worries, and eating disorders.

Body Image and Self-Concept

Perception of one's body image and attractiveness is related to adolescents' level of self-esteem, especially for girls (Berk, 1999; Harter, 1990). People who consider themselves attractive tend to be more self-confident and satisfied with themselves.

Physical appearance is very important to adolescents. In general, they dwell on and worry about what they look like to the point of distraction. Girls generally tend to be more critical of and dissatisfied with their physical appearance than boys (Newman & Newman, 1999). This is especially true concerning weight. Eighty-five percent of girls express worry about weight control compared to 30 percent of boys (Newman & Newman, 1999). This is probably due to the extreme importance placed on females' appearance in this culture.

Girls are more specific about what they see wrong with their bodies and appearance (Tobin-Richards, Boxer, & Petersen, 1983). For example, when asked what she feels is wrong with her body, a girl might say, "My thighs are too fat and my rump sticks out too much. I'd really like to fit into a size 7 jeans, but can't get under a size 9. Can girls my age have cellulite?" Boys, on the other hand, when asked the same question might respond something like, "Aww, I don't know," or "I guess I'd like to be stronger."

Girls also tend to have higher frequencies of depression (Newman & Newman, 1999). This may be due to their intensified levels of self-criticism. Before puberty, boys and girls display similar levels of depression; however, among adolescents, depression rates for girls are double those of boys (Berk, 1999).

Weight, Women, and Eating Disorders

Lott (1987) addresses the general issue of women's situation within our culture. She posits that virtually all applicable research and information point to the fact that women spend much more time than men criticizing their own physical appearance and worrying about their weight. She asserts:

> [W]omen's preoccupation with appearance is normative in our society, that it results from social pressure, from the greater punishments experienced by obese women than men, and from the strong relationship between women's judged attractiveness and thinness. . . . Most women regard . . . [their] weight as a crucial index of acceptability and attractiveness. (p. 266)

In view of this intense concern, women manifest the vast majority of eating disorders, most of which begin in adolescence. In general, eating disorders are extremely serious disturbances in eating patterns considered mental disorders by the American Psychiatric Association (APA) (APA, 2000). Due to their frequency, anorexia nervosa and bulimia are of special concern during adolescence.

Anorexia nervosa is a condition where an individual "refuses to maintain a minimally normal body weight," defined as less than 85 percent of the expected body weight (APA, 2000, p. 583). People with this disorder have an inaccurate perception of their own body's appearance whereby they see themselves as "fatter" than they really are. Along with this, they experience an intense

worry about gaining weight even though they are exceptionally thin.

It is estimated that 90 percent of those affected with anorexia nervosa are females (APA, 2000). These women, often adolescents and young women, become so obsessed with being thin that their need to control and limit their weight essentially takes over their lives. It is estimated that 0.5 percent of women have anorexia nervosa (APA, 2000). These estimates may be low because they include only those females who have been diagnosed according to APA criteria. Many more people might exhibit less severe symptoms of the disorder. Prevalence among males is approximately one-tenth that of females (APA, 2000).

Bulimia nervosa is a condition characterized by repeated episodes of binge eating (consuming huge amounts of calories), severe lack of control over eating behavior, and the use of extreme methods to get rid of calories (e.g., forcing oneself to vomit [purging], using laxatives or enemas, and undergoing intensive, rigorous exercise) (APA, 2000). Like in anorexia nervosa, people with bulimia nervosa have a distorted perception of their physical appearance. They, too, see themselves as being "fatter" than they should be, regardless of whether they are overweight, underweight, or at normal weight.

Bulimia nervosa appears to be even more common than anorexia nervosa. An accurate prevalence of bulimia nervosa is difficult to establish. Bulimics tend to guard this "secret" carefully, and they often appear "normal" in terms of weight. However, bulimia nervosa can also take control of people's lives. It is estimated that about 1 to 3 percent of women have bulimia nervosa; males appear to manifest this disorder only one-tenth as frequently as females (APA, 2000).

Eating disorders are discussed in much greater depth in Chapter 8. There the dynamics of such disorders will be explored. However, because concern about weight is so critically significant to young women and the effects of this concern so potentially lethal, the issue needs to be identified here. These concerns and conditions clearly illustrate the intimate interactions of the biological, psychological, and social subsystems operating developmentally within any one individual (micro system).

Critical Thinking About Weight and Body Image

What do *you* think about these concerns and issues? Is it right or fair to place so much importance on external physical appearance, especially as such emphasis concerns weight? Is it equitable that the burden of weight control rests even more heavily on women than on men? How have these concerns about weight and physical appearance affected you and your own aspects of biological, psychological, and social development?

Early and Late Maturation in Boys

Some adolescents mature earlier than others, some much later. Some are lucky enough to fall within the average range of maturation. These average maturers experience their physical changes at roughly the same time as many of their peers. Average maturers are able to conform to the peer group, at least in this physical respect. They have others to talk to and relate to about their physical and sexual changes.

A number of long-term studies concerning early and late maturation in boys have revealed fairly consistent results (Crockett & Petersen, 1987; Jones & Bayley, 1950; Jones, 1957, 1965). Those who mature earlier than most of their peers have the advantages of increased size and athletic ability. Peers are more likely to look up to them. Lefrancois (1999) summarizes the psychological effects on early maturers: "Early maturing boys are typically better adjusted, more popular, more confident, more aggressive, and more successful in heterosexual relationships. In addition, they appear to have clear advantages with respect to self-concepts" (p. 316).

It's important not to assume that early maturers will automatically become team quarterbacks and class presidents (or gang leaders, for that matter). Many other factors such as individual personalities and environmental influences also affect an individual's development. Papalia and her associates (2001) caution that there is some evidence that early maturers can also be "more worried about being liked, more cautious, more reliant on others, and more bound by rules and routines" (p. 416). Early maturers may suffer more pressure from both peers and adults. Peers are more likely to look up to them for exemplary behavior and leadership. Similarly, adults are more likely to treat early maturers as if they were older than they are. Adults tend to place higher expectations on them.

Late-maturing boys, on the other hand, are perceived as being less physically attractive and not as poised. They also appear to be more tense and are more likely to engage in immature, attention-getting behavior. Late maturers may be denied the respect and attention given more mature-looking boys. Acting-out behavior may provide late maturers a means of expressing themselves and of getting at least some attention and recognition, even though it may not be very positive.

By adulthood, the differences between early and late maturers become much less clear. So many other elements are involved in a person's development, including those that are cognitive and social, that it is difficult to predict the effects of any one variable like maturation rate.

Early and Late Maturation in Girls

There is increasing evidence that early-maturing girls, in contrast to early-maturing boys, are initially disadvantaged, compared to average and late-maturing girls (Brooks-Gunn & Paikoff, 1993; Siegel, 1982; Stattin & Magnusson, 1990). They tend to have lower self-esteem and a lower self-concept in terms of body image (Alsaker, 1992; Dubas & Petersen, 1993). Early-maturing girls are more likely to get involved in smoking cigarettes and drinking; experience depression, eating disorders, academic problems, and behavioral difficulties; become more distanced and independent from parents at an earlier age; involve themselves with older peers including men; and participate in earlier sexual experiences (Brooks-Gunn, 1996; Gariulo et al., 1987; Graber & Brooks-Gunn, 1998;

© Bob Daemmrich

Maturation rates vary drastically, as these 2 girls, both in the same grade, illustrate, and can significantly affect self-esteem.

Magnusson, Stattin, & Allen, 1985; Simmons & Blyth, 1987; Stattin & Magnusson, 1990). Perhaps their lack of life experience, level of cognitive development, and naiveté put them at risk of having to make serious "adult" choices before they are ready to accept the consequences of behavior or even acknowledge such consequences (Peterson, 1993).

However, there is also some indication that the disadvantages of early maturation disappear in later adolescence (Lefrancois, 1999). Early-maturing girls in the fifth or sixth grade may feel out of place when compared to their peers. It may be difficult for them to communicate about their new physical development with other girls who have not experienced these developments. However, as early as the seventh grade, the picture changes. Early maturers rapidly gain prestige as their classmates also begin to develop breasts and to menstruate. These higher levels of prestige tend to be maintained throughout the rest of adolescence.

Evidence regarding the long-term results of early maturation for girls is conflicting. Perhaps, as with boys, the picture is much more complicated than simply focusing on the life results caused by one specific variable, such as early maturation.

🌿 Young Adulthood

It is difficult to pinpoint the exact time of life we are referring to when we talk about young adulthood. The transition into adulthood is not a clear-cut dividing line. People become voting adults by age 18. However, in most states, they are not considered adult enough to drink alcoholic beverages until 21. A person cannot become a U.S. senator until age 30 or president until age 35. All this presents a confusing picture of what we mean by adulthood.

Various theorists have tried to define young adulthood. Buhler (1933) clustered adolescence and young adulthood together. He felt that this period included the ages from 15 to 25. During this time, people focus on establishing their identities and on idealistically trying to make their dreams come true. Buhler saw the next phase as young and middle adulthood. This period lasts from approximately ages 23 to 45 or 50. This group focuses on attaining realistic, concrete goals and on setting up a work and family structure for life.

Levinson and his colleagues (1974) broke up young adulthood into smaller slices. They believed that in the process of developing a life structure, people go through stable periods separated by shorter transitional periods. The stage from ages 17 to 24 is characterized by leaving the family and becoming independent. This is followed by a transitional phase from ages 22 to 28, which involves entering the adult world. The age 30 transition focuses on making a decision about how to structure the remainder of life. A settling-down period then occurs from about ages 32 to 40.

For our purposes, we will arbitrarily consider young adulthood as including the ages from 18 to 30. This is the time following the achievement of full physical growth when people are establishing themselves in the adult world. Specific aspects of young adulthood addressed in this chapter will include physical development, health status, and the effects of lifestyle on health.

Physical Development

Young adults are in their physical prime. Maximum muscular strength is attained between the ages of 25 and 30, and generally begins a gradual decline after that. After age 30, decreases in strength occur mostly in the leg and back muscles. Some weakening also occurs in the arm muscles.

Top performance speed in terms of how fast tasks can be accomplished is reached at about age 30. Young adulthood is also characterized by the highest levels of manual agility. Hand and finger dexterity decrease after the mid-30s (Troll, 1985).

Sight, hearing, and the other senses are their keenest during young adulthood. Eyesight is the sharpest at about age 20. A decline in visual acuity isn't significant until age 40 or 45, when there is some tendency toward *presbyopia* (farsightedness). At that point you start to see people read their newspapers by holding them 3 feet in front of them.

Hearing is also sharpest at age 20. After this there is a gradual decline in auditory acuity, especially in sensitivity to higher tones. This deficiency is referred to as *presbycusis*. Most of the other senses, namely touch, smell, and taste, tend to remain stable until approximately age 45 or 50.

Health Status

Young adulthood can be considered the healthiest time of life. Young adults are generally healthier than when they were children, and they have not yet begun to suffer the illnesses and health declines that develop in middle age. More than 93 percent of people aged 15 to 44 perceive their health as being either good or excellent (U.S. Department of Health and Human Services [USDHHS], 1996). There is significant interest on the part of many in all socioeconomic classes in measures that promote health. For example, running and other forms of exercising, health foods, and weight control have become very popular.

Despite the fact that young adulthood is generally a healthy time of life, health differences can be seen between men and women. For example, women of all ages tend to report more illnesses than do men (Lefrancois, 1999). However, this may be attributed to health issues related to gender, (such as contraception, pregnancy, or an annual Pap test), rather than more general reasons of poor health. Perhaps women are also more conscientious about preventive health care in general. Highlight 6.1 discusses the important health issue of breast cancer.

Of all the acute or temporary pressing health problems occurring during young adulthood, approximately one half are caused by respiratory problems. An additional 20 percent are due to injuries. The most frequent chronic health problems occurring in young adulthood include spinal or back difficulties, hearing problems, arthritis, and

Highlight 6.1

Breast Cancer

According to the American Cancer Society, 1 in 9 women will develop breast cancer during her lifetime (Kelly, 2001; Kirk & Okazawa-Rey, 2001). This rate has increased from 1 in 10, which was evident in 1987, and 1 in 11 in 1981 (Silverberg, 1981). Part of the increase is attributed to the fact that more and more women are getting regular mammograms (low-dose X-ray photographs of the breast). Mammograms have enabled earlier detection and better reporting of cancer. They often detect cancers too small to feel with the fingers.

New machines for breast-cancer detection are currently being developed and tested. Many women find mammograms distasteful because breasts must be uncomfortably squeezed between clear plates and then be exposed to radiation. One recently patented machine, the computed tomography laser mammography (CTLM) "uses laser imaging technology to create a three-dimensional image of breast tissue—an image that can be sliced and turned upside down and inside out to more carefully inspect suspicious masses" (Schrof, 1998, p. 67). The machine never touches the breast and no radiation is used.

Being knowledgeable about the issue of breast cancer is especially important for you in helping your female clients become aware of risks, prevention, and treatment. If you are a female, it's important for your own health. If you are a male, it's important for the women who are close to you.

Benign Lumps

Eighty percent of all breast lumps are benign, usually taking one of two forms. First, there are cysts, which are "fluid-filled sacs"; the other common form of benign lump is a fibroadenoma, which is a "solid, rounded tumor" (Crooks & Baur, 2002, p. 111).

Symptoms

A number of symptoms other than identification of a tumor can indicate malignancy. Tumors can assume a number of shapes and forms. Generally, any change in the external appearance of the breasts should make one suspicious. For instance, one breast becoming significantly larger or hanging significantly lower than the other is a potential warning sign. Discharges from the nipple or nipple discoloration are additional indications. Dimpling or puckering of the nipple or skin of the breast should be noted. Finally, any swelling of the upper arm or lymph nodes under the arm should be investigated.

Risk Factors

A number of risk factors are involved in getting breast cancer. Approximately 10 percent of all cases result from genetic factors (Ezzell, 1994). Researchers have identified two genes labeled BRCA1 on chromosome 17 and BRCA2 on chromosome 13 that, when mutated, appear to cause breast cancer (Ezzell, 1994; Marx, 1996; Miki et al., 1994; Scully et al., 1996; Struewing et al., 1997). When one of the genes is defective, women face a 60 percent possibility of developing breast cancer by age 50 and 85 percent likelihood by age 65 (Miki et al., 1994; Wooster et al., 1994). Increased potential for ovarian cancer has also been linked to gene BRCA1 (Kelly, 2001).

A number of other high-risk factors for breast cancer have been identified. Age is one. From birth to age 40, 1 in 217 women will develop breast cancer, 1 in 50 at age 50, 1 in 24 at age 60, and 1 in 14 at age 74 (Rathus et al., 2002). Other risk factors include: a family history of breast cancer; exposure to environmental toxins like pesticides; prolonged exposure to estrogen; heavy drinking of alcohol; a long menstrual history; obesity; and physical inactivity (Byer et al., 2002; Crooks & Baur, 2002; Rathus et al., 2002). Remember that these factors only increase risk, not condemn a person to getting breast cancer. In 80 percent of all breast cancers, there is no clearly established risk factor or cause (Heck & Pamuk, 1997; Pritchard, 1997).

Treatment of Breast Cancer

In the event that a suspicious lump is detected, a number of options can be pursued. First, needle aspiration can be used to attempt drawing the fluid out of the lump. If fluid can be removed, the lump is likely to be a cyst. If the lump subsequently disappears, it was a cyst. There is no need for further alarm.

Another means of examining a lump involves a biopsy. Here a small section of tissue is surgically removed and examined for cancer cells. A new technique becoming available is stereotactic biopsy, which uses x-ray images to pinpoint an abnormality and a needle to remove small cores of tissue for analysis. This technique is less invasive than surgical tissue removal, and there is little or no pain, minimal scarring, and quick recovery.

If it has been established that a lump is cancerous, several alternative treatments are available. First, there are surgeries of increasing complexity and severity. The simplest surgical procedure is a lumpectomy, in which only the tumor and a small portion of the surrounding tissue are removed. This allows for the least disruption of

Highlight 6.1

Breast Cancer (continued)

the breast's external appearance. The next alternative is a *partial mastectomy,* in which a portion of the breast containing the cancerous tumor is taken out along with some of the muscle tissue right below it and breast skin above it. The third option is a *simple mastectomy.* Here, the entire breast is removed, sometimes along with some of the lymph nodes under the arm. Although some of us find it offensive to use the term "simple" in this context ("It's simple for you to say my breast should be removed."), the term refers to the fact that the musculature in the chest will remain pretty much intact after this procedure. Removal of muscle tissue usually impairs arm movements. The fourth surgical alternative is a *modified radical mastectomy* where the breast, lymph nodes, the covering over the chest muscles, and sometimes one of the chest muscles are removed. Finally, as the name implies, the most extreme surgical procedure, a *radical mastectomy,* involves removal of the breast, the skin, the chest muscles, and all lymph nodes under the arm.

The surgical procedure chosen depends on a number of factors. One, of course, is how far the cancer has progressed. All cancerous cells must be removed. In the past, the most common procedure by far was the most severe, namely, the radical mastectomy. Now, less severe options are available and often effective. It should be emphasized that breasts are given tremendous significance in this society. Additionally, external appearance and physical shape are highly acclaimed. A woman's perception of herself, of how others perceive her, and of the effects on her sexual relationships all can be severely affected by breast removal.

After a mastectomy, reconstructive surgery is an option. This involves plastic surgery to implant an artificial breast filled with a saline solution and to make it look as natural as possible. It is estimated that more than 100,000 breast implants are performed each year (Strong et al., 2002). The extent of reconstructive surgery required depends on how much of the breast and other tissue remains after removing cancerous tissue. Women should give careful consideration to the pros and cons of this course of action. Reconstructive surgery can boost a woman's self-image and adjustment. Potential negative consequences include scarring, infection, implant leakage, and disappointing results in terms of breast appearance.

In addition to surgery, several other treatments exist for breast cancer. Radiation is used as the major means of treatment for very early cancers and to supplement surgery and prevent recurrence. *Chemotherapy* is administered when cancer has spread to the lymph nodes. Such a spread of cancer cells implies that other organs may be involved. *Hormonal therapy* is used to prevent recurrence of breast cancer in women whose cancer growth was stimulated by estrogen.

Researchers are currently exploring transplant therapy, "high-dose chemotherapy accompanied by a transplant of stem cells, precursors of disease-fighting immune-system cells" (Kluger, 1999, p. 68). Chemotherapy not only kills cancer cells, but also seriously depletes the immune system. Transplants involve harvesting immune cells produced from bones or "stem cells from the bloodstream—both of which give rise to new immune cells—before they begin chemotherapy. When the treatment is done, these cells are reinfused into the body, in the hope that the immune system will rebound" (Kluger, 1999, p. 69). Gene therapy is also being explored, in which "genetically engineered cells containing normal BRCA1 genes are injected into the woman" with one possible result being to shrink already existing tumors (Ezzell, 1994; Hyde & DeLamater, 2000).

Early Detection of Breast Cancer

There are three primary recommendations for early detection of breast cancer. The first involves seeing a health-care practitioner regularly, and having an annual Pap smear (examination of a small scraping of cells from the cervix), a pelvic examination (a check of the genital and reproductive areas for abnormalities), and a breast palpation (a manual checking of the breasts).

The second recommendation for breast cancer detection involves regular mammograms. The meaning of "regular" varies according to a woman's age. Every woman between ages 35 and 40 should have a mammogram to establish a baseline. This early mammogram can be compared with later ones to identify any changes in breast tissue. Women with high risk factors, such as having close female family members with breast cancer, may prompt a physician to begin doing mammograms much earlier. During her 40s, a woman should have one every 1 to 2 years. Finally, she should have a mammogram every year after age 50. Two newer methods of viewing breasts are still being evaluated and are not yet readily available. The first of these, *computer-generated diagnosis,* is the use of a program to scan mammogram film so as to identify white spots that indicate cancer (Fischman, 2001). The second, *digital mammography,* sends X-ray images to "an electronic detector" ("[i]nstead of capturing them on film") that theoretically provides higher contrast and a sharper image of breast tissue (Park, 2001, p. 58). It should be emphasized, however, that many cancers cannot currently be detected by mammography, so the third recommendation for breast cancer detection, a monthly breast self-examination, is important. If a woman checks regularly, she will be able to detect minor, subtle changes in her breasts. She can develop much greater expertise in checking herself than a physician or other health professional who checks her only once a year or less often.

It is best to do a breast self-examination 7 to 10 days after a menstrual period ends, because the breasts are least likely to be swollen at that time. After menopause, it is suggested that women perform examinations on the first day of each month, an easy pattern to remember. A breast self-examination can be done in three phases. First, in the shower, use the flat pads of the three middle fingers to check for lumps. Using fingertips can easily push lumps away and out of touch. Both superficial and deeper pressure should be used. Superficial pressure will detect tiny lumps that will slip away from the fingers when greater pressure is used. Deeper pressure gets at mid-level tissues. Because cancer can also occur in the lymph nodes under the arm, areas near the armpit and the collarbone should also be checked. About one-half of all tumors occur in this area. See Figure 6.1a, which illustrates

Figure 6.1 Breast Cancer Detection

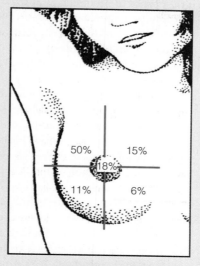 

(a) Where cancer tends
to develop

(b) The spiral method
of breast self-examination

the likelihood that cancer will develop in any particular area of the breast.

Breast self-examinations should be systematic to make certain no areas of the breast are missed. A common technique, the *spiral method* is illustrated in Figure 6.1b. It makes certain she has not missed some portion of the breast.

A woman should start at the top of the breast and follow the line as indicated, up into the armpit, around, up to the collarbone, and then back down to the breast. At least three smaller circles should then be made around the breast, ending up at the nipple. This should be done twice, once with light pressure and once with deeper pressure.

The second phase of the breast self-examination entails observing the breasts in a mirror. The woman should look for any changes in size or shape. She should lift her arms above her head and then shrug her shoulders. She should bend over to see if her breasts hang evenly. Finally,

she should check her nipples for any discharge. The third phase of the breast self-examination involves lying down and once again using either the spiral method or the grid method. A folded towel should be placed under the midback so that the breast tissue is more evenly distributed.

A Final Note

Breast cancer is a critically important issue. Some important principles for women to remember include:

1. Women should become experts on their bodies. They should perform monthly breast self-examinations. The earlier a lump is found, the smaller it will probably be, and the easier it will be to treat.

2. In the event that a lump is found, women should be knowledgeable about alternative remedies. They should consider the pros and cons of each.

hypertension. These chronic problems occur even more frequently in families of lower socioeconomic status. For example, young African Americans experience hypertension more frequently than their white counterparts (Kirk & Okazawa-Rey, 2001; Krieger & Sidney, 1996; USDHHS, 1992).

Lifestyle and Good Health

Good health doesn't just happen. It is related to specific practices and to a person's individual lifestyle. People begin developing either beneficial or harmful health habits at an early age. Several simple, basic habits have been found to prolong life. People who follow all of them tend

to live longer than people who follow only some of them. As a matter of fact, a clear relationship seems to exist between the number of the suggested habits followed and the state of overall health.

These positive health habits include eating breakfast and other meals regularly. Snacking on high-fat and high-sugar foods should be avoided. Moderate eating in order to maintain a normal, healthy weight is important. Smoking and heavy alcohol consumption are dangerous to health and should be avoided. Moderate exercise and adequate sleep also contribute to good health.

Excessive consumption of alcohol has very negative effects on health. Alcoholics are people who have a continual and compulsive need for alcohol. Physical dependence occurs when body tissues become dependent on the continuous presence of alcohol. Approximately three-quarters of all alcoholics show some impaired liver function. Cirrhosis of the liver is eventually developed by about 8 percent of all alcoholics. Cirrhosis involves gradual deterioration of the liver tissue until it no longer can adequately perform its normal function. These functions include converting food to usable energy. Other effects of alcoholism include cancer, heart problems and heart failure, a variety of gastrointestinal disorders including ulcers, damage to the nervous system, psychoses, and others.

Adolescents' use of alcohol has remained at a consistently high rate since 1979; 55 percent of eighth graders indicate they have "tried alcohol," 25 percent relate that they've gotten "drunk at least once in their lives," and 8 percent state "that the first time they got drunk they were in sixth grade" (Newman & Newman, 1999, pp. 341–342).

Cigarette smoking is another activity that is clearly associated with health problems. Many of the deaths related to smoking are due to heart disease. Cigarette smoke contains nicotine, which acts as a stimulant. As nicotine enters the lungs, it is quickly absorbed by the small blood vessels in the lungs and immediately transported throughout the body. As a stimulant it causes both an increased heart rate and increased blood pressure. Over time the heart will be overworked and eventually be damaged.

Lung cancer is another major cause of death attributed to smoking. Cigarette tars and other particles in the smoke gradually accumulate in the tubes and air sacs of the lungs. This causes a gradual change in the lung tissue's normal cells. Eventually these affected cells may reproduce new cells that are different from the original ones. The new cancerous cells reproduce more cancerous cells that eventually kill off the normal cell tissue. The result is the growth of a malignant tumor that invades the lung and spreads to other parts of the body.

Adolescent smoking is a serious problem. Subject to extreme peer pressure, adolescents find it easy to begin smoking, but very hard to quit (Santrock, 1999). The rate of adolescent smoking, high in the 1970s, somewhat less in the 1980s, has gained momentum once again during the 1990s (Johnston, O'Malley, & Bachman, 1997). One survey reveals that 19 percent of eighth graders and 28 percent of tenth graders report having smoked in the prior 30 days (Santrock, 1999). The rate of smoking by high school seniors has increased by more than 20 percent since 1992, with more than one-third of them indicating they have smoked within the past 30 days (Santrock, 1999).

Stress is another variable related to health problems. There is a strong relationship between stress and illness (Holmes & Rahe, 1976; Longstreth & Wolde-Tsadik, 1993). The more stress a person is experiencing, the greater is the chance of becoming ill. Interestingly stress is caused not only by negative occurrences such as the death of a close relative, but also by new, positive occurrences. These include outstanding personal achievements and even vacations. Apparently change in general causes stress. Adjustment to new situations required expending energy. This additional energy is apparently related to stress regardless of whether the adjustment is to a happy or a sad occasion.

Once again, it must be emphasized that one's capacity to establish and follow positive health habits depends on one's accessibility to resources. A poor person does not have the available choices that a middle- or upper-class person does. A poor person can't join the local health club or the racquet club in order to get adequate exercise. First, such places probably don't exist in the area. Second, there certainly is no money for such extravagances. Third, these places often have explicit or implicit requirements regarding their members' background, financial status, appearance, and social standing.

Poor people are also likely to suffer additional stress related to their lack of resources. They may be worrying about what to feed their kids near the end of the month when money has run out. Maybe they're worried about having their phone disconnected or their electricity turned off because they couldn't pay the bills.

Some behaviors have been found to be positively related to good health. For example, physical exercise helps to prevent heart disease, reduce stress and anxiety, enhance mental health, strengthen muscles, maintain a healthy bone structure, lower blood pressure, and extend life (Papalia et al., 2001; Santrock, 2002b).

Diet has also been found to affect health. Being overweight increases risks of heart disease, high blood pressure, and other health problems. On the other hand, choosing a well-balanced diet, limiting food intake, and avoiding foods that are infused with salt and fat can promote good health, especially in conjunction with exercise. For instance, limiting cholesterol intake decreases the risks of heart disease (Lipid Research Clinics Program, 1984a, 1984b). Cholesterol is "a soft, fat-like substance found among the fats in the bloodstream (American Heart Association, 1984, p. 1). It can collect in arteries, thereby stalling blood flow. Extreme blockages can arrest the blood flow into the heart and, ultimately, cause a heart attack. Eating foods low or lacking in cholesterol can significantly decrease these risks.

Health is obviously related to the incidence of death. Spotlight 6.1 discusses the differential death rates and causes of death experienced by different groups.

Spotlight on Diversity 6.1 — Differential Incidence of Death

The leading causes of death among all young adults in the United States aged 15 to 24 are accidents, homicide and legal intervention, suicide, and cancer, respectively; among people aged 25 to 44, the leading causes of death are accidents, cancer, heart disease, and suicide (U.S. Census Bureau, 2001). When dividing people into racial and gender groups, some differences emerge. Death rates for men aged 15 to 24 are almost three times higher than those for women (U.S. Census Bureau, 2001).

Racial differences also occur. For instance, the death rate for African American males aged 15 to 24 is almost double that of their white counterparts (U.S. Census Bureau, 2001). The incidence of violent death in the two groups contributes to this difference. Murder is the number one cause of death for young African American men: Recent census data report that African American men aged 15 to 19 are 7 times more likely to die from a homicide than their white peers, and those aged 20 to 24 are almost 9 times more likely. Furthermore, "[t]he U.S. homicide rate is 4 times higher than Western Europe's, 6 times higher than Great Britain's, and 7 times higher than Japan's" (Mooney, Knox, & Schacht, 2002, p. 93). You might ask yourself why you live in such a violent society.

Kirk and Okazawa-Rey (2001) comment on the health and likelihood of death for women of color as compared to white women:

Among the top ten causes of death for African American women and Latinas are conditions connected to pregnancy and childbirth, not found in the top ten causes of death for White women [a fact that is probably at least partially due to their decreased access to adequate health care]. Significantly more (25 percent more) African American women die in their twenties than to White women of that age as a result of HIV/AIDS, maternal mortality, drug use, and homicide . . . Native American women aged 15 to 24 show a 50 percent higher death rate than White women of the same age for similar reasons. . . . Native American women have lower life-expectancy rates compared with the overall population,

and they have high mortality rates due to violence, alcoholism, treatable diseases like diabetes and tuberculosis, as well as suicide . . . Taken as a whole, the health of African American women, Native American women, and Latinas is significantly worse than that of White women and Asian American women. (p. 361)

The difference in the death rates of people of color and whites reflects a significant difference in environment. Of course, there are people of virtually every ethnic and racial background who are poor. However, in the United States, if you are African American or a member of a number of other minority groups, including Latinos/Latinas and Native Americans, you are more likely to be poor than if you are white. This is a complicated issue. However, much of the difference in circumstances is due to a long history or prejudice and discrimination. If you're poor, you're more likely to be living in the crowded urban center of a city than in the suburbs. If you're poor and live in the inner city where the crime rate is higher, you are most likely to be a homicide victim.

If you are poor, you are also more likely not to have employment that provides adequate health insurance. You're more likely to find yourself in a position where you can't go to a doctor when you're sick because you have no money and no insurance. Young adulthood is supposed to be the healthiest time of life, and it is for most people. However, overall health status varies drastically depending on environment and living conditions. It's important for social workers to be aware of the impact that poor environments can have no people.

Poverty is often linked to nonmajority status. Many "minorities" have been physically abused, burdened by the abuse of others' power, and treated unfairly. The result is the likelihood of a poor standard of living, including a poor health status with more health problems. Instead of asking what people can do to get out of poor environments, social workers need to ask how these environments can be changed to improve the living conditions of the oppressed people.

🌿 Significant Issues and Life Events

Certain significant experiences and life events tend to characterize adolescence and young adulthood. Some issues are of special concern to people in this age group. Several of these issues have been selected for discussion here. They were chosen on the basis of their relevance and impact on the physical well-being of young people. Because adolescence is a period of sexual development, sexuality will be emphasized. The issues include sexual activity in adolescence, unplanned pregnancy, teenage fatherhood, motivation for pregnancy, sex education, sexually transmitted

diseases, and contraception. Highlight 6.2 discusses young people's experience with masturbation.

Sexual Activity in Adolescence

Two major trends have characterized adolescent sexual activity in recent years. First, the proportion of teenagers who have sexual intercourse has increased dramatically. Second, the age at which first intercourse occurs has become younger. Both of these trends are more true for girls than for boys.

In the 1940s, Kinsey (1948, 1953) found that about one-third of all females and almost three-quarters of all

Highlight 6.2

Masturbation

Masturbation refers to self-stimulation of the genitals that causes sexual arousal. It appears that masturbation begins fairly early. About half of all males and almost one-third of all females report that they began masturbating by age 13 (Janus & Janus, 1993; Leitenberg, Detzer, & Srebnik, 1993). African American and Latino youths are less likely to masturbate than white teens (Belcastro, 1985; Cortese, 1989; Strong & DeVault, 1997).

Girls tend to masturbate less frequently than do boys (Crooks & Baur, 2002), about once a month, compared to boys, who masturbate two to three times per week (Hass, 1979; Hyde & DeLamater, 2000). By the end of adolescence, almost all males and about three-quarters of all females have masturbated (Crooks & Baur, 2002). Such gender differences may be related to sex roles and sexual expectations of men and women. They may also have to do with the fact that the sex drive of females tends to develop relatively later than that of males.

It's important to address the issue of masturbation. As we've already established, it is very common among adolescents. However, it is also looked down on. The numerous slang terms used to describe it are very uncomplimentary. Perhaps the traditional negative attitude about masturbation can best be expressed by the statements of H. R. Stout in the 1885 edition of *Our Family Physician*:

When the evil has been pursued for several years, there will be an irritable condition of the system; sudden flushes of heat over the face; the countenance becomes pale and clammy; the eyes have a dull, sheepish look; the hair becomes dry and split at the ends; sometimes there is pain over the region of the heart; shortness of breath; palpitation of the heart (symptoms of dyspepsia show themselves); the sleep is disturbed; there is constipation; cough; irritation of the throat; finally the whole man becomes a wreck, physically, morally, and mentally.

After such a tirade, it would be a wonder if a person would dare to masturbate. This presents quite a contradiction and a source of confusion for adolescents. They are actually participating in the activity of masturbation. Yet, there is some tendency for it to be considered an unappealing and even disgusting behavior. Negative feelings can include anxiety, defensiveness, embarrassment, and guilt (Byer et al., 2002; Hyde & DeLamater, 2000).

Adolescents need to understand that masturbation is not abnormal or harmful. In a period of their lives when they are coping with many physical changes and new life situations, they do not need to be burdened with unnecessary confusion and even guilt. Masturbation is a normal means of relieving sexual tension and other stress, allowing a means of self-discovery, learning to control sexual needs and impulses, and fighting isolation and loneliness (Barbach, 1980; Clifford, 1978; Sorenson, 1973). Masturbation is even a prescribed means of treatment for sexual dysfunction. Women with orgasmic dysfunctions (that is, the inability to experience orgasms) are counseled to use masturbation. This helps them overcome anxiety and understand their sexual responses. This information can later be transferred to a partner.

Spotlight on Diversity 6.2 Racial and Other Differences in Adolescent Sexual Activity

In the United States, significantly different patterns of adolescent sexual intercourse exist among various racial groups. For example, African-American teenagers are more likely to have sexual intercourse than their white and Hispanic counterparts (CDC, 1996; Kissinger et al., 1997). About 24 percent of African American adolescents report having intercourse before age 13 compared to 5.7 percent of whites and 8.8 percent of Hispanics (CDC, 1996). Similarly over 73 percent of African American, almost 58 percent of Hispanic, and almost 49 percent of white youths reported having had sexual intercourse by the time they left high school.

Differences in patterns of sexual activity may relate more to poverty than to race or ethnicity (Crooks & Baur, 2002). African American females raised in affluent homes are more likely to abstain from sexual activity than those raised in poorer environments (Brewster, 1994; Leadbeater & Way, 1995; Murry, 1996). Other variables associated with having earlier sexual intercourse include alcohol use, high stress levels, having mothers who had sex at an early age, lower grade-point average, and spending greater amounts of unsupervised time at home (Harvey & Spigner, 1995; Hyde & DeLamater, 2000; Mott et al., 1996).

males under age 25 reported that they had had nonmarital intercourse. Today, by tenth grade, 46 percent of all women and 50 percent of all men indicate that they have had sexual intercourse; 66 percent of girls and 67 percent of boys have had intercourse by tenth grade (Byer et al.,

2002; Crooks & Baur, 2002; Centers for Disease Control [CDD], 1996).

Men's expressed motivation for engaging in sexual intercourse often includes "pleasure, fun, and physical reasons, whereas women's motives are more often based on love, commitment, and emotions" (Allgeier & Allgeier, 2000, p. 291; Buss, 1999).

Spotlight 6.2 discusses some racial and other differences in adolescent sexual activity.

Unplanned Pregnancy in Adolescence

About 22 percent of teenage girls, or more than 1 in 5, in the United States become pregnant each year (Alan Guttmacher Institute, 1999). Over 80 percent of these pregnancies are unintentional (McAnulty & Burnette, 2001). Of all teenage pregnancies, 56 percent result in live births; 30 percent, in abortion; and 14 percent, in miscarriages or stillbirths (Alan Guttmacher Institute, 1999). The birthrate for single adolescent women in the United States is the second highest in the Western world, second only to the Russian Federation; it is over 8 times higher than Japan's and almost twice as high as Canada's (Singh & Darroch, 2000). Although it is still high, the rate of births for teens has actually decreased since the early 1990s (Curtin & Martin, 2000). This is probably a result of increased use of contraception (Alan Guttmacher Institute, 1999).

The vast majority of babies born to single teens remain at home with their young mothers. Only 5 percent of the children are placed for adoption (Downs et al., 1996). This places these young women in a very different situation than that of most of their peers. Adolescence and young adulthood is the usual time of life for meeting and socializing with friends, dating, possibly selecting a mate, obtaining an education, and making a career choice. The additional responsibility of motherhood poses serious restrictions on the amount of freedom and time available to do these other things. Additionally, such young women are most often ill-prepared for motherhood. They are usually in the midst of establishing their own identities and learning to care for themselves.

Pregnant teenagers are less likely to marry than they have been in the past. Apparently, young women no longer experience the pressure that they "have to" marry the baby's father. Divorce rates in teen marriages significantly exceed those of women who marry later (Lefrancois, 1999; Newman & Newman).

There are a number of other strikingly negative consequences to teen pregnancy. First, such pregnancies are marked by increased physical risks, both to the child and to the mother (Crooks & Baur, 2002; Papalia et al., 2001). Such problems include prolonged labor, anemia, toxemia, hemorrhaging, miscarriage, and, in the extreme, the pregnant teen's death. The babies have a much greater chance either of being premature or of having a lower than normal birth weight. They are twice as likely to suffer from neurological defects. A related finding concerning maternal and child health is that many teenage mothers are poverty stricken and receive very little prenatal health care (Children's Defense Fund, 1995; Papalia et al., 2001; Strong et al., 2002). This contributes to the health risks of the mothers and their babies.

Other longer term research indicates that negative effects continue long after the baby's birth. Teen mothers are much less likely to finish high school than their peers who are not mothers (Papalia et al., 2001; Stevens-Simon, Kelly, & Singer, 1996). Adolescent mothers are also more likely than nonmothers to be poor and to receive social services (Meschke, Bartholomae, & Zentall, 2000; Papalia et al., 2001; Roye & Balk, 1997; Strong et al., 2002). Later in life they are more likely than their peers without children to be unemployed or underemployed (Davtyan, 2000; Roye & Balk, 1997). Teen mothers tend to have poorer parenting skills and are more likely to abuse their children compared to more mature mothers (Coley & Chase-Landsdale, 1998; Felsman et al., 1987; Lamb, Hopps, & Elster, 1987; Strong & DeVault, 1997). Thus, the added stress and responsibility of motherhood tend to take a toll on teen mothers. Raising a child demands time, energy, and attention. Time taken to care for a baby must be subtracted from the time available for school and recreational activities. There are potentially serious impacts on the mental health and daily functioning of young mothers.

Long-term studies also reveal negative effects on the children themselves. As the children of teen mothers mature, they tend to have more emotional, intellectual, and physical problems than their counterparts born to adult mothers (Byer et al., 2002; Crooks & Baur, 2002; Furstenberg et al., 1987; Klein & Cordell, 1987). More specifically, these children tend to perform more poorly in school and have lower IQs than other children (Kinard & Reinherz, 1987; Roye & Balk, 1997; Trussell, 1988). Academic difficulties do not diminish with time; children born to teen mothers tend to be low achievers even in high school (Brooks-Gunn & Furstenberg, 1986).

The consequences of teenage parenthood are emphasized here to provide a realistic perspective on teen pregnancy. Teenagers need to be at least intellectually aware of the impacts of motherhood. They need this information in order to make more realistic decisions for themselves concerning their sexual activity and their use of birth control. The other reason to focus on the consequences of teenage pregnancy concerns helping young mothers who already have their babies. Social workers need to understand the problems of teenage parenthood. This is needed to help young mothers realistically appraise their situations, make decisions about what to do for themselves, and get involved with the supportive services they need.

Teenage Fathers

The single father's paternal rights and needs merit some attention. The male teenager's role of biological father is distinguished from the role of the mother's potential husband. As with teenage mothers, teenage fathers tend to do less well educationally and economically than other males (Marsiglio, 1986; Masters et al., 1995; Nock, 1998). For those feeling obliged to support their family, many opportunities are denied them. They are more likely to leave school and have less education than others their age. They are also more likely to have lesser skilled, more poorly paying jobs than their peers. Finally, if the teenage parents marry, marital problems are more frequent and divorce is more likely. In other words, teenage fathers, like teenage mothers, have both more disadvantages and greater difficulties surviving than do their peers.

Almost half of all babies of teenage mothers have fathers who are at least age 20 (Newman & Newman, 1999; Sonenstein, 1986). Those fathers who are teenagers themselves should not be neglected. There are often assumptions that teen fathers are "irresponsible, selfish, and uninterested in their partners and children" (Strong & DeVault, 1997, p. 183). However, many adolescent fathers remain integrally involved with the mother during her pregnancy and demonstrate emotional involvement with her and the baby (Hatcher et al., 1998; Newman & Newman, 1999).

A teenage father has a role in relationship to his child. He not only has feelings concerning the existence of the child, but he also has attachments and responsibilities. It is not helpful to be punitive about what he's done wrong. Rather, it is important to help him to express his feelings, to more clearly define his role, and to contribute where he can in taking over responsibilities for his child.

Highlight 6.3 illustrates the potential effects of teenage fatherhood.

Why Do Teens Get Pregnant?

Adolescents often do not use contraception conscientiously, and frequently don't use it at all (Crooks & Baur, 2002; Hatcher et al., 1998; Strassberg & Mahoney, 1988). Most adolescents fail to use any kind of contraception the first few times they have sex (Crooks & Baur, 2002). Even when sexual activity is not new to them, most adolescents fail to use a reliable birth control method consistently (Byer & Shainberg, 1994; Crooks & Baur, 2002; Poppen, 1994). Many adolescents, particularly those who are

younger, fail to use contraception (Strong, DeVault, & Sayad, 1999). Twenty-four percent of teenage women state they do not use any method the first time they have intercourse (Trussell et al., 1998). Why don't teens use birth control?

There are a number of reasons. When asked, adolescents often reveal a deep sense of privacy about sexual behavior and feel embarrassed talking about it with partners, friends, or parents (Trussel et al., 1998). Thus, a young woman may feel extremely uncomfortable talking to a partner about such intimate issues as putting on a condom or placing a diaphragm in her vagina. Another fear may be giving her partner a wrong impression. If she appears to know a lot about contraception, she may fear her partner will think her too knowledgeable and experienced.

Many adolescents express that most teenagers have neither ample knowledge about birth control methods nor adequate access to obtain contraception (Trussel, 1998). Other adolescents adhere to erroneous myths (Crooks & Baur, 2002; Levinson, 1995; Trussell, 1988). For instance, many teens inaccurately believe that they are not old enough to conceive, that "the first time" doesn't count, that they must have intercourse much more frequently than they do in order to conceive, that it is perfectly safe to have sex during certain times of the month, and that withdrawal before ejaculation is an effective birth control method.

Another reason for not using birth control involves a type of psychological avoidance. Adolescents are most likely to use some type of contraception when they are involved in a relationship that has some consistency over time (Baker, Thalberg, & Morrison, 1988; Crooks & Baur, 2002; Glei, 1999). Some young women may illogically feel that if they ignore the issue of potential pregnancy, it will cease to exist. If they don't think about their own sexual activity, then they don't have to worry about it.

There are yet other reasons why teens may not use birth control (Harris et al., 1986). They might not like the bother of using contraception. They might feel sexual activity is more pleasurable without it. They may worry that parents will find out. They may feel invulnerable to pregnancy, that it's something that only happens to other people. Finally, they may simply think that they want to get pregnant.

Macro System Treatment of Sex Education

A heated controversy often develops over the issue of providing teens with information about sex. This is true even in the age of AIDS (acquired immunodeficiency syndrome) (Gibbs, 1991). The fear is that giving adolescents information about sexuality will encourage them to start

Highlight 6.3

Portrait of a Single Father

Gary didn't know what to do. Linda had just ruined his day and probably his life. She had just told him that she was pregnant. How could this happen? What could he do?

Gary, a 17-year-old high school sophomore, had never done very well in school and had even flunked sixth grade once. Ever since then, he'd been taking "Special Ed" classes and was just barely squeaking by.

He had always considered himself a freak. He liked to do a lot of drugs, that is, whenever he had the money to get them. He also liked to listen to booming rock and was intimately familiar with radio station WROK's top ten hits. His uniform included well-patched blue jeans, construction worker boots, and 18-inch long, somewhat scraggly, greasy hair.

Beneath this exterior, Gary was an extremely sensitive person. He really cared about other people, although sometimes he had trouble showing it. This thing about Linda and a baby had really shaken him up. He really loved Linda. In fact, she was the best thing that had ever happened to him. She actually cared about him. It seemed like nobody had ever done that before. Gary really didn't have much self-confidence. The fact that Linda cared simply amazed him.

Gary lived with his mother and younger sister, Hillary, aged 11. He cared about Hillary but they really didn't have much in common. There was too much of an age difference. Sometimes they stuck up for each other, though, when their mother went out with some new boyfriend and came home drunk. That happened pretty often. His mother was really something else. It seemed like she loved him, but she had always had a horrible problem accepting responsibility. A lot of times he felt like he had to take care of her, instead of vice versa. No, she wasn't one to depend on much.

Another problem was that they were dirt poor. He could never remember having a lot of things. For years he had wanted to learn how to play the guitar. He picked one up 2 years ago at a sleazy neighborhood auction, but it never really sounded like much. The other problem, of course, was that he felt he had absolutely no talent. He often thought the guitar looked good, though, sitting on an old peach crate in his basement room, his place of retreat.

Sometimes Gary thought about his father out in Utah. Although he had only actually seen him once in the last 10 years, he talked to him sometimes on the phone on holidays. His big dream was to go out and live with his dad and his dad's new family. Gary liked nature and camping. He thought that Utah would be the perfect place to go to and get away. In his more somber moments, he realized this was only a dream. His dad was pleasant enough on the phone, but he knew he really didn't care. It was fun to think about sometimes, though. Sometimes when he got a better batch of drugs, he'd just sit in his room and think. He dreamed of all the wonderful things he'd do in Utah. That's what it was though, just a dream.

Gary dreamed a lot. He didn't have much hope for the future. He thought that was pretty hopeless. One of his teachers asked him once if he ever thought about going to college. College, hah! How could he ever afford to go to college. He couldn't even afford a Super Kmart guitar. The other problem was how poorly he always did in school. He stopped really studying years ago. Now he was so far behind he knew he'd never catch up. He didn't like to think much about the future. There was no future in it.

But now Gary's problem was Linda—Linda and the baby. It's funny how he already thought of it as a baby even though it wasn't born yet. He liked the thought of having something that was really his. He liked Linda, too, and he didn't want to lose her. She was crying when she told him she was pregnant. He bet she'd like it if they lived together, or maybe even got married. Then he could move out of his mother's apartment. He could be free and on his own. He could drop out of school. School wasn't much anyhow. Maybe he could get that second-shift job slinging burgers at the local hamburger shack. That wouldn't be too bad. He could see his friends there. They could have a good time.

Yeah, that's what he'd do. He'd do a good thing for once in his life. He'd marry Linda and be a father. Maybe everything would be all right then. Maybe they'd all live happily ever after.

Epilogue

Gary and Linda did get married 4 months later. They had a 6-pound, 8-ounce baby boy who they named Billy. The problem was that things really didn't get any better. They didn't change much at all. Gary was still poor. Now, however, he was poor but with adult responsibilities. He still couldn't afford a guitar. He had to go to work at the hamburger shack every day at 5:00 P.M. just like he used to have to go to school every morning. There wasn't much money for him and Linda to have any fun with. As a matter of fact, there wasn't much money to do anything much at all. Their small apartment was pretty cramped. Sometimes the baby's crying drove him almost crazy. He and Linda weren't doing too well either. When they weren't fighting, they weren't talking. Things hadn't changed much at all; he still didn't have much hope for the future.

Commentary

This case example isn't meant to portray the thoughts of a typical or representative teenage father. For example, Gary was very poor. In reality teenage parents originate in all socio-economic levels. However, this example is intended to illustrate the lack of experience and information adolescents often have available to them. Without information it's difficult to make insightful, well-founded decisions. A major job of a social worker is to help young people in a situation like this rationally think through the alternatives available to them. Potential services need to be talked about and plans need to be made. Young people often need both support and suggestions regarding how to proceed. They need to examine their expectations about the future and make certain that they're being realistic.

experimenting sexually. An underlying assumption is that adolescents won't think about sex or be interested in it unless someone around them brings up the subject.

Two fallacies can be pointed out in this approach. First, it assumes that adolescents have little or no access to sexual information other than that which adults choose to give. In reality, most teenagers say they've learned the most about sex from TV, magazines, and their friends (Hyde & DeLamater, 2000; Masters et al., 1995).

Obviously, adolescents are functioning within a complex environment that exposes them to many new ideas. They are not locked up in a sterile cage. A tremendous emphasis is placed on sexuality and sexual behavior by the media. Television, magazines, newspapers, and books are filled with sexual episodes and anecdotes. Adolescents indeed have numerous exposures to the concept of sex.

A second fallacy is that adolescents will automatically try anything they hear about. If a parent tells a young person that some people are murderers, will the young person go out and try murdering someone? Of course not. Although adults, especially parents, might wish they had such control over adolescents, they do not.

Perhaps an analogy concerning sex education could be made to the situation of buying a used Chevy van. An analogous assumption would be that it would be better to have no information about how the van works before buying it and hope for the best. This is ludicrous. In this situation you would want as much information as possible to make the best decision about whether to buy the van or not. It would be wise to take the van to a mechanic to have it thoroughly evaluated. You would both need and want information. People, including adolescents, need as much information as possible in order to make responsible decisions about their own sexual behavior and avoid ignorant mistakes. It is illogical to deprive them of information and have them act on the basis of hearsay and chance.

One primary source of information about sex is friends, and yet friends probably don't know much more about sex than they do. Information that is available from friends is likely to be vague and inaccurate. Just because adolescents use sexual terms does not mean they are very knowledgeable about sexuality.

Another aspect of the sex education controversy is the idea that sex education should be provided by parents in the home. This is a good idea; however, most children receive no sex education in the home (Hyde & DeLamater, 2000). There may be several reasons for this. Adolescents may feel uncomfortable talking about such intimacy with parents, and vice versa. Many young people have extreme difficulty envisioning their parents and grandparents being involved in sexual scenarios. Similarly, parents often don't relish the picture of their children involved in such acts either. Parents may fear that by talking about it, they will encourage children to have sex, a fallacy we have already discussed. Parents may also fear their own ignorance. What if their children ask them questions they can't answer? An implication of these concerns is that it is probably easier to avoid the issue altogether.

Public opinion polls consistently indicate that 80 percent of adults in America support the provision of sex education in schools (Gordon, 1992). Additionally, when sex education is made available, only 3 percent of parents refuse to allow their children to participate (Caron, 1998). Sex educators do not want to take the parents' place as sex educators (Dickman, 1982). Rather, they want to ensure that children have adequate and accurate information about sex. Many times parents are uncomfortable or embarrassed talking about sex with their children. One student shared her 8-year-old son's reaction to her own discomfort in talking to him about sex. As she was trying to explain to him some of the basics of human reproduction, he put his hand on her arm and said, "It's okay, Mom, I get the general idea."

With the extensive publicity given to AIDS in the past few years, more schools have opted or have been required to provide sex education programs. Only 20 states plus the District of Columbia require sex education in the schools as of 1999; however, 35 states require that schools provide education concerning sexually transmitted diseases and HIV (human immunodeficiency virus), which causes AIDS (Allgeier & Allgeier, 2000). However, a wide range of course content can be included in a sex education curriculum. A sex education course can focus only on physical content. Specific topics such as birth control may or may not be covered. Community, parental, and moral values may or may not be integrated into the curriculum. Masters and his associates (1995) urge that "sex education should cover the problems surrounding sexuality, but it should also discuss such aspects of sex as love, intimacy, and interpersonal responsibility" (p. 223).

Sex education can both increase the amount of information teenagers have about sexuality and alter their sexual behavior. For example, a Johns Hopkins University study of students in an inner-city senior high school found that providing an extensive sex education curriculum in addition to furnishing free contraception and birth control counseling resulted in 30 percent fewer pregnancies; additionally, girls chose to postpone having sexual relations for significantly longer periods of time (Zabin et al., 1986). Other research supports the relationship between sex education programs and decreased pregnancy rates (Singh, 1986; Strong & DeVault, 1994; Zelnik & Kim, 1982).

It is each individual's responsibility and our professional aim as social workers to assist people in making the best choices possible in their unique situations. The choice to become sexually active also has potential positive and negative consequences. Positively, one can potentially gain warmth, love, and physical enjoyment from sexual activity. Negatively, however, one can either procreate an unwanted pregnancy or contract a sexually transmitted disease.

Spotlight 6.3 explores the provision of culturally sensitive sex education to Cherokee people.

Sex Education in the Age of AIDS

When AIDS was identified in the early 1980s, the two highest risk groups in the United States were intravenous drug users and gay or bisexual men (Strunin & Hingson, 1987). However, now the spread of infection in the

general heterosexual population is of enormous concern. AIDS transmission is increasing significantly among adolescents and young adults (CDC, 1997b). Consider the following facts (Strong et al., 2002):

- Of the 40,000 people in the United States who are thought to contract HIV each year, one-half are aged 13–24.

- A quarter of a million people in this age group are unaware that they are HIV positive.

- African Americans and Latinos make up 49 percent of reported AIDS cases for people aged 13–19, yet represent only 15 percent of the total population. People of color make up 65 percent of AIDS cases in the 12–24 age group.

(Because AIDS can impact people throughout their life spans, it will be covered in greater depth in Chapter 10).

AIDS merits intense concern when talking about sex education with adolescents and young adults. In the

---

| Spotlight on Diversity 6.3 | Empowerment through Sex Education for Native Americans |

Goodman (1998) cautions that most sex education curricula espouse a limited unilateral view of the world, thereby failing to adequately serve people of color. She describes a case study focusing on a small community in the Cherokee Nation where an empowerment model proposed by Freire (1970, 1985) was used to develop sex education curricula.

Freire suggests that any teaching should occur within a context where community members are active participants in developing and approving content. The process involves three phases. First, developers of curricula should explore the community's needs by actively communicating with residents and observing interaction, expectations, and activities. Second, developers should talk with community members about what principles and values preside over community customs and behavior, thereby identifying recommendations for change. During this phase, community members should be actively recruited to lead discussions and provide input. Third, Freire proposes taking action to solve identified problems.

This model was applied to developing a sex education curriculum in a small Cherokee community of about 200 families in Oklahoma. Goodman (1998) describes the community as consisting of families living in subsidized housing "built on both sides of a state highway" in addition to "two small gas stations/convenience stores, a school, and a church. The community has a reputation for being violent and is located in a county that rumor says has the most unsolved murders of any county in the United States. The county is poor and has one of the highest teen pregnancy rates" in the state (p. 137).

The participatory research process included conducting discussion groups, interviews, and surveys throughout the Cherokee Nation in addition to holding various meetings and seminars. Identified issues during phase 1 were: the huge gap between the community's needs for education about healthy sexual decision making and what was actually being done to meet these needs; school issues including prejudice and discrimination; teen pregnancy; the absence of men in many families' lives; and the influence of drugs on sexual behavior. Phase 2 involved focusing discussion of each identified issue to determine how to address it.

Phase 3 entailed putting community recommendations into action. After-school sex education training sessions were held for teachers. A special Saturday program was provided for male Cherokee youth aged 9 to 13 stressing topics like "talking about tough issues, making good sexual decisions, AIDS, and feeling proud to be Indian" (Goodman, 1998, p. 140). Other project results included improving community members' knowledge about the access to the appropriate social services, developing a video, initiating an Alateen program,[1] and acquiring access to a tribal substance-abuse counselor for individual assessments.

1. Alateen is an organization providing support for teenage children living in a family with an alcoholic. As in Al-Anon, members meet regularly to discuss the facts about alcoholism, provide mutual support and coping suggestions, improve personal attitudes, and reduce family tension.

1980s, it was established that adolescents generally had inadequate information about AIDS and that they did not feel they were vulnerable to contracting the disease (McGill, Smith, & Johnson, 1989; Price, Desmond, & Kukulka, 1985; Simkins & Kushner, 1986; Taylor-Nicholson, Wang, & Adams, 1989).

It appears that adolescents today are better informed about the prevention and contraction of AIDS than in years past (Hyde & DeLamater, 2000). In view of the extensive publicity given to AIDS, many more schools have developed or intensified their sex education programs. One study reviewed 40 published research reports evaluating the effectiveness of AIDS education programs (Kim et al., 1997). Results indicate that such educational programs significantly improve participants' knowledge about HIV and AIDS—7 of the 12 studies that measured attitudinal change found that participants "increased positive attitudes toward prevention and negative attitudes toward risk" (Hyde & DeLamater, 2000, p. 619). Further, 6 of the 10 studies exploring attitudes toward condom use revealed participants' increased intentions to use condoms in the future.

The U.S. Department of Health and Human Services (1986a, pp. 17–18) makes the following recommendations for selecting material to use in educational programming about AIDS:

1. *Teach about high-risk behaviors.* Because of their high rates of sexual activity, adolescents should know which behaviors are the most dangerous and which are the safest. They should be taught and encouraged to take responsibility for their own safety. For instance, using condoms during sexual intercourse makes transmission of contaminated body fluids less likely, although avoidance of intercourse is the safest course of all. Likewise, young people should be aware of the dangers of sharing needles when using illicit drugs.

2. *Present the facts in a straightforward manner.* The facts about AIDS, its transmission, and its prevention should be taught honestly and directly. This is true even when talking about explicit sexual behavior and condom use. Responsible behavior should be clearly defined in adolescents' minds. It is important that AIDS educators themselves be comfortable in talking about these potentially anxiety-producing topics.

3. *Convey values about responsibility and respect for oneself and for the well-being of others.* The importance of values should be emphasized throughout AIDS education. Behaviors can be discussed within the context of evaluating alternatives. For examples, adolescents can be helped to evaluate the potential positive and negative consequences of sexual behavior and drug use. They can be encouraged to establish a firm set of values about what they feel is right and wrong. One focus involves enhancement of self-esteem.

A New York Board of Education "Kids on the Block" team of puppeteers performs plays educating school-age children about AIDS. This particular story concerns a 24-year-old woman with HIV, who is talking to a teenage friend.

© Allan Clear

They have the right to control their behavior and not be subject to the oppressive pressure of peers. They can also be helped to examine the consequences of their own behavior on others.

4. *Select appropriate materials.* Depending on the age level, children and adolescents need different types of information. For example, in kindergarten through third grade, the main intent is to alleviate children's fear of AIDS and lay the groundwork for more advanced discussions about sexuality later in grade 6 (National Coalition of Advocates for Students [NCAS], 1987). In grades 4 and 5, the thrust should be similar, but with greater weight placed on acknowledgment that people have sexual feelings and that individuals and their families have personal values (NCAS, 1987). Finally, in grades 6 through 12, a major objective should be teaching to protect themselves from HIV (NCAS, 1987). It is beyond the scope of this text to detail an entire AIDS or sex education curriculum. However, numerous excellent curriculum development aids are available.

5. *Promote parental involvement.* AIDS education addresses a broad range of sensitive topics. Parents should be integrally involved in planning and developing the curriculum. They should be fully aware of what and how content will be presented. For instance, one means of soliciting parental involvement is to form a task force including both parents and educators. Subsequently, other parents can be invited to attend previews of the proposed educational programming prior to presenting it to students.

Sexually Transmitted Diseases (STDs)

Sexually transmitted diseases, often referred to as STDs, are infections that people can contract through sexual relations. They include some conditions that can also be transmitted in other ways not involving sexual contact. In the past STDs were referred to as venereal diseases (VD). The term STD is preferable because it doesn't sound quite as negative as VD.

We've already established that young people are choosing to become sexually active earlier. It's critical that they have as much information as possible in order to make up for their lack of experience. They need to make responsible decisions both for themselves and for their partners. They need information about what common STDs are, how they are transmitted, what could be their effects, if and how they can be cured, and, perhaps most importantly, how they can be prevented. Discussion here will focus on information about some of the most

common STDs. These include gonorrhea, chlamydial infections, syphilis, and genital herpes. AIDS will be discussed in much greater detail later in Chapter 10.

Gonorrhea. It is estimated that 650,000 people contract gonorrhea each year (Byer et al., 2002; Cates, 1999). Gonorrhea (also called "clap" and "drip") is easily transmitted by various sexual contacts including intercourse, oral stimulation of the genitals, and possibly even kissing. A woman has a 50 percent and a man 20 percent chance of contracting gonorrhea by having intercourse with a contagious person one time (Allgeier & Allgeier, 2000). It's also been established that the gonorrhea organism can live up to 2 hours on materials like wet toilet paper or on toilet seats (Allgeier & Allgeier, 2000; Neinstein, Goldering, & Carpenter, 1984).

A man's symptoms include a yellowish, puslike discharge secreted from the opening at the tip of the penis. Urination is usually quite painful. About 10 percent of men have no symptoms. Symptoms may first appear as early as 1 day or as late as a month after contraction.

Most women, on the other hand, as many as 80 percent, have mild or no noticeable symptoms (Allgeier & Allgeier, 2000). This is because in the vast majority of cases, the infection invades the cervix. Thus, a woman is not as likely as a man either to notice the discharge or to experience pain. The bad thing about this is that without symptoms, a woman won't know she has it. If she doesn't know she has it, she won't seek treatment and, therefore, will continue to be contagious.

If unchecked, gonorrhea usually spreads from the cervix, up the uterus, and into the fallopian tubes. It then can cause pelvic inflammatory disease and possibly sterility if the fallopian tubes become blocked with scar tissue. Because men feel pain as a symptom, they are much more likely to seek treatment. Otherwise, the organisms can move into other sexually related organs, causing pain and possibly fever. Sterility is possible, although it occurs infrequently. Other possible results of gonorrhea include infection and the resulting inflammation of other organs such as the heart, brain, or joints.

Diagnosis of gonorrhea involves obtaining a sample of the discharge on a cotton swab and identifying bacteria on a slide, under a microscope, or growing a laboratory culture of the bacteria. Treatment entails administering antibiotics such as ceftriaxone. People remain contagious to others until they are cured.

Chlamydial Infections. Chlamydial infections are now the most common STDs in the United States; 2 to 4 million new infections are diagnosed annually (Byer et al.,

2002; Cates, 1998). Chlamydia is a specific type of bacterium that invades and lives in the cells of an infected person. A number of diseases can result. Among the most common are mucopurulent cervicitis in women and nongonococcal urethritis, or NGU (also referred to as nonspecific urethritis, or NSU) in men.

Mucopurulent cervicitis is "an infection of the cervix which causes a discharge" (Denney & Quadagno, 1992, p. 531). If not treated, long-term effects for women may include cervical damage, pelvic inflammatory disease, infected fallopian tubes, and potentially sterility. About 40 percent of women experience no symptoms (Mundy, Thomas, & Taylor-Robinson, 1986). Therefore, as with gonorrhea, many women do not seek treatment. NGU is an infection of a man's urethra. It is usually, although not always, caused by chlamydia. Symptoms usually include a thin, clear discharge and pain upon urination. If not treated, it can lead to infertility.

Chlamydial infections can easily be passed back and forth between sexual partners even when one has been cured. People contracting chlamydial infections are supposed to refer all previous sexual partners for treatment. It should be noted that as many as 40 percent of all people contracting gonorrhea also have a chlamydial infection (CDC, 1993). Diagnosis of a chlamydial infection can be done using a variety of techniques including scraping cells from the genitals and growing a culture. Treatment commonly involves the administration of antibiotics such as azithromycin or doxycycline.

Syphilis. Syphilis is contracted by approximately 20,000 people each year in the United States (Cates, 1998). Although it is not as common as either gonorrhea or chlamydial infections, syphilis is much more deadly. Syphilis is transmitted during sexual intercourse and through blood transfusions. Also, a fetus may get it from its mother.

The symptoms progress through four phases. The first is the *primary stage*. Most notable during this phase is the appearance of a round, crater-like sore, which, despite its very unpleasant appearance, is painless. The chancre, as this lesion is called, marks the spot where the bacteria initially penetrated the body. Most frequently, syphilis enters the body through a mucous membrane, around the tip of the penis, in the vagina, or at the cervix. Syphilis can, however, also be contracted through a cut anywhere on the skin. The chancre usually appears within 2 to 4 weeks after syphilis has been contracted. Within several weeks the chancre disappears.

The *secondary stage* begins with a rash that spreads all over the body. It neither itches nor hurts. This stage begins 1 week to 6 months after the chancre disappears. By this time, the bacteria have spread throughout the body. A number of other symptoms may characterize this stage, including sore throat, hair loss, headaches, weight loss, nausea, joint pains, and fever. Most of these symptoms could also characterize a number of other illnesses. This might mask the fact that a person has syphilis. The individual might not seek treatment at all or seek treatment for some other illness.

Another aspect of the disease makes it difficult to pin down and diagnose. The time periods during which these generalized symptoms occur vary greatly and can be long. It's difficult to relate the symptoms of a disease like syphilis to a time perhaps 6 months earlier when it was contracted. These symptoms may last from 2 weeks to sporadic appearance for 6 months.

The *latent stage* begins sometime after all secondary-stage symptoms have disappeared. No symptoms occur during this stage. The bacteria concentrate in some organ of the body like the brain, spinal cord, or bones. Fifty to 70 percent of all people who contract syphilis remain in this stage forever and live out their lives in a normal way. After about 1 year in this stage, they are no longer contagious. One exception is a pregnant woman, who may pass the disease on to her child.

However, the rest of the people who progress to the latent stage enter the final *late stage* of syphilis. During this phase the bacteria viciously attack the organs where they've concentrated. The heart, eyes, brain, spinal cord, digestive organs, liver, or endocrine glands may be involved. The results can include "paralysis, insanity, blindness, and death" (Masters et al., 1995, p. 515).

Blood tests are usually used to diagnose syphilis, although a number of other tests can also be used. Penicillin is the preferred treatment, although antibiotics such as tetracycline are also effective.

Genital Herpes. Genital herpes is caused by a virus and is characterized by small, painful blisters. Other symptoms may include headache, fever, muscular aches, and painful urination. Approximately 200,000 people contract genital herpes each year, adding to the estimated 40 million people already infected (Cates, 1998).

The technical name for genital herpes is *herpes simplex virus type 2* (HSV-2). Except for minor differences in its genetic code, this virus closely resembles herpes simplex virus type 1 (HSV-1), which causes fever blisters or cold sores often found in and around the mouth. Approximately 85 percent of the herpes sores found on people's genitals result from HSV-2; the remainder, from HSV-1

(Gunby, 1983). Likewise, 15 percent of herpes found around the mouth is HSV-2 and the remaining 85 percent HSV-1. Either virus, if it affects the genitals, can be referred to as genital herpes. Transmission from mouth to genitals or vice versa can occur during oral-genital sex. It can also occur by touching fingers to infected areas and subsequently touching other receptive mucous membranes such as those in the genital area or in the mouth.

The first outbreak of genital herpes usually lasts an average of 12 days and frequently is the most painful and uncomfortable; this outbreak typically occurs 2 to 20 days after exposure to the virus (Crooks & Baur, 2002; Denney & Quadagno, 1992). After the initial outbreak, recurrences vary from one individual to another. That is, outbreaks will vary greatly in frequency, duration, and severity. Some people never experience another outbreak. Others experience them regularly. For some people, outbreaks seem to be related to high levels of stress.

One of the most serious consequences of herpes is that it may be passed on to a developing fetus through the placenta. Although this occurrence is not common, herpes can cause birth defects. Herpes also may be contracted by the newborn during delivery if contact is made with an infected cervix or vagina. Mothers who have herpes are often urged to have a cesarean section performed so that the baby avoids contagion. Another serious aspect of herpes is that it appears to be related to cancers of the vulva and cervix. Because both of these cancers are usually responsive to treatment, women with herpes are encouraged to have gynocological examinations and Pap smears every 6 months.

Because herpes is a virus, there is no cure. Like a bad cold or flu, which are also caused by viruses, a cure has not been found. Although not a cure, the drug acyclovir (trade name: Zovirax), and others in pill form, are effective in preventing recurrence and suppressing symptoms (Gershengorn & Blower, 2000). Acyclovir is also available in ointment form. When used on a long-term basis, the drug seems to diminish the number and severity of outbreaks. However, such long-term use runs the danger of encouraging the development of new, mutated strains of the virus that would be more resistant to the drug's effects.

A woman's chances of contracting herpes if she has sexual intercourse with an infected man is 80 to 90 percent (Straus et al., 1985). A man, on the other hand, has a 50 percent chance of contracting the disease from an infected woman (Masters et al., 1995). Herpes is most contagious during an outbreak of painful blisters. The blisters should not be touched. However, there is increasing evidence that herpes can also be transmitted when no symptoms are apparent (Stanberry, 2000; Wald et al., 2000).

Other STDs. A number of other STDs may occur. However, it is beyond the scope of this text to address them all in detail. For instance, pubic lice or "crabs" are tiny creatures who live at the base of pubic hair and feed on blood. They can cause severe itching. A prescription drug sold under the brand name Kwell in the United States and Kwellada in Canada kills pubic lice within 24 hours. Genital warts are yet another STD. The warts have a texture resembling cauliflower and are found on the genitals. They can be treated with a solution of Podophyllin mixed with alcohol, which causes the warts to fall off within several days or weeks. There appears to be a relationship between genital warts and cervical cancer.

Preventing STDs. Suggestions for preventing STDs include using condoms because they prevent contact between the penile tissues and a woman's genital tissues or a partner's anal tissues. A condom or a "dental dam" (a small sheet of plastic that can be placed over a woman's genitalia during oral sex) can help prevent STD transmission between mouth and genitalia during oral sex. Spermicides have also been found to help kill some STDs. Washing the genital areas with soap and water before sexual contact can help. Urinating both before and after intercourse can also help clear the urethra of bacteria.

These are specific behaviors that people can follow to help prevent contracting an STD. However, perhaps suggestions concerning thought and choice are the most effective. Masters and his associates (1995, p. 534) make six suggestions for preventing the transmission of STDs. First, each person should "be informed." Know what STDs are and how they can be contracted. Second, each individual should "be observant." This doesn't necessarily mean one should say, "Well, excuse me, dear, but may I please take a moment to examine your genitals for symptoms of STDs?" However, it does mean that being aware and watching for symptoms may help a person avoid contracting a disease. Third, "be selective." Choose sexual partners carefully. A partner who has had several other sexual partners recently can significantly increase his or her risk of having an STD. Fourth, "be honest." That means if a person has an STD, he or she should tell a prospective partner about it. It also means that if someone is worried about a potential partner having an STD, that person should ask about it. Fifth, "be cautious." Follow the suggestions mentioned earlier, such as using condoms for protection. Sixth, if a person thinks he or she might have an STD, that person should "be promptly tested and treated."

Major Methods of Contraception

Anyone who is considering becoming sexually active and who is not intentionally trying to conceive a child needs accurate and specific information about contraceptive methods.[2] This includes adolescents. Without adequate information, responsible decisions cannot be made. Information helps to prevent people from taking unnecessary risks. We've already established the importance of sex education. Information concerning contraception is especially important. The risk of unplanned pregnancy and the resulting impact on the lives of adolescents is too critically important to ignore.

Major methods of contraception are described in the following sections. Their levels of effectiveness are indicated, and the advantages and disadvantages of each method are explored. No one best method of birth control exists for everybody. Each individual must select a method according to how it fits with his or her lifestyle. Some methods are easier to use than others. Some methods require responsible adherence to a schedule. Other methods are best suited for persons who have only occasional sexual contacts.

The Pill. Birth control pills or oral contraceptives are one of the most effective forms of contraception other than sterilization. There are two major types of birth control pills. Various companies produce more than 40 brands of these two types of pills (McCammon et al., 1998). The most commonly used type of birth control pill combines a synthetic estrogen and a progestin (both primary female hormones). The *combined pill* targets a 28-day menstrual cycle and is distributed in monthly packs.

Combined pills are taken in one of two ways. The most commonly used brands of combined pills are sold in packages of 21 pills, which should be taken daily until they are used up. A woman then refrains from starting her next monthly pack of pills for 7 days. During this time she will have her menstrual period. Other brands of combined pills come in packs of 28 pills. These include placebos or ineffective sugar pills for the last 7 days of the cycle. This serves to reinforce a woman's habit of taking one pill each day.

2. An excellent resource for further information regarding contraceptive methods is *Contraceptive Technology,* by R. H. Hatcher et al. (eds.) (New York: Ardent Media, 1998).

Combined pills prevent the ovaries from ovulating, or releasing a ripened egg ready for fertilization. In a sense, they trick the body into thinking that the woman is pregnant. A pregnant woman temporarily stops ovulating in order to prevent multiple pregnancies. Combined pills also thicken cervical mucus, making it more difficult for sperm to enter the uterus. They alter the endometrium (the lining of the uterus, part of which is sloughed off during menstruation) and hamper the ability of sperm to fertilize an egg (Hatcher & Guillebaud, 1998).

Combined pills are *theoretically* 99.9 percent effective, which is considered excellent (Hatcher & Guillebaud, 1998). Theoretical effectiveness rates refer to the number of women out of 100 in whom pregnancy is prevented. A theoretical effectiveness rate of 100 percent means that for every 100 women, none should become pregnant.

However, the combined pill's *actual* effectiveness rate is approximately 95 percent (Hatcher & Guillebaud, 1998). Actual effectiveness refers to how effective the method is in actual use. The differences between the two rates probably can be explained by human error. For example, forgetting to take a pill one day increases the chance of pregnancy. Or, with other birth control methods, failing to use them every time a person has sexual intercourse decreases the actual effectiveness rate.

The other major type of birth control pill is usually referred to as the *mini-pill,* which provides a lower dosage of hormones than the combined pill. Its theoretical effectiveness rate is 99.5 percent, but its actual effectiveness rate can be as low as 95 percent (Hatcher & Guillebaud, 1998). Mini-pills contain only artificial progestin, and women who take them may continue to ovulate. Mini-pills cause changes in the interior uterine lining, the consistency of cervical mucus, and the functioning of the fallopian tubes so that it is more difficult for an egg to be fertilized and implanted on the uterine wall. Mini-pills can provide a good contraceptive alternative. There are indications that such pills pose fewer health risks than do combined pills (Ortiz, 1989; Strong, et al., 2002). Both combined pills and mini-pills should be taken regularly at approximately the same time each day.

Today's birth control pills have relatively lower dosages of hormones than they did 2 decades ago. This is to minimize unpleasant side effects. However, the fact that they are low-dosage pills makes it more important that they be taken at approximately the same time each day. Otherwise, there is a chance that their pregnancy-inhibiting abilities will be decreased to the point that they will not work. With combination pills, it is important that the hormonal levels maintained by the pill do not drop to a level that makes ovulation possible. Once ovulation occurs, pregnancy is possible. With mini-pills, if the internal reproductive environment is not kept hostile enough to prevent fertilization and implantation, pregnancy may occur.

Ortiz (1989) cautions that "even the best organized woman will forget a pill once in a while" (p. 206). She suggests: "If you forget one pill, take two the next day. If you forget two pills in a row, catch up by taking two each for the next two days, and use a back-up method such as the condom for the rest of the cycle. If you forget three pills in a row, your protection for that cycle is probably lost, so stop taking them and wait for your period. Then start again. Use another form of birth control, such as condoms or foam, until you start the pills again. If you are on the mini-pill, keep on taking the pills but use another method of contraception as well until after your next period" (p. 206).

Advantages of taking either form of birth control pill are numerous. They are very effective. They are fairly easy to use, in that they must simply be swallowed daily. Nothing needs to be inserted into the vagina. No complicated process is involved. Nothing interferes with the spontaneity of a sexual encounter. Those who are frequently sexually active are always prepared. Birth control pills have been found to prevent ovarian cancer and endometrial cancer, decrease the risk of developing benign breast tumors, and even improve acne (Hatcher & Guillebaud, 1998).

Disadvantages to taking birth control pills include undesirable side effects such as nausea, headaches, constipation, water retention and the resulting swelling, minor increases in blood pressure, and irregular vaginal discharges. These side effects resemble those of the first trimester of pregnancy. This is because they are due to similar changes in hormonal levels. These symptoms usually disappear after 2 to 3 months, like they do in pregnancy. Changing brands of birth control pills sometimes helps because different brands often have minor variations in hormonal dosages. Such variations affect various women differently. Additionally, women taking the combined pill who suffer more severe side effects might consider trying the mini-pill. Negative consequences tend to be less severe with the mini-pill.

Another disadvantage to taking birth control pills is possible weight gain due to increased water retention. Some women indicate that they have an increased incidence of vaginal infections due to changes in their vaginal mucus. Additionally, because the pill is a prescription drug, cost is somewhat prohibitive.

Birth control pills should not be taken when a woman is pregnant because there are some indications that they can cause damage to a fetus. Nor should pills be taken during breast-feeding because they "cause a decrease in the amount and quality of milk produced" (Ortiz, 1989, p. 205). Birth control pills also have interactive effects with some other drugs, such as insulin, blood-thinning medications, and some tranquilizers. Some medications such as antibiotics and some tranquilizers can decrease the pill's effectiveness. Thus, any woman taking birth control pills should check with her physician regarding possible interactive effects with any other drugs she may be taking.

The most serious health risks in taking the pill are cardiovascular problems, such as an increased chance of blood clots in the circulatory system. The danger is that the clot can cause damage to the lungs or the brain. A second cardiovascular danger is the increased risk of having a heart attack. However, this is true primarily for women who smoke, lead an exceptionally sedentary lifestyle, are overweight, are over age 50, are hypertensive, suffer from diabetes, or have elevated cholesterol (Hatcher & Guillebaud, 1998).

Because of the associated cardiovascular problems, women over age 35 are discouraged from taking the pill. This is especially true for those who smoke (Planned Parenthood Association of Wisconsin, undated).

In the past, questions have been raised regarding the relationship between the pill and cancer. There is no credible evidence that the pill causes cancer (Hatcher & Guillebaud, 1998). As a matter of fact, we have established that birth control pills actually protect women against some kinds of cancer, particularly ovarian cancer and cancer of the uterine lining (Hatcher & Guillebaud, 1998).

The possible relationship between birth control pills and breast cancer has also been an issue. However, some large-scale research has shown this not to be the case (Cancer and Steroid Hormone study, 1986; Hatcher et al., 1998; Lipnick et al., 1986).

There should be a note of caution here, however. It is too early to make a definite statement that birth control pills never cause cancer under any circumstances. Some forms of cancer may take 20, 30, or even 40 years to develop. Longer term research is necessary to counter this possibility.

Birth control pills have some positive side effects. Women who take the pill tend to have a decreased menstrual flow, have less painful cramping, and menstruate on a more regular basis (Hatcher & Guillebaud, 1998; Mishell, 1982). When pill users fall prey to pelvic inflammatory disease, the condition is usually less severe (Hatcher & Guillebaud, 1998).

One fear about the pill has proven to be unfounded, namely, that women who take the pill will have difficulty getting pregnant later. Although it appears that women must usually wait about 3 months after stopping the pill in order to get pregnant, no long-term effects in fertility have been found (Maier, 1984).

One important aspect to consider before using the pill as a means of contraception is a person's general approach to life. In other words, a person must be notably responsible and conscientious in order to take the pill regularly every day. Many people, despite their good intentions, find it difficult to follow a regimented procedure. Women who are only occasionally sexually active might also find it unappealing to take the pill every day.

The Emergency Contraceptive Pill (The Morning-After Pill). Despite the controversy over newer chemical methods of abortion (such as RU 486 and methotrexate, discussed in Chapter 2), several methods of postcoital contraception already exist legally in the United States (Van Look & Stewart, 1998). A *postcoital method* is a type of birth control "used after a pregnancy is confirmed or suspected" (Carroll & Wolpe, 1996, p. 429). The most frequently used method "is a regimen of combined oral contraceptive pills (called ECPs, for emergency contraceptive pills)" (Van Look & Stewart, 1998, p. 277). Typically, treatment involves taking one dose within 72 hours of sexual intercourse and another dose 12 hours later. Taken before ovulation they "inhibit or delay ovulation to prevent fertilization, and they may possibly alter the endometrium to prevent fertilization" (Van Look & Stewart, 1998, p. 281). ECPs may also hinder the mobility of sperm or ova. There are questions regarding the effectiveness of ECPs if taken after ovulation or fertilization have already occurred.

Effectiveness of ECPs is difficult to determine because it's impossible to establish how often women would have become pregnant without treatment. Additionally, a woman's fertility varies significantly depending on the day of her menstrual cycle. She is most fertile "beginning 6 days before ovulation and ending the day after ovulation" (Van Look & Stewart, 1998, p. 281). Even during this period, her pregnancy risk is only 10 to 30 percent. Considering available research, it is estimated that the effectiveness of ECPs is at least 75 percent, and quite possibly greater than 80 percent (Van Look & Stewart, 1998; Trussell, 1998).

Side effects of ECPs include nausea for 30 to 50 percent of women taking them and vomiting for 15 to 25 percent (Van Look & Stewart, 1998). Other side effects include "fatigue, breast tenderness, headache, abdominal pain, and dizziness" (Van Look & Stewart, 1998, p. 284). These effects usually do not last more than

a day or two following treatment. Mifepristine (RU 36), discussed in Chapter 2, tends to produce less nausea and vomiting and fewer side effects than ECPs (Van Look & Stewart, 1998).

ECPs are approved for birth control purposes only. However, physicians are not prohibited from using these drugs for purposes other than contraception such as to inhibit ovulation or prevent fertilization. The Food and Drug Administration (FDA) examined pertinent research and stated in the *Federal Register* that "certain combined oral contraceptives . . . are safe and effective for use as postcoital emergency contraception" (FDA, 1997). The American College of Obstetricians and Gynecologists has specified how ECPs should be administered in its "Practice Patterns" (1996). Also, the clinical guidelines of the International Planned Parenthood Federation describes the use of ECPs. Thus, it appears that ECPs are being employed extensively to inhibit ovulation, prevent fertilization, and possibly prevent implantation of a fertilized egg. Van Look and Stewart (1998) suggest that "these new policies should provide important encouragement for health care professions to prescribe emergency contraception" (p. 280).

Progestin-only pills are also available to induce abortions in other countries, although they are not available in the necessary dosage in the United States (Van Look & Stewart, 1998). In the past, diethylstilbestrol (more commonly referred to as DES), a high-dosage estrogen substance, was given to women twice daily for 5 days following intercourse to expel an embryo. Although DES was fairly effective, side effects were severe, including linkages to cancer developing in the children of women who used it (Carroll & Wolpe, 1996; Hatcher et al., 1994). It might be noted that pregnancy will likely be prevented if a copper-releasing intrauterine device (IUD) is inserted in the uterus within 5 to 7 days after intercourse occurred. However, women choose to use this much less frequently than chemical methods (Hatcher et al., 1994; Webb & Morris, 1993).

Hormonal Implants: Norplant. The first significantly new birth control method the Food and Drug Administration (FDA) has approved in 25 years is a hormonal implant called Norplant. The implant consists of six small tubes containing levonorgestrel, a synthetic female hormone, which are placed underneath the skin in the upper arm. The hormones are gradually absorbed by the body over a 5-year period, after which the nonbiodegradable implants must be removed.

A major advantage of Norplant is its effectiveness. The implants appear to approach 100 percent in both theoretical and actual effectiveness rates, making it the most effective reversible contraceptive ever sold (Hatcher, 1998). Thus, Norplant provides an effective long-term contraceptive method that involves virtually no effort after initial insertion.

Disadvantages includes menstrual irregularity, weight gain, breast tenderness, and depression (Hatcher, 1998). Many women also experience either an increased number of light bleeding days during menstruation or cessation of menstrual flow altogether (Hatcher, 1998). Other possible disadvantages include "headaches, nervousness, nausea, and dizziness" (Allgeier & Allgeier, 2000, p. 238). One other potential disadvantage is that this form of birth control can clearly be seen, in a sense advertising that one is on birth control. Kuiper and her associates (1997) conducted focus groups with teenagers in which hormone implant usage was discussed. The researchers found that many young women expressed concerns about whether friends would think that implants might look strange or "gross." Worse yet, some teens worried about appearing as if they were easy targets for sexual action. Although Norplant usage among teens has decreased (Allgeier & Allgeier, 2000), about 88 percent of women using Norplant continue usage after 1 year, and half of these continue for 3 years (Hatcher, 1998).

The World Health Organization has issued some words of caution about hormonal implants and injections although research has established no definitive relationship with potential problems (Hatcher, 1998; World Health Organization, 1996). Concerns include potential harm to a fetus; possible relationship to breast cancer; interaction with other medications; potential liver problems in some women; effects on cardiovascular functioning; and complications with diabetes.

Hormonal Injections: Depo-Provera. Depo-Provera is the most commonly used hormonal injection method for contraception. It is a long-acting progestin that is injected once every 12 weeks, although it probably provides an even longer period of protection. It works very much like Norplant and has a theoretical and actual effectiveness rate approaching 100 percent (Hatcher, 1998). Advantages and disadvantages are similar to those of Norplant. However, it does not have the visibility problem. Women are more likely to experience cessation of menstrual flow during menstruation with Depo-Provera than with Norplant (Hatcher, 1998). One study found that about half of women taking Depo-Provera stopped menstruation completely after 1 year (Strong, DeVault, & Sayad, 1999). More than 59 percent of women taking Depo-Provera continued after 1 year, 41.5 percent after

2 years, 30.2 percent after 3 years, and 24.1 percent after 4 (Hatcher, 1998).

The Diaphragm. The diaphragm is one of the *barrier* methods of birth control. This means that the device acts as a barrier to keep sperm from reaching and fertilizing the egg. The diaphragm is a circular thin piece of rubber stretched over a flexible ring of wire. It is shaped like a dome. A woman inserts it by pushing it with her fingers up into the vagina to cover the cervix.

Before insertion, approximately one teaspoonful of spermicidal cream or jelly should be placed at the bottom of the dome. Then using her finger, she should spread a small amount of cream or jelly around the rim to maximize the potential for contacting sperm. These substances kill any sperm that manage to get around the diaphragm's barrier. The diaphragm can be placed in the vagina up to 6 hours before intercourse. Then, it should be left in the vagina at least 6 to 8 hours after intercourse to make certain that all of the sperm are disposed of. An additional application of spermicide must be inserted after each act of intercourse. The diaphragm should be checked for holes before each use, which can be done by holding it up to the light.

The diaphragm, when used with a spermicide, can be a very effective form of birth control. Its theoretical effectiveness rating is 94 percent; the rate is 80 percent (Hyde & DeLamater, 2000; F. Stewart; 1998).

Failures may be due to slippage while in use or the development of tiny holes in the diaphragm itself. Additional failures may be due to its inconvenience and difficulty in use. That is, it takes time to prepare for use and insert before every sexual encounter. Sometimes a woman may not have it with her when she needs it. At other times, she may not use it with a spermicide. This greatly decreases its effectiveness. Sometimes it might not be used because it would interfere with spontaneity.

A major advantage of the diaphragm is its safety factor. That is, it causes virtually no health problems. No chemicals are forced into the body. No device is inserted into delicate organs to cause irritation. The only potential difficulty suffered by only a small minority of people is an allergic reaction to a particular brand of spermicide.

Another advantage is its relatively reasonable cost. The diaphragm does require a visit to a physician. Different women need different sizes. After this initial evaluation, a diaphragm is prescribed. It can then be used over a long period of time, provided it is not damaged. In the case of a weight gain or loss of 10 pounds or more, a woman should be reexamined to make certain that her diaphragm still fits.

For individuals who are only occasionally sexually active, the diaphragm need only be used when needed. A person does not have to undergo the ongoing health risks involved in other contraceptive methods when contraception is not needed all of the time.

The major disadvantages of the diaphragm include its relatively complicated method of use and its potential interruption of spontaneity. A person must be willing to go through the correct procedure consistently for it to be an effective birth control method. As is indicated by the relatively high failure rate, this is not always so easy.

The Cervical Cap. The cervical cap, made of a soft plastic or rubber, resembles the diaphragm. Smaller and deeper than a diaphragm, the cap fits snugly over the cervix and is held in place by suction. Like a diaphragm, it acts to keep sperm from entering the uterus. Its theoretical effectiveness rate resembles that of the diaphragm (Hyde & DeLamater, 2000). However, the rate varies greatly depending on whether a woman has had a baby (i.e., she is *parous*) or has never given birth (i.e., she is *nulliparous*). The theoretical and actual effectiveness rates for parous women are 74 and 60 percent, respectively; for nulliparous women, these respective rates are 91 and 80 percent, quite a striking difference (F. Stewart, 1998).

Cervical caps must be fitted to each individual woman's cervix. Women usually can be fitted with one of the available standard sizes. As with the diaphragm, spermicidal jelly or cream should be used, although in a somewhat lesser amount. The cap should be left in the vagina 6 to 8 hours after intercourse. At the latest, it should be removed after 72 hours. Leaving the cervical cap in longer poses risks of disagreeable odor and of toxic shock syndrome (Hyde & DeLamater, 2000).

Advantages and disadvantages related to the cervical cap are similar to those of the diaphragm. Although insertion and removal is a bit more difficult than that of the diaphragm, the cervical cap is smaller and less likely to be felt during sexual intercourse.

The Contraceptive Sponge. The contraceptive sponge, currently available over the Internet, is a soft, cuplike sponge device that can be inserted into the vagina and covers the cervix. It is saturated with a spermicide to provide additional protection. Before insertion, it should be moistened with tap water. It should be left in the vagina at least 6 hours after sexual intercourse and can be left there up to 24 hours.

The sponge's effectiveness is based on three principles. First, it acts like a barrier to prevent sperm from entering the cervix. Second, the chemical spermicide it contains acts to kill sperm. Third, its potential for absorbing sperm is also thought to be beneficial. Like the cervical cap, it is significantly more effective for women who have never had children than for those who have had children. Its theoretical and actual effectiveness for women who have not had children are 91 and 80 percent, respectively; the respective rates for women who have borne children are 72 and 60 percent (F. Stewart, 1998).

The Condom. A condom, also called a prophylactic or rubber, is a thin sheath made of latex rubber that fits over the penis. Some are made of the thin tissue of a lamb's

A variety of birth control methods: the pill, the sponge, contraceptive foam, the condom, and the diaphragm. Anyone who wants to be sexually active without conceiving children needs to become educated on the specific uses of contraceptives.

© T. J. Florian /Rainbow

intestine; these tend to be more expensive. The condom is initially rolled up into a little circular packet. This packet must be unrolled and placed on the penis. Because it fits rather snugly, it acts as another of the barrier methods of birth control. After ejaculation, sperm are contained in the rubber sheath. They are never allowed to enter the vagina. Some condoms have a small bulge at the tip to allow room for semen. Otherwise, some empty space must purposefully be left at the tip of the condom so that there is a place to hold the semen.

Condoms are available with a number of variations. Some are lubricated. They come with slightly different textures and a variety of colors.

The theoretical effectiveness of a condom is 97 percent (Warner & Hatcher, 1998). The effectiveness level approaches 100 percent when the condom is used in conjunction with a contraceptive foam.

The actual effectiveness rate of the condom is 86 percent (Warner & Hatcher, 1998). Once again, this decrease in actual effectiveness can be attributed to human error. The condom must be held at the base of the penis as the penis is withdrawn from the vagina. This is to make sure that none of the sperm is spilled and can enter the vagina. Condoms should not be reused.

There are many notable advantages to using the condom. First of all, it is the only nonsurgical means giving the male some direct responsibility for contraception. Condoms are readily available at a relatively low cost. They don't require a prior physical examination or a medical prescription. They are small and easy to carry for use at any time. They cause no side effects, and serve to prevent venereal disease. Latex condoms "lubricated with the spermicide nonoxynol-9" provide the best protection against sexually transmitted diseases (Denney & Quadagno, 1992, p. 224).

Of course, their use has been given much publicity and encouragement over the past few years as a method to help prevent the spread of AIDS. (AIDS and its spread will be discussed much more thoroughly later in Chapter 10.) (Note, though, that condoms made from lambs' intestines do not protect one from some STDs such as AIDS.) One interesting advantage for some men is that the snug fit helps to maintain an erection for a longer period of time in the cases where this is desirable.

One disadvantage of using the condom is the minor intrusion of spontaneity when placing it on the penis. It is also important that it be withdrawn shortly after ejaculation to avoid spilling semen. Some young men have indicated that they hesitate to carry condoms with them. They feel it looks to a prospective partner as if they were expecting to have intercourse, which might give a bad impression. However, the important thing is to evaluate the potential risks that are involved. The costs of an unwanted pregnancy must be weighed against risking a poor impression.

Female Condoms. The female condom, available since 1994, provides another barrier form of contraception. It consists of two rings connected by latex. One ring fits over the cervix; the latex protects the cervix from contact with either the penis or semen. The other ring rests outside the vagina; here the latex forms a pouch for the penetrating penis, thus protecting the penis from vaginal contact. The interior is covered with a lubricant to facilitate penile penetration. It can be inserted up to 8 hours before sexual intercourse and should not be reused. A female condom should never be used together with a male condom because they might stick together "causing slippage or displacement of one or both devices" (F. Stewart, 1998, p. 372). The theoretical effectiveness rate is 95 percent, although the actual rate is 79 percent (F. Stewart, 1998).

The IUD (Intrauterine Device). The IUD is a plastic device that is placed in a woman's uterus. IUDs have been made in various shapes. They need to be inserted by a physician or trained health professional. Because of alleged health problem claims and the resultant lawsuits, IUD use in the United States dropped significantly during the 1980s (Hyde & DeLamater, 2000). An estimated 106 million women now use IUDs worldwide, although only 1 percent of women of reproductive age in the United States use IUDs; most U.S. users are older, 90 percent being in their 30s and 40s (G.K. Stewart, 1998b).

Two types of IUDs are currently available in the United States, both of which are T-shaped. The CU T 380A or Copper-T (with the brand name of Paragard) contains copper, and the Progesterone T (with the brand name Progestasert) contains progesterone.

A third IUD, Lng 20-IUD or the levonorgestrel IUD, which releases hormones directly into the uterus for up to 5 years, is used in other countries and may be available in the United States soon. It also assumes a T-shape. There is some evidence "that it will be the most effective of all IUDs" and will "have fewer side effects associated with it" (Kelly, 2001, p. 32b; Sivin, Stern, & International Committee for Contraceptive Research, 1994; G. K. Stewart, 1998b).

It is thought that IUDs "work primarily by preventing sperm from fertilizing ova" (G. K. Stewart, 1998b, p. 512). Apparently, they generate changes in the uterus and fallopian tubes that hinder sperm from entering the fallopian tube to fertilize the egg; this altered environment may also cause the egg to "move more swiftly through the fallopian tube, reducing the chances of fertilization" (Hyde & DeLamater, 2000, p. 193; G. K. Stewart, 1998b). The hormones released by both the Progestasert and the levonorgestrel IUD add to the interference by thickening cervical mucus, further altering the uterine environment, and slowing down sperm (G. K. Stewart, 1998b). The tiny amount of copper emitted by the Copper-T is thought to have a similar effect (Hyde & DeLamater, 2000). Theorectical effectiveness for the Copper-T, Progestasert, and levonorgestrel IUDs is 99.4 percent, 98.5 percent, and 99.1 percent, respectively; actual effectiveness rates for them are a respective 99.2, 98, and 99.9 percent (G. K. Stewart, 1998b).

The IUD is attached to a string that hangs out of the cervix. A woman must check this string regularly to be assured that the IUD is still in place. She can check the IUD by inserting her finger into the vagina and feeling if the string is still there.

After initial insertion, a woman should check the string regularly. Between 2 percent and 10 percent if IUDs are expelled within the first year after insertion (G. K. Stewart, 1998b). During this time, the string should be checked before each sexual encounter. Women are also encouraged to use an additional form of birth control during this period to better ensure protection against pregnancy. After 3 months, women should check the string at least once a month to ensure that the IUD is still in place.

A major advantage of the IUD is its ease of use. Additionally, it provides continuous protection at a high level of effectiveness. Despite the initial cost of insertion, the extended length of use over time makes the cost relatively reasonable. It is also easily reversible. Upon removal a woman can become pregnant immediately.

IUDs also have a number of disadvantages (G. K. Stewart, 1998b). The first serious potential consequence is pelvic inflammatory disease (PID). PID refers to an infection located in either the uterus or the fallopian tubes. Although PID can have many causes, the IUD appears to increase risk both during the first few weeks after initial insertion and if the woman is exposed to and contracts STDs. Women who have more than one sexual partner or whose partners have increased risk of acquiring an STD assume a greater risk for developing PID.

A second disadvantage of IUD use involves menstrual problems such as painful menstruation, excessive bleeding, or spotting at different times of the month. Approximately 10 to 15 percent of IUD users discontinue use because of such problems.

A third disadvantage of IUD use involves complications in the event that pregnancy does occur. Resulting problems include spontaneous abortions, ectopic pregnancies, or PID. A fourth potential problem is perforation of the uterus, although this occurs in only 1 in 1,000 insertions.

One other issue concerns the questionable use of IUDs by nulliparous women. G. K. Stewart (1998b) warns that "because of the slight increased risk of PID in IUD users, women who wish to bear children in the future should consider more suitable contraceptive methods" (p. 520). PID, especially long-term, severe, or multiple cases of, can cause scar tissue resulting in infertility.

It seems like we've listed a lot of potential disadvantages. However, many IUD users swear by them as an easy, effective, safe, and long-term means of avoiding pregnancy.

Vaginal Spermicides. Spermicides are chemical contraceptives that function in two ways. First, the chemicals act to kill sperm. Second, the substance itself acts as a barrier that inhibits sperm from entering the uterus. Spermicides are available in creams, jellies, and foams that are squeezed or thrust into a tube, which in turn is inserted into the vagina. Other spermicides include suppositories, tablets, and thin, tissuelike sheets of spermicide, either of which is placed directly into the vagina. Some condoms are lubricated with a spermicide.

Advantages of spermicides include their relative ease of use, their ready availability, their low cost, their use only when needed, and their lack of health risks. An increasing body of research also indicates that spermicides may help to prevent some STDs including gonorrhea, genital herpes, and AIDS (Cates & Raymond, 1998). Despite these advantages, the actual effectiveness rate of spermicides ranges from less than 5 to more than 50 percent for regular users, depending on what study you review (Cates & Raymond, 1998). However, spermicides used in conjunction with other forms of contraception can be very effective. For instance, spermicides used along with a condom approach the effectiveness of the pill, both theoretically and actually.

Withdrawal. Withdrawal, or coitus interruptus, refers to withdrawing the penis before ejaculating into the vagina. Although it has often been considered a relatively ineffective method of birth control, in actuality its effectiveness resembles that of the barrier methods of contraception.

Theoretical effectiveness is 96 percent and actual effectiveness 81 percent (Kowal, 1998). One problem with this method is that a few drops of semen are expelled by a pair of glands called the Cowper's glands before the full ejaculation. Both urine and semen pass through the urethra. Urine is acidic. An acidic environment is not conducive for sperm. It is thought that these few drops of liquid are discharged before ejaculation in order to clear the urethra of some of its acidic quality and better prepare it for sperm. However, sometimes live sperm remain in the urethra. These can be transported out through the tip of the penis by the Cowper's glands' secretion and still impregnate a woman.

Major advantages of withdrawal are that no extraneous devices or substances are needed and it's free. A primary disadvantage is that its "effectiveness depends largely on the man's ability to withdraw prior to ejaculation" (Kowal, 1998, p. 304). In the heat of emotion it may be difficult for some men to exercise great control over ejaculation.

Fertility Awareness Methods. Fertility awareness methods (formerly sometimes referred to as the rhythm method) refer to monitoring a woman's ovulation cycle and initiating sexual relations only during the safe times of her cycle. Because so many variables are involved, it's difficult to calculate theoretical effectiveness. However, it is estimated that actual effectiveness is about 75 percent (Jennings, Lamprecht, & Kowal, 1998). Fertility awareness methods "are considered effective when they are used correctly. However, they are not effective when used incorrectly because, with incorrect use, unprotected intercourse takes place when the woman is potentially fertile" (Jennings et al., 1998, p. 309). The actual effectiveness rate for couples using no methods and relying on chance is 15 percent (Jennings et al., 1998).

There are at least three types of fertility awareness. Due to their complicated procedures, we will not address them in detail here. The *calendar method* is the simplest of the three. It involves counting the days of the menstrual cycle and trying to determine when ovulation occurs. The idea is to have intercourse only when it is certain that the woman is not ovulating.

A second method is the *basal body temperature method*. A woman's body temperature undergoes minor predictable variations depending on where she is in her ovulatory cycle. Using this method involves taking her temperature every morning as soon as she wakes up. A problem with this method is that the major temperature differential occurs only after ovulation has taken place. By this time pregnancy prevention could be too late.

A third type of fertility awareness method is the *cervical mucus method*. It necessitates that a woman examine her cervical mucus throughout her menstrual cycle. The consistency, amount, and clarity of the mucus tends to change predictably depending on where she is in her ovulatory cycle.

Sterilization. Sterilization is one of the most common forms of family planning methods used in the world; more than one million sterilizations are performed annually in the United States alone (Stewart & Carignan, 1998). It is considered to be permanent, although it can be reversed in some cases.

Sterilization for women involves a *tubal ligation,* in which the fallopian tubes leading from the ovaries to the uterus are severed. Hence, sperm are unable to reach the egg. Sterilization for men entails a *vasectomy;* a small section of the vas deferens is removed near the place where the scrotum is attached to the body. The vas deferens is the tube that transports sperm from the testicles to the urethra. Thus, sperm are not ejaculated. "Vasectomy continues to be simpler, safer, less expensive, and more effective than female sterilization" (Stewart & Carignan, 1998, p. 549).

Many young people ask whether sterilization interferes with sexual responsiveness. They wonder if having a vasectomy means that a man will not be able to ejaculate or have an orgasm. This, of course, is not the case. Most of the milky liquid contained in semen is produced by the seminal vesicles and the prostate gland, other organs that feed into the vas deferens later in the ejaculation process. This liquid is still ejaculated, but without any sperm in it. Because sperm are so tiny, the volume of semen ejaculated is virtually unaffected. Sterilization has no effect on either men's or women's ability to respond sexually or enjoy sexual activity.

Contraceptive Methods of the Future. In view of current concerns about contracting AIDS and other STDs, researchers "emphasize development of methods that are more user friendly, effective, and female controlled so women may better protect themselves" (Gabelnick, 1998, p. 616). The following are contraceptive methods being investigated for future use (Denney & Quadagno, 1992; Gabelnick, 1998):

1. *New and improved barrier methods.* Lea's Shield is an "oval silicone rubber device" resembling a diaphragm that is used with spermicide (F. Stewart, 1998, p. 376). Lea's Shield comes in only one size and has "a one-way valve to allow air to escape during placement, thus creating a suction to keep the

device against the cervix" (Gabelnick, 1998, p. 616). It is already marketed in Canada and Europe. Researchers are also exploring new and improved materials and designs for diaphragms, latex male condoms, and female condoms.

2. *Small vaginal rings containing hormones.* A ring is inserted in the upper part of the vagina and left there for several days. It is not supposed to be felt or to disrupt sexual activity. It works by changing the cervical mucus so that sperm cannot swim up through the cervix into the uterus.

3. *Immunizations and vaccines to inhibit fertilization and implantation.* Vaccines for women would obstruct fertilized eggs from implanting on the uterine walls. Vaccines for men would employ hormones to inhibit sperm production.

4. *Oral contraceptives for men.* Some substances have been found to interfere with sperm production.

5. *Frameless IUDs.* Such IUDs would eliminate "any pressure against the uterus and thus should minimize cramping" (Gabelnick, 1998, p. 619). One such device under investigation is a polypropylene thread that attaches copper-releasing material to the interior of the uterus. Another is a "biodegradable cone" also anchored in the uterus (Gabelnick, 1998, p. 619).

❧ Summary

Numerous physical changes mark adolescence. These include a growth spurt and the development of primary and secondary sex characteristics. Adolescents have strong psychological reactions to their physical changes. Eating disorders characterizing primarily females are anorexia nervosa and bulimia. It is important for adolescents to feel they are physically attractive.

Adolescents mature at different rates. Male adolescents who mature early tend to be more self-confident and are more apt to assume leadership positions among their peers. They are more apt to be perceived as physically attractive and are treated more like adults. Early-maturing girls on the other hand, appear to be initially disadvantaged. However, these drawbacks disappear as girls get older.

Young adulthood, from ages 18 through 30, is the healthiest time of life. Some lifestyles contribute to good health, while others such as alcohol use and cigarette smoking have a negative effect on health. Early detection of breast cancer is important because 1 in 9 women will get it sometime in their life.

Significant issues and life events that concern adolescents and young adults include: sexual activity in adolescence, unplanned pregnancy, teenage fatherhood, motivation for pregnancy, sex education, methods of contraception, and sexually transmitted diseases. Of those pregnant adolescents who choose to have their babies, the vast majority keep them.

Sex education is important because it allows adolescents to make responsible decisions about their sexual behavior. Sex education curricula should be responsive to the needs and values of diverse racial and ethnic groups. This is especially true in this age of AIDS. In addition to AIDS, millions of young people contract other sexually transmitted diseases each year, including gonorrhea, chlamydial infections, syphilis, and genital herpes.

Adolescents tend not to use birth control when they first become sexually active. There is no one best method of contraception for all people. Methods include oral contraception ("the pill"), emergency contraceptive pills, Norplant, Depo-Provera, the diaphragm, the cervical cap, the condom, the contraceptive sponge, the female condom, the intrauterine device, vaginal spermicides, withdrawal, fertility awareness methods, and sterilization. Each person should evaluate the pros and cons of each method to determine the most effective method for him or her.

InfoTrac College Edition Keywords

adolescence	AIDS	puberty	sexually transmitted diseases
adolescent sexual activity	contraception	sex education	unplanned pregnancy

On the Internet

Centers for Disease Control and Prevention— Division of Sexually Transmitted Diseases

http://www.cdc.gov/nchstp/dstd/dstdp.html

The Division of STD Prevention at the Centers for Disease Control and Prevention provides national leadership through research, policy development, and support of effective services to prevent sexually transmitted diseases (including HIV infection) and their complications, such as enhanced HIV transmission, infertility, adverse outcomes of pregnancy, and reproductive tract cancer.

National Breast Cancer Foundation

http://www.nationalbreastcancer.org/

The National Breast Cancer Foundation's mission is to save lives by increasing awareness through education and by providing mammograms for those in need.

Pregnancy Centers Online

http://www.pregnancycenters.org/

You will find wonderful and caring online counselors at Pregnancy Centers Online.

Planned Parenthood

http://www.plannedparenthood.org/

Planned Parenthood believes in the fundamental right of each individual, throughout the world, to manage his or her fertility, regardless of the individual's income, marital status, race, ethnicity, sexual orientation, age, national origin, or residence. Planned Parenthood believes that respect and value for diversity in all aspects of the organization are essential to our well-being.

CHAPTER 7

Psychological Systems and Their Impacts on Adolescence and Young Adulthood

"Teen Alcoholism Shows Dramatic Increase"

"Twenty-Two-Year-Old Hangs Self in Kenosha Jail"

"$400,000 Worth of Cocaine Found in College Drug Bust"

"Teen Mother Shoots Infant Daughter, Husband, and Self"

"Four Killed by Drunk Teen Driver"

These statements might all be seen in newspaper headlines. They refer to tragedies that involve adolescents and young adults. Although the media often address sensationalistic and tragic events, the fact that such things are occurring merits our attention. What psychological variables operate to help cause such happenings?

A PERSPECTIVE

This chapter will focus on some of the major psychological growth tasks and pitfalls confronting adolescents and young adults. Psychological systems involve such aspects of growth and development as forming an identity and developing a personal morality. An individual's psychological system interacts with biological and social systems to affect behavior.

We have already addressed some of the interactions between biological and psychological systems. For example, maturation rate and body weight (which relate to an individual's biological system) can affect body image and self-concept (which relate to the psychological system). Knowledge of psychological milestones normally negotiated during adolescence and young adulthood is important for the overall assessment of behavior and functioning. Additionally, this chapter will discuss two categories of critical issues that affect many persons in this age group: suicide and assertiveness.

This chapter will:

▶ Explore identity formation in adolescence by examining Erikson's eight stages of psychosocial development and Marcia's categories of identity.

▶ Explain and evaluate Kohlberg's theory of moral development, present Gilligan's alternative model for women, and describe Fowler's seven-stage model concerning spirituality and the development of faith.

▶ Examine some critical issues of life events, including suicide and assertiveness, that have special impacts on adolescents and young adults.

🌿 Identity Formation

Personal identities crystallize during adolescence. Through experimentation and evaluation of experience and ideas, the adolescent should establish some sense of who he or she really is. In other words, people get to know themselves during adolescence.

Erik Erikson (1950, 1968) proposed a theory of psychological development comprising eight stages. This theory focuses on how personalities evolve throughout life as a result of the interaction between biologically based maturation and the demands of society. The emphasis is on the role of the social environment in personality development. The eight stages are based partly on the stages proposed by Freud and partly on Erikson's studies in a wide variety of cultures. Erikson writes that the society within which one lives makes certain psychic demands at each stage of development. Erikson calls these demands *crises*. During each psychosocial stage, the individual must seek to adjust to the stresses and conflicts involved in these crises. The search for identity is a crisis that confronts people during adolescence.

Although Erikson's psychosocial theory addresses development throughout the life span, it is included here because of the importance of identity formation during adolescence. After the entire theory is discussed, its application to adolescence will be explored in greater depth.

© Kit Hedman / Jeroboam

Reflection on one's identity operates on many levels. A Navajo youngster here views herself in the company of her grandmother. Her grandmother probably "reflects" on her sense of self.

Highlight 7.1

Erikson's Eight Stages of Development

Stage	Crisis	Age	Important Event
1	Basic trust versus basic mistrust	Birth to 18 months	Feeding
2	Autonomy versus shame and doubt	18 months to 3 years	Toileting
3	Initiative versus guilt	3 to 6 years	Locomoting
4	Industry versus inferiority	6 to 12 years	School
5	Identity versus role confusion	Adolescence	Peer relationship
6	Intimacy versus isolation	Young adulthood	Love relationship
7	Generativity versus stagnation	Maturity	Parenting and creating
8	Ego integrity versus despair	Old age	Reflecting on and accepting one's life

The stages are described in Highlight 7.1, "Erikson's Eight Stages of Development."

Erikson's Psychosocial Theory

Each stage of human development presents its characteristic crises. Coping well with each crisis makes an individual better prepared to cope with the next. Although specific crises are most critical during particular stages, related issues continue to arise throughout a person's life. For example, the conflict to trust versus mistrust is especially important in infancy. Yet, children and adults continue to struggle with whether or not to trust others.

Resolution of each crisis is an ideal, not necessarily a reality. The degree to which crises in earlier stages are resolved will affect a person's ability to resolve crises in later stages. If an individual doesn't learn how to trust in stage 1, that person will find it very difficult to attain intimacy in stage 6.

Stage 1: Basic Trust versus Basic Mistrust. For infants up to 18 months of age, learning to trust others is the overriding crisis. To develop trust, one must understand that some people and some things can be depended on. Parents provide a major variable for such learning. For instance, infants who consistently receive warm, loving care and nourishment learn to trust that these things will be provided to them. Later in life, people may apply this concept of trust to friends, an intimate partner, or their government.

Stage 2: Autonomy versus Shame and Doubt. The crisis of autonomy versus shame and doubt characterizes early childhood, from 18 months to 3 years. Children strive to accomplish things independently. They learn to feed themselves and to use the toilet. Accomplishing various tasks provides children with feelings of self-worth and self-confidence. On the other hand, if children of this age are constantly downtrodden, restricted, or punished, shame and doubt will emerge instead. Self-doubt will replace the self-confidence that should have developed during this period.

Stage 3: Initiative versus Guilt. Preschoolers aged 3 to 6 years must face the crisis of taking their own initiative. Children at this age are extremely active physically; the world fascinates them and beckons them to explore it. They have active imaginations and are eager to learn. Preschoolers who are encouraged to take initiative to explore and learn are likely to assimilate this concept for use later in life. They will be more likely to feel confident in initiating relationships, pursuing career objectives, and developing recreational interests. Preschoolers who are consistently restricted, punished, or treated harshly, are more likely to experience the emotion of guilt. They want to explore and experience, but they are not allowed to. Instead of learning initiative, they are likely to feel guilty about their tremendous desires to do so many things. In reaction, they may become passive observers who follow the lead of others instead of initiating their own activities and ideas.

Stage 4: Industry versus Inferiority. School-age children 6 to 12 years old must address the crisis of industry versus inferiority. Children in this age group need to be productive and succeed in their activities. In addition to play, a major focus of their lives is school. Therefore, mastering academic skills and material is important. Those who do learn to be industrious master activities. Comparison with peers becomes exceptionally important.

Children who experience failure in school, or even in peer relations, may develop a sense of inferiority.

Stage 5: Identity versus Role Confusion. Adolescence is a time when young people explore who they are and establish their identity. It is the transition period from childhood to adulthood when people examine the various roles they play (for example, child, sibling, student, Catholic, Native American, basketball star), and integrate these roles into a perception of self, an identity. Some people are unable to integrate their many roles and have difficulty coping with conflicting roles; they are said to suffer from *role confusion*. Such persons feel confused and uncertain about their identity.

Stage 6: Intimacy versus Isolation. Young adulthood is characterized by a quest for intimacy, which involves more than the establishment of a sexual relationship. Intimacy includes the ability to share with and give to another person without being afraid of sacrificing one's own identity. People who do not attain intimacy are likely to suffer isolation. These people have often been unable to resolve some of the crises of earlier psychosocial development. Various types of intimate relationships and how people experience them will be discussed in more detail in Chapter 8.

Stage 7: Generativity versus Stagnation. Mature adulthood is characterized by the crisis of generativity versus stagnation. During this time of life, people become concerned with helping, producing for, or guiding the following generation. Generativity involves a genuine concern for the future beyond one's own life track, although it does not necessarily involve procreating one's own children. Rather, it concerns a drive to be creative and productive in a way that will aid people in the future. Adults who lack generativity become self-absorbed. They tend to focus primarily on their own concerns and needs rather than on those of others. The result is stagnation, that is, a fixed, discouraging lack of progress and productivity.

Stage 8: Ego Integrity versus Despair. The crisis of ego integrity versus despair characterizes old age. During this time of life, people tend to look back over their years and reflect on them. If they appreciate their life and are content with their accomplishments, they are said to have *ego integrity,* that is, the ultimate form of identity integration. Such people enjoy a sense of peace and accept the fact that life will soon be over. Others who have failed to cope successfully with past life crises and have many regrets experience despair.

Implications of Identity Formation in Adolescence

Achieving genital maturity and rapid body growth signals young people that they will soon be adults. They therefore begin to question their future roles as adults. The most important task of adolescence is to develop a sense of identity, a sense of "Who I am." Highlight 7.2 poses some questions to help you explore and articulate your sense of identity. Making a career choice is an important part of this search for identity.

The primary danger of this period, according to Erikson, is identity confusion. This confusion can be expressed in a variety of ways. One is to delay acting like a responsible adult. Another is to commit oneself to poorly thought-out courses of action. Still another way is to regress into childishness to avoid assuming the responsibilities of adulthood. Erikson views the cliquishness of adolescence and its intolerance of differences as defenses against identity confusion. Falling in love is viewed as an attempt to define identity. Through self-disclosing intimate thoughts and feelings with another, the adolescent is articulating and seeking to better understand his or her identity. Through seeing the reactions of a loved one to one's intimate thoughts and feelings, the adolescent is testing out values and beliefs and is better able to clarify a sense of self.

Adolescents and young adults experiment with roles that represent the many possibilities for their future identity. For instance, students take certain courses to test out their future career interests. They also experiment with a variety of part-time jobs to test occupational interests. They date and go steady to test relationships with the opposite sex. Dating also allows for different self-presentations with each new date. Adolescents and young adults may also experiment with drugs—alcohol, tobacco, marijuana, cocaine, and so on. Many are confused about their religious beliefs and seek in a variety of ways to develop a set of religious and moral beliefs with which they can be comfortable. They also tend to join, participate in, and then quit a variety of organizations. They experiment with a variety of interests and hobbies. As long as no laws are broken (and health is not seriously affected) in the process of experimenting, our culture gives teenagers and young adults the freedom to experiment in a variety of ways in order to develop a sense of identity.

Erikson (1959) uses the term *psychosocial moratorium* to describe a period of free experimentation before a final sense of identity is achieved. Generally, our society allows adolescents and young adults freedom from the daily expectations of role performance. Ideally, this moratorium

Highlight 7.2

How to Determine Who You Are

Forming an identity essentially involves *thinking* about, and arriving at, answers to the following questions: (1) What do I want out of life? (2) What kind of person do I want to be? (3) Who am I? The most important decisions you make in your life may well be in arriving at answers to these questions.

Answers to these questions are not easy to arrive at. They require considerable contemplation and trial and error. But if you are to lead a fulfilling life, it is imperative to find answers to give direction and meaning to your life. Without answers, you are apt to muddle through life by being a passive responder to situations that arise, rather than a continual achiever of your life's goals.

Knowing who you are and where you are going is important both for clients and for you as a practitioner. The following questions may be a useful tool in pursuing that quest:

1. What do I find satisfying, meaningful, and enjoyable? (Only after you identify what is meaningful and gratifying, will you be able to consciously seek involvement in activities that will make your life fulfilling, and avoid those activities that are meaningless or stifling.)

   music, learning love

2. What is my moral code? (One possible code is to seek to fulfill your needs and to seek to do what you find enjoyable, doing so in a way that does not deprive others of the ability to fulfill their needs.)

3. What are my spiritual beliefs?

4. What are my employment goals? (Ideally, you should seek employment in which you find the work stimulating and satisfying, that you are skilled at, and that earns you enough money to support your lifestyle.)

5. What are my sexual mores? (All of us should develop a consistent code that we are comfortable with and that helps us to meet our needs without exploiting others. There is no one right code— what works for one may not work for another, due to differences in lifestyles, life goals, and personal values.)

6. Do I desire to have a committed relationship? (If yes, to what type of person and when? How consistent are your answers here with your other life goals?)

7. Do I desire to have children? (If yes, how many and when? How consistent are your answers here with your other life goals?)

8. What area of the country/world do I desire to live in? (Variables to be considered are climate, geography, type of dwelling, rural or urban setting, closeness to relatives or friends, and characteristics of the neighborhood.)

9. What do I enjoy doing with my leisure time?

10. What kind of image do I want to project to others? (Your image will be composed of your dressing style and grooming habits, your emotions, personality, assertiveness, capacity to communicate, material possessions, moral code, physical features, and voice patterns. You need to assess your strengths and shortcomings honestly in this area, and seek to make needed improvements.)

11. What type of people do I enjoy being with, and why?

12. Do I desire to improve the quality of my life and that of others? (If yes, in what ways, and how do you hope to achieve these goals?)

13. What types of relationships do I desire to have with relatives, friends, neighbors, and with people I meet for the first time?

14. What are my thoughts about death and dying?

15. What do I hope to be doing 5 years from now, 10 years, 20 years?

To have a fairly well-developed sense of identity, you need to have answers to most, but not all, of these questions. Very few persons are able to arrive at rational, consistent answers to all the questions. Having answers to most of them will provide a reference for developing your views to the yet unanswered areas.

Honest, well-thought-out answers to these questions will go a long way toward defining who you are. Again, what you want out of life, along with your motivation to achieve these goals, will primarily determine your identity. The above questions are simple to state, but arriving at answers is a complicated, ongoing process. In addition, expect some changes in your life goals as time goes on. Environmental influences change (for example, changes in working conditions). Also, as personal growth occurs, changes are apt to occur in activities that you find enjoyable and also in your beliefs, attitudes, and values. Accept such changes. If you have a fairly good idea of who you are, you will be prepared to make changes in your life goals, which will give continued direction to your life. Your life is shaped by events that are the results of decisions you make and decisions that are made for you. Without a sense of identity, you will not know what decisions are best for you. With a sense of identity, you will be able to direct your life toward goals you select and find personally meaningful.

allows young people the freedom to experiment with values, beliefs, and roles so that they can best fit into society so as to maximize their personal strengths and gain positive recognition from the community.

The crisis of identity versus role confusion is best resolved through integrating earlier identifications, present values, and future goals into a consistent self-concept. A sense of identity is achieved only after a period of questioning, reevaluation, and experimentation. Efforts to resolve questions of identity may take the young person down paths of emotional involvement, overzealous commitment, alienation, rebellion, or playful wandering.

Many adolescents are idealistic. They see the evils and negatives in our society and in the world. They cannot understand why injustice and imperfection exists. They yearn for a much better life for themselves and for others and have little understanding of the resources and hard work it takes for advancements. They often try to change the world and their efforts are genuine. If society can channel their energies constructively, adolescents' contributions can be meaningful. Unfortunately, some become disenchanted and apathetic after being continually frustrated with obstacles.

Importance of Achieving Identity. Adolescents and young adults struggle with developing a sense of who they are, what they want out of life, and what kind of people they want to be. Arriving at answers to such questions is among the most important tasks people face in life. Without answers, a person will not be prepared to make such major decisions as which career to select; deciding whether, when, or whom to marry; deciding where to live; and deciding what to do with leisure time. Unfortunately, many people muddle through life and never arrive at well-thought-out answers to these questions. Those who do not arrive at answers are apt to be depressed, anxious, indecisive, and unfulfilled.

The Formation of Identity. Identity development is a lifelong process. During the early years one's sense of identity is largely determined by the reactions of others. A long time ago, Cooley (1902) coined this labeling process as resulting in the *looking-glass self*—that is, persons develop their self-concept in terms of how others relate to them. For example, if a neighborhood identifies a teenage male as being a troublemaker or delinquent, neighbors are then apt to distrust him, accuse him of delinquent acts, and label his behavior as such. This labeling process, the youth begins to realize, also results in a type of prestige and status, at least from his peers. In the absence of objective ways to gauge whether he is in fact a delinquent, the youth will rely on the subjective evaluations of others. Thus, gradually, he is apt to begin to perceive himself as a delinquent, and begin to enact the delinquent role.

Labels have a major impact on our lives. If a child is frequently called stupid by his or her parents, that child is apt to develop a low self-concept, anticipate failure in many areas (particularly academic), put forth little effort in school and in competitive interactions with others, and end up failing.

Because identity development is a lifelong process, positive changes are probably possible even for those who view themselves as failures. In identity formation, it is important to remember that what we want out of the future is more important than past experience in determining what the future will be. The past is fixed and cannot be changed, but the present and the future can be. Although the past may have been painful and traumatic, it does not follow that the present and the future must be so. We are in control of our lives, and we largely determine what our future will be.

Marcia's Categories of Identity

Marcia (1980, 1991) has done a substantial amount of research on the Eriksonian theory of psychosocial development. He identifies four major ways in which people cope with identity crises: (1) identity achievement, (2) foreclosure, (3) identity diffusion, and (4) moratorium. People may be classified into these categories on the basis of three primary criteria: first, whether the individual experiences a major crisis during identity development; second, whether the person expresses a commitment to some type of occupation; and, third, whether there is commitment to some set of values or beliefs.

Identity Achievement. To reach the stage of identity achievement, people undergo a period of intense decision making. After expending much effort, they develop a personalized set of values and make their career decisions. The attainment of identity achievement is usually thought of as the most beneficial of the four status categories.

Foreclosure. People who fall into this category are the only ones who never experience an identity crisis as such. They glide into adulthood without experiencing much turbulence or anxiety. Decisions concerning both career and values are made relatively early in life. These decisions are often based on the values and ideas of their parents rather than their own. For example, a woman might become a traditional housewife and mother, not because she makes a conscious choice, but because she assumes it's what she is expected to do. Likewise, a man might become a Democratic millwright in a shipbuilding factory simply because his father was also a Democratic millwright and it seemed a good way of life.

It's interesting that the term *foreclosure* is used to label this category. Foreclosure involves shutting someone out from involvement, as one would foreclose a mortgage and bar a person who mortgaged his or her property from reclaiming it. To foreclose one's identity implies shutting off various other opportunities to grow and change.

Identity Diffusion. People who experience identity diffusion suffer from a serious lack of decision and direction. Although they go through an identity crisis, they never resolve it. They are not able to make clear decisions concerning either their personal ideology or their career choice. These people tend to be characterized by low self-esteem and lack of resolution. For example, such a person might be a drifter who never stays more than a few months in any one place and defies any serious commitments.

Moratorium. The moratorium category includes people who experience intense anxiety during their identity crisis, yet have not made decisions regarding either personal values or a career choice. However, moratorium people experience a more continuous, intense struggle to resolve these issues. Instead of avoiding the decision-making issue, they address it almost constantly. They are characterized by strong, conflicting feelings about what they should believe and do. For example, a moratorium person might struggle intensely with a religious issue, such as whether there is a god. Moratorium people tend to have many critical, but as yet unresolved, issues.

Critical Thinking: The Evaluation of Theory and Application to Client Situations

Both Erikson's and Marcia's theories provide interesting insights into people's behavior and their interaction with others. Both provide a framework for better understanding "normal" life crises and events. For example, stage 2 of Erikson's psychosocial theory focuses on ages 18 months to 3 years. Most of this period is frequently referred to as "the terrible twos." Understanding that children in this age group are striving to achieve some autonomy and control over their environment during this time interval helps us also understand that their behavior is full of action and

| Spotlight on Diversity 7.1 | | Race, Culture, Ethnicity, and Identity Development |

Questions might be raised regarding the extent to which Erikson's and Marcia's theories apply to all people. This includes various racial and ethnic groups. For instance, some cultures emphasize respect for and deference to older family members. Young people are expected to conform until they, too, become older and "wiser." To what extent, then, is it important for each individual to struggle in order to achieve a strikingly unique and independent personality? Must this particular aspect of behavior be stressed to a great extent? Or, should the ability to assume a strong identification with the family and cultural group be given precedence?

Approximately one-third of adolescents in the United States belong to an ethnic group that is a "minority"; these include such groups as African Americans, Native Americans, Hispanics, and Asian Americans (Kail & Cavanaugh, 2000). It is very important that young people establish an ethnic identity along with their individual identity (Phinney, 1990). This involves identifying with their ethnic group, feeling that they belong, and

A proud father at the Jewish celebration of Passover. It is very important that young people establish an ethnic identity along with their individual identity. This involves identifying with their ethnic group, feeling that they belong, and appreciating their cultural heritage.

© Andrew Brilliant/Jeroboam

exploration. Children should not be reprimanded for the types of behavior that are normal and natural during this stage of development. Such insight can better prepare social workers for helping parents develop age-appropriate expectations and behavior management techniques.

Marcia's emphasis on the acquisition of coping skills also provides insights for work with clients. Those people who are trapped in foreclosure, identity diffusion, or moratorium identity crises may benefit from help in the resolution of these crises. Social workers can give feedback in addition to helping people formulate and evaluate new alternatives. Acknowledgment of the existence of such crises and understanding their dynamics are the first steps toward resolution.

Both Marcia's and Erikson's theories emphasize the importance of identity formation. Looking at adolescence and young adulthood with some understanding of the forces at work can help social workers better understand the dynamics of human behavior within the social environment. For instance, strife between parents and children is common during adolescence. It is also understandable. Parents try to maintain some control with their leadership roles. Adolescents struggle to define themselves as individuals and to become independent. Knowing that these are natural occurrences provides clues to insights social workers can give to clients regarding their feelings and behaviors. The struggle for control can be identified and discussed. Parental restrictiveness and adolescent rebelliousness can be examined. New behavioral options for interaction can be explored.

Traditional theories of identity development such as Erickson's and Marcia's have limitations due to their Westernized perspective on how people *should* develop. For example, traditional Asian and Native American cultures generally emphasize interdependence instead of stressing the development of an independent identity. Spotlight 7.1 explores some of the issues concerning cultural background and identity development. Spotlight 7.2

appreciating their cultural heritage. Older adolescents are more likely to have established an ethnic identity than younger ones (Phinney & Chavira, 1992). The former apparently have had more time to explore aspects of their culture, develop their cognitive ability, and think about who they are.

Spencer and Markstrom-Adams (1990) conducted a review of the literature concerning how a person's ethnic and racial differences affect self-concept and identity development. They studied variables such as a person's skin color, speaking a language other than English, physical appearance relating to racial identity, and stereotypes about ethnic and racial social status. They found that these variables significantly impacted how young people felt about themselves. Other research supports the idea that adolescents of diverse ethnic backgrounds gain sharp awareness of how the majority white culture evaluates their ethnic and racial status (Comer, 1988). They begin to understand how prejudice and discrimination can negatively influence their future career and life options (Spencer & Dornbusch, 1990). It also appears that college students belonging to ethnic and racial minorities are more likely to explore their ethnic identities than are white youth. Additionally, nonwhite young people who have given their ethnic identity and the issues involved serious thought have higher self-esteem than their peers who have not resolved their ethnic identity crisis (Phinney & Alipura, 1992).

Phinney (1989) suggests a parallel development for children from diverse ethnic groups that coincides with Marcia's four coping strategies for identity development. A person with a *diffused identity* demonstrates little or no involvement with his or her ethnic and cultural heritage and may be unaware of or disinterested in cultural issues. A person with *foreclosed identity* has explored his or her cultural background to a minor extent. However, his or her feelings about ethnic identity are vague. He or she most likely simply adopts the ideas of parents or other relatives without giving them much thought. Someone with a *moratorium identity* displays an active pursuit of ethnic identity. This state reflects an ethnic identity crisis. Finally, a person who has *achieved an ethnic identity* has struggled with its meaning and come to conclusions regarding how this ethnic identity is an integral part of his or her life. Cross and Fhagen-Smith (1996) summarize how Phinney's model relates to ethnic identity development:

> The . . . model states that ethnic and racial minorities enter adolescence with poorly developed ethnic identities (diffusion) or with an identity "given" to them by their parents (foreclosure). They may sink into an identity crisis, during which the conflicts and challenges associated with their minority status are sorted out (moratorium), and should all go well, they achieve an ethnic identity that is positive and gives high salience to ethnicity (achieved ethnicity). (p. 111)

Moratorium is reflected in the thoughtful words of a Mexican American adolescent who stated, "I want to know what we do and how our culture is different from others. Going to festivals and cultural events helps me to learn more about my own culture and about myself" (Phinney, 1990, p. 44). Likewise, an Asian American teen describes his feelings about his ethnic identity achievement, "I have been born Filipino and am born to be Filipino. . . . I'm here in America, and people of many different cultures are here, too. So I don't consider myself only Filipino, but also American" (Phinney, 1989, p. 44).

Spencer and Markstrom-Adams (1990) provide a number of suggestions for encouraging positive identity development for adolescents in ethnically diverse groups. These include: encouraging community and extended family support for young people; providing resources to schools, teachers, and services relating to good physical and mental health; urging young people to complete their education so that a wider career choice is available to them; and emphasizing the significance and value of their ethnic and cultural heritage.

Spotlight on Diversity 7.2 — Lesbian and Gay Adolescents

Lesbian and gay adolescents in this culture suffer even more extreme obstacles to identity development than their heterosexual peers. Perhaps their biggest obstruction is the constant oppression of homophobia. *Homophobia is an extreme and irrational fear and hatred for lesbian and gay people simply because they are lesbian and gay.* (Chapter 13 addresses sexual orientation and homophobia in greater detail.) Homophobia and the oppressive reactions of others to homosexuality isolates lesbian and gay youth. On the one hand, lesbian and gay adolescents are trying to establish individual identities, just as heterosexual adolescents are. On the other hand, lesbian and gay youth are severely discouraged from expressing and establishing their sexual identities. The question should be raised, To what extent do Erikson's and Marcia's theories concerning identity development apply to these young people? Do these theories go far enough to explain the serious crises lesbian and gay people go through?

Kaplan and Saperstein (1985) stress the isolation young lesbian and gay people feel. If they "come out"[1] and reveal their homosexuality, they are ostracized and demeaned. On the other hand, if they cautiously hide their true feelings and identity, they risk depression, avoidance behaviors such as drug or alcohol abuse, and rebellious acting out, such as running away or truancy. Kaplan and Saperstein (1985) suggest that social work practitioners be especially sensitive to the issues facing lesbian and gay adolescents. First, social workers need to evaluate their own homophobic attitudes. They

should work to develop a caring, empathic, nonjudgmental perspective that can be communicated to their lesbian and gay clients. Second, social workers "need to pay attention to the 'coming out' process as it may be a cause of acting-out behavior, for example, truancy or homelessness" (p. 18). Such youth may need help in answering a variety of questions: Should they come out or not? What should they say? Whom should they tell? How will people react? Additionally, workers can help lesbian and gay youth become connected with others of their own sexual orientation. Many cities have helplines, support groups, speakers bureaus, and activities available for lesbian and gay young people. If no such resources exist in a worker's area, might it not be possible for the worker to develop them?

In summary, it appears that Erikson's and Marcia's theories have only limited relevance for lesbian and gay identity development. The theories can be applied to a certain extent; they indicate that all young people go through an identity crisis. However, they do little to focus on the special issues of lesbian and gay young people.

It is up to you as a social worker to scrutinize theories closely and use what you can from them. However, it is just as important to recognize limitations of theories.

1. "Coming out" refers to "the process of self-identification as a lesbian woman or a gay man, followed by revelation of one's sexual orientation to others" (Barker, 1999, p. 88).

---

explores the special issues involved in identity development for lesbian and gay adolescents.

We established in an earlier chapter that social workers need to evaluate theory and determine for themselves what theoretical concepts and frameworks are most suited for their own practice with clients. Questions to keep in mind while doing this include:

1. How does the theory apply to client situations?

2. What research supports the theory?

3. To what extent does the theory coincide with social work values and ethics?

4. Are other theoretical frameworks or concepts available that are more relevant to practice situations?

Moral Development

Young adulthood is filled with avid quests for intimate relationships and other major commitments involving career and life goals. A parallel pursuit is the formulation

of a personal set of moral values. *Morality* involves a set of principles regarding what is right and what is wrong. Many times these principles are not clearly defined in black or white, but involve various shades of grey. There is no one absolute answer. For example, is the death penalty right or wrong? Is it good or bad to have sexual intercourse before marriage?

Moral issues range from very major to minor day-to-day decisions. Although moral development can take place throughout life, it is especially critical during adolescence and young adulthood. These are the times when people gain the right to make independent decisions and choices. Often, the values developed during this stage remain operative for life.

Kohlberg's Theory of Moral Development

Lawrence Kohlberg (1963, 1968, 1969, 1981a, 1981b) has proposed a series of three levels, and six stages, through which people progress as they develop their moral

Highlight 7.3

Kohlberg's Three Levels and Six Stages of Moral Development

Level/Stage	Description
Level 1: Preconventional (Conventional Role Conformity)	Controls are external. Behavior is governed by receiving rewards or punishments.
Stage 1: Punishment and obedience orientation	Decisions concerning what is good or bad are made in order to avoid receiving punishment.
Stage 2: Naive instrumental hedonism	Rules are obeyed in order to receive rewards. Often favors are exchanged.
Level 2: Conventional (Role Conformity)	The opinions of others become important. Behavior is governed by conforming to social expectations.
Stage 3: "Good boy/girl morality"	Good behavior is considered to be what pleases others. There is a strong desire to please and gain the approval of others.
Stage 4: Authority-maintaining morality	The belief in law and order is strong. Behavior conforms to law and higher authority. Social order is important.
Level 3: Postconventional (Self-Accepted Moral Principles)	Moral decisions are finally internally controlled. Morality involves higher-level principles beyond law and even beyond self-interest.
Stage 5: Morality of contract, of individual rights, and of democratically accepted law	Laws are considered necessary. However, they are subject to rational thought and interpretation. Community welfare is important.
Stage 6: Morality of individual principles and conscience	Behavior is based on internal ethical principles. Decisions are made according to what is right rather than what is written into law.

Source: Adapted from Kohlberg (1968, 1981a; 1981b).

framework. These six stages are clustered within three distinct levels, as shown in Highlight 7.3.

The first level, the *preconventional* or *premoral* level, is characterized by giving precedence to self-interest. People usually experience this level from ages 4 to 10. Moral decisions are based on external standards. Behavior is governed by whether a child will receive a reward or punishment. The first stage in this level is based on avoiding punishment. Children do what they are told to in order to avoid negative consequences. The second stage focuses on rewards instead of punishment. In other words, children do the "right" thing in order to receive a reward or compensation. Sometimes this involves an exchange of favors: "I'll scratch your back if you'll scratch mine."

Level 2 of Kohlberg's theory is the *conventional* level, in which moral thought is based on conforming to conventional roles. Frequently, this level occurs from ages 10 to 13. There is a strong desire to please others and to receive social approval. Although moral standards have begun to be internalized, they are still based on what others dictate, rather than on what is personally decided.

Within Level 2, stage 3 focuses on gaining the approval of others. Good relationships become very important. Stage 4, "authority-maintaining morality," emphasizes the need to adhere to law. Higher authorities are generally respected. "Law and order" are considered necessary in order to maintain the social order.

Level 3, the *postconventional* level, concerns developing a moral conscience that goes beyond what others say. At this level, people contemplate laws and expectations and decide on their own what is right and what is wrong. They become autonomous, independent thinkers. Behavior is based on principles instead of laws. This level progresses beyond selfish concerns. The needs and well-being of others become very important. At this level, true morality is achieved.

Within Level 3, stage 5 involves adhering to socially accepted laws and principles. Law is considered good for the general public welfare. However, laws are subject to interpretation and change. Stage 6 is the ultimate attainment. During this stage, one becomes free of the thoughts and opinions expressed by others. Morality is completely internalized. Decisions are based on one's personal conscience, transcending laws and regulations. Examples of people who attained this level include Martin Luther King Jr. and Gandhi.

Critical Thinking: Evaluation of Kohlberg's Theory

Many questions have been raised concerning the validity and application of Kohlberg's theory (Kurtines & Gewirtz, 1991; Puka, 1991). For one thing, Kohlberg places primary emphasis on how people think, not what they do. Presidents and kings talk about the loftiest moral standards, but what they do is often another matter. President Richard Nixon espoused high moral standards but was forced to resign after his cover-up of the Watergate break-in and theft of Democratic party documents was brought to light. Many times difficult moral decisions must be made in crisis situations. If you find yourself in a burning building with a crowd of people, how much effort will you expend to save others before yourself? What is the discrepancy between what you think is right and what you would really do in such a situation?

A second criticism of Kohlberg's theory is that dilemmas are posed in an abstract manner that requires a high level of verbal competence in order to answer them (Lefrancois, 1999). Children, then, may be at a disadvantage because of their poorer ability to use language in understanding the proposed moral dilemmas and adequately expressing complex answers. Children may be more capable of higher moral reasoning than Kohlberg predicts. Children of 6 or 7 typically consider not only a person's actions but also the motivation behind such actions (Darley & Shultz, 1990). Are young children really premoral? Even before entering school, children can distinguish between telling the truth and lying (Bussey, 1992). At that early age they already begin to evaluate their own and other people's behavior in terms of what is right and what is wrong (Buzzelli, 1992).

A third criticism of Kohlberg's theory is that it is culturally biased (Kail & Cavanaugh, 2000; Miller, 1991; Santrock, 1999). Even Kohlberg (1978) himself has conceded that stage 6 may not be applied across all cultures, societies, and situations. Snarey (1987) studied research on moral development in 27 countries and found that Kohlberg's schema does not incorporate the higher moral ideals that some cultures embrace. Examples of higher moral reasoning that would not be considered such within Kohlberg's framework include "values related to communal equity and collective happiness in Israel, the unity and sacredness of all life forms in India, and the

relation of the individual to the community in New Guinea" (Santrock, 1999, p. 322).

Moral Development and Women: Gilligan's Approach

A major criticism of Kohlberg's theory is that virtually all of the research on which it is based used only men as subjects. Gilligan (1982; Gilligan & Attanucci, 1988; Gilligan, Brown, & Rogers, 1990) maintains that women fare less well according to Kohlberg's levels of moral development because they tend to view moral dilemmas differently than men. Kohlberg's theory centers on a *justice perspective* in which "individuals stand alone and independently make moral decisions" (Newman & Newman, 1999; Santrock, 1999, p. 323). In contrast, Gilligan maintains that women are more likely to adopt a *care perspective* that "views people in terms of their connectedness with others and emphasizes interpersonal communication, relationships with others, and concern for others" (Newman & Newman, 1999; Santrock, 1999, p. 323). In other words, women tend to view morality in terms of personal situations.

Women often have trouble moving from a very personalized interpretation of morality to a focus on law and order. This bridge involves a generalization from the more personal aspects of what is right and wrong (how individual moral decisions affect one's own personal life) to morality within the larger, more impersonal society (how moral decisions, such as those instilled in law, affect virtually everyone). Kohlberg has been criticized because he has not taken into account the different orientation and life circumstances common to women.

Gilligan and her associates (1982; Gilligan & Attanucci, 1988; Gilligan et al., 1990) reason that women's moral development is often based on their personal interest and commitment to the good of others close to them. Frequently, this involves giving up or sacrificing one's own well-being for others. Goodness and kindness are emphasized. This contrasts with a common male focus on assertively making decisions and exercising more rigid moral judgments.

Gilligan initially targeted 29 women who were receiving pregnancy and abortion counseling. She postulated that pregnancy and birth was an area in women's lives in which they could emphasize choice, yet it still was an intimate area to which they could relate. Gilligan interviewed the women concerning their pregnancies. She arrived at a sequence of moral levels that relate specifically to women. She found that women tend to view morality "in terms of selfishness versus responsibility and as an obligation to exercise care and avoid hurting others. They viewed people who care for each other as the most responsible, and people who hurt someone else as selfish and immoral. . . . While men tend to think more in terms of justice and fairness, women tend to think more about their responsibilities to specific people" (Papalia & Olds, 1995, p. 425).

Gilligan describes the following levels and transitions of moral development for women.

Level 1: Orientation to Personal Survival.

This level focuses purely on the woman's self-interest. The needs and well-being of others are not really considered. At this level, a woman focuses first on personal survival. What is practical and best for her is most important.

Transition 1: Transition from Personal Selfishness to Responsibility.

This first transition involves a movement in moral thought from consideration only of self to some consideration of the others involved. During this transition, a woman comes to acknowledge the fact that she is responsible not only for herself but also for others, including the unborn. In other words, she begins to acknowledge that her choice will impact others.

Level 2: Goodness as Self-Sacrifice.

Level 2 involves putting aside one's own needs and wishes. The well-being of other people becomes important. The "good" thing to do is to sacrifice herself so that others may benefit. A woman at this level feels dependent on what other people think. Often a conflict occurs between taking responsibility for her own actions and feeling pressure from others to make her decisions.

Transition 2: From Goodness to Reality.

During this transitional period, women begin to examine their situations more objectively. They draw away from depending on others to tell them what they should do. Instead, they begin to take into account the well-being of everyone concerned, including themselves. Some of the concern for personal survival apparent in Level 1 returns, but in a more objective manner.

Level 3: The Morality of Nonviolent Responsibility.

Level 3 involves women thinking in terms of the repercussions of their decisions and actions. At this level, a woman's thinking has progressed beyond mere concern for what others will think about what she does. Rather, it involves accepting responsibility for making her own decisions. She places herself on an equal plane with others, weighs the various consequences of her potential actions, and accepts the fact that she will be responsible for these

consequences. The important principle operating here is that of minimizing hurt, both to herself and to others.

Gilligan's sequence of moral development provides a good example of how morality can be viewed from different perspectives. It is especially beneficial in emphasizing the different strengths manifested by men and women. The emphasis on feelings, such as direct concern for others, is just as important as the ability to decisively make moral judgments.

Critical Thinking: Evaluation of Gilligan's Theory

Research provides some support for the difference in moral perspectives between females and males (Bussey & Maughan, 1982; Hanson & Mullis, 1985; Santrock, 1999). For example, Skoe and Gooden (1993) asked 46 11- and 12-year-old males and females to respond to three established everyday scenarios that posed ethical dilemmas. Additionally, they asked each adolescent to describe one personalized incident. For example, one of the contrived situations involved friend A accepting friend B's invitation to dinner. However, friend A then receives another invitation, from friend C, to attend a major rock concert of a favorite group—and with excellent seats! The adolescent subject was asked to discuss what friend A should do. The adolescents' responses were then rated according to a scale developed to reflect their status on Gilligan's proposed levels and transitions of moral development.

Findings revealed that the girls were significantly more likely than boys to express concern about maintaining friendships and not emotionally injuring other people. Boys, on the other hand, were more prone to express concern about their own predicament and talk about more general issues like staying out of trouble. When asked to initiate more individualized scenarios, girls were more likely to talk about their interpersonal relationships with people very close to them. Boys tended to choose situations that did not involve themselves personally or else addressed a more philosophical issue altogether.

Application of Theory to Client Situations

Social work has a sound foundation of professional values expressed in the National Association of Social Workers (NASW) Code of Ethics. Ethics involve making decisions about what is right and what is wrong. Ethics provide social workers with guidelines for practice with clients.

Gilligan emphasizes the relationship between responsibility and morality. People develop morally as they gradually become more capable and willing to assume responsibility. Morality provides the basis for making ethical

Studies show that girls are more likely than boys to confide in intimate friends.

decisions. Gilligan "bases the highest stage of decision making on care for and sensitivity to the needs of others, on responsibility for others, and on nurturance" (Rhodes, 1985, p. 101). This principle is central to the NASW Code of Ethics. Gilligan's theory can provide some general ethical guidelines to which we can aspire in our day-to-day practice with clients. Social workers should strive to be sensitive to the needs of their clients. They should assume responsibility for effective practice with clients. Finally, they should provide help and nurturance to meet their clients' needs.

Fowler's Theory of Faith Development

Spirituality is an important aspect of human diversity. It shapes major dimensions of many people's lives and can provide a significant source of strength. As Spotlight 7.3 explains, spirituality can serve as a major source of empowerment that social workers must address.

James Fowler (1981) proposed a theory of faith development in which people progress through seven stages "that parallel Piaget's . . . stages of intellectual growth" (Beckett & Johnson, 1995, p. 1393). The theory is based on 359 intensive interviews conducted in Boston, Chicago, and Toronto. Most respondents were white (97.8%) and Christian (more than 85%), with ages ranging from 3.5 to 84 years. Generally, findings revealed that the older people were, the more likely they were to attain higher levels of faith, although relatively few people progressed to stages five or six.

Fowler describes faith as something more than religious doctrines or practices. Faith may not even involve God. Rather, faith is "an integral, centering process, underlying the formation of beliefs, values, and meanings" that gives "direction to people's lives," "links them" to others, provides a broader, more meaningful "frame of reference," and helps them tackle life's obstacles (Fowler, 1996, p. 32).

In faith development, people progress from an "undifferentiated" phase in the first 2 years of life to a "universalizing" stage in middle age and beyond (Beckett & Johnson, 1995). During each respective life period, an individual depends on a new focal point of power (for example, another person or a philosophical viewpoint), grows close to a higher power, and becomes more concerned about the welfare of other people.

Stage 1: Primal or Undifferentiated Faith (Birth to 2 years). All people begin to develop their views of faith and the world from scratch. Infants learn early on whether their environment is safe or not, whether they can trust or not. Are they being cared for in warm, safe, secure family environments? Or are they being hurt, neglected, and abused? People begin to develop their use of language to express thought and distinguish between themselves and others. They start to develop relationships and ideas about what those relationships mean.

Stage 2: Intuitive-Projective Faith (Ages 2 to 6). Children aged 2 to 6 continue developing their ability to glean meaning from their environments. What children are exposed to in terms of spiritual language and experiences is what they conceptualize on their faith. During stage 2, children are egocentric and manifest preoperational thought patterns. Their view of faith and religion lacks in-depth conceptualization and application to life

---

Spotlight on Diversity 7.3 Empowerment Through Spiritual Development

We have defined *spirituality* as "the views and behaviors that express a sense of relatedness to something greater than the self" (Beckett & Johnson, 1995, p. 1393). Spirituality rises above concern over worldly things such as possessions and expands consciousness to a realm beyond the physical environment. It is a "universal aspect of human culture" (Canda, 1989; Cowley & Derezotes, 1994) that concerns "developing a sense of meaning, purpose, and morality" (Canda, 1989, p. 39). It can provide people with strength to withstand pain and guidance to determine what life paths to take.

Cowley and Derezotes (1994) question how social workers can implement "the core social work value" of demonstrating respect for people's diverse values and convictions "without an understanding of their deepest beliefs," namely, those of a spiritual nature (p. 32). Sermabeikian (1994) stresses that "spirituality as a

weapon in . . . [clients'] coping arsenal is precisely why spirituality must be acknowledged. Strengthening clients' abilities to develop viable strategies to both meet basic needs and maintain mental health is a social work goal" (p. 178). Therefore, it's important for social workers to appreciate clients' spiritual beliefs, which influence their thoughts, feelings, and actions (Beckett & Johnson, 1995).

Spirituality is often manifested in the form of *religion*, which is the formal institutional expression of spiritual beliefs and practices (Canda, 1989). Sermabeikian (1994) explains that "although spirituality is expressed in religion, as well as philosophy and culture, it transcends ideologies, rights, dogma, and institutions" (p. 180). Chapter 15 discusses several predominant religions including Judaism, Christianity, Islam, and Buddhism more thoroughly.

---

experiences. Their view of faith is that it is out there someplace; it is whatever they're exposed to. For instance, to Herman, whose parents adhere to strict Wisconsin Synod Lutheran Church beliefs, faith is going to church, singing hymns, attending Sunday school, and saying bedtime prayers every night. If asked where God is, he says, "Everywhere," because that's what he's been told.

Stage 3: Mythic-Literal Faith (Ages 6 to 12). Development of conceptual thought continues over this period. Stories are especially important as ways to help children develop their thinking about life and relationships. Individuals can be deeply moved by dramatic representations and spiritual symbolism "such as the wearing of special garments and the circling of the ka'ba seven times during Muslim's annual pilgrimage to Mekkah"[2] (Hutchinson, 1999, p. 169). The concrete operations period helps children distinguish between what is real and what is not. During this stage, children think more seriously about aspects related to faith, although they tend to take what they are told literally. For example, they may think of the wafers used in Christian Holy Communion ceremonies as the actual "body" of Christ instead of symbolic representation of the body. Children become more organized in their thinking but are not yet very creative nor capable of critical thinking.

2. The ka'ba is "a small stone building in the court of the Great Mosque at Mecca that contains a sacred black stone and is the goal of Islamic pilgrimage and the point toward which Muslims turn in praying" (*Webster's*, 1995, p. 637).

Stage 4: Synthetic-Conventional Faith (Ages 12 and Older). During this stage, individuals develop their ability to conceptualize and apply information in new ways. They are exposed to much more of the world through social, school, and media experiences. On the one hand, people in this stage strive to conform. On the other, they begin to evolve their unique identities. They no longer perceive the world as literally as they did in stage 3, but "symbols that evoke deep meaning and loyalty are not seen as separate from what they symbolize. For example, a Jewish person in this faith stage experiences the salt water and bitter herbs used in the Passover supper as direct representations of the tears and bitterness of slavery" (Hutchinson, 1999, p. 170). During this stage, people have not yet critically evaluated the fundamental basis of their faith. Rather, they adhere to conventional ideology.

Stage 5: Individuative-Reflective Faith (Early Adulthood and Beyond). Critical thinking about the meaning of life characterizes stage 5. People confront conflicts in values and ideas, and they strive to establish their individualized belief system. For example, a young adult will seriously consider the extent to which her own personal beliefs coincide with conventional religious practices and beliefs. If her church condemns abortion, does she agree or not? If her church denies membership to lesbian and gay people, does she support this or not? Stage 5 marks the construction of a more detailed belief system that reflects an individual's critical evaluation of the physical and spiritual world.

Stage 6: Conjunctive Faith (Midlife and Beyond).

Only one-sixth of all respondents in Fowler's study reached stage 6, conjunctive faith, and then never before age 30. The concept that characterizes this phase is integration. Individuals have confronted the conflicts between their own views and conventional ones and have accepted the fact that such conflicts exist. They have integrated their own beliefs into their perception of the physical and spiritual universe. They have accepted the fact that diversity and opposites characterize life. Good exists along with evil. Happiness dwells beside sadness. Strength subsists alongside weakness. Spiritual beliefs assume a deeper perspective. Religious symbols may assume new profundity of meaning. For instance, in this stage an individual "may view the cross displayed during religious services as both a symbol of the crucifixion of Christ and a representation of sacrifice or death and rebirth" (Hutchinson, 1999, p. 1720).

Stage 7: Universalizing Faith (Midlife and Beyond).

Universalizing faith is characterized by selfless commitment to justice on behalf of others. During stage 6, people confront discrepancies and unfairnesses, integrating them into their perception of how the world operates. However, the self remains the primary reference point. An individual accepts and appreciates his own vulnerability, and seeks his own continued existence and salvation. Stage 7, however, reflects a deeply spiritual concern for the greater good, the benefit of the masses, above oneself. Such commitment may involve becoming a martyr on behalf of or devoting one's life to some great cause at the expense of personal pleasure and well-being. Only a tiny minority of people may reach this point. Martin Luther King Jr., Mother Teresa, and Joan of Arc are examples.

Critical Thinking: Evaluation of Fowler's Theory

Fowler provides a logically organized theory concerning the development of faith. It follows Piaget's proposed levels of cognitive development, advancing from the more concrete to the more abstract. It makes sense that people increase their ability to think critically, integrate more difficult concepts, and develop deeper, more committed ideas and beliefs as their lives and thinking progress.

However, at least three criticisms of the theory come to mind. First, the sample on which it was based is very limited concerning race and religious orientation. Questions can be raised regarding the extent to which it can be applied universally to non-Christian faiths worldwide.

Second, concepts of human diversity, oppression, and discrimination are not taken into account. There is an inherent assumption that all people start out with a clean slate. In reality, some are born richer, some poorer, some in high-tech societies, others in third-world environments. To what extent does people's exposure to more ideas and greater access to the world's activities and resources affect the development of faith? Are all people provided an equal opportunity to develop faith? Do oppression and discrimination affect one's spirituality and the evolution of faith?

A third criticism is the difficulty of applying Fowler's theory to macro situations. How does the development of faith from an individual perspective fit into the overall scheme of the macro environment? How does faith development potentially affect organizational, community, and political life?

Spirituality and Social Work Practice

Sermabeikian (1994) describes spirituality and its relationship to social work practice:

> Spirituality is a human need; it is too important to be misunderstood; avoided; or viewed as regressive, neurotic, or pathological in nature. Social workers must recognize that a person's spiritual beliefs, values, perceptions, feelings, and ideals are intrinsically connected to religious, philosophical, cultural, ethnic, and life experiences. It is important that the practitioner acknowledge that spirituality in a person's life can be a constructive way of facing life's difficulties. . . . Developing practice skill in addressing spirituality begins with acceptance of the values, beliefs, and attitudes that are fundamental to the client. When the client chooses to use spiritual perspectives, practitioner empathy and encouragement of client self-determinations should follow. Clients may choose to pursue self-help group membership, church involvement, prayer, meditation, or commitment to a social action or cause. The practitioner should be willing to incorporate goals in treatment that include spiritual values for the accomplishment of tasks. (pp. 181–182)

One cautionary note is that social workers should take great care not to impose their own personal spiritual values upon clients. It is crucial to view spirituality from the client's perspective, not your own.

◣ Significant Issues and Life Events: Suicide and Assertiveness

Each phase of life tends to be characterized by issues that receive considerable attention and concern. Two issues command special attention as they relate to adolescence and youth. These are suicide and assertiveness. Although these issues continue to elicit concern with respect to any age group, they have a special critical quality for those whose lives are just beginning. Young lives terminated at such an early age represent tragic and regrettable losses of potential. Likewise, lives marked by either docile meekness and nonassertiveness on the one hand, or pushy, self-serving aggression on the other can be thwarted, damaging, or nonproductive.

Each of these issues may be viewed either from a psychological or a social perspective. They will arbitrarily be addressed in this chapter, which focuses on the psychological aspects of adolescence and young adulthood.

❦ Suicide

Why do people decide to terminate their lives? Is it because life is unbearable, painful, hopeless, or useless? Suicide can occur during almost any time of life. However, it might be considered especially critical in the years of adolescence and youth. This is the time of life when people could enjoy being young and fresh and looking forward to life's wide variety of exciting experiences. Instead, many young people decide to take their own lives.

Incidence of Suicide

Suicide is one of the most critical health problems in the United States today. Consider these frightening facts: Almost 31,000 deaths are due to suicide in the United States each year (U.S. Census Bureau, 2001). The number of suicides has tripled over the past 30 years (Berk, 1999; Santrock, 1999). The suicide rate is lowest in childhood and highest in old age, although it jumps sharply during adolescence (Berk, 1999). Suicide is the third leading cause of death for people age 15 through 24, surpassed only by accidents and homicides (U.S. Census Bureau, 2001). No one knows how many of those accidents were really suicides.

Some national surveys reveal that 6 to 13 percent of adolescents say they have tried to commit suicide, although few have received any physical or mental health treatment for it (Garland & Zigler, 1993; Newman & Newman, 1999). Another national Gallup poll indicated that 15 percent of adolescents had considered committing suicide at one time or another (Ackerman, 1993; Newman & Newman, 1999). One in 10,000 adolescents actually succeeds in committing suicide, and white adolescents are more likely to commit suicide than African American adolescents (Kail & Cavanaugh, 2000). Suicide

Many pressures and anxieties are exerted on adolescents. Young people are not sure that they will find a job with which they can support themselves when they get out of school.

rates for Native American youth, especially Apaches, are higher than for their white counterparts (Henry et al., 1993; Newman & Newman, 1999).

Causes of Adolescent Suicide

No specific recipe of variables contributes to any individual adolescent's suicide probability. However, adolescents who threaten or try to commit suicide tend to experience problems in three main arenas: increased stress, family issues, and psychological variables (particularly depression) (Goldman & Beardslee, 1999; Kirk, 1993; Moscicki, 1999).

Increased Stress. Many teenagers today express concern over the multiple pressures they have to bear. To some extent, these pressures might be related to current social and economic conditions. Many families are breaking up. Pressures to succeed are great. Many young people are worried about what kind of job they will find when they get out school. Peer pressure to conform and to be accepted socially is constantly operating. Suicidal adolescents may lose any coping powers they may have had and simply give up.

A range of significant events might increase stress and jar adolescents into suicidal thinking. Unwanted pregnancy or even fear of unwanted pregnancy is an example. Other stressful events include losses such as the death of someone close, divorce, or family relocation (Kirk, 1993; Moscicki, 1999; Swedo et al., 1991; Wagner, 1997). Even the stress resulting from declining grades in school might contribute to suicide (Goldman & Beardslee, 1999).

Problems in peer relationships can contribute to stress. An adolescent may feel unwanted or isolated, that he or she simply does not fit in. Or, an adolescent might experience devastating trauma after being "dumped" by a girlfriend or boyfriend. Adolescents' lack of experience in coping with such situations may make it seem like life is over after losing "the one and only person" they love. Many adolescents have not yet had time to work through such experiences and learn that they can survive emotional turmoil.

Evidence suggests that teenagers who are overachievers experience greater stress and, therefore, are more likely to commit suicide (Jobes, Berman, & Martin, 1999; U.S. Congress, 1984). Overachievers may expect too much of themselves and respond to pressure from parents, school, and friends in an overly zealous manner. One teenager comes to mind. Terri was a popular high school cheerleader. She had been Homecoming Queen last fall. She was an A student and editor of the yearbook. When she killed herself, everyone was surprised. Most of the people around her felt that she had everything and wondered why she threw it all away. They said it was such

a shame. Apparently, she had hidden her inner turmoil very well. Perhaps she was just tired of working (and playing) so hard. Or, maybe, no matter how she seemed to others, she never measured up to her own expectations for herself. At any rate, no one will ever know. We all probably know of someone like Terri. (Chapter 14 will discuss stress and stress management in greater detail.)

Family Issues. Turbulence and disruption at home contribute to the profile of an adolescent suicide (Goldman & Beardslee, 1999; Hodgman, 1992; Moscicki, 1999; Swedo et al., 1991; Tishler, 1992). There might be serious communication problems, parental substance abuse, parental mental health problems, or physical or sexual abuse (Bagley, Bolitho, & Bertrand, 1997; Kirk, 1993). One of the two best predictors for adolescent suicide among males is an incohesive family relationship; the other is depression (Goldman & Beardslee, 1999; Meneese, Yutrzenka, & Vitale, 1992; Moscicki, 1999). Lack of a stable home environment contributes to the sense of loneliness and isolation for both boys and girls. Highlight 7.4 describes a young woman who struggled to cope with family and other issues, but failed.

Psychological Variables. Psychological variables, usually relating to depression, make up the third arena for problems leading to suicidal thoughts. One such factor is low self-esteem (Dacey & Travers, 2002; Goldman &

Highlight 7.4

Joany—A Victim of Suicide

Joany, age 15, was one of the "fries." People said that she used a lot of drugs and was wild. She did poorly in school, when she did manage to attend. Her appearance was striking. Her hair was cropped short, somewhat unevenly, and was characterized by a different color of the rainbow every day, including purple, green, and hot pink. Short leather miniskirts, heavy chainlike jewelry, and dark, exaggerated makeup were also part of her style. She hung around with a group who looked and behaved much like herself. More studious, straight, upper-middle-class, college-bound peers couldn't understand why she behaved that way. It was easy for them to point and snicker at her as she walked down the high school halls.

One day she came to school looking almost normal, noted one of her straight classmates, Karen. Karen had at times felt sorry for Joany in the past when people made fun of her. Today Joany was wearing an unobtrusive skirt and sweater. More noticeably, her hair was combed in a much

more traditional manner than usual. Today Joany finally looked like she fit in with her other classmates. Karen called out a compliment to her as she was walking down the hall, laughing with some of her other weird-looking friends. Joany turned, smiled, gave a hurried thanks, and returned to her active conversation with the others.

The next day the word spread like wildfire throughout the student population. Joany, it seemed, had hanged herself in her parents' basement. The rumor was that she was terribly upset because her parents were getting a divorce. No one really knew why she had killed herself. People didn't understand the sense of hopelessness and desolation she felt. Nor did anyone know why she did not turn to friends or family or school counselors for help. There seemed to be so many unanswered questions.

All that remained of Joany several months later was an oversized picture of her on the last page of the high school yearbook. It was labeled "In Memoriam."

Beardslee, 1999). When people don't feel strong internally, they find it very difficult to muster the support necessary to cope with outside pressures.

Feelings of helplessness and hopelessness may also contribute to suicide potential (Goldman & Beardslee, 1999; Hutchinson, 1999; Swedo et al., 1991). As adolescents struggle to establish an identity and function independently of their parents, it's no wonder that many feel helpless. They must abide by the rules of their parents and schools. They suffer from peer pressure to conform to the norms of their age group. They are seeking acceptance by society and a place where they will fit in. At the same time, an adolescent must strive to develop a unique personality, a sense of self that is valuable for its own sake. At times such a struggle may indeed seem hopeless.

Impulsivity, or a sudden decision to act without giving much thought to the action, is yet another variable related to adolescent suicide (Papalia et al., 1998; Slap et al., 1989). Confusion, isolation, and feelings of despair may contribute to an impulsive decision to end it all.

Adolescents today face a hard transition into adulthood. Social values are shifting. Peer pressure is immense.

Adolescents have not had time to gain life experience and so tend to behave impulsively. Any trivial incident may become a crisis. Every moment of the day can feel like the end of the world if something goes wrong.

Suicidal Symptoms

Patterson and his associates (1983) cite various risk factors that are related to a person's actual potential of carrying through with a suicide. They propose a mechanism for evaluating suicide potential, which is called the "SAD PERSONS" scale. Each letter in the acronym corresponds to one of the high-risk factors.

It should be emphasized that any of the many available guidelines to assess suicide potential are just that—guidelines. People who actually threaten to commit suicide should be believed. The very fact that they are talking about it means that they are thinking about actually doing it. However, the following variables are useful as guidelines for determining risk, that is, how high the probability is that they actually will attempt and succeed at suicide. Highlight 7.5 cites a number of actual suicide notes that reflect these symptoms.

Highlight 7.5

Suicide Notes

The following are suicide notes written by people of various ages shortly before they successfully committed suicide.

Whomever—I wrote this sober, so it is what I planned, sober or drunk. I love you all and please don't feel guilty because it is what I planned drunk or sober. Life still happens whether it is today or tomorrow. But after 23 years I would think that I could have met a person that I would mean more than personal advantage. If only I meant something. People just don't seem to care. Is it that I give the impression that I don't care? I wish and want to know. I feel so unimportant to everyone. As though my presence does not mean anything to anybody. I wish so much to be something to someone. But I feel the harder I try the worse I do. Maybe I just have not run into the right person. I am still 6 feet underground. My mind just didn't want any of it obviously. Make sure———goes to mom. No matter what I do, in my life, I still am going to die. By someone else's hands OR MY OWN.

(Female, age 23, died of a gunshot wound.)

I can't put up with this shit. I'm sorry I have to do this, but I have nothing left.
   P.S. Closed casket please.
   Give my guns to———
(Male, age 25, died of a gunshot wound.)

Mom and Dad
   don't feel bad—I have problems—don't feel the blame for this on you———
(Male, age 18, died of a gunshot wound.)

Please forgive me for leaving you. I love you very much, but could not cope with my health problems plus financial worries etc. Try to understand and pray for me.
   I wish you all the best and that you will be able to find the happiness in life I could not.

Love and Kisses

I can't take the abuse, the hurt, the rejection, the isolation, the loneliness. I can't deal with all of it. I can't try anymore. The tears are endless. I've fallen into a bottomless pit of despair. I know eternal pain and tears . . .
   No one knows I'm alive or seems to care if I die. I'm a terrible, worthless person and it would be better if I'd never been born. Tabby was my only friend in the world, and now she's dead. There's no reason for me to live anymore. . . .
   Mom and Dad, I hate you!

Love Tommy

Source: Recorded in "A Cry for Help: Teen Suicide," prepared and presented by Tom Skinner, Edison Junior High School, Janesville, WI. Reprinted by permission of the Rock County Coroner's Office, Beloit, WI.

Sex. Among adolescents, females are much more likely to try to kill themselves than males (Lewinsohn et al., 2001). However, males are three times more likely to succeed in their attempts. Adolescents of either gender may have serious suicide potential. However, greater danger exists if the person threatening suicide is a male. One reason for this is that males are more likely to choose a more deadly means of committing suicide such as firearms or a hanging (Berk, 1999).

Age. Although a person of almost any age may attempt and succeed at suicide, the risks are greater for some age groups than for others. Statistics indicate that people who are aged 15 to 24 or younger, or men aged 75 or older are in the high-risk groups (Dacey & Travers, 2002).

Depression. Depression contributes to a person's potential to commit suicide. *Depression,* technically referred to as *depressive disorder,* is a psychiatric condition characterized by a disheartened mood; unhappiness; a lack of interest in daily activities; an inability to experience pleasure; pessimism; significant weight loss not related to dieting or weight gain; insomnia; an extremely low energy level; feelings of hopelessness and worthlessness; a decreased capacity to focus and make decisions; and a preoccupation with thoughts about suicide and one's own death. Being depressed doesn't involve simply feeling bad. Rather, it involves a collection of characteristics, feelings, and behaviors that tend to occur in conjunction with each other.

Previous Attempts. People who have tried to kill themselves before are more likely to succeed than people who are trying to commit suicide for the first time (Harvard Medical School, 1986, 1996; Kirk, 1993; Linehan, 1999; Sheafor et al., 2000).

Ethanol and Other Drug Abuse. People who abuse alcohol and other drugs are much more likely to commit suicide than people who do not (Clerici, Carta, & Cazzullo, 1994; Linehan, 1999; Moscicki, 1999). Such substance abuse is involved in one-third or more of all adolescent suicides (Garland & Zigler, 1993; Papalia et al., 1998).

Rational Thinking Loss. People who suffer from mental or emotional disorders, such as depression or psychosis, are more likely to kill themselves than those who do not. Hallucinations, delusions, extreme confusion, and anxiety all contribute to an individual's risk factor. If a person is not thinking realistically and objectively, emotions and impulsivity are more likely to take over.

Social Supports Lacking. Loneliness and isolation have already been discussed as primary contributing factors. People who feel that no one cares about them may feel useless and hopeless. Suicide potential may be especially high in cases in which a loved one has recently died or deserted the individual who's threatening suicide.

Organized Plan. The more specific and organized an individual's plan regarding when and how the suicide will be undertaken, the greater the risk. Additionally, the more dangerous the method, the greater the risk. For instance, the presence of a firearm increases suicide risk (Jobes et al., 1999; Sheafor et al., 2000). A plan to use the loaded rifle you have hidden in the basement tomorrow evening at 7:00 P.M. is more lethal than a plan of somehow getting some drugs and overdosing sometime. Several questions might be asked when evaluating this risk factor. How much detail is involved in the plan? Has the individual put a lot of thought into the specific details regarding how the suicide is to occur? Has the plan been thought over before? How dangerous is the chosen method? Is the method or weapon readily available to the individual? Has the specific time been chosen for when the suicide is to take place?

No Spouse. Single people are much more likely to commit suicide than married people. People who have never married are twice as likely; divorced and widowed people have the highest suicide rates of all (Harvard Medical School, 1986). Generally, single people have a greater chance of feeling lonely and isolated.

Sickness. People who are ill are more likely to commit suicide than those who are healthy (Moscicki, 1999). This is especially true for those who have long-term illnesses, which place substantial limitations on their lives. Perhaps in some of these instances, their inability to cope with the additional stress of sickness and pain eats away at their overall coping ability.

Other Symptoms. Other characteristics operate as warning signals for suicide. For example, rapid changes in mood, behavior, or general attitude are other indicators that a person is in danger of committing suicide (Kail & Cavanaugh, 2000). A potentially suicidal person may be one who has suddenly become severely depressed and withdrawn. Or, a person who has been depressed for a long period of time and suddenly becomes strikingly cheerful may also be in danger. Sometimes in the latter instance, the individual has already made up his or her mind to commit suicide. In those instances, the cheerfulness

Spotlight on Diversity 7.4

Suicide and Adolescent Hispanic Females

We have established the importance of understanding and focusing on the many aspects of cultural, racial, and ethnic diversity to better understand people's behavior. This is also true when evaluating suicide potential. The suicide rate for adolescent Hispanic females is about twice as high as for their non-Hispanic white and African American female peers (CDC, 1996). Zayas and associates (2000) propose an "integrative model" for understanding suicide attempts by adolescent Hispanic females that reflects their cultural context and immediate environment (p. 53).

One of the integrative model's dimensions is *sociocultural*. One aspect of this concerns the degree to which the adolescents' families are acculturated, that is, have accepted and adopted the cultural patterns and behaviors manifested by the dominant cultural group. Discrepancies in acculturation between daughters and parents are apparent in Hispanic families with suicidal female adolescents (Zayas et al., 2000). Daughters strive to adopt customs and values evident in the overriding non-Hispanic culture, whereas parents maintain their allegiance to values, beliefs, and behavior characterizing their original cultural heritage. The result may be high levels of family stress and conflict, contributing to the adolescent's anguish and suicide potential.

A second dimension involved in the integrative model is *family domain*. Regardless of racial and ethnic background family discord including "low cohesiveness, familial and marital conflict and violence, low parental support and warmth, [and] parent-adolescent conflict" contribute to suicide potential (Zayas et al., 2000). With respect to female Hispanic adolescents, Zayas and associates (2000) explain that "traditionally structured (that is, patriarchal and male-dominated) Hispanic families tend to emphasize restrictive, authoritarian parenting, especially with regard to girls. This traditionalism may affect a family's capacity to respond flexibly to a daughter during a developmental move toward autonomy and individualism, even when the father is absent" (p. 57). As daughters strive for independence and are faced with inflexibility, conflict may result. This, in turn, may contribute to young women's distress and suicide potential.

Still another dimension stressed in the integrative model involves a *psychological domain*. We have established that depression is one factor contributing to suicidal potential. Zayas and his associates (2000) explain that "among adolescents who attempt suicide, a key factor in coping is how they manage anger. Because of the cultural prohibitions on women's direct expressions of anger, the adolescent Hispanic female also may be socialized by her own more tradition-bound parents to suppress her anger. . . . [As a result] having limited abilities cope with anger and lacking appropriate problem-solving skills may interact to trigger the suicide attempt" (p. 59).

---

may stem from relief that the desperate decision has finally been made.

Suddenly giving away personal possessions that are especially important or meaningful is another warning signal of suicide potential (Dacey & Travers, 2002; Kirk, 1993). It is as if once the decision has been made to commit suicide, giving things away to selected others is a way of finalizing the decision. Perhaps it's a way of tying up loose ends, or of making certain that the final details are taken care of.

Note that other variables can also contribute to suicide potential. Spotlight 7.4 explores the relatively high rate of suicide for Hispanic females, compared to their non–Hispanic white and African American female counterparts.

How to Use the SAD PERSONS Scale

Patterson and colleagues (1983, p. 348) suggest a framework for using the SAD PERSONS scale when evaluating suicide potential. The scale itself is presented in Highlight 7.6. One point is assigned to each condition that applies to the suicidal person. For example, if a person is depressed, he or she would automatically receive a score

Highlight 7.6

The SAD PERSONS Scale

S (Sex)
A (Age)
D (Depression)
P (Previous Attempt)
E (Ethanol Abuse)
R (Rational Thinking Loss)
S (Social Supports Lacking)
O (Organized Plan)
N (No Spouse)
S (Sickness)

Source: W. M. Patterson, H. H. Dohn, J. Bird, and G. A. Patterson, "Evaluation of Suicidal Patients: The SAD PERSONS Scale," *Psychosomatics* 24(4): 343–349. Used by permission of the Academy of Psychosomatic Medicine.

of 1. Depression in addition to alcoholism would result in a score of 2, and so on. Although the SAD PERSONS scale was developed specifically to teach medical students how to evaluate suicidal potential, social workers might use it in a similar manner. It may be helpful in assessing the intensity of treatment an individual might need. The following decision-making guidelines are recommended:

Total Points	Proposed Clinical Actions
0 to 2	Send home with a follow-up.
3 to 4	Close the follow-up; consider hospitalization.
5 to 6	Strongly consider hospitalization, depending on confidence in the follow-up arrangement.
7 to 10	Hospitalize or commit.

Zero to 2 points indicate a mild potential that still merits some follow-up and attention. On the other hand, a score of 7 to 10 indicates severe suicide potential. These cases would merit immediate attention and action. Hospitalization or commitment are among available options. Scores ranging from 3 to 6 represent a range of serious suicide potential. Although people with these scores need help and attention, the immediacy and intensity of that attention may vary. In each case, professional discretion would be involved.

The SAD PERSONS scale was developed to aid physicians in training. It is most likely that such physicians will not be proficient in addressing mental health problems themselves. Thus, there is an emphasis on referral to someone else and on hospitalization. Social workers, on the other hand, may often be called upon to work with suicidal people. Some guidelines are described below.

Guidelines for Helping Suicidal People

Two levels of intervention are possible for dealing with a potentially suicidal person. The first involves addressing the immediate crisis. The person threatening to commit suicide needs immediate help and support literally to keep him or her alive. The second level would address the other issues that worked to escalate his or her stress. This second level of intervention might involve longer-term treatment to address issues of longer duration that were not necessarily directly related to the suicide crisis.

For example, consider a 15-year-old male who is deeply troubled over the serious problems his parents are currently experiencing in their marriage. This preoccupation, in addition to his normally shy personality, has alienated him from virtually any social contacts with his peers. The result is a serious consideration regarding whether life is worth it or not. The first priority is to prevent the suicide. However, this young man also needs to address and resolve the problems that caused the stress in the first place, namely, his parents' conflicts and his lack of friends. Longer-term counseling or treatment might be necessary.

Reactions to a Suicide Threat. You get a phone call in the middle of the night from an old friend you haven't heard from in a while who says she cannot stand living anymore. Or, a client calls you late Friday afternoon and says that he is planning to shoot himself. What do you do? Specific suggestions for how to treat the potentially suicidal person include the following.

- *Remain calm and objective* (Kirk, 1993). Don't allow the emotional distress being experienced by the other person to contaminate your own judgment. The individual needs help in becoming more rational and objective. The person does not need someone else who is drawn into the emotional crisis.

- *Be supportive.* Jobes and his colleagues (1999) suggest that "[c]onnecting with the pain can be achieved through careful and thoughtful listening, emotional availability, and warmth; it may be shown by eye contact, posture, and nonverbal cues that communicate genuine interest, concern, and caring" (p. 143). They note further that it is vital to "respect the depth and degree of pain reported by a youth. Self-reports of extreme emotional pain and trauma should not be dismissed as adolescent melodrama. The experience of pain is acute and real to adolescents and potentially life-threatening. . . . [Y]oung people tend to be present oriented and lack the years of life experience that may provide the perspective needed to endure a painful period" (p. 144).

- *Identify the immediate problem* (Jobes et al., 1999; Sheafor et al., 2000). Help the person clearly identify what is causing the excessive stress. The problem needs to be recognized before it can be examined. The individual may be viewing an event way out of perspective. For example, a 16-year-old girl was crushed after her steady boyfriend of 18 months dropped her. In this instance, the loss of her boyfriend overshadowed all of the other things in her life—her family, her friends, her membership in the National Honor Society, and her favorite activity, running. She needed help focusing on exactly what had caused her stress, namely the loss of her boyfriend. To her, it felt like she had lost her whole life which was a gross distortion of reality.

- *Identify strengths* (Jobes et al., 1999). It is helpful to identify and emphasize the person's positive qualities. For example, the individual might be pleasant, unselfish, hard-working, conscientious, bright, attractive, and so on. People who are feeling suicidal and most likely focusing on the "bad things" they perceive about themselves. They forget their positive characteristics.

- *Decrease isolation* (Jobes et al., 1999). Another source of strength lies in people close to the suicidal person. Who can that person turn to for emotional support and help? These people may include family, friends, a religious leader, a guidance counselor, or a physician—people the person trusts and can communicate with.

- *Explore past coping mechanisms* (Roberts, 1999). When the person has hit rough spots before, how has he or she dealt with them? You can emphasize how the person has survived such tough times before. Suicidal people may be in a rut of negative, depressing thoughts. They may be blind to anything but their immediate crisis. Sometimes, people in this suicidal rut have hit their lowest emotional point. Their perspective is such that they feel that life has *always* been as bad as this, and that it always will be as bad as this (see Figure 7.1). A suicidal person has probably been "up" before and probably will be "up" again. Many times this "sense of history" can be pointed out and used beneficially. If possible, help the person understand that suicide is a permanent,

fatal option in response to a temporary crisis. (Sheafor et al., 1997, p. 396).

- *Latch on to the will to live* (Kirk, 1993; Sheafor et al., 2000). The very fact that the suicidal person came to talk to you indicates that he or she is reaching out. Especially with adolescents, there is almost always ambivalence about wanting to die. On the one hand, they want to die, but on the other hand, they want to live. It is helpful to identify and concentrate on that part of them that clutches at life.

- *Avoid clichés.* Don't argue with the suicidal person about the philosophical values of life versus death (Sheafor et al., 2000). Don't use clichés like, "There's so much that life has to offer you," or, "Your life is just beginning." This type of approach only makes people feel like you're operating on a different wavelength, and don't understand how they feel. People who threaten suicide have real suicidal feelings. They're not likely to be exaggerating them or making them up. What they need is objective, emphatic support (Kirk, 1993).

- *Examine potential options* (Jobes et al., 1999; Kirk, 1993). One of the most useful and concrete things that can be done for suicidal people is to help them get the help they need. Because suicidal people tend to be isolated, this help often involves referring them to the various resources—both personal

Figure 7.1 Life's Ups and Downs

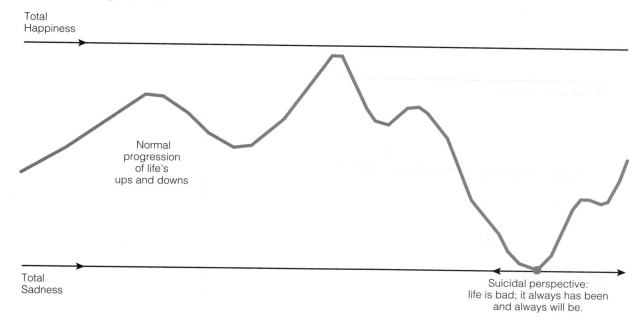

and professional—that are available. Referrals to police or a hospital emergency room can be helpful when an emergency situation arises. Finally, professionals in mental health are available to provide long-term help to people in need.

Professional Counseling of Suicidal People. Jobes and his associates (1999) suggest at least 5 steps social workers or counselors consider when working with, and establishing a plan of action with, suicidal clients:

1. Make the environment safe. Take away, or make minimally available, the means by which the person was contemplating suicide—depending on the plan, this might include removing pills or guns. It might also include making certain supportive people remain with the client.

2. "Negotiate safety" (p. 146). Jobes and his associates (1999) explain: "Generally, the concrete goal of these negotiations is to ensure the patient's physical safety by establishing that the patient will not hurt him- or herself for a specific period of time. The more concrete and specific the understanding, the better. Typically, the patient will agree to maintain his or her safety until the next clinical contact, at which point a new understanding can be negotiated" (p. 146). Although such an agreement does not guarantee safety, it serves as one means of bolstering support.

3. Plan for future support. The suicidal client should have continuity of social and professional support. This includes scheduling future counseling sessions, making follow-up calls to ensure that the client is all right, and planning meetings and events the client can look forward to.

4. Minimize loneliness and seclusion. Jobes and his associates (1999) reflect: "The patient must not be left alone in the midst of a suicidal crisis. It is critical that a trustworthy friend or family member remain with the patient through the crisis phase. Efforts must be made to mobilize friends, family, and neighbors, making them aware of the importance of ongoing contact with the suicidal youth" (p. 146).

5. Provide more intensive care via hospitalization. If it's not possible to stabilize the client and his or her environment to keep the client safe, hospitalization may be necessary.

A Cautionary Note. It's important to realize that suicide prevention may not always be possible (Fiske, 2002; Sheafor et al., 2000). All you can do is your very best

to help a suicidal person hold on to life. The ultimate decision lies with him or her whether to continue living or not.

Community Responses to Suicide: Prevention and Crisis Intervention

Community resources are critical for successful suicide prevention. You cannot refer people for help if the appropriate services don't exist. If resources are not available, you as a social worker may need to advocate for new programs or to expand services within your own or other agencies. A community system can address suicide prevention in many ways. Four are discussed here: task forces for suicide prevention, crisis lines, peer-helping programs in schools, and training programs for community professionals.

Creation of a *suicide prevention task force* provides a potentially effective means to evaluate the need for services and decide what types of services to offer. A *task force* is a group established for a specific purpose, usually within the context of an organization or community, that pursues designated goals and disbands when these goals have been achieved (Kirst-Ashman & Hull, 2002). A task force can be made up of interested individuals within an organization or a cross-section of professionals and citizens within a community. The task force group can then make decisions regarding how the agency or community can best meet the community's need for suicide prevention services. It can answer a number of questions and decide on a plan of action. Who are the potential clients? Are there services already existing within the community that can best meet the suicide prevention need? If not, what types of programs should be initiated? What resources are available to develop such programs?

For example, the Task Force on Suicide in Canada was established in 1980. This group addressed the needs of the entire country instead of smaller community systems. Its members represented each of the 12 regions of the country. The group's purpose was to "gather and analyze the available data, to present its findings in a concise yet comprehensive report and to make recommendations where necessary and appropriate. Specific dimensions of the problem investigated include: Coroner/Medical examiner's certification procedures [to determine the cause of death]; . . . [incidence of suicide; causes of suicide]; high risk groups, primary prevention strategies; existing programs and services; the suicide prevention training of mental health professionals; and a number of insurance and legal issues" (Syer-Solursh, 1984, p. 1).

Crisis telephone lines are another approach to suicide prevention. Such crisis lines can be for a specific type of crisis (such as domestic violence or suicidal potential) or provide crisis intervention and referral information for virtually any type of crisis. An advantage of either type of crisis line is that people thinking about suicide can call anonymously for help at the time they need such help the most. People working on crisis lines need thorough training in suicide prevention. Additionally, such lines should have staff available at all hours of the day. Imagine the reaction of the person contemplating suicide who is told to leave her message at the sound of the beep. Finally, crisis lines should be well publicized. People must know about them to use them.

Another example of a community system's approach to suicide prevention is the establishment of a *peer-helping program* within a school setting. One such program is "Link-Up" in Minneapolis, Minnesota (Keys, 1990). Students identified by teachers and peers as being at risk are encouraged to join. Students who are functioning well academically and socially are also recruited as participants. Students meet in a group for 1 hour weekly over the course of 4 or 5 weeks. The goal for at-risk students is to enhance self-esteem, develop more effective life coping skills, and get support from their peers. Emphasis is on developing friendships and networking with peers rather than on peer counseling. Program participants are encouraged to reach out to each other, enjoy recreational activities together, introduce each other to other new friends, and generally improve the overall social and educational environment.

The fourth example of a community system's response to the suicide problem is the development and provision of *suicide prevention training programs for community professionals and other caregivers.* Caregivers include professionals such as social workers, psychologists, psychiatrists, and counselors. Caregivers may also include any others that potentially suicidal people may turn to for help. These include clergy, family members, nurses, teachers, and friends. Training as many caregivers as possible significantly increases the chance for a potentially suicidal person to make contact with someone who can help.

❧ Empowerment through Assertiveness and Assertiveness Training

Assertiveness involves behavior that is both straightforward and yet not offensive. The behavior can be either verbal or nonverbal. Assertiveness involves taking into account both your own rights and the rights of others. It sounds simple, but for many people appropriate assertiveness is difficult to master. For instance, consider the two people

sitting in front of you in a movie theater who are talking loudly. How should you react? Should you ignore them even though it's the scariest portion of the latest horror film? Should you scream, "Shut up!"? Or, should you tap one of them gently on the shoulder and politely ask the person to please be quiet?

Your best friend asks to borrow your car. Your friend emphasizes it'll only be for one time and it's needed for *such an important reason!* You happen to know that your friend is not a very good driver, has gotten two speeding tickets in the past 6 months, and sometimes drives after drinking. Should you say, "No way! You know what a horrible driver you are"? Should you say, "Sure"? Should you say, "Well, okay, I guess so"? Or, should you say, "No. You know I don't let other people drive my car. Would it help if I drive you somewhere?"

Many times it's difficult to look at a situation objectively and take the feelings and needs of all concerned into account. Often, it's especially difficult for adolescents and young people who are still getting to know themselves and establishing their own identities. On the other hand, they want to fit in socially and respond to the feelings of others.

Assertiveness involves specific skills that can be taught. This, of course, is referred to as *assertiveness training.* Adolescents and young people may find assertiveness skills especially valuable as they decide how to react in new situations, especially when under social pressure. For example, they might struggle regarding how to respond in sexual situations: *What do I want to do versus what does my partner want to do?* Another example involves decisions about taking drugs: *Everyone is doing it; what should I do?* Here we will discuss, in more depth, the meaning of assertiveness and some concepts involved in assertiveness training.

Most people remember occasions on which they wish they could have been more assertive. Yet, at those moments they felt very uncomfortable doing so. On the other hand, many people have also experienced situations in which they "lost it," and exploded in a loud burst of anger. An example is a newly married 22-year-old woman who is "at her wits' end" with her husband's best friend. He continues to make derogatory racial slurs against almost anyone who is not white, of a certain religious group, and of European heritage. The young woman, a newly graduated social worker, tries everything she can think of to turn the friend's comments off. She tries ignoring him. She tries to change the subject. Yet, she doesn't want to offend the man. After all, he is her husband's best friend. Finally, something snaps and she screams, "I can't stand it anymore. I think you're a disgusting bigot. Just shut up!" This outburst does little for their relationship.

The Relevance of Assertiveness

Assertiveness and assertiveness training is included here for three reasons. First, appropriate assertiveness is an important skill to be acquired in adolescence and young adulthood. When someone uses an assertive approach, that person values both his or her own rights and the rights of others. Assertiveness is a critical aspect of establishing both a personal identity and a moral perspective toward other people.

A second reason for including assertiveness is its importance in working with clients. As a social work practitioner, you must recognize your own professional and personal rights in order to communicate effectively with clients and get your job done. On the other hand, you must also recognize, respect, and appreciate your clients' rights and needs. An assertive approach enables you to take both your rights and your clients' rights into consideration. (These rights are discussed in Highlight 7.7.) In assessing human behavior, you must seek to understand why people behave the way they do. Observing human behavior from an assertiveness perspective helps you focus on who is getting their needs met and who is not. It allows you to identify who is pushing others around inappropriately and who is being pushed.

The third reason for including assertiveness here is its significance for clients. Not only must you assess human behavior as part of the intervention process, you must also work with clients to plan and achieve positive changes. Many clients may benefit from using an assertiveness perspective to understand their own actions and the effects of these actions on others. In your role as educator, you can teach your clients assertiveness principles to enhance their own interpersonal effectiveness.

Nonassertive, Assertive, and Aggressive Communication

On an assertiveness continuum, communication can be rated as nonassertive, assertive, or aggressive. Assertive communication involves verbal and nonverbal behavior that permits speakers to make points clearly and straightforwardly. *Assertive* speakers take into consideration both their own value system and the values of whoever is receiving their message. They consider their own points to be important; yet, they also consider the points and reactions of the communication's receiver important.

For example, the president of the Student Social Work Club asks Maria to take notes at a meeting three meetings in a row. The club's secretary, who is supposed to take notes, is absent all three times. Maria is willing to serve, but feels it's unfair to ask her to do the work every time instead of letting others help, too. Maria assertively states to the club president, "This is the third meeting in a row that you've asked me to take notes. I'm happy to help out, but I feel that it's fair to share this task with other club

Highlight 7.7

Each of Us Has Certain Assertive Rights

Part of becoming assertive involves believing that we are worthwhile people. It's easy to criticize ourselves for our mistakes and imperfections. And it's easy to hold our feelings in because we're afraid that we will hurt someone else's feelings or that someone will reject us. Sometimes feelings that are held in too long will burst out in an aggressive tirade. This applies to anyone, including our clients.

A basic principle in social work is that each individual is a valuable human being. Everyone, therefore, has certain basic rights.

The following are eight of your, and your clients', assertive rights:

1. You have the right to express your ideas and opinions openly and honestly.
2. You have the right to be wrong. Everyone makes mistakes.

3. You have the right to direct and govern your own life. In other words, you have the right to be responsible for yourself.
4. You have the right to stand up for yourself without unwarranted anxiety and make choices that are good for you.
5. You have the right *not* to be liked by everyone. (Do you like *everyone* you know?)
6. You have the right to make requests and to refuse them without feeling guilty.
7. You have the right to ask for information if you need it.
8. Finally, you have the right to decide not to exercise your assertive rights. In other words, you have the right to choose not to be assertive.

Source: Most of these rights are adapted from Lynn Z. Bloom, Karen Coburn, and Joan Pearlman, *The New Assertive Woman* (New York: Dell, 1976), and from Kathryn Apgar and Betsy Nicholson Callahan, *Four One-Day Workshops* (Boston: Resource Communications, Inc, and Family Service Association of Greater Boston, 1980).

members. Why don't you ask someone else to take notes this time?"

Aggressive communication involves bold and dominant verbal and nonverbal behavior in which a speaker presses his or her point of view as taking precedence above all others. Aggressive speakers consider only their views as important and devalue what the receiver has to say. Aggressive behaviors are demanding and most often annoying. Consider, for example, the man who barges in at the return desk in front of 17 other people standing in line and demands *service!*

Nonassertive communication, on the other hand, is the opposite of aggressive. Speakers devalue themselves. They feel that what the other person involved thinks is much more important than their own thoughts. For example, for lunch one day Cassie orders a hamburger well done. The waitress brings her a burger that's practically dripping blood. However, Cassie is afraid of what the waitress will think if she complains. She doesn't want to be seen as a "bitch." So, instead of assertively telling the waitress that the hamburger is much too rare, Cassie douses it in ketchup and forces herself to eat half of it.

There is no perfect recipe for what to say to be assertive in any particular situation. The important thing is to take into consideration both your own rights and the rights of the person you are talking to. Following are a few examples.

Situation 1. A 16-year-old woman is on her first date with a young man she likes. After a movie and pizza, they drive around a bit and find a secluded spot in the country where he pulls over and parks. The woman does not want to get sexually involved with the young man. She thinks this is too soon in their relationship. What will he think of her? She doesn't know him well enough yet to become intimate. What can she say?

Nonassertive Response: She says nothing and lets him make his sexual advances.

Aggressive Response: "Get your slimy hands off me, you pervert!"

Assertive Response: "I like you, Harry, but I don't think we know each other well enough yet to get involved this way. Would you please take me home now?"

Situation 2. Biff, Clay's supervisor at Stop'n'Shop, tells Clay that he needs him to work several extra hours the upcoming weekend. Biff has often asked Clay to work extra time on weekends. However, he doesn't ask any of the other workers to do so. Clay thinks this is unfair. He needs his job, but he hates to work extra hours on weekends. What can he say?

Nonassertive Response: "Okay."

Aggressive Response: "No way, Jose! Get off my butt, Biff!"

Assertive Response: "You know I like my job here, Biff. However, I'm sorry, but I can't work extra hours next weekend. I've already made other plans."

Situation 3. Dinah Lee and Hannah, both 18, "hang around" with the same group of friends. However, they don't like each other very much. Dinah Lee approaches Hannah one day and says, "It's too bad you're gaining so much weight." What can Hannah say?

Nonassertive Response: "Yes, you're right. I'm trying to go on a diet."

Aggressive Response: "I'm not nearly as fat or ugly as you are, Buzzard Breath!"

Assertive Response: "No, I haven't gained any weight. I think that was a very inappropriate thing to say. It sounded as if you were just trying to hurt my feelings."

The Advantages of Assertiveness

Developing assertiveness skills has many benefits. For one thing, you can gain more control over your interpersonal environment. Assertiveness may help you avoid uncomfortable or hostile interactions with others. You will probably feel that other people understand you better than they did before. Your self-concept can be enhanced as the result of your gain in control and interpersonal effectiveness. Appropriate assertiveness helps to alleviate building up undue tension and stress and diminish such psychosomatic reactions as headaches or stomach upsets. Finally, other people may gain respect for you, your strength, and your own demonstration of respect for others. People may even begin to use you as a role model for their own development of assertive behavior.

Assertiveness Training

Assertiveness training leads people to realize, feel, and act on the assumption that they have the right to be themselves and express their feelings freely. Assertive responses generally are not aggressive responses. The distinction between these two types of interactions is important. For example, a woman has an excessively critical father-in-law. Intentionally doing things that will bother him (bringing up topics that she knows will upset him, forgetting Father's Day and his birthday, not visiting) and getting into loud arguments with him would be considered "aggressive" behavior.

On the other hand, an effectively assertive response would be to counter criticism by saying, "Dad, your criticism deeply hurts me. I know you're trying to help when you give advice, but I feel that you're criticizing me. I'm an adult, and I have the right to make my own decisions and mistakes. The type of relationship that I'd like to have with you is a close adult relationship and not a father-child relationship."

As we know, social work is practical. Therefore, you can use the suggestions provided to enhance both your client's assertiveness and your own. Alberti and Emmons (1976a, 1976b, 2001) developed the following 13 steps to help establish assertive behavior:

1. Examine your own actions. How do you behave in situations requiring assertiveness? Do you think you tend to be nonassertive, assertive, or aggressive in most of your communications?

2. Make a record of those situations in which you felt you could have behaved more effectively, either more assertively or less aggressively.

3. Select and focus on some specific instance when you felt you could have been more appropriately assertive. Visualize the specific details. What exactly was said? How did you feel?

4. Analyze how you reacted. Examine closely your verbal and nonverbal behavior. Alberti and Emmons (1976a, pp. 31–32) cite the following seven aspects of behavior that are important to monitor. They include:

    a. *Eye contact.* Did you look the person in the eye? Or did you find yourself avoiding eye contact when you were uncomfortable?

    b. *Body posture.* Were you standing up straight or were you slouching? Were you leaning away from the person sheepishly? Were you holding your head up straight as you looked the person in the eye?

    c. *Gestures.* Were your hand gestures fitting for the situation? Did you feel at ease? Or, were you tapping your feet or cracking your knuckles? In the beginning of his term, people often criticized former President George H. Bush for moving his arms and hands around during his public speeches. This tended to give the public the impression that he was frantic. Professional coaches

helped him gain control of this behavior and present a calmer public image.

    d. *Facial expressions.* Did you have a serious expression on your face? Were you smiling or giggling uncomfortably, thereby giving the impression that you were not really serious?

    e. *Voice tone, inflection, volume.* Did you speak in a normal voice tone? Did you whisper timidly? Did you raise your voice to the point of stressful screeching? Did you sound as if you were whining?

    f. *Timing.* It is best to make an appropriately assertive response just after a remark is made or an incident happens. It's also important to consider whether a particular situation requires assertiveness. At times it might be best to remain silent and just "let it go." For example, it might not be wise to criticize your professor for being a "dreary bore" in a class presentation you are giving that your professor is simultaneously grading.

    g. *Content.* What you say in your assertive response is obviously important. Did you choose your words carefully? Did your response have the impact you wanted it to have? Why or why not?

5. Identify a role model and examine how he or she handled a situation requiring assertiveness. What exactly happened during the incident? What words did your model use that were particularly effective? What aspects of his or her nonverbal behavior helped to get points across?

6. Identify a range of other assertive responses that could address the original problem situation you targeted. What other words could you have used? What nonverbal behaviors might have been more effective?

7. Picture yourself in the identified problematic situation. It often helps to close your eyes and concentrate. Step by step, imagine how you could handle the situation more assertively.

8. Practice the way you envisioned yourself being more assertive. You could target a real-life situation that remains unresolved. For example, perhaps the person you live with always leaves dirty socks lying around the living room or drinks all your soda and forgets to tell you the refrigerator is bare. Or you can ask a friend, teacher, or counselor to help you role-play the situation. Role playing provides effective mechanisms for practicing responses before you have to use them spontaneously in real life.

9. Once again, review your new assertive responses. Emphasize your strong points and try to remedy your flaws.

10. Continue practicing steps 7, 8, and 9 until your newly developed assertive approach feels comfortable and natural to you.

11. Try out your assertiveness in a real-life situation.

12. Continue to expand your assertive behavior repertoire until assertiveness becomes part of your personal interactive style. You can review the earlier steps and try them out with an increasingly wider range of situations.

13. Give yourself a pat on the back when you succeed in becoming more assertive. It's not easy changing long-standing patterns of behavior. Focus on and revel in the good feelings you experience as a result of your successes.

Application of Assertiveness Approaches to Social Work Practice

Helping clients learn to be more assertive is appropriate in a wide range of practice situations. For example, teenagers may need to develop assertiveness skills to ward off the massive peer pressure engulfing them. This means more than "just saying no" to drugs, sex, or any other activity they feel pressured to participate in. Assertiveness training involves helping people identify alternative types of responses in uncomfortable situations. Finally, assertiveness training concerns working out and practicing these alternative responses ahead of time so that they become easier and more natural.

Other examples of clients needing assertiveness training include a shy, reserved client who needs to ask his landlord to do some repairs needed in the client's apartment. Still another client might need help becoming more assertive in preparation for a job interview.

Workers themselves need to develop assertiveness skills in order to advocate for services on the behalf of their clients. Good communication skills and a respect for others are basic necessities for social work practice. You can lead your clients through each step in assertiveness training to become more competent and effective communicators.

✔ Summary

Personal identities crystallize during adolescence. Erikson proposed eight stages of psychosexual development that include basic trust versus basic mistrust, autonomy versus shame and doubt, initiative versus guilt, industry versus inferiority, identity versus role confusion (which occurs during adolescence), intimacy versus isolation, generativity versus stagnation, and ego integrity versus despair. Marcia's four categories of identity include identity achievement, foreclosure, identity diffusion, and moratorium. There are questions regarding the applicability of Erikson's and Marcia's theories to people of all racial, cultural, and ethnic backgrounds. Kohlberg's theory of moral development has three levels: preconventional, conventional, and postconventional. Gilligan's theory on moral development, which is more relevant to women, establishes three levels: orientation to personal survival; goodness as self-sacrifice; and the morality of nonviolent responsibility, in addition to the two transitions involved. Fowler proposes a seven-stage theory of faith development in spirituality that parallels Piaget's stages of intellectual growth.

Two issues that are especially significant in adolescence and young adulthood are suicide and assertiveness. Potential causes of suicide include feelings of helplessness, loneliness, impulsivity, lack of a stable environment, and increased external and internal pressures. People need to distinguish between nonassertive, aggressive, and assertive styles of interaction. Both social workers and their clients have specific assertive rights, which are based on a feeling of self-worth. Assertiveness can be learned and used by social workers and clients by practicing the 13 steps of assertiveness training.

InfoTrac College Edition Keywords

adolescent suicide	faith development	moral development	spiritual development
empowerment	identity formation	psychosocial theory	spirituality

On the Internet

Association for Moral Education

http://www.amenetwork.org/

The Association for Moral Education (AME) was founded in 1976 to provide an interdisciplinary forum for professionals interested in the moral dimensions of educational theory and practice. The association is dedicated to fostering communication, cooperation, training, curriculum development, and research that links moral theory with educational practice. It supports self-reflective educational practices that value the worth and dignity of each individual as a moral agent in a pluralistic society.

The Development of Faith—James Fowler

http://www.bluewitch.com/tardev/fowler.htm

The work of pastoral specialist James Fowler integrates the stages of human faith development with the more secular stages of cognitive development.

Gay Student Center

http://gaystudentcenter.studentcenter.org/

The Student Center Network, since its inception in late 1995, has always been very supportive of the gay community. Gay, lesbian, and bisexual students have been active at all of our sites. Yet, many gay/les/bi students urged the organization to put together a special site like this.

#1 Teenage Suicide.Com

http://www.1-teenage-suicide.com/

The Web site contains statistics, risk factors, and resources pertaining to teenage suicide and depression.

CHAPTER 8

Social Systems and Their Impacts on Adolescence and Young Adulthood

Laura Sardina is 19 years old and is wondering what the future holds for her. She lives with her parents and has a job as a hotel maid, for which she receives the minimum hourly wage. She has frequent arguments with her mother, and both of her parents have encouraged her to get a better-paying job so that she can become self-supporting and move out of the house. She realizes that a minimum-wage job will not enable her to live in an apartment, buy a car, buy clothes and food, and have sufficient money for entertainment.

Laura was raised in a middle-class family. Her brother is attending college to become a minister. Religion has always been an important aspect of Laura's parents' lives, but not of Laura's. She detests going to church. Her parents have often called her "stupid" and negatively compared her to her brother who they believe can do no wrong. This disparagement of Laura has in many ways become a self-fulfilling prophecy. She repeated a grade in elementary school, seldom studied, and often received failing grades.

In school she saw herself as a failure and hung out with other students who viewed themselves as failures. In high school, she frequently skipped school and partied. Eight weeks before graduation, she was expelled for skipping too much school. Her parents and the school system had tried numerous times to motivate Laura to apply herself in school; she even had a number of individual sessions with three different social workers and a psychiatrist.

Laura's parents are especially irate when she leaves home for 3 to 4 days at a time and parties in an abandoned house in the inner city of Milwaukee. She has lied to her parents about her sexual activities, when the truth is she has a variety of partners. Fortunately, she is taking birth control pills. Some of Laura's male friends are putting pressure on her to become a prostitute so that there will be more money to buy drugs and party. Laura and her friends have had several encounters with the police for shoplifting, running away from home, drinking liquor under age, kicking police officers while being arrested, and high-speed auto chases after radar detected they were speeding.

Laura is asking herself a number of questions: Should she prostitute herself? Or, should she stop associating with her friends and try to make peace with her parents by seeking a high school education and a better-paying job? Whenever she has tried in the past to achieve the middle-class goals of her parents she has been criticized by them as being a failure. She wonders what are her chances of making it this time? The one thing she has found enjoyable in life is partying with her friends, but she realizes her friends are getting her in trouble with the police. She is worried that cutting ties with her friends will result in living a life in which she will be continually rejected and put down by others. She wants a better-paying job but realizes her chances are not good, especially because she hasn't completed high school. She wants a one-to-one relationship with a caring male, but because she has a low self-concept, the only thing she feels that males will find attractive about her is sexual intercourse. This has been a factor in her having multiple sex partners. She is increasingly concerned that being so sexually active is not right and may result in her acquiring a sexually transmitted disease (such as AIDS). What should she do about all of these concerns? She is deeply perplexed and confused.

A PERSPECTIVE

This chapter will focus primarily on the social changes and social problems encountered by adolescents and young adults. The social growth from puberty to roughly age 30 involves a number of passages: from being dependent on parents to becoming more independent, from adjusting to puberty to establishing a sexual identity, from beginning to date to usually marrying, from being a child with parents to parenting children, from earning money from baby-sitting to selecting a career and starting one's life work, from buying baseball gloves and playing ball to buying a car and traveling, from drinking soda to drinking beer and hard liquor and experimenting with drugs. The pressures and stresses of this time period produce many casualties who suffer from a variety of problems.

This chapter will:

▶ Describe the social system changes that adolescents and young adults undergo.
▶ Describe the following lifestyles and family forms that young adults may enter into: marriage, cohabitation, single life, parenthood, and the life of a childless couple.
▶ Describe some major problems encountered by this age group: emotional and behavior problems, crime and delinquency, delinquent gangs, and eating disorders.
▶ Present theoretical material on the causes and treatments of these problems.
▶ Provide material on social work with groups—including theories about group development and theories about group leadership.

❧ Social System Changes in Adolescence and Young Adulthood

During adolescence and young adulthood, people move from dependence on parents to adult independence, establish peer relationships and intimate relationships, and choose a personal lifestyle involving decisions about career, marriage, and children.

Movement from Dependence to Independence

Young people often are in a conflict between wanting to be independent of their parents but on another level realizing their parents are providing for many of their wants and needs: food, shelter, clothes, emotional support, spending money, and so on. Many young people see their parents as having shortcomings and conclude they know more than their parents. Yet, when their car breaks down and they have no idea of how to fix it, mom or dad almost always knows what to do to get it fixed.

In the pursuit of independence, adolescents often rebel against their parents' attempts to guide them and reject their views as being out of date and stupid. They sometimes do things to shock them as if to say "See, I'm my own person, and I'm going to live my life my way!" Interestingly, once young people become more independent in their 20s and have to pay their own bills, they tend to have a greater appreciation for their parents' knowledge. Mark Twain noted (as quoted in Papalia & Olds, 1981, p. 375), "When I was fourteen my father knew nothing, but when I was twenty-one, I was amazed at how much the old man had learned in those seven years."

Children who are raised in families in which the parents have provided opportunities to learn self-reliance, responsibility, and self-respect tend to make a smoother transition from dependency to adulthood interdependence. Children who are raised in families where the parents are overly permissive or take little interest in their children's behavior tend to have greater difficulty making the transition to adulthood. These young people lack structure or a system of standards and values to gauge whether their behavior is suitable and their decisions are appropriate. Children who have overly protective parents also have difficulty making this transition; they usually do not learn how to assume responsibilities or make important decisions.

Some parents are wary about their children growing up. In particular, some fathers and mothers become alarmed and uncomfortable when their "little girl" starts dating. Many parents worry their daughter may become sexually involved and pregnant, which they believe will interfere with their dreams and hopes for her having a good life. When teenagers assert their right to becoming more independent, it changes the components of the family system. Any change in the components of the system will create tension within the family. This tension is expressed by teens with such statements as, "You don't understand me," "Get off my back," "I know what I'm doing—don't treat me like a baby," and "Chill out."

Parents may feel hurt by what they perceive as a lack of appreciation or gratitude. Common areas of conflict between parents and adolescents are: performing home chores; use of time; attitude toward studies; expenditures of money; morals and manners; choice of friends; clothes selection; use of phone; dating practices; and use of car.

How should parents seek to cope with thrusts of independence from their teenagers? A key is seeking to keep the lines of communication open. All teenagers need help, even if they sometimes do not recognize this need or seem ungrateful for help that is given. Teenagers need to feel that their parents are a resource they can turn to. If communication is severed, teenagers have only their peers to turn to—and the suggestions and advice from another teenager are apt to be less constructive (and potentially more destructive) in resolving a dilemma than suggestions from a responsible adult. Keeping the lines of communications open is admittedly easier said than done. It requires work! Highlight 8.1 offers some techniques for effective communication between adults and young people.

The task of becoming independent involves attaining emotional, social, and economic independence. Emotional independence involves progressing from emotional dependence on parents or on others, to increased independence while still being able to maintain close emotional ties; it involves moving from a parent-child relationship to an adult-adult relationship. Emotional independence involves becoming self-reliant with the knowledge that, "I am put together well enough emotionally that I can fend for myself, but I am willing to share my feelings with others and let them become part of me." Emotional independence involves receiving and sharing and being interdependent, without being emotionally dominated or overwhelmed.

Social independence involves becoming self-directed rather than other-directed. Many adolescents are *other-directed* because they are so strongly motivated for social acceptance that much of what the group says is what adolescents think and do. *Self-directed* people think things out for themselves and make decisions based on their personal interests. Becoming socially independent does not mean becoming selfish. Socially independent people realize their best interests are served by becoming involved in

Highlight 8.1

Interaction in Families: Effective Communication Between Parents and Children

Thomas Gordon (1970), in his book *Parent Effectiveness Training,* identified the following four communication techniques designed to improve relationships between parents and their children.

Active Listening

This technique is recommended for use when a child indicates he or she has a problem. For example, when a 16-year-old daughter looks in a mirror and states, "I'm fat and ugly—everyone but me has a boyfriend." For such situations Gordon recommends that the parent use *active listening.*

The steps involved in active listening are these: The receiver of a message tries to understand what the sender's message means or what the sender is feeling. The receiver then puts this understanding into his or her own words and returns this understanding for the sender's verification. In using this approach, the receiver does *not* send a message of his or her own, such as asking a question, giving advice, expressing feelings, or giving an opinion. The aim is to feed back only what he or she feels the sender's message meant. An active listening response to the 16-year-old girl in the above example might be, "You want very much to have a boyfriend and think the reason you don't is related to your physical appearance." An active listening response involves either *reflecting feelings* or *restating content.*

Dr. Gordon lists a number of advantages for using active listening. It facilitates problem solving by young people, which fosters the development of responsibility. By talking a problem through, a person is more apt to identify the root of the problem and arrive at a solution than by merely thinking about a problem. When a teenager feels his or her parents are listening, a by-product is that he or she will be more apt to listen to the parents' point of view. In addition, the relationship between parent and youth is apt to be improved because children feel they are being heard and understood. Finally, the approach helps a teen to explore, recognize, and express his or her feelings.

Certain parental attitudes are required to use this technique. The parent must view the young person as being a separate person with his or her own feelings. The parent must be able to accept the youth's feelings, whatever they may be. The parent should genuinely want to be helpful and must want to hear what the child has to say. Additionally, the parent must have trust in the child's capacities to handle problems and feelings.

"I"-Messages

Many occasions arise when a young person causes a problem for the parent. For example, a son may turn up the stereo so high that the music is irritating, or he may stay out after curfew hours, or he may recklessly drive an auto. Confronted with such situations, many parents send either a solution message (they order, direct, command, warn, threaten, preach, moralize, or advise), or a put-down message (they blame, judge, criticize, ridicule, or name-call). Solution and put-down messages can have devastating effects on a child's self-concept and are generally counterproductive in helping a child become responsible.

Solution and put-down messages are primarily *you-messages:* "You do what I say," "Don't you do that," "Why don't you be good," "You're lazy," "You should know better."

Dr. Gordon advocates that parents should instead send *I-messages* for those occasions when a teenager is causing a problem for the parent. For example, consider a parent who is riding in a car with the son driving and exceeding the speed limit. Instead of the parent saying, "Slow down, you idiot, before you get us killed," Dr. Gordon urges the parent to use an I-message: "I feel frightened when driving this fast."

I-messages, in essence, are nonblaming messages that communicate only how the sender of the message believes the receiver is adversely affecting the sender. I-messages do not provide a solution, nor are they put-down messages. It is possible to send an I-message without using the word *I* ("Driving this fast really frightens me"). The essence of an I-message involves sending a nonblaming message of how the parent feels the child's behavior is affecting the parent.

You-messages are generally put-downs that either convey to youths that they should do something or that convey to them how bad they are. In contrast, I-messages communicate to young people much more honestly the effect of the behavior on the parent. I-messages are also more effective because they help teenagers learn to assume responsibility for their own behavior. An I-message tells a teenager that the parent is trusting the teen to respect the parent's needs and that the parent is trusting him or her to handle the situation constructively.

You-messages frequently lead to an argument between parent and youth; I-messages are much less likely to do so. I-messages lead to honesty and openness in a relationship, and generally foster intimacy. Teenagers, as well as adults, often do not know how their behavior affects others. I-messages produce startling results; parents frequently report that their teenagers express surprise upon learning how their parents really feel.

Note that I-messages will work only if the youth does not want his actions to adversely affect his parent. If the youth does not want to cause discomfort in his parent, he will seek to change his adversive behavior when informed by an I-message of how he is adversely affecting his parent. However, if the youth enjoys causing discomfort in her parent, then the use of an I-message by the parent is apt to result in an *increase* in the youth's adversive behavior because she is now more fully aware of how to cause discomfort in the parent.

No-Lose Problem Solving

In every parent-teenager relationship, there are inevitable situations where the youth continues to behave in a way that interferes with the needs of the parent. Conflict is part of life and is not necessarily bad. Conflict is bound to occur because people are different and have different needs and wants, which at times do not match. What is important is not how frequently conflict arises, but how the conflicts get resolved. Generally in a conflict between parent and youth, a power struggle is created.

In many families the power struggle is typically resolved by one of two win-lose approaches. Most parents try to resolve the conflict by having the parent win and the young person lose. Psychologically, parents almost always are recognized as having greater authority. The outcome of the parent winning is that it creates resentment in the teenager toward his parents, leads to low motivation for him to carry out the solution, and does not provide an opportunity for him to develop self-discipline and self-responsibility. Such teenagers are likely to react by becoming either hostile, rebellious, and aggressive, or submissive, dependent, and withdrawing.

In other families, fewer in number, the win-lose conflict is resolved by the parents giving in to their teenagers out of fear of frustrating them or fear of conflict. In such families teenagers come to believe their needs are more important than anyone else's. They generally become self-centered, selfish, demanding, impulsive, and uncontrollable. They are viewed as being spoiled by others, have difficulty in interacting with peers, and also do not have respect for property or feelings of others.

Of course, few parents use either approach exclusively. Oscillating between the two approaches is common. There is evidence that both approaches lead to the development of emotional problems in children (Gordon, 1970).

Gordon seriously questions whether power is necessary or justified in a parent-teenager relationship. For one reason, as teenagers grow older, they become less dependent, and parents gradually lose their power. Rewards and punishments that worked in young years become less effective as youths grow older. Teenagers resent those who have power over them, and parents frequently feel guilty after using power. Gordon believes that parents continue to use power because they have had little experience in using nonpower methods of influence.

Gordon suggests a new approach, the *no-lose* approach to solving conflicts. The approach involves parents and youth solving their conflicts by finding their own unique solutions acceptable to both.

The no-lose approach is simple to state—each person in the conflict treats the other with respect, neither person tries to win the conflict by the use of power, and a creative solution acceptable to both parties is sought. The two basic premises to no-lose problem solving are (a) that all people have the right to have their needs met and (b) that what is in conflict between the two parties involved is not their *needs* but their *solutions* to those needs.

Gordon (1970, p. 237) lists the six steps in the no-lose method as:

Step 1: Identifying and defining the needs of each person.

Step 2: Generating possible alternative solutions.

Step 3: Evaluating the alternative solutions.

Step 4: Deciding on the best acceptable solution.

Step 5: Working out ways of implementing the solution.

Step 6: Following up to evaluate how it worked.

This approach motivates youths to carry out the solution because they participated in the decision. It develops their thinking skills and a sense of responsibility. It requires less enforcement, eliminates the need for power, and improves relationships between parents. It also develops their problem-solving skills.

Collisions of Values

Collisions of values are common between parents and their children, particularly as the children become adolescents and young adults. Likely areas of conflict include values about sexual behavior, clothing, religion, choice of friends, education, plans for the future, use of drugs, hairstyles, and eating habits. In these areas emotions run strong, and parents generally seek to influence their offspring to follow the values the parents hold as important. Teenagers, on the other hand, often think their parents' values are old-fashioned and declare that they want to make their own decisions about these matters.

Gordon identifies three constructive ways in which parents and teenagers can seek to resolve these conflicts. (For the sake of simplicity, we will use the term *mother* in describing what should be done—a father or a teenager can also use these same techniques.)

The first way a mother can influence her offspring's values is to model the values she holds as important. If she values honesty, she should be honest. If she values responsible use of alcohol, she should exhibit a responsible model. If she values openness, she should be open. She needs to ask herself if she is living according to the values she professes. If her values and behavior are incongruent in certain areas, she needs to change either her values or behavior in the direction of congruency. Congruence between behavior and values is important if she wants to be an effective model.

The second way she can influence her teenagers' values is to act as a consultant to them. There are some do's and don'ts of a good consultant. First of all, a good consultant finds out whether the other person would like her consultation. If the answer is "yes," she then makes sure she has all the available pertinent facts. She then shares these facts—once—so that the young person understands them. She then leaves him or her the responsibility for deciding whether to follow the advice, or not. A good consultant is neither uninformed nor a nag; otherwise she is not apt to be used as a consultant again.

The third way for a mother to reduce tensions over values issues is to modify her values. By examining the values held by her teenagers, she may realize their values have merit, and she may move toward their values or at least toward an understanding of why they hold them as values.

Note that all of these techniques for more effective communication can be used to improve communication and relationships in practically all interactions, such as adult-adult and counselor-client. The techniques are much broader in application than just a parent-teenager interaction.

Source: Adapted from Charles Zastrow, *The Practice of Social Work*, 2nd ed. (Homewood, IL: Dorsey, 1985). Used with permission of Dorsey Press.

political, civic, educational, religious, social, and community affairs.

Economic independence involves earning sufficient money to meet one's financial needs. Many older teenagers and young adults do not have special skills, and therefore obtaining good-paying jobs to meet their financial needs is very difficult. Economic independence also involves learning to limit one's desires and purchases to ability to pay. To become economically independent it is necessary to develop at least one marketable set of skills that one can offer an employer in exchange for a job. Interestingly, the more money that people earn, the more material items they usually desire; from their improved financial position, they see a whole new set of material items that they "just have to have."

Interaction in Peer Group Systems

Adolescents have a strong *herd* drive and desire to be accepted by their peers. Peers are an important influence on adolescents. Some studies indicate that peers are more of a factor than parents in determining whether a youth will become involved in serious juvenile delinquency (Papalia et al., 1998, p. 391). However, a study by Patterson, DeBaryshe, and Ramsey (1989) indicates that the strongest predictor of delinquency is the family's supervision and discipline of children. The process of becoming delinquent, this study found, starts out in childhood and has its roots in troubled parent-child interactions. Children get certain payoffs for antisocial behavior: they get attention or their own way by acting up, and they avoid punishment by lying or by cheating on school tests. Children's antisocial behavior interferes with their school work and their ability to get along with their classmates. As a result, these children—unpopular and nonachieving—seek out other antisocial children. These children influence each other and learn new forms of problem behavior from one another.

The particular kind of peer group that an adolescent selects depends on a variety of factors: socioeconomic status (most peer groups are bound by social class); values derived from parents; the neighborhood one lives in; the nature of the school; special talents and abilities; and the personality of the adolescent. Once an adolescent becomes a member of a peer group, the members of that subgroup influence each other in their social activities, study habits, dress, sexual behavior, use or nonuse of drugs, vocational pursuits, and hobbies.

Not all adolescents join cliques. Some prefer to be loners. Some are already pursuing what they believe will be their life goals. Some may be busy baby-sitting for younger children in the family. Some prefer having only one or two close friends. Some are excluded from the cliques that exist in their area.

Adolescents tend to identify with other teenagers, rather than with adults or younger children. This identification may be due to teens believing that most other teens share their personal values and interests, whereas younger and older people have more divergent interests and values. Compared to people in their 40s and 50s, adolescents view themselves as being less materialistic, more idealistic, healthier sexually, and better able to understand friendships and what is important in life. Spotlight 8.1 describes issues about ethnic-group identity that face minority adolescents.

Friends and peer groups help adolescents and young adults make the transition from parental dependence to independence. Friends give each other emotional support and serve as important points of reference for young people to compare their beliefs, values, attitudes, and abilities. In a number of cases friendships forged during adolescence endure throughout life.

Intimacy versus Isolation

Erikson (1950) theorized that after young people develop a sense of identity, they next face the psychosocial crisis of intimacy versus isolation, which generally occurs in young adulthood (roughly during the 20s). *Intimacy* is the capacity to experience an open, tender, supportive relationship with another person, without fear of losing one's own identity in the process of growing close. In such a relationship the partners are able to understand, cognitively and emotionally, each other's points of view. An intimate relationship permits the sharing of personal feelings as well as the disclosure of ideas and plans that are not fully developed. There is respect for each other and mutual enrichment in the interactions. Each person perceives an enhancement of his or her well-being through the stimulating interactions with the other.

Intimacy involves being empathetic and able to give and receive pleasure within the relationship. Although intimacy is often established within the context of a marital relationship, marriage itself does not produce intimacy. In some marriages there is considerable intimacy (including sharing and mutual respect). However, in empty-shell marriages and in marriages with considerable conflict, there is very little intimacy. There are additional contexts where intimacy is apt to develop. The work setting is one of these, where close friendships are often formulated. Close friendships are also apt to develop through membership in social and religious organizations.

Traditional socialization patterns in our society create different problems for males and females in the

Spotlight on Diversity 8.1

Ethnic-Group Identity for Minority Adolescents

One of the most challenging aspects of establishing group identity for minority adolescents is the formation of an ethnic-group identity. Ethnic identity involves not only knowing that one is a member of a certain ethnic group, but also recognizing that some aspects of one's thoughts, actions, and feelings are influenced by one's ethnic identity. One's ethnic group thus becomes a significant reference group whose values, goals, and outlook are taken into account as one makes important choices in life. Ethnic identity varies among individuals within a group, and varies across ethnic groups. One reason for the variation is that some minority adolescents have had more exposure to the cultural norms and values of their ethnic group than other minority adolescents.

In the United States a history of discrimination, violence, and negative imagery has been associated with a number of ethnic groups, including African Americans, Native Americans, Latinos, and Asian Americans. Minority adolescents most struggle with the negative stereotypes that are associated with their own ethnic groups.

Issues of ethnic identity may not become salient until early adolescence. Newman and Newman (1999, p. 340) note:

As minority children grow up, they tend to incorporate many of the ideals and values of the Anglo culture. Suddenly in adolescence, however, they may find themselves excluded from it. At that time, peer groups become more structured. Sanctions against cross-race

friendships and dating relationships become more intense. Minority adolescents may encounter more overt rejection and failure in academic achievement, employment, and school leadership. They may find that their family and ethnic-group values are actually in conflict with the values of the majority culture. These minority adolescents may also feel that they have to choose between their ethnic-group identity and membership in a nonminority group. In some cases, commitment to an ethnic-group identity takes the place of membership in some other peer group. In other instances, minority youths are rejected by their Anglo peers. They may then flounder, not having established a clear ethnic identity, and may struggle through a period of bitter rejection.

The more fully immersed minority adolescents are in the values and traditions of their ethnic culture, the more likely it is that they will experience a dual identity—for example, viewing themselves as an American and a Japanese American. Newman and Newman (1999, p. 340) note: "Over time, and with the benefit of exposure to reading, conversations, and interactions with people from other subgroups, young people begin to synthesize a sense of how their ethnic identity fits into their overall personal identity and how it will influence the quality of their relationships with members of their own and other ethnic groups."

---

establishment of intimacy. Boys are taught to be restrained in expressing their feelings and personal thoughts. They are also socialized to be competitive and self-reliant. They are raised to believe that they should be sexually aggressive and seek to "go as far as possible" in order to demonstrate their virility to their male friends. Males are thus unprepared for intimate heterosexual relationships—which require that they express their feelings, be supportive rather than competitive, and have a commitment to continuing the relationship rather than piling up sexual trophies.

Traditionally, girls are socialized to be better prepared for the emotional demands of intimacy. They are socialized to express their feelings and personal thoughts and to be nurturant. They may, however, enter an intimate relationship with inappropriate expectations based on traditional gender-role stereotypes. For example, they may expect their partner to be stronger or more resourceful than he is. (The women's movement has changed gender-role expectations and socialization practices for males and females; hopefully, the difficulties that men and women experience in forming intimate relationships will be reduced in future years.)

The negative pole of the crisis of young adulthood is isolation. People who resist intimacy continually erect

barriers between themselves and others. Some people view intimacy as a blurring of the boundaries of their own identity and therefore are reluctant to become involved in intimate relationships. Some people are so busy seeking or maintaining their identity that they cannot share and express themselves in an intimate relationship.

Isolation may also result from situational factors. A young person may be so involved in studying to get into medical school that he or she may not have the time for an intimate relationship. Or, a teenage female may become pregnant, deliver and start raising the child, and then have few opportunities to become involved in a close relationship with an adult.

Isolation may also result from diverging spheres of activity and interest. An example of how isolation may develop in a traditional marriage involves Bill and Mary Ramsey. They married while in their early 20s, after dating for 4 years and enjoying doing many activities together. They were very much in love. They both wanted a traditional marriage. In their early years of marriage, they had two children, and Mary was content to stay at home to raise them. In her leisure time she interacted with the other wives in the neighborhood. Bill, on the other hand, worked as an insurance agent and spent his leisure hours hunting, fishing, and attending spectator sporting events with male friends. As the years passed, Mary and Bill had less and less in common. Isolation became increasingly evident in their lack of mutual understanding and their lack of support for each other's needs and life goals.

Empowerment of Homeless Youth

Youth in poverty often experience a special sense of powerlessness and hopelessness that is even more intensified for those who are homeless. Although no one knows exactly how many young people are homeless in the United States, this has been established as a significant problem (Coleman & Kerbo, 2002). Homeless youth tend to experience many serious difficulties including those that are health-related and those involving the mental health, substance abuse, and unemployment of other family members, especially parents (Coleman & Kerbo, 2002). Few resources and supports exist for such young people in their immediate social environments.

Rees (1998) proposes that social workers can help homeless youth become more empowered by helping them progress through four stages. The stages are based on the ability of youth to express themselves and their experiences through biographical storytelling. Stage 1 involves "understanding powerlessness" (p. 137). Young people must be allowed to express their despair, disappointment, fear, and hurt before social workers and others rush in to help them. They must get their feelings out before they can begin to focus on positive change.

Stage 2 is "awareness and mutual education" (p. 138). After expressing feelings, homeless youth should be encouraged to talk about their experiences, as painful as they have been. Articulating and sharing experiences can help young people organize their thoughts and identify themes characterizing their lives. Rees (1998) comments that "this stage of dawning awareness gives practitioners a chance to encourage young people to construct their stories so they can begin to think of different choices in their lives. Usually their stories reconstruct experiences of powerlessness. . . . Such spelling out is a crucial part of empowerment" (p. 139).

Stage 3 is "dialogue and solidarity" (p. 140). After telling their stories, continuing to exchange information and share feelings with others provides opportunities to learn from and support each other. Such discourse can involve their rights to education, services, income, housing, and legal assistance. They can help each other begin to formulate plans for empowering themselves and demanding access to resources. Together, homeless youth can establish solidarity, supporting each other in their quest for empowerment.

Stage 4 is "action and political identity" (p. 141). This involves a sense of self-confidence in one's ability to make progress, seek changes in conditions, and improve one's overall quality of life. Political identity is the sense that one has the right and power to seek improvements in life. Effects can include an improved self-concept, more effective communication skills, better relationships with professionals and family, and more productive interactions

Adolescents seek to conform to their peers.

with resource providers and legal system representatives. Rees (1998) furnishes two example of homeless youth experiencing empowerment. Sean's empowerment involved seeing that his future could become more than an early, violent death. He gained confidence in his ability to advocate for himself with health-care professionals, the police, and resource providers. Dean indicated that for the first time he had some hope that someday he would get a job and even live in a home of his own, things he never thought were possible before. He began to like himself more and eagerly participated in a job training program.

Interaction in Family Systems: Choosing a Personal Lifestyle

Most people make decisions during their young adult years about how they want to live their adult years. (As time goes on, it is important to remember that a person has a right to make changes in the following decisions.) Decisions about lifestyles include whether to marry or stay single; whether or not to have children; what kind of career to pursue; what area of the country to live in; whether to live in an apartment, duplex, or house; and so on. In choosing a lifestyle, what is actually experienced by many is not a matter of ideal choice, but rather a result of opportunities. In other words, financial resources, personal deficiencies, discrimination, and so on may greatly prevent or modify free choice. In addition, unexpected life events (such as unplanned pregnancy, divorce, or death of a spouse) can greatly alter a person's lifestyle and family living arrangements. In regard to lifestyles and family forms, we will take a brief look at the following areas: marriage, cohabitation, single life, parenthood, and the life of a childless couple.

Marriage

Throughout recorded history, regardless of the simplicity or sophistication of the society, the family has been the basic biological and social unit in which most adults and children live. In addition, all past and present societies sanction the family through the institution of marriage. Clayton (1975) suggests that one of the primary reasons for instituting the custom of marriage was to enable the two partners to enjoy sexuality as fully as possible with a minimum of anxieties and hazards. The natural sex drive of men and women needs to be satisfied, yet control needs to be exercised over the spread of sexually transmitted diseases. Children that result from sexual relationships need to be raised and cared for.

Close to 92 percent of all adults will get married in our society. More than 90 percent of all married couples will have children (Papalia et al., 2001). In our society people marry for a variety of reasons including desire for children, economic security, social position, love, parents' wishes, escape, pregnancy, companionship, sexual attraction, common interests, and adventure. Other reasons for marrying include societal expectations, and the psychological need to feel wanted more than anyone else by someone and to be of value to another person. Highlight 8.2

Highlight 8.2

Theories about Why People Choose Each Other as Mates

The reasons that people choose each other as partners are complex and vary greatly. Certainly such factors as religion, age, race, ethnic group, social class, and parental pressure influence the choice of mates. In addition, many theories suggest additional factors. Some of these theories are summarized here. No theory fully identifies all of the factors involved in mate selection, and mate selection may involve aspects of more than one theory.

Propinquity theory asserts that being in close proximity is a major factor in mate selection. This theory suggests we are apt to select a mate with whom we are in close association, such as at school or at work, or whom we meet through neighborhood, church, or recreational activities (Rubin, 1973).

Ideal mate theory suggests we choose a mate who has the characteristics and traits we desire in a partner.

This theory is symbolized by the statement, "He's everything I've ever wanted."

Congruence in values theory holds that our value system consciously and unconsciously guides us in selecting a mate who has similar values (Grush & Yehl, 1979).

Homogamy theory suggests that we select a mate who has similar racial, economic, and social characteristics.

Complementary needs theory holds that we either select a partner who has the characteristics we wish we had ourselves or someone who can help us be the kind of person we want to be.

Compatibility theory asserts that we select a mate with whom we can enjoy a variety of activities. This is someone who will understand us, accept us, and with whom we feel comfortable in communicating because that person has a similar philosophy of life.

presents some theories as to why people choose whom they do as mates. In our impersonal and materialistic society, marriage helps meet the need to belong because it helps to provide emotional support and security, affection, love, and companionship.

Predictors of Marital Success. A number of studies have sought to identify factors associated with marital happiness and marital unhappiness (Kail & Cavanaugh, 2000; Kornblum & Julian, 2001; Papalia et al., 2001; Santrock, 1999). Some factors are associated in a predictive manner with whether the marriage will be happy or not. Other factors are related to whether an already existing marriage is happy or not. The findings in these studies are summarized in Highlight 8.3.

Benefits of Marriage. Marriage leads to the formation of a family, and the family unit is recognized as the primary unit in which children are to be produced and raised. The marriage bond thus provides for an orderly replacement of the population. The family is the primary institution for the rearing of and socializing of children.

Marriage also provides an available and regulated outlet for sexual activity. Failure to regulate sexual behavior would result in clashes between individuals due to jealousy and exploitation. Every society has rules that

Highlight 8.3

Predictive Factors Leading to Marital Happiness/Unhappiness

Factors for Marital Happiness

Premarital Factors
Parents' marriage is happy
Personal happiness in childhood
Mild but firm discipline by parents
Harmonious relationship with parents
Gets along well with the opposite sex
Acquainted for more than 1 year before marriage
Parental approval of the marriage
Similarity of age
Satisfaction with affection of partner
Love
Common interests
Optimistic outlook on life
Emotional stability
Sympathetic attitude
Similarity of cultural backgrounds
Compatible religious beliefs
Satisfying occupation and working conditions
A love relationship growing out of companionship rather than infatuation

Self-insight and self-acceptance
Awareness of the needs of one's partner
Coping ability
Interpersonal social skills
Positive self-identity
Holding common values

Factors during Marriage
Good communication skills
Equalitarian relationship
Good relationship with in-laws
Desire for children
Similar interests
Responsible love, respect, and friendship
Sexual compatibility
Enjoying leisure-time activities together
Companionship and an affectional relationship
Capacity to receive as well as give

Factors for Marital Unhappiness

Premarital Factors
Parents divorced
Parent or parents deceased
Incongruity of main personality traits with partner
Acquainted less than 1 year before marriage
Loneliness as a major reason for marriage
Escape from one's own family as major reason for marriage
Marriage at a young age, particularly under age 20
Predisposition to unhappiness in one or the other spouse
Intense personal problems

Factors during Marriage
Husband more dominant
Wife more dominant
Jealous of spouse
Feeling of superiority to spouse
Feeling of being more intelligent than spouse
Living with in-laws
Whining, acting defensively, being stubborn, and withdrawing by walking away or not talking to spouse
Domestic violence

regulate sexual behavior within family units (for example, incest taboos).

A marriage is also an arrangement to meet emotional needs of the partners, such as affection, companionship, approval, encouragement, and reinforcement for accomplishments. (Interestingly, Highlight 8.4 indicates that emotional needs are better satisfied over the long term by rational love than by romantic love.) If people do not have such affective needs met, emotional, intellectual, physical, and social growth will be stunted. (Our high divorce rate indicates that this ideal of achieving an emotionally satisfying relationship is not easily obtained.) Married people of all ages tend to report somewhat higher rates of satisfaction about their lives than people who are single, divorced, or widowed (Papalia et al., 1998, p. 453). Two alternative factors may be operating here—either a number of people do find happiness in marriage, or else happy people are more apt to be married.

Marriage also correlates with good health. Married people live longer, particularly men (Papalia et al., 1998). But we cannot conclude that marriage *confers* health. Healthy people may be more interested in getting married, may be better marriage partners, and may attract mates more easily. Or, married people may lead safer, healthier lives than single people.

Widowed and divorced men have shorter life expectancies than single men, whose life expectancy is closest to the rate of married men (Hu & Goldman, 1990). Perhaps widowed and divorced men have shorter life expectancies because they feel they have less to live for.

The marriage relationship encourages personal growth; it provides a setting for the partners to share their innermost thoughts. In a marriage, a lot of decisions need to be made. Should the husband and wife both pursue careers? Do they want children? How will the domestic tasks be divided? How much time will be spent with relatives? Should they buy a new car or a house? Should a vacation be taken this year; if so, where? Problems in these areas can erupt into crises that, if resolved constructively, can lead to personal growth. Through successful resolution, people often learn more about themselves and are better able to handle future crises. However, if the problems remain unresolved, conflict may fester and considerable discord result.

Highlight 8.5 summarizes some useful guidelines for building and maintaining a successful marriage. (This chapter focuses on heterosexual marriages. Chapter 13 provides some material on gay and lesbian marriages.)

Cohabitation

Cohabitation is the open living together of an unmarried couple. Most such couples live together for a relatively short time (less than 2 years) before they either marry or separate (Papalia et al., 2001). For some, cohabitation serves as a trial marriage. For others it offers a temporary or permanent alternative to marriage. And for many young people, it has become the modern equivalent of dating and going steady.

People who cohabitated before marriage do not have better marriages than those who did not. In fact, some research shows that couples who lived together before getting married report lower-quality marriages and a lower commitment to the institution of marriage—and a greater likelihood of divorce than noncohabiting couples (Papalia et al., 2001).

Why do couples decide to live together without a marriage ceremony? The reasons are not fully clear. Many people want close intimate and sexual arrangements but are not ready for the financial and long-term commitments of a marriage. With our society being more accepting of cohabitation than in the past, some couples appear to be choosing this living arrangement. To some extent, they can have friendship, companionship, and a sexual relationship, without the long-term commitment of marriage. Living with someone helps many young adults to learn more about themselves, to better understand what is involved in an intimate relationship, and to grow as a person. Cohabitating may also help some people clarify what they want in a mate and in a marriage.

Cohabitating also has its problems, some of which are similar to those encountered by newlyweds: adjusting to an intimate relationship, working out a sexual relationship, overdependency on the partner, missing what one did when living alone, and seeing friends less. Other problems are unique to cohabitation, such as explaining the relationship to parents and relatives, discomfort about the ambiguity of the future, and a desire for a long-term commitment from one's partner.

Closely related to cohabitating is a relationship in which the man and woman maintain separate addresses and domiciles, but live together for several days a month (perhaps on weekends). This latter form is more of a trial honeymoon than a trial marriage. When people live together for only a few days a month, they are apt to seek to put their best foot forward.

In some recent instances courts have decided that cohabitating couples who dissolve their nonmarital living arrangements have certain legal obligations to one another. For example, some courts (under certain circumstances, such as an oral agreement between the two individuals to pool their earnings) view assets acquired during the time the couple was living together as being "marital property," which then is divided (sometimes not equally) between the two individuals after the relationship is dissolved.

Highlight 8.4

Romantic Love versus Rational Love

Achieving a gratifying, long-lasting love relationship is one of our paramount goals. The experience of feeling in love is exciting, adds meaning to living, and psychologically gives us a good feeling about ourselves. Unfortunately, few people are able to maintain a long-term love relationship. Instead, many people encounter problems with love relationships, including: falling in love with someone who does not love them; falling out of love with someone after an initial stage of infatuation; being highly possessive of someone they love; and having substantial conflicts with the loved one because of differing sets of expectations about the relationship. Failures in love relationships are more often the rule than the exception.

The emotion of love, in particular, is often viewed (erroneously) as being a feeling over which we have no control. A number of common expressions connote or imply that love is a feeling beyond our control: "I fell in love," "It was love at first sight," "I just couldn't help it," and, "He swept me off my feet." It is more useful to think of the emotion of love as being primarily based on our self-talk (that is, what we tell ourselves) about a person we meet. *Romantic love* can be diagrammed as follows:

Event
Meeting or becoming acquainted with a person who has *some* of the overt characteristics you want in a lover.

Self-Talk
"This person is attractive, personable; has all of the qualities I admire in a lover/mate."

Emotion
Intense infatuation, being romantically in love; a feeling of being in ecstasy.

Romantic love is often based on self-talk that stems from intense unsatisfied desires and frustrations, rather than on reason or rational thinking. Unsatisfied desires and frustrations include extreme sexual frustration, intense loneliness, parental and personal problems, and extensive desires for security and protection.

A primary characteristic of romantic love is to idealize the person with whom we are infatuated; that is, we notice this person has some overt characteristics we desire in a lover and then conclude that this person has *all* the desired characteristics.

A second characteristic is that romantic love thrives on a certain amount of distance. The more forbidden the love, the stronger it becomes. The more social mores are threatened, the stronger the feeling. (For example, couples who live together and then later marry often report living together was more exciting and romantic.) The more effort necessary to be with each other (e.g., traveling long distances), the more intense the romance. The greater the frustration (e.g., loneliness or sexual needs), the more intense the romance.

The irony of romantic love is that, if an ongoing relationship is achieved, the romance usually withers. Through sustained contact, the person in love gradually comes to realize what the idealized loved one is really like—simply another human being with certain strengths and limitations. When this occurs, the romantic love relationship either turns into a rational love relationship, or the relationship is found to have significant conflicts and dissatisfactions and ends in a broken romance. For people with intense unmet desires, the latter occurs more frequently.

Romantic love thus tends to be of temporary duration and based on make-believe. A person experiencing romantic love never loves the real person—only an idealized image of the person.

Rational love, in contrast, can be diagrammed in the following way.

Event
While being aware and comfortable about your own needs, goals, identity, and desires, you become well acquainted with someone who fulfills, to a fair extent, the characteristics you desire in a lover/spouse.

Self-Talk
"This person has many of the qualities and attributes I seek in a lover/spouse. I admire this person's strengths, and I am aware and accepting of his or her shortcomings."

Emotion
Rational love

The following are ingredients of a rational love relationship: You are clear and comfortable about your desires, identity, and goals in life. You know the other person well. You have accurately and objectively assessed the loved one's strengths and shortcomings and are generally accepting of the shortcomings. Your self-talk about this person is consistent with your short- and long-term goals. Your self-talk is realistic and rational, so that your feelings are not based on fantasy, excessive desires, or pity. You and this person are able to communicate openly and honestly, so that problems can be dealt with when they arise and so that the relationship can continue to grow and develop. Rational love also involves giving and receiving; it involves being kind, showing affection, knowing and doing what pleases the other person, communicating openly and warmly, and so on.

Because love is based on self-talk that causes feelings, it is we who create love. *Theoretically,* it is possible to love anyone by making changes in our self-talk. On the other hand, if we are in love with someone, we can gauge the quality of the relationship by analyzing our self-talk to determine the nature of our attraction and to determine the extent to which our self-talk is rational and in our best interests.

Source: Charles Zastrow, *You Are What You Think: A Guide to Self-Realization* (Chicago: Nelson-Hall, 1993).

Highlight 8.5

Guidelines for Building and Maintaining a Happy Marriage

A successful and satisfying marriage requires ongoing work by each partner. The following are some useful guidelines on how to achieve and maintain a successful marriage:

1. Keep the lines of communication open. Learn to bite the bullet on minor or unimportant issues. Voice the concerns that are important to you, but in a way that does not attack, blame, or threaten the other person. Seek to use I-messages, which were described earlier in this chapter in Highlight 8.1.

2. Seek to foster the happiness, personal growth, and well-being of your spouse as much as you seek to foster your own happiness and personal growth.

3. Seek to use the no-lose problem-solving technique to settle conflicts with partners (as described in Highlight 8.1), rather than the win-lose technique. Be tolerant and accepting of trivial shortcomings and annoyances.

4. Do not try to possess, stifle, or control your partner. Also, do not seek to mold your partner into a carbon copy of your opinions, values, beliefs, or of your personal likes and dislikes.

5. Be aware that everyone has up and down mood swings. When your partner is in a down cycle, seek to be considerate and understanding.

6. When arguments occur—and they will—try to fight fair. Limit the discussion to the issue, and keep past events and personality traits out of the fight.

7. Be affectionate, share pleasant events, be a friend and a good listener.

Single Life

Some people choose to remain single; they like being alone and prefer not being with others much of the time. Others end up being single because they do not find a partner they want to marry or because they are in relationships with a partner who chooses not to marry. Historically, there was a greater expectation that people would marry than at the present time. Now, people are freer to make decisions about whether to marry and what kind of lifestyle to seek.

Single people have fewer emotional and financial obligations. They do not need to consider how their decisions and actions will affect a spouse and children. They are freer to take economic, physical, and social risks. They can devote more time to the pursuit of their individual interests.

Studies reviewed by Papalia and her associates (2001) reported the following advantages of being single as listed by respondents who were not married: satisfaction of being self-sufficient, increased career opportunities, an exciting lifestyle, mobility, sexual availability, the freedom to change, opportunities to have a variety of experiences, opportunities to play a variety of roles, and opportunities to have friendships with a variety of people. Reported disadvantages of being single include: wondering how single people fit into the social world of mostly married people; lack of companionship; concerns about how well friends and family accept unmarried adults; and concerns about how being single affects self-esteem.

Parenthood

The birth of a baby is a major life event. (See Highlight 8.6 for material on parental gender preferences.) Caring for a baby changes lifestyles of parents and also changes the marriage. For some, caring for a child (who is totally dependent) is a troublesome crisis. For others, caring for a baby is viewed as a fulfillment and an enhancement of life. For many couples, parenthood has troublesome aspects, while it also enhances their lives.

What are some of the problem areas of parenthood? The birth of a baby signals to parents that they are now adults and no longer children; they now have responsibilities not only to themselves, but also in caring for someone who needs 24-hour care. A baby demands a huge amount of time and attention.

Women generally assume the majority of both household and child-care responsibilities. Levinson (1996) has found that the more the division of labor in a marriage changes from egalitarian to traditional, the more marital happiness declines, especially for nontraditional wives.

Thompson and Walker (1989) found that one-third of mothers view mothering as both enjoyable and meaningful, a third find it unpleasant and not meaningful, and another third report mixed experiences. Fathers tend to treasure and to be emotionally committed to their children, but they generally report less enjoyment in looking after them than mothers do.

Highlight 8.6

Parental Gender Preferences

In most countries boys are generally preferred to girls. Although it is the male's sperm that determines the gender of the child,* in many developing countries and countries where the status of women is low, a woman's capacity to remain married may depend on her producing sons. In some of these countries, boys are fed better, given better medical care, and receive more schooling. The death rate for female children is significantly higher than for male children because female children are more apt to be neglected.

In the United States, couples who want only one child usually desire a boy. Those who want two, generally desire one of each; and those who prefer three usually want two boys and one girl. Men, in particular, tend to have a strong preference for a boy. The reasons a couple desires a boy or a girl vary. Those couples desiring a boy generally prefer someone to carry on the family name and bring honor to the family; those who prefer a girl want someone who is easier to raise, is lovable, is fun to dress, and is able to help with the housework (Santrock, 1999).

*Sperm carrying the X chromosome will produce a female; sperm carrying the Y chromosome will produce a male.

Why do people have children? Historically, in agricultural and preindustrial societies children were an economic asset; their labor was important in planting and harvesting crops and in tending domestic animals. Parents wanted large families to help with the work. When parents became elderly, children tended to provide much of the care. Because children were an economic asset, values were gradually established that it was natural and desirable for married couples to want to have children. Motherhood became invested with a unique emotional aura. Some psychological theories reflected this aura by asserting that women (interestingly, not men) had a nurturing instinct that could only be fulfilled by having and caring for children. (It now appears the supposed nurturing instinct was in reality a value that was largely learned by women through socialization practices.)

Today, children are an economic liability, rather than an economic asset. In our society there is an expectation that Social Security and other retirement programs will care for elderly parents, rather than this being a responsibility of their children. Children can have negative, as well as positive, effects on lifestyles and on marital relationships. For these and other reasons, married couples in our society over the years have gradually decided to have fewer children. Now most couples usually want zero to three children. Contraception devices now make such wishes a reality.

Parenthood has many rewards and many joyful moments. Some of the rewards include having someone to love and return that love, the joy of playing and interacting with a child, watching and helping a child grow and develop, and socializing with other parents.

Parenthood also has many demands and stresses, including discipline problems, increased responsibilities, financial demands, interference with previous lifestyles, cleaning up messes, trying to accomplish some task while stepping over a child, running time-consuming errands, planning a schedule around a child's needs, listening to a crying or whining child, changing diapers, interrupted rest and sleep, fatigue, and concerns about being able to give less attention to personal appearance.

Children are less likely to lower marital satisfaction in families where the parents desired to have children, and where the parents have outside resources for helping to care for the children. In marriages that deteriorate after parenthood, one or both partners tend to have low self-esteem, and the husbands were likely to be less sensitive (Belsky & Rovine, 1988). The partners in deteriorating marriages were also more likely to be younger and less educated, to earn less money, and to have been married for fewer years.

Even when parenting has a negative influence on marital satisfaction, it often has a positive effect on the self-concepts of the parents and on their work roles. Thus, parenting appears to contribute to the personal development of an individual.

The Group for the Advancement of Psychiatry (1973) views parenting as a developmental process and has identified the following four stages:

1. *Anticipation:* This stage occurs during pregnancy when the expectant parents think about how they will raise their children, how their lives will change, and the meaning of parenthood. Some expectant parents have ambivalent feelings about what lies ahead. During this stage the expectant parents begin the process of viewing themselves as their children's parents, instead of being their parents' children.

2. *Honeymoon:* This stage occurs after the birth of the first child and lasts for a few months. Parents

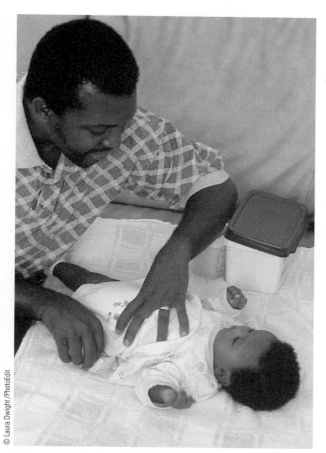

Fathers generally report less enjoyment in looking after children than mothers do, but fathers who enjoy parenting usually see it as being one of their most important life roles.

are often very happy about having and holding a baby. It is also a time of adjustment and learning, as attachments are formed between parents and child, and family members learn new roles in relation to one another.

3. *Plateau:* This stage occurs from infancy through the teenage years. Frequent adjustments must be made by the parents, as parents adapt their parenting behavior to the level of the child.

4. *Disengagement:* This stage occurs at the time when the child disengages (for example, when the child marries). Because the child disengages, the parents should also change their behavior and disengage from the child. Relationships change from parent-child in nature to adult-adult.

These stages illustrate the fact that children have a great effect on parents. The Group for the Advancement of Psychiatry (1973) also notes that parents often judge their parenting on how well their children turn out. When children fulfill their expectations, the parents usually pat themselves on the back for a job well done. The danger of this approach is that if the children fall short of meeting parental expectations (which sometimes are unrealistic), parents are apt to conclude they failed. Parents need to realize the final product is not entirely under their control because children are influenced by many other factors that are external to the family.

Childless Couples

Having children is recognized legally and religiously as being one of the central components of a marriage. In our society there still continues to be a value that something is wrong with a couple if they decide not to have children. This value, however, is no longer as strongly held as it once was. Perhaps in the future this value will cease to exist due to the problem of overpopulation and the high cost of raising children. The average cost of raising a child from birth to age 18 is estimated to be $161,000 in low-income families, $225,000 in middle-income families, and $315,000 in upper-income families (Kail & Cavanaugh, 2000).

Married couples may decide not to have children. Some feel they do not have what it takes to be good parents. Some have heavy commitments to their careers or to their hobbies and do not want to take time away from them to raise a family. Others feel that having children would be an intrusion into their marital relationship. Still others enjoy the freedom to travel, to make spur-of-the-moment plans, and do not want their lifestyle changed. Some feel choosing not to have children is desirable in order to avoid contributing to the problem of overpopulation.

Unwanted children are adversely affected in a variety of ways; they are more apt to be abused, have more frequent illnesses, receive poorer school grades, and have more behavior problems than children whose births are desired (Kail & Cavanaugh, 2000). Such findings suggest that if couples do not want to have children, it is probably in their best interest and that of society for them not to do so.

✹ Social Problems

In addition to going through normal phases of social development (such as developing an identity and choosing a lifestyle), a number of situations and life crises tend to occur in adolescence and young adulthood. The following material will focus on certain social problems: eating disorders; emotional and behavioral problems; crime and delinquency; and delinquent gangs. The latter two can be viewed as macro system problems because large systems are often involved in the planning and carrying out of criminal activity, and large systems are involved in investigating, prosecuting, preventing, and curbing criminal activity.

Eating Disorders

Eating disorders are occurring in epidemic proportions. Although they have existed for a long period of time, the dramatic increase in the number of individuals affected is now a major concern for mental health professionals. The majority of people who have an eating disorder are female. The three primary eating disorders are anorexia nervosa, bulimia nervosa, and compulsive overeating. All three are serious disorders that create life-threatening health problems.

Anorexia Nervosa. *Anorexia nervosa* means "loss of appetite due to nerves." This definition is inaccurate, because people with anorexia do not actually lose their appetite until the late stages of their starvation. Until then, they do feel hungry, but they just do not eat. Anorexia nervosa is a disorder characterized by the excessive pursuit of thinness through voluntary starvation. The predominant features of this disorder include excessive thinness, intense fear of gaining weight or becoming fat, a distorted body image in which anorexics view themselves as being overweight, and amenorrhea (cessation of menses) in females.

Anorexics refuse to accept the fact that they are too thin. They eat very little, even when experiencing intense hunger. They insist they need to lose even more weight. They erroneously believe that an ultrathin body is a perfect body, and that achieving such a body will bring happiness and success. As they lose weight, their health deteriorates and they tend to become increasingly depressed. Symptoms of physical deterioration include reduced heart rate, lowered blood pressure, lowered body temperature, increased retention of water, fine hair growth on many parts of their body, amenorrhea in females, and a variety of metabolic changes (Koch et al., 2001). Even while their health is deteriorating, anorexics stubbornly cling to the belief that through controlling their body weight, they can gain control of their lives.

On the surface someone who is prone to develop anorexia appears to be a model child. She is eager to please, well-behaved, a good student, and someone who appears to get along well with her peers. She rarely asks for help, and she is unlikely to indicate that anything is wrong. Behind this mask is an insecure, self-critical perfectionist who feels she is unworthy of any praise that she receives.

She is also apt to be concerned about whether other people like her.

The development of this disorder usually proceeds according to the following pattern.

Step 1: It begins with a diet. Dieting for these individuals usually begins just before or just after a major change occurs—such as beginning of puberty, breaking up with a boyfriend, or leaving home for college.

Step 2: Dieting creates a feeling of control. At first the person feels better about herself because dieting is something she can do successfully. Soon, however, food and the fear of becoming fat become the major concerns in life.

Step 3: Exhausting exercise is added. The anorexic exercises excessively, such as running 10 miles before eating.

Step 4: Health begins to fail. Weight loss and malnutrition begin, leading to mental and physical deterioration. Although the person may sense something is wrong, she refuses to conclude that she needs to start eating more. Anorexia can lead to the shrinking of internal organs, including the brain, heart, and kidneys. As the heart muscle weakens, the chances of irregular heart rhythm and congestive heart failure increase. Other complications include muscle aches and cramps, swelling of joints, constipation, difficulty urinating, inability to concentrate, digestive problems, and injuries to nerves and tendons. In addition, loss of fat and muscle tissue makes it difficult for the body to keep itself warm, which leads to the sensation of feeling "cold." The unusual growth of fine body hair (especially on the arms and legs) on anorexics may be the body's response to seek to make up for heat loss.

A large number of anorexics engage in excessive exercise for prolonged periods of time in an attempt to lose more weight. They prefer solitary activities (such as running and exercise machines) over team sports. At mealtimes, to avoid conflicts with others over eating so little, they are apt to say that they already have eaten, or, if they are forced to be at the table with others, they may dispose of their food by slipping it into a container under the table. Because they are always hungry, anorexics are preoccupied with food, grocery shopping, nutritional information, and cooking. They may collect cookbooks and memorize calorie charts.

Anorexics, even in warm weather, tend to wear several layers of bulky clothing, or sweaters and baggy pants, to warm their cold bodies and to conceal their thinness. (Their thinness often brings questions or criticisms from relatives and friends, so wearing bulky clothing is a way to avoid being questioned.) Anorexics usually deny they need help with their eating patterns because they insist their bodies are normal and attractive.

Anorexics tend to maintain rigid control over nearly all aspects of their lives. To avoid criticism, they often withdraw from others and are introverted. They often develop compulsive rituals involving exercise, food, housekeeping, studying, and other aspects of their lives. A favorite ritual is to weigh themselves several times a day. They may cut their small morsels of food into tiny pieces and then spend extended time eating each piece. They find security in discipline and order. To achieve greater control of their lives they tend to avoid social activities, sexual relationships, parties, and friends.

Some anorexics occasionally yield to their hunger pangs and eat—and perhaps even binge. After eating and binging, they are apt to feel guilty because they failed in their efforts to always follow a restricted diet.

Anorexics tend to think in black-and-white terms. They view themselves, and others, as being right or wrong, successes or failures, beautiful or ugly, fat or thin, and so on. They do not deal well with complexity or shades of gray. Anorexics seek to be perfectionists in all aspects of their lives: relationships, school or job responsibilities, personal appearance, and so on.

Ninety-five percent of those affected with anorexia nervosa are females (Koch et al., 2001). Onset usually occurs during adolescence, although the onset can occur from prepuberty to the early 30s. Estimates of the number of teenage females affected by this disorder range from one in 100 to one in 800 (Koch et al., 2001). Although this disorder is found in all ethnic and socioeconomic groups, especially vulnerable are overly perfectionistic "model" children from upper-middle and upper-class backgrounds.

To prevent death through starvation, hospitalization is frequently needed for anorexics. Studies estimate mortality rates of between 5 and 18 percent of anorexics, due to a variety of medical complications (Koch et al., 2001). The complications include heart attack, kidney damage, liver impairment, malnutrition, and starvation. Starvation weakens the body's immune system, which leaves the anorexic vulnerable to pneumonia and other infections. Suicide following severe depression is also a danger. The mortality rate for anorexia nervosa is thought to be higher than for any other psychiatric disorder (Koch et al., 2001).

Bulimia Nervosa. The term *bulimia* is derived from a Greek word meaning "ox-like hunger." But the binge-purge cycle that is characteristic of bulimics is triggered not by physical hunger but by emotional upset.

Binge-eating is the rapid, uncontrolled consumption of large amounts of food. A binge may last from a few minutes to several hours. Purging is the process of getting rid of the food eaten during a binge. The most frequent method of purging is self-induced vomiting. Other methods of purging include strict dieting or fasting, vigorous exercise, diet pills, and abuse of diuretics and laxatives. Some bulimics chew food to enjoy the taste and then spit it out to avoid calories and weight gain. Estimates of the incidence of bulimia nervosa among high school and college-age females range between 4.5 and 18 percent (Koch et al., 2001).

The development of bulimia tends to proceed according to the following pattern:

Step 1: A diet is started. The person wants to lose weight and improve self-esteem. However, dieting increases hunger and leads to a craving for sweet, high-calorie food.

Step 2: Overeating begins. The overeating is often triggered by stress such as anger, depression, loneliness, frustration, and boredom. Food helps to relieve hunger and also is a comfort for emotional pain.

Step 3: Guilt develops. The person feels guilty about gaining weight in a society where "thin is in."

Step 4: Purging is discovered. The person discovers that self-induced vomiting or other forms of purging will allow her to binge but not gain weight.

Step 5: A binge-purge habit takes hold. Binge eating and purging become a way of coping with life and emotional pain. Bulimics tend to fear that others will discover their habit and view it as being disgusting.

The average bulimic binge involves between 1,000 and 5,500 calories, although daylong binges of more than 50,000 calories occur in some bulimics. (The average American's food intake is about 3,000 calories a day.) Bulimics tend to binge on high-calorie junk foods, such as sweets and fried foods. Bulimics generally feel considerable shame about their binging and purging, but continue to resort to the binge-purge cycle as a way to relieve the pain of their daily problems.

Most bulimics are within a normal weight range, although some are somewhat overweight or underweight. Obesity in adolescence may be a contributing factor in the development of the disorder in some bulimics. The parents of bulimics are often overweight, and close relatives of bulimics have a higher-than-chance frequency of alcoholism and depression (Koch et al., 2001).

The usual age of onset for bulimia nervosa is late adolescence or early adulthood. Alcohol and other substance abuse is fairly common among bulimics. This is because the psychological dynamics that lead a person to abuse alcohol or drugs are similar to the dynamics that lead a person to be bulimic. Substance abuse may be easier to treat than bulimia, however, because a substance abuser can completely abstain from using alcohol or drugs, but a bulimic needs to continue to eat (which acts as a trigger to binging) in order to survive.

Because bulimia nervosa is seldom incapacitating, the disorder can go undetected by family and friends for years. Physical complications, however, begin to develop. Chronic vomiting can lead to gum disease and innumerable cavities, due to the hydrochloric acid content of vomit. Vomiting can also lead to severe tearing and bleeding in the esophagus. Chronic vomiting may result in a potassium deficiency, which then may lead to muscle fatigue, weakness, numbness, erratic heartbeat, kidney damage, and in severe instances, paralysis or death. Digestive problems range from stomach cramps, nausea, ulcers, and colitis, to a fatal rupturing of the stomach. Sore throats are also common. Bulimia can also lead to diabetes.

Dehydration and electrolyte imbalance can occur and in some cases cause cardiac arrhythmias and even death. Psychotropic drugs (such as tranquilizers and antidepressant drugs) may affect the body differently due to changes in body metabolism. For bulimics who are substantially below normal weight, physical complications associated with anorexia nervosa may also occur.

Both anorexia and bulimia lead to serious health problems. Stating the obvious, nutritious meals are needed for good health and survival. Anorexics risk starvation, and both bulimics and anorexics risk serious health problems. Fat synthesis and accumulation are necessary for survival. Fatty acids are a major source of energy. When fat levels are depleted, the body must draw on carbohydrates (sugar). When sugar supplies dwindle, body metabolism decreases, which often leads to drowsiness, inactivity, pessimism, depression, dizziness, and fatigue.

Although a few bulimics at times binge with friends, usually bulimics binge alone and secretly. Because binging leads to guilt, anxiety, and fear of weight gain, the process of purging serves as a reinforcer for binging because purging often results in a sense of again being in control with a flat stomach. However, many bulimics feel shame and personal disgust about their binging-purging cycle.

Bulimics tend to be people-pleasers who crave affection, attention, and approval from others. Unlike anorexics, they usually have active social lives with a number of friends and acquaintances. However, they are often filled with self-doubt and insecurity. Although they want close personal relationships, they also tend to fear such relationships, partly because they fear their eating disorder is more apt to be discovered. Many bulimics are sexually promiscuous, partly because they want affection and have low self-esteem. Some bulimics may shoplift and steal food. Most bulimics feel they do not have decent control of their lives, and feel especially out of control around food. They worry that once they begin to eat, they will be unable to refrain from binging. Bulimics are more likely to ask for help for their eating disorder than anorexics.

Compulsive Overeating. *Compulsive overeating* is the irresistible urge to consume excessive amounts of food for no nutritional reason. In most cases, compulsive overeating is a response to a combination of familial, psychological, cultural, and environmental factors. Compulsive overeating results in excessive accumulation of body fat. Compulsive eaters are overweight. Estimates are that one of five Americans are overweight (Koch et al., 2001).

Treatment is recommended for persons whose body weight is more than 20 percent over ideal body weight (Koch et al., 2001). The more overweight a compulsive overeater is, the greater the health risks. Being overweight is correlated with such health problems as hypertension, elevated cholesterol levels, and diabetes. People who are overweight are also prone to heart attacks and other heart diseases.

Compulsive overeaters have many of the characteristics that are commonly found in bulimics. (A key distinguishing factor between the two disorders is that bulimics frequently engage in purging, whereas compulsive overeaters seldom, if ever, do.) Similar to bulimics, compulsive overeaters tend to binge in an effort to temporarily escape painful problems in their lives. Compulsive overeaters generally feel considerable shame and embarrassment about their eating patterns and their weight. Alcohol and other substance abuse are common. Like bulimics, compulsive overeaters tend to be people pleasers who crave attention and approval from others and who are often filled with self-doubt and insecurity. Overeaters have a high incidence of depression and are apt to have a low self-esteem. Age of onset of the disorder is usually during adolescence.

Compulsive overeaters are apt to display one or more of the following:

1. Frequent diet plan failures. Overeaters attempt and fail at numerous diet plans. They are apt to try nearly every new diet fad briefly, believing that their latest effort will be the one that achieves permanent weight loss. No diet fad really works for them. Repeated diet failures result in a sense of hopelessness and self-deprecation.

2. Avoidance of health warning signs. Being excessively overweight eventually leads to health problems, such as diabetes and hypertension. Compulsive overeaters tend to ignore early warning signs of health problems, choosing instead to continue binging rather than making a commitment to developing healthier eating patterns.

3. Social isolation. Overeaters often feel shame and guilt about being overweight, and as a result they may seek to reduce interpersonal contact. For some, avoiding interactions with others becomes a dominant behavioral pattern.

4. Nutritional ignorance. Compulsive overeaters often lack adequate knowledge of basic nutrition. Many have a distorted view of what constitutes a well-balanced and healthy diet.

5. Selective eating amnesia. Compulsive overeaters are unlikely to conscientiously count their calorie intake. They are also apt to binge several times a day without keeping track of the frequency of their binging.

6. Overeating as a response to unwanted emotions. When overeaters feel unwanted emotions such as loneliness, frustration, insecurity, anger, and depression, they are apt to ease the pain of these emotions through binging. Binging temporarily takes their mind off their concerns, so this does work—but only during the short time while they are eating. After binging, overeaters are not only apt to feel the pain of their original unwanted emotions, which now return, but also to feel shame and guilt over their excessive eating.

Interrelationships among Eating Disorders. As noted above, there are a number of differences among these three eating disorders, but there are also interrelationships. Some people have symptoms of both anorexia and bulimia, and are identified as having the disorder *anorexia bulimia*. Many of those who have anorexia bulimia occasionally move back and forth between being anorexic and bulimic. In addition, some overeaters occasionally have episodes of purging, and at times fit the criteria for being bulimic. Koch and his associates (2001) indicate that it is important to conceptualize these three eating disorders as existing on a continuum, ranging from being overly thin to being excessively overweight:

Eating disorders seem to exist on a continuum. On one end are the people with anorexia, who achieve drastic weight loss by severely restricting food intake. In the middle are the anorexic bulimics, who eat and binge on occasion, but still maintain a much lower than normal weight by a combination of strict dieting and purging. Also included are normal-weight bulimics who binge and purge but are not significantly underweight. These bulimics usually diet when they are not bingeing and may repeatedly gain and lose ten or more pounds because of their eating behaviors. At the other end of the continuum, the binge eater will repeatedly eat excess amounts of food, gaining significant amounts of weight without engaging in any of the purging behavior associated with anorexia or bulimia nervosa. Individuals may move back and forth along this continuum, alternatively restricting or bingeing, depending on the circumstances in their lives. (p. 435)

Causes. Many factors contribute to the development of an eating disorder. The factors differ from one individual to another. Some bulimics and compulsive overeaters may be genetically predisposed to these disorders. Depression or alcoholism tends to be present in parents or other family members. People with an eating disorder tend to feel inadequate and worthless. Their low self-esteem combined with their quest for perfectionism leads them to be intolerant of any flaws. They tend to compare themselves to others, and usually conclude "I'm not good enough." A significant number of anorexics and bulimics have been victimized by molestation, rape, and incest (Koch et al., 2001).

Anorexics and bulimics have some similarities. Both are likely to have been brought up in middle-class, upwardly mobile families, where their mothers are overinvolved in their lives and their fathers are preoccupied with work outside the home. For the most part, bulimics and anorexics were "good children," eager to comply and eager to achieve in order to obtain the love and approval of others. Both tend to have a distorted body image in which they view themselves as being fatter than others view them. Both have an obsessive concern with food. Their parents tended to be overprotective and did not allow them to become more independent and learn from their mistakes. Their parents still treat them as if they were young children rather than teenagers and young adults. A smaller number of anorexics and bulimics come from nonsupportive and nonnourishing families that were demanding, critical, and rejecting. Others with an eating disorder were raised by parents who combined obsessive concern with criticism and rejection, which places the children in a double bind of wanting to protest but feeling guilty because their parents are so "caring." Still others were raised by parents who have good parenting skills and show love and act appropriately with their children. In such families other factors lead to the development of an eating disorder.

Bulimics are often overachievers, and in college tend to attain high academic averages. Purging for bulimics often becomes a purification rite because it is frequently viewed as a way to overcome self-loathing. They tend to believe they are unlovable and inadequate. Through purging, they feel completely fresh and clean again. These feelings of self-worth are only temporary. They are extremely sensitive to minor insults and frustrations, which are often used as excuses to initiate another food binge.

Impacts of Social Forces.   One reason for the increased incidence of anorexia and bulimia may be the increasing value that our society places on being slim and trim. Why are bulimics and anorexics primarily women? Koch and his associates (2001) make a strong case that there are many more pressures on women to be thin than on men. Our socialization practices also overemphasize the importance of women being slender.

Eating disorders have become epidemic in the United States in the past 30 years. Before that time, society allowed all people, and especially women, to be rounder and heavier. Weight-gain products and breast enhancers were popular products that were purchased by thin women who wanted to look like Marilyn Monroe. However, norms for what is attractive have changed. Koch and his associates (2001) note:

> The American culture is saturated with direct and indirect messages about the virtues of a thin, lean body. Television, movies, magazines, and advertisements regularly equate thinness with popularity, success, and happiness. Research has shown a direct correlation between the influence of mass media and the distorted, low self-images that many eating-disordered individuals suffer.
>
> Despite the media's lure of thinness, medical research and life insurance statistics indicate that people are healthier, live longer, and function better when they have a degree of roundness and fatty reserves beyond that allowed by fashion. Vulnerable people who believe they will be happy and admired when they are thin can precipitate an eating disorder when their bodies rebel against a restricting diet.
>
> Researchers believe an eating disorder may develop after prolonged dieting when individuals try to achieve or maintain a body size that is in direct conflict with their biology. They maintain that one's weight is genetically predetermined. This weight is referred to as the body's set point, and family history is the best indication of what a person's set point weight should be. According to the set point theory, efforts to reduce body weight below set point [are] resisted by an increase in appetite and lethargic behavior, and a reduction in basic metabolic rate, all designed to increase body weight. (p. 438)

Treatment.   Because eating disorders are complex and serious, professional intervention is generally needed. Treatment for an eating disorder usually has the following three goals: (1) resolution of the psychosocial and family dynamics that led to the development of the eating disorder; (2) provision of medical services to correct any medical problems that resulted from starving, binging and purging, or being obese; and (3) reestablishment of normal weight and healthy eating behavior.

Many anorexics and bulimics who enter treatment for eating disorders want to be treated for their unhealthy eating habits, but still want to be very thin. These two objectives are incompatible. Unless anorexics and bulimics truly comprehend that ultrathinness is unhealthy, they will soon return to their old behaviors. Treatments must be comprehensive and multifaceted because eating disorders are complex and multidimensional. Each person's unique circumstances need to be carefully assessed so that the specific needs of each client can be treated.

The client may be treated on an inpatient or outpatient basis. Hospitalization of a person with an eating disorder is sometimes needed. Inpatient care should be considered for anorexics when weight loss continues or when there is an absence of weight gain after a reasonable length of time in outpatient treatment. It should be considered for bulimics who are unable to break the binge-purge cycle after a reasonable period of time in outpatient treatment. If a client with an eating disorder indicates suicidal thoughts or severe self-destructive behavior, inpatient care should be seriously considered. Hospitalization is usually necessary when physical complications require close medical supervision (for example, when an anorexic is in danger of severe heart dysfunction, or when a bulimic needs treatment for dehydration and electrolyte imbalance). A compulsive overeater may occasionally need to be hospitalized for medical conditions such as heart disease or problems associated with diabetes. Because hospitalization severely disrupts a person's life, it should be used only when necessary.

Individual psychotherapy is a prominent part in practically all comprehensive treatment of people who have an eating disorder. Goals of individual therapy include the establishment of healthy eating patterns, increased self-esteem, increased sense of power and control over one's life, resolution of negative and unwanted emotions such as guilt and depression, and resolution of internal conflicts and personal problems. Individual psychotherapy may also have the goals of reducing stress, increasing assertiveness, and exploring relationship issues and career options.

Because family dynamics are usually contributing factors to an eating disorder, family therapy is also important, particularly if the affected person is living at home. Other family members are always affected, and sometimes victimized, by the turmoil experienced by the individual with the eating disorder. Through therapy, family members are better able to understand the dynamics of the eating disorder and can make changes that provide increased support for the affected person. The family therapist seeks to improve family functioning, which facilitates the recovery of the individual. Family sessions are also helpful to eating disordered individuals who are struggling with issues of separation from their primary family.

Group therapy is also an important intervention. It may be provided in a variety of forms, including self-help, psycho-educational, and behavioral therapy. Through group interaction, members are able to put their problems in perspective because they see that others have problems as serious as theirs. Groups also enable members to test out more appropriate interaction patterns. Members can also share their unwanted emotions and problematic behaviors, and discover ways to think and act in more realistic ways. Groups also provide interpersonal support. Groups are useful in confronting members about the health hazards of their eating patterns. Group treatment provides an arena for diminishing feelings of isolation and secrecy, sharing successful techniques for better coping with common problems, demystifying eating disorders, expressing feelings, obtaining feedback from other members, and facilitating realistic goal setting.

Nutritional counseling is an essential component of any treatment plan. A registered dietician can provide information about proper nutrition and the body's need for nutritious food. The dietician can provide information on the physiology of dieting and weight management, and can help the affected person to establish healthier eating patterns as well.

Because some persons with an eating disorder are depressed, antidepressant medication is sometimes beneficial. Such medication is prescribed by a psychiatrist or physician. Couples therapy is sometimes needed when there is significant conflict in a couple's relationship. Some elementary, secondary, and higher education school systems are now developing prevention programs that seek to inform students about the risks of eating disorders and to identify services for students who are beginning to develop an eating disorder.

Emotional and Behavioral Problems

Emotional problems (involving unwanted feelings) and behavioral problems (involving irresponsible actions) are two comprehensive labels covering an array of problems.

Emotional difficulties include depression, feelings of inferiority or isolation, feeling guilty, shyness, having a low self-concept, having a phobia, and excessive anxiety. Behavioral difficulties include being sadistic or masochistic, being hyperactive, committing unusual or bizarre acts, being overly critical, being overly aggressive, abusing one's child or spouse, being compulsive, committing sexual deviations, showing violent displays of temper, attempting suicide, and being vindictive.

Everyone at one time or another, will experience emotional and/or behavioral problems. Severe emotional or behavioral problems have been labeled as mental illnesses by certain members of the helping professions. The two general approaches to viewing and diagnosing people who display severe emotional disturbances and abnormal behaviors are the medical model and the interactional model.

Medical Model. The medical model views emotional and behavioral problems as a mental illness, comparable to a physical illness. The medical model applies medical labels (schizophrenia, paranoia, psychosis, insanity) to emotional problems. Adherents of the medical approach believe the disturbed person's mind is affected by some generally unknown, internal condition. That condition, they assert, might be due to genetics, metabolic disorders, infectious disease, internal conflicts, unconscious use of defense mechanisms, and traumatic early experiences that cause emotional fixations and hamper psychological growth.

The medical model has a lengthy classification of mental disorders that are defined by the American Psychiatric Association (see Highlight 8.7).

Numerous mental disorders are defined in *DSM-IV-TR* (American Psychiatric Association, 2000).

The medical model arose in reaction to the historical notion that the emotionally disturbed were possessed by demons, were mad, and were to blame for their disturbances. These people were "treated" by being beaten, locked up, or killed. The medical model led to viewing the disturbed as in need of help; it stimulated research into the nature of emotional problems and promoted the development of therapeutic approaches.

The major evidence for the validity of the medical model approach comes from studies that suggest that some mental disorders, such as schizophrenia, may be influenced by genetics (heredity). The bulk of the evidence for the significance of heredity comes from studies of twins. For example, identical twins have been found by studies to have a *concordance* rate (that is, if one has it, both have it) for schizophrenia of about 50 percent (Rosenhan & Seligman, 1995). The rate of schizophrenia in the general population is about 1 percent (Rosenhan & Seligman,

Highlight 8.7

Major Mental Disorders According to the American Psychiatric Association

Disorders Usually Diagnosed in Infancy, Childhood, or Adolescence

These include, but are not limited to, mental retardation, learning disorders, communication disorders (such as stuttering), autism, attention-deficit/hyperactivity disorders, and separation-anxiety disorder.

Delirium, Dementia, and Amnestic and Other Cognitive Disorders

These include delirium due to alcohol and other drug intoxication, dementia due to Alzheimer's disease or Parkinson's disease, dementia due to head trauma, and amnestic disorder.

Substance-Related Disorders

This category includes mental disorders related to abuse of alcohol, caffeine, amphetamines, cocaine, hallucinogens, nicotine, and other mind-altering substances.

Schizophrenia and Other Psychotic Disorders

This category includes delusional disorders and all forms of schizophrenia (such as paranoid, disorganized, and catatonic).

The essential feature of a delusional disorder is the presence of one or more delusions that persist for at least 1 month. A *delusion* is something that is falsely believed or propagated. An example is the persecutory type in which an individual erroneously believes he or she is being conspired against, cheated, spied on, followed, poisoned or drugged, harassed, or obstructed in the pursuit of long-term goals.

Schizophrenia encompasses a large group of disorders, usually of psychotic proportion, manifested by disturbances of language and communication, thought, perception, affect, and behavior that last longer than 6 months.

Mood Disorders

These include emotional disorders such as depression and bipolar disorders. A bipolar disorder is a major affective disorder with episodes of both mania and depression, which was formerly called *manic-depressive psychosis*. Bipolar disorders may be subdivided into manic, depressed, or mixed types, on the basis of current symptoms.

Somatoform Disorders

These are psychological problems that manifest themselves as symptoms of physical disease (for example, hypochondria). Hypochondria is a chronic preoccupation with shifting health concerns and symptoms, a fear or conviction that one has a serious physical illness, the search for medical treatment, inability to accept reassurance, and either hostile or dependent relationships with caregivers and family.

Anxiety Disorders

This category includes phobias, posttraumatic stress disorder, generalized anxiety disorder, acute stress disorder, and substance-induced anxiety disorder. A phobia is characterized by an obsessive, persistent, unrealistic, intense fear of an object or situation. A few common phobias are *acrophobia* (fear of heights), *algophobia* (fear of pain), and *claustrophobia* (fear of closed spaces).

Dissociative Disorders

This category includes problems in which part of the personality is dissociated from the rest, such as dissociative identity disorder (formerly called multiple personality disorder).

Sexual and Gender Identity Disorders

This category includes sexual dysfunctions (such as hypoactive sexual desire, premature ejaculation, male erectile disorder, male and female orgasmic disorders, and vaginismus), exhibitionism, fetishism, pedophilia (child molestation), sexual masochism, sexual sadism, voyeurism, and gender identity disorders (such as cross-gender identification).

Eating Disorders

This category includes anorexia nervosa, bulimia nervosa, and compulsive overeating.

Sleep Disorders

This classification includes insomnia and other problems with sleep (such as nightmares and sleepwalking).

Impulse-Control Disorders

These disorders relate to the inability to control certain undesirable impulses (for example, kleptomania, pyromania, and pathological gambling).

Adjustment Disorders

These involve difficulty in adjusting to the stress created by such common events as unemployment or divorce.

Personality Disorders

This category refers to an enduring pattern of inner experience and behavior that deviates markedly from the expectations of the individual's culture, is pervasive and inflexible, has an onset in adolescence or early adulthood, is stable over time, and leads to distress or impairment. Examples of these disorders include the following:

- *Paranoid:* a pattern of distrust and suspiciousness, such that others' motives are interpreted as malevolent.

- *Schizoid:* a pattern of detachment from social relationships and a restricted range of emotional expression.

- *Schizotypal:* a pattern of acute discomfort in close relationships, cognitive or perceptual distortions, and eccentricities of behavior.

- *Antisocial:* a pattern of disregard for, and violation of, the rights of others.
- *Borderline:* a pattern of instability in interpersonal relationships, self-image, affects, and impulsivity.
- *Histrionic:* a pattern of excessive emotionality and attention seeking.
- *Narcissistic:* a pattern of grandiosity, need for admiration, and lack of empathy.
- *Avoidant:* a pattern of social inhibition, feelings of inadequacy, and hypersensitivity to negative evaluation.
- *Dependent:* a pattern of submissive and clinging behavior related to an excessive need to be taken care of.

- *Obsessive-Compulsive:* a pattern of preoccupation with orderliness, perfectionism, and control.

Other Conditions

This category covers a variety of other disorders that may be a focus of clinical attention. The category includes parent-child relational problems; partner relational problems; sibling relational problems; child victimization of physical abuse, sexual abuse, and neglect; adult victimization of physical and sexual abuse; malingering; bereavement; academic problems; occupational problems; identity problems; and religious or spiritual problems.

Source: *DSM-IV-TR (Diagnostic and Statistical Manual of Mental Disorders),* 4th ed., text revision (Washington, D.C.: American Psychiatric Association, 2000).

1995). So when one identical twin is schizophrenic, the other is fifty times more likely than the average to be schizophrenic. This suggest a causal influence of genes, but not genetic determination, because concordance for identical twins is only 50 percent, not 100 percent.

Interactional Model. Critics of the medical (mental illness) model assert that such medical labels have no diagnostic or treatment value and frequently have an adverse labeling effect.

Thomas Szasz (1961a) was one of the first authorities to assert that mental illness is a myth—that it does not exist. Szasz's theory is an *interactional model,* which focuses on the processes of everyday social interaction and the effects of labeling on people. Beginning with the assumption that the term *mental illness* implies a "disease of the mind," he categorized all of the so-called mental illnesses into three types of emotional disorders and discussed the inappropriateness of calling such human difficulties mental illnesses:

1. *Personal disabilities,* such as excessive anxiety, depression, fears, and feelings of inadequacy. Szasz said that such so-called mental illnesses may appropriately be considered mental (in the sense in which thinking and feeling are considered mental activities) but they are not diseases.

2. *Antisocial acts,* such as bizarre homicides and other social deviations. Homosexuality used to be in this category, but was removed from the American Psychiatric Association's list of mental illnesses in 1974. Szasz said such antisocial acts are social deviations and are neither mental nor diseases.

3. *Deterioration of the brain with associated personality changes.* This category includes the disorders labeled as mental illnesses in which personality changes result following brain deterioration from such causes as arteriosclerosis, chronic alcoholism, general paresis, or serious brain damage following an accident. Common symptoms are loss of memory, listlessness, apathy, and deterioration of personal grooming habits. Szasz said these disorders can appropriately be considered diseases, but are diseases of the brain (i.e., brain deterioration that specifies the nature of the problem) rather than diseases of the mind.

Szasz (1961b) asserted that the notion that people with emotional problems are mentally ill is as absurd as the belief that the emotionally disturbed are possessed by demons:

> The belief in mental illness as something other than man's trouble in getting along with his fellow man, is the proper heir to the belief in demonology and witchcraft. Mental illness exists or is "real" in exactly the same sense in which witches existed or were "real." (p. 87)

The point that Szasz and many others are striving to make is that people do have emotional problems, but they do not have a mystical, mental illness. Terms that describe behavior, they believe, are very useful. For example, depression, anxiety, an obsession, a compulsion, excessive fear, hallucinations, or feelings of being a failure describe personal problems that people have. But they assert the medical terms (such as schizophrenia and psychosis) are not useful because there is no distinguishing symptom that would indicate whether a person has, or does not have, the illness. In addition, Caplan (1995) points out that there is considerable variation between cultures regarding what is defined as a mental illness. The usefulness of the medical model is also questioned because psychiatrists frequently disagree on the medical diagnosis to be assigned to those who are disturbed (Caplan, 1995).

In a dramatic study, psychologist David Rosenhan (1973) demonstrated that professional staff in mental hospitals could not distinguish insane patients from sane patients. Rosenhan and seven normal associates went to 12 mental hospitals in five different states claiming they were hearing voices; all eight were admitted to these hospitals. After admission these pseudopatients stated they stopped hearing voices and acted normally. The hospitals were unable to distinguish their sane status from the insane status of other patients. The hospitals kept these pseudopatients hospitalized for an average of 19 days, and all were then discharged with a diagnosis of "schizophrenia in remission."

The use of medical labels has severe adverse effects (Rosenhan & Seligman, 1995). The person labeled mentally ill believes that he or she has a disease for which unfortunately there is no known cure. (Frequently the therapist believes this as well.) The label gives the labeled person an excuse for not taking responsibility for his or her actions (for example, innocent by reason of insanity). Because no cure is known, the disturbed frequently idle away their time waiting for someone to discover a cure, rather than assuming responsibility for their behavior, examining the reasons why there are problems, and making efforts to improve. Other undesirable consequences of being labeled mentally ill are: the labeled persons may lose some of their legal rights; they may be stigmatized in their social interactions as being dangerous, unpredictable, untrustworthy, or of weak character; and they may find it more difficult to secure employment or receive a promotion (Rosenhan & Seligman, 1995).

The question of whether mental illness exists is important. The assignment of mental illness labels to disturbed people has substantial implications for how the disturbed will be treated, for how others will view them, and for how they will view themselves. Cooley's "looking glass self-concept" (1902) applies here. The looking glass says we develop our self-concept in terms of how other people react to us. If someone is labeled mentally ill, other people are apt to react to him as if he were mentally ill, and that person may well define himself as being different, crazy, and begin playing that role. Authorities who adhere to the interactional model raise a key question: "If we relate to people with emotional problems as if they were mentally ill, how can we expect them to act in emotionally healthy and responsible ways?"

Adherents of the interactional approach believe that people get labelled mentally ill for two reasons—they may have an intense unwanted emotion, or they may be engaged in dysfunctional (or deviant) behavior. Assigning a mental illness label to unwanted emotions or dysfunctional behaviors does not tell us how the emotions or behaviors originated nor how to treat such emotions and behaviors. The following section, based on a rational therapy approach, does both. It gives us an approach for identifying the sources of unwanted emotions and dysfunctional behaviors, and it provides strategies for changing these unwanted emotions and dysfunctional behaviors.

Assessing and Treating Unwanted Emotions: Application of Theory to Client Situations. A variety of theoretical frameworks can be used for assessing and treating emotional problems. (A summary of these frameworks is in Zastrow, 1999.) The rational therapy approach, described here, is one of the more useful approaches. The primary developer of rational therapy is Albert Ellis (1962).

Many people erroneously believe that emotions are primarily determined by experiences (that is, by events that happen to us). Rational therapy has demonstrated that the primary cause of all of our emotions is what we tell ourselves about events that happen to us.

All emotions occur according to the following format:

Events
(Our experiences.)

↓

Self-Talk
(The set of evaluating thoughts we give ourselves about facts and events that happen to us.)

↓

Emotions
(May include remaining calm.)

This basic principle is not new. The stoic philosopher Epictetus wrote in *The Enchiridion* in the first century A.D.: "Men are disturbed not by things, but by the view which they take of them" (quoted in Ellis, 1979, p. 190). An example will illustrate this process:

Event
Jane Adams studies extensively for her first human behavior exam, takes the exam, and receives a C.

Jane's Self-Talk

"Gee, this is awful. I studied so hard for this exam, and bombed out. It sure looks like I'm going to fail this course. Human behavior is not for me. I'm simply dumber than other students. Since this is a required course in the social work major, it looks like I'll never make it as a social worker. I'm a failure. Maybe I should drop out of college right now, rather than continuing to waste my money, when I'll never graduate anyway."

Jane's Emotions

Depressed, feeling of being a failure, disgusted with self.

If on the other hand, Jane tells herself the following about receiving a C, her emotions will be very different:

Event

Jane Adams studies extensively for her first human behavior exam, takes the exam, and receives a C.

Jane's Self-Talk

"Wow—I just got by on this exam. Nearly half the class got a C or lower on the exam, so it looks like I'm doing about as well as others. All I need is a grade of C in this course to pass and fulfill the requirement. I see where I made some mistakes that I shouldn't have made, so I think I will be able to do better on the next exam. I'll also talk with the instructor to get some ideas on how I can improve in this course. I feared I flunked this exam, and I wound up doing better than I expected. I'm progressing satisfactorily in the social work major, and I think I can do better."

Jane's Emotions

Mildly anxious about receiving a C, relief that the exam was not flunked, optimistic about improving her grade on the next exam, and optimistic about passing the course and continuing in the social work major.

The most important point about this process is that our self-talk determines how we feel, and by changing our self-talk we can change any unwanted emotion. An unwanted emotion can be defined as either an emotion we want to change or an emotion we have that others have become significantly concerned about—for example, excessive depression that has continued since a loved one died several years earlier. It is possible that an emotion that is generally viewed as being positive can be an unwanted emo-

tion. For example, if you find you are feeling happy at a funeral, you may want to change the emotion. Also, emotions generally viewed as negative can be a wanted emotion in certain situations, for example, sadness at a funeral.

Changing Unwanted Emotions. There are only five ways to change an unwanted emotion, and only the first three of them are constructive. These three are: getting involved in meaningful activity, changing the negative and irrational thinking that underlies the unwanted emotion, and changing the distressing event.

Meaningful Activity. The first constructive way to change an unwanted emotion is to get involved in some meaningful or enjoyable activity. When we become involved in activity that is meaningful, it provides satisfaction and structures and fills time, thereby taking our mind off a distressing event.

Practically all of us encounter day-to-day frustrations and irritations—having a class or two that are not going too well, having a job with irritations, or having a blah social life. If we go home in the evening and continue to dwell on the irritations, we will develop such unwanted emotions as depression, anger, frustration, despair, or feeling of being a failure. (Which of these emotions we will have will directly depend on what we tell ourselves.)

By having an escape list of things we enjoy doing, we can nip unwanted emotions in the bud. Everyone should develop an escape list of things they enjoy doing: taking a walk, golfing, going to a movie, shopping, doing needlework, visiting friends, exercising, and so on. By getting involved in things we enjoy, we take our minds off our day-do-day concerns and irritations. The positive emotions we will instead experience will directly stem from the things we tell ourselves about the enjoyable things we are doing.

In urging people to use an escape list, we are not suggesting that people should avoid trying to change unpleasant events. If something can be done to change an unpleasant event, all constructive efforts should be tried. However, we often do not have control over unpleasant events and cannot change them. Yet we always have the capacity to control and change what we tell ourselves about unpleasant events. It is this latter focus that is often helpful in learning to change our unwanted emotions.

Changing Self-Talk. A second approach to changing unwanted emotions is to identify and then change the negative and irrational thinking that leads to unwanted emotions. Maultsby (1975) developed an approach, called *rational self-analysis* (RSA), that is very useful for learning

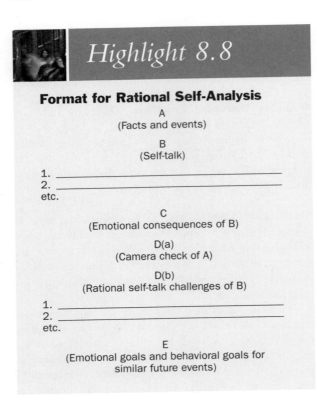

Highlight 8.8

Format for Rational Self-Analysis

A
(Facts and events)

B
(Self-talk)

1. _____
2. _____
etc.

C
(Emotional consequences of B)

D(a)
(Camera check of A)

D(b)
(Rational self-talk challenges of B)

1. _____
2. _____
etc.

E
(Emotional goals and behavioral goals for
similar future events)

to challenge and change irrational thinking. An RSA has six parts, as shown in Highlight 8.8.

The goal in doing an RSA is to change any unwanted emotion (anger, love, guilt, depression, hate, and so on). An RSA is done by recording the event and self-talk on paper. Under Part A (facts and events), simply state the facts or events that occurred. Under Part B (self-talk), write all of your thoughts about A. Number each statement in order (1, 2, 3, 4, and so on). Also write either good, bad, or neutral after each self-talk statement to show yourself how you believed each statement reflected on you as a person. (The RSA example presented in Highlight 8.8 illustrates the mechanics of doing an RSA.)

Under Part C (emotional consequences) write simple statements describing your gut reactions/emotions stemming from your self-talk in B. Part D(a) is to be written *only* after you have written sections A, B, and C. Part D(a) is a "camera check" of the A section. Reread the A section and ask yourself, "If I had taken a moving picture of what I wrote was happening, would the camera verify what I have written as facts?" A moving picture would probably have recorded the facts, but not personal beliefs or opinions. Personal beliefs or opinions belong in the B section. A common example of a personal opinion

mistaken as a fact is: "Marty made me look like a fool when he laughed at me while I was trying to make a serious point." Under D(a) (camera check of A), correct the opinion part of this statement by writing only the factual part: "I was attempting to make a serious point when Marty began laughing at what I was saying." Then add the personal opinion part of the statement to B (that is, "Marty made me look like a fool").

Part D(b) is the section designed to challenge and change negative and irrational thinking. Take each B statement separately. Read B-1 first and ask yourself if it is inconsistent with any of the five questions for rational thinking. It will be *irrational* if it does one of or more of the following:

1. Does not fit the facts. For example, you tell yourself no one loves you after someone has ended a romantic relationship—and you still have several close friends and relatives who love you.

2. Hampers you in protecting your life. For example, if you decide you can drive 30 miles home when you are intoxicated.

3. Hampers you in achieving your short- and long-term goals. For example, you want to do well in college and you have two exams tomorrow, which you haven't studied for, but instead you decide to go out and party.

4. Causes significant trouble with other people. For example, you think you have a right to challenge anyone to a fight whenever you interpret a remark as being an insult.

5. Leads you to feel emotions that you do not want to feel.

If the self-talk statement is rational, merely write, "That's rational." If, on the other hand, the self-talk statement meets one or more of the guidelines for irrational thinking, then think of an alternative "self-talk" to that B statement. This new self-talk statement is of crucial importance in changing your undesirable emotion. It needs to be rational and to be a self-talk statement you are willing to accept as a new opinion for yourself. After writing down this D(b-1) self-talk in the D(b) section, then consider B-2, B-3, and so on in the same way.

Under Part E write down the new emotions you want to have in similar future A situations. In writing these new emotions, keep in mind that they will follow from your self-talk statements in your D(b) section. This section may also contain a description of certain actions you intend to take to help you achieve your emotional goals when you encounter future A's.

In order to make a rational self-analysis work, you have to put effort into challenging the negative and irrational thinking with your rational debates whenever you start thinking negatively. With effort, you can learn to change any unwanted emotion. This capacity is one of the most important abilities you have. (Once you gain skill in writing out an RSA, you will be able to do the process in your head without having to write it out.) An illustration of writing an RSA is displayed in Highlight 8.9.

This process of challenging negative and irrational thinking *will* work to change unwanted emotions if you put the needed effort into it. Just as dieting is guaranteed to lose weight, so is this approach guaranteed to change unwanted emotions. Both, however, require an effort and commitment to use the process in order to make it work.

Changing the Distressing Event. A third way to change unwanted emotions is to change the distressing event. Some distressing events can be changed by directly confronting the events and taking constructive action to change them. For example, if we are let go from a job, we can seek another; when we find one we will feel better. Or, if we are receiving some failing grades, one way of constructively handling the situation is to meet individually with the instructors of these courses to obtain their suggestions on how to do better. If suggestions are received that appear practical and have merit, we will feel better.

Not all distressing events can be changed. For example, we may have a job that we like but be forced to interact with an employee who displays behaviors we dislike. If we cannot change their behaviors, the only other constructive option is to "bite the bullet" and seek to adapt to the circumstances. However, when it is feasible and practical to change distressing events, we should seek to do so. If we are successful we are apt to feel better because we will then give ourselves more positive self-talk about the changed events.

Destructive Ways to Change Unwanted Emotions. Unfortunately, some people turn to two other ways to change unwanted emotions. One of these ways is seeking to temporarily relieve intense unwanted emotions through the use of alcohol, other drugs, or food. Unfortunately many people seek to relieve unwanted emotions through the use of such mind-altering drugs as alcohol, cocaine, tranquilizers, and so on. When the effects of the drug wear off, the problems and unwanted emotions still remain, and there is a danger that through repeated use a person will become dependent on the drug.

Some people overeat for the same reasons. Such people are apt to become overweight or bulimic—or both.

The only other way to relieve unwanted emotions is a sure-fire way—a bullet to the head (or some other form of suicide). This way is the ultimate destructive approach to changing unwanted emotions.

Assessing and Changing Deviant Behavior: Application of Theory to Practice. Our thinking determines both our emotions and our actions, as depicted in the following diagram:

Events

↓

Self-Talk

↓

Emotions

↓

Actions

To demonstrate this principle, reflect on the last time you did something bizarre or unusual. What self-talk statements were you giving yourself (that is, what were you thinking) prior to and during the time you did what you did?

Thinking processes determine behavior. The reasons behind unusual or dysfunctional behavior can always be identified by determining what the perpetrator was thinking prior to and during the time the act is being committed. Examples of cognitions that lead to dysfunctional behavior are the following:

Cognition: A 17-year-old sees an unlocked Camaro and thinks, "Hey, this is really a neat car to take a ride in. Let me cross the starting wires, and take it for a drive."
Behavior: car theft

Cognition: A 27-year-old male is on his second date, is in his date's apartment, and thinks, "She is really sexy. Since I've now wined and dined her twice, it's now time for her to show her appreciation to me. She wants it as much as I do. I'll show her what a great lover I am. She may protest a little, but I'll overcome that with force. Once we get involved sexually, she'll be emotionally attracted to me."
Behavior: date rape

Cognition: A 31-year-old bartender thinks, "Cocaine gives me such a great high. Unfortunately I don't make the kind of money to buy as much as I need. I have no

Highlight 8.9

A Rational Self-Analysis of Emotions Associated with Ending a Marriage

A 41-year-old college student sought counseling about her deteriorating relationship with her estranged husband and her son. After the woman discussed her feelings in some depth, the counselor instructed her to combat her unwanted emotions by using rational debates to counter her negative and irrational self-talk. These rational debates were generated by the following rational self-analysis. (Names and other identifying information have been changed.)

A Facts and Events	D(a) Camera Check of A
On March 14, 1998, I separated from my husband because our marriage wasn't working. The marriage was causing me extreme pain, and my husband refused to go to counseling with me. Three weeks after the separation, he filed for a divorce. Since the hearing on April 19, 1998, he has refused to cooperate in following through on his decision to get a divorce. He has refused to have the house and furniture assessed. He has postponed the divorce trial three times. In February 1999 my attorney notified me that my husband has cancer and is in Memorial Hospital. The trial was postponed again. Both my husband and son blame me for the divorce and for my husband's illness. My son has refused to see me or have any relationship with me since I moved out last March.	This is all factual.

B My Self-Talk	D(b) My Rational Debates of B
B-1. "It's not fair. I want out of this marriage. It has dragged on for over a year." (bad)	D(b)-1. "Life isn't always fair. I will make the best of the situation and accept the inconvenience.
B-2. "Blair is doing this purposely to keep me from living my own life." (bad)	D(b)-2. "Blair may be stalling the divorce, but I can and will live my own life."
B-3. "I caused Blair's cancer because I separated from him. It's all my fault." (bad)	D(b)-3. "I didn't cause the cancer. I'm not that powerful. His illness isn't my fault."
B-4. "I'll never see my son again because he blames me for his father's illness." (bad)	D(b)-4. "I am not seeing my son now, but I don't know what the future may hold. Time heals many wounds."
B-5. "I have no right to be enjoying myself with Scott. I don't deserve to be happy." (bad)	D(b)-5. "I have the right to live my own life and to enjoy my relationship with Scott. I deserve a healthy relationship."
B-6. "I may never get a divorce. If Blair goes into remission, the trial will be rescheduled; and if he has a relapse, it will be postponed again. This situation can drag on forever." (bad)	D(b)-6. "I will eventually be free. It may drag on longer than I'd like; however, I doubt it will go on forever."
B-7. "I am a bad person for becoming involved with Scott when Blair may be dying." (bad)	D(b)-7. "I am not a bad person. I'm a person who has the right to go forward and develop a new relationship that meets my needs. What is happening to Blair has nothing to do with me."
B-8. "People will think I'm awful for enjoying myself and my life." (bad)	D(b)-8. "What people think is not my concern. What is more important is what I think. I think it is okay to enjoy my life and to live it to the fullest."
B-9. "I'm a bad mother because Paul won't see me." (bad)	D(b)-9. "I'm not a bad mother. I am a good mother. Paul's choice of sides in this divorce has nothing to do with whether I'm a good or a bad mother."

B My Self-Talk	D(b) My Rational Debates of B
B-10. "If Blair dies, I won't have maintenance, so I won't have enough money to get through school." (bad)	*D(b)-10.* "If Blair dies, I'll find other options. I can get more student loans. I could get a full-time job and go to school part-time. I will reach my goals of graduating with a B.S. degree and going to graduate school."

C My Emotions	E My Emotional and Behavioral Goals
I feel depressed, guilty, hurt, angry, controlled, disappointed, sad, lonely, and frustrated. (very, very bad)	To stop feeling depressed and guilty, and to get rid of my other unwanted emotions. To feel comfortable in dating Scott. To feel sufficiently relaxed to concentrate on my studies. To do whatever is reasonable to restore my relationship with Paul. To do whatever is reasonable to facilitate the ending of my marriage to Blair.

other choice but to buy more than I use, and then sell some of it for a profit."

Behavior: drug trafficking

Cognition: A 16-year-old female who has run away from home thinks, "Now what am I going to do? Where am I going to stay? Where will I get enough money to eat? Maybe I can find some guys on the street who will give me a place to stay and some money. They'll probably want to jump on me—but that's O.K. That's better than going back home and being beaten by my father when he's drunk."

Behavior: prostitution

Cognition: A 48-year-old bookkeeper of a retail computer firm thinks, "This is an awful financial mess I'm in. I've got so many bills: mortgage payments, gambling debts, and tuition payments for two kids in college. Hopefully I can win at the next poker game. But I need a stake. The only way to get a it is to take a couple grand from this company and pay the money back in a few weeks. With me handling the books, no one will ever miss it."

Behavior: embezzlement

The cognitions underlying each dysfunctional behavior may vary considerably among perpetrators. For example, possible cognitions for shoplifting a shirt might be: "This shirt would look really nice for the wedding I'm going to on Saturday. Since I'm buying a number of other items from this store, they still will make a profit from me

even if I take this without paying for it." Another may be: "This will be a challenge to see if I can get away with taking this shirt. I'll put it on in the fitting room and put my own shirt and coat on over it, and no one will see me walk out of the store with it. I'll act real casual as I walk out of the store." Or: "My son really needs a decent shirt. He doesn't have any nice ones to wear. I don't get enough money from being on public assistance to buy my children what they need. I know my son is embarrassed to wear the rags that he has. I'll just stick this shirt under my coat and walk out with it."

Assessing human behavior is largely a process of identifying the cognitions that underlie unwanted emotions or dysfunctional behavior. The stages of this process are as follows:

Step 1: Identify as precisely as possible the unwanted emotions and/or dysfunctional behavior that a client has.

Step 2: Identify the cognitions or thinking patterns that the client has during the time when he or she is having unwanted emotions or is displaying dysfunctional behavior. There are two primary ways of identifying these cognitions. One way is to ask the client what he was thinking prior to and during the time when he was having unwanted emotions or displaying dysfunctional behavior. If this approach does not work (perhaps because the client refuses to divulge what he was thinking), a second approach is to obtain information about the client's life circumstances at that time. Once these life circumstances are identified, the professional conducting the assessment needs to place herself mentally into the life circumstances of the perpetrator, and then reflect on the kinds of cognitions that would lead to specific unwanted emotions or dysfunctional behavior. For example, if the client is a 16-year-old female who has run away from home and is unemployed, it is fairly easy to identify (to some extent) the kinds of cognitions that would lead her to turn to prostitution.

A deduction from the principle that thinking processes determine dysfunctional behaviors and unwanted emotions is that in order to change these outcomes it is necessary for the affected person to change his or her thinking patterns. These concepts are illustrated in Highlight 8.10.

Macro System Problems: Crime and Delinquency

A life event or social problem frequently experienced during adolescence or young adulthood is crime or delinquency. A crime is a violation of the criminal law. Practically everyone occasionally breaks the law. For example, if a person drives a car, it is likely that person has intentionally or unintentionally broken such laws as speeding, driving the wrong way on a one-way street, or making an illegal turn. Many people have also committed such offenses as jaywalking, taking something of value from

work, and perhaps some liquor violations. If a criminal is defined as someone who has violated the law, then in a broad sense we are all criminals.

The people who tend to get arrested and spend time in jail or prison are those who generally commit more serious crimes—such as armed robbery, burglary, or rape. On rare occasions, a person may be arrested, charged, and convicted of a crime he or she did not commit. This has adverse effects on the person's emotional well-being, trust in the justice system, reputation, and finances.

Adolescents and young adults commit the bulk of crimes and are by far the most arrested age group in our society (Kornblum & Julian, 2001). Juveniles can be arrested for committing all of the same crimes as adults. However, they can also be arrested for violating an additional set of laws involving *status offenses*—that is, acts that are defined as illegal if committed by juveniles but not if committed by adults. Status offenses include running away from home, being truant from school, violating curfew, having sexual relations, being ungovernable, and being beyond the control of parents.

When arrested, juveniles are generally treated differently than adults. The juvenile court tries to act in the best interests of the child, as parents should act. Juvenile courts (in theory) have a *treatment orientation*. In adult criminal proceedings, the focus is on charging the defendant with a specific crime, holding a public trial to determine if the defendant is guilty as charged, and if found guilty, punishing the wrongdoer via a sentence. In contrast, the focus in juvenile courts is on the current physi-

Highlight 8.10

Our Thinking Determines Our Behavior and Our Emotions

One of the authors was describing to a class the concept that our thinking primarily causes our emotions and our actions. A male student voluntarily self-disclosed the following:

What you're saying makes a lot of sense. It really applies to something that happened to me. I was living with a female student who I really cared about. I thought, though, that she was going out on me. When I confronted her about it, she always said I was paranoid and denied it.

Then one night I walked into a bar in this town and I saw her in a corner hugging and kissing some other

guy. I told myself things like, "She really is cheating on me. Both of them are playing me for a fool." Such thinking led me to be angry.

I also told myself, "I'm going to set this straight. I'm going to get even with them. I'll break the bottoms off these two empty beer bottles and then jab each of them with the jagged edges." I proceeded to knock off the bottoms on the bar, and then started walking toward them. I got to within 8 feet of them and they were still arm in arm and didn't see me. I began, though, to change my thinking. I thought that if I jabbed them, the end result would be that I would get 8 to 10 years in prison, and I concluded she isn't worth that. Based on this thinking I decided to drop the beer bottles, walk out, and end my relationship with her—which is what I did.

cal, emotional, psychological, and educational needs of the children as opposed to punishment for their past misdeeds. Reform or treatment of the juvenile is the goal, even though the juvenile or his family may not agree that the court's decision is in the juvenile's best interest.

Of course, not all juvenile court judges live up to these principles. In practice, some juvenile judges focus more on punishing, rather than treating, juvenile offenders. Court appearances by children can have adverse labeling effects, such as youths viewing themselves as delinquent and then continuing to break the law.

Why do people violate the law? There are many theories about crime causation. (For a review of these theories, see Coleman & Kerbo, 2002). Crime is a comprehensive label covering a wide range of offenses, such as drunkenness, possession of narcotics, rape, auto theft, arson, shoplifting, attempted suicide, purse snatching, incest, gambling, prostitution, fraud, false advertising, homicide, and kidnapping. Obviously, since the nature of these crimes varies widely, the motives or causes underlying each must vary widely.

The self-talk theory as described by Zastrow and Navarre (1979), in essence, asserts the reasons for any criminal act can be identified by discovering what the offender was thinking prior to and during the time when the crime was being committed. This theory is a derivation from rational therapy which was described earlier in this chapter. A case example of this theory is presented in Highlight 8.11.

Macro System Problems: Delinquent Gangs

Juvenile gangs have existed for many decades in the United States and in other countries. In recent years in the United States there have been increases in the number of gangs, the number of youths belonging to gangs, gang youth drug involvement, and gang violence. Violent, delinquent urban gang activity has become a major social problem. The scientific knowledge base about delinquent gangs is very limited. There is no universal agreement on definitions of "gangs," or of the types of groups that should be labeled as gangs (Regulus, 1995). In addition, no agreed-upon recording system exists, and no data on gang offenses are collected in systematic ways by governmental agencies.

The inadequacy of the knowledge base about delinquent gangs is a major obstacle to developing effective intervention strategies. The lack of consensus among investigators is indicated by the numerous and diverse categories that have been used by different investigators to classify gangs: corner group, social club, conflict group, pathological group, athletic club, industrial association, predatory organization, drug addict group, racket organization, fighting-focused group, defensive group, unconventional group, criminal organization, turf group, heavy metal group, punk rock group, satanic organization,

Highlight 8.11

Self-Talk Explanation for Multiple Forgeries

Self-talk theory asserts the reasons for any criminal act can be identified by discovering what the offender was thinking prior to and during the time when the crime was being committed. The theory focuses on identifying the underlying *motives* for committing a crime.

While in jail, a 28-year-old male gave the following explanation of why he forged checks.

In my early years I worked on an assembly line in a manufacturing plant. The money was good, but I hated the work, so I quit. When my money ran out, I wrote some bad checks, and people took them without asking many questions. I used the money to party and enjoy life. When the checks bounced, no one put much pressure on me to pay them back because I was unemployed. That gave me an idea. Since I hated the only kind of work I could get, it dawned on me that I might be able to live the good life by forging checks. I decided to give it a whirl. For the past 4 years I've been forging checks. It's

amazing the way people take bad checks without asking many questions. I dress in an expensive suit, show some fake credit cards, and people take the checks. Once, I even had a set of checks printed up with the name 'I.O. Yew,' and people took them. I've traveled all over Europe and the United States in the past 4 years on bad or forged checks. Three times I've been arrested and put in jail. But no local community wants to keep me in jail very long—it's more expensive for society to keep me locked up than to leave me on the outside. I see jail as a necessary inconvenience. It's not that bad. It's free room and board, and I enjoy talking to most inmates.

When I get out of here I know what my next check cashing scheme will be. I'm going to have some checks printed up that look like payroll checks for a large company, such as I.B.M. Everybody takes payroll checks from nationally known companies without asking questions. I've even told the sheriff here about this plan. He apparently enjoys talking to me. He just laughed and shook his head. I get along well with people. They'll be letting me out soon—you'll see.

skinheads, ethnic or racial group, motorcycle club, and scavenger group (Goldstein, 1991).

Morales's Classification. An illustration of one categorization is provided by Morales (2002), who classified youth gangs into four types: criminal, conflict, retreatist, and cult/occult.

According to Morales (2002), the primary goal of criminal gangs is material gain through criminal activities. Criminal activities include theft of property from persons or premises, extortion, fencing, and obtaining and selling illegal substances (particularly drugs). Drug trafficking of rock cocaine is presently a major source of income for criminal gangs.

Conflict gangs are turf-oriented and will engage in violent conflict with individuals or rival groups that invade their neighborhood or that commit acts that they consider degrading or insulting. Respect is highly valued and defended. Hispanic gangs are heavily represented among conflict gangs. The Code of the Barrio mandates that gang members watch out for their neighborhood and that gang members must be willing to die for their neighborhood.

Retreatist gangs focus on getting "high" or "loaded" on alcohol, cocaine, marijuana, heroin, or other drugs. Individuals tend to join this type of gang in order to secure continued access to drugs. In contrast to criminal gangs that become involved with drugs for financial profit, retreatist gangs become involved with drugs for consumption.

Some gangs become involved in "devil worship." These groups are often referred to as occult groups. *Occult* means keeping something secret or hidden, or a belief in supernatural or mysterious powers. However, not all occult groups are involved in criminal activity or in devil worship. Unlike the gangs mentioned earlier, which are primarily composed of juveniles, the majority of occult groups are composed of adults.

Contradictions in Conceptualizing Gangs. Contradictions abound in conceptualizing delinquent gangs. Gangs are believed to be composed largely of ethnically homogeneous adolescents (African American, Hispanic, and Asian youths); yet some gangs composed of white youths exist. Most gang members are believed to be between ages 12 and 18, yet recent evidence indicates some gangs include and may be controlled by adults (Huff, 1993). Gangs are believed to be composed of males; yet some gangs have female members, and a few gangs consist exclusively of females (Regulus, 1995). Gangs are believed to be primarily involved in drug trafficking; yet some delinquent gangs have other illegal foci, such as burglary, robbery, larceny, or illegal drug consumption. Gang activity is thought to be primarily located in large, inner city, urban areas; yet gang activity is flourishing in many smaller cities and in some suburbs (Regulus, 1995).

At the present time there are inadequate statistical data on the number of gangs, the number and characteristics of members, and their criminal activities. No uniform definition of a gang-related offense exists across police jurisdictions (even within the same state or city).

Sociological Theories: Applications of Theories to Gangs. Numerous attempts to explain why youths join gangs and why gangs engage in delinquent or criminal activities have been made. These explanations include biological, psychological, and sociological theories (see

Three female gang members flash hand signals and exhibit tattoos.

Goldstein, 1991, for a review). No consensus exists as to which theories are most useful, and insufficient research has been conducted to ascertain the validity of the theories. In order to illustrate the existing theories, we will summarize four of them: differential association theory, anomie theory, deviant subcultures theory, and control theory.

Edwin Sutherland (Sutherland & Cressey, 1970) advanced his famous *theory of differential association* in 1939. This theory asserts that criminal behavior is the result of a learning process that primarily stems from small, intimate groups—family, neighborhood peer groups, and friends. In essence, the theory states, "A person becomes delinquent because of the excess of definitions favorable to violation of law over definitions unfavorable to violation of law" (p. 76). People internalize the values of the surrounding culture. When the environment includes frequent contact with criminal elements and infrequent contact with noncriminal elements, a person is apt to engage in delinquent or criminal activity. Past and present learning experiences in intimate personal groups define whether a person should violate laws; for those deciding to commit crimes, the learning experiences also include which crimes to commit, the techniques of committing these crimes, and the attitudes and rationalizations for committing them. Thus, a youth whose most admired person is a member of a gang involved in committing burglaries or in drug trafficking will seek to emulate this model, will receive instruction from gang members in committing these crimes, and will also receive approval from the gang for successfully committing these crimes.

Robert Merton (1968) applied *anomie theory* to delinquency and crime. This approach views delinquent behavior as resulting when an individual or a gang is prevented from achieving high-status goals in a society. Merton begins by noting that every society has both approved goals (for example, wealth and material possessions) and approved means for attaining these goals (going to college, getting a job). When certain members of society want these goals but have insufficient access to the approved means for attaining them, a state of anomie results. (*Anomie* is a condition in which the acceptance of the approved standards of conduct is weakened.) Unable to achieve the goals through society's legitimately defined channels, the individuals' and gangs' respect for these channels is weakened, and they seek to achieve the desired goals through illegal means. Merton asserts that higher crime rates are apt to occur among those groups discriminated against (that is, those groups facing additional barriers to achieving the high-status goals). These groups include the poor and racial minorities. Societies with high crime rates (such as the United States) differ from those with low crime rates because, according to Merton, they tell all their citizens that they can achieve, but in fact they block achievement for some of these people.

Deviant subcultures theory is another explanation for delinquent gang behavior. This theory asserts that some groups have developed their own attitudes, values, and perspectives that support criminal activity. Walter Miller (1958), for example, argues that American lower-class culture is more conducive to crime than middle-class culture. He asserts that lower-class culture is organized around six values—trouble, toughness, excitement, fate, smartness (ability to con others), and autonomy—and allegiance to these values produces delinquency. Miller concludes that the entire lower-class subculture is deviant in the sense that any male growing up in it will accept these values and almost certainly violate the law.

Albert Cohen (1955) advanced another subculture theory. He contends that gangs develop a delinquent subculture that represents solutions to the problems of young male gang members. A gang gives them a chance to belong, to amount to something, to develop their masculinity, to fight middle-class society. In particular, the delinquent subculture, according to Cohen, can effectively solve the status problems of working-class boys, especially those who are rejected by middle-class society. Cohen contends that the main problems of working-class boys revolve around status.

Control theories (Hirschi, 1969) ask the question, "Why do people *not* commit crimes?" Theories in this category assume that all people would "naturally" commit crimes and therefore must be constrained and controlled by society from breaking the law. Control theorists have identified three factors for preventing crime. One is the internal controls through the socialization process that society builds up in an individual; it is believed that developing a strong conscience and a sense of personal morality will prevent most people from breaking the law. A second factor is thought to be a strong attachment to small social groups, such as the family, which prevents individuals from breaking the law, because they fear rejection and disapproval from the people who are important to them. A third factor is that people do not break the law because they fear arrest and incarceration. Control theories assume that the basic nature of humans is asocial or evil. Such an assumption has never been proved.

Hirschi (1969) suggests that the prospects of delinquent behavior decline because the adolescent is controlled by social bonds such as affective ties to parents, involvement in school activities, success in school, high educational and occupational aspirations, and belief in the moral rightness of conventional norms. The weaker the social bonding, the greater the likelihood that an adolescent will become involved in delinquent gang activities. Social bonding is weakened by such factors as parental criminality, parental difficulties such as excessive drinking and extensive unemployment, inadequate parental supervision and monitoring, parental rewarding of deviant behavior, parental modeling of aggressive behavior, and inadequate parental warmth.

Social Work Roles and Intervention Programs. A wide variety of programs have attempted to reduce delinquent gang activities. These have included detached worker programs, in which workers join gangs and seek to transform antisocial into prosocial attitudes and behaviors; formal supervision of those gang members adjudicated delinquent through juvenile probation departments; placement of delinquent gang members in group homes, residential treatment facilities, or reform schools; drug treatment of gang members who have a chemical addiction; programs to support and strengthen families, particularly single-parent families in urban areas; and programs to prevent dropping out of school and to provide academic support (Goldstein & Huff, 1993).

The outcomes of such interventions have not been sufficiently researched. The factors that lead adolescents to join delinquent gangs and to then engage in delinquent activities are multifaceted and highly complex. It is clear that delinquent gang activities are on the increase in our society. The reasons for this increase are largely unknown. Also unknown are the most effective programs to reduce delinquent gang activities.

Of all the helping professions, it would appear that social work is best suited from the perspective of knowledge, values, and skills to develop intervention strategies to use with gangs. Gangs as a focus for practice find the social worker intervening with individuals, groups, families, organizations, and the community (that is, micro, mezzo, and macro level intervention).

Social workers intervene on a one-to-one level with a delinquent gang member in a variety of settings—as a juvenile probation officer, as a counselor at a group home or residential treatment facility, as a school social worker in a school setting, and as an alcohol and drug counselor in a chemical dependency treatment program. On a one-to-one level, social workers may assume the following roles: *enabler, counselor, educator, case manager,* and *broker.*

Social workers intervene on a mezzo level with a delinquent gang with a group approach; the worker is viewed as a "detached worker" or "gang group worker." Working with gangs requires that the social worker spend a considerable amount of time in the gang's immediate environment rather than in the agency, hence the term "detached worker" or "street worker." Spergel (1995) found that most gangs are receptive to a worker engaging the gang as a group within the purposes of social work practice, and that a social worker can help urban gangs to change from being a destructive force to being a constructive contributor to the community while maintaining the gang's right to self-determination. In working with gangs, a worker can function in the roles of *group facilitator, educator, enabler,* and *advocate* in helping the gang obtain needed resources. The worker can also function as a *negotiator* or a *mediator* when there is intragang conflict or when there is a conflict between rival gangs. At a mezzo level a worker may also work with the families of gang members to assist them in being constructive forces in curbing their children's delinquent behavior.

Spergel (1995) presents documentation that gangs primarily develop in those local communities that are often socially disorganized and/or impoverished. Gang members typically come from families where the parents lack effective parenting skills, where the school systems give little attention to students who are falling behind in their studies, where youths are exposed to adult crime groups, and where youths feel there is practically no opportunity to succeed through the legitimate avenues of education and a good paying job. Spergel (1995) asserts that youths join gangs for many reasons—security, power, money, status, excitement, and new experiences—particularly under conditions of social deprivation or community instability. In essence, he presents a community disorganization approach to understanding the attraction of joining a gang.

In a very real sense, a delinquent gang is created because the needs of youths are not being met by the family, neighborhood, or traditional community institutions (such as the schools, police, and recreational and religious institutions). A social worker can function as an *analyst* and *evaluator* of community conditions that are conducive to the formation of gangs. A worker can also function as an *initiator* and an *advocate* for social policy changes. Some useful changes suggested by Spergel (1995) are a reduced access to handguns; improved educational resources; access to recreation, job training, jobs, family counseling, drug rehabilitation, and mobilization of community groups and organizations to restrain gang violence (such as neighborhood watch groups). Social policy changes are also needed at state and national levels in order to funnel more resources to urban centers. Funds are needed to improve the quality of life for city residents, including youths, so that the needs of youths are met in ways other than through gang involvement. Social workers have an obligation to advocate for such local, state, and national changes in social policy.

Regulus (1995) asserts that community mobilization appears to be the most effective strategy to reduce gang problems. Regulus (1995) defines this approach:

Community mobilization is a strategy that attempts to integrate and coordinate the collective resources of citizens and organizations in gang control. In the broadest sense, community mobilization attempts to harness the combined efforts of governmental agencies, schools, police and criminal justice agencies, youth agencies, indigenous grassroots organizations, churches, and so on within a community. (p. 1052)

❦ Empowerment Through Social Work with Groups

Today it is not uncommon to find social workers as both group leaders and participants in a myriad of settings, helping solve or ameliorate human or social problems, and planning for and creating change. We have established that empowerment is the "process of increasing personal, interpersonal, or political power so that individuals can take action to improve their life situations" (Gutierrez, 1990, p. 149). Groups can provide forceful and effective means to accomplish these ends. Johnson and Johnson (1997) define a *group* as: ". . . two or more individuals in face-to-face interaction, each aware of his or her membership in the group, each aware of the others who belong to the group, and each aware of their positive interdependence as they strive to achieve mutual goals." (p. 12)

From this description we can see that the members of a group relate to one another within a context of sensing they form a distinct entity, that they share a common goal or purpose, and that they have confidence that together they can accomplish as much or more than would be possible working separately. This commonality is characteristic of a wide variety of groups dealing with a multitude of societal problems. The beginning social worker is likely to be surprised at the diversity of groups in existence and excited by the challenge of practicing social work in groups. This section gives an introduction to social work with groups—including types of groups, theories about group development, and theories about group leadership.

Types of Groups

The following types of groups are frequently encountered in social work practice: recreation, recreation–skill, educational, task, problem-solving and decision-making, focus, self-help, socialization, therapy, and encounter. This list is not an exhaustive one.

Recreation Groups. The objective of recreation groups is to provide activities for enjoyment and exercise. Often such activities are spontaneous and the groups are practically leaderless. The group service agency (such as the YMCA, or neighborhood center) may offer little more than physical space and the use of some equipment. Spontaneous playground activities, informal athletic games, and an open game room are examples. Some group agencies providing such physical space claim that recreation and interaction with others helps build character and prevent delinquency among youth by providing an alternative to the street.

Recreation-Skill Groups. The objective of a recreation-skill group is to improve a set of skills while providing enjoyment. In contrast to recreational groups, this group has an adviser, coach, or instructor; also there is more of a task orientation. Examples of activities include golf, basketball, needlework, arts and crafts, and swimming. Competitive team sports and leagues may emerge. Frequently such groups are led by professionals with recreational training rather than social work training. Social service agencies providing such services include the YMCA, YWCA, Boy Scouts, Girl Scouts, neighborhood centers, and school recreation departments.

Educational Groups. The focus of educational groups is to help members acquire knowledge and learn more complex skills. The leader generally is a professional person with considerable training and expertise in the subject area. Examples of topics include childrearing practices, assertiveness training, techniques for becoming a more effective parent, preparing to be an adoptive parent, and training volunteers to perform a specialized task for a social service agency. Educational group leaders often function in a more didactic manner and frequently are social workers. These groups may resemble a class, with considerable group interaction and discussion being encouraged.

Task Groups. Task groups are formed to achieve a specific set of tasks or objectives. The following are examples of task groups that social workers are apt to interact with or become involved in. *A board of directors* is an administrative group charged with responsibility for setting the policy governing agency programs. A *task force* is a group established for a special purpose and is usually disbanded after the task is completed. A *committee* of an agency or organization is a group that is formed to deal with specific tasks or matters. An *ad hoc committee,* like a task force, is set up for one purpose and usually ceases functioning after completion of its task.

Problem-Solving and Decision-Making Groups. Both providers and consumers of social services may become involved in groups concerned with problem solving and decision making. There is considerable overlap between task groups and these groups; in fact, problem-solving and decision-making groups can be considered a subcategory of task groups.

Providers of services use group meetings for objectives such as developing a treatment plan for a client or a group of clients, deciding how to best allocate scarce resources, deciding how to improve the delivery of services to clients, arriving at policy decisions for the agency, deciding how to improve coordination efforts with other agencies, and so on.

Potential consumers of services may form a group to study an unmet need in the community and to advocate the development of new programs to meet the need. Data on the need may be gathered, and the group may be used as a vehicle either to develop a program or to influence existing agencies to provide services. Social workers may function as stimulators and organizers of such group efforts as well as participants.

In problem-solving and decision-making groups, each participant normally has some interest or stake in the process and may gain or lose, depending on the outcome. Usually, there is a formal leader, although other leaders sometimes emerge during the process.

Focus Groups. Closely related to task groups and problem-solving and decision-making groups are focus groups. Focus groups are formed for a variety of purposes: to identify needs or issues, to generate proposals to resolve an identified issue, to test reactions to alternative approaches to an issue, and so forth. A *focus group* is a specially assembled collection of people who respond through a semistructured or structured discussion to the concerns and interests of the person, group, or organization that invited the participants. Members of the group are invited and encouraged to bring up their own ideas and views.

A *representative group* is a version of the focus group. Its strength is that its members have been selected specifically to represent different perspectives and points of view in a community. At its best, a representative group is a focus group that reflects the diversity in the community and seeks to bring these diverse views to the table. At its worst, it is a front group manipulated by schemers to make the community think that it has been involved.

Self-Help Groups. Self-help groups are becoming increasingly popular in our society and are often successful in helping individuals with certain social or personal problems. Katz and Bender (1976) provide a comprehensive definition of *self-help groups:*

Self-help groups are voluntary, small group structures for mutual aid and the accomplishment of a special purpose. They are usually formed by peers who have come together for mutual assistance in satisfying a common need, overcoming a common handicap or life-disrupting problem, and bringing about desired social, and/or personal change. The initiators and members of such groups perceive that their needs are not, or cannot be, met by or through existing social institutions. Self-help groups emphasize face-to-face social interactions and the assumption of personal responsibility by members. They often provide material assistance as well as emotional support; they are frequently cause-oriented, and promulgate an ideology or values through which members may attain an enhanced sense of personal identity. (p. 9)

Powell's (1987) classification of self-help groups conveys the varieties and focuses of self-help groups that now exist.

1. *Habit disturbance organizations:* These organizations focus on a problem that is specific and concrete. Examples include Alcoholics Anonymous, Smokestoppers, Overeaters Anonymous, Gamblers Anonymous, Take Off Pounds Sensibly (TOPS), Women for Sobriety, Narcotics Anonymous, and Weight Watchers.

2. *General purpose organizations:* These organizations address a wide range of problems and predicaments. Examples are Parents Anonymous (for parents of abused children); Emotions Anonymous (for persons with emotional problems); the Compassionate Friends (for persons who have experienced a loss through death); and GROW, an organization that works to prevent the hospitalization of mental patients through a comprehensive program of mutual aid. In contrast to habit disturbance organizations, general purpose organizations address a wider range of problems and predicaments.

3. *Lifestyle organizations:* These organizations seek to provide support for and advocate for the lifestyles of people whose members are viewed by society as being different (and the dominant groups in society are generally indifferent or hostile to that difference). Examples of this category include Widow-to-Widow Programs; Parents Without Partners; ALMA (Adoptees' Liberty Movement Association); FLAG (Parents and Friends of Lesbians and Gays); the National Gay and Lesbian Task Force;

and the Gray Panthers (an intergenerational group that advocates for the elderly).

4. *Physical-handicap organizations:* These organizations focus on major chronic diseases and conditions. Some are for people with conditions that are relatively stable, some for conditions that are likely to get worse, and some for terminal illnesses. Examples of this category include Make Today Count (for the terminally ill and their families); Emphysema Anonymous; Lost Chord clubs (for those who have had laryngectomies); stroke clubs; Mended Hearts; the Spina Bifida Association, and Self-Help for Hard of Hearing People.

5. *Significant-other organizations:* The members of these organizations are parents, spouses, and close relatives of troubled and troubling persons. Very often, members of significant-other groups are last-resort caregivers. Significant-others contend with dysfunctional behavior. Through sharing their feelings, they obtain a measure of relief. In the course of sharing, they may also learn about new resources or new approaches. Examples of such organizations include Al-Anon, Gam-Anon, Toughlove, and the National Alliance for the Mentally Ill.

Many self-help groups stress (1) a confession by members to the group that they have a problem, (2) a testimony by members to the group recounting their past experiences with the problem and their plans for handling the problem in the future, and (3) support. That is, when a member feels an intense urge of a recurrence (such as to drink or to abuse a child), he or she calls a member of the group, and that member comes over to stay with the person until the urge subsides.

Such self-help groups are successful for several other reasons. The members have an internal understanding of the problem, which helps them help others. Having experienced the consequences of the problem, they are highly motivated to finding ways to help themselves and their fellow sufferers. The participants also benefit from the *helper therapy principle:* the helper gains psychological rewards by helping others (Riessman, 1965). Helping others makes a person feel good and worthwhile; it also enables the helpers to put their own problems into perspective as they see that others' problems may be as serious, or even more serious, than their own.

When people help each other in self-help groups, they tend to feel empowered as they are able to control important aspects of their lives. When help is given from the outside (from an expert or a professional), there is a danger that dependency may develop, which is the opposite

effect of empowerment. Empowerment increases motivation, energy, personal growth, and an ability to help that goes beyond helping oneself or receiving help.

Some self-help groups advocate for the rights and lifestyles of people whose members are viewed by society as being different. One such group is the National Gay and Lesbian Task Force. Some self-help groups (such as the National Association for Retarded Citizens) raise funds and operate community programs. Many people with a personal problem use self-help groups in the same way others use social agencies. An additional advantage is that self-help groups generally are able to operate with a minimal budget. Hundreds of these groups are now in existence. Social workers often act as brokers in linking clients to appropriate self-help groups.

Socialization Groups. The objective of socialization groups generally is to develop or change attitudes and behaviors of group members to become more socially acceptable. Social skill development, increasing self-confidence, and planning for the future are other goals. Illustrations include working with a group of predelinquent youth in group activities to curb delinquency trends, a youth group of diverse racial backgrounds to reduce racial tensions, a group of pregnant young females at a maternity home to make plans for the future, a group of elderly residents at a nursing home to remotivate them and get them involved in various activities, and a group of boys at a correctional school to help them make plans for returning to their home community. Leadership of such groups requires considerable skill and knowledge in using the group to foster individual growth and change. These leadership roles are frequently filled by social workers. (The RAP framework, which can be used for leading multiracial groups, is presented in Spotlight 8.2.)

Therapy Groups. Therapy groups are generally composed of members with rather severe emotional or personal problems. Similar to one-to-one counseling, the goal of therapy groups is generally to have members explore their problems in depth and then to develop one or more strategies for resolving them.

Leadership of therapy groups generally requires considerable skill, perceptiveness, knowledge of human behavior and group dynamics, group counseling capacities, and ability to use the group to bring about behavioral changes. Among other skills, the group leader needs to be highly perceptive about how each member is being affected by what is being communicated. Considerable competence is needed to develop and maintain a constructive atmosphere within the group. The group

Spotlight on Diversity 8.2

The RAP Framework for Leading Multiracial Groups

Whenever people of different races interact in a group, the leader should assume that race is an issue, but not necessarily a problem. Race is an issue in a multiracial group because it is a very apparent difference among participants and one that is laden with considerable social meaning. The leader of a multiracial group should not attempt to be color-blind, because being color-blind leads to ignoring important dynamics related to race.

In leading a multiracial group, Davis, Galinsky, and Schopler (1995) urge that the leader use the RAP framework. RAP stands for *recognize, anticipate,* and *problem-solve.* Each element will be briefly described in the sections that follow.

Recognize

Recognizing crucial ethnic, cultural, and racial differences in any group requires the leader to be both self-aware and aware of the racial dynamics of the group. A leader of a multiracial group needs to:

- Be aware of personal values and stereotypes.
- Recognize racial, ethnic, and cultural differences among the members.
- Respect the norms, customs, and cultures of the populations represented in the group.
- Become familiar with resources (community leaders, professionals, agencies) in the community that are responsive to the needs of the racial components of the group. These resources can be used as consultants by the leader when racial issues arise and may also be used as referral resources for special needs of particular members.
- Be aware of various forms of institutional discrimination in the community and of their impact on various population groups.
- Be aware of racial tensions in the community that may concern members of the group. Such tensions may directly impact interactions among members of different races in the group.

Anticipate

Anticipating how individual members will be affected by racial issues prepares the leader to respond preventively and interventively when racial issues arise. The leader should anticipate potential sources of racial tension in the group when the members formulate their group goals, and when the leader structures the group's work. Because relationships between members and race-laden outside issues (i.e., outside of the group) change over time, anticipating racial tensions is an ongoing leadership responsibility. To anticipate tensions and help members deal effectively with them, the leader should

- Seek to include more than one member of any given race. If the group has a solo member, the leader should acknowledge the difficulty of this situation for that member and should make it clear that that member is not expected to serve as the representative of his or her race.

- Develop a leadership style that is culturally appropriate to the group's specific racial configuration. This requires that the leader become knowledgeable about the beliefs, values, and cultures of the various racial components of the group.
- Treat all members with respect and equality in both verbal and nonverbal communications.
- Help the group formulate goals responsive to the concerns and needs expressed by all the members.
- Seek to empower members to obtain their rights, particularly if they are being victimized by institutional discrimination or other forms of racism in the community.
- Acknowledge in initial contacts with members and in initial sessions that racial and ethnic differences do exist in the group and that any issues that arise in the group regarding race must be openly discussed—even if discussing such issues and differences is uncomfortable.
- Encourage the development of norms of mutual respect and appreciation of diversity.
- Announce in initial sessions that at times people do and say things that are racially inappropriate. When this occurs, these comments and actions will be thoroughly discussed in order to resolve the issues and to work toward an appreciation of differences.

Problem-Solve

When incidents related to racial issues do arise, the leader must intervene to resolve the issues. The leader should:

- Use a problem-solving approach. Briefly, this approach involves identifying the issues and needs of each party, generating alternatives to meet those needs, evaluating the merits of each of these alternatives, and selecting and implementing the most promising alternative.
- Use conflict-resolution approaches (described in Chapter 12). These approaches include role reversal, empathy, inquiry, I-messages, disarming, stroking, and mediation.
- Use interventions and goals that are culturally acceptable and appropriate for all members of the group.
- Provide some rules when involving members in problem solving and conflict resolution (for example, no name calling).
- Assist members in being assertive in confronting and dealing with problems related to race.
- Be prepared to advocate outside the group on a member's behalf when that member is being victimized by discrimination and oppression in the community.

therapist generally uses one or more therapy approaches as a guide for changing attitudes and behaviors; these approaches include psychoanalysis, reality therapy, learning theory, rational therapy, transactional analysis, client-centered therapy, and psychodrama.

Group therapy is being used increasingly in social work. It has several advantages over one-to-one therapy. The *helper therapy* principle (in which members interchange roles and sometimes become the helper for someone else's problems) is generally operative. In such roles, members receive psychological rewards for helping others. Groups also help members put their problems into perspective as they realize others have equally serious problems. Groups also help members who are having interaction problems test out new interaction approaches. Research has shown that it is generally easier to change the attitudes of an individual in a group than in one-to-one counseling (Johnson & Johnson, 1997). Research on conformity has found group pressure can have a substantial effect on changing attitudes and beliefs (Johnson & Johnson, 1997). Furthermore, group therapy permits the social worker to help more than one person at a time, with potential savings in the use of professional effort.

Encounter Groups. Encounter groups and sensitivity-training groups (these terms are used somewhat synonymously) refer to a group experience in which people relate to each other in a close interpersonal manner, and self-disclosure is required. The goal is to improve interpersonal awareness.

Barker (1999) defines a sensitivity group as:

A training and consciousness-raising group rather than one that meets to resolve psychosocial or mental disorders. Such groups typically consist of 10 to 20 members and a leader, called a trainer or facilitator. The members participate in discussions and experiential activities to demonstrate how groups function, to show how each member tends to affect others, and to help them become more aware of their own and other people's feelings and behaviors. (p. 434)

An encounter group may meet for a few hours or for as long a period as a few days. Once increased interpersonal awareness is achieved, it is anticipated that attitudes and behaviors will change.

In the encounter group, the leader usually does not act like a leader. He or she frequently starts with a brief statement encouraging the group members to participate, to be open and honest, and to expect things to be different. Group members may begin by taking off their shoes, sitting in a circle on the floor, and holding hands with their eyes closed. The leader then encourages them to feel intensely the sensations they are experiencing, the size and texture of the hands they are holding, and so forth.

Other structured exercises or experiences may be planned to help the group focus on the "here-and-now" experience. For example, pairs may go for "trust walks" in which each person alternatively is led around with his eyes closed.

The goal of sensitivity groups provides an interesting contrast to that of most therapy groups. In therapy, the goal is to have all members explore personal or emotional problems and then develop a strategy to resolve the problems. In comparison, sensitivity groups seek to foster increased personal and interpersonal awareness and then develop more effective interaction patterns. Sensitivity groups generally do not attempt to identify and change specific emotional or personal problems (such as drinking problems, feelings of depression, sexual dysfunctions, and so on). The philosophy behind sensitivity groups is that with increased personal and interpersonal awareness, people will be better able to cope with specific personal problems that arise.

In our society sensitivity groups are used for a variety of purposes: to train professional counselors to be more perceptive and effective in interpersonal interactions with clients and with other professionals; to train people in management positions to be more effective in their business interactions; to help clients with overt relationship problems become more aware of how they affect others and to help them develop more effective interaction patterns; and to train interested citizens in becoming more aware and effective in their interactions.

Models of Group Development over Time

Groups change over time. Numerous models or frameworks have been developed to describe the changes that occur in groups over time. Here we will describe the following models of group development: (1) the Garland, Jones, and Kolodny model; (2) the Tuckman model; and (3) the Bales model.

Garland, Jones, and Kolodny Model. Garland, Jones, and Kolodny (1965) developed a model that identifies five stages of development in social work groups. This model seeks to describe the kinds of problems that commonly arise as groups begin to form and continue to develop. Understanding of these problems, it is theorized, enables the designated leader to anticipate and respond to the reactions of group members more effectively. The conceptualization of Garland and his colleagues (1965) appears particularly applicable to socialization groups, therapy groups, and encounter groups. To a lesser extent, the model is also applicable to self-help groups, problem-solving and decision-making groups, educational groups, recreation-skill groups, and task groups.

Closeness (that is, the question of how near group members will allow themselves to become to one another emotionally) is the central focus of the model. The question of closeness is reflected in *struggles* that occur at five levels of growth of the group: preaffiliation, power and control, intimacy, differentiation, and separation.

In the first stage, *preaffiliation,* members are ambivalent about joining the group. Interaction is guarded. Members test out, often through approach and avoidance behavior, whether they really want to belong to the group. New situations are often frightening, and the members try to protect themselves from being hurt or taken advantage of in such new situations. They attempt to maintain a certain amount of distance and get what they can from the group without risking much of themselves. Individuals are aware that group involvement will make demands that may be frustrating or even painful. On the other hand, members are also attracted to the group because they generally have had satisfying experiences in other groups, and this group offers the hope of similar rewards. In the first stage the leader should seek to increase the attractions toward the group "by allowing and supporting distance, gently inviting trust, facilitating exploration of the physical and psychological milieu, and by providing activities if necessary and initiating group structure" (Garland & Frey, 1973, p. 3). The first stage gradually ends when members come to feel fairly safe and comfortable with the group and view the rewards as being worth a tentative emotional commitment.

The second stage, *power and control,* emerges as the characteristics of the group begin to develop. Patterns of communication within the group emerge, alliances and subgroups begin to appear, members begin to take on certain roles and responsibilities, norms and methods for handling group tasks develop, and membership questions arise. Such processes are necessary for the group to conduct its business. However, these processes lead to a struggle as the members establish their places within the group. Each member seeks power, partly for self-protection and partly to attempt to gain greater control over the rewards to be received from the group. In this struggle, the group leader is a major source of gratification. The leader is perceived as having the greatest power to influence the direction of the group and to give or withhold emotional and material rewards. At this point members realize that the group is becoming important to them.

The second stage is a transitional stage, with certain basic issues needing to be resolved: Does the group or the leader have primary control over the group's affairs? What are the limits of the power of the leader and of the group? To what extent will the leader use his or her power?

This uncertainty results in anxiety among group members and considerable testing by them to gauge the limits and establish norms for the power of both the group and the group leader. Rebellion is not uncommon, and the dropout rate in groups is often highest at this stage. During this struggle the leader should: (1) seek to help the members understand the nature of the power struggle; (2) give emotional support to weather the discomfort of uncertainty; and (3) help the group establish norms to resolve the uncertainty. It is very important that group members develop trust in the leader so he or she will maintain a safe balance of shared power and control. When this trust is achieved, group members make a major commitment to become involved in the group.

In the third stage, *intimacy,* the likes and dislikes of intimate relationships are expressed. The group becomes more like a family, with sibling rivalry arising between members and the leader sometimes even being referred to as a parent. Feelings about the group at this stage are more openly expressed and discussed. The group is now viewed as a place where growth and change take place. Individuals feel free to examine and make efforts to change personal attitudes, concerns, and problems. Group tasks are also worked on, and there is a feeling of "oneness" or cohesiveness within the group. Struggle or turmoil during this stage leads the members to explore and make changes in their personal lives and to examine "what this group is all about."

During the fourth stage, *differentiation,* there is increased freedom for members to experiment with new and alternative behavior patterns. There is a recognition of individual rights and needs and a high level of communication among members. At this stage the group is able to organize itself more efficiently. Leadership is more evenly shared and roles are more functional. Power problems are now minimal, and decisions are made and carried out on a less emotional and more objective basis. Garland and Frey (1973) noted:

> This kind of individualized therapeutic cohesion has been achieved because the group experience has all along valued and nurtured individual integrity. . . .
>
> The worker assists in this stage by helping the group to run itself and by encouraging it to act as a unit with other groups or in the wider community. During this time the worker exploits opportunities for evaluation by the group of its activities, feelings, and behavior. (p. 5)

The differentiation stage is analogous to a healthy functioning family in which the children have reached adulthood and are now becoming successful in pursuing their own lives; relationships are more between equals, members are mutually supportive, and members are able to relate to each other in ways that are more rational and objective.

The final stage is *separation*. The purposes of the group have been achieved, and members have learned new behavioral patterns to enable them to move on to other social experiences. Termination is not always easily accomplished. Members may be reluctant to move on and may even display regressive behavior in an effort to prolong the safety of the group. Members may also express anger over ending the group or even psychologically deny the end is near. Garland and Frey (1973) suggested the leader's role should be the following:

> To facilitate separation the worker must be willing to let go. Concentration upon group and individual mobility, evaluation of the experience, help with the expression of the ambivalence about termination, and recognition of the progress which has been made are his major tasks. Acceptance of termination is facilitated by active guidance of members as individuals to other ongoing sources of support and assistance. (p. 6)

Tuckman Model. Tuckman (1965) reviewed more than 50 studies of mostly therapy and sensitivity groups, of a limited duration, and concluded that these groups go through five predictable developmental stages: forming, storming, norming, performing, and adjourning.

Forming: In this stage members become oriented toward each other, work on being accepted, and learn more about the group. During this stage there is a period of uncertainty in which members try to determine their place in the group and the rules and procedures of the group.

Storming: In this stage conflicts begin to arise as members resist the influence of the group and rebel against accomplishing the task. During this stage members often confront their various differences, and the management of conflict becomes the focus of attention.

Norming: In this stage the group establishes cohesiveness and commitment, and in the process discovers new ways to work together. Norms are also set for appropriate behavior.

Performing: In this stage the group works as a unit to achieve its goals. The group develops proficiency in achieving its goals and becomes more flexible in its patterns of working together.

Adjourning: In this stage the group disbands. The feelings that members experience are similar to those in the "separation stage" of the Garland, Jones, and Kolodny model.

Bales Model. The stages described in the Garland, Jones, and Kolodny model and in the Tuckman model are sequential-stage models; both models specify sequential stages of group development. In contrast, Bales (1965) developed a *recurring-phase* model. Bales asserted that groups continue to seek an equilibrium between task-oriented work and emotional expressions to build better relationships among group members. (Task roles and social/emotional roles performed by members in a group are discussed in the next section of this chapter.) Bales asserts that a group tends to oscillate between these two concerns. Sometimes it focuses on identifying and performing the work tasks that must be conducted in order for the group to achieve its goals. At other times the group focuses on building the morale, and improving its social-emotional atmosphere.

Note that the sequential-stage perspective and the recurring-phase perspective are not necessarily contradictory. Both are useful for understanding group development. The sequential-stage perspective assumes that a group is apt to move through various phases while dealing with basic themes that surface as they become relevant to the group's work. The recurring-phase perspective assumes that the issues underlying the basic themes are never completely resolved but tend to recur later.

Task and Maintenance Roles

All groups, whether organized for therapeutic reasons, for problem solving, or for other objectives, rely on the performance of a variety of roles by their members. The group's needs generally require that both task roles and group-building roles be performed satisfactorily. *Task roles* are those that are needed to accomplish the specific goals set by the group; *maintenance roles,* include those that serve to strengthen social/emotional aspects of group life.

Johnson and Johnson (1975) summarized task roles as follows:

Information and opinion giver: Offers facts, opinions, ideas, suggestions, and relevant information to help group discussion.

Information and opinion seeker: Asks for facts, information, opinions, ideas, and feelings from other members to help group discussion.

Starter: Proposes goals and tasks to initiate action within the group.

Direction giver: Develops plans on how to proceed and focuses attention on the task to be done.

Summarizer: Pulls together related ideas or suggestions and restates and summarizes major points discussed.

Coordinator: Shows relationships among various ideas and harmonizes activities of various subgroups and members.

Diagnoser: Figures out sources of difficulties the group has in working effectively and the blocks to progress in accomplishing the group's goals.

Energizer: Stimulates a higher quality of work from the group.

Reality tester: Examines the practicality of ideas, evaluates alternative solutions, and applies them to real situations to see how they will work.

Evaluator: Compares group decisions and accomplishments with group standards and goals.

The Johnsons (1975) also identified the group maintenance roles, which strengthen social/emotional bonds within the group:

Encourager of participation: Warmly encourages everyone to participate, giving recognition for contributions and demonstrating openness to ideas of others; is friendly and responsive to group members.

Harmonizer and compromiser: Persuades members to analyze constructively their differences in opinions, searches for common elements in conflicts, and tries to reconcile disagreements.

Tension reliever: Eases tensions and increases the enjoyment of group members by joking, suggesting breaks, and proposing fun approaches to group work.

Communication helper: Shows good communication skills and makes sure that each group member understands what other members are saying.

Evaluator of emotional climate: Asks members how they feel about the way in which the group is working and about each other, and shares own feelings about both.

Process observer: Watches the process by which the group is working and uses the observations to help examine group effectiveness.

Standard setter: Expresses group standards and goals to make members aware of the direction of the work and the progress being made toward the goal and to get open acceptance of group norms and procedures.

Active listener: Listens and serves as an interested audience for other members, is receptive to others' ideas, goes along with the group when not in disagreement.

Trust builder: Accepts and supports openness of other group members; reinforces risk taking and encourages individuality.

Interpersonal problem solver: Promotes open discussion of conflicts between group members in order to resolve conflicts and increase group togetherness.

Hersey and Blanchard (1977) developed a situational theory of leadership that serves as a guideline for when effective leaders should focus on task behaviors, when they should focus on maintenance behaviors, and when they should focus on both. In essence, the theory asserts that when members have low maturity in terms of accomplishing a specific task, the leader should engage in high-task and low-maintenance behaviors. Hersey and Blanchard refer to this situation as *telling,* because the leader's behavior is most effective when he or she defines the members' roles and tells them how, when, and where to do needed tasks. The task maturity of members increases as their experience and understanding of the task increases. For moderately mature members, the leader should engage in high-task and high-maintenance behaviors. This combination of behaviors is referred to as *selling,* because the leader should not only provide clear direction as to role and task responsibilities, but should also use maintenance behaviors to get the members to psychologically buy into the decisions that have to be made.

Also, according to Hersey and Blanchard, when group members' commitment to the task increases, so does their maturity. When members are committed to accomplishing the task and have the ability and knowledge to complete the task, the leader should engage in low-task and high-maintenance behaviors, referred to as *participating.* Finally, for groups in which members are both willing and able to take responsibility for directing their own task behavior, the leader should engage in low-task and low-maintenance behaviors, referred to as *delegating.* Delegating allows members considerable autonomy in completing the task.

Leadership Theories

There are at least four major approaches to leadership theory: trait, position, style, and distributed functions.

The Trait Approach. Aristotle observed, "From the hour of their birth some are marked for subjugation, and others for command" (quoted in Johnson & Johnson, 1987, p. 39). As implied by this comment, this approach to leadership has been in existence for centuries. The *trait approach* assumes that leaders have personal characteristics or traits that make them different from followers. It also implies that leaders are born, not made, and that leaders emerge naturally rather than being trained. The trait approach has also been called the *great person theory* of leadership.

Two postulated leadership traits that have received considerable attention are charisma and Machiavellianism.

Charisma. Johnson and Johnson (1987, p. 43) defined charisma as "an extraordinary power, as of working miracles." Johnson and Johnson (1987) gave the following definition of a charismatic leader:

> *The charismatic leader must have a sense of mission, a belief in the social-change movement he or she leads, and confidence in oneself as the chosen instrument to lead the movement to its destination. The leader must appear extremely self-confident in order to inspire others with the faith that the movement he or she leads will, without fail, prevail and ultimately reduce their distress. (p. 44)*

Some charismatic leaders appear to inspire their followers to adore and be fully committed to them. Other charismatic leaders offer their members the hope and promise of deliverance from distress.

Charisma has not been precisely defined and its components have not been fully identified. The qualities and characteristics that any charismatic leader has will differ somewhat from those of other charismatic leaders. The following leaders all have been referred to as charismatic, yet they differed substantially in personality characteristics: John F. Kennedy, Martin Luther King Jr. Julius Caesar, General George Patton, Confucius, Gandhi, and Winston Churchill.

One difficulty with the charisma approach to leadership is that people who are viewed as charismatic tend to express this quality in a variety of ways. A second difficulty is that many leaders do well as leaders without being viewed as having charisma. For example, many group therapists are very effective in leading groups, even though they are not viewed as charismatic.

Machiavellianism. Niccolò Machiavelli (1469–1527) was an Italian statesman who advocated that rulers use cunning, craft, deceit, and duplicity as political methods for increasing their power and control. (Machiavelli was not the originator of his approach; some earlier theorists had conceptualized leadership in terms of manipulation for self-enhancement. However, the term *Machiavellianism* has become associated with the notion that politics is amoral and that any unscrupulous means can justifiably be used in achieving political power.) Machiavellian

leadership is based on the concepts that followers: (1) are basically fallible, gullible, untrustworthy, and weak; (2) are impersonal objects; and (3) should be manipulated in order for the leader to achieve his or her goals.

Christie and Geis (1970) concluded that Machiavellian leaders have four characteristics: (1) They have little emotional involvement in interpersonal relationships, because it is emotionally easier to manipulate others when viewing them as impersonal objects; (2) they are not concerned about conventional morality and take a utilitarian (what they can get out of it) rather than a moral view of their interactions with others; (3) they have a fairly accurate perception of the needs of their followers, which facilitates their capacity to manipulate them; and (4) they have a low degree of ideological commitment, they focus on manipulating others for personal benefit rather than for achieving long-term ideological goals.

While a few leaders may have Machiavellian characteristics, most do not. Few groups would ever function effectively or efficiently with Machiavellian leaders.

In recent years the trait theory of leadership has declined in popularity, partly because research results have raised questions about its validity. For example, different leadership positions often require different leadership traits. The characteristics of a good leader in the military differ markedly from those of a good group therapy leader. Moreover, traits found in leaders have also been found in followers. Though qualities such as high intelligence and a well-adjusted personality may have some correlation with leadership, many highly intelligent people never get top leadership positions, and some highly intelligent leaders (Adolf Hitler, for example) have been emotionally unstable. The best rule for leader selection involves choosing individuals with the necessary skills, qualities, and motivation to help a group accomplish its goals.

The Position Approach. Most large organizations have several levels of leadership, such as president, vice-president, manager, and supervisor. The *position approach* defines leadership in terms of the authority of a particular position and has focused on studying the behavior of people in high-level positions. At times, the training and personal background of leaders have also been examined.

Studies using the position approach, however, have revealed little consistency in how people assume leadership positions. Obviously, some individuals may become leaders with little related training (in family businesses, for example), whereas others spend years developing their skills. Also, what is viewed as "desirable" leadership behavior in one position may be considered "undesirable" behavior in a different type of position. For example, a drill sergeant in basic military training is not expected to be empathetic, but a sensitivity group leader is. It is difficult to compile a list of leadership traits using this approach. Not surprisingly, the position approach has shown that what constitutes leadership behavior depends on the particular requirements of the position.

It is also difficult to define which behaviors of a designated leader are leadership behaviors and which are not. Certainly not all of the behaviors of a designated authority figure are leadership behaviors. For instance, an inexperienced individual in a position of authority can mask incompetence with an authoritarian attitude. Also, leadership behavior among group members who are not designated leaders is difficult to conceptualize with the position approach, because the position approach focuses only on behaviors of designated leaders.

The Style Approach. Because research on the trait approach was turning out contradictory results, Lewin, Lippitt, and White (1939) took a *leadership style approach.* These researchers described and studied three leadership styles: authoritarian, democratic, and laissez-faire.

Authoritarian leaders have more absolute power than democratic leaders. They alone set goals and policies, dictate the activities of the members, and set major plans. They hand out rewards and punishments, and they alone know the succession of future steps in the group's activities. In contrast, democratic leaders seek maximum involvement and participation of every member in all decisions affecting the group. They seek to spread responsibility rather than to concentrate it.

Authoritarian leadership is generally efficient and decisive. One of the hazards, however, is that group members may do what they are told out of necessity and not because of any commitment to group goals. The authoritarian leader who anticipates approval from subordinates for accomplishments achieved may be surprised to find backbiting and bickering common in the group. Unsuccessful authoritarian leadership is apt to generate factionalism, behind-the-scenes jockeying and maneuvering for position among members, and lead to a decline in morale.

Democratic leadership, in contrast, is slow in decision making and sometimes confusing, but frequently proves to be more effective because of strong cooperation that generally emerges with participation in decision making. With democratic leadership, interpersonal hostilities between members, dissatisfactions with the leader, and concern for personal advancement all become issues that are discussed and acted on. The danger is that the private, behind-the-scenes complaining of the authoritarian approach becomes public conflict in a democratic approach.

Once this public conflict has been resolved in a democratic group, however, a strong personal commitment develops that motivates members to implement group decisions rather than to subvert them. The potential for sabotage in an authoritarian group is high, and therein lies the advantage of the democratic style.

The democratic leader knows that some mistakes are inevitable, and that the group will suffer from them. Yet, such mistakes require the leader's ability to stand by without interfering because to do otherwise might harm the democratic process and impede the progress of the group in developing the capacity to make decisions as a group.

In some situations authoritarian leadership is more effective, whereas in others democratic leadership is more effective (Hare, 1962). As in any situation, the group will be more effective when members' expectations about the behavior appropriate for that situation are met. Where group members anticipate a democratic style, as they do in educational settings, classrooms, or discussion groups, the democratic style usually produces the most effective group. When members anticipate forceful leadership from their superiors, as in industry or military service, a more authoritarian form of leadership results in a more effective group.

In the *laissez-faire* style, there is very little participation by the leader. The group members are primarily left to function (or flounder) with little input from the designated leader. There are a few conditions in which group members function best under laissez-faire style: when the members are committed to a course of action, have the resources to implement it, and need a minimum of designated leader influence to work effectively.

Because different leadership styles are required in different situations (even with the same group), research interest in recent years has switched to the distributed functions approach.

The Distributed-Functions Approach. With this approach, leadership is defined as the performance of acts that help the group reach its goals and maintain itself in good working order (Johnson & Johnson, 1975). The functional approach to leadership seeks to discover what tasks are essential to achieve group goals under various circumstances and how different group members should take part in these actions.

The *distributed-functions approach* disagrees with the great person theory of leadership. It asserts *any member* of a group will at times be a leader by taking actions that serve group functions. With this approach, leadership is viewed as being specific to a particular group in a particular situation. For example, telling a joke may be a useful leadership function in certain situations if it relieves tension, but telling a joke when other members are revealing intense personal feelings in a therapy group may be counterproductive and therefore not be a leadership function.

The functional approach defines leadership as occurring whenever one member in a group influences other members to help the group reach its goals. Because at times all group members influence other group members, each member in a group exerts leadership. A difference exists in most groups between being a designated leader (such as a president or chairperson) and engaging in leadership behavior. A *designated leader* has certain responsibilities (such as calling meetings and leading the discussion), whereas the term *leadership* means one member is influencing other group members to help the group reach its goals.

The functional approach asserts that leadership is a learned set of skills that anyone with certain minimal requirements can acquire. Responsible membership is the same thing as responsible leadership; both involve doing what needs to be done to help the group maintain itself and accomplish its goals. This approach asserts that people can be taught the skills and behaviors that help the group accomplish its tasks.

Like any member of a group, the designated leader may be called on or may be forced to adopt one or more of the task specialist or maintenance specialist roles discussed earlier in this chapter. Indeed, the leader has a special obligation to be alert for such occasions and to assume or to assist others to assume whichever roles are timely and appropriate. The leader's contribution to the group is not limited, however, by the assumption of specified roles. Each leader is responsible for a variety of functions. The needs and developmental stage of a group may at different times require a leader who can assume any of the previously described roles as well as those that follow:

Executive: being the top coordinator of the activities of a group.

Policymaker: establishing group goals and policies.

Planner: deciding the means by which the group will achieve its goals.

Expert: serving as the source of readily available information and skills.

External group representative: being the official spokesperson for the group.

Controller of internal relations: controlling the structure as a way to control in-group relations.

Purveyor of rewards and punishments: determining promotions, demotions, and assigning pleasant or unpleasant tasks.

Arbitrator and mediator: acting as both judge and conciliator with the power to reduce or to increase factionalism within the group.

Exemplar: serving as a model of behavior to show what the members should be and do.

Ideologist: serving as the source of the beliefs and values of the members.

Scapegoat: serving as the target for ventilating members' frustrations and disappointments.

❦ Summary

This chapter focuses on the social changes and social problems encountered by adolescents and young adults. Young people during this time period face the social developmental tasks of moving from parental dependence to adult interdependence, establishing peer relationships, forming intimate relationships with others, and choosing a personal lifestyle. Choosing a personal lifestyle partly involves making career decisions. Young adults may also enter into a variety of family living arrangements, including: marriage, cohabitation, single life, parenthood, and childless couples.

Social problems centered in adolescence and young adulthood include emotional and behavioral problems, crime and delinquency, delinquent gangs, and eating disorders. There are a wide variety of emotional and behavioral problems. There are two models of conceptualizing such problems: the medical model, which views emotional and behavioral problems as being mental illnesses, and an interactional model, which holds mental illness does not exist.

Adolescents and young adults commit the bulk of crimes. Juvenile courts have more of a treatment orientation than the adult criminal justice system. Delinquent gang activity has become a major social problem in the United States; but the scientific knowledge base about delinquent gangs is limited.

Eating disorders (anorexia nervosa, bulimia nervosa, and compulsive overeating) have recently been recognized as a serious problem. Anorexics eat very little food, bulimics binge and purge, and overeaters binge.

The rational therapy approach provides a useful way to assess and treat unwanted emotions and dysfunctional behaviors. This approach asserts that thinking patterns primarily determine all emotions and behaviors, and that assessing human behavior is largely a process of identifying the cognitions that underlie unwanted emotions or dysfunctional behaviors. Furthermore, the approach asserts that in order to change dysfunctional behaviors or unwanted emotions it is necessary for the affected person to change his or her thinking patterns.

Doing social work with groups is a typical activity for today's social workers. Types of groups frequently encountered in practice include recreation, recreation-skill, educational, task, problem-solving and decision-making, focus, self-help, socialization, therapy, and encounter groups.

Three models of group development explain how groups change over time. The Garland, Jones, and Kolodny model hypothesizes five stages: preaffiliation, power and control, intimacy, differentiation, and separation. The Tuckman model conceptualizes groups as having the following stages: forming, storming, norming, performing, and adjourning. Bales developed a recurring-phase model in which he asserted that groups continue to seek an equilibrium between task-oriented work and emotional expressions to build better relationships among group members.

All groups have task roles and maintenance roles that need to be performed by members. Task roles are needed to accomplish the specific goals set by the group; maintenance roles strengthen the social or emotional aspects of group life.

The theory of leadership highlighted in this chapter is distributed functions. With this approach, leadership is defined as the performance of acts that help the group reach its goals and maintain itself in good working order. Leadership occurs when one member influences other members to help the group reach its goals. Because all group members at times influence other group members, each member in a group exerts leadership. Three other approaches to leadership theory are the trait approach, the position approach, and the style approach.

InfoTrac College Edition Keywords

delinquency
eating disorders

empowerment
ethnic identity

homeless youth
medical model

self-talk

On the Internet

Anorexia Nervosa and Related Eating Disorders, Inc.

http://www.anred.com/

ANRED is a nonprofit organization that provides information about anorexia nervosa, bulimia nervosa, binge eating disorder, and other less-well-known food and weight disorders. The Web site's material includes self-help tips and information about recovery and prevention.

Justice for Kids and Youth (Department of Justice)

http://www.usdoj.gov/kidspage/index.html

This Web page provides information for kids and youth on different aspects of justice—like Internet crimes, drug prevention, and laws that protect their rights.

Parent Effectiveness Training

http://www.thomasgordon.com/aboutdtg.asp

Widely recognized as a pioneer in teaching communication skills and conflict-resolution methods to parents, teachers, youth, organization managers, and employees, Dr. Thomas Gordon is the founder and guiding light of Gordon Training International.

CHAPTER 9

Gender Roles and Sexism

Girls are pretty. Boys are strong.

Girls are emotional. Boys are brave.

Girls are soft. Boys are tough.

Girls are submissive. Boys are dominant.

These ideas refer to some of the traditional stereotypes about men and women.

Stereotypes are "preconceived and relatively fixed ideas about an individual, group, or social status. These ideas are usually based on superficial characteristics or overgeneralizations of traits observed in some members of the group" (Barker, 1999, p. 465). The problem with such fixed images is that they allow no room for individual differences within the group. One of the major values adhered to in social work is that each individual has the right to self-determination. Clinging to stereotypes violates this basic value.

Stereotypes about men and women are especially dangerous because they affect every one of us. To expect all men to be successful, strong, athletic, brave leaders places an impractical burden on them. To expect all women to be sweet, submissive, pretty, and born with a natural love of housekeeping places tremendous pressure on them to conform.

Sexism is "prejudice or discrimination based on sex, especially discrimination against women," that involves "behavior, conditions, or attitudes that foster stereotypes of social roles based on sex" (Webster's, 1995, p. 1073). Prejudice involves negative attitudes and prejudgments about a group. Discrimination involves the actual treatment of that group's members in a negative or unfair manner. Aspects of diversity directly affect how individuals function and interact with other systems in the social environment.

The aspect of diversity addressed here is gender. Because men in our society have traditionally held the majority of positions of power, this chapter will focus on the state and status of women as victims of sexism.

This chapter will:

▶ Identify and discuss traditional gender role expectations and stereotypes as they affect people over the life span.
▶ Assess the impacts of sexism on both men and women.
▶ Examine some of the differences between men and women, including personality, abilities, and communication styles.
▶ Discuss and examine the issues of economic inequality, sexual harassment, sexist language, rape and sexual assault, battered women, and the empowerment of women.
▶ Present strategies for combating sexism and achieving sexual equality.

◊ Gender Role Stereotypes

From the moment they're born, boys and girls are treated very differently. Girls are wrapped in pink blankets and parents are told that they now have "a beautiful little girl." Boys, on the other hand, are wrapped in blue blankets and parents are told that they now are the proud parents of "a bouncing baby boy." The process of gender stereotyping continues through childhood, adolescence, and adulthood. Gender stereotyping involves expectations about how people should behave based on their gender. Female stereotypes include being "nurturant, supportive, intuitive, emotional, . . . needful, dependent, tender, timid, fragile, . . . childlike, . . . passive, . . . obedient, . . . [and] . . . submissive"; in stark contrast male stereotypes include being "powerful, creative, intelligent, rational, independent, self-reliant, strong, courageous, daring, responsible, . . . forceful, . . . authoritative, . . . [and] successful" (Ruth, 1998, p. 153). These stereotypes have

nothing to do with an individual's personality, his or her own personal strengths and weaknesses, or likes and dislikes. Note, however, that gender stereotypes held by many in this culture do not apply equally to all racial and ethnic groups. For example, the traditional gender role for African American women includes both strength and independence (Strong et al., 1999).

A major problem with gender-based stereotypes is that they often limit people's alternatives. Pressure is exerted from many sources for people to conform to gender-based expectations. This pressure affects the individual and affects the alternatives available to him or her.

For example, until 1920, when women finally were allowed to vote, concrete political input was not available to them. Before that time, the political macro system (the U.S. government) dictated that women could not vote. Gender-based stereotypes about women that helped maintain that law may have included these: that women were not bright enough to partake in decision making;

that women belonged in the home, caring for husband and children, not in the hectic world of politics; and that women were destined to be the virtuous upholders of purity and human dignity (Rothman, 1978)—qualities not to be "muddied" in the political arena. Whatever the reasons, women were simply not allowed to vote.

In order to understand and assess human behavior one must be aware of the pressures that gender-based stereotypes bring to bear on people. Social workers need to understand how human diversity affects behavior. Gender is one critical type of diversity. Gender-based differences and stereotypes will be examined within the contexts of childhood, adolescence, and adulthood.

Childhood

We established in Chapter 4 that females and males are treated differently from the moment they are born. Even parents who state that they consciously try to avoid imposing gender stereotypes on their children nevertheless do treat girls and boys differently (Carroll & Wolpe, 1996; Crooks & Baur, 2002; Bernstein et al., 2003). Thus, it's difficult to separate out any inborn differences from those that are learned.

Parents generally treat male children in a more physical manner than female children. Parents also tend to communicate to male and female children differently (Byer et al., 2002; Lott, 1994). For example, they tend to respond positively to boys who behave actively and to girls who talk calmly or touch gently.

Boys are discouraged from crying (Lott, 1994; McCammon, Knox, & Schact, 1993). If 6-year-old Susie falls, skins her knee, and comes into the house crying, her mother might respond, "You poor thing. Did you hurt yourself? It's okay now. Let me kiss it and make it better." If 6-year-old Bill falls, skins his knee, and runs into the house, his mother might respond, "Now, now, Bill, big boys don't cry. It'll be okay. Let me put a Band-aid on it." Even very little boys are often encouraged to be strong, brave, and bereft of outward emotion. A tragic result of this is that as adults, males often maintain this facade. This sometimes creates problems in adult love and sexual relationships where men are expected to express their feelings and communicate openly.

Gender differences are demonstrated in how children play (Szegedy-Maszak, 2001). Boys are more aggressive than girls. Additionally, children tend to choose gender-related toys. Boys are drawn to "masculine" toys such as guns and trucks, whereas girls tend to prefer "feminine" playthings like Barbies.

Adolescence

Because it is a time of change, adolescence can be difficult. Bodies change drastically, sexual desires emerge, peers exert tremendous pressure to conform, personal identities are struggling to surface, and conflicts with parents are rampant. In addition to these other issues, adolescents must deal with powerful pressures to conform to gender stereotypes exerted by parents, peers, teachers, and the media (Lips, 1995; McCammon et al., 1998).

Masters, Johnson, and Kolodny (1995) indicate that male adolescents are expected to abide by three basic rules. First, they must achieve success at athletics. Second, they have to become enthralled with girls and sex. Third, they don't dare show any interest in feminine things or manifest any feminine behavior. Young men who violate these rules are subject to social ostracism and ridicule. The reasons for these pressures to conform are probably twofold. The first reason is that masculinity and femininity are often seen as two opposite extremes. If a male shows any signs of leaning toward feminine behavior, he may be shifted into the feminine category. The second reason is to avoid any suspicion that he may be homosexual (see Chapter 13).

Adolescent girls, on the other hand, have problems of their own. Lott (1994) describes three cultural themes that are predominant in shaping young women's gender roles. It should be noted that the cultural themes explained here are heterosexual in orientation. It is excessively difficult for young women who are lesbians to survive and thrive under pressure to live in a world pushing them to appeal to men (Lott, 1994; Weitz, 1995).

First, despite advances and changes on many levels over the past decades, "the search for Mr. Right is as primary and important" a cultural theme for today's teenagers as ever (Lott, 1994, p. 69). Beginning in adolescence, women "are faced with pressures to balance their achievement needs against their desire for relationship, and for marriage and family" (Lips, 1995, p. 139). Therefore, many young women tend first to determine how work and family roles can be combined; their second task, then is to orient themselves toward a career that will accommodate their family responsibilities (Corder & Stephan, 1984; Lips, 1995). This may be one reason why "most adolescent women rule out occupations that are high in prestige or in required commitment" and "continue to base their occupational choices on gender-stereotyped perceptions of family roles" (Lips, 1995, pp. 140–141).

A female adolescent gets messages from many sources, including parents and teachers, that achievement in a career may detract from her ability to fulfill her gender role expectations as a woman (Lips, 1995; Lott, 1994; Reskin & Hartman, 1986; Sherman, 1982). For example, one 17-year-old female high school senior happened to be 6 feet tall, beautiful, and poised. She was also ranked fourth academically in a class of 467 students at a prestigious suburban high school. Her high school guidance counselor emphatically urged her to think about selling fashion clothing for some large department store. No mention was made of becoming an astrophysicist, a corporation attorney, or a brain surgeon. According to the guidance counselor, those were professions more oriented toward men. But the fact is that a person's gender role and achievement are two totally unrelated concepts. One has nothing to do with the other. The young woman, by the way, eventually became an occupational therapist.

A second cultural theme engulfing young women is the importance of being popular and feminine (Lott, 1994). Early on, they learn that the way to achieve this involves "dressing in the latest fashion, covering up blemishes, being friendly and available, and smiling" (p. 72). Much behavior is oriented toward attracting men. One unfortunate consequence is that female adolescents are often considered foolish and captivated by shallow frivolities

such as shopping and making themselves beautiful (Lott, 1994; Freedman, 2001). One marketing survey completed by teenage girls revealed that what they preferred doing more than anything else was shopping; school and volunteer activities were last on the list (Patinkin, 1987).

A third cultural theme for socializing young women concerns being flexible, considerate, and taking care of others (Lott, 1994). Establishing a unique identity yet retaining responsibility for taking care of others presents quite a dilemma for young women. Where should they concentrate their efforts and attentions? Should they develop their own personalities, interests, and careers? Or, should they focus on making others happy and satisfying others' needs?

Spotlight 9.1 describes the importance of cross-cultural influences on gender role development.

Adulthood

Women are taught that they should be fulfilled by becoming wives and mothers (Lips, 1995; Lott, 1994). Men, on the other hand, are taught that their main source of self-satisfaction should come from their jobs

Spotlight on Diversity 9.1 — Cross-Cultural Perspectives on Gender Role Development

Gender role socialization, of course, varies depending on one's cultural background. Differences in roles between men and women are exaggerated in some cultures and diminished in others. Huang and Ying (1998) describe the values associated with a Chinese heritage: "Gender and birth position were . . . associated with certain duties and privileges. Sons were more highly valued than daughters; family lineage was passed through the male, while females were absorbed into the families of their husbands. The first-born son, the most valued child, received preferential treatment as well as more familial responsibilities. The prescriptive roles for daughters were less rewarding; females often did not come into positions of authority or respect until they assumed the role of mother-in-law" (p. 38).

China continues to enforce the policy that most couples may have only one child. Because male infants are valued much more highly than females, many parents choose to give their infant girl up for adoption and try again for a boy (Schoof, 1999).

Ramirez (1998) describes the gender role socialization of many Mexican Americans: "Differences in sex-role socialization are clearly evident in this culture and become especially prominent at adolescence. The adolescent female is likely to remain much closer to the home than the male and to be protected and guarded in her contacts with others beyond the family, so as to preserve her femininity and innocence. The adolescent male, following

the model of his father, is given much more freedom to come and go as he chooses and is encouraged to gain worldly knowledge outside the home in preparation for the time when he will assume the role of husband and father" (p. 220).

African Americans, on the other hand, are often taught to assume more egalitarian roles (Strong, et al., 2002). Hines and Boyd-Franklin (1996) describe the gender roles characterizing many African American women: "African American women, who often are more actively religious than their mates, tend to be regarded as 'all sacrificing' and the 'strength of the family.' Their identity often is tied to their role as mothers. . . . Historically, they have worked outside the home, sometimes as the sole wage earners, particularly in times of high unemployment" (p. 69).

Remember, however, not to make automatic assumptions. Just because an individual belongs to an ethnic or racial group, that individual does not automatically conform to the gender role traits that often characterize that group. The idea is to be sensitive to differences and appreciative of diverse strengths. Any individual may experience some degree of *acculturation*,—"an ethnic person's adoption of the dominant culture in which he or she is immersed. There are several degrees of acculturation; a person can maintain his or her own traditional cultural beliefs, values, and customs from the country of origin [or cultural heritage] to a greater or a lesser extent" (Lum, 2000, p. 201).

(McCammon et al., 1993; Stockard & Johnson, 1992). The pressures and expectations resulting from both of these stereotypes often create serious problems. A woman who devotes herself entirely to being a wife and homemaker makes herself entirely dependent on her husband. If her husband dies, becomes ill, or leaves her, such a woman is in a vulnerable position. About one out of two marriages in the United States ends in divorce (Kail & Cavanaugh, 1996; U.S. Department of Commerce, 1990).

There are at least four disadvantages for women that are associated with traditional gender role socialization and stereotypes (Lott, 1994; McCammon et al., 1993). For one thing, women tend to be treated differently and less positively than men by the educational system (Sapiro, 1999). Ultimately, as we will discuss, women tend to enter fields where they make significantly less money than men do (McCammon et al., 1998; Steiger & Wardell, 1995). Numerous studies reveal that teachers tend to give more attention to boys than to girls (American Association of University Women, 1992; Bailey, 1993; Saltzman, 1994; Sapiro, 1999) Significant research has investigated how schools tend to drive "girls away from science, technology, and mathematics" (Sapiro, 1999). One study found that 73 percent of female scientists felt they had been discriminated against on the basis of gender, compared with only 13 percent of male scientists (Sonnert & Holton, 1996).

A second disadvantage of gender role stereotyping for women is the potential stress generated from the demands and contradictions inherent in the traditional female gender role. For example, female college students are more likely than their male counterparts to experience stress in at least three areas (Gillespie & Eisler, 1992; McAnulty & Burnette, 2001). First, they tend to worry that they aren't beautiful enough, especially that they're too fat. Second, they worry that they're too assertive. Third, they're concerned that they fail to be as nurturant and supportive as they're supposed to be.

A third disadvantage for women is that even when they do work outside the home, which most do, they are still expected to do the majority of the housework and child care (Faludi, 1991; Golding, 1990; Grant, 1988; Lott, 1994; Ruth. 1998; Sapiro, 1999). This is true regardless of social class, the status of the woman's job, or rural or urban residence. When more time and energy are devoted to home and family, there is simply less time and energy left to contribute to outside work and career. Often, this expectation is related to experiencing less marital satisfaction than their spouses (Basow, 1992; McCammon et al., 1993). McCammon and associates (1993) comment that this is at least partially due to how women "experience role overload; they are expected to

keep their husbands, children, and employers happy, to keep a clean house, and to keep up the correspondence with her (and his) parents" (p. 299).

For example, Sharon and Dick, who were both professionals in their late 30s, married late and chose to have no children. They lived in a tiny duplex for several years to save money so that they might buy a new home. Finally, they made it. They had saved enough, and it was moving day. They asked Dick's parents to help them move. That was a big mistake. For years Sharon and Dick both worked long hours outside of the home in their jobs. They had divided the housework up by room. Sharon had the kitchen, the extra bedroom, which was her office, and the bathroom to keep clean. Dick, on the other hand, had the bedroom and the living room as his domain. When the large pieces of furniture were moved out, Sharon made the mistake of walking into the bedroom, Dick's domain, as Dick's father was sweeping large dust balls around the floor. He barked abrasively at Sharon, "You better not let your new house get this dirty! This is disgusting!" Sharon's father-in-law and the world made housecleaning Sharon's responsibility and burden as the wife. Any uncleanliness was clearly considered her fault. This was despite the fact that she had never been in the least bit domestically oriented. Housework always had bored her to tears.

A fourth disadvantage of gender role stereotyping for a woman is that her value "is often defined by men in terms of her body and appearance" (Lott, 1994; McCammon et al., 1993, p. 299). Men prefer women who look like "Barbies" with large breasts and hourglass figures (Furnham, Hester, & Weir, 1990; Handy. 1999; Turner, 1999). Lott (1994) stresses the interchangeability of female beauty by describing a cartoon in which a director on a movie set is trying to stage a scene. A tall, muscular, dark-haired, prominent-chinned hero roosts on a bed, impatiently awaiting his damsel. Meanwhile, the director has placed his arm around a naked woman with huge breasts and an hourglass figure. But, her face is a blank space. Hence, the director bellows, "Makeup, please!" The emphasis on being beautiful becomes more intense as women age. Even women who approach the ideal image of beauty to begin with find it hard to keep it up.

Men, too, experience lack of freedom and negative consequences from gender role stereotyping. McCammon and her associates (1993) cite three repercussions. First, men are pressured to establish an identity through their work. In essence, a man is an engineer, a salesman, a mortician, a dentist, or in some other career. A man holding a job with lesser status is often thought to be a lesser person. Related to occupation is how much money a man makes. Men who make less money are thought of as less masculine than men who make more money (Rubenstein, 1990).

A second negative impact on men of gender role stereotyping is the pressure not to express emotions (Crooks & Baur, 2001; McCammon et al., 1993). Men are taught that they should not cry, and that they should be strong and decisive. They should especially withhold any emotional demonstrations associated with weakness, such as depression, fear, and sadness (Blier & Blier-Wilson, 1989; Crooks & Baur, 1999). Intimacy is more difficult for men than women, perhaps due to how they were socialized (Masters et al., 1995). This may relate to the idea that displaying emotion displays weakness. Therefore, revealing true intimate feelings may be seen as a sign of weakness to be avoided.

A third negative consequence of gender role stereotyping for men involves the fact that they have an average life span that is significantly less than that of women. For instance, white females live more than 5 years longer than white males and African American females live over 7 years longer than their male counterparts (U.S. Census Bureau, 2001). Biology, of course, is involved. However, the implications of traditional gender role pressure is also apparent (Harrison, Chin & Ficarrotto, 1992). McCammon and associates (1993) explain:

> The traditional male role emphasizes achievement, competition, and suppression of feelings, all of which may produce stress. Not only is stress itself harmful to physical health, it also may lead to compensatory behaviors, such as smoking, alcohol and drug abuse, and dangerous risk taking. (p. 302)

The ongoing problem for both men and women is that gender stereotypes pressure people to conform. They don't allow much room for individuality and creativity. If we become more flexible and gender stereotypes dissolve, maybe people will be more objective in assessing themselves and not feel pressured to be something they're not. Abolishing gender stereotypes may give us all the freedom to develop more realistic expectations and to live the way we choose.

ᘒ Male/Female Differences

Some differences do emerge between males and females. To what extent they are due to biological predisposition or to environmental effects is unknown. Some of these differences are evident in abilities and in communication styles.

Ability Level

Although there are no differences between male and females in terms of intellectual ability or IQ, there has been heated debate for many years regarding the differences in males' and females' verbal ability. Males have traditionally been thought to have better mathematical ability and females better verbal ability. However, later research has raised some serious questions about the extent of these differences and even whether significant differences exist at all.

A recent U.S. Department of Education (2000) study found that boys scored a little higher on math and science tests. However, girls were better students overall, in addition to being better readers and writers. Still other research found virtually no differences between boys and girls in verbal ability (Hyde & Linn, 1988; Rosen, 1995).

Interestingly, some research indicates small differences between girls' and boys' mathematical ability in early elementary school (Robinson et al., 1996). Another study found that these differences actually intensify *after* adolescence (Burkham, Lee, & Smerdon, 1997). However, an analysis of 100 studies, published between 1962 and 1988, found no significant differences in this regard (Hyde, 1996; Hyde, Fennema, & Lamon, 1990).

There is some evidence that boys, as early as age 4, tend to score higher than girls in tests measuring visual and spatial ability (Livesey & Intili, 1996; Papalia et al., 2001). Other research on adults in both Ghana and Norway found similar differences between genders (Amponsah & Krekling, 1997). However, still other research, analyzing 286 studies of spatial ability, found no significant differences between boys and girls prior to adolescence (Voyer, Voyer, & Bryden, 1995).

Is this confusing? What really is true? The debate continues. At its core is the nature-nurture controversy. To what extent are such abilities innate and to what extent are they the result of the differential treatment of boys and girls? The important thing is not to make assumptions regarding an individual's ability on the basis of gender. The fact is that some girls score higher on mathematical achievement tests than the majority of boys; some boys score higher on verbal achievement tests than the majority of girls (Deaux, 1984). In general, differences are small and appear to be decreasing (Coon, 2001; Lips, 1995; Lott, 1994).

Communication Styles

Another area in which differences between males and females are evident is verbal and nonverbal communication style (Henley & Freeman, 1995; Lott, 1994). Contrary to popular belief, men spend more time talking than women do (Hyde, 1994). Men also interrupt conversations more than women do (Henley & Freeman, 1995; Hyde, 1994; Turner & Rubinson, 1993).

Women are more likely to give information or make self-disclosures than men are (Henley & Freeman, 1995; Hyde & DeLamater, 2000). Self-disclosure can place a person in a vulnerable or inferior position. It involves increasing the other person's power (Henley & Freeman, 1984). The person who receives the information can choose to criticize the discloser or can give the information to other people.

It is interesting to note that the less people adhere rigidly to traditional gender role stereotypes, the more flexible they are in their levels of self-disclosure (Gerdes et al., 1981; Sollie & Fischer, 1985). They are more likely to vary their amount of self-disclosure depending on the situation, how much others are sharing about themselves, and the topic they're discussing.

Nonverbal behavior also differs between men and women. Men more frequently touch other people, while women are most likely to be the ones who are touched (Henley & Freeman, 1995; Hyde, 1994). Touching has also been found to be associated with status (Henley & Freeman, 1995). Persons of higher status are much more likely to touch persons of lower status than the other way around. The fact that women are more likely to be touched implies that somehow they are perceived to have a lower status.

Another difference in communication styles is that women often tend to be coy in their behavior. Henley and Freeman (1984) define being coy as involving gestures of submission including lowering the eyes from another's gaze, falling silent when interrupted or pointed at (or not beginning to speak at all), and cuddling to the touch. These may be considered by some to be typically "feminine" behaviors. Picture the stereotypical nineteenth-century Southern belle fluttering at every eligible man. Being coy, along with its sexual connotations, conveys deference, dependence, and a sense of needing leadership and protection.

Although many of these differences in communication styles are subtle and minor, in combination they mean a lot. Many of women's most salient issues involve unfairness and victimization due to sexism. To begin to examine the issues and to initiate change, some of the foundations of sexism need to be understood. Changes in these behaviors, when they're all considered together, may bring about significant adjustments in gender role expectations and the distribution of power.

People as Individuals

Men and women are more similar than dissimilar. The differences we refer to are differences in treatment and differences in what people have learned. Sexism needs to be addressed because it's unfair. It causes people to be treated differently because of their gender when there are no objective reasons for differential treatment.

Each individual, whether male or female, has the right to make choices. Cutting through and obliterating gender stereotypes and sexism will give people as individuals more freedom. Each individual will then have a better chance of being the way he or she naturally is comfortable being. The idea is to confront the hidden rules that pressure people to conform on the basis of gender. Women can then be assertive without being pushy. Men won't have to be strong all of the time and will be freer to express their feelings. Tasks and the burdens of leadership can then be shared or divided on the basis of mutual decision making. The best of each individual's personality traits can then blossom and be nurtured.

Significant Issues and Events in the Lives of Women

Women have been the victims of sexism in many striking and concrete ways. Historically, they have had fewer rights and have been financially less well off to a significant degree. They are victims of life events (rape and domestic violence) that rarely touch the lives of men.

The issues addressed here were selected on the basis of prevalence, severity, and current relevance. They include economic inequality, sexual harassment, sexist language, sexual assault, battered women, and the empowerment of women.

Economic Inequality

It is a well-known fact that women generally earn less than men. Today, women earn about 76 percent of what men earn (U.S. Census Bureau, 2001). The wage gap between women and men becomes even worse when race is taken into account. That is, women of color are significantly more disadvantaged than white women. Spotlight 9.2 indicates that Hispanic women earn less than African American women and both groups earn less than white women. Also, consider that for all races women earn significantly less than men do at every educational level. The median weekly

	All Races	White	African American	Hispanic
Females	$491	$500	$429	$364
Males	$646	$669	$503	$414

Spotlight on Diversity 9.2

Gender/Racial Comparison of Median Weekly Earnings

Source: U.S. Census Bureau, "Full-time Wage and Salary Workers—Number and Earnings: 1985 to 2000," *Statistical Abstract of the United States: 2001,* 121st ed. (Washington, DC: Government Printing Office), p. 403.

Economic inequality is a long-standing sexist issue. Today, women earn about 76 percent of what men earn.

© Lou Dematteis/Jeroboam

earnings[1] for women with a bachelor's degree or more are 55 percent of what men with a college education or more earn; similarly, the median income for women with a high school education is 59 percent of what correspondingly educated men earn (U.S. Census Bureau, 2001).

1. The *median* is "the middle number in a given sequence of numbers" (Nichols, 1999, p. 822).

A number of reasons have been given for gender-based salary differences. A major one is that women and men tend to be clustered in different kinds of occupations. Occupations more likely to be characterized by men usually pay higher salaries. See Table 9.1.

The majority of American women work outside the home (U.S. Census Bureau, 2001). Their work is critical to their livelihood and, in many cases, to their self-concept. As we have noted, however, women tend to be clustered in occupations that historically are relatively low paying. More than 70 percent of working women are employed in occupations made up of more than 80 percent women; these included nurses and health technicians, elementary and secondary school teachers, salesclerks, clerical workers, apparel and textile workers, and service workers (including waitresses, maids, and dental assistants) (Thornborrow & Sheldon, 1995; U.S. Census Bureau, 1998; U.S. Department of Labor, 1991). Men, on the other hand, tend to work in better paying occupations as physicians, managers, engineers, lawyers, and construction workers.

Perhaps an even more striking finding is that for most job categories (including those that are viewed as being feminine and those viewed as being masculine) women earn less than men in the same job category while doing the same work. For example, the percentages of women's earnings as compared to men's in the following job categories are: 80 percent for computer programmers, 73 percent for bookkeepers, 76 percent for cooks, 61 percent for office managers, and 58 percent for salespersons (Lott, 1994; U.S. Census Bureau, 1998; U.S. Department of Labor, 1991). Other studies have found similar gender differences in salary for physicians, engineers, accountants, lawyers, and other professional specialties (Schreiner, 1984; U.S. Census Bureau, 1998; *U.S. News and World Report,* 1996).

The same picture of wage inequity is found in social work. Female social workers earn about 80 cents for every dollar earned by male social workers (Lott, 1994). Huber

Table 9.1	Employment Positions Held by Women		
Female-Dominated Professions	**Percent Female**	**Male-Dominated Professions**	**Percent Female**
Secretaries	99.0	Automobile mechanics	0.5
Dental hygienists	98.6	Firefighters	1.0
Dental assistants	98.1	Carpenters	1.4
Child-care workers	96.9	Loggers	1.4
Receptionists	96.8	Construction workers	1.8
Cleaners and servants	95.8	Airplane pilots	2.1
Registered nurses	95.8	Mechanics and repairers	2.8
Bookkeepers	91.0	Truck drivers	3.1
Bank tellers	91.0	Material moving equipment operators	4.8
Nursing aides	88.7	Clergy	5.6
Dieticians	90.8	Police officers	5.7
Data-entry keyers	93.6	Engineers	5.8
Telephone operators	90.4	Dentists	6.7
Librarians	87.3	Farm operators	12.1
Elementary school teachers	83.3	Architects	12.7
Textile machine operators	82.1	Lawyers	15.3
Cashiers	84.4	Surveying technicians	17.5

Source: U.S. Census Bureau, *Statistical Abstract of the United States*, 2001, 121st ed. (Washington, DC: Government Printing Office), pp. 380–382.

and Orlando (1995) report on their research findings for social workers holding master's degrees:

> *Male social workers who responded to a survey reported receiving about $8,000 more annually than female social workers. Differences persisted when other factors were controlled: age, years of experience, number of hours worked per week, method of practice (administrative versus direct practice), and field of practice (for example, children and families versus mental health). (p. 585)*

Additionally, Gibelman and Schervish (1993) found support for a "glass ceiling" in social work on the basis of gender. They analyzed the demographics of NASW's membership and found that "male social workers disproportionately hold managerial positions, assume such positions earlier in their careers, and earn more money in these positions than do their female counterparts" (p. 443).

Academia is another area characterized by gender role discrepancies in status and earnings. Generally speaking, "the higher the rank, the fewer the women" (Fox 1995, p. 231). Women teaching in colleges and universities comprise 53 percent of lecturers, 36 percent of assistant professors, 25 percent of associate professors, and only 14 percent of full professors (Sapiro, 1999). Women are also more likely than men to hold part-time appointments; this status often results in their becoming "permanent,

marginally employed faculty who exist on the fringes of academic life" (Fox, 1995, p. 232).

Women also have less direct political power in terms of the actual number of political offices they hold. As of this writing, 73 women are serving in the U.S. Congress, making up 13.6 percent (Center for American Women and Politics, 2002). Of these, 13 are U.S. senators, making up 13 percent of the 100 senators. The remaining 60 serve in the House of Representatives, making up 13.8 percent of the 435 U.S. representatives. Despite the fact that the number of women holding national public office does not approach their proportion of the total population (almost 51 percent) (U.S. Census Bureau, 2002), these figures reflect an all-time high (Center for American Women and Politics, 2002).

Women tend to do a bit better in state governments. For example, although only 5 individuals, or 10 percent, of the 50 state governors are women, women make up 22.6 percent of state legislators (Center for American Women in Politics, 2002).

The statistics reflect ways in which women are disadvantaged and undervalued in our society. People who hold important political positions have significant power and control over other people's lives. What do you think are the reasons for never having elected a woman as president of the United States?

❧ Sexual Harassment

Ann's boss states that if she doesn't have sex with him, she won't make it through her 6-month probationary period. She really needs the job. She doesn't know what to do.

Barbara's male supervisor likes to sneak up behind her and surprise her by putting his arms around her. This makes her feel very uncomfortable. However, he's responsible for scheduling her hours, evaluating her, and giving her raises. She is terrified of confronting him.

Harry really needs to get a good grade in his course with Dr. Getsom, a female professor, in order to keep his scholarship and stay in school. So far he has a "D+" in the course. When he goes to see Dr. Getsom, she likes to touch him a lot and acts very friendly. Last Thursday she said she would "see what could be done about helping him with his grade" if they'd start dating. He feels trapped. He doesn't know what to do.

One of the other financial assistance workers in the county social services department really annoys Buella. The man is constantly telling dirty jokes about women. Additionally, he whistles at any woman under 25 who passes his desk.

Sexual harassment is a serious form of sex discrimination that recently has gained public attention. It affects business, industrial, academic, and public work environments. The number of sexual harassment complaints filed with the federal Equal Employment and Opportunity Commission (EEOC) "has more than doubled, from 6,883 in 1991 to 15,889 in 1997" (Ahmad, 1998, p. 61).

Sexual harassment is illegal. Title VII of the Civil Rights Act of 1964 outlaws discrimination on the basis of sex along with discrimination on the basis of race. Legal precedents have been established, which include sexual harassment as a form of sex discrimination (Maypole & Skaine, 1983). In 1991, the Civil Rights Act "was amended to allow juries to award compensatory and punitive damages" to people seeking legal action concerning sexual harassment in employment-related civil cases[2] (Ahmad, 1998, p. 61). Additionally, individual state laws can prohibit sexual harassment and provide legal recourse to victims.[3] Title IX of the Higher Educational Amendments of 1972 specifically prohibits sex discrimination from

taking place on university campuses. Finally, individual agencies, organizations, or universities may have established policies prohibiting sexual harassment.[4]

The Definition of Sexual Harassment

Sexual harassment involves unwelcome sexual advances, requests for sexual favors, and other verbal or physical conduct of a sexual nature under the following conditions: First, submission to such conduct is required as a condition of employment or education. Second, submission to such conduct is used as a basis for decisions that affect an individual's employment or academic achievement. Such conduct results in a hostile, intimidating, or anxiety-producing work or educational environment.[5]

Sexual harassment occurs when a female employee is made to tolerate the regular touching of her arms, waist, neck, or buttocks by her male supervisor in order to ensure that she gets good supervisory reviews. Sexual harassment exists when a female administrative assistant is pressured to become sexually involved with the vice-president she works for if she wants to keep her job. Sexual harassment also is evident when a male college professor likes to touch young male students in suggestive ways and refers to them as "pretty boys."

Sexual harassment almost always involves elements of unequal power and coercion. Sometimes it involves promising a victim a reward or threatening a punishment on the basis of the victim's sexual cooperation. Other times it involves becoming overly and inappropriately personal with a victim, either by sharing intimacies or prying into the victim's personal life.

Although most victims are women, sexual harassment can be directed at either males or females. In this respect it can be considered a human rights issue. A member of either gender may be the victim of harassing, offensive behavior of a sexual nature. For example, consider the case of Joseph Oncale, who filed a sexual harassment suit against Sundowner Offshore Services, a Houston firm that drills for oil in the Gulf of Mexico. Cloud (1998) described the situation:

Oncale had worked on offshore rigs before (and does today), but says he never encountered such abusive treatment as when

---

2. Civil court cases "relate to private rights and to remedies [such as cash awards] sought by action or suit distinct from criminal proceedings" (*Webster's*, 1995).

3. For example, the state of Wisconsin's Fair Employment Act, as amended in 1978, prohibits sexual harassment.

4. For example, the University of Wisconsin System's Board of Regents has stated in its Resolution #2384 of May 8, 1981, that sexual harassment "is unacceptable and impermissible conduct which will not be tolerated."

5. The definition of sexual harassment is taken from Resolution #2384 of the Board of Regents of the University of Wisconsin System, dated May 8, 1981. The Equal Employment Opportunity Commission has published a similar definition of sexual harassment in "Guidelines on Discrimination because of Sex, Title VII, Sec. 703," *Federal Register,* 45 (April 11, 1980).

he signed on with Sundowner in 1991. He claims, for instance, that three male co-workers held him down in a shower and shoved a bar of soap between his buttocks. One of them threatened rape, he says. He quit and later was found to have posttraumatic stress. (p. 55)

After the case was thrown out by an appeals court, the U.S. Supreme Court later ruled unanimously that "men who sexually harass other men (and women who harass women) are discriminating against them and thus breaking the law" (Cloud, 1998, p. 55). A key is that the harassment must involve dissimilar treatment of men and women.

A relatively clear example involves harassment of gay or lesbian people. They can be targets of inappropriate sexual advances, threats, and promises when such overtures involve someone of their same gender or the opposite gender.

Sexual harassment can also take place when verbal remarks make the work or academic atmosphere offensive or stifling. Sexual remarks that are not related to the work at hand can interfere with productivity and performance. For example, female students might be forced to endure derogatory remarks from a male instructor that focus on women's anatomy or on their inferior ability. Or female employees might force themselves to tolerate their supervisor's annoying behaviors. These might include a male's constant reference to women as "girls," his comments that "it must be that time of month" whenever a woman is moody, his remarks about how he likes "his girls" to wear short skirts, and his placing of pictures of naked women on the office bulletin board. Any of these behaviors disrupts a positive, productive working environment.

Strengthening the Definition: A Macro System Response

A U.S. Supreme Court decision in late 1993 reinforced the seriousness of a hostile and offensive working environment as one aspect of sexual harassment (Kaplan, 1993; Sachs, 1993). Teresa Harris waited 6 years for the Supreme Court to hear her case after filing a sexual harassment case against her former employer, Charles Hardy, president of a Nashville truck rental company. Harris had been a rental manager in Hardy's employ. She accused Hardy of asking her and other female employees to retrieve coins out of his front pants pocket, suggesting that Harris "accompany him to the local Holiday Inn to negotiate her raise," and "regularly [responding] to her with remarks like, 'You're a woman; what do you know?'" (Sachs, 1993, p. 44). He also "called her a 'dumb ass woman'" and "suggested she won an account by having sex with a client" (Kaplan, 1993, p. 34).

Although lower courts found that Hardy's behavior "was not so severe as to be expected to seriously affect her psychological well-being," the Supreme Court unanimously ruled in her favor (Sachs, 1993, p. 44). Justice Sandra Day O'Connor wrote on behalf of the Court that it rejected the former "psychological injury" standard courts typically upheld. In prior cases, people filing charges had to prove that they had suffered severe psychological injury in order to win cases and collect damages (Kaplan, 1993). The new standard makes that unnecessary. Now "an employer has broken the law if a 'reasonable person' would find the workplace so filled with sexual improprieties that it had become a hostile and abusive environment" (Sachs, 1993, p. 44). It is interesting that Supreme Court Justice Clarence Thomas agreed with the verdict but did not utter a single word about the case (Sachs, 1993).

The U.S. Supreme Court has made even more recent rulings that determine appropriate "new parameters of behavior in the school or workplace" (Lavelle, 1998, p. 30). The three relevant cases involved "a lifeguard who was threatened and assaulted with vulgarities by her supervisors; a sales agent who was urged to submit to the sexual demands of a boss who could make life 'very hard or very easy' for her; and a 14-year-old student accosted by a teacher who visited her home on the pretext of returning a book" (Lavelle, 1998, p. 30). The three new rules both facilitate a complainant's ability to file and win a sexual harassment lawsuit and provide some protection for companies that develop strong prevention and disciplinary programs.

The first rule is that an employee can successfully claim sexual harassment even though she has been treated well on the job. This contrasts with the old rule that dictated that "to prove harassment, a worker has to show that because she resisted sexual advances she was punished in terms of salary, assignments or promotions" (Lavelle, 1998, p. 30).

The second newly established principle is that a manager can be held accountable for a harasser's action, if the company does not have a strong system of handling harassment issues. This deviates from the prior rule that a manager is probably not held responsible for a harasser's behavior if he "isn't informed that one of his employees is harassing other workers" (Lavelle, 1998, p. 31). In short, it is now management's job to know and handle harassment problems.

The third new standard is that a victim of harassment must tell someone "with decision-making power" if she is being harassed (Lavelle, 1998, p. 31). This deviates from the old rule that she should inform some other person (a friend or colleague, for example).

Highlight 9.1

Sexual Harassment Allegations Plague Those in High Places

The media are bombarding the public with charges of sexual harassment. The Anita Hill/Clarence Thomas clash paved the way for many complaints to be brought out into the open (Bingham & Wolfberg, 1992). One case involved Senator Bob Packwood, who "resigned [from his 27 year U.S. Senate career] just hours after the Senate Ethics Committee voted unanimously that he be expelled from the Senate. The Committee released 10 volumes of evidence that detailed Packwood's habitual, aggressive sexual advances toward female members of his staff" (AASECT, Oct. 1995a, p. 8). More than two dozen aides and other women stepped forward to accuse Packwood of various acts of sexual harassment from 1969 to 1990 (Smolowe, 1995; Thomas & Rosenstiel, 1995). A primary factor in the investigation was the fact that Packwood attempted to alter and delete items in his personal diary that revealed his sexual escapades (Thomas & Rosenstiel, 1995). One 1989 entry in this diary reported an office rendezvous with a female staffperson he refers to as "S-1," a "very sexy thing with bright eyes and hair and ability to shift her hips." Thomas & Rosenstiel (1995) describe his notation: "After a few glasses of wine that evening, I finally said to her, 'S-1, would you like to dance?' She says, 'I'd love to.' So I slipped around the side of this gigantic desk and we danced. . . . Well, I won't bore you with all the details of the evening. S-1 and I made love, and she has the most stunning figure—big breasts. . . . They stand at attention" (p. 32).

The extensive 33-month investigation dragged on due to Packwood's lack of repentance and continuing denial. Smolowe (1995) explains: "Instead of quickly coming clean on the sexual-misconduct charges, he essentially denied knowledge of his lewd behavior by blaming alcohol and charging his accusers of lying, a maneuver that served only to bring forward new complainants and to persuade the committee to investigate charges that Packwood was intimidating potential witnesses" (p. 45). Because he resigned instead of being dismissed, Packwood will retain both his pension and health benefits worth $88,922 annually (Smolowe, 1995).

Another incident involved Paula Corbin Jones's accusation of sexual harassment against President Bill Clinton. Jones accused the president of inviting her "to a room in the Excelsior Hotel and urged her [to] perform oral sex on him" (AASECT, June 1994, p. 14). She sought "$700,000 in damages for alleged violation of her civil rights, defamation and emotional distress" (Cooper & Ferguson, 1994, p. 26). In rebuttal, Clinton stated that he "doesn't remember meeting Jones and that he didn't do anything inappropriate" (AASECT, June 1994, p. 14). Ultimately, a U.S. District court threw out Jones's sexual harassment lawsuit. The judge ruled "that even if Clinton had crudely propositioned Jones in a hotel room back in 1991, his actions constituted 'boorish and offensive' behavior rather than sexual harassment. The judge rejected the contention that [Jones] had suffered irreparable personal and professional harm as a result of the incident" (AASECT, 1998, p. 7). The judge continued "that in order to have a viable case, Jones had to prove that her refusal

The Extent of Sexual Harassment

An accurate profile of when, where, how, and to whom sexual harassment occurs does not exist. However, some surveys suggest that it is quite prevalent in a variety of settings. Renzetti and Curran (1995) indicate that women "routinely experience sexual harassment in the workplace. Studies in the United States and Great Britain reveal that from one-fifth to four-fifths of female workers have experienced sexual harassment at work" (p. 270). Research reveals that between 20 and 49 percent of faculty women and about 30 percent of female students have been subjected to some form of sexual harassment (Cole, 1990; Dzeich & Weiner, 1990; Martin, 1995; Reilly, Lott, & Gallogly, 1986; Rubin & Borgers, 1990; Sandler & Hall, 1986). Only 2 to 3 percent of female undergraduates experienced the most severe forms of *sexual* harassment such as being offered a better grade in return for sexual favors or being threatened in some way. However, a large number of women encountered less severe forms

of sexual harassment such as verbal abuse or being touched inappropriately (Reilly et al., 1986; Sandler & Hall, 1986).

One of the most massive studies to date was undertaken by the U.S. Merit Systems Protection Board (MSPB, 1981). A stratified random sampling procedure was used to involve more than 23,000 federal employees. Of the female employees surveyed, 42 percent stated that they were victims of sexual harassment of some kind during the 2-year period before the survey. Only 1 percent reported being victims of actual sexual assault. However, 29 percent indicated that "severe sexual harassment" had occurred to them. This included harassing telephone calls, unsolicited touching and embracing, and unwanted pressure to participate in sexual activities. An additional 12 percent experienced "less severe harassment." This included inappropriate sexual jokes and comments, leering looks, and excessive pressure to date the harasser. Interestingly enough, women were not the only ones to consider

to have sex with Clinton resulted in 'tangible job detriment' or the creation of a hostile work environment" (AASECT, 1998, p. 7).

Mention is merited regarding White House intern Monica Lewinsky and her sexual relationship or lack of sexual relationship (depending on the definition) with Clinton. How did the complicated scenario impact the treatment of sexual harassment? Clinton was impeached by the U.S. House of Representatives, which accused "the President of lying under oath to Kenneth Starr's grand jury about his affair with Lewinsky" (Lacayo, 1999, pp. 61). Lewinsky, had stated that she had oral sex with Clinton on several occasions. He had responded that his relationship with her did not fall under his definition of sexual relations. Clinton was eventually acquitted.

Thomas and Hosenball (1999) raise concerns that the scandal "has already done harm to the fight against sexual harassment. Several workplace consultants say they've seen an increase in harassment defendants' going on the offensive—threatening to countersue their accusers for violating their privacy" (p. 31). According to Dennis M. Brown, a partner at Littler Mendelson, the country's largest firm specializing in employment issues, "The natural reaction of a defendant is to minimize [his or her conduct]. But since the Jones case, some think the appropriate defense strategy is to lie about it. They say everything they're hearing says that everyone lies about sex, so, 'Why should I be the idiot who tells the truth and gets hung?'" (Thomas & Hosenball, 1999, p. 31).

Still another incident concerns Navy Capt. Everett L. Greene, 47, who is accused by Lt. Mary Felix, 28, and ex-Lt. Pamela Castrucci, 30, of making unwanted advances toward them (Thompson, 1995; Vistica, 1995). Both women stated that Greene made them "feel uneasy by sending them suggestive cards and gifts and calling them on the telephone" (Thompson, 1995, p. 42). The Navy dismissed the sexual harassment charges made by Castrucci (Vistica, 1995). However, Felix's case, filed in the spring of 1993, was pursued. Vistica (1995) explains the case:

> Greene . . . the navy's director of equal opportunity . . . became close to . . . Felix, who was working on a sexual-harassment hot line in his office. After Felix confided in Greene that her boyfriend had given her sexually transmitted diseases, Greene wrote her a poem called "I'll Be There." ("Whenever you need to be adored, I'll be there.") Over several months in 1993, Greene jogged and lifted weights with Felix and sent her letters and small gifts, including an old pair of men's running shorts. (p. 36)

Driving together on the way home after work one evening, Felix consoled Greene after he became upset while talking about his wife. Later, Greene sent Felix a card thanking her "for making one of my dreams come true" (Vistica, 1995, p. 36). Another of Greene's letters to Felix stated, "What you offered to do with me was very special, very precious. I wanted you just as much, if not more, than you wanted me" (Vistica, 1995, p. 36). Felix indicated that she never sought any kind of sexual involvement with Greene and that his letters horrified her. She "described her frustration over Green's attentions. 'I didn't want to believe this was happening. . . . He was a married man, my boss and old enough to be my father'" (Thompson, 1995, p. 42). Greene's response to these accusations was that both Felix and Castrucci "had confused his concern for their well-being with harassment" (p. 42).

themselves victims of sexual harassment; 15 percent of the men in the MSPB study felt that they also had been harassed.

Several variables made victimization more likely according to the MSPB research. Youth was one variable. A woman under age 20 was twice as likely to be sexually harassed as one between age 20 and 40. A second variable was marital status. Divorced and single women were more likely to be harassed than women who were married or widowed. Finally, education appeared to be a variable related to sexual harassment. Contrary to what might be expected, sexual harassment was more likely to occur to women with higher levels of education. Perhaps this finding was due to the fact that more highly educated women were more aware of sexual harassment issues and also to the fact that they assumed job positions traditionally not held by women.

Sexual harassment appears to be a serious problem. Despite the lack of a definitive profile of its occurrence, sexual harassment occurs frequently in a variety of employment and educational settings. Highlight 9.1 discusses sexual harassment allegations that plague those in high places.

Effects of Sexual Harassment

Negative psychological effects of sexual harassment include "fear of retaliation, fear of not being believed, feelings of shame and humiliation, a belief that nothing can or will be done, and a reluctance to cause problems for the harasser. In many ways, a woman who reports sexual harassment is viewed as a troublemaker or whistle-blower and is treated accordingly" (Koss et al., 1994; Stout & McPhail, 1998, p. 196).

Many women, therefore choose to try to ignore sexual harassment. In reality, the vast majority of sexually harassed women do not file a complaint (Stout & McPhail, 1998). One recent major study indicated that only about 6 percent of respondents pursued a formal complaint process (U.S. Merit Systems Protection Board, 1995).

Sexual harassment incurs financial costs as well. From 1991 to 1997 "monetary awards in federal sexual harassment suits rose from $7.1 million to $49.4 million" (Ahmad, 1998, p. 61). Additional costs for the federal government include job turnover costs such as hiring and training new employees, costs due to absenteeism and increased health problems, and reduced worker productivity due to emotional stress. The personal and emotional costs placed on the victims themselves cannot even be measured.

Highlight 9.2 provides some suggestions for confronting sexual harassment.

Highlight 9.2

Confronting Sexual Harassment

Victims of sexual harassment have several alternative routes available to them. Alternatives include ignoring the harassing behavior, avoiding the harasser, or asking the harasser to stop (Martin, 1995). The U.S. Merit Systems Protection Board (1981) study found that ignoring the behavior had virtually no effect. Asking the harasser to stop, however, effectively stopped the harassment in half of the cases.

Avoiding the harasser is another option. A severe shortcoming of this approach is that the victim is the one who must expend the effort. The ultimate avoidance measure is actually quitting the job or dropping the class in order to avoid contact with a sexual harasser. This is the least fair (and potentially most damaging) alternative to the victim. Further, it does nothing to re-educate the harasser, prevent harassment from recurring, or prepare the victim to deal with it in subsequent incidents.

There are, however, several other ways to help victims confront sexual harassment. In many cases, using these strategies will stop harassment. First, a victim needs to know his or her rights. A call to the Equal Employment Opportunity Commission (EEOC), the federal agency designated to address the issue of sexual harassment, is helpful. Many women can obtain necessary information about their rights and the appropriate procedures to follow for filing a formal complaint.

Many states also have state laws that make sexual harassment illegal. Such states often have agencies or offices that victims may call for help and information. Additionally, organizations and agencies also have specific policies against sexual harassment. Filing a formal complaint through established procedures is often an option.

However, most victims choose not to pursue the formal complaint route (Martin, 1984; U.S. Merit Systems Protection Board, 1981, 1995). Some victims fear reprisal or retaliation; others don't want to be labeled troublemakers. Still others don't choose to expend the time and effort necessary in carrying out a formal process. Most victims simply want the harassment to end so that they can work peacefully and productively.

In addition to knowing your rights, the following suggestions can be applied to most situations where sexual harassment is occurring.

1. *Confront your harasser.* Tell the harasser which specific behaviors are unwanted and unacceptable.

If you feel you cannot handle a direct confrontation, write the harasser a letter. It is helpful to criticize the harasser's behavior rather than the harasser as a person. The intent is to stop the harassment and maintain a pleasant, productive work environment. There is also the chance that the harasser was not aware that his or her behavior was offensive. In this case, giving specific feedback is frequently effective.

2. *Be assertive.* When giving the harasser feedback, look him or her directly in the eye. Look like you mean what you're saying. Don't smile. Rather, look the harasser directly in the eye, stand up straight, adopt a serious expression, and calmly state, "Please stop touching me by putting your arms around me and rubbing my neck. I don't like it." This is a serious matter. You need to get a serious point across.

3. *Document your situation* (Farley, 1978). Record every incident that occurs. Note when, where, who, and what was said or done, what you were wearing, and any available witnesses. Be as accurate as possible. Documentation does not have to be elaborate. Simple handwritten notes that state the facts will suffice. It is also a good idea to keep copies of your notes in another location.

4. *Talk to other people about the problem.* Get support from friends and colleagues. Sexual harassment often erodes self-confidence. Victims do not feel they are in control of the situation. Emotional support from others can bolster self-confidence and give victims the strength needed to confront sexual harassment. Frequently, sharing these problems with others will also allow victims to discover they're not alone. Corroboration with other victims will not only provide emotional support, but it will also strengthen a formal complaint if that option needs to be taken sometime in the future. We have already established that telling someone with decision-making power is important in the event a suit is filed.

5. *Get witnesses.* Look around when the sexual harassment is occurring and note who can observe it. Talk to these people and solicit their support. Try to make arrangements for others to be around you when you anticipate that sexual harassment is likely to occur.

❦ Sexist Language

One form of sexual harassment involves making verbal remarks that establish an offensive or stifling work or educational environment. Such language can include jokes with inappropriate sexual connotations. It can also include derogatory comments about ability based on gender. For example, a male professor might say to his students, "Girls don't usually do very well in this major. They're usually not as bright as men. They just run off and get married anyway." Such a comment is discriminatory. The professor is making an unfounded, unfair prediction. He is not attending to each student's ability to perform on an individual basis.

Many times English words themselves reflect an aura of sexism and unfairness. For instance, the word *man* seems to occur everywhere. Consider such words and phrases as *mankind, chairman, salesman, congressman,* and the *best man for the job.* Such terms often imply that women are included, but in a subsidiary way.

Another example of how sexism has infiltrated the English language is in the proper titles for men and women. On reaching adulthood, a man becomes a "Mr." for the remainder of his life. This is a polite term that makes no reference to the status of a man's personal life. A woman, however, traditionally starts as a "Miss." Following that tradition she becomes a "Mrs." upon marriage, which clearly establishes her marital status. At least

it establishes the fact that at one time or another she has been married.

Highlight 9.3 offers some suggestions for replacing sexist language in everyday conversation.

❦ Rape and Sexual Assault

The most intimate violation of a person's privacy and dignity is sexual assault. Sexual assaults involve any unwanted sexual contact where verbal or physical force is used. Although the legal definition of rape varies from one state to another, it is basically "sexual intercourse without mutual desire. It is generally seen as forced (or threat of forced) penetration of a body orifice, including the mouth, rectum, and vagina, and the use of objects or other body parts, such as fingers" (Byer & Shainberg, 1994, p. 630).

Throughout their lives the fear of assault and rape lingers in the minds of women. It is an act of violence over which they may feel they have neither control nor protection. Several aspects of sexual assault and rape will be addressed here to give an understanding of the effects on women and how women might best cope with the fact that rape exists. Note that we will refer to people who have survived sexual assault as *survivors,* not *victims.* Instead of focusing on a woman's weakness, which the word

Highlight 9.3

Using Nonsexist Language

There are ways to minimize the use of sexist language. Frequently, all it takes is becoming accustomed to a different way of phrasing words and sentences. The following are some suggestions aimed at maximizing fairness and objectivity through language.

1. Replace the word *man* with other more inclusive terms such as *human* or *person.* For example, *mankind* can become *humankind,* *chairman* can become *chairperson* or *chair,* and the *nature of man* can become the *nature of humankind.*

2. Use the term *Ms.* instead of *Miss* and *Mrs.* Ms. and Mr. are equivalent terms.

3. Try to phrase sentences so that the masculine pronouns *he, him,* and *his* can be avoided. This can be done in several ways. First, pronouns can be eliminated altogether. For example, "The average American likes to drink *his* coffee black" can be

changed to: "The average American likes black coffee."
    Second, statements can frequently be rephrased into the plural: "Average Americans like their coffee black."
    Third, masculine pronouns can be replaced with *one, you,* or *his or her.* For example: "The average American likes to drink his or her coffee black."

4. Avoid using patronizing and derogatory stereotypes. These include phrases such as *sweet young thing, the little lady, bubble-brained blonde, henpecked husband, frustrated spinster, nagging mother-in-law, dirty old man,* and *dumb jock.*

Many good suggestions can be found for using nonsexist language. However, the main idea is for a person to be sensitive to what he or she is saying. Subtle implications need to be examined in order to communicate accurately and objectively. This is especially true for social workers and is pertinent to what they say and write.

victim implies, we will use the term *survivor* to emphasize a woman's survival strengths (McHugh, 1993).

Incidence of Rape

Approximately 2,000 rapes (or about one every 5 minutes) are committed in the United States every day (Shaw & Lee, 2001). Among women college students, at least one-quarter have experienced some type of violence (Elliott & Brantley, 1997; Kelly, 1998; Shaw & Lee, 2001). One study indicated that nearly 18 percent of all women in the United States "have been victims of rape or attempted rape" (AASECT, 1999b, January, p. 7; Kirk & Okazawa-Rey, 2001). The number of rapes reported to authorities thus "is a vast underestimate of the actual number of assaults committed each year" (Allgeier & Allgeier, 2000, p. 449). It is estimated that the number of reported rapes range from 8 to 16 percent of those actually committed (Crooks & Baur, 1999; Koss, 1988; National Victim Center, 1992).

Spotlight 9.3 presents some racial and cultural differences in the incidence of violence against women.

Women fail to report being raped for many reasons. Survivors whose bodies have been brutally violated often desperately want to forget that the horror ever happened. To report it means dwelling on the details and going over the event again and again in their minds. Other survivors fear retribution from the rapist. If they call public attention to him, he might do it again to punish them. No police officer will be available all of the time for protection.

Other survivors feel that people around them will think less of them because they've been raped. It's almost as if a part of them has been spoiled, a part that they would prefer to hide from other people. Rape is an ugly crisis that takes a great amount of courage to face.

Theoretical Views of Rape

There are at least three theoretical perspectives on why rape occurs (Albin, 1977; Baron & Straus, 1989; Hyde & DeLamater, 2000; Ward, 1995). These include theories on victim precipitation of rape, the psychopathology of rapists, and the feminist perspective. The intent is not to state which one is the best theory but to present three different ways of conceptualizing rape.

Victim-Precipitated Rape. This perspective assumes that the survivor is actually to blame for the rape—that the woman "asked for it." Perhaps she was wearing provocative clothing or subconsciously desired to be raped.

An unfortunate example of how destructive this perspective can be is provided by a young female student who came to her instructor seeking help for her friend. Her friend, age 18, had attended a local festival during the prior summer. The woman somehow got separated from her friends and found herself talking and flirting with two men about age 20. Because it had been a hot July day, the woman was wearing a halter top and jeans. Suddenly, before she realized what had happened, the men shoved her into the car and swept her away to a city apartment. There they raped her throughout the night.

Spotlight on Diversity 9.3	**Cultural Differences in the Incidence of Violence Against Women**

Shaw and Lee (2001) report the following facts:

- Among Asian/Pacific Islander women, 6.8 percent reported being raped at some point in their lifetime; 17.7 percent of White women, 18.8 percent of African American women, 24.4 percent of mixed race women, and 34.1 percent of Native American/Native Alaskan women reported being raped. Among Hispanic women, 19.6 percent reported being raped.[*]

- Among Asian/Pacific Islander women, 49.6 percent reported being physically assaulted at some point in their lifetime; 51.3 percent of White women, 52.1 percent of African American women, 57.5 percent of mixed race women, and 61.4 percent of Native American/Native Alaskan women reported physical assault. Among Hispanic women, 53.2 percent reported physical assault.[*]

- Native American/Native Alaskan women were most likely to report rape and physical assault. Asian/Pacific Islander women were least likely to report victimization, although many did talk about violence as a significant concern.[*]

- Women of all races and Hispanic and non-Hispanic women were about equally vulnerable to violence by an intimate.[**]

- Rape/sexual assault rates increased as household income decreased.[**]

[*]Statistics are from the National Violence Against Women Survey.
[**]Statistics are from the National Crime Victimization Survey (p. 396).

The next morning the men put her into the car and dropped her off at the festival entrance. In terror and tears, she called her father and, sobbing, explained to him what had happened. His response to her was, "I told you not to ask for it. Why do you have to dress like that?" The woman was crushed.

This father had adopted the victim-precipitated view of rape. He immediately assumed it was his daughter's fault. Unfortunately, the young woman did not recover very well. What she had really needed from her father was support and help. What she got was blame. Six months later the young woman found herself terrified of men. Her reaction was so extreme that on the following New Year's Eve at midnight, she could not bear to watch people give each other New Year's kisses. She rushed from the room crying.

The instructor listening to the story strongly suggested that the young rape survivor get counseling help. She needed to work through her feelings and put the blame where it belonged, namely, on her attackers.

Many male students have also found the victim-precipitated view offensive. The implication is that men are animalistic and cannot control their own impulses. Various men have indicated that they find this you-know-how-men-are point of view as degrading as women might find the you-know-how-women-are perspective. Neither perspective takes into account individual differences or personal morals and values.

Rapist Psychopathology. A second theoretical perspective concerns rapist psychopathology. This view proposes that the rapist is emotionally disturbed or mentally unbalanced. He rapes because he is sick. This view places virtually none of the blame on society or on social attitudes.

The Feminist Perspective on Rape. The feminist perspective emphasizes that rape is the logical reaction of men who are socialized to dominate women. Rape is seen as a manifestation of men's need to aggressively maintain power over women. It has little to do with sexuality. Sexuality only provides a clear-cut means for exercising power. Rape is seen as a consequence of attitudes toward women that are intimately intertwined throughout the culture. The feminist perspective sees rape as a societal problem, rather than only an individual one.

Herman (1984) elaborates on this view. She points out that both aggressors and survivors are brought up to believe that sexual aggression is natural. As a result, survivors often blame themselves. The rationale is that they should have expected to be raped. They should have been prepared or have done something to prevent it.

An analogous situation concerning self-blame is the example of a woman who has her purse snatched while shopping on a Saturday afternoon. If the self-blame concept were applied, it would follow that the woman would blame herself for the incident. She would chastise herself by saying that she never should have taken her purse with her to shop in the first place. Maybe she should shop only through the home-shopping channel from now on. Of course, taking that course of action would be absurd. It was not the woman's fault. It was the purse snatcher who broke the law. He is the one who should be held responsible.

The feminist view holds that society is wrong for socializing people to assume that male sexual aggression is natural. Socializing women to consider themselves weak and nurturant also contributes to the problem. It fosters a victim mentality, that is, an expectation that it's natural for women to be victims. The feminist perspective emphasizes that these attitudes need to be changed. Only then can rape as a social problem disappear.

Common Myths about Rape

Various myths about rape need to be examined and corrected. Women need accurate information in order to make responsible decisions. They need to learn what types of conditions and circumstances prompt rape so that they may be avoided.

One myth is that rapes tend to occur in dark alleys. Although some circumstances such as hitchhiking or walking home alone in the dark tend to increase the chances of being raped, there is a good chance of being raped right in one's own home. According to Lott (1994, p. 165), "the single most common place of attack is in a woman's own residence—approximately 30 percent of all reported cases."

In cases occurring indoors, especially in their own homes, survivors are very likely to know the rapist. This presents a problem because people tend to feel safe when they're in their own homes with a person they know. However, knowledge of this fact is important if it helps people be more cautious.

One incident emphasizes the importance of caution. A 20-year-old female student sheepishly approached her instructor and finally blurted out that she had been raped at a party the past Saturday night. Although it was not in her home, it was in the home of a good friend of hers. Apparently, people attending the party were drinking and not concerning themselves with the noise level. The student found herself talking with a young male lawyer while sitting on the bed in one of the bedrooms. Suddenly, the lawyer closed and locked the door. He pinned her to the bed and began to rape her. She was awestruck that this could be happening. Although he was not a good friend, he was an acquaintance of hers. They shared several mutual friends. After all, he was even a lawyer. She resisted to the best of her ability. She was too ashamed to scream.

As she was talking about the incident several days later, her main concern was what her friends would think about her if they ever found out. Although she dreamed about getting revenge, she didn't want to jeopardize her reputation. As she continued to relate her story, her instructor discussed her feelings, the potential physical ramifications, and possible legal alternatives. Her instructor also helped the student gain a more objective perception of the incident. It was especially important for this survivor to place the blame where it belonged, namely on the rapist. Finally, her instructor referred her to counseling to give her a chance to work out and deal with the feelings about such a horrible experience.

Another myth is that only strangers are potential rapists (Koss, 1992; Masters et al., 1995; McCammon et al., 1993; Strong et al., 1999). One study indicated the over three-quarters of all women aged 18 and older who reported that they had been raped named their significant other or a "date" as the perpetrator (Kirk & Okazawa-Rey, 2001; National Institute of Justice and Centers for Disease Control and Prevention, 1998). This is known as *acquaintance* or *date rape*. Acquaintance rapes are particularly prevalent on college campuses.

Additional Facts about Rape

Age of Victims. Women have been raped at ages younger than 6 months and as old as 93 years (Herman, 1984), but most rapes involve younger women. One study indicated that "nearly half of all rape victims are under 17 years old" (AASECT, 1999b, January, p. 7). Another study used police reports collected from eleven states and the District of Columbia (AASECT, 1994, August). Data indicated that the younger the woman, the more likely she will be raped by someone she knows rather than a stranger. Data also indicated "that girls under age twelve account for 16 percent of reported rapes. One in five victims under twelve is raped by her father. However, Justice Department statisticians and other experts say that the actual percentages of underage girls who are raped is definitely much higher because this population is the least likely of all victims to come forward" (AASECT, 1994, August, p. 12). Other sources indicate that women aged 16 to 24 are three times more likely to be raped than are women of other ages (Harlow, 1991; McCammon et al., 1993).

It appears that young women are at the greatest risk of rape, although it's important to stress that rape may occur at virtually any age. Highlight 9.4 proposes suggestions for rape prevention.

Profile of a Rapist

There is no clearly defined profile of a rapist in terms of "occupation, education, marital status, previous criminal record, and motivation for committing rape" (Hyde & DeLamater, 2000, p. 452). However, at least four variables can predispose men to rape (Malamuth, 1998; Malamuth et al., 1991). First, rapists tend to come from hostile, violent family environments (Malamuth, 1998; Malamuth et al., 1991). Perhaps they learned to demonstrate anger violently after witnessing or experiencing battery or sexual abuse.

Second, perpetrators are more likely to have a history of delinquency (Malamuth, 1998; Malamuth et al., 1991). Delinquency, of course, is also associated with hostile home environments. It makes sense that a potential rapist might associate "with delinquent peers who, for example, encourage hostile attitudes and rationalizations for committing illegal acts and reward a tough, aggressive image" (Hyde & DeLamater, 2000, p. 452).

A third factor characterizing perpetrators is sexual promiscuity (Malamuth, 1998; Malamuth et al., 1991). Rapists might perceive that the violent subjugation of women enhances their self-esteem and status, especially within an angry or violent delinquent peer group.

The fourth variable often characterizing rapists is a "hostile, masculine personality" defined as one "rejecting anything feminine such as nurturance, and emphasizing power, control, and 'macho' characteristics" (Hyde & DeLamater, 2000, p. 453). Rapists often harbor anger toward women (Hall & Barongan, 1997), which can be behaviorally expressed in violent sexual behavior. Related to this is a lack of empathy—that is, the condition of being in tune with how others feel and conveying to others this understanding (Dean & Malamuth, 1997). Rapists tend to be self-centered (Dean & Malamuth, 1997). They often maintain hardened attitudes toward women, viewing them as sexual objects (Crooks & Baur, 1993; Malamuth, 1986).

Situational characteristics may also play a role in sexual assault. Alcohol is often involved (Crooks & Baur, 1999; McCammon et al., 1998). Extreme examples of social disruption characterized by the breakdown of legitimate social control may also contribute to rape potential (Hyde & DeLamater, 2000). Throughout history, women have been raped by attacking warriors and soldiers (Crooks & Baur, 1999). The recent war in Bosnia, part of

Highlight 9.4

Suggestions for Rape Prevention

Rape is not the survivor's fault. Women do not have control over being attacked. However, women can take some measures to minimize their chances of being assaulted. Most of these suggestions are simply matters of common sense. It is unfortunate that women must be extra cautious, must plan ahead, and sometimes must change patterns of behavior in minor ways. However, it is necessary.

The following suggestions are included among those made by Women Organized Against Rape (WOAR)* in order to avoid being raped.

The first suggestion is to be aware of the things around you. Notice the people and cars in your immediate surroundings. Think ahead about what areas might be especially dangerous in your usual walking routes. If you have to travel through such areas, think ahead about what you would do if you were attacked. Try to stay in well-lighted areas and walk in the middle of the sidewalk. Walking in the middle of the street when there is little traffic is also a possibility. If you can, use different routes to get where you are going, especially at night. Avoid establishing a predictable pattern for a potential assailant.

Also try to be aware of your own behavior. Notice how you're standing or walking, and how you might appear to other people. Always walk with an air of confidence and strength. Try not to appear confused, vulnerable, or preoccupied, because attackers often look for such people. Walking with others or taking public transportation are other options.

If you think someone is following you, don't be afraid to look behind you. You might want to cross the street or travel in another direction. If you continue to have the feeling that someone is following you, it's best to go to the nearest lighted store or house and call a friend or the police for help. Don't hesitate to scream for help if you feel you are in danger. Screaming such words as "fire" or "police" is usually better than screaming words like "help" or "rape."

Some specific suggestions can also be followed for avoiding sexual assault when you are in situations involving driving your car. First of all, try to park in well-lighted areas and have your car keys ready to use. Check the backseat before getting in. While driving, keep your car doors locked and your windows partly rolled up. If approached by someone while at a stoplight, put your hand on your horn and be ready to blow it. It's also a good idea to keep at least a quarter tank of gas in the car whenever you drive to avoid running out of gas in potentially dangerous situations.

If you should have car trouble, pull over to the side of the road and stay in the car with doors locked and windows raised. When no one is around, get out and raise the car's hood to alert others to your distress. It's best to wait until police come to assist you. In the event that a man should stop and volunteer help, roll your window down only slightly and ask that he call for police help. Although such persons offering assistance may have only the best intentions, there is no way to know for sure.

Hitchhiking is very dangerous and should be avoided. The best way to prevent sexual assault when hitchhiking is simply not to hitchhike at all.

There are also ways to maintain your safety at home. Outside entrances and hallways should all be well lighted. Doors should have good dead-bolt locks instead of simple key locks which offer virtually no protection. Windows should also have locks so that potential assailants cannot enter in that manner. Women who live by themselves or with other women should use only their first initials on the mailboxes, which helps prevent potential assailants from targeting women. It's also very helpful to know your neighbors even if you live in a large, relatively impersonal apartment complex. You should know where you can go for help if you need it. Don't allow strangers in your home. If a man knocks on your door and says he's a serviceman, ask for identification and have him slide it under the door, or call his company for identification.

In the event of an attack, there are some guidelines that may help to lessen the probability of being raped (McCammon et al., 1998; Sexual Assault Treatment Center, 1979). The first suggestion is simply to run. It's more advantageous to get angry instead of scared and to react immediately. Screaming loudly is also suggested.

Traditional weapons such as guns or knives usually do not provide an effective defense. It's too easy for the attacker to take them away and use them on the victim. Rather, carrying ordinary objects such as whistles, keys, rings, umbrellas, or hat pins is helpful. To fight back, aim for the face, including eyes, ears, nose, and mouth, which are more sensitive to pain. Pulling hair is another option, and loud screams in the attacker's ear will stun him. Biting or kicking sometimes is effective. A kick aimed at his knees may be more effective in order to knock an attacker off balance, because he will be most likely to protect his genitals first.

*WOAR is located at 1233 Locust Street, Philadelphia, PA 19107; telephone: (215) 985-3315.

---

the former Yugoslavia, provides an example. Attacking Serbs raped, killed, and drove out thousands of ethnic Albanians in the pursuit of "ethnic cleansing."

Some research has compared rapists (men who revealed that they have forced women to have sexual intercourse with them) with nonrapists. Kanin (1985) studied male college students who fell into these two categories. Men who raped reported that they applied much more pressure to women in order to have sex. For example, almost 80 percent of the rapists indicated that they had tried to get a woman drunk in order to have sex with her; this is compared with 23 percent of the nonrapists.

Approximately 86 percent of the rapists recounted telling a woman that they "loved" her in order to persuade her to have sex with them; this is compared to 25 percent of the nonrapists. It should be noted that although the rapists were significantly more coercive, about one-quarter of the "normal" men studied (that is, nonrapists) reported using such pressuring techniques.

Rapist were more likely to have a peer group that both endorsed violent sex and pressured them to expand their sexual experience. Finally, 86 percent of the rapists reported that they thought rape was appropriate under some circumstances; this is compared with 19 percent of the nonrapists. Once again, note that almost one-fifth of the nonrapists felt that rape might be appropriate under some conditions. What does this say about our society's attitudes?

Other research has supported the fact that peer group acceptance of rape and hardened attitudes toward women as sexual objects tend to characterize men who rape (Crooks & Baur, 1993; Malamuth, 1986). They also tend to display animosity toward women in general, accept physical violence as a means of attaining their ends, demonstrate involvement in a high level of sexual activity, and express hostility, superiority, and anger in sexual situations (Cate & Lloyd, 1992). Men who rape often have low levels of self-esteem and are socially inadequate (Crooks & Baur, 1993).

Finally, there is growing evidence that exposure to pornography that depicts violent sexual behavior with women can make men insensitive to women as human beings. These men may become less likely to view sexual assault as a criminal offense and be more likely to rape (Crooks & Baur, 1993; Donnerstein & Linz, 1984). It should be pointed out that it appears to be the violent nature of this pornography, and not the pornography itself, that is related to subsequent rape (Scott & Schwalm, 1988).

One study of 2,000 college men revealed that men's sexual behavior toward women may be categorized into four types (Koss et al., 1985). *Sexually assaultive* men, who comprised 4.3 percent of the sample, admitted to having forced women to have sexual intercourse with them by threatening harm or by using actual physical violence. Another 4.9 percent were *sexually abusive*. These men had sexually assaulted women by using force, but did not have sexual intercourse with them. The third group, *sexually coercive* men, tried to verbally intimidate women into sexual contact, using such ploys as threatening emotional withdrawal. Finally, 59 percent of the men were *sexually nonaggressive*. These men felt that they never had used force and that their sexual interaction had always been desired by both them and their partners. The researchers were unable to classify the remaining 9.4 percent. In summary, almost one-third of these 2,000 young men had used some kind of force or extreme pressure to solicit sexual cooperation from their female partners. Thus, the idea that it is appropriate to force women into sexual activity appears to be fairly common.

Date Rape. We've already established that women are in danger both of being raped by someone they know and in a place where they feel safe. We've also established that it seems many men feel that it is appropriate or expected or at least tolerable to force women to have sex with them. Dates provide the perfect opportunity. The frightening fact is that the vast majority of date rapes go unreported. For example, the study by Koss and her associates (1985), mentioned earlier, found that many of the female survivors of sexual assault did not label it as such. Somehow,

A perfectly normal-seeming and trustworthy "date" could become a rapist.

© R. W. Jones/CORBIS

because they had been "in love" with the perpetrator, rape was within the realm of acceptable behavior.

Another dynamic of date rape involves the misconception that although her words say, "No, no," her eyes say, "Yes, yes." In other words, there is a mythical idea that women really love being raped, that they "really want it." Related to this is the idea that "she shouldn't have started it or let it go so far if she wasn't ready to go all the way." These misconceptions trap women. Women can't win under these conditions. On the one hand, there's the idea that "all she needs is a good————," which implies that all women really want to have their animal sexual drives released by sex with a "good" man. So, the man, of course, is expected to try to release these imprisoned sexual drives. Women, in return, are expected to respond and to participate in some kind of sexual interaction with men they really care about. However, date rape dynamics lead men to think that once a woman becomes involved in the developing sexual interaction, she loses her right of choice to stop. She's expected to finish what she has allowed to start.

A serious current issue involves the use of a "date-rape drug" call Rohypnol. Highlight 11.4 (in Chapter 11) discusses how it is used.

Consider an article in *TV Guide:* Waggett (1989) pleads with afternoon and night-time soap operas to stop making their rapists into heroes who even marry their victims. He reports:

> *Ross from* All My Children *had engaged in a brief affair with his father's fiancee, Natalie. . . . When Natalie's slip of the tongue cost Ross his marriage and his position in his father's company, Ross raped her in a drunken rage. Natalie pressed charges, and Ross went to prison. . . . Ross immediately changed from criminal to hero. He broke out of jail to rescue his adopted daughter, Julie . . . from an escaped convict. He worked undercover in the prison to uncover an arsonist. On furlough for a wedding, he risked his life to save his family and friends from a bomb. (p. 11)*

The point is not that rapists are worthless scum. From a helping professional's perspective, they are people who have problems, cause damage, and need help. However, the trouble is that, in so many instances, the act of rape is glamorized and associated with such positive behaviors and results.

Survivors' Reactions to Rape

Women can experience serious psychological effects that can persist for a half year or more following a rape (Burgess & Holmstrom, 1974a, 1974b, 1988; Hyde &

DeLamater, 2000; Turner & Rubinson, 1993). They call these emotional changes the *rape trauma syndrome,* "now considered to be a specific aspect of posttraumatic stress disorder" (Byington, 1995, p. 2139; Hyde & DeLamater, 2000). Post-traumatic stress disorder (PTSD) is "a psychological reaction occurring after a highly stressing event that is usually characterized by depression, anxiety, flashbacks, recurrent nightmares, and avoidance of reminders of the event" (Webster's, 1995, p. 911). The rape trauma syndrome has two basic phases. The first is the acute phase, which involves the woman's emotional reactions immediately following the rape and up to several weeks thereafter. The survivor reacts in one of two ways (Masters et al., 1995). She may show her emotions by crying, expressing anger, or showing fear. On the other hand, she may try to control these intense emotions and keep them from view. Emotions experienced during the acute phase range from humiliation and guilt to shock to anger and desire for revenge (Lott, 1994).

Additionally, during this phase women will often experience physical problems including difficulties related directly to the rape, such as irritation of the genitals or rectal bleeding from an anal rape (Hyde & DeLamater, 2000). Physical problems also include stress-related discomforts such as headaches, stomach difficulties, or inability to sleep.

The two primary emotions experienced during the acute phase are fear and self-blame. Fear results from the violence of the experience. Many rape survivors report that during the attack they felt their life had come to an end. They had no control over what the attacker would do to them and were terrified. Such fear can linger. Oftentimes survivors fear that rape can easily happen again. The second emotion, self-blame, results from society's tendency of blaming the victim as discussed in the theory of victim-precipitated rape and the feminist perspective on rape.

The second stage of the rape trauma syndrome is the long-term reorganization and recovery phase. The emotional changes and reactions of this phase may linger on for years. Nadelson and her associates (1982) found that three-fourths of rape survivors felt that the rape had changed their lives in one way or another. Reported reactions included fear of being alone, depression, sleeplessness, and, most frequently, an attitude of suspicion toward other people. Other long-term changes that sometimes occur include avoiding involvement with men (Masters et al., 1995) and suffering various sexual dysfunctions such as lack of sexual desire, aversion to sexual contact, or difficulties in having orgasms (Becker & Kaplan, 1991; Masters et al., 1995).

It is very important for survivors of rape to deal with even the most negative feelings and get on with their lives. In some ways rape might be compared to accepting the death of a loved one. The fact that either has occurred cannot be changed. Survivors must learn to cope. Life continues.

Suggestions for Counseling Rape Survivors

Three basic issues are involved in working with a survivor of rape. First, she is most likely in a state of emotional upheaval. Her self-concept is probably seriously shaken. Various suggestions for helping a rape survivor in such a traumatic emotional state will be provided. Second, the rape survivor must decide whether to call the police and press charges. Third, the rape survivor must assess her medical status following the rape, for example, injuries or potential pregnancy.

Emotional Issues. Collier (1982) suggests that counseling survivors of rape involves three major stages. First, the counselor or social worker needs to provide the survivor with immediate warmth and support. The survivor needs to feel safe; she needs to feel free to talk. She needs to ventilate and acknowledge her feelings before she can begin to deal with them. To the extent possible, the survivor should be made to feel she is now in control of her situation. She should not be pressured to talk, but rather encouraged to share her feelings.

Although it is important for the survivor to talk freely, it is also important that she not be grilled with intimate, detailed questions. She will have to deal with those enough if she reports the incident to the police.

Frequently, the survivor will dwell on what she could have or should have done. It is helpful to emphasize what she did right. After all, she is alive, safe, and physically not severely harmed. She managed to survive a terrifying and dangerous experience. It is also helpful to indicate that she reacted normally, as anyone else in her situation would most probably have reacted. This does not mean minimizing the incident. It does mean objectively talking about how traumatizing and potentially dangerous the incident was. One other helpful suggestion for dealing with a rape survivor is to help her place the blame where it belongs, namely on the rapist. He chose to rape her. It was not her doing.

The second stage of counseling, according to Collier, involves eliciting support from others. This support may include that of professional resources such as local rape crisis centers as well as support from people who are emotionally close to the survivor. Doege (2002) tells the story of Alice, a survivor of an exceptionally brutal rape by two men, and explains how difficult it was for her to deal with her friends' negative reactions:

> *"Why are all my friends acting so weird?" Alice wondered in the weeks after the attack. "I need to talk about this, but they can't."*
>
> *One close friend, a male coworker, went on a three-day drinking binge after learning what happened. Months later, he still was deeply troubled and prone to occasional sullen periods when they were together.*
>
> *Another friend—one she had been planning to meet the night she had been abducted—learned about the rapes the next day, and didn't talk to Alice again for 10 months. (p. 3L)*

Sometimes those close to the survivor need to be educated. They need to know that what the survivor needs is warmth and support, and to feel loved. They must understand that she needs to talk about her feelings when she's ready. Questions that emphasize her feelings of self-blame (such as why she didn't fight back or why she was wearing a low-cut blouse) should be completely avoided.

Collier's third stage of counseling involves rebuilding the survivor's trust in herself, in the environment around her, and in her other personal relationships. Rape weakens a woman. It destroys her trust in herself and in others. This stage of counseling needs to focus on the survivor's objective evaluation of herself and her situation. Her strong points need to be clarified and emphasized so that she may gain confidence in herself.

The survivor also needs to look objectively at her surrounding environment. She cannot remain cooped up in her apartment for the rest of her life. It is impractical and unfair. She can take precautions against being raped, but needs to continue living a normal life.

Finally, the survivor needs to assess her other personal relationships objectively. Just because she was intimately violated by one aggressor, this has nothing to do with the other people in her life. She needs to concentrate on the positive aspects of her other relationships. She must not allow the fear and terror she experienced during that one horrible incident to color and taint other relationships. She must clearly distinguish the rape from her other relationships.

A raped woman may initially want to talk with another woman. However, it might also be important to talk to men, including those close to her. It is important for the survivor to realize that not all men are rapists. Sometimes there is a male partner. His willingness to let the survivor express her feelings, and in return offer support and empathy, is probably the most beneficial thing that can be done for the survivor (Crooks & Bauer, 1993; Masters et al., 1995).

Reporting to the Police. The initial reaction to being raped might be to call the police and relate the incident. However, many survivors choose not to do this. There are numerous reasons why this is so, including fear that the rapist will try to get revenge, fear of public embarrassment and derogation, an attitude that it won't matter anyway because most rapists get off free, and fear of the legal process and questioning (Masters et al., 1995). It's financially expensive and emotionally draining to take a rape case to court (Herman, 1984). In reality, even when they are persistent, women have found it difficult to have rapists prosecuted. In many cases, as we've already discussed, police determine that the case is unfounded. In cases in which police do believe that a rape occurred, only half of the alleged rapists are apprehended and arrested (Herman, 1984). Even then, few rapists are actually convicted (Byington, 1995).

Some positive changes are occurring (Byington, 1995). In many states information about the survivor's past sexual history is no longer permissible for use in court. When such information is introduced, it can serve to humiliate and discredit the survivor. Some states have more progressive laws. Wisconsin,[6] for example, has established four degrees of sexual assault in addition to forbidding the use of the survivor's past sexual conduct in court. According to Wisconsin law the severity of the crime and the corresponding severity of punishment is based on the amount of force used by the rapist and on the amount of harm done to the survivor. A wife is also able to prosecute her husband for sexual assault when sexual relations are forced on her.

Despite the potential difficulties in reporting a rape, the fact remains that if the survivor does not report it, the rapist will not be held responsible for his actions. A rape survivor needs to think through the various alternatives that are open to her and weigh their respective positive and negative consequences in order to come to this often difficult decision.

In the event that a survivor decides to report, she should not take a shower. Washing will remove vital evidence. However, survivors often feel defiled and dirty, and it is a logical initial reaction for them to want to cleanse themselves and try to forget that the incident ever occurred. In counseling situations, it's important to emphasize the reason for not washing immediately.

6. See Wisconsin State Statute 940.225.

Reporting a rape should be done within 48 hours at the absolute longest. The sooner the rape is reported and the evidence gathered, the better the chance of being able to get a conviction.

Medical Status of the Victim. A third major issue that rape survivors need to address is their medical status following the assault. At some point the survivor needs to attend to the possibility of pregnancy. She should be asked about this issue at an appropriate time and in a gentle manner. She should be encouraged to seek medical help both for this possibility and for screening sexually transmitted diseases, including HIV. The negative possibilities should not be emphasized. However, the survivor needs to attend to these issues at some point. And the survivor should, of course, be urged to seek immediate medical care for any physical injury.

❧ Battered Women

Terms associated with wife beating include *domestic violence, family violence, spouse abuse,* and *battered women.* Strong and DeVault (1983) describe battering as a catch-all term that includes, but is not limited to, the practices of slapping, punching, knocking down, choking, kicking, hitting with objects, threatening with weapons, stabbing, and shooting. The *battered woman syndrome* implies the systematic and repeated use of one or more of the above against a woman by her husband or lover.

Some of the myths about battered women include the following (Roberts, 1996):

- Battered women aren't really hurt that badly.
- Beatings and other abuses just happen; they aren't a regular occurrence.
- Women who stay in such homes must really enjoy the beatings they get.
- Wife-battering only occurs in lower-class families.

As many as half of all women will suffer from "violence at some time in their marriage" (Gibbs, 1998, p. 326). In the vast majority of heterosexual partner-abuse cases—over 90 percent—men abuse women (Dziegielewski et al., 1996; Papalia et al., 2001). Although some women abuse their male partners, the dynamics in these cases are often different. Because women are generally smaller and weaker than men, they are much more likely to experience serious harm than men (Davis, 1995; Gibbs, 1998; Kurz, 1993; Lott, 1994; Renzetti & Curran,

1995). "Given the differences in size, strength, and resources between husbands and wives, some have questioned the appropriateness of labeling wives' abusive behavior towards their husbands 'battery'" (Renzetti & Curran, 1995, p. 238). Of all women treated in hospital emergency rooms, between 22 and 35 percent are there to receive treatment for injuries incurred during domestic violence incidents (Davis, 1995; Dziegielewski et al., 1996; Gibbs, 1995; Randall, 1990). Battering women is so prevalent that women are more likely to be beaten in their own homes than police officers are likely to be assaulted on the job (U.S. Department of Justice, 1994; U.S. House of Representatives, 1988). Women "suffer more from domestic violence than from all other crimes combined" (AASECT, November 1994, p. 10; Renzetti & Curran, 1995).

Battered women don't like to be beaten. They may initially experience "shock, disbelief, and denial, followed by terror, then attempts to reestablish the level of safety previously believed to have existed, followed by depression with intermittent inner-directed rage and outbursts of anger" (Harway, 1993, p. 38). Women go to domestic-violence programs for help to stop the beatings and maintain their marriages. They don't enjoy the pain and suffering, but for reasons that will be discussed later, they tolerate it.

Wife battering is not limited to poor families or families of particular racial, ethnic, or cultural backgrounds (Davis, 1995). Battered wives come from virtually every socioeconomic level. However, three factors are "associated with higher rates of wife abuse: (1) poverty, (2) underemployment and unemployment, and (3) employment in a blue-collar job" (Davis, 1995, p. 782).

The Abusive Perpetrator

A series of traits tend to characterize men who batter their female partners. They tend to adhere to common masculine gender role stereotypes such as failing to display emotion or sensitivity to others, because they perceive these as reflecting weakness (Shaw & Lee, 2001). Batterers likely feel it's important to maintain male dominance in society and keep women under control; "gender-based violence against women is still widely considered normal, acceptable, and justifiable" (Sapiro, 1999, p. 191; Shaw & Lee, 2001).

Low self-esteem often characterizes abusers (Chornesky, 2000; Hamberger & Hastings, 1988). This, in conjunction with the need to control, can generate extreme jealousy, resulting in abuse and even murder (Kail & Cavanaugh, 2000).

Although battering occurs in all classes and at all socioeconomic levels, stress from job loss or poverty, or emotional distress like depression, can contribute to the potential for violence; even family holidays like Thanksgiving and Christmas can initiate enough stress to trigger abusive incidents (Bennett, 1995; Davis, 1995; Kirk & Okazawa-Rey, 2001; Sapiro, 1999). It can also be "very stressful for some men to have wives with higher-status occupations because the men have learned that they are supposed to be superior to their wives" (Sapiro, 1999, p. 191). Alcohol use is linked to violent

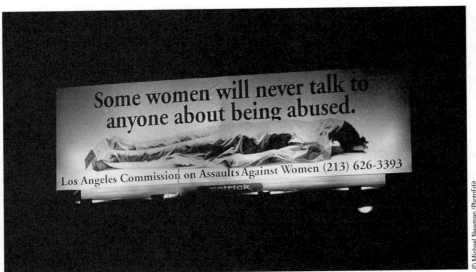

A battered woman sees herself as having significantly less power in her relationship with an abusive man than does a woman with a partner who is nonviolent. This billboard, showing a dead woman, encourages victims of domestic violence to ask for help.

© Michael Newman/PhotoEdit

episodes (Chornesky, 2000; Kirk & Okazawa-Rey, 2001; Sapiro, 1999).

Finally, many abusers experienced abuse themselves as children or observed abusive behavior displayed by parents (Davis, 1995; Sapiro, 1999). For instance, a male child can learn abusive behavior by observing the behavior modeled by his own father. As an adult the man may learn he can gain satisfaction by battering because it gives him control over something in his life.

The Battering Cycle

Three basic phases tend to characterize battery in an intimate relationship (Davis, 1995; Lott, 1994; Walker, 1979). The first phase involves building up stress and tension. The woman tries to make things okay and avoid confrontations. There may be a few minor abusive incidents.

The second phase in the battering cycle is the explosion. This is when the battering occurs. This is generally the shortest of the three phases, but it may last for up to several days.

The third phase involves making up. Because a man's tension has been released, he now adamantly states that he is truly sorry for what he has done. He swears he will never do it again. The battered woman relents and believes him. He is forgiven and all seems well, that is, until the cycle of violence begins again.

Why Does She Stay?

Women stay in the battering environment for many reasons (Davis, 1995; Forte et al., 1996; Roberts, 1996b; Walker, 1979, 1988). Approximately half of the women who seek help from shelters and even those who initiate separation through the courts eventually return to their abusive home situations (Lott, 1994). The reasons they remain or return include economic dependence, lack of self-confidence, lack of power, fear of the abuser, adherence to traditional beliefs, guilt, fear of isolation, fear for their children, and love.

Economic Dependence. Many battered women stay with the perpetrator for economic reasons (Davis, 1995; Roberts, 1996b). Many are financially dependent on the abuser as the primary wage earner for themselves and their children. Although battering occurs at all socioeconomic levels, it is more likely to happen in families with fewer resources.

Lack of Self-Confidence. Domestic violence involves not only physical abuse but also sexual abuse and psychological abuse (Burstow, 1992; Davis, 1995). Psychological abuse may entail regular tirades by battering men who criticize and blast survivors with derogatory remarks. Bit by bit, such treatment eats away at women's self-esteem and shrinks self-confidence. Perpetrators tend to claim that their female partners couldn't survive without them, and after an extended period of time, many of these women start to believe them. In some ways, psychological abuse is similar to the brainwashing of war prisoners (Davis, 1995).

It takes initiative and courage to muster the self-confidence required to leave a painful situation and strike out for the unknown. The unknown is frightening. At least if the domestic violence survivor remains in the home, she knows she has a place to stay. Often, it takes 5 to 7 attempts at leaving an abuser before a survivor permanently succeeds (Doege, 2002).

Lack of Power. A battered woman views herself as having significantly less power in her relationship with an abusive man than does a woman with a partner who is nonviolent (Forte et al., 1996). Battered women see their relationships as almost completely dominated by the perpetrator. Batterers' systematic regimen of intimidation, criticism, and violence places women in a vulnerable and difficult position. However, it should be noted that even in the face of such adversity, which for many is daily torture, these woman utilize their strengths; Burstow (1992) explains:

> They are not simply submitting, even where submission is key and even though submission is expectable and blameless. They are also making active and critical decisions about how to cope and survive on a moment-to-moment basis. They are deciding to hide certain things. They are deciding to duck. They are deciding not to duck. They are each in her own way also resisting. They are actively and passively resisting violation, whether that resistance takes the form of numbing themselves so that they will not feel the pain, finding ways of avoiding the abuser's ire, or saying no. (p. 153)

Fear of the Abuser. It is logical for a battered woman to fear brutal retaliation by the perpetrator if she leaves him. A man who has dealt with stress by physical brutality might do so again if his female partner leaves him. The battered woman might even fear death at the hands of an abandoned male partner. One myth is that battered women stay in their relationships because they *like* being beaten. This is not true. For reasons discussed here, they tolerate their circumstances in order to survive.

The following excerpt from a novel describes what it's like to be under an abusive partner's thumb:

> For seventeen years. There wasn't one minute when I wasn't afraid, when I wasn't waiting. Waiting for him to go,

waiting for him to come. Waiting for the fist, waiting for the smile. I was brainwashed and braindead, a zombie for hours, afraid to think, afraid to stop, completely alone. I sat at home and waited. I mopped up my own blood. I lost all my friends, and most of my teeth. He gave me a choice, left or right; I chose left and he broke the little finger on my left hand. Because I scorched one of his shirts. Because his egg was too hard. Because the toilet seat was wet. Because because because. He demolished me. He destroyed me. (Doyle, 1996, pp. 176–177, cited in Chornesky, 2000, pp. 491–492)

Adherence to Traditional Beliefs. Because battered women tend to believe in traditional gender role stereotypes, they often view their male partners as caretakers and providers. They tend to shun the alternatives of separation or divorce. It's often difficult for them to think about what they would do on their own. A battered woman may believe that it is her responsibility to nurture and maintain her relationship with the abuser and may blame herself for problems in that relationship (Harway, 1993; Renzetti & Curran, 1992). A battered woman will typically report that terminating her relationship with the abuser would hurt her more than him and that by doing that she has more to lose than he does (Forte et al., 1996).

Guilt. Many battered women feel that it is their own fault that they are abused (Harway, 1993; Renzetti & Curran, 1992). They tend to believe in men being the dominant decision makers and leaders of the family, and they feel women should be submissive and obedient. To some extent this guilt may be due to their husbands telling them that they're to blame for causing trouble. Perhaps because of their low self-esteem, it's easy for them to be critical of themselves. Their beliefs in traditional gender role stereotypes may cause them to wonder how they have failed in their nurturant role of wife.

Fear of Isolation. Battered women often try to keep the facts of their battering a secret. They may feel isolated from friends and family. Frequently, the perpetrator strongly discourages his female partner's interactions with friends and family. He criticizes them. He makes it as difficult as possible for her to communicate with them. He gradually gets her to cut others off. When the abuser becomes everything to the survivor, losing him means that she would be all alone.

Fear for Her Children. A battered woman usually fears for her children's safety. First, she might be worried about her ability to support them financially on her own. Second, she may firmly adhere to the traditional belief that children need a father. She may think that a father who

abuses his wife is better than no father at all. Third, she may even fear losing custody of her children. The abuser may threaten to take them away from her. She may have little knowledge of the complicated legal system and may believe that he can and will do it.

Love. Many battered women still love their abusive husbands. Many who seek help would prefer to remain in their relationships if the battering could be stopped (Chornesky, 2000). Walker (1979) cited one elderly woman's reactions to the death of her husband, who had battered her throughout their 53-year marriage. The woman stated, "We did everything together. . . . I loved him; you know, even when he was brutal and mean. . . . I'm sorry he's dead, although there were days when I wished he would die. . . . He was my best friend. . . . He beat me right up to the end. . . . It was a good life and I really do miss him."

Community Responses to Battered Women: Their Alternatives

Despite the difficulties in dealing with domestic violence, definite intervention strategies can be undertaken. They involve police departments, shelters, and specific counseling approaches.

The Police and Battered Women. It is likely that police officers will be the first outside means of intervention in episodes of domestic abuse. Many police departments, despite their previously mentioned reluctance, are taking an increasingly active interest in addressing family violence (Roberts, 1996c; Saunders, 1995). Because of the seriousness of the issue and the high potential for fatality and injury, they are acknowledging that something must be done. For example, training programs targeting domestic violence are being developed for police personnel (Roberts, 1996c). One thrust of such programs is the development of specialized interpersonal skills for dealing with such situations.

Legally, however, most states still consider battery a form of assault. Thus, it must be subject to the same requirements for prosecution as other assaults—that is, observation by a witness, filing an official complaint, and issuing a warrant for arrest (Renzetti & Curran, 1992). Some states have implemented mandatory arrest laws in which police must remove people who have been violent. Other states provide for the removal of the batterer from the home in order to avoid harm to the spouse and children. There is some evidence that such policies do help to thwart recurrent violent episodes (Dutton, 1987). However, there is also evidence that such laws frequently are not enforced (Ferraro, 1989).

Shelters for Battered Women. The most immediate need of a battered woman who seeks to flee her situation is a place to go. For this purpose, shelters have been developed around the country. Late 1973 marked the opening of the first U.S. shelter for battered women, Rainbow Retreat, in Phoenix, Arizona (Hutchins & Baxter, 1980). Unfortunately these shelters are usually overcrowded. Most can take in fewer than half of the women who approach them for help (Renzetti & Curran, 1992).

All such programs provide a safe place where battered women can go to obtain temporary shelter. There is a range in philosophies adopted by such shelters (Dziegielewski et al., 1996; Hutchins & Baxter, 1980). At one end of the continuum are the more traditionally oriented agencies that emphasize the traditional values of keeping the family together. They orient themselves toward helping women resolve their problems with their mates, stopping the battering, and enabling these women to return safely home.

At the other end of the continuum are those shelters adopting a purely feminist perspective. For these, "wife abuse is seen as a social problem, rooted in sexism and manifested in the suffering of countless individual women. The women are regarded as victims in need of immediate protection and long-term life change. Some of the refuges with this philosophy actively encourage permanent separation of the couple" (Hutchins & Baxter, 1980, p. 207). Here the idea is that women need not be dependent on men, especially those who have been abusive to them. Rather, such women need to nurture confidence in themselves and to develop their own alternatives.

Many shelters, however, adopt philosophies somewhere in between the purely traditional and the purely feminist. These shelters encourage women to think through their own individual situations, evaluate their own alternatives, and make their own decisions concerning what they feel is best for them.

Counseling Strategies. The following are some basic suggestions gathered from a range of sources regarding how social workers and counselors can help battered women (Burstow, 1992; Petretic-Jackson & Jackson, 1996; Register, 1993).

The Initial Interview. A battered woman is probably very anxious during her initial meeting with a social worker or counselor. She may be worried about what to say. The counselor should try to make the survivor as comfortable as possible and emphasize that she doesn't have to talk about anything she doesn't want to.

The survivor may also feel that the counselor will be judgmental and critical. Resnick emphasizes that it is important that the counselor put personal feelings aside and not pressure the battered woman into any particular course of action. This may be especially difficult when the counselor has strong feelings that the survivor should leave the abusive situation. A basic principle is that it is the survivor's decision as to what she will choose to do. In those cases in which the survivor chooses to return home, it may be useful for the counselor to help her clarify the reasons behind the decision.

Confidentiality may also be an issue for the battered woman. She may be fearful of the abuser finding out that she is seeking help and of his possible retaliation. The counselor needs to assure her that no information will be given to anyone without her consent. In the event that the survivor does need a place to go, it should be made clear to her that the shelter is available.

The survivor may show some embarrassment at being a "battered woman." The label may make her feel uncomfortable. The counselor should make an effort to downplay any embarrassment by emphasizing that the woman is a survivor of victimization and that her situation has nothing to do with her character or with her intrinsic human value.

Offer Support. A battered woman has probably been weakened both physically and emotionally. She needs someone to empathize with her and express genuine concern. She needs some time to sit back, experience some relief, and think.

Encourage Expression of Feelings. Many battered women will display a range of emotional reactions including helplessness, fear, anger, guilt, embarrassment, and even doubts about her sanity. The counselor needs to encourage the survivor to get all of these emotions out in the open. Only then will she be able to deal with them. The counselor can then help the survivor to look objectively at various aspects of her situation and help get control of her own life.

Focus on Strengths. One aspect of counseling that is very easy to forget is focusing on the survivor's strengths. A battered woman will probably be suffering from low self-esteem. She probably needs help in identifying her positive characteristics.

Furnish Information. Most survivors probably don't have much information about how they can be helped. Information about available legal, medical, and social services may open up alternatives to them to better enable them to help themselves.

Review Alternatives. A battered woman may feel trapped. She may be so overwhelmed that alternatives other than surviving in her abusive situation may not even have occurred to her. Her alternatives may include returning to the marriage, getting counseling help for both herself and her partner, temporarily separating from him, establishing other means of financial support and independent living conditions for herself, or filing for divorce.

A battered woman is often overwhelmed and confused. One of the most helpful things a counselor can do is to help her sort through her various problems. A survivor cannot do everything at once. However, she can begin getting control of her life by addressing one issue at a time and making decisions step by step.

Establish a Plan. One other important counseling technique is helping the survivor establish a plan of action. She needs to clearly understand and define what she chooses to do. This choice may include formulating major goals such as divorcing her husband. It may involve setting smaller subgoals such as developing a list of existing day-care centers she can call to find out available child-care options.

Advocate. An advocate can seek out information for a survivor of domestic violence and provide her with encouragement. An advocate can also help the survivor get in touch with legal, medical, and social service resources and find her way through bureaucratic processes. Perhaps, an even more critical aspect of advocacy involves changing legal macro systems. Duprey and associates (1996) explain:

> *Effective intervention requires some fundamental changes in current police and court practices. In many communities advocates for battered women pushed for pro-arrest policies, a more aggressive approach to prosecution, and sentences geared toward victim safety. Advocates promoted civil processes that complemented the criminal court response and pushed for a coordination of civil and criminal approaches to ensure the maximum protection for victims. (p. 10)*

❧ Working with Women

Social workers can help women regain their senses of having power and of being in control of their lives. Lott (1987, p. 277) asserts that the "personal traits that have clearly been shown to relate positively to measures of self-esteem or subjective well-being are the same for women as for men; and include assertiveness, independence, self-responsibility, and efficacy, characteristics typically included in the stereotype of masculinity." Social workers can help women build up their self-confidence and self-esteem. Positive qualities can be identified and emphasized. Social workers can help women recognize the

various alternatives available to them and evaluate the pros and cons of each. Decision-making and problem-solving skills can be taught. Success at using such skills breeds more success. Once women have learned the process of making their own decisions and solving their own problems, they can apply these skills to more decisions and more problems. This can help to build their feelings of being in control.

Social workers can teach women about assertiveness and how to develop assertiveness skills. They can provide practice situations and guide their female clients through more effective ways of handling difficult or uncomfortable situations. Assertiveness improves personal interactions, which in turn builds confidence.

Social workers can also encourage women to express their anger instead of holding it in. The real causes and targets of their anger can be identified. Once causes are recognized, social workers can "help the client learn to deal with anger directly through verbal and nonverbal communications styles, negotiation, confrontation, alliances and networks, compromises and resoluteness" (Collier, 1982, p. 277). Women can be helped to address the situations that cause their anger. If a woman is angry with her spouse, she can be taught how to express her feelings effectively so that whatever is happening to cause the anger can be changed.

Finally, social workers can encourage women to take care of themselves. The qualities they like about themselves can be nurtured. Women can learn that they have the right to their own time for themselves and to participate in activities they enjoy.

All of these suggestions are related to each other. Each one enhances the accomplishments of the others. Becoming more assertive enhances one's sense of control. An increased sense of control improves self-esteem. Greater self-esteem increases one's confidence in being assertive. The overall intent is to establish a confident, competent sense of self which is every person's right. Spotlight 9.4 proposes some basic suggestions for combatting sexism in terms of changing cultural values in the macro social environment.

❧ Summary

Traditional gender role stereotypes pressure males to be strong, dominant, successful, and career-oriented, and females to be nurturant, passive, and beautiful homebodies. The socialization process and gender role stereotyping have led to a number of problems. There is sex discrimination in employment, with men earning significantly more than women. There are double standards of conduct

Spotlight on Diversity 9.4 — Strategies for Empowering Women and Achieving Sexual Equality

In many ways problems discussed in this chapter are simply manifestations of the core problem of sexism: Sexism involves misinformation and attitudes that result in behavior that discriminates against women. Some basic suggestions for combating sexism involve supplying accurate information, revising attitudes, and changing behavior.

■ Become conscious of the gender role stereotypes affecting people from birth on. Don't force boys to be little men who must be actively aggressive and never dare cry when they're sad or hurting. Likewise, don't force girls to be little ladies who must wear frilly pink dresses, play with dolls, and be passive and submissive. The concept of androgyny may be helpful here. *Androgyny* refers to the capacity to have both traditionally feminine and masculine characteristics and qualities at the same time. It does not mean that men should be like women, or that women should be like men. Instead, androgyny implies that each individual, regardless of gender, be allowed to develop positive personal qualities. It means that males could be freer to express their emotional feelings and develop their communication skills. It also means that women could be freer to be assertive and have a greater share in leadership and decision making.

■ Throughout life place less emphasis on the need to conform with gender-based stereotypes. If less pressure were placed on men to be dominant, successful leaders, perhaps the midlife crisis would no longer exist for most men. (A midlife crisis is the internal discord and, sometimes, changed behaviors experienced by people in middle age as they reassess their perspective on life, which is different from that of a younger person. It involves examining goals and facing mortality.) Likewise, if

less emphasis were placed on women to be beautiful, docile homemakers, perhaps they would be happier, more self-satisfied, and more comfortable in their relationships with men.

■ To combat the discriminatory effects of sexism on women, encourage women to develop their assertiveness skills, enhance their self-confidence, and learn to develop and appreciate analytical and spatial manipulation skills. (Lack of these skills seems to be barring women from many of the more profitable career alternatives.) Encourage both males and females to pursue whatever interest they have from early on. Females should be encouraged to develop their mathematical ability. Males should be equally encouraged to develop their domestic skills.

■ Encourage more freedom in adult domestic relationships. Allow couples to negotiate both household tasks and outside work career goals without external pressure and criticism. Encourage men and women to share in child-care tasks. Doing so would allow children to know their fathers better and fathers to know their children. Don't criticize men who opt to stay home and manage the house or women who choose to work outside the home. Allow people the freedom to live their lives the way they want.

■ Confront laws and regulations that are discriminatory and restrictive on the basis of gender. Raise questions about them if you feel they're unfair. Vote for legislators and support administrators who adopt nonsexist stances. If necessary, fight for your own rights and advocate for the rights of your clients.

---

for males and females. There are power struggles between males and females, because men are socialized to be dominant in interactions with women, whereas women increasingly seek equalitarian relationships. Gender role stereotyping is pervasive in our society and can be found in childrearing practices, the educational system, language, the mass media, the business world, and marriage and family patterns. It is important to note that significant cultural differences exist in gender role expectations.

Several significant issues and life events related to sexism are: economic inequality, sexual harassment, the use of sexist language, rape and sexual assault, and battered women.

One aspect of economic inequality involves women and men tending to be clustered in different types of jobs. Men tend to earn significantly more than women regardless of job category.

Sexual harassment involves unwelcome sexual advances, requests for sexual favors, and other verbal or physical conduct of a sexual nature occurring under certain employment or educational conditions. The courts continue to address various dimensions of sexual harassment, which reportedly occurs frequently. Suggestions for confronting sexual harassment include confronting your harasser, being assertive, documenting occurrences, talking to others about the problem, and getting witnesses. Sexist language should be avoided.

Sexual assaults involve any unwanted sexual contact in which verbal or physical force is used. Theoretical views of rape include the victim–precipitated, rapist psychopathology, and feminist perspective. Sexual assault often occurs indoors, even in one's own home, by people who are known to the survivors. Date rape is common, especially on college campuses. Rape survivors tend to experience a rape trauma syndrome involving both an acute phase and a long-term reorganization phase. Suggestions for counseling rape survivors concern emotion issues, reporting to the police, and medical status.

Battering is a catchall term reflecting various types of physical and emotional abuse. As many as half of all women will suffer from violence sometime during their married lives. Phases characterizing the battering cycle are build up of tension, the explosion, and making up.

Women stay in abusive relationships because of economic dependence, lack of self-confidence, lack of power, fear of the abuser, adherence to traditional beliefs, guilt, fear of isolation, fear for the children, and love. Many police departments are taking an increasingly active interest in addressing family violence. Shelters for battered women have been developed around the country. Social workers and others can help battered women by using a range of counseling strategies.

InfoTrac College Edition Keywords

battered women	date rape	rape	sexual assault
comparable worth	economic inequality	sexist language	sexual harassment

On the Internet

New Brunswick, Canada Human Rights Commission— Sexual Harassment Information

http://www.gnb.ca/hrc-cdp/e/sexharas.htm

This site focuses on sexual harassment regulations in New Brunswick, Canada, and what you can do if you are sexually harassed. It includes information for employers, educators, and the general public.

Center for the Prevention of Sexual and Domestic Violence

http://www.cpsdv.org/

The center is an interreligious educational resource addressing issues of sexual and domestic violence. The goal is to engage religious leaders in the task of ending abuse, and to prepare human services professionals to recognize and attend to the religious questions and issues that may arise in their work with women and children in a crisis. The emphasis is on education and prevention.

Employment Policy Foundation—Comparable Worth

http://www.epf.org/documents/CompWorth.html

Comparable Worth is an attempt to set wage rates for job categories by an administrative method. Points would be assigned to all jobs; then pay would be equalized for those in supposedly underpaid jobs that also happen to be dominated by women.

Resources and Networking for Gender Equity in Early Childhood (RANGE)

http://www.edfac.unimelb.edu.au/LED/RANGE/index.htm

RANGE is an informal network of early-childhood professionals who are committed to gender equity in early childhood. Some of the people involved work in tertiary education, some in children's services, and some in resource and training agencies.

CHAPTER 10

Biological Systems and Their Impacts on Middle Adulthood

Patrick and Laura Bailey have been married for 23 years and have had relatively few serious conflicts. They have one daughter, who is in college. Patrick is 50 years old, and has been a bus driver for the city of Milwaukee for the past 11 years. Laura, age 48, has been a carrier for Federal Express for the past 13 years. They have a family income in excess of $60,000 a year. Their early years together were a financial struggle; the past 10 years, however, have been better. Except for the monthly mortgage payment on their small house, they have no major outstanding debts to pay. They are active in church activities and enjoy taking walks, gardening, playing softball, and bowling. For the past five summers they have been spending their vacations traveling to various places in the United States in their Chevrolet Lumina van.

A PERSPECTIVE

Middle adulthood has been referred to as the prime time of life. Patrick and Laura Bailey illustrate this. Most people at this age are in fairly good health, both physically and psychologically. They are also apt to be earning more money than at any other age and have acquired considerable wisdom through experiences in a variety of areas. However, middle adulthood also has developmental tasks and life crises. This chapter will examine human biological subsystems in middle adulthood and discuss how they impact people's lives.

The chapter will:

► Describe the physical changes in middle adulthood, including those affecting physical appearance, sense organs, physical strength and reaction time, and intellectual functioning.

► Describe the midlife crises associated with female menopause and male climacteric.

► Summarize sexual functioning in middle age.

► Describe AIDS—its causes, effects, origin; how it is contracted, and how the spread of this devastating disease can be prevented. Also discussed is AIDS discrimination, and helping persons with AIDS.

The Age Span of Middle Adulthood

Middle age has no distinct biological markers. The beginning of middle adulthood has been identified by different writers as ranging from 30 to 40. The ending of this age period has been viewed as ranging from ages 60 to 70. Somewhat arbitrarily, this text will view the age limits for the beginning and ending of middle adulthood as ranging from age 30 to age 65. This period indeed covers a large number of years.

Physical Changes in Middle Age
Changes in Physical Functioning

Most middle-aged people are in good health and have substantial energy. Small declines in physical functioning are barely perceptible. At age 48, for example, Althea Lawrence, who jogs, may notice it takes her a little longer to run the course. These decreases in physical functioning may be sufficient to make people feel they are aging.

People age at different rates, and the decline of the body systems is gradual. A major change is a reduction in reserve capacity, which serves as a backup in times of stress and during a dysfunction of one of the body's systems. Common physiological changes in middle age include diminished ability of the heart to pump blood; the gastrointestinal tract secretes fewer enzymes, which increases the chances of constipation and indigestion; the diaphragm weakens, which results in an increase in the size of the chest; reduced kidney functioning; and in some males, the prostate gland (the organ surrounding the neck of the urinary bladder) enlarges, which can cause urinary and sexual problems.

In addition to gradual reductions in energy levels, middle-aged adults also have less capacity to do physical work. A longer time period is needed to recoup strength after an extended and strenuous period of activity. Working full time at a job and socializing into the wee hours of the morning is harder. Recovering from colds and other common ailments generally takes longer. It takes longer for pain in joints and muscles to subside after extensive physical exercise. Middle-aged adults are best at tasks that require endurance rather than rapid bursts of energy; they need to make adjustments in their physical activities to compensate for these changes in energy level.

Health Changes

In the early 40s a general slowing down in metabolism usually begins. Individuals who reach this age either begin to gain weight or have to compensate by eating less and exercising more.

Health problems are more apt to arise. Signs of diabetes may occur; and the incidence of gallstones and kidney stones increases. Hypertension, heart problems, and cancer also have higher rates of occurring during the middle adult years as compared to the younger years. Back problems, asthma, arthritis, and rheumatism are also more common. But because nearly all these ailments can be treated, middle-aged adults need to have periodic physical examinations in order to detect and treat these illnesses in their early stages of development.

One major health problem during middle age is hypertension, or high blood pressure. The disorder predisposes people to heart attacks and to strokes. The disorder affects about 40 percent of adults in the United States, and is more prevalent among African Americans and poor people (Papalia et al., 2001). Fortunately, the disorder is now often detected by blood pressure screening, and can generally be effectively treated with medication. An emerging health problem for this age group is AIDS, which is adversely affecting many people.

The three leading causes of death for those between the ages of 35 and 54 are, in order: cancer, heart disease, and accidents. Between ages 55 and 64 the leading causes are: cancer, heart disease, and strokes (Papalia et al., 2001).

The typical middle-aged American is quite healthy. About 83 percent of people 45 to 64 years old report their health to be good, very good, or excellent. Only 17 percent consider themselves in fair or poor health (USDHHS, 1996).

Changes in Physical Appearance

Gradual changes in appearance take place. Some people become alarmed when they discover these changes. Gray hairs begin to appear. The hair may thin. Wrinkles gradually appear. The skin may become dry and lose some of its elasticity. There is a redistribution of fatty tissues; males, for example, are apt to develop a "tire" around their waist, and the breasts of women may decrease in size. Minor ailments develop that cause a variety of twinges.

Some studies with interesting results have been conducted on personal appearance. Knapp & Hall (1998) review studies in which slides of both women and men were shown to subjects. The studies have found that those judged to be physically attractive were also judged to be brighter, richer, and more successful in their social and career lives.

Having a physically attractive body has become a cult in our society. Americans spend thousands of hours and millions of dollars on grooming themselves, exercising, and dieting. The body-beautiful cult leads those who judge themselves to be attractive to feel that they are superior to those they judge to be less attractive physically.

The Double Standard of Aging

Gray hairs, coarsened skin, and "crow's feet" wrinkles are considered attractive in men; they are viewed as signs of distinction, experience, and mastery. Yet, the same physical changes in women are viewed as unattractive indicators that they are "over the hill." There is also a tendency in our society for many men to view such women as having less value as a sexual and romantic partner and even as a business associate or prospective employee (Knapp & Hall, 1998). For example, some middle-aged television

anchorwomen allege they have been discharged from their positions because normal changes in their physical features are considered "unattractive."

The physical changes that generally occur with age appear to have more of an effect on a husband's sexual responsiveness to his wife than on a wife's responsiveness to her husband. In a study of 1,509 married men and women 55 years old or less, Margolin and White (1987, p. 25) conclude: "Men who believe that their spouse is declining in physical attractiveness, but that they themselves are not are more likely than other men to report sexual problems in their marriage. . . . No such pattern exists for women." These men tended to become less interested in their wives sexually, and were more apt to be unfaithful.

In a different area, career advancement, men are more apt than women to feel old before their time if they have not achieved career or financial success. More pressure is placed on men in our society in regard to having a successful career.

Changes in Sense Organs

A gradual deterioration occurs in the sense organs during middle adulthood. Middle-aged adults are apt to develop problems with their vision that may force them to wear bifocals, reading glasses, or contact lenses. As the lens of the eye becomes less elastic with age, its focus does not adjust as readily. As a result, many people develop *presbyopia*—which means they become farsighted. They have an inability to focus sharply for near vision and thus need reading glasses. The psychological impact of being required to wear glasses may be minor or can be fairly serious if the person is fearful about growing older.

During middle age there is also a gradual hardening and deterioration of the auditory nerve cells. The most common deterioration in middle adulthood is *presbycusis,* which is a reduction in hearing acuity for high frequency tones. Middle-aged men generally have significantly greater losses of high frequency tones than middle-aged women. Sometimes the hearing loss is enough so that a hearing aid is needed. There are generally some minor changes in taste, touch, and smell as a person grows older. Most of these changes are so gradual that a person makes adjustments without recognizing that changes are occurring.

Changes in Physical Strength and Reaction Time

Physical strength and coordination are at their maximum in the 20s and then decline gradually in middle adulthood. Generally these declines are minor. Manual

Highlight 10.1

An Identity Crisis: When the Applause Stops

Chuck Walters excelled in sports in grade school and high school. In high school he lettered in basketball, football, and baseball. In his senior year he was 6 feet 1 inch tall and weighed about 220 pounds. He was a halfback on the football team and scored ten touchdowns in eight games. He was an outfielder on the baseball team and batted .467, hitting thirteen home runs. Especially good at basketball, he was quick and averaged 23.4 points a game.

He was recruited by a number of universities for both his football and basketball skills. He chose to accept a basketball scholarship at a major midwestern university. As a bonus for accepting a scholarship, an alumnus bought him a Pontiac Firebird. He was also given a summer job as a construction worker by another alumnus, which paid well and didn't require much work. Chuck had concentrated on sports and partying in high school and college. In college he chose the easiest major he could find (Physical Education) and only occasionally went to class. By taking the minimum number of credits needed to maintain his basketball eligibility and by having a tutor, he managed to make his grades and play varsity basketball. He loved college. He had plenty of money, a new car,

many dates, and was worshipped on campus as being a hero. He thought this was the way to live. In his junior year he averaged 16.7 points as a guard, and in his senior year he was an all-conference selection and averaged 22.3 points a game.

He also began experimenting with cocaine. He loved being applauded and adulated. He thought the merry-go-round would keep whirling around. To his surprise, he wasn't drafted by the pros. So he went to Europe to play basketball, hoping to excel so that some pro team would give him a try-out. He played in Europe for 5 years and was traded several times. At age 30 he was finally cut.

This cut led to a major identity crisis. He realized the applause and adulation were now coming to a screeching halt. He drank and used cocaine to excess in order to try to numb the pain of his loss. He had failed to graduate from college, having only junior standing when his scholarship eligibility ran out. He had been carried in college by his tutor because his reading and writing skills were at the tenth-grade level. He now fears he has no salable skills and is worried his money may soon run out. He can no longer support his extravagant lifestyle. At the present time he is considering trying to get some fast money by smuggling cocaine into the United States. His cocaine habit is costing him $100 per day. What should he do? He doesn't know, but he's dulling the pain with cocaine.

laborers and competitive athletes (boxers, football players, weightlifters, wrestlers, ice skaters) are most apt to be affected by these gradual declines. As Highlight 10.1 illustrates, some sports figures who have been applauded and worshiped by fans may experience an identity crisis in middle adulthood when they no longer are as competitive. Their lifestyle and identity have been based on excelling with athletic skills, and as those skills are fading they need to find new interests and another livelihood.

Simple reaction time reaches its optimum at around age 25 and is maintained until around age 60, when the reflexes gradually slow down. As people grow older they learn more and are generally better at a number of physical tasks in middle adulthood than they were in their 20s. Such tasks include driving ability, hunting, fishing, and golf. The improvement that comes from experience outweighs minor declines in physical abilities. The same is true in other areas. Skilled industrial workers are most productive in their 40s and 50s, partly because they are more careful and conscientious than younger workers. Middle-aged workers are less likely to have disabling injuries on the job—which is probably due to learning to be careful and learning to use good judgment. An

additional factor in reduced accident rates for this age group may be a reduction in the abuse of mind-alerting substances among middle-aged workers.

Changes in Intellectual Functioning

Contrary to the notion that "You can't teach an old dog new tricks," mental functions are at a peak in middle age. Middle-aged adults can continue to learn new skills, new facts, and can remember those they already know well. Unfortunately, many middle-aged people do not fully use their intellectual capacities. Many settle into a job and family life and are less active in using their intellectual capacities than they were in their younger years, when they were attending school or when they were learning their profession or trade. Some middle-aged adults are unfortunately trapped by the erroneous belief that they can't learn anything new.

If a person is mentally active, that person will continue to learn well into later adulthood. Practically all cognitive capacities show no noticeable declines in middle adulthood. Adults who mistakenly believe that they completed their education in their 20s are apt to show declines in their intellectual functioning in middle adulthood. There is truth in the adage, "What you do not use, you will begin to lose."

In regard to specific intellectual capacities, there are variations. People in middle adulthood who use their verbal abilities regularly (either on the job or through some other mental stimulation such as reading) further develop their vocabulary and verbal abilities. There is some evidence that middle-aged adults may be slightly less adept at tests of short-term memory, but this is usually compensated by wisdom gained from a variety of past experiences (Papalia et al., 2001). If middle-aged adults are mentally active, their IQ scores on tests are apt to show slight increases.

Creative productivity is at its optimum point in middle age. Scientists, scholars, and artists have their highest rate of output generally in their 40s—and their productivity tends to remain high in their 60s and 70s (Papalia et al., 2001). There are different age peaks for different types of creative production. In general, the more unique, original, and inventive the production, the more likely it is to have been created in the 20s and 30s rather than later in life. The more a creative act depends on accumulated development, however, the more likely it is to occur in the later years of life.

Middle-aged adults tend to think in an integrative way. That is, they tend to interpret what they see, read, or hear in terms of its personal and psychological meaning. For example, instead of accepting what they read at face value (as younger people are apt to do), middle-aged adults filter information through their own learning and experience. This ability to interpret events in an integrative way has a number of benefits. It enables a person to better identify scams and "con games," because an integrative thinker is less naive. It enables many adults to come to terms with childhood events that once disturbed them. It enables middle-aged people to create inspirational legends and myths by putting truths about the human condition into symbols that younger generations can turn to for guidelines in leading their lives. Papalia and her associates (2001) note that people need to be capable of integrative thought before they can become spiritual and moral leaders.

Integrative thinking also enables people in their 40s and 50s to be at the peak of their *practical problem-solving capacities*. People in this age group are best able to arrive at quality solutions for everyday problems and crises, such as what is wrong with an automobile that fails to start, how to repair a hole in drywall in a house, and what types of injuries require medical attention.

In the past decade an increasing proportion of middle-aged adults have been returning to college. Some want an additional degree to move up a career ladder. Some seek training that will help them to perform their present jobs better. Some are preparing to seek a new career. Some are taking courses to fill leisure time and to learn about subjects they find challenging. Some attend to expand their knowledge in special-interest areas, such as photography or sculpturing. Some want to expand their interests in preparation for retirement years. Professionals in rapidly expanding fields (such as computer science, law, health care, gerontological social work, engineering, and teaching) need to keep up with new developments. (Social work practitioners often take workshops and continuing education courses to keep abreast of new treatment techniques, new programs, and changes in social welfare legislation.) In our modern, complex society it is essential that learning continues throughout one's life span.

Life is more meaningful if one's intellectual capacities are being challenged and used. College instructors are generally delighted to have returning students in their classes, because such students have a wealth of experiences to share and are usually highly committed to learn. Compared to younger students, they are less apt to major in "having a good time."

When middle-aged adults return to college, they often need a few weeks to get used to the routine of taking notes in classes, writing papers, and studying for exams. A few courses, such as mathematics and algebra, tend to be particularly difficult because returning students have forgotten some of the basic concepts they learned years ago. Because people at age 50 learn at nearly the same rate and in the same way as they did at age 20, most returning students do well in their courses.

Colleges are not the only places that offer adult education courses. Courses are also provided by vocational and technical centers, businesses, labor unions, professional societies, community organizations, and government agencies. The concept of lifelong education has been a boon for many colleges and universities.

In middle adulthood there is generally only a small amount of deterioration in physical capacities, and almost no deterioration in potential for mental functioning. Cognitive functioning may actually increase well into later adulthood (Lefrancois, 1999). The sad fact is that many people are not sufficiently active, both mentally and physically. As a result, their actual performance, physical and mental, falls far short of their potential performance.

❦ Female Menopause

Menopause is the event in every woman's life when she stops menstruating and can no longer bear children. The median age when menopause occurs is 51 years, although

Spotlight on Diversity 10.1 — Cultural Differences in Women's Experience of Menopause

The importance of doing cross-cultural research on widely held beliefs is indicated in a study by Lock (1991) that compares Japanese women's experience of menopause to that of Canadian women. Vast differences were found. Only 12.6 percent of Japanese women who were beginning to experience irregular menstruation reported experiencing hot flashes in a 2 week period compared to 47.4 percent of Canadian women. Fewer than 20 percent of Japanese women had ever had a hot flash compared to almost 65 percent of Canadian women.

There is no specific Japanese word for a hot flash, which is surprising, because the Japanese language makes many subtle distinctions about all kinds of body states. This lack of a word for a hot flash supports the finding of a low incidence of what most Western women report as the most troubling symptom of menopause.

Chornesky (1998) notes that Mayan women in Mexico do not report having any symptoms related to menopause. Chornesky (1998) also indicates symptoms of menopause are uncommon among Native American women. Interestingly, in Native American cultures menopause is viewed as an important rite of passage signifying entrance into the highly respected state of elderhood, and opening up the opportunity to assume important new social rules. For example, in the Lakota Sioux tribe, only after menopause can a Lakota woman become a midwife or a medicine woman and assume roles that are equal to those of men in tribal affairs (Chornesky, 1998).

What does this research tell us? It emphasizes the importance of conducting cross-cultural studies on biological phenomena. The findings also mean that it would be a mistake to use a list of menopausal symptoms drawn up in one country to assess women in another country. The findings also suggest the possibility of biological interpopulation variations in physical symptoms, such as hot flashes. Finally, the research suggests that different cultures view events (such as menopause) differently.

---

the event may occur in some women as young as 36, or may not occur until a woman is in her mid 50s. The time span ranging from 2 to 5 years during which a woman's body undergoes the physiological changes that bring on menopause is called the *climacteric*. There is some evidence of a hereditary pattern for the onset of menopause, because daughters generally begin and end menopause at about the same age and in the same manner as their mothers. Menopause is caused by a decrease in the production of estrogen, which leads to a cessation of ovulation.

Menopause begins with a change in a woman's menstrual pattern. This pattern varies between women. Periods may be skipped and become irregular. There may be a general slowing down of flow of blood during menstruation. There may be irregularity in the amount of blood flow and in the timing of periods. Or, there may be an abrupt cessation of menstruation. The usual pattern is skipped periods, with the periods occurring farther and farther apart.

During menopause a number of biological changes occur. The ovaries become smaller and no longer secrete eggs regularly. The fallopian tubes (having no more eggs to transport) become shorter and smaller. The vagina loses some of its elasticity and becomes shorter. The uterus shrinks and hardens. The hormone content of urine changes. All of these changes are biologically related to cessation of functioning of the reproductive system.

The reduction of activity of the ovaries affects other glands and may produce disturbing symptoms in some women. A majority of women undergoing menopause encounter few, if any, disturbing symptoms. As Spotlight 10.1 indicates, the symptoms of menopause may even vary among cultures.

The most common symptom of menopause is the "hot flash," which affects approximately 50 percent of menopausal women (Hyde & DeLamater, 2000). A hot flash generally occurs quite rapidly, involves a feeling of warmth over the upper part of the body (very similar to generalized blushing), and is usually accompanied by perspiring, reddening, and perhaps dizziness. Some women have hot flashes infrequently (once a week or less), while others may have them every few hours. A hot flash may last just a few seconds and be fairly mild, or it may last for 15 minutes or more. They tend to occur more often during sleep than during waking hours. A hot flash while sleeping tends to awaken the woman, which contributes to insomnia.

Hot flashes appear to be due to a malfunction of temperature control mechanisms in the hypothalamus (Hyde & DeLamater, 2000). Estrogen deficiency contributes to this malfunction, and therefore estrogen therapy provides relief for the discomfort associated with hot flashes. Hot flashes generally disappear spontaneously after a few years even without estrogen treatment. Deciding whether to receive estrogen treatment is largely a subjective decision for each woman.

Other changes may occur during menopause, most of which are due to reduced estrogen. The hair on the scalp

Highlight 10.2

Osteoporosis

Osteoporosis is a thinning and weakening of the bones. As a result of a drop in blood calcium level, bones become thin and brittle, with a consequent reduction in bone mass. Osteoporosis is a major factor leading to broken bones in later life. Women are much more susceptible to osteoporosis, particularly women who are white, thin, and smokers, and those who do not get enough exercise or calcium. Women who have had their ovaries surgically removed in middle age are also more susceptible to osteoporosis.

One of the dangers of osteoporosis is fractures of the vertebrae, which can lead to those affected becoming stooped from the waist up, with a height loss of 4 inches or more. Osteoporosis also often leads to hip fractures in elderly women.

Osteoporosis is preventable. The most important preventive measures include exercising, getting more calcium, and avoiding smoking. Exercise appears to stimulate new bone growth. It should become part of the daily routine early in life, and continue at moderate levels throughout life. Weight-bearing exercises (such as jogging, aerobic dancing, walking, bicycling, and jumping rope) are particularly beneficial in increasing bone density.

Most women in the United States drink too little milk and eat few foods rich in calcium. It is recommended that women should get between 1,000 and 1,500 milligrams (or more) of calcium daily, beginning in their youth (Papalia et al., 2001). Dairy foods are calcium-rich. To avoid high-cholesterol dairy products, low-fat milk and low-fat yogurt are recommended. Other foods rich in calcium include canned sardines and salmon (if eaten with the bones still present), oysters, and certain vegetables, such as broccoli, turnips, and mustard greens.

A somewhat controversial approach to preventing osteoporosis is the administration of estrogen (a hormone) to women who are at high risk for developing osteoporosis, such as those who have had their ovaries removed at a fairly young age. Research about the benefits and risks of hormone-replacement therapy (HRT) is contradictory. Some studies indicate HRT may increase the risks of breast cancer and cancer of the lining of the uterus. Other studies indicate that HRT does not increase the risks of these types of cancer. A major study in 2002 found that women who received HRT, rather than a placebo, suffered more strokes, more heart attacks, more blood clots, and had higher rates of invasive breast cancer (Spake, 2002).

---

and external genitalia may become thinner. The labia may lose their firmness. The breasts may lose some of their firmness and become smaller. There is a tendency to gain weight, and the body contour may change, though some women lose weight. Itchiness, particularly after showering, may occur. Headaches may increase, and insomnia may occur. Some muscles, particularly in the upper legs and arms, may lose some of their elasticity and strength. Growth of hair on the upper lip and at the corners of the mouth may appear. Many of these symptoms can be minimized by the use of estrogen replacement therapy and regular exercise. In approximately one of four women who are postmenopausal, the decrease in estrogen leads to osteoporosis (see Highlight 10.2).

A variety of psychological reactions also accompany menopause, but certainly not every woman encounters psychological difficulties. If a woman is well adjusted emotionally before menopause, she is unlikely to experience psychological difficulties (Hyde & DeLamater, 2000).

The psychological reactions that a woman has about menopause are determined by her interpretations of this life change. If a woman sees this change as simply being one of many life changes, she is not apt to have any adverse difficulties. She may even view menopause as being a posi-

tive event, for she no longer has to bother with menstruation or worry about getting pregnant.

On the other hand, if a woman views menopause negatively, she is apt to develop such emotions as anxiety, depression, feelings of low self-worth, and lack of fulfillment. Some women believe menopause is a signal they are losing their physical attractiveness, which they further erroneously interpret as meaning an ending of their sex life. Some no longer feel needed, especially if their children have left the nest and they have a low-paying, boring job — or no job at all. Some are widowed, separated or divorced, and regret still having to "scrimp and save to make ends meet." For many women this is a time of reexamining the past; if the past is interpreted as having been something other than what they had desired, they feel unfulfilled and cheated. Even worse, if they appraise the chances for a better life to be nil, they are apt to be depressed and have a low sense of self-worth. If they viewed their main role in life as being a mother and raising children, they now may feel a sense of rolelessness; and if their children fall far short of meeting their hopes and expectations, they are apt to view themselves as a failure. Some women seek to relieve their problems through alcohol. Others seek out understanding lovers.

Some isolate themselves, while others cry much of the time and are depressed.

There is no clear-cut way to identify the exact time when menopause ends. Most authorities agree that the climacteric can be considered as ending when there has been no menstrual period for 1 year. (Some women may go several months during menopause before having one of their last periods.) Physical symptoms of menopause usually end when ovulation ceases.

Some doctors urge that some type of birth control be continued for 2 years after the last period in order to prevent pregnancy. "Change-of-life" babies are rare because conception, although possible, is unlikely to occur. Middle-aged pregnancies do present increased health risks. The child has a higher chance of having a birth defect. For example, the risk of Down syndrome is greatest with older parents; the chances rise from 1 such birth in 2,000 among 25-year-old mothers to 1 in 40 for women over 45 (Papalia et al., 2001). Spontaneous abortions are more common in women who become pregnant after the age of 40. In addition, older women are more apt to have a prolonged labor due to the loss of elasticity of the vagina and the cervix. All in all, menopause does not appear to have serious consequences for most women.

❧ Male Climacteric

In recent years there has been considerable discussion about "male menopause." In a technical sense the term male menopause is a misnomer, as menopause means the cessation of the menses. The term *male climacteric* is more accurate. It should be noted that men who have gone through male climacteric still retain the potential to reproduce.

Sometime between the ages of 35 and 60 men reach an uncertain period in their lives that has been termed a *midlife crisis*. It is a time of high risk for divorce, for extramarital affairs, for career changes, for accidents, and even for suicide attempts. All men experience it to some degree and emerge a bit changed, for better or for worse. It is a time of questions: "Is what I'm doing with my life really satisfying and meaningful? Would I be better off if I had pursued a different vocation or career? Do I really want to be married to my wife?"

Male climacteric is a time when a man reevaluates his marriage and his family life. This period of reassessment is often characterized by nervousness, decrease in sexual activity, depression, decreased memory and concentration, decreased sexual interests, fatigue, sleep disturbances, irritability, loss of interest or self-confidence, indecisive-

ness, numbness and tingling, fear of impending danger, and/or excitability. Other possible symptoms are headaches, vertigo, constipation, crying, hot flashes, chilly sensations, itching, sweating, and/or cold hands and feet.

A man going through male climacteric usually encounters some event that forces him to examine who he is and what he wants out of life. During this crisis he looks back, as well as ahead, on his successes and failures, his degree of dependency on others, the outcomes of his dreams, and his capabilities for what lies ahead. Depending on what he sees and how he deals with it, this experience can be either exhilarating or demoralizing. He sees the disparity between youth and age, between hope and reality.

Male climacteric is caused by a combination of biological and psychological factors. As a male grows older, his hair thins and begins to turn gray. He develops more wrinkles and tends to develop a "tire" around his waist. His physical energy gradually decreases, and he can no longer run as fast as he once did. There are changes in his heart, his prostate, his sexual capacity, his chest size, his kidneys, his hearing, and his gastrointestinal tract.

The production of testosterone gradually decreases. Testosterone is an androgen that is the most potent naturally occurring male hormone. It stimulates the activity of male secondary sex characteristics, such as hair growth and voice depth, and helps to prevent deterioration in the sex organs in later life. The male sex glands are essential for the vitality of youth. These glands are the first glands to suffer when aging occurs. Two of the more subtle changes (as compared to hair loss, wrinkles, slowing blood circulation, and more sluggish digestion) are a decline in the number of sperm in an ejaculation and a reduction of testosterone present in the plasma and urine. The testes lose their earlier vigorous functioning and produce decreasing amounts of hormones. Older men generally take a longer time to achieve an erection. It also takes a longer time before an erection can be regained after an orgasm.

Some men do have greater hormonal fluctuations at climactric. Hyde and DeLamater (2000) summarize studies that have found evidence of monthly cycles in some men with hormonal fluctuations in a 30-day rhythm.

While biological changes (including the diminishing production of sex hormones) play an important part in male climacteric, perhaps even more important is the problem of being middle-aged in a culture that worships youth. Many of the problems associated with male climacteric are due to psychological factors.

There is the fear of aging, which is intensified by the awareness that mental and physical capacities are declining, including sexual capacities. Also involved is the fear of failure, either in a job or in the man's personal life. Fear of women may be a part of this. A man may think that his sexual prowess is waning, and then may fear women's greater sexual capacities. He may also have a fear of failing in his sexual activities. The man with self-doubts is especially susceptible to the fear of rejection. He is very sensitive to derogatory comments about his age, his physique, or his thinning hair. A fear of death may be apparent as he realizes he has probably lived at least half of his life. All of these fears are apt to have an adverse impact on his emotional and sexual functioning.

A significant part of male climacteric is due to depression, which is often brought on when a man fears aging and recognizes that his sexual powers are waning (Hyde & DeLamater, 2000). He also realizes that he will never achieve the successes that he envisioned for himself years earlier. His bouts with depression may be so profound that he may contemplate suicide. Depression during this midlife crisis may also be triggered by a reevaluation of childhood dreams, conflicts in need of resolution, new erotic longings and fantasies, sadness over opportunities lost, and a new questioning of values. All of this is coupled with a search for new meaning in life. He realizes half of his life may be gone, and time becomes more precious. He worries about things undone, and there does not seem to be enough time for everything. He has the feeling of missing out on a big chunk of life. The man who is engaged in activities outside his daily job is a less likely candidate for depression. It is unbalanced to be so busy with getting ahead that the pleasures of life are missed. To recapture some of his former enthusiasm and perhaps to shake some of his unsettling doubts and fears, he may drive himself to work harder, to exercise more, or to seek younger women.

A man at midlife is also apt to experience a growing dissatisfaction with his job. He feels a sense of entrapment as the pressure to pay bills forces him to continue working at a job that he finds increasingly boring and unfulfilling. Along these lines is the fact that his personal identity is deeply entwined with his work roles. His job has provided him with an opportunity to define his self with others, to enter into a stable set of relationships with colleagues and/or clients, and to explain his place in the world. Now he questions that place. Occupational aspirations may change several times during this period. The emphasis may shift from measuring success in terms of achievement to measuring it in terms of economic security. Also at this time, movement up the occupational ladder is largely completed. If he has not achieved his work goals by age 40 or 50, he may realize he may never achieve them; he may even be demoted one or two steps down the occupational ladder.

Midlife Crisis: True or False?

The ease or panic with which a man faces his mid-years will depend on how he has accepted his faults and his strengths throughout life. The man who has developed a strong affective bond with his family will fare better than the man who followed a more isolated and career-oriented course. To age gracefully is to realize that he has done the best he could with his life.

Many physicians will prescribe antidepressant therapy and counseling, along with requesting the support and understanding of family and close friends (Hyde & DeLamater, 2000). Men who undergo a midlife crisis need to realize that there is still a great deal of pleasure and satisfaction to be gotten out of life. This is not the end; there are still things left for them to do.

Women go through similar psychological worries (for example, the empty-nest syndrome). Recent research indicates a declining proportion of women are affected by the empty-nest syndrome because more women are emphasizing careers. Midlife is a time of reassessment for both sexes as people in this age group look over their lives. It is a time of reprioritizing one's life. With the right attitude, this time period can become a time of reappraisal, renewed commitment, and growth.

But the realization of slow deterioration in one's physical capacities and of a disparity between one's earlier dreams and present reality is apt to be a crisis for many people.

Some health evidence shows that midlife is a time of crisis for many people. Hypertension, peptic ulcers, and heart disease are most often diagnosed in middle-aged patients. The rate of first admissions for alcoholism treatment for middle-aged individuals is higher than for younger adults (U.S. Census Bureau, 1998). These statistics suggest that middle adulthood can be a period of stress and turmoil.

Thus, it appears that midlife is a time of transition and change. For some it is a crisis, but not for others (Hyde & DeLamater, 2000). For some women, menopause is a precipitating factor that sets off a midlife crisis; for other women some of the symptoms may be uncomfortable, but an identity crisis is not precipitated. For some men and women, their children leaving home precipitates an identity crisis, while other men and women delight in seeing their children grow and develop, and experience a new sense of freedom in being able to travel more and in being able to pursue more vigorously special interests and hobbies. Most men and women look forward to the departure of the youngest child.

Men who undergo a midlife crisis are apt to have had adjustment problems for a long time. Kaluger and Kaluger (1984, p. 541) conclude: "Midlife crises may be the result of unadjusted adolescents and young adults who grow up to be unadjusted middle-aged adults rather than the result of a universal crisis confined to midlife."

❧ Sexual Functioning in Middle Age

Sexual expression is an important part of life for practically all age groups. In this section we will focus on sexual functioning during middle adulthood—in marriage, in extramarital relationships, for those who are divorced or widowed, and for people who never married.

Sex in Marriage

A close relationship exists between overall marital satisfaction and sexual satisfaction, particularly for men (Hyde & DeLamater, 2000). These two factors probably influence each other. Marital satisfaction probably increases the pleasure derived from sexual intercourse; and a satisfying sexual relationship probably increases the satisfaction derived from a marriage. Women are much more likely to be orgasmic in very happy marriages than in less happy marriages (Hyde & DeLamater, 2000).

Generally speaking, marriage partners report satisfaction with marital sex. Clements (1994) conducted a survey of 1,049 men and women aged 18 to 65. For men, satisfaction was highest in the 18 to 24 age group and decreased slightly as men grew older. For women, satisfaction was highest in the 35 to 44 age group. These findings are consistent with studies that have found that a man's sex drive reaches its peak at a relatively young age, whereas that of a woman tends to peak in her late 30s or early 40s. (Hyde & DeLamater, 2000).

The median frequencies of coitus by age groups as found in the Clements (1994) study are presented in Figure 10.1. The frequency of coitus is highest when the individuals are in their 20s and 30s, and then gradually declines to about once a week in couples over age 55. It is important to note that there is wide variation in these average frequencies, and it is a serious mistake for people to judge themselves or to judge their marriage by the frequency of marital sex.

Hyde and DeLamater (2000) note that for women there is a strong correlation between the frequency of

Figure 10.1 **Median Frequency of Coitus by Age Groups**

People should not seek to assess their sex life by median figures. Some couples enjoy sex more frequently, and others less frequently. The important aspect of sex is that of satisfaction and comfort, not frequency.

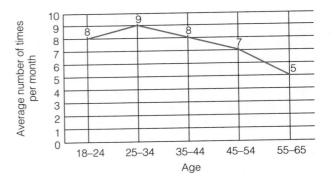

Source: Clements (1994).
Note: The median numbers have been rounded to the nearest whole number.

intercourse and satisfaction with marital sex. There is also a strong correlation between a wife's ability to communicate her sexual desires and feelings to her husband and the quality of marital sex.

After the birth of their first child, couples report less sexual satisfaction on the average than childless couples (Hyde & DeLamater, 2000). The presence of children in a family generally functions as an inhibition to sexual relations. Contrary to popular belief, the highest frequencies of sexual intercourse occur in childless couples. Many adjustments, pressures, and problems can be associated with parenthood.

For some couples the birth of the first child produces difficulties, particularly if the pregnancy was unplanned. Wives usually experience the most stress after the birth of the first child. They are apt to be concerned about their physical appearance, have increased responsibilities that lead to fatigue, and sometimes feel neglected by their husbands as the husband-wife interactions and social activities tend to decline. The arrival of more children tends to further lessen sexual satisfaction in the marriage. The frequency of sexual intercourse appears to be negatively related to the number of children in a family (Hyde & DeLamater, 2000). To some extent the reduction of sexual activity and sexual gratification with parenthood are offset by the increased gratifications that most parents receive from being parents—watching and helping their children grow and develop, and feeling pride in performing parental roles.

Married couples now use a greater variety of sexual techniques than couples in earlier generations. The female-on-top position is increasingly being used, because it gives the female greater control over stimulation of the clitoris than the man-on-top position. Oral sex has also become more popular. Couples today also spend a longer time making love. Most couples now spend between 15 minutes and an hour having sex (Schrof, 1994). This change may reflect a greater awareness by married men and women that women are more likely to enjoy sex more and to be orgasmic if intercourse is unhurried.

A study of 3,432 Americans by the University of Chicago's National Opinion Center found that the more active a person's sex life, the more likely it is that the person masturbates: 60 percent of the men and 40 percent of the women in the study had masturbated in the previous year; 25 percent of the men and 10 percent of the women reporting they masturbated in the previous week (Schrof, 1994). Sex therapists generally view masturbation to be a normal and useful sexual outlet.

Extramarital Sexual Relationships

Different studies have found a wide variance in the percent of men and women who report having had an affair while they were married: 10 to 25 percent of husbands, and 5 to 15 percent of wives reported having affairs (Hyde & DeLamater, 2000). For males, the frequency of extramarital coitus decreases with age, whereas with females there is a gradual increase up to around age 40. These sex differences may reflect differences in the peaking of the sex drive. Wives with full-time jobs outside of the home are more apt to have extramarital affairs than wives who do not have jobs. Wives with full-time jobs have an increased opportunity to become acquainted with a variety of men who are not known by the husband.

Spouses become involved in extramarital coitus for a variety of reasons. In some cases marital sex may not be satisfying. The spouse's partner may have a long-term illness or a sexual dysfunction, or the couple may be separated. The extramarital affair may represent an attempt to obtain what is missing in the marriage. Some seek extramarital involvements to obtain affection, to satisfy curiosity, to find excitement, or to add to their list of sexual conquests. Some become involved in extramarital affairs to get revenge for feeling wronged by their spouse. Some want to punish their spouse for not being more affectionate or appreciative. In many cases there are a combination of reasons for an extramarital affair.

In regard to extramarital sexual relationships, Nass, Libby, and Fischer (1984) note:

physical acts are invested with symbolic meaning by the people involved. To have intercourse—still the main focus of ideas about sex—with someone outside our central relationship means quite different things to different people. To some,

it's a serious infringement on a love commitment. Sex outside marriage may be viewed as a breach of a monogamous legal and/or religious contract. At the opposite extreme some people applaud any close relationship. They believe that it is good to express the warmth, love, or sexual desire they feel for others. In their minds such feelings may enhance life in the central relationship rather than detract from it. (p. 207)

Some surveys have examined why a high percentage of married couples do not have an extramarital affair. The most mentioned reason is that it would be a betrayal of trust in the love relationship. Other stated reasons are that it would damage the marital relationship; that it would hurt the spouse; and that the probable benefits of an affair are not worth the consequences (Hyde & DeLamater, 2001).

In most cases extramarital affairs are carried out in secret. Sometimes the spouse later discovers the affair. Typical reactions to the affair are summarized by Maier (1984) through his experiences as a marriage counselor:

Among the most common feelings expressed by a spouse after such a discovery are anger and a sense of being deceived and betrayed. In addition, the affair is often seen as a symbolic insult to the spouse's affection and sexual adequacy. Certain subcultures consider it appropriate to seek some type of revenge or retribution.

Generally speaking, isolated sexual experiences are less disturbing to spouses than prolonged extramarital affairs. Brief sexual encounters can sometimes be written off as temporary reactions to sexual frustration; however, longer affairs are seen as greater threats to the marital love relationship. (p. 322)

The discovery of an extramarital affair may lead to a divorce, but not always. Sometimes the discovery of an affair is a crisis that forces a couple to recognize that problems (sexual or nonsexual) exist in their marriage, and the couple then seek to work on these to improve the marriage. Some spouses reluctantly accept and adjust to the affair without saying much. They may be financially dependent on their partner, or they may have a low sense of self-worth and have made adjustments to being emotionally abused by their spouse in the past. Others show little reaction because they realize a divorce is expensive, socially degrading, and may result in loneliness. In such marriages the relationship may become devitalized with the partners having little emotional attachment to each other.

A few spouses react to an extramarital affair by gradually entering into a consensual extramarital relationship. In such a relationship extramarital sexual relationships are permitted and even encouraged by both partners. One type of consensual extramarital sex arrangement is *mate swapping.* In this arrangement two or more couples get together and exchange partners, either retiring to a separate place to have sexual relations or having sex in the same room with various combinations of partners.

Sex Following Divorce

A great majority of formerly married persons become sexually active within a year after divorce. When matched for age, divorced men have a slightly higher frequency of coitus than married men. Divorced men also tend to have a variety of partners (Hyde & DeLamater, 2001). Divorced women also generally have a fairly active sex life, although the incidence of postmarital sex tends to be lower than when they were married. They also tend to have smaller number of partners than divorced men (Hyde & DeLamater, 2001). Divorced women report a higher frequency of orgasm than they experienced in marital sex (Hyde & DeLamater, 2001). Divorced men also report that sexual relationships are satisfying.

These results should not be interpreted as meaning that sex following a divorce is more satisfying than marital sex. People who have a satisfying sexual relationship may be less likely to get a divorce. People who get a divorce are probably not as likely to give high ratings to their sexual relationship when they were married.

Divorced people today are less concerned about hiding their sexual relationships from their children than were divorced people a generation ago. Divorced people apparently now have more liberal views on sexuality than in the past.

Sex in Widowhood

Ending a marriage by divorce can be traumatic, but a marriage ended by the death of one's spouse is usually more traumatic. In a divorce a spouse has input into the decision to part, but most widows and widowers have no input and wish their partner was still alive. They have to adjust not only to being single, but also to the death of a loved one.

Widowers are more likely than widows to establish a new sexual relationship. In middle and later adulthood there are substantially more single women than single men. There is greater cultural acceptance of older men dating younger women, than vice versa. Cultural patterns also encourage widowers to establish new sexual relationships, whereas widows feel pressure to be sexually loyal to their deceased spouse. Widows also tend to receive more emotional support from friends and family; and therefore, may feel less need to form a new sexual relationship.

Sex among the Never-Married

Very little research has been conducted on the sexual lifestyles of never-married adults. The attitudes of singles about their status vary widely. Some plan never to marry. Some want to marry, but haven't found the right partner, or have found someone they want to marry but that person refuses to marry. Some desperately seek a partner.

The lifestyles of the never-married vary tremendously. Some contently become celibate. Others are highly involved in the singles scene—living in apartments for single people, going to singles bars, and joining singles clubs. Some singles have numerous sexual partners. Some singles, on the other hand, become involved in their careers or hobbies, and though they occasionally may date, they do not want the restrictions of a marriage. Some singles are content to date someone steadily for a few years, and when that relationship sours, they move on to another. Some occasionally cohabit with the opposite sex. Some become addicted to alcohol or to some other drug, and spend relatively little time in romantic relationships.

Celibacy

A small minority of people choose to abstain from sexual intercourse. Certain religious leaders (such as Buddhist monks and Roman Catholic nuns and priests) are required to remain celibate. In other cases, individuals choose to abstain for a variety of reasons. They may not want the entanglements of sexual relationships. They may have a low sex drive. They may enjoy other ways, such as masturbation, of expressing their sexuality. They may fear acquiring a sexually transmitted disease, or have a sexually transmitted disease and do not want to risk passing on the disease to someone else. They may be in a conflictive relationship with a partner and, therefore, may not desire to become sexually intimate. They may have a partner who has a low sex drive or one who is physically incapable of intercourse.

Although some people find abstinence to be very difficult, others experience it as satisfying. Periods of celibacy may be important for self-exploration and recovery from broken romances.

❧ People Living with AIDS: A Population-at-Risk

The remainder of this chapter will focus on AIDS (acquired immunodeficiency syndrome). AIDS is a devastating disease that has the potential to kill more people than any other. It is a contagious, presently incurable disease that targets the body's immune system and greatly reduces the body's capacity to defend itself against disease.

AIDS became headline news in 1985 when it was revealed that Rock Hudson (the prominent actor) had contracted AIDS—he died from the disease a few months after the public release of the news. Since 1985, AIDS has continued to periodically make national headlines. The public was stunned in 1991 when NBA star Magic Johnson announced he had tested positive for HIV, the virus causing AIDS (see Highlight 10.3).

Highlight 10.3

Magic Johnson, An American Hero, Joins the Battle Against the Aids Virus

On November 18, 1991, millions of people throughout the world were stunned when Earvin "Magic" Johnson announced at a news conference that he had contracted the AIDS virus. He also announced his retirement from the Los Angeles Lakers and the National Basketball Association after 12 superb seasons. He added, "I will now become a spokesman for the HIV virus."

Thirteen years earlier, Magic Johnson had made his first appearance in the public eye by leading Michigan State, as a sophomore, to the NCAA (National Collegiate Athletic Association) championship. At 6 feet 9 inches, he could play every position, including center.

In his 12 years with the Los Angeles Lakers, he led the Lakers to five world championships, and in the process acquired three Most Valuable Player awards. Magic Johnson is not only one of the most talented individuals ever to play basketball, he is also charismatic and has an appealing smile. A few days after the news conference Johnson indicated he believes he became infected with the virus from sexual intercourse with a female. He further acknowledged that over the years he has had a large number of female partners.

A few days after Johnson's news conference, he appeared on the *Arsenio Hall Show* and stated, "You don't have to feel sorry for me because if I die tomorrow, I've had the greatest life." His main message to Hall's audience and to the general public: "Practice safe sex, start using condoms and be aware. . . . Please put your thinking caps on and put your cap on down there" (gesturing below his belt).

In 1991, fears about the disease ran rampant. Johnson triggered a storm of criticism when he tried to stage a comeback in 1992, for possibly endangering the health of his teammates and other players. Four years later, in February 1996, Johnson ended his retirement, and returned to play for the Los Angeles Lakers. His comeback unleashed bearhugs from his teammates, and an avalanche of support from across the country. The change in public opinion about his comeback in 1996 versus 1992 is a remarkable sign of growing compassion and understanding by the public of persons infected by HIV. (Johnson retired at the end of the 1996 season "on his own terms.")

Johnson is still robust and healthy—more than ten years after he announced that he is HIV positive.

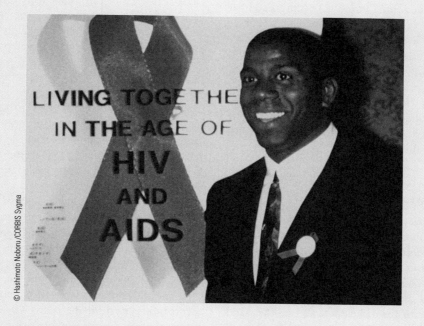

© Hashimoto Noboru/CORBIS Sygma

What Causes AIDS?

AIDS is caused by a type of virus called HIV, an abbreviation for human immunodeficiency virus. A virus is a protein-coated package of genes that invades a healthy body cell and alters the normal genetic apparatus of the cell, causing the cell to reproduce the virus. In the process, the invaded cell is often killed. The HIV virus falls within a special category of viruses called *retroviruses,* so named because they reverse the usual order of reproduction within the cells they infect.

In recent years it has become clear that more than one virus is linked with the development of AIDS. The first virus to be identified, and the one that causes the largest number of AIDS cases, has been designated as human immunodeficiency virus type 1 (HIV-1). This virus appears to be one of the most virulent member of the growing family of AIDS and AIDS-related viruses. HIV is a formidable enemy in that it is constantly changing, or mutating, and is present in multiple strains. To simplify our discussion of AIDS in the following pages, we refer to the infectious agent simply as HIV.

The HIV virus invades cells involved in the body's normal process of protecting itself from disease and causes these cells to produce more of the virus. Apparently HIV destroys normal white blood cells, which are supposed to fight off diseases invading the body. As a result, the body is left defenseless and can fall prey to other infections. The virus devastates the body's immune or defense system so that other diseases occur and eventually cause death. Without a functioning immune system to combat germs, the affected person becomes vulnerable to bacteria, fungi, malignancies, and other viruses that may cause life-threatening illnesses, such as cancer, pneumonia, and meningitis.

HIV is a tiny delicate shred of genetic material. As far as scientists know, it can live in only a very limited environment. It prefers one type of cell—the T-helper cell in human blood. Outside of blood and other bodily fluids, the virus apparently dies.

How Is AIDS Contracted?

Documented ways in which the AIDS virus can be transmitted are: by sexual intercourse with someone who has HIV, by using hypodermic needles that were also used by someone who has the virus, and by receiving contaminated blood transfusions or other products derived from contaminated blood. Babies may also contract the AIDS virus before or at birth from their infected mothers and through breast milk.

HIV has been isolated in semen, blood, vaginal secretions, saliva, tears, breast milk, and urine. Only blood, semen, vaginal secretions, and to a much lesser extent, breast milk have been identified as capable of transmitting the AIDS virus (Lloyd, 1995). Many experts doubt whether there is enough of the virus present in tears and saliva to be transmitted in these fluids. Experts rule out casual kissing or swimming in pools as a means of contracting AIDS. Sneezing, coughing, crying, or handshakes also have not proven to be dangerous. Only the exchange of body fluids (for example, through anal, oral, or genital intercourse) permits infection. The virus is very fragile and cannot survive long without a suitable environment, nor is it able to penetrate the skin. In summary, evidence has not been found to show that AIDS can be spread through any type of casual contact. You cannot get AIDS from doorknobs, toilets, or telephones.

Few lesbians have contracted AIDS. Lesbians are at low risk unless they use intravenous drugs or have unsafe sexual contact with people in high-risk groups. Female-to-female transmission *is* possible, however, through vaginal secretions or blood.

Women who use sperm for artificial insemination from an infected donor are also at risk of infection. Donors should be screened by licensed sperm banks as a preventive measure.

When a person is exposed to the virus, the virus usually becomes inactive. Once it is in a person's body it apparently needs help to stay active. Such help might include a history of infections with certain other viruses, general poor health, the abuse of certain recreational drugs (such as butyl nitrite), malnutrition, and genetic predisposition. For those who develop AIDS, the mortality rate is nearly 100 percent. In the early 1980s the AIDS virus was transmitted in some cases through blood transfusions. (Tennis player Arthur Ashe was exposed to HIV in this way.) Blood that is used in blood transfusions is now tested for the presence of antibodies to the AIDS virus; therefore, it is unlikely that the virus will be transmitted by transfusions. But because antibodies do not form immediately after exposure to the virus, a newly infected person may unknowingly donate blood after becoming infected but before his or her antibody test becomes positive. As an added precaution, donated blood is heat-treated to inactivate HIV. There is no risk of contracting the AIDS virus by being a blood donor.

Most people infected by HIV will eventually develop AIDS. The length of time between initial infection of HIV and the appearance of AIDS symptoms is called the incubation period for the virus. The average incubation period (before the development of recent drugs used to treat the disease) was estimated to be 7 to 11 years (Lloyd, 1995). There is considerable variation in this incubation period, ranging from a few months (particularly for babies who are HIV-positive) to 20 years or more.

Another major health problem involves people who are HIV-positive but have no symptoms of AIDS. Most of these individuals have not been tested for the AIDS virus and therefore are unaware they have the virus. These people can infect others, although they experience no life-threatening symptoms themselves. The following are high-risk factors in contracting AIDS:

- Having multiple sex partners without using safe sex practices (such as using condoms). The risk of infection increases according to the number of sexual partners one has, male or female. In considering the risks of acquiring AIDS a person should heed this warning: "When you have sex with a new partner, you are having sex not only with this person but also with all of this person's previous sexual partners."

- Sharing intravenous needles because HIV may be transmitted by reusing contaminated needles and syringes.

- Having anal intercourse with an infected person.

- Having sex with prostitutes; prostitutes are at high risk because they have multiple sex partners and are more apt to be intravenous drug users.

Sexually active, heterosexual adolescents and young adults are increasingly becoming a high-risk group for contracting HIV. Persons in this age group tend to be sexually active with multiple sex partners, which increases the risk of contracting HIV. The risk of male-to-female transmission through sexual intercourse is higher than that of female-to-male. As noted, the risk of woman-to-woman transmission through sexual contact appears to be low, but has not yet been determined. Having multiple sexual partners increases the likelihood that transmission will occur.

Lloyd (1990) describes the ways in which sexual transmission of HIV can be prevented or reduced:

Only two methods of completely preventing sexual transmission have been identified: (1) abstaining from sex or (2) having sexual relations only with a faithful and uninfected partner. The risk of infection through sexual intercourse can be reduced by practicing what has been called "safer sex," which is using a condom for all sexual penetration (vaginal, oral, and anal) whenever there is any doubt about a sexual partner's HIV status; engaging in nonpenetrative sexual activity; limiting the number of sexual partners; and avoiding sexual contact with people such as prostitutes who have had many partners. (p. 19)

Although some people believe any contact with someone who is HIV-positive guarantees illness and death, such fears are not justified. Body fluids (such as fresh blood, semen, urine, and vaginal secretions) infected with the virus must enter the bloodstream in order for the virus to be transmitted from one person to another. Male homosexuals account for so many AIDS cases because they are apt to engage in anal intercourse. Anal intercourse often results in tearing the lining of the rectum, which allows infected semen to get into the bloodstream. Sharing a needle during mainlining a drug with someone who is carrying the virus is also dangerous because there is transmission of blood. The reason sharing intravenous drug needles poses such a risk of the transmission of HIV is that a small amount of the previous user's blood is often drawn into the needle and then injected directly into the bloodstream of the next user.

At the present time, there is no evidence that the virus can be spread by "dry" mouth-to-mouth kissing. Although unproven, there is a theoretical risk of transmitting HIV through vigorous "wet" or deep tongue kissing, because infected blood may be transmitted from one person to the other.

Diagnosis

Several tests have been developed to determine if a person has been exposed to the AIDS virus. These tests do not directly detect the virus, but only the antibodies a person's immune system develops to fight the virus. Two of the most widely used tests are called the ELISA and the Western blot. ELISA stands for "enzyme-linked immunosorbent assay." ELISA can be used in two important ways. First, donated blood can be screened to prevent the AIDS virus from being transmitted by blood transfusions. Second, individuals who fear they may be carriers of the virus can be tested. For a person who has been infected with HIV, it generally takes 2 to 3 months before enough antibodies are produced to be detected by the test.

ELISA is an extremely sensitive test and therefore is highly accurate in detecting the presence of antibodies. It rarely gives a negative result when antibodies are present. However, it has a much higher rate of false positive results. That is, it indicates that antibodies are present when in reality they are not. Therefore, it is recommended that positive results on the ELISA be confirmed by another test called the Western blot or immunoblot. This test is much more specific and less likely to give a false positive. Because the Western blot is expensive and difficult to administer, it can't be used for mass blood screening as can the ELISA. It must be emphasized that neither test can determine if a person already has AIDS or will actually develop it. The tests only establish the presence of antibodies that indicate exposure to the virus.

Origin of AIDS

The origin of AIDS is unknown, although there have been a variety of speculations. (We probably never will be able to identify the origin, particularly now that AIDS exists throughout the world.) One theory postulates that the virus first developed in Africa in the 1970s. Samples of blood taken from Ugandan children in 1973 appeared to contain antibodies for the AIDS virus or a virus very similar to it. The presence of antibodies imply that these children had been exposed to the virus. Furthermore, the sudden appearance of AIDS may have resulted from the fast-paced urbanization of portions of Africa. Previously isolated enclaves harboring the disease might suddenly have been exposed to the outside world. Some authorities have found that some species of monkeys have the AIDS virus, and there is speculation that the virus may have been transmitted to humans perhaps through a monkey bite or perhaps through eating monkey meat.

Another theory is that some military research unit (sponsored by the government of some unknown country) may have developed the virus as a way to exterminate large numbers of the population of "enemy" countries. Somehow, the virus may have escaped during experimental tests.

Another theory links the birth of AIDS to polio vaccine (Curtis, 1992). In 1957, an experimental oral vaccine for polio was developed by Dr. Hilary Koprowski of Philadelphia's Wistar Institute. This vaccine was made from weakened polio viruses grown in a culture of monkey kidney cells. Several monkey viruses have been known to contaminate such cultures (vaccine makers now have processes to eliminate these contaminants). The people of the African nation of Zaire became the first large group to receive this experimental polio vaccine. Extrapolating from a number of coincidences—the testing of the vaccine in the very site where AIDS is thought to have originated; Koprowski's recollection that he cultured the virus in the tissue of green monkeys (a species that harbors a virus similar to HIV)—has led some authorities to speculate that the polio vaccine was contaminated with a virus that evolved into the deadly HIV. (There is no reason to worry about standard present-day polio vaccines; they are rigorously screened for contamination.)

Some feel that the advent of AIDS in the United States can be traced to a single individual (Shilts, 1987), Gaetan Dugas, a Canadian airline steward. As early as 1979, it was noted that several men began to suffer from a rare form of skin cancer named Kaposi's sarcoma, a disease that the body's immune system could normally resist easily. By 1981 it was established that AIDS had invaded the United States. Investigation of many of these men and their lives revealed that either they or someone with whom they had sexual relations had also been sexually involved with Dugas. Allegedly, Dugas was noted for exceptional pride in his appearance and his ability to attract many lovers. He reportedly continued to have sexual relations with men even after he understood his diagnosis and knew such behavior could be fatal to these partners. Dugas died on March 30, 1984. This was only one month after he turned 31 and almost 4 years after he sought a doctor's help to remove an unattractive purple spot near his ear, the beginning of his first bout with Kaposi's sarcoma.

The fact that Dugas was gay is inconsequential. It cannot be proven that he was the first person to bring AIDS to the United States. The fact that he knowingly continued to practice unsafe sex without regard for the lives of others is the significant and deadly part of the story. AIDS appears to have spread significantly throughout the heterosexual community. Dugas provides an excellent lesson for all people who choose to be sexually active—namely, that it is an absolute necessity that they be concerned about the well-being of other people. The gay community merits credit for providing the first major impetus in the fight against AIDS. Many gay people banded together, brought the issue of AIDS to the attention of the general public, advocated for research, identified and lauded the use of safer sex practices, closed down facilities such as bathhouses where men met for sexual encounters, and helped people afflicted with the disease.

The Effects of HIV

Persons with the AIDS virus are now classified as being either HIV-asymptomatic (without symptoms of AIDS) or HIV-symptomatic (with symptoms of the syndrome). HIV invades particularly a group of white blood cells (lymphocytes) called T-helper cells, or T-4 cells. These cells, in turn, produce cells that are critical to the body's immune response in fighting off infections. When HIV attacks T-4 helper cells, it stops them from producing immune cells, which fight off disease. Instead, HIV changes T-4 cells so that they begin producing HIV. Eventually, the infected person's number of healthy T-4 cells is so reduced that infections cannot be fought off.

Once a person is infected with HIV, several years are apt to go by before symptoms of AIDS appear.

Initial symptoms include dry cough, abdominal discomfort, headaches, oral thrush, loss of appetite, fever, night sweats, weight loss, diarrhea, skin rashes, tiredness, swollen lymph nodes, and lack of resistance to infection. (Many other illnesses have similar symptoms, so it is irrational for persons to conclude they are developing AIDS if they have some of these symptoms.) As AIDS progresses, the immune system is less and less capable of fighting off "opportunist" diseases, making the infected person vulnerable to a variety of cancers, nervous system degeneration, and infections caused by other viruses, bacteria, parasites, and fungi. Ordinarily, opportunistic infections are not life threatening to people with healthy immune systems, but they are frequently fatal to people with AIDS, whose immunological functioning has been severely compromised.

The serious diseases that afflict persons with AIDS include Kaposi's sarcoma (an otherwise rare form of cancer that accounts for many AIDS deaths), pneumocystic carinii pneumonia (a lung disease that is also a major cause of AIDS deaths), and a variety of other generalized opportunistic infections, such as shingles (herpes zoster), encephalitis, severe fungal infections that cause a type of meningitis, yeast infections of the throat and esophagus, and infections of the lungs, intestines, and central nervous system. The incidence of tuberculosis, a disease once nearly eradicated in the United States, has escalated rapidly in recent years due largely to the epidemic of HIV infection and AIDS.

Initially, HIV infection was diagnosed as AIDS only when the immune system became so seriously impaired that the infected individual developed one or more severe, debilitating diseases, such as Kaposi's sarcoma or pneumocystic carinii pneumonia. However, on April 1, 1992, the Centers for Disease Control and Prevention broadened its definition of AIDS: now, anyone who is infected with HIV and has a helper T-cell count of 200 cells per cubic millimeter of blood or less is said to have AIDS, regardless of other symptoms that person may or may not have. (Normal helper T-cell counts in healthy people not infected with HIV range from 800 to 900 per cubic millimeter of blood.)

AIDS is a syndrome, not one specific disease. AIDS simply makes those infected by the virus increasingly more vulnerable to any disease that might come along. The disease process of AIDS involves a continuum whereby those affected become more and more vulnerable to devastating diseases.

In some patients AIDS may attack the nervous system and cause damage to the brain. The deterioration, called AIDS-dementia complex, occurs gradually over a period of time (sometimes a few years). Several specific intellectual functions may be affected by AIDS. These include inability to concentrate; forgetfulness; inability to think quickly and efficiently; visuospatial problems, which make it difficult to get from place to place or to perform complex and simultaneous tasks; and slowed motor ability. It is interesting that language capacity and the ability to learn, difficulties that characterize people with Alzheimer's disease, do not seem to be affected.

People tend to react in a variety of ways when they are first informed they have HIV infection or AIDS. Certain patterns of reaction, however, have been observed. Lloyd (1990) notes a typical reaction progresses through the following stages: shock; denial; crisis; transition; fear; depression; panic; guilt; anger; self-pity; bargaining; search for meaning, and fighting to a stage of sense of self, positive action, and acceptance. People with HIV infection or AIDS may experience losses in physical strength, health, career development, community standing, control over decision making, and the opportunity to have children,

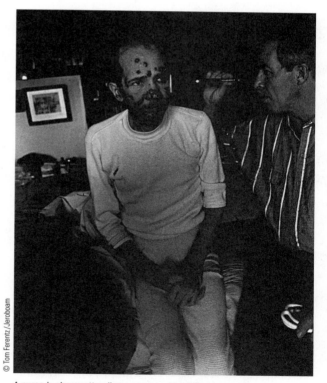

© Tom Ferentz/Jeroboam

A nurse is shown attending a person with AIDS at home. The sores are caused by Kaposi's sarcoma. Research has revealed that Kaposi's sarcoma may be caused by a little-known strain of herpes virus, which has been found in patients both with and without HIV infection.

among others. Friends and family also feel loss and some-times anger toward the person with HIV infection, which often is followed by guilt about these feelings.

Unfortunately, those who have AIDS are further vic-timized as they have to deal with the public hysteria and powerful prejudice against gays. Because gay men were some of the first people identified as suffering from AIDS in the United States, some people have associated having AIDS with being gay. Prejudice and discrimination make staying alive even more difficult.

Treatment and Prevention of AIDS

At this time there is no cure for AIDS. There are a mul-titude of hurdles to overcome in combatting the disease. AIDS is caused by a form of virus, and even with modern technology, we don't know how to cure a virus. The common cold is caused by virus; despite millions of dol-lars spent on research in the hopes of finding an effective cure, such a treatment has not yet been found for this common ailment. Currently, serious research is being undertaken to understand, prevent, and fight AIDS.

Prevention can be pursued in two major ways. First, people can abstain from activities and behaviors that put them at risk for contracting the disease. Second, scientists can work on developing a vaccine to prevent contracting the disease, similar in a way to vaccines that prevent polio or measles. A vaccine might either block the virus from attacking a person's immune system or bolster the im-mune system so that HIV is unable to invade it.

Drugs are being studied in the hope of fighting AIDS after it has already been contracted. However, serious problems are being encountered. For one thing, many of the drugs have serious toxic effects on the people who take them. Additionally, it is difficult and time-consuming to test drugs and get them to the point where they can be tested on humans. Animal-rights activists have protested using monkeys and orangutans for testing that inevitably results in their deaths. Testing drugs is enormously costly. Only since about 1990 have substantial funds been chan-nelled into AIDS research. Until the middle 1980s, AIDS was frequently seen as a disease contracted only by drug abusers and gay men. There seemed to be an attitude that "people were getting only what they deserved." Many gay people were outraged and demanded that national atten-tion be given to fighting a disease that was killing people, regardless of who they were. Nonetheless, the early resist-ance to providing money for research has set back progress in overcoming the disease. Finally, there is the major prob-lem that the virus mutates and changes form. This further complicates finding a cure.

The drug called AZT (azidothymidine) has been found to delay the progress of the disease in some people (Lloyd, 1995). First synthesized in 1964 and initially de-veloped as a cancer drug, AZT helps to extend life and provide hope. It does not cure AIDS, and there are some serious difficulties with the drug. AZT or Retrovir (its brand name) must be taken every 4 hours both night and day. People often experience very uncomfortable side ef-fects. These include nausea, headaches, anemia, lowered white blood cell counts, liver function changes, kidney effects, and bone marrow damage. The longer the drug is taken, the more likely the person is to experience side ef-fects with increasing severity. Additionally, the drug is very difficult to manufacture, involving 17 chemical steps plus 6 more steps to make it marketable. The result is scarcity and high costs. Nonetheless, the existence of a drug that at least can delay the effects of such a devastat-ing disease has lifted the black curtain of pessimism that has shrouded AIDS.

Other drugs to combat the AIDS virus are being de-veloped. In 1991, the Food and Drug Administration ap-proved DDI (didanosine) for treatment of adults and chil-dren with advanced AIDS who cannot tolerate or are not helped by AZT (Scanlan, 1991). In 1995 and 1996, the Food and Drug Administration approved several drugs called protease inhibitors, which fight HIV by deactivat-ing an enzyme the virus needs to be able to infect human blood cells (Brink, 1996). Combining AZT with some of these protease inhibitors is delaying substantially the pro-gression of AIDS in people who are HIV-infected (Hyde & DeLamater, 2000).

To avoid getting the AIDS virus, former Surgeon General C. Everett Koop (1987, p. 27) recommends: "The most certain way to avoid getting the AIDS virus and to control the AIDS epidemic in the United States is for individuals to avoid promiscuous sexual practices, to maintain mutually faithful monogamous sexual relation-ships, and to avoid injecting illicit drugs." It is advisable to use a condom when having sexual intercourse with a new partner until it is certain that the person does not test positive to HIV. One cannot acquire AIDS from someone who is not infected by HIV.

Impacts of Social and Economic Forces: AIDS Discrimination and Oppression

People who test positive to HIV or who have AIDS often are victimized by discrimination. Many Americans have a "them and us" mentality about those who test positive to HIV or who have AIDS. They want to have no contact with anyone who has HIV. They erroneously think casual

Spotlight on Diversity 10.2 — Aids in Africa

AIDS is likely to have its most devastating impact in Africa. Each day more than 5,000 people die of AIDS-related diseases in Africa (Coleman & Kerbo, 2002, p. 181). In future years the number of people dying daily from this disease is apt to increase in Africa. It is anticipated that life expectancy in Africa will drop dramatically—to as low as 29 years in some countries (Coleman & Kerbo, 2002). Over a quarter of the population of Botswana, Swaziland, and Zimbabwe are infected with the HIV virus, and several other countries have HIV infection rates of around 20 percent (Coleman & Kerbo, 2002). Already, over 13 million children in Africa are orphaned by AIDS (Coleman & Kerbo, 2002). In the next 10 years it is estimated that the number of AIDS deaths in Africa will exceed all of those killed in both World War I and World War II, and will be far greater than the 20 million people that were killed by the infamous bubonic plague that devastated Europe in the fourteenth century (Coleman & Kerbo, 2002, p. 181). One reason the AIDS picture in Africa appears bleak is because most of the infected people are poor, and therefore simply cannot afford the expensive new drugs that often hold the HIV infection at bay.

social contact may put them at risk. As a result, those having the AIDS virus are apt to be shunned, risk losing their jobs, and often are abandoned by family, spouse, lovers, and friends. In some communities where it becomes public knowledge that a child has the AIDS virus, parents of other children have reacted by not allowing their children to attend the same school and by prohibiting their children from having any contact with the child who is HIV-positive.

Spotlight 10.2 summarizes material on the social and economic impact of AIDS in Africa.

Professional Values and AIDS

Social work has traditionally supported and advocated for oppressed and disenfranchised groups in our country—African Americans, Hispanics, the poor, the elderly, gays and lesbians, and women. Social workers have an ethical obligation to combat the numerous injustices connected with AIDS. AIDS is not a "gay disease" or an intravenous-drug-users disease. It is a human disease.

It should be noted that in June 1998 the U.S. Supreme Court ruled that people infected by HIV (including those having AIDS) are covered by the 1990 Americans with Disabilities Act, which protects those with a disability against discrimination in jobs, housing, and public accommodations.

Ethical Dilemmas: Confidentiality

The major social concerns and controversies encompassing AIDS are far too numerous for all of them to be addressed here. The focus will be on a select few. The intent is to provide a perspective for how massive and complicated the issues are.

A core concern, and one that has many offshoots, is that of confidentiality. Once a person has been positively diagnosed as having antibodies to HIV and is, therefore, contagious, who else should have access to this information? For instance, consider Harvey, who has just been positively diagnosed. He has been dating Chris steadily for about a year and a half. Although she is under the impression that the relationship is monogamous, Harvey has had approximately two dozen sexual encounters with other women since he and Chris first had intercourse. Harvey adamantly states that he does not want Chris to know about his other sexual experiences. Because Harvey is contagious, Chris is in a high-risk group for developing AIDS. Should Chris be told about Harvey's test results?

Should Harvey be forced to tell her and, if so, how can he be forced? Should Harvey's positive test results be reported to a public health agency? If results are reported, what if Shirley, an administrative assistant working for the agency who happens to know Chris and Harvey, sees the results? Should Shirley alert Chris? If Shirley tells Chris about the results, should Shirley be legally prosecuted for breaking confidentiality? Should Chris be forced to be tested so that she can take precautions from spreading the contagion? If Chris is forced, who will pay for the testing? Should she be required to pay? What about the other women with whom Harvey's had sexual contact? Should Harvey be required to tell them of his positive test results? If so, should they be required to be tested?

The dispute focuses on the individual's rights to confidentiality and privacy versus the rights of others to know about their vulnerability and possible condition. Few states have laws that specify when, if, and how social workers and others in the helping professions who become aware of an infected person and the potential harm to his or her intimate others should notify these other people at risk. Ryan and Rowe (1988) suggest that "workers must continue to use their professional judgment in determining whether they should disclose this information to interested third parties by weighing failure to notify against the potential for harm" (p. 328). There are no easy answers.

An HIV-infected person who acts irresponsibly is potentially life threatening to sexual or drug-injecting partners. Whether social workers (and other health professionals) have an ethical duty to inform partners when the infected and diagnosed person refuses to do so has not been determined. The principle argument for breaking confidentiality and informing someone placed unknowingly at risk by the actions of another person derives from the California State Supreme Court case *Tarasoff* v. *Regents of the University of California* (1975). In this case a university student informed his psychiatrist that he was going to shoot his girlfriend. The psychiatrist informed the campus police of this threat but did not inform the intended victim or her parents. Shortly afterward the student murdered his girlfriend. Her parents sued the psychiatrist, and the California Supreme Court ruled that a helping professional has a duty to warn the intended victim.

At the time this is being written neither court decisions nor the social work code of ethics provide guidance as to whether *Tarasoff* can or should be used as justification for helping professionals in HIV-related cases to warn and breach confidentiality. Some authorities have argued that a risk of infecting an unnamed person at some unspecified future time is not sufficient grounds for breaching confidentiality. Other authorities argue that an HIV-infected person poses a threat to the well-being of another person and that this threat is sufficient grounds for invoking *Tarasoff* as a precedent.

The scenario of Harvey and Chris depicted earlier is really not so farfetched. Research studies have found that a significant percentage of men and women have lied about or understated the number of past sexual contacts they have had, and have denied engaging in high-risk behaviors for acquiring HIV (such as engaging in anal intercourse, being sexually involved with persons who were intravenous drug users, and having multiple sex partners without using condoms) when they have engaged in such behaviors (Lloyd, 1995). In addition, in surveys of people being tested anonymously for infection with the AIDS virus, a significant percentage of men and women have stated they do not intend to inform their sexual partners of a positive result (Lloyd, 1995).

Lise Van Susteren, a psychiatrist in private practice, describes her dilemma with a client who tested positive for HIV antibodies. Her client was "deeply disturbed" and yet continued to have numerous sexual partners (Van Susteren, 1989). He neither told his partners of his condition, nor used any precautions, such as condoms. He knew he was contagious and that the result of his behavior could be that people could die. He had a stormy emotional history and had been in and out of mental hospitals. Van Susteren was appalled at his behavior. She struggled with the issue of her patient's confidentiality. Finally, she had him voluntarily committed to a mental hospital and shared her concerns with the staff there. Despite knowledge of his condition, the client was discharged. Van Susteren approached many people for help including a magistrate, a judge, the U.S. District Attorney's office, and hospital staff. All was to no avail. None of them felt they could take the initiative and stop the man's destructive behavior. There were no directives for what could be done. Despite the fact that the client was hospitalized again at a later date, he was once again discharged. Van Susteren ends her story by lamenting that "no one has wanted to take a stand on this controversial issue." She raises the question, "How many people will suffer the consequences?"

With this confidentiality issue, two values clash. First, a client who is suffering from this incurable disease should have any privacy concerns about disclosure to others respected. Second, because it is a terminal disease that is sexually transmitted, any sexual partners who are unknowingly at risk of becoming infected certainly should be made aware of the danger that is imposed. This issue can be restated in another way. Government has two very important responsibilities in regards to HIV infection— and these responsibilities conflict. On the one hand, the state is obligated to protect individual rights (such as confidentiality of health information) and defend its citizens from discrimination and injustice. Hyde and DeLamater (1997) note:

> To have AIDS, or even to be thought to have the disease, has caused many individuals to be fired from their jobs, divorced parents to lose custody or visitation rights, people to lose health insurance coverage or even to be deprived of medical care, and children to be barred from attending school; these people have also endured all sorts of informal harassment and discrimination. (p. 73)

On the other hand, the government is equally obligated to protect the health and welfare of the population (including sexual partners who are unknowingly at risk of becoming infected).

Ethical Dilemmas: HIV Testing

An issue related to confidentiality is mandatory testing for antibodies to the AIDS virus. Who should be tested, and what should be done with the results? At this point there are many other questions involved before these issues can be resolved. Should all health-care officials be required to be tested? Should public employees? What about private industry? Should all university students be tested as a prerequisite for admission? If so, should students be required to pay for the testing as part of their tuition?

There are many ramifications to testing. People have lost jobs, been thrown out of residences and schools, and been denied services that they desperately needed. For instance, some physicians and other health-care professionals have refused to serve people with AIDS. Morticians have refused to prepare the bodies of persons with AIDS for burial. People with AIDS need to have their rights protected, including their right of free choice. Mandated testing does not guarantee protection from discrimination.

In regard to mandatory testing of certain populations, Hyde and DeLamater (2000) note:

> So far, testing is legally required of all military recruits, Job Corps entrants, would-be immigrants, and, in some states, prison inmates. None of these requirements has been invalidated by the courts. There are proposals to test other high-risk groups, such as people with STDs or all pregnant women. The issue is especially important in the case of pregnant women, because the baby of an HIV-positive woman has a 33 percent probability of being born infected. There is now a treatment regimen, if started early enough in pregnancy, reduces the infant's risk by two-thirds. However, some fear that widespread mandatory testing—of, for example, all fertile women or all who seek treatment for other STDs—will only serve to keep away those who most need testing and treatment, or drive them underground. (p. 604)

An important issue is that of the distinction between confidential and anonymous testing. In *confidential testing,* the identity of the person being tested is recorded, although not made public. Questions have been raised with confidential testing regarding who has (or should have) access to a person's positive results—those having access may include secretaries in testing sites, the state's communicable disease center, the person's physician, and even insurance companies. With confidential testing there is a danger that those who have access to a positive test result for the tested person may then discriminate against the person. For example, an insurance company may seek to find an excuse to cancel a health or life insurance policy. *Anonymous testing,* on the other hand, involves no identification. An individual goes in for testing, uses a code word or number, and returns approximately 2 weeks later to receive testing results. Names are neither mentioned nor recorded. A drawback of anonymous testing is that the state's communicable disease center is not informed of a positive test result for a tested individual and therefore is unable to contact and encourage past and present sexual partners of that person to be tested for HIV.

Another controversial issue is that of home testing. Testing packets are now available for home use. An individual can prick a finger for a blood sample, submit the sample by mail for anonymous testing, and then call the testing laboratory a week later to obtain results. Testing may be anonymous because code numbers can be used; no names are involved. A positive thing about this is the maintenance of confidentiality. However, several problems are also involved. The accuracy of home testing has been questioned. Additionally, it is generally recommended that counseling is necessary both before and after testing because of the critical implications of the test result. Although some people maintain that counseling can be provided over the phone, this type of contact seems pretty weak in view of a positive test result and its impact on a person. People need to be prepared to receive a positive result and to know what to do and expect next. In view of a negative result, people need to examine their prior behaviors to decrease or minimize their risks.

Macro System Responses to AIDS

Health-care costs are another mammoth issue. Being sick is expensive. Being very sick is very expensive. Many people who have AIDS have found their resources increasingly exhausted. People with AIDS tend to get sick very fast because of their immune system's vulnerability. If they have a job, sick days are easily used up. If they get too sick for too long, they lose their jobs. When they lose their jobs, they probably will also lose their health insurance. Any savings can be quickly used up in hospital, physician, and drug expenses. People then turn to overburdened public assistance and Medicaid systems for help.

Yet another issue concerning health care directly involves the providers of such care. A number of people in the health-care professions either refuse to treat people with AIDS or treat them very differently than their other patients. For example, one medical attendant would talk to a person with AIDS only when wearing surgical clothing including gown, gloves, and mask. Under no circumstances would he touch or shake hands with a person having AIDS. How would such behavior make a person with AIDS feel? Such a person may already be feeling isolated and scourged. Such differential treatment could make anyone feel much like a leper must have felt in Biblical times.

Other health-care issues involve nursing homes. Some homes refuse to admit people with AIDS. Is this fair or right? Such discrimination is legally prohibited by the 1990 Americans with Disabilities Act—but it often takes years to process such charges of discrimination through the court system. Most persons with AIDS have immediate medical and housing needs and cannot wait years for the court system to process such a case.

Solutions to discrimination against persons with AIDS in the health-care system must involve educating people about AIDS and preparing them to work with people who have it. Health-care professionals need to learn what is safe and what is not safe. They need to work on their own fears and personal conflicts. It is unlikely that making new laws and mandating to people how they must behave will be enough.

In 1991, the American public was shocked when it was revealed that Florida resident Kimberly Bergalis had apparently contracted the AIDS virus from her dentist while receiving dental services. An extensive investigation led to the conclusion that four other dental patients also contracted the AIDS virus from the same dentist. Exactly how these patients became infected with the AIDS virus is unknown. Nationwide, very few people have contracted the AIDS virus from health-care workers such as dentists, physicians, or nurses. Because five patients are believed to have contracted the AIDS virus from the Florida dentist (who later died from AIDS), some authorities have questioned whether this dentist intentionally engaged in dental procedures that put his patients at risk (Findlay, 1991). The risk of contracting the AIDS virus from infected health-care workers is minimal.

However, the danger of patients becoming infected by health-care workers has led the American Medical Association, the American Dental Association, and the Centers for Disease Control and Prevention to recommend that health-care workers who know they are infected should stop doing certain "at risk" procedures. The only time for concern is when a health-care procedure exposes some of the patient's blood to the blood of an infected health-care worker.

Actually, health-care workers are at a greater risk of contracting the AIDS virus from infected patients than vice versa. Drawing blood from an infected patient, for example, can result in an accidental needle prick to the health-care worker, and perhaps transmission of the AIDS virus. Substantially more health-care workers have contracted the AIDS virus from infected patients than patients have contracted the virus from health-care workers.

The risk of transmission of the virus between health-care workers and patients has raised a number of complex questions. When should patients be informed that one of their health-care providers has the AIDS virus? Are there circumstances or medical conditions that would warrant health-care workers being informed that a patient is HIV-positive? Most patients and health-care workers who are HIV-positive are unaware they are infected. Are there circumstances or medical conditions for which HIV testing of either patients or health-care workers should be mandated?

Many other issues have not even been mentioned here. There are opposing views regarding the conditions under which children with AIDS can go to school. Likewise, there are opposing views whether free needles should be distributed to intravenous drug users. Will this procedure prevent them from sharing needles and thereby contracting AIDS, or will it only encourage their antisocial drug abusing behavior? Another controversial issue is whether condoms should be distributed at no charge to adolescents at school. Proponents of distribution say it will help prevent the spread of AIDS, while opponents claim it promotes sexual promiscuity.

All of these matters merit serious attention and consideration. A picture of Japanese-American citizens forced into concentration camps during World War II might flash before one's eyes. In those days irrational fear resulted in acts of discrimination against U.S. citizens. Basic individual rights were violated. Those people who are unfortunate enough to contract this deadly disease deserve attention and compassion. (For a fuller discussion of the effects of organizational systems on clients, see the section on the Systems Impact Model in Chapter 1.)

Social Work Roles: Empowering Persons Living with AIDS

In regard to the role of social work in helping persons with AIDS, Lloyd (1990) notes:

Given the epidemiology and demography of HIV and AIDS, it is doubtful that social workers can practice anywhere without being directly or indirectly involved with people affected by HIV infection and AIDS. Therefore, all social workers should be knowledgeable about HIV transmission and prevention, capable of adapting practice methods to needs of those affected by HIV or AIDS, and committed to applying social work values to ensure that people are not discriminated against in the workplace, social service agencies, or health care facilities because of their HIV status. (p. 13)

Social workers have numerous roles to play in empowering persons with AIDS and in preventing and/or

© Caroline Kroon

At Housing Works in New York City, a community-based, minority-controlled, not-for-profit organization that provides housing, supportive services, and advocacy for homeless families and individuals living with AIDS and HIV, a teacher (hand on head) encourages a student to read through her response to a poem by Sylvia Plath on suicide. Literature helps her students cope with their own experiences regarding their life prospects.

reducing the transmission of HIV. Social workers practicing with people affected by AIDS should use the same professional skills they would use in working with any other group. Services provided by social workers include: testing and counseling people for HIV infection, educating the general public and high-risk groups to reduce risk behavior for HIV infection, assisting HIV-affected persons to remain active and productive, encouraging HIV-affected persons to reduce the risk of passing the infection on to others, and providing support and information to family and friends of persons with HIV. Services to persons with AIDS include information and education, crisis intervention, case management, facilitating support groups, facilitating therapy and bereavement groups, brokering needed services and resources, facilitating support networks, advocacy, financial and legal assistance, linkage to Social Security entitlements, providing services to AIDS-specialized foster family homes, and finding living arrangements for homeless HIV-infected babies.

Empowerment is a key concept for social workers helping persons with AIDS. Empowerment involves feeling good about ourselves and feeling that we have some control and direction over our lives. Empowerment is clearly related to hope. It used to be that most people with AIDS died within 2 years of diagnosis. In recent years research has found that treating persons who are HIV-infected with a "cocktail" combination of the drug AZT and some of the protease inhibitor drugs is delaying substantially the progression of AIDS, and thereby extending their lives. This medical advance assists in conveying to persons who are HIV-infected that there is realistic hope for living a quality life for many years.

Persons with AIDS should never be referred to as victims. Rather, they should be referred to as people *living with* AIDS, with an emphasis on living. The word *victim* implies helplessness, powerlessness, and lack of control. People with AIDS need to be viewed as people capable of empowerment, not as hopeless victims. Hope should be maintained. Many people with AIDS have years of living fruitful lives ahead of them. Much research and effort is being directed at combatting the disease.

Maintaining a meaningful quality of life is important for persons living with AIDS. Strengths should be emphasized. Part of this involves focusing on the positive instead of the negative aspects of life. Almost any situation in life can be looked at either positively or negatively. Take, for example, a couple who built a spacious new home with cathedral ceilings, which was just what they had always wanted. It had taken years of thrift and saving to build a home that was "just perfect." However, perfection was not to last. One morning they woke up and saw a 3-foot-long crack extending down from one of their beautiful "just perfect" skylights. With changes in the weather, they learned, walls typically shift in homes with cathedral ceilings and cracks may result. Fixing the cracks wouldn't help as it is a basic structural problem that caused the cracks. They would simply return with the passage of time. The man and the woman each had a choice of how to think about the crack. The man chose to dwell on how awful the crack looked. Whenever visitors came, he showed them the crack and complained about the construction company's incompetence. The woman chose to ignore the crack and instead concentrated on all the other wonderful aspects of their brand new home—the spaciousness, the large picture windows, and how comfortable the home really was. You might guess who was the happier person of the two.

This story highlights the importance of focusing on the positive aspects of any particular situation. Something wrong can be found about virtually any situation. The winner of a $10,000 gift certificate from a major department store must pay thousands of dollars in taxes on the money before a cent can be "spent." Women who take pride in their long fingernails inevitably break one off. There is always something that one's boyfriend, girlfriend, or spouse doesn't do exactly as one wishes. Although these examples are silly when compared to the literal life or death situation encompassing AIDS, they still illustrate the point. People with AIDS need to work all the harder on identifying, concentrating on, and enjoying the day-to-day positive happenings in their lives.

Haney (1988) emphasizes that positives can come from any negative experience. Working through difficulties makes people stronger and wiser. He lists some of the positives that he has experienced since contracting AIDS. These include "learning to accept (his) limitations; learning to cope by getting in touch with (his) strengths; experiencing a clarity of purpose; learning to live one day at a time; learning to focus on the good in (his) life here and now; and the incredibly moving experience of having complete support from (his) family, friends, lover, people (he) hardly know(s), and sometimes even complete strangers" (p. 252).

Empowerment can come from reconnections (Haney, 1988). Having AIDS often results in people feeling isolated and disconnected from their old lives. Social workers can help people with AIDS to reconnect with other people. Support systems are essential. These can include families, friends, intimate others, or coworkers. Lines of communication need to be maintained. Of course, people with AIDS have strong feelings about their condition, but so do people close to them. Fear, guilt, anger, depression, hopelessness, feelings of abandonment, and many other emotions may be involved. Regardless of how people feel, it is crucial to bring these feelings out in the open so that significant others learn how to cope with them instead of hiding them and withdrawing from the person with AIDS.

The person living with AIDS should also be encouraged to express his or her feelings openly, even when they are negative. Suicidal thoughts and plans should be discussed openly and the potential for suicide assessed. (See Chapter 7 for a more extensive discussion of how to assess and treat suicidal people.) Sometimes medications to curb anxiety and depression are helpful.

Support groups provide another excellent means of enhancing empowerment. People can talk with others in similar situations. They need no longer feel so alone. They can see that other people understand their concerns and feelings. Additionally, such groups provide excellent channels for gaining information on how others have worked out similar problems. A common social work role is that of *facilitator* of such groups. The acquisition of coping skills can help empower people with AIDS. Social workers can help to identify and emphasize coping skills used in the past.

It is important for people with AIDS to deal not only with life but also with death. Moynihan, Christ, and Silver (1988) stress that people with AIDS need to learn how to cope with their fears of death. (Coping with death will be addressed in much greater detail later in Chapter 15.) Spiritual issues may be involved. Helping people with AIDS discuss plans for what will happen after their death can be useful. In a way this may help them gain greater control. They may need to write up a will or make funeral arrangements. They may want to finish unsettled business or settle conflicts they have with others. A useful concept for working with people who are addressing death is the idea of making them the "star of their own death." In other words, instead of avoiding the issues that concern them because it makes us uncomfortable, emphasize that they have the right to make decisions and settle their affairs. Encourage them to talk openly about these matters and have as much control over them as possible.

One specific aspect of AIDS that is helpful for social workers to know about is the AIDS-dementia complex. It has already been pointed out that the symptoms of this complex, which is experienced by many people with AIDS, include forgetfulness, the inability to concentrate, visuospatial problems, difficulties performing complex tasks, and slowed motor ability. Buckingham and Van Gorp (1988) present a number of implications for social work practice when dealing with AIDS-dementia. First, they suggest the use of a variety of environmental aids. Some aids (such as reminder notes and calendars) can help to minimize the effects of forgetfulness. Living arrangements should allow easy access for people with motor impairments. Additionally, situations that would require quick thinking and decisions should be identified and avoided.

Second, structure can help people living with AIDS-dementia continue to function. A familiar environment and people available to help with daily tasks (such as giving medication and presenting meals) are important. These, too, help fight forgetfulness.

Third, the difference between initiation and motivation should be stressed. People living with AIDS-dementia often are motivated to complete a task but have trouble starting out. Once started, they can frequently carry it out themselves.

Fourth, people who help take care of those with AIDS-dementia should be well educated about what the condition involves. These helpers should know what the person is and is not capable of in order to have appropriate expectations.

Additional recommendations include having a clinical assessment for depression performed and providing psychotherapy in those cases in which it would be useful. Legal contracts and estate planning should also be initiated before the dementia progresses to the point that these are no longer feasible.

Taylor-Brown (1995) suggests that the social work roles of educator, advocate, mediator, social broker, and enabler can all be applied to working with persons with AIDS. As an *educator,* the social worker can supply persons with AIDS and those close to them with information about the disease so that they are better prepared to cope with their situations. The *advocate* role allows the social worker to speak out on behalf of clients. A social worker can help clients to fight for their rights, especially in those cases in which discrimination is occurring. As a *mediator,* the social worker may become a go-between between the person with AIDS and others with whom he's in conflict. For example, the client may have been shunned by his family or fired from his job. A social worker might help both sides better understand the concerns of the other and come to some mutually agreeable plan.

In the *broker* role a social worker can help the person with AIDS come into contact with needed health, financial, and social support sources. Finally, as *enabler,* the social worker may help the client cope with his situation. A social worker can help the client to express his feelings, look closely at his relationships, and make plans to do the best he can with each day of his life.

Highlight 10.4 describes some situations involving people living with AIDS in which social workers might be able to provide help.

Highlight 10.4

Persons Living with Aids

The following are scenarios of people who have been diagnosed as having AIDS or as testing positive to HIV. In what ways could empowerment take place? In what ways could social workers be helpful? What laws and social policies would be helpful to them in their situations?

Mary has AIDS. She's 38 years old and used to have a lucrative Milwaukee law practice. She had been dating Norm and having intercourse with him for a year and a half before he told her that he was bisexual, that he had tested positively for having AIDS antibodies, and that she had better get tested, too. She dropped him immediately. The first time she went in for a test, the results were negative. However, the physician told her to come in once again in 3 months just to be sure. The second time she tested positive. Her rage was almost uncontrollable. It wasn't fair! She didn't "sleep around!" She didn't use intravenous drugs! Now Mary rarely leaves her apartment. She's terrified of being vulnerable to the multitude of diseases running rampant among all of the people out there. She knows that people are much more dangerous to her than she is to them. Her savings are declining. She can't afford to worry about the future.

Harry has been diagnosed positive for having AIDS antibodies in his system. Harry is only 22 and likes to party. He can hardly remember how many women he's had sexual intercourse with over the past 2 years. He's tall and handsome. Women have always found him attractive, and he's always left the birth control responsibility to them. He thought they all must be on the pill anyway. He never thought of using a condom. He thought AIDS was a gay disease. He found out it is not. He doesn't know if or when he'll actually come down with AIDS, but he does know he's potentially contagious. He's very scared.

Bill has AIDS. He's 28. He's been feeling very run-down for the past few months and finally went in to have the purple splotches of skin on his back checked. It is Kaposi's sarcoma. He's been together with Mike for almost 3 years, a relationship they've committed to as being permanent. However, before he met Mike, Bill dated a lot of men. He didn't think about things such as "safer sex" 3 years ago. He must've gotten AIDS from one of his many intimate partners. He wonders who. Now he's worried about Mike. They haven't been practicing "safer sex" either because they're monogamous. What if Mike has it, too? He truly loves Mike and prays that Mike is all right. Mike's going in for his test results tomorrow. Bill is very worried.

Tonya has AIDS. She's 19. She comes from a very poor side of town where living is tough. It seemed everybody was "into" using intravenous drugs. "Shooting up" was easy. Heroin let her escape. Needles were expensive so she shared them with her friends. Now she's very sick. She's in the hospital with some kind of strange pneumonia. This time deep down she doesn't think she'll ever make it home again.

Cheryl has AIDS. She's 2 months old. She got it from her mother, who also has it. Cheryl's very weak now. She probably won't live very long.

Persons who are HIV-positive, or who have AIDS, are a protected group under the 1990 Americans with Disabilities Act. Social workers have a role in informing persons who are HIV-positive that they are legally protected against discrimination; and social workers have a role in educating the general public that it is illegal to discriminate against persons who are HIV-positive.

✿ Summary

For many people, middle adulthood is the prime of life— most middle-aged adults are in good health (both physically and psychologically) and tend to earn more money than at any other age. Middle adulthood covers a range of years; somewhat arbitrarily, the authors consider middle adulthood to range from age 30 to age 65. Some decline in physical capacities occurs in middle adulthood. There is also a higher incidence of health problems than in younger years. Cognitive functioning may actually increase during middle adulthood. The sad fact is that many people fail to be sufficiently active both mentally and physically so that their actual performance *mentally* falls short of their potential performance.

Female menopause is the event in every woman's life when she stops menstruating and can no longer bear children. For a few women menopause is a serious crisis, but for many it is just another of life's developmental changes. It appears that many males reach an uncertain period in their lives, which is referred to as a midlife crisis. The ease or panic with which a man faces his midyears will depend on how he has accepted his weaknesses and strengths throughout life.

A man's sex drive reaches its peak in the early 20s, while that of a woman tends to peak in her 30s or early 40s. There appears to be a close relationship between overall marital satisfaction and sexual satisfaction.

AIDS is a contagious and presently incurable disease that destroys the body's immune system. AIDS is caused by the HIV virus. The two primary ways in which AIDS is now being spread are by sexual intercourse with someone who is HIV-positive and by using hypodermic needles that were also used by someone who is HIV-positive. Presently, the best way to stop the spread of AIDS is through educating people to avoid exposing themselves to known risks. People who test positive to HIV or who have AIDS often are additionally victimized by discrimination.

InfoTrac College Edition Keywords

AIDS/HIV   AIDS in Africa   climacteric   HRT   male climacteric   menopause   midlife crisis

On the Internet

AIDS

http://www.avert.org/

AVERT is a leading U.K.-based AIDS Education and Medical Research charity. It is responsible for a wide range of education and medical research work, with the overall aim of preventing people from becoming infected with HIV; improving the quality of life of those already infected; and, through medical research, working to develop a cure for AIDS.

Divorce

http://www.divorcesource.com/

Divorcesource.com is not only a resource for vital divorce-related information, but it also carries a supportive atmosphere through The Interactive Support Community and The Chat Rooms. You may want to think of the site as one enormous online divorce-support group that caters to people facing divorce (or related issues), who desire pertinent information and want to share questions, find answers, and learn from other's experiences.

Male Menopause

http://www.midlife-passages.com/page25.htm/

This Web site is dedicated to issues affecting the health of midlife men and women, including preventive health care, nutrition, menopause, and the relationships between common medical problems and menopause. It discusses gynecological problems, including the use of hormones and surgery.

National Osteoporosis Foundation

http://www.nof.org/

The National Osteoporosis Foundation (NOF) is the leading non-profit, voluntary health organization dedicated to promoting lifelong bone health that can reduce the widespread prevalence of osteoporosis and associated fractures; it also works to find a cure for the disease through programs of research, education, and advocacy.

CHAPTER 11

Psychological Systems and Their Impacts on Middle Adulthood

It is Saturday night on Michigan Avenue in Chicago, and Doug and Debbie Peepers are engaged in a favorite activity on a warm summer evening: strolling down this "Gold Coast" street and watching the thousands of other people who are also strolling and people watching. Americans have a fascination with people watching. While strolling, Doug and Debbie enjoy discussing why people do what they do. For example, they look at the elderly bag lady dressed in a moth-eaten red plaid overcoat, knee-high nylon hose, and ancient, blue sneakers. They wonder what happened in her past that resulted in her now living on the street. Is she the victim of some tragic story? Where is her family, or doesn't she have any? Likewise, Doug and Debbie look at the sleek, jet-set millionaire pulling up to the curb in his Maserati Biturbo so that a fastidious, uniformed doorman can help him out of the car. The millionaire is striking with his fashionable haircut, glowing gold jewelry, and well-cut clothes. Doug and Debbie wonder if he is a self-made computer magnate displaced from Silicon Valley, or if he's the product of generations of wealth.

A PERSPECTIVE

Figuring out the underlying reasons that cause others' actions often has substantial payoffs. If a salesperson knows what motivates people to buy a certain product, he or she can then structure the sales pitch around this focus. If a social worker knows why a father is abusing his child, the worker then knows what has to be changed to stop the abuse. If a mother knows what discipline techniques will be effective with her children, she is then better prepared to curb unwanted behavior in her children.

The primary focus of this human behavior and social environment text is to provide theoretical frameworks that will help the reader to observe and assess human behavior. The systems impact model described in Chapter 1 provides a model for identifying a multitude of variables that influence human behavior.

Debbie Peepers is a computer programmer, and her husband, Doug, is a mechanical engineer. Although they have had little formal training in assessing human behavior, playing amateur psychologist is one of their favorite leisure activities. As with anything else, assessments of human behavior are apt to be more accurate when one has greater knowledge and awareness of the significant cues to attend to. Professional social workers who will be planning interventions with people and organizations have a special need to develop their assessment skills. Middle adulthood provides as critical a stage as earlier developmental periods to examine some of the psychological dynamics of human behavior. Because there is a paucity of psychological theories specifically directed at middle adulthood, the primary focus of this chapter will be on describing contemporary theories and models for assessing human behavior throughout the life span.

This chapter will:

▶ Describe Erikson's and Peck's theories of psychological development during middle adulthood.
▶ Describe Levinson's theories of life structure, life eras, and transitions during adulthood.
▶ Summarize Maslow's theory on hierarchy of needs.
▶ Discuss human behavior in terms of game analysis and script analysis.
▶ Describe nonverbal communication cues.
▶ Summarize Glasser's control-theory explanation of human behavior.
▶ Describe Gawain's theories about intuition and how human behavior is affected by intuition.
▶ Examine the issue of chemical substance abuse.

Generativity versus Stagnation

Erikson's (1963) seventh life-stage developmental crisis is generativity versus stagnation. Generativity involves a concern and interest in establishing and guiding the next generation. The crisis of generativity versus stagnation is perceived by a middle-aged adult to involve a commitment to improve the life conditions of future generations. The achievement of generativity involves a willingness to care about the people and the things that one has produced. It also involves a commitment to protecting and enhancing the conditions of one's society.

The achievement of generativity is important for the survival and development of any society. It involves having the adult members dedicating themselves to contributing their skills, resources, and creativity to improve the quality of life for the young.

The contributions may be monumental, as were Martin Luther King Jr.'s and Gandhi's to equality and human rights. For most people, however, the contributions are less well known—for example, the work done by volunteers for human service organizations. Adults serve on school boards, are active members of parent-teacher associations, serve on local government boards, are active in church activities, and so on. In each of these roles, adults have opportunities to positively influence the quality of life for others. To some extent it is a reciprocity situation—when these adults were younger they were recipients of such services from other adults; now they are providers of such services.

The opposite of generativity is stagnation. Stagnation indicates a lack of psychological movement or growth. Some adults are self-centered and seek to maximize their pleasures at the expense of others; such people are stagnated because they have difficulty in looking beyond their own needs or experiencing satisfaction in taking care of others. Having children does not necessarily guarantee generativity; adults who are unable to cope with raising children or with maintaining a household are likely to feel a sense of stagnation. Burnout has been identified as being one of the signs of stagnation (Davis et al., 2000).

Different individuals manifest stagnation in different ways. A narcissistic individual who generally relates to others in terms of how others can serve him may be fairly happy until the physical and psychological consequences of aging begin to occur. Such individuals often then experience an identity crisis when they realize their beautiful bodies and other physical attributes are waning. Many of these individuals experience a conversion to finding other meanings in living. For example, they coach Little League teams or become active in church activities.

On the other hand, a depressed person is likely to perceive himself or herself as having insufficient resources to make any contribution to society. Such a person is apt to have low self-esteem, to be pessimistic about opportunities for improvement in the future and therefore to be unwilling to invest effort in self-improvement or in seeking to help others.

Peck's Theories of Psychological Development

Peck (1968) asserted that there are four psychological advances critical to successful adjustment in middle adulthood:

1. *Socializing versus sexualizing in human relationships.* Peck suggests it is psychologically healthy for middle-aged adults to redefine the men and women in their lives so that they value them as individuals, friends, and companions, rather than primarily as sex objects.

2. *Valuing wisdom versus valuing physical powers.* Peck views wisdom as the capacity to make wise choices in life. He suggests that well-adjusted middle-aged adults are aware that the wisdom they now have more than compensates for decreases in stamina, physical strength, and youthful attractiveness.

3. *Emotional flexibility versus emotional impoverishment.* Emotional flexibility is the capacity to shift emotional investments from one activity to another, and from one person to another. Middle-aged adults are apt to experience breaking of relationships due to the deaths of friends, parents, and other relatives and the growing independence of children and their moving out of the home. Physical limitations may also necessitate a change in activities.

4. *Mental flexibility versus mental rigidity.* By middle age, most people have completed their formal years of education and have been sufficiently trained for their jobs or careers. They have also arrived at a set of beliefs about an afterlife, religion, politics, desirable forms of entertainment, and so on. Some middle-aged adults stop seeking new information and ideas and become set in their ways and closed to new ideas. Such people are apt to be stymied in their intellectual growth and are apt to view life as mundane, unfulfilling, and unrewarding. Others are apt to continue to seek new experiences and be challenged by additional learning opportunities. They use their prior experiences and answers they've already arrived at as provisional guides to the solution of new issues. Such people are likely to view life as being meaningful, rewarding, and challenging.

Levinson's Theories of Life Structure, Life Eras, and Transitions for Men

Levinson (1978) and his colleagues studied 40 men aged 35 to 45 who had the following careers and occupations: business executives, academic biologists, novelists, and hourly workers in industry. These men were interviewed and given personality tests. From this data, Levinson constructed some developmental theories of life changes in adulthood.

The concept of *life structure* is at the heart of Levinson's theory. This term is defined as "the underlying pattern or design of a person's life at a given time" (Levinson, 1986,

p. 6). A person's life structure shapes and is shaped by the person's interactions with the environment. Components of the life structure include the people, institutions, things, places, and causes that a person decides are most important, as well as the dreams, values, and emotions that make them so. Most people build their life structures around their work and their families. Other important aspects in one's life structure may include religion, racial identification, ethnic heritage, societal events (such as wars and economic depressions), and hobbies.

According to Levinson, life involves a number of passages: from the freedom of childhood to entering school; from school to the work world; from not dating to dating; from dating to breaking up or marrying; from marrying to divorce; and so on. Levinson sees some structure to these series of life passages. He asserts that people shape their life structures during the following four overlapping eras (each of which is 20 to 30 years in length):

1. *Preadulthood* (birth to age 22) is the formative time from conception to the end of adolescence.

2. *Early adulthood* (age 17 to age 45) is the era in which people make choices that significantly influence their lives, and the era in which people display the greatest energy and experience the most stress.

3. *Middle adulthood* (age 40 to age 65) is the era in which people tend to have reduced biological capacities but increased social responsibilities.

4. *Late adulthood* (age 60 and beyond) is the final phase of life.

There are transitional periods within some of these eras, and there are also transitional periods of about 5 years each that connect these eras. These transitional periods are displayed in Table 11.1. This table shows the approximate ages when these transitions occur. (The transitions do not consume all the time in these periods because there are periods of stability in each transitional period.)

During these transitional periods, men review the life structures they built and explore options for restructuring their lives. According to Levinson, people spend nearly half their adult lives in transition. These transitional periods are described in the following sections.

Early adult transition (ages 17 to 22). During this transition (which may take 3 to 5 years) men move from preadulthood into adulthood. A person moves out of his or her parents' home and becomes more financially and emotionally independent. Going to college or joining the military service serves as a transitional institutional situation between being a child in a family and reaching full adult status.

Table 11.1	Eras and Transitional Periods in Levinson's Theories of Adult Development (Males)
Eras	**Transitions**
1. Preadulthood (ages 0 to 22)	Early adult transition (ages 17 to 22)
2. Early adulthood (ages 17 to 45)	Entry life structure for early adulthood (ages 22 to 28) Age-30 transition (ages 28 to 33) Culminating life structure for early adulthood (ages 33 to 40) Midlife transition (ages 40 to 45)
3. Middle adulthood (ages 40 to 65)	Entry life structure for middle adulthood (ages 45 to 50) Age-50 transition (ages 50 to 55) Culminating life structure for middle adulthood (ages 55 to 60) Late adult transition (ages 60 to 65)
4. Late adulthood (age 60 and beyond)	

Entry life structure for early adulthood (ages 22 to 28). This phase has been called "entering the adult world." During this phase a young person becomes an adult and builds the entry life structure for early adulthood. Aspects of this phase often include: involvement with work, which may lead to a career choice; intimate relationships with others, which may lead to marriage and children; choosing a home; involvement with social and civic groups; and relationships with family and friends.

Two important features of this phase are a *dream* and a *mentor*. During this phase men often have a dream of their future, which is usually viewed in terms of a career. The vision of becoming a highly successful corporate president or a famous writer spurs them on and energizes their work activities. A man's success during these apprenticeship years is strongly influenced by finding a mentor. A mentor is older (usually by about 8 to 15 years). The relationship with the mentor is a friendship with adult equality, but the mentor also performs the fatherly tasks of teaching, caring, criticizing, helping, and offering constructive suggestions in both career and personal matters.

Age-30 transition (ages 28 to 33). During this phase men take another look at their lives. They may review whether the commitments made during the previous decade were premature, or they may consider making strong commitments for the first time. Some men move fairly effortlessly through this transition. Others experience crises in which they decide their present life structures are intolerable, yet have grave difficulty in formulating better ones. Marriage conflicts may erupt during this phase, and divorce is common. Work responsibilities may shift as the man is promoted, changes jobs, or settles into his job after a period of uncertainty. Some men seek counseling to help clarify their goals.

Culminating life structure for early adulthood (ages 33 to 40). This phase is ushered in by a period of "settling down." The person makes a concerted effort to realize youthful dreams. The apprenticeship is over. During this phase men make deeper commitments to family, work, and other important aspects of their lives. They set specific goals for themselves (such as a certain level of income and moving into their own house) with a set timetable. They work at formulating a niche in society, by anchoring their lives in terms of career, family, and community involvement. They also work on advancing themselves to build a better life, become more creative, improve their skills, and so on. In the middle to late 30s, toward the end of the settling-down period, comes a phase called "becoming one's own man" (BOOM). During BOOM a man often becomes independent of his mentor and may be at odds with his wife, boss, children, friends, lover, or coworkers. During this phase a man chafes under the authority of those who have power and influence over him, and seeks to break away and speak with his own voice. However, he also fears a loss of respect from significant others during this period.

Midlife transition (ages 40 to 45). This transition is focused on a person completing the work of early adulthood while learning the ropes of middle adulthood. Similar to all other transitional periods, this transition is both an ending and a beginning. During this period men (now more acutely aware of their mortality) question nearly every aspect of their lives. Many men find this is a time of moderate or severe crisis. People in this stage undergo a midlife reappraisal that often involves emotional turmoil. Previous values are reviewed. Such a review is often healthy; through examining the choices that they made early in life, they have the opportunity to focus on aspects of themselves that may have been neglected. Those who successfully negotiate this phase come to terms with the dreams of their youth and emerge with a more realistic view of themselves. Many men at this stage experience a midlife crisis (described in Chapter 10). People

A man at midlife feels older than the younger generation, but is not yet ready to call himself middle-aged. A person at this age needs to integrate his need for separateness and his need for attachment to others. People at this age need to become "more compassionate, more reflective and judicious, less tyrannized by inner conflicts and external demands, and more genuinely loving of themselves and others" (Levinson, 1986, p. 5). People

who fail in this task lead lives that become increasingly stagnant and trivial.

Entry life structure for middle adulthood (ages 45 to 50). During this transition a man in his mid-40s begins a life structure that may involve new choices: perhaps a new wife or a different way of relating to his wife, or perhaps a new career or a restructuring of his present work. The most successful people often find middle age to be the most gratifying and creative time of life as they utilize opportunities that arise to allow new facets of their personalities to flower. Those who are unsuccessful in resolving the tasks of midlife lead a constricted life or they keep busy in an organized but unfulfilling lifestyle.

Age-50 transition (ages 50 to 55). This transition is likely to be an especially difficult time for men whose midlife transition has been relatively smooth. Most men experience a moderate crisis at this time. It is another time at which men review where they have come from, and make plans for where they are heading.

Culminating life structure for middle adulthood (ages 55 to 60). This phase is generally a stable transition in which men finish the framework of their life structure for middle adulthood. During this phase those who are able to rejuvenate themselves enrich their lives and generally, find the 50s a time period of great fulfillment.

Late adult transition (ages 60 to 65). This is a major transitional turning point, as it is a time for ending middle age and preparing for late adulthood.

Note that Levinson primarily studied middle-aged men. As a result, he has only limited and speculative information of the transitions and adjustments that occur in late adulthood. However, an important finding of Levinson is that life is a series of passages—from periods of stability to periods of instability. This cycle continues throughout life.

Various researchers have applied Levinson's theories to women's lives, as discussed in Spotlight 11.1.

✿ Maslow's Hierarchy of Needs

Abraham Maslow (1954, 1968, 1971) viewed humans as having tremendous potential for personal development. He believed it was human nature for people to seek to know more about themselves and to strive to develop their capacities to the fullest. He viewed human nature as basically good and saw the striving for *self-actualization* as a positive process because it leads people to identify their abilities, to strive to develop them, to feel good as they become themselves, and to be beneficial to society. Yet he believed that very few people fully attain a state of

Spotlight on Diversity 11.1

Application of Levinson's Theories to Women: An Evaluation

Papalia and Olds (1992) reviewed four unpublished dissertations describing studies that used women subjects and Levinson's research design. The four investigators interviewed a total of 39 women from 28 to 53 years old. The women were primarily white, although eight respondents were African American. Most respondents were employed, but some were not. The studies had a mix of married and unmarried respondents, with and without children.

These studies tend, in general, to support the idea that women undergo similar kinds of age-linked changes as men, but they found some important differences, which are summarized as follows:

The Mentor: Women were substantially less likely to have a mentor. Many of the women identified role models during their 20s, but only four had a true mentor relationship. If these women's patterns are typical, many women may be hampered in their career for lack of a mentor.

The Love Relationship: Levinson found men want a "special woman" who helps them pursue their dreams. In the studies on women, all 39 respondents sought a "special man," but these women mostly saw themselves as supporting their special man's dreams, rather than wanting a special man who would support them in achieving *their* goals.

The Dream: Most respondents had dreams (goals they wanted to achieve in life). But their dreams were more vague, more complex, more tentative and temporary, and less career oriented than those of men. Most women's dreams were split between achievement and relationships. Women were more likely to define themselves in relation to others—husbands, children, parents, or colleagues. While men tend to "find themselves" by separating from their families of origin and pursuing their own interests, women tend to develop their identity through the responsibilities and attachments of relationships.

While men dream of achievements in occupations or careers, women dream of a mix of family and career interests. Although many female respondents sought to help their "special man" achieve his goals, others began at about age 30 making greater demands on their husbands to accommodate their interests and goals in regard to career, marriage, and raising children.

Levinson and Levinson (1996) completed a study in which 45 women were intensively interviewed. The women ranged in age from 35 to 45 years. The study was designed to focus on three subgroups: (1) 15 homemakers drawn randomly from the city directory of New Haven, Connecticut; (2) 15 women who had careers in major corporate financial organizations in New York City; and (3) 15 women faculty members in colleges and universities. The latter two groups were struggling to combine career and family.

A major finding of the study was that women, similar to men, go through a predictable, age-linked series of developmental stages, moving from one period to the next via transitions that are often painful and turbulent. Levinson concludes that his conception of life cycle, eras, and periods in life structure development provides a framework for the study of both men and women.

Yet, Levinson found a number of profound differences between how men and women develop throughout their lives. Many of these differences relate to the phenomenon he calls *gender splitting*—the rigid division between male and female. Gender splitting includes such dimensions as differences in traditional gender role expectations between men and women, the splitting between the female homemaker and the male provisioner, and the splitting of the personal qualities identified as "feminine" and "masculine." (Levinson notes that the evolution of society in the past few centuries has been gradually reducing the splitting.)

The women in the homemaker sample sought, at a young age, to lead predominantly traditional, family-centered lives. They entered marriage with the belief that their primary role was to continue the traditional family, and the wife's role was to be the homemaker, have children, and do most of the domestic tasks. They viewed the husband's role as occupying the dominant family position and being the provisioner—devoting himself to outside work and bringing back the resources needed to sustain the family. These women were in for a shock. Only 1 homemaker of the 15 by midlife was not working outside the home. Fifty percent were legally divorced, and most of the rest were psychologically divorced. Most of these women were currently in the workforce, and several of those who had legally divorced were in a second marriage. At midlife, motherhood was becoming a less central component of their life structure. Many of these women, as they developed in their 30s and 40s, became more independent and sought to exist on more equal terms with men. Thus, young women who actively sought at a young age to have a traditional, family-centered life tended to seek to establish a more modern lifestyle, which Levinson called the "anti-traditional figure." Levinson concludes that a traditional marriage is no longer viable in our culture.

The women who had careers, in contrast, attempted even at a young age to modify the traditional pattern. A recurrent theme in their lives was the intense conflict between the "traditional homemaker figure" and the "internal anti-traditional figure." These women struggled with being everything to everyone and seeking to have everything. They spoke of excitement and joy and playfulness and challenge. But they were constantly plagued by exhaustion, worries about their children, and exasperation with their spouses who failed to do their fair share in helping with the household responsibilities and raising the children.

The study reveals considerable hardships for both the homemakers and the "career women"—anguish, stressful and traumatic experiences, marital difficulties, problems in raising their children, problems at work, and difficulties in personal relationships. The difficulties and anguish reported by these female subjects appear more pronounced than those reported by Levinson in his earlier study of men.

self-actualization. Rather, Maslow saw most people as being in a constant state of striving to satisfy their needs.

Maslow identified a hierarchy of needs that motivate human behavior. When people fulfill the most elemental needs, they strive to meet those on the next level, and so forth, until the highest order of needs is reached. In ascending order, these needs are:

1. *Physiological:* Food, water, oxygen, rest, and so on.
2. *Safety:* Security; stability; and freedom from fear, anxiety, threats, and chaos. A social structure of laws and limits assists in meeting these needs.
3. *Belongingness and love:* Intimacy and affection provided by friends, family, and lover.
4. *Self-esteem:* Self-respect, respect of others, achievement, attention, and appreciation.
5. *Self-actualization:* The sense that one is fulfilling one's potential and is doing what one is suited for and capable of. This need results in efforts to create and to learn. A fully developed, self-actualized person displays high levels of all of the following characteristics: acceptance of self, of others, and of nature; seeks justice, truth, order, unity, and beauty; has problem-solving abilities; is self-directed; has freshness of appreciation; has a richness of emotional responses; has satisfying and changing relationships with other people; is creative; and has a high sense of moral values.

Maslow's hierarchy of needs is illustrated in Figure 11.1. The needs at each level must be fairly well satisfied before the needs at the next level become important. Thus, physiological needs must be fairly well satisfied before

Figure 11.1 Maslow's Hierarchy of Needs

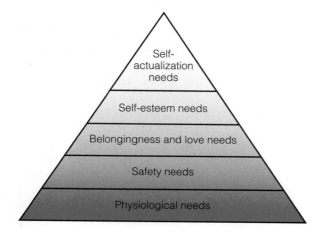

safety needs become important, and so on. As applied to social work practice, Maslow's theory indicates that social workers must first help clients meet basic needs (e.g., physiological needs). Once clients' basic needs are met, higher level needs can be dealt with.

Maslow did not offer an age-stage approach to development. Striving for self-actualization is seen as a universal process that can be observed at nearly all ages. However, it is likely that there is some progression among age groups. Infants probably have a strong emphasis on physiological needs. As a person gradually grows older, safety needs are emphasized, and then belongingness and love needs, and so on. Because middle-aged adults have had a variety of learning experiences and tend to be at the peak of their earning potential, they tend to have a greater opportunity to focus on meeting self-actualization needs. However, such crises as unemployment, prolonged illness, and broken relationships can switch the emphasis to a lower area of need.

✿ Game Analysis and Script Analysis

Analyzing human behavior in terms of games and scripts provides another useful theoretical framework for understanding human behavior. Both game analysis and script analysis were developed by Eric Berne, who is recognized as being the founder of transactional analysis (TA), which is a psychotherapy approach. (See Dusay & Dusay, 1984, for a summary of TA.)

Game Analysis

A game can be defined as a set of transactions with a gimmick—that is, a hidden scheme for attaining an end (Berne, 1964). In a game one or more participants are consciously or unconsciously striving to achieve an ulterior outcome by using a hidden scheme. For example, in the following exchange a salesperson uses a gimmick to sell the product:

> *Salesperson:* "This one is better, but it may be out of your price range."
> *Male customer:* "That's the one I'll take."

The salesperson arouses the customer's pride by telling him that he may be unable to afford the better, but more expensive item. Psychologically, the customer says to himself, "I'll buy the expensive item just to show that arrogant so-and-so that I'm as good as anyone."

People who are attempting to achieve a hidden outcome may or may not be aware of their intentions—or aware of the gimmick they are using. For instance, a husband who has a vague fear that his wife may desert him may not be aware he is playing a game when he says to her, "Honey, why don't you quit work and stay home to take care of the house? I can earn enough to support both of us." He may not be aware that he wants his wife to stay home so that she becomes financially dependent on him, and so that she has less opportunity to meet other men.

Although some games may lead to substantial financial loss or mental anguish for some participants, not all games are necessarily undesirable. For instance, an individual having a strong need for social approval may perform many altruistic and charitable deeds.

A game may also be repeated over and over. A few people, for instance, continually play "One-up." For some, playing a certain game may become so much a part of their personality that it can aptly be called their style of life. An alcoholic who denies that he has a drinking problem is an example of this. Some people are involved in playing games that have destructive outcomes for themselves and for others. Often people are unaware that a destructive game is being played. For example, a problem drinker who drinks an average of three to four drinks a day to escape from day-to-day concerns may be unaware of the negative consequences to her health and interpersonal relationships.

Two levels of communication—social and psychological—are involved in games. The social level is *overt* or *manifest*, and the psychological level is *covert* or *latent*. Prochaska (1979) gave the following example of these two levels of communication in a game:

> . . . *if a woman asks a man, "Why don't you come by my place to see my collection of sculptures?" and the man responds, "I'd love to. I'm really interested in art," they may be . . . communicating a message at a different level, such as . . . , "Boy, I'd really like to get you alone in my apartment" and, "I'd sure love to look at your curves." (pp. 237–238)*

For a game to progress, at least one of the participants has to pull a switch, as described in this example by Prochaska (1979):

> *For the payoff to occur, one of the players has to pull a switch. In this case, after fixing drinks and sitting close on the couch examining a reproduction of Rodin's* The Kiss, *the woman still seems to be sending a seductive communication. The man's vanity convinces him to proceed, and he puts his hand on her leg, only to be rebuffed by a slap on the face and an irate "What kind of woman do you think I am?"*

> *The couple has just completed a heavy hand of RAPO.[1] Besides gaining mutual recognition, excitement, and some structured time together, there is also a strong emotional payoff for each. The woman is able to proudly affirm her position in life that she is OK, while feeling angry toward men for not being OK, just as her mother always said. The payoff for the man is to feel depressed and thereby reaffirm his conviction that he is not OK. (p. 238)*

Examples of Games. Berne (1964) listed a large number of psychological games in *Games People Play*. People tend to have a repertoire of favorite games they play; many people base their social relationships on finding suitable partners to play the corresponding opposite roles. The following are common games.

In the game, "Why don't you? Yes, but . . . ," a person consistently asks for suggestions or advice, and then consistently rejects any that is offered. The other participant in this game assumes that the principal player is attempting to solve a real problem in a concrete manner, so he offers suggestions. The principal player is able to get at least two payoffs—one is attention from other people, and the other comes from being able to put others down by implying "That's really a dumb suggestion." The other participant may get a payoff through telling himself "I must be a warm, caring person because this person respects and trusts me enough to share this problem with me."

In the "One-up" game, one person seeks to top whatever someone else says. If the conversation is about big fish, the one-upper always has a story about how he caught a mammoth fish. If the topic is about bad grades received, the one-upper seeks to amaze everyone with how bad his or her grades are. If jokes are being told, the one-upper begins by saying, "I've got one that'll top that. Have you heard about . . ."

"Wooden leg" is a game in which people attempt to manipulate others to not expect too much from them because of such "wooden legs" as having a physical disability, being raised in a dysfunctional family, having had a tragic romance, having emotional problems such as being depressed, and so on. Closely related, "If it weren't for . . ." is a cop-out game in which players seek to rationalize not succeeding at tasks and goals.

A person who plays "Poor me" is seeking sympathy and may at times try to get others to do things for him or her. Closely related is someone who plays "Ain't it awful" by taking a negative view of events. Such a person is usually seeking attention and sympathy. In the game "There

---

1. Eric Berne defines RAPO in its milder forms as "kiss off" or "indignation."

I go again," the player seeks to excuse away his or her ineffective behavior without taking responsibility.

Some clients enjoy playing "Confession" where they seek to tell all their personal troubles in the hope of receiving recognition and help from others. Some unhappily married men get together and enjoy discussing "Wives are a pain" as a way of ventilating their unhappiness. Some unhappily married wives enjoy discussing "Men aren't worth it" as a way of ventilating their frustrations. Parents enjoy discussing "Look how hard I've tried" when a home situation is particularly uproarious and hostile as a way to relieve their frustrations that the goals for their family have not been achieved. Many people seek to avoid assuming responsibility for their failures and shortcomings by placing the blame on others in the "It's all them" game.

Some individuals who have received few positive strokes end up seeking a lot of negative strokes, which to them is better than receiving no strokes. One game that is played to receive negative strokes is "Kick me" in which the player seeks to do things that will elicit negative reactions from others.[2]

People who enjoy creating trouble for others are apt to play "Let's you and him/her fight," with the payoff being the spectator pleasure they receive in watching others tangle.

People who receive psychological rewards in analyzing others and in giving advice often play "Psychiatry." A person who seeks to see how many different sexual relationships he or she can have often seeks to play "Love 'em and leave 'em." Traditionally, men in our society have been socialized to play "Mr. Macho" and women "Miss America."

"Monday morning quarterbacks" seek to make themselves feel important by telling you what you should have done differently after things have not turned out well for you.

The number of different games that can be played is best described as infinite. Only a few of the more typical ones have been summarized here.

Application of Game Analysis to Practice. *Game analysis* is a treatment technique in which a counselor enables clients to gain insight into some of their interactions through the use of game concepts. The kinds of games that are the main focus of game analysis are those that lead to undesirable outcomes for clients.

The social worker's role in analyzing games is to teach clients the terminology of game analysis. This perhaps can best be accomplished on the first occasion in which a worker helps a client gain insight into a game. The social worker needs to point out to the client that playing games is not necessarily undesirable. This may be therapeutically valuable because some clients may feel that playing games has an exploitative connotation. Such a feeling may cause resistances to examining games. These resistances may be reduced by informing clients that everyone plays games, some with beneficial outcomes, and some with undesirable outcomes. Social workers must help clients recognize those games that are destructive for them or for other players and also enable them to gain insight into how these games are being played.

Clients should be encouraged to explore new ways of responding after they are aware of how their role in a game leads to undesirable consequences. Clients need help in assigning specific names to those undesirable games they are playing. Using colloquial names for games is often advantageous as they may be more precise and have more meaning for clients. Social workers can teach people the kind of games they need to play in order to achieve their goals. For example, a person seeking a job may need to learn to play "How to get an interview," and "How to sell yourself in an interview." Or, a couple who is frequently feuding may need to learn "How to fight fairly" and "How to get what you want in a relationship through giving."

Game analysis appears to be a useful therapeutic approach for three reasons. First, one of the important functional values of naming something (in this case a certain kind of game) is that it increases clients' capacities to identify when similar transactions are occurring in the future. Once clients recognize and have insight into a game that is causing them difficulty, they are in a better position to cease their destructive behavior and to explore alternative modes of behavior. Second, analyzing behavior in terms of games is apt to be intriguing to clients and, therefore, may lead to greater personal involvement in therapy and increase their motivation to resolve their difficulties. Third, game analysis provides clients with a methods of analyzing certain problematic interactions. After learning how to analyze such interactions, clients should be better able to analyze other problematic games beyond those specifically discussed in counseling.

Life Scripts

Every person has *life scripts* (plans) that are formed during childhood and are based on early beliefs about oneself and others. These plans are developed from early interactions

---

2. Transactional analysis makes an important psychological point by asserting that in the absence of receiving positive strokes, a person will seek negative strokes. *Strokes* are forms of human recognition. Positive strokes include greetings, smiles, approval, cheers, and applause. Negative strokes include cold looks, disapproval, criticism, and frowns.

with parents and others and are largely determined by the pattern of strokes that are received. (See the definition of strokes in footnote 2.)

Many details of a life script are supplied by parental opinions, suggestions, and encouragements: Examples include: "She's such a cute girl, everyone loves her," "He's stupid and will never amount to much," "He'll be famous some day," "He sure is nutty," "All the girls will want to date him." Fairy tales, myths, TV shows, early life experiences, and children's stories are also important sources of life scripts. While outside influences are important contributing factors, the life script is still the creation of a young child. One's life script may be either winning or losing, success or failure, exciting or dull. Each script also includes specific roles, such as heroes and heroines, villains and victims, and so on.

Harris (1969) theorized that each person chooses one of four general life scripts in regard to how he or she views himself or herself in comparison with others. These four scripts are:

1. I'm OK—You're OK.

2. I'm OK—You're not OK.

3. I'm not OK—You're OK.

4. I'm not OK—You're not OK.

People who decide to use "I'm OK—You're OK" tend to be productive, law-abiding people who are successful and who have positive, meaningful relationships with others.

People who decide to use "I'm OK—You're not OK" predispose themselves to succeed at the expense of others. This type of person may be a criminal, a ruthless business executive, or a destructive lover who "loves 'em and leaves 'em."

People who decide to use "I'm not OK—You're OK" feel inferior in the presence of those they judge as superior. Such a life script frequently leads to withdrawal from others as a way to avoid being reminded of not being OK. Withdrawal is not the only alternative. The person can write a counterscript based on lines borrowed from early authority figures: "I can be OK if . . ." The person is then driven to achieve the "if" contingencies. Examples of such contingencies include: making huge sums of money, being submissive, or being entertaining by making others laugh. Such a person strives to meet these contingencies in order to receive approval from others.

People who decide to use "I'm not OK—You're not OK" tend to be the most unhappy and disturbed. Prochaska (1979) states:

The extreme withdrawal of schizophrenia or psychotic depression is their most common fate. They may regress to an infantile state in the primitive hope that they may once again receive the strokes of being held and fed. Without intervention from caring others, these individuals will live out a self-destructive life of institutionalization, irreversible alcoholism, senseless homicide, or suicide. (p. 241)

Decisions about life scripts are generally made early in childhood. James and Jongeward (1971) provide an incident in the life of a client, age 43, that led her to conclude "I'm not OK, and men are not OK either":

My father was a brutal alcoholic. When he was drunk he would hit me and scream at me. I would try to hide. One day when he came home, the door flew open and he was drunker than usual. He picked up a butcher knife and started running through the house. I hid in a coat closet. I was almost four years old. I was so scared in the closet. It was dark and spooky, and things kept hitting me in the face. That day I decided who men were—beasts, who would only try to hurt me. I was a large child and I remember thinking, "If I were smaller, he'd love me" or "If I were prettier, he'd love me." I always thought I wasn't worth anything. (pp. 84–85)

Based on this script, she married an alcoholic at age 23 and, for the next 20 years, lived her life drama of feeling worthless and living with a "beast."

Scripts (as in a play in a theater) are plans that we learn and then carry around in our heads. These scripts are plans for directing what we need to do to complete our activities and to accomplish our goals. Scripts are also devices for helping us to remember what we have done in the past.

One area in which our behavior is largely guided by scripts is sexual behavior. Sexual scripts result from elaborate prior learning of an etiquette of sexual behavior. Scripts tell us who are appropriate sexual partners, what sexual activity is expected, where and when the sexual activity should occur, and what should be the sequence of the different sexual behaviors.

Scripts vary greatly from one culture to another. Powdermaker (1933) provided the following description of a script about female masturbation that is generally followed by the Lesu of the South Pacific:

A woman will masturbate if she is sexually excited and there is no man to satisfy her. A couple may be having intercourse in the same house, or near enough for her to see them, and she may thus become aroused. She then sits down and bends her right leg so that her heel presses against her genitalia. Even young girls of about six years may do this quite casually as they sit on the ground. The women and men talk about it freely, and there is no shame attached to it. It is a customary position for women to take, and they learn it in childhood. They never use their hands for manipulation. (pp. 276–277)

A life script and a theatrical script have many similarities. Each has a cast of characters, dialogue, themes and plots, acts and scenes, and generally both move toward a climax. Often, however, a person is unaware or only vaguely aware of the life scripts he or she is acting out. Public stages on which people act out their scripts include home, social gatherings, church, school, office, and factory. As Shakespeare wrote, "All the world's a stage."

As children grow they learn to play roles—villains, law enforcers, heroes, heroines, victims, and rescuers—and seek others to play complementary roles. Through playing roles, children integrate new themes and parts into their roles and gradually develop their life scripts. The particular scripts that are developed are substantially influenced by the reactions they receive from significant people in their lives.

Cultural Scripts and Family Scripts. Individuals follow scripts and so do families and cultures. Cultural scripts are expected patterns of behavior within a society. (See Spotlight 11.2 for material that notes that cultural scripts are a determinant of sexual behavior.) In regard to cultural scripts, James and Jongeward (1971) note:

Script themes differ from one culture to another. The script can contain themes of suffering, persecution, and hardship (historically the Jews); it can contain themes of building empires and making conquests (as the Romans once did). Throughout history some nations have acted from a "topdog" position of the conqueror; some from an "underdog" position of the conquered. In early America, where people came to escape oppression, to exploit the situation, and to explore the unknown, a basic theme was "struggling for survival." In many cases this struggle was acted out by pioneering and settling. (p. 70)

Women in our society have been socialized to have different life scripts than men. American girls and women traditionally were expected to be affectionate, passive, conforming, sensitive, intuitive, dependent, and "sugar and spice and everything nice." They are supposed to be primarily concerned with domestic life, to be nurturing, to instinctively love to care for babies and young children, to be deeply concerned about their personal appearance, and to be self-sacrificing for their family. They should not appear to be ambitious, aggressive, competitive, or more intelligent than men. They are expected to be ignorant of and uninterested in sports, economics, or politics. In relationships with men they should not initiate the relationship. These traditional scripts for women are changing in our society, largely as a result of the women's rights movement.

Males also have a number of traditional gender role expectations in our society. A male is expected to be tough,

---

Cultural Scripts Are a Determinant of Sexual Behavior

Sexual scripts result from elaborate prior learning in which we acquire an etiquette of sexual behavior. According to this script approach, little in sexual activity is spontaneous. Scripts tell us who appropriate sexual partners are, what sexual activity is expected, where and when the activity should occur, and what the sequence of the different sexual behaviors should be.

Scripts vary greatly from one culture to another. Marshall and Suggs (1971) describe the cultural scripts that are a significant factor in determining sexual behavior in Mangaia. Mangaia is an island in the South Pacific. The Mangaians have elaborate rituals that use sex for pleasure and for procreation.

Mangaian boys around the age of 7 or 8 are instructed how to masturbate. At about age 13, they have a superincision ritual (in which a slit is made on the full length of the skin on the top part of the penis). This ritual initiates them into manhood. As part of this ritual, they are also given instruction in how to kiss, how to bring a female partner to orgasm several times before they have an orgasm themselves, and how to perform cunnilingus. Approximately 2 weeks later, each boy is introduced to sexual intercourse with an experienced woman. She demonstrates intercourse in various positions and further instructs him on how to delay ejaculation to have simultaneous orgasms with his partner.

Mangaian girls also receive sexual instruction from adult women. Thereafter, Mangaian boys and girls actively seek each other out, and many have coitus nearly every night. Teenage girls are raised to believe virility in a male is proof of his desire for her. In particular, a male is expected to be able to vigorously continue the in-and-out action of intercourse for 15 to 30 minutes or longer while the female moves her hips back and forth in a rhythmic motion. Any male who is unable to perform this act is looked down on.

By age 20, the average male is likely to have had ten or more female partners, and the average "nice" female will have had three or four successive male partners. Mangaian parents encourage such sexual experiences because they want their daughters and sons to find a marriage partner with whom they are sexually compatible. At around age 18, Mangaians typically have sex every night. Men are brought up to believe that bringing their partner to orgasm is one of the chief sources of sexual pleasures for a man.

Families have scripts that provide directions for the behavior of each member.

© Elizabeth Crews/The Image Works

fearless, logical, self-reliant, independent, and aggressive. He should have definite opinions on the major issues of the day and is expected to make authoritative decisions at work and at home. He is expected to be strong, to never be depressed, vulnerable, or anxious. He is not supposed to be a sissy, or feminine. He is expected not to cry or openly display emotions. He is expected to be the provider and to be competent in all situations. He is supposed to be physically strong, self-reliant, athletic, to have a manly air of confidence and toughness, to be aggressive, to be brave, to always be in a position to dominate any situation. He is supposed to initiate relationships with women and is expected to be dominant in relationships with them.

The women's movement has initiated changes in these gender role scripts. The ultimate result would be to take pressure off both men and women to conform to rigid gender role stereotypes. Each individual, either male or female, would then be free to develop the personality characteristics and strengths naturally fitting that person.

In our society (as well as in other large and complex societies) there are a number of subcultures, and each subculture has its own scripts. Street gangs, dentists, and college students, to name only a few of the subcultures, have their own subcultural scripts. For example, common aspects of scripts for college students include cramming at the last moment for exams, procrastination, partying, idealism, shortage of money, and expectation of success, happiness, and money following graduation.

Families also have scripts. These scripts provide a set of directions for family members. Examples include:

We Winships have always been pillars of the community.

We Navarres have always been rowdy.

We Hubbards have always been in trouble with the police.

We Schoemakers have always been gamblers.

We Hepps have never had to ask for a handout from anyone.

We Rices have always been Democrats.

If a family member does not live up to the script expectation, he or she is often viewed as a deviant. The importance of scripts in determining human behavior is emphasized by Berne (1964):

Nearly all human activity is programmed by an ongoing script dating from early childhood, so that the feeling of autonomy is nearly always an illusion—an illusion which is the greatest affliction of the human race because it makes awareness, honesty, creativity, and intimacy possible for only a few fortunate individuals. For the rest of humanity, other people are seen mainly as objects to be manipulated. They must be invited, persuaded, seduced, bribed or forced into playing the proper roles to reinforce the protagonist's position and fulfill his script. (p. 310)

There are an infinite number of script themes. A few of the more common themes are the following:

"I have to be loved by everyone."

"I've got to be perfect."

"My purpose in life is to save sinners."

"People will love me only if I make them laugh."

"My life will always be one big party."

"I'm cut out to be a leader."

"I'll never get anywhere."

"I will never let anyone get the best of me."

"I'm headed for fame and fortune."

James and Jongeward (1971) provide the following example of how a life script is played:

> . . . a woman, who had taken the position, "Men are bums," marries a sequence of bums. Part of her script is based on "Men are not OK." She fulfills her own prophecy by nagging, pushing, complaining, and generally making life miserable for her husband (who has his part to play). Eventually, she manipulates him into leaving. Then she can say, "See, I told you. Men are bums who leave you when the going gets rough." (pp. 84–85)

Often people play games as part of their life scripts. A person who has a script of being a Casanova plays the game "Love 'em and leave 'em." A person who has a script of "I won't let anyone get the best of me" is apt to play "One-up." A person who has a script of "I'll always find a way to seduce people into helping me" is apt to play "Poor me."

Application of Script Analysis to Practice. *Script analysis* is a treatment technique in which a counselor enables clients to gain insight into the scripts they are acting out through the use of script concepts. The types of scripts that are the primary focus of script analysis are those that lead to undesirable outcomes for clients or for others.

The counselor's role in analyzing scripts is to (1) teach clients the terminology of script analysis; (2) point out to clients that everyone is playing a variety of scripts, and that scripts largely determine human behavior (and that some scripts have beneficial outcomes, while others have undesirable outcomes); (3) help clients to recognize those scripts that have undesirable outcomes; (4) help clients to assign names to the scripts they are playing so that they can be more readily identified when they are being acted out in the future; and (5) help clients develop new, desirable scripts to act out, and encourage and teach clients more effective ways of responding in the future.

Mezzo System Interactions: Nonverbal Communication

In seeking to assess human behavior, it is also important to attend to nonverbal communication. Sigmund Freud (quoted in Knapp & Hall, 1992) noted, "He that has eyes to see and ears to hear may convince himself that no mortal can keep a secret. If his lips are silent, he chatters with his finger tips; betrayal oozes out of him at every pore" (p. 391).

It is impossible not to communicate. No matter what we do, we transmit information about ourselves. Even an expressionless face communicates messages. As you are reading this, stop for a minute and analyze what nonverbal messages you would be sending if someone were observing you. Are your eyes wide open or half closed? Is your posture relaxed or tense? What are your facial expressions communicating? Are you occasionally gesturing? Do you occasionally roll your eyes? What would an observer deduce you are now feeling from these nonverbal cues?

At times nonverbal cues (such as sweating, stammering, blushing, and frowning) convey information about feelings that we desire to hide. Through developing skill in reading nonverbal communication, we will be more aware of what others are feeling and better able to interact effectively. Because feelings stem from thoughts, nonverbal cues such as blushing also transmit information about what people are thinking.

The Functions of Nonverbal Communication

Nonverbal communication interacts with verbal communication. Nonverbal communication has the following functions in relation to verbal communication:

1. Nonverbal messages may *repeat* what is said verbally. A husband may say he is really looking forward to becoming a father and repeat this happy anticipation with glowing facial expressions.

2. Nonverbal messages may *substitute* for verbal ones. If a close friend has just failed an important exam, you can get a fairly good idea what he or she is thinking and feeling by looking at the facial expressions.

3. Nonverbal messages may *accent* verbal messages. If someone you are dating says he or she is angry and upset with something you did, the depth of these feelings may be emphasized by pounding a fist and pointing an accusing finger.

4. Nonverbal messages may serve to *regulate* verbal behavior. Looking away from someone who is talking

to you is a way of sending a message that you are not interested in talking.

5. Nonverbal messages may *contradict* verbal messages. An example of such a double message is someone with a red face, bulging veins, and a frown on the face, yelling, "Me—angry? Hell no, what makes you think I'm upset?" When nonverbal messages contradict verbal messages, the nonverbal messages are often more accurate. When receivers perceive a contradiction between nonverbal and verbal messages, they usually believe the nonverbal (Adler & Towne, 1981, p. 257).

Although nonverbal messages can be revealing, they can also be unintentionally misleading. Think of the times when people have misinterpreted your nonverbal messages. Perhaps you tend to say little when you first wake up, and others have interpreted this as meaning that you are preoccupied with a personal concern. Perhaps you have been quiet on a date because you are tired or because you're thinking about something that has recently happened. Has your date at times misinterpreted such quietness to mean you are bored or unhappy with the relationship? When you have been thinking deeply about a subject, have you had an expression on your face that others have interpreted as being a frown? Nonverbal behavior is often difficult to interpret. A frown on the face, for example, may represent a variety of feelings: being tired or angry; feeling rejected, confused, unhappy, irritated, disgusted, bored; or simply being lost in thought. Nonverbal messages should not be interpreted as facts but as clues that need to be checked out verbally to determine what the sender is thinking and feeling.

The remainder of this section will examine some examples of how we communicate nonverbally. Many of the examples are taken from white, middle-class American nonverbal communication. Nonverbal communication is strongly culture based. In other words, the identical nonverbal behavior may be interpreted differently depending on the cultural/ethnic/racial background of the observer. For example, a comfortable interpersonal distance may be 6 inches in some cultures and 6 feet in others. Awareness of these differences is especially critical when communicating with clients of different cultural/ethnic/racial backgrounds. Such awareness is the only thing that makes accurate understanding possible. To illustrate, direct eye contact by a social worker is usually considered desirable by white clients but is considered rude and intimidating by many Native Americans. Kissing between adult males is usually interpreted as indicating a gay relationship in our culture, but such kissing is a greeting custom in some European cultures. Adult males who wear skirts in our culture are viewed as weird, but kilts (knee-length pleated skirts) are commonly worn by men in Scotland and by Scottish regiments in the British armies. (An example of the importance of nonverbal communication is presented in Highlight 11.1.)

Posture

In picking up nonverbal cues from posture, one needs to note the overall posture of a person and the changes in posture. We tend to take relaxed postures in nonthreatening

Highlight 11.1

Nonverbal Behavior Among Poker Players

Oswald Jacoby noted that poker players use nonverbal messages extensively. He divided poker players into three classes: (1) naive players, (2) tricky players, and (3) unreadable players.

Naive players: These players are usually beginning players who possess few skills. When they look worried, they probably are. When they have a mediocre hand, they take a long time to bet. When they like their hand, they bet quickly. When they dislike their hand, they frown and scowl and look like bad luck has bit them. When they bluff, they look a little guilty. When they have a really good hand they immediately seek to raise the bet. This naiveness is seldom found in veteran players. Naive players reveal their hands by their

body language. Players of this type usually quit poker at an early stage because they generally lose.

Tricky players: Most poker players fall into this category. Tricky players act opposite of the way they really feel. When they have a poor hand they exude confidence, and when they have a good hand they tremble a little and look nervous as they bet. Sometimes they do a triple cross by acting the way they feel their hand is.

Unreadable players: Unreadable players have no consistency. They will randomly exude confidence or look nervous, and such nonverbal messages will give no clue to the nature of their hand. Unreadable players are excellent players.

Source: Oswald Jacoby, *Oswald Jacoby on Poker* (New York: Doubleday, 1974).

situations and to tighten up when under stress. Some people never relax, and their rigid posture shows it.

Watching the degree of tenseness has been found to be a way of detecting status differences. In interactions between a higher status person and a lower status person, the higher status person is usually more relaxed, while the lower-status person is usually more rigid and tense (Knapp & Hall, 1998). For example, note the positions that are usually assumed when a faculty member and a student are conversing in the faculty member's office.

Teachers and public speakers often watch the posture of listeners to gauge how the presentation is going. If members in the audience are leaning forward in their chairs, it is a sign that the presentation is going over well. The audience slumping in their chairs is a cue that the presentation is beginning to bomb.

Body Orientation

Body orientation is the extent to which we face toward or away from someone with our head, body, and feet. Facing directly toward someone signals an interest in starting or continuing a conversation, while facing away signals a desire to end or avoid conversation. The phrase "turning your back" on someone concisely summarizes the message that is sent when you turn away from someone. Can you remember the last time someone signaled that he or she wanted to end a conversation with you by turning away from you?

Gestures

Most of us are aware that our facial expressions convey our feelings. When we want to hide our true feelings, we concentrate on controlling our facial expressions. We are less aware that our gestures also reveal our feelings, and we put less effort into controlling our gestures when we want to cover up our feelings. As a result, gestures are sometimes better indicators of how we really feel.

People who are nervous tend to fidget. They may bite their fingernails, tap their fingers, rub their eyes or other parts of their body, bend paperclips, or tap a pencil. They may cross and uncross their legs. They may rhythmically swing one leg or move one foot back and forth.

Many gestures provide cues to a person's thoughts and feelings. Clenched fists, whitened knuckles, and pointing fingers signal anger. When people want to express friendship or attraction, they tend to move closer. Hugs can represent a variety of feelings: physical attraction, good to see you, best wishes in the future, and friendship. Shaking hands is a signal of friendship and a way of saying, "Hello" or, "Good-bye."

Albert Scheflen (1974) notes that a person's sexual feelings can be signaled through gestures. He describes preening behavior, which is designed to send a message that the sender is attracted to the receiver. Preening behavior includes rearranging one's clothing, combing or stroking one's hair, and glancing in a mirror. Scheflen cites a number of invitational preening gestures that are specific to women: exposing or stroking a thigh, protruding the breast, placing a hand on the hip, and exhibiting a wrist or palm. Naturally, these gestures do not always suggest sexual interest; they may occur for a variety of other reasons. (It is interesting to note that comparable research has not been conducted on males. Conducting this research only on women may indicate a sexist bias.)

Gestures are also used in relation to verbal messages for a variety of purposes: repeating, substituting, accenting, contradicting, and regulating. Some people literally speak with their hands, arms, and head movements. Many people are unaware of the number of gestures they use, and then (if videotaped) are surprised to view the extent to which they communicate with gestures.

Touching

Rene Spitz (1945) demonstrated that young children need direct physical contact, such as being cuddled, held, and soothed. Without such direct physical contact, the emotional, social, intellectual, and physical development of children will be severely stunted. Spitz observed that in the nineteenth century high proportions of children died in some orphanages and other child-care institutions. The deaths were not found to be due to poor nutrition or inadequate medical care, but instead to lack of physical contact with parents or nurses. From this research came the practice of nurturing children in institutions—picking the baby up, holding her close, playing with her, and carrying her around several times a day. With this physical contact, the infant mortality rate dropped sharply in institutions.

Knapp and Hall (1998) describe findings that suggest that eczema, allergies, and certain other medical problems are in part caused by a person's lack of physical contact with a parent during infancy. Physical stimulation of children will facilitate their intellectual, social, emotional, and physical development.

Adults also need physical contact. People need to know that they are loved, recognized, and appreciated. Touching (through holding hands, hugging, pats on the back) are ways of communicating warmth and caring. Unfortunately, we have been socialized to refrain from touching, except in sexual contacts.

Touching someone is in fact an excellent way of conveying a variety of messages, depending on the context. A hug at a funeral will connote caring, while a hug when meeting someone connotes, "It's good to see you." A hug between parent and child conveys "I love you," whereas a hug on a date may have sexual meanings. A number of therapists have noted that communication and human relationships would be vastly improved if people reached out and touched others more—with hugs, squeezes of the hand, kisses, and pats on the back. Touch is crucial for the survival and development of children, and touch is just as crucial for adults, to assure them that they are worthwhile and loved.

Clothing

Clothes keep us warm and cover certain areas of our body so we are not arrested for indecency. But clothes have many other functions. Certain uniforms tell us what a person does and who we can receive services from: for example, uniforms of police officers, firefighters, nurses, physicians, and waiters. People intentionally and unintentionally send messages about themselves by what they wear. Clothes give messages about our occupations, personality, interests, sexuality, groups we identify with, social philosophies, religious beliefs, status, values, mood, age, nationality, and personal attitudes. For example, the way an instructor dresses sends messages to the class as to the kind of atmosphere he or she is seeking to create.

Any given item of clothing can convey several different meanings. For example, the tie a man selects to wear may reflect sophistication or nonconformity. In addition, the way the tie is worn (loosened, tightly knotted, thrown over one's shoulder, soiled and wrinkled) may provide additional information about the wearer.

A problem often encountered by women is that they lack a socially dictated business uniform. Men wear ties and suits in bland, dark colors. Women interested in developing professional and business careers are still seeking clothing that will convey the best impression. Often they must choose between masculine-looking, unattractive, bland clothing and clothing that is more colorful and aesthetically attractive but considered "unprofessional" in some settings.

Clothes also affect our self-image. If we feel we are well dressed in a situation, we are apt to be more self-confident, assertive, and outgoing. If we feel we are poorly dressed in a situation, we are apt to feel more reserved, less confident, and be less assertive. When we're feeling at a low tide, dressing up will make us feel better about ourselves and raise our spirits.

There is a real danger of misreading nonverbal messages. We often stereotype others on skimpy information, and frequently our interpretations are in error—which may lead to serious adverse consequences. One of the authors remembers a client he interviewed in a correctional facility who for the previous 4 years had lived in an elegant fashion, traveled all over Europe and North America, and stayed in the finest hotels. He financed this lifestyle by writing bad checks. He stated that whenever he needed money, he would carefully dress in an expensive suit and would have no trouble cashing his bogus checks.

Personal Space

Each of us carries around a kind of invisible bubble of personal space wherever we go. The area inside this bubble is perceived as our private territory. The only people we are comfortable in allowing to enter our private territory are those we are emotionally close to. We feel we are being invaded when strangers and people we are not emotionally close to enter our private territory.

Edward Hall (1969) identified four distances or zones that we set in our daily interactions. We use these distances to guide us in setting the type of interactions we want to have with others. The particular zone we choose depends on the context of the conversation, how we feel toward the other person, and what our interpersonal goals are. These zones include the intimate zone, the personal zone, the social zone, and the public zone.

Intimate Zone. The *intimate zone* begins with skin surface and goes out about 18 inches. We generally let only people we are emotionally very close to enter this boundary, and then mostly in private situations—comforting, conveying caring, making love, and showing love and affection. When we voluntarily let and want someone to enter this zone, it is a sign of trust. We lower our defenses. Think about the dates you have. If the person moves within this zone and sits tight against you, it is a signal that he or she is comfortable with the relationship and may want it to progress further. On the other hand, if the person seeks to maintain a safe distance of 2 or more feet, the person is still sorting out the relationship or wants a more distant relationship.

When someone moves into this intimate zone without our wanting them to, we feel invaded and threatened. Our posture becomes more upright, and our muscles tense. We may move back, and avoid eye contact, as a way of signaling we want a more distant relationship. When we are forced to get close to strangers (on crowded buses and elevators), we tend to avoid eye contact and try not

The personal zone ranges from about 18 inches to 4 feet. People in public usually maintain this distance.

to touch others, probably as a way of conveying, "I'm sorry I'm forced to invade your territory. I'll try not to bother you."

Personal Zone. The *personal zone* ranges from about 18 inches to approximately 4 feet. This is the distance at which couples stand in public. Interestingly, if someone of the opposite sex at a party stands this close to someone we are dating or are married to, we tend to become suspicious of that person's intentions. Also, if we see our spouse or date move this close to someone of the opposite sex at a party, we also may become suspicious and sometimes jealous.

The far range of the personal zone (from about 2½ to 4 feet) is the distance in which we convey that we are seeking to keep the other person at arm's length. It is the distance just beyond the other person's reach. Interactions at this distance may still be reasonably close, but they are much less personal than the ones that occur at a closer distance. Sometimes the communication at an arm's length distance represents a testing out by people regarding whether they want the relationship to become emotionally closer.

Social Zone. The *social zone* ranges from about 4 feet to about 12 feet. Business communications are frequently exchanged in this zone. The closer part of this zone (from 4 to about 7 feet) is the distance at which people who work together usually converse, and it is the distance at which salespeople and customers usually interact.

The 7-to-12-foot range is the distance for more impersonal and formal situations. For example, this is the distance at which our boss talks to us from behind his or her desk. If we were to pull our chair around to the boss's

side of the desk in order to sit closer, a very different kind of relationship would be signaled. Furniture arrangement in an office also conveys signals about the type of relationship the officeholder wants to have. For example, an office in which the officeholder has a desk between the customer/client/student suggests that a formal and impersonal interaction is being sought. An office in which a desk is not used as a barrier suggests that a warmer, less formal interaction is allowed.

Public Zone. The *public zone* runs outward from 12 feet. Teachers and public speakers often use a distance of 12 to 18 feet from their audience. In the farther distances of public space (beyond 25 feet) two-way communication is very difficult. Any speaker who voluntarily chooses to have considerable distance from the audience is not interested in having a dialogue.

Territoriality

Territoriality is behavior characterized by identification with an area in such a way as to indicate ownership and defense of this territory against those who may invade it (Knapp & Hall, 1998). Many animals will strike back against much larger organisms if they feel their territory is being invaded.

Territoriality also exists in humans. There are even things we feel we own that we really do not own. Students tend in each class to select a certain seat to sit in. If someone else should happen to sit in your chosen seat, do you feel your territory is being invaded?

What we acquire as property is a strong indicator of our interests and values. The things we acquire are often topics of conversation—cars, homes, leisure-time equipment, plants, clothes. These material things also communicate messages about our status. Wealthy people acquire more property. Interestingly, we generally grant more personal space and greater privacy to people of higher status. For example, we will knock at the boss's office and wait for an invitation to walk in before entering. With people of a status similar to ours or of a lower status, we frequently walk right in.

Facial Expressions

For most people, the face and eyes are the primary sources of nonverbal communication. Facial expressions often are mirrors that reflect our thoughts and feelings. Yet, facial expressions are a complex source of information for several reasons. First, they can change rapidly. Slow motion films have found that a fleeting expression can come and go in as short a time as a fifth of a second (Knapp & Hall, 1998). In addition, researchers have found that there are at least eight distinguishable positions of the eyes and lids, at least eight positions for the eyebrows and forehead, and at least ten for the lower face (Knapp & Hall, 1998). Multiplying these different combinations together leads to several hundred different possible combinations. Therefore, compiling a directory of facial expressions and their corresponding emotions is almost impossible.

Ekman and Friesen (1975) have identified six basic emotions that facial expressions reflect—fear, surprise, anger, happiness, disgust, and sadness. These expressions appear to be recognizable in all cultures. People seeing photos of these expressions are quite accurate in identifying these emotions. Therefore, although facial expressions are complex, these six emotions can fairly accurately be identified (Knapp & Hall, 1998).

A word of caution should be noted about reading facial expressions. Because people are generally aware that their facial expressions reflect what they are feeling and thinking, they may seek to mask their facial expressions for a variety of reasons. For example, a person who is angry and doesn't want others to see the anger, may seek to hide this feeling by smiling. Therefore, in reading facial expressions we should be aware that the sender may be seeking to conceal his or her real thoughts and feelings.

The eyes are also great communicators. When we want to end a conversation, or avoid a conversation, we look away from the other person's eyes. When we want to start a conversation we often seek out the other's eyes. We may wait until the receiver looks at us as a signal to begin. The eyes also communicate dominance and submission. When

a high-status person and a low-status person are looking at each other, the low-status person tends to look away first. Downcast eyes signal submission or giving in. (Downcast eyes may also signal sadness, boredom, or fatigue.)

Good salespeople are aware that eyes are a sign of involvement. They seek to catch our eye. When they know they have caught our eye, they begin their pitch and seek to maintain eye contact. They know there are social norms in our society, such as the courtesy of hearing what a person has to say once we allow the person to begin speaking. These social norms trap us into hearing the sales pitch once eye contact has been made. Good salespeople watch eyes in a store in another way. They observe what items we are most looking at, and then seek to emphasize those items in their sales pitch.

Eye expressions suggest a wide range of human emotions. Wide open eyes suggest wonder, terror, frankness, or naiveté. Raised upper eyelids may mean displeasure. A constant stare connotes coldness. Eyes rolled upward suggest another's behavior is unusual or weird.

When we become emotionally aroused or interested in something, the pupils of our eyes dilate. Some counselors are so sufficiently skilled in reading pupil dilation that they can tell when they touch on a subject that a client is sensitive about.

Voice

The tone of one's voice often has more influence than the actual words spoken. The same word or phrase may have many meanings. Therefore, the way we say the word is the meaning we give to the word. For example, Knapp and Hall (1992, p. 327) show how the meaning of the following sentence is changed by the word that is emphasized.

He's giving this money to Herbie. (HE is the one giving the money, nobody else.)

He's *giving* this money to Herbie. (He is GIVING, not lending the money.)

He's giving *this* money to Herbie. (The money being exchanged is not from another fund or source; it is THIS money.)

He's giving this *money* to Herbie. (Money is the unit of exchange, not a check.)

He's giving this money to *Herbie*. (The recipient is Herbie, not Eric or Bill or Rod.)

When we ask a question, we usually raise our voice at the end of the sentence. When we make a declarative statement, we usually lower our voice at the end of the sentence. Sometimes we intentionally manipulate our voice to contradict the verbal message.

In addition to emphasizing certain words in a sentence, one's voice can communicate in many other ways. These ways include length of pauses, tone, pitch, speed, volume, and disfluencies (such as stammering or saying, "Uh," "um," and "er"). All of these factors together have been called *paralanguage*. Paralanguage deals with how something is said and not with what is said (Knapp & Hall, 1998).

Using paralanguage we can communicate the exact opposite of what the verbal message is. You might practice through changing your voice how you would seek to convey literally, and then sarcastically, messages such as:

"I really like you."

"I'm having a perfectly wonderful time."

"You're really terrific."

When paralanguage and the verbal message are contradictory, the former will carry more meaning. When there is a contradiction between words and the way something is said, subjects usually interpret the message in terms of the way it is said (Knapp & Hall, 1998).

An excellent way to learn more about the way you are using paralanguage is to videotape one of your conversations or speeches, and then watch the replay. Such a process will also give you valuable feedback about your other forms of nonverbal communication.

Physical Appearance

Although it is common to hear people say that only inner beauty really counts, research shows that outer beauty (physical attractiveness) plays an influential role in determining responses for a broad range of interpersonal interactions. College professors tend to give higher grades to females who are physically attractive than to those who are less attractive. In one study, attractive females were more effective in modifying the attitudes of male students on national issues than were less attractive females. Attractive persons, regardless of sex, are rated high on credibility, which greatly increases their ultimate persuasiveness in a variety of areas—sales, public speaking, counseling, and so on (Knapp & Hall, 1998). Conversely, unattractive defendants are more likely to be judged guilty in courtrooms and more likely to receive longer sentences (Knapp & Hall, 1998). The evidence is clear that *initially* we respond much more favorably to those perceived as physically attractive than those seen as less attractive. Attractiveness serves to open doors and create greater opportunities.

Physically attractive people have been found to outstrip less attractive people on a wide range of socially desirable evaluations, including personality, popularity, success, sociability, persuasiveness, sexuality, and often happiness (Knapp & Hall, 1998). For example, attractive women are more apt to be helped and less likely to be the objects of aggressive (nonsexual) acts.

Less attractive people are at a disadvantage from early childhood on. Teachers, for example, interact less (and less positively) with unattractive children. Physical attractiveness is also a crucial factor in determining who we decide to date and who we decide to marry. In many situations practically everyone prefers the most attractive date regardless of her or his own attractiveness and regardless of being rejected by the most attractive date (Knapp & Hall, 1998).

Unattractive men who are seen with attractive women are judged higher in a number of areas than are attractive men who are seen with attractive partners (Bar-Tal & Saxe, 1976). They are judged as making more money, as being more successful in their occupation, and as being more intelligent. Apparently, the evaluators reasoned that unattractive males must have to offset this imbalance by succeeding in other areas to be able to obtain dates with attractive women.

Being physically attractive does *not* mean that a person will *be* more intelligent, more successful, better adjusted, and happier than less attractive people. Attractiveness *initially* opens more opportunities to be successful, but after a door is opened, it is performance that determines outcome.

The shape of one's body suggests certain stereotypes that may or may not be accurate. People who are overweight are judged to be older, more old-fashioned, less strong physically, more talkative, less good looking, more agreeable and good natured, more trusting of others, more dependent on others, and more warmhearted and sympathetic. People who are muscular are rated as being stronger, better-looking, younger, more adventurous, more self-reliant, more mature in behavior, and more masculine.

People with a thin physique are rated as younger, more suspicious of others, more tense and nervous, less masculine, more pessimistic, quieter, more stubborn, and more inclined to be difficult. Both overweight people and very thin people have been found to be discriminated against when seeking to obtain jobs, buy life insurance, adopt children, and be accepted into college. Being tall is a strong advantage in the business world for men but not for women. Shorter men are shortchanged on salaries and job opportunities (Knapp & Hall, 1998).

We have considerable capacity to improve our physical appearance. Dieting, exercising, learning to manage stress, learning to be assertive, getting adequate sleep, improving grooming habits, and improving choice of clothes will substantially improve physical appearance. Improving physical appearance will open more doors and create more opportunities.

The Environment

Perhaps all of us have been in immaculate homes that have "un-living rooms" with furniture coverings, plastic lamp coverings, and spotless ashtrays that send off-putting nonverbal messages: do not get me dirty, do not touch, do not put your feet up, and stay alert to avoid a mistake. In such homes we are not able to relax; their owners wonder why guests don't relax and have a good time. They are unaware that the environment is communicating messages that lead guests to feel uncomfortable.

The attractiveness of a room shapes the kind of communication that takes place and also influences the happiness and energy of people working in it. When people are in an unattractive room they tend to become tired and bored and take longer to complete assigned work than when in an attractive room. When people are in a pleasant room, they display a greater desire to work, and they communicate many more feelings of comfort, importance, and enjoyment. Workers do a better job and generally feel better in an attractive environment (Knapp & Hall, 1998).

The color of rooms apparently affects mood and productivity. In one study children who were given an IQ test scored about 12 points higher in rooms they described as beautiful than they did in rooms they described as having ugly colors (Knapp & Hall, 1998). The beautiful rooms appeared to stimulate alertness and creativity. Friendly words and smiles increased in the beautiful rooms, and irritability and hostility decreased. The most arousing colors are, in order, red, orange, yellow, violet, blue, and green. The pastel colors of pink, baby blue, and peach are thought to have a calming effect. Some prison and jail administrators are now painting cells in pastel colors, hoping that it will have a calming and relaxing effect on inmates.

Businesses have found that they can control the rate of customer turnover by environmental design. Dim lighting, comfortable seats, and subdued noise levels will encourage customers to talk more and spend more time in a bar or restaurant (Knapp & Hall, 1998). If the goal is to run a high-volume business (as in a fast-food place) businesses can encourage customer turnover by bright lights, uncomfortable seats, and high noise levels (for example, by having poor soundproofing). Chairs can be constructed to be comfortable, or they can be made uncomfortable by putting pressure on the sitter's back. Airports seek to get travelers into the restaurants and bars where they will spend money by having comfortable chairs, tables where people can converse, and dim lighting. They discourage travelers from sitting in waiting areas by using bright lighting and by having uncomfortable chairs bolted shoulder to shoulder in rows facing outward, which makes conversation and relaxation more difficult.

Casino owners in Las Vegas build their facilities without windows or clocks so that customers will be less aware of how long they have been gambling. The aim is to keep people gambling as long as possible. Without windows, some customers are unaware that they are gambling into the next day.

The shape and design of buildings affect interaction patterns in many ways. In apartment buildings people who live near stairways and mailboxes have more contact with neighbors than those who live in less heavily traveled parts of the building. Access to neighbors increases communication. Fences, rows of trees, and long driveways increase privacy.

As indicated earlier, types and placement of furniture in offices convey messages as to whether the officeholder wants informal, relaxed communication or formal, to-the-point communication. A round table, for example, suggests the officeholder is seeking to have the communication be seen as equalitarian, whereas a rectangular table suggests the communication should recognize status and power differentials. With a rectangular table, the high-status people generally sit at one end of the table. If the meeting is between parties of equal strength, one contingent tends to sit on one side, and the other on the other side, rather than intermingling the members. A classroom in which the chairs are in a circle suggests the instructor wants to create an informal, discussion atmosphere. A classroom with the chairs in rows suggests the instructor wants to create a formal, lecture-type atmosphere.

❦ Control Theory

William Glasser (1984) developed a *control-theory* explanation of human behavior. A major thrust of the theory is that we have pictures in our heads of what reality is like, and pictures of how we would like the world to be. Glasser asserts that "all our behavior is our constant attempt to reduce the difference between what we want (the pictures in our heads) and what we have (the way we see situations in the world)" (p. 32).

An example may illustrate the process. Keith Fitzpatrick (age 37) has been dating Sonja Noddelson (age 38) off and on for 3½ months. Keith was divorced 19 months ago; Sonja has never been married. Gradually Keith discovers he is becoming more and more attached to Sonja. He develops a picture of them making a commitment to each other and perhaps getting married in a year or two. This picture motivates him one night when they are having dinner to inform her that he increasingly feels attracted to her, and he asks how she views their relationship. Sonja indicates that she enjoys being with him, but also wants her independence. She adds she is occasionally dating others. Keith's reaction to the last statement is to feel "crushed" as he realizes there is a wide discrepancy between the way he wants their relationship to be and what Sonja wants. After several moments of small talk, Keith regains his composure. He concludes that he will try a variety of strategies to entice Sonja into making a commitment to him.

In the next few weeks Keith wines and dines Sonja. He also observes what she likes and dislikes. He tries to present himself in the way that he thinks she likes. For example, she mentions she detests men who drink and smoke to excess. So he cuts down on his drinking when he is with her and also announces to her that he has given up smoking. He discovers she likes theatrical plays, so (even though he dislikes such plays) he buys tickets and takes her to some plays and then tells her that he really loves going to them.

When Sonja mentions she has had a date with someone else, he feels hurt and jealous. In an attempt to also make her feel jealous, he then asks someone else on a date. Afterwards, he informs Sonja that the date really went well (even though it didn't).

Keith also shows his interest in her by sending her cards and flowers. Three weeks later, when he asks her to go with him to Thanksgiving dinner at his parents' house, she indicates she thinks that will give the wrong impression. At this point Keith feels he has put a lot into this relationship and realizes that Sonja is remaining rather uninvolved. To attempt to force her to make more of a commitment to him, he displays, by his verbal and nonverbal communication, that he is angry and that he thinks she has an obligation to go with him. He adds that his folks will be disappointed if she fails to attend.

Unfortunately for Keith, Sonja has learned in the past that it is a mistake to be controlled in relationships by guilt trips and obligations. She tactfully and politely informs Keith that she not only will not go with him to the Thanksgiving dinner, but that their present dating relationship is not working, and, therefore, she no longer will date him. Keith immediately gives up the tactics of anger and making her feel obligated to go. Instead, he pleads with her to continue dating him. However, Sonja adheres to her decision. When Keith realizes this latest strategy is not going to work, he feels he has to regain some of his honor in this lost cause. He resorts to name calling, four-letter words, and pointing out her faults as he perceives them.

At this point, their relationship ends in an uproar. In this example, all of Keith's efforts to achieve the picture of an ongoing relationship with Sonja fail. After the uproar, he starts dating others, hoping to find someone who comes close (as Sonja did) to having the characteristics contained in his mental picture of an ideal mate.

How do we develop the pictures that we believe will satisfy our needs? Glasser asserts that we begin to create our picture albums at an early age and that we spend our whole lives enlarging these albums. Essentially what happens is that whenever what we do gets us something that satisfies a need, we store the picture of what satisfied us in our personal picture album. Glasser (1984) gives the following example of this process by describing how a hungry child added chocolate-chip cookies to his picture album:

Suppose you had a grandson and your daughter left you in charge while he was taking a nap. She said she would be right back, because he would be ravenous when he awoke and she knew you had no idea what to feed an 11-month-old child. She was right. As soon as she left, he awoke screaming his head off, obviously starved. You tried a bottle, but he rejected it—he had something more substantial in mind. But what? Being unused to a howling baby, and desperate, you tried a chocolate-chip cookie and it worked wonders. At first, he did not seem to know what it was, but he was a quick learner. He quickly polished off three cookies. She returned and almost polished you off for being so stupid as to give a baby chocolate. "Now," she said, "he will be yelling all day for those cookies." She was right. If he is like most of us, he will probably have chocolate on his mind for the rest of his life. (p. 19)

When this child learned how satisfying chocolate-chip cookies are, he placed the picture of these cookies in his personal picture album.

Glasser notes that when he uses the term *pictures,* he means *perceptions* from the five senses of sight, hearing, touch, smell, and taste. When we get hungry, or thirsty, or have some other needs or wants, we select one or more pictures from our albums and then seek to obtain what that picture represents. For example, if we are really hungry we may select a picture of a prime rib dinner (or lobster, or two hamburgers) from our album and then seek to obtain what our picture represents.

The pictures in our albums do not have to be rational. Anorexics have a picture that they are too fat and so they starve themselves to come closer to their irrational picture of unhealthy thinness. Alcoholics have a picture of themselves satisfying many of their needs through alcohol. Child molesters have pictures of satisfying their sexual needs through sexual activities with young children. Rapists have pictures of satisfying their power and perhaps sexual needs through sexual assault. To change a picture, we have to replace it with another that will at least reasonably satisfy the need in question. People who are unable to replace a picture may endure a lifetime of misery. Some battered women, for example, endure brutal beatings in marriage because they do not believe they can replace their husbands in their albums.

Glasser notes that whenever there is a difference between the picture we now see and the picture we want, a *signal* is generated by this difference, which starts us behaving in a way to obtain the picture we want. We examine our behavioral systems and select from these behaviors one or more that we judge as being the best available behaviors to reduce this difference. These behaviors include not only straightforward problem-solving efforts, but also such manipulative strategies as becoming angry, pouting, and trying to make others feel guilty. People who are acting irresponsibly or ineffectually have either failed to select responsible behaviors that they have in their behavioral repertoires or have not yet learned responsible courses of action for the particular situation they are facing.

❦ Intuition

The cerebrum (the area of conscious mental processes of the brain) is composed of two cerebral hemispheres. The right hemisphere has been called the *right brain,* and the left hemisphere has been called the *left brain.* Anatomically, the two hemispheres appear to be quite similar, but there is abundant evidence that their functions are by no means identical (Gleitman, 1986). Movements of the left side of the body are under the control of the right hemisphere; movements of the right side of the body are controlled by the left hemisphere.

The left hemisphere of the brain ordinarily controls language and speech functions. It appears the left hemisphere is also more centrally involved in rational thought processes, logic, deduction, and mathematical skills. In contrast, the right hemisphere may be more centrally

involved in creativity, musical abilities, intuition, and feelings. (It should be noted that research on the location of different functions is somewhat speculative, and further, that there is considerable overlap in functions across the two hemispheres.)

The self-talk approach, described in Chapter 8, demonstrates that humans, by thinking rationally, can learn to better control their emotions and their actions, and obtain better control of their lives. However, Gawain (1986) theorizes that it is also important for humans to develop and use their intuition.

A strong body/personality structure is not created by eating certain foods, doing certain exercises, or following anybody's rules or good ideas. It is created by trusting your intuition and learning to follow its direction. (p. 18)

Gawain asserts that it is important for all of us to learn to trust our intuitive knowledge. She states:

Most of us have been taught from childhood not to trust our feelings, not to express ourselves truthfully and honestly, not to recognize that at the core of our being lies a loving, powerful, and creative nature. (1986, p. 69)

Through reeducating ourselves to listen to and trust our intuition, Gawain asserts that we will gain integrity, creativity, and wholeness. Learning to trust this inner voice may feel risky at first, because we are no longer playing it safe, doing what we "should" do, pleasing others, deferring to outside authority, or following rules.

An important step toward identifying and following your intuition is simply taking time (perhaps several times a day) to relax and listen to your "gut feelings." The inner voice of intuition will present itself in a variety of ways, including images, feelings, and words. When you have an important decision to make, your true feelings will more easily be identified if you are very relaxed. When you are relaxed (perhaps through using meditation or some other relaxation technique) your intuition will inform you which alternative is in your best interest. Frequently your intuition will inform you of creative alternatives that you previously were unaware of.

Human intuition is similar (and perhaps identical) to the instinct in geese that guides them to fly south in fall and north in spring. It is similar to the instinct in dogs that makes them wary upon seeing a bear in the wild—even when they have never seen a bear before.

Your intuition can assist you in making such major decisions as whether to stay in college, choosing a career, whether to end a romantic relationship, what kind of automobile to purchase, what hobbies to pursue, and so on. Your intuition can also lead you to be a more creative, productive, contented, and fulfilled person.

🌿 Chemical Substance Use and Abuse

The remainder of this chapter will focus on a critical issue affecting, in one way or another, nearly every person in our society—chemical substance use and abuse. Nearly everyone has one or more relatives or friends who are abusing alcohol or some other drug. Some of the readers of this text may be personally struggling with this issue. We begin our discussion with some examples.

There was going to be a big party at Evelyn's on Saturday night. Georgia, a high school junior, couldn't wait to go. Everybody was going to be there. Evelyn said she had some great hash. Georgia didn't like to smoke all that much. However, people would think that there was something wrong with her if she didn't, and that was the last thing she wanted.

Marty, aged 15, liked to drink a couple of six packs on the weekend. After all, his father did, and Marty was almost an adult.

Virgil, aged 18, liked to get high because then he could forget about all his problems. He wouldn't have to think about his alcoholic mother and all the problems she and his father were having. He wouldn't have to worry about all the pressures he had in school. He wouldn't even have to think about how his girlfriend recently dumped him. He just couldn't wait until the next chance he had to get high.

Drugs have become part of our daily lives. We use drugs to relax, to increase our pleasure, to feel less inhibited, to get rid of unwanted emotions, to keep awake, and to fall asleep. Practically all Americans use drugs of one kind or another. People have coffee in the morning, soda (which has caffeine) during the day, cocktails before dinner, and aspirin to relieve pain.

When the Pilgrims set sail for America, they loaded on their ships 14 tons of water—plus 10,000 gallons of wine and 42 tons of beer (Robertson, 1980). Ever since, Americans have been widely using and abusing drugs.

Pharmacologically, a drug is any substance that chemically alters the function or structure of a living organism. Such a definition includes food, insecticides, air pollutants, water pollutants, acids, vitamins, toxic chemicals, soaps, and soft drinks. Obviously, this definition is too broad to be useful. For our purposes, a definition based on context is more useful. In medicine, for example, a drug is any substance that is manufactured specifically to relieve pain or to treat and prevent diseases and other medical conditions.

Here drugs will be addressed within the context most useful for social workers. We will focus on drugs that can dramatically impact human behavior and have serious consequences on people's lives. For our purposes, then, a *drug* is any habit-forming substance that directly affects the brain and the nervous system; it is a chemical substance that affects moods, perceptions, bodily functions, or consciousness and that has the potential for misuse as it may be harmful to the user.

Drug abuse is the regular or excessive use of a drug when, as defined by a group, the consequences endanger relationships with other people, are detrimental to a person's health, or jeopardize society itself. All of the drugs mentioned earlier are types of chemicals. Another way of referring to drug abuse is *chemical substance abuse*. Drug or chemical substance intake becomes abusive when an individual's mind and/or body are affected in negative or harmful ways.

Both legal drugs, such as alcohol and tobacco, and prescription drugs are frequently abused. Among the most abused prescription drugs are sedatives, tranquilizers, painkillers, and stimulants. Americans are obsessed with taking pills. Many prescribed drugs have the potential to be psychologically and physiologically addicting. Drug companies spend millions in advertising to convince customers that they are too tense, too irritable, take too long to fall asleep, that they should lose weight, and so on. These companies then assert that their medications will relieve these problems. Unfortunately, many customers accept this easy symptom-relief approach and end up dependent on pills, rather than making the necessary changes in their lives to be healthy. Such changes include exercise, stress management techniques, positive thinking, and a healthy diet.

Illegal drugs such as cocaine and heroin are also frequently abused. People use them to distort their own realities. They can be used to attain unrealistic "highs" or to escape unpleasant life situations. However, as we will see, heavy drug use can often result in serious physical deterioration and slave-like psychological and physical dependence.

This section will describe a variety of legal over-the-counter, prescription, and illegal drugs and will examine various issues of drug use and treatment. Finally, the relationship between knowledge about drug use and assessment in social work practice will be proposed.

Specific Drugs—What They Are and What They Do

Knowing what a specific drug is and what it does to a person is important both in treatment and in considering its use and abuse. Specific drugs discussed here include depressants, stimulants, narcotics, hallucinogens, marijuana,

Highlight 11.2

Drugs of Abuse: Facts and Effects

| Drug | Dependence Potential | | Tolerance | Duration of Effects (in hours) | Usual Methods of Administration | Possible Effects | Effects of Overdose | Withdrawal symptoms |
	Physical	Psychological						
Narcotics Opium	High	High	Yes	3 to 6	Oral, smoked	Euphoria; drowsiness; respiratory depression; constricted pupils; nausea	Slow and shallow breathing; clammy skin; convulsions; coma; possible death	Watery eyes; runny nose; yawning; loss of appetite; irritability; tremors, panic; chills and sweating; cramps; nausea
Morphine	High	High	Yes	3 to 6	Injected, smoked			
Heroin	High	High	Yes	3 to 6	Injected, sniffed			
Depressants Alcohol	High	High	Yes	1 to 12	Oral	Slurred speech; disorientation; drunken behavior; loss of coordination; impaired reactions	Shallow respiration; cold and clammy skin; dilated pupils; weak and rapid pulse; coma; possible death	Anxiety; insomnia; tremors; delirium; convulsions; possible death
Barbiturates	High	High	Yes	1 to 16	Oral, injected			
Tranquilizers	Moderate	Moderate	Yes	4 to 8	Oral			
Quaalude	High	High	Yes	4 to 8	Oral			
Stimulants Caffeine	High	High	Yes	2 to 4	Oral	Increased alertness; excitation; euphoria; dilated pupils; increased pulse rate and blood pressure; insomnia; loss of appetite	Agitation; increase in pulse rate and blood pressure; loss of appetite; insomnia	Apathy; long periods of sleep; irritability; depression; disorientation
Cocaine	Possible	High	Yes	2	Injected, sniffed		Agitation; increase in body temperature; hallucinations; convulsions; tremors; possible death	
Crack	Possible	High	Yes	2	Smoked			
Amphetamines	Possible	High	Yes	2 to 4	Oral, injected			

tobacco, and anabolic steroids. Highlight 11.2 summarizes information about these drugs.

Depressant Drugs. Depressant drugs are those that slow down bodily functioning and activity. Alcohol, barbiturates, tranquilizers, and Quaalude all fall within this category.

Alcohol. *Alcohol* is a colorless liquid found in beer, wine, brandy, whiskey, vodka, rum, and other intoxicating beverages. The type of alcohol found in beverages is ethyl alcohol; it is also called grain alcohol because most of it is made from fermenting grain.

Who Drinks? The American adult consumes an average of 33.9 gallons of beer, 3.01 gallons of wine, and 1.9 gallons of distilled spirits a year (Kornblum & Julian, 2001). The vast majority of teenagers and adults in our society drink.

Several factors are related to whether an individual will drink and, if so, how much. These variables include biological factors, socioeconomic factors, gender, age, religion, urban-rural residence, and cultural influences (Kornblum & Julian, 2001):

- *Biological Factors:* Close relatives of an alcoholic are four times more likely to become alcoholics themselves, and this tendency holds true even for chil-

Drug	Dependence Potential		Tolerance	Duration of Effects (in hours)	Usual Methods of Administration	Possible Effects	Effects of Overdose	Withdrawal symptoms
	Physical	Psychological						
Butyl nitrate	Possible	Unknown	Probable	Up to 5	Inhaled	Excitement; euphoria; giddiness; loss of inhibitions; aggressiveness; delusions; depression; drowsiness; headache; nausea	Loss of memory; confusion; unsteady gait; erratic heartbeat and pulse; possible death	Insomnia; decreased appetite; depression; irritability; headache
Amyl nitrate	Possible	Unknown	Probable	Up to 5	Inhaled			
Hallucinogens LSD	None	Degree	Yes	Variable	Oral	Illusions and hallucinations; poor perception of time and distance	Longer, more intense "trip" episodes; psychosis; possible death	Unknown
Mescaline and Peyote		Unknown			Oral, injected			
Psilocybin psilocin					Oral			
PCP					Oral, injected, smoked			
MDMA (ecstasy)					Oral, injected			
Cannabis Marijuana Hashish	Degree unknown	Moderate	Yes	2 to 4	Oral, smoked	Euphoria; relaxed inhibitions; increased appetite; disoriented behavior; rate increased heart and pulse rate	Fatigue; paranoia; possible psychosis; time disorientation; slowed movements	Insomnia; hyperactivity; decreased appetite
Nicotine (Tobacco)	High	High	Yes	2 to 4	Smoked, chewed	Increased alertness; excitation; euphoria; dilated pupils; increased pulse rate and blood pressure; insomnia; loss of appetite	Agitation; increase in pulse rate and blood pressure; loss of appetite; insomnia	Apathy; long periods of sleep; irritability; depression
Anabolic steroids	None	High	Unknown	Unknown	Oral	Moodiness; depression; irritability	Unknown	Unknown

dren who were adopted away from their biological families at birth and raised in a nonalcoholic family. Such findings clearly suggest that drinking and alcoholism are due in part to biological factors. Some Asian populations have highly negative reactions to alcohol, which tend to diminish their risk of becoming alcoholics. On the other hand, some ethnic groups (such as Native Americans in the Western Hemisphere) have a lower tolerance for alcohol than other groups do, which places them at a greater risk for alcoholism.

■ *Socioeconomic factors:* Drinking is more frequent among younger men who are positioned at higher socioeconomic levels, and less frequent among older women at lower levels.

- *Gender:* Men are more likely to use and abuse alcohol than are women. Still, recent decades have seen a dramatic increase in alcoholism among adult women. Why? One explanation is that cultural taboos against heavy drinking among women have weakened. Another explanation is that increased drinking is related to the changing roles of women in our society.

- *Age:* Older people are less likely to drink than younger people, even if they were drinkers in their youth. Heavy drinking is most common at ages 21 to 30 for men and ages 31 to 50 for women.

- *Religion:* Nonchurchgoers drink more than regular churchgoers. Heavy drinking is more common among Episcopalians and Catholics, whereas conservative and fundamentalist Protestants are more often nondrinkers or light drinkers. Fewer Jews are heavy drinkers.

- *Urban-rural residence:* Urban residents are more likely to drink than rural residents.

Recently, there has been a marked decline in drinking, especially of hard liquor, in many segments of the American public (Kornblum & Julian, 2001). For example, some business executives have switched from martini luncheons to jogging and working out. In recent years the federal government has put considerable financial pressure on states to raise the drinking age to 21; if a state does not raise the age, federal highway funds are withheld. All states have now raised the drinking age to 21. Many secondary schools, colleges, and universities have initiated alcohol awareness programs. Many businesses and employers have developed Employee Assistance Programs, which are designed to provide treatment services to alcoholics and problem drinkers. Many states have passed stricter drunk driving laws, and police departments and the courts are more vigorously enforcing such laws. Organizations such as Mothers Against Drunk Driving and Students Against Drunk Driving have been fairly successful in creating greater public awareness of the hazards of drinking and driving. A cultural norm is emerging in many segments that it is stylish not to have too much to drink. Despite these promising trends, rates of alcohol use and abuse in the United States remain extremely high.

What Alcohol Does. Many drinkers believe alcohol is a stimulant, because it relaxes tensions, lessens sexual and aggressive inhibitions, and seems to facilitate interpersonal relationships. However, it acts as a depressant to the central nervous system, because it reduces functional activity of this system. Its chemical composition and effects are very similar to ether (an anesthetic used in medicine to induce unconsciousness).

Alcohol slows down mental activity, reasoning ability, speech ability, and muscle reactions. It distorts perceptions, slurs speech, lessens coordination, and slows down memory functioning and respiration. In increasing quantities, it leads to stupor, sleep, coma, and finally death. A hangover (the aftereffects of too much alcohol) includes having a headache, thirst, muscle aches, stomach discomfort, diarrhea, and nausea. Alcohol can seriously affect how one drives an automobile. Behavior resulting from excessive alcohol intake can also negatively interfere in family, friend, and work relationships.

The effects of alcohol vary with the percentage of alcohol in the bloodstream as it passes through the brain. Generally, the effects are observable when the concentration of alcohol in the blood reaches one-tenth of a percent. Five drinks (with each drink being 1 ounce of 86-proof alcohol, or 12 ounces of beer, or 3 ounces of wine) in 2 hours for a 120-pound person will result in a blood alcohol concentration of one-tenth of a percent, which is the legal criterion in most states for being intoxicated.

Alcohol also has long-term effects on a person's health. Alcoholics have a life expectancy that is 10 to 12 years less than that of nonalcoholics (Kornblum & Julian, 2001). The life span is shorter for several reasons. One is that alcohol, over an extended period of time, gradually destroys liver cells and replaces the cells with scar tissue. When the scar tissue is extensive, a medical condition occurs called *cirrhosis*. This is the eighth most frequent cause of death in the United States, leading to about 25,000 deaths per year (Kornblum & Julian, 2001). Also, although it has no nutritional value, alcohol contains a high number of calories. As a result, heavy drinkers have a reduced appetite for nutritious food and thus frequently suffer from vitamin deficiencies and are more susceptible to infectious diseases. Heavy drinking also causes kidney problems, contributes to a variety of heart ailments, is a factor in diabetes, and also appears to contribute to cancer. In addition, heavy drinking is associated with thousands of suicides annually (Kornblum & Julian, 2001).

However, for some as yet unknown reason, the life expectancy for light-to-moderate drinkers exceeds that for nondrinkers. Perhaps an occasional drink helps people to relax and thereby reduces the likelihood of life-threatening stress-related illnesses developing.

Alcohol also can seriously affect sexual response. The effects of alcohol vary considerably. A small amount of alcohol may reduce inhibitions and anxiety, thereby improving responsiveness. A large amount of alcohol, however, acts as a depressant and reduces sexual arousal, thereby causing sexual dysfunction (Hyde, 1994). Male alcoholics who are exposed to repeated high doses of alcohol frequently have sexual dysfunctions, including erectile dysfunction and loss of sexual desire. Women who have consumed small amounts of alcohol (compared with controls who have consumed none) report greater sexual arousal and more pleasurable orgasms, although their orgasms are slightly delayed. However, when a large amount of alcohol is consumed (and the state of being intoxicated is approached), an orgasm takes significantly longer to occur, and women report that the orgasm is less intense. Although a high proportion of recovering alcoholics still experience some form of sexual dysfunction, the majority of alcohol-related sexual problems will disappear after a few months of abstinence.

Combining alcohol with other drugs can have disastrous, and sometimes fatal, effects. Two drugs taken together may have a *synergistic interaction*—that is, they interact to produce an effect much greater than either would cause alone. For example, sedatives such as barbiturates (often found in sleeping pills) or Quaaludes taken with alcohol can so depress the central nervous system that a coma or even death may result.

Other drugs tend to create an *antagonistic response* to alcohol—one drug negates the effects of the other. Many doctors now caution patients not to drink while taking certain prescribed drugs because the alcohol will reduce, and even totally negate, the beneficial effects of those drugs.

Whether drugs will interact synergistically or antagonistically depends on a wide range of factors: the properties of the drugs, the amounts taken, the amount of sleep of the user, the kind and amount of food that has been eaten, and the user's overall health and tolerance. The interactive effects may be minimal one day and extensive the next.

When used by pregnant women, alcohol may gravely affect the unborn child by causing mental retardation, deformities, stunting of growth, and other abnormalities. This effect has been named the *fetal alcohol syndrome.*

Withdrawal from alcohol, once the body is physically addicted, may lead to the DTs (delirium tremens) and other unpleasant reactions. The DTs include rapid heartbeat, uncontrollable trembling, severe nausea, and profuse sweating.

Barbiturates. *Barbiturates,* another type of depressant, are derived from barbituric acid, and depress the central nervous system. Barbiturates were first synthesized in the early 1900s, and there are now more than 2,500 different barbiturates. They are commonly used to relieve insomnia and anxiety. Some are prescribed as sleeping pills, and others are used during the daytime by tense and anxious persons. They are also used to treat epilepsy and high blood pressure, and to relax patients before or after surgery. Barbiturates are illegal, unless obtained by a physician's prescription.

Taken in sufficient doses, barbiturates have effects similar to alcohol. Users experience relief from inhibitions, have a feeling of euphoria, feel "high" or in good humor, and are passively content. However, these moods can change rapidly to gloom, agitation, and aggressiveness. Physiological effects include slurred speech, disorientation, staggering, appearance of being confused, drowsiness, and reduced coordination.

Prolonged heavy use of barbiturates can cause physical dependence, with withdrawal symptoms similar to those of heroin addiction. Withdrawal is accompanied by body tremors, cramps, anxiety, fever, nausea, profuse sweating, and hallucinations. Many authorities believe barbiturate addiction is more dangerous than heroin addiction, and it is considered to be more resistant to treatment than heroin addiction. Abrupt withdrawal (*cold turkey,* the sudden and complete halting of drug use) can cause fatal convulsions.

Barbiturate overdose may cause convulsions, coma, poisoning, and sometimes death. Barbiturates are particularly dangerous when taken with alcohol, because alcohol acts synergistically to magnify the potency of the barbiturates. Accidental deaths due to excessive doses are frequent. Barbiturates are also the number one drug used for suicide. A number of famous people have fatally overdosed on barbiturates.

Barbiturates are generally taken orally, although some users also inject them intravenously. Use of barbiturates, like alcohol, may also lead to traffic fatalities.

Tranquilizers. Yet another type of depressant is the group of drugs classified as tranquilizers. Common brand names are Librium, Miltown, Serax, Tranxene, and Valium. Tranquilizers reduce anxiety, relax muscles, and are sedatives. Users have moderate potential of becoming physically and psychologically dependent. The drugs are usually taken orally, and the effects last for 4 to 8 hours. Side effects include slurred speech, disorientation, and behavior resembling being intoxicated. Overdoses are possible, with the effects including cold and clammy skin, shallow respiration, dilated pupils, weak and rapid pulse, coma, and possibly death. Withdrawal symptoms are similar to those from alcohol and barbiturates and include anxiety, tremors, convulsions, delirium, and possibly death. Highlight 11.3 discusses depressants that are used as so-called "date-rape drugs."

Highlight 11.3

Date-Rape Drugs

In the mid-1990s Rohypnol became known as the date-rape drug. A number of women were sexually assaulted after the drug was slipped into one of their drinks (both alcohol and nonalcoholic drinks). Rohypnol often causes blackouts, with complete loss of memory. Female victims who were slipped the drug and then raped often cannot remember any details of the crimes.

Rohypnol is a sedative that is related to Valium, but ten times stronger. Rohypnol is legally available in more than 60 countries for severe insomnia. It is illegal in the United States (many drugs—such as cocaine and heroin—are too, but are widely used and abused). Much of the illegal Rohypnol in the United States is smuggled in from Mexico and Colombia.

Rohypnol is also popular with teens and young adults (both males and females) who like to combine it with alcohol for a quick punch-drunk hit. Another reason for its popularity is that it's relatively inexpensive—often being purchased on the street for $1 to $5 per pill. In some jurisdictions, drivers are now being tested for Rohypnol when they appear drunk but register a low alcohol level.

(It should be noted, Rohypnol is also addictive, and there is a potential for lethal overdosing.)

Because of the ease through which Rohypnol can be slipped into a drink, rape crisis centers are urging women to *never* take their eyes off their drink. In 1997 the marketer of Rohypnol, Hoffman-LaRoche, announced it intended to sell only a new version of Rohypnol—one that would cause any liquid that it is slipped into to change to blue. Even with this change being made, people (particularly women) need to beware—other sedatives have similar effects.

Gamma hydroxy butyrate (GHB) is another drug that is increasingly being used as a date-rape drug. GHB is a central nervous system depressant that is approved as an anesthetic in some countries. It can be readily made at home from chemicals purchased in stores. It is made from a mixture of chemicals normally used for cleaning, such as lye. Just one gram of this liquid home-brew provides an intoxicating experience equivalent to 26 ounces of whisky. Similar to Rohypnol, GHB is slipped into a drink of intended victims.

Quaalude. Methaqualone (better known by its patent name Quaalude) has effects similar to barbiturates and alcohol, although it is chemically different. It has a reputation as a love drug, as users believe it makes them more eager for sex and enhances sexual pleasure. These effects are probably due to the fact that it lessens inhibitions. Quaalude also reduces anxiety and gives a feeling of euphoria.

Users can become both physically and psychologically dependent on Quaalude. Overdose can result in convulsions, coma, delirium, and even death—most deaths occur when the drug is taken together with alcohol, which vastly magnifies the drug's effects. Withdrawal symptoms are severe and unpleasant. Abuse of the drug may also cause hangovers, fatigue, liver damage, and temporary paralysis of the limbs.

Stimulants. In this section we will examine drugs that are classified as stimulants. Stimulants are substances that produce a temporary increase in a person's activity level or efficiency. They include caffeine, amphetamines, cocaine, crack, amyl nitrate, and butyl nitrate.

Caffeine. Caffeine is a stimulant to the central nervous system. It is present in coffee, tea, cocoa, and many soft drinks. It is also available in tablet form (for example, No-Doz). Caffeine is widely used—practically all

Americans use it daily. It reduces hunger, fatigue, and boredom, and improves alertness and motor activity. The drug appears addictive, as many users develop a tolerance for it. A further sign that it is addictive is that heavy users (for example, habitual coffee drinkers) will experience withdrawal symptoms of mild irritability, headaches, and depression.

Excessive amounts of caffeine cause insomnia, restlessness, and gastrointestinal irritation. Excessive doses can even, surprisingly, cause death.

Because caffeine has the status of a "nondrug" in our society, users are not labeled criminals, there is no black market for it, and no subculture is formed to give support in obtaining and using the drug. Because caffeine is legal its price is low compared to other drugs. Users are not tempted to resort to crime to support their habit. Some authorities assert that our approach to caffeine should serve as a model for the way we react to other illegal drugs (such as marijuana) that they feel are no more harmful than caffeine (Kornblum & Julian, 2001).

Amphetamines. Another type of stimulant, amphetamines, are often called "uppers" because of their stimulating effect. When prescribed by a physician, they are legal. Some truck drivers have obtained prescriptions in order to stay awake and more alert while making a long haul. Dieters have received prescriptions to help them lose weight, and they often find that the pills tend to give them more self-confidence and buoyance. Others who have used amphetamines to increase alertness and performance for relatively short periods of time include college students, athletes, astronauts, and executives. Additional nicknames for this drug are speed, ups, pep pills, black beauties, and bennies.

Amphetamines are synthetic drugs. They are similar to adrenalin, a hormone from the adrenal gland that stimulates the central nervous system. The better known amphetamines include dexedrine, benzedrine, and methedrine. Physical reactions to amphetamines are extensive: consumption of fat stored in body tissues is accelerated, heartbeat is increased, respiratory processes are stimulated, appetite is reduced, and insomnia is common. Users feel euphoric, stronger, and have an increased capacity to concentrate and to express themselves verbally. Prolonged use can lead to irritability, deep anxiety, and an irrational persecution complex that can lead to sudden acts of violence.

Amphetamines are usually taken orally in tablet, powder, or capsule form. They can also be sniffed or injected. "Speeding" (injecting the drug into a vein) produces the most powerful effects and can also cause the greatest harm. An overdose may cause a coma, with possible brain damage, and, in rare cases, death. Speeders may also develop hepatitis, abscesses, convulsions, hallucinations, delusions, and severe emotional disturbances. Another danger is that, when sold on the street, the substance may contain impurities that are health hazards.

An amphetamine high is often followed by mental depression and fatigue. Continued amphetamine use leads to psychological dependence. It is unclear whether amphetamines are physically addictive, as the withdrawal symptoms are uncharacteristic of withdrawal from other drugs. Amphetamine withdrawal symptoms include sleep disturbances, apathy, decreased activity, disorientation, irritability, exhaustion, and depression. Some authorities believe such withdrawal symptoms indicate that amphetamines may be physically addicting.

One of the legal uses of certain amphetamines is in the treatment of *hyperactivity* in children. Hyperactivity (also called hyperkinesis) is characterized by a short attention span, extensive motor activity, restlessness, and mood shifts. Little is known about the causes of this condition. As children become older, even without treatment, the symptoms tend to disappear. Interestingly, some amphetamines (Ritalin is a popular one) have a calming and soothing effect on hyperactive children—the exact opposite effect occurs when Ritalin is taken by adults. It should be noted that treating uncontrollable children

with amphetamines has sometimes been abused. Some of the children for whom Ritalin was prescribed were not really hyperactive. They were normal children who simply refused to submit to what their teachers and parents considered appropriate childhood behavior. As a result, these children were labeled as troublemakers and were introduced to the world of taking a mood-altering drug on a daily basis.

One amphetamine that has had increasing illegal use in recent years is methamphetamine hydrochloride, known on the street as "meth" or "ice." In liquid form it is often referred to as "speed." Under experimental conditions, cocaine users often have difficulty distinguishing cocaine from methamphetamine hydrochloride. There is a danger this drug may be increasingly abused, as the "high" lasts longer than that from cocaine and the drug can be synthesized relatively easily in laboratories from products that are sold legally in the United States. As a "last resort," methamphetamine hydrochloride (Desoxyn) is legally used to treat obesity as one component of a weight-reduction regimen. There is, however, a serious side effect of this drug when used for weight reduction: The user's appetite returns with greater intensity after withdrawal from the drug.

Cocaine and Crack. Cocaine is obtained from the leaves of the South American coca plant. It is rapidly replacing other illegal drugs in popularity. Although legally classified as a narcotic, it is in fact not related to the opiates from which narcotic drugs are derived. It is a powerful stimulant and antifatigue agent.

In the United States, it is generally taken by sniffing and is then absorbed through the nasal membranes. The most common method is sniffing up through a straw or a rolled-up bank note, known as "snorting." It may also be injected intravenously, and in South America the natives chew the coca leaf. It may be added in small quantities to a cigarette and smoked. Cocaine has been used medically in the past as a local anesthetic, but other drugs have largely replaced it for this purpose.

Cocaine constricts the blood vessels and tissues, and thereby leads to increased strength and endurance. It also is thought by users to increase creative and intellectual powers. Other effects include a feeling of euphoria, excitement, restlessness, and a lessened sense of fatigue.

Larger doses, or extended use, may result in hallucinations and delusions. A peculiar effect of cocaine abuse is "formication," the illusion that ants, snakes, or bugs are crawling on or into the skin. Some abusers have such intense illusions that they literally scratch, slap, and wound themselves trying to kill these imaginary creatures.

Physical effects of cocaine include increased blood pressure and pulse rate, insomnia, and loss of appetite. Heavy users may experience weight loss or malnutrition due to appetite suppression. Physical dependence on cocaine is considered to be a low to medium risk. However, the drug appears to be psychologically habituating. Termination of use usually results in intense depression and despair, which drives the person back to taking the drug. Additional effects of withdrawal include apathy, long periods of sleep, extreme fatigue, irritability, and disorientation. Serious tissue damage to the nose can occur when large quantities of cocaine are "sniffed" over a prolonged period of time. Regular use may result in habitual sniffing, and sometimes leads to an anorexic condition. High doses can lead to agitation, increased body temperature, and convulsions. A few people who overdose may die if their breathing and heart functions become too depressed.

Crack, also called "rock," is obtained from cocaine by separation of the adulterants from the cocaine by mixing it with water and ammonium hydroxide. The water is then removed from the cocaine base by means of a fast drying solvent, usually ether. The resultant mixture resembles large crystals, similar to rock sugar. Crack is highly addictive. Some authorities claim that one use is enough to lead to addiction. Users generally claim that after they have finished one dose, they crave another.

Crack is generally smoked, either in a specially-made glass pipe, or mixed with tobacco or marijuana in a cigarette. The effects are similar to those of cocaine, but the "rush" is more immediate, and the drug gives an intensified high.

An overdose is more common when crack is injected than when it is smoked. Withdrawal effects include an irresistible compulsion to have the drug, as well as apathy, long periods of sleep, irritability, extreme fatigue, depression, and disorientation.

Communal use of needles spreads AIDS. Cocaine and crack can have serious effects on the heart, straining it with high blood pressure, with interrupted heart rhythm, and with raised pulse rates. Cocaine and crack may also damage the liver. Severe convulsions can cause brain damage, emotional problems, and sometimes death. Smoking crack may also damage the lungs. Babies born to crack users face a series of significant physical and behavioral problems, described in Highlight 11.4.

Amyl Nitrate and Butyl Nitrate.
Amyl nitrate (poppers) is prescribed for patients who risk certain forms of heart failure. It is a volatile liquid that is sold in capsules or small bottles. When the container is opened, the chemical begins to evaporate (similar to gasoline). If the vapor is sniffed, the user's blood vessels are immediately dilated

and heart rate increases. These physical changes create feelings of mental excitation (head rush) and physical excitation (body rush). The drug is supposedly sold only by prescription, but (as with many other drugs) the illicit drug market distributes it.

Butyl nitrate is legally available in some states without a prescription and has an effect similar to amyl nitrate's. Trade names under which it is sold are Rush and Locker Room. Similar to amyl nitrate, butyl nitrate vapor is sniffed. It is available at some sexual aid and novelty stores.

Both of these drugs have been used as aphrodisiacs and as stimulants while dancing. The drugs have some short-term, unpleasant side effects that may include fainting, headaches, and dizziness. A few deaths have been reported due to overdoses. Both drugs are classified as stimulants.

Narcotics. The most commonly used narcotic drugs in the United States are the opiates (such as opium, heroin, and morphine). The term *narcotic* means sleep-inducing. In actuality, drugs classified as narcotics are more accurately called *analgesics,* or painkillers. The principal effect produced by narcotic drugs is a feeling of euphoria.

The opiates are all derived from the opium poppy. The opium poppy grows in various parts of the world: Turkey, Southeast Asia, and Colombia have, in the recent past, been major sources of the opiates. The drug opium is the dried form of a milky substance that oozes from the seed pods after the petals fall from the flowers. It has been used for centuries.

Morphine is the main active ingredient of opium. It was first identified early in the 1800s, and has been used extensively as a painkiller. Heroin was first synthesized from morphine in 1874. It was once thought to be a cure for morphine addiction, but later was also found to be addictive. Heroin is a more potent drug than morphine.

Opium is usually smoked, although it can be taken orally. Morphine and heroin are either sniffed (snorted) or injected into a muscle or into a vein (called "mainlining"), which maximizes the drugs' effects.

Opiates affect the central nervous system and produce feelings of tranquility, drowsiness, or euphoria. They produce a sense of well-being that makes pain, anxiety, or depression seem unimportant. Blaze-Gosden (1987) notes that opiates

have been described as giving an orgasmlike rush or flash that lasts briefly but memorably. At the peak of the euphoria, the user has a feeling of exaggerated physical and mental comfort and well-being, a heightened feeling of buoyancy and bodily health, and a heightened feeling of being competent, in control, capable of any achievement, and being able to cope. (p. 95)

Highlight 11.4

Crack Babies

In recent years crack cocaine use by pregnant women has sharply increased. As a result, thousands of babies have been born that have been adversely affected by their mother's use of crack cocaine.

Cocaine causes blood vessels in a pregnant woman to constrict, thus reducing the vital flow of oxygen and other nutrients to the fetus. Because fetal cells multiply swiftly in the first months, an embryo deprived of a proper blood supply by a mother's early and continuous use of cocaine is apt to be adversely impacted cognitively. Such babies when born tend to look quite normal, but are apt to be undersized, and the circumference of their head tends to be unusually small—a trait associated with lower IQ scores. Only the most intensive care after birth will give these babies a fighting chance to have a "normal" life.

In rare cases during the later months of pregnancy heavy crack use can lead to an embolism (a blood clot) that lodges in a fetal vessel and completely disrupts the blood supply to an organ or a limb. The result is a deformed arm or leg, a missing section of an intestine or kidney, or other deformities.

Cocaine exposure affects brain chemistry as well. The drug alters the actions of neurotransmitters, the messengers that travel between nerve cells and help control a person's mood and responsiveness. Such changes may help explain the behavioral problems, including impulsiveness and moodiness, seen in cocaine-exposed children as they mature.

Repeated use of crack cocaine while pregnant in combination with other drugs can adversely impact the fetus in a variety of ways. (The other drugs that are used can also damage the fetus.) The children born to pregnant mothers who used crack cocaine have become known as "crack babies" and "crack kids." A few of them have severe physical deformities from which they will never recover. In others, the damage can be more subtle, showing up as behavioral problems that may sabotage their schooling and social development. Many of these children look and act like other children, but their early exposure to cocaine makes them less able to overcome negative influences, such as a disruptive home life.

Crack children often ring up huge bills for medical treatment and other care. Some grow up in dysfunctional families and increasingly display behavioral and emotional disorders as they grow older. The injury during gestation is often compounded after birth by an environment of neglect, poverty, and violence. Even after mothers give birth to drug-impaired children, their addiction to crack cocaine is so strong that many tend to continue using the drug.

How can such children be helped? What seems to work is a combination of the social services carrot and the legal stick. The best way to rescue a crack child is to rescue the mother as well. The most successful programs for addicted mothers offer a variety of assistance beginning with detoxification, then extending to pediatric services for the child, psychological and job counseling for the mother, and extensive parenting classes. Crack children often need extensive medical services, social services, and specialized educational services. All of these services need to be backed up with the threat of legal intervention, including threat of removal of the child to foster care through the protective services system.

Some studies have shown that cocaine-exposed infants can catch up in weight, length, and head circumference by 1 year of age (Papalia et al., 2001). They may also catch up in other ways, so it is important for people who care for such children and for policy makers not to give up on them—they can be helped after birth.

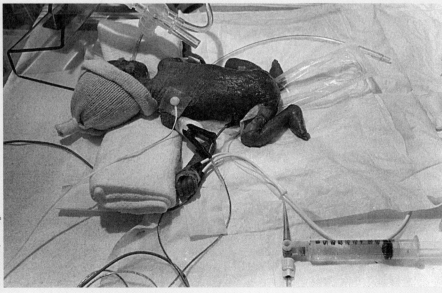

This mother of this premature baby at Interfaith Hospital in Brooklyn, New York, used cocaine and alcohol.

© John Griffin / The Image Works

Overdoses can cause convulsions and coma, and, in rare cases, death by respiratory failure. All opiates are now recognized as highly addictive.

Opiate addiction occurs when the user takes the drug regularly for a period of time. Whether addiction will occur depends on the opiate drug taken, the strength of the dosages, the regularity of use, the characteristics of the user, and the length of time taken—sometimes as short as a few weeks. Users rapidly develop a tolerance, and may eventually need a dose that is up to one hundred times stronger than a dose that would have been fatal during the initiation to the drug (Abadinsky, 1989).

The withdrawal process is very unpleasant. Symptoms include chills, cramps, sweating, nervousness, anxiety, running eyes and nose, dilated pupils, muscle aches, increased blood pressure, severe cramps, sometimes extreme nausea, and a fever. Most addicts are obsessed with securing a fix to avoid these severe withdrawal symptoms.

Addiction to opiates is extremely difficult to break, partly because an intense craving for the drug may recur periodically for several months afterward. Most opiate addicts are under 30, of a low socioeconomic status, and poorly educated. A disproportionate number are African Americans. Distribution and addiction to narcotic drugs occur primarily in large urban centers.

Heroin is the most widely abused opiate. In addition to the above-mentioned effects, heroin slows the functioning parts of the brain. The user's appetite and sex drive tend to be dulled. After an initial feeling of euphoria, the user generally becomes lethargic and stuporous. Contrary to popular belief, most heroin users take the drug infrequently and do not, as a rule, become addicted (Abadinsky, 1989), although frequent use is highly addictive.

When heroin was first discovered in the late 1880s, it was initially used as a painkiller, as a substitute for morphine, and as a drug taken by many to experience euphoria. A fair number of people became addicted, and in the early 1900s laws were passed to prohibit its sale, possession, and distribution.

Heroin abuse continues to be regarded by some Americans as our most serious drug problem. This stereotype does not appear warranted because only a tiny fraction of the U.S. population has ever tried heroin. In addition, such drugs as alcohol and barbiturates contribute to many more deaths.

One reason heroin has the reputation it does is because users are thought to be "dope fiends" who commit many violent crimes, and who reject the values of contemporary society. Addicts, however, are unlikely to commit violent crimes such as rape or aggravated assault. They are more apt to commit crimes against property (shoplifting, burglary, pickpocketing, larceny, and robbery) in order to support their habit (Kornblum & Julian, 1998). Prostitution among female addicts is also common. Because the severe withdrawal symptoms begin about 18 hours after the last fix, addicts who have experienced these symptoms will do almost anything to avoid them.

Unsanitary injections of heroin may cause hepatitis and other infections. Communal use of needles can spread AIDS. Also, the high cost of maintaining a heroin habit—often over $100 daily—may create huge financial problems for the user.

Because the price of illicit narcotic drugs is so high, organized crime has made huge profits in the smuggling and distribution of these drugs. Often, such drugs are diluted with dangerous impurities, which pose serious health hazards for the users. And, unfortunately, addicts are often economically forced into illegal activities to maintain their daily supply in order to avoid the withdrawal symptoms.

Hallucinogens. Hallucinogens were popular as psychedelic drugs in the late 1960s. These drugs distort the user's perceptions, creating hallucinations consisting of sensory impressions of "sights and sounds" that do not exist. The six hallucinogens most commonly used in this country are mescaline (peyote), psilocybin, psilocin, LSD, PCP, and ecstasy. All are taken orally—for example, in capsule form, on a sugar cube, or licked from the back of a stamp.

Peyote is derived from a cactus plant. Mescaline is the synthetic form of peyote. Psilocybin and psilocin are found in approximately 90 different species of mushrooms. They have been called "magic mushrooms." Both peyote and psilocybin have had a long history of use by certain Native American tribes. Members of the Native American Church, a religious organization, have won the legal right to use peyote on ceremonial occasions (Robertson, 1980).

By far the most popular hallucinogen is LSD (lysergic acid diethylamide). LSD is a synthetic material derived from a fungus (ergot) that grows on rye and other plants. It is one of the most potent drugs known; a single ounce will make up to 300,000 doses.

The effects of LSD vary a great deal depending on the expectations and psychological state of the user, and the context in which it is taken. A given person may experience differing reactions on different occasions. The effects that can be experienced include the apparent "seeing" of sounds; "hearing" of color; colors seeming unusually bright and shifting kaleidoscopically; exaggerations of color and sound; and objects appearing to expand and contract. Users become highly suggestible and easily manipulated.

Bizarre hallucinations are also common. The experience may be peaceful or may result in panic. Some users have developed severe emotional disturbances that resulted in long-term hospitalization. Usually a "trip" will last 6 to 16 hours. Physical reactions include increased heartbeat, goose bumps, dilated pupils, hyperactivity, tremors, and increased sweating. Aftereffects include acute anxiety or depression. Flashbacks sometimes occur after the actual drug experience. Flashbacks may happen at any time and place, with no advance warning. If the user is driving a car when a flashback occurs, a life-threatening condition is present for the user and for others in the vicinity.

There is no evidence of physical or psychological dependence on LSD among users. Users do develop tolerance to the drug very rapidly as the effects can only be achieved in the future by larger doses. Cessation of use, even for a few days, will restore sensitivity to the drug, enabling the user to take smaller quantities to experience the effects.

Phencyclidine (better known as PCP) was developed in the 1950s as an anesthetic. This medical use was soon terminated because patients displayed symptoms of severe emotional disturbance after receiving the drug. PCP is used legally today to tranquilize elephants and monkeys, as they apparently do not have the adverse side effects.

PCP is primarily used by young people who are often unaware of its hazards. It is usually smoked, often after being sprinkled on a marijuana joint. It may also be sniffed, swallowed, or injected.

PCP is a very dangerous drug. It distorts the senses, disrupts balance, and leads to an inability to think clearly. Effects produced are similar to those of hallucinogens. Larger amounts of PCP may cause a person to become paranoid, lead to aggressive behavior, and may cause the user to display temporary symptoms of severe emotional disturbance. Continued use can lead to prolonged emotional disturbance. Overdose can result in coma or even death. Research has not yet concluded whether PCP induces physical and/or psychological dependence. The drug has a potential to be used (and abused) extensively, as it is relatively easy to prepare in a home laboratory, with the ingredients and recipes being widely available. An additional danger of PCP is that even one-time users sometimes have flashbacks in which the hallucinations are re-experienced, even long after use has ceased.

The effects and dangers of mescaline, psilocybin, and psilocin are similar to those of LSD and PCP. The latter two, however, are the most potent of these hallucinogens.

Ecstasy was developed and patented in the early 1900s as a chemical forerunner in the synthesis of pharmaceuticals. Chemically, ecstasy is similar to a stimulant, amphet-amine, and to a hallucinogen, mescaline, as it can produce both stimulant and psychedelic effects. Effects last for approximately 3 to 6 hours, although confusion, depression, sleep problems, anxiety, and paranoia have been reported to occur even weeks after the drug is taken. Ecstasy is used, sometimes, by young adults at all-night dance parties, such as "raves." The stimulant effects of ecstasy enable users to dance for extended periods.

Ecstasy use in high doses can be extremely dangerous. It can lead to dehydration, hypertension, and heart or kidney failure. It can cause a marked increase in body temperature. Chronic use of ecstasy can produce long-lasting, perhaps permanent damage to the neurons that release serotonin, and consequent memory impairment.

Tobacco. The use of tobacco has now become recognized as one of the most damaging drug habits in the United States. Smoking can cause emphysema, cancer of the mouth, ulcers, and lung cancer, and it reduces life expectancy. It significantly increases the risk of strokes and heart disease, particularly in women who use birth control pills. Smoking by a pregnant woman sometimes leads to miscarriages, premature births, and the child being born underweight. Yet, in spite of these widely publicized hazards, about 25 percent of the adult population continues to smoke (Noah, 1997).

Tobacco is the number-one killer drug. It contributes to far more deaths than all other drugs combined (Noah, 1997). Tobacco is estimated to contribute to more than 400,000 deaths per year in the United States. This is more than double the number of deaths attributed to alcohol abuse and hundreds of times the number of deaths due to cocaine. Most of the tobacco-related deaths are the results of diseases such as heart disease and lung cancer. However, over 2,000 deaths per year result from fires caused by careless smoking (Noah, 1997). There is also substantial evidence that "passive smoking" (breathing the smoke from others' cigarettes, cigars, or pipes) is also hazardous to health. One source of evidence for this is that young children whose parents smoke have a higher incidence of pneumonia and other respiratory disorders than young children whose parents do not smoke (Noah, 1997).

In 1988, the then surgeon general of the United States, C. Everett Koop, declared that tobacco is as addictive as heroin or cocaine (Rosellini, 1988). Koop noted that people addicted to tobacco are drug addicts. The attitudes of Americans toward tobacco use are gradually becoming more negative. In the early 1990s a movement developed that is increasingly viewing tobacco as a dangerous drug, and nonsmokers are increasingly considering smokers to

Despite vigorous anticigarette campaigns, the proportion of adolescent smokers has remained the same for the last 10 years.

be pariahs. Some authorities are now predicting that cigarettes will someday be outlawed in many countries.

Tobacco is highly habit-forming. Nicotine is the primary drug in tobacco. Nicotine has remarkable capacities—it can act as a depressant, a stimulant, or a tranquilizer. Smokers quickly develop a tolerance for nicotine and often gradually tend to increase consumption to one or two packs or more a day.

Special clinics and a variety of other educational and therapeutic programs help people quit smoking. Withdrawal from use leads users to become restless, irritable, depressed, and to have an intense craving to smoke.

At the same time that the government is widely publicizing the hazards of drugs, the Department of Agriculture is subsidizing tobacco farmers. Educational programs urge people not to smoke, while tobacco companies are permitted to advertise that cigarette smoking is "cool" and "sexy," connoting rugged manliness in men and social sophistication in women. Studies show that only a minority of smokers who make determined efforts to quit actually succeed (Noah, 1997).

In the biggest civil settlement in U.S. history, tobacco companies agreed in 1998 to pay more than $240 billion to the 50 states to settle claims against the industry for health-care costs blamed on tobacco-related illnesses. The payments to the states will be distributed over 25 years (payments began in 2000). A portion of the funds will go to a foundation to study how to reduce teen smoking. A major objective of the deal is to discourage children from smoking by restrictions on advertising and by imposing sharp limits on the ways that cigarettes are marketed.

Marijuana. Marijuana, or "grass" or "pot," comes from a variety of the hemp plant, *Cannabis sativa*. This hemp plant grows throughout the world, and its fibers are legally used to produce rope, twine, paper, and clothing.

The main use of the plant now, however, centers on its dried leaves—marijuana—and on its dried resin—hashish. Both may be taken orally, but are usually smoked. Hashish is several times more potent than marijuana.

The effects of marijuana (and hashish) vary, as with any other drug, according to the mood and personality of the user, according to circumstances, and according to the quality of the drug. The effects are rather complicated and may induce a variety of emotions.

Many of the effects are produced because marijuana has sedative properties and creates in the user a sense of relaxed well-being and freedom from inhibition. There may also be mild hallucinations that create a dreamy state in which the user may experience fantasies. Smokers become highly suggestible and may engage in actions (such as sexual activities) in which they would not otherwise be involved. The drug may induce feelings of joyousness, hilarity, and sociability. It may lead to talkativeness, disconnected ideas, a feeling of floating, and laughter. It may also intensify sensory stimulation, create feelings of enhanced awareness and creativity, and increase self-confidence. A person may gradually experience some of these emotions, followed by others.

The threat of physical dependence is rated low, while the threat of psychological dependence is rated as moderate. Withdrawal, however, may be very unpleasant for the user who may suffer from insomnia, hyperactivity, and loss of appetite.

The short-term physical effects of marijuana are minor: a reddening of the eyes, dryness of the throat and the mouth, and a slight rise in heart rate. There is some evidence that continued use by young teenagers will result in these users becoming apathetic, noncompetitive, and uninterested in school and other activities.

Frequent users may have impairments of short-term memory and concentration, and of judgment and coordination. They may find it difficult to read, or to understand what they read, or to follow moving objects with their eyes. Users may feel confident that their coordination, reactions, and perceptions are quite normal while they are still experiencing the effects of the drug; under these conditions such activities as driving a vehicle may have tragic consequences for them and for others.

An overdose of the active ingredients of cannabis can lead to panic, fear, confusion, suspiciousness, fatigue, and sometimes aggressive acts. One of the most frequently voiced concerns about marijuana is that it will be a "stepping-stone" to using other drugs. About 60 percent of marijuana users "progress" to using other drugs (*Hope Health Letter,* 1991). However, other factors, such as peer pressure, are probably more crucial determinants of what mind-altering drugs people will "progress" to use.

The attempt to restrict the use of marijuana through legislation has been described as a "second prohibition," which has had results similar to those of the first, because a large number of people are using the drug in a disregard of the law. The unfortunate effect of laws that attempt to regulate acts (crimes as defined by law) without victims is that they criminalize the private acts of many people who are otherwise law abiding. Such laws also foster the development of organized crime and the illicit drug market.

For years, debates have raged about the hazards of long-term marijuana use. Some studies claim it may cause brain damage, chromosome damage, irritation of the bronchial tract and lungs, and a reduction in male hormone levels. These findings have not been confirmed by other studies, and so the controversy rages on.

In 1982 the National Academy of Sciences completed an extensive, 15-month study on marijuana. The study found no evidence that marijuana causes permanent changes in the nervous system and concluded that the drug probably does not break down human chromosomes. It also found that marijuana may be useful in treating glaucoma, asthma, certain seizure disorders and spastic conditions, and in controlling severe nausea caused by cancer chemotherapy. The study warned, however, that the drug presents a variety of short-term health risks and justifies "serious national concern." One of the reversible, short-term health effects is impairment of motor coordination, which adversely affects driving or machine-operating skills. The drug also impairs short-term memory, slows learning abilities, and may cause periods of confusion and anxiety. The study also found evidence that smoking marijuana may affect the lungs and respiratory system in much the same way that tobacco smoke does, and may be a factor in causing bronchitis and precancerous changes. Thus, the study found some evidence that marijuana may lead to certain adverse, long-term health problems. The major recommendation was that "there be a greatly intensified and more-comprehensive program of research into the effects of marijuana on the health of the American people" (National Academy of Sciences, 1982). Such extensive research has not yet been conducted.

In 1996 voters in California and Arizona approved the medical use of marijuana—for example, for treating symptoms of AIDS, cancer, and other diseases. However, the Clinton administration threatened sanctions against doctors who prescribed it. In 1997 a panel of experts convened at the National Institutes of Health stated that marijuana shows promise in treating painful symptoms of some diseases and urged that its medical use should be studied further (Leary, 1997). A total of nine states soon passed legislation that allowed marijuana to be used for medical purposes.

In 2001 the U.S. Supreme Court ruled that federal law definitely classifies the use of marijuana as illegal, and that marijuana has no medical benefits worthy of an exception. The high court did not strike down state laws allowing medical use of marijuana, but it left those distributing the drug for that purpose open to prosecution. The controversy over the medical use of marijuana will probably continue to be an issue.

Anabolic Steroids. Anabolic steroids are synthetic male hormones. Although steroids have been banned for use by athletes in organized sports competition, steroids are still being used by some athletes, bodybuilders, and teenagers who want to look more muscular and brawny. From early childhood, many boys have been socialized to believe that the ideal man looks something like Mr. Universe.

Many adolescents who use steroids want to be sports champions. Steroids are derivatives of the male hormone testosterone. Some young male bodybuilders who use steroids to promote tissue growth and to endure arduous workouts routinely flood their bodies with 100 times the testosterone they produce naturally (Schrof, 1992). Most steroid users are middle class and white.

Steroid-enhanced physiques are a hazardous prize. Steroids can cause temporary acne and balding, upset hormonal production, and damage the heart and kidneys. Doctors suspect they may contribute to liver cancer and atherosclerosis (Toufexis, 1989). For teens, the drugs can stunt growth by accelerating bone maturation. Male steroid users have also experienced a shrinking of the testicles, impotence, a yellowing of the skin and eyes, and the development of female-type breasts. In young boys, steroids can have the effect of painfully enlarging the sex organs. In female users, the voice deepens permanently, breasts shrink, periods become irregular, the clitoris swells in size, and hair is lost from the head but grows on the face and body.

Steroid drug users are prone to moodiness, depression, and irritability. Users are apt to experience difficulty in tolerating stress. Some males (who had been easygoing prior to steroid use) experience raging hostility after prolonged use, which is displayed in a variety of ways—ranging from being obnoxious to continually provoking physical fights. Some users become so depressed that they commit suicide.

Steroid users generally experience considerable difficulty in terminating steroids after prolonged use. One reason is that bulging biceps and ham-hock thighs soon fade when steroid use is discontinued. Concurrent with the decline in muscle mass is the psychological feeling of being less powerful and less "manly." Most users who try to quit wind up back on the drug. A self-image that relies on a steroid-enhanced physique is difficult to change.

Dependence on Alcohol and Other Drugs

Habit-forming drugs can lead to *dependence,* which is a tendency or craving for the repeated use or compulsive use (not necessarily abuse) of a chemical. This dependence may be physical, psychological, or both. When physical dependence occurs, the user will generally experience bodily withdrawal symptoms when drug use is discontinued. Withdrawal may take many forms and range in severity from slight tremblings to fatal convulsions.

When psychological dependence occurs, the user feels psychological discomfort if use is terminated. Dependent users also tend to believe that they will use the chemical for the rest of their lives as a regular part of social/recreational activities. They also question whether the desired emotional state can be achieved without the use of the chemical, and they have a preoccupation with thinking and talking about the chemical and activities associated with using it.

Users also generally develop a *tolerance* for some drugs, which means they have to take increasing amounts over time to achieve a given level of effect. Tolerance partly depends on the type of drug, because some drugs (such as aspirin) do not create tolerance.

Drug addiction is difficult to define. In a broad sense addiction refers to an intense craving for a particular substance. The problem is this definition could be applied to an intense craving for a variety of substances—pickles, ice cream, potato chips, strawberry shortcake. To avoid this problem we will define *addiction* as an intense craving for a drug that develops after a period of heavy use.

Why Do People Use and Abuse Alcohol and Other Drugs? The effects of using drugs are numerous, ranging from feeling light-headed to death through over-dosing. Drug abuse may lead to deterioration in health, relationship problems, automobile accidents, child abuse and spouse abuse, loss of job, low self-esteem, loss of social status, financial disaster, divorce, and arrests and convictions.

A distinction needs to be made between responsible drug use and drug abuse. Many drugs do have beneficial effects when used responsibly; aspirin relieves pain, alcohol helps people relax, tranquilizers reduce anxiety, antidepressant drugs reduce depression, amphetamines increase alertness, morphine is a painkiller, and marijuana is useful in treating glaucoma. Irresponsible drug use is abuse, which was defined earlier in this chapter.

Why do people abuse drugs? The reasons are numerous. Drug companies widely advertise the beneficial effects of their products. The media (such as television and movies) glamorize the mind-altering effects. Many popular songs highlight drinking. Taverns and cocktail lounges have become centers for socializing, and promote drinking. Through such channels, Americans have become socialized to accept drug usage as a part of daily living. Socialization patterns lead many people to use drugs, and for some the use is a stepping-stone to abuse.

Attitudes toward drug use also encourage abuse. For example, some college students believe that they should get blitzed or stoned after a tough exam. Ryne Duren (1985), former pitcher for the New York Yankees, asked this question: "I started becoming an alcoholic at age four, even though I had my first drink at age nine—how can this be?" Duren went on to explain that at a very young age he became socialized to believe that a real man was "someone who could drink others under the table," and that the way to have fun was to get high on alcohol.

People abuse drugs for a variety of reasons. Some people build up a tolerance to a drug, and then increase the dosage to obtain a high. Physical and psychological dependence usually leads to abuse. People with intense unwanted emotions (such as intense loneliness, anxiety, feelings of inadequacy, guilt, depression, insecurity, and resentment) may turn to drugs to relieve the intensity of their unwanted emotions. For many abusers their drug of choice becomes their best friend because they tend to personalize it and value it more highly than they value their friends. The drug is something that they can always count on to relieve pain or give them the kind of high they desire. Many abusers become so highly attached to their drug that they choose to continue using it even though it leads to deterioration of health, divorce, discharges from jobs, automobile accidents, alienation from children, loss of friends, depletion of financial resources, and court appearances. Drug abusers usually feel they need their drug as a crutch to make it through the day.

Abusers develop an intimate relationship with their drug of choice. Even though this relationship is unhealthy, the drug plays a primary role in the abuser's life, dictates a certain lifestyle, fills a psychological need, and more often than not takes precedence over family, friends, and work. Most abusers *deny* their drug usage is creating problems for them, because they know that admitting they have a drug problem means they will have to end their relationship with their best friend, and they deeply believe they need their drug to handle their daily concerns and pressures. Drug abusers are apt to use the following defense mechanisms in order to continue using drugs. They *rationalize* adverse consequences of drug abuse (such as the loss of a job) by twisting or distorting reality to explain the consequences of their behavior while under the influence. They *minimize* the adverse consequences of their drug use. They use *projection* to place the blame for their problems on others; for example, "If you had a wife like mine, you'd drink too."

Theories about Drug Use. There are also a variety of theories as to why people use drugs. *Biological theories* assert that physiological changes produced by the drugs eventually generate an irresistible craving for the drug. Some biological theories also postulate that some people are predisposed by their genetic structure to abuse certain types of drugs. For example, some authorities believe that genes play a role in predisposing some people to alcoholism. *Behavioral theories* hold that people use drugs because they find them pleasurable and continue to use them because doing so prevents withdrawal distress. *Interactionist theories* maintain that drug use is learned from interaction with others in our culture. For example, people drink alcohol because drinking is widely accepted. Interactionist theories assert that those who use such illegal drugs as marijuana or cocaine have contact with a drug subculture that encourages them to experiment with illegal drugs.

Interaction in Family Systems: A Theoretical Approach to Drug Abuse

Wegscheider (1981) maintains that chemical dependency is a family disease that involves and affects each family member. Although she focuses on the families of alcoholics, much of what she says also frequently applies to the families of other types of chemical substance abusers.

She cites several rules that tend to characterize the families of drug abusers. First, the dependent person's alcohol use becomes "the most important thing in the

family's life" (Wegscheider, 1981, p. 81). The abuser's top priority is getting enough alcohol, and the family's top priorities are the abuser, the abuser's behavior, and keeping the abuser away from alcohol. The goals of the abuser and of the rest of his or her family are at completely opposite poles.

A second rule in an alcoholic family is that alcohol is not the cause of the problem. Denial is paramount. A third family rule maintains that the dependent person is really not responsible for his or her behavior and that the alcohol causes the behavior. There is always someone or something else to blame. Another rule dictates that no one should rock the boat, no matter what. Family members strive to protect the family's status quo, even when the family is miserable. Yet other rules concern forbidding discussion of the family problem either within or outside of the family, and consistently avoiding stating one's true feelings. Wegscheider maintains that these rules act to protect the dependent person from taking responsibility for his or her behavior, and that the rules actually serve to maintain the drinking problem.

Wegscheider goes on to identify several roles that are typically played by family members. In addition to the chemically dependent person, there is the chief enabler, the family hero, the scapegoat, the lost child, and the mascot.

The chief enabler's main purpose is to assume the primary responsibility for family functioning. The abuser typically continues to lose control and relinquishes responsibility. The chief enabler, on the other hand, takes more and more responsibility and begins making more and more of the family's decisions. A chief enabler is often the parent or spouse of the chemically dependent person.

Conditions in families of chemically dependent people often continue to deteriorate as the dependent persons lose control. A positive influence is needed to offset the negative. The family hero fulfills this role. The family hero is often the person who does well at everything he or she tries. The hero works hard at making the family look like it is functioning better than it is. In this way the family hero provides the family with self-worth.

Another typical role played by someone in the chemically dependent family is that of the scapegoat. Although the alcohol abuse is the real problem, a family rule mandates that this fact must be denied. Therefore, the blame must be placed elsewhere. Frequently, another family member is blamed for the problem. The scapegoat often behaves in negative ways that draw attention to him or her (for example, the person gets caught for stealing, runs away, becomes extremely withdrawn). The scapegoat's role is to distract attention away from the dependent person and onto something else. This role helps the family avoid addressing the problem of chemical dependency.

Often, there is also a lost child in the family. This is the person who seems rather uninvolved with the rest of the family, yet never causes any trouble. The lost child's purpose is to provide relief to the family from some of the pain it is suffering. At least there is someone in the family who neither requires much attention, nor causes any stress. The lost child is simply just there.

Finally, chemically dependent families often have someone playing the role of mascot. The mascot is the person who probably has a good sense of humor and appears not to take anything seriously. Despite how much the mascot might be suffering inside, he or she provides a little fun for the family.

In summary, chemical dependency is a problem affecting the entire family. Each family member is suffering from the chemical dependency, yet each assumes a role in order to maintain the family's status quo and to help the family survive. Family members are driven to maintain these roles no matter what happens. The roles eventually become associated with survival.

The Application of Theory to Client Situations: Treatment for the Chemically Dependent Person and His or Her Family

One of the first tasks in treatment is for the chemically dependent person to take responsibility for his or her own behavior. The abuser must acknowledge that he or she has a problem before beginning to solve it. Several concepts involving working with the family are critical (Wegscheider, 1981). Family members must first come to realize the extent of the problem. They need to identify the chemical abuse as their major problem. Additionally, they need to learn about and evaluate their family dynamics. They need to evaluate their own behavior and break out of the roles that were maintaining the dependent person's abuse. The chief enabler, in particular, must stop making excuses and assuming the dependent person's responsibility. If the dependent one is sick from a hangover and cannot make it to school or work the next day, it must be the dependent one's responsibility, not a parent's or spouse's, to call in sick.

Family members eventually learn to confront the chemically dependent person and give him or her honest information about his or her behavior. For instance, they are encouraged to tell the dependent exactly how he or she behaved while having a blackout. If the dependent person hit another family member while drunk, this fact

needs to be confronted. The confrontation should occur not in an emotional manner but rather in a factual one.

The family also needs to learn about the progression of the disease. We've already discussed some characteristics of drug dependence. Figure 11.2 portrays the typical progression of an alcoholic's feelings and behavior. At first only occasional relief drinking occurs. Drinking becomes more constant. The dependent person then begins to drink in secret and to feel guilty about drinking. Memory blackouts begin to occur and gradually increase in frequency. The dependent person feels worse and worse about his or her drinking behavior, but seems to have less and less control over it. Finally, the drinking begins to seriously affect the person's work, family, and social relationships. A job may be lost or all school classes flunked. Perhaps, family members leave or throw the dependent person out. The dependent person's thinking becomes more and more impaired.

Eventually, the dependent person hits rock bottom. Nothing seems to be left but despair and failure, and the dependent person admits complete defeat. It is at this point that the dependent person may make one of two choices. Either he or she will continue on the downward spiral to a probable death related to alcohol or may desperately struggle. Typically during this period, the dependent one will make some progress only to slip back again. Vicious cycles of drinking and stopping are often apparent.

Finally, the dependent person may express an honest desire for help. A dependent person on the path to recovery will stop drinking. Meeting with other people who are also alcoholics or addicts is also very helpful. Support from others at this time in the process of recovery is especially critical.

Alcoholics Anonymous (AA) is a self-help organization that has provided the support, information, and guidance necessary for many dependent people to continue on in their recovery. The nationwide group is made up of recovering alcoholics. The organization's success seems to rest on several principles. First, other people who really understand are available to give the recovering dependent person friendship and warmth. Each new member is given a sponsor who can be called for support at any time during the day or night. Whenever the dependent person feels depressed or tempted, there is always the sponsor to turn to.

AA provides the recovering alcoholic with a new social group and activities. The recovering alcoholic can no longer participate in the drinking activity. Old friends with well-established drinking patterns usually become difficult to associate with; often social pressure is applied to drink again. AA provides a respite from such pressure

FIGURE 11.2 Alcohol Addiction and Recovery

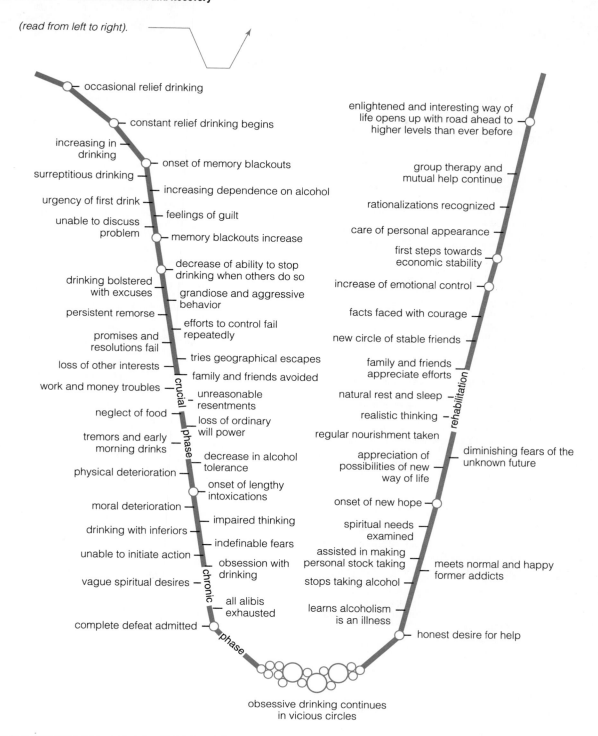

(read from left to right).

occasional relief drinking

constant relief drinking begins

increasing in drinking

surreptitious drinking

onset of memory blackouts

urgency of first drink

increasing dependence on alcohol

unable to discuss problem

feelings of guilt

memory blackouts increase

decrease of ability to stop drinking when others do so

drinking bolstered with excuses

grandiose and aggressive behavior

persistent remorse

efforts to control fail repeatedly

promises and resolutions fail

tries geographical escapes

loss of other interests

family and friends avoided

work and money troubles

unreasonable resentments

neglect of food

loss of ordinary will power

tremors and early morning drinks

decrease in alcohol tolerance

physical deterioration

onset of lengthy intoxications

moral deterioration

impaired thinking

drinking with inferiors

indefinable fears

unable to initiate action

obsession with drinking

vague spiritual desires

all alibis exhausted

complete defeat admitted

crucial phase

chronic phase

enlightened and interesting way of life opens up with road ahead to higher levels than ever before

group therapy and mutual help continue

rationalizations recognized

care of personal appearance

first steps towards economic stability

increase of emotional control

facts faced with courage

new circle of stable friends

family and friends appreciate efforts

natural rest and sleep

realistic thinking

regular nourishment taken

appreciation of possibilities of new way of life

onset of new hope

spiritual needs examined

assisted in making personal stock taking

stops taking alcohol

learns alcoholism is an illness

honest desire for help

diminishing fears of the unknown future

meets normal and happy former addicts

rehabilitation

obsessive drinking continues in vicious circles

Source: M. M. Glatt, "Group Therapy in Alcoholism," British Journal of Addiction 54 (2). Used by permission of the Society for the Study of Addiction, Edinburgh, Scotland

Highlight 11.5

An AA Meeting

Alcoholics Anonymous is a remarkable human organization. Its chapters now cover every part of the United States and most of the world. There is more caring and concern among the members for one another than in most other organizations. Group members work together to save the lives of each other and to restore self-respect and sense of worth. AA has helped more people overcome their drinking problems than all other therapies and methods combined.

AA is supported entirely by voluntary donations from the members at meetings. There are no dues or fees. Each chapter is autonomous, and free of any outside control by the AA headquarters in New York City or by any other body. There is no hierarchy in the chapters. The only office is that of the group secretary. This person chooses a chairperson for each meeting, makes the arrangements for meetings, and sees that the building is open, the chairs are set up, and the tea and coffee put on. The group secretary holds office for only a limited time period; after a month or two the secretary's responsibilities are transferred to another member.

The only requirement for membership in AA is a desire to stop drinking. All other variables (such as economic status, social status, race, religion) do not count. Members can even attend meetings while drunk, as long as they do not disturb the meeting.

AA meetings are held in a variety of physical locations—churches, temples, private homes, business offices, schools, libraries, or banquet rooms of restaurants. The physical location is thus unimportant.

When a newcomer first arrives, he or she will usually find people setting up chairs, placing ashtrays, putting free literature on a table, and making coffee. Other members will be socializing in small groups. Someone is apt to introduce himself or herself and other members to the newcomer. If someone is shy about attending the first meeting alone, he or she can call AA and someone will take the person to the meeting and introduce him or her to the other members.

When the meeting starts, everyone sits down around tables or in rows of chairs. The secretary and/or chairperson, and one or more speakers, sit at the head of the table or on a platform if the meeting is in a hall.

The chairperson opens with a moment of silence, which is followed by a group recitation of a nondenominational prayer. The chairperson then reads or gives a brief description of Alcoholics Anonymous and may read or refer to a section of the book *Alcoholics Anonymous*

(a book that describes the principles of AA and gives a number of case examples).

Then, the chairperson usually asks if anyone is attending for the first, second, or third time. The new people are asked to introduce themselves according to the following: "Hello, my name is [first name], and this is my first [second, third] meeting." Those who do not want to introduce themselves are not pressured to do so. New members are the lifeblood of AA, and are the most important people at the meeting in the members' eyes. (All the longer-term members remember their first meeting and how frightened and inhibited they felt.)

If the group is small, the chairperson usually then asks the longer term members to introduce themselves and say a few words. If the group is large; the chairperson asks volunteers among the longer term members to introduce themselves by saying a few words. Each member usually begins by saying, "My name is [first name]; I am an alcoholic" and then discloses a few thoughts or feelings. (The members do not have to say they are alcoholic, unless they choose to do so. Each member sooner or later generally chooses to say this, to remind himself or herself that he or she is an addictive drinker who is recovering and that alcoholism is a lifelong disease, which must be battled daily.) Those who introduce themselves usually say whatever they feel will be most helpful to the newcomers. They may talk about their first meeting, or their first week without drinking, or something designed to make the newcomers more comfortable. Common advice for the newcomers is to get the phone numbers of other members after the meeting so that they can call a member when they feel a strong urge to drink. AA considers such help as vital in recovering. The organization believes members can remain sober only through receiving the help of people who care about them and who understand what they are struggling with.

AA members want newcomers to call when they have the urge to drink, at any time day or night. The members sincerely believe that by helping others they are helping themselves to stay sober and grow. Members indicate that such calling is the newcomer's ace in the hole against the first drink, if everything else fails. They also inform newcomers that it is good to call others when lonely, just to chat.

In his own words, a newcomer explains how AA began to help him:

> *Here's what happened to me. When I finally hit bottom and called AA for help, a U.S. Air Force officer came to tell me about AA. For the first time in my life, I was*

and the opportunity to meet new people, if such an opportunity is needed. For more on AA, see Highlight 11.5.

AA also helps the recovering person to understand that alcoholism is a disease. This means that the alcoholic cannot cure himself or herself. He or she need no longer feel guilty about being an alcoholic. What must be done is to

stop drinking. AA also encourages introspection. Members are encouraged to look inside themselves and face whatever they see. They are urged to acknowledge that they have flaws and will never be perfect. This perspective often helps people to stop fleeing from the pain of reality and hiding in alcohol or drugs. It helps them to redefine

talking to someone who obviously really understood my problem, as four psychiatrists had not, and he took me to my first meeting, sober but none too steady. It was amazing. I went home afterward and didn't have a drink. I went again the next night, still dry, and the miracle happened a second time. The third morning my wife went off to work, my boys to school, and I was alone. Suddenly I wanted a drink more than I had ever wanted one in my life. I tried walking for a while. No good. The feeling was getting worse. I tried reading. Couldn't concentrate. Then I became really desperate, and although I wasn't used to calling strangers for help, I called Fred, an AAer who had said that he was retired and would welcome a call at any time. We talked a bit; he could see that talking on the phone wasn't going to be enough. He said, "Look, I've got an idea. Let me make a phone call, and I'll call you back in ten minutes. Can you hold on that long?" I said I could. He called back in eight, asking me to come over to his house. We talked endlessly, went out for a sandwich together, and finally my craving for a drink went away. We went to a meeting. Next morning I was fine again and now I had gone four days without a drink.[1]

After such discussion, speakers may describe their life of drinking, how drinking almost destroyed their life, how they were introduced to AA, their struggles to remain sober one day at a time, how AA has helped them, and what their life is now like.

At the end of a meeting the chairperson may ask the newcomers if they wish to say anything. If they do not wish to say much, that is okay. No one is pressured to self-disclose what they do not want to reveal.

Meetings usually end after the chairperson makes announcements. (The collection basket for donations is also passed around. New members are not expected, and frequently not allowed, to donate any money until after the third meeting. If someone cannot afford to make a donation, none is expected.) The group then stands, usually holding hands, and repeats in unison the Lord's Prayer. Those who do not want to join in this prayer are not pressured to do so. After a meeting the members socialize. This is a time for newcomers to meet new friends and to get phone numbers.

AA is a cross-section of people from all walks of life. Anonymity is emphasized. It is the duty of every member to respect the anonymity of every person who attends. Concern for anonymity is a major reason for two kinds of meetings in AA, open and closed. Anyone is welcome at open meetings. Only people with drinking problems are allowed at closed meetings. Therefore, if a person feels uncomfortable going to an open meeting and has a drinking problem, then closed meetings are an alternative.

Members do not have to believe in God to get help from AA. Many members have lost, or never had, a faith in God. AA does, however, assert that faith in some higher power is a tremendous help in recovery because such a belief offers a source of limitless power, hope, and support whenever one feels one has come to the end of one's resources.

How does AA help? New members, after years of feelings of rejection, loneliness, misunderstanding, guilt, and embarrassment, find they are not alone. They feel understood by others who are in similar predicaments. Instead of being rejected, they are welcomed. They see that others who had serious drinking problems are now sober, apparently happy that way, and are in the process of recovering. It gives them hope that they do not need alcohol to get through the day and that they can learn to enjoy life without alcohol. They find that others sincerely care about them, want to help them, and have the knowledge to do so.

At meetings they see every sort of personal problem brought up and discussed openly, with suggestions for solutions being offered from others who have encountered similar problems. They can observe that group members bring up "unspeakable" problems without apparent embarrassment, and that others listen and treat them with respect and consideration. Such acceptance gradually leads newcomers to share their personal problems and to receive constructive suggestions for solutions. Such a disclosure leads individuals to look more deeply into themselves and to ventilate deep personal feelings. With the support of other members, newcomers gradually learn how to counter strong desires to drink, through such processes as calling other members.

Newcomers learn that AA is the means of staying away from that first drink. AA also serves to reduce the stress that compels people to drink by providing a comfortable and relaxed environment and by having members helping each other to find ways to reduce the stresses encountered in daily living. AA meetings and members become a safe port that is always there when storms start raging. AA helps members to be programmed from negative thinking to positive thinking. The more positive a member's thinking becomes, the more stress is relieved, the better he or she begins to feel about himself or herself, the more the compulsion to drink decreases, and the more often and more effectively the person begins to take positive actions to solve his or her problems.

1. Clark Vaughan, *Addictive Drinking* (New York: Penguin, 1984), pp. 75–76.

expectations for themselves and to gain control. Within this context, people often can also acknowledge their strengths. They can learn that they do have some control over their own behavior and that they can accomplish things for themselves and for others.

Organizations are also available to provide support for other family members and to give them information and suggestions. For example, Al-Anon is an organization for the families of alcoholics, and Al-Ateen is specifically for teenagers within these families. Likewise, self-help organizations similar to AA, such as Narcotics Anonymous, exist to help other types of chemical substance abusers.

Today a range of treatment approaches are available to chemical substance abusers. Types of facilities and treatment include inpatient and outpatient treatment programs at community mental health centers, chemical abuse rehabilitation centers and medical hospitals, halfway houses, and chemical treatment programs such as Antabuse. When Antabuse is taken, a person who then drinks an alcoholic beverage will soon become flushed, his or her pulse will quicken, and he or she will feel nauseated, often to the point of regurgitation.

Treatment programs almost always advocate that abusers abstain totally from their drug of choice in the future, because research indicates that even one use will return the abuser to drug abuse. It should also be noted that when abusers complete a treatment program they are urged to view themselves as *recovering,* rather than being cured, because they continually must work on abstaining in order to avoid the temptations of using.

It is important that those receiving treatment also make lifestyle changes. The social activities of users almost always revolve around using the drug of choice; to successfully abstain, recovering abusers need to form new friendships and establish drug-free social activities and interests. Making such lifestyle changes is extremely difficult. Many recovering addicts fail in making these changes and then return to using their drug of choice.

Roles assumed by social workers in treating addicts and family members include counselor, group facilitator, broker, program initiator, and educator. The role of a social worker in confronting denial is described in Highlight 11.6.

Understanding and Treating Codependency

Codependent people are so trapped by a loved one's addiction that they lose their own identity in the process of obsessively managing the day-to-day trauma created by the addict. Codependency is unhealthy behavior learned amid chaos. Some codependent people are as dysfunctional as the addict, if not more so. Living with addiction triggers excessive caretaking, suppression of one's needs, a feeling of low self-worth, and strained relationships. The life and identity of a codependent person becomes "enmeshed" with the everyday problems of living with an addict.

Many codependent people grow up in a dysfunctional family. (Some are adult children of alcoholics.) They

---

Highlight 11.6

Working With Alcoholic Clients: The Problem of Denial

Michael Jacobs (1981) has written an excellent handbook of counseling strategies for alcoholic persons. He addresses a variety of problems commonly encountered when working with alcoholic clients and suggests intervention strategies to deal with each. One specific problem—namely, that of denial—and the accompanying intervention strategies will be summarized here. Jacobs suggests:

> During the early phases of treatment it can be difficult to differentiate between clients who genuinely do not believe they have a problem and those who privately fear they can no longer control their drinking. One surefire way of losing clients before the distinction can be made is to demand total abstinence. Even if clients are willing to return, they are likely to be hostile and resistant, because the counselor has unwittingly compelled them to entrench their denial more deeply. Early confrontation with deniers is most ill-advised. (p. 10)

Jacobs continues that goals of the first sessions should be very basic. For instance, the client might simply agree to return for the next session. We have already established the need to help the dependent person accept responsibility for his own behavior and its effects. When working with persons who deny they are alcoholics, any confrontation should be as "unthreatening" as possible (p. 10). For instance, the social worker might ask, "If you were to stop drinking, do you think your life would be any different? If so, in what ways?," or, "Do you ever get the feeling you're having trouble controlling your drinking?"

More direct use of confrontation should be used only after a stronger relationship between worker and client has been established. It is crucial to time the confrontation well. A problem at work related to alcohol or a crisis in the marriage might provide exceptionally good possibilities for confronting the client about the effects of his drinking. For instance, the social worker might then say, "It looks like you're having a serious problem. Let's look at how it's related to drinking."

Many times it's tedious to work with a genuine denier. Jacobs (1981) warns that sometimes the client will choose to discontinue treatment when the worker places greater demands on him for self-assessment. However, "the counselor can take solace in knowing that he or she has done all that can be reasonably expected" (p. 12). The bottom line is that it is the client's choice and responsibility.

In conclusion, Jacobs notes that insight-oriented therapy, especially that which addresses reasons for drinking, is generally unsuccessful with the denial problem. On the other hand, becoming involved in a group therapy situation may encourage deniers to assess themselves and their problem, as they compare themselves to others.

marry or become romantically involved with someone who abuses alcohol or some other drug. To some extent, the addict fills the needs of the codependent ones—needs such as caretaking, loneliness, and addiction to destructive behavior such as excessive partying and thrill seeking. Codependency can be viewed as a normal reaction to abnormal stress.

If the addict terminates the use of his or her drug of choice, the codependent's dysfunctional behaviors generally continue, unless he or she receives treatment. There are a variety of treatment approaches for codependent people—individual psychotherapy, self-help groups (such as Al-Anon and Adult Children of Alcoholics), and codependency therapeutic groups. For many codependent people, treatment involves recognition that they have a life and an identity separate from the addict; that the addict alone is responsible for his or her drug abuse; and that their life and the addict's will improve by terminating their caretaking and enabling behaviors. Through treatment, many codependent people regain (or gain for the first time in their life) their own identity. Treatment is designed to banish the self-destructive habits that sabotage the codependent people's happiness.

Roles assumed by social workers in treating codependent people include: counselor; educator (through conveying information about addiction and codependency); facilitator (through leading treatment groups); broker (through linking codependent people to self-help groups and to other human service resources); and program initiator (through being a catalyst in developing needed new programs to serve codependent people in communities where treatment programs for codependent ones are scarce or nonexistent).

The Relationship Between Knowledge and Assessment

Considerable attention has been given to the issue of chemical substance abuse. It was selected because it is especially critical and widespread. For social workers to be able to intervene and help facilitate another person's recovery from chemical dependency, a base of knowledge is necessary. Social workers need to know some of the dynamics involved in the behavior of chemically dependent individuals and families, and they need to understand the concept of enabling. Only then can they assess a family accurately and know at what point intervention is needed. With this base of knowledge, skills can be applied to help family members stop their enabling and their maintenance of false rules. Social work skills can also be used to encourage the family to realign responsibility.

Other family members need to relinquish it to the chemically dependent person. In summary, the examination of such a major life issue should provide social workers with a starting point on which to begin problem assessment. The intent is to provide a map or guide to begin the process of intervention.

A Treatment Model From Another Culture: The Dutch Approach

The United States primarily uses a punitive approach with anyone found guilty of possessing or using prohibited drugs. Some advocates of a treatment approach to the drug problem point to the Netherlands as a possible model.

Coleman & Kerbo (2002, p. 412) describe the Dutch approach:

> Dutch drug policy is an interesting combination of four elements. The first is the official tolerance of "soft drugs" (marijuana and hashish—a condensed form of marijuana). Although sale is technically illegal, many cafes openly sell marijuana without fear of arrests or fines. The second is a tough enforcement effort aimed at the dealers of hard drugs, such as heroin and cocaine, that are often smuggled into Rotterdam, the world's largest port. The third element of Dutch policy is the decriminalization of all users. No one is jailed for merely using or possessing small amounts of any drug. Finally, the Dutch have made treatment and maintenance programs easily available to all addicts.

What have been the effects of this approach? The Netherlands, since the program's inception a number of years ago, has seen a sharp decline in the number of heroin addicts and an increase in their average age (indicating that fewer younger people are becoming addicted). In addition, the Netherlands has not experienced the cocaine epidemic that happened in the United States. Critics of this approach are skeptical that this treatment approach would work in the United States. They claim the Netherlands is less susceptible to drug abuse because it has less of a poverty problem (as the country has a much more generous welfare system), and it does not have large and deteriorating urban areas (Coleman & Kerbo, 2002). Critics also note that the Netherlands has the additional problem of "drug tourism"—an increasing number of travelers are specifically coming to the Netherlands to buy marijuana.

❦ Summary

Erikson asserted that middle-aged adults face the developmental crisis of generativity versus stagnation. Peck theorized there are four psychological advances that are critical to successful adjustment in middle adulthood: (1) emphasizing socializing rather than sexualizing in human relationships; (2) valuing wisdom rather than physical powers; (3) having emotional flexibility rather than emotional impoverishment; and (4) having mental flexibility rather than mental rigidity. Levinson theorizes that people shape their life structures during four overlapping eras: preadulthood, early adulthood, middle adulthood, and late adulthood. There are transitional periods within some of these eras, and there are also transitional periods that connect these eras. According to Levinson, people spend nearly half their adult lives in transition.

This chapter also describes contemporary theories and models for assessing human behavior throughout the life span. Maslow's theory of a hierarchy of needs has an ascending order of needs: physiological, safety, belongingness and love, self-esteem, and self-actualization. Analyzing human behavior in terms of games and life scripts provides another useful approach for understanding human behavior. In seeking to assess human behavior it is important to understand nonverbal communication.

Glasser's control theory asserts that all human behavior is an attempt to reduce the differences between the pictures of what we want and the way we perceive situations in the world. Gawain asserts that it is important for all of us to learn to trust our intuitive knowingness.

The chapter ends with an examination of the critical issue of chemical substance abuse. Chemical substances include alcohol, barbiturates, tranquilizers, Quaalude and PCP, amphetamines, cocaine and crack, amyl and butyl nitrate, narcotics, hallucinogens, tobacco, marijuana, and anabolic steroids. As part of the treatment process, chemically dependent persons need to assume responsibility for their behavior.

InfoTrac College Edition Keywords

Alcoholics Anonymous
codependency

control theory
crack-addicted babies

date-rape drugs
nonverbal communication

On the Internet

Alcohol and Drug Abuse Information

http://www.well.com/user/woa/

The "Web of Addictions" is dedicated to providing accurate information about alcohol and other drug addictions, as well as to providing a resource for teachers, students, and others who need factual information about abused drugs.

Cross-Cultural Communication

http://www.nwrel.org/cnorse/booklets/ccc/table4.html

Examples of verbal and nonverbal communication contrasts among some African Americans and some Anglo Americans.

Date Rape Drugs

http://www.4woman.gov/faq/rohypnol.htm?src=ng

The "date rape" drug is the common name for Rohypnol, generically called flunitrazepam. Rohypnol is manufactured by Hoffman-LaRoche and prescribed as a sleeping pill in countries outside the United States. It is used as a short-term treatment for insomnia, as a sedative hypnotic and a preanesthetic. It has physiological effects similar to Valium (diazepam), but is approximately ten times more potent. It is used also as an illicit drug, often in combination with other drugs, such as heroin, cocaine, and alcohol. Common names for Rohypnol include the following: rophies, roofies, R2, roofenol, Roche, roachies, la rocha, rope, rib, circles, Mexican valium, roach-2, roopies, and ropies. A similar drug is known as clonazepam (Klonopin in the United States and Rivotril in Mexico).

Eric Berne

http://www.itaa-net.org/ta/bernehist.htm

Berne defined certain socially dysfunctional behavioral patterns as "games." Berne proposed that dysfunctional behavior is the result of self-limiting decisions made in childhood in the interest of survival. Such decisions culminate in what Berne called the "life script," the preconscious life plan that governs the way life is lived out.

CHAPTER 12

Social Systems and Their Impacts on Middle Adulthood

George Andrus is spending 55 hours a week getting his insurance business going and uses his leisure time working around his house. Jenny Savano recently got a divorce, is trying to raise her three children on a meager monthly public assistance grant, and is attending a vocational school to receive training as a secretary. Tom and Eleanor Townsend have their careers well established, their two children have grown and left home, and they enjoy traveling to such exotic places as the Greek Isles. Joan Sarauer spends much of her day caring for her husband, who is dying of emphysema. Carmen and Carlos Garcia attend church every Sunday and take leadership roles in church activities during the week.

A PERSPECTIVE

There is obviously considerable variation in the major social interests of middle-aged adults. However, there are some fairly common themes: settling into a career; raising children and maintaining a household; participating in some hobbies; becoming grandparents; adjusting to relationship changes with a spouse and children after the children leave home; and socializing with friends.

This chapter will:

▶ Describe three major sociological theories about human behavior: functionalism, conflict theory, and interactionism. These theories are macro system theories.

- ▶ Discuss three social problems that middle-aged adults may encounter: poverty, unemployment, empty-shell marriages, and divorce. Single-parent families, blended families, and mothers working outside the home, will also be discussed.
- ▶ Present material on assessing and intervening in family systems.
- ▶ Summarize material on social work with organizations, including several theories of organizational behavior.
- ▶ Describe liberal, conservative, and developmental perspectives on human service organizations.

✿ Macro Social System Theories

The systems impact model, described in Chapter 1, emphasizes how people interact with various sized systems within their social environments. These interactions have major impacts on human behavior. We have defined a macro system as one that is larger than a small group. We have established that culture, communities, institutions, and organizations are examples of macro systems. To maximize their effectiveness, social workers must understand and assess the impacts of macro systems on their clients.

Micro system theories, on the other hand, seek to make sense of the effects of group life on individuals. Prominent theories of this type include Erikson's theory, which was summarized in Chapter 7, and the learning theory, summarized in Chapter 4.

This chapter will first describe several theories addressing macro social systems. These theories explore how macro systems function and propose explanations for how these systems influence human behavior. Macro system theories seek to make sense of the behavior of large groups of people and the workings of entire societies. We begin by looking at the three most prominent macro system theories in sociology: functionalism, conflict theory, and interactionism. (Note that these theories are applicable to all age groups, not only middle-aged adults.)

Advocates of these various theories often disagree with one another, as each theory has certain merits and shortcomings. The theories vary in their usefulness for analyzing any particular issue or problem individuals encounter within their social environments. Having a knowledge of a range of contemporary theories enables the social worker to effectively select the theory or theories that are most useful in understanding a particular human behavior, problem, or issue. Often, the greatest understanding results from combining and critically thinking about a combination of these theories.

The Functionalist Perspective

In recent years *functionalism* has been one of the most influential sociological theories. The theory was originally developed by Emile Durkheim, a French sociologist, and was refined by Robert K. Merton, Talcott Parsons, and many others. The theory views society as a well-organized system in which most members agree on common values and norms. Institutions, groups, and roles fit together in a unified whole. Members of society do what is necessary to maintain a stable society because they accept its regulations and rules.

Society is viewed as a system composed of interdependent and interrelated parts. Each part makes a contribution to the operation of the entire system. The various parts are involved in a delicate balance, and a change in one part affects the other parts.

A simple way to picture this approach is to use the analogy of a human body. A well-functioning person has thousands of parts, each having a specific function. The heart pumps blood, the lungs draw oxygen into the body and expel carbon dioxide, the stomach digests food for energy, the muscles move bodily parts to perform a variety of functions, and the brain coordinates the activities of the various parts. Each of these parts is interrelated in complex ways to the others and is also dependent on them. Each performs a vital function, without which the entire system might collapse, as in the case of heart failure.

Functionalism asserts that the components of a society, similar to the parts of the human body, do not always work the way they are supposed to work. Things get out of whack. When a component of a society interferes with efforts to carry out essential social tasks, that part is said to be *dysfunctional*. Often, changes in society introduced to correct a particular imbalance may produce other imbalances, even when things are going well. For example, developing effective contraceptives and making these readily available is quite effective in preventing unwanted pregnancies. However, contraceptives may also be a factor leading to increased premarital and extramarital sexual relationships—which is viewed as a problem by some groups.

According to the functionalist perspective, all social systems have a tendency toward equilibrium—maintenance of a steady state, or particular balance, in which the parts of the system remain in the same relationship to one another. The approach asserts that systems have a tendency to resist social change; change is seen as disruptive unless it occurs at a slow pace. Because society is composed of interconnected parts, a change in one part of the system will lead to changes in at least some of the other parts. The introduction of the automobile into our society, for example, led to drastic changes: people being able to commute long distances to work; vacation travel to distant parts of the country; the opening of many new businesses (service stations, car dealerships, etc.); and sharp increases in air pollution and traffic fatalities.

Some of the functions and dysfunctions of a social system are *manifest,* that is, obvious to everyone. For example, a manifest function of police departments is to keep crime rates low. Other functions and dysfunctions are *latent*—hidden and unintended. Sociologists have discovered that when police departments label people they arrest with such stigmatizing labels as "criminal," "outlaw," and "delinquent," a hidden consequence is that those who are so labeled may actually commit more crimes over the long run than they would if they had never been arrested in the first place. Thus, police departments (in trying to curb crime) may unintentionally, at times, contribute to an increase in crime.

According to functionalists, social problems occur when society, or some part of it, becomes disorganized. *Social disorganization* occurs when a large organization or an entire society is imperfectly organized to achieve its goals and maintain its stability. When disorganization occurs, the organization loses control over its parts.

Functionalists see thousands of potential causes of social disorganization. However, underlying all these causes is rapid *social change,* which disrupts the balance of society. In recent years more technological advances (such as the development of telephones, computers, television, robots, heart transplants, the Internet) have occurred in less time than at any other time in human history. These advances have led basic institutions (such as the family and the educational system) to undergo drastic changes. Technological advances have occurred at such a pace that other parts of the culture have failed to keep pace. This *cultural lag* between technological changes and our adaptation to

them is viewed as one of the major sources of social disorganization.

Examples of such social disorganization abound. The development of nuclear weapons has the potential to destroy civilization. Advances in sanitation and medical technology have lengthened life expectancy but have also contributed to a worldwide population explosion. Advances in artificial insemination have led to surrogate motherhood, which our society has not yet decided whether to encourage or discourage. The development of technological advances in performing abortions has led to the capacity to terminate pregnancies quite safely on request, but has also led to a national controversy about the desirability of legalized abortions.

Critics of functionalism assert that it is a politically conservative philosophy, as it takes for granted the idea that society as it is (the status quo) should be preserved. As a result, basic social injustices of society are ignored. Critics also argue that the approach is value laden, because one person's disorganization is another person's organization. For example, some people view divorce as being functional, because it is a legal way to terminate a relationship that is no longer working.

Functionalism has also been criticized as being a philosophy that works for the benefit of the privileged social classes, while perpetuating the misery of the poor and those who are being victimized by discrimination.

The Conflict Perspective

The *conflict theory* views society as a struggle for power among various social groups. Conflict is thought to be inevitable and in many cases actually beneficial to society. For example, most Americans would view the struggle of the "freedom fighters" during the revolutionary war as being highly beneficial to our society. (England, however, viewed them as ungrateful insurgents.)

The conflict perspective rests on an important assumption: members of society highly value certain things (such as power, wealth, and prestige), and most of these valued resources are in scarce supply. Because of their scarcity, conflict theory asserts that people—either individually or in groups—struggle with one another to attain them. Society is thus viewed as an arena for the struggle over scarce resources.

Struggle and conflict may take many forms: competition, disagreements, court battles, physical fights and violence, and war. If the struggles usually involved violence, then nearly everyone would be involved in violent activities, and society would be impossible. As a result, norms have emerged that determine what types of conflict are allowable for which groups. For example, participating in a labor strike or acquiring a higher education is an approved way of competing for the limited money available in our society, whereas robbery is not an acceptable way.

From the conflict perspective, social change mainly involves reordering the distribution of scarce goods among groups. Unlike functionalism, which views change as potentially destructive, the conflict approach views change as potentially beneficial. Conflict can lead to improvements, advancements, the reduction of discrimination against oppressed groups, and the emergence of new groups as dominant forces in society. Without conflict, society would become stagnant.

Functionalism and conflict theory differ in another way. Functionalists assert that most people obey the law because they believe the law is fair and just. Conflict theorists assert that social order is maintained by authority backed by the use of force. They assert that the privileged classes hold legal power and use the legal system to make others obey their will. They conclude that most people obey the law because they are afraid of being arrested, imprisoned, or even killed if they do not obey.

Functionalists assert that most people in society share the same set of values and norms. In contrast, conflict theorists assert that modern societies are composed of many different groups with divergent values, attitudes, and norms—and, therefore, conflicts are bound to occur. The abortion issue illustrates such a value conflict. Pro-life groups and traditional Roman Catholics believe that the human fetus at any stage after conception is a living human being and, therefore, aborting a pregnancy is murder. In contrast, pro-choice advocates assert that an embryo for the first few months after conception is not yet a human being because it is unable to survive outside the womb. They also assert that if the state were to forbid a woman to obtain an abortion that she desires, the state would be violating her right to control her life.

Not all conflicts stem from disagreements over values. Some conflicts arise in part *because* people share the same values. In our society, for example, wealth and power are highly valued. The wealthy spend considerable effort and resources to maintain their position, whereas the poor and oppressed groups vehemently advocate for equal rights and a more equitable distribution of income and wealth. Labor unions and owners in many businesses are in a continual battle over wages and fringe benefits. Republicans and Democrats continually struggle with one another in the hopes of gaining increased political power.

In contrast to functionalism being criticized as too conservative, conflict theory has been criticized as too radical. Critics say that if there were as much conflict as these theorists claim, society would have disintegrated long ago. Conflict theory has also been criticized as encouraging oppressed groups to revolt against the existing power structure, rather than seeking to work within the existing system to address their concerns.

The Interactionist Perspective

The *interactionist approach* focuses on individuals and the processes of everyday social interaction between them rather than on larger structures of society, such as the educational system, the economy, or religion. Interactionist theory views behavior as a product of each individual's social relationships. Cartwright (1951) noted:

How aggressive or cooperative a person is, how much self-respect or self-confidence he has, how energetic and productive his work is, what he aspires to, what he believes to be true and good, whom he loves or hates, and what beliefs or prejudices he holds—all these characteristics are highly determined by the individual's group memberships. In a real sense, they are products of groups and of the relationships between people. (p. 383)

The interactionist theory asserts that human beings interpret or define each other's actions instead of merely reacting. This interpretation is mediated by the use of symbols (particularly words and language).

Interactionists study the socialization process in detail because it forms the foundation for human interaction. The approach asserts that people are the products of the culture and social relationships in which they participate. Coleman and Cressey (1984) summarize this approach:

People develop their outlook on life from participation in the symbolic universe that is their culture. They develop their conceptions of themselves, learn to talk, and even learn how to think as they interact early in life, with family and friends. But unlike the Freudians, interactionists believe that an individual's personality continues to change throughout life in response to changing social environments.

The work of the American philosopher George Herbert Mead has been the driving force behind the interactionists' theories of social psychology. Mead noted that the ability to communicate in symbols (principally words and combinations of words) is the key feature that distinguishes humans from other animals. Individuals develop the ability to think and to use symbols in the process of socialization. Young children blindly imitate the behavior of their parents, but eventually they learn to "take the role of the other," pretending to be "Mommy" or "Daddy." And from such role taking children learn to understand the interrelationships among different roles and to see themselves as they imagine others see them.

Eventually, Mead said, children begin to take the role of a generalized other. In doing so, they adopt a system of values and standards that reflect the expectations of people in general, not just those in the immediate present. In this way reference groups as well as actual membership groups come to determine how the individual behaves. (p. 21)

Cooley (1902) observed that it is impossible to make objective measures of most aspects of our self-concept—such as how brave, likable, generous, attractive, or honest we are. Instead, in order to gauge the extent to which we have these qualities, we have to rely on the subjective judgments of the people we interact with. In essence, Cooley asserted, we learn what kind of person we are by seeing and hearing how others react to us; in effect, the reactions of others become a mirror or "looking glass" that we use to judge our own qualities.

Another important concept is that social reality is what a particular group agrees it is. Social reality is not a purely objective phenomenon.

The interactionist theory views human behavior as resulting from the *interaction* of a person's unique, distinctive personality and the groups he or she participates in. Groups are a factor in shaping one's personality, but the personality is also shaped by the person's unique qualities.

The reality we construct is mediated through symbols. We respond to symbolic reality, not physical reality. Sullivan and his colleagues (1980) describe the importance of symbols in shaping our reality:

Symbols are the principal vehicles through which expectations are conveyed from one person to another. A symbol is any object, word, or event that stands for, represents, or takes the place of something else. Symbols have certain characteristics. First, the meaning of symbols derives from social consensus— the group's agreement that one thing will represent something else. A flag represents love of country or patriotism; a green light means go, not stop; a frown stands for displeasure. Second, the relationship between the symbol and what it represents is arbitrary—there is no inherent connection. There is nothing about the color green that compels us to use that, rather than red, as a symbol for go; a flag is in reality a piece of cloth for which we could substitute anything, as long as we agreed that it stood for country. Finally, symbols need not be tied to physical reality. We can use symbols to represent things with no physical existence, such as justice, mercy, or God, or to stand for things that do not exist at all, such as unicorns.

A direct offshoot of the interactionist perspective is the labeling theory. This theory holds that the labels assigned to a person have a major impact on that person's life. Labels often become self-fulfilling prophecies. If a child is continually called "stupid" by his or her parents, that child is apt to develop a low self-concept, anticipate failure in many areas (particularly academic), put forth little effort in school and in competitive interactions with others, and end up failing. If a teenage girl gets a reputation as being promiscuous, adults and peers may label her as such, with other girls then shunning her, and teenage boys ridiculing her, and perhaps some seeking to date her for a one-night stand. If a person is labeled an ex-con for spending time in prison, that person is likely to be viewed with suspicion, have trouble finding employment, and be stigmatized as being dangerous and untrustworthy, even though the person may be conscientious and hardworking. Scheff (1966) has developed a labeling theory to explain why some people develop a career of being mentally ill. He asserts the act of labeling someone mentally ill is the major determinant for their acting as if they were mentally ill. Once labeled, others interact with them as if they were mentally ill, which leads them to view themselves as being mentally ill, and they then enact this role.

The most common criticism of the interactionist theory is that the theory is so abstract and vaguely worded that it is nearly impossible either to prove or to disprove it (Coleman & Cressey, 1984).

❧ Poverty: Impacts of Social and Economic Forces

The functionalist, conflict, and interactionist perspectives are further illustrated by discussing how each of these theories explains poverty. Poverty is a problem of major macro system consequence. It dramatically affects a majority of social welfare resource recipients.

The Rich and the Poor

Poverty and wealth are closely related. In most countries of the world, wealth is concentrated in a small percentage of the population. Abundance for a few is created by depriving others.

There are two ways of measuring the extent of economic inequality. *Income* refers to the amount of money a person makes in a given period. *Wealth* is a person's total assets—real estate holdings, cash, stocks, bonds, and so forth.

The distribution of wealth and income is highly unequal in our society. Similar to most countries, the United States is characterized by *social stratification*—that is, it has social classes, with the upper classes having by far the greatest access to the pleasures that money can buy. As Spotlight 12.1 indicates, the income disparities between the very rich and very poor are astounding.

Although this chapter focuses on poverty in the United States, it is important to note that there is a growing gap between the rich and the poor throughout the world. (Kornblum & Julian, 2001). Kornblum and Julian (2001) note:

These growing disparities between rich and poor throughout the world have a direct bearing on the situation of the poor in the United States, because American jobs are being "exported" to areas where extremely poor people are willing to accept work at almost any wage. World poverty also contributes to environmental degradation, political instability, and violence, which drain resources that could be used to meet the nation's domestic needs. (p. 222)

In the United States, the wealthiest 1 percent of all households hold about 40 percent of all personal wealth (Kornblum & Julian, 2001). *Net worth* refers to the value of all assets minus debts; assets include savings and checking accounts, automobiles, real estate, and stocks and bonds. The distribution of income is also unequal. The wealthiest 20 percent of households in the United States receive over 50 percent of all income, whereas the poorest 20 percent receive less than 5 percent of all income (Kornblum & Julian, 2001).

In the words of a pastoral letter issued by a committee of Roman Catholic bishops, "The level of inequality in income and wealth in our society. . . . must be judged morally unacceptable" (quoted in Kornblum & Julian, 2001, p. 225). Paul Samuelson (1980), an economist,

provides a dramatic metaphor of the disparity between the very rich and most people in the United States:

If we made an income pyramid out of a child's blocks, with each layer portraying $1,000 of income, the peak would be far higher than the Eiffel Tower, but almost all of us would be within a yard of the ground. (p. 34)

Given the huge wealth of the richest 20 percent, it is clear that a simple redistribution of some of the wealth from the top one-fifth to the lowest one-fifth could easily wipe out poverty. Of course, that is not politically acceptable to members of the top fifth, who have the greatest control of the government.

In contrast, millions of Americans regularly do not get enough to eat because they are poor. The brain of an infant grows to 80 percent of its adult size within the first 3 years of life. If supplies of protein are inadequate during this period, the brain stops growing, the damage is irreversible, and the child will be permanently retarded (Robertson, 1980).

Coleman and Cressey (1990) describe the effects of having, and not having, wealth:

The poor lack the freedom and autonomy so prized in our society. They are trapped by their surroundings, living in run-down, crime-ridden neighborhoods that they cannot afford to leave. They are constantly confronted with things they desire but have little chance to own. On the other hand, wealth provides power, freedom, and the ability to direct one's own fate. The wealthy live where they choose and do as they please, with few economic constraints. Because the poor lack education and money for travel, their horizons seldom extend beyond the confines of their neighborhood. In contrast, the world

---

| **Spotlight on Diversity 12.1** | **Personal Income Disparities Are Astounding** |

In some countries in the world, the average per capita income is less than $500 per year. In the United States over 34 million people (about 13% of the population) are living in poverty. (In 2001 the poverty threshold for a family of four was $17,184.)

In the fall of 1997, Kevin Garnett signed a 6-year deal, for $123 million, with the Minnesota Timberwolves (a professional team in the National Basketball Association). The deal, a $20.5 million average annual salary, was (at the time) the richest long-term sports contract. Kevin Garnett was only 20 years old when he signed. He joined the NBA after high school, without ever attending (or playing basketball in) college.

In the fall of 2000, Alex Rodriguez signed a 10-year-deal, for $252 million, with the Texas Rangers (a

professional baseball team). The deal of over $25 million per year then became the richest long-term sports contract.

In one year (June 1998 to June 1999), the personal worth of Bill Gates (then the richest person in the world) rose $39 billion, from $51 billion to $90 billion. During this 1-year period, he made an astounding average of $750 million per week, which is over $100 million per day! (Bill Gates is the chairman of the Microsoft Corporation.)

Sources: U.S. Bureau of the Census, *Statistical Abstract of the United States: 2001* (Washington, DC: Government Printing Office, 2001); Eric R. Quinones, "Rich Get Richer: Forbes Lists 170 Billionaires," *Wisconsin State Journal*, Oct. 14, 1997, p. 2A; William Kornblum & Joseph Julian, *Social Problems*, 10th ed. (Upper Saddle River, NJ: Prentice-Hall, 2001).

of the wealthy offers the best education, together with the opportunity to visit places that the poor haven't even heard of.

The children of the wealthy receive the best that society has to offer, as well as the assurance that they are valuable and important individuals. Because the children of the poor lack so many of the things everyone is "supposed" to have, it is much harder for them to develop the cool confidence of the rich. In our materialistic society people are judged as much by what they have as by who they are. The poor cannot help but feel inferior and inadequate in such a context. (p. 161)

The Problem

About 13 percent of the population in the United States is living below the poverty line (Kornblum & Julian, 2001). The *poverty line* is the level of income that the federal government considers sufficient to meet basic requirements of food, shelter, and clothing. One of the alarming elements about poverty is that the rate of poverty in recent years has been increasing. In addition, there are many people who do not fall under the government's poverty line, but still have very limited income and a living standard that is similar to those below the poverty line.

Poverty does not simply mean that poor people in the United States are living less well than people of average income. It means eating diets largely of beans, macaroni and cheese, or, in severe cases, even dog and cat food. It may mean not having running water, living in substandard housing, and being exposed to rats, cockroaches, and other vermin. It means not having sufficient heat in the winter and being unable to sleep because the walls are too thin to deaden the sounds from the neighbors living next

door. It means being embarrassed about the few ragged clothes that one has to wear. It means great susceptibility to emotional disturbances, alcoholism, and victimization by criminals, as well as a shorter life expectancy. It means few opportunities to advance oneself socially, economically, or educationally. It often means slum housing, unstable marriages, and little opportunity to enjoy the finer things in life—traveling, dining out, movies, plays, concerts, sports events.

The infant mortality rate of the poor is almost double the rate of the affluent (Kornblum & Julian, 2001). The poor have less access to medical services and receive lower-quality care from health-care professionals. The poor are exposed to higher levels of air pollution, water pollution, and unsanitary conditions. They have higher rates of malnutrition and disease. Schools in poor areas are of lower quality and have fewer resources. As a result the poor achieve less academically and are more apt to drop out of school. They are more apt to be arrested, indicted, imprisoned, and given longer sentences. They are less likely to receive probation, parole, or suspended sentences (Kornblum & Julian, 2001).

Poverty also often leads to despair, low self-esteem, and stunting of physical, social, emotional, and intellectual growth. A second level of damage from poverty occurs from the *feeling* that lack of financial resources is preventing one from having equal opportunities and from the *feeling,* then, that one is a second-class citizen. Poverty hurts deeply when it leads to viewing oneself as inferior or second-class.

We like to think that America is a land of equal opportunity and that there is considerable upward class

The poverty rate in the United States is increasing. Children raised in poor families are likely to remain poor in their adult years.

© Spencer Grant /PhotoEdit

Highlight 12.1

The Ideology of Individualism

Wealth is generally inherited in this country. There are few individuals who actually move up the social status ladder. Having wealth opens up many doors (through education and contacts) for children of the wealthy to make large sums of money when they become adults. For children living in poverty, there is little chance to escape when they become older.

Yet, there is the myth of individualism which is held by many. It states that the rich are personally responsible for their success, and that the poor are to blame for their failure. The main points of this myth are:

1. Each individual should work hard and strive to succeed in competition with others.

2. Those who work hard should be rewarded with success (seen as wealth, property, prestige, and power).

3. Because of widespread and equal opportunity, those who work hard will, in fact, be rewarded with success.

4. Economic failure is an individual's own fault and reveals lack of effort and other character defects.

The poor are blamed for their circumstances in our society. Blaming the poor has led to a stigma being attached to poverty, particularly to those who receive public assistance (welfare).

---

mobility for those who put forth the effort (see Highlight 12.1). The reality is the opposite of the dream. Extensive research has shown that poverty is almost inescapable. Children raised in poor families are themselves apt to live in poverty in their adult years. Most people have much the same social status as their parents had. Movement to a higher social status is an unusual happening in practically all societies—including the United States (Kornblum & Julian, 2001).

Who Are the Poor?

An encouraging trend is that the proportion of people below the poverty line has gradually been decreasing in the last 80 years. Prior to the twentieth century a majority of the population lived in poverty. President Franklin D. Roosevelt (1937) stated, "I see one-third of a nation ill-housed, ill-clad, ill-nourished." In 1962, one-fifth of the population were living in poverty (U.S. Census Bureau, 1982). Now about 13 percent of the people are estimated to be below the poverty line. Since 1978, the proportion of the population who are poor has increased slightly.

Poverty is concentrated among certain population categories, including one-parent families, children, the elderly, large-size families, people of color, and the homeless. Attainment of less than a ninth-grade education is a good predictor of poverty. Completing high school, however, is not a guarantee that one will earn wages adequate to avoid poverty, as many of the poor have graduated from high school. A college degree is an excellent predictor of avoiding poverty, as only a small proportion of those with a college degree live in poverty (Kornblum & Julian, 2001).

Being unemployed is also associated with poverty. People who live in rural areas have a higher incidence of poverty than people who live in urban areas. In rural areas there is high unemployment, work tends to be seasonal, and wages are low. The Ozarks, Appalachia, and the South have pockets of rural poverty with high rates of unemployment (Kornblum & Julian, 2001).

People who live in urban, deteriorated areas constitute the largest geographical group in terms of numbers of poor people. The decaying cities of the Northeast and Midwest have particularly large deteriorated areas. Poverty is also extensive on Native American reservations and among seasonal migrant workers. Spotlight 12.2 tells a tragic story of urban poverty.

Although poverty is concentrated in certain population categories, Rank and Hirschl (1999) found that many more Americans are directly impacted by poverty than what is widely believed. They found that by age 35, nearly one-third of the U.S. population will have experienced a year in poverty. By age 65, more than half of all Americans will have spent a year below the poverty line, and by age 85, two-thirds will have done so. The reality is that the majority of Americans will encounter poverty firsthand during adulthood.

What Causes Poverty?

There are a number of possible causes of poverty, including unemployment, poor physical health, emotional problems, drug addiction, low education level, racial and

| **Spotlight on Diversity 12.2** | **Poverty Perpetuates Poverty** |

The following summary of Marcee Calvello's life describes how poverty and dismal living conditions lead to despair, hopelessness, and failure.

Marcee Calvello was born and raised in New York City. Her father had trouble holding a job because he was addicted to cocaine, and her mother was an alcoholic who divorced her husband when Marcee was 3 years old. Marcee's mother at first sought to provide a better home for Marcee and her three brothers. She worked part-time and also went on AFDC. However, her addiction to alcohol consumed most of her time and money. Neighbors reported that the children were living in abject neglect, and Protective Services removed Marcee and her brothers to foster care. Marcee was placed in a series of foster homes—a total of 17 different homes. In one of these homes her foster father sexually assaulted her, and in another a foster brother assaulted her. Being moved from foster home to foster home resulted in frequent school changes. Marcee grew distrustful of the welfare system, school teachers and administrators, males, and anyone else who sought to get close to her.

When she turned 18, the state no longer paid for her care in foster care. She got a small efficiency apartment that cost her several hundred dollars a month. Because she had dropped out of school at age 16, she had few marketable job skills. She worked for a while at some fast-food restaurants. The minimum wages she received were insufficient to pay her bills. Eight months after she moved into her apartment she was evicted. Unable to afford another place, she started living in the subway system of New York City. She soon lost her job at McDonald's because of poor hygiene and an unkempt appearance.

Unable to shower and improve her appearance, she has not been able to secure another job. For the past 2 years she has been homeless, living on the street and in the subway. She has given up hope of improving her situation. She now occasionally shares IV needles and has been sexually assaulted periodically by men at night in the subway. She realizes she is at high risk for acquiring the AIDS virus but no longer cares very much. Death appears to be, to her, the final escape from a life filled with victimization and misery.

sexual discrimination, budgeting problems and mismanagement of resources, and mental retardation.

This list is not exhaustive. However, it serves to show that (1) there are a large number of causes of poverty; (2) eliminating the causes of poverty would require a wide range of social programs; and (3) poverty interacts with almost all other social problems—emotional problems, alcoholism, unemployment, racial and sexual discrimination, medical problems, crime, gambling, and mental retardation. The interaction between poverty and these other social problems is complicated. These social problems are contributing causes of poverty. Yet, for some social problems, poverty is also a contributing *cause* of those problems (such as emotional problems, alcoholism, and unemployment). And, being poor intensifies the effects (the hurt) of all social problems.

To some extent, poverty is passed on from generation to generation. This cycle of poverty is diagrammed in Figure 12.1.

The Culture of Poverty: Evaluation of the Theory and Its Application to Client Situations

Why is poverty passed on from one generation to another? Some authorities argue that the explanation is due to a "culture of poverty." Oscar Lewis (1966), an anthropologist, is a chief proponent of the cultural explanation.

Lewis examined poor neighborhoods in various parts of the world and concluded that the poor are poor because they have a distinct culture or lifestyle. The key elements of Lewis's cultural explanation follow.

The culture of poverty arises after extended periods of economic deprivation in highly stratified capitalistic societies. Such deprivation is brought about by high rates of unemployment and low wages for those who are employed. Economic deprivation leads to the development of attitudes and values of despair and hopelessness. Lewis described these attitudes and values as follows:

The individual who grows up in this culture has a strong feeling of fatalism, helplessness, dependence and inferiority; a strong present-time orientation with relatively little disposition to defer gratification and plan for the future, and a high tolerance for psychological pathology of all kinds. (p. 23)

Once developed, this culture continues to exist, even though the economic factors that created it (for example, lack of employment opportunities) no longer exist. These attitudes, norms, and expectations of the poor serve to limit their opportunities and prevent their escape. A major reason they remain locked into their culture is that they are socially isolated. They have few contacts with groups outside their own culture and are hostile to the institutions (for example, social services and education) that might be able to help them escape poverty. They reject

Figure 12.1 A Macro System Problem: The Cycle of Poverty

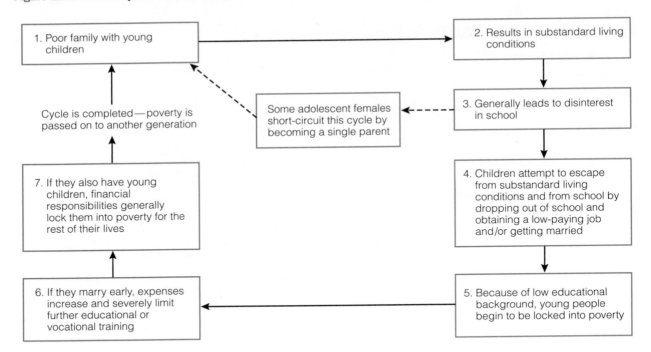

such institutions because they perceive them as belonging to the dominant class. Furthermore, because they view their financial circumstances as private matters and hopeless, and because they lack political and organizational skills, they do not take collective action to try to resolve their problems.

The culture-of-poverty theory is controversial and has been widely criticized. Leacock (1971) argued that the distinctive culture of the poor is not the cause but the result of their continuing poverty. She agreed that the poor tend to emphasize instant gratification, which involves spending and enjoying one's money while it lasts. But she argued that instant gratification is a result of being poor rather than the cause, because it makes no sense to defer gratification when a person is pessimistic about the future. Deferred gratification is a rational response only when one is optimistic that postponing pleasure today by saving the money will reap greater benefits in the future. Studies have found that when inner-city residents are able to obtain a stable, good-paying job, they display the middle-class value of deferred gratification (Farley, 1992). Because of poverty, Leacock argues, the poor are forced to abandon middle-class attitudes and values, because such values are irrelevant to their circumstances. If they had stable, good-paying jobs, they would likely take on the values of the middle class.

In an even stronger indictment, Ryan (1976) criticized the culture of poverty theory as simply being a classic example of *blaming the victim*. Blaming the poor for their circumstances is a convenient excuse, according to Ryan, for avoiding developing the programs and policies thought necessary to eradicate poverty. The real culprit is the social system that allows poverty to exist. Ryan said bluntly that the poor are not poor because of their culture, but because they do not have enough money.

Pro and con arguments for the culture of poverty theory continue to persist. There are many reasons, both external and internal, why a person may be poor. External reasons include high rates of unemployment; racial discrimination; automation, which throws people out of work; lack of job training programs; sex discrimination; a shortage of programs to eradicate poverty; and inflation. Internal reasons include having a physical or mental disability, being alcoholic, having obsolete job skills, becoming a parent at an early age, dropping out of school, and being uninterested in taking available jobs.

Poverty Is Functional

Obviously, poverty causes many problems, mainly to the poor themselves, but also to the affluent. However, realizing that poverty has some functions helps us to understand

Volunteers are shown working at a food distribution center for the poor.

why some decision makers are not actively seeking to eradicate poverty.

The 11 functions the poor provide for affluent groups are summarized by Sullivan and his colleagues (1980, p. 390):

1. They are available to do the unpleasant jobs that no one else wants to do.

2. By their activities, they subsidize the more affluent. (An example of such an activity is domestic service for low pay.)

3. Jobs are established for those people, such as social workers, who provide services to the poor.

4. The poor purchase goods, such as those of poor quality, that otherwise could not be sold.

5. They serve as examples of deviance that are frowned on by the majority and that thereby support dominant norms.

6. They provide an opportunity for others to practice their "Christian duty" of helping the less fortunate.

7. They make mobility more likely for others because they are removed from the competition for a good education and good jobs.

8. They contribute to cultural activities by providing, for example, cheap labor for the construction of monuments and works of art.

9. They create cultural forms (for example, jazz and the blues) that are often adopted by the affluent.

10. They serve as symbolic opponents for some political groups and as constituents for others.

11. They often absorb the costs of change (for example, by being the victims of unemployment that results from technological advances).

Also, denigrating the poor has the psychological function, for some Americans, of making them feel better about themselves.

Partly because poverty is functional, our society makes only a halfhearted effort to eradicate or at least reduce it. To eliminate it would mean a redistribution of income from the rich to the poor. Because the rich control the political power, they have generally been opposed to proposals that would eliminate poverty, such as guaranteed annual income programs.

Our country has the resources to eliminate poverty—but not the will. In the twentieth century, we found billions of dollars in resources within a few months to pay for a war, but we are not willing to allocate similar funds to improve living conditions for the homeless and millions of other people who are living in poverty in this country.

Application of Functionalism to Poverty

Functionalists view poverty as being due to dysfunctions in the economy. A wide range of dysfunctions have been identified, some of which will be mentioned here. Rapid industrialization has caused disruption in the economic system. For example, people who lack job skills are forced into menial work at low wages. Then when automation comes, they are discharged, without having work, money, or marketable job skills. Some products produced by industry also become outdated—such as steam engines, milk bottles, and horse-drawn carriages. When such products become obsolete, workers lose their jobs. In addition, work training centers and apprenticeship programs may continue to produce graduates whose skills are no longer in demand. For example, there no longer is a job market for people who are trained to repair adding machines and manual typewriters, and direct telephone calling is sharply reducing the number of people needed as telephone operators.

Functionalists also note that the welfare system, which is intended to solve the problem of poverty, has a number of dysfunctions. Social welfare programs are sometimes established without sufficient funds to meet the needs of potential clients. Some bureaucrats are reluctant to bend the rules to help a deserving family that is technically ineligible for assistance. Social welfare programs at times have design dysfunctions in meeting the needs of recipients. For example, in the past, mothers of young children in some states were eligible for public assistance only if the fathers were out of the home. Consequently, some unemployed men were forced to desert their families so their children could be fed and sheltered.

Additional problems in the welfare system are caused by inadequate information systems that fail to inform the poor about benefits to which they are entitled (in addition to the deliberate withholding of information due to prejudice). Job training and educational programs sometimes train people for positions in which there are no employment openings.

According to functionalists, the best way to deal with poverty is to make adjustments to correct these dysfunctions.

Many functionalists view some economic inequality (that is, poverty) as being functional. Because the poor are at the bottom of the stratification system, they receive few of the material and social rewards in the society. Functionalists view the threat of being at the bottom of the heap as an important mechanism for motivating people to perform. According to functionalists, poverty becomes a social problem when it no longer performs the function of motivating people to make productive contributions to society. Poverty is also functional as the poor do the demeaning, difficult, and low-paying jobs that are essential but that no one else wants to do.

Application of the Conflict Theory to Poverty

Conflict theorists assume that, because there is such enormous wealth in modern societies, no one in such societies should go without their essential needs being met. These theorists assert that poverty exists because the power

structure wants it to exist. They assert that the working poor are being exploited, by being paid poverty-level wages so that their employers can reap higher profits. The unemployed are also seen as the victims of the power structure. Wealthy employers oppose programs to reduce unemployment (such as educational and job training programs) because they do not want to pay the taxes to support them.

Wealthy people are apt to cling to the ideology of individualism, because they tend to view unemployment and poverty as stemming from a lack of effort rather than from social injustice or from circumstances beyond the control of the individual. As a result, the wealthy ignore the economic and political foundations of poverty, and instead get involved in charitable efforts for the poor, which leaves them feeling they have done good deeds. Conflict theorists see charity and government welfare programs as a force in perpetuating poverty and economic inequality, as such programs quell political protests and social unrest that threaten the status quo. Conflict theorists also assert that many poor people eventually come to accept the judgments passed on them by the rest of society and adjust their aspirations and self-esteem downward.

Conflict theorists do not see poverty as either essential or functional. They see poverty as arising because some groups benefit from the poverty of others. From the conflict perspective, poverty becomes a social problem when some group feels the existing distribution of resources is unjust and that something should be done about it.

Conflict theorists believe that poverty can best be dealt with by the poor becoming politically aware and organizing to reduce inequality through government action. These theorists view poor people's adjustments to poverty as being a set of chains that must be broken. Most conflict theorists believe poverty can be significantly reduced only through political action that receives at least some support from concerned members of the power structure.

Application of Interactionist Theory to Poverty

Interactionists emphasize the subjective nature of poverty. Poverty is viewed as being relative, because it depends on what it is compared to. Most poor people in the United States presently have a higher standard of living than middle-class people did 200 years ago. Poor people in this country are also substantially better-off than poor people in Third World countries.

The main reference for poor people in this country is their poor neighbors. A successful person in some neighborhoods is someone who knows where the next meal is coming from, and a big success may be someone who gets a job on an assembly line. People with such attitudes become trapped in their own beliefs. Another value that traps them is instant gratification, in which they are not inclined to defer immediate rewards so that long-range goals, such as a college education, can be reached.

Interactionists view poverty as a matter of shared expectations. The poor are negatively judged by influential groups. Those who are the objects of such labeling are stigmatized and may begin to behave in accordance with those expectations. Interactionists emphasize that poverty is not just a matter of economic deprivation, but involves the person's self-concept. For example, a third-generation welfare recipient is apt to view himself or herself much more negatively than a person working his or her way through college, even though both have the same income.

To resolve the poverty problem, interactionists urge that the stigma associated with poverty be eliminated. Positive changes in the poverty problem will not occur until the poor are convinced that they no longer are doomed to live in poverty. The poverty trap can be sprung with improved public assistance programs that bring the poor up to an adequate standard of living, *combined* with programs that provide opportunities to move up the socioeconomic ladder, and programs that encourage the poor to redefine their social environment.

❦ Family Mezzo System Problems

The systems impact model described in Chapter 1 emphasizes the effects of both macro and mezzo systems on human behavior. The first part of this chapter has emphasized the importance of understanding macro social systems when assessing human behavior. It is equally important to understand people's interactions with mezzo systems—small groups, including families. This section will examine problems and living arrangements in families.

Empty-Shell Marriages

In empty-shell marriages the spouses feel no strong attachments to each other. Outside pressures keep the marriage together. Such outside pressures include: business reasons (for example, an elected official wanting to convey a stable family image); investment reasons (for example, husband and wife may have a luxurious home and

other property that they do not want to lose by parting); and outward appearances (for example, a couple living in a small community may remain together to avoid the reactions of relatives and friends to a divorce). In addition, a couple may believe that ending the marriage would harm the children or may believe that getting a divorce would be morally wrong.

Cuber and Harroff (1971) identified three types of empty-shell marriages. In a *devitalized relationship* husband and wife lack any real interest in their spouse or their marriage. Boredom and apathy characterize this marriage. Serious arguments are rare.

In a *conflict-habituated relationship* husband and wife frequently quarrel in private. They may also quarrel in public or put up a facade of being compatible. The relationship is characterized by considerable conflict, tension, and bitterness. Highlight 12.2 provides strategies for couples—and people in general—to resolve interpersonal conflicts.

In a *passive-congenial relationship* the partners are not happy, but are content with their lives and generally feel adequate. They may have some interests in common, but these interests are generally insignificant. The spouses contribute little to each other's real satisfactions. This type of relationship generally has little overt conflict.

The number of empty-shell marriages is unknown—it may be as high as the number of happily married couples. The atmosphere in empty-shell marriages is without much fun or laughter. Members do not share and discuss their problems or experiences with each other. Communication is kept to a minimum. There is seldom any spontaneous expression of affection or sharing of a personal experience. Children in such families are usually starved for love and reluctant to have friends over because they are embarrassed about having their friends see their parents interacting.

The couples in these marriages engage in few activities together and display no pleasure in being in one another's company. Sexual relations between the partners, as might be expected, are rare and generally unsatisfying. Visitors will note that the partners (and often the children) appear insensitive, cold, and callous to each other. Yet, closer observation will reveal that the family members are highly aware of each other's weaknesses and sensitive areas, and manage to frequently mention these areas in order to hurt one another.

Both spouses have to put considerable effort into making a marriage work in order to prevent an empty-shell marriage from gradually developing. The number of empty-shell marriages ending in divorce is unknown. It is likely that a fair number eventually do.

Highlight 12.2

Conflict Resolution Strategies

Conflict, an antagonistic state or action involving divergent ideas or interest, is inevitable in interpersonal relationships. There is an erroneous belief in our society that conflicts always produce negative results and therefore should be avoided. But since people have divergent interests, beliefs, values, and goals, it is inevitable that conflicts will occur in our work settings and in our private lives. Conflicts are not only a natural component of any interpersonal relationship, but often desirable, because they have a number of potential payoffs. Conflicts produce lively discussions. When constructively handled, conflicts motivate the people involved to define issues more sharply, to search harder for resolution strategies, and to work harder in implementing solutions. Conflict, when handled effectively, can lead to greater commitment to the relationship of the people involved, raise morale, and increase communication and cooperation. Successful resolution of conflict can lead to personal growth and facilitate innovation and creativity.

However, ineffective management of conflict can lead to deterioration of rapport between the people involved, distrust, and perhaps alienation and burnout. Unfortunately, some organizations have norms that urge front-line service providers to suppress their suggestions for changes. Such norms are at times informally communicated by agency management taking adverse actions (such as dismissal, demotion, assignment to onerous tasks, and no salary raises) against those who press for changes. Efforts to suppress suggestions for changes by agency management usually result in lower morale, lower productivity, and less commitment to the agency's mission by the staff.

Following are a variety of strategies for resolving conflicts: the win-lose approach, the problem-solving approach, the role reversal, empathy, inquiry, being assertive, I-messages, disarming, stroking, and mediation. This section ends with a discussion of what to do if none of these strategies work.

Win-Lose Approach

With the win-lose approach, the two sides engaged in the conflict attempt to sell their own solution without really listening to the other side. Each side denies the legitimacy of the other's interests and concerns. Sometimes each side seeks to form a power block of supporters.

In win-lose situations, both sides usually end up losing. The losing side is not motivated to carry out the winning decision. The losing side is apt to resent the winning side, and then search for subtle ways to get even. In a win-lose situation, distrust increases between the two opposing sides, communication becomes more limited and inaccurate, and rapport deteriorates.

Problem-Solving Approach

The problem-solving approach asserts that it is almost always possible for both sides to have their needs met in a conflict situation. This approach is based on two basic premises: both sides have the right to have their needs met; and what is in conflict between the two sides is almost never their needs but their solutions to those needs.

The six steps in the problem-solving approach are:

1. Identify and define the needs of each opposing side.
2. Generate possible alternative solutions.
3. Evaluate the merits and shortcomings of the alternative solutions.
4. Decide on the best acceptable solution.
5. Work out ways of implementing the solution.
6. At a later date, evaluate how well the solution is working.

The advantages of this approach are numerous. Both sides fulfill their needs. The resentment, hostility, and subversive actions of a win-lose situation are avoided. Open communication is increased, and trust between the parties is enhanced. Both sides are more prepared to constructively handle conflicts in the future, as they now have had experience in doing so. A cooperative, problem-solving approach also promotes creativity. The problem-solving approach often generates a new perspective on a problem, and innovative alternatives for resolving the conflict are often arrived at.

Role Reversal

A useful strategy in resolving conflict is role reversal. The basic rule for role reversal is: *Each person expresses his or her opinions or views only after restating the ideas and feelings of the opposing person.* These ideas and feelings should be restated in one's own words rather than parroted or mimicked in the exact words of the other person. It is advisable to begin the restatement with words such as, "Your position is . . . ," "You seem to be saying . . . ," or, "You apparently feel. . . ." Approval or disapproval, blaming, giving advice, interpreting, or persuading should be avoided.

In addition, nonverbal messages should be consistent with the verbal paraphrasing and should convey interest, openness, and attentiveness to the opposition's ideas and feelings. Above all, role reversal should be the expression of a sincere interest in understanding the other person's feelings, ideas, and position.

Role reversal can result in a reevaluation and a change of attitude concerning the issue by both parties. The approach has also been found to increase cooperative behavior between role reversers, to clarify misunderstandings, to change win-lose situations into problem-solving situations, and most important, to allow the issue to be perceived from the other person's frame of reference.

Empathy

A closely related technique to role reversal is the expression of empathy. *Empathy* involves putting yourself in the shoes of the person you are in conflict with, and expressing your understanding of what he is thinking and saying. Some examples of phrases that are useful in helping you get started in expressing empathy are:

"What you seem to be saying is . . . ," "I take it that you think . . . ," and, "I sense you feel———about this issue."

When expressing empathy, it is essential to mirror what was said in a nonjudgmental way to grasp the essence of what the other person is thinking or feeling. Similar to role reversal, the use of empathy facilitates open communication, assists in clarifying misunderstandings, increases cooperative behavior, and facilitates the process of no-lose problem solving.

Inquiry

If you are in conflict with someone, and you are confused regarding his or her thoughts and feelings, the inquiry technique is often useful. This technique involves using gentle, probing questions to learn more about what the other person is thinking and feeling. Tone of voice is very crucial in the inquiry technique, as asking a question sarcastically or defensively is apt to result in defensive responses from the person.

Being Assertive

There are three basic styles of interacting with others: nonassertive, aggressive, and assertive. (See Chapter 7 for an expanded discussion of these terms.) Simply stated, assertive behavior is being able to express yourself in a confident, nonaggressive manner. The assertive approach in discussing issues with someone you are in conflict with is almost always more effective than the nonassertive approach or the aggressive approach. With the nonassertive approach you fail to express your thoughts and concerns. An aggressive approach usually results in an escalation of the conflict.

"I"-Messages

When conflicts arise, most people respond with you-messages. There are two types of you-messages: a solution message and a put-down message. A solution message orders, directs, commands, warns, threatens, preaches, moralizes, or advises. A put-down message blames, judges, criticizes, ridicules, or name-calls. Examples of you-messages include: "You stop that," "Don't do that," "I hate you," and, "You should know better." You-messages tend to inhibit open communication.

I-messages, in contrast, tend to foster open communication. I-messages are nonblaming messages that simply communicate how the sender of the message believes the receiver is affecting the sender. I-messages do not provide a solution, and they do not criticize. It is possible to send an I-message without using the word *I*. For example, when the driver is speeding at a reckless rate, an I-message that does not use "I" is, "Driving this fast really frightens me." The essence of I-messages involves sending a nonblaming message of how the sender feels the receiver is affecting him or her.

You-messages are generally counterproductive because people do not like to be ordered or criticized. You-messages frequently result in an ongoing struggle between the two people involved.

In contrast, I-messages communicate much more honestly the effect of behavior. I-messages tend to be more effective because they help the other person to assume responsibility for his behavior. An I-message conveys to the person with whom you are in conflict that you are trusting him or her to respect your needs and that you are trusting him or her to handle the conflict constructively. I-messages are much less likely to produce an argument. They tend to facilitate honesty, openness, and

more cordial relationships. (See Chapter 8 for an expanded discussion of I-messages.)

Disarming

When you are in conflict with someone, a frequently effective strategy in moving toward resolving the conflict is the disarming technique. This technique involves finding some truth in what the other person (or side) is saying and then expressing this "agreement"—even if you feel that what the other person is saying is largely wrong, unreasonable, irrational, or unfair. There is always a grain of truth in what the other person is saying, even if it sounds obnoxious and insulting. By the use of disarming, the other person won't feel so dogmatic and will have less of an urge to insist that he or she is right and you are wrong. As a result, he or she is apt to be more willing to examine the merits of your point of view. If you want respect, you first have to give respect. This technique helps you to listen to the other person first and facilitates more open (rather than defensive) communication thereafter.

In using the disarming technique, it is important that you be genuine in what you say, and express your agreement in a sincere way.

Stroking

A closely related technique to disarming is stroking. *Stroking* is saying something genuinely positive to the person (or side) you are in conflict with, even in the heat of battle. Stroking tells the other person that you respect him or her, even though both of you may be angry with each other. During an argument or conflict we have a tendency to feel the need to reject the other person before we get rejected (so we can save face). Often we overreact, and differences of opinion become blown out of proportion. To prevent this rejection, all we need to do is let the other person know that, although we are at odds, you still think highly of him or her. This makes it easier for the other person to open up and to listen, as he or she feels less threatened.

Mediation

In the past two decades, mediation has increasingly been used to resolve conflicts. *Mediation* involves the intervention of an acceptable impartial, neutral third party who has no authoritative decision-making power to assist contending parties in voluntarily reaching their own mutually acceptable settlement of issues in dispute. Mediation leaves the decision-making power in the hands of the people in conflict. Mediation is a voluntary process in that the participants must be willing to accept the assistance of the intervenor if the dispute is to be resolved. Mediation is usually initiated when the partners no longer believe that they can handle the conflict on their own and when the only means of resolution appears to involve impartial third-party assistance.

One of the major techniques a mediator uses is a caucus. At times a mediator, or either party, may stop the mediation and request a caucus. In a caucus the two parties are physically separated from each other and there is no direct communication between them. The mediator meets with one of the parties or with both parties individually. There are many reasons for calling a caucus: to vent intense emotions privately, to clarify misperceptions, to reduce unproductive or repetitive negative

Highlight 12.2

Conflict Resolution Strategies (continued)

behavior, to clarify a party's interests, to provide a pause for each party to consider an alternative, to convince an uncompromising party that the mediation process is better than going to court, to uncover confidential information, to educate an inexperienced disputant about the processes of mediation, or to design alternatives that will later be brought to a joint session.

In a caucus some parties are willing to express possible concessions privately. Usually such concessions are conditional on the other party's making certain concessions. By the use of caucuses, a mediator can go back and forth relaying information from one party to the other and seek to develop a consensus.

What If These Strategies Don't Work?

If used appropriately, these strategies will help resolve interpersonal conflicts in the vast majority of cases. When these strategies fail to work, you can probably correctly conclude that the person you are in conflict with does not really want to resolve the conflict. Perhaps the other person is a very hostile person who wants to generate conflicts to meet his or her personal needs by venting his or her anger and hostility. Or, perhaps the other person wants to be in conflict with you in order to make your life uncomfortable.

What can you do when you become aware that the other person really wants to sustain the conflict with you? Using the Law of Requisite Variety is an option. This law states that if you continue to creatively come up with new ways of responding to the "daggers being thrown" at you, eventually the other person will grow tired of the turmoil and will finally decide to "bury the hatchet." Here are two examples:

Janice and Pete Palmer were married about a year ago. Unknown to Janice, Pete was having lunch about once a month with a former partner (Paula), whom he had dated over a 3-year period. Seven months ago Janice walked into a restaurant at noon and saw her husband with Paula. In a fit of rage, Janice stomped out. That evening she and Pete had a major uproar about this. Pete claimed Paula was just a friend, and that nothing romantic was occurring. Janice yelled and screamed. Pete indicated he would stop having lunch with Paula. But he didn't keep his promise. About once a month he continued to see Paula, and when Janice found out, there was a major argument. Janice suggested a number of resolution options, including marriage counseling. Pete refused to go to counseling and also indicated he had decided that he was going to continue having lunch with Paula (the win-lose approach).

Then one day Janice ran into one of her former partners—Dave. Dave invited Janice for lunch or dinner. A lightbulb went on for Janice—she accepted the invitation and made plans for dinner. She went home and gleefully told Pete she ran into Dave (who Pete knew had dated Janice in the past). Pete became very jealous and tried to talk Janice out of having dinner with Dave. Janice said "No way." Pete was in anguish during the time Janice and Dave were having dinner. When Janice came home, Dave politely said he had called Paula that evening to inform her he was canceling their next scheduled lunch, and that he felt it was best that they no longer meet for lunch. Pete then asked Janice if she also would no longer get together with Dave—she indicated "Yes." Through this experience, Pete and Janice learned to respect and appreciate each other to a greater extent.

Vicki Stewart was a secretary for an attorney, Randy Fuller, who frequently criticized her and never complimented her. The harder she sought to perform well, the more it seemed she was criticized. She tried a variety of resolution strategies—discussing the conflict with him, discussing it with his supervisor, and making a point of complimenting him to set a good example. Nothing worked. Finally, she decided on a new approach. Mr. Fuller's grammar and spelling were atrocious. Ms. Stewart always improved the spelling and grammar when given rough drafts from Mr. Fuller and the other attorneys in the office. When Mr. Fuller gave her a rough draft of a legal brief for the state supreme court, Ms. Stewart typed it as is and sent it after Mr. Fuller signed it (he frequently signed such documents without proofreading them). When Mr. Fuller finally read the brief 3 weeks later, he was first angry, and then discussed the matter with his supervisor. His supervisor at first laughed, and then informed Mr. Fuller that in order to avoid a similar situation in the future, he needed to show appreciation to Ms. Stewart. After a few more days of reflecting about it, Mr. Fuller decided it was in his personal interest to display more respect and appreciation to Ms. Stewart.

Divorce

Our society places a higher value on romantic love than most other societies do. In societies where marriages are arranged by parents, being in love generally has no role in mate selection. In our society, however, romantic love is a key factor in forming a marriage.

Children in this country are socialized from an early age to believe in the glories of romantic love. Magazines, films, TV programs, and books portray "happy-ending"

romantic adventures. All of these romantic stories suggest that every normal person falls in love with that one special person, gets married, and lives happily ever after. This happily-ever-after ideal rarely happens.

About one of two marriages ends in divorce (Kornblum & Julian, 2001). This high rate has gradually been increasing. Before World War I divorce was comparatively rare.

Divorce usually leads to a number of difficulties for those involved. First, those who are divorcing face emotional concerns, such as a feeling that they have failed, concern over whether they are able to give and receive love, a sense of loneliness, concern over the stigma attached to divorce, concern about the reactions of friends and relatives, concern over whether they are doing the right thing by parting, and concern over whether they will be able to make it on their own. Many people feel trapped because they believe they cannot live with their spouse and cannot live without him or her. Dividing up the personal property is another area that frequently leads to bitter differences of opinions. If there are children, there are concerns about how the divorce will affect them.

Other issues also need to be decided. Who will get custody of the children? Joint custody is now an alternative. With joint custody, both parents have joint responsibility for decision making involving the children, and they may (or may not) share equally in the physical custody of the children. If one parent is awarded custody, controversies are apt to arise over visiting rights, and how much (if any) child support should be paid. Both spouses often face the difficulties of finding new places to live, making new friends, doing things alone in our couple-oriented society, trying to make it on their own financially, and thinking about the hassles of dating.

Studies show that going through a divorce is very difficult (Papalia et al., 2001). People are less likely to perform their jobs well and more likely to be fired during this period. Divorced people have a shorter life expectancy. Suicide rates are higher for divorced men.

Divorce per se is no longer automatically assumed to be a social problem. In some marriages where there is considerable tension, bitterness, and dissatisfaction, divorce is sometimes a solution. It may be a concrete step that some people take to end the unhappiness and to begin leading a more productive and gratifying life. It is also increasingly being recognized that a divorce may be better for the children, as they no longer may be subjected to the tension and unhappiness in a marriage that has gone sour.

The rising rate of divorce does not necessarily mean that more marriages are failing. It may simply mean that in marriages that have gone sour, more people are dissolving the marriage than continuing to live unhappily.

Reasons for Divorce. The reason people decide to divorce may have nothing to so with specific "bad" qualities of the marriage partners. Rather, a major reason people divorce is disappointment with each other. In other words, partners simply do not measure up to their spouse's expectations. Over time such disappointment

and disillusionment lead to the decision to divorce. (Highlight 12.3 provides a framework for people to analyze their love relationships.)

It is interesting to note that the same individual might be considered horrendous by one spouse but wonderful by the next, depending on the expectations of each spouse. Take Nick, for instance. His first wife, Judy, found him to be cold, noncommunicative, and unaffectionate. She lamented that he refused to sit with her on the couch, hold hands, and watch television as they relaxed in the evening. She once indicated that the purchase of a single-person reclining chair caused the demise of their marriage because they could no longer sit together. After the divorce, however, his second wife Karen felt that Nick was very, very affectionate, even though he demonstrated the same or at least very similar behavior toward her. She loved having her independence in the evenings and having television sets in separate rooms. To Karen, with her love of horror movies and Nick's love of "Wall Street Week in Review," living in this more independent manner was much more appealing.

There are many sources of marital breakdown, including alcoholism, economic strife caused by unemployment or other financial problems, incompatibility of interests, infidelity, jealousy, verbal or physical abuse of spouse, and interference in the marriage by relatives and friends.

As noted earlier, many people marry because they believe they are romantically in love. If this romantic love does not grow into rational love (see Chapter 8 for a description of rational love), the marriage is apt to fail. Unfortunately, young people are socialized in our society to believe that marriage will bring them continual romance, resolve all their problems, be sexually exciting, be full of adventure, and always be as wonderful as the courtship. (Most young people only need to look at their parent's marriage to realize such romantic ideals are seldom attained.) Unfortunately, living with someone in a marriage involves carrying out the garbage, washing dishes and clothes, being weary from work, putting up with the partner's distasteful habits, changing diapers, dealing with conflicts over such things as how to spend a vacation, and differences in sexual interests. Making a marriage work requires that each spouse put considerable effort into making it successful.

Another factor that is contributing to an increasing divorce rate is the unwillingness of some men to accept the changing status of women. Many men still prefer a traditional marriage where the husband is dominant, and the wife plays a supportive (subordinate role) as child-rearer, housekeeper, and emotional supporter of her husband. Many women no longer accept such a status and demand

Highlight 12.3

Analyzing Love Relationships

Cameron-Bandler (1985) developed the following frame-work for understanding the various stages of a love rela-tionship. Cameron-Bandler also gave suggestions for im-proving love relationships. Knowing when to get out of a destructive relationship is as important as knowing how to improve a healthy relationship.

1. *Attraction/Infatuation:* All of us have in mind a pic-ture of our ideal date or mate. This picture may include a variety of characteristics about such items as: physical appearance, color of hair, color of eyes, age, height, weight, personality, hobbies, personal interests, religion, musical interests, sports, education, career interests, family background, financial security, and sexual values and interests. Such pictures vary from person to person. When we meet someone who comes close to having the characteristics we desire, we tell ourselves that this is an "ideal" potential partner. We feel strongly attracted to the person and are in a stage of infatuation. After a few dates, the infatuation may intensify. Cameron-Bandler notes that this is "a fun time, full of intensity and excite-ment and romance" (p. 119).

2. *Appreciation:* In this stage the two persons are a couple who are seriously dating, living together, or even married. They are delighted to be together. They focus on the positive qualities of each other. They appreciate each other, rather than taking one another for granted. Cameron-Bandler says:

This phase can be based on a wide range of illusion or varying degrees of knowledgeable understanding of each other's wants and needs. The extent to which it is based on knowledgeable understanding is the extent to which it can be depended upon to last. (p. 120)

There are three basic elements for achieving and maintaining appreciation in a relationship. First, each partner has to know what he or she needs and wants in a relationship. Second, each partner must know what specifically fulfills these needs and wants. Third, each person must be able to elicit these fulfilling behaviors, lovingly, from his or her partner.

3. *Habituation:* Habituation is the stage of becoming accustomed to something. It involves being comfortable and secure with dependability and familiarity. For people who seek security, habituation is viewed as equaling safety and commitment. However, for people seeking ad-venture, habituation can be viewed as equaling boredom. Cameron-Bandler notes, "The phase of habituation can be a very positive one, provided it cycles back to appreci-ation and includes an occasional trip back to attraction" (p. 121).

Partners in this state of a relationship are advised to engage in old and new activities that they enjoy. One sug-gestion is for the partners to commit two weekends each year for enhancing the relationship. The partners first agree on how much money will be spent for each week-end. Then one of the partners arranges the activities that are designed to meet his or her fantasies of how he or she wants to spend time with the partner. A few weeks later the other partner similarly arranges for his or her fantasy weekend. Among other benefits, these weekends serve as a learning experience for each partner as to the other's previously unexpressed or newly formed desires.

4. *Expectation:* Cameron-Bandler writes, "The differ-ence between duty and pleasure often rears its ugly head in the phase of expectation" (p. 122). Many of the things that one did and were appreciated by one's partner now become an expectation. For example, at first A expressed

an equalitarian marriage in which making major deci-sions, doing the domestic tasks, raising the children, and bringing home paychecks are shared responsibilities.

About 60 percent of the adult women in the United States are now in the labor force (U.S. Census Bureau, 2001). This increase in the percentage of working women means women are no longer as dependent financially on their husbands. Women who are financially able to sup-port themselves are more likely to seek a divorce if their marriage goes sour.

Another factor contributing to the increasing divorce rate is the growth of individualism. Individualism involves the belief that people should seek to develop their inter-ests and capacities to the fullest, to seek to fulfill their own needs and desires. With individualism the interests of the individual take precedence over the interests of the fam-ily. People in our society have increasingly come to accept individualism as a way of life. In contrast, people in more

traditional societies and in extended families are social-ized to put the interests of the group first, with their own individual interests being viewed as less important. In extended families people view themselves as members of a group first and as individuals second. With the grow-ing belief in individualism, people who conclude that they are unhappily married are much more apt to dissolve the marriage and seek a new life.

Another reason for the rise in the divorce rate is the growing acceptance of divorce in our society. With less of a stigma attached to a divorce, more people who are un-happily married are now ending the marriage.

An additional factor in the increasing divorce rate is that modern families no longer have as many functions as in traditional families. Education, food production, en-tertainment, and other functions once centered in the family, are now largely provided by outside agencies. In earlier times, the end of a marriage was far more likely to

intense appreciation when B shopped for groceries and cooked on certain evenings. Now these tasks have become expected duties, and B receives frowns and criticisms when they aren't done. This stage in a relationship is usually signaled by more complaints than compliments. Each partner focuses on what the other is not doing, rather than on what he or she is doing to benefit the relationship. One way of seeking to halt further deterioration in a relationship when this stage is reached is an intervention in which each partner is encouraged to once again treat the other as a lover instead of as a spouse.

5. *Disappointment/Disillusionment:* Unless the couple works on their relationship, disappointment and disillusionment soon follow expectation. In this stage the partners become increasingly disappointed because each is failing to fulfill the other's expectations. In this stage partners are apt to say their mate has started some bad habits; however, closer investigation usually shows the mate has been engaging in the undesirable behavior all along. In this stage the partners still remember the past as being wonderful and want things to be "the way they used to be." A relationship at this stage can be improved by a mutual commitment from each partner to put forth efforts to elicit those fulfilling behaviors, lovingly, from his or her partner.

6. *Threshold/Perceptual Reorientation:* The threshold is reached when one or both partners decide the relationship is over. The partner reaching this stage has a memory change—from remembering past pleasurable experiences to remembering primarily past unpleasant memories. Such partners are no longer able to *feel* the good times, even when they think about earlier good times. Sometimes the threshold is reached by the occurrence of a minor event that, like the straw that broke the camel's back, leads a partner to conclude the relationship is over. The partner reaching this threshold has a perceptual reorientation of discounting the partner's positive qualities and instead seeks to find evidence

in the partner's behaviors that warrant terminating the relationship.

7. *Verification:* In this stage the partner who has decided to end the relationship focuses on observing the other's behaviors and qualities to find evidence that warrants termination. Sometimes, during this phase one or both partners experience the feeling that "I can't live with him/her and I can't live without him/her." Considerable emotional energy is generated by anyone with this feeling, because he or she is under intense stress.

Usually one of the partners reaches this stage sooner than the other. One wants out, and the other seeks to maintain the relationship. The person seeking to maintain it may engage in a variety of behaviors such as seeking to please the partner, attempting to make the other partner feel guilty, seeking to have a child in order to "lock" the partner into the relationship, flirting with others to make the partner jealous, or threatening suicide. Relationships at this stage are not fun. The partner who wants out has the most "power" as he or she decides whether the relationship continues or ends.

8. *Termination:* At this stage one or both partners decide to end the relationship. This stage is usually a painful experience for both. Property must be divided. Goodbyes are said—sometimes with considerable anger and animosity. If children are involved, custody and child support arrangements need to be worked out. If the couple is married, the legal divorce process must be gone through. In addition, each person has to work on forming a new life without the former partner.

We often tend to treat strangers with more respect than the people close to us. If a stranger does something we dislike, we usually ignore it or politely express our concerns. But if someone we love does something we dislike, we are apt to criticize and attempt to "train" the partner to meet our expectations. A major suggestion for improving intimate relationships is to seek to treat a partner with the same kind of respect given to strangers.

---

deprive both spouses of much more than each other's company. Because family members performed so many functions for one another, divorce in the past meant a father being without a wife as a partner in educating the children and doing the farm work, and meant a mother being without a husband to plow the fields and raise crops to feed their children. Today, when emotional satisfaction is the bond that holds marriage together, the waning of love and failure to meet one another's expectations for marriage leave few reasons for a marriage to continue. (Highlight 12.4 provides facts about divorce.)

Consequences of Divorce. Both members of the couple, even the person who initiated the divorce, experience grief at the loss. Typical patterns of behavior must be changed. Even the loss of negative behavior patterns causes stress, because new ways of interacting must be established. There is a tendency to feel that the old ways,

even when they were bad, at least were predictable. The unknown is scary to many people. This makes any kind of change more difficult.

Feelings are often strong and varied after a divorce. People may feel anger and anxiety. Things didn't work out as they had planned. It's easy to think of how unfair it all is and to blame the other partner for the failure. People may also feel self-blame and guilt.

A major result of divorce for women generally is a sharp decline in their standard of living. Divorced women and their children usually experience an immediate and sharp drop in their standard of living, whereas the husband's drop in standard of living is usually much less severe. Such discrepancies are often due to the way property is legally divided. For instance, the man frequently gets half of all property. The half allotted to the woman must be shared with her children. Because divorce most frequently results in a severe drop in income for a divorced

Highlight 12.4

Facts about Divorce

Age of spouses: Divorce is most likely to occur when the partners are in their 20s.

Length of engagement: Divorce rates are higher for those having a brief engagement.

Age at marriage: People who marry at a very young age (particularly teenagers) are more apt to divorce.

Length of marriage: Most divorces occur within 2 years after marriage. There is also an increase in divorce shortly after the children are grown—this may be partly because some couples wait until the children are ready to leave the nest before dissolving an unhappy marriage.

Social class: Divorce occurs more frequently at the lower socioeconomic levels.

Education: Divorce rates are higher for those with fewer years of schooling. Interestingly, divorce occurs more frequently when the wife's educational level is higher than the husband's.

Residence: Divorce rates are higher in urban areas than in rural areas.

Second marriages: The more often individuals have divorced, the more likely they are to divorce again.

Religion: The more religious individuals are, the less apt they are to become divorced. Divorce rates are higher for Protestants than for Catholics or Jews. Divorce rates are also higher for interfaith marriages than for single-faith marriages.

Sources: James W. Coleman and Harold R. Kerbo, *Social Problems*, 11th ed. (Upper Saddle River, NJ: Prentice-Hall, 2002, pp. 40–42); and William Kornblum and Joseph Julian, *Social Problems*, 10th ed. (Upper Saddle River, NJ: Prentice-Hall, 2001, pp. 350–354).

---

woman, she and her children must often move to much less expensive housing.

Usually, divided assets do not include occupational assets such as years of experience in full-time employment, health insurance, and future earning-power potential. In families in which the man had been the primary breadwinner, a woman is at a serious disadvantage after divorce. Even women who work outside of the home during the marriage are likely to be in professions earning less money than professions traditionally occupied by men. Also, they are more likely to have lost career time due to pregnancy and child-care leaves and are more likely to have worked part-time.

For older women who have not worked outside of the home, the results are even more serious. They have had no opportunity to acquire skills and experience that are traditionally valued in the workplace. Nor have they been able to acquire access to benefits such as retirement and health insurance. Because of their age, they find it difficult to get jobs that can support them.

In 86 percent of divorce cases, mothers are awarded custody of the children (Papalia et al., 2001). Fathers are usually court ordered to pay child support. But the amounts awarded are generally insufficient to meet the financial needs of the children. In addition, many divorced fathers fail to pay the full amount of child-support payments, and some do not make any court-ordered child-support payments. As a result, the income for the divorced mother and her children often plunges below the poverty level. In many cases taxpayers wind up supporting the mother and her children through the welfare system.

Children of Divorce. Annually, over 1 million children under the age of 18 experience a divorce in their family (U.S. Census Bureau, 2001). Many unknowns must be confronted by children involved in a divorce. For instance, there will often be a change of home environment, frequently to a home that is not as nice as the old one. Another issue children must cope with is custody. Legal custody refers to the fact that one or both parents (the latter in the case of joint custody) maintain all rights and responsibilities regarding the child.

Kaluger and Kaluger (1984) note that society places two conflicting demands on parents who are contemplating a divorce:

One is that the couple's first concern should be with their parental roles and that they should try to put aside their marital problems, which imply that marriage roles are secondary to parental roles. Yet, in a society that places great emphasis on personal ego-need satisfaction in marriage, the placing of marriage in a secondary position may be difficult for the married person to accept. (p.298)

A basic question that parents contemplating divorce ask themselves is: "Which would be better for the children—that we remain unhappily married or we end the marriage and thereby end the conflict and tension?"

© Evan Johnson/Jeroboam

In general, children grow up and become better adjusted when they have a good relationship with one parent than when they grow up in a two-parent home where there is discord and discontent.

A key to answering this question depends on what life will be like after the divorce. In general, children grow up and become better adjusted when they have a good relationship with one parent than when they grow up in a two-parent home with discord and discontent. An inaccessible, rejecting, or hostile parent is worse than an absent one (Papalia et al., 2001).

Within 5 years after a divorce, three-quarters of all divorced people are remarried (Papalia et al., 2001). Therefore, most children of divorce eventually return to living in a family having an adult male and female.

The breakup of a marriage is traumatic not only for the parents but also for the children. Children appear to react more severely to a divorce than they do to the death of a parent, as suggested by the fact that children of divorce are more likely to get into trouble with the law than those in which a parent has died (Coleman & Kerbo, 2002). This delinquent behavior appears to be more of a reaction to the discontent in the home that caused the divorce, rather than a reaction to the separation and divorce itself, because children from intact homes where there is considerable conflict are also more likely to commit delinquent acts.

When parents end a marriage, the children are apt to be fearful of the future, to feel guilty for their own (usually fantasized) role in causing the breakup, to be angry at both parents, and to feel rejected by the parent who moves out. They may become irritable, accident-prone, depressed, bitter, hostile, disruptive, or even suicidal. They may suffer from skin disorders, inability to concentrate, fatigue, loss of appetite, and insomnia. They may also show less interest in their school work and their social lives (Papalia et al., 2001).

Immediately after a breakup there is considerable disruption and disorganization in family life. The parents have a variety of stresses to deal with—including economic pressures (partly the result of now maintaining two households), restrictions on recreational and social activities (more so for the mother, especially if she is unemployed), and the needs for affectionate and intimate relationships. A number of changes also occur in parent-child interactions. Divorced parents make fewer demands on the children, are less consistent in discipline, communicate less effectively with them, and have less control over them. These differences are greatest during the first year after the breakup. The first 2 years after a breakup tend to be stressful for everyone in the family.

A child's reaction to a divorce is affected by a variety of factors, including the age and sex of the child, the length of time of severe discord in the marriage, and the length of time between the first separation and the formal divorce. A key factor in how traumatic the divorce will be for the child is how well the parents deal with the child's concerns, fears, questions, and anxieties. It is much more traumatic when parents do not explain that the breakup is not the child's fault and if the divorce and custody arrangements are hotly contested.

Another factor that increases the trauma is when one or both of the parents seek to turn the child against the other parent. Transferring anger and bitterness about the breakup to the child also increases the child's trauma. The many feelings children of divorce may experience include pain, confusion, anger, hate, bitter disappointment, a sense of failure, and self-doubt.

Children need to work through at least six major issues in order to maintain positive emotional adjustment. First, children need to accept the fact that their parents' marriage is over. They need to understand that their parents will no longer be together and that their access to one or both parents will be changed. Second, children need to withdraw from any conflicts their parents might be having and get on with their own lives and activities. Third, children need to cope with their loss. This might include their loss of contact with a parent, home situation, family rules, or family routines. Fourth, children need to acknowledge and cope with their strong feelings of anger at their parents and of self-blame. They need to forgive all involved, stop dwelling on what went wrong, and attend to the present and future. Fifth, children need to understand that the situation is a permanent one. They need to relinquish any dreams they might have that their parents will get together someday. Sixth, children need to maintain a realism about their own relationships with other people. They need to understand and accept that just because their parents' relationship failed, it does not mean their own close relationships with other people will fail.

Although the period during and immediately following the divorce is traumatic for both parents and children, the negative effects appear to lessen after 2 years. The worst disturbance seems to occur during the first year after the divorce. It seems that after a while the single-parent family is able to make adjustments to the new financial and social situation and regain its homeostasis. Over time, fathers also tend to become less and less available to their children. Perhaps children learn to accept their mother as the primary, single family leader. They have to (and do) adjust to the fact that a father is not always available.

A critical variable affecting children's adjustment to a divorce is the way the parents handle both the divorce and their children's feelings. For example, children react more negatively if the divorce proceedings are drawn out and bitter. Children also suffer when parents use them as a buffer between each other and a means of transmitting hostility because this only fosters children's confusion and resentment. As Highlight 12.5 indicates, the effects of a divorce on children depend largely on what happens after the divorce.

The best thing parents can do is be open with the children about the fact that the marriage has failed. Children should not be made to feel that it was their fault. Parents should clearly take responsibility for their decision to part. Finally, parents should continue to be supportive of their children and understand that the children are suffering

pain and loss, too. Children need to be heard; they need to be able to express their anger, unhappiness, and shock. Only then can all family members begin to accept the new situation and start moving forward.

Lefrancois (1999) reviewed a number of studies on the effects on children of parental separation and divorce. One large body of research (conducted 20 to 40 years ago) generally found divorce has significant negative effects on school achievement, behavior, adjustment, self-concept, and relations with both the remaining parent and the departed parent. Several explanations have been given for this including: absence of one of the parents (the remaining parent has to struggle to raise the children alone), problems associated with the children adjusting to the remaining parent (who may be in emotional turmoil over the breakup of the marriage), continuing conflict between the two parents, and economic hardship. More recent investigations (Lefrancois, 1999), however, are finding less negative effects of divorce on children than were found in earlier studies. Apparently, the impact of divorce was far stronger in the 1950s and 1960s than it is now. Why? Perhaps divorces then were less culturally acceptable and therefore both children and parents affected by divorce were more likely to have faced disapproval and less support from family members, the school system, and the community.

Social Work Roles: Marriage Counseling. The primary social service for people who are considering a divorce, or who have an empty-shell marriage, is marriage counseling. (Those who do obtain a divorce may also need counseling to work out adjustment problems—such as adjusting to a single person's life. Generally such counseling is one-on-one but, at times, may include the ex-spouse and the children, depending on the nature of the problem.)

Marriage counseling is provided by a variety of professionals, including social workers, psychologists, guidance counselors, psychiatrists, and members of the clergy. Marriage counseling is provided (to a greater or lesser extent) by most direct social service agencies.

Marriage counselors generally use a problem-solving approach in which (1) problems are identified; (2) alternative solutions are generated; (3) the merits and shortcomings of the alternatives are examined; (4) the clients select one or more alternatives to implement; and (5) the extent to which the problems are being resolved by the alternatives are later assessed. Because the spouses "own" their problems, they are the primary problem solvers.

A wide range of problems may be encountered by married couples. A partial list of such problems includes sexual problems, financial problems, communica-

Highlight 12.5

The Effects of a Divorce on Children Depend on What Happens after the Divorce

The Haag Family

Mary Beth and Doug Haag obtained a divorce after 9 years of marriage. They had two children, John (8 years old) and David (4 years old). The divorce process was filled with a fair amount of emotional trauma, because both partners were uncertain whether to end the marriage. But both partners were honest in answering their children's questions about the divorce and made crystal clear to them that they were in no way at fault for the marriage ending. Mary Beth and Doug decided to each take custody of a child, partly because John wanted to live with Doug. Doug took custody of John, and Mary Beth took custody of David. The reasons for separating the children were carefully explained to them. The children frequently visited each other on weekends, holidays, and during the summer. Telephone calls between the children were frequent and encouraged.

Mary Beth and Doug respected each other after the divorce and no longer fought. Doug was an accountant, and Mary Beth, an elementary school teacher; both earned enough so that neither was in serious financial difficulty. Doug was married a year and a half later to a woman who understood the harmonious relationship that had developed between Doug and Mary Beth after the divorce.

Mary Beth occasionally dates, but largely concentrates her free time on attending college to obtain her master's degree and on spending time with David. The home environment is now much better for all the Haags than it was in the final years of a marriage that was filled with bitterness and hostility.

The Denny Family

Robert and Corine Denny divorced after 13 years of marriage. Robert, a dentist, asked for the divorce because he was involved with one of his dental assistants. Corine was furious when she found out. Because she had stayed home to raise the children for the last 12 years, she got the larger part of the divorce settlement. She received the house, the year-old Buick, custody of the three children, and $1,200 per month in child support. The reasons for the divorce were never fully explained to the children, because the parents wanted to hide the fact that Robert had been dating someone else for 2 years prior to the divorce. As a result, the children assumed they were responsible for causing the tension and arguments before the divorce and felt guilty because they thought they were responsible for their parents' separation.

Corine became depressed after the divorce and sought to drown her misery in vodka. She also began going out with a woman friend who was also divorced. Frequently she brought men home to stay overnight. Her standard of living dropped sharply. She refused to look for a job or seek job training and sought to live off of the child support payments. When the children visited their father (which was infrequent, because Corine tended to sabotage such visits), Robert sought to dazzle his children with how well his life was now going. Both Robert and Corine sought to use the children as pawns to get back at each other. Corine viewed Robert as someone who had destroyed her comfortable life. Robert viewed Corine as an irresponsible lush.

The children suffered greatly. Their grades dropped sharply in school. They were embarrassed about having friends over because their house was a mess and they never knew when their mother would be intoxicated. The oldest daughter, Jill (12 years old), began skipping school and is now sexually active without using birth control. Bob, 10 years old, was recently caught for shoplifting and is on informal supervision at the juvenile probation department. Dennis, 8 years old, has withdrawn. He spends most of his free time watching rock videos on TV. In school he makes practically no effort, has few friends, and is receiving Ds and Fs in all his classes.

---

tion problems, problems with relatives, interest conflicts, infidelity, conflicts on how to discipline and raise children, and drug abuse problems. Marriage counselors seek to have spouses precisely identify their problems and then use the problem-solving format to resolve the issues. At times, some couples may rationally decide a divorce is in their best interests.

Marriage counselors try to see both spouses together during sessions. Practically all marital conflicts involve both partners and, therefore, are best resolved when both partners work together on resolving the conflicts. (If the spouses are seen separately, each spouse is apt to become suspicious of what the other is telling the counselor.) By seeing both together, the counselor can facilitate communication between the partners and have the partners work together on resolving their concerns. Seeing both partners together allows each partner the opportunity to refute what the other is saying. Only in rare cases is it desirable to hold an individual session with a spouse. For example, if one of the partners wants to work on unwanted emotions dealing with an incestual relationship in the past, meeting individually with that spouse might be desirable. When an individual session is held, the other spouse should be informed of why the session is being held and of what will be discussed. If the other spouse is not informed, there is a danger that he or she will suspect that negative information is being related, which will increase the distrust of both the spouse and the counselor.

Because practically all marital conflicts involve both partners and, therefore, are best resolved when the partners work together on resolving their conflicts, marriage counselors try to see both spouses together.

If some of the areas of conflict involve other family members (such as the children), it may be desirable to include these other family members in some of the sessions. For example, if a father is irritated because his 14-year-old daughter is often disrespectful to him, the daughter may be invited to the next session to work on this subproblem.

The self-help organization Parents Without Partners serves divorced people, unwed mothers or fathers, and stepparents. It is partially a social organization but also an organization to help members with adjustment problems of raising a family alone. Social workers may function as brokers in linking divorcing parents to this organization.

A recent development in social services is divorce mediation, which helps spouses who have decided to obtain a divorce to resolve such issues as dividing the personal property, resolving custody and child support issues, and working out possible alimony arrangements. Some social workers are now receiving specialized training to provide divorce mediation services.

Single-Parent Families

More than 30 percent of all children in the United States are raised in homes with only one parent present. Several reasons account for this: divorce, desertion, death of a spouse, and births outside of marriage. About 90 percent of these families are headed by women. The rate of female-headed homes in African American families is nearly three times that in white families and is over 60 percent (Papalia et al., 2001). These rates have significantly increased over the past two decades. The traditional family configuration (two parents, one a mother

who remains in the home to provide full-time child care) is becoming less and less common.

Just what effect does being raised in single-parent homes have on children? Obviously, a single parent must fulfill all of the responsibilities of running a home, instead of being able to share them with a partner. A single parent wrestles with responsibilities and tasks equal to two full-time jobs in the traditional two-parent family. As described earlier, research reviewed by Lafrancois (1999) parallels the findings of divorce on the adjustment of children: 20 to 40 years ago, children raised in single-parent families were found to be significantly more likely than those raised in two-parent families to experience behavioral, social, emotional, or academic problems.

It must be taken into consideration that this research was done during a time when a father's absence was considered an anomaly. Female-headed, single-parent families are much more common today. Possible negative influences on children, such as feeling different from other children or being stigmatized for their family situations, may no longer have as much adverse impact.

In contrast to research that has found negative effects of single-parent families, other research portrays a more positive picture. For instance, Rutter (1983) found that children grew up and became better adjusted in single-parent families, where they had a positive relationship with their parent, than in two-parent families that were ridden with strife. Likewise, Hetherington (1980) found that a parent who is unapproachable, belligerent, and rejecting can cause more harm to a child than a parent who is not there at all. In summary, it appears that how the available parent feels toward and treats the child are more important than simply having two bodies present in the home.

Poverty affects single-parent families significantly more than two-parent families. Differences in the average income levels of single-parent, female-headed families and two-parent families are striking and deplorable. Thirty-seven percent of female-headed families are living in poverty, compared to 12 percent for two-parent families (U.S. Census Bureau, 2001).

White mothers who live in poverty most likely have been married. Their current single status results from divorce, separation, or death of a spouse. African American mothers in poverty, however, are more likely to have borne their children without having been married (U.S. Census Bureau, 2001). See Highlight 12.6 for information on TANF, which is designed to assist single-parent families, as well as other low-income families.

Blended Families

One of two marriages now ends in divorce (U.S. Census Bureau, 2001). A number of divorcees have had children while married. Most people who obtain a divorce remarry in a few years. Some people are marrying for the first time, but have parented a child while single. A variety of blended families are now being formed in our society. In *blended families* one or both spouses have biologically parented one or more children with someone else prior to the current marriage. In many blended families the newly married couple gives birth to additional children. In some blended families the children are biologically a combination of "his, hers, and theirs."

Many terms are used for two families that are joined together by the marriage of one parent to another: stepfamilies, blended families, reconstituted families, and nontraditional families. Regardless of which term is used, blended families involve complex situations. Conditions depend on variables like the number of children each member of the couple brings into the marriage and the existing relationships already established among members in the previously separate families.

In blended families a number of adjustments have to be made. The husband or wife (or both) have to adjust to raising children that are biologically parented by someone else. The children in blended families have to form relationships with other children in their family who are biologically half-brothers and half-sisters. The children in such families also often have to adjust to a prior divorce that has occurred. Many of the children in blended families have to form relationships with a biological parent who is absent from the home and with a new stepparent. A man or woman who marries a divorced person and brings children into the marriage often has to form a

relationship with the ex-spouse, as the ex-spouse is apt to have visitation rights and an impact on the family. If ex-spouses are still feuding, they are apt to use the children as "pawns" to create problems, which then generate extensive strife and turmoil in families.

Blended families are increasing in number and proportion in our society. The family dynamics and relationships are much more complex than in the traditional nuclear family. Blended families are, in short, burdened by much more baggage than are two adults who are childless and marrying for the first time. Blended families must deal with stress that arises from the losses (as a result of divorce or death) experienced by both adults and children, which can make them afraid to love and to trust. Previously established bonds between children and their biological parents may interfere with the formation of ties to the stepparent. If children go back and forth between two households, conflicts between stepchildren and stepparents may be intensified.

Some difficulties in adjustment can be anticipated (Lefrancois, 1999). They include jealousies arising between new siblings. Jealousies may focus on the sharing of parental attention with the new spouse and with new siblings. Another issue for children is the adjustment to a new parent, who may have new ideas, values, rules, and expectations. Yet another adjustment involves sharing space and properties when children aren't used to sharing with these new people or to sharing at all. Finally, if one member of the couple comes into the marriage with no childrearing experience, an adjustment is apt to be necessary by all family members to allow time for the new parent to learn and adapt.

People come into a blended family with ideas and issues based on past experiences. Old relationships and ways of doing things still have their impacts. In discussing blended families, Stuart and Jacobsen (1985) suggest that marrying a new partner involves marrying a whole new family. A blended family differs somewhat from a traditional family in that more people are involved—for example, ex-spouses, former in-laws, as well as an assortment of cousins, uncles, and aunts. The married couple can have both positive and negative interactions with this large supporting cast. If a prior marriage has ended bitterly, the unresolved emotions that remain will affect the present relationship.

The area of greatest stress for most stepparents is that of child rearing. A stepchild, used to being raised in a somewhat different way, may balk at having to conform to a new set of rules. The stepchild may also have difficulty accepting the stepparent as one who has the right to parent him or her. Such a difficulty is more likely to arise

Highlight 12.6

Temporary Assistance to Needy Families (TANF)

In 1996 President Bill Clinton and the Democrats and Republicans in Congress compromised on welfare reform and passed the Personal Responsibility and Work Opportunity Reconciliation Act. This act abolished the AFDC (Aid to Families of Dependent Children) program, and replaced it with TANF. No longer is cash assistance to the poor an entitlement. It is now a short-term program and a variable one among the states. Key provisions of TANF are the following:

- The federal guarantee of cash assistance for poor families with children (under the AFDC program) is ended. Each state now receives a capped block grant (lump sum) to run its own welfare and work programs.

- The head of every family has to work within 2 years, or the family loses its benefits. After receiving welfare for 2 months, adults have to perform community service unless they have found regular jobs. (States can choose not to have a community service requirement.)

- Lifetime public welfare assistance is limited to 5 years. (States can establish stricter limits.) Hardship exemptions from this requirement are available for up to 20 percent of the recipients in a state.

- States can provide payments to unmarried teenage parents only if a mother under 18 is living at home, or in another adult-supervised setting, and attends high school or an alternative educational or training program as soon as the child is 12 weeks old.

- States are required to maintain their own spending on public welfare at 75 percent of their 1994 level, or 80 percent if they failed to put enough public welfare recipients to work.

- States cannot penalize a woman on public welfare who does not work because she cannot find day care for a child under 6 years old.

- States are required to deduct from the benefits of welfare mothers who refuse to help identify the fathers. States may deny Medicaid to adults who lose welfare benefits because of a failure to meet work requirements.

- A woman on public welfare, who refuses to cooperate in identifying the father of her child, must lose at least 25 percent of her benefits.

- Future legal immigrants who have not yet become citizens are ineligible for most federal welfare benefits and social services during their first 5 years in the United States. SSI benefits and food stamp eligibility ended for noncitizens, including legal immigrants, receiving benefits in 1996.

Since each state has considerable leeway in designing its own version of TANF, it is accurate to indicate that there are 50 versions of TANF. Taking advantage of the flexibility allowed by the federal legislation, some states modified TANF services by setting stricter time limits on how long someone living in poverty could receive cash assistance. For example, Georgia and Florida set their limits at 48 months; Montana and Indiana, at 24 months; and Utah, at 36 months. Cash amounts given to TANF participants vary widely from one state to another, with Alabama and Mississippi on the low end, and California and New York on the high end.

A number of studies have been conducted, and are continuing to be conducted, on the effects of Temporary Assistance to Needy Families. (The long-term effects on children in these families will not be known for many years, as follow-up studies will have to be conducted, when the children grow up and become adults, in order to determine the long-term effects of TANF on children.) Initial results of the early studies are the following:

1. More single mothers are working. An initial positive result was that the number of Americans on cash assistance plummeted in the first few years of the program.

2. Most mothers who leave the welfare rolls find jobs, but a large minority do not. Moreover, some of those who find jobs soon lose them and do not again appear on the welfare rolls.

3. Incomes are rising at the top, but not at the bottom. Some former welfare recipients are making successful transitions to work, often after many years of welfare dependency. Yet, even the more successful jobholders experience economic hardship and often must ask for help from family and friends. Jencks and Swingle (2000) note:

Some single mothers can't manage both employment and parenthood simultaneously. Even those who have the energy and skill to juggle work and parenthood often earn so little that they cannot make ends meet without additional help. If such help is not available, the long-term impact of welfare reform on both single mothers and their

---

if the stepchild feels sad because the missing parent is not present. If the husband and wife disagree about how to raise children, the chances of conflict are substantially increased. Stepparents and stepchildren also face the problem of adjusting to the habits and personalities of each

other. Stepparents should not rush into establishing a relationship with stepchildren; a gradual effort at establishing a relationship is more likely to result in a trusting and positive relationship. Lefrancois (1999) notes that becoming a stepparent is usually more difficult for a woman be-

children could well turn out to be like the long-term impact of deinstitutionalization on the mentally ill: good for some but terrible for others. This is a worst-case scenario. But it is a possibility we should bear in mind as states keep cutting their welfare rolls. (p. 51)

4. There have been significant increases in the proportion of poor people, especially single mothers and their children, who are not covered by health insurance. Once people leave welfare to begin working, they may not be eligible for Medicaid, and their employer may not offer health insurance.

5. Almost all mothers who are working state they prefer work to welfare.

6. Many working mothers report problems finding satisfactory child care. There is some evidence that young children are being left alone, sometimes for long periods. Will welfare reform end up helping parents, but hurting their children?

7. The TANF program was implemented at a time when the nation's economy was booming. If a serious recession occurs, no one knows what will happen to TANF participants if few jobs are available.

8. The people who have been kicked off the welfare rolls are pushing down wages for low-skilled workers in the United States. People desperate for food and shelter are working for lower wages than those, currently employed, who may lose their jobs to former welfare recipients.

9. States now have many more choices in determining whom they will assist, what requirements they will impose upon those who receive aid, and what noncash supports those families will receive. As a result, there is much more disparity between states with TANF, as compared to AFDC. With this disparity between states, two children in identical situations in different states now live with very different realities. One may have household resources above the poverty level, stable and high-quality child care, and health insurance, while the other may have none of these.

10. TANF has transformed the central question of American welfare policy—from how much to give single mothers who do not work, to how to support work among low-income families with children.

11. Teenage birthrates have fallen in recent years. One motivation for the passage of the 1996 Welfare Reform Act was the desire to change policies that conservatives claim reward early

childbearing by single mothers. The Welform Reform Act denies public assistance payments to teenage mothers, except under the following conditions: States can provide payments to unmarried teenage parents only if a mother under 18 is living at home, or in another adult-supervised setting, and if she attends high school or an alternative educational or training program as soon as the child is 12 weeks old. The underlying reason behind denying welfare payments to most teenage mothers is to send a message to teenagers that having babies will not be financially rewarded.

Researching the effects of TANF on children is very difficult. Schorr (2001) notes:

How family arrangements were affected will be murky; how children are making out will not be known in a reliable way. Researching these issues is difficult. (p. 72)

Some children will be better-off. Their mother (and father) may be gainfully employed. A few of these working parents may rise in socioeconomic status, and may have an increased self-worth, and a higher living status. Eventually, these families will have more total income than when they received cash assistance. In such families, the children are apt to be proud of their working mother (or parents), and such children are apt to follow their mother's (parents') example.

On the other hand, many children may be worse-off under TANF than under AFDC, Schorr (2001) notes:

[A]s a result of welfare reform, many children are moved about—arbitrarily, as it seems to them, aimlessly—into daycare; from their mother to a grandmother; to a county foster home, and, with luck, back home again; from one school to another or to no school at all; even into the street or to a shelter for the homeless. They may not eat as well as they once did; they may be deprived of medical care. Viewed educationally, it is as if they were being schooled to become poor adults—untrained, insecure, truculent. (p. 47)

There is a serious danger that many TANF recipients will be trapped into long-term poverty. TANF programs provide almost no opportunities, via paid benefits, for TANF recipients to attain a higher level of education than high school. As a result, TANF recipients are likely to obtain minimum-wage jobs that lead to "dead-end work," (work involving poor pay, scant fringe benefits, and little opportunity for advancement). The education offered to TANF recipients does not prepare or qualify them for higher-end work.

The 1935 Social Security Act created a social safety net of programs for children and others in need. It is, as yet, too early to determine whether TANF has ripped *major holes* in this social safety net.

cause children tend to be emotionally closer to their biological mother and have spent more time with her than with the father.

Three myths about blended families can also be addressed (Janzen & Harris, 1986). First, there is the myth of the "wicked stepmother." This involves the idea that

the stepmother is not really concerned about what is best for the children, but is more concerned about her own well-being. The story of "Cinderella" comes to mind. Here, the "wicked stepmother" cruelly keeps Cinderella from going to the ball in the hope that her own biological daughters will have a better chance at nabbing the handsome prince. In reality, stepmothers have been found to establish very positive and caring relationships with their stepchildren, provided that the stepmothers have a strong self-concept and the support of their husband (Papalia et al., 2001).

A second myth about blended families is that "step is less" (Wald, 1981). In other words, this myth asserts that stepchildren will never hold the same place in the hearts of parents that biological children do. This myth does not take into account the fact that people can learn to love each other and are motivated to bind members of their new family together.

The third myth about blended families is that the moment they become joined as one family, they will have "instant love" for each other (Wald, 1981). Relationships take time to develop and grow. The idea of instantly having strong love bonds for each other does not make sense. People involved in any relationship need time to get to know each other, test each other out, and grow to feel comfortable with each other. Kail and Cavanaugh (2000) reviewed the research literature on stepparenthood and concluded: (1) Integration tends to be easier in families that have been split by divorce than by death, perhaps because the children realize the first marriage is not working out; (2) stepparents and stepchildren come to the blended family with unrealistic expectations that love and togetherness will rapidly occur; (3) children tend to see a stepparent of the opposite sex as playing favorites with their own children; (4) most children continue to miss and admire the absent biological parent; (5) male children tend to more readily accept a stepparent, particularly if the new parent is also a male; and (6) adolescents have greater difficulty accepting a stepparent than young children or adult children.

Stepfamilies need to pursue at least four tasks in order to achieve integration (Visher, 1982; Visher & Visher, 1983). The first task involves acknowledging that losses from old relationships do exist. In addition to the bad times suffered in these prior relationships, there are also memories of the good times. Recalling how good things used to be may elicit feelings of sadness that these times are gone and anger that they can be no more. As Janzen and Harris (1986) put it, "In this case, help is usually needed to assist stepfamily members in sorting out feelings, identifying sources of sadness and anger, and looking at the new family as an opportunity to develop and share meaningful relationships, without being disloyal to friends and relatives or desecrating pleasant memories from previous experiences" (p. 284).

A second task for stepfamilies is the creation of new customs and traditions. New ways of doing things need to be established to replace the old ways used in the old family structures. New traditions involve a combination of values and activities enjoyed by all new blended family members. For instance, one side of a newly blended family member celebrated at home on New Year's Eve and the other side celebrated the New Year on New Year's Day. A completely new tradition might be established where the family spends the New Year's holiday at a resort and celebrates both on New Year's Eve and New Year's Day.

A lobster bake offers an opportunity for new members of a blended family to work on alliances.

© Sara Gray/Getty Images

The third task for blended families involves establishing new alliances within the family. Alliances may involve not only the spouses' relationship with each other, but also relationships among siblings and between parents and children. Spending time on activities together is one of several ways of working on alliances.

The fourth task for blended families is integration. Parents have the responsibility of providing organization for the family. Children need to have their limits defined and consistently upheld. One of the difficulties is that children are faced with a new stepparent attempting to gain control, when they have not yet enjoyed many supportive and positive experiences with this new individual. It is important, therefore, for the new stepparent to provide nurturance and positive feedback to stepchildren, in addition to making rules and maintaining control.

Berman (1981) and Visher and Visher (1983) give the following suggestions to help parents in blended families increase the chances of positive relationships developing between adults and children:

1. Maintain a courteous relationship with the former spouse or spouses. Children adjust best after a divorce when there are harmonious relationships between former spouses. Problems are intensified when former spouses continue to insult each other and when the children are used as weapons for angry former spouses to hurt each other.

2. Understand the emotions of their children. Although the newly wed adults in a recently formed blended family may be fairly euphoric about their relationship, these adults need to be perceptive and responsive to the fears, concerns, and resentments of their children.

3. Allow time for loving relationships to develop between stepparents and stepchildren. Stepparents need to be aware that their stepchildren will probably have emotional ties to their absent biological parent, and that the stepchildren may resent the breakup of the former marriage. Some children may even feel they are responsible for their biological parents separating. Some may try to make life difficult for the stepparent so that he or she will leave, with the hope that the biological parents will then reunite. Stepparents need to be perceptive and understanding of such feelings, and patiently allow their stepchildren time to work out their concerns and to bond.

4. New rituals, traditions, and ways of doing things that seem right and enjoyable for all members of the blended family need to be developed. Sometimes it is helpful to move to a new house or a new apartment that does not hold memories of a past life. Leisure time should be given structure so that the children spend time alone with the biological parent of the family, some time alone with the stepparent, some time with both of these parents together, and some time perhaps with the absent parent or parents. The new spouses also need time to be alone. New rituals need to be developed for holidays, birthdays, and other special days.

5. Seek social support. Parents in blended families should seek to share their concerns, feelings, frustrations, experiences, coping strategies, and triumphs with other stepparents and stepchildren. Such sharing allows parents in blended families to view their own situations more realistically and to learn from the experiences of others.

Mothers Working Outside the Home

A major break with tradition has occurred with the surge of married women entering the workforce over the past several decades. In 1948, only 11 percent of all married women with children under age 6 were in the labor force. In 2001 this figure was over 60 percent (U.S. Census Bureau, 2001). When we look at the percentage of married women working outside of the home with children under 18, the figure jumps to 70 percent. Single mothers are also likely to enter the labor force; 61 percent of single mothers with children work outside of the home. Most working mothers work full time.

Many questions have been raised concerning the effects of working mothers (and single working custodial fathers) on the social and emotional development of children. The traditional view stressed the importance of a stable, supportive, caregiver being available consistently to meet the needs of children. In other words, it was important for a mother to remain in the home and coordinate the family's care and activities. However, research indicates that women need not have to remain home in order to maintain a well-adjusted family.

Reviews of the research on working mothers and their children conclude that if the mother is satisfied with her job and the provision for child care is reasonably good and suitable, there is no adverse effect on the child's development (Papalia et al., 2001). Many contemporary researchers emphasize the positive effects of a mother's employment on her entire family.

Some questions have been raised concerning the effects on children under age 3 when mothers work outside the home. These questions tend to revolve around the issue of maternal deprivation (that is, that infants are emotionally deprived if they do not have enough contact with their mother). Concerns were initially raised after some very early research indicated that institutionalized infants suffered negative effects. This research related these negative effects to the fact that the mother was absent. However, could these effects have been due to the fact that the infants received inadequate care and very little attention from anyone? It may not necessarily be that they specifically missed their mother.

There is no simple answer to the question about the effects on children of their mothers working. Children need consistent nurturance, guidance, and care. Home conditions vary widely. Not all biological mothers provide adequate care and attention to their young children. Also the conditions under which a mother works vary tremendously. Some mothers love their jobs; others hate having to work. The level of the mother's overall satisfaction with life must affect the child.

Indications are that good child care, that is, child care that provides the child with consistent attention and care, does not harm a child. Much of the research on the effects on children of mothers working was performed in good facilities with high-quality care. Many parents find it very difficult to get good child care. This is due to many reasons, including cost, location, hours available, type of care, and age restrictions on children. Substantial concerns exist when the single mother works outside the home (or when both parents work outside the home) and the children receive poor child care or no care. It seems that the ideal solution is to make enough good alternative care available so that mothers can work with the knowledge that their children are well cared for.

One other related issue concerns the role of the father in caring for children in those cases where a father is present in the home. Can't the father be a primary participant in child care? It's interesting that the term maternal deprivation is commonly used, while the parallel term paternal deprivation is not. In reality, mothers, whether they work outside of the home or not, generally maintain the primary responsibility for child care in our society.

Child rearing is most often seen as the mother's responsibility. However, perhaps this idea was more credible when few women worked outside of the home. Perhaps changing attitudes to encourage shared parenting would be in the best interest of families.

The "Sandwich" Generation

Many middle-aged adults are "sandwiched" between two generations—their parents and their children. This puts great demands and pressures on them. Because the elderly are the fastest growing age group in terms of numbers in our society, an increasing proportion of middle-aged adults find themselves providing care for their parents as well as their children. Some middle-aged adults have their children and a parent or two living with them. People find it very difficult to find the time and resources to respond to the needs and demands of their work, their children, and their parents. Papalia and Olds (1998) identify the following stresses and demands faced by adult children when their parents' dependency on them becomes evident:

> Adults who have been looking forward to the waning of responsibility for their children and who sense keenly that their own remaining years are limited may fear that caring for their parents will deprive them of any chance to fulfill their dreams.
>
> Adult children may be torn between love and resentment, between duty to parents and duty to spouses and children, and between wanting to do the right thing and not wanting to change their lives. Such children may feel disappointment, anger, or guilt. Anxiety over the anticipated end of a parent's life may be tinged with worry about one's own mortality. (p. 526)

For members of the sandwich generation who are working outside the home, flexible work schedules can help alleviate the stresses associated with both caregiving responsibilities and work responsibilities. The Family and Medical Leave Act, adopted in 1993, guarantees family caregivers some unpaid leave. In addition, some large corporations provide time off for caregiving.

❧ Assessing and Intervening in Family Systems

Families are characterized by multiple ongoing interactions. When social workers intervene with families there is much to observe and understand. The dimensions of family interaction that will be discussed here include communication, family norms, and problems commonly faced by families. In addition, two prominent family assessment instruments will be described: the ecomap and the genogram.

Verbal and Nonverbal Communication

Communication involves transmitting information from one person to another. To do this, a common system of symbols, signs, or behavior is used. Verbal communication involves the use of words and will be addressed first.

The first phase of verbal communication involves the translation of thoughts into words. The information sender must know the correct words and how to put them together. Only then will the information have the chance of being effectively received. The sender may be vague or inaccurate with the message, and interruptions and distractions may detract from the communication process.

The information receiver then must be receptive to the information. That is, she or he must be paying attention both to the sender and to the sender's words. The receiver must understand what the specific words mean. Inaccuracies or problems at any point in this process can stop the information from getting across to the receiver. At any point distortions may interfere.

Verbal communication patterns inside the family include who talks a lot and who talks only rarely. They involve who talks to whom and who defers to whom. They also reflect the subtle and not so subtle qualities involved in family members' relationships.

The sender also transmits nonverbal messages along with the verbal messages. These include facial expressions, body posture, emotions displayed, and many other subtle aspects of communication. Somewhere between verbal and nonverbal aspects of communication are voice inflection, intonation, and loudness. All this gives the receiver additional information about the intent and specific meaning of the message that's being sent. Sometimes the receiver will attribute more value to the nonverbal aspects of the message than the verbal.

For example, a 17-year-old son asks his father, "Dad, can I have the car next Saturday night?" Dad, who's in the middle of writing up his tax returns (which are due in 2 days), replies, "No, Harry." Harry interprets this to mean that his father is an authoritarian tyrant who does not trust him with the family car. Harry stomps off in a huff. However, what Dad really meant was that he and Mom need the car this Saturday because they're taking their best friends, the Jamesons, out for their twentieth wedding anniversary. Dad was also thinking that perhaps the Jamesons wouldn't mind driving. Or maybe he and Harry could work something out to share the car. At any rate, Dad really meant that he was much too involved with the tax forms to talk about it and would rather do it during dinner.

This is a good example of ineffective communication. The information was vague and incomplete, and neither person clarified his thoughts or gave feedback to the other. There are endless variations to the types of ineffective communication that can take place in families. Social workers often can help to clarify, untangle, and reconstruct communication patterns.

One especially important aspect of assessing messages is whether they are congruent or incongruent. Communication is *incongruent* when two or more messages contradict

each other's meaning. In other words, the messages are confusing. Contradictory messages within families disturb effective family functioning.

Nonverbal messages can sometimes contradict verbal messages. For example, a recently widowed woman says, "I'm sorry Frank passed away," with a big grin on her face. The information expressed by the words indicates that she is sad. However, her accompanying physical expressions show that she is happy. Her words are considered socially appropriate for the situation. However, in this particular case, she seems relieved to get rid of "the old buzzard" and happy to be the beneficiary of a large life insurance policy.

The double message reflected by the widow's verbal and nonverbal behavior provides a relatively simple, clearcut illustration of potential problem communication within families. However, congruence is certainly not the only important aspect of nonverbal communication. All of the principles of nonverbal communication discussed in Chapter 11 can be applied to communication within families.

Family Norms

Family *norms* are the rules that specify what is considered proper behavior within the family group. Many times the most powerful rules are those that are not clearly and verbally stated. Rather, these are implicit rules or repeated family transactions that all family members understand but never discuss. It's important for families to establish norms that allow both the entire family and each individual member to function effectively and productively.

Every family differs in its individual set of norms or rules. For example, Family A has a relatively conservative set of norms governing communication and interpersonal behavior. Although the norms allow frequent pleasant talk among family members, it is always on a superficial level. The snowy winter weather or the status of the new variety of squash grown in the garden is fair game for conversation. However, nothing more personal is ever mentioned. Taboo subjects include anything to do with feelings, interpersonal relationships, or opinions about careers or jobs. On one occasion, for example, a friend asked the family matriarch what her son and daughter-in-law would name their soon-to-be-born first baby. With a shocked expression on her face, she replied, "Oh, my heavens, I haven't asked. I don't want to interfere."

Family B, on the other hand, has a vastly different set of norms governing communication and behavior. Virtually everything is discussed and debated, not only among the nuclear family members but among several generations. Personal methods of birth control, stances on abortion, opinions on capital punishment, and politics number among the emotionally heated issues discussed. Family members frequently talk about their personal relationships, including who is the favorite grandchild and who tends to fight all the time with rich-old Aunt Harriet. The family is so open that price tags are left on gifts.

The rules of behavior that govern Family B are very different from those of Family A. Yet, in each family, the members consider their family's behavior to be normal. Members of each family may find it inconceivable that families could be any other way.

In families with problems, however, most frequently the family rules do not allow the family or the individual members to function effectively and productively. Ineffective norms need to be identified and changed. Positive, beneficial norms need to be developed and fostered.

The following is an example of a family in which there was an implicit, invalid, and ineffective norm functioning. The norm was that no one in the family would smoke cigarettes. A husband, wife, four children, and two sets of grandparents composed this family. Although never discussed, the understanding was that no one had ever or would ever smoke. One day the husband found several cigarette butts in the ashtray of the car typically used by his wife. He thought this odd but said nothing. Over the next 6 months, he frequently found cigarette butts in the same ashtray. Because no one in the family smoked, he deduced that these butts must belong to someone else. He assumed that his wife was having an affair with another man, which devastated him. However, he said nothing about it and suffered in silence. His relationship with his wife began to deteriorate. He became sullen, and spats and conflicts became more frequent. Finally, in a heated conflict, he spit out his thoughts and feelings about the cigarette butts and her affair. His wife expressed shocked disbelief. The reality was that it was she who smoked the cigarettes, but only when no one else was around. Her major time to be alone was when she was driving to and from work. She took advantage of this time to smoke, but occasionally forgot to empty the ashtray. She told him the entire story, and he was tremendously relieved. Their relationship improved and prospered.

This example illustrates how an inappropriate norm almost ruined a family relationship. Such a simple thing as the wife being a "closet smoker" had the potential for destroying a marital relationship. In this instance, a simple correction in communication solved the problem. The interesting thing is that eventually the entire family learned of this incident. The wife still smokes but still insists on doing it privately. The family now functions effectively with an amended family rule that accepts smoking.

Social workers need to identify and understand family norms so that inappropriate, ineffective norms can be changed. At any point, a social worker can point out such an ineffective norm to family members, help them clarify alternative solutions and changes, and help them assess which is the best solution for them.

Family System Assessment: The Ecomap

An *ecomap* is a paper-and-pencil assessment tool used by practitioners to assess specific troubles and plan interventions for clients. The ecomap is a drawing of the client/family in its social environment. An ecomap is usually jointly drawn by the social worker and the client. It helps both the worker and the client achieve a holistic or ecological view of the client's family life and the nature of the family's relationships with groups, associations, organizations, other families, and individuals. It has been used in a variety of situations, including marriage and family counseling, and adoption and foster care home studies. The ecomap has also been used to supplement traditional social histories and case records. It is a shorthand method for recording basic social information. The technique helps users (clients and practitioners) gain insight into clients' problems and better sort out how to make constructive changes. The technique provides a "snapshot view" of important interactions at a particular point in time. The primary developer of the technique is Ann Hartman (1978).

A typical ecomap consists of a family diagram surrounded by a set of circles and lines used to describe the family within an environmental context. The ecomap user can create her or his own abbreviations and symbols (see Figure 12.2).

To draw an ecomap, a circle (representing the client's family) is placed in the center of a large, blank sheet of paper (see Figure 12.3). The composition of the family is indicated within the family circle. A number of other circles are drawn in the area surrounding the family circle. These represent the other systems (that is, the groups, other families, individuals, and organizations) with which the family ordinarily interacts.

Different kinds of lines are drawn to describe the nature of the relationships that the members of the client family have with the other systems. The directional flow of energy (indicating giving and/or receiving of resources and communication between the client family members and the significant systems) is expressed by the use of arrows. A case example of the use of an ecomap follows.

Figure 12.2 **Commonly Used Symbols in an EcoMap**

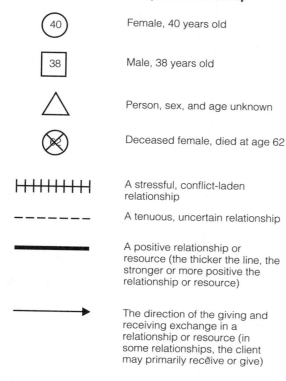

40	Female, 40 years old
38	Male, 38 years old
△	Person, sex, and age unknown
⊗	Deceased female, died at age 62
╫╫╫╫╫	A stressful, conflict-laden relationship
– – – – – –	A tenuous, uncertain relationship
▬▬▬	A positive relationship or resource (the thicker the line, the stronger or more positive the relationship or resource)
⟶	The direction of the giving and receiving exchange in a relationship or resource (in some relationships, the client may primarily receive or give)

Barb and Mike Haynes are referred to the Adult Services Unit of the Greene County Human Services Department by Dean Medical Clinic. The clinic has been treating Mike's mother, Ruth Haynes, for Alzheimer's disease since she was diagnosed with the disorder 4 years ago. For the past three years she has been living with Barb and Mike Haynes. She now requires round-the-clock care, because during the evening hours she has trouble sleeping, wanders around the house, and starts screaming when she becomes lost in the house and confused. Dean Medical Clinic refers Barb and Mike Haynes to the Adult Services Unit to explore alternative caregiving arrangements.

Barb and Mike Haynes meet with Maria Garcia, Adult Services Worker. They indicate that they feel a moral obligation to continue caring for Ruth in their home, because Ruth spent most of her adult years caring for Mike and his brother and sister when they were children. Barb and Mike also indicate that they have a 2-year-old child, Erin, at home. This is a second marriage for both Barb and Mike, and they are paying for Mike's son, Brian, to attend the state university. With such expenses, both believe they need to continue to work because of their financial obligations. Mike's oldest sister, Mary Kruger, is a single parent who has two children in high school. Mary Kruger

Figure 12.3 **Setting Up an EcoMap**

An ecomap is an assessment tool for depicting the relationships and interactions between a client family and its social environment. The largest circle in the center depicts the client family. The surrounding circles represent the significant groups, organizations, other families, and individuals that make up the family's social environment.

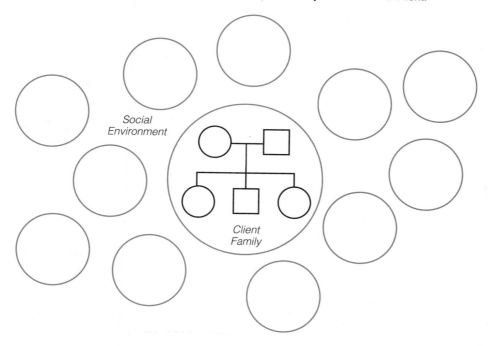

has a visual disability but has been able to be the primary caregiver for Ruth and Erin during the daylight hours when Mike and Barb are working outside the home. Recently, Mary informed Mike and Barb that caring for Ruth is becoming too difficult for her and that some kind of alternative care is needed. Ms. Garcia suggests adult day care for Ruth may be a useful resource during the daytime.

Mike adds that it is emotionally devastating to see his mother slowly deteriorate. He indicates he is in a double bind; he feels an obligation to care for his mother but

doing so is causing major disruptions in his family life. The stress has resulted in marital discord with Barb, and he adds that both he and Barb have increasingly become "short" in temper and patience with Erin.

At this point, Ms. Garcia suggests it may be helpful to graphically diagram their present dilemma. Together, the Hayneses and Ms. Garcia draw the ecomap shown in Figure 12.4. While drawing the map, Mike inquires whether Ruth's medical condition might soon stabilize. Ms. Garcia indicates that temporarily Ruth may

Figure 12.4 Sample EcoMap: Barb and Mike Haynes

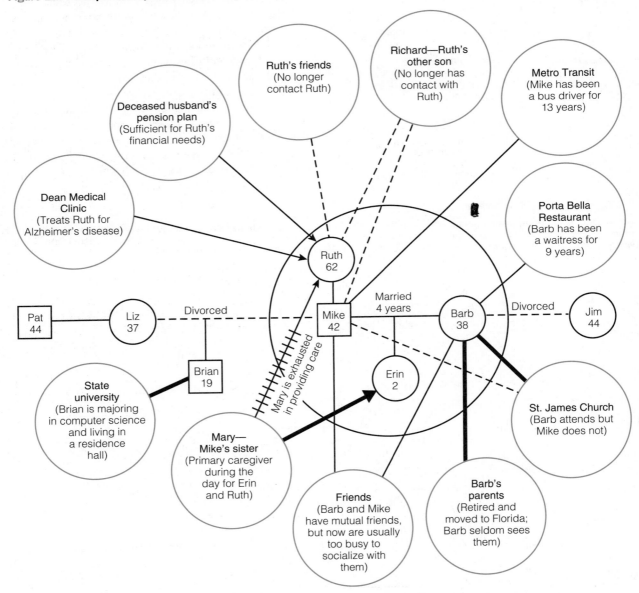

occasionally appear to stabilize but that the long-term prognosis is gradual deterioration in mental functioning and in physical capabilities. The ecomap helps Mike and Barb see that even though they are working full time during the day and spending the remainder of their waking hours caring for Erin and Ruth, they are becoming too emotionally and physically exhausted to continue doing all of this. During the past 3 years, they have also ceased socializing with friends. Now they seldom have any time to spend even with Brian. Feeling helpless and hopeless, they inquire if some other care arrangement is available besides a nursing home. They indicate that Ruth has stated on numerous occasions, "I'd rather die now than be placed in a nursing home." Ms. Garcia states that there are some high-quality adult group homes in the area. The Hayneses are given the addresses.

After visiting a few of the care facilities, Barb and Mike ask Ruth to stay for a few days at one they particularly like. At first Ruth is opposed to going for a "visit." But after being there a few days, she adjusts fairly well, and soon concludes (erroneously, but no one objects) that it is a home she bought and that the people on the staff are her "domestic employees." Ruth's adjustment eases the guilt that Barb and Mike feel in placing Ruth in a care facility, and this results in substantial improvements in their marital relationship and in their interactions with Erin, Brian, and their friends.

A major value of an ecomap is that it facilitates both the worker's and the client's view of the client's family from a systems and an ecological perspective. Sometimes, as happened in the case of the Hayneses, the drawing of the ecomap helps clients and practitioners gain greater insight into the social dynamics of a problematic situation.

Family System Assessment: The Genogram

A *genogram* is a graphic way of investigating the origins of a client's problem by diagramming the family over at least three generations. The client and the worker usually jointly construct the family genogram. The genogram is essentially a family tree. Murray Bowen is the primary developer of this technique (Kerr & Bowen, 1988). The genogram is a useful tool for the worker and family members to examine problematic emotional and behavioral patterns in an intergenerational context. Emotional and behavioral patterns in families tend to repeat themselves; what happens in one generation will often occur in the next. Genograms help family members to identify and understand family relationship patterns.

Figure 12.5 shows some of the commonly used symbols. Together, the symbols provide a visual picture, for at least three generations, of a family tree including the family members; their names, ages, and gender; marital status; sibling positions, and so on. When relevant, additional items of information may be included, such as

Figure 12.5 **Commonly Used Genogram Symbols**

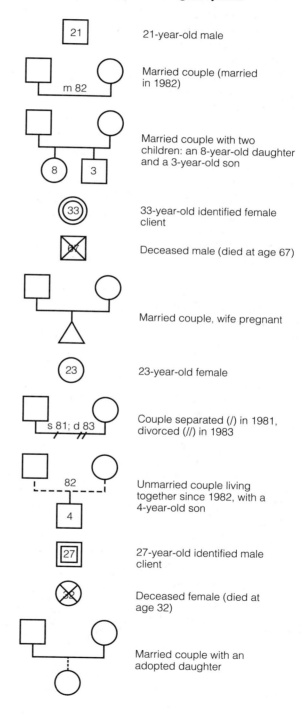

21-year-old male

Married couple (married in 1982)

Married couple with two children: an 8-year-old daughter and a 3-year-old son

33-year-old identified female client

Deceased male (died at age 67)

Married couple, wife pregnant

23-year-old female

Couple separated (/) in 1981, divorced (//) in 1983

Unmarried couple living together since 1982, with a 4-year-old son

27-year-old identified male client

Deceased female (died at age 32)

Married couple with an adopted daughter

emotional difficulties, behavioral problems, religious affiliation, ethnic origins, geographic locations, occupations, socioeconomic status, and significant life events. The use of the genogram is illustrated in the following case example.

Chris Witt makes an appointment with Kyle Nolan, a social worker in private practice. Chris is distraught. He indicates his wife, Karen, and two children are currently at Sister House, a shelter for battered women. Chris states he and his wife had a "scuffle" 2 days ago, and she bruised her face. Yesterday, when he was at work, she left home with the children and went to Sister House. He adds that she has contacted an attorney and is now seeking a divorce.

Mr. Nolan inquires as to the specifics of the "scuffle." Chris says he came home after having a few beers. His dinner was cold, and he "got on" Karen for not cleaning up the house. He adds that Karen then started mouthing off, and he slapped her to shut her up. Mr. Nolan inquires whether such incidents had occurred in the past. Chris indicates, "A few times," and adds that getting physical with Karen is the only way for him to "keep her in line." He says he works all day long in his small business as a concrete contractor, while his wife sits at home watching soap operas. He feels she is not doing her "fair share" and the house usually looks like a "disaster."

Mr. Nolan asks Chris if he feels getting physical with his wife is justifiable. He responds, "Sure," and adds that his dad frequently told him to "spare the rod, and spoil both the wife and the kids." Mr. Nolan asks Chris if his dad was at times abusive to him when he was a child. Chris indicates that he was and adds that to this day he detests his dad for being abusive to him and to his mother.

Mr. Nolan then suggests that together they draw a "family tree," focusing on three areas: episodes of heavy drinking, episodes of physical abuse, and traditional versus modern gender stereotypes. Mr. Nolan explains that a *traditional gender stereotype* includes the husband as being the primary decision maker, the wife as being submissive to him, and the wife as being primarily responsible for domestic tasks. The *modern gender stereotype* involves an equalitarian relationship between husband and wife. After an initial reluctance (Chris expresses confusion as to how such a "tree" would help get his wife back), Chris agrees. The resulting genogram is presented in Figure 12.6.

The genogram helps Mr. Witt to see that he and his wife are products of family systems that have strikingly different values and customs. In his family, the males tend to drink heavily, have a traditional view of marriage, and tend to use physical force in interactions with their

spouses and children. Upon questioning, Chris mentions that he has, at times, struck his own children. Mr. Nolan asks Chris how he feels about repeating the same patterns of abuse with his wife and children that he despised his father for using. Tears come to his eyes, and he says one word, "Guilty."

Mr. Nolan and Chris discuss courses of action that Chris might take to change his family interactions and how he might best approach his wife to request that she and the children return. Chris agrees to attend AA (Alcoholics Anonymous) meetings and a therapy group for batterers. After a month of attending these weekly meetings, Chris contacts his wife and asks her to return. Karen agrees to return *if* Chris stops drinking (most of the abuse occurred when he was intoxicated) and *if* he agrees to continue to attend group therapy and AA meetings. Chris readily agrees. Karen's parents express their disapproval of her returning.

For the first few months, Chris Witt is on his best behavior, and there is considerable harmony in the Witt family. Then one day Chris has to fire one of his employees. Feeling bad, he stops afterward at a tavern and drinks until he is intoxicated. When he finally arrives home, he starts to verbally and physically abuse Karen and the children. This is the final straw for Karen. She takes the children to her parents' house, where they stay for several days until they are able to find and move into an apartment. She also files for divorce and follows through in obtaining one.

In many ways this is not a "success" case (in reality, many cases are not). The genogram, however, was useful in helping Mr. Witt realize that he had acquired, and was acting out, certain dysfunctional family patterns. Unfortunately, he was not yet fully ready to make lasting changes. Perhaps sometime in the future he will be more committed to making changes. At the present time, he has returned to drinking heavily.

The ecomap and the genogram have a number of similarities. With both techniques, users gain insight into family dynamics. Some of the symbols used in the two approaches are identical. There are also differences. The ecomap focuses attention on a family's interactions with groups, resources, organizations, associations, other families, and other individuals. The genogram focuses attention on intergenerational family patterns, particularly those that are problematic or dysfunctional.

Family Problems and Social Work Roles

Thorman (1982) points out that although each family is unique, conflicts and problems within families tend to be clustered in four major categories. First, there are marital

Figure 12.6 **Sample Genogram: The Chris and Karen Witt Family**

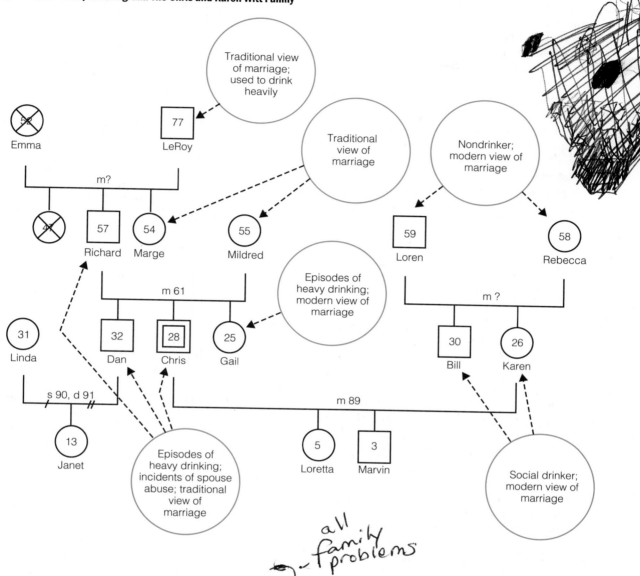

problems between the husband and wife. Second, there are difficulties existing between parents and children. Third, there are the personal problems of individual family members. Finally, there are stresses imposed on the family by the external environment.

Family problems do not necessarily fall neatly into one or another of these categories. Frequently, families experience more than one category of problems. Nor are these problem categories mutually exclusive. Many times one problem will be closely related to another. Consider, for instance, the wife and mother of a family who is a department store manager and the primary breadwinner for her family. The store at which she has been working for the past 11 years suddenly goes bankrupt and out of

business. Despite massive efforts, she is unable to find another job with similar responsibilities and salary. This can be considered a family problem caused by stresses in the environment. However, this is also a personal problem for the wife and mother. Her sense of self-worth is seriously diminished by her job loss and inability to find another position. She becomes cranky, short-tempered, and difficult to live with. The environmental stress she is experiencing causes her to have difficulties relating to both her children and spouse. The entire family system becomes disturbed.

A family therapy perspective sees any problem within the family as a family group problem, not as a problem on the part of any one individual member (Okun &

Rappaport, 1980). Social workers, therefore, need to assess the many dimensions of the problem and the impacts on all family members.

Marital problems between the husband and wife present the first category of problems typically experienced by families. Although problems between spouses impact all family members, intervention may target a subsystem of the family—in this case, the marital subsystem. In other words, a social worker may work with only these two instead of the entire family to solve a specific problem. When the marital pair gets along better, the entire family will be positively affected. A marital problem case example follows.

Bill and Linda Lechnir, both in their mid-30s, had a communication problem. They had been married for 1 year. The marriage occurred after a lengthy dating period filled with strife. A primary source of stress was Linda's desire for a permanent commitment of marriage and Bill's unwillingness to make such a commitment. In view of Linda's threats to leave him, Bill finally decided to get married.

Before the marriage, another source of difficulty was the amount of time that Bill and Linda spent together. They each owned their own condominiums and lived separately. Bill was involved in a physical fitness program, working out at a health club 4 nights a week, including Fridays. Bill also had numerous close friends at the club with whom he enjoyed spending his time. Linda was infuriated that Bill restricted the time he spent with her to only the days when he didn't work out at the club. Her major concern, however, remained Bill's inability to make a commitment. Linda felt that things would change once they got married.

After marriage, things did not change very much. Although Linda and Bill now lived together, he still worked out at the club with his friends 4 nights a week, and Linda was still infuriated. In a discussion the two expressed their feelings. Linda said, "I hate all the time Bill spends at the club. I resent having him designate the time he thinks he can spend with me. I feel like he's putting my time into little boxes." Bill responded, "My physical health is very important to me. I love to work out at the club. What should I do—stay home every night and become a couch potato watching television?"

One way of assessing this couple's communication is evaluating the intent (what the speaker wants to have communicated to the receiver) and the actual impact of the communication (what the listener actually hears). Many times the intent and impact of communication are different. One therapeutic goal is to improve the accuracy and quality of communication, that is, the extent to which the intent of the speaker and the impact upon the listener resemble each other.

Although other difficulties existed in the relationship that are too lengthy to describe here, we will address some of the issues involved in this simple communication. After further meetings and discussion, the following scenario developed. Linda verbally states that she is intensely unhappy that Bill goes to the health club. The impact on Bill is that he feels Linda is trying to tell him what to do. He loves Linda but is wary of losing his independence and what he sees as his identity. When Linda places demands on him, he becomes even more protective of his time.

Linda's intent in her communication is very different than her impact; she feels Bill thinks the club and his friends are more important than she is. This is related to her basic lack of self-esteem and self-confidence.

Bill's response to Linda's statement also has serious discrepancies between its intent and impact. Bill states that he loves to work out. The impact on Linda (that is, what she is hearing Bill say) is that he likes the club and his friends more than he likes her. Bill's actual intent is to tell Linda his physical health and appearance are important to him. He also wants to communicate that his sense of independence is also important to him. He loves her and wants to be committed to her. Yet, this long-term fear of commitment is related to his actual fear that he will lose his identity in someone else's. He's afraid of losing his right to make choices and decisions. He fears being told what to do.

Eventually, Bill and Linda used a problem-solving approach to resolve this issue. Through counseling, the accuracy of their communication gradually improved. Each learned how to communicate personal needs. Instead of their old standoff, they began to identify and evaluate alternatives. Their final solution involved several facets. First, Bill would continue to go to the club to work out on 3 nights each week. Fridays, however, would be spent with Linda; it became clear that she was particularly annoyed at not being able to go out with Bill on Friday nights. Linda, who also was an avid believer in physical fitness, would occasionally go with Bill to the health club to work out. This gave her a sense of freedom to join him when she chose to. The important thing was that she no longer felt restricted. In reality, she rarely went with him to the club. Linda also chose to take some postgraduate courses in her field on those evenings when Bill visited the club. She enjoyed such activities, and they enhanced her sense of professional competence. The personal issues of Bill's need to feel free and Linda's lack of self-esteem demanded ongoing efforts by both spouses. Enhanced communication skills helped them communicate their ongoing needs.

Richard B. Stuart developed a "Couple's Pre-Counseling Inventory," which is used to assess a couple's problems (1983). Each member of the couple is asked to fill out the questionnaire separately. Later, answers can be shared during counseling, and misconceptions each has about how the other person feels can be clarified. Areas that are evaluated include: happiness with the relationship; caring behaviors liked, and perceptions of caring behaviors liked, by the partner; communication; how conflict is managed; how moods and other aspects of personal life are managed; sexual interaction; how children are managed; willingness to make changes; marital history; and specific goals each person wants to pursue.

Such an instrument provides an excellent mechanism for assessment because misconceptions between partners can be clearly pinpointed. For instance, under the topic of "Sexual Interaction," members of the couple are asked to respond to a variety of statements and indicate their levels of satisfaction with the issue involved. The range is from 5, which means "very satisfied," to 1, which means "very dissatisfied." One statement concerns "the length of our foreplay." If one partner is very satisfied and the other very dissatisfied, this is clearly an area that needs to be addressed.

The second major type of family problem involves relationships between parents and children, including parents' difficulties controlling their children and, especially as children reach adolescence, communication problems.

There are many perspectives on child management and parent/child communication techniques. Two major approaches are the application of learning theory and Parent Effectiveness Training (PET), developed by Thomas Gordon (1970). Practitioners can help parents improve their control of children by assessing the individual family situations and teaching parents some basic behavior modification techniques. Behavior modification involves the application of learning theory principles to real-life situations. Practitioners also can teach use of PET techniques. (The application of learning theory principles to positive parenting was discussed in Chapter 4 and PET was described in Chapter 8.)

Personal problems of individual family members make up the third category of problems typically experienced by families.

Sometimes a family will come to a practitioner for help and identify one family member as being "the problem." However, a basic principle of family therapy is that the entire family "owns" the problem (Thorman, 1982). Sometimes one family member becomes the scapegoat for a malfunction of the entire family system. The social worker is responsible for helping the family define the problem as a family problem rather than blaming an individual. Treatment goals will most likely involve restructuring various family relationships.

For example, a family of five came in for treatment. The family consisted of a 48-year-old husband and father, a 45-year-old wife and mother, and three children: Bob, aged 19; Ralph, 16; and Rosie, 12. The family lived in a small rural Wisconsin town. The father was a successful businessman involved in local politics. The mother was a homemaker who did not work outside the home. Bob was a freshman at the University of Wisconsin–Madison. The identified client was Ralph. For the past year, Ralph had been stealing neighbors' cars and running down mailboxes. To say the least, this behavior annoyed the townspeople. The family came to counseling as a last resort.

After several sessions of family members pointing blaming fingers at Ralph, Rosie quietly commented to her parents, "Well, you never say anything about his problem" and proceeded to point at Bob. Suddenly, as if a floodgate had been opened, the entire family situation came pouring out. Rosie was referring to her parents' difficulties in accepting Bob's recent announcement that he was gay. Bob was going through a difficult period as he was "coming out"—making lifestyle decisions and relating to old friends and family members. His father was terrified that the local townspeople, who were severely homophobic (see chapter 13), would find out. He feared he would lose his social status and that his political career would be damaged. Bob's mother turned out to be an alcoholic, a secret the family kept well guarded. The parents had not had a sexual relationship for 10 years and now slept in separate bedrooms. The father was a harsh, stern man who felt it necessary to maintain what he considered absolute control over family members, including his wife. Highly critical of his family, he never risked sharing his own feelings. Finally, Rosie was having serious problems both with her grades and attendance in school. She was also sexually active with a variety of young men. Both she and her parents lived in constant fear that she would become pregnant.

As it turned out, Ralph was one of the better-adjusted individuals in the family. He attended school regularly, had a B average, and was active in sports before being suspended for his delinquent behavior. This family provides a good illustration of a family-owned problem. The entire family system was showing disturbances. Ralph was the scapegoat, the identified client, largely because his behavior was more public. All Ralph was doing was calling attention to the family's deeper problems.

The fourth category of problems frequently found in families includes problems caused by factors outside the family. These problems can include inadequate income, unemployment, poor housing, inadequate access to means of transportation and places for recreation, and lack of job opportunities. Included in the multitude of other potential problems are poor health, inadequate schools, and dangerous neighborhoods.

To begin addressing these problems, social workers need effective brokering skills. That is, they need to know what services are available, and how to make a connection between families in need and these services.

Many times appropriate services will be unavailable or nonexistent. Social workers will need to advocate, support, or even help to develop appropriate resources for their clients. Services that do not exist, for example, will need development. Unresponsive agency administrations will need to be confronted. Legal assistance may be needed. There are no easy solutions to solving such nationwide problems as poverty or poor health care. This is an ongoing process, and political involvement may be necessary. Such environmental stresses pose serious problems for families, and social work practitioners cannot ignore them.

❦ Social Work with Organizations

As defined in Chapter 1, organizations are "(1) social entities that (2) are goal directed, (3) are designed as deliberately structured and coordinated activity systems, and (4) are linked to the external environment" (Daft, 1998, p. 11). *Social entities* involve groups of people, all having their own strengths, needs, ideas, and quirks. Organizations are *goal directed* in that they exist to accomplish some purpose or meet some need. As an *activity system,* an organization is made up of a coordinated series of units accomplishing different tasks yet working together to achieve some common end. Finally, organizations are in constant interaction with other people, decision makers, agencies, neighborhoods, and communities in the *external social environment* as they strive to achieve goals.

Is is imperative that social workers have an extensive knowledge of organizations. As Chapter 1 of this text indicates, working with organizations is one of the systems in which social workers are expected to have expertise. Highlight 12.7 expands on the importance of social workers being skilled in understanding and analyzing organizations. Several theories of organizational behavior are presented in this section. These different theories provide a variety of perspectives for viewing and analyzing organizations.

The Autocratic Model

The autocratic model has been in existence for thousands of years. During the Industrial Revolution, this model was the prominent model of how an organization should function. The model depends on *power*. Those who are in power act autocratically. The message to employees is, "You do this—or else"; an employee who does not follow orders is penalized, often severely.

An autocratic model uses one-way communication— from the top to the workers. Management believes that it knows what is best. The employee's obligation is to follow orders. Employees have to be persuaded, directed, and pushed into performance, and this is management's task. Management does the thinking, and the workers obey the directives. Under autocratic conditions, the workers' role is *obedience* to management.

The autocratic model does work in some settings. Most military organizations throughout the world are formulated on this model. The model was also used successfully during the Industrial Revolution, for example, in building great railroad systems and in operating giant steel mills.

The autocratic model has a number of disadvantages. Workers are often in the best position to identify shortcomings in the structure and technology of the organizational system, but one-way communication prevents feedback to management. The model also fails to generate much of a commitment among the workers to accomplish organizational goals. Finally, the model fails to motivate workers to put forth an effort to further develop their skills (skills that often would be highly beneficial to the employer).

The Custodial Model

Many decades ago, when the autocratic model was the predominant model of organizational behavior, some progressive managers began to study their employees and soon found that the autocratic model often resulted in the employees feeling insecure about their continued employment. Employees also had feelings of aggression toward management. Because the employees could not directly express their discontent, it was expressed indirectly. Some vented their anger on their families and neighbors, and the entire community suffered. Others sabotaged production. Davis and Newstrom (1989) described sabotage in a wood-processing plant:

> *Managers treated workers crudely, sometimes even to the point of physical abuse. Since employees could not strike back directly for fear of losing their jobs, they found another way to*

Highlight 12.7

Analyzing a Human Services Organization

It is essential that a social worker understand and analyze not only the agency/organization that she or he works for but also the other agencies and organizations that she or he interacts with. Some questions that are useful in analyzing an agency or organization are the following:

1. What is the mission statement of the organization?
2. What are the major problems of the organization's clients?
3. What services are provided by the organization?
4. How are client needs determined?
5. What percentage of clients are people of color, women, gays or lesbians, elderly, or members of other at-risk populations?
6. What was the total cost of services of this organization in the past year?
7. How much money is spent on each program?
8. What are the organization's funding sources?
9. How much money and what percentage of funds are received from each source?
10. What types of clients does the organization refuse?
11. What other organizations provide the same services in the community?
12. What is the organizational structure? For example, does the organization have a formal chain of command?

13. Is there an informal decision-making process and structure at the organization? (That is, are there people who are quite influential and thus exert more influence than would be expected for their formal positions in the bureaucracy of the organization?)
14. How much input do the direct service providers at the organization have on major policy decisions?
15. Does the organization have a board that oversees its operations? If so, what are the backgrounds of the board members?
16. Do employees at every level feel valued?
17. What is the morale among employees?
18. What are the major unmet needs of the organization?
19. Does the organization have a handbook of personnel policies and procedures?
20. What is the public image of the organization in the community?
21. What has been the rate of turnover in recent years among the staff at the organization? What were departing staff members' major reasons for leaving?
22. Does the organization have a process for evaluating the outcomes of its services? If so, what is the process, and what are the outcome results?

---

do it. They symbolically fed their supervisor to a log-shredding machine! They did this by purposely destroying good sheets of veneer, which made the supervisor look bad when monthly efficiency reports were prepared. (p. 31)

In the 1890s and 1900s some progressive employers thought that if these feelings could be alleviated, employees might feel more like working, which would increase productivity. To satisfy the employees' security needs, a number of companies began to provide welfare programs—examples include pension programs, child-care centers at the workplace, health insurance, and life insurance.

The custodial approach leads to employee dependence on the organization. According to Davis and Newstrom (1989), "If employees have ten years of seniority under the union contract and a good pension program, they cannot afford to quit even if the grass looks greener somewhere else!" (p. 31).

Employees working under a custodial model tend to focus on their economic rewards and benefits. They are happier and more content than under the autocratic model, but they do not have a high commitment to helping the organization accomplish its goals. They tend to give *passive cooperation* to their employer. The model's most evident flaw is that most employees are producing substantially below their capacities. They are not motivated to advance to higher capacities. Most such employees do not feel fulfilled or motivated at their place of work. In summary, contented employees (which the custodial model is designed to generate) are not necessarily the most productive.

The Scientific Management Model

One of the earliest and most important schools of thought on the management of functions and tasks in the workplace was based on the work of Frederick Taylor (1947).

Taylor was a mechanical engineer, an American industrialist, and an educator. He focused primarily on management techniques that would lead to increased productivity. He asserted that many organizational problems in the workplace involved misunderstandings between managers and workers. Managers erroneously thought that workers were lazy and unemotional, and they mistakenly believed they understood workers' jobs. Workers mistakenly thought that managers cared most about exploiting them.

To solve these problems, Taylor developed the *scientific management model,* which focused on the need for managers to conduct a scientific analysis of the workplace. One of the first steps was to conduct a careful study of how each job could best be accomplished. An excellent way to do this, according to Taylor, was to identify the best worker for each job and then carefully study how he or she did the work. The goal of this analysis was to discover the optimal way of doing the job—in Taylor's words, the "one best way." Once this best way was identified, tools could be modified to better complete the work, workers' abilities and interests could be fitted to particular job assignments, and the level of production that the average worker could sustain could be gauged.

Once the level of production for the average worker was determined, Taylor indicated that the next step was to provide incentives to increase productivity. His favorite strategy for doing this was the piece-rate wage, in which workers were paid for each unit they produced. The goals were to produce more units, reduce unit cost, increase organizational productivity and profitability, and provide incentives for workers to produce more.

Taylor's work has been criticized as having a "technicist" bias, because it tends to treat workers as little more than cogs in a wheel. No two workers are exactly alike, so the "one best way" of doing a job is often unique to the person doing it. In fact, forcing the same work approach on different workers may actually decrease both productivity and worker satisfaction. In addition, Taylor's approach has limited application to human services providers. Because each client is unique, each situation case has to be individualized, and therefore it is difficult (if not impossible) to specify the "one best way" to provide service.

The Human Relations Model

In 1927 the Hawthorne Works of the Western Electric Company in Chicago began a series of experiments designed to discover ways to increase worker satisfaction and worker productivity (Roethlisberger & Dickson, 1939). Hawthorne Works manufactured telephones on the assembly-line basis. Workers needed no special skills, and

they performed simple, repetitive tasks. The workers were not unionized, and management sought to find ways to increase productivity. If job satisfaction could be increased, employees would work more efficiently, and productivity would then increase.

The company tested the effects on productivity of a number of factors: rest breaks, better lighting, changes in the number of work hours, changes in the wages paid, improved food facilities, and so on. The results were surprising. Productivity increased, as expected, with improved working conditions; but it also increased when working conditions worsened. This latter finding was unexpected and led to an additional study.

The investigators discovered that participation in the experiments was extremely attractive to the workers. They felt they had been selected by the management for their individual abilities, and so they worked harder, even when working conditions became less favorable. In addition, the workers' morale and general attitude toward work improved, because they felt they were receiving special attention. By participating in this study, the workers were able to work in smaller groups and became involved in making decisions. Working in smaller groups allowed them to develop a stronger sense of solidarity with their fellow workers. Being involved in decision making decreased their feelings of meaninglessness and powerlessness about their work.

In sociological and psychological research, the results of this study have become known as the *Hawthorne effect.* In essence, when subjects know they are participants in a study, this awareness may lead them to behave differently and substantially influence the results.

The results of this study, and of other similar studies, led some researchers to conclude that the key variables impacting productivity are social factors. Etzioni (1964) summarized some of the basic tenets of the human relations approach:

- The level of production is set by social norms, not by physiological capacities.
- Noneconomic rewards and sanctions significantly affect the behavior of the workers and largely limit the effect of economic incentive plans.
- Workers do not act or react as individuals but as members of groups.
- The role of leadership is important in understanding social factors in organizations, and this leadership may be either formal or informal.

Numerous studies have provided evidence to support these tenets (Netting, Kettner, & McMurtry, 1993).

Workers who are capable of greater productivity often will not excel because they are unwilling to exceed the "average" level set by the norms of the group, even if this means earning less. These studies have also found that attempts by management to influence workers' behavior are often more successful if targeted at the group as a whole, rather than at individuals. Finally, the studies have documented the importance of informal leadership in influencing workers' behavior in ways that can either amplify or negate formal leadership directives. This model asserts that managers who succeed in increasing productivity are most likely responsive to the workers' social needs.

One criticism of the human relations model is (surprisingly) that it tends to manipulate, dehumanize, oppress, and exploit workers. The model leads to the conclusion that management can increase productivity by helping workers become content, rather than by increasing economic rewards for higher productivity. The human relations model allows for concentrated power and decision making at the top. It is not intended to empower employees in the decision-making process or to assist them in acquiring genuine participation in the running of the organization. The practice of dealing with people on the basis of their perceived social relationships within the workplace may also be a factor in perpetuating the "good-old-boys" network; this network has disadvantaged women and people of color over the years. Another criticism of the human relations approach is that a happy workforce is not necessarily a productive workforce, because the norms for worker production may be set well below the workers' levels of capability.

Theory X and Theory Y

Douglas McGregor (1960) developed two theories of management. He theorized that management thinking and behavior are based on two different sets of assumptions, which he labeled Theory X and Theory Y.

Theory X managers view employees as being incapable of much growth. Employees are perceived as having an inherent dislike for work and attempting to evade work whenever possible. Therefore, X-type managers believe they must control, direct, force, or threaten employees to make them work. Employees are also viewed as having relatively little ambition, wishing to avoid responsibilities, and preferring to be directed. Theory X managers therefore spell out job responsibilities carefully, set work goals without employee input, use external rewards (such as money) to force employees to work, and punish those who deviate from established rules.

Because Theory X managers reduce responsibilities to a level at which few mistakes can be made, work usually becomes so structured that it is monotonous and distasteful. These Theory X assumptions, of course, are inconsistent with what behavioral scientists assert are effective principles for directing, influencing, and motivating people. Theory X managers are, in essence, adhering to an autocratic model of organizational behavior.

In contrast, *Theory Y managers* view employees as wanting to grow and develop by exerting physical and mental effort to accomplish work objectives to which they are committed. These managers believe that the promise of internal rewards, such as self-respect and personal improvement, are stronger motivators than external rewards (money) and punishment. They also believe that under proper conditions, employees will not only accept responsibility but seek it. Most employees are assumed to have considerable ingenuity, creativity, and imagination for problem solving. Therefore, they are given considerable responsibility to test the limits of their capabilities. Mistakes and errors are viewed as necessary phases of the learning process, and work is structured so that employees have a sense of accomplishment and growth.

Employees who work for Y-type managers are generally more creative and productive, experience greater work satisfaction, and are more highly motivated than employees who work for X-type managers. Under both management styles, expectations often become self-fulfilling prophecies.

The Collegial Model

A useful extension of Theory Y is the *collegial model*, which emphasizes the team concept. It involves employees working closely together and feeling a commitment to achieving a common purpose. Some organizations— such as university departments, research laboratories, and most human services organizations—have a goal of creating a collegial atmosphere to facilitate achieving their purposes. (Sadly, many such organizations are unsuccessful in creating such an atmosphere.)

Creating a collegial atmosphere is highly dependent on management's building a feeling of partnership with employees. When such a partnership develops, employees feel needed and useful. Managers are then viewed as joint contributors rather than as bosses. Management is the *coach* who builds a better team. Davis and Newstrom (1989) described some of the approaches to developing a team concept:

> *The feeling of partnerships can be built in many ways. Some organizations have abolished the use of reserved parking*

spaces for executives, so every employee has an equal chance of finding one close to the workplace. Some firms have tried to eliminate the use of terms like "bosses" and "subordinates," feeling that those terms simply create perceptions of psychological distance between managers and nonmanagers. Other employers have removed time clocks, set up "fun committees," sponsored company canoe trips, or required managers to spend a week or two annually working in field or factory locations. All of these approaches are designed to build a spirit of mutuality, in which every person makes contributions and appreciates those of others. (p. 34)

If the sense of partnership is developed, employees produce quality work and seek to cooperate with co-workers, not because management directs them to do so, but because they feel an internal obligation to produce high-quality work. The collegial approach thus leads to a sense of *self-discipline*. In this environment, employees are more apt to have a sense of fulfillment, to feel self-actualized, and to produce higher-quality work.

Theory Z

William Ouchi described the Japanese style of management in his 1981 best-seller *Theory Z*. In the late 1970s and early 1980s, attention in the U.S. business world became focused on the Japanese approach to management, as markets long dominated by U.S. firms (such as the automobile industry) were taken over by Japanese industries. Japanese industrial organizations had rapidly overcome their earlier reputation for poor-quality work and were setting worldwide standards for quality and durability.

Theory Z asserted that the theoretical principles underlying Japanese management went beyond Theory Y. According to Theory Z, a business organization in Japan is more than the profitability-oriented entity that it is in the United States. It is a way of life. It provides lifetime employment. It is enmeshed with the nation's political, social, and economic network. Furthermore, its influence spills over into many other organizations, such as nursery schools, elementary and secondary schools, and universities.

The basic philosophy of Theory Z is that involved and committed workers are the key to increased productivity. Ideas and suggestions about how to improve the organization are routinely solicited, and implemented where feasible. One strategy for accomplishing this is the *quality circle,* where employees and management routinely meet to brainstorm about ways to improve productivity and quality.

In contrast to American organizations, Japanese organizations tend not to have written objectives or organizational charts. Most work is done in teams, and decisions are made by a consensus. The teams tend to function without a designated leader. Cooperation within units, and between units, is emphasized. Loyalty to the organization is also emphasized, as is organizational loyalty to the employee.

Experiments designed to transplant Japanese-style management to the United States have resulted in mixed success. In most cases American organizations have concluded that Theory Z probably works quite well in a homogeneous culture that has Japan's societal values, but some components do not fit well with the more heterogeneous and individualistic character of the United States. In addition, some firms in volatile industries (such as electronics) have difficulty balancing their desire to provide lifetime employment with the need to adjust their workforces to meet rapidly changing market demands.

✿ Management by Objectives

Fundamental to the core of an organization is its purpose—that is, the commonly shared understanding of the reason for its existence.

Management theorist Peter Drucker (1954) proposed a strategy for making organizational goals and objectives the central construct around which organizational life is designed to function. In other words, instead of focusing on employee needs and wants, or on organizational structure, as the ways to increase efficiency and productivity, Drucker proposed beginning with the desired outcome and working backward. The strategy is first to identify the organizational objectives or goals and then to adapt the organizational tasks, resources, and structure to meet those objectives. This management by objectives (MBO) approach is designed to focus the organization's efforts on meeting these objectives. Success is determined, then, by the degree to which stated objectives are reached.

This approach can be applied to the organization as a whole, as well as to internal divisions or departments. When the MBO approach is applied to internal divisions, the objectives set for each division should be consistent and supportive of the overall organizational objectives.

In many areas, including human services, the MBO approach can also be applied to the cases serviced by each employee. Goals are set with each client, tasks to meet these goals are then determined, and deadlines are set for the completion of these tasks. The degree of success of each case is then determined at a later date (often when a case is closed) by the extent to which stated goals were achieved.

An adaptation of the MBO approach, called strategic planning and budgeting (SPB), became popular in the 1990s, and is still widely used. The process involves first specifying the overall vision or mission of an organization, then identifying a variety of more specific objectives or plans for achieving that vision, and, finally, adapting the resources to meet the specific high-priority objectives or plans. Organizations often hire outside consultants to assist in conducting the SPB process.

One major advantage of the MBO approach for an organization (or its divisions) is that it produces clear statements (made available to all employees) about the objectives and the tasks that are expected to be accomplished in specified time periods. This type of activity tends to improve cooperation and collaboration. The MBO approach is also useful because it provides a guide for allocating resources and a focus for monitoring and evaluating organizational efforts.

An additional benefit of the MBO approach is that it creates diversity in the workplace. Prior to this approach, those responsible for hiring failed to employ women and people of color in significant numbers. As affirmative action programs were developed within organizations, the MBO approach was widely used to set specific hiring goals and objectives. The result has been significant changes in recruitment approaches that have enabled a number of women and other minorities to secure employment.

Total Quality Management

The theorist most closely associated with developing the concept of total quality management (TQM) is W. Edwards Deming (1986). Deming was a statistician who formed many of his theories during World War II, when he instructed industries on how to use statistical methods to improve the quality of military production. Deming taught the Japanese his theories of quality control and continuous improvement following World War II, and he now is recognized, along with J. Juran (1989) and others, with laying the groundwork for Japan's industrial and economic boom.

Total quality management has been defined by Omachonu and Ross (1994) as "the integration of all functions and processes within an organization in order to achieve continuous improvement of the quality of goods and services. The goal is customer satisfaction" (p. 1). TQM is based on a number of ideas. It means thinking about quality in terms of all functions of the enterprise and is a start-to-finish process that integrates interrelated functions at all levels. It is a systems approach that considers every interaction between the various elements of the organization.

TQM asserts that the management of many businesses and organizations makes the mistake of blaming what goes wrong in an organization on individual people, not on the system. TQM, rather, believes in the "85/15 Rule," which asserts that 85 percent of the problems can be corrected by changing systems (structures, rules, practices, expectations, and traditions that are largely determined by management), and that less than 15 percent of the problems can be solved by individual workers. When problems arise, TQM asserts that management should look for causes in the system and work to remove them before casting blame on workers.

TQM further maintains that customer satisfaction is the main purpose of the organization. Therefore, quality includes continuously improving all the organization's processes that lead to customer satisfaction. The customer is seen as part of the design and production process, as the customer's needs continually must be monitored.

In recent years numerous organizations have adopted a TQM approach to improve their goods and services. One of the reasons that quality is being emphasized more is because consumers are increasingly shunning mass-produced, poorly made, disposable production. Companies are realizing that in order to remain competitive in global markets, quality of products and services is essential. Ford's motto, "Quality Is Job One," symbolizes the emphasis on quality.

There are a variety of approaches to TQM, largely because numerous theoreticians (business gurus) have advanced somewhat diverse approaches. Hower (1994) gives the following summary of the key principles of TQM:

- employees asking their external and internal customers what they need, and providing more of it;
- instilling pride into every employee;
- concentrating on information and data (a common language) to solve problems, instead of concentrating on opinions and egos;
- developing leaders, not managers, and knowing the difference;
- improving every process (everyone is in a process), checking this improvement at predetermined times, then improving it again if necessary;
- helping every employee enjoy his or her work while the organization continues to become more productive;
- providing a forum or open atmosphere so that employees at all levels feel free to voice their opinions when they think they have good ideas;

- receiving a continuous increase in those suggestions, and accepting and implementing the best ones;

- utilizing the teamwork concept, because teams often make better decisions than individuals;

- empowering these teams to implement their recommended solutions and learn from their failures;

- reducing the number of layers of authority to enhance this empowerment;

- recognizing complaints as opportunities for improvement. (p. 10)

These principles give the reader an idea of the "flavor" of TQM.

Summary Comments about Models of Organizational Behavior

Any of these models can be successfully applied in some situations. The question of which model to apply, in order to obtain the highest productivity, depends on the tasks to be completed the on employee needs and expectations. For example, the autocratic model will probably work well in military operations, where quick decisions are needed to respond to rapidly changing crises and where military personnel expect autocratic leadership. However, this model does not generally work well in human services organizations, in which employees are expecting the Theory Y style of managers.

✇ Value Orientations in Organizational Decision Making

In theory, the task of making decisions about an organization's objectives and goals would follow a definite rational process. This process would include identifying the problems, specifying resource limitations, weighing the advantages and disadvantages of proposed solutions, and selecting the resolution strategy with the fewest risks and the greatest chance of success. In practice, however, subjective influences (particularly on value orientations) can impede the rational process.

Most people tend to believe that decisions are made primarily on the basis of objective facts and figures. However, values and assumptions form the bases of most decisions, and facts and figures are used only in relation to these values and assumptions. Consider the following list of questions. What do they indicate about how we make our most important decisions?

- Should abortions be permitted or prohibited during the first weeks following conception?

- Should homosexuality be viewed as a natural expression of sexuality?

- When does harsh discipline of a child become child abuse?

- Should the primary objective of imprisonment be rehabilitation or retribution?

Answers to these questions are usually not based on data uncovered after careful research; they are based on individual beliefs about the value of life, personal freedom, and protective social standards. Even everyday decisions are based largely on values.

Practically every decision is also based on certain assumptions. Without assumptions, nothing can be proved. Assumptions are made in every research study to test any hypothesis. For example, in a market research survey, analysts *assume* that the instruments they use (such as a questionnaire) will be valid and reliable. It cannot even be proved the sun will rise in the east tomorrow without *assuming* that its history provides that proof.

Every decision maker in an organization brings not only his or her objective knowledge and expertise to the decision-making process, but also his or her value orientations. *Value orientation* means an individual's own ideas about what is desirable and worthwhile. Most values are acquired through prior learning experiences in interactions with family, friends, educators, organizations such as the church, and anyone else who has made an impression on a person's thinking.

The philosopher Edward Spranger (1928) believed that most people eventually come to rely on one of six possible value orientations. While it is possible for a person to hold values in all six orientations, each person tends to lean more heavily toward one type in the decision-making process. The six value orientations are:

Theoretical: A person with a theoretical orientation strives toward a rational, systematic ordering of knowledge. Personal preference does not count as much as being able to classify, compare, contrast, and interrelate various pieces of information. The theoretical person places value on simply knowing what exists—and why.

Economic: an economic orientation places primary value on the utility of things, and practical uses of knowledge are given foremost attention. Proposed plans of action are assessed in terms of their costs and benefits. If the costs outweigh the benefits, the economically oriented person is not likely to support the plan.

Aesthetic: An aesthetic orientation is grounded in an appreciation of artistic values, and personal preferences for form, harmony, and beauty are influential in making decisions. Because the experience of single events is considered an important end in itself, reactions to aesthetic qualities will frequently be expressed.

Social: A social orientation is an empathetic one that values other people as ends in themselves. Concern for the welfare of people pervades the behavior of the socially oriented decision maker, and primary consideration is given to the quality of human relationships.

Political: A political orientation involves a concern for identifying where power lies. Conflict and competition are seen as normal elements of group activity. Decisions and their outcomes are assessed in terms of how much power is obtained, and by whom, because influence over others is a valued goal.

Religious: A person with a religious orientation is directed by a desire to relate to the universe in some meaningful way. Personal beliefs about an "absolute good" or a "higher order" are employed to determine the value of things, and decisions and their outcomes are placed into the context of such beliefs.

✍ Liberal, Conservative, and Developmental Perspectives on Human Service Organizations

In regard to value orientation, three diverse views that have major impacts on human services organizations are the liberal, conservative, and developmental perspectives. Politicians and decision makers often make their decisions on human service issues in terms of whether they adhere to a liberal philosophy or to a conservative philosophy. The Republican party is considered to be relatively conservative, and the Democratic party is considered to be relatively liberal. This discussion will focus on liberalism and conservatism in their pure forms. In reality, many people espouse a mixture of both views. For example, some Democrats are primarily conservative in ideology and some Republicans are primarily liberal in ideology.

Note that the three dimensions described below— conservative, liberal, and developmental—are portrayed in a purist fashion, implying that proponents rigidly adhere to the prescribed views. As with Democrats and Republicans, in real life most people reflect a unique combination of these views.

Conservative Perspective

Conservatives (a term derived from the verb *to conserve*) tend to resist change. They emphasize tradition and believe rapid change usually results in more negative than positive consequences. In economic matters, conservatives feel that the government should not interfere with the workings of the marketplace. They encourage the government to support (for example, through tax incentives) rather than regulate business and industry in society. A free market economy is thought to be the best way to ensure prosperity and fulfillment of individual needs. Conservatives embrace the old adage, "That government governs best which governs least." They believe that most government activities constitute threats to individual liberty and to the smooth functioning of the free market.

Conservatives generally view individuals as being autonomous—that is, as being self-governing. Regardless of what a person's situation is, or what problems he or she has, each person is thought to be presently responsible for his or her own behavior. People are thought to choose whatever they are doing, and they therefore are viewed as being responsible for whatever gains or losses result from their choices. Conservatives view people as having free will, and thus, as able to choose to engage in behaviors such as hard work that help them get ahead, or activities such as excessive leisure that contribute to failing (or being poor). Poverty and other personal problems that people have are seen as being the result of laziness, irresponsibility, or lack of self-control. Conservatives believe that social welfare programs force the hard-working, productive citizens to pay for the consequences of the irresponsible behavior of recipients of social welfare services.

Conservatives generally advocate the residual approach to social welfare programs (Wilensky & Lebeaux, 1965). The residual view holds that social welfare services should be provided only when an individual's needs are not properly met through other societal institutions, primarily the family and the market economy. Social services and financial aid should not be provided until all other measures or efforts have failed and the individual's or family's resources are fully used up. In addition, this view asserts that funds and services should be provided on a short-term basis (primarily during emergencies) and should be withdrawn when the individual or the family again becomes capable of being self-sufficient.

The residual view has been characterized as "charity for unfortunates." Funds and services are not seen as a right (something that one is entitled to) but as a gift, and the receiver has certain obligations; for example, in order to receive financial aid, recipients may be required to perform certain low-grade work assignments. Under the residual view, there is usually a stigma attached to receiving services or funds.

Conservatives believe that dependency is a result of personal failure, and they also believe it is natural for inequality to exist among humans. They assert that the family, religious organizations, and gainful employment should be the primary defenses against dependency. Social welfare, they believe, should be only a temporary function that is used sparingly. Prolonged social welfare assistance, they believe, will lead recipients to become permanently dependent.

Conservatives believe charity is a moral virtue and that the "fortunate" are obligated to help the "less fortunate" become productive, contributing citizens in society. If government funds are provided for health and social welfare services, conservatives advocate that such funding should go to private organizations, which are thought to be more effective and efficient than public agencies in providing services. Conservatives tend to believe that the federal government is not a solution to social problems but is part of the problem. They assert that federally funded social welfare programs tend to make recipients dependent on the government, rather than assisting recipients to become self-sufficient and productive.

Conservatives revere the "traditional" nuclear family and try to devise policies to preserve it. They see the family as a source of strength for individuals, and as the primary unit of society. Accordingly, they oppose abortion, sex education in schools, rights for homosexuals, public funding of day-care centers, birth control counseling for minors, and other measures that might undermine parental authority or support alternative family forms such as single parenthood.

Liberal Perspective

In contrast, liberals believe change is generally good as it brings progress; moderate change is best. They view society as needing regulation to ensure fair competition between various interests. In particular, the market economy is viewed as needing regulation to ensure fairness. Government programs, including social welfare programs, are viewed as necessary to help meet basic human needs. Liberals advocate government action to remedy social deficiencies and to improve human welfare conditions. Liberals feel government regulation and intervention are often necessary to safeguard human rights, to control the excesses of capitalism, and to provide equal chances for success. They emphasize egalitarianism and the rights of minorities.

Liberals generally adhere to an *institutional* view of social welfare. This view holds that social welfare programs are "accepted as a proper legitimate function of modern industrial society in helping individuals achieve self-fulfillment" (Wilensky & Lebeaux, 1965, p. 139). Under this view, there is no stigma attached to receiving funds or services; recipients are viewed as entitled to such help. Associated with this view is the belief that an individual's difficulties are due to causes largely beyond his or her control (for example, a person may be unemployed because of a lack of employment opportunities). With this view, when difficulties arise, causes are sought in the environment (society) and efforts are focused on improving the social institutions within which the individual functions.

Liberals assert that because society has become so fragmented and complex, and because traditional institutions (such as the family) have been unable to meet human needs, few individuals can now function without the help of social services (including such services as work training, job-location services, child care, health care, and counseling). Liberals believe that the personal problems encountered by someone are generally due to causes beyond that person's control. Causes are generally sought in that person's environment. For example, a child with a learning disability is thought to be at risk only if that child is not receiving appropriate educational services to accommodate his or her disability. In such a situation, liberals would seek to develop educational services to meet his or her learning needs.

Liberals view the family as an evolving institution, and therefore they are willing to support programs that assist emerging family forms—such as single-parent families and same-sex marriages.

Developmental Perspective

Liberals for years have criticized the residual approach to social welfare as being incongruent with society's obligation to provide long-term assistance to those who have long-term health, welfare, social, and recreational needs. Conservatives, on the other hand, have been highly critical of the institutional approach as they claim it creates a welfare state in which many recipients then decide to become dependent on the government to meet their health, welfare, social, and recreational needs—without seeking to work and without contributing in other ways to the well-being of society. It is clear that conservatives will attempt to stop the creation of any major social program that moves the country in the direction of being a welfare society. They have the necessary legislative votes to stop the enactment of programs that are "marketed" to society as being consistent with the institutional approach.

Is there a view of social welfare that can garner the support of both liberals and conservatives? Midgley (1995) contends that the *developmental view* (or perspective) offers an alternative approach that appears to have appeal to liberals, conservatives, and to the general public. Midgley (1995, p. 25) defines this approach as a "process of planned social change designed to promote the well-being of the population as a whole in conjunction with a dynamic process of economic development."

This perspective has appeal to liberals as it is a perspective that supports the development and expansion of needed social welfare programs. The perspective has appeal to conservatives as it asserts that the development of certain social welfare programs will have a positive impact on the economy. The general public also would be apt to support this development perspective. Many voters oppose welfarism, as they believe it causes economic problems (for example, recipients choosing to be on the government dole, rather than contributing to society through working). Asserting, and documenting, that certain proposed social welfare programs will directly benefit the economy is attractive to voters.

Midgley and Livermore (1997) note that the developmental approach is, at this point in time, not very well defined. The approach has its roots in the promotion of the growth of social programs in developing (Third World) countries. Advocates for social welfare programs in developing countries have been successful in getting certain social welfare programs enacted by asserting, and documenting, that such programs will have a beneficial impact on the overall economy of the country. Midgley and Livermore (1997) note, "The developmental perspective's global relevance began in the Third World in the years of decolonization after World War II" (p. 576). The developmental approach was later used by the United Nations in its efforts in developing countries to promote the growth of social programs, as the United Nations asserted such programs had the promise of improving the overall economies of these countries.

What are the characteristics of the developmental approach? It advocates social interventions that contribute positively to economic development. It thus promotes harmony between economic and social institutions. The approach regards economic progress as a vital component of social progress, and it promotes the active role of government in economic and social planning (which is in direct opposition to the residual approach). Finally, the developmental approach focuses on integrating economic and social development for the *benefit of all* members of society.

The developmental approach can be used in advocating for the expansion of a wide range of social welfare programs. It can be argued that any social program that assists a person in becoming employable contributes to the economic well-being of a society. It can also be argued that any social program that assists a person in making significant contributions to his or her family, or to his or her community, contributes to the economic well-being of a society, as functional families and functional communities are good for businesses. Members of functional families tend to be better employees, and businesses desire to locate in communities that are prospering and that have low rates of crime and other social problems.

A few examples will be cited to illustrate how the developmental approach can be used to advocate for the expansion of social welfare programs. It can be argued that the following programs will be beneficial for the economy as they will assist unemployed single parents in obtaining employment: job training, quality child-care programs for the children of these parents, and adequate health insurance for these parents and their children so that health care is provided to keep them healthy. All of these programs will facilitate the parents being able to work. It can be argued that providing mentoring programs and other social services in school systems will assist at-risk children in staying in school and eventually contributing to society when they become adults by their then obtaining employment, and by the contributions they then are apt to make to their families and to the communities in which they live. It can be argued that rehabilitative programs in the criminal justice system will assist correctional clients in becoming contributing members to society. It can be argued that the following programs will help those with issues in these areas to better handle these issues, and thereby increase the likelihood they will becoming contributors to the economy and to the well-being of society: alcohol and other drug-abuse treatment programs, nutritional programs, eating disorder intervention programs, stress management programs, and grief management programs.

❦ Summary

Three macro system theories in sociology offer contrasting explanations of human behavior—functionalism, conflict theory, and interactionism. Functionalism views society and other social systems as composed of interdependent and interrelated parts. In contrast, conflict theory is more radical, and views society as being a struggle for scarce resources among individuals and social groups. Interactionist theory views human behavior as resulting from the interaction of a person's unique, distinctive personality and the groups she or he participates in. The chapter also described the following social problems that middle-aged adults (and other age groups) may encounter—poverty, empty-shell marriages, and divorce. Those most vulnerable to being poor include one-parent families, children, the elderly, large size families, people of color, the homeless, those without a high school education, and those living in urban slums.

Three types of empty-shell marriages are: devitalized relationships, conflict-habituated relationships, and passive-congenial relationships. About one of two marriages end in divorce. Although a divorce is traumatic for everyone in the family, it appears children become better adjusted when raised in a single-parent family in which they have a good relationship with that parent, than when they are raised in a two-parent family which is filled with discontent and tension.

Becoming more common in our society are single-parent families, blended families, and mothers working outside of the home. Poverty affects single-parent families significantly more than two-parent families. The formation of a blended family requires substantial adjustments by a number of people, including: the spouses, the children, the former spouses, and close relatives and friends. Because an increasing number of mothers are working outside of the home, our society needs to expand its effort to make good child-care arrangements available to the children in these families.

Problems faced by families tend to be clustered in the following four categories: marital problems between the husband and the wife; conflicts between the parents and the children; personal problems of individual family members; and stresses imposed on the family by the external environment. Two family system assessment techniques are the ecomap and the genogram.

This chapter also summarized material on social work with organizations. A number of theories provide a variety of perspectives for viewing and analyzing organizations. The theories covered include the autocratic model, the custodial model, the scientific management model, the human relations model, Theory X, Theory Y, the collegial model, Theory Z, management by objectives, and total quality management. Any of these models can be applied successfully in some situations.

Values and assumptions (rather than facts and figures) form the bases of most decisions in organizations. Six value orientations frequently have an impact on decision making: theoretical, economic, aesthetic, social, political, and religious.

In regard to value orientations, three diverse views that have major impacts on human service organizations are the conservative, liberal, and developmental perspectives. Politicians and decision makers often make their decisions on human service issues in terms of whether they adhere to a liberal or conservative philosophy. Conservatives generally advocate the residual approach to social welfare programs, whereas liberals generally follow an institutional view of social welfare. The developmental perspective offers an alternative approach that appears to have appeal to liberals, conservatives, and to the general public. It advocates social interventions that contribute positively to economic development.

InfoTrac College Edition Keywords

children of divorce	functionalist perspective	interactionist approach	Theories X, Y, and Z
culture of poverty	infant mortality rate	TANF	

On the Internet

Conflict Resolution Network (CRN)

http://www.crnhq.org/

Its vision is to create a conflict-resolving community in a culture of peace and social justice. Conflict Resolution builds stronger and more cohesive organizations and more rewarding relationships. So it makes Conflict Resolution skills, strategies, and attitudes more readily and universally accessible. Most CRN material can be freely reproduced, provided that its copyright notice appears on each page.

GenoPro (Genogram)

http://www.genopro.com/genogram/

A genogram (pronounced *jen-uh-gram*) is a pictorial representation of family relationships across several generations. It can be a convenient organizing device to help you identify patterns or develop hypotheses about family functioning. **Primarily used by mental health experts,** the genogram can help identify positive and negative influences surrounding an individual.

National Law Center on Homelessness and Poverty

http://www.nlchp.org/

The National Law Center on Homelessness and Poverty was established in June 1989. It is governed by a nine-member board of directors that includes lawyers, activists, researchers, and homeless and formerly homeless people. Based in Washington, D.C., the Law Center works with a wide variety of groups around the country.

TANF

http://www.acf.dhhs.gov/programs/ofa/

The Office of Family Assistance (OFA) is located in the United States Department of Health and Human Services, Administration for Children and Families, and oversees the Temporary Assistance for Needy Families (TANF) Program which was created by the Welfare Reform Act of 1996. TANF became effective on July 1, 1997, and replaced what was then commonly known as welfare: Aid to Families with Dependent Children (AFDC) and the Job Opportunities and Basic Skills Training (JOBS) programs.

CHAPTER 13

Sexual Orientation

John had been attending the state university for more than a year now. He didn't have a chance to visit his parents in their small midwestern town very often. When he did get home, his visits were usually limited to holidays. Thanksgiving, during his sophomore year, had finally rolled around, and he found himself hopping on the Greyhound bus headed for Slab City, Wisconsin, his home.

This trip home was a problem for him. No matter how often or how deeply he mulled it over in his mind, he couldn't find an answer. He had something to tell his parents that he didn't think they would like very much. Over the past year John had come to realize something about himself. He had come out; he was gay.

As he watched the countryside roll by from his bus seat, he thought about his childhood, about his high school friends, and even about the girl he had gone steady with for 2½ years during high school. What would they think if they found out?

He had never really been interested in girls. Sure, he pretended to be. Once a guy got labeled a "fag," he might as well run off to a monastery. He had always been pretty bright. He had learned really fast how men were supposed to act. As all-conference fullback on the high-school football team, he became quite adept at telling the appropriate locker room dirty jokes and at exaggerating the last weekend's conquests with women. He often wondered why he had to pretend so hard. The others seemed to really get into it. They seemed genuinely enthralled with the ideas of big-breasted women and sex. He never dared mention the fact that he'd rather spend time with Dan or Chuck. He certainly never came close to mentioning any of his secret fantasies.

He even asked Millie to go steady with him. She was a nice girl, in addition to being cute and extremely popular. With her he didn't feel the pressure of constantly having to push for sex. Typically, every Saturday night they'd go to a movie or a basketball game or something like that. Then afterwards they'd "neck" in the driveway for just a bit. That couldn't last too long anyway because Millie's parents were pretty strict and imposed a midnight curfew. She was in by midnight, or else. He always had to put a little bit of a move on her and try to get to second base. At that point she always stopped him, told him she loved him, and firmly stated she was waiting for marriage. What a relief.

At college things were different. He had chosen the state university for a variety of reasons. He found that a person could do a lot of hiding among 40,000 other students. He also found that there were other men who felt just like he did. There was an exceptionally active gay rights group that sponsored a spectrum of social and recreational activities for gay men. Through one of these activities, he had met Hank. Lately they had been spending a lot of time together. He had never felt so comfortable in a relationship before. He found he could talk to Hank about his most intimate thoughts. He also discovered how much he enjoyed expressing his affection for Hank both verbally and physically.

John was jolted from his reverie as the bus pulled up to the local bus stop. He could see his parents waiting to pick him up. There was his father with a big smile on his face, waving at the son he was so proud of. John smiled, waved back, and thought, "Oh, boy. Well, here goes." He stepped off the bus.

Although most people have a sexual orientation toward the opposite gender, many do not. Many are attracted to members of the same gender and some to both genders.

For whatever reasons, the idea of homosexuality, which involves having a sexual orientation for members of the same gender, frequently elicits a strong negative emotional response. As future professional social workers, you need to identify and address this negative response. The National Association of Social Workers' (NASW) Code of Ethics specifies that "social workers [should] respect and promote the right of clients to self-determination and assist clients in their efforts to identify and clarify their goals" (NASW, 1996, 1.02). Additionally, it specifies that "social workers should obtain education about and seek to understand the nature of social diversity and oppression with respect to race, ethnicity, national origin, color sex, *sexual orientation,* age, marital status, political belief, religion, and mental or physical disability" (NASW, 1996, 1.04c). The NASW Policy Statement on "Lesbian, Gay, and Bisexual Issues" states that "NASW is committed to advancing policies and practices that will improve the status and well-being of all lesbian, gay, and bisexual people" (NASW, 2000, p. 197). Clearly, determination of one's sexual orientation is a person's right.

A PERSPECTIVE

This chapter will provide information about various aspects of homosexuality. The intent is to encourage readers to examine their own feelings and reactions. Understanding the effects of diverse sexual orientations on human behavior is necessary for objective, professional social work practice. Assessing one's own values toward people's diverse sexual orientations is a major step in developing professional social work values.

This chapter will:

▶ Define and explain the meanings of homosexuality, transgender people, and bisexuality, and discuss the terms used to refer to lesbian and gay people.

▶ Report estimates of how many people are lesbian and gay, and discuss some of the theories attempting to explain why people have diverse sexual orientations.

▶ Address the issue of discrimination against lesbian and gay people and discuss the concept of homophobia.

▶ Review some of the myths and stereotypes about gay and lesbian people.

▶ Describe lesbian and gay lifestyles, including lesbian and gay relationships, sexual interaction, lesbian and gay pride, and sense of community.

▶ Identify some of the life situations and crises affecting lesbian and gay people, such as legal issues, violence against them, coming out, ethnicity, adolescence, aging, and AIDS.

✿ Homosexuality and Bisexuality

A man is committed to prison and has sexual relations with other men. Is he a homosexual? A very shy, lonely woman who has never dated any men is approached by a lesbian friend. The lonely woman decides to have an affair with her friend. Is she a homosexual? Two 14-year-old male adolescents experiment with each other by hand-stimulating each other to orgasm. Are they homosexuals? While having sexual intercourse with his wife, a man frequently fantasizes about having sexual relations with other men. He has never had any actual sexual contact with a man in his adult life. Is he a homosexual?

The answers to these questions are not so easy. Placing people in definite, distinct categories is difficult. It is not always easy to draw a clear distinction between a heterosexual and a homosexual. It may make us feel more secure and in control to cordon off the world into neat and predictable little boxes of black or white. However, in reality the world is an endless series of shades of gray.

People frequently like to polarize others as being either heterosexual or homosexual. Perhaps such labeling makes situations appear to be predictable. If a person is labeled a heterosexual, then many assume that they know a lot of things about that person. For example, if a person is labeled a heterosexual female, then she is probably unassertive, sweet, demure, and emotional. She will date men and probably marry and become a mother and homemaker. If a person is a homosexual male, then he will probably frequently flick his wrists and become a hairdresser. In reality things are not so predictable and clear.

The problem with these neat categories is that they foster stereotypes. A stereotype is a fixed mental image of a group that is frequently applied to all its members. Often the characteristics involved in the mental picture are unflattering. Stereotypes refuse to take into account individual differences. They negate the value and integrity of the individual. Highlight 13.1 identifies some of the stereotypes characterizing lesbian and gay people.

Highlight 13.1

Stereotypes About Gay and Lesbian People

Lesbian and gay people are not only the victims of homophobia, but also the targets of derogatory, inaccurate stereotypes. Some of the more common ones are that gay and lesbian people like to assume either a male or female role, that they are potential child molesters, and that they have AIDS (Berger & Kelly, 1995; Hyde, 1994). All of these stereotypes are false.

The Queen and the Butch

A prevalent stereotype about gay and lesbian people is that gay men typically look extremely feminine and that lesbians appear very masculine. Words that are used to refer to effeminate gay males include *swish, nellie,* and *queen.* Words that are used to refer to masculine-looking lesbians include *dyke* and *butch.* In truth these are stereotypes and are not accurate in most instances (Berger & Kelly, 1995; Byer & Shainberg, 1994; Hyde, 1994; McCammon, Knox, & Schacht, 1998; Tully, 2001).

Byer and Shainberg (1994) explain: "These stereotypes may sometimes prove accurate, but they do not apply to the majority of homosexual people. There are gay men and lesbian women who do fit the stereotypes in terms of mannerisms, but there are also many heterosexual people who fit these same stereotypes. Appearances are unreliable bases on which to judge a person's sexual orientation" (p. 386). With the breakdown of some of the traditional gender roles, identifying lesbians and gay men by appearance is difficult.

The stereotypes about how gay and lesbian people look is the result of confusion between two central concepts—gender identity and sexual orientation. *Gender identity* refers to a person's internal psychological self-concept of being either a male or a female. *Sexual orientation* refers to "a person's erotic and emotional orientation toward members of his or her own gender or members of the other gender" (Hyde, 1994, p. 728). These concepts should not be confused. For example, whether a man prefers to have sexual relations with another man has nothing to do with his own feeling that he is a man. Most gay men think of themselves as being men (Storms, 1980, 1981). They do not think of themselves as being women, nor do they want to become women. Therefore, a gay man can look and act like any other man, yet still be attracted to men. Gender identity and sexual orientation should not be confused with respect to women either. A woman may feel like a woman and think of herself as a woman, yet still be attracted to women (Hyde, 1994). The two concepts are separate and distinct.

Playing Male and Female Roles

Another common stereotype about gay and lesbian people is that in any particular pair, one will choose a "masculine" dominant role and the other a "feminine" submissive role. As with most heterosexual couples, this is usually not the case (Berger & Kelly, 1995; Hyde, 1994; McCammon, Knox, & Schacht, 1998). Any individual, homosexual or heterosexual, may play a more dominant or more submissive role depending on his or her particular mood, activity, or the interaction involved. People are rarely totally submissive or totally dominant.

The Myth of Child Molesting

One other derogatory stereotype targeting gay and lesbian people is that they are inclined to molest children (Tully, 2001). This stereotype is especially damaging for homosexual teachers in that it can cause them to lose their jobs. Evidence indicates that the vast majority of child molestation is done by men whose victims are female children (Berger & Kelly, 1995). Gay men are no more likely to molest children than their heterosexual counterparts (Berger & Kelly, 1995; Hyde, 1994; McCammon, Knox, & Schacht, 1998). There are indications that lesbians are much less likely to molest children than heterosexual or gay men (Hyde, 1994).

The Stereotype "If They're Gay, They Must Have AIDS"

AIDS has commanded extensive media attention over the past few years. This concentration has focused on such issues as what the disease involves and what portions of the population are involved. Because gay men were among the first groups hit by the epidemic, the public has some tendency to identify them with the virus. In reality, the spread of AIDS is growing in other population groups. For example, for all reported cases in the United States, the proportion of men contracting AIDS from other men has declined between 1990 and 2001; however, the heterosexual contraction rate has risen during that same period (McAnulty & Burnette, 2003). Increases are especially true for women: "the proportion of female adults and adolescent with AIDS [in the U.S.] increased from 7 percent of all cases in 1985 to nearly 30 percent in 2000" (Centers for Disease Control, 2000; McAnulty & Burnette, 2003, p. 463). Worldwide, about half the people who have AIDS are women (Brown, 2002).

Even seniors are not immune. Approximately 13 percent of people with AIDS are seniors (Marcus, 2002). Marcus (2002) explains: "A larger senior population is having more sex later in life, a pattern that is enhanced by the popularity of Viagra and the promise of potency drugs for women. In addition, greater numbers of older people are being screened for HIV. . . . In Dade County, Fla., for example, almost 20 percent of people with AIDS are seniors, giving the county one of the highest rates in the country for the 50 plus segment. . . . Forty-four percent of senior women in Florida with AIDS, and 18 percent of men over 50 there, are known to have been infected through heterosexual sex" (p. 41).

Gay men have been extremely active in AIDS prevention, education, and advocacy for research and resources. They have strived to saturate gay communities with information about safer sex and to provide mutual support. AIDS is virtually unknown among lesbians, except those who are IV drug users, a high-risk group (Hyde, 1994).

AIDS is not a "gay disease." Its transmission has nothing to do with being gay. Sexual and other behaviors (such as sharing IV drug needles) can put anyone at greater risk. Both heterosexual and gay and lesbian people need to be aware of and avoid high-risk behaviors.

What Does Being a Homosexual Mean?

The concept of homosexuality is complex. It is difficult to formulate a definition that reflects its many facets (Berger & Kelly, 1995). A simplistic definition of a *homosexual* is a person who is attracted primarily to people of the same gender to satisfy "sexual and affectional needs" (Shernoff, 1995, p. 1075). This involves *sexual orientation,* "a person's erotic and romantic attraction to one or both sexes" (McAnulty & Burnette, 2001, p. 617). Berger and Kelly (1995), however, emphasize that "to understand the complexities of sexual orientation, it is necessary to view homosexuality as an identity formation process that occurs over time" (p. 1065).

Three distinct stages are involved in this process (Berger, 1983; Berger & Kelly, 1995). The first stage is *sexual encounter,* when a person has physical contact and involvement with another person of the same gender. The second stage is *social reaction,* which refers to how other people label the person as homosexual. The third stage, *identity,* involves a series of happenings. Initially, a person experiences uneasiness and confusion when confronting discrepancies. For example, behavior and feelings for others of the same gender may conflict with a person's identity as a heterosexual being. As time passes, however, "the individual begins to label himself or herself as a gay

person and confronts the question of how to manage the new identity."

An important aspect of any definition of "homosexual" is that above all else, a homosexual is a person. In the eyes of some heterosexuals the sexuality of a lesbian or gay person often takes precedence over all other aspects of his or her personality, and the person becomes lost or invisible (see Figure 13.1). Most people are taught *homophobia,* the irrational "hatred, fear, or dislike of homosexuals and bisexuals" (Morales, 1995, p. 1089). These feelings warp their perception of homosexuals. The homosexuality is seen as prominent, at the expense of all other aspects of the lesbian or gay person's personality. A more realistic view is one in which homosexuality is seen in context. The fact that a person is lesbian or gay is only one slice in a person's personality pie. A realistic perspective allows the many various aspects of the person's personality to be acknowledged and appreciated.

Another aspect of the definition of homosexual is that the homosexual is attracted *primarily* to people of the same gender to satisfy sexual and affectional needs. A gay male is attracted to and would choose to have an intimate sexual and affectional relationship with another male rather than a female. A lesbian or female homosexual would opt to have such an intimate involvement with another female

Figure 13.1 The Personality Pie

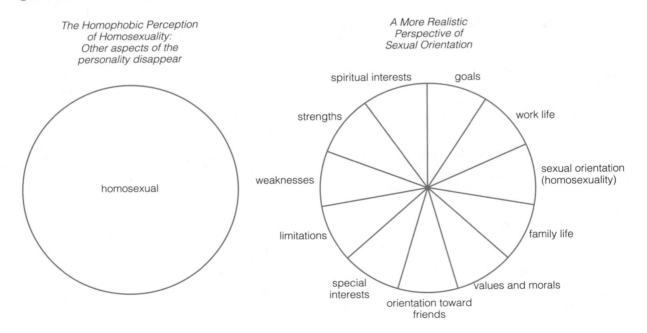

instead of a male. This part of the definition excludes people who under certain circumstances engage in homosexual activities. For instance, prisoners and other institutionalized persons might establish homosexual relationships with others simply because persons of the opposite gender are unavailable. These people will typically return to heterosexuality when the opportunity arises.

The word *homosexual* is derived from the Greek root *homo,* meaning "same." The word *homosexual* itself, however, was not used until the late 1800s (Karlen, 1971). Terms used to refer to lesbian and gay people can be confusing. Both women and men with same-gender orientations have been labeled homosexuals. Gay men prefer the term *gay* instead of *homosexual* because it has neither the direct sexual connotations nor the demeaning implications frequently associated with the word *homosexual.*

The word *lesbian* refers to female homosexuals. Around the year 600 B.C., a woman named Sappho lived on the Greek island of Lesbos in the Aegean Sea (from which the term *lesbian* is derived). Although Sappho was married, she remains famous for the love poems she wrote to other women.

Many people who are not lesbian or gay use the term *gay* to refer both to lesbians and gay men. However, many lesbians have expressed concern that men are given precedence over women when this term is used by itself to refer to both genders. Therefore, throughout this chapter we will differentiate between the terms *lesbian* and *gay,* giving them equal status. Although we have established specific definitions of *lesbian, gay,* and *homosexual,* many who use these terms do not have a clear picture of what they actually mean. All three words may refer to a person with slight, moderate, or substantial interest in or sexual experience with persons of the same gender. Heterosexual people are often referred to as *straight.*

Note that sometimes the concepts of sexual orientation and gender identity are confused, when they are really distinctly separate concepts. *Gender identity* is one's perception of oneself as being either male or female. Some people assume that gay men really want to be women and that lesbians desire to be men. This is false. A gay man's gender identity is male. He identifies himself as a man and feels like a man. Similarly, a lesbian's gender identity is female, which is how she perceives herself. Gay men and lesbians are simply romantically attracted to (i.e., have a *sexual orientation* toward) their same gender instead of the opposite gender, as heterosexuals are.

Some people, however, regardless of whether they are gay or heterosexual, feel that their biological gender identity is wrong. Spotlight 13.1 discusses another dimension of human diversity—transgender people.

Definition of Bisexual

A *bisexual* person is sexually attracted to members of either gender. A bisexual is indeed a person who is "sexually involved with or attracted to members of both sexes" (Strong et al., 1999, p. 175).

We have already initiated the idea that homosexuality is not such a clearcut concept. Bisexuality is even less clearly defined. In the first major study of sexuality in our era, Kinsey, Pomeroy, and Martin (1948) found that it was very difficult to categorize people in terms of being homosexual, bisexual, or heterosexual. They found many people who considered themselves as being heterosexual had had homosexual experiences at some time during their lives. For example, 37 percent of the men in his sample of 5,300 had had at least one sexual experience with another male, to the point of orgasm, after reaching age 16. In a study of 5,940 women, Kinsey and his associates (1953) found that between 8 and 20 percent had had some type of homosexual contact between ages 20 and 35. A significantly smaller percentage of each group had exclusively homosexual experiences throughout their lifetimes. The *Encyclopedia of Social Work* indicates that "despite sampling flaws, the Kinsey et al. studies [1948, 1953] are still considered the most comprehensive and generally reliable research available" (Gochros, 1995, p. 300).

Because Kinsey and his associates found it so difficult to place people into distinct categories, namely those of homosexual and heterosexual, they developed a six-point scale that placed people on a continuum concerning their sexual experiences (see Figure 13.2). A rating of 0 on the scale meant that the individual was exclusively heterosexual—the person had never had any type of homosexual experience. On the other hand, a score of 6 on the scale indicated exclusive homosexuality—this individual had never experienced any form of heterosexual behavior. Those persons scoring 3 would have equal homosexual and heterosexual interest and experience.

More recent researchers have discovered similar difficulties in clearly categorizing people in terms of their sexual orientation. Storms (1980, 1981) suggests that the Kinsey scale still failed to provide an accurate description. He developed a two-dimensional scheme to reflect sexual orientation (see Figure 13.2). The two dimensions involved reflect homoeroticism (sexual interest in and/or experience with those of the same gender) and

Spotlight on Diversity 13.1   Transsexual and Transgender People

Transsexual people are those whose gender identity is the opposite of their biological gender. It is frequently said that they "feel trapped in the body of the opposite gender," when their true gender identity is not their biological one. Often transsexual people prefer to be referred to as *transgender* people because the term *transsexual* emphasizes "sex," and gender identity involves so many more facets of an individual's personality and life circumstances. However, the term *transgender* is also used to refer to a broader spectrum of people—namely, "those whose appearance and behaviors do not conform to the gender roles ascribed by society for people of a particular sex" (Crooks & Baur, 2002, p. 62). These include people who prefer to dress in the clothing generally worn by the opposite gender and adopt behaviors commonly exhibited by that gender. Such preferences occur in a wide range of degrees. Transsexual and transgender people involve complex concepts. Here we will use the term *transgender* to mean "transsexual" as defined above.

Many transgender people pursue surgery to enhance their physical appearance as people of the opposite gender—a process that usually involves four steps. First, they enter counseling to make certain that they are aware of their true feelings and that they understand the potential ramifications of changing genders. Second, they undergo a "real-life test" where they actually live and undertake their daily activities as a person of the opposite gender. Third, they receive extensive hormone treatments to align their bodies with the opposite gender as much as possible—a process that they must continue for the rest of their lives. For example, female-to-male transgender people would take male hormones to encourage facial and body hair growth, while male-to-female transgender people would take female hormones to encourage the softening of body tissue and the redistribution of body fat. The fourth step involves undergoing surgery where genitals and other areas of the body are surgically altered to more closely resemble the opposite gender. Of course, changes are primarily cosmetic because construction of internal organs is impossible. Genital tissue is used to create a penislike organ and scrotum for female-to-male transgender people, and a vaginal canal and labia for male-to-female transgender people. Other physical alterations might include breast implants or breast removal, or decreasing the size of a biological male's Adam's apple.

In the past, male-to-female operations were more common, but today female-to-male operations are catching up in frequency. Female-to-male surgery is generally more complex. In view of the physical pain and discomfort, in addition to the high cost, many transgender people choose not to pursue surgery.

The NASW (2000) Policy Statement on "Transgender and Gender Identity Issues" reads as follows: "NASW recognizes that there is considerable diversity in gender expression and identity among our population. NASW believes that people of diverse gender—including those sometimes called 'transgender'—should be afforded the same respect and rights as any other person. NASW asserts that discrimination and prejudice directed against any individuals are damaging to the social, emotional, physical, and economic well-being of the affected individuals, as well as society as a whole, and NASW seeks the elimination of the same both inside and outside the profession" (p. 302).

heteroeroticism (sexual interest in and/or experience with those of the opposite gender).

Additionally, Storms's scheme portrays sexual interest in general. Those individuals who express high interest in both sexes are placed in the upper right–hand corner. They are considered bisexuals. Those persons who have a very low sexual interest in either gender are placed in the lower left–hand corner. They are considered asexual. Persons with primary sexual interest in the same gender, the homosexuals, are placed in the upper left–hand corner. Similarly people with primary sexual interest in the opposite gender, the heterosexuals, are placed in the lower right–hand corner.

Numbers of Lesbian and Gay People

It's difficult, if not impossible, to state exactly how many people are lesbian or gay. However, it may be useful to consider the numbers of people who have adopted a primarily lesbian or gay orientation over an extended period of time.

Based on Kinsey's work, "many authors have used 10 percent as the proportion of men who are gay" (Berger & Kelly, 1995, p. 1066). Kinsey found that, although more than one-third of American men had homosexual experiences leading to orgasm during their adolescent or adult lives, only 10 percent of men were exclusively homosexual for a 3-year period between ages 16 and 55. Only about 4 percent were gay throughout their lives.

Supposedly, two to three times as many men as women have a homosexual orientation. Although Kinsey found that 19 percent of American women had homosexual experiences by the age of 40, only 2 to 3 percent of these remained lesbian throughout their lives.

Many lesbian and gay organizations maintain that they make up 10 percent of the population. One lesbian and gay organization is called "The Ten Percent Society."

Figure 13.2 Conceptualizations of Homosexuality and Heterosexuality

The homophobic conceptualization: a "black or white" perspective

heterosexual   homosexual

Kinsey's (1953) six-point scale

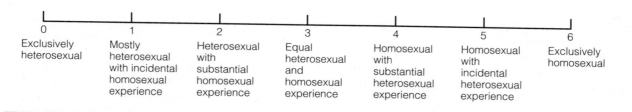

0	1	2	3	4	5	6
Exclusively heterosexual	Mostly heterosexual with incidental homosexual experience	Heterosexual with substantial homosexual experience	Equal heterosexual and homosexual experience	Homosexual with substantial heterosexual experience	Homosexual with incidental heterosexual experience	Exclusively homosexual

Storms's (1980) two-dimensional conceptualization

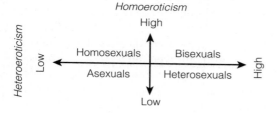

Source: A. C. Kinsey, W. B. Pomeroy, and C. E. Martin (eds.), *Sexual Behavior in the Human Male*. Adapted by permission of the Kinsey Institute for Research in Sex, Gender & Reproduction, Inc., Bloomington, IN.; Adapted from M. D. Storms, "Theories of Sexual Orientation," *Journal of Personality and Social Psychology* 38(1980): 783–792.

However, more recent surveys have revealed that only 1 to 2 percent of the total population is lesbian or gay (Barringer, 1993; Berger & Kelly, 1995; Billy et al., 1993; Painton, 1993). The Kinsey research posed some methodological problems that make it difficult to compare them with more recent research. For example, Kinsey and his colleagues included a large number of prisoners and volunteers from gay organizations (Masters et al., 1995). They also "included feelings and fantasies in their definition of homosexuality, whereas some recent surveys focused exclusively on sexual behavior" (Berger & Kelly, 1995). Still other sources indicate that between 2.5 and 3 percent of Americans are lesbian or gay people (Rogers, 1993; Tully, 1995).

The controversy regarding the actual number of lesbian and gay people continues (Berger & Kelly, 1995; Rogers, 1993; Tully, 1995). Regardless of whether lesbian and gay people make up 1 to 10 percent of the population, they are a sizable minority group.

Why Are Some People Lesbians or Gays?

Although various theories have been proposed to explain why people are gays or lesbians, none has been proven. (A similar question could be asked, "Why are people heterosexual?") No one can give a definitive answer concerning why some people are homosexual and others heterosexual. Some of the primary hypotheses will be reviewed here. They fall under the umbrellas of biological and psychosocial theories. Evaluation of theory, interactionist theory, ethical issues related to theory, and other recent research will also be discussed.

Biological Theories

The biological theories attempting to explain homosexuality can be clustered under three headings: genetic, anatomical (brain), and hormonal. They are based on the idea that homosexuality is caused by physiological factors over which individuals have no control.

Genetic Factors. The genetic explanation for homosexuality supports the idea that people's sexuality is programmed through their genes. Bailey and Pillard compared groups of identical twins, fraternal twins, and brothers who were adopted (1991). Identical twins develop from the splitting of a single fertilized egg. They are therefore genetically identical. Fraternal twins, on the other hand, develop concurrently from two separate eggs that were fertilized from two separate sperm. They are only as genetically similar as any brothers might be. Brothers who are adopted, unless they are family members, have no genetic commonality. The researchers found that when one brother was gay, 52 percent of the identical twins were also gay. Among only 22 percent of fraternal twins and 11 percent of adoptive brothers were both brothers gay. The researchers concluded that this provides evidence for a genetic link. They indicated that the degree of genetic contribution to homosexuality could vary from 30 to 70 percent.

Another study looked at 108 lesbians who had either identical or fraternal twin sisters, and at another 32 lesbians who had adopted sisters (Bailey et al., 1993). They found that among almost half of the identical twins, both were lesbians. However, only 16 percent of fraternal twins and 6 percent of the unrelated sisters were both lesbians. These results support the idea that there is a genetic component to homosexuality.

A study by the National Cancer Institute's Laboratory of Biochemistry explored the family trees of 76 gay men to identify gay and bisexual family members (Hamer et al., 1993; Pool, 1993). They found that 13.5 percent of identified gay men's brothers were also gay. This was significantly greater than the 2 percent likelihood of having a gay brother in the general population. Interestingly, the preponderance of gay relatives was on the mother's side of the family. This led researchers to consider a potential maternal genetic link on the X chromosome, because the X chromosome in men is inherited only from their mothers.

This finding, in turn, led to another study (Bower, 1993). Forty pairs of gay brothers were recruited, and genes on their X chromosomes examined. Thirty-three of the 40 pairs displayed the same configuration of DNA on a designated stretch of their X chromosomes. As a result, the researchers suggested "that these families possessed a maternally transmitted gene that predisposed them to homosexuality" (p. 37). However, they cautioned that "genes may play a role in at least some cases of homosexuality, but the seven pairs of brothers who did

not both inherit the crucial bit of X chromosome also provide an opening to study how the environment influences sexual orientation" (p. 37).

Brain (Anatomical) Factors. LeVay (1991, 1996) studied the brains of 41 cadavers: 19 of gay men, 16 of supposedly heterosexual men, and 6 of supposedly heterosexual women. He found that the anterior hypothalamus (a marble-sized cluster of cells that regulates sexual activity in addition to appetite and body temperature) in gay men was only half the size as that in heterosexual men.

However, there are a number of concerns about these findings (Masters et al., 1995). First, the sample size was exceptionally small. Second, the gay men studied had died of AIDS. Therefore, brain differences might have been due to AIDS-related brain afflictions, which are common. Third, male "heterosexuals" were labeled as such on the basis of an assumption. Their sexual orientation was assumed, not verified. Finally, the brain differences do not indicate whether they were "a cause or consequence of sexual orientation" (p. 381). Therefore, more research is needed to confirm the findings.

Hormonal Factors. Hormonal theories of heterosexuality suggest that hormonal type and level cause homosexuality. One subset of hormonal theories concerns differences in hormonal levels during adulthood. Tourney (1980) examined studies, completed since 1969, that were oriented toward this issue. (Earlier studies were not included because of their methodological problems.) He found that results were extremely contradictory. Some studies indicate that gay men have lower levels of testosterone than heterosexual men; other studies found the opposite; and yet other research found no differences at all.

Another subset of the hormonal theories indicates that abnormal hormonal levels during the prenatal period may result in homosexuality (Berger & Kelly, 1995). Ehrhardt (1985), for example, studied 30 women whose mothers had been administered a synthetic hormone, DES or diethylstilbestrol during their pregnancies. These women were found to manifest a higher-than-average level of lesbian and bisexual activity than women whose mothers had not taken DES during pregnancy. However, these findings cannot be taken to be indicative of a clear cause–effect relationship. Three-quarters of the women, clearly the large majority, were heterosexual despite the DES. Another problem with this research is that results from a sample with possible biological abnormalities due to the DES cannot be generalized to the "normal" population.

There has been a recent surge of interest in hormonal theories of homosexuality. This probably coincides with the development of increasingly more sensitive and accurate technology for hormonal measurements. Many experts feel that there is a greater likelihood that hormones influence the predisposition of sexual orientation to one gender or the other prenatally rather than postnatally (Byer et al., 1988; Masters et al., 1988). However, no clear cause–effect relationship has been established. Hormonal levels vary from one individual to another, and, indeed, within the same individual over time. Human hormones are not yet clearly understood. Whatever causes homosexuality and heterosexuality is likely to be a much more complex process.

Psychosocial Theories

Psychosocial or behavioral theories emphasize that homosexual behavior is learned, just as any other type of behavior is learned. Early in life, homosexual behavior might be positively reinforced by pleasurable experiences and thereby strengthened. Or, such behavior may be punished by negative, punitive experiences and, as a result, be weakened.

For instance, a child who has several positive sexual contacts with members of the same gender might be positively reinforced or encouraged to seek out more such contacts. Similarly, a child who has a negative experience with a member of the same gender might be discouraged from having more such encounters.

The Evaluation of Theory: What Is the Answer?

The answer to why people are gay is a multifaceted one. Genetic rationales have major shortcomings. For example, we discussed the research finding concerning identical twins. If, as some researchers postulate, genetic rationales explain some component or percentage of why people are gay, then what explains the remaining components or percentages? If people are gays or lesbians because of some hormonal impact (perhaps prenatally), why aren't all people lesbians or gays who experienced similar hormonal impacts?

At least two major shortcomings can be cited with respect to psychosocial theories of homosexuality that emphasize the learning process. First, there is a tremendous amount of negative feedback about homosexuality. Children learn early that being called a "fag" is not a compliment. How homosexual behavior would be reinforced and would increase in frequency, in view of such punitive circumstances, might be questioned.

Second, learning theory implies that a person must first have a homosexual experience. Then, if the experience was positively reinforcing or personally rewarding,

the person would seek out more such experiences. However, might it not be the case that individuals who have homosexual desires seek out sexual experiences with the same gender in the first place? In other words, might not the desire for sexual contact with the same gender be there even before any actions ever occur?

Interactionist Theory

Storms (1981) has proposed a theory that focuses on the interaction of biological predisposition and the effects of the environment. He poses that the development of a homosexual orientation is related to the rate at which people mature during preadolescence. Children tend to play and interact with people of the same gender during preadolescence. This same-sex interaction reaches its peak at about age 12, after which heterosexual interactions begin to develop. Heterosexual dating may start around age 15. Storms suggests that the sex drive for some people emerges earlier than for others. If children who mature earlier are still in same-sex groupings, they may have positive sexual experiences with persons of the same gender during this time. They may develop a pattern whereby they remain oriented toward the same gender. They never become interested sexually in the opposite gender. This is where the environment plays a part. If these children happen to have positive sexual same-sex experiences, they may continue with that same sexual orientation. If early maturers do not have these experiences, they continue later to develop a heterosexual orientation as they begin interacting with people of the opposite gender.

Many experts agree that homosexuality probably results from some mixture of both biological and psychosocial variables. As yet we don't know what that mixture is (Crooks & Baur, 2002; Gooren, Fliers, & Courtney, 1990; McCammon et al., 1998). There is still no clearly established reason why people are lesbians or gays.

Ethical Issues Related to Theory

Some lesbian and gay people have expressed ethical concerns regarding proving any theory about homosexuality involving a biological component. On the one hand, many express relief at the thought that others might consider their homosexuality not to be their "own fault." If there's a medical basis, the general public might become more accepting of lesbians and gay men. Gelman and his colleagues (1992) found that people were generally more accepting of lesbian and gay people if they felt such people were "born that way" instead of *choosing* or *learning* that lifestyle.

On the other hand, if specific genetic or hormonal "ingredients" are found for homosexuality, lesbian and gay people might be considered defective by society at large. Taking this one step further, society at large might decide to make biological "corrections" prenatally. Might this mean changing what a person was meant to be into something else? Might potential parents be more likely to abort a fetus determined to be lesbian or gay if they learn about the homosexuality early in the gestational process? There are no easy answers to these questions in our technological age.

Other Research on the Origins of Homosexuality

Bell and his colleagues (1981) undertook a massive investigation through the Alfred C. Kinsey Institute for Sex Research concerning the causes of homosexuality. They studied 979 lesbians and gay men, and compared them to 477 heterosexual women and men. Study participants were asked extensive questions about many aspects of their lives. A statistical method called *path analysis* allowed the researchers to explore possible casual relationships between variables, such as prenatal characteristics and family relationships, and the development of sexual orientation.

Despite the fact that the research offers some of the most extensive and methodologically sound findings available, none of the aforementioned theories that explain homosexuality were supported. If anything, several of the variables proposed by these other theories were found not to be related to homosexuality. For instance, no relationship was found between being gay and having been seduced by a person of the same gender when young. The researchers found no ultimate answers, but they did identify some interesting aspects about being lesbian or gay. Three findings are of special significance.

First, sexual orientation appears to emerge by the time both males and females reach adolescence. This is the case even when people have little or no sexual experience. Second, lesbian and gay people have a similar amount of heterosexual experience during childhood and adolescence when compared to heterosexual people. There was one basic difference, however. Despite the fact that lesbian and gay people participate in heterosexual activity, they do not enjoy it very much.

The third major finding of the study involves the concept of gender nonconformity during childhood. *Gender nonconformity* refers to a child's preference for play and activities that our society generally assumes appropriate for children of the opposite gender. For example, little girls usually choose to play with Barbie dolls and play dishes, whereas little boys generally prefer "GI Joes" and toy bulldozers. A little girl who only plays with tanks and footballs or a little boy who only plays with Barbie dolls would be examples of gender nonconformity. Gender nonconformity was a much stronger causal factor for gay men than for lesbians. Other factors such as family relationships have a stronger causal relationship with lesbianism.

This research indicates that sexual orientation develops very early in life. It also suggests that whether a person is gay or lesbian or heterosexual is not a matter of choice. Just as a heterosexual person might be sexually attracted to another heterosexual person, so is a lesbian or gay person sexually attracted to another of the same gender. It appears that it would be just as impossible for a lesbian or gay person to turn heterosexual as it would be for a heterosexual person to begin choosing sexual partners of the same gender.

The fact that many lesbian and gay people externally assume heterosexual roles for appearance' sake is also logical. Numerous homophobic stigmas are placed on gay or lesbian people. They are often subjected to serious discrimination. In evaluating the consequences of the various alternatives open to them, some lesbian and gay people may decide that it is too difficult to survive openly as a gay/lesbian person (e.g., hold a job, relate to family members, participate in community activities). A lesbian or gay person with a heterosexual facade is burdened with pretending to be someone she or he is not. Such pretense can violate individual dignity and freedom. Spotlight 13.2 discusses discrimination and the impact of homophobia upon gay and lesbian people.

✿ Lesbian and Gay Lifestyles

What is it like to be a lesbian or gay person? How would life be different or similar if you awoke tomorrow morning and discovered that you were homosexual? What would happen to your relationships with family, friends, and colleagues?

No one typical lifestyle is practiced by all lesbians and gay people. Lesbians and gay men have lives that are just as varied as those of heterosexuals. Being a gay man in Dickeyville, Wisconsin, is different from being a gay man in a San Francisco suburb. Being a white lesbian mother receiving public assistance in Utah is different from being an African American upper-class lesbian mother in Boston. However, some common patterns emerge in the lives of lesbian and gay people. Several issues reflected by these patterns are addressed here.

Spotlight on Diversity 13.2

Discrimination and the Impacts of Homophobia

"Did you ever hear the one about the dyke who . . ."

"Harry sure has a 'swishy' way about him. You'd never catch me in the locker room alone with that guy."

"They're nothing but a bunch of lousy faggots."

Our common language is filled with derogatory terms referring to lesbian and gay people. Just as other diverse groups are subject to arbitrary stereotypes and to discrimination, so are gay and lesbian people. Because of negative attitudes and the resulting discriminatory behavior, alternatives for lesbian and gay people are often different and limited. There are often other negative consequences. Other, non-sexually related aspects of their lives are affected because of their sexual orientation.

For example, a male third-grade teacher may live in fear that the parents of his students will discover he's living with another man. He loves his job, which he's had for 9 years. If parents put pressure on the school administration about his homosexuality, he may get fired. He may never get another teaching job again.

Another example is provided by a female college student who expends massive amounts of energy to disguise the fact that she's a lesbian. She attends a state university in a small, midwest, rural town. She is terribly lonely. She keeps hoping that that special someone will walk into her life. However, she doesn't dare let her friends know she's lesbian or she really will be isolated. There wouldn't be anyone to talk to or to go to have dinner with. They would just never understand. People have committed suicide for less.

Lesbian and gay people are frequently the victims of homophobia. *Homophobia* is the irrational "hatred, fear, or dislike of homosexuals and bisexuals" (Morales, 1995, p. 1089) that many people have. Morales explains that "the U.S. military, medical, mental health, educational, and religious establishments historically have taken antihomosexual stances. Furthermore, homophobia . . . is taught early by most families" (p. 1085).

Some feel that the term homophobia is too strong because the word *phobia* means "an intense and persistent fear of an object or situation" (Barker, 1999, p. 361; Blumenfeld, 1992). *Antihomosexual* or *antigay* stance, *prejudice,* or *discrimination* might be alternate terms. In reality, homophobia is likely a continuum. People probably vary markedly regarding the depth of their negative feelings about lesbian and gay people. Regardless of what it's called, the fact is that many people harbor seriously negative perceptions and prejudice against lesbian and gay people (Berger & Kelly, 1995; Longres & Fredriksen, 2000; Morales, 1995; Tully, 2001; Woodman, 1995).

It is not clear how homophobia originated. Maier (1984) postulates that it may be people's attempts to deny homosexual feelings in themselves. Perhaps the more strongly homophobic people are, the more they are working to deny such feelings in themselves. Regardless of the cause, the manifestations of homophobia are all around us. In the past homosexuality was considered an illness. Not until 1974 did the American Psychiatric Association remove it from the list of mental illnesses. Whitham and Mathy (1986) potently describe the extent of homophobia:

Not only are homosexuals criminalized, victimized, and labeled pathological, they are also regarded by some religious groups as sinners deserving to be put to death, a view reminiscent of the Inquisition. There are very few, if any, groups in American society which evoke more hostility than homosexuals. (p. 180)

Today there are many indications of homophobia. In one survey, 71 percent of the people interviewed felt that sexual relations between adults of the same sex was *always* wrong; 40 percent indicated that a gay man should not be allowed to teach in college (Davis & Smith, 1991). The Roman Catholic church has decried homosexual behavior as sinful. In many Protestant churches, although not all denominations, gay/lesbian people are not allowed to join the clergy (Sheler, 1999). Lesbian and gay people have been denied or lost jobs and housing purely on the basis of their sexual orientation. Violence against lesbian and gay people has risen dramatically in the past few years.

A potentially serious negative effect would be to internalize such negative attitudes. In other words, a gay/lesbian person might think, "If being homosexual is bad, and I am homosexual, then that means that I am bad, too."

The *Encyclopedia of Social Work* (Morales, 1995; Shernoff, 1995; Tully, 1995; Woodman, 1995) stresses the importance of social workers confronting their own homophobia and learning more about the special issues of lesbian and gay clients. Morales (1995) explains: "Obviously, social workers need to address their own homophobia to become competent in addressing the needs of lesbian and gay parents and their children in their practice methods. Social workers who cannot do so must not offer services to this client system and must question their role in the profession" (p. 1093).

Shernoff (1995) comments: "Once the social worker recognizes that he or she is prejudiced toward gay men [and lesbians] or ignorant about the unique issues that affect them, the social worker must acquire reliable, accurate, state-of-the-art information about the contemporary gay community" (p. 1082). Woodman (1995) further explains the social work role: "Social workers must be aware of their own attitudes and biases; knowledgeable about lesbian [and gay] issues; informed about resources; flexible in designing intervention strategies with an ecological perspective and an empowerment approach; . . . and ready for problem solving with homophobic social institutions" (p. 1597).

Gay people in a close-coupled relationship differ little from their heterosexual counterparts.

© Bruce Ayers/Getty Images

Lesbian and Gay Relationships

Individual relationships and lifestyles vary among lesbian and gay people just as they do among heterosexuals (Longres & Fredriksen, 2000; Tully, 2001). For example, lesbians "may live alone, in couples, with children, with friends, with heterosexual husbands, or in a variety of relationship patterns" (Tully, 1995, p. 1592). As with heterosexuals, many lesbian and gay people live with a significant other as a couple. Additionally, many have children (McLeod, Crawford, & Zechmeister, 1999). When examining heterosexual married, heterosexual couples, and gay male and lesbian couples, there are "striking similarities across family forms in terms of what is valued, issues to be negotiated, problems confronted, problem-solving strategies adopted, and so on. For example, all types of couples closely associate money and power" (Laird, 1995, pp. 1607–1608).

Lesbians are as likely as heterosexual women to live in a relationship as a couple (Laird, 1995). "Given the lack of legal sanction or social recognition," lesbians' relationships are often marked by "stability and longevity" (p. 1608).

There is some evidence that gay men have a greater number of partners than heterosexual men and that gay partners are more likely to accept nonmonogamy than their heterosexual counterparts (Berger & Kelly, 1995; Moses & Hawkins, 1982). There is also evidence that many gay men do establish long-term relationships (Crooks & Baur, 2002; McCammon et al., 1993). For example, some research indicated that between 40 and 60 percent of gay men are involved in same-gender relationships (Kurdek, 1995; McAnulty & Burnette, 2003). In fact there is some indication that the quality of gay relationships has been similar to that of their heterosexual

counterparts (Green, Bettinger, & Zachs, 1996; Kurdek, 1995; Ossana, 2000). Osanna (2000) remarks: "The correlates of relationship quality are similar for all couples: appraisals that the relationship includes many rewards and few costs; personality characteristics such as high expressiveness; partner's placing higher value on security, permanence, shared activities, and togetherness; less belief that disagreement is destructive; higher mutual trust; better problem-solving and conflict resolution skills; more frequent shared or egalitarian decision making; and greater satisfaction with perceived social support" (p. 277).

Major social and legal obstacles that prevent lesbian and gay people from establishing long-term relationships do exist. For example, gay and lesbian marriages are illegal in every state. Even if gays and lesbians are very much in love with each other and want to spend their lives together, social obstacles might exist, such as pressure from family and heterosexual friends to form heterosexual relationships, marry, and have children.

Sexual Interaction

Many people find it hard to imagine what lesbian and gay people do sexually. After all, they don't have the "necessary" ingredients of both penis and vagina. The fact is that lesbian and gay people engage in the same types of activities that heterosexuals also enjoy (McCammon et al., 1998; Peplau, Veniegas, & Campbell, 1996). These include hugging, kissing, touching, fondling of the genitals, and oral sex.

The physiological responses of gay and lesbian people are exactly the same as those of heterosexuals. They become aroused or excited, enter a plateau stage of high arousal, have an orgasm, and go through a period of resolution during which the body returns to its normal, unaroused state. The process is the same for all people, male or female, gay or heterosexual.

One difference between gay and lesbian people and straight people is that gay and lesbian people tend to be more open to new techniques, take more time, and pay more attention to the ways in which they interact sexually (Allgeier & Allgeier, 2000; Masters et al., 1988). This may be partly due to the fact that there are fewer conventions or traditional rules about how sexual relations should be accomplished. For example, heterosexual men tend to quickly reach for their partner's breasts and then move on directly to stimulating her genitals; lesbians, on the other hand, will tend to spend much more time kissing, holding, and caressing each other before any genital touching occurs (Masters, Johnson, & Kolodny, 1979; McCammon et al., 1993).

It's interesting that a major thrust of much sex theory for heterosexual couples is to slow down and enjoy the many various aspects of sexual interaction and to avoid being so goal oriented (Annon, 1976; Masters et al., 1995). Perhaps many heterosexual couples could learn a thing or two from lesbian and gay couples (Allgeier & Allgeier, 2000).

❧ Significant Issues and Life Events

As members of a diverse group, lesbian and gay people are victims of stereotypes and homophobia. Discrimination may frequently limit the alternatives available to them. Social workers and other human service professionals need to be aware of the special issues and life events confronting lesbian and gay people. In order to help clients define and evaluate the alternatives available to them, social workers must understand the effects of certain life events. Significant issues and life events of gay and lesbian people are examined here. Additionally, social work with gay and lesbian people is addressed.

The Impacts of Social and Economic Forces: Legal Issues

For hundreds of years, laws have existed to suppress homosexuality. Although some progress has been made by and on behalf of lesbian and gay people in the last decade, homosexual acts are still illegal in many states (Crooks & Baur, 2002). The laws in this country have developed over the past two centuries to "support and protect heterosexuality and nuclear family relationships"; the result is that many of the legal rights of lesbians and gay men have been ignored (Schwaber, 1985, p. 92). However, in the 1990s, lesbian and gay communities have been "sufficiently large and vocal to emerge as a powerful political interest group" (Berger & Kelly, 1995, p. 1070). Spotlight 13.3 discusses the importance of a sense of community among gay and lesbian people.

Six issues will be addressed concerning where lesbian and gay people are treated differently than heterosexual people under the law. The issues include employment, the military, personal relationships and finances, child custody and visitation, and criminal (sodomy) laws.

Employment. Not until 1976 was the federal government's personnel manual changed to forbid discrimination against lesbian and gay people in hiring or terminations unless the public agency involved could prove that homosexual behavior affected work completion (Dale, 1993). This means that most federal government agencies cannot discriminate against lesbian and gay people purely on the basis of their sexual orientation. However, these rules don't apply to state and local job positions. For example, police departments and public schools have often succeeded in driving out lesbian and gay employees (Dale, 1993).

Other than for federal government jobs, there are no federal statutes that prohibit employers from discriminating against lesbian and gay people. They are not considered to be one of the groups such as racial minorities included under the equal protection clause of the U.S. Constitution. Some states, cities, and counties have implemented legislation that protects the rights of lesbian and gay people in specific ways. Several states have passed laws prohibiting some kinds of discrimination based on sexual orientation (Berger & Kelly, 1995). Other states have established executive mandates that effectively do the same thing; numerous smaller localities have enacted "antidiscrimination civil rights ordinances or executive orders" to combat discrimination (p. 1071). The types of discrimination these laws and regulations usually address include "public and private employment, public accommodations, insurance practices, housing, credit, and education" (Berger & Kelly, 1995, p. 1071; Dale, 1993).

Some major companies have implemented personnel policies granting benefits to partners of lesbian and gay employees (Berger & Kelly, 1995; Tully, 1995). However, the vast majority of private employers do not operate under these guidelines (Kantrowitz, 1996). Many employers will not hire people who are lesbian or gay, and they may fire people simply because they are lesbian or gay.

Spotlight on Diversity 13.3

Gay and Lesbian Pride and a Sense of Community

All people, gay, lesbian, and heterosexual, need places to socialize, to feel free, to be themselves, and to feel that they belong. Gay and lesbian pride and the sense of community are important concepts (van Wormer et al., 2000). One young man summarized these concepts well by joyously stating:

> As someone who has recently "come out," I have acquired a sense of pride in my homosexuality; a part of me I have run and hidden from for twenty of my twenty-five years. I owe much gratitude to many people in the gay community who have given me the courage to stand up for who I am. I am proud to call these people my gay brothers, the first real friends I have ever had. I'm not ashamed—I'm proud to be gay. My sense of gay pride has made me realize that I'm as good as any other person on this earth and deserving of the same basic human dignity and respect all human beings are entitled to. ("What Does Gay/Lesbian Pride Mean to You?," 1985, p. 2)

Heterosexual innuendos, expectations, values, and ideas saturate our society. One gay man said he always felt he had to be watchful and cautious in heterosexual groups. He carefully censored what he said to protect himself from homophobic attacks on himself and his lifestyle.

Within the lesbian and gay communities, lesbians and gay men can be themselves. They can let down their protective facades. They can be with other people who understand what it's like to be gay in a heterosexually oriented world. This is not to say that many lesbians and gay men have not openly and proudly proclaimed their sexual orientation. This is so despite the fact that it means they expose themselves to homophobic criticism, prejudice, and discrimination. In a way, by doing this, they are advocating for individual freedom and the end of discrimination.

In this homophobic world, there are a multitude of lesbian and gay activities and organizations. These range far beyond crisis lines and support groups. There are sports teams and organizations, choral groups, churches, bookstores, newspapers, magazines, advocacy groups, and computer dating services all oriented toward lesbians and gay men. The sense of community has developed and grown far beyond that of the gay bar.

Interestingly, the results of a 1996 *Newsweek* poll revealed that 84 percent of respondents supported providing equal job opportunities for lesbian and gay people (Kaplan & Klaidman, 1996). This represents an increase from 74 percent of respondents in a poll done 2 years earlier.

The Military. Lesbian and gay people historically have been prohibited from joining the CIA, the FBI, and the armed forces (McCrary & Gutierrez, 1979/80; Tully, 1995). Leonard Matlovich perhaps provides one of the most publicized examples of discrimination against gay/lesbian people by the military. As the son of an Air Force sergeant, Matlovich was raised on Air Force bases. Upon his high school graduation, he immediately joined the Air Force. He received numerous decorations for his service, which included fighting in Vietnam. He was also labeled superior in his evaluations.

Years later, at age 30, Matlovich acknowledged that he was gay and became involved in gay activities. When he related this to his superiors, he was discharged with a "general discharge," a type of discharge considered less than honorable. He eventually took his case to court. He "later collected $160,000 in back pay when the Air Force could not rebut his claim to an exemption from the no-gays policy." In late 1992, the U.S. Supreme Court "upheld a lower court ruling that demanded the services provide a 'rational basis' for the ban on gays" (*Newsweek*, 1993, p. 54).

In January 1993, President Clinton announced a plan to revoke the 50-year-old ban on gay and lesbian people in the military. However, Congress so eroded the plan that the final version entailed an uncomfortable "don't ask, don't tell, don't pursue" guideline (Gelman, 1993, p. 28). This meant that military personnel are supposed to pretend, with an "out of sight, out of mind" approach, that homosexuality doesn't exist. Many questions are raised regarding whether this policy has helped or hindered gay and lesbian military personnel. One study by the Servicemembers Legal Defense Network, a legal aid organization, reported the following findings (AASECT, 2002, April):

- Military discharges for gay and lesbians are at their highest rate in 15 years.

- Antigay harassment is up 23 percent, with 1,075 antigay harassment cases being reported—up from 871 in 2000 (AASECT, 2002, April).

- 1,250 gay men and lesbians were discharged from the military in 2001, after they had announced their sexual orientation or homosexual behavior—up from 1,212 discharges in 2000.

A newspaper article reflects on the perspective of many military leaders (*Milwaukee Journal*, Nov. 11, 1992):

Such a change would be one of the most far-reaching social changes imposed on the armed services since Harry Truman ordered blacks integrated into the military in 1948. . . . Little was being done to prepare the nation's 1.8 million troops for such a major change. The subject is so sensitive "no one wants to deal with it," said one officer, speaking on conditions of anonymity. . . . About 14,000 troops have been kicked out of the service during the last 10 years because they were homosexual . . . Both four-star generals [the chairman of the Joint Chief of Staff and the chief of staff of the Army] contend the issue affects the readiness of the troops for battle, their morale and their rights to privacy. (pp. A1, A3)

Personal Relationships and Finances. In no state in the nation can lesbian and gay people legally marry. Heterosexual unions are characterized by, hopefully, much celebration and legal support. Families and friends hold wedding showers, give gifts, and make the wedding itself a major social event. Lesbian and gay people, however, do not have this legal alternative. With few exceptions in some municipalities and companies, "partners" cannot be included in health insurance policies; nor can they file joint tax returns. Laws concerning these issues are

generally referred to as "domestic partnership" legislation (Berger & Kelly, 1995; Tully, 1995).

Vermont has passed a law allowing gay and lesbian people to form "civil unions" that provide essentially the same rights and responsibilities as those inherent in a heterosexual marriage (AASECT, 2000, May, April). Such rights include "child custody, probate court, workers' compensation, and family leave benefits" (AASECT, 2000, April, p. 6). However, these rights are not transferable to other states should the couple move. Factions criticizing the civil union legislation claim it "undermine[s] traditional marriage," "goes against God's will," and reeks of "social rape" and "moral rot" (AASECT, 2000, May, p. 9).

California and Hawaii have domestic partnership legislation that provides some rights, although they are not nearly as far-reaching as those in the Vermont law (AASECT, 2000, April). An attempt in California at passing legislation mirroring that in Vermont was recently dropped "in the face of heavy criticism" (AASECT, 2002, February, p. 7). Nevada and Nebraska passed constitutional amendments forbidding same-gender marriage (AASECT, 2000, December).

Without the sanction of marriage, except in Vermont, if a lesbian or gay person becomes critically ill and needs hospitalization, his or her partner may be denied visiting

Two gay men are shown kissing after their wedding ceremony in Bohnes, California. The man at the right was one of the two ministers who conducted the ceremony. In California, as in every other state, marriage of lesbians or gays is not "legal." Vermont did recently pass a "civil unions" law that recognizes lesbian and gay relationships. This law gives lesbian and gay couples all the legal privileges provided for married couples—except a "marriage" certificate.

privileges. A gay or lesbian lover and partner has no legal rights because he or she does not fall under the legal definition of family under these circumstances. Lesbian and gay people are encouraged, therefore, to draw up a legal document involving the medical power of attorney; these may address "visitation rights, the right to be consulted, and to give or withhold consent about medical decisions, and in case of death, the right to personal effects and the right to dispose of the body" (Schwaber, 1985, p. 92).

Wills are another source of difficulty for many lesbian and gay people. Lesbian and gay partners have no rights to any inheritance if there is no will. All inheritance will be given to legal family members. Therefore, lesbian and gay people are strongly encouraged to have a will made. Wills may clearly specify what possessions will go to which people. Even with a will, however, relatives may still challenge it under the concept of "undue influence" (Peters, 1982). Lesbian and gay people are, therefore, encouraged to update their wills from time to time. Each time they should ascertain that the will accurately reflects their current assets and is well documented.

On a different and, in a way, more positive note, after the September 11 terrorist attacks, federal and independent relief organizations did provide benefits to gay partners of victims, just as those agencies did for spouses of heterosexual married victims (AASECT, 2001, November). A spokesperson for the American Red Cross indicated that his agency understood "that families come in many different forms" including "committed relationships and domestic partnerships" (p. 7). Remember, however, that domestic partners still can't receive other types of government benefits such as Social Security or workers' compensation.

Child Custody and Visitation Rights. Lesbian and gay parents have experienced major difficulties in custody debates over their children because of their sexual orientation. Numerous courts have denied parents custody simply because of being lesbians or gays (Berger & Kelly, 1995). On the other hand, some state courts have ruled that child custody could not be denied purely on the basis of parental homosexuality unless it was proven that such sexual orientation would hurt the child (Berger & Kelly, 1995).

State court rulings often are in opposition. For example, Hetter (1995) explains:

> *The Virginia Supreme Court ruled . . . [in April 1994] that sexual orientation can be a basis for denying child custody or visitation. But a Wisconsin judge . . . [in summer 1995]*

> *granted visitation rights to the nonbiological parent of a child from a same-sex couple who split up. With gays having their own children, states are still split over legal recognition of such families. California banned adopting by gay couples in March [1995]. In July [1995], a lesbian couple in Illinois was granted joint adoption rights to a child one of them had conceived. Many more cases are coming down the pipeline, as more gays decide to raise children. (pp. 71, 74)*

Cases have been cited where even when a lesbian mother receives custody of her child, she must abide by personal restrictions imposed by the courts. One example is a San Francisco mother who was awarded custody of her three children (Lewis, 1980). The court mandated that as a condition for custody the mother see her female lover only at specified times: when her children were at school or when they visited their father. The question must be raised whether such conditions would have been imposed had her lover been a male.

Judges presiding over custody disputes can make arbitrary judgments concerning what is in the child's best interests (Moses & Hawkins, 1980). Some judges may have homophobic ideas, which have the potential of influencing their decisions.

There are several myths about lesbian and gay parenthood that might influence people against lesbian and gay parents. First, there is the misconception that lesbian or gay parents will influence their children to become gays or lesbians. No verification exists for this myth or for the worry "that daughters will be more masculine and sons more feminine than children from 'normal' families" (Laird, 1995, p. 1609; see also Morales, 1995; Moses & Hawkins, 1982). Second, there is the idea that children will be damaged by growing up in lesbian or gay homes. All indications are that children growing up in such households flourish as well as those raised in heterosexual homes (Laird, 1995; Moses & Hawkins, 1982; Woodman, 1995). Third, some people mistakenly believe that gay and lesbian people's parenting skills are inadequate. No evidence bears this out (Moses & Hawkins, 1982). Finally, "fears about children of lesbians and gay men being sexually abused by adults, ostracized by peers, or isolated in single-sex homosexual communities are unfounded" (Laird, 1995, p. 1609).

It's interesting that the American Association of Pediatrics "endorsed its support of gay and lesbian parents to adopt a partner's children" (AASECT, 2002, March, p. 10). It maintained that it is in the best interest of children, and their security, that they live with legal parents. Only seven states and the District of Columbia permit such adoptions, while three states legally ban them (AASECT,

2002, March). Several suggestions can be made to human service professionals to help lesbian and gay people fight and win battles concerning child custody (Moses & Hawkins, 1982). First of all, the parent must realize that although progress has been made, the odds for gaining custody are still not very good. The parent needs to realize that such cases usually take considerable time and energy. Court cases also frequently cause burdensome stress for both parent and children, and are expensive. Teaching the client such skills as assertiveness, stress management, and problem solving are frequently useful. Another suggestion is to make certain to get a highly competent attorney. Referring the lesbian or gay parent to support groups is also helpful. Finally, educating the parent by providing reading material is often beneficial.

Criminal Law. In many states homosexual activities, both public and private, are specifically illegal. There is significant variation regarding both possible penalties (some include jail terms) and the extent to which these laws are enforced. In many places, certain intimate sexual acts between any two consenting adults are technically illegal and can be prosecuted. Such legislation is often referred to as *sodomy* law. Sodomy is "copulation with a member of the same sex or with an animal," or "noncoital and especially anal or oral copulation with a member of the opposite sex" (*Webster's,* 1995, p. 1116). That reflects quite a range of activity.

"According to the National Gay and Lesbian Task Force, 32 states and the District of Columbia have no sodomy law [as many states have repealed laws in recent years], five states prohibit same-gender sodomy, and 13 states forbid opposite and same-gender sodomy" (AASECT, 2000, July, p. 7). Although enforcement of sodomy laws is relatively rare, they act against lesbian/gay rights. People use them as a reason to discriminate against gay people, who, they say, are more likely to participate in such "criminal" behavior.

The Future of Lesbian and Gay Rights. Although lesbian and gay people are not treated equally under the law, the great progress that has been made should be emphasized. Some states and localities are adopting equal housing and employment legislation for lesbian and gay people. Homosexuality is no longer considered a psychiatric illness. Most of the federal government agencies can no longer discriminate against gay/lesbian people. Lesbian and gay people, through their advocacy and hard work, have achieved a great deal.

Their struggle for equality is sometimes characterized by the phrase "Remember Stonewall!" Stonewall was a gay bar in New York City's Greenwich Village. On June 28, 1969, police stormed and raided the bar, an incident not unusual in those times. How the gay people at the bar responded, though, was indeed unusual. They fought back. The struggle continued in the street for hours.

People involved in gay/lesbian liberation have provided much impetus to progress made in gay and lesbian legal rights. Such groups exist in many communities, especially in urban settings. Group meetings often provide opportunities to discuss issues, plan political interventions, and get help and support concerning personal difficulties such as employment discrimination. Additionally, they provide a means of becoming acquainted with other lesbian and gay people and with the gay and lesbian community in general.

Social workers need to attend to gay and lesbian rights issues. Not only is an objective, open-minded attitude and belief in individual self-determination necessary, but an *advocacy* stance is also critical. Unfair, discriminatory rules in public and private agencies can be confronted. Attention can be called to any discrimination that does occur. Political candidates who encourage gay and lesbian rights can be supported. Finally, others including friends, family, and professional colleagues can be educated about gay and lesbian rights and encouraged to support them.

Community Responses: Violence Against Lesbian and Gay People

A Phoenix gay bar explodes when it is attacked with a firebomb.

Two lesbians are thrown out of their apartment after their landlady spied at them through their own apartment window and discovered their sexual orientation. Later, when the two women tried to address the issue through court action, they were assaulted by the landlady's son and his friends. The group beat up and attacked one of the women with a knife, resulting in serious injuries.

A station wagon filled with five men passes by three gay teenagers. At first the men in the wagon only scream out verbal assaults to the three. However, as the situation intensifies, one of the men in the car hauls out a golf club and hits a gay teenager in the head, fracturing his skull.

"In October [1998] Matthew Shepard, a gay college student, was pistol whipped, beaten and left tied to a fence near Laramie, Wyoming, for 18 hours. Shepard died of his injuries four days later. Sources close to Russell Henderson, 21, and Aaron McKinney, 21, claimed that originally the two men had only intended to rob Shepard, but that awareness of his sexual orientation drove them to violence" (AASECT, 1998, November, p. 1).

More and more frequently, such hideous incidents are being reported in the daily press. David Wertheimer (1988), executive director of the New York City Gay and Lesbian Anti-Violence Project, reports the significant increase of violent attacks on lesbians and gay men in recent years. He cites one study that reports that 22 percent of all gay men surveyed had been "punched, hit, kicked, or beaten simply because they were perceived to be gay"; he continues that more than one-third of the lesbians surveyed said that they had either been "sexually harassed or assaulted based on the assumption they were lesbians" (p. 52). He indicated that his own Anti-Violence Project had observed an 83 percent increase in such victimization within one year.

Wertheimer cites seven types of victimization. These include verbal harassment, which occurs most frequently; threatening behavior, such as being followed by harassers or being warned that attacks are forthcoming; physical attacks by groups of men, which can result in emotional and physical injury; assaults associated with AIDS and the resentment toward gay and lesbian people related to it; sexual assaults of women and men; assaults and discrimination by police; and even murder. Homophobia seems to form the foundation for these attacks.

What can be done to curb and halt such victimization of lesbians and gay men? Wertheimer proposes four potential solutions. First, gay and lesbian civil rights legislation must be passed. Discrimination on the basis of sexual orientation must be clearly illegal. People must get the message that such behavior will not be tolerated. Victims need to feel safe in reporting abusive incidents.

Wertheimer's second suggestion involves the passage of laws that specifically address crimes committed because of hatred and prejudice toward specific groups. Such legislation would protect not only lesbian and gay people but others subjected to prejudice because of their gender, race, ethnic status, religion, or beliefs.

The third proposal involves educating the police, and people working in the criminal justice system, about homophobia, gay and lesbian victimization, and the needs and rights of gay people. Education could include training employees to have greater empathy for lesbian and gay people, and to be more sensitive to their situations. This would encourage lesbian and gay victims to report crimes instead of fearing harassment and retribution from authorities.

Finally, Wertheimer's fourth suggestion for combating gay and lesbian victimization is to establish crisis centers for victims. Such resources would resemble the centers that have already been developed to help heterosexual victims of sexual assault and domestic violence.

Coming Out

"Coming out of the closet," or "coming out" refers to the process of a person acknowledging publicly that she or he is lesbian or gay. It is frequently a long and difficult process in view of the homophobia and stereotypes enveloping us (Swigonski, 1995).

Lesbian and gay people usually become aware of the fact that they are different from most others in terms of sexual orientation before the age of 20 (Moses & Hawkins, 1982). The process of coming out itself frequently takes 1 to 2 years. It should be noted, however, that there is great variation regarding how any specific individual comes out. In other words, for some people it might take much longer, and they might come out much later in life. For many people, especially adolescents who do not have much independence and are subject to severe peer pressure, the coming out period may be very difficult.

One way to describe coming out is to identify the four stages involved (Boston Women's Health Book Collective, 1984). The stages include (1) coming out to oneself; (2) getting to know other people within the gay and lesbian community; (3) sharing with family and friends that one is lesbian or gay; and (4) coming out of the closet—that is, openly and publicly acknowledging one's sexual orientation.

Moses and Hawkins (1982) describe the first stage of the process—namely, coming out to oneself, and elaborate on its implications. It involves thinking about oneself as a person who is lesbian or gay instead of as one who is heterosexual. The term used for this is *signification*. They suggest that there is often a period of identity shifting, during which individuals experiment with the label. They may begin conceptualizing themselves as lesbian or gay and begin thinking about what such a label will mean concerning their own lifestyle.

Part of the signification process involves accepting a label about which society has had so many negative things to say. Some people feel much better about themselves after applying a label of being lesbian or gay. It seems such a label helps in the process of establishing a self-identity. It also seems to give people permission to think and feel honestly about themselves. They then feel they can pursue new thoughts and experiences they feared and avoided before.

Moses and Hawkins (1982) suggest some excellent intervention strategies for human service professionals when helping lesbian and gay clients during their coming out period. To begin with, it is important to provide the client with information about what being lesbian or gay is really like. Chances are that the client thinks in terms of

Some parents feel compelled to "come out" in support of their gay or lesbian children.

© Rick Gerharter

some of the same stereotypes and has some of the same homophobic responses that many others in society do. A gay man who is coming out may need to be educated about the difference between gender identity and choice of sexual partner. He would also need to understand that homosexuality is not an illness.

The issue of self-concept may need to be addressed in counseling. Many times it is initially difficult for lesbian and gay people to distinguish between society's somewhat negative view of gay and lesbian people and their own views of themselves. They need to understand that they will not suddenly become different people with odd habits. Rather, they can be helped to see that different options are available to them, which may provide them with greater freedom to be themselves.

Another suggestion is the realistic identification and evaluation of the alternatives open to a lesbian or gay person. Signification may have advantages and disadvantages. Advantages might include the decreased fear and anxiety that result from pretending to be someone you're not. Another advantage might be the blossoming of new possibilities for social activities and support systems with other lesbian and gay people. Referrals to local organizations would be helpful here.

Disadvantages also need to be confronted. These might include the discrimination in employment and social settings sometimes suffered by lesbian and gay people. Another disadvantage might be the potential loss of some friends and family members. Any anxiety about potential risks in telling people needs to be explored.

The second phase of the coming out process involves actually meeting and getting to know other lesbian and

gay people. According to Lewis (1984, p. 467), this involves searching for "community—a place to belong." The best way to curb fears and rid oneself of stereotypes is to meet other lesbian and gay people and find out that the horrible things one has heard simply are not true. It's important to establish a social support system made up of people who understand what it is like to come out and who can easily talk to about it.

The third phase of coming out involves telling friends and family. Most people come out to friends first, because it seems to be more difficult to tell family members (Boston Women's Health Book Collective, 1984). However, it's also difficult *not* to tell family members.

Moses and Hawkins (1982) make specific suggestions for coming out to friends and family. First, the potential consequences need to be realistically examined. They emphasize that it may not be necessary to tell all close friends, relatives, and colleagues if the consequences for the lesbian or gay person are likely to be negative.

For example, a young man, a junior in college, has recently come out. His relationship with his father has always been marginal in that they have never communicated well and do not feel close to each other. However, they do attend family functions together and participate in the family system with other family members. The father has often made derogatory statements about gay people for as long as the son can remember. In this case, it may serve no purpose to come out to the father, because the relationship will probably not be improved. On the other hand, coming out may cause the son much painful criticism and potential ostracism from the family unit.

The fourth phase of coming out involves publicly acknowledging that one is a lesbian or a gay person. As with friends and family, it's important to evaluate the potential positive and negative consequences of each alternative. That is, one must carefully consider if letting it be known that one is a lesbian or a gay will be to one's advantage or disadvantage in any particular setting.

Many people choose not to come out of the closet. We've already discussed the criticism, rejection, and discrimination lesbian and gay people experience. Perhaps each individual needs to consider what's best personally. Those on one side of the issue emphasize that discrimination victimizes people unfairly and that each individual must decide for herself or himself what is best. Moses and Hawkins (1982) reflect that many consider this a conservative approach. Those on one side of the issue proclaim that one cannot be free to be oneself without honesty and openness to everyone. Spotlight 13.4 discusses some issues involving ethnicity and sexual orientation.

A reality-oriented approach involves looking at all available alternatives. The positive and negative consequences for each alternative must be evaluated. The idea is to assist clients in making decisions that are in their best interests. Highlight 13.2 addresses one woman's exploration of her self-identity and sexual orientation.

Spotlight on Diversity 13.4 **Ethnicity and Sexual Orientation**

It is critically important for social workers to assess "the impact of differences in class, ethnicity, health status, rural or urban background, and stage of gay identity formation, in addition to the individual's psychodynamics, ego strengths, and social supports" in order to help clients most effectively (Shernoff, 1995, p. 1077). Appreciation of people's individual strengths and differences is the key. For example, a 45-year-old Hispanic gay male living in a sparsely populated rural environment in Texas will experience very different life circumstances and issues than an 18-year-old African American gay male living in a bustling urban Los Angeles neighborhood. Likewise, a 24-year-old Asian American lesbian living in uptown Manhattan will experience life very differently from a 78-year-old Native American lesbian living in northern Montana.

African American and Hispanic gay men may have difficulty experiencing a comfortable level of acceptance both in their ethnic communities and in the primarily white gay community (Tully, 2000; van Wormer et al., 2000). This is also true for gay men who are Asian American and Native American (Shernoff, 1995). On the one hand, white gay organizations may be racist or unresponsive to the needs of other ethnic groups despite reflecting the same sexual orientation. On the other hand, various ethnic and racial communities may be homophobic resulting from a range of cultural traditions (van Wormer et al., 2000).

Nonwhite gay men may see their racial and ethnic communities as safe havens from the oppressive white majority culture. Therefore, they may be less likely to divulge openly their sexual orientation for fear of losing that support (Morales, 1995). It can be very helpful for them to seek linkage and support from other gay men of similar racial and ethnic heritage who better understand the problems resulting from membership in two "minority" groups (Shernoff, 1995).

A special issue for gay Hispanic men involves their traditional religion and folk beliefs (Shernoff, 1995). Many Hispanic people are strongly influenced by "the impact of conservative Catholicism and its emphasis on traditional values (which strongly reject gay love or sexual expression)" (p. 1077). Additionally, many gay Hispanics place serious significance on the concept of *espiritismo,* or spiritualism (Shernoff, 1995). Social workers must be aware of such issues and explore the significance they have for clients.

Asian American gay men may see their sexual orientation as being incompatible with traditional values espoused by their culture. As a result, many may be pressured to adopt a dual identity, one concerning their racial heritage and one their sexual orientation (Shernoff, 1995). Social workers may help them to think through their situations and make effective decisions regarding what choices and plans are best for them.

Tafoya and Rowell (1988) indicate that "Native American gay and lesbian clients often combine elements of common gay experiences with the uniqueness of their own ethnicity. To treat them only as gay and to ignore important cultural issues may bring . . . [counseling] sessions to a quick end with little accomplished" (p. 63).

Lesbians of diverse ethnic and racial backgrounds experience similar pressures to that suffered by gay men with diverse ethnic and racial heritage; this is due to their membership in more than one diverse group (Almquist, 1995; Hunter College Women's Studies Collective, 1995; Smith, 1995). Lesbians of nonwhite radical backgrounds confront a type of "triple jeopardy"; they suffer not only from racism and sexism but also from heterosexism (Greene, 1994). "Just as the experience of sexism is 'colored' by the lens of race and ethnicity for women of color, so is the experience of heterosexism similarly filtered for lesbian women of color" (p. 395). Furthermore, "for racially oppressed groups, lesbianism may seem like a betrayal of . . . [their] ethnic community. Among African Americans and Native Americans, for example, reproductive sexuality may be viewed as contributing to the survival of a group subject to racist genocide attempts" (Hunter College Women's Studies Collective, 1995, p. 151). In other words, lesbianism may be viewed as a betrayal to one's racial heritage, because lesbians don't form traditional heterosexual pairs oriented toward reproduction and increasing racial numbers.

Lesbian and Gay Adolescents. Lesbian and gay adolescents have to deal with not only their identity development in general but also their identity as a lesbian or gay male in a heterosexual world. This frequently occurs during adolescence when their sexual selves start to awaken. Most gay men indicate they realized that they were gay between ages 9 and 15 (Berger & Kelly, 1995). Social workers should pay particular attention to lesbian and gay adolescents during this time in their lives. (Chapter 7 addressed some of the issues facing adolescents concerning the special circumstances of their identity development.) Boes and van Wormer (2002), noting that adolescents "are sometimes treated as if they were less than human," go on to explain:

Struggling to survive in environments (school, home, church) that are more often than not hostile to their very being, gay and lesbian youth have many intense personal issues to resolve.

Among the most pressing issues . . . are:

- *The turmoil involved in coming out to yourself, discovering who you are and who you are not.*
- *Deciding who to tell, when, and how to tell it.*
- *Rebuilding relationships and grieving rejections when the truth is known.*
- *Developing new and caring support systems.*
- *Protecting oneself from a constant onslaught of attacks of one who is openly out or from the guilt feelings accompanying the secrecy and deception of being in the closet (p. 621).*

Lesbian and gay adolescents are six times more likely to attempt suicide than their heterosexual counterparts (Rotheram-Borus, Hunter & Rosario, 1994). A major suggestion for working with lesbian and gay youth is to avoid minimizing or denying the young person's developing identity and sexual orientation. Rather, help to

Highlight 13.2

Cheryl's Exploration of Her Self-identify and Sexual Orientation

Cheryl, aged 19, worked as a sales clerk at Shopko, the local discount store. Although she still lived with her parents primarily for financial reasons, she was starting to make her own decisions. She debated moving into an apartment with several female friends, and whether she should attend the local technical school or college part-time. These were not the issues she addressed, however, as she came in for counseling.

Cheryl hesitantly explained that she was very anxious about the sexual feelings she was having lately. Although she was steadily dating her high school sweetheart, he did not interest her sexually. She was thinking more and more about her sexual attraction toward other women. She had had these feelings for as long as she could remember. Lately she was becoming obsessed about them. She was very worried that she might be a lesbian.

On further discussion, she expressed fears about what being a lesbian would be like. She was concerned about starting to look too masculine and about becoming sex-starved for other women. Cheryl's counselor provided some information about what being lesbian or gay is really like. They discussed and discarded some of Cheryl's negative stereotypes. The counselor referred Cheryl to some written material on lesbianism and to some local organizations so Cheryl could get more information.

As counseling progressed, Cheryl began to nurture her weakened self-image. Her years of anxiety and her efforts to hide her feelings had taken an emotional toll. Her counselor helped her to work through her confusion about all the negative things she'd heard about gays and her perception of herself. Cheryl began to look at herself more

realistically. She began to focus on her personal strengths. These included her good sense of humor, her pleasant disposition, and her desire to become more independent and establish a career for herself. She found that these attributes and her personal identity had nothing to do with the negative stereotypes she had previously heard about homosexuality.

Finally, her counselor helped her to define and evaluate the various alternatives open to her. For the first time, she explored the possibility of breaking up with her boyfriend. She considered the possibility of pursuing a sexual relationship with one of the women she had recently met at a gay and lesbian rights organization meeting. She was already beginning to develop friendships with other women she'd met in a lesbian support group.

After several months of counseling, Cheryl had made some decisions. She had gone through the signification process. She had moved out of her parents' home and into an apartment with several female friends, none of whom were lesbians. After much fear and trepidation, she had come out to them. To her relief, they indicated that although they were surprised, it made no difference concerning their friendship. She had broken off with her boyfriend and had started a sexual relationship with another woman. Not only did she have no regrets about her new romantic situation, but she felt extreme relief, satisfaction, and a new sense of freedom.

Cheryl still had not decided whether to come out to her parents. She was still working on that. Nor had she yet decided what career route would be best for her. However, her new sense of self-identity provided her with new confidence and strength. The future looked hopeful and exciting instead of dull and restrictive.

empower them by taking their thoughts and feelings seriously and providing them with the information and support they need.

Three principles should guide social workers when trying to help lesbian and gay youth (Woodman, 1995). First, simply admit to yourself that some adolescents, perhaps many with whom you work and come into contact, are lesbian or gay. Second, increase your own awareness and that of your agency regarding how to provide accessible services to lesbian and gay youth. Third, do not allow antigay, homophobic sentiment to get in the way of providing lesbian and gay youth with the services they need. Such services may include "special advocacy efforts, peer support groups, recreational programs, and other resources to counter the isolation and despair that are all too common among gay and lesbian adolescents" (Laird, 1995, p. 1611).

Lesbian and Gay Parents

Many lesbian and gay people have children (Henry, 1993; Laird, 1995; Morales, 1995). It's impossible to give an exact number because no accurate numbers exist of how many people are homosexual (Henry, 1993). Estimates of lesbian and gay adults with children vary from 1.5 to 5 million; it is also estimated that the number of children raised in lesbian or gay homes is between 8 and 10 million (Laird, 1995). Children of lesbian and gay people "are most often born to parents in heterosexual marriages who subsequently come out" (Henry, 1993, p. 67). One-fifth to one-third of gay men marry at some time during their lives (Berger & Kelly, 1995). During the past decade lesbians have increasingly turned to bearing children through artificial or donor insemination (Henry, 1993; Laird, 1995). Many lesbian and gay people also attempt adoption, but this is often unsuccessful due to prejudice against their sexual orientation (Henry, 1993; Ingrassia & Rossi, 1994). In one national poll, 65 percent of those surveyed felt that lesbian and gay partners should not be allowed to adopt children (Ingrassia & Rossi, 1994).

Even when a lesbian or gay parent gains custody of a child, there still may be problems to overcome. For instance, lesbian and gay parents must deal with the ongoing "societal disapproval and scorn" they face because of their sexual orientation (Morales, 1995, p. 1090). Losing a job or an apartment might have a much greater impact on lesbians with children than lesbians who aren't parents. Much more may be at stake when the welfare, support and living conditions of children must also be taken into consideration. Many people believe that the children of

Susan and Eileen are lesbian mothers raising their son Kevin together. Susan (left) is Kevin's biological mother.

lesbian and gay people "will face social discrimination and perhaps even ridicule and isolation" because of their parents' sexual orientation (Laird, 1995, p. 1609).

Several suggestions can be made to social workers and other human service professionals in their efforts to help lesbian and gay people cope with parenthood (Moses & Hawkins, 1982). First, social workers can help the lesbian or gay parent identify and appreciate the joys of parenthood. It might be all too easy to get lost in the additional problems of being lesbian or gay and miss all of the normal pleasures of raising children.

Second, social workers can help lesbian and gay parents address the issue of coming out to children. Practitioners can help parents identify the various alternative ways of sharing information about their sexual orientation with children and evaluate the potential positive and negative consequences of each. Probably "no best way" exists "for parents to reveal their sexual identity to their children" (Morales, 1995, p. 1090). Lesbian and gay parents may use any of a number of approaches. Some hide their sexual orientation from their children because they fear custody battles or the effects such knowledge will have on children. Others encourage secrecy on the child's part, although such concealment can create quite a strain for children (van Wormer et al., 2000).

Still other lesbian and gay parents feel it is important to come out to their children as soon as possible. Berzon (1978) recommends that parents adopt such an open attitude. There are some advantages to this approach. First, it may avoid family stresses and problems in communication that could result from hiding such an important aspect about the parents. It might make daily living much more comfortable when the lesbian or gay parent can openly interact with and express affection toward a partner, without excluding the children. Finally, sharing the truth with children might prevent them from finding out about it from someone else—which might cause them surprise and shock. Children would wonder why their parents hadn't told them, and this secrecy might convey a very negative perspective about being lesbian or gay.

However, it should be remembered that every lesbian or gay family situation is unique. A social worker's role can be to help parents determine the best way to come out to children in their particular family system.

A third way social workers can assist lesbian or gay parents involves dealing with new partners. When a lesbian or gay parent finds a partner and decides to live with her or him, a social worker can help that parent address many of the same issues that need to be dealt with when a new heterosexual partner joins a household. Issues about child management need to be discussed. Expectations regarding how money will be shared or spent, how daily routines will be organized, and how the adults will act in front of the children need to be clarified openly.

Fourth, many lesbian and gay parents worry about the prejudice and discrimination their children might experience because of the parents' sexual orientation. Social workers can help such parents identify and evaluate ways to help children with these issues. Parents can learn to help their children think through situations and determine when to talk about their parents' sexual orientation and when not to (Laird, 1995).

Wolf (1979) suggests teaching children situational ethics. The idea here is for lesbian and gay parents to be open about their sexual orientation. Children then can learn about being lesbian or gay in a positive sense. However, at the same time, a lesbian or gay parent can teach a child that it is more appropriate to refer to and talk about sexual orientation in some situations than in others. For example, it is perfectly appropriate to be open about mother's female partner at home with the family. However, more discretion might be necessary when the child is giving a report before his or her class at school.

That children learn when certain behavior is appropriate or inappropriate is a normal part of growing up. One means of teaching the concept of appropriateness is to teach about individual differences (Moses & Hawkins, 1982). Children understand that each person is different. Every individual has his or her own ideas and beliefs. Each lives a distinctly unique life. Differences in sexual orientation are simply another type of human difference. Because people have divergent ideas about sexual orientation, they might be prejudiced. Therefore, it is not always wise to raise the issue.

As Lesbians and Gay Men Age

"The adage 'Nobody loves you when you're old and gray' has been modified by lesbian women and gay men to read, 'Nobody loves you when you're old and *gay*'" (Baron & Cramer, 2000, p. 207). The negative stereotypes of elderly homosexual people involve a man who "becomes effeminate, an 'old queen,' while a woman becomes a heartless, cruel, and 'masculine' witch" (Berger, 1985, p. 53). The stereotype continues that because elderly lesbians and gay men lose their youthful appearance, they are rejected by other lesbian and gay people as well as by homophobic heterosexuals. They become lonely, isolated, saddened human beings.

Contrary to this stereotype, the research indicates that what happens is just the opposite. There are two major summary statements about older lesbian and gay people. First, most are relatively well-adjusted (Lee, 1991; Longres & Fredriksen, 2000; Tully, 1992; van Wormer et al., 2000). Furthermore, many have numerous gay and lesbian friends and a few heterosexual ones, have some ties with the gay and lesbian community and its support network, and have an age-appropriate sexual and emotional relationship with a longtime partner. The second major summary statement is that both the adjustment levels and the psychosocial needs of older lesbian and gay people are more similar to those of heterosexuals than dissimilar. As gay and lesbian people age, they are exposed to most of the same conditions and have most of the same needs as elderly heterosexuals (Berger, 1985).

If anything, lesbian and gay people may adjust better to aging than heterosexual people based on two principles. These are "mastery of independence" and "mastery of stigma" (Berger, 1985; Moses & Hawkins, 1982). The concept of "mastery of independence" means that being independent is nothing new to lesbian and gay people. Heterosexuals tend to be more involved with their traditional family systems and often have difficulties coping with the death of a spouse and other peers. In a sense heterosexual people have been sheltered during their lives. Lesbian and gay people, however, have had to fend for themselves and experience a lifetime of independence. Because their lifestyle did not fit with the traditional heterosexual one, they always had to reach out to others and forge new paths and relationships. Coping with the "aloneness" of old age theoretically might not be as great a shock to lesbian and gay people as it is to heterosexuals.

The second concept that conveys an advantage to older gay men and lesbians involves "mastery of stigma." This means that lesbian and gay people are probably better at coping with the stigma of old age because they have experience coping with stigma and rejection (Longres & Fredrikson, 2000). Coping with one stigma, namely homosexuality, helps prepare them to cope with another, namely aging.

Berger (1985, p. 56) indicates that elderly homosexual people and heterosexual people have two major concerns, "good health and good finances"; he continues that in addition lesbian and gay people have three more problems specifically related to being lesbian or gay: "institutional problems, legal problems, and emotional needs." Institutional problems many times involve being placed in a nursing home or having to be hospitalized. A person's lover and closest friends may neither be allowed input into whether and where the person is placed, nor even allowed admission to see the person. As was discussed under legal issues, the traditionally defined family can often take over and deny access to the lesbian or gay person's companion.

We have also already established that the legal system frequently ignores gay and lesbian relationships. If a will is not clearly written, well established, updated, and well documented, a lesbian or gay partner may lose much of what the couple worked for. The biological, legal "family" may claim all.

The emotional needs of elderly gay and lesbian people are much like the emotional needs of elderly heterosexuals. They need social contacts, human warmth, and self-respect. However, lesbian and gay people have the additional pressure of battling the heterosexual bias that the world should be a heterosexual world. For instance, consider a social worker who can't understand why a client would want to take a leave from work and apply for public assistance in order to care for a very close "friend." Lesbians and gays must wage constant battle either to explain or defend themselves and their behavior.

Berger (1985) makes several suggestions to social workers for their interventions with lesbian and gay clients. First, social workers need to know something about what homosexuality is like and also about the local gay and lesbian communities. Second, social workers must confront their own biases and ideas about homosexuality and sexuality of the elderly. Third, social workers can both work to develop new services for older lesbian and gay people and also help them receive better service from existing traditional agencies.

Gay and Lesbian People and AIDS

AIDS was discussed in depth earlier in Chapter 10. Although initially many people labeled it a gay disease, it is now spreading among heterosexuals at a greater rate than among gay people. Therefore, in Chapter 10 AIDS was discussed as a condition that could affect anyone, heterosexual or gay or lesbian. Because gay men were among the first to contract the disease in this country, a few comments will be made here about its impact on them.[1]

Before the existence of AIDS was acknowledged in the United States, many people had already been exposed to and contracted it. Most of the people first exposed here were gay men. As a result, many gay people have seen dozens of their friends die from it. The emotional impact on the gay community has been awesome.

Little attention was initially given to AIDS. Many saw it as something that happened to homosexuals, drug addicts, and other "bad" people. Homophobic responses by heterosexual people and the idea that AIDS is a punishment for bad behavior may have been a contributing factor to the relative inaction on the part of the government. Meanwhile, many gay men along with their friends, families, and lovers, were suffering desperately from the disease.

Gay people can be thanked for much of the publicity about AIDS, the new resources directed to research for a cure, and the strong emphasis on prevention. Gay people were infuriated that the crisis was ignored by the government. The implication was that those contracting the disease weren't that important anyway and that they deserved it. As a result, people in the gay and lesbian community banded together, wrote letters to legislators, marched, advocated for people with the disease, and demanded that it be given some attention.

Gay people also took major steps to initiate a massive campaign aimed at prevention. They circulated information and provided people with information in any way they could think of. For instance, brochures emphasizing the need for safer sex practices were distributed at gay bars. Gay people abruptly slowed the spread of the disease within their own communities.

Any social worker who works with a gay or lesbian client needs to be aware of the ramifications and emotional impacts AIDS has had. Those close to the client have likely dealt with many of the economic and social issues involved with AIDS. These include not only serious illness, but poverty when personal resources have been depleted, social isolation, insurance and public-assistance

---

1. AIDS is virtually unknown among lesbians (except those who are IV drug users, a separate high-risk group).

Spotlight on Diversity 13.5 — Social Work with Lesbian and Gay People: Promoting Optimal Well-Being

Social work has at least two important thrusts concerning working with lesbian and gay people. One involves the individual practitioner's attitudes and skills. The other concerns agencies' provision of services to gay and lesbian people.

Counseling

Josephine Stewart, who chaired the NASW National Committee on Lesbian and Gay Issues, has made several suggestions for social work practitioners working with lesbian and gay clients (*NASW Practice Digest,* 1984). For one thing, it is very important to confront one's own homophobia. One of the worst things a practitioner can do is negatively label a lesbian or gay client and criticize that client for her or his sexual orientation. This contradicts the basic social work value of the client's right to self-determination. A negatively biased practitioner can unknowingly work against a client's development and maintenance of a positive self-image. Alternatives involving a lesbian or gay lifestyle and resources available in the gay and lesbian communities might be ignored or even rejected.

Another suggestion for working with lesbian and gay people is to become familiar both with the lesbian and gay lifestyles and with the lesbian and gay communities (Moses & Hawkins, 1982; *NASW Practice Digest,* 1984). This knowledge is necessary in order to help clients identify and evaluate the various alternatives available to them. It's also helpful to know people within the gay or lesbian community who can update a practitioner on new events and resources.

Agency Provision of Services

The other issue concerning social work with lesbian and gay people involves agencies' provision of services. Lesbian and gay people need various services that address specific aspects of lesbian and gay life. These might include lesbian support groups, groups for gay men who are in the process of coming out, legal advice for lesbian or gay parents seeking child custody, or couple counseling for lesbian or gay partners. Such services can be provided by agencies focusing on and serving only lesbian and gay people, or the services can be mainstreamed into traditional agencies. Either way has advantages.

Segregated services rapidly destroy preconceptions about lesbian and gay inferiority. Having their own services implies that lesbian and gay people are important and numerous enough to merit services equivalent to others. Segregated services also provide greater exposure for the gay or lesbian community.

There also are advantages of mainstreaming services into already existing social service agencies (*NASW Practice Digest,* 1984). First, a large traditional agency can provide a wider variety of services and serve more specific individual needs. For example, a lesbian mother might have easy access to agency-provided parent effectiveness training, even though it has nothing to do with her sexual orientation.

Second, lesbian and gay people do not have to be segregated from the rest of society. They can go to a social service agency just as heterosexual people can. No stigma need be involved.

Third, mainstreaming provides the opportunity for heterosexual practitioners to interact with practitioners who are familiar with the issues of gay or lesbian life and serve a gay or lesbian clientele. This provides an excellent opportunity for practitioners to learn from each other. Stereotypes can be addressed and homophobic responses confronted.

Regardless of where services are provided for lesbian and gay people, the fact is that they are needed. Social workers need to apply social work values to lesbian and gay clients. They need to learn about resources available for lesbian and gay people and make appropriate referrals. They also need to educate others about the special issues confronting lesbian and gay people. Finally, many times social workers need to act as advocates for the rights of lesbian and gay people. Sexual orientation needs to be addressed as simply another aspect of human diversity. Sexual orientation should be respected instead of denied. Political candidates in favor of gay and lesbian rights need to be supported. Agencies that discriminate against lesbian and gay people need to be confronted, educated, and pressured to provide needed services in a fair and unbiased manner.

---

problems, and problems getting medication. Sensitivity to these issues can only help social workers better serve their clients' needs. Spotlight 13.5 continues to address the promotion of optimal well-being for all lesbian and gay people, not just those who are HIV-positive.

❧ Summary

A homosexual person is someone who is attracted primarily to people of the same gender to satisfy sexual and affectional needs. A bisexual is a person who is sexually involved with or attracted to members of either gender. Transgender people are those whose gender identity is the opposite of their biological gender. Because of the large numbers of people who have homosexual experiences at some time during their lives, most people do not fall within the distinct categories of gay or lesbian or heterosexual. Although various theories attempt to explain why people become lesbian or gay, no definite causes have been established. Most experts agree that homosexuality probably results from some mixture of biological and psychosocial variables.

Lesbian and gay people are frequently the victims of homophobia, the irrational hostility and fear that many people have toward homosexuality. A number of inaccurate stereotypes exist in our culture. There is no one type of lifestyle adopted by all lesbian and gay people, just as there is no single lifestyle for all heterosexuals.

Two important concepts for many gay men and lesbians are "gay and lesbian pride" and "a sense of community." Several significant issues and life events tend to characterize the lives of lesbian and gay people. Some laws permit discrimination against gay people. Homophobia has produced increasing violence against gay men and lesbians in recent years. "Coming out," or acknowledging that one is lesbian or gay, sometimes is difficult in view of the homophobic fears and negative stereotypes about homosexuality.

It is very important for social workers to focus on the issues involved in racial and ethnic diversity when working with lesbian and gay people. Adolescence can be an especially difficult time for lesbian and gay people. Many lesbian and gay people are parents and must address coming out to their children. Lesbian and gay people face many, but not all, of the same issues as heterosexuals during the aging process.

Although the gay and lesbian communities have made tremendous strides in curbing the spread of AIDS, the emotional and economic impacts on many gay people have been devastating. To work with lesbian and gay people, social workers need to confront their own homophobia and to familiarize themselves with the lesbian and gay communities.

InfoTrac College Edition Keywords

bisexuality   gay and lesbian parents   gay stereotypes   homophobia   homosexuality   lesbian and gay people

On the Internet

Citizens Against Homophobia

http://www.actwin.com/cahp/

Citizens Against Homophobia is a group that uses mass media campaigns to reduce homophobia.

Gay Student Center

http://gaystudentcenter.studentcenter.org/

The Student Center Network, since its inception in late 1995, has always been very supportive of the gay community. Gay, lesbian, and bisexual students have been active at all of its sites. Yet, many gay/les/bi students urged them to put together a special site like this.

International Journal of Transgenderism

http://www.symposion.com/ijt/

The new International Journal of Transgenderism (IJT) can serve as an important vehicle for the transmission of scholarly work in the area of transgenderism.

CHAPTER 14

Biological Systems and Their Impacts on Later Adulthood

LeRoy was a muscular, outgoing teenager. He was physically bigger than most of his class-mates and starred in basketball, baseball, and football in high school. In football he was selected as an all-state linebacker in his senior year. At age 16, he began drinking at least a six-pack of beer each day, and at 17 he began smoking. Because he was an athlete, he smoked and drank on the sly. Since LeRoy was good at conning others, he found it fairly easy to smoke, drink, party, and still play sports. That left little time for studying, but LeRoy was not interested in that, anyway. He had other priorities.

LeRoy received a football scholarship and went on to college. He did well in football and majored in "partying." His grades suffered, and when his college eligibility in football was used up, he dropped out of college. Shortly after dropping out, he married Rachel Rudow, a college sophomore. She soon became pregnant and also dropped out of college. LeRoy was devastated after leaving college. He had been a jock for 10 years, the envy of his class-mates. Now he couldn't get a job with status. After a variety of odd jobs, he obtained work as a road-construction worker. He liked working outdoors and also liked the macho-type guys with whom he worked, smoked, drank, and partied.

LeRoy and Rachel had three children, but he was not a good husband. He was seldom at home, and when he was, he was often drunk. After a stormy 7 years of marriage (in-cluding numerous incidents of physical and verbal abuse), Rachel moved out and got a di-vorce. She and the children moved to Florida, along with her parents, so that LeRoy could not continue to harass her and the children. LeRoy's drinking and smoking increased. He was smoking over two packs each day, and he sometimes also drank a quart of whiskey.

A few years later he fathered an out-of-marriage child for whom he was required to pay child support. At age 39, he married Jane, who was only 20. They had two children and stayed married for 6 years. Jane eventually left because she became fed up with being assaulted when LeRoy was drunk. LeRoy now had a total of six children to help support and he seldom saw any of them. LeRoy continued to drink and also ate to excess. His weight went up to 285 pounds, and by age 48 he was no longer able to keep up with the other road-construction workers. He was discharged by the construction company.

The next several years saw LeRoy taking odd jobs as a carpenter. He didn't earn much, and he spent most of what he earned on alcohol. He was periodically embarrassed by being hauled into court for failure to pay child support. He was also dismayed because he no longer had friends who wanted to get drunk with him. When LeRoy was 61, the doctor discovered he had cirrhosis of the liver and informed him he wouldn't live much longer if he continued to drink. Since LeRoy's whole life centered on drinking, he chose to continue to drink. LeRoy also noticed that he had less energy and frequently had trouble breathing. The doctor indicated that he probably had damaged his lungs by smoking and now had a form of emphysema. The doctor lectured LeRoy on the need to stop smoking, but LeRoy didn't heed that advice either. His health continued to deteriorate, and he lost 57 pounds. At age 64, while drunk, he fell over backward and fractured his skull. He was hospitalized for 3½ months. The injury permanently damaged his ability to walk and talk. He is now confined to a low-quality nursing home. He is no longer allowed to smoke or drink. He is frequently angry, impatient, and frustrated. He no longer has friends. The staff detests working with him; his hygiene habits are atrocious, and he frequently yells obscenities. LeRoy frequently expresses a wish to die to escape his misery.

ElRoy's early years were in sharp contrast to his brother LeRoy. ElRoy had a lean, almost puny, muscular structure and did not excel at sports. LeRoy was his parents' favorite, and also dazzled the young females in school and in the neighborhood. ElRoy had practically no dates in high school and was viewed as a prude. He did well in math and the natural sciences. He spent much of his time studying and reading a variety of books and liked taking radios and electrical appliances apart. At first, he got into trouble because he was not skilled enough to put them back together. However, he soon became known in the neighborhood as someone who could fix radios and electrical appliances.

He went on to college and studied electrical engineering. He had no social life but graduated with good grades in his major. He went on to graduate school and obtained a master's degree in electrical engineering. On graduating, he was hired as an engineer by Motorola in Chicago. He did well there and in 4 years was named manager of a division. Three years later he was lured to RCA with an attractive salary offer. The group of engineers he worked with at RCA made some significant advances in television technology.

At RCA, ElRoy began dating a secretary, Elvira McCann, and they were married when he was 36. Life became much smoother for ElRoy after that. He was paid well and enjoyed annual vacations with Elvira to such places as Hawaii, Paris, and the Bahamas. ElRoy and Elvira wanted to have children, but could not. When ElRoy was in his early 40s, they adopted two children, both from Korea. They bought a house in the suburbs and a sailboat. ElRoy and Elvira occasionally had some marital disagreements but generally got along well. In their middle adult years, one of their adopted sons, Kim, was tragically killed by an intoxi-cated automobile driver. That death was a shock and very difficult for the whole family to come to terms with. But the intense grieving gradually lessened, and after a few years ElRoy and Elvira put their lives back together.

Now, at age 67, ElRoy is still working for RCA and loving it. In a few years he plans to re-tire and move to the Hawaiian island of Maui. ElRoy and Elvira have already purchased a condominium there. Their surviving son, Dae, has graduated from college and is working for a life insurance company. ElRoy is looking forward to retiring so that he can move to Maui, and can get more involved in his hobbies—photography and making model railroad dis-plays. His health is good, and he has a positive outlook on life. He occasionally thinks about his brother and sends him a card on his birthday. Since ElRoy never had much in common with LeRoy, he seldom visits him.

A PERSPECTIVE

Later adulthood is often the age of recompense (our return for the way we lived earlier). How we live in our younger years largely determines how we will live in our later years. This chapter will:

► Define later adulthood.
► Describe the physiological and mental changes that occur in later adulthood.
► Present contemporary theories on the causes of the aging process.
► Describe common diseases and major causes of death among the elderly.
► Present material on stress management and on other ways to maintain good physical and mental health throughout life.

❧ What Is Later Adulthood?

Later adulthood is the last major segment of the life span. Sixty-five has usually been cited as the dividing line be-tween middle age and old age (Santrock, 1999). There is nothing magical or particularly scientific about 65. Wrin-kles do not suddenly appear on the sixty-fifth birthday, nor does hair suddenly turn gray or fall out. In 1883, Germany set 65 as the criterion of aging for the world's first modern social security system (Sullivan et al., 1980).

When our Social Security Act was passed in 1935, the United States followed the German model by selecting 65 as the age of eligibility for retirement benefits.

The elderly are an extremely diverse group, spanning an age range of over 30 years. Looking at this biologically, psychologically, and sociologically, there are a number of differences for example, between Sylvia Swanson, age 65, and her mother, Maureen Methuselah, age 86. Sylvia owns and operates a boutique, making frequent buying trips to Paris, Mexico City, and San Francisco, while Maureen

Senescence may involve reduced agility and increasing unsteadiness of the hands.

© David Phillips/Photri

has been a resident of a nursing home since the death of her husband 13 years ago.

Gerontologists—doctors who specialize in medical care of the elderly—have attempted to deal with these age-related differences among the elderly by dividing later adulthood into two groups: *young-old*—ages 65 to 74 years; and *old-old*—ages 75 and above (Santrock, 1999).

Our society tends to define old age mainly in terms of chronological age. In primitive societies, old age was generally determined by physical and mental conditions rather than by chronological age. Such a definition is more accurate than ours. Everyone is not in the same mental and physical condition at age 65. Aging is an individual process that occurs at different rates in different people, and socio-physchological factors may retard or accelerate the physiological changes. As Spotlight 14.1 indicates, people can continue to live productive lives long past the age of 65.

Senescence

The process of aging is called *senescence*. Senescence is the normal process of bodily change that accompanies aging. Senescence affects different people at different rates and affects various parts of the body. Some parts of the body resist aging more than others. In this section we will look at the aging process in later adulthood.

Appearance. Changes in physical appearance include increased wrinkling, reduced agility and speed of motion, stooping shoulders, increasing unsteadiness of the hands and legs, increased difficulty in moving, thinning of hair, and the appearance of varicose veins. Wrinkling of the skin is caused by the partial loss of elastic tissue and of the fatty layer of the skin.

Senses. The acuity of the senses generally deteriorates in later years. The sense of touch declines with age due to drying, wrinkling, and toughening of the skin. The skin also has increased sensitivity to changes in temperature. Since the automatic regulation of bodily functions responds at a slower rate, elderly persons often "feel the cold more." Exposure to cold and to poor living conditions may cause abnormally low body temperature, which is a serious problem for some elderly. They cannot cope as well as younger people with heat, either, and therefore cannot work as effectively in moderately high temperatures as younger people can.

The sense of hearing gradually deteriorates. The ability to hear very high tones is generally affected first. As time goes on, the level of auditory acuity becomes progressively lower. Many of the elderly find it difficult to follow a conversation when there is a competing noise, as from a radio, television, or other people talking. An impairment in hearing is five times as common in persons aged 65 to 79 as it is in individuals between the ages of 45 and 64 years. Men are more apt to experience hearing impairments than women (Santrock, 1999). People who have a hearing impairment are apt to feel lonely and isolated, as they cannot as readily join in conversations.

Spotlight on Diversity 14.1

Internationally Noted Individuals Prove that Age Need not be a Barrier to Being Productive

At 100, Grandma Moses was still painting.

At 99, twin sisters Kin Narita and Gin Kanie recorded a hit CD single in Japan and starred in a television commercial.

At 94, Bertrand Russell was active in international peace drives.

At 93, George Bernard Shaw wrote the play *Far-fetched Fables.*

At 93, actress Dame Judith Anderson gave a one-hour benefit performance.

At 91, Eamon De Valera served as president of Ireland.

At 91, Adolph Zukor was chairman of Paramount Pictures.

At 91, Hulda Crooks climbed Mount Whitney, the highest mountain in the continental United States.

At 90, Pablo Picasso was producing engravings and drawings.

At 89, Albert Schweitzer headed a hospital in Africa.

At 89, Arthur Rubinstein gave one of his greatest recitals in New York's Carnegie Hall.

At 88, Michelangelo did architectural plans for the Church of Santa Maria degli Angeli.

At 88, Konrad Adenauer was chancellor of Germany.

At 87, Mary Baker Eddy founded the *Christian Science Monitor.*

At 85, Coco Chanel was the head of a fashion design firm.

At 84, W. Somerset Maugham wrote *Points of View.*

At 82, Leo Tolstoy wrote *I Cannot Be Silent.*

At 81, Benjamin Franklin effected the compromise that led to the adoption of the U.S. Constitution.

At 81, Johann Wolfgang von Goethe finished *Faust.*

At 80, George Burns won an Oscar for his role in *The Sunshine Boys.*

At 77, Ronald Reagan was finishing his second term as president of the United States.

These internationally noted individuals prove that age need not be a barrier to making major contributions in life. Unfortunately, the discrimination against the elderly in our society prevents many of the elderly from having a meaningful and productive life.

Sometimes such an impairment and the feelings of isolation facilitate the development of personality quirks that result in their being more difficult to get along with, which further increases their loneliness. (We see once again how the physical and social environment can affect emotional development.)

Vision also declines. Most people over age 60 need glasses or contact lenses to see well. The decline in vision is usually caused by a deterioration of the lens, cornea, retina, iris, and optic nerve. The power of the eye to adjust to different levels of light and darkness is reduced, and color perception is also reduced. The elderly are likely to have 20/70 vision or less, are not as able to perceive depth as others are and cannot see as well in the dark, a problem that keeps many of them from driving at night. Half of the legally blind persons in the United States are over 65 (Papalia et al., 2001).

In many of the elderly, the eyes eventually appear sunken due to a gradual loss of orbital fat. The blink reflex is slower, and the eyelids hang loosely because of reduced muscle tone.

Cataracts are a common concern of the elderly. A cataract is a clouding of the lens of the eye, or of its capsule, that obstructs the passage of light. The consequences of a cataract for visual functioning depend on its location. The most common form of a cataract involves hardening of cell tissues in the lens. Cataracts prevent light from passing through and can thus cause blurred vision and blindness. In severe cases double vision may result. Cataracts generally can be surgically removed and a substitute lens implanted. More than half of the elderly develop cataracts (Papalia et al., 2001). Fortunately, with the development of corrective lenses and new surgical techniques for removing cataracts and implanting artificial lenses, many vision losses are fully or partially restored.

A frequent cause of blindness among the elderly is glaucoma, which occurs when fluid pressure in the eye builds up. This pressure, if untreated, damages the eye internally. If this disease (which seldom has early symptoms) is detected through routine vision checkups, it can be treated and controlled with eyedrops, medication, surgery, or laser treatments.

Macular degeneration, which is age-related, is the leading cause of functional blindness in the elderly. This condition occurs when the center of the retina gradually loses the ability to sharply distinguish fine details. Smokers are about 2½ times as likely to develop this condition (Papalia et al., 2001).

The senses of taste and smell have reduced functional capability during advancing years. Much of this reduced sensitivity appears to be related to illness and poor health rather than to a deterioration of sense organs due to age. Taste is very often based on what people can smell. More than four out of five persons over 80 years of age have major impairments in smell, and more than half have practically no sense of smell at all (Papalia et al., 2001). Because food loses its taste for those who have serious impairments in smell and taste, those affected eat less and are often undernourished.

The vestibular senses, which function to maintain posture and balance, also lose some of their efficiency. As a result, the elderly are more prone to fall than younger adults. The elderly are also more apt to suffer from dizziness, which increases the likelihood they will fall.

Teeth. As people grow older, their gums gradually recede, and the teeth increasingly take on a yellowish color. Periodontal disease (a disease of the gums) becomes an increasing problem. Many of the elderly eventually lose many of their teeth; the problem is more severe for people from low income levels, who often have financial and transportation barriers to receiving dental care (Santrock, 1999). Having teeth replaced with dentures takes several weeks to get adjusted to, and the person is not able to eat or sleep as well during this adjustment period. Poor teeth or the use of dentures may also be traumatic as it drives home the fact that the person is aging physically. A person's disposition can be adversely affected. On the other hand, for some people dentures improve their appearance and may lead to an improved self-concept. Many of the facial evidences of later adulthood may be prevented by proper dental care throughout life or by using dentures. Dental health is related to a combination of innate tooth structure and lifelong eating and dental health habits.

Voice. In later adulthood the voice may become less powerful and more restricted in range. Public speaking and singing abilities generally deteriorate earlier than normal speaking skills. All of these changes are partly due to the hardening and decreasing elasticity of the laryngeal cartilages. Speech often becomes slower and pauses become longer and more frequent. If there are pathological changes in the brain, slurring may occur.

Skin. The skin in many of the elderly becomes somewhat splotchy, paler in color, and loses some of its elasticity. Some of the subcutaneous muscle and fat disappears, resulting in the skin hanging in folds and wrinkles.

Psychomotor Skills. The elderly can do most of the same things that younger people can do, but they do them more slowly. A key factor in the high accident rates of the elderly is a slowdown in the processing of information by the central nervous system (Papalia et al., 2001). It takes the elderly longer to assess their environment, longer to make a decision after assessment, and then longer to implement the right action. This slowness in processing information shows up in many aspects of the elderly's lives. Their rate of learning new material is slowed, and the rate at which they retrieve information from memory is reduced.

Have you ever been irritated when an elderly person was driving a car slowly in front of you? Perhaps you even blasted your car horn to attempt to hurry that person along. We need to remember the elderly are probably functioning at the fastest pace that is safe for them.

The slower processing times and reaction times have practical implications for drivers. The elderly have higher accident rates than middle-aged adults. Their rates are similar to those for teenagers (Papalia et al., 2001). However, the reasons for these relatively high accident rates differ. Teenagers frequently have accidents because they tend to be more reckless and often take risks. The elderly tend to have accidents because of being slower in getting out of the way of potential problems and because of less efficient sensorimotor coordination. The elderly have as great a need to drive as others. Being able to drive often means the difference between actively participating in society or facing a life of enforced isolation. Papalia and Olds (1992) suggest what needs to be done:

> *For the protection of themselves and others, older drivers' vision, coordination, and reaction time need to be retested regularly. Older drivers can compensate for any loss of ability by driving more slowly and for shorter distances, by choosing easier routes, and by driving only in daylight. In many communities, defensive driving courses are given for senior citizens to help them continue to drive as long as possible. (p. 481)*

Physical exercise and mental activity appear to reduce losses in psychomotor skills, such as in the areas of speed, strength, and stamina. Regular exercise also helps to maintain the circulatory and respiratory systems and helps people be more resistant to physical ailments that might be fatal, such as heart attacks.

Intellectual Functioning. The notion that there is a general intellectual decline in old age is largely incorrect. Most intellectual abilities hold up well with age. The elderly do tend to achieve somewhat lower scores on IQ tests than younger people, and the scores of the elderly

Being able to drive one's own car means the difference between actively participating in society or facing a life of enforced isolation.

© Frank Siteman /Stock Boston

gradually decline as the years pass (Santrock, 1999). In explaining such differences Papalia and associates (2001) note that a distinction needs to be made between *performance* and *competence*. It could well be that while the elderly show a decline in performance on IQ tests, their actual intellectual competence may not be declining. Their lower performance on IQ tests could be due to a variety of factors. With their diminished capacities to see and hear, they have more difficulty perceiving instructions and executing tasks. Due to their reduced powers of coordination and agility, they may perform less well. They may be more fatigued, and fatigue has been found to suppress intellectual performance. Speed is a component of many IQ tests, and the elderly have a decline in speed because it takes them longer to perceive, longer to assess, and longer to respond (Santrock, 1999). In addition, when elderly people know they are being timed, their anxiety increases as they are aware that it takes them longer to do things than it used to; such increased anxiety may actually lower performance (Papalia et al, 2001).

There are still other factors in the elderly's IQ test performance. IQ tests include items that are designed to test intelligence in younger people; as a result, some of the items may be less familiar to older people—which lowers their scores. The elderly are consistently more cautious than the young; this may hinder their performance on IQ tests, which generally emphasize risk taking and speed. The elderly are more apt to have self-defeating attitudes about their abilities to solve problems; such attitudes may become self-fulfilling prophecies on IQ tests.

The reduced performance by the elderly on IQ tests may also be partly due to a lessening of continuing intellectual activity in later adulthood. It appears that the reduced use of one's intellectual capacities results in a reduction of intellectual ability. Such a proposition underscores the need for the elderly to remain intellectually active.

A *terminal drop* in intelligence—that is, a sudden drop in intellectual performance—occurs a few weeks or a few months before death from a terminal illness (Papalia et al., 2001). A terminal drop is not limited to the elderly; it is also found in younger people who have a terminal illness.

It is not possible at this time to draw definite conclusions as to whether intellectual functioning actually declines in later adulthood. IQ scores do go down, but that does not mean intellectual competence declines, for the reasons cited. Continuing intellectual activity serves to maintain intellectual capacities. Further information about myths surrounding intellectual and physical functioning of the elderly is presented in Highlight 14.1.

Height and Joints. The maximum height of a person is reached by the late teens or early 20s. In future years there is little or no change in the length of the individual bones. In elderly persons there may be a small reduction in overall height due to a progressive decline in the discs between the spinal vertebrae. The bones of the body also become less dense and more brittle due to changes in chemical composition. Such changes increase the risk of breakage. Joint movements also become stiffer and more restricted,

Highlight 14.1

Values and Aging: The Myth of Senility

Senility can be defined as an irreversible mental and physical deterioration associated with later adulthood. Many people erroneously believe that every elderly person will eventually become senile. This is simply not accurate. Although the physical condition of the elderly deteriorates somewhat, the elderly can be physically active until they are near death. Furthermore, the vast majority of the elderly show no signs of mental deterioration (Santrock, 1999).

Senility is not a true medical diagnosis, but a wastebasket term for a range of symptoms that, minimally, include memory impairment or forgetfulness; difficulty in maintaining attention and concentration; a decline in general intellectual grasp and ability; and a reduction in emotional responsiveness to others.

Those elderly persons who appear disoriented and confused are apt to be suffering from one or more of over a hundred illnesses, many of which are treatable. Infections, an undiagnosed hardening of the blood vessels in the brain, Alzheimer's disease, anemia, brain tumors, and thyroid disorders—these are only a few of the medical conditions that can cause a person to have senilelike symptoms.

---

and the incidence of disease (such as arthritis) affecting the joints increases with age. The elderly need to stay physically active to exercise their joints, as the joints will increase in stiffness if there is little activity.

Homeostasis. Homeostasis becomes less efficient in later adulthood. The stabilizing mechanisms become sluggish, and the physiological adaptability of the person is reduced. The heart and breathing rates take longer to return to normal. Wounds take longer to heal. The thyroid gland shrinks, resulting in a lower rate of basal metabolism. The pancreas loses part of its capacity to produce enzymes that are used in protein and sugar metabolism.

Muscular Structure. After age 30, there is a gradual reduction in the power and speed of muscular contractions, and the capacity for sustained muscular effort decreases. After the age of 50, the number of active muscle fibers gradually decreases, resulting in the older person's muscles being reduced in size. The hand grip strength of a 75-year-old man is only about 55 percent that of a 30-year-old man (Santrock, 1999). The ligaments tend to harden and contract, and sometimes result in a hunched-over body position. The reflexes respond more slowly, and incontinence (loss of bowel or bladder control) sometimes occurs. Involuntary smooth muscles that are part of the autonomic system show much less deterioration than other muscle groups.

Nervous System. Although there is little functional change in the nerves with increasing age, some of the nerve tissue is gradually replaced by fibrous cells. Reflex and reaction times of an older person become slower. The total number of brain cells may decrease, but the brain continues to function normally unless its blood supply is blocked. The brain weight of an average 75-year-old person is similar to that of a middle-aged person (Santrock, 1999). People with certain medical conditions (such as cerebral arteriosclerosis) will have progressive deterioration of brain tissue. If such deterioration takes place, the person may have a loss of recent and/or past memories; may become apathetic; may be less coordinated in body movements; may give less attention to grooming habits; and may have some personality changes (such as being more irritable, confused, and frustrated). In many of the elderly the cortical area of the brain that is responsible for organizing the perceptual processes gradually shows degenerative changes.

Digestive System. With increased age, there is a reduction in the amount of enzyme action, gastric juices, and saliva, which upsets the digestion process. Complaints about digestive disorders are among the most common complaints of the elderly. Since the digestive system is highly sensitive to stress, to emotional disturbances, and to anxieties that accompany old age, many of the digestive disorders may be due to these factors rather than to age per se. The regularity of bowel movements is also more of a problem in later adulthood, resulting in diarrhea or constipation.

Respiration. As people age, their lungs decrease in size, resulting in a decrease of oxygen utilization. Some air sac membranes are replaced by fibrous tissue, which obstructs the normal exchange of gases within the lungs. The maximum breathing capacity and maximum oxygen intake in a 75-year-old are about 40 percent of those of a 30-year-old (Santrock, 1999). Moderate exercise throughout life is important for keeping oxygen intake and blood flow at their highest levels, thereby slowing down the aging process.

Heart. The heart and the blood vessels are the bodily parts in which aging produces the most destructive changes. The heart and arteries are the weakest link in the chain of life, as most of the other organs would probably last for 150 years if they received an adequate blood supply (Kail & Cavanaugh, 2000). The heart is affected by aging in a variety of ways. It shrinks in size, and the percentage of fat in the heart increases. The heart muscles tend to become stringy and dried out. Deposits of a brown pigment in the cells of the heart partly restrict the passage of blood and interfere with the absorption of oxygen through the heart walls. The elasticity in the valves of the heart is reduced, and deposits of cholesterol and calcium in heart valves also decrease valve efficiency.

The heart of an older person pumps only 70 percent as much blood as that of a younger person (Santrock, 1999). The rhythm of the heart becomes slower and more irregular. Deposits of fat begin to accumulate around the heart and interfere with its functioning. Blood pressure also rises. These changes are not necessarily dangerous, provided the heart is properly treated. A nutritious diet, moderate exercise, adequate sleep, and a positive mental attitude will help keep the heart functioning properly.

In later life the coronary artery has a tendency to harden and become narrow, which may lead to a partial blockage. The coronary artery is the site of many heart attacks that are brought on by increased emotional stress or physical effort. Hardening of the coronary artery may also increase blood pressure and may reduce the flow of blood to many parts of the body. Poor circulation of blood may cause a variety of problems. For example, poor circulation to the brain may lead to brain deterioration and to personality changes. Poor circulation to the kidneys may result in kidney problems and even kidney failure.

Reserve Capacity. Under ordinary circumstances, people do not use their body systems and organs to their limits. This backup capacity (which allows organs and body systems to respond at greater levels during times of stress) has been called *reserve capacity*. Younger adults have reserve capacities that put forth four to ten times as much effort as usual (Papalia et al., 2001). Reserve capacity helps to preserve homeostasis.

As people age, their reserve capacities decrease. As a result, the elderly cannot respond to stressful demands as rapidly as younger adults. An elderly person who used to be able to mow the lawn, and then go water-skiing, may now exhaust the capacity of the heart by mowing the lawn. Young people usually recover fairly rapidly from the flu or pneumonia, while the elderly may succumb to these illnesses. Because the elderly no longer have fast reflexes, vigorous heart action, and quick-responding muscles, they are at a great risk of being victims of certain accidents (for example, traffic accidents that occur while crossing the street). As the reserve capacity continues to diminish, those affected become less able to care for themselves and more dependent on others.

Sexuality: Conceptualizing Sexual Response. Masters and Johnson (1966) identified four stages of sexual response in females and males: excitement, the plateau stage, orgasm, and resolution. There are many similarities in the physical responses of men and women. These include the two major body changes that result from individual stimulation—myotonia, or muscle tension; and vasocongestion, or blood engorgement.

In *excitement,* blood flows into the erectile tissue of the penis (vasocongestion), resulting in erection. The scrotum (the sac surrounding the testicle) becomes thicker, more wrinkled, and the testicles move up closer to the body.

Plateau response is characterized by the continuation of erection, although it often waxes and wanes during sex play with a partner. The testicles become fully elevated, rotate toward the front, and become blood-engorged, causing expansion in their size. The Cowper's gland secretes a small amount of clear fluid that comes out at the tip of the penis. The purpose of this fluid is generally thought to be to cleanse the urethra of urine, thereby neutralizing the chemical environment for the passage of sperm.

The *orgasm* stage in men consists of two phases. The first is ejaculatory inevitability, a short period during which the stimulation sufficient to trigger orgasm has occurred and the resulting ejaculation becomes inevitable. The second phase, ejaculation, results from rhythmic contractions (myotonia) forcing sperm and semen through the urethra. Simultaneous with this is the very pleasant physical sensation of orgasm.

The final stage, *resolution,* represents a return to the unstimulated state. In resolution, the penis loses its erection and the testicles lose their engorgement and elevation.

In women, the *excitement* stage of sexual response ushers in many changes. The process of vaginal lubrication begins. This response is analogous to the male erection; it is caused by sexual stimulation and is, physiologically, a blood-engorgement response. The uterus and cervix begin to move up and away from the vagina. The clitoris and labia minora (inner lips) enlarge and the labia majora (outer lips) spread. Breast size increases slightly and the nipples become erect.

In the *plateau* stage, the uterus continues in its movement up and back, the vagina lengthens and balloons at the rear, and the outer third of the vagina contracts, causing a gripping effect. The clitoris retracts under its hood, making it seem to disappear.

At *orgasm*, the uterus and vagina become involved in wavelike muscular contractions. This response, as well as the subjective pleasure of orgasm, are very similar to the experience of the male.

In *resolution*, the cervix and uterus drop to their normal position and the outer third of the vagina returns to normal, followed by the inner two-thirds. The clitoris and the breasts also return to normal.

There are many involuntary *extragenital* physical responses in men and women. These include muscle tension responses such as facial grimaces, spastic contractions of the hands and feet, and pelvic thrusting. Extragenital blood-engorgement responses include sex flush, blood pressure and heart-rate increases, and perspiration on the soles of the feet and the palms of the hands.

The effects of aging on sexual response are summarized in Figures 14.1 and 14.2.

Values and Sexuality. A common misconception is that older people lose their sexual drive. It is true that both sexual interest and sexual activity gradually decline among the elderly (Hyde & DeLamater, 2000). However, an extensive study (Brecher, 1984) on sexual patterns among the elderly indicates that many elderly continue to engage in sexual activity. Sixty-five percent of married women, and 59 percent of married men, over 70 years old

Figure 14.1 Effects of Aging on Sexual Response in Men

Bodily processes slow down *but they do not stop*. A natural slowing down *does not* mean a loss of interest. *Regularity* of sexual release is most important in maintaining sexual response capability in later years.

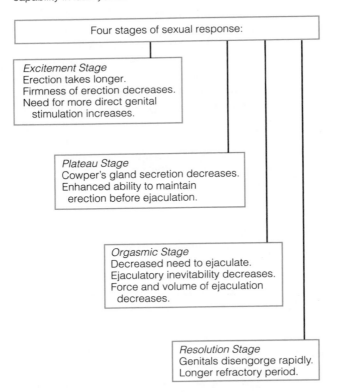

Figure 14.2 Effects of Aging on Sexual Response in Women

Bodily processes slow down *but they do not stop*. A natural slowing down *does not* mean a loss of interest. *Regularity* of sexual release is most important in maintaining sexual response capability in later years.

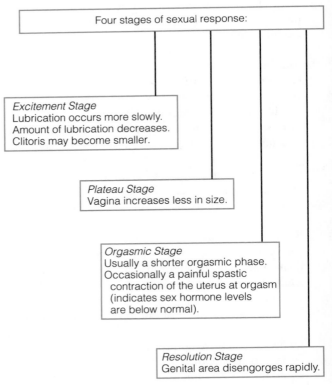

reported in the study that they continue to have sex with their spouse. In addition, 33 percent of the women, and 43 percent of the men, over 70 reported they still masturbate.

In a sample of healthy 80- to 102-year-olds, 62 percent of the men and 30 percent of the women reported that they still engage in sexual intercourse (Bretschneider & McCoy, 1988). There does not seem to be any age beyond which all people are sexually inactive.

The elderly who are in fairly good health are physiologically able to be sexually active into their 70s and beyond. As far as sexuality is concerned, in older years there is truth to the saying, "If you don't use it, you'll lose it." Studies have found that those who were most active sexually during youth and middle age usually maintained their sexual vigor and interest longer into old age.

If sexual behavior declines in later years, it probably is due to social rather than physical reasons. The most important deterrents to sexual activity, when one is older, are the lack of a partner; boredom with one's partner; overindulgence in drinking or eating; poor physical or mental health; fear of poor performance; negative attitudes toward menopause; and negative attitudes toward sex, such as the erroneous belief that sex is inappropriate for the elderly (Hyde & DeLamater, 2000). Other factors deter sexual activity. One is the lack of privacy in many living arrangements, such as in nursing homes. The fear of death due to a stroke or a heart attack deters some of the elderly from sexual activity. A variety of feelings—guilt, anxiety, depression, or hostility—also deter sexual activity. Because of some of these reasons, there is usually more interest in sex than there is sexual activity. (This is true, however, for practically all age groups.)

As noted in Figure 14.1, elderly men normally take longer to develop an erection and to ejaculate, may need more manual stimulation, and may experience longer intervals between erections. Erections may be smaller and less firm and may subside more quickly after ejaculation. Erectile dysfunction may increase, particularly in men with hypertension, heart disease, or diabetes (Papalia et al., 2001). Erectile dysfunction is often treatable; for example, the drug Viagra (an erectile-enhancing drug) is now widely used by men affected by erectile dysfunction.

Attitudes of younger adults, as to what is appropriate sexual behavior for the elderly, commonly create problems. Many younger people express beliefs that it is inappropriate for an unmarried elderly person to become romantically involved with someone. A widower or widow may face strong opposition to remarrying from other family members. Negative views are often strongest when an elderly person becomes involved with someone younger who has the potential to become an heir if the older person dies.

Older people tend to feel less sexual tension, experience less physical intensity, and have less frequent sexual relations. The increased muscle tone and the sexual flush that accompany arousal are still present, but to a lesser degree. Both young and old people in our society need to recognize that sexual expression among the elderly is normal and healthy. Older people need to accept their own sexuality without shame or embarrassment. Younger people need to avoid ridiculing or telling jokes about older persons who show signs of healthy sexuality.

The elderly, like other age groups, have a right to sexual expression as long as they do not hurt anyone. Think about how angry you feel if someone tries to control your sexual activity. Few efforts are made to control the sexual expressions of middle-aged people. It seems absurd for society to put restrictions on people as they move from middle adulthood to later adulthood. Being touched and receiving affection is something that everyone needs, at all ages, to promote feelings of self-worth and personal satisfaction.

Many of the current living arrangements for the elderly (group homes, nursing homes, and foster homes) have overlooked the need for privacy. Nursing homes, for example, place two women or two men in a small room. Housing arrangements should give older men and women chances to socialize, with ample privacy. Physicians, when possible, should avoid prescribing drugs that interfere with sexual functioning. When such a drug needs to be prescribed, the patient should be alerted about its effects. Social workers and other health professionals should discuss sexual activity in a matter-of-fact way. For example, a person with heart problems may be too embarrassed to raise questions about the health risks of being sexually active. A social worker could initiate a conversation about this person's fears.

What Causes Aging?

Everyone who lives to later adulthood will experience some of the physiological changes that are described in the preceding discussion. But what causes these changes? No one knows all of the reasons. A number of theories have been developed that involve biological, sociological, environmental, and psychological factors. Most of the theories involve biological factors.

Genetic Theories. These theories hypothesize that aging occurs due to damage or changes in the genetic information involved in the formation of cellular proteins.

Such changes cause cells to die, which results in aging. The following theories have been classified as genetic theories.

The cellular genetic theory of DNA damage asserts that damages or changes to DNA molecules alter the genetic information and result in the cell being unable to manufacture essential enzymes. (DNA molecules in each cell contain the genetic information of each person. Amazingly, each cell of the body is literally a blueprint of the composition of a person.) Without essential enzymes, it is theorized that aging occurs as cells gradually die.

The running-out-of-program theory asserts that there is a set amount of basic genetic material (DNA molecules) in each cell. As the cells age, the DNA is used up and the cells die. Gerhard and Cristofalo's (1992) research supports this theory, as their findings showed human cells will divide only a limited number of times, usually about 50. This limit controls the life span, which they estimate to be about 110 years for humans.

The somatic-mutation-by-radiation theory postulates that aging occurs due to abnormal chromosomes developing after exposure to radiation.

The error theory of aging asserts that aging is due to an accumulation of errors involved in the transmission of information from the DNA molecule to the final protein product. Such an accumulation of errors results in an "error catastrophe," which eventually leads to the death of the cells.

Nongenetic Cellular Theories. This category of theories postulates that changes take place in cellular proteins after they had been formed. Such changes cause some cells to die, which results in aging. The following theories have been classified as nongenetic cellular theories.

The deprivation theory assumes that aging is caused by vascular changes that deprive cells of essential nutrients and oxygen.

The accumulation theory asserts that aging results from the accumulation of harmful substances in the cells of an organism. When the accumulation builds up, the cells eventually begin to die. The specific substances involved have not as yet been identified.

The wear-and-tear theory asserts that cells begin to die after long use and exposure to stressful elements during the process of living. In this theory the human body is comparable to a machine whose parts eventually wear out. For example, the cells of the brain and heart do not replace themselves when damaged—those cells, when damaged, usually die.

The free-radical theory hypothesizes that there are chemicals, called free radicals, that contain oxygen in a highly activated state and that react with other molecules in their vicinity. Such reactions are postulated to damage and kill some cells.

The cross-linkage theory asserts that cross-linkages or bonds develop between molecules or between components of the same molecules. These bonds supposedly change the chemical and physical properties, which cause some cells to function improperly and gradually die.

Physiological Theories. These theories explain aging as being due to either the breakdown of an organ system or an impairment in physiological control mechanisms. The following theories have been classified as physiological theories.

The single organ system theory asserts that aging is due to an essential system breaking down. The precise system that is thought to control aging has not been identified, but various systems have been suggested. Those suggested include the thyroid gland, which is involved with metabolism; sex glands that regulate hormone secretions; the cardiovascular system, which controls oxygen and blood flow; and the pituitary gland, which regulates secretions from other glands.

The endocrine control system theory postulates that hormones control the aging process. There is evidence that hormones are involved in puberty and menopause. There is also evidence that the functions of the endocrine system decline with age.

The stress theory asserts that aging is due to the accumulation of the effects of the stresses of living. Each stress encountered is thought to leave a small residual of accumulants and impairments, which results in bodily systems then aging. This theory is consistent with clichés about how stressful events will turn a person's hair gray or cause the hair to fall out.

The immunological theory assumes that changes in the immune system result in aging. The immune system protects the body from invading bacteria, microorganisms, and atypical mutant cells that may form. As a person grows older, it is hypothesized that fewer antibodies are produced, which decreases the protective ability of the immune system. Gradually, invading microorganisms begin to engulf and digest body cells, which results in aging.

The control-mechanisms theory of the central nervous system asserts that mechanisms in the central nervous system are responsible for aging. A variety of mechanisms may be involved. For example, the mechanisms that control the autonomic nervous system may function less effectively, causing the autonomic nervous system to gradually degenerate. Or control mechanisms may cause the endocrine system to function less effectively, resulting in a gradual reduction in the function of practically every body system.

Evaluation of Theories of Aging. Everyone grows old, so the conclusion is obvious that nature has a built-in mechanism that promotes aging. We still do not know what this mechanism is. As yet, sufficient evidence has not been presented to prove which (if any) theory is valid.

Factors That Influence the Aging Process

Aging is a complex process. There seem to be many variables that accelerate and decelerate the process. A person who has a serious, long-term illness, or a severe disability, will often age much faster and earlier than someone who is healthy (Kail & Cavanaugh, 2000). The precise reasons why such conditions accelerate the aging process are not known. More rapid aging in such individuals may be due to decreased exercise, or to unknown biochemical changes, or to greater stress.

A large number of "biological insults" hastens the aging process. Such "insults" include accidents, broken bones, severe burns, severe psychological stress, and severe alcohol or drug abuse. Poor eating habits also accelerate aging (Santrock, 1999).

Environmental factors influence the aging process. Being physically and mentally active tends to slow down the aging process. Inactivity speeds it up. A positive outlook (positive thinking) tends to slow down the aging process. Insecurity, the lack of someone to talk to, negative thinking, and being in a strange environment tend to accelerate the aging process (Kail & Cavanaugh, 2000). Prolonged exposure to excessive heat or cold will also speed up the aging process (Santrock, 1999).

Genetic inheritance also plays a role. People whose parents lived a long time have a longer life expectancy than people whose parents lived a shorter period of time (assuming that they died from natural causes). Our bodies apparently have a genetic time clock. Some individuals have a longer time than others. Within a family group, the rate of aging shows a high positive correlation with genetic factors for the different family members. It seems that some kind of timing device causes tissues and organ systems to break down at specific times. This timing device can be accelerated or decelerated by a variety of factors. Highlight 14.2 lists 10 health practices that are known to promote longevity.

◖ Diseases and Causes of Death among the Elderly

Most older persons have at least one chronic condition and may have multiple conditions. The most frequently occurring chronic conditions are arthritis, hypertension, hearing impairments, heart disease, orthopedic impairments, cataracts, diabetes, visual impairments, and sinusitis (AARP, 2000). Older persons see their doctors more frequently, spend a higher proportion of their income on prescribed drugs, and, once in the hospital, stay longer. As might be expected, the health status of the old-old (75 and over) is worse than that of the young-old.

The medical expenses of an elderly person average four times more than those of a young adult (AARP, 2000). One of the reasons medical costs are high is that the elderly suffer much more from long-term illnesses—such as cancer, heart problems, and diabetes.

Physical affection promotes self-worth and personal satisfaction for people of all ages.

© Bill Backmann/PhotoEdit

Highlight 14.2

Health Practices and Longevity

The following 10 health practices have been found to be positively related to good health and longevity:

1. Eating breakfast.
2. Eating regular meals and not snacking.
3. Eating moderately to maintain normal weight.
4. Exercising moderately.
5. Not smoking.
6. Drinking alcohol moderately or not at all.
7. Regularly sleeping seven to eight hours a night.
8. Avoiding the use of illegal drugs.
9. Learning to cope with stress.
10. Leading a healthy sexual life.

Source: John W. Santrock, *Life-Span Development* (Madison, WI: Brown and Benchmark, 1995), pp. 527–531.

Highlight 14.3

Leading Causes of Death Among the Elderly

Cause of death	Of those who died, the proportion who died of this cause
1. Diseases of the heart	34.6%
2. Malignant neoplasms (cancer)	21.8
3. Cerebrovascular diseases (stroke)	7.9
4. Chronic obstructive pulmonary diseases (lung diseases)	5.9
5. Pneumonia	4.7
6. Diabetes	2.6
7. Accidents	1.9
8. All other causes	20.6
Total	100.0%

Source: U.S. Bureau of the Census, *Statistical Abstract of the United States: 2001* (Washington, DC: Government Printing Office), p. 82.

The physical process of aging is a factor in the elderly having a higher rate of health problems. However, research in recent years has demonstrated that personal and social stresses also play major roles in causing diseases. The elderly face a wide range of stressful situations: death of family members and friends, retirement, loneliness, changes in living arrangements, reduced income, loss of social status, and a decline in physical capacities and physical energy. Medical conditions also may result from inadequate exercise, substandard diets, cigarette smoking, and excessive drinking of alcohol.

A special problem for the elderly is that when they become ill, their illness is often imposed on an assortment of preexisting chronic illnesses and on organ systems that no longer are functioning very well (because their reserve capacities are diminished). The health of elderly patients is thus more fragile, and even a relatively minor illness such as a flu can lead to major consequences, or even death.

The most common conditions that limit the activities of the elderly are high blood pressure, heart conditions, rheumatism, arthritis, orthopedic impairments, and emotional disorders. Some of these disorders, such as heart problems, high blood pressure, and arthritis, begin to appear among people in their 30s. Highlight 14.3 lists the leading causes of death among the elderly.

The discussion of these health problems needs to be put in context. The elderly have higher rates of illnesses than younger people, but it needs to be emphasized that a majority of the elderly are reasonably healthy. People over 65 do have a health advantage over younger persons in a few areas—they have fewer flu infections, colds, and acute digestive problems. The reasons are unclear.

They may be more immune to common germs, or they may go out less and, therefore, be less exposed to germs. (Information about Alzheimer's disease, an illness that affects many elderly persons, is presented in Highlight 14.4.)

Highlight 14.4

Alzheimer's Disease

Tony Wiggleworth is 68 years old. Two years ago, his memory began to falter. As the months went by, he even forgot what the day of his wedding to Rose was like. His grandchildren's visits slipped from his memory in 2 or 3 days.

The most familiar surroundings have also become strange to him. Even his friends' homes seem like places he has never been before. When he walks down the streets in his neighborhood, he frequently becomes lost.

He is now quite confused. He has difficulty speaking and can no longer do such elementary tasks as balancing his checkbook. At times, Rose, who is taking care of him, is uncertain whether he knows who she is. All of this is very baffling for Tony. Until he retired 3 years ago, he had been an accountant and had excelled at remembering facts and details.

Tony has Alzheimer's disease. Although the disease sometimes strikes in middle age, most sufferers are over 65. About 4 million Americans have Alzheimer's; 5 to 10 percent of all people over 65 have it, but 47% of those 85 and over have it (Boerenstein, 2000).

Alzheimer's disease is a degenerative brain disorder that gradually causes deterioration in intelligence, memory, awareness, and ability to control bodily functions. In its final stages, Alzheimer's leads to progressive paralysis and breathing difficulties. The breathing problems often result in pneumonia, the most frequent cause of death for Alzheimer's victims. Other symptoms of Alzheimer's include irritability, restlessness, agitation, and impairments of judgment. Although most of those affected are over 65, the disease occasionally strikes people in middle age.

A woman comforts her mother, a victim of Alzheimer's disease, in a private care facility in northern California.

© Evan Johnson / Jeroboam

Highlight 14.4

Over a period lasting from as few as 5 years to as many as 20, the disease destroys brain cells. The changes in behavior that are displayed by those afflicted have a degree of variation. Brownlee (1991) notes:

> One sufferer refuses to bathe or change clothes, another eats fried eggs without utensils, a third walks naked down the street, a fourth has the family's beloved cats put to sleep, while yet another mistakes paint for juice and drinks it. The outlandish acts committed by Alzheimer's patients take as many forms as there are people who suffer the disease. Yet, in every case, the bizarre behavior serves as a sign that the sufferer is regressing towards unawareness, a second childishness. (p. 40)

Researchers in recent years have made tremendous strides in identifying the causes of Alzheimer's disease. At least three different genes have been identified as being linked to the disease, and there may be more genes involved. Yet, having one or more of these genes does not necessarily mean one will develop this disorder. Therefore, researchers believe there must be some as yet unidentified "triggers." Possible triggers are viral infections, biochemical deficiencies, high levels of stress, toxic substances, exposure to radiation, and nutritional deficiencies. Scientists are aware that genetic tendencies are a contributing factor because relatives of Alzheimer's patients have an increased risk of having the disease (Papalia et al., 1998).

An examination of the brains of victims have found a distinctive tangle of protein filaments in the cortex, the part of the brain responsible for intellectual functions. This research shows that there are biochemical causes for the disease and leads to the conclusion that aging does not automatically include senility.

Diagnosing the disease is difficult because the disorder has symptoms that are nearly identical to other forms of dementia. The only sure diagnosis at the present time is the observation of tissue deep within the brain, which can be done only by autopsy after death. Doctors usually diagnose the disease in a living person by ruling out other conditions that could account for the symptoms.

The most prominent early symptom of the disease is memory loss, particularly for recent events. Other early symptoms (which are often overlooked) are the reduced ability to play a game of cards, a reduced performance at sports, and sudden outbreaks of extravagance. More symptoms then develop—irritability, agitation, confusion, restlessness, and impairments of concentration, speech, and orientation. As the disease progresses, the symptoms become more disabling. The caregiver or caregivers eventually have to provide 24-hour care—which is a tremendous burden for caregivers. As the disease progresses in its final stages, a nursing home placement is often necessary. Near the end, the patient usually cannot recognize family members, cannot understand or use language, and cannot eat without help.

Brownlee (1991) briefly describes the mental and physical trauma that patients' caregivers and family members experience:

> They live in a private hell, one that cannot be discussed with neighbors and friends in too much detail because the details are so devastating. They grieve even as their loved ones plunge them into a maelstrom of unreality, where mothers streak through the living room wearing nothing but a shower cap and garter belt and grandfathers try to punch their baby granddaughters. (p. 48)

In addition, the patient's inability to reciprocate expressions of caring and affection robs relationships of intimacy.

Scientists are now investigating a number of hypotheses as to what triggers Alzheimer's. One intriguing finding is that victims of Down syndrome (a severe form of mental retardation due to a chromosome defect) who survive into their 30s frequently develop symptoms indistinguishable from Alzheimer's. Such a similarity may provide a clue as to what triggers Alzheimer's. A recent clue is the discovery of fragments of amyloid in brains of persons who died from the disorder. Amyloid is a very tough protein that in normal amounts is necessary for cell growth throughout the body. Some researchers hypothesize that abnormal patches of this protein in the brain set up a chain reaction that progressively destroys brain cells. This amyloid protein is an abnormal product formed from a larger compound called the amyloid precursor protein, or APP.

Researchers are attempting to develop a test to detect Alzheimer's disease in its early stages. If Alzheimer's disease can be detected in its early stages, people would be better able to plan for their future care and make arrangements for their families while they still retain control of their mental faculties. Furthermore, if in fact Alzheimer's disease results from an accumulation of the amyloid protein, and if the early accumulation of this protein can be detected, then it is likely that drugs can be developed to treat the disorder by blocking the formation of amyloid in the brain. There are high hopes that the causes of Alzheimer's can be found soon and treatment developed.

In December 2000, it was announced that scientists have developed an experimental vaccine that can ward off memory loss in mice stricken with a disease similar to Alzheimer's. The studies used strains of mice that develop lots of a myloid plagues in their brains. It was also announced that preliminary results in human patients indicated that the vaccine was safe (Ritter, 2000). More research is needed to determine whether the vaccine will stop the progression of Alzheimer's in humans.

At the present time there is no cure for the disease. Patients with Alzheimer's receive some relief from drugs that reduce depression and agitation and help them sleep. Both vitamin E and selegiline (a drug used to treat Parkinson's disease) seem to slow the progress of Alzheimer's disease. The number of drugs available to fight effects of Alzheimer's was approaching 60 by December 2000 (Ritter, 2000). Exercise, physical therapy, proper nourishment, and proper fluid intake are also beneficial. Memory aids assist somewhat in everyday functioning. Especially helpful to patients and their families are emotional and social support provided by groups and professional counseling.

Life Expectancy

The average life expectancy in ancient Rome and during the Middle Ages was between 20 and 30 years. Some people lived to be 70 or 80, but infant mortality was very high, and famine, diseases, and wars took the lives of many more. The life expectancy for Americans has gradually been increasing due to better sanitation, nutrition, and disease control. In the middle of the nineteenth century, Americans lived for an average of 40 years. At the turn of the twentieth century, the average was 49 years. The average life expectancy in 2001 was 76 years (U.S. Census Bureau, 2001). These gains have resulted from improvements in infant survival, medical care, diets, and sanitation. A particularly significant factor leading to these gains has been the immunization effort against many diseases that used to kill (such as whooping cough, polio, and diphtheria), and the development of antibiotics that reduce the severity of such illnesses as strep throat, bronchitis, and pneumonia.

Two life events have been found to be significant in predicting the death of an elderly person: death of a spouse and moving to a nursing home (Newman & Newman, 1999). A partial explanation for the effects of these life events is that those who lose a spouse, or are moved to a nursing home, may no longer have the will to live—which hastens their death. For those moved to a nursing home, an additional, partial explanation for a higher death rate is that such individuals may be in poorer health and therefore more apt to die.

Significant sex differences are found in life expectancies. In 2000, females in the United States had a life expectancy at birth of 80 years while males had a life expectancy of only 74 years (U.S. Census Bureau, 2001). There appear to be both environmental and biological reasons for the higher mortality rates among men. Environmental factors are demonstrated by the fact that men are more likely to die from suicide, accidents, and homicides (U.S. Census Bureau, 2001). Men are also more likely to die from lung cancer, heart disease, emphysema, and asthma, all of which have been linked to such environmental causes as smoking and alcohol abuse (U.S. Census Bureau, 2001). A partial explanation for sex differences in mortality rates is that sex role stereotypes allow women to be much more expressive of their feelings than men. It may be that the suppression of feelings leads to anger, frustration and other unwanted emotions being bottled up inside, all of which increase stress, result in an increased number of stress-related disorders in men, and then shorten their life span.

Biological factors are probably also involved in leading to higher mortality rates among men. The higher mortality rate among males in the fetal stage and in infancy supports the notion of an inborn difference in resistance.

The fact that there are many more women over age 65 than men means that women are much more apt to be widows than men are apt to be widowers. In 2000 there was a sex ratio, among those who were 65 and over, of 141 women for every 100 men (AARP, 2000). Since there is a social custom in our society for males to marry someone younger, husbands are even more likely to die before their wives. Women are thus much more likely than men to spend their later years alone.

A number of factors have been found to influence life expectancy (Santrock, 1999). Factors associated with a longer life expectancy are the following:

1. Parents and grandparents lived to 80 or more.
2. Being married for most adult years.
3. Not being overweight.
4. Exercising regularly (such as jogging or walking briskly three times a week).
5. Light drinking (one or two drinks a day).
6. Not smoking.
7. Being basically happy and content with life.
8. Graduating from college.
9. Living in a rural environment.
10. Having regular medical checkups and regular dental care.
11. Routinely using stress management techniques.

Factors associated with a shorter life expectancy are the following:

1. Parents and grandparents died of an illness fairly early in their lives—such as a heart attack or a stroke before age 50.
2. Parents or grandparents had diabetes, thyroid disorders, breast cancer, cancer of the digestive system, asthma, or chronic bronchitis.
3. Being unmarried for most adult years.
4. Overweight.
5. Not exercising regularly.
6. Having a sedentary job.
7. Heavy drinking (more than four drinks per day).
8. Smoking—cigarettes, pipe, or cigars.
9. Being aggressive, intense, and competitive.
10. Often being unhappy, or worried, or feeling guilty.

Longevity: Cross-Cultural Research on Centenarians

A centenarian is a person who is 100 years old, or even older. Why do some people live to be 100 or older? As yet, we do not know the answers. We do know that the number of centenarians in the world is increasing significantly. There are now an estimated 70,000-plus centenarians in the United States (Papalia et al., 2001). Research on the reasons why some people live to be centenarians is beginning.

One possibility involved in this trend is exceptional genes, which may offer protection against dread diseases of old age, such as Alzheimer's and cancer. There are undoubtedly also some environmental and cultural factors. We do know that some centenarians are vegetarians, and that others eat a lot of red meat. Some were athletes, and some engaged in little strenuous activity. One personality characteristic that appears to be shared by this group is the ability to manage stress (Perls et al., 1999).

Infusino and his associates (1996) studied 40 centenarians living in a remote region of Italy (the Calabrian region). Most of these people continued to perform physical tasks and activities associated with daily life. They also had very low levels of depression, and were functioning well mentally. Significantly, they continued to feel important and valued in their culture.

Sadly, our society has tended to devalue the contributions of the elderly in our society. Lefrancois (1999) states that, in our society: "little is asked of the individual for the first twenty or so years of life, a contribution is expected during the middle thirty or thirty-five years, and after age sixty or sixty-five, little more is expected. This *discontinuity* between productive and nonproductive life, is, in effect, a clear social signal that differentiates between being useful and being useless, between being culturally valued and not being valued, between being wanted and not being wanted" (p. 496). Is the feeling of being valued one of the factors that increases one's life expentancy?

11. Not completing high school.

12. Living in an urban environment that has moderate to high levels of smog.

13. Frequent illness.

14. Experiencing high levels of stress without routinely using stress management techniques.

15. Engaging in activities that are high risk for the AIDS virus.

(See Spotlight 14.2 for research on some reasons why people live to be 100.)

✿ Wellness: The Impact of Different Systems on Health

The preceding section echoes, over and over, a central theme: Elderly people are apt to experience little physical or mental deterioration (until near death) if they have a nutritious diet, are successful in managing stress, and stay mentally and physically active. A real key to good mental and physical health in later years is having a lifestyle throughout life that incorporates health-maintenance principles. Health is indeed one of our most important resources.

Traditionally, the health profession in this country has focused on treatment of diseases rather than on prevention. The Chinese approach to medicine has focused on helping patients maintain good health. The holistic concept of treating the whole person is gaining ground in America. There is now greater emphasis on prevention, wellness, and treating a patient psychologically and socially as well as physically.

Physical Exercise

For people who have had poor health-maintenance habits, it is nearly never too late to change. Many studies have shown that elderly persons benefit from a variety of exercise programs that include walking, swimming, and weight lifting. There is also evidence that, as people grow older, continued exercise reduces the degree of physical and mental slowness that occurs in many of the elderly. Before middle-aged and older adults embark on an exercise program (if they have been relatively inactive for a number of years), they should have a physical examination to identify heart conditions and other medical problems that may be aggravated by exercise.

Mental Activity

Just as physical exercise maintains the level of physiological functioning, mental exercise maintains good cognitive functioning. There are some age-related declines in cognitive functioning (described earlier), but if a person is

Regular physical activity can increase longevity. Dr. Jane Ellen McAllister is shown mowing the lawn at the age of 90. Dr. McAllister was the first black woman to receive a Ph.D. from Columbia University's Teachers College. She taught for 50 years at historically black colleges and universities. She died in January 1996 at the age of 96.

© David Rae Morris

mentally active, the declines begin to appear at a later age and are less severe.

Our society needs to put more emphasis on ensuring that the elderly are exposed to intellectual stimulation. Some nursing homes and retirement communities now have daily programs that provide such stimulation; national issues or local issues are discussed, and guest speakers on a variety of subjects are sometimes brought in.

One innovative program is Elderhostel, which offers low-cost courses, often held on college campuses, designed for people over 55. People sign up for 1-, 2-, or 3-week sessions to study a variety of topics at a relaxed pace. Some public universities also have provisions for those over 65 to attend regular classes with either reduced or no tuition. The elderly have generally responded well to adult education courses. Some want to update earlier studies, and others want to pursue educational programs to enrich their lives. Others want to acquire basic learning skills or attain a high school or college diploma.

Traveling is yet another way for the elderly to stay mentally active. Some organizations, such as the American Association of Retired Persons (AARP) and Elderhostel, offer travel tours within the United States and to other parts of the world.

Most authorities on aging now believe that an intellectual decline in later adulthood is largely a myth. It thus appears that our society is largely wasting a precious resource—an elderly population with extensive experience, training, and intelligence. Our society needs to develop more educational programs to help the elderly

maintain their intellectual functioning, and we must find additional ways to allow the elderly to be productive, contributing members to society.

Sleep Patterns

Many of the elderly have one or more sleep disturbances, such as insomnia; difficulty in falling asleep; restless sleep; falling asleep when company is present, frequently awakening during the night; and feeling exhausted or tired after a night of fitful sleep.

What is a healthy sleep pattern for the elderly? The stereotype that the elderly need more sleep appears to be erroneous. It appears that the elderly in fairly good health require no more sleep than those in middle adulthood (Santrock, 1999).

Sleep disturbances that the elderly experience tend to be a result of anxiety, depression, worry, or illness. Restless sleep is common for those who are inactive, those who catnap too much, and those who have physical discomforts (such as arthritic pains).

Some normal changes occur in sleep patterns for the elderly. Deep sleep virtually disappears. The elderly generally take a longer time to fall asleep and have more frequent awakenings. More important, the elderly distribute their sleep somewhat differently. They generally have several catnaps of 15 to 60 minutes during the day. Catnaps are normal, and caution should be used in attempting to use sleep medication to keep an elderly person asleep for 8 hours throughout the night, as they need less sleep when they have catnaps. People develop their sleep patterns according to their physical needs and according to the responsibilities and activities they have.

Nutrition and Diet

The majority of the elderly have inadequate diets (Newman & Newman, 1999). Because of the relationship between diet and cardiac problems, physicians recommend that the elderly have low-fat, high-protein diets.

The elderly are the most undernourished group in our society (Papalia et al., 2001). A number of reasons can be given for chronic malnutrition of the elderly: a lack of money; transportation problems; a lack of incentives to prepare a nutritious meal when one is living alone; inadequate cooking and storage facilities; a decreased or altered sense of taste; poor teeth and lack of good dentures; and a lack of knowledge about proper nutrition.

Some of the elderly have a tendency to overeat. One way for people to occupy their free time is to eat, and most of the elderly have a lot of free time. The caloric requirements decrease somewhat in the later years, and the excess calories that are consumed turn into fat, which increases the risks of heart disease and other medical conditions.

To improve the nutritional health of the elderly, some programs have been developed. Many communities, with the assistance of federal funds, now provide meals for the elderly at group eating sites. These meals are generally provided four or five times a week and usually are luncheon meals. These programs improve the nutrition of elderly persons and offer opportunities for socialization. Meals on Wheels is a service that delivers hot and cold meals directly to housebound recipients who are incapable of obtaining or preparing their own meals, but who can feed themselves.

Stress and Stress Management

Learning how to manage stress is important for the physical and emotional health of all age groups. Because of its importance, we will discuss, in considerable detail, stress and techniques to manage stress.

Stress is a contributing factor in a wide variety of emotional and behavioral difficulties, including anxiety, child abuse, spouse abuse, temper tantrums, feelings of inadequacy, physical assaults, explosive expressions of anger, feelings of hostility, impatience, stuttering, suicide attempts, and depression (Romas & Sharma, 1995).

Stress is a contributing factor in most physical illnesses (Davis et al., 2000). These illnesses include hypertension,

heart attacks, migraine headaches, tension headaches, colitis, ulcers, diarrhea, constipation, arrhythmia, angina, diabetes, hay fever, backaches, arthritis, cancer, colds, flu, insomnia, hyperthyroidism, dermatitis, emphysema, Raynaud's disease, alcoholism, bronchitis, infections, allergies, and enuresis. Stress-related disorders have now been recognized as being our number-one health problem (Romas & Sharma, 1995).

Becoming skillful in learning how to relax is important in treating and facilitating the recovery from both emotional and physical disorders. The therapeutic value of learning how to manage stress has been dramatically demonstrated by Simonton and Matthews-Simonton (1978), who have had considerable success in treating terminal cancer patients by instructing them on how to manage and reduce stress.

The increased recognition of stress management in treating physical and emotional disorders is gradually altering the traditional physician–patient relationship. Instead of being passive participants in the treatment process, patients are increasingly being taught (by social workers and other health professionals) how to prevent illness and how to speed up the recovery from illness by learning stress management strategies (Romas & Sharma, 1995).

People who are successful in managing stress have a life expectancy that is several years longer than those who continually are at high stress levels (Romas & Sharma, 1995). Effective stress management is a major factor in enabling people to live fulfilling, healthy, satisfying, and productive lives (Davis et al., 2000).

Conceptualizing Stress. Stress can be defined as the physiological and emotional reactions to stressors. A stressor is a demand, situation, or circumstance that disrupts a person's equilibrium (internal balance) and initiates the stress response. There are an infinite variety of possible stressors: loss of a job, a loud noise, toxic substances, retirement, arguments, the death of a spouse, a move to a nursing home, hot or cold weather, serious illness, a lack of a purpose in life, and so on. For every second we are alive, our bodies are responding to stressors that call for adaptation or adjustment. Our bodily reactions are continually striving for homeostasis, or balance.

Selye (1956), one of the pioneer researchers on stress, found that the body reacts to all stressors in the same way, regardless of the source of stress. This means that the body reacts to positive stressors (for example, a romantic kiss) in the same way it reacts to negative stressors (for example, an electric shock). Selye found that the body has a three-stage reaction to stress: (1) the alarm phase,

(2) the resistance phase, and (3) the exhaustion phase. Selye called this three-phase response the *general adaptation syndrome* (GAS).

In the alarm phase the body recognizes the stressor and responds by preparing to fight or flee. The body's reactions are numerous and complex. Briefly, the body sends messages from the hypothalamus (a section of the brain) to the pituitary gland to release its hormones. These hormones trigger the adrenal glands to release adrenaline. The release of adrenaline and other hormones results in:

- increased breathing and heartbeat rates;
- a rise in blood pressure;
- increased coagulation of blood, which minimizes potential loss of blood in case of physical injury;
- diversion of blood from the skin to the brain, the heart, and contracting muscles;
- a rise in serum cholesterol and blood fat;
- decreased mobility of the gastrointestinal tract;
- dilation of the pupils.

These changes result in a huge burst of energy, better vision and hearing, and increased muscular strength—all changes that increase our capacities to fight or to flee. (A major problem of the fight–or–flight reaction for us is that we often cannot deal with a threat by fighting or by fleeing. In our complex, civilized society, fighting or fleeing generally runs counter to sophisticated codes of acceptable behavior. The fight–or–flight response was once functional for primitive humans, but now seldom is.)

In the resistance phase (the second phase) bodily processes seek to return to homeostasis. The body seeks, during this phase, to repair any damage caused by the stressors. In handling most stressors, the body generally goes through only the two phases of alarm and repair. During a lifetime a person goes through these two phases hundreds of thousands of times.

The third phase, exhaustion, occurs only when the body remains in a state of high stress for an extended period of time. If the body remains at a high level of stress, it is unable to repair damage that has occurred. If exhaustion continues, a person is apt to develop a stress-related illness.

There are two components of a stressor—experiences or events that are encountered and our thoughts and perceptions about these events (Davis et al., 2000). (See Highlight 14.5.)

Stress is heavily dependent on what a person thinks about events. The following example shows how a person's thinking about a positive event can be a source of negative stress.

Stressor
{
Event:
↓
Ms. Wilcox's thinking about this event:
↓
}

Glenda Wilcox (age 75) is informed by her granddaughter that her level of alertness is fantastic.

"What a backhanded compliment! She expects me to become senile and is surprised I haven't yet. Young people are so inconsiderate. But I wonder if there is truth in what she's implying? Will I soon begin to lose my mind and have to leave my house and live my remaining years in confusion in a nursing home? It seems there are things I'm starting to forget more frequently than I did in the past."

Stress
{
Emotion:
↓
Physiological reaction:
}

Anger, anxiety, worry, alarm.

The alarm stage of the GAS is occurring. If it is sustained and intensive, conditions exist for a stress-related illness to develop.

Not all stress is bad. Life without stress would be boring. Selye (1974) indicates stress is often "the spice of life," and that it is impossible to be alive without experiencing stress. Dreaming even produces some stress. Stress at times is often beneficial to us. It stimulates and prepares us to perform a wide variety of tasks. Students, for example, often find they need to feel a moderate level of stress before they can study for an exam—too little stress results in their being unable to concentrate and may even result in their falling asleep, while too high a level of stress results in too much anxiety and interferes with their concentration. High levels of the alarm phase of the GAS are very desirable during emergencies where physical strength is needed—such as in lifting a heavy object that has fallen on someone.

The kind of stress that is harmful has been called *distress* by Selye (1974). Long-term distress occurs when we continue to think negatively about events that have

Highlight 14.5

Conceptualizing Stressors, Stress, and Stress-related Illnesses

Stressors	Events or experience	(For example, being forced to retire from a job held for 27 years)
	↓	
	A certain kind of thinking	(For example, "What will I do now with all of my time? My work has been my life. Life is over for me now. All I have left to do is die. My income now will be sharply reduced—how will I pay my bills? The company has no right to force me to retire! This is unfair.")

	↓	
Stress	Emotional reactions	Fear, anxiety, worry, alarm, depression, anger
	↓	
	Physiological reactions	The alarm stage of the general adaptation syndrome occurs, and the body prepares for fight or flight. Adrenaline and other hormones increase the heartbeat and rate of breathing, increase perspiration, raise blood sugar levels, dilate the pupils, and slow digestion. The process results in greater muscular strength, a huge burst of energy, and better vision and hearing.
	↓	
	Stress-related disorder	If the body remains at a high level of stress for a prolonged period, a stress-related disorder will develop.

happened to us. When unpleasant events occur, we always have a choice to think negatively or positively. If we continue to think negatively about the situation, our thinking keeps the body under a high level of stress—which can then lead to a stress-related illness. On the other hand, if we think positively about the situation, our thinking enables the body to relax and repair any damage that was done. In addition, when we are relaxed, the immune system is much more effective in combating potential illnesses. (In the alarm phase the functioning of the immune system is sharply reduced, as bodily resources are primarily focused on facilitating the fight-or-flight response.)

There are a number of signals, presented in Table 14.1, that we can use to measure levels of stress. Most of us use these signals to judge whether our friends are under too much stress. But most of us fail to use these same signals to determine when our own stress level is too high. For our emotional and physical health, we need to give more attention to monitoring these signals in ourselves.

Empowerment Approaches to Stress Management: Application of Theory. Of the five major categories of approaches to stress management, only three are constructive in terms of empowering a person and helping her gain greater control over her life. The three constructive

approaches are: (1) changing the distressing event; (2) changing one's thinking about the distressing event; and (3) taking one's mind off the distressing event, usually by thinking about something else.

There are also two destructive ways that some people use to relieve stress. One involves resorting to alcohol, other drugs, or food. Perhaps the major reason for abusing alcohol and other drugs is to seek relief from stress and unwanted emotions. Drugs will provide temporary relief, but the next day a person's problems still remain, and there is a serious danger that drug abuse may become a destructive habit. Compulsive overeating is also an unhealthy way of temporarily relieving stress.

The second destructive way of escaping stress is suicide. We will focus mostly on constructive ways to relieving stress.

Changing a Distressing Event. When distressing events occur, it is desirable to confront them directly to try to improve the situation. If an elderly person is concerned about what to do with his or her time after retiring, the person needs to work on finding meaningful and enjoyable activities to become involved in. If a person is concerned about a deterioration in health, it is desirable to see a physician and receive medical treatment. Many

Table 14.1	Stress Signals

A number of signals can be used to measure whether we are at a good level of stress, or whether we are at too high a level of stress. Based on these signals, you have to use your own judgment to determine whether your stress is too high.

Good level	Too High
1. *Behaviors*	High-pitched, nervous laughter
Creative, makes good decisions	Lack of creativity
Friendly	Poor work quality
Generally successful	Overdrinks or overeats
Able to listen to others	Smokes to excess
Productive—gets a lot done	Stutters
Appreciates others, is perceptive of others, and recognizes contributions of others	Inability to concentrate
	Easily startled by small sounds
Smiles, laughs, jokes	Impatient
	Easily irritated
	Unpleasant to be around
	Puts others down
	Engages in wasted activity and motion
2. *Feelings*	Resentful, bitter, dissatisfied, angry
Feeling of confidence	Timid, tense, anxious, fearful
Feeling of being calm, relaxed	Paranoid
Feelings of pleasure and enjoyment	Weary, depressed, fed up
Feelings of excitement and exhilaration	Feelings of inadequacy or failure
	Confused, swamped, overwhelmed
	Feelings of powerlessness or helplessness
3. *Body Signals*	Loss of appetite, diarrhea, or vomiting
Restfulness	Prone to accidents
Absence of aches and pains	Frequent need to urinate
Coordinated body reactions	Trembling, nervous tics
Unaware of body, which is functioning smoothly	Feelings of dizziness or weakness
Good health, absence of stress-related illnesses	Frequent colds and flu
	High blood pressure
	Tight or tense muscles
	Asthma or breathing irregularities
	Skin irritations, itches, and rashes
	Sleep problems
	Upset stomach and ulcers
	Various aches and pains—muscle aches, backaches, neck aches, and headaches

distressing events can be improved by confronting them head on, and taking constructive action to change them.

Changing One's Thinking about a Distressing Event. Some events cannot be changed. For example, Juan Garcia (age 64) has experienced such a severe deterioration in his eyesight that he no longer is able to drive his truck (by which he earned a living) or even a car. Ophthalmologists have informed him that his eyesight will slowly continue to deteriorate and that the condition is not reversible. Since Juan cannot change the situation, the only constructive alternative is to accept it and find meaningful activities unrelated to driving. It is counterproductive to complain or get upset about something that cannot be changed. Acceptance of the situation will also improve Juan's disposition.

One of the structured techniques for changing one's thinking about a distressing event is to challenge and change the negative and irrational thinking through a rational self-analysis, as described in Chapter 8.

When unpleasant events occur, we have a choice to take either a positive or a negative view. If we take a negative view we are apt to experience more stress, and also apt to alienate friends and acquaintances.

Akin to *positive thinking* is having a philosophy of life that allows us to take crises in stride, to travel through life at a relaxed pace, to look at the scenery with enjoyment, to approach work in a relaxed fashion so as to permit greater creativity, to enjoy and use leisure time to develop more fully as a person, and to find enjoyment in each day.

Every person needs someone to share good times with and to talk with about personal difficulties. *Sharing concerns with someone* helps to vent emotions. The listener may be a neighbor, friend, member of the clergy, or professional counselor. Talking a concern through often helps in two ways to reduce stress. It may lead to a new perspective on how to resolve the distressing event, or it may help by changing one's thinking about the distressing event to a more positive and rational attitude.

Closely related to discussing a distressing event with someone is having a social support group. Support groups allow people to share their lives, to have fun with others, to let their hair down, and to be a resource for help when emergencies and crises arise. Possible support groups include friends in a retirement community, one's family, one's coworkers, a church group, a community group, and so on.

Taking One's Mind Off the Distressing Event, Usually by Thinking about Something Else. There are a variety of ways to stop thinking about a distressing event.

1. *Relaxation Approaches.* Deep-breathing relaxation, imagery relaxation, progressive muscle relaxation, meditation, and biofeedback are effective techniques for reducing stress and inducing the relaxation response (becoming relaxed). For each of these techniques, the relaxation response is facilitated by sitting in a comfortable position, in a quiet place, with closed eyes (Davis et al., 2000).

Deep-breathing relaxation helps you to stop thinking about day-to-day concerns and to concentrate your thinking on your breathing processes. For 5 to 10 minutes, slowly and gradually inhale deeply and exhale, while telling yourself something like, "I am relaxing, breathing smoother. This is soothing, and I'm feeling calmer, renewed, and refreshed." Continued practice on this technique will enable you to become more relaxed whenever you are in a tense situation—such as prior to giving a speech.

Imagery relaxation involves switching your thinking from your daily concerns to focusing your thinking (for 10 to 15 minutes) on your ideal relaxation place. It might be lying on a beach beside a scenic lake in the warm sun. It might be relaxing in warm water, while you read a magazine. Savor all the pleasantness, the peacefulness—focus on everything that you find calming, soothing, relaxing. Sense your whole body becoming refreshed, revived, and rejuvenated.

Progressive muscle relaxation is based on the principle that a person cannot be anxious if the muscles are relaxed (Jacobson, 1938). The approach is learned by having a person tighten and then relax a set of muscles. While relaxing the muscles, the person is advised to concentrate on the relaxed feeling while noting that the muscles are becoming less tense. Watson and Tharp (1973) give a brief description of the initial steps in this procedure:

Make a fist with your dominant hand (usually right). Make a fist and tense the muscle of your (right) hand and forearm: tense it until it trembles. Feel the muscles pull across your fingers and the lower part of your forearm. . . . Hold this position for five to seven seconds, then . . . relax. . . . Just let your hand go. Pay attention to the muscles of your (right) hand and forearm as they relax. Note how those muscles feel as relaxation flows through (twenty to thirty seconds). (pp. 182–183)

The procedure of tensing and then relaxing is continued for three or four times until the hand and forearm are relaxed. Next, other muscle groups are tensed and relaxed in the same manner, one group at a time. These groups might include: left hand and forearm, right biceps, left biceps, forehead muscles, upper lip and cheek muscles, jaw muscles, chin and throat muscles, chest muscles, abdominal muscles, back muscles between the shoulder blades, right and left upper leg muscles, right and left calf muscles, and toes and arches of the feet. With practice, the capacity to relax, simply by visualizing the muscles, is developed.

A variety of meditative approaches are being used today. (Deep-breathing relaxation and imagery relaxation are two forms of meditation.) Benson (1975) has identified four basic components common to meditative approaches that induce the relaxation response: (1) being in a quiet environment free from external distractions; (2) being in a comfortable position; (3) having an object to dwell on, such as a word, sound, chant, phrase, or imagery of a painting (Benson suggests the word *one*); and (4) having a passive attitude in which you stop thinking about day-to-day concerns. This last component, Benson asserts, is the key element in inducing the relaxation response.

Biofeedback equipment provides mechanical feedback to a person about her or his level of stress. Such equipment informs people about levels of stress that they are usually unaware of until a markedly high level is reached. For example, a person's hand temperature may vary from 10 to 12 degrees in an hour's time, with an increase in temperature indicating an increase in becoming calm and relaxed. Biofeedback equipment measures the levels of functioning of numerous physiological processes, such as blood pressure, hand temperature, muscle tension, heartbeat rate, and brain waves. With biofeedback training, a person is first instructed in recognizing high levels of anxiety or tenseness. Then the person is instructed on how to reduce such high levels by either closing the eyes and adopting a passive letting-go attitude or by thinking about something pleasant or calming. Often, relaxation approaches are combined with biofeedback to elicit the relaxation response. Biofeedback equipment provides immediate feedback to a person about the kind of thinking that is effective in reducing stress (Davis et al., 2000).

2. *Exercise.* Since the alarm phase of the general adaptation syndrome automatically prepares us for large muscle activity, it makes sense to exercise. Through exercising, we use up fuel in the blood, reduce blood pressure and heartbeat rate, and reverse the other physiological changes set off during the alarm state of the general adaptation syndrome. Exercising helps keep us physically fit so that we have more physical strength to handle stressful crises. Exercising also reduces stress and relieves tension, partly by switching our thinking from our daily concerns to the exercise we are involved in. For these reasons we need to have an exercise program. A key to making ourselves exercise daily is seeking a program we enjoy. A wide variety of exercises are available, including walking, jogging, weight lifting, kick boxing, jumping rope, swimming, and so on.

3. *Pleasurable Goodies.* Pleasurable goodies relieve stress, change our pace of living, are enjoyable, make us feel good, and are, in reality, personal therapies. What is a "goody" (pleasurable experience) to one person may not be to another. Common goodies are: being hugged, listening to music, going shopping, taking a bath, going to a movie, having a glass of wine, taking part in family and religious get-togethers, taking a vacation and singing. Such goodies add spice to life and remind us we have worth.

Personal pleasures can also be used as payoffs to ourselves for jobs well done. Most of us would not seek to shortchange others for doing well; so we ought not to shortchange ourselves. Such rewards are a motivator to move on to new challenges.

Having enjoyable activities beyond work and family responsibilities are also pleasurable goodies that relieve stress. Research has found that stress reduces stress—that is, an appropriate level of stressful activities in one area helps reduce excessive stress in others (Davis et al., 2000). Getting involved in enjoyable outside activities switches our negative thinking from our daily concerns to positive thoughts about the enjoyable activities. Therefore, it reduces stress if we become involved in activities we enjoy. Such activities may include golf, tennis, swimming, scuba diving, flying lessons, and traveling.

Application of Theory to Client Situations. Social workers are one of the groups of helping professionals, along with psychologists, psychiatrists, and guidance counselors, who are involved in developing and providing stress-management programs. Social workers have a variety of roles in stress management. They can serve as *educators* in providing stress-management educational programs to individuals and groups. Some physicians now refer patients experiencing high levels of stress, or those who have stress-related illnesses, to such programs. Social workers can incorporate relaxation training and biofeedback training in their *counseling* sessions with clients, particularly those experiencing high levels of stress; if highly stressed clients learn to relax, they are often more effective in solving their difficulties. Social workers can serve as *brokers* in referring highly stressed individuals to stress-management programs, and they can serve as *group facilitators* in leading therapeutic groups that emphasize stress management. Social workers can also serve as *initiators* and *consultants* in developing stress-management programs in schools, businesses, and industries, and in medical settings.

❦ Summary

Later adulthood begins at around 65. This age group is an extremely diverse one, spanning an age range of over 30 years. Later adulthood is an age of recompense, as it is a time when people reap the consequences of the kind of life they have lived. The process of aging affects different persons at different rates. Nature appears to have a built-in mechanism that promotes aging, but it is not known what this mechanism is.

There are a variety of factors that accelerate the aging process: poor diet, overwork, alcohol or drug abuse, prolonged illnesses, severe disabilities, prolonged stress, negative thinking, exposure to prolonged hot or cold conditions, and serious emotional problems. Factors that slow down the aging process include a proper diet, skill in relaxing and managing stress, being physically and mentally active, a positive outlook on life, and learning how to control unwanted emotions.

The elderly are much more susceptible to physical illnesses than younger people; yet, a majority of the elderly are reasonably healthy. The two leading causes of death are diseases of the heart and cancer. Alzheimer's disease, a malady that affects many older adults, was described. The chapter ends with a discussion of the effects of stress, and describes a variety of stress-management techniques.

InfoTrac College Edition Keywords

Alzheimer's disease   death of elderly   life expectancy   senescence   senility   sexuality and aging   stress management

On the Internet

Administration on Aging

http://www.aoa.dhhs.gov/

The site is designed to serve you—whether you are an older American, a caregiver, a professional in the field of aging, a member of our national aging network, a representative of the media, or anyone with an interest in our nation's large and growing aging population.

Alzheimer Society of Canada

http://www.alzheimer.ca/

The first organization of its kind in the world, the Alzheimer Society of Canada was founded in 1978. Its mission is to alleviate the personal and social consequences of Alzheimer's disease, and promote the search for a cause and cure for the disease.

Huffington Center on Aging—Centenarians

http://www.hcoa.org/centenarians/centenarians.htm

The center aims to improve the quality of life of older people through programs of research, education, and service.

Macular Degeneration Foundation

http://www.eyesight.org/

Dedicated to serving the interests of those affected by macular degeneration and related low-vision conditions.

CHAPTER 15

Psychological Systems and Their Impacts on Later Adulthood

Mrs. Sandra Lombardino is 69 years old. Except for being overweight and having arthritis, she is in fairly good health. She is personable, well groomed, kind, and articulate. She retired 2 years ago from her job as an elementary school teacher; she was well liked by students and her fellow teachers in her 33 years of teaching. She raised four children, all of whom have started careers and families of their own.

Mrs. Lombardino would like to use her retirement years to travel and do volunteer work. She has worked hard for many years and has looked forward to enjoying her retirement.

She is increasingly frustrated because her husband's demands and offensive behavior are destroying her retirement dreams. Her husband, Benedito, has a number of health-care needs. Benedito used to be a carpenter and at one time was a good athlete. But he has been a heavy drinker for over 40 years. When drunk, he has been physically and verbally abusive to his wife and to his children. His children left home to escape from him as soon as they were financially able to do so. The children love their mother but despise their father.

In many ways Sandra Lombardino has been a martyr. She took a marriage vow to have them live together for better or worse until death. She has fulfilled that vow, in spite of the urging of her friends and relatives to seek a divorce. Several years ago, Benedito was discovered to have cirrhosis of the liver and had to stop working. He now receives a monthly disability check. Despite his illness, Benedito has continued to drink heavily and has developed high blood pressure and diabetes. He is grossly overweight and is often incontinent. The drinking and illnesses have caused brain deterioration, and he now has difficulty walking, talking, and grooming himself, and he frequently hallucinates. His behavior has resulted in a loss of friends. Benedito has been pressured into attending a number of alcoholism treatment programs, including Alcoholics Anonymous, but he has always re-turned to drinking.

Sandra Lombardino is in a quandary about what she should do. She is angry that she now has to spend most of her waking hours caring for someone who is obnoxious and verbally abusive to her. She resents not being able to travel and not being able to leave home in or-der to do volunteer work. Sometimes she wishes her husband would die, so that she could get on with her life. At other times she feels guilty about wishing her husband would die.

She has contemplated getting a divorce, but such a process would mean her husband would get half of the property that she has worked so many years to acquire. She has also considered placing Benedito in a nursing home, but she feels an obligation to care for him and realizes that the expenses of a nursing home would deplete her life savings. Mrs. Lombardino feels that the cruelest injustice would be for her to die before her husband dies, so that she would be robbed of her chances to achieve her retirement dreams.

A PERSPECTIVE

People need to make a number of psychological adjustments at all ages for their lives to be meaningful and fulfilling. Later adulthood is no exception.

This chapter will:

► Describe the developmental tasks of later adulthood.
► Present theoretical concepts about developmental tasks in late adulthood.
► Summarize theories of successful aging.
► Discuss the impact of key life events on the elderly.
► Present guidelines for positive psychological preparations for later adulthood.
► Summarize material on grief management and death education.

❦ Developmental Tasks of Later Adulthood

Most of the developmental tasks that the elderly en-counter are psychological in nature. We will discuss a number of these tasks, using a couple, Douglas and Norma Polser, as an example.

1. *Retirement and lower income.* In 1987, Douglas Polzer retired from being a road-construction

foreman in Dubuque, Iowa. Two years earlier, his wife, Norma, had retired from the post office. Retirement brought a number of changes to their lives. For several months after retiring, Douglas had difficulty in finding things to do with his time. His work had been the center of his life. He seldom saw his former coworkers, and he had practically no hobbies or interests. When he was working, he always had many stories to tell about unusual situations that happened. He no longer had much to talk about. Another problem for the

Polzers was that they now had a lower standard of living. Their main sources of income are Social Security benefits and Norma's federal pension.

2. *Living with one's spouse in retirement.* Prior to retiring, Norma and Douglas did not see each other very much. Both worked during the week, and Norma worked on Saturday. Each tended to socialize with his or her coworkers. Norma and Douglas tended to annoy each other if they were together a lot.

   Since Douglas retired, both were generally at home. Since Norma had always done most of the domestic tasks, she kept busy. Finding things to do was not very difficult for her.

   For the first few months after Douglas retired, he followed Norma around the house telling her how she should do her work. That didn't go over very well. They got on each other's nerves and had a number of arguments. As time passed, Douglas became more interested in fishing, taking walks, and getting together with his retired friends. Gradually, with Douglas being gone more, the arguments faded.

3. *Affiliating with individuals of one's own age group or with associations for the elderly.* The Polzers joined the Senior Citizens Leisure Club in Dubuque. Norma participated more frequently than Douglas. The club has a variety of activities: luncheons, speakers, bus tours, painting and craft sessions, bowling, and golf. The club also has a small library.

4. *Maintaining interest in friends and family ties.* Norma and Douglas have formed a number of new friendships with members they met in the club. Through conversing with such friends, Norma and Douglas have been able to gain new perspectives on the adjustments they had to make.

   Most of the Polzers' friends, prior to retiring, were coworkers. After retirement, they gradually saw less and less of these friends, since their interests were growing in different directions. These former friends still talk a great deal about what was happening at work, and both Norma and Douglas now found such conversations boring.

   The Polzers usually got together on Sunday with their son, Kirk, and his family, who lived in Dubuque. Their daughter, Devi, had left home at age 17 to marry. After she had three children, she obtained a divorce and was on public assistance for 4 years until she remarried. She is now living in California and has had two more children. The Polzers seldom see her, but their relationship with her has improved since her adolescent years. Doug and Norma wish they could see Devi and her children more.

5. *Continuing social and civic responsibilities.* Douglas has continued to be a volunteer night watchman for the county fair that is held for 4 days during the summer. Since they retired, Doug and Norma have been more active in attending their church and participating in church activities; Doug has become an elder for the church and Norma has become more active in the ladies' aid society.

6. *Coping with illness and the loss of a spouse and/or friends.* After 4 years of retirement, life was going fairly smoothly for the Polzers. Then in 1991 Doug had a stroke that left him partially paralyzed. Doug's and Norma's lives changed radically. Douglas almost never went outside the house. He became irritable, incontinent, and needed constant attention. Visiting-nurse services provided some help, and so did the Polzers' son and daughter-in-law. But the major burden was Norma's. She was forced to drastically reduce her church and club activities. For the next 2 years she spent most of her time caring for Douglas. He never said "Thank you," and he verbally abused her. At times Norma wished he would die. Then in 1993 he did.

   Norma's world again changed. For the first time in many years, she was living alone. Douglas's death was very hard for her. She felt guilty since she had wished Douglas would die. Initially, she was lonely. But, as the months began to pass, she gradually started putting her life back together. She became active again in the church and in the seniors' leisure club. Sharing her grief with other club members helped. As the years passed, more of her friends died, and Norma found herself attending more funerals.

7. *Finding satisfactory living arrangements at the different stages of later adulthood.* After Douglas died, Norma became depressed and had less energy. Kirk helped, but he had his own family, career, and home to care for. Norma realized she was slowing down physically. After 2 years, Kirk began to encourage her to sell the house and move into an apartment complex that was especially built for the elderly. Norma resisted for over a year. Then, in 1996, Norma slipped on a stairway and broke her leg. She had to crawl to the telephone. Kirk

came and took her to the emergency room where her leg was put in a cast. When she got out of the hospital, Kirk took her to his home. Norma's house was put up for sale.

Having to leave her house was almost as great a loss as when Douglas died. She spent 2 months with Kirk's family, but she did not get along with Kirk's wife. Each had different ways of doing things and different ideas on how children should be raised. When relationships became severely strained, Norma moved to an apartment for the elderly. The move meant that many cherished possessions had to be discarded. Norma began to realize that if her mental or physical condition deteriorated further, her next move would be to a nursing home; at times she thought she would rather die than enter a nursing home. The move also meant Norma had to establish new relationships. Fortunately, the move went smoother than Norma had hoped, and she was warmly welcomed by the staff and the residents.

8. *Adjusting to changing physical strength and health and overcoming bodily preoccupation.* For many years Norma had struggled to get used to gray hairs, wrinkles, and all the other physical changes of aging. Her arthritis often caused swelling and pain in her joints, and she no longer had as much energy and stamina as in the past.

9. *Reappraising personal values, self-concept, and personal worth in light of new life events.* A major adaptation task of the elderly is to conduct an evaluative life review. During this review they reflect on their failures and accomplishments, their disappointments and satisfactions, and hopefully come to a reasonably positive view of their life's worth. The failure to arrive at a positive view can result in a case of overt psychopathology.

After Norma became settled in her apartment, she again had a lot of free time. She was now 76 years old, and her health was declining. She spent a lot of time thinking about the past. She had enjoyed the early years of retirement, but she acknowledged that the 5 years since Douglas's first stroke had been rocky.

10. *Accepting the prospect of death.* It is now 2003 and Norma has been living in her apartment for 7 years. Her arthritis is worse, and she has cataracts. But her last 7 years have been fairly uneventful. Kirk and his family visit almost every Sunday, and she has made a number of friends at her apartment

complex. She has attended a number of funerals, and still occasionally mourns the death of Douglas, especially on holidays and on their wedding anniversary. Norma feels her life has been fairly full and meaningful. These assessments have also led her to think about her eventual death. She worries about the pain she may experience and is fearful about slowly deteriorating. To avoid being kept alive after her mental capacities have deteriorated, she has signed a "living will," which declares that if she becomes unconscious for a prolonged period of time, she does not want heroic measures to be used to keep her alive. She is fully aware and accepting of the fact that she will die in the not-too-distant future. Since her life has been full and positive, she is prepared for death. Her religion asserts there is a life after death; she is uncertain whether an afterlife exists, but if it does, she is hoping to be reunited with Douglas, and to see many of her friends who have died.

❧ Theoretical Concepts about Developmental Tasks in Later Adulthood

In this section we will examine various theoretical concepts relating to the developmental tasks of later adulthood.

Integrity versus Despair

The final stage of life, according to Erikson (1963), involves the psychological crisis of *integrity versus despair.* The attainment of integrity comes only after considerable reflection about the meaning of one's life. *Integrity* refers to an ability to accept the facts of one's life and to face death without great fear. The elderly who have achieved a sense of integrity view their past in an existential light. They have a feeling of having achieved a respected position during their lifetime and have an inner sense of completion. They accept all of the events that have happened to them, without trying to deny some unpleasant facts or to overemphasize others. Integrity involves an integration of one's past history with one's present circumstances, and a feeling of being content with the outcome. In order to experience integrity, the elderly must incorporate a lifelong sequence of failures, conflicts, and disappointments into their self-image. This process is made more difficult by the fact that the role of the elderly is devalued in our society. There are a lot of negative attitudes expressed in our society that (often erroneously) suggest the elderly are incompetent, dependent, and old-fashioned. The death of close friends and relatives and the gradual deterioration of physical health make it additionally difficult for the elderly to achieve integrity.

The opposite pole of integrity is despair. *Despair* is characterized by a feeling of regret about one's past and includes a continuously nagging desire to have done things differently. Despair makes an attitude of calm acceptance of death impossible, as those who despair view their life as incomplete and unfulfilled. Either they seek death as a way of ending a miserable existence, or they desperately fear death because it makes any hope of compensating for past failures impossible. Some of the elderly who despair commit suicide.

Men, particularly elderly men, are more apt to commit suicide than are women (U.S. Census Bureau, 2001). The highest rate of suicide is found not among male adolescents or male young adults, but among elderly men (U.S. Census Bureau, 2001). One of the reasons the suicide rate among elderly men is so high is that men are more apt than women to view their chosen career as providing the primary source of meaning in life; when men with this perspective then retire, they are more apt to despair and to select suicide as a way to end their misery.

Three Key Psychological Adjustments

Peck (1968) suggests that there are three primary psychological adjustments that must be made in order to make later adulthood meaningful and gratifying. The first adjustment involves shifting from a work-role preoccupation to *self-differentiation*. Since retirement is a crucial shift in one's life, a new role must be acquired. The elderly person has to adjust to the fact that she or he will no longer go to work and needs to find a new identity and new interests. People who are in the process of making this adjustment must spend time assessing their personal worth. (A woman whose major work has been being a wife and a mother faces this adjustment when her children leave home or her husband dies.) A crucial question to resolve at this point is: "Am I a worthwhile person insofar as I can do a full-time job or can I be worthwhile in other different ways . . . ?" (Peck, 1968, p. 90). In making this adjustment, people need to recognize that they are richer and more diverse than the sum of their tasks at work.

A second adjustment involves shifting from body preoccupation to *body transcendence*. Health problems increase for the elderly, and energy levels decrease. One's physical appearance also shows signs of aging such as graying and thinning of hair and increasing wrinkles. Many older people become preoccupied with their state of health and their appearance. Others, however, transcend these concerns and are able to enjoy life in spite of declining health. Those who make this transcendence have generally learned to define comfort and happiness in terms of satisfying social relationships or creative mental activities.

The third adjustment involves shifting from self-preoccupation to *self-transcendence*. The inevitability of death must be dealt with. Although death is a depressing prospect, Peck (1968) indicates a positive acceptance can be achieved by shifting one's concerns from "poor me" to, "What can I do to make life more meaningful, secure, or happier for those who will survive me?"

Life Review

Most older persons conduct an evaluative life review in which they assess their past life and consider the future in terms of the inevitability of death. Frenkel-Brunswik (1970) referred to this life review as "drawing up the balance sheet of life." The two key elements in this review are: concluding that the past was meaningful and learning to accept the inevitability of death. Those who psychologically achieve this are apt to be content and comfortable with their later years; those who conclude that life has been empty, and who do not as yet accept death, are apt to despair.

During a life review, a reconsideration of previous experiences and their meaning occurs, often with a revision or an expanded understanding taking place (Haight, 1991). This reorganization of the past may provide a more valid picture for the individual, providing a new and significant meaning to his or her life.

Self-Esteem

Self-esteem (the way people regard themselves) is a key factor in overall happiness and adjustment to life. According to Cooley's (1902) "looking glass self" concept, people develop their sense of who they are in terms of the ways that others relate to them. If elderly people are treated by others as if they are old-fashioned, senile, dependent, and incompetent, they are apt to view themselves in the same way. With losses of friends and relatives through death, the loss of the work role, and a decline in physical appearance and in physical abilities, the elderly are vulnerable to a lowering of self-esteem.

In order for the elderly to feel good about themselves, they need feedback from others indicating that they are worthwhile, competent, and respected. Like people in all other age groups, the elderly thrive by demonstrating their competence. People tend to feel competent when they exert control over their own lives. The more options they have, the more in control they are, and the higher their self-esteem will be.

Privacy is a factor in furthering competence and self-esteem. People who have a private place to go can decide when they want to be with other people and when they want to be alone. In a nursing home, those who have a private room can retreat to it whenever they find something distasteful, or too noisy, or whenever they want to rest. A private room gives them a way to control their environment.

Life Satisfaction

Life satisfaction is a sense of psychological well-being in general or of satisfaction with life as a whole. Life satisfaction is a widely used index of psychological well-being in older adults. Older adults who are in good health and have an adequate income are more likely to be content with their lives than those who have poor health and limited incomes (Santrock, 1999). The elderly who have an extended social network of friends and family are more satisfied than those who are socially isolated (Santrock, 1999). An active lifestyle is also associated with psychological well-being in older adults—those who play golf, go out to dine, go to the theater, travel, exercise regularly, go to church, go to meetings, and are actively involved in the community, are more content with their lives than those who stay at home and lead a sedentary lifestyle (Santrock, 1999).

Low Status and Ageism

The elderly suffer psychologically because our society has been generally unsuccessful in finding something important or satisfying for them to do. It is not the elderly but, rather, the younger age groups who determine the status and position of the elderly in a society. The young and the middle-aged not only determine the future for the elderly; they also determine their own future, as they will someday be old.

In most primitive and earlier societies, the elderly were respected and viewed as useful to their people to a much greater degree than is the case in our society. Industrialization and the growth of modern society have robbed the elderly of their high status. Prior to industrialization, older people were the primary owners of property. Land was the most important source of power; therefore, the elderly controlled much of the economic and political power. Now, people earn their living in the job market, and the vast majority of the elderly own little land and are viewed as having no salable labor. In earlier societies, the elderly were also valued because of the knowledge they possessed. Their experiences enabled them to supervise planting and harvesting and to pass on knowledge about hunting, housing, and crafts. The elderly also played key roles in preserving and transmitting the culture. But the rapid advances of science and technology have tended to limit the value of the technological knowledge of the elderly, and books and other memory-story devices have made the elderly less valuable as storehouses of culture and records.

Our society does not allow many of our elderly to experience their later years positively. We don't respect the elderly for their experience and wisdom, but instead dismiss their ideas as being irrelevant and outdated.

The low status of the elderly is closely associated with ageism. The term *ageism* refers to having negative images of, and attitudes toward, people simply because they are old. Today, the reaction to the elderly by many people is a negative one. Ageism is similar to sexism or racism as it involves discrimination and prejudice against all members of a particular social category. Children's books do not usually have elderly characters, and those that do usually portray the elderly unfavorably. The prejudice against the elderly is shown in everyday language by the use of such terms as "old biddy," and "old fogey." (The triple jeopardy of being female, African American, and old is discussed in Spotlight 15.1.)

Ageism is an additional burden that the elderly encounter. Some of the elderly, particularly among the young-old, are able to refute ageism stereotypes by being productive and physically and mentally active. Unfortunately for others, ageism stereotypes become self-fulfilling prophecies. The elderly are treated as if they are incompetent, dependent, and senile; such treatment lowers their self-esteem, and some end up playing the roles suggested by the stereotypes. Ageism adversely impacts on the elderly and restricts the roles and alternatives available to them.

Depression and Other Emotional Problems

The older person is often a lonely person. Most people 70 years of age or older are widowed, divorced, or single. When someone has been married for many years and his or her spouse dies, a deep sense of loneliness usually occurs that seems unbearable. The years ahead often seem full of emptiness. It is not surprising, then, that depression

Spotlight on Diversity 15.1

Triple Jeopardy: Being Female, African American, and Old

The poverty rate for elderly females is almost double that of elderly males (Kornblum & Julian, 2001). Despite their positive status in the African American family and culture; African American women over the age of 70 are the poorest population group in the United States (Kornblum & Julian, 2001).

Three out of five elderly African American women live alone; most of them are widowed (Kornblum & Julian, 2001). The poverty rate of this age group is related to ageism, sexism, and racism. When they were young, these women tended to hold very low-paying jobs—some were not even covered by Social Security. In the case of domestic service, their income was not apt to be reported by their employers.

Even though many of these women are struggling financially, socially, and physically, Schaefer (1996) notes they have shown remarkable adaptiveness, resilience, coping skills, and responsibility. Extensive family networks help them cope, providing them with the essentials of life and giving them a sense of being loved. African American churches have provided avenues for meaningful social participation, social welfare services, feelings of power, and a sense of internal satisfaction. These women also tend to live together in ethnic minority communities, which gives them a sense of belonging. They also tend to adhere to the American work ethic and view their religion as a source of strength and support. Nonetheless, the incomes and health of older African American women (as well as of other ethnic minority individuals) are important concerns in our aging society.

© Joseph Sorrentino

Being female, African American, and old is a triple jeopardy. Many women in this category are the financially poorest of all citizens. This woman in southern Delaware is pumping water from a well. Her trailer has no running water and the washing machine is located outside.

---

is the most common emotional problem of the elderly. Symptoms of depression include feelings of uselessness, of being a burden, of being unneeded, of loneliness, and of hopelessness. Somatic symptoms of depression include a loss of weight and appetite, fatigue, insomnia, and constipation. It is often difficult to determine whether such somatic symptoms are due to depression or to an organic disorder.

Depression can alter the personality of an elderly person. Depressed people may become apathetic, withdrawn, and show a slowdown in behavioral actions. An elderly person's reluctance to respond to questions is apt to be due to depression rather than to the contrariness of old age (Newman & Newman, 1999).

Those who have had unresolved emotional problems earlier in life will generally continue to have them when older. Often, these problems will be intensified by the added stresses of aging.

Two major barriers to good mental health in the later years are failure to bounce back from psychosocial losses (such as the death of a loved one) and failure to have meaningful life goals. Later adulthood is a time when there are drastic changes thrust on the elderly that may create emotional problems: loss of a spouse, loss of friends and relatives through death or moving to another place, poorer health, loss of accustomed income, and changing relationships with children and grandchildren.

Unfortunately, there is an erroneous assumption that *senility* and *mental illness* are inevitable and untreatable. On the contrary, the elderly respond well to both individual and group counseling (Atchley, 1988). In addition, even many 90-year-olds show no sign of senility. Senility is by no means an inevitable part of growing old.

Spirituality and Religion

Spirituality and religion are important components in the lives of the elderly—as they are in the lives of people in all age groups. In recent years there has been a renewal of interest, in the social work profession, in recognizing the importance of spirituality and religion.

Religion has been found to be an important factor that promotes emotional well-being in later life. Koenig, George, and Siegler (1988) asked 100 well-educated white women and men, aged 58 to 80, to describe the worst events in their lives and how they dealt with them. Heading the list of coping strategies were behaviors associated with religion—including praying, placing trust and faith in God, getting help and strength from God, having friends from church, participating in church activities, reading the Bible, and receiving help from a minister. Koenig, Kuale, and Ferrel (1988), in a study of 836 older adults, found that people who were religious had higher level of morale, had a better attitude toward aging,

and were more satisfied and less lonely, than those who were not affiliated with any religion. Women and people who were over 75 showed the highest correlations between religion and well-being in this study.

The church has always been important to most African Americans. Elderly African Americans who feel supported by their church tend to have high levels of emotional well-being and to report a higher level of life satisfaction (Coke, 1992).

As people grow older and reflect about death and the meaning of their lives, they are apt to focus more on spiritual matters. Many religious institutions have outreach programs to identify and to offer services to older persons. (Spotlight 15.2 presents information on four prominent world religions, which will help you work with clients from differing spiritual backgrounds.)

❧ Theories of Successful Aging

Three theories about how to age successfully are the activity theory, the disengagement theory, and the social reconstruction syndrome theory.

Activity Theory

The activity theory asserts that the more physically and mentally active people are, the more successfully they will age. Components of this theory were discussed at length in Chapter 14. One component of the theory asserts that

These elderly are praying before the Muslim Day parade on September 25, 1994, at 41st Street and Madison Avenue in New York City.

© Clark Jones

Spotlight on Diversity 15.2 Spirituality and Religion

A major thrust of social work education is to prepare students for a culturally sensitive practice. Since religion and spirituality play important roles in all cultures, it is essential that social workers comprehend the influence of religion and spirituality in human lives. The Educational Policy and Accreditation Standards (2001) of the Council on Social Work Education now require that accredited baccalaureate and master's programs provide practice content in this area, so that students will develop approaches and skills for working with clients with differing spiritual backgrounds.

Spirituality and religion are separate, though often related, dimensions. *Spirituality* can be defined as "the general human experience of developing a sense of meaning, purpose, and morality" (Miley, 1992, p. 2). Key components of spirituality are: the personal search for meaning in life; having a sense of identity (discussed in Chapter 7); and having a value system. In contrast, the term *religion* is used to refer to formal institutional contexts of spiritual beliefs and practices.

Social work has its historical roots in religious organizations. Social work originated under the inspiration of the Judeo-Christian religious traditions of its philanthropic founders. Jewish scriptures and religious law requiring the emulation of God's caring have inspired social welfare activities for many centuries. Similarly, the Christian biblical command to love one's neighbor as oneself has been interpreted as a moral responsibility for social service and inspired the development of charity organizations and philanthropy in the United States during the nineteenth century.

Social workers need to train for an effective practice with religiously oriented clients, as many of the social issues today have religious dimensions—including abortion, use of contraceptives, acceptance of gays and lesbians, cloning, reproductive technology, roles of women, prayer in public schools, and physician-assisted suicide. Social workers need to have an appreciation and respect for religious beliefs that differ from their own chosen beliefs. There is a danger that those who believe that *their* religion is the "one true religion" will tend to view people with divergent religious beliefs as ill-guided, evil, mistaken, or in need of being "saved." More wars have been fought over religious differences than for any other cause.

Furman (1994) notes, "The goal of incorporating religious and spiritual beliefs in social work curricula should include a broad array of knowledge of many different religious and spiritual beliefs, primarily to expand students' understanding and sensitivity" (p. 10). As a beginning effort to move in this direction, this box summarizes information on four prominent world religions: Judaism, Christianity, Islam, and Buddhism. These religions were selected because of their prominence. You should be aware that there are hundreds of religions in the world. Practicing social workers need to have a knowledge and appreciation of the religious beliefs and value systems of their clients.

Judaism

Judaism is the religion of the Jews. Jews believe in one God, the creator of the world. The Hebrew Bible is the primary text of Judaism. (The Hebrew Bible was adopted by Christians as part of their sacred writings, and they now call it the Old Testament.) God is believed to have revealed his law (Torah) to the Jewish people; part of this law was the Ten Commandments, which were given to Moses by God. The Jews believe that God chose them to be a light to all humankind.

Next in importance to the Hebrew Bible is the Talmud, an influential compilation of rabbinic traditions and discussions about Jewish life and law. The Talmud consists of the Mishnah (the codification of the oral Torah) and a collection of early rabbinical commentaries. Various later commentaries and the standard code of Jewish law and ritual (Halakhah), produced in the later Middle Ages, have been important in shaping Jewish practice and thought.

Abraham (who lived roughly 2,000 years before Christ) is viewed as an ancestor or father of the Hebrew people. According to Genesis, he came from the Sumerian town of Ur (now part of modern Iraq) and migrated with his family and flocks via Haran (the ancient city of Nari on the Euphrates) to the "Promised Land" of Canaan, where he settled at Shechem (modern Nablus). After a sojourn in Egypt, he lived to be 175 years old and was buried with his first wife, Sarah. By Sarah he was the father of Isaac (whom he was prepared to sacrifice at the behest of the Lord) and the grandfather of Jacob ("Israel"). By his second wife, Hagar (Sarah's Egyptian handmaiden), he was the father of Ishmael, the ancestor of twelve clans. By his third wife, Keturah, he had six sons who became the ancestors of the Arab tribes. He was also the uncle of Lot. Abraham is regarded by Judaism, Christianity, and Islam as an important ancestor or father of their religion.

All Jews see themselves as members of a community whose origins lie in the time in which Abraham lived. This past lives on in rituals. The family is the basic unit of Jewish ritual, although the synagogue has come to play an increasing important role. The Sabbath, which begins at sunset on Friday and ends at sunset on Saturday, is the central time of religious worship. The synagogue is the center for community worship and study. Its main feature is the "ark" (a cupboard) containing the handwritten scrolls of the Pentateuch (the five books of Moses in the Hebrew Bible, comprising Genesis, Exodus, Leviticus, Numbers, and Deuteronomy). A rabbi is primarily a teacher and a spiritual guide.

There is an annual cycle of religious festivals and days of fasting. The first of these is Rosh Hashanah, the Jewish New Year, which falls in September or October. During this New Year's celebration, a ram's horn is blown as a call to repentance and spiritual renewal. The holiest day in the Jewish year is Yom Kippur, the Day of Atonement, which comes at the end of 10 days of penitence following Rosh Hashanah; Yom Kippur is a day devoted to fasting, prayer, and repentance for past sins. Another important festival is Hanukkah, held in December, commemorating the rededication of Jerusalem after the victory of Judas Maccabees over the Syrians. Pesach is the Passover festival, occurring in March or April, and commemorating the exodus of the Israelites from Egypt; the festival is named after God's passing over the house of Israelites when he killed the first-born children of Egyptian families.

Christianity

Christianity is a religion practiced in numerous countries, centered on the life and work of Jesus of Nazareth, and developing out of Judaism. The earliest followers were Jews, who, after the death and resurrection of Jesus, believed him to be the Messiah or Christ, as promised by the prophets in the Old Testament. He was declared to be the Son of God. During his life he chose 12 men as disciples, who formed the nucleus of the church. This communion of believers believed that Jesus would come again to inaugurate the "Kingdom of God." God is believed to be one in essence but threefold in person, comprising the Father, the Son, and the Holy Spirit or Holy Ghost (known as the Trinity). The Holy Spirit represents the touch or "breath" of God that inspires people to follow the Christian faith. The Bible is thought to have been written under the Holy Spirit's influence.

Jesus Christ was the son of Mary and Joseph, yet also the Son of God, created by a miraculous conception by the spirit of God. He was born in Bethlehem (near Jerusalem), but began his ministry in Nazareth. The main records of his ministry are the New Testament Gospels, which show him proclaiming the coming of the kingdom of God and, in particular, the acceptance of the oppressed and the poor into the kingdom. The duration of his public ministry is uncertain, but from John's Gospel, one gets the impression of a 3-year period of teaching. He was executed by crucifixion under the order of Pontius Pilate, a Roman ruler. The date of his death is uncertain, but is considered to be when Jesus was in his early 30s.

At the heart of the Christian faith is the conviction that through Jesus' death and resurrection, God has allowed humans to find salvation. Belief in Jesus as the Son of God, along with praying for forgiveness of sin, brings forgiveness of all sin. Many Christians believe that those who ask for forgiveness of their sins will join God in heaven, while nonbelievers who do not ask for forgiveness of their sins will be consigned to hell.

The Gospel of Jesus was proclaimed at first by word of mouth, but by the end of the first century A.D., it was written down and became accepted as the authoritative scripture of the New Testament. Through the witness of the 12 earliest leaders (apostles) and their successors, the Christian faith, despite sporadic persecution, spread through the Greek and Roman worlds, and in 315 A.D., was declared by Emperor Constantine to be the official religion of the Roman Empire. It survived the breakup of the empire and the "Dark Ages" of Europe, largely through the work of groups of monks in monasteries in Europe and of the Eastern Christian church headquartered in Constantinople. The religion helped form the basis of civilization in medieval Europe. Since the Middle Ages, major divisions of Western Christianity have formed as a result of differences in doctrine and practice.

Islam

Islam is the Arabic word for "submission" to the will of God, Allah. Islam is also the name of the religion originating in Arabia during the seventh century through the prophet Muhammad. Followers of Islam are known as Muslims, or Moslems.

Muhammad was born in Mecca. He was the son of Abdallah, a poor merchant of the powerful tribe of Quaraysh, hereditary guardians of the shrine of Mecca. Muhammad was orphaned at 6 and raised by his grandfather and uncle. His uncle, Abu Talib, trained him to be a merchant. At the age of 24 he entered the service of a rich widow, Khadijah, whom he eventually married. They had six children. While continuing as a trader, Muhammad became increasingly drawn to religious contemplation. Soon he began to receive revelations of the word of Allah, the one and only God. These revelations given to Muhammad by the angel Gabriel over a period of 20 years, were eventually codified into the Quran (Koran). The Quran commanded that the numerous idols of the shrine should be destroyed and that the rich should give to the poor. This simple message attracted some support but provoked a great deal of hostility from those who felt their interests threatened. When his wife and uncle died, Muhammad was reduced to poverty, but he began making a few converts among the pilgrims to Mecca. Muhammad eventually migrated to Hegira. The name of this town was changed to Medina, "the city of the prophet." This migration marks the beginning of the Muslim era. After a series of battles with warring enemies of Islam, Muhammad was able to take control of Mecca, which recognized him as the chief and prophet. By 360 A.D. he had control over all of Arabia. Two years later he fell ill and died in the home of one of his nine wives. His tomb in the mosque at Medina is venerated throughout Islam.

The religion of Islam embraces every aspect of life. Muslims believe that individuals, societies, and governments should all be obedient to the will of God as set forth in the Quran. The Quran teaches that there is one God who has no partners. He is the Creator of all things and has absolute power over them. All persons should commit themselves to lives of praise-giving and grateful obedience to God, as everyone will be judged on the Day of Resurrection. Those who have obeyed God's commandments will dwell forever in paradise, while those who have sinned against God and have not repented will be condemned eternally to the fires of hell. Since the beginning of time, God has sent prophets (including Abraham, Moses, and Jesus) to provide the guidance necessary for the attainment of an eternal reward.

There are five essential religious duties, known as "the pillars of Islam": (1) the *Shahadah* (profession of faith) is the sincere recitation of the two-fold creed: "There is no god but God" and "Muhammad is the Messenger of God." (2) the *Salat* (formal prayer) must be performed at fixed hours five times a day while facing toward the holy city of Mecca. (3) Alms-giving through the payment of *Zakat* ("purification") is regarded primarily as an act of worship and is the duty of sharing one's wealth out of gratitude for God's favor, according to the uses stated in the Quran. (4) There is a duty to fast (*Saum*) during the month of Ramadan. (Ramadan is the ninth month of the Muslim year; Muslims abstain from eating and drinking between sunrise and sunset.) (5) The pilgrimage (*hajj*) to Mecca is to be performed if at all possible at least once during one's lifetime.

Shariah is the sacred law of Islam, and applies to all aspects of life, not just religious practices. This sacred law is found in the Quran and the *Sunnah* (the sayings and acts of Muhammad).

Buddhism

Buddhism originated in India about 2,500 years ago. The religion derived from the teachings of Buddha (Siddharta Gautama). Buddha is regarded as one of a continuing series of enlightened beings.

Buddha was born the son of the rajah of the Sakya tribe in Kapilavastu, north of Benares. His personal name was Gautama. At about age 30, he left the luxuries of the court, his beautiful wife, and all earthly ambitions. He became an ascetic, and he practiced strict self-denial as a measure of personal and spiritual discipline. After several years of severe austerities, he saw, in meditation and contemplation, the way to enlightenment. For the next 4 decades, he taught, gaining many followers and disciples. He died at Kusinagara in Oudh.

The teachings of Buddha are summarized in the Four Noble Truths, the last of which asserts the existence of a path leading to deliverance from the universal human experience of suffering. A central tenet of Buddhism is the law of Karma, by which good and evil deeds result in appropriate rewards or punishments in this life or in a succession of rebirths. It is believed that the sum of a person's actions is carried forward from one life to the next, leading to an improvement or a deterioration in that person's fate. Through a proper understanding of the law of karma, and by obedience to the right path, humans can break the chain of karma.

The Buddha's path to deliverance is through morality (Sila), meditation (Samadhi), and wisdom (Panna). The goal is Nirvana, which is the "blowing out" of the fires of all desires and the absorption of the self into the infinite. All Buddhas are greatly revered, with a place of special accordance being given to Gautama.

There are two main branches of Buddhism, dating from its earliest history. Theravada Buddhism adheres to the strict and narrow teachings of the early Buddhist writings; in this branch, salvation is possible for only the few who accept the severe discipline and effort to achieve it. Mahayana Buddhism is more liberal and makes concessions to popular piety; it teaches that salvation is possible for everyone. It introduced the doctrine of the bodhisattva (or personal savior). A bodhisattva is one who has attained the enlightenment of a Buddha but chooses not to pass into nirvana and voluntarily remains in the world to help lesser beings attain enlightenment; this view emphasizes charity toward others. Mahayana Buddhism asserts that all living beings have the inner potential of the Buddha nature. The Buddha nature is a kind of a spiritual embryo that holds out the promise to all people that they can eventually become Buddhas because they all have the potential for Buddhahood.

Source: *Dictionary of Beliefs and Religions*, edited by Rosemary Goring (New York: Larousse, 1994).

A volunteer teaches a class in English as a second language. The more physically and mentally active the elderly are, the more successfully they will age.

© Lawrence Migdale

the sexual response can be maintained in later adulthood by being sexually active. There is considerable evidence that being physically and mentally active helps to maintain the physiological, psychological, and intellectual functions of the elderly.

Disengagement Theory

Cummings and Henry (1961) coined the term *disengagement* to refer to a process whereby people respond to aging by gradually withdrawing from the various roles and social relationships they occupied in middle age. Such a disengagement is claimed to be functional for the elderly as they are thought to gradually lose the energy and vitality to sustain all the roles and social relationships they held in younger years.

Societal Disengagement Theory. The disengagement theory refers not only to the elderly withdrawing from society, but also to society withdrawing from the elderly, or *societal disengagement* (Atchley, 1983). It is claimed to be functional for our society (which values competition, efficiency, and individual achievement) to disengage from the elderly, who have the least physical stamina and the highest death rate. Societal disengagement occurs in a variety of ways: employers may seek to force the elderly to retire; the elderly may not be sought out for leadership positions in organizations; their children may involve them less in making family decisions; and the government may be less responsive in meeting their needs as compared to people who are younger. Societal disengagement is often unintended and unrecognized by employers, younger relatives, and other younger members of society. Disengagement theory also asserts that the elderly welcome this withdrawal and contribute to it.

Evaluation of the Disengagement Theory. The disengagement theory has generated considerable research over the years. There is controversy regarding whether disengagement is functional for the elderly and for our society. Research has found that some people do voluntarily disengage as they grow older (Papalia et al., 2001). However, critics assert that disengagement is related less to old age itself than to the factors associated with aging, such as retirement, poor health, death of a spouse and of close friends, and impoverishment. For example, when people are forced to retire, they tend to disengage from coworker friendships, union activities, professional friendships, and reading in their field. Once retired, they also have less money to spend on entertainment, so disengagement from some activities is forced on them.

Disengagement is neither universal nor inevitable. Contrary to the theory's predictions, most older persons maintain extensive associations with friends, and active involvement in voluntary organizations (such as church groups and fraternal organizations). Also, after retiring, some of the elderly develop new interests, expand their circle of friends, join clubs, and do volunteer work. Others rebel against society's stereotypes and refuse to be treated as if they had little to offer to society. Many of these people are marshaling political resources to force society to adapt to their needs and skills.

The disengagement theory at times advocates the exact opposite of the activity theory. The activity theory asserts it is beneficial for the elderly to be physically and mentally active, while the disengagement theory asserts it is beneficial to withdraw from a variety of activities.

Ethical Issues. A severe criticism of the disengagement theory is that it may be used to justify society's failure to help the elderly maintain meaningful roles. It may also be used to justify ageism. The disengagement theory may, at best, be merely a description of the age/youth relationships (and reactions to them), which we should combat as we try to combat ageism.

Social Reconstruction Syndrome Theory

This theory was developed from the *social breakdown syndrome* that was conceptualized by Zusman (1966). Zusman indicated social breakdown occurs for the elderly because of the effects of labeling. Society has unrealistic expectations that all adults should work and be productive; other people label the elderly as incompetent or lacking in some ways; the elderly accept the label and view themselves in terms of the label; they then learn behavior consistent with the label and downplay their previous skills. As a result, they become more dependent and incompetent, and feel inadequate.

Kuypers and Benston (1973) assert that this negative interaction between the elderly's environment and self-concept explains many of the problems of aging in our society. To break the vicious cycle of this labeling process, they recommend the *social reconstruction syndrome,* which includes three major recommendations. First, our society should liberate the elderly from unrealistic standards and expectations. The belief that self-worth depends on a person's productivity has adverse consequences for those who are retired. Kuypers and Benston (1973) recommend that society be reeducated to change these unrealistic standards. Fischer (1977) specifies the direction such reeducation should take:

> The values of our society rest upon a work ethic—an ethic of doing—that gives highest value to people in the prime of their productive years. We should encourage a plurality of ethics in its place—not merely an ethic of doing, but also an ethic of feeling, an ethic of sharing, an ethic of knowing, an ethic of enduring, and even an ethic of surviving. (p. 33)

The second recommendation of Kuypers and Benston (1973) is to provide the elderly with the social services they need. Such services include transportation, medical care, housing, help with housekeeping, and programs that provide physical and mental activity.

The third recommendation is to find creative ways to give the elderly more control over their lives. For example, providing home health services, along with other services, may assist the elderly in living independently and thereby having a sense of control over their lives.

🌿 The Impact of Life Events on the Elderly

We will discuss a number of life events that impact on life in later adulthood. These events directly affect the behavior of the elderly and often limit the alternatives available to them.

Marriage

Because people are living longer, many marriages are lasting longer as well. Today, fiftieth wedding anniversaries are much more common than they were in the past. But divorces are more common, too.

Couples who are still married in their later years are less likely than younger couples to see their marriages as full of problems (Papalia et al., 2001). There could be a variety of reasons. They may well have worked out their major conflicts. Since divorce is now quite accessible, those marriages that survive many years may be the happier and more conflict-free ones. Or, the difference may

be one of development, as people learn to better cope with crises and conflicts.

Being in love is still important for successful marriage in late adulthood (Papalia et al., 2001). Spouses at this age also value open expression of feelings, companionship, respect from one another, and common interests.

Gilford (1986) found that people over age 70 tend to consider themselves less happily married than those aged 63 to 69; perhaps decline in physical health aggravates the strains on marriage. Gilford also found that elderly women tend to be less satisfied with marriage than are elderly men, partly because women generally expect more warmth and intimacy from marriage than men do.

Married elderly people are happier than the unmarried, and considerably happier than the widowed and the divorced. The extent to which elderly people, particularly women, are satisfied with their marriage influences their overall sense of well-being. Health and satisfaction with one's standard of living also positively correlate with an overall sense of well-being. Chronic illness has a negative impact on the morale of couples, even when only one member is ill. The healthy partner may become depressed, angry, or frustrated with the responsibilities of taking care of the ill spouse and maintaining the household. The poor health of one spouse may also reduce the opportunities for enjoyable activities, may drain financial resources, and may reduce sexual involvement. Other crises and life events (such as retirement) can also generate considerable marital turmoil and conflict.

Fiftieth wedding anniversaries are more common now than in the past.

© Lonny Shavelson

Poor health can also lead to role changes in the lives of elderly couples. The spouse who first develops a serious life-threatening illness is usually the husband—as women tend to be younger than their spouses and to live longer. If one spouse develops an illness (such as Alzheimer's disease) where there is progressive deterioration of mental and physical capacities, the other spouse has to take on increasing decision-making and caregiving responsibilities. Gilford (1986) found that spouses (especially wives) who must care for mates with disabilities may experience anger, isolation, and frustration. They are also more apt to develop a chronic illness themselves.

Death of a Spouse

The death of a spouse is traumatic at any age. It is more apt to occur in later adulthood, as death rates are considerably higher in this age group. The surviving spouse faces a variety of emotional and practical problems. The survivor has lost a lover, a companion, a good friend, and a confidant. The more intertwined their lives have become, the deeper the loss is apt to be felt. In most marriages, household maintenance responsibilities are divided. The survivor now finds he or she has a lot more tasks to do, some of which were never learned.

The survivor's social life changes also. At first, relatives, friends, and neighbors usually rally to give the survivor sympathy and emotional support. But gradually they return to their own lives, leaving the widower or widow to form a new life. Friends and relatives are apt to grow tired of listening to the survivor talk about his or her loss and grief, and they may withdraw emotional and practical help. The survivor may have to make such decisions as moving to a smaller place that is easier to maintain, and going to social events alone. Some survivors withdraw because they feel like a "fifth wheel," especially with other couples.

Widowhood

Because women tend to live longer than men, and tend to be younger than their husbands, they are more likely to be widowed. The effects of widowhood are poignantly summarized by a 75-year-old widow, "As long as you have your husband, you're not old. But once you lose him, old age sets in fast" (quoted in Papalia et al., 1992, p. 514).

Widowed people of both sexes have higher rates of depression and mental illness than married people. Men are more likely to die within 6 months of a wife's death, and women are more apt to develop a chronic illness after a husband's death (Papalia et al., 2001).

People who adjust best to widowhood are those who keep busy, perhaps by taking on new, paying positions, or volunteer work or by becoming more deeply involved in other activities (such as seeing friends often or taking part in community programs). Participating in support groups for widowed people is also beneficial (Papalia et al., 2001).

Never Married

Only about 5 percent of older men and women have never been married (U.S. Census Bureau, 2001). Papalia and her associates (2001) cite research indicating that those who have never been married tend to be more independent, have fewer social relationships, and express less concern about their age than older persons who have been married.

Remarriage

Our society has generally opposed the idea of the elderly dating and remarrying. We think of younger people hugging and kissing each other, but such behavior by an elderly couple is often met with stares or crude remarks. Children of the elderly are sometimes opposed to their mother's or father's remarrying. (They may be concerned about inheritance, or they may believe starting a new relationship is being unfaithful to or dishonoring the parent who has died.) Yet, remarriage in later adulthood is increasing (Papalia et al., 2001, p. 701).

For a variety of reasons, our society should change its negative attitude about remarriage in later adulthood. Married elderly people are happier than those who are widowed or divorced. They have companionship, can share interests, provide emotional support, and can assist each other in household maintenance tasks. It is also cost-effective for society to support the single elderly in remarrying as they are then less likely to need financial assistance and social services and are less likely to be placed in nursing homes (Papalia et al., 2001).

Family System Relationships

There is a popular belief that the elderly disengage somewhat from their adult children and their grandchildren. There is also a belief that there is a generation gap (conflict in values) between the elderly and younger family members. These beliefs suggest that the elderly may have strained and somewhat unfavorable family relationships.

Research reviewed by Kail and Cavanaugh (2000), however, suggests that most elderly persons' family relationships are generally quite positive. The findings suggest that family relationships with the elderly are substantially better than generally believed.

In most instances, the elderly and their adult children do not live together for a variety of reasons. Many younger people live in small quarters that make it inconvenient to house another person. The elderly are reluctant to move in as they fear they will have little privacy. They may fear that there will be somebody else's rules to follow and that they may not have visitors when they wish. They may resent having to account to their children for how they spend their time. They may fear their children may put pressure on them to make lifestyle changes, such as giving up smoking, changing their eating habits, and reducing the intake of alcoholic beverages. They may also fear inconveniencing or becoming a burden to their children's families. And, many simply do not want to leave their own home, where they feel comfortable and have pleasant memories.

Although most of the elderly do not live with their children, they tend to live close to them and to see them frequently. Most of the elderly do not want to live with their children. Of the few who do, most are female and widowed (Santrock, 1999).

As discussed earlier, our society's views about the contributions of the elderly are exactly opposite to those held by most primitive societies. In primitive societies the advice and knowledge of the elderly were actively sought, and the elderly usually lived with their children and received needed care. In our society middle-aged adults tend to feel that their first priorities are to meet their own needs and the needs of their children. The fact that many adults would rather see their parents cared for in a nursing home than living with them suggests that they do not feel as great an obligation to their parents as do members of primitive societies. The question of whether to place one's partially incapacitated elderly parent in a nursing home, or to provide care in one's own home, is a question that many middle-aged adults struggle with.

Most older people see their children quite often—an average of once or twice a week. Most older persons feel closer, emotionally, to their children than they did when they were in their middle years. They tend to live near at least one adult child and to help their children in a number of ways. When they need help themselves, their children are the first people they tend to ask for help (Papalia et al., 2001). Older people in good health report feeling close to family members and have frequent contact with their families (Field et al., 1993).

How Parents Help Children. Parents are usually the primary caregivers for adult children who have a mental illness, have a moderate cognitive disability, or who have some other disability. Parents of divorced adults see their children more often after the divorce than they did before, and often take them into their homes.

In a study of 29 healthy, white, midwestern middle-class, and working-class married couples who were aged 60 and over, Greenberg and Becker (1988) found that the subjects' children were a daily topic of conversation. "Although they had left home years ago, these children remained psychologically present in their parents' thoughts and conversations" (p. 789). These parents helped their children in a variety of ways—inviting divorced daughters to live with them, helping care for grandchildren, helping with household projects, paying for treatment for drug abuse, and lending or giving money for a variety of purposes.

Suitor and Pillemer (1988) found that when an adult moves into the home of his or her elderly parents, the parents report that they get along quite well. Such harmony may be explained in at least two ways. People who get along with others are those most likely to choose to live together. In addition, older parents may exaggerate the harmony in an effort to make reality match their wishes. When parents and children do *not* get along very well, the parents' marriage is sometimes adversely affected. Grandparents who are providing care to their grandchildren or to their adult children refute the societal myth that older adults are freed from active parenting and its stresses.

Grandparenthood

Neugarten and Weinstein (1964) identified five major styles of grandparenting in our society. The *fun seeker* is a playmate to the grandchildren in a mutual relationship that both enjoy. The *distant figure* has periodic contact with the grandchildren, generally on birthdays and holidays, but is quite uninvolved with their lives. The *surrogate parent* assumes considerable caretaking responsibilities, usually because the grandchildren's parents are working, or because the mother is single and working. The *formal figure* leaves all child-rearing responsibilities to the parents and limits his or her involvement with the grandchildren to providing special treats and occasional babysitting. The *reservoir of family wisdom* takes on an authoritarian role and dispenses special resources and skills.

The tacit "norm of noninterference" by grandparents tends to evaporate in times of trouble faced by their adult children and their grandchildren. Grandparents tend to perform the role of family "watchdogs." They stay on the fringes of the lives of their children and grandchildren, with varying degrees of involvement. During times of crisis (such as serious illness, money problems, or divorce), they tend to become much more involved by stepping in and playing more active roles. During good times they are less involved, but they are still watching.

Some gender differences have been found to exist in the degree of grandparenting. Cherlin and Furstenberg (1986) found that grandmothers tend to have closer and warmer relationships with their grandchildren and are more apt to serve as surrogate parents than are grandfathers. The same study also found that the mother's parents are likely to be closer to the grandchildren than the father's parents and are more apt to become involved during a crisis. Thomas (1986) found that grandmothers tend to be more satisfied with grandparenting than are grandfathers.

Great-Grandparenthood

Because the elderly are living longer, four and even five generations of families are becoming more common. Future research will need to focus on the relationships that develop. An exploratory study by Doka and Mertz (1988) indicates that great-grandparents view great-grandchildren as a source of diversion and as evidence of their own longevity and of their family's renewal and continued survival.

Because of age, declining health, and the scattering of families, great-grandparents tend to be less involved than grandparents in a child's life. The great-grandparents who have the most intimate connections with their great-grandchildren are those who live nearby; such great-grandparents often help their grandchildren and great-grandchildren with gifts, loans, and baby-sitting.

❧ Guidelines for Positive Psychological Preparation for Later Adulthood

Growing old is a lifelong process. Becoming 65 does not destroy the continuity of what a person has been, is now, and will be. Recognition of this fact should lessen the fear of growing old. For those who are financially secure and in good health, and who have prepared thoughtfully, later adulthood can be a period of at least reasonable pleasure and comfort, if not luxury.

Some may be able to start small home businesses, based on their hobbies, or become involved in meaningful activities with churches and other organizations. Others may relax while fishing or slowly traveling around the country. Still others may continue to pursue such interests as gardening, woodworking, reading, needlework, painting, weaving, and photography.

Our lives depend largely on our goals and our efforts to achieve these goals. How we live prior to retiring will largely determine whether later adulthood will be a nightmare or will be gratifying and fulfilling. The importance of being physically and mentally active throughout life was discussed in Chapter 14. Here are some factors that are closely related to satisfaction in later adulthood:

1. *Close personal relationships.* Having close relationships with others is important throughout life. The elderly who have close friends are more satisfied with life. Practically everyone needs a person to whom one can confide one's private thoughts or feelings. The elderly who have a confidant are better able to handle the trials and tribulations of aging. Through sharing their deepest concerns, people are able to ventilate their feelings and to talk about their problems and possibly arrive at some strategies for handling such problems. Those who are married are more likely than the widowed to have confidants, and the widowed are more likely to have confidants than those who have never married. For those who are married, the spouse is apt to be the confidant, especially for the men.

2. *Finances.* Health and income are two factors closely related to life satisfaction in later adulthood. When people feel good and have money, they can be more active. Those who are active—who go out to eat, go to meetings or museums, go to church, go on picnics, or travel—are happier than those who tend to stay at home. Saving money for later years is important, and so is learning to manage or budget money wisely.

3. *Interests and hobbies.* Psychologically, people who are traumatized most by retirement are those whose self-image and life interests center on their work. People who have meaningful hobbies and interests look forward to retirement in order to have sufficient time for these activities.

4. *Self-identity.* People who are comfortable and realistic about who they are and what they want from life are better prepared to deal with stresses and crises that arise.

5. *Looking toward the future.* A person who dwells on the past or rests on past achievements is apt to find the older years depressing. On the other hand, a person who looks to the future generally has interests that are alive and growing and is therefore able to find new challenges and new satisfaction in later years. Looking toward the future involves planning for retirement, including deciding where you would like to live, in what type of housing and

community, and what you look forward to doing with your free time.

6. *Coping with crises.* If a person learns to cope effectively with crises in younger years, these coping skills will remain useful when a person is older. Effective coping is learning to approach problems realistically and constructively.

🌿 Grief Management and Death Education

In the remainder of this chapter, we will discuss reactions to death in our society, including social work roles in grief management and guidelines for relating to a dying person and to survivors.

Death in Our Society: The Impact of Social Forces

People in primitive societies handle death better than we do. They are more apt to view death as a natural occurrence, partly because they have a shorter life expectancy. They also frequently see friends and relatives die. Because they view death as a natural occurrence, they are better prepared to handle the death of loved ones. (Spotlight 15.3 illustrates the cultural-historical context of death and bereavement.)

In our society we tend to shy away from thinking about death. The terminally ill generally die in institutions (hospitals and nursing homes), away from their homes. Therefore, we are seldom exposed to people dying. Many people in our society seek to avoid thinking about death. They avoid going to funerals and avoid conversations about death. Many people live as if they believe they will live indefinitely.

We need to become comfortable with the idea of our own eventual death. If we do that, we will be better prepared for the deaths of close friends and relatives. We will also then be better prepared to relate to the terminally ill and to help survivors who have experienced the death of a close friend or relative.

Funerals are needed for survivors. Funerals help initiate the grieving process so that people can work through their grief. (Delaying the grieving process may intensify the eventual grief.) For some, funerals also serve the function of demonstrating that the person is dead. If survivors do not actually see the dead body, some may mystically believe that the person is still alive. For example, John F. Kennedy was assassinated in 1963 and had a closed-casket funeral. Because the body was not shown, rumors abounded for many years that he was still alive.

The sudden death of a young person is more difficult to cope with, for three reasons. First, we do not have time to prepare for the death. Second, we feel the loss as more severe because we feel the person is missing out on many of the good things in life. Third, we do not have the opportunity to obtain a sense of "closure" in the relationship; we may feel we did not have the opportunity to tell the person how we felt about him or her, or we did not

Spotlight on Diversity 15.3 — The Cultural-Historical Context of Death and Bereavement

Cultural customs concerning the disposal and remembrance of the dead, the transfer of possessions, and even expressions of grief vary greatly from culture to culture. Often, religious or legal prescriptions about these topics reflect a society's view of what death is and what happens afterward.

In ancient Greece, bodies of heroes were publicly burned as a symbol of honor. Public cremation is still practiced by Hindus in India and Nepal. In contrast, cremation is prohibited under Orthodox Jewish law, as it is believed that the dead will rise again for a "last judgment" and the chance for eternal life. To this day, some of the Polynesians that live in the Tahitian Islands bury their parents in the front yard of their parents' home as a way of remembering them.

In Malayan society (which prospered several centuries ago in Mexico and Central America), death was seen as a gradual transition. At first a body was given only a provisional burial. Survivors continued to perform mourning rites until the body decayed to the point where it was thought the soul left it and transcended into the spiritual realm.

In Japan, religious rituals expect survivors to maintain contact with the deceased. Families keep an altar in their homes that is dedicated to their ancestors; they offer them cigars and food and talk to the altar as if they were talking to their deceased loved ones. In contrast, the Hopi (Native American tribe) fear the spirits of the deceased and try to forget, as quickly as possible, those who have died.

Some modern cultural customs have evolved from ancient ones. The current practice of embalming, for example, evolved from the *mummification* practice in ancient Egypt and China (about 3,000 years ago) that was designed to preserve a body so that the soul could eventually return to it.

get the opportunity to resolve interpersonal conflicts. (Because the grieving process is intensified when closure does not occur, it is advisable to actively work toward closure in the relationships we have with others.)

Children should not be sheltered from death. They should be taken to funerals of relatives and friends and their questions answered honestly. It is a mistake to say, "Grandmother has gone on a trip and won't be back." The child will wonder if others who are close will also go on a trip and won't come back; or, the child may be puzzled about why grandmother won't return from the trip. It is much better to explain to children that death is a natural process. It is desirable to state that death is unlikely to occur until a person is elderly, but that there are exceptions—such as an automobile accident. Parents who take their children to funerals almost always find the children handle the funeral better than they expected. Funerals help children learn that death is a natural process.

It is generally a mistake for survivors to seek to appear strong and emotionally calm following the death of a close friend or relative. Usually such survivors want to avoid dealing with their loss, and there is a danger that when they do start grieving they will experience intense grief—partly because they will feel guilty about denying that they are hurting, and partly because they will feel guilty because they deemphasized (by hiding their pain and feelings) the importance of the person who died.

Many health professionals (such as medical doctors) find death difficult to handle. Health professionals are committed to healing. When someone is found to have a terminal illness, health professionals are apt to experience a sense of failure. In some cases they experience guilt because they cannot do more, or because they might have made a mistake that contributed to a terminal illness. Therefore, do not be too surprised if you find that some health professionals do not know what to say or do when confronted by terminal illness.

The Grieving Process

Nearly all of us are currently grieving about some loss that we have had. It might be the end of a romantic relationship, or moving away from friends and parents, or the death of a pet, or failing to get a grade we wanted, or the death of someone.

It is a mistake to believe that grieving over a loss should end in a set amount of time. The normal grieving process is often the life span of the griever. When we first become aware of a loss of great important to us, we are apt to grieve intensively—by crying or by being depressed. Gradually, we will have hours, then days, then weeks, then months where we will not think about the loss and will not grieve. However, there will always be something that reminds us of the loss (such as anniversaries), and we will again grieve. The intense grieving periods will, however, gradually become shorter in duration, occur less frequently, and gradually decrease in intensity.

Two models of the grieving process will be presented here: the Kübler-Ross (1969) model and the Westberg (1962) model. Some people believe the Kübler-Ross model better describes the grieving process, while others assert that the Westberg model does. These models help us to understand the grief we feel from *any* loss.

The Kübler-Ross Model

Stage One: Denial. During this stage, in the Kübler-Ross model, we tell ourselves, "No, this can't be. There must be a mistake. This just isn't happening." Denial is often functional as it helps cushion the impact of the loss.

Stage Two: Rage and Anger. During this stage we tell ourselves, "Why me? This just isn't fair!" For example, terminally ill patients resent the fact that they will soon die while other people remain healthy and alive. During this stage God is sometimes a target of the anger. The terminally ill, for example, blame God as unfairly imposing a death sentence.

Stage Three: Bargaining. During this stage people with a loss attempt to strike bargains to regain all or part of the loss. For example, the terminally ill may bargain with God for more time. They promise to do something worthwhile or to be good in exchange for another month or year of life. Kübler-Ross indicates that even agnostics and atheists sometimes attempt to bargain with God during this stage.

Stage Four: Depression. During this stage those having a loss tell themselves, "The loss is true, and it's really sad. This is awful. How can I go on with life?"

Stage Five: Acceptance. During this stage the person fully acknowledges the loss. Survivors accept the loss and begin working on alternatives to cope with the loss and to minimize its impact.

The Westberg Model

Shock and Denial. According to the Westberg model, many people, when informed of a tragic loss, are so numb, and in a state of such shock, that they are practically devoid of feelings. It could well be that when emotional pain is unusually intense, a person's response system experiences "overload" and temporarily "shuts down," so that he or she feels hardly anything, and the person then acts as if nothing has happened. Such denial is a way of avoiding the impact of a tragic loss.

Emotions Erupt. As the realization of the loss becomes evident, the person expresses the pain by crying, screaming, or sighing.

Anger. At some point a person usually experiences anger. The anger may be directed at God for causing the loss. The anger may be partly due to the unfairness of the loss. If the loss involves the death of a loved one, there is often anger at the dead person for what is termed "desertion."

Illness. Since grief produces stress, stress-related illnesses are apt to develop, such as colds, flu, an ulcer, tension headaches, diarrhea, rashes, insomnia, and so on.

Panic. Because the grieving person realizes he or she does not feel like the "old self," the person may panic and worry about going insane. Nightmares, unwanted emotions that appear uncontrollable, physical reactions, and difficulties in concentrating on day-to-day responsibilities—these contribute to the panic.

Guilt. The grieving person may blame himself or herself for having done something that contributed to the loss, or feel guilty for not doing something that might have prevented the loss.

Depression and Loneliness. At times the grieving person is apt to feel very sad about the loss and also has feelings of isolation and loneliness. The grieving person may withdraw from others, who are viewed as not being supportive or understanding.

Reentry Difficulties. At this point the grieving person makes efforts to put his or her life back together. Reentry problems are apt to arise: the person may resist letting go of attachments to the past, and loyalties to memories may hamper the pursuing of new interests and activities.

Hope. Gradually, hopes of putting one's life back together return and begin to grow.

Affirming Reality. The grieving person puts his or her life back together again, and the old feeling of having control of one's life returns. The reconstructed life is not the same as the old, and memories of the loss remain. However, the reconstructed life is satisfactory. The grieving person resolves that life will go on.

Figure 15.1 is a graphic representation of the Westberg model.

Evaluation of Models of the Grieving Process. Kübler-Ross and Westberg note that some people continue grieving and never do reach the final stage (the acceptance stage in the Kübler-Ross model, and the affirming reality stage in the Westberg model). Kübler-Ross and Westberg also caution that it is a mistake to rigidly believe everyone will progress through these stages as diagrammed. There is often considerable movement back and forth in these stages. For example, in the Kübler-Ross model, a person may go from denial and depression, to anger and rage, then back to denial; then to bargaining; then again to depression, and back to anger and rage, and so on.

How to Cope with Grief. The following suggestions are given to help those who are grieving:

- Crying is an acceptable and valuable expression of grief. Cry when you feel the need. Crying releases tension that is part of grieving.

- Talking about your loss, and about your plans, is very constructive. Sharing your grief with friends, family, the clergy, a hospice volunteer, or a professional counselor is advisable. You may seek to become involved with a group of others having

Figure 15.1 Westberg Model of the Grieving Process

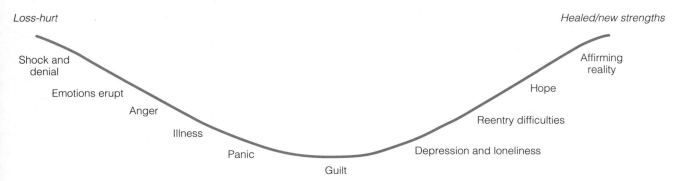

Loss-hurt

Shock and denial

Emotions erupt

Anger

Illness

Panic

Guilt

Depression and loneliness

Reentry difficulties

Hope

Affirming reality

Healed/new strengths

similar experiences. Talking about your grief eases loneliness, allows you to ventilate your feelings. Talking with close friends gives you a sense of security and brings you closer to others you love. Talking with others who have similar losses helps put your problems into perspective. You will see you are not the only one with problems, and you will feel good about yourself when you assist others in handling their losses.

- Death often causes us to examine and question our faith or philosophy of life. Do not become concerned if you begin questioning your beliefs. Talk about them. For many, a religious faith provides help in accepting the loss.

- Writing out a rational self-analysis on your grief will help you to identify irrational thinking that is contributing to your grief (see Chapter 8). Once any irrational thinking is identified, you can relieve much of your grief through rational challenges to your irrational thinking.

- Try not to dwell on how unhappy you feel. Become involved and active in life around you. Do not waste your time and energy on self-pity.

- Seek to accept the inevitability of death—yours and that of others.

- If the loss is the death of a loved one, holidays and the anniversaries of your loved one's birth and death can be stressful. Seek to spend these days with family and friends who will give you support.

- You may feel that you have nothing to live for and may even think about suicide. Understand that many people who encounter severe losses feel this way. Seek to find assurance in the fact that a sense of purpose and meaning will return.

- Intense grief is very stressful. Stress is a factor that leads to a variety of illnesses, such as headaches, colitis, ulcers, colds, and flu. If you become ill, seek a physician's help, and tell him or her that your illness may be related to grief you are experiencing.

- Intense grief may also lead to sleeplessness, sexual difficulties, loss of appetite, or overeating. If a loved one has died, do not be surprised if you dream the person is still alive. You may find you have little energy and cannot concentrate. All of these reactions are "normal." Do not become worried that you are going crazy or losing your mind. Seek to take a positive view. Eat a balanced diet, get ample rest, and exercise moderately. Every person's grief

is individual—if you are experiencing unusual physical reactions (such as nightmares) try not to become overly alarmed.

- Medication should be taken sparingly and only under the supervision of a physician. Avoid trying to relieve your grief with alcohol or other drugs. Many drugs are addictive and may stop or delay the necessary grieving process.

- Recognize that guilt, real or imagined, is a normal part of grief. Survivors often feel guilty about things they said or did, or feel guilty about things they think they should have said or done. If you are experiencing intense guilt, it is helpful to share it with friends or with a professional counselor. It might also be helpful to write a rational self-analysis of the guilt (see Chapter 8). Learn to forgive yourself. All humans make mistakes.

- You may find that friends and relatives appear to be shunning you. If this is happening, they probably are uncomfortable around you as they do not know what to say or do. Take the initiative and talk with them about your loss. Inform them about ways in which you would like them to be supportive of you.

- If possible, put off making major decisions (changing jobs, moving) until you become more emotionally relaxed. When you're highly emotional, you're more apt to make undesirable decisions.

Application of Grief Management Theory to Client Situations

Most people are grieving about one or more losses—the end of a romantic relationship, the death of a pet, or the death of a loved one. Social workers may take on a variety of roles in the areas of grief management and death education: They can be *initiators* of educational programs in schools, churches, and elsewhere for the general public. They can be *counselors* in a variety of settings (including hospices, nursing homes, and hospitals) in which they work, on a one-to-one basis, with the terminally ill and with survivors. They can be group *facilitators* and lead grief management groups (including bereavement groups for survivors) in settings such as hospitals, hospices, mental health clinics, and schools. They may also serve as *brokers* in linking individuals who are grieving, or who have unrealistic views about death and dying, with appropriate community resources.

In order for social workers to be effective in these roles, they need to become comfortable with the idea of their own eventual death. They also need to develop skills

When a person's spouse dies, he or she is apt to feel sad, lonely, and isolated. Gradually, the grieving person reaches out to others.

for relating to the terminally ill and to survivors. The following sections summarize some guidelines in these areas. The material is useful not only for social workers but also for anyone (including yourself) who has contact with a dying person or with survivors.

How to Relate to a Dying Person

First, you need to accept the idea of your own eventual death and view death as a normal process. If you cannot accept your own death, you will probably be uncomfortable talking to someone who is terminally ill and will not be able to discuss the concerns that the dying person has in an understanding and positive way. The questions in Highlight 15.1 will help you assess your attitudes toward the reality of death.

Second, convey verbally that you are willing to talk about any concerns that the other person has. Touching or hugging the dying person is very helpful. Remember the person has a right not to talk about concerns if he or she so chooses. What you want to convey is that you are emotionally ready and supportive, that you care, and that you are available.

Third, answer the dying person's questions as honestly as you can. If you do not know an answer, seek out a person who will accurately provide the requested information. Evasion or ambiguity, in response to a dying person's questions, only increases his or her concerns. If there is a

chance for recovery, this should be mentioned. Even a small margin of hope can be a comfort. Do not, however, exaggerate the chances for recovery.

Fourth, a dying person should be allowed to accept the reality of the situation at his or her own pace. Relevant information should not be volunteered, nor should it be withheld. People who have a terminal illness have a right to have access to all the relevant information. A useful question that may assist a dying person is, "Do you want to talk about it?"

Fifth, if people around the dying person are able to accept the death, the dying person is helped to accept the death. Therefore, it is therapeutic to help close family members and friends to accept the death. Remember, they may have a number of concerns that they want to share, and they may need help to do this.

Sixth, if you do have trouble about certain subjects involving death, inform the dying person of your limitations. This takes the guesswork out of the relationship.

Seventh, the religious or philosophical viewpoint of the dying person should be respected. Your own personal views should not be imposed.

How to Relate to Survivors

These suggestions are similar to the suggestions on relating to a dying person. It is very helpful to become accepting of the idea of your own death. If you are comfortable about your own death, you will be better able to calmly listen to the concerns being expressed by survivors.

It is helpful to initiate the first encounter with a survivor by saying something like, "I'm sorry," and then touching or hugging the person. Then convey that if he or she wants to talk or needs help, you're available. Take your lead from what the survivor expresses. You should seek to convey that you care, that you share his or her loss, and that you're available if he or she wants to talk.

It is helpful to use active listening with both survivors and persons who are terminally ill. In using active listening, the receiver of a message feeds back only what he or she feels was the intent of the sender's message. In using this approach, the receiver does *not* send a message of his or her own—such as a question, giving advice, personal feelings, or an opinion.

It is frequently helpful to share with a survivor pleasant and positive memories you have about the person who has died. This conveys that you sincerely care about and miss the deceased person and also that the deceased person's life had positive meaning. Relating your memories will often focus the survivor's thoughts on pleasant and positive memories of his or her own.

Highlight 15.1

Questions about Grief, Death, and Dying

Arriving at answers to these questions is one way to work toward becoming more confortable with your own eventual death.

1. Which of the following describe your present conception of death?
   a. Cessation of all mental and physical activity
   b. Death as sleep
   c. Heaven-and-hell concept
   d. A pleasant afterlife
   e. Death as being mysterious and unknown
   f. The end of all life for you
   g. A transition to a new beginning
   h. A joining of the spirit with an unknown cosmic force
   i. Termination of this physical life with survival of the spirit
   j. Something other than what is on this list

2. Which of the following aspects of your own death do you find distasteful?
   a. What might happen to your body after death
   b. What might happen to you if there is a life after death
   c. Concerns about what might happen to your dependents
   d. The grief that it would cause to your friends and relatives
   e. The pain you may experience as you die

   f. The deterioration of your body before you die
   g. All your plans and projects coming to an end
   h. Something other than what is on this list

3. If you could choose, what age would you like to be when you die?

4. When you think of your own eventual death, how do you feel?
   a. Depressed
   b. Fearful
   c. Discouraged
   d. Purposeless
   e. Angry
   f. Pleasure in being alive
   g. Resolved as you realize death is a natural process of living
   h. Other (specify)

5. For what, or for whom, would you be willing to sacrifice your life?
   a. An idea or moral principle
   b. A loved one
   c. In combat
   d. An emergency where another life could be saved
   e. Not for any reason

6. If you could choose, how would you prefer to die?
   a. A sudden, violent death
   b. A sudden but nonviolent death

Continue to visit the survivors if they show interest in such visits. It is also helpful to express your caring and support through a card, a little gift, or a favorite casserole. If a survivor is unable to resume the normal functions of living, or remains deeply depressed, suggest seeking professional help. Joining a survivor's self-help group is another possible suggestion.

The religious or philosophical viewpoint of survivors should be respected. You should not seek to impose your views on the survivors.

How to Become Comfortable with the Idea of Your Own Eventual Death

Perhaps the main reason people are uncomfortable about death is that in our culture we are socialized to avoid seeing death as a natural process. We would be more comfortable with the idea of our own death if we would more openly talk about it and actively seek answers to questions and concerns that we have. Comfort with the idea of our own death helps us be more supportive in relating to and understanding those who are dying. If you are uncomfortable about death, including your own eventual death, there are a number of suggestions for things you can do to become more comfortable.

Identify what your concerns are and then seek answers to these concerns. A number of excellent books provide information on a wide range of subjects involving death and dying. Many colleges, universities, and organizations provide workshops and courses on death and dying. If you have intense fears related to death and dying, you may consider talking to authorities in the field, such as professional counselors, or to clergy with experience and training in grief counseling.

c. A quiet and dignified death

d. Death in the line of duty

e. Suicide

f. Homicide victim

g. Death after you have achieved your life goals

h. Other (specify)

7. If it were possible, would you want to know the exact date on which you would die?

8. Would you want to know if you had a terminal illness?

9. If you had 6 more months to live, how would you want to spend the time?

   a. By satisfying hedonistic desires such as sex

   b. By withdrawing

   c. By contemplating or praying

   d. By seeking to prepare loved ones for your death

   e. By completing projects and tying up loose ends

   f. By considering suicide

   g. Other (specify)

10. Have you seriously contemplated suicide? What are your moral views of suicide? Are there circumstances under which you would take your life?

11. If you had a serious illness and the quality of your life had substantially deteriorated, what measures do you believe should be taken to keep you alive?

    a. All possible heroic medical efforts should be taken

    b. Medical efforts should be discontinued when there is practically no hope of returning to a life with quality

    c. Other (specify)

12. If you are married, would you prefer to outlive your spouse? Why?

13. How important do you believe funerals and grief rituals are for survivors?

14. If it were up to you, how would you like to have your body disposed of after you die?

    a. Cremation

    b. Burial

    c. Donation of your body to a medical school or to science

    d. Other (specify)

15. What kind of funeral would you prefer?

    a. A church service

    b. As large as possible

    c. Small with only close friends and relatives present

    d. A lavish funeral

    e. A simple funeral

    f. Whatever your survivors want

    g. Other (specify)

16. Have you made a will? Why or why not?

17. Were you able to arrive at answers to most of these questions? Were you uncomfortable in answering these questions? If you were uncomfortable, what were you feeling, and what made you uncomfortable? For the questions you do not have answers to, how might you arrive at answers?

Taboos against talking about death and dying need to be broken in our society. You may find that tactfully initiating discussions about death and dying with friends and relatives will be helpful to you, and to people close to you.

It is probably accurate that we will never become fully accepting of the idea of our own death, but we can learn a lot more about the subject and obtain answers to many of the questions and concerns we have. In talking about death, it is advisable to avoid using euphemisms such as "passed on," "gone to heaven," and "taken by the Lord." It is much better to be accurate and say the person has died. Using euphemisms gives an unrealistic impression of death and is part of an avoidance approach to facing death. Fortunately, an open-communications approach about death is emerging in our society.

Additional ways to become more informed about death and dying are: attending funerals; watching quality films and TV programs that cover aspects of dying; providing support to friends or relatives who are terminally ill; being supportive to survivors; talking to people who do grief counseling to learn about their approach; keeping a journal of your thoughts and concerns related to death and dying; and planning the details of your own funeral. Some persons move toward becoming more comfortable with their own death by studying the research that has been conducted on near-death experiences, as described in Highlight 15.2.

Mwalimu Imara (1975) views dying as having a potential for being the final stage of growth. Learning to accept death is similar to learning to accept other losses—such as the breakup of a romantic relationship or leaving a job we cherished. If we learn to accept and grow from the losses we encounter, such experiences will help us in facing the deaths of loved ones and our own eventual death.

Highlight 15.2

Life after Life

Raymond Moody (1975) interviewed a number of people who had near-death experiences. These people had been pronounced clinically dead, but, then shortly afterward, were revived. Moody provides the following composite summary of typical experiences that are being reported. (It is important to bear in mind that the following narrative is not a representation of any one person's experience; rather, it is a composite of the common elements found in many accounts.)

A man is dying and, as he reaches the point of greatest physical stress, he hears himself pronounced dead by his doctor. He begins to hear an uncomfortable noise, a loud ringing or buzzing, and at the same time feels himself moving very rapidly through a long dark tunnel. After this, he suddenly finds himself outside of his own physical body, but still in the immediate physical environment, and he sees his own body from a distance, as though he is a spectator. He watches the resuscitation attempt from his unusual vantage point and is in a state of emotional upheaval.

After a while, he collects himself and becomes more accustomed to his odd condition. He notices that he still has a "body," but one of a very different nature and with very different powers from the physical body he has left behind. Soon other things begin to happen. Others come to meet and to help him. He glimpses the spirits of relatives and friends who have already died, and a loving, warm spirit of a kind he has never encountered before—being of light—appears before him. This being asks him a question, nonverbally, to make him evaluate his life and helps him along by showing him a panoramic, instantaneous playback of the major events of his life. At some point he finds himself approaching some sort of barrier or border, apparently representing the limit between earthly life and the next life. Yet, he finds that he must go back to the earth, that the time for his death has not yet come. At this point he resists, for by now he is taken up with his experiences in the afterlife and does not want to return. He is overwhelmed by his intense feelings of joy, love, and peace. Despite his attitude, though, he somehow reunites with his body and lives.*

Later he tries to tell others, but he has trouble doing so. In the first place, he can find no human words adequate to describe this unearthly episode. He also finds that others scoff, so he stops telling other people. Still, the experience affects his life profoundly, especially his views about death and its relationship to life.

No one is sure why such experiences are being reported. A variety of explanations have been suggested (Siegel, 1981). One is that it suggests there may be a pleasant afterlife. This explanation gives comfort to those who dislike seeing death as an absolute end. Another explanation, however, is that these near-death experiences are nothing more than hallucinations triggered by chemicals released by the brain or induced by lack of oxygen to the brain. Scientists involved with near-death research acknowledge that so far there is no conclusive evidence that these near-death experiences prove there is life after death.

Source: Raymond A. Moody, Jr., *Life after Life* (New York: Bantam Books, 1975), pp. 21–23. Reprinted by permission of the copyright owner, Mockingbird Books, St. Simon's Island, GA.

Having a well-developed sense of identity (that is, who we are and what we want out of life) is an important step in learning to become comfortable with our own eventual death. If we have a well-developed blueprint of what will give meaning and direction to our lives, we are emotionally better prepared to accept the fact that we will eventually die.

❧ Summary

A number of psychological, developmental adjustments must be made by the elderly, such as adjusting to retirement and lower income and to changing physical strength and health. Theoretical concepts about developmental tasks in later adulthood include: integrity versus despair; shifting from work-role preoccupation to self-differentiation; shifting from body preoccupation to body transcendence; shifting from self-occupation to self-transcendence; conducting a life review; the importance of self-esteem; the significance of having a high level of life satisfaction; the negative effects of low status and ageism; the prevalence of depression and other emotional problems; and the significance of spirituality and religion.

Three theories of successful aging are: the activity theory, the disengagement theory, and the social reconstruction syndrome theory. Suggestions for positive psychological preparations by younger adults for later adulthood include: forming close personal relationships, preparing financially, having interests and hobbies, forming a positive self-identity, looking toward the future, learning to cope with crises, and learning to cope with death.

The chapter ends with guidelines on grief management and death education, relating to a dying person, relating to survivors, and becoming more comfortable with the idea of one's own eventual death.

Infotrac College Edition Keywords

activity theory	ageism	disengagement theory	grief management
African American elderly	death customs	elderly/depression	spirituality

On the Internet

Asociacion Nacional Pro Personas Mayores

http://www.aoa.gov/directory/139.html

Asociacion Nacional Pro Personas Mayores (ANPPM) is a national, private, nonprofit organization that focuses on the needs of older Hispanic people and other low-income elderly as a way of bringing about social change that will impact the Hispanic community and the nation.

Beyond Indigo

http://www.death-dying.com/index.php

Provides the most updated information available regarding issues surrounding the death and dying process.

Hospice Net

http://www.hospicenet.org/

For patients and families facing life-threatening illness.

National Caucus and Center on Black Aged, Inc.

www.ncba-aged.org

The National Caucus and Center on the Black Aged (NCBA) is a nonprofit organization dedicated to improving the quality of life of the Black elderly.

National Resource Center on Native American Aging

http://www.und.nodak.edu/dept/nrenaa

The National Resource Center on Native American Aging serves the elderly Native American population of the United States. The center is committed to increasing awareness of issues affecting American Indian. Alaskan Native, and Native Hawaiian elders, and to being a voice and advocate for their concerns.

CHAPTER 16

Social Systems and Their Impacts on Later Adulthood

On July 14, 1996, David Pearsall had his seventieth birthday, and it was a day to remember. It was not only his birthday but also his last day of work at the company he worked for, Quality Printers. That evening, the owners of Quality Printers gave a retirement party for Dave. He received a gold watch, and the owners and many of his fellow printers gave testimonial speeches about how much Dave had contributed to the morale and productivity of the company. Dave was deeply honored, and tears occasionally came to his eyes.

Dave felt strange waking up the next morning. He was used to getting up early to go to work. Work had become the center of his life. He even socialized with his fellow printers. This morning he had nothing planned and nothing to do. He lay in bed thinking about what the future would hold for him. Dave had generally muddled through life. His father had helped him obtain a position as a printer, and Dave seldom gave much attention to planning for the future. For example, while he thought it would be nice to retire, he had given little consideration to it.

Dave got up, looked in a mirror, and noticed his thinning, gray hair, the wrinkles on his face and hands, and the tire around his waist. In concluding that the best part of his life had passed by, he anxiously wondered what the future would hold for him, and he contemplated what he should do with all of his time—he had no idea.

For the next few weeks, he followed his wife, Jeanette, around the house. Dave began giving Jeanette suggestions on how she could be more efficient and productive around the house. After a few weeks of such advice, Jeanette angrily told Dave to "get off her back." He visited the print shop where he used to work but soon realized everyone was too busy to spend time talking with him. He also stopped socializing with these printers, since they tended to talk about work. He felt useless. As the months went by, he spent most of his time *sitting at home and watching TV. Occasionally, he went to a neighborhood bar, where he drank to excess.*

Dave and his wife never gave much attention to long-range financial planning. They both had worked for many years and tended to spend their paychecks shortly after they received them. When they bought their house in 1991, they gave little thought to how they would make their mortgage payments after retiring. Dave had hoped the Social Security system would take care of his bills.

Dave and Jeanette were in for a shock when they retired. The monthly Social Security checks were much less than they had anticipated. They stopped going out to eat, to movies, and to ballgames. A few months after Dave retired, they realized they no longer could make the mortgage payments. They put the house up for sale and sold it 4½ months later, at a price lower than what the house was worth. Both were sad about leaving their home, but financially they had no other choice. They moved into a two-bedroom apartment. Both became even more inactive, as they no longer had yard work and now had fewer home maintenance tasks. One neighbor frequently played a stereo late into the night, and the Pearsalls had trouble sleeping.

In February 1998, Jeanette had a major heart attack. She was in the hospital for nearly two weeks and was then placed in a nursing home. Dave missed the companionship of his wife and became deeply depressed. He wished she could come home, but her medical needs wouldn't allow that, so he visited her every day. Since Dave had never learned to cook much, and because he was depressed, his diet consisted mainly of cheese sandwiches and TV dinners. In November 1998, Jeanette died of another heart attack.

Dave now became even more depressed. He no longer shaved or bathed. He no longer cleaned his apartment, and neighbors began to complain about the odors. Dave gave up the will to live. He seldom heard from his son, Donald, who was living in a distant city. Dave sought to drown his unhappiness in whiskey. One night, in January 2003, he passed out in his apartment with a lighted cigarette in his hand, which set his couch on fire. Dave died of smoke inhalation.

Dave's later years raise some questions for our society. Have we abandoned the elderly to a meaningless existence? Is it a mistake for the elderly to count on the Social Security system to meet their financial needs when they retire? How can our society provide a more meaningful role for the elderly?

A PERSPECTIVE

This chapter will focus on the social problems encountered by the elderly. The plight of the elderly has now become recognized as a major problem in the United States. The elderly face a number of personal problems: high rates of physical illness and emotional difficulties, poverty, malnutrition, lack of access to transportation, low status, lack of a meaningful role in our society, elder abuse, and inadequate housing. To a large extent, the elderly are a minority group. Similar to other minority groups, the elderly are victims of job discrimination and are subjected to prejudice that is based on erroneous stereotypes.

This chapter will:

▶ Summarize the specific problems faced by the elderly and the causes of these problems.

▶ Describe the current services to meet these problems and identify gaps in these services.

▶ Discuss the emergence of the elderly as a significant political force in our society.

▶ Present a proposal to provide the elderly with a meaningful, productive, social role in our society.

❦ The Elderly: A Population-at-Risk

Human societies have different customs for dealing with the incapacitated elderly. Some societies abandoned their enfeebled old. The Crow, Creek, and Hopi tribes, for example, built special huts away from the tribe where the old went to die. The Eskimos left the incapacitated elderly in snowbanks or they went off in a kayak. The Siriono of the Bolivian forest simply left them behind when they moved on in search of food (Moss & Moss, 1975). Even today, the Ik of Uganda leave the elderly and disabled to starve to death (Kornblum & Julian, 2001). Generally, the primary reason such societies have been forced to abandon the elderly is scarce resources.

Although we might consider such customs to be barbaric and shocking, have we not also abandoned the elderly? We urge them to retire when many are still productive. All too often, when a person is urged to retire, his or her status, power, and self-esteem are lost. Also, in a physical sense, we seldom have a place for large numbers of older people. Community facilities—parks, subways, libraries—are oriented to serving children and young people. Most housing is designed and priced for the young couple with one or two children and an annual income of over $40,000. If the elderly are not able to care for themselves (and if their families are unable or unwilling to care for them), we store them away from society in nursing homes. Our abandonment of the elderly is further indicated by our taking little action to relieve the financial problems of the elderly—one in six of the elderly have incomes close to or below the poverty line (AARP, 2000). (In one sense, our abandonment of the elderly is more barbaric than that of tribal societies who are forced by survival pressures to abandon the elderly.) Our treatment of the elderly has only recently come to be viewed as a major social problem.

The elderly are subjected to various forms of discrimination—for example, job discrimination. Older workers are erroneously believed to be less productive. Unemployed workers in their 50s and 60s have greater difficulty finding new jobs and remain unemployed much longer than younger unemployed workers. The elderly are given no meaningful role in our society. Our society is youth-oriented and deplores growing old. Our society glorifies physical attractiveness and, thereby, shortchanges the elderly. The elderly are viewed as out of touch with what's happening, and their knowledge is seldom valued or sought. Intellectual ability is sometimes thought to decline with age, even though research shows intellectual capacity, barring organic problems, remains essentially unchanged until very late in life (Lefrancois, 1999).

The elderly are erroneously thought to be senile, resistant to change, inflexible, incompetent workers, and a burden on the young. Given opportunities, elderly individuals usually prove such prejudicial concepts to be wrong. They generally react to prejudice against them in the same way that racial and ethnic minorities react—by displaying self-hatred and by being self-conscious, sensitive, and defensive about their social and cultural status (Kornblum & Julian, 2001). As we have mentioned previously, individuals who frequently receive negative responses from others eventually tend to come to view themselves negatively.

❦ Problems Faced by the Elderly

As the systems impact model reflects, individuals are dramatically affected by their interactions with other micro, mezzo, and macro systems. The following section will address a range of problems suffered by the elderly within the macro system context. This involves two dimensions. The

Estelline Robinson mopping the floor of her kitchen. The elderly may face many problems such as severe financial constraints, physical disabilities, and perceptual limitations.

first concerns problems elderly people as individual micro systems suffer within the macro environment. These include poverty, malnutrition, health difficulties, elder abuse, and lack of transportation. The other dimension of problems affecting elderly people focuses on the macro systems providing them with support and services. Often, cost is of chief concern. For example, the general population might experience rapidly rising taxes to cover a range of services for the elderly, including medical care. Examining both perspectives can enhance your understanding of human behavior in preparation for assessment and practice.

A point to remember is that unlike other minorities, the elderly have problems that we all encounter eventually (assuming we do not die prematurely). By the time most of today's college students reach middle age (presumably their peak earning years), a larger proportion of the adult population will be retired, because the elderly have the highest rate of population growth in our society. Those who are retired depend heavily on Social Security, Medicare, and other government programs to assist in meeting their financial and medical needs. If we do not face and solve the problems of the elderly now, we will be in dire straits in the future.

Emphasis on Youth: The Impacts of Social and Economic Forces

Our society fears aging more than most other societies do. Our emphasis on youth is illustrated by our dread of getting gray hair and wrinkles or becoming bald and by our being pleased when someone guesses our age to be younger than it actually is. We place a high value on youthful energy and action. We like to think we are doers. But why is there such an emphasis on youth in our society?

Industrialization resulted in a demand for laborers who are energetic, agile, and strong. Rapid advances in technology and science have made obsolete past knowledge and certain specialized work skills. Pioneer living and the gradual expansion of our nation to the west required brute strength, energy, and stamina. Competition has always been emphasized and has been reinforced by a social interpretation of Darwin's theory of evolution, which highlighted survival of the fittest, though Darwin meant those that "fit" their environment, not those that were young and healthy. The cultural tradition of overvaluing youth in our society has resulted in our devaluation of the elderly. Spotlight 16.1 discusses the status of the elderly in China and Japan and lists factors associated with high status for the elderly.

The Increasing Elderly Population

There are now over ten times as many people age 65 and older than there were in 1900. Table 16.1 shows that the percentage of older people has steadily been increasing.

Table 16.1	Composition of U.S. Population Aged 65 and Older					
	Year					
	1900	**1950**	**1970**	**1980**	**1990**	**2000**
Number of older persons (in millions)	3	12	20	25	31	35
Percent of total population	4	8	9.5	11	12	13

Source: U.S. Census Bureau, *Statistical Abstract of the United States: 2001* (Washington, DC: Government Printing Office, 2001).

Spotlight on Diversity 16.1 | **High Status for the Elderly in China, Japan, and Other Countries**

For many generations the elderly in Japan and China have experienced higher status than the elderly in the United States. In both of these countries the elderly are integrated into their families much more than in the United States. In Japan, more than 75 percent of the elderly live with their children, while in the United States most of the elderly live separately from their children (Santrock, 1999). The elderly in Japan are accorded respect in a variety of ways. For example, the best seats in a home are apt to be reserved for the elderly, cooking tends to cater to the tastes of the elderly, and individuals bow to the elderly.

However, Americans' images of the elderly in Japan and China are somewhat idealized. Japan is becoming more urbanized and Westernized. As a consequence, the proportion of the elderly living with their children is decreasing, and the elderly there are now often employed in lower-status jobs (Santrock, 1999).

Five factors have been identified as predicting high status for the elderly in a culture (Santrock, 1999):

1. Older persons are recognized as having valuable knowledge.
2. Older persons control key family and community resources.
3. The culture is more collectivistic than individualistic.
4. The extended family is a common family arrangement in the culture, and older persons are integrated into the extended family.
5. Older persons are permitted and encouraged to engage in useful and valued functions as long as possible.

Several reasons can be given for the phenomenal growth of the older population. The improved care of expectant mothers and newborn infants has reduced the infant mortality rate. New drugs, better sanitation, and other medical advances have increased the life expectancy of Americans from 49 years in 1900 to 76 years in 2001 (Kornblum & Julian, 2001).

Another reason for the increasing proportion of the elderly is that the birthrate is declining—fewer babies are being born, while more adults are reaching later adulthood. After World War II, a baby boom lasted from 1947 to 1960. Children born during these years flooded schools in the 1950s and 1960s. Then they moved into the labor market. Very soon, this generation will begin to reach retirement. After 1960, there was a baby bust, a sharp decline in birthrates. The average number of children per woman went down from a high of 3.8 in 1957 to the current rate of about 2.0 (U.S. Census Bureau, 2001).

The increased life expectancy, along with the baby boom followed by the baby bust, will significantly increase the median age of Americans in future years. The median age is indeed increasing dramatically. The long-term implications are that the United States will undergo a number of cultural, social, and economic changes.

The Fastest-Growing Age Group Is the Old-Old

As our society is having more success in treating and preventing heart disease, cancer, strokes, and other killers, more and more elderly are living into their 80s and beyond. People aged 75 and over constitute the fastest-growing age group in the United States.

The older population itself is getting older. In 1999 the 65–74 age group (18.2 million) was eight times larger than in 1900, but the 75–84 group (12.1 million) was 16 times larger, and the 85+ group (4.2 million) was 34 times larger (AARP, 2000).

Those who are 75 and over are creating a number of problems and difficult decisions for our society. Many of the old-old suffer from multiple chronic illnesses. Common medical problems of the old-old include arthritis, heart conditions, hypertension, osteoporosis (brittleness of the bones), Alzheimer's disease, incontinency, hearing and vision problems, and depression. The old-old with major health problems are putting strains on family resources. The old-old need more of such community help as Meals on Wheels, home health care, special busing, and homemaker services. The older an elderly person becomes, the higher the probability that he or she will become a resident of a nursing home. Although only about 5 percent of the elderly are currently in a nursing home, the percentage increases dramatically with age, ranging from 1 percent for persons 65–74 years to 5 percent for persons 75–84 years, and 15 percent for persons 85 years and older (AARP, 2000). The cost to society for such care is high—over $40,000 a year per person to provide nursing-home care (AARP, 2000). Despite the widespread image of families dumping aged parents into nursing homes, most frail elderly still live outside institutional walls, being cared for by a spouse, a child, or a relative.

Some middle-aged people are now simultaneously encountering demands to put children through college and to support an aging parent in a nursing home.

"Can we afford the very old?" is a favorite conference topic for doctors, bioethicists, and other specialists. Rising health-care costs and superlongevity have ignited controversy over whether to ration health care to the very old. For example, should people over age 75 be prohibited from receiving liver transplants or kidney dialysis? Discussion of euthanasia (the practice of killing individuals who are hopelessly sick or injured) has also been increasing. In 1984, Governor Richard Lamm of Colorado created controversy when he asserted the terminally ill have a duty to die. Dr. Eisdor Fer (quoted in Otten, 1984) stated:

> The problem is age-old and across cultures. Whenever society has had marginal economic resources, the oldest went first, and the old people bought that approach. The old Eskimo wasn't put on the ice flow; he just left of his own accord and never came back. (p. 10)

Early Retirement: The Impacts of Social and Economic Forces

The maintenance of a high rate of employment in our society is a major goal. One instrument that our society used in the past to keep the workforce reduced to a level in line with demand was mandatory retirement at a certain age, such as 65 or 70. In 1986, Congress (recognizing that mandatory retirement was overtly discriminatory against the elderly) outlawed most mandatory retirement policies. In many occupations, the supply of labor is exceeding the demand. An often-used remedy for the oversupply of available employees is the *encouragement* of ever-earlier retirement. Even though employers can no longer force a worker to retire, many exert subtle pressures on their older employees to retire.

Many workers who retire early supplement their pension by obtaining another job, usually at a lower status. Nearly 90 percent of Americans 65 and older are retired, even though many are intellectually and physically capable of working (U.S. Census Bureau, 2001). Our Social Security program supports early retirement at the age of 62. Pension plans of some companies and craft unions make it financially attractive to retire as early as 55. Perhaps the extreme case is the armed forces, which permit retirement on full benefits after 20 years of service or as early as age 38.

While early retirement has some advantages to society, such as reducing the labor supply and allowing younger employees to advance faster, there are also some disadvan-

tages. For society, the total bill for retirement pensions is already huge and still growing. For the retiree, it means facing a new life and status without much preparation or assistance. While our society has developed education and other institutions to prepare the young for the work world, it has developed few comparable institutions to prepare the elderly for retirement.

In our society, we still view people's worth partly in terms of their work. People often develop their self-image in terms of their occupation. Because the later years generally provide no exciting new roles to replace the occupational roles lost on retirement, retirees cannot proudly say, "I am a . . ." Instead, they must say, "I *was* a . . ." The more a person's life revolves around work, the more difficult retirement is apt to be. Retirement often diminishes people's social contacts and their status and places them in a *roleless role*. People who were once valued as salespeople, teachers, accountants, barbers, or secretaries are now considered noncontributors in a roleless role on the fringe of society.

There are several myths about the older worker that have been widely believed by employers and the general public. Older workers are thought to be less healthy, clumsier, more prone to absenteeism, more accident-prone, more forgetful, and slower in task performance (Papalia et al., 2001). Research has shown these beliefs to be erroneous. Older workers have lower turnover rates, produce at a steadier rate, make fewer mistakes, have lower absenteeism rates, have a more positive attitude toward their work, and exceed younger employees in health and low on-the-job injury rates. However, when older workers do become ill, they usually take a somewhat longer time to recover (Papalia et al., 2001).

A key question regarding early retirement is the age at which people *want* to retire. Gerontologists have studied this question. Younger workers generally state they prefer to retire before age 65. Older workers indicate they desire to retire later than the conventional age of 65 (Newman & Newman, 1999). The explanation for this difference appears to be partly economic. Since Social Security benefits and pension plans are usually insufficient to provide the same standard of living as when a person was working, the elderly see an economic need to continue working beyond age 65. An additional explanation is sociopsychological. With retirement often being a roleless role in our society, older workers may gradually identify more and more with their work and prefer it over retirement.

Adjustment to retirement varies for different people. Retirees who are not worried about money and who are healthy are happier in retirement than those who miss their income and do not feel well enough to enjoy their leisure time. Many recent retirees relish the first long stretches of leisure time they have had since childhood. After a while, however, they may begin to feel restless, bored, and useless. Schick (1986) found that the most satisfied retirees tend to be physically fit people who are using their skills in part-time volunteer or paid work.

Retirement appears to have little effect on physical health, but it sometimes affects mental health. Bossé, Aldwin, Levenson, and Ekerdt (1987) found that retirees are more likely than workers to report depression, obsessive-compulsive behavior, and physical symptoms that have no organic cause. Workers who are pressured to retire before they want to may feel anger and resentment, and may feel out of step with younger workers. Also, workers who defer retirement as long as possible because they enjoy their work may feel that no more work is an immense loss when they are pressured to retire. On the other hand, some people's morale and life satisfaction remain stable through both working and retirement years.

The two most common problems associated with retirement are adjusting to a reduced income and missing one's former job. Those who have the most difficulty in adjusting tend to be rigid or overly identify with their work by viewing their job as their primary source of satisfaction and self-image. Those who are happiest are able to replace job prestige and financial status with values stressing self-development, personal relationships, and leisure activities.

The golden age of leisure following retirement appears to be largely a myth. Life in retirement is apt to be sedentary, with TV viewing and sleep outranking such traditional leisure time activities as gardening, travel, sports, clubs, and other pastimes.

Financial Problems of the Elderly

Many of the elderly live in poverty. A fair number lack adequate food, essential clothes and drugs, and perhaps a telephone in the house to make emergency calls. One in six of the elderly have incomes close to or below the poverty line (AARP, 2000). Only a small minority of the elderly have substantial savings or investments.

The financial problems of the elderly are compounded by additional factors. One factor is the high cost of health care, as previously discussed. A second factor is inflation. Inflation is especially devastating to those on fixed incomes. Most private pension benefits do not increase in size after a worker retires. For example, if living costs rise annually at 3.5 percent, after 20 years a person on a fixed pension would be able to buy only one-half as many goods and services as he or she could at retirement (*U.S. News & World Report,* 1979). Fortunately, in 1974, Congress enacted an automatic escalator clause in Social Security benefits, providing a 3 percent increase in payments when the Consumer Price Index increased a like amount. However, Social Security benefits were never intended to make a person financially independent—it is

Retirees who have previously enjoyed affluence, travel, and education are more likely to enjoy retirement.

© David Lissy/Photri

nearly impossible to live comfortably on monthly Social Security checks.

The most important source of income for the vast majority of the elderly is Social Security benefits, primarily the Old-Age Survivors, Disability, and Health Insurance Program (OASDHI). This program is described later in this chapter.

The importance of financial security for the elderly is emphasized by Sullivan and his associates (1980):

Financial security affects one's entire life-style. It determines one's diet, ability to seek good health care, to visit relatives and friends, to maintain a suitable wardrobe, and to find or maintain adequate housing. One's financial resources, or lack of them, play a great part in finding recreation (going to movies, plays, playing bridge or bingo, etc.) and maintaining morale, feelings of independence, and a sense of self-esteem. In other words, if an older person has the financial resources to remain socially independent (having her own household and access to transportation and medical services), to continue contact with friends and relatives, and to maintain her preferred forms of recreation, she is going to feel a great deal better about herself and others than if she is deprived of her former style of life. (pp. 357–58)

The Social Security System

The Social Security system was not designed to be the main source of income for the elderly. It was originally intended as a form of insurance that would *supplement* other assets when the retirement, disability, or death of a wage-earning spouse occurred. Yet, many of the elderly do not have investments, pensions, or savings to support them in retirement, and therefore, Social Security has become the major source of income for these elderly.

The Social Security system was instituted in the United States in 1935. Money is paid into the system from Social Security taxes on employers and employees. In 1935, life expectancy was only somewhat over 60 years of age. Life expectancy, however, increased to 76 in 2001. Social Security taxes have sharply increased in recent years, but the proportion of the elderly is increasing in our society. Some projections have the Social Security fund being depleted around 2020.

The *dependency ratio* is the ratio between the number of working people and the number of nonworking people in the population. As the proportion of elderly people increases, the nonworkers will represent a greater and greater burden on the workers. Authorities predict that by the year 2020 the dependency ratio will decline from the current level of about three workers for every nonworking person to a ratio of about two to one (Kornblum & Julian, 2001).

Some problems now exist with the system. First, the benefits are too small to provide the major source of income for the elderly. Even with payments from Social Security included, an estimated 80 percent of retirees are now living on less than half of their preretirement annual income. And the monthly payments from Social Security are generally below the poverty line (Kornblum & Julian, 2001). Second, it is unlikely that the monthly benefits will be raised much. Our society faces some hard choices about keeping the Social Security system solvent in future years. Benefits might be lowered, but this would further impoverish the recipients. Social Security taxes might be raised, but there is little public support for this. The annual rate paid by workers for Social Security taxes has been rising significantly each year since 1970.

The future of the Social Security system is unclear. The system is likely to continue to exist, but reduced benefits are possible. Young people are well-advised to plan for retirement through savings and investments that are independent of the Social Security system and will supplement Social Security payments.

Death

Preoccupation with dying, particularly with the circumstances surrounding it, is an ongoing concern of the elderly. For one reason, they see their friends and relatives dying. For another, they realize they've lived more years than they have left.

The elderly person's concern about dying is most often focused on the disability, the pain, or the long periods of suffering that may precede death. People generally would like a death with dignity. They would prefer to die in their own homes, with little suffering, with mental faculties intact, and with families and friends nearby. The elderly are also concerned about the costs of their final illness, the difficulties they may cause others by the manner of their death, and whether their resources will permit a dignified funeral.

In modern America most people die in nursing homes or hospitals surrounded by medical staff (Kornblum & Julian, 2001). Such deaths often occur without dignity. Fortunately, the hospice movement has been developing in recent years to attempt to foster death with dignity. A hospice is a program that is designed to allow the terminally ill to die with dignity—to live their final weeks in a way they want. Hospices originated among European religious groups in the Middle Ages who welcomed travelers who were sick, tired, or hungry (Sullivan et al., 1980).

Hospices serve patients in a variety of settings—in hospitals, in nursing homes, and in the dying person's home. Medical services and social services are provided in

Highlight 16.1

Critical Thinking About An Ethical Issue: Should Assisted Suicide Be Legalized?

The technology of life-support equipment can keep people alive almost indefinitely. Respirators, artificial nutrition, intravenous hydration, and so-called miracle drugs not only sustain life but also trap many of the terminally ill in a degrading mental and physical condition. Such technology has raised a variety of ethical questions. Do people who are terminally ill and in severe pain have a right to die by refusing treatment? Increasingly, through "living wills," patients are able to express their wishes and refuse treatment. However, does someone in a long-term coma, who has not signed a living will, have a right to die? How should our society decide when to continue and when to stop life-support efforts? Courts and state legislatures are presently working through the legal complexities governing death and euthanasia.

Should assisted death or assisted suicide be legalized? As of 2001, only the Netherlands permitted physicians to give qualifying terminally ill patients a lethal dose of drugs. There is considerable controversy about assisted suicide in the United States. Hemlock Society founder Derek Humphry has written a do-it-yourself suicide manual that has become a best-seller. (The Hemlock Society promotes active voluntary euthanasia.) Michigan doctor Jack Kevorkian made national news by building a machine to help terminally ill people end their lives and by assisting a large number of them to do so.

In the Netherlands an informal, *de facto* arrangement made with prosecutors over 25 years ago allows physicians there to help patients die, as long as certain safeguards are followed. The patient, for example, has to be terminally ill, in considerable pain, and mentally competent; she or he must also repeatedly express a wish to die.

Oregon's Death with Dignity Act was passed by voters in 1994. It allows doctors to prescribe lethal drugs at the request of terminally ill patients who have less than 6 months to live. Doctors may only prescribe a lethal dose, not administer it.

People in favor of assisted suicide argue that unnecessary, long-term suffering is without merit and should not have to be endured. They argue that people have a right to a death with dignity, which means a death without excessive emotional and physical pain and without excessive mental, physical, and spiritual degradation. They see assisted suicide as affirming the principle of autonomy—upholding the individual's right to make decisions about his or her dying process. Allowing the option of suicide for the terminally ill is perceived as the ultimate right of self-determination.

Opponents assert that suicide is, at best, unethical and, at worst, a mortal sin for which the deceased cannot receive forgiveness. They view assisted suicide as assisted murder. They assert that modern health care can provide almost everyone a peaceful, pain-free, comfortable, and dignified end to life. Opponents believe that most terminally ill persons consider suicide not because they fear death but because they fear dying—pain, abandonment, and loss of control (all of which a hospice is designed to alleviate). Moreover, assisted-suicide legislation could easily result in a number of unintended consequences: The terminally ill might believe they have a *duty*

---

hospices, and extensive efforts are made to allow the terminally ill to spend their remaining days as they choose. Hospices sometimes have educational and entertainment programs, and visitors are welcome. Pain relievers are extensively used, so that the patient is able to live out his or her final days in relative comfort.

Hospices view the *disease,* not the patient, as terminal. Their emphasis is on helping people use the time that is left, rather than trying to keep people alive as long as possible. Many hospice programs are set up to assist people in living their remaining days at home. In addition to medical and visiting nurse services, hospices have volunteers to help the patient and family members with such services as counseling, transportation, filling out insurance forms and other paperwork, and respite care (that is, staying with the patient to provide temporary relief for family members).

Highlight 16.1 raises the ethical issue regarding whether assisted suicide should be legalized.

Elder Abuse

A shocking way for the elderly to spend their final years is by being victims of *elder abuse*—neglect, physical abuse, or psychological abuse of dependent older persons. The perpetrator may be the son or daughter of the elderly victim, a caregiver, or some other person. Although elder abuse can occur in nursing homes and in other institutions, it is most often suffered by frail elderly living with their spouses or their children. Because of problems in defining elder abuse, as well as the fact that the abuse is grossly underreported, estimates of the number of cases each year range from 600,000 to more than 1 million. The number abused may involve as many as 5 percent of the older population (Papalia et al., 2001).

An example of elder abuse is related by Koch and Koch (1980):

In Chicago, a nineteen-year-old woman confessed to torturing her eighty-one-year-old father and chaining him to a toi-

to die, in order to avoid being a financial and emotional burden to their families and to society. A health-care system intent upon cutting costs could give subtle, even unintended, encouragement to a patient to die. Relatives of a terminally ill person receiving expensive medical care may put pressure on the person to choose physician-assisted suicide to avoid eroding the family's finances. There is concern that, if competent people are allowed to seek death, then pressure will grow to use the treatment-by-death option with adults in comas or with others who are mentally incompetent (such as the mentally ill and those who have a severe cognitive disability). Finally, many people worry that if the "right to die" becomes recognized as a basic right in our society, then it can easily become a "duty to die" for the elderly, the sick, the poor, and others devalued by society.

Some authorities have sought to make a distinction between *active* euthanasia (assisting in suicide) and *passive* euthanasia (withholding or withdrawing treatment). In many states it is legal for physicians and courts to honor a patient's wishes to not receive life-sustaining treatment.

A case of passive euthanasia involved Nancy Cruzan. On January 11, 1983, when this Missouri woman was 25, her car overturned. Her brain lost oxygen for 14 minutes following the accident, and for the next several years she was in a "persistent vegetative state," with no hope of recovery. A month after the accident, her parents, Joyce and Joe Cruzan, gave permission for a feeding tube to be inserted. In the months that followed, however, the parents gradually became convinced there was no point in keeping Nancy alive indefinitely in such a hopeless condition.

In 1986 they were shocked when a Missouri state judge informed them that they could be charged with murder for removing the feeding tube. The Cruzans appealed the decision all the way to the U.S. Supreme Court, requesting the Court to overturn a Missouri law that specifically prohibits withdrawal of food and water from hopelessly ill patients. In July 1990 the Supreme Court refused the Cruzans' request that their daughter's tube be removed but ruled that states could sanction the removal if there is "clear and convincing evidence" that the patient would have wished it. Cruzan's family subsequently found other witnesses to testify that Nancy would not have wanted to be kept alive in such a condition.

A Missouri judge decided that the testimony met the Supreme Court's test. The tube was disconnected in December 1990, and Nancy Cruzan died several days later, on December 26.

At the present time, 10,000 Americans are in similar vegetative conditions, unable to communicate. Many of these individuals have virtually no chance to recover. Right-to-die questions will undoubtedly continue to be raised in many of these cases.

In June 1997 the U.S. Supreme Court ruled that terminally ill people do not have a constitutional right to doctor-assisted suicide. The Court upheld laws in New York and Washington states that make it a crime for doctors to give life-ending drugs to mentally competent but terminally ill patients who no longer want to live. The judges in their ruling made it clear their decision does not permanently attempt to resolve the assisted-suicide issue, and they in fact urged that debate continue about this issue.

Do you believe that the terminally ill have a right to die by refusing treatment? Do you believe that assisted suicide should be legalized? If you had a terminally ill close relative who was in intense pain and asked you to assist her or him in acquiring a lethal dose of drugs, how would you respond? Would you be willing to help? Or would you refuse?

---

let for seven days. She also hit him with a hammer when he was asleep: "I worked him over real good with it. Then after I made him weak enough, I chained his legs together. After that, I left him and rested. I watched TV for a while." (p. 14)

Adult children may abuse their parents for a variety of reasons. They may be responding to the stress of their own personal problems or to the stress of the time, energy, and finances needed to care for another person. They may be paying back their parent for having been abusive to them when they were younger. They may be upset with their elderly parent's emotional reactions, physical impairments, lifestyle, or personal habits. They may be intentionally abusing the parent to force him or her to move out of their home. When the elderly person is living with the abuser, finding alternative living arrangements is often necessary.

The typical victim is an elderly person in poor health who lives with someone. Papalia and her associates (2001) note that the abuser is more likely to be a spouse than a child, partly because substantially more of the elderly live with spouses than with their children. The risk of elder abuse is substantially increased when the caregiver is depressed (Paveza et al., 1992).

The varied forms of mistreatment of the elderly are typically grouped into the following four categories:

- *Physical abuse*—the infliction of physical pain or injury, including bruising, punching, restraining, or sexually molesting.

- *Psychological abuse*—the infliction of mental anguish, such as intimidating, humiliating, and threatening harm.

- *Financial abuse*—the illegal or improper exploitation of the victim's assets or property.

- *Neglect*—including deliberate failure or refusal to fulfill a caretaking obligation, such as denial of food or health care, or abandoning the victim (Gelles, 1997).

Every state is mandated by the federal government to provide adult protective services similar to those provided for children. This program serves adults—primarily the elderly and adults with physical or mental disabilities—who are being neglected or abused. (This program is described in more detail later in this chapter.)

Where the Elderly Live

We have heard so much about nursing homes in recent years that few people realize that 95 percent of the elderly do not live in nursing homes or any other kind of institution. Over 70 percent of all elderly males are married and live with their wives. Because females tend to outlive their spouses, over 40 percent of women over age 65 live alone. Nearly 80 percent of older married couples maintain their own households—in apartments, mobile homes, condominiums, or their own houses. In addition, nearly half of the single elderly (widows, widowers, divorced, never married) live in their own homes (AARP, 2000). When the elderly do not maintain their own households, they most often live in the homes of relatives, primarily children.

The elderly who live in rural areas generally have a higher status than those living in urban areas. People living on farms can retire gradually. People whose income is in land, rather than a job, can retain importance and esteem to an advanced age.

However, almost three-fourths of our population live in urban areas, and the elderly often live in poor-quality housing. At least 30 percent of the elderly live in substandard, deteriorating, or dilapidated housing (Kornblum & Julian, 2001). Many of the elderly in urban areas are trapped in decaying, low-value houses needing considerable maintenance and often surrounded by racial and ethnic groups different from their own. Many of the urban elderly live in the urban inner cities in hotels or apartments with inadequate living conditions. Their neighborhoods may be decaying and crime ridden, where they are easy prey for thieves and muggers.

Fortunately, many mobile-home parks, retirement villages, and apartment complexes geared to the needs of the elderly have been built throughout the country. Many such communities for the elderly provide a social center, security protection, sometimes a daily hot meal, and perhaps help with maintenance.

Transportation

Many of the elderly do not drive. Some cannot afford the cost of a car, while others have physical limitations that prevent them from driving and maintaining a car. The lack of convenient, inexpensive transportation is a problem faced by most elderly.

Crime Victimization

Having reduced energy, strength, and agility, the elderly are vulnerable to being victimized by crime, particularly robbery, aggravated assault, burglary, larceny, vandalism, and fraud. Many of the elderly live in constant fear of being victimized, although reported victimization rates for the elderly are lower than rates for younger people. The actual victimization rates for the elderly may be considerably higher than official crime statistics indicate, because many of the elderly feel uneasy about becoming involved with the legal and criminal justice systems. Therefore, they may not report some of the crimes they are victims of. Some of the elderly are afraid of retaliation from the offenders if they report the crimes, and some of the elderly dislike the legal processes they have to go through if they press charges.

Some of the elderly are hesitant to leave their homes for fear they will be mugged or for fear their homes will be burglarized while they are away.

Malnutrition

The elderly are the most uniformly undernourished segment of our population (Papalia et al., 2001). Chronic malnutrition of the elderly exists because of transportation difficulties in getting to grocery stores; lack of knowledge about proper nutrition; lack of money to purchase a well-balanced diet; poor teeth and lack of good dentures, which greatly limit the diet; lack of incentives to prepare an appetizing meal when one is living alone; and inadequate cooking and storage facilities.

Health Problems and Cost of Care

As noted earlier, the proportion of the elderly in our society is increasing dramatically, and the old-old (aged 75 and over) is the most rapidly growing age group in our society. Today, there is a crisis in health care for the elderly. There are a variety of reasons for this crisis.

As described in Chapter 14, the elderly are much more apt to have long-term illnesses. In the 1960s the Medicare and Medicaid programs were created to pay for much of their medical costs. Due to the high costs of these programs, the Reagan-Bush administrations in the 1980s said we could no longer pay the full costs of that care, and as a result there have been cuts in eligibility for payment and limits set for what the government will pay for a variety of medical procedures.

A national debate is raging over how to reduce the rate of increase of the funds the federal government spends on Medicare and Medicaid. (These programs are described later in this chapter.) One faction asserts that limits have to be set on the annual amount being spent on these programs in order to keep the programs solvent. Another faction claims that these programs are providing essential medical care to the elderly and to the poor—and that setting additional limits on funds will result in sharp reductions in health-care services provided to the elderly and to the poor, which will mean more serious untreated illnesses and higher death risks for these two at-risk populations.

When we look at the quality of health-care services provided to the elderly, it is important to note that physicians are primarily trained in treating the young, and generally less interested in serving the elderly. As a result, when the elderly become ill, they often do not receive quality medical care. For example, Hugh Downs (1985) in an ABC news report described the case of an 82-year-old woman who was shuffled from one hospital to another over a 3-month period of time, and finally dumped in a county hospital—where she eventually died of a single grossly neglected bedsore.

Medical conditions of the elderly are often misdiagnosed, as physicians receive little specialized training in the unique medical conditions of the elderly. Many of the elderly who are seriously ill do not get medical attention. One of the reasons physicians are not interested in treating the elderly is the problem of reimbursement. The Medicare program sets reimbursement limits on a variety of procedures that are provided to the elderly. As a result, most physicians prefer to work with younger patients, where the fee-for-service system is much more profitable.

There have also been restrictions put on hospital payments under Medicare. In the past, the payment system covered whatever the expenses came to. To curtail rampant costs, the federal government in the 1980s set flat payments for categories of illness, which were called "Diagnostic Related Groups" or DRGs. With this system, instead of reimbursing hospitals for the actual cost of treating Medicare patients, the government now pays a set fee for each medical condition. For the medical community it's a simple message: If a hospital spends less on a patient than the fixed amount, it makes money. If it spends more, it must absorb the loss. A perverse, unintended consequence of DRGs is that many seriously ill elderly patients

are being discharged prematurely (Kornblum & Julian, 2001). With the DRG system, hospitals that have a social conscience and continue to treat the elderly beyond the length of time allowed by the DRG regulations must cover the expenses themselves, and thereby face bankruptcy.

In addition, the elderly who live in the community often have transportation difficulties in getting medical care. And those living in nursing homes sometimes receive inadequate care, as some health professionals assume such patients no longer have much time to live, and therefore the professionals are less interested in providing high-quality medical care. Medical care for the elderly is becoming a national embarrassment.

Cultural Differences in Seeking Health Care: The Case of Elderly Mexican Americans

Significant variations exist for different ethnic and cultural populations both in access to health care and how such care is welcomed and received (Applewhite, 1996; Green, 1999). Sensitivity to and appreciation of cultural differences is essential in providing effective health care. Applewhite (1996) explains, for example:

"This is especially true for elderly Mexican Americans, many of whom retain a strong attachment to indigenous values, including those about health care. Culturally specific beliefs and attitudes about folk healing play an essential role in elderly Mexican Americans' approach to their own health and use of health care resources" (p. 455).

Folk healing or *curanderismo* is "a set of health beliefs and practices derived from ethnic and historical traditions that have as their goal the amelioration or cure of psychological, spiritual, and physical problems" (Applewhite, 1996, p. 455). Health care must not only be responsive to the needs of elderly Mexican Americans, but also work in conjunction with traditional cultural values concerning health care such as *curanderismo*. Members of ethnic populations may not seek out or accept health care that conflicts with their value and belief systems. One traditional Hispanic disease concept, for instance, is *mal ojo,* or "the evil eye"; "the result of dangerous imbalances in social relationships". . . . Its symptoms include headaches, sleeplessness, drowsiness, restlessness, fever, and, in severe cases, vomiting. . . . Particularly if one has been the subject of covetous glances, admiring attention, or intense interest by another, *mal ojo* can result" (Green, 1999, p. 61). Furthermore, it is the belief that "*mal ojo* is resolved, balance is restored, when the unwitting perpetrator of the disease touches the victim, assuring that there is no intent of inappropriate desire to control the other" (Green, 1999, p. 62).

Applewhite (1996) recommends that social workers and health-care professionals be respectful of clients' cultural beliefs before making health-care referrals and recommendations. It is important to assess the extent to which elderly Mexican Americans adhere to such beliefs, as this varies from one person to another. Applewhite (1996) concludes, "Ultimately, traditional folk healing represents a time-honed alternative to conventional medicine that helps maintain healthful lifestyles for people who are tied to their ancestral cultures. Viewed in this way, social workers and other health care professionals can separate myths from realities to serve elderly Mexican Americans more effectively" (p. 466).

✤ Current Services: Macro System Responses

Present services and programs for the elderly are primarily maintenance in nature, as they are mainly designed to meet basic physical needs. Nonetheless, there are a number of programs, often federally funded, to provide services needed by the elderly. Before we briefly review many of these programs, we will look at the Older Americans Act of 1965, which set objectives for programs that serve the elderly.

Older Americans Act of 1965

The Older Americans Act of 1965 created an operating agency (Administration on Aging) within the Department of Health, Education, and Welfare (as of 1980, the Department of Health and Human Services). This law and its amendments are the basis for financial aid by the federal government to assist states and local communities to meet the needs of the elderly. The objectives of the act are to secure for the elderly:

- an adequate income
- best possible physical and mental health
- suitable housing
- restorative services for those who require institutionalized care
- opportunity for employment
- retirement in health, honor, and dignity
- pursuit of meaningful activity
- efficient community services

- immediate benefit from research knowledge to sustain and improve health and happiness
- freedom, independence, and the free exercise of individual initiative in planning and managing their own lives (U.S. Department of Health, Education, and Welfare, 1970)

Although these objectives are commendable, in reality they have not been realized for many of the elderly. However, some progress has been made. Many states have offices on aging, and some municipalities and counties have established community councils on aging. A number of universities have established centers for gerontology, which focus on research on the elderly and training of students for working with the elderly in such disciplines as nursing, psychology, medicine, sociology, social work, and architecture. (*Gerontology* is the scientific study of the aging process from physiological, pathological, psychological, sociological, and economic points of view.) Government research grants are being given to encourage the study of the elderly and their problems. Publishers are now producing books and pamphlets to inform the public about the elderly, and a few high schools are beginning to offer courses to help teenagers understand the elderly and their circumstances.

A number of programs, often federally funded and administered at state or local levels, provide funds and services needed by the elderly. Some of these programs are briefly described in the following sections.

Old Age, Survivors, Disability, and Health Insurance (OASDHI)

The OASDHI social insurance program[1] was created by the 1935 Social Security Act. OASDHI is usually referred to as Social Security by the general public. It is an income insurance program designed to partially replace income lost when a worker retires or becomes disabled. Cash benefits are also paid to survivors of insured workers.

Payments to beneficiaries are based on previous earnings. Rich as well as poor are eligible if insured. Benefits are provided to fully insured workers at age 65 or older (age 62 if somewhat smaller benefits are taken). Dependent husbands and wives over 62 and dependent children under 18 are also covered under the benefits. (There is no

---

1. Social insurance programs are financed by a tax on employees, or on employers, or on both. In contrast, public assistance benefits are paid from general government revenues (such as revenues through income taxes). In our society, receiving social insurance benefits is generally considered a right, while receiving public assistance is usually considered charity and is stigmatized.

age limit on disabled children who become disabled before 18.)

Participation in this insurance program is compulsory for most employees, including the self-employed. The program is generally financed by a payroll tax (FICA—Federal Insurance Contributions Act) assessed equally to employer and employee. The rate has gone up gradually. Eligibility for benefits is based on the number of years in which Social Security taxes have been paid and the amount earned while working.

Supplemental Security Income (SSI)

Under the SSI program, the federal government makes monthly payments to people in financial need who are 65 years of age or older or to persons of any age who are legally blind or disabled. In order to qualify for payments, applicants must have no (or very little) regular cash income, own little property, and have little cash or few assets (such as jewelry, stocks, bonds, or other valuables) that could be turned into cash.

The SSI program became effective on January 1, 1974. The word *supplemental* in the program's name is used because, in most cases, payments supplement whatever other income may be available to the claimant. Since OASDHI monthly payments are often low, SSI sometimes supplements even that income source.

SSI provides a guaranteed minimum income (an income floor) for the elderly, the legally blind, and the disabled. Administration of SSI has been assigned to the Social Security Administration. Financing of the program is through federal tax dollars, primarily income taxes.

Medicare

In 1965 Congress enacted the Medicare program (Title XVIII of the Social Security Act). Medicare helps the elderly pay the high cost of health care. It has two parts: hospital insurance (Part A) and supplementary medical insurance (Part B). Everyone 65 or older who is entitled to monthly benefits under the Old Age, Survivors, and Disability Insurance program gets Part A automatically, without paying a monthly premium. Nearly everyone in the United States 65 or older is eligible for Part B; Part B is voluntary, and beneficiaries are charged a monthly premium. Disabled people under age 65 who have been getting Social Security benefits for 24 consecutive months or more are also eligible for both Part A and Part B, effective in the 25th month of disability.

Part A—hospital insurance—helps pay for time-limited care in a hospital, in a skilled nursing facility (home), and for home health visits (such as visiting nurses). Coverage is limited to 150 days in a hospital and to 100 days in a skilled nursing facility. If patients are able to be out of a hospital or nursing facility for 60 consecutive days following confinement, they are again eligible for coverage. Covered services in a hospital or skilled nursing facility include the cost of meals and a semiprivate room, regular nursing services, drugs, supplies, and appliances. Part A also covers home health care on a part-time or intermittent basis if beneficiaries meet the following conditions: they are homebound, in need of skilled nursing care or physical or speech therapy, and services are ordered and regularly reviewed by a physician. Finally, Part A covers up to 210 days of hospice care for a terminally ill Medicare beneficiary.

Part B—supplementary medical services—helps pay for physicians' services, outpatient hospital services in an emergency room, outpatient physical and speech therapy, and a number of other medical and health services prescribed by a doctor, such as diagnostic services, X-ray or other radiation treatments, and some ambulance services.

Each Medicare beneficiary has the choice of selecting, from an "alphabet soup" of health plans, which plan he or she will be in. The variety of plans includes preferred provider organizations, provider service organizations, point-of-service plans, private fee-for-service plans, and medical savings accounts. (It is beyond the scope of this text to give detailed descriptions of these plans. Details can be obtained from your local Social Security Administration office.)

Medicaid

This program was established in 1965 by Title XIX of the Social Security Act. Medicaid primarily provides medical care for recipients of public assistance. It enables states to pay hospitals, nursing homes, medical societies, and insurance agencies for services provided to recipients of public assistance. Many of these recipients are indigent elderly, some of whom are in nursing homes. The federal government shares the expenses with the states on a 55–45 basis for recipients of public assistance. Medical expenses that are covered under Medicaid include diagnosis and therapy performed by surgeons, physicians, and dentists; nursing services in the home or elsewhere; and medical supplies, drugs, and laboratory fees.

Medicaid benefits vary from state to state. The original legislation encouraged states to include coverage of all self-supporting persons whose marginal income made them unable to pay for medical care. However, this inclusion is not mandatory, and the definition of medical indigence has generally been considered by states to provide insurance coverage primarily to recipients of public assistance.

Food Stamps

The food stamp program is designed to combat hunger. Food stamps are available to public assistance recipients and to other low-income families, including the elderly, who qualify. These stamps are then used to purchase groceries.

Adult Protective Services

One of the types of services that is offered in practically all communities, usually by human services departments, is adult protective services. Although it is offered widely, the public is largely unaware of it. About 1 in every 20 elderly people probably needs some form of protective services, and this proportion is expected to increase as the proportion of people over age 75 increases (Papalia et al., 2001). Protective services are for adults who are being neglected or abused or for adults whose physical or mental capacities have substantially deteriorated. The aim of adult protective services is to help the elderly, and adults with disabilities, meet their needs in their own home if possible. Alternative placements include foster care, group home care, and elderly housing units (such as apartments for the elderly). Services provided include homemaker services, counseling, rehabilitation, medical services, visiting nursing services, Meals on Wheels, and transportation.

Highlight 16.2 illustrates some of the help that an adult protective services agency might offer.

Additional Programs

Additional programs for the elderly include the following:

- *Meals on Wheels* provides hot and cold meals to housebound recipients who are incapable of obtaining or preparing their own meals, but who can feed themselves.
- *Senior-citizen centers,* golden-age clubs, and similar groups provide leisure time and recreational activities for the elderly.
- *Special bus rates* reduce bus transportation costs for the elderly.
- *Property tax relief* is available to the elderly in many states.
- *Housing projects* for the elderly are built by local sponsors with financing assistance by the Department of Housing and Urban Development.

- *Reduced rates* at movie theaters and other places of entertainment are often offered voluntarily by individual owners.
- *Home health services* provide visiting nurse services, physical therapy, drugs, laboratory services, and sickroom equipment.
- *Nutrition programs* provide meals for the elderly at group eating sites. (These meals are generally provided four or five times a week and usually are luncheon meals.)
- *Homemaker services* provide household tasks that the elderly are no longer able to do for themselves.
- *Day-care centers* for the elderly provide activities that are determined by the needs of the group.
- *Telephone reassurance* is provided by volunteers, often older persons, who telephone elderly people who live alone. (Such calls are a meaningful form of social contact for both parties and also ascertain whether any serious problems have arisen that require emergency attention.)
- *Nursing homes* provide residential care and skilled nursing care when independence is no longer practical for the elderly who cannot take care of themselves or for the elderly whose families can no longer take care of them.
- *Congregate housing facilities* are private or government-subsidized rental apartment complexes, remodeled hotels to meet the needs of independent older adults, or mobile-home parks designed for older adults. They provide meals, housekeeping, transportation, social and recreational activities, and sometimes health care.
- *Group homes* provide housing for some elderly residents. A group home is usually a house that is owned or rented by a social agency. Employees are hired to shop, cook, do heavy cleaning, drive, and give counseling. Residents take care of much of their own personal needs and take some responsibility for day-to-day tasks.
- *Assisted-living facilities* allow the elderly to have semi-independent living. The elderly in such a facility live in their own rooms or apartments. Residents receive personal care (bathing, dressing, and grooming), meals, housekeeping, transportation, and social and recreational activities.
- *Foster-care homes* are usually single-family residences where the owners of the home take in an unrelated older adult and are reimbursed for providing housing, meals, housekeeping, and personal care.

Highlight 16.2

Adult Protective Services

The Dodge City Human Services Department received a complaint from a neighbor of Jack and Rosella McArron that the McArrons were living in health-threatening conditions and the Mr. McArron was frequently abusing his wife.

Vincent Rudd, adult protective service worker, investigated the complaint. When he arrived at the door, Jack McArron appeared in shabby, dirty clothes with a can of beer in his hand and refused entry to Mr. Rudd. Mr. Rudd heard someone moaning in the background, so he went to the nearest service station where he called the police department. Together, Mr. Rudd and a police officer returned to the McArrons. The officer informed Mr. McArron that a protective services complaint had been made, and that an investigation must be made. Mr. McArron grudgingly let the officer and Mr. Rudd in.

The inside of the house had the appearance of having been hit by a cyclone. Newspapers and dirty clothes were heaped together in piles on the floor. The dining room table was covered by dust, cigarette butts, beer cans, whiskey bottles, and dirty dishes. The plumbing was not working. Cockroaches were seen. The house had a wood-burning stove that was covered with dirt and a burned crust. At the very least the place appeared to be a firetrap. There was a stench that was largely due to urine.

Mr. McArron appeared to be intoxicated. Mrs. McArron was found moaning in the bedroom. Mr. McArron stated that she had arthritis and had slipped on the stairway. He further stated that her demands and her behavior were driving him to drink. Her hair was greasy and appeared not to have been washed for months. She was wearing a torn nightgown that smelled of urine. She was very thin, wrinkled, and had a variety of cuts and bruises. Her mutterings were difficult to understand, but she seemed to be saying that her husband had been battering her for months.

She was taken to a hospital where she spent 2½ weeks. (She was found to be 66 years old, and her husband, 69.) At first she wouldn't eat, so she was fed intravenously. After several days she became more alert. Daily baths improved her appearance. It became clear that she had frequently been abused by her husband for more than a decade. She was also found to have severe arthritis and diabetes. In the hospital she stated she did not want to return to live with her husband because of the beatings. She was placed in a foster home.

The neighbors of the McArrons were interviewed; it was found that Jack McArron had had a drinking problem for years and that the neighbors seldom saw him sober. The neighbors were afraid of what he might do when intoxicated. He frequently beat his wife and was loud and obnoxious, and the neighbors were fearful he might kill someone while driving under the influence. Mr. McArron was taken to a 30-day drug treatment center. Records showed he had been admitted to this center on seven previous occasions. This time a physician found evidence that Mr. McArron was suffering from brain deterioration due to chronic alcoholism. He seemed to be paranoid as he talked about his neighbors being gangsters. He stated that they were stealing his possessions. As the days went by, he started blaming the police and protective services for kidnapping his wife and talked about getting her back. He stated, "I'm goin' lookin' for her with my shotgun, and I'll blast anyone who gets in my way." With his increasing paranoid statements, the staff was reluctant to let Mr. McArron return to his home, as it was felt that if he became intoxicated he could be dangerous. His mental capacities were deteriorating, and he was found to have a severe case of cirrhosis of the liver. As a result, procedures were followed to have a court declare him incompetent, to appoint a younger cousin as guardian, and to place Mr. McArron in a nursing home.

After Mrs. McArron had been in the foster home for several weeks, she said that she wanted to return to live with her husband. She was informed that her husband was in a nursing home. She visited him on several occasions and became increasingly depressed about his deteriorating condition. She began talking about wanting to die. About a year and a half later, she did die of a massive heart attack. Her husband's condition in the nursing home has continued to deteriorate.

Vincent Rudd often thought about this case. It seemed that the intervention that resulted in Jack and Rosella being separated from each other was in some way a factor in facilitating both their mental and emotional deterioration. Breaking a husband-wife bond had unexpected adverse consequences. But what were the alternatives? They seemed to be killing each other by living together. Mr. Rudd realized intervention in social work is a matter of judgment, and all anyone can do is give it his or her best shot.

■ *Continued-care retirement communities* are long–term housing facilities which are designed to provide a full range of accommodations and services for affluent elderly people as their needs change. A resident may start out living in an independent apartment; then move into a congregate housing unit with such services as cleaning, laundry, and meals; then move to an assisted–living facility; and finally move into an adjoining nursing home.

■ *Nursing Home Ombudsman Programs* investigate and acts on concerns expressed by residents in nursing homes.

Nursing Homes

Nursing homes were created as an alternative to expensive hospital care and are substantially supported by the federal government through Medicaid and Medicare. About

A nursing home protest by Gray Panthers.

© Don Ivers/Jeroboam

1.5 million older people now live in extended-care facilities, making nursing homes a billion-dollar industry. There are more patient beds in nursing homes than in hospitals (AARP, 2000).

Nursing homes are classified according to the kind of care they provide. At one end of the scale, there are residential homes that provide primarily room and board, with some nonmedical care (such as help in dressing). At the other end of the scale are nursing-care centers that provide skilled nursing and medical attention 24 hours a day. The more skilled and extensive the medical care given, the more expensive the home. The costs per resident average more than $3,000 a month (AARP, 2000). Although only about 5 percent of the elderly live permanently in nursing homes, many spend some time convalescing in them.

One scandal after another characterizes care in nursing homes. Patients have been found lying in their own feces or urine. Food may be so unappetizing that some residents refuse to eat it. Some homes have serious safety haz-

ards. Boredom and apathy are common among staff as well as residents.

A study in 2001 found that a third of the nursing homes in the United States have been cited by state inspectors as being abusive to residents in 1999 and 2000 (*U.S. News & World Report,* August 13, 2001).

A number of nursing homes fail to meet food sanitation standards and have problems administering drugs and providing personal hygiene for residents (Kornblum & Julian, 2001). In 1987, investigators for the U.S. Senate Special Committee on Aging found that conditions in one out of ten nursing homes were "shockingly, dangerously bad." The study found neglect, medical maltreatment, and, in a few isolated cases, even beatings and rape. The study found that in California between 1985 and 1986, 79 patients died as a direct result of neglect (Robinson, 1988).

Robinson (1988) conducted a nationwide investigation of nursing homes in 1988 and concluded: "I learned that the majority of nursing homes are safe, well-run institutions that take good care of the sick people entrusted to them. Some are superb" (pp. 13–14). But he also noted a number of horrors and abuses in some of the homes. The abuses included giving new and unapproved drugs to patients without their consent, giving patients heavy doses of tranquilizers to keep them docile, kickbacks given to nursing home administrators from druggists, stealing funds from patients, submitting phony cost reports to Medicare, sexual abuse by staff of some patients, and charging patients thousands of dollars to gain admission to a home.

At the present time, people of all ages tend to be prejudiced against nursing homes, even those that are well run. The average senior citizen looks at a nursing home as a human junkyard. There is some truth to the notion that most nursing homes are places where the elderly wait to die. (An alternative to nursing home care is the community options program, which is described in Highlight 16.3.)

The cost of care for impoverished nursing home residents is largely paid by the Medicaid program. Since the federal government has set limits on what will be reimbursed under Medicaid, other problems may arise. There may be an effort to keep salary and wage levels as low as possible and the number of staff to a minimum. A nursing home may postpone repairs and improvements. Food is apt to be inexpensive, such as macaroni and cheese, which is high in fats and carbohydrates. Congress has mandated that every nursing home patient on Medicaid is entitled to a monthly personal spending allowance. The homes have control over these funds, and some homes keep this money.

A danger of nursing home care is the potential abuse of the residents by staff members. In a telephone survey of

Highlight 16.3

Community Options Program: Providing Alternatives To Nursing Home Placement

The Community Options Program (COP) is an innovative Wisconsin program that provides alternatives to nursing home placement. COP is funded by the state and the federal government and is administered by county social services departments.

To qualify for the program a person must have a long-term or irreversible illness or disability and be a potential or current resident of a nursing home or a facility for the developmentally disabled. The person must also have income and assets that are below the poverty line. If these eligibility guidelines are met, a social worker and a nurse assess applicants for their social and physical abilities and disabilities to determine the types of ser-

vices needed. If an alternative to nursing home placement is available, is financially feasible, and, most important, is preferred by an applicant, a plan for services is drawn up, and a start date for in-home or in-community services is determined.

A wide variety of services may be provided that are designed to be alternatives to placement in nursing homes. Typical services that are provided include homemaker services, visiting nurse services, home-delivered meals, adult foster care, group home care, and case management. COP is a coordinated program that makes use of a number of resources from a variety of agencies. Wisconsin is finding that the program is not only cost effective in comparison to nursing home care but also preferred over nursing home care by service recipients. (A number of other states now offer COP or similar programs.)

---

577 nurses and nurses' aides, Pillemer and Moore (1989) heard of many instances of abuse by staff. Over one-third of the respondents stated they had seen other staff members physically abusing patients—pushing, shoving, pinching, hitting, or kicking them, throwing things at them, or restraining them more than was necessary. Ten percent acknowledged committing one or more of these acts themselves. Psychological abuse was even more common, with 81 percent of the respondents indicating they had seen other staff members yelling at patients, insulting them, swearing at them, isolating them unnecessarily, threatening them, or refusing to give them food. Forty percent of the respondents acknowledged committing such abuse themselves.

Complaints about the physical facilities of nursing homes include not enough floor space or too many people in a room. The call light by the bed may be difficult to reach, or the toilets and showers may not be conveniently located. And the building may be in a state of decay.

While the quality of nursing home care ranges from excellent to awful, nursing homes are needed, particularly for those requiring round-the-clock health care for an extended time. If nursing homes were abolished, other institutions such as hospitals would have to serve the elderly. Life in nursing homes need not be bad. Where homes are properly administered, residents can expand their life experiences.

The ideal nursing home should be lively (with recreational, social, and educational programming), safe, hygienic, and attractive. It should offer stimulating activities

and opportunities to socialize with people of both sexes and all ages. It should offer privacy so that (among other reasons) residents can be sexually active. It should offer a wide range of therapeutic, social, recreational, and rehabilitative services. The best-quality care tends to be provided by larger nonprofit facilities that have a high ratio of nurses to nurse's aides (Pillemer & Moore, 1989).

Social Work with the Elderly

Social work education is taking a leading role in identifying the problems of the elderly and is developing gerontological specializations within the curricula. Social workers are a significant part of the staff of most agencies serving the elderly. Some states, for example, are now requiring that each nursing home employ a social worker.

Some of the services in which social workers have expertise in providing to the elderly are as follows:

- *Brokering services.* In any community there are a wide range of services available, but few people are knowledgeable about the array of services or the eligibility requirements. The elderly are in special need of this broker service, because some have difficulty with transportation and communication and others may be reluctant to request needed assistance to which they are entitled.

- *Case management or care management services.* Social workers are trained to assess the social service needs of a client and the client's family. When appropriate, the social worker case-manages by arranging, coordinating, monitoring, evaluating, and advocating for a package of multiple services to meet the often complex needs of an elderly client. Common functions of most case management programs for the elderly include case finding, prescreening, intake, assessment, goal setting, care planning, capacity building, care-plan implementation, reassessment, and termination.

- *Advocacy.* Because of shortcomings in services to the elderly in our society, social workers need at times to advocate for needed services for the elderly.

- *Individual and family counseling.* Counseling interventions focus on examination of the elderly client's needs and strengths, the family's needs and strengths, and the resources available to meet the identified needs.

- *Grief counseling.* The elderly are apt to need counseling for role loss (such as retirement or loss of self-sufficiency); loss of a significant other (such as a spouse, a child, or an adult sibling); and loss due to chronic health or mental health conditions.

- *Adult day-care services.* Social workers provide individual and family counseling, outreach and broker services, supportive services, group work services, and care-planning services for the elderly being served by adult day-care services.

- *Crisis intervention services.* Social workers providing crisis intervention seek to stabilize the crisis situation and connect the elderly person and the family to needed supportive services.

- *Adult foster-care services.* Foster care and group homes are designed to help the older person remain in the community. Social workers providing foster care match foster families with an older person and monitor the quality of life for those living in foster-care settings.

- *Adult protective services.* Social workers in adult protective services assess whether elderly adults are at risk for personal harm or injury owing to the actions (or inactions) of others. At risk circumstances include physical abuse, material (financial) abuse, psychological abuse, and neglect (in which caregivers withhold medications or nourishment, or fail to provide basic care). If abuse or neglect is determined, then adult protective service workers develop, implement, and monitor a plan to stop the maltreatment.

- *Support and therapeutic groups.* In some settings social workers facilitate the formation of support groups and therapeutic groups for the elderly or for family members (some of whom may be caregivers). Support and therapeutic groups are useful for such issues as adjusting to retirement, coping with illnesses such as Alzheimer's disease, dealing with alcohol or other drug abuse, coping with a terminal illness, and coping with depression and other emotional difficulties.

- *Respite care.* Social workers are involved with the recruitment and training of respite-care workers, as well as in identifying families in need of these services. When an older person requires 24-hour at-home care, respite services allow caregivers (such as the spouse or other family members) time away from caregiving responsibilities, which alleviates some of the stress involved in providing 24-hour-a-day care.

- *Transportation and housing assistance.* Social workers operate as brokers for finding appropriate housing in the community and for arranging safe transportation services.

- *Social services in hospitals and nursing homes.* Social workers in these settings provide: assessment of social needs; health education for the older person and the family; direct services (such as counseling) to the elderly person, the family, and significant others; advocacy; discharge planning; community liaison; participation in program planning; consultation on developing a therapeutic environment in the facility; and participation in developing care plans that maximize the older person's potential for independence.

(Obviously, there is some overlap in these services provided by social workers to the elderly.)

Because the elderly population is the most rapidly growing age group in our society, it is anticipated that services to the elderly will significantly expand in the next few decades. This expansion will generate a number of new employment opportunities for social workers.

❧ The Elderly Are a Powerful Political Force

Most programs for the elderly are designed to maintain the elderly at their current level of functioning, rather than having the higher goal of enhancing their social, physical, and psychological well-being. In spite of all the maintenance programs available for the elderly, key problems remain to be solved. A high proportion of the elderly do not have meaningful lives, respected status, or adequate income, transportation, living arrangements, diet, or health care. The elderly are victims of ageism. How can we defend urging people to retire when they are still productive? How can we defend the living conditions within some of our nursing homes? How can we defend our restrictive attitudes toward sexuality among the elderly? How can we defend providing services to the elderly that are limited to maintenance and subsistence? Moss and Moss (1975) comment, "Just as we are learning that black can be beautiful, so we must learn that gray can be beautiful too. In so learning, we may brighten the prospects of our old age" (p. 79).

In the past, prejudice has been most effectively combated when those being discriminated against joined together for political action. It seems apparent that if major changes in the elderly's role in society are to take place, they will have to be made through political action.

The elderly are, in fact, increasingly involved in political activism and in some cases, even radical militancy. A prominent organization is the American Association of Retired Persons. This group lobbies for the interests of the elderly at local, state, and federal levels of government.

An action-oriented group that has caught the public's attention is the Gray Panthers. This organization argues that a fundamental flaw in our society is the emphasis on materialism and on the consumption of goods and services, rather than on improving the quality of life for all citizens (including the elderly). The Gray Panthers seek to end ageism and to advance the goals of human freedom, human dignity, and self-development. This organization uses social action techniques, including getting the elderly to vote as a bloc for their concerns. Founder of the group, Maggie Kuhn (quoted in Butler, 1975), stated, "We are not mellow, sweet old people. We have got to effect change, and we have nothing to lose" (p. 341).

Another reason the elderly are a powerful political group is that they tend to be more likely to vote than the young (Kornblum & Julian, 2001). And the elderly will be more politically active in the future because the composition of the elderly population is changing. The average educational level of this population has been steadily increasing (U.S. Census Bureau, 2001). The coming generation of elderly will be better educated, better informed, and more politically conscious.

Significant steps toward securing a better life for the elderly have been made in the last 35 years: increased Social Security payments, enactment of the Medicare and

© Elizabeth Crews/Stock Boston

An elderly Hispanic man campaigns for senior citizens' rights at a rally in Sacramento, California. Older adults in America are politically organized and influential.

Medicaid programs, the emergence of hospices, and the expansion of a variety of other programs for the elderly. With the elderly becoming a powerful political bloc, we are apt to see a number of changes in future years to improve the status of the elderly in our society.

Changing a Macro System: Finding a Social Role for the Elderly

As we have discussed, the elderly face a variety of problems. The elderly have a roleless role in our society and are the victims of ageism. How can these problems be combated?

In a nutshell, it would seem essential to find a meaningful productive role for the elderly. At present, early retirement programs and the stereotypic expectations of the elderly often result in the elderly being unproductive, inactive, dependent, and unfulfilled. To develop a meaningful role for the elderly in our society, the productive elderly should be encouraged to continue to work and the expectations of the elderly should be changed.

The elderly who want to work and are still performing well should be encouraged to continue working past age 65 or 70. Also, if an elderly person wants to work half-time or part-time, this should be encouraged. For example, two elderly persons working half-time could fill a full-time position. New roles might also be created for the retired elderly to be consultants in the areas where they possess special knowledge and expertise. For those who do retire, there should be educational and training programs to help them develop their interests and hobbies into new sources of income.

Working longer in our society would have a number of payoffs for the elderly and for society. The elderly would continue to be productive, contributing citizens. They would have a meaningful role. They would continue to be physically and mentally active. They would have higher self-esteem. They would begin to break down the stereotypes of the elderly being unproductive and a financial burden on society. They would be paying into the Social Security system rather than drawing from it.

In our materialistic society perhaps the only way for the elderly to have a meaningful role is to be productive, either as paid workers or as volunteers. The elderly face the choice (as do younger people) between having adequate financial resources through productive work or inadequate financial resources as a result of not working.

Objections to such a system may be raised by those who maintain that some of the elderly are no longer productive. This may be true, but some younger people are also unproductive. What is needed to make the proposed system work is jobs having realistic, objective, and behaviorally measurable levels of performance. Those at any age who do not meet the performance levels should be informed about the deficiencies and be given training to meet the deficiencies. If the performance levels still are not met, discharge processes should be used as a last resort. (For example, if a tenured faculty member is deficient in levels of performance—as measured by student-course evaluations, peer-faculty evaluations of teaching, record of public service, record of service to the department and to the campus, and record of publications— that faculty member should be informed of the deficiencies. Training and other resources to meet the deficiencies should be offered. If the performance levels then do not improve to acceptable standards, dismissal proceedings would be initiated. Some colleges and universities are now moving in this direction.)

In the productivity system that is being suggested, the elderly would have an important part to play. They would be expected to continue to be productive within their capacities. By being productive, they would serve as examples to counter the current negative stereotypes of the elderly.

Another objection we have heard to this new system is that the elderly have worked most of their lives and deserve to retire and live in leisure with a comfortable standard of living. It would be nice if the elderly really had this option. However, that is not realistic. Most of the elderly do not have the financial resources after retiring to maintain a high standard of living. Most elderly retirees experience sharply reduced incomes and standards of living. The choice in our society is really between working and thereby maintaining a comfortable standard of living, or retiring and having a lower standard of living.

We are already seeing the elderly heading in a more productive direction. A number of organizations have been formed to promote the productivity of the elderly. Three examples are the Retired Senior Volunteer Program, the Service Corps of Retired Executives, and the Foster Grandparent Program.

The *Retired Senior Volunteer Program (RSVP)* offers people over age 60 the opportunity of doing volunteer service to meet community needs. RSVP agencies place volunteers in hospitals, schools, libraries, day-care centers, courts, nursing homes, and a variety of other places.

The *Service Corps of Retired Executives (SCORE)* offers retired businessmen and businesswomen an opportunity to help owners of small businesses and managers of community organizations who are having management problems. Volunteers receive no pay but are reimbursed for out-of-pocket expenses.

The *Foster Grandparent Program* employs low-income older people to provide personal care to children who live in institutions. Such children include those with a developmental disability and those who have emotional or behavioral difficulties. Foster grandparents are given special assignments in child care, speech therapy, physical therapy, or as teacher's aides. This program has been shown to be of considerable benefit to both the children and to the foster grandparents (Atchley, 1988). The children served become more outgoing and have improved relationships with peers and staff. They have increased self-confidence, improved language skills, and decreased fear and insecurity. The foster grandparents have an additional (small) source of income, increased feelings of vigor and youthfulness, an increased sense of personal worth, a feeling of being productive, and a renewed sense of personal growth and development. For society, foster grandparents provide a vast pool of relatively inexpensive labor that can be used to do needed work in the community.

The success of these programs illustrates that the elderly can be productive in both paid and volunteer positions. Atchley (1988) makes the following recommendations for using elderly volunteers:

First, agencies must be flexible in matching the volunteer's background to assigned tasks. If the agency takes a broad perspective, useful work can be found for almost anyone. Second, volunteers must be trained. *All too often agency personnel place unprepared volunteers in an unfamiliar setting. Then the volunteer's difficulty confirms the myth that you cannot expect good work from volunteers. Third, a variety of placement options should be offered to the volunteer. Some volunteers prefer to do familiar things; others want to do* anything but familiar *things. Fourth, training of volunteers should not make them feel that they are being tested. This point is particularly sensitive among working-class volunteers. Fifth, volunteers should get personal attention from the placement agency. There should be people (perhaps volunteers) who follow up on absences and who are willing to listen to the compliments, complaints, or experiences of the volunteers. Public recognition from the community is an important reward for voluntary service. Finally, transportation to and from the placement should be provided. (p. 216)*

Summary

People 65 and older now comprise over one-tenth of our population and are the fastest-growing age group in our society. The elderly tend to encounter a number of problems in our society: low status, lack of a meaningful role, an emphasis on youth, health problems, inadequate income, inadequate housing, transportation problems, elder abuse, malnutrition, crime victimization, emotional problems (particularly depression), and concern with circumstances surrounding dying. A majority of the elderly depend on the Social Security system as their major source of income. Yet, monthly payments are inadequate.

In many ways, the elderly are victims of ageism. But increasingly, the elderly are politically active and organized to work toward improving their status.

In order to provide the elderly with a productive, meaningful role in our society they should be encouraged to work (either in paid work or as volunteers) as long as they are productive and have an interest in working to maintain their standard of living. Helping the elderly to stay productive in their lives is predicted to have a number of personal payoffs for them and to be highly beneficial to society.

InfoTrac College Edition Keywords

adult protective services	early retirement	elderly problems	Medicare	Older Americans Act
assisted suicide	elder abuse	malnutrition/elderly	nursing homes	Social Security

On the Internet

AARP (American Association of Retired Persons)

http://www.aarp.org/

AARP is a nonprofit membership organization dedicated to addressing the needs and interests of persons 50 and older. Through information and education, advocacy and service, AARP seeks to enhance the quality of life for all by promoting independence, dignity and purpose.

Care for the Elderly in Sweden and Japan

http://www.yamanoi.net/ronbun/index.htm

A report regarding the situation and the problem of the care for the elderly in Japan, which is compared with the Swedish elderly care.

Gray Panthers

http://www.graypanthers.org/

The Gray Panthers is a national organization of intergenerational activists dedicated to social change. It is a blend of age and youth in action. For almost 30 years, the Gray Panthers has worked to make America a better place to live for the young, the old, and everyone else.

National Center on Elder Abuse

http://www.elderabusecenter.org/

The National Center on Elder Abuse (NCEA) consists of a partnership of six agencies: the National Association of State Units on Aging (NASUA); the American Bar Association (ABA) Commission on Legal Problems of the Elderly; the Clearinghouse on Abuse and Neglect of the Elderly (CANE); the Institute on Aging (IOA), San Francisco Consortium for Elder Abuse Prevention; the National Association of Adult Protective Services Administrators (NAAPSA); and the National Committee for the Prevention of Elder Abuse (NCPEA). Each agency retains responsibility for distributing the publications it produces for NCEA.

Social Security Administration

http://www.ssa.gov

The official Web site of the Social Security Administration.

Abadinsky, H. (1989). *Drug abuse: An introduction*. Chicago: Nelson-Hall.

Abadinsky, H. (1995). *Drug abuse: An introduction* (2nd ed.). Chicago: Nelson-Hall.

Ackerman, G. L. (1993). A congressional view of youth suicide. *American Psychologist, 48,* 183–184.

Adame, D. D., Taylor-Nicholson, M. E., Wang, M., & Abbas, M. A. (1991, Fall). Southern college freshmen students: A survey of knowledge, attitudes, and beliefs about AIDS. *Journal of Sex Education and Therapy, 17*(3), 196–206.

Adams, G., Adams-Taylor, S., & Pittman, K. (1989). Adolescent pregnancy and parenthood: A review of the problem, solutions, and resources. *Family Relations, 38,* 223–229.

Adler, N. E. (1989, March 16). Testimony before the U.S. House of Representatives on the medical and psychological impact of abortion on women. Washington, DC: American Psychological Association.

Adler, N. E., David, H. P., Major, B. M., Roth, S. H., Russo, N. F., & Wyatt, G. E. (1990). Psychological factors in abortion. *American Psychologist, 47,* 41–44.

Adler, N. E., & Tschann, J. M. (1993). The abortion debate: Psychological issues for adult women and adolescents. In S. Matteo (Ed.), *American women in the nineties: Today's critical issues*. Boston: Northeastern University Press.

Adler, R. B., & Towne, N. (1981). *Looking out/looking in* (3rd ed.). New York: Holt, Rinehart and Winston.

Adorno, T. W., Frenkel-Brunswik, E., Devinson, J. J., & Sanford, R.N. (1950). *The authoritarian personality*. New York: Harper & Row.

Afek, D. (1990). Sarah and the women's movement: The experience of infertility. *Women and Therapy, 10,* 195–203.

Ahearn, F. L., Jr. (1995). Displaced people. In R. L. Edwards (Editor-in-chief), *Encyclopedia of social work* (Vol. 1, pp. 771–780). Washington, DC: NASW Press.

Age need not be a barrier to making major contributions. (1980, September 1). *U.S. News & World Report*, pp. 52–53.

Ahmad, S. (1998, March 2). Get your sex insurance now: Companies are rushing to buy policies to protect themselves from sex harassment suits. *U.S. News & World Report*, p. 61.

After one year, Thomas-Hill hearings still echo across the land. (1992, October 8). *Milwaukee Journal*, p. A14.

AIDS kids beat odds against survival. (1994, April 14). *Edmonton Journal*, p. C7.

Alan Guttmacher Institute. (1981). *Safe and legal: 10 years' experience with legal abortion in New York State*. New York: Alan Guttmacher Institute.

Alan Guttmacher Institute. (1999). *Teen sex and pregnancy*. New York: Alan Guttmacher Institute.

Alberti, R. E., & Emmons, M. L. (1976a). *Assert yourself—It's your perfect right: A guide to assertive behavior*. San Luis Obispo, CA: Impact.

Alberti, R. E., & Emmons, M. L. (1976b). *Stand up, speak out, talk back!* New York: Pocket Books.

Alberti, R. E., & Emmons, M. L. (2001). *Your perfect right* (8th ed.). Atascadero, CA: Impact.

Albin, R. S. Psychological studies of rape. (1977). *Signs, 3,* 423–435.

Algozzine, R. (1976). What teachers perceive—children receive. *Communication Quarterly, 24,* 41–47.

Alinsky, S. (1969). *Reveille for radicals*. New York: Basic Books.

Alinsky, S. (1972). *Rules for radicals*. New York: Random House.

Allgeier, A. R., & Allgeier, E. R. (1995). *Sexual interactions* (4th ed.). Lexington, MA: D. C. Heath.

Allgeier, E., & Allgeier, A. R. (1984). *Sexual interactions* (1st ed.). Lexington, MA: D. C. Heath.

Allgeier, E., & Allgeier, A. R. (2000). *Sexual interactions* (5th ed.). Lexington, MA: D. C. Heath.

Almeida, R. (1996). Hindu, Christian, and Muslim families. In M. McGoldrick, J. Giordano, & J. K. Pearce (Eds.), *Ethnicity & family therapy* (2nd ed., pp. 395–423). New York: Guilford.

Almquist, E. M. (1995). The experiences of minority women in the United States: Intersections of race, gender, and class. In J. Freeman (Ed.), *Women: A feminist perspective* (5th ed., pp. 573–606). Mountain View, CA: Mayfield.

Alsaker, F. D. (1992). Pubertal timing, overweight, and psychological adjustment. *Journal of Early Adolescence, 12*(4), 396–419.

Alter, J. (1996, October 7). When facts get aborted: The fight over partial-birth abortion illustrates the practical limits of unflinching principle. *Newsweek*, p. 67.

American Academy of Pediatrics (AAP). (1986). *How to be your child's TV guide: Guidelines for constructive viewing*. Elk Grove Village, IL: AAP.

AAP, Committee on Children with Disabilities and Committee on Drugs. (1996). Education for children with attentional disorders. *Pediatrics, 98,* 301–304.

American Association of Retired Persons (AARP). (1990). *A profile of older Americans: 1990*. Washington, DC: AARP.

AARP. (1997). *A profile of older Americans: 1997*. Washington, DC: AARP.

AARP. (2000). *A profile of older Americans, 2000*. Washington, DC: AARP.

American Association of Sex Educators, Counselors, and Therapists (AASECT). (1993, May). Abortion update. *Contemporary Sexuality, 27*(8), 7–8.

AASECT. (1993, August). Abortion issues update. *Contemporary Sexuality, 27*(5), 6–7.

AASECT. (1993, September). Studies in short. *Contemporary Sexuality, 27*(9), 9.

AASECT. (1993, October). Sexuality and the law. *Contemporary Sexuality, 27*(10), 8–9.

AASECT. (1994, May). Sexuality and the law. *Contemporary Sexuality, 28*(5), 12–13.

AASECT. (1994, June). Sexuality and the law. *Contemporary Sexuality, 28*(6), 13–14.

AASECT. (1994, July). Abortion update. *Contemporary Sexuality, 28*(7), 6.

AASECT. (1994, August). Studies in short. *Contemporary Sexuality, 28*(8), 12–13.

AASECT. (1994, September). Sexuality and the law. *Contemporary Sexuality, 28*(9), 8–9, 15.

AASECT. (1994, October). Sexuality and the law. *Contemporary Sexuality, 28*(10), 12.

AASECT. (1994, November). Studies in short. *Contemporary Sexuality, 28*(11), 10–11.

AASECT. (1994, December). Sexuality and the law. *Contemporary Sexuality, 28*(12), 16.

AASECT. (1995a, February). Sexuality and the law. *Contemporary Sexuality, 29*(2), 9.

AASECT. (1995b, February). Studies in short. *Contemporary Sexuality, 29*(2), 7–8.

AASECT. (1995, March). Studies in short. *Contemporary Sexuality, 29*(3), 6–7.

AASECT. (1995, April). Sexuality and the law. *Contemporary Sexuality, 29*(4), 9.

AASECT. (1995, August). International update. *Contemporary Sexuality, 29*(8), 8–9.

AASECT. (1995, September). Sexuality and the law. *Contemporary Sexuality, 29*(9), 6.

AASECT. (1995a, October). Sexuality and the law. *Contemporary Sexuality, 29*(10), 8.

AASECT. (1995b, October). Studies in short. *Contemporary Sexuality, 29*(10), 5–6.

AASECT. (1995, November). Sexuality and the law. *Contemporary Sexuality, 29*(11), 85–6.

AASECT. (1995, December). Sexuality and the law. *Contemporary Sexuality, 29*(12), 6.

AASECT. (1997, March). Sexuality and the law. *Contemporary Sexuality, 31*(3), 4–6.

AASECT. (1997, June). Sexuality and the law. *Contemporary Sexuality, 31*(6), 9.

AASECT. (1998, January). Studies in short. *Contemporary Sexuality, 32*(1), 11–12.

AASECT. (1998, November). Homophobia: Six perspectives. *Contemporary Sexuality, 32*(11), 1–9.

AASECT. (1999a, January). Sexuality and the law. *Contemporary Sexuality, 33*(1), 11–14.

AASECT. (1999b, January). Studies in short. *Contemporary Sexuality, 33*(1), 5–8.

AASECT. (1999, March). Sexuality and the law. *Contemporary Sexuality, 33*(3), 5–7.

AASECT. (1999, April). Sexuality and the law. *Contemporary Sexuality, 33*(4), 3, 4, 8.

AASECT. (2000, April). Vermont House passes "civil union" measure for same-sex couples. *Contemporary Sexuality 34*(4), 6.

AASECT. (2000, May). Big strides in gay civil unions, parental rights. *Contemporary Sexuality 34*(5), 9.

AASECT. (2000, December). Gay marriage banned in 2 states. *Contemporary Sexuality, 34*(12), 8.

AASECT. (2000, July). Minnesota's sodomy law challenged. *Contemporary Sexuality, 34*(7), 7.

AASECT. (2001, November). Gay partners get relief after Sept. 11 terrorist attack. *Contemporary Sexuality, 35*(11), 7.

AASECT. (2002, February). Calif. civil union bill dropped. *Contemporary Sexuality 36*(2), 7.

AASECT. (2002, March). Pediatricians group backs gay parents. *Contemporary Sexuality, 36*(3), 10.

AASECT. (2002, April). "Don't ask, don't tell" spurs rise in gay troop discharges. *Contemporary Sexuality 36*(4), 9.

American Association of University Women. (1991). Shortchanging girls, shortchanging America. Washington, DC: Greenberg-Lake Analysis.

American Association of University Women. (1992). *How schools shortchange girls.* Washington, DC: AAUW Educational Foundation.

American Association of Obstetricians and Gynecologists. (1996). *ACOG practice patterns: Emergency oral contraception.* Washington, DC: American Association of Obstetricians and Gynecologists.

American Heart Association (AHA). (1984). *Cholesterol and your heart.* Dallas, TX: AHA.

AHA. (1995). *Silent epidemic: The truth about women and heart disease.* Dallas: AHA.

American Psychiatric Association. (1994). *Diagnostic and statistical manual of mental disorders (DSM-IV)* (4th ed.). Washington, DC: American Psychiatric Association.

American Psychiatric Association. (2000). *Diagnostic and statistical manual of mental disorders, text revision (DSM-IV-TR)* (4th ed.). Washington, DC: American Psychiatric Association.

American Psychiatric Association. (2001). *Publication Manual of the American Psychological Association* (5th ed.). Washington, DC: American Psychological Association.

Amponsah, B., & Krekling, S. (1997). Sex differences in visual-spatial performance among Ghanaian and Norwegian adults. *Journal of Cross-Cultural Psychology, 28,* 81–92.

Annon, J. S. (1976). *The behavioral treatment of sexual problems: Brief therapy.* New York: Harper & Row.

Antonarakis, S. E., & Down Syndrome Collaborative Group. (1991). Parental origin of the extra chromosome in trisomy 21 as indicated by analysis of DNA polymorphisms. *New England Journal of Medicine, 324,* 872–876.

Apgar, K., & Callahan, B. C. (1980). *Four one-day workshops.* Boston: Resource Communications.

Apgar, V. (1958). The Apgar scoring chart. *Journal of the American Medical Association, 32,* 168.

Apparent per capital ethanol consumption—United States, 1977–1986. (1989). *Morbidity and Mortality Weekly Report, 38*(46), 800–803.

Applewhite, S. L. (1996). Curanderismo: Demystifying the health beliefs and practices of elderly Mexican Americans. In P. L. Ewalt, E. M. Freeman, S. A. Kirk, & D. L. Poole (Eds.), *Multicultural issues in social work* (pp. 455–468). Washington, DC: NASW Press.

Arehart-Triechel, J. (1977, April 11). It's never too late to start living longer. *New York Magazine,* p. 38.

Arlow, J. A. (1995). Psychoanalysis. In R. J. Corsini & D. Wedding (Eds.), *Current Psychotherapies* (5th ed.). Itasca, IL: Peacock.

Atchley, R. C. (1983). *Aging: Continuity and change.* Belmont, CA: Wadsworth.

Atchley, R. C. (1988). *Social forces and aging* (5th ed.). Belmont, CA: Wadsworth.

Au, K. H. (1997). A sociocultural model of reading instruction: The Kamehameha Elementary Education Program. In S. A. Stahl & D. A. Hayes (Eds.), *Instructional models in reading* (pp. 181–202). Mahwah, NJ: Erlbaum.

Austin, C. D. (1995). Adult protective services. In R. L. Edwards (Ed.), *Encyclopedia of social work* (19th ed., Vol. 1). Washington, DC: NASW Press.

Baer, B. L., & Federico, R. C. (1978). *Educating the baccalaureate social worker.* Cambridge, MA: Ballinger.

Bagley, C., Bolitho, F., & Bertrand, L. (1997). Sexual assault in school, mental health, and suicidal behaviors in adolescent women in Canada. *Adolescence, 32,* 361–394.

Bailey, J. M., & Pillard, R. (1991). A genetic study of male sexual orientation. *Archives of General Psychiatry, 48,* 1089–1096.

Bailey, J. M., et al. (1993). Heritable factors influence sexual orientation in women. *Archives of General Psychiatry, 50,* 217–223.

Bailey, S. M. (1993). The current status of gender equity research in American schools. *Educational Psychologist, 28,* 321–329.

Baillargeon, R. (1987). Object permanence in 3½–4½-month-old infants. *Developmental Psychology, 23*(5), 655–664.

Baker, S., Thalberg, S., & Morrison, D. (1988). Parents' behavioral norms as predictors of adolescent sexual activity and contraceptive use. *Adolescence, 28,* 278–281.

Baldwin, W., & Cain, V. S. (1980). The children of teenage parents. *Family Planning Perspectives, 12,* 34.

Bales, R. F. (1965). The equilibrium problem in small groups. In A. Hare, E. Borgatta, & R. Bales (Eds.), *Small groups: Studies in social interaction.* New York: Knopf.

Balgopal, P. R. (1995). Asian Americans overview. In R. L. Edwards (Ed.), *Encyclopedia of social work* (19th ed., Vol. 1). Washington, DC: NASW Press.

Baltes, P., & Schaie, K. (1974, October). Aging and IQ: The myth of the twilight years. *Psychology Today,* 35–38.

Bandura, A. (1965). Influence of models' reinforcement contingencies in the acquisition of imitative responses. *Journal of Personality and Social Psychology, 1,* 589–95.

Barbach, L. G. (1980). *Women discover orgasm.* New York: Free Press.

Barker, L. M. (1994). *Learning and behavior: A psychobiological approach.* New York: Macmillan.

Barker, L. M. (1997). *Learning and behavior: Biological, psychological, and sociocultural perspectives* (2nd ed.). Upper Saddle River, NJ: Prentice-Hall.

Barker, R. L. (1991). *The social work dictionary.* Silver Spring, MD: National Association of Social Workers.

Barker, R. L. (1995). *The social work dictionary* (3rd ed.). Washington, DC: NASW Press.

Barker, R. L. (1999). *The social work dictionary* (4th ed.). Washington, DC: NASW Press.

Barnett, W., Freudenberg, N., & Wille, R. (1992). Partnership after induced abortion—A prospective controlled study. *Archives of Sexual Behavior, 21*(5), 443–455.

Baron, A., & Cramer, D. W. (2000). Potential counseling concerns of aging lesbian, gay, and bisexual clients. In R. M. Perez, K. A. DeBord, & K. J. Bieschke (Eds.), *Handbook of counseling and psychotherapy with lesbian, gay, and bisexual clients* (pp. 207–223). Washington, DC: American Psychological Association.

Baron, L., & Straus, M. A. (1989). *Four theories of rape in American society.* New Haven, CT: Yale University Press.

Barringer, F. (1993, April 15). Sex survey of American men finds 1 percent are gay. *New York Times,* p. 1A.

Bar-Tal, D., & Saxe, L. (1976). Perceptions of similarity and dissimilarity of physically attractive couples and individuals. *Journal of Personality and Social Psychology, 33,* 772–781.

Barth, R. P. (1995). Adoption. In R. L. Edwards (Ed.), *Encyclopedia of social work* (19th ed., Vol. 1). Washington, DC: NASW Press.

Bartlett, H. M. (1970). *The common base of social work practice.* New York: NASW.

Baruth, L. G., & Manning, M. L. (1991). *Multicultural counseling and psychotherapy: A life-span perspective.* New York: Macmillan.

Baruth, L. G., & Manning, M. L. (1999). *Multicultural counseling and psychotherapy: A lifespan perspective.* Upper Saddle River, NJ: Merrill.

Basow, S. A. (1992). *Gender: Stereotypes and roles* (3rd ed.). Pacific Grove, CA: Brooks/Cole.

Bass, D. (1995). Runaways and homeless youths. In *Encyclopedia of social work* (Vol. 3, pp. 2060–2067). Washington, DC: NASW Press.

Bates, J. E. (1987). Temperament in infancy. In J. D. Osofsky (Ed.), *Handbook of infant development* (2nd ed.). New York: Wiley.

Baumrind, D. (1971). Current patterns of parental authority. *Developmental Psychology Monographs, 4*(1, Pt. 2).

Baumrind, D. (1972). An exploratory study of socialization effects on black children: Some black-white comparisons. *Child Development, 43,* 261–267.

Baumrind, D. (1989). Rearing competent children. In W. Damon (Ed.), *Child development today and tomorrow.* San Francisco, CA: Jossey-Bass.

Baumrind, D. (1991). Parenting styles and adolescent development. In R. M. Lerner, A. C. Peterson, & J. Brooks-Gunn (Eds.), *Encyclopedia of adolescence.* New York: Garland.

Baumrind, D. (1991a). Effective parenting during the early adolescent transition. In P. A. Cowan & E. M. Hetherington (Eds.), *Advances in family research* (Vol. 2). Hillsdale, NJ: Erlbaum.

Baumrind, D. (1991b). The influence of parenting syle on adolescent competence and substance use. *Journal of Early Adolescence, 11*(1), 56–95.

Baumrind, D. (1993). The average expectable environment is not good enough: A response to Scarr. *Child Development, 38,* 291–327.

Baumrind, D. (1996). The discipline controversy revisited. *Family Relations, 45,* 405–414.

Bays, L., & Freeman-Longo, R. (1989). *Why did I do it again?* (Workbook 2). Brandon, VT: Safer Society Press.

Bechham, D., Lopez, D., Palacios-Jimenez, L., Patti, V., & Shernoff, M. (1973). *When a friend has AIDS.* New York: Chelsea Psychotherapy Associates.

Beck, D. (1973). *Progress on family problems.* New York: Family Service Associations of America.

Beck, J., & Davies, D. (1987). Teen contraception: A review of perspectives on compliance. *Archives of Sexual Behavior, 16,* 337–368.

Becker, J. V., & Kaplan, M. S. (1991). Rape victims: Issues, theories, and treatment. *Annual Review of Sex Research, 2,* 267–292.

Beckett, J. O., & Johnson, H. C. (1995). Human development. In R. L. Edwards (Ed.), *Encyclopedia of social work* (19th ed., Vol. 2). Washington, DC: NASW Press.

Beckwith, L., & Rodning, C. (1991). Intellectual functioning in children born preterm: Recent research. In L. Okagake & R. J. Sternberg (Eds.), *Directors of development: Influences on the development of children's thinking.* Hillsdale, NJ: Erlbaum.

Beeler, N. G., Rycus, J. S., & Hughes, R. C. (1990). *The effects of abuse and neglect on child development: A training curriculum.* Washington, DC: Child Welfare League of America.

Begley, S., Brant, M., Springen, K., & Rogers, A. (1995, September 4). The baby myth. *Newsweek,* pp. 38–47.

Begley, S., & Rosenberg, D. (1995, September 11). Abortion by prescription. *Newsweek,* p. 76.

Beitchman, J. H., Zucker, K. J., Hood, J. E., DaCosta, G. A., Akman, D., & Cassavia, E. (1992). A review of the long-term effects of child sexual abuse. *Child Abuse and Neglect, 16*(1), 101–118.

Belcastro, P. (1985). Sexual behavior differences between black and white students. *Journal of Sex Research, 21*(1), 56–67.

Bell, A. P., Weinberg, M. S., Martin, S., & Hammersmith, S.K. (1981). *Sexual preference.* Bloomington: Indiana University Press.

Bellak, A. O. (1984). Comparable worth: A practitioner's view. In *Comparable worth: Issue for the 80's.* Vol. 1. Washington, DC: U.S. Commission on Civil Rights.

Belloc, N. B., & Breslow, L. (1972). Relationship of physical health status and health practices. *Preventive Medicine, 1*(3), 409–421.

Belsky, J., Lang, M., & Huston, T. L. (1986). Sex typing and division of labor as determinants of marital change across the transition to parenthood. *Journal of Personality and Social Psychology, 50,* 517–522.

Belsky, J., & Rovine, M. J. (1988). Nonmaternal care in the first year of life and the security of infant-parent attachment. *Child Development, 59,* 157–167.

Benedetti, J., Corey, L., & Ashley, R. (1994). Recurrence rates in genital herpes after symptomatic first-episode infection. *Annals of Internal Medicine, 121,* 847–854.

Benjamin, L. (1991). *The black elite: Facing the color line in the twilight of the twentieth century.* Chicago, IL: Nelson-Hall.

Bennett, E. C. (1992). The black population in the United States. *Current Population Reports* (Series P-20, No. 464). Washington, DC: U.S. Government Printing Office.

Bennett, L. W. (1995). Substance abuse and the domestic assault of women. *Social Work, 40*(6), 760–771.

Benson, H. (1975). *The relaxation response.* New York: Avon.

Benson, M. D., et al. (1986). Sex education in the inner city. *Journal of the Medical Association, 255,* 43–47.

Berg, I. K., & Jaya, K. P. (1993). Different and same: Family therapy with Asian-American families. *Journal of Marital and Family Therapy, 19*(1), 31–38.

Berger, R. M. (1983). What is a homosexual? A definitional model. *Social Work, 28,* 132–135.

Berger, R. M. (1985). Rewriting a bad script: Older lesbians and gays. In H. Hidalgo et al. (Eds.), *Lesbian and gay issues: A resource manual for social workers.* Silver Spring, MD: NASW.

Berger, R. M., & Kelly, J. J. (1995). Gay men overview. In R. L. Edwards (Ed.), *Encyclopedia of social work* (19th ed., Vol. 2, pp. 1064–1075). Washington, DC: NASW Press.

Berk, L. E. (1999). *Infants, children, and adolescents* (3rd ed.). Boston: Allyn & Bacon.

Berliner, L., & Elliott, D. M. (2002). Sexual abuse of children. In J. E. B. Myers, L. Berliner, J. Briere, C. T. Hendrix, C. Jenny, & T. A. Reid (Eds.), *The APSAC handbook on child maltreatment* (2nd ed., pp. 55–78). Thousand Oaks, CA: Sage.

Berman, C. (1981). *Making it as a stepparent: New roles/new rules.* New York: Bantam.

Bermant, G. (1976). Sexual behavior: Hard times with the Coolidge effect. In M. H. Siegel & H. P. Ziegler (Eds.), *Psychological research: The inside story.* New York: Harper & Row.

Berne, E. (1964). *Games people play.* New York: Grove Press.

Bernstein, D. A., & Nash, P. W. (2002). *Essentials of psychology* (2nd ed.). Boston: Houghton Mifflin.

Bernstein, D. A., Penner, L. A., Clarke-Stewart, A., & Roy, E. J. (2003). *Psychology* (6th ed.). Boston: Houghton Mifflin.

Berscheid, E., & Walster, E. H. (1974). Physical attractiveness. In L. Berkowitz (Ed.), *Advances in experimental social psychology* (Vol. 7). New York: Academic Press.

Berzon, B. (1978). Sharing your lesbian identity with your children. In G. Vida (Ed.), *Our right to love: A lesbian resource book.* Englewood Cliffs, NJ: Prentice-Hall.

Beyette, B. (1986, October 17). Teen sex-education campaign launched. *Los Angeles Times,* pp. 20, 22.

Bibby, R. W., & Posterski, D. C. (1985). *The emerging generation: An inside look at Canada's teenagers.* Toronto: Irwin.

Bierman, E., & Hazzard, W. (1973). Biology of aging. In D. Smith & E. Bierman (Eds.), *The biologic ages of man.* Philadelphia: Saunders.

Bierman, K. L., & Furman, W. (1984). The effects of social skills training and peer involvement on the social adjustment of preadolescents. *Child Development, 55,* 151–162.

Billingsley, A. (1993). *Climbing Jacob's ladder: The enduring legacy of African-American families.* New York: Simon and Schuster.

Billy, J. O., Tanfer, K., Grady, W. R., & Klepinger, D. H. (1993). The sexual behavior of men in the United States. *Family Planning Perspectives, 25*(2), 52–60.

Bingham, C., & Wolfberg, A. (1992, December 7). A way on sexual harassment. *Newsweek,* p. 28.

Birren, J. E. (1974). Translations in gerontology—from lab to life: Psychophysiology and speed of response. *American Psychologist, 29*(11), 808–815.

Bishop, J. (1971). *The days of Martin Luther King, Jr.* New York: Putnam.

Black, R. D. (1991). Women's voices after pregnancy loss: Couple's patterns. *Social Work in Health Care, 16*(2), 19–36.

Blatchford, P., & Mortimore, P. (1994). The issue of class size for young children in schools: What can we learn from research? *Oxford Review of Education, 20,* 411–428.

Blaze-Gosden, T. (1987). *Drug abuse.* Birmingham, UK: David and Charles.

Blier, M. J., & Blier-Wilson, L. A. (1989). Gender differences in self-rated emotional expressiveness. *Sex Roles, 21,* 287–295.

Bloom, L. Z., Coburn, K., & Pearlman, J. (1976). *The new assertive woman.* New York: Dell.

Blumenfeld, W. J. (Ed.). (1992). *Homophobia: How we all pay the price.* Boston: Beacon Press.

Boes, M., & van Wormer, K. (2002). Social work with lesbian, gay, bisexual, and transgendered clients. In A. R. Roberts & G. J. Greene (Eds.), *Social work desk reference* (pp. 619–623). New York: Oxford.

Bolumar, F. (1996). Smoking reduces fecundity: A European multi-center study on infertility and subfecundity. *American Journal of Epidemiology, 143,* 578–587.

Boodman, S. (1994, October 8). "Miracle" babies face physical, intellectual disabilities—study. *Edmonton Journal,* p. E2.

Bootzin, R. R., Epstein, D., Engle-Friedman, M., & Salvio, M. A. (1996). Sleep disturbances. In L. L. Carstensen, B. A. Edelstein, & L. Dornbrand (Eds.), Chap. 21 (pp. 398–420). Thousand Oaks, CA: Sage.

Boskin-White, M., & W. C. White.(1983). *Bulimarexia.* New York: Norton.

Bossé, R., Aldwin, C. M., Levenson, M. R., & Ekerdt, D. J. (1987). Mental health differences among retirees and workers: Findings from the normative aging study. *Psychology and Aging, 2,* 383–389.

Boston Women's Health Book Collective. (1984). *The new our bodies, ourselves.* New York: Simon and Schuster.

Boston Women's Health Book Collective. (1992). *The new our bodies, ourselves* (Rev. ed.). New York: Simon and Schuster.

Botwinick, J. (1966). Cautiousness in advanced age. *Journal of Gerontology, 21,* 347–353.

Botwinick, J. (1970). Geropsychology. *Annual Review of Psychology, 21,* 239–272.

Bouchard, T. J., Jr. (1968). Current conceptions of intelligence and their implications for assessment. In P. McReynolds (Ed.), *Advances in psychological assessment* (Vol. 1). Palo Alto, CA: Science and Behavior Books.

Bourque, L. B. (1989). *Defining rape.* Durham, NC: Duke University Press.

Bower, B. (1993, July 17). Genetic clue to male homosexuality emerges. *Science News, 144,* p. 37.

Boyte, H. C. (1989). People power transforms a St. Louis housing project. Occasional papers. Chicago: Community Renewable Society.

Bracken, M., et al. (1990). Association of cocaine use with sperm concentration, motility and morphology. *Fertility and Sterilization, 53,* 315–322.

Brassard, M., Germain, R., & Hart, S. (1987). *Psychological maltreatment of children and youth.* Elmsford, NY: Pergamon.

Braungart, J. M., Plomin, R., Defries, J. C., & Fulker, D. W. (1992). Genetic influence on tester-rated infant temperament as assessed by Bayley's infant behavior record: Nonadoptive and adoptive siblings and twins. *Developmental Psychology, 28*(1), 40–47.

Braverman, P., & Strasburger, V. (1994, January). Sexually transmitted diseases. *Clinical Pediatrics,* 26–37.

Brazelton, H. M. (1973). Neonatal behavioral assessment scale. In *Clinics in developmental medicine* (No. 50). Philadelphia: Lippincott.

Brazelton, T. B., Nugent, J. K., & Lester, B. M. (1987). Neonatal behavioral assessment scale. In J. D. Osofsky (Ed.), *Handbook of infant development* (2nd ed.). New York: Wiley.

Brecher, E. M. (1984). *Love, sex, and aging.* Mount Vernon, NY: Consumers Union.

Bretschneider, J. G., & McCoy, N. L. (1988). Sexual interest and behavior in healthy 80- and 102-year olds. *Archives of Sexual Behavior,* 109–130.

Breuer, J., & Freud, S. (1895). *Studies in hysteria.* London: Hogarth Press.

Brewster, K. (1994). Race differences in sexual activity among adolescent women: The role of neighborhood characteristics. *American Sociological Review, 59,* 408–424.

Bricker-Jenkins, M., & Hooyman, N. (Eds.). (1986). *Not for women only: Social work practice for a feminist future.* Silver Spring, MD: NASW Press.

Bricker-Jenkins, M., & Lockett, P. W. (1995). Women: Direct practice. In R. L. Edwards (Ed.), *Encyclopedia of social work* (19th ed., Vol. 3, pp. 2529–2539). Washington, DC: NASW Press.

Bridges, K. M. B. (1932). Emotional development in early infancy. *Child Development, 3,* 324–341.

Bright, P. (1987). Adolescent pregnancy and loss. *Maternal-Child Nursing Journal, 16,* 1–12.

Brink, S. (1996, February 12). Beating the odds. *U.S. News & World Report,* pp. 60–68.

Brock, C., et al. (1990). Frequency of asymptomatic shedding of herpes simplex virus in women with genital herpes. *Journal of the American Medical Association, 263,* 418–422.

Brody, G. H., Stoneman, Z., & McCoy, J. K. (1994). Forecasting sibling relationships in early adolescence from child temperaments and family processes in middle childhood. *Child Development, 65,* 771–784.

Bromley, D. B. (1974). *The psychology of human aging* (2nd ed.). Middlesex, UK: Penguin.

Bronstein, P., Clauson, J., Stoll, M. F., & Abrams, C. L. (1993). Parenting behavior and children's social, psychological, and academic adjustment in diverse family structures. *Family Relations, 42,* 268–276.

Bronstein, P., & Paludi, M. (1988). The introductory course from a broader human perspective. In P. A. Bronstein & K. Quina (Eds.), *Teaching a psychology of people.* Washington, DC: American Psychological Association.

Brooks-Gunn, J. (1988). Pubertal processes and the early adolescent transition. In W. Dumon (Ed.), *Child development today and tomorrow.* San Francisco, CA: Jossey-Bass.

Brooks-Gunn, J. (1996, March). The uniqueness of the early adolescent transition. Paper presented at the meeting of the Society for Research on Adolescence, Boston.

Brooks-Gunn, J., & Furstenberg, F. F. (1986). The children of adolescent mothers: Physical, academic, and psychological outcomes. *Developmental Review, 6,* 224–251.

Brooks-Gunn, J., & Paikoff, R. L. (1993). Sex is a gamble, kissing is a game: Adolescent sexuality and health promotion. In S. G. Millstein, A. C. Petersen, & E. O. Nightingale (Eds.), *Promoting the health of adolescents.* New York: Oxford University Press.

Brown, B. (1977). *Stress and the art of biofeedback.* New York: Harper & Row.

Brown, B. S. (1977). The decriminalization of marijuana. In *Hearings of the House Select Committee on Narcotic Abuse,* March 14, 1977, First session, 95th Congress. Washington, DC: U.S. Government Printing Office.

Brown, D. (December 1, 2002). 50% of those with HIV are women. *Milwaukee Journal and Sentinel,* p. 27A.

Brown, S. S. (1985). Can low birth weight be prevented? *Family Planning Perspectives, 17*(3), 112–118.

Browne, A., & Finkelhor, D. (1986). Initial long-term effects: A review of the research. In D. Finkelhor, S. Araji, A. Browne, S. D. Peters, & G. E. Wyatt (Eds.), *A Sourcebook on Child Sexual Abuse.* Beverly Hills, CA: Sage.

Brownlee, S. (1991, August 12). Alzheimer's: Is there hope? *U.S. News & World Report,* pp. 40–49.

Buckingham, S. L., & Van Gorp, W. G. (1998, June). AIDS dementia complex: Implications for practice. *Social Casework, 29*(6), 375–376.

Budiansky, S. (1988, April 18). The new rules of reproduction. *U.S. News & World Report,* pp. 66–69.

Buhler, C. (1933). *Der menschliche, lebenslauf al pschologishes problem.* Leipzig: Verlag von S. Herzel.

Burgess, A. W., & Holmstrom, L. L. (1974a). Rape trauma syndrome. *American Journal of Psychiatry, 131,* 981–896.

Burgess, A. W., & Holmstrom, L. L. (1974b). *Rape: Victims of crisis.* Bowie, MD: Robert J. Brady.

Burgess, A. W., & Holmstrom, L. L. (1988, January). Treating the adult rape victim. *Medical Aspects of Human Sexuality,* pp. 36–43.

Burkham, D. T., Lee, V. E., & Smerdon, B. A. (1997). Gender and science learning early in high school: Subject matter and laboratory experiences. *American Educational Research Journal, 34,* 297–331.

Burstow, B. (1992). *Radical feminist therapy: Working in the context of violence.* Newbury Park, CA: Sage.

Bush, S. (1976, October). Beauty makes the beast look better. *Psychology Today,* pp. 15–16.

Buss, A. H., & Plomin, R. (1986). The EAS approach to temperament. In R. Plomin & J. Dunn (Eds.), *The study of temperament: Changes, continuities, and challenges.* Hillsdale, NJ: Erlbaum.

Buss, D. M. (1999). *Evolutionary psychology: The new science of the mind.* Boston: Allyn & Bacon.

Bussey, K. (1992). Lying and truthfulness: Children's definitions, standards, and evaluative reactions. *Child Development, 63,* 129–137.

Bussey, K., & Maughan, B. (1982). Gender differences in moral reasoning. *Journal of Personality and Social Psychology, 42,* 701–706.

Butler, R. N. (1975). *Why survive? Being old in America.* New York: Harper & Row.

Butler, R. N., & Lewis, M. (1977). *Aging and mental health: Positive psychosocial approaches* (2nd ed.). St. Louis: Mosby.

Buzzelli, C. A. (1992). Young children's moral understanding: Learning about right and wrong. *Young Children, 47,* 48–53.

Byer, C. O., & Shainberg, L. W. (1988). *Dimensions of human sexuality* (2nd ed.). Dubuque, IA: W. C. Brown.

Byer, C. O., & Shainberg, L. W. (1994). *Dimensions of human sexuality* (4th ed.). Madison, WI: Brown and Benchmark.

Byer, C. O., Shainberg, L. W., & Galliano, G. (Revised by S. P. Shriver). (2002). *Dimensions of human sexuality* (6th ed.). Boston: McGraw-Hill.

Byington, D. B. (1995). Sexual assault. In *Encyclopedia of social work* (19th ed., Vol. 3, pp. 2136–2141). Washington, DC: NASW Press.

Cameron-Bandler, L. (1985). *Solutions.* San Rafael, CA: Future Pace.

Cancer and Steroid Hormone Study, Centers for Disease Control, and National Institute of Child Health and Human Development. (1986). Oral contraceptive use and the risk of breast cancer. *New England Journal of Medicine, 315,* 405–411.

Cancer Society says more women in U.S. will develop breast cancer. (1991, January 25). *Milwaukee Journal.*

Canda, E.R. (1989). Religious content in social work education: A comparative approach. *Journal of Social Work Education, 25*(1), 36–45.

Caplan, P. J. (1995). *They say you're crazy.* Reading, MA: Addison-Wesley.

Caputo, L. (1985). Dual diagnosis: AIDS and addiction. *Social Work, 30*(4), 361–364.

Carey, R. G., & Bucher, B. B. (1986). Positive practice overcorrection: Effects of reinforcing correct performance. *Behavior Modification, 10,* 73–92.

Carlson, E., Ginerman, A., Keiding, N., & Skakketaek, N. E. (1992). Evidence for decreasing quality of sperm during the past 30 years. *British Medical Journal, 305,* 609, 613.

Carmichael, S., & Hamilton, C. V. (1967). *Black power: The politics of liberation in America.* New York: Vintage Books.

Carnes, P. (1983). *Out of the shadows: Understanding sexual addiction.* Minneapolis: Comp Care.

Caron, S. L. (1998). *Cross-cultural perspectives on human sexuality.* Needham Heights, MA: Allyn & Bacon.

Carroll, J. L., & Wolpe, P. R. (1996). *Sexuality and gender in society.* New York: HarperCollins.

Carroll, J. L., Volk, K. D., & Hyde, J. S. (1985). Differences between males and females in motives for engaging in sexual intercourse. *Archives of Sexual Behavior, 14,* 18–28.

Carson, S. A., & Buster, J. E. (1993). Ectopic pregnancy. *New England Journal of Medicine, 329,* 1174–1181.

Carter, B., & McGoldrick, M. (1999). *The expanded family life cycle: Individual, family, and social perspectives* (3rd ed.). Boston: Allyn & Bacon.

Carter, E. A., & McGoldrick, M. (1980). *The family life cycle: A framework for family therapy.* New York: Gardner Press.

Carter, E. A., & McGoldrick, M. (1989). Overview: The changing family life cycle—a framework for family therapy. In B. Carter and M. McGoldrick (Eds.), *The changing family life cycle: A framework for family therapy* (2nd ed.). Boston: Allyn & Bacon.

Carter, B., & McGoldrick, M. (1999). Overview: The expanded family life cycle. In B. Carter & M. McGoldrick (Eds.), *The expanded family life cycle* (3rd ed., pp. 1–26). Boston: Allyn & Bacon.

Cartwright, D. (1951). Achieving change in people: Some applications of group "dynamics theory." *Human Relations, 4,* 381–392.

Castex, G. M. (1994). Providing services to Hispanic/Latino populations: Profiles in diversity. *Social Work, 39*(3).

Cate, R. M., & Lloyd, S. A. (1992). *Courtship.* Newbury Park, CA: Sage.

Cates, W., Jr. (1998). Reproductive tract infections. In R.A. Hatcher, J. Trussell, F. Stewart, W. Cates Jr., G. K. Stewart, F. Guest, & D. Kowal (Eds.), *Contraceptive technology* (17th ed.). New York: Ardent Media.

Cates, W., Jr., & Ellertson, C. (1998). Abortion. In R. A. Hatcher, J. Trussell, F. Stewart, W. Cates Jr., G. K. Stewart, F. Guest, & D. Kowal (Eds.), *Contraceptive technology* (17th ed.). New York: Ardent Media.

Cates, W., Jr., & Raymond, E. G. (1998). Vaginal spermicides. In R. A. Hatcher, J. Trussell, F. Stewart, W. Cates Jr., G. K. Stewart, F. Guest, & D. Kowal (Eds.), *Contraceptive technology* (17th ed., pp. 357–369). New York: Ardent Media.

Cates, W., Jr. (1999). Estimates of the incidence and prevalence of sexually transmitted diseases in the United States. *Sexually Transmitted Disease, 26* (suppl), S2–S7.

Cattell, R. B. (1971). *Abilities: their structure, growth, and action.* Boston: Houghton Mifflin.

Ceci, S. J. (1991). How much does schooling influence general intelligence and its cognitive components? A reassessment of the evidence. *Developmental Psychology, 27*(5), 703–722.

Center for American Women in Politics. *Women in elected office—2002 fact sheet summaries.* Available at http://www.rci.rutgers.edu/~cawp/facts/cawpfs.html (accessed on August 30, 2002).

Centers for Disease Control. (1988, September 26). *AIDS Weekly Surveillance Report.*

Centers for Disease Control. (1992a). Ectopic pregnancy—United States, 1988–89. *Morbidity and Mortality Weekly Report, 41,* 591–594.

Centers for Disease Control and Prevention. (1992b). The second 100,000 cases of Acquired Immunodeficiency Syndrome—United States. *Morbidity and Mortality Weekly Report, 41,* 28–29.

Centers for Disease Control. (1993). Recommendations for the prevention and management of chlamydia trachomatis infections. *Morbidity and Mortality Weekly Report, 42,* RR-12.

Centers for Disease Control. (1996). Youth risk behavior surveillance—United States, 1995. *Morbidity and Mortality Weekly Report, 45,* 41 (Table 10).

Centers for Disease Control. (1997a). HIV/AIDS and college students.

Centers for Disease Control. (1997b). *HIV/AIDS surveillance report, 9*(2), 1–44.

Centers for Disease Control and Prevention. (2001). *HIV/AIDS surveillance report, 31*(1), 1–22.

Chasnoff, I. J., et al. (1989). Temporal patterns of cocaine use in pregnancy: Perinatal outcomes. *Journal of the American Medical Association, 261*(12), 1741–1744.

Chasnoff, I. J., Griffith, D. R., Freier, C., & Murray, J. (1992). Cocaine/polydrug use in pregnancy: Two-year follow-up. *Pediatrics, 89*(2), 284–289.

Chavez, G. F., Mulinare, J., & Cordero, J. F. (1989). Maternal cocaine use during early pregnancy as a risk factor for congenital urogenital anomalies. *Journal of the American Medical Association, 26*(2), 795–798.

Cherlin, A., & Furstenberg, F. F. (1986). Grandparents and family crisis. *Generations, 10*(4), 26–28.

Chess, W. A., & Norlin, J. M. (1988). *Human behavior and the social environment: A social systems model.* Boston: Allyn & Bacon.

Chess, W. A., & Norlin, J. M. (1991). *Human Behavior and the Social Environment: A Social Systems Model.* Boston: Allyn & Bacon.

Chestang, L. (1972). Character development in a hostile environment. Occasional Paper No. 3. Chicago: School of Social Science Administration, University of Chicago.

Children's Defense Fund. (1995). *The state of America's children yearbook, 1995.* Washington, DC: Children's Defense Fund.

Chilman, C. S. (1987). Abortion. In *Encyclopedia of social work* (Vol. 1). New York: NASW.

Chilman, C. S. (1993). Hispanic families in the United States: Research perspectives. In H. P. McAdoo (Ed.), *Family ethnicity: Strength in diversity.* Newbury Park, CA: Sage.

Chornesky, A. (1998, Spring). Multicultural perspectives on menopause and the climacteric. *Affilia,* pp. 31–47.

Chornesky, A. (2000). The dynamics of battering revisited. *Affilia, 15*(4), 480–501.

Christie, R., & Geis, F. (1970). *Studies in Machiavellianism.* New York: Academic Press.

Christopher, F., & Cate, R. (1984). Factors involved in premarital decision making. *Journal of Sex Research, 20,* 363–376.

Chumlea, W. C. (1982). Physical growth in adolescence. In B. B. Wolman (Ed.), *Handbook of developmental psychology.* Englewood Cliffs, NJ: Prentice-Hall.

Circirelli, V. (1994). Sibling relationships in cross-cultural perspective. *Journal of Marriage and the Family, 56,* 7–20.

Clayton, R. R. (1975). *The family, marriage and social change.* Lexington, MA: D. C. Heath.

Clements, M. (1994, August 7). Sex in America today. *Parade Magazine,* pp. 4–6.

Clerici, M., Carta, I., & Cazzullo, C. L. (1994). Drug addiction behaviors, attempted suicide and adolescent crisis. *Psychologie Medicale, 26,* 33–36.

Clifford, R. E. (1978). Subjective sexual experience in college women. *Archives of Sexual Behavior, 7,* 183–197.

Cloud, J. (1998, March 16). Harassed or hazed: Why the Supreme Court ruled that men can sue men for sex harassment. *Time,* p. 55.

Cohen, A. (1955). *Delinquent boys: The culture of the gang.* New York: Free Press.

Cohen, N. A. (1992). The continuum of child welfare services. In N. A. Cohen (Ed.), *Child welfare: A multicultural approach,* (pp. 39–83). Needham Heights, MA: Allyn & Bacon.

Coke, M. M. (1992). Correlates of life satisfaction among elderly African-Americans. *Journal of Gerontology, 47,* 316–320.

Cole, E. K. (Ed.). (1990). *Sexual harassment on campus: A legal compendium.* Washington, DC: National Association of College and University Attorneys.

Cole, G. F. (1992). *The American system of criminal justice* (6th ed.). Pacific Grove, CA: Brooks/Cole.

Coleman, J. W., & Cressey, D. R. (1984). *Social problems* (2nd ed.). New York: Harper & Row.

Coleman, J. W., & Cressey, D. R. (1990). *Social problems* (4th ed.). New York: Harper & Row.

Coleman, J. W., & Cressey, D. R. (1993). *Social problems* (5th ed.). New York: HarperCollins.

Coleman, J. W., & Cressey, D. R. (1995). *Social problems* (8th ed.). Englewood Cliffs, NJ: Prentice-Hall.

Coleman, J. W., & Cressey, D. R. (1999). *Social problems* (4th ed.). New York: Longman.

Coleman, J. W., & Kerbo, H. R. (2002). *Social problems* (8th ed.). Upper Saddle River, NJ: Prentice-Hall.

Coles, R., & Stokes, G. (1985). *Sex and the American teenager.* New York: Harper & Row.

Coley, R., & Chase-Landsdale, P. (1998). Adolescent pregnancy and parenthood. *American Psychologist, 53,* 152–166.

Collier, H. V. (1982). *Counseling women.* New York: Free Press.

Comer, J. P. (1988). Educating poor minority children. *Scientific American, 259,* 42–48.

Commission of the Council on Social Work Education (CSWE). (2002). *Glossary to Educational Policy and Accreditation Standards.* Alexandria, VA: CSWE.

Cook, C. A. L., Selig, K. L., Wedge, B. J., & Gohn-Baube, E. A. (1999, March). Access barriers and the use of prenatal care by low-income, inner-city women. *Social Work, 44*(2), 129–139.

Cooley, C. H. (1902). *Human nature and the social order.* New York: Scribner's.

Coon, D. (2001). *Introduction to psychology: Gateways to mind and behavior* (9th ed.). Belmont, CA: Wadsworth.

Coon, D. (2002). *Psychology: A journey.* Belmont, CA: Wadsworth.

Cooper, M., & Ferguson, G. (1994, May 16). The new FOBs: Foes of Bill. *U.S. News & World Report,* pp. 26–31.

Corder, J., & Stephan, C. W. (1984). Females' combinations of work and family roles: Adolescents' aspirations. *Journal of Marriage and the Family, 46,* 391–402.

Corey, L., & Spear, P. G. (1986). Infections with herpes simplex virus—part two. *New England Journal of Medicine, 314,* 749–757.

Corsini, R. J., & Wedding, D. (1995). *Current psychotherapies* (5th ed.). Itasca, IL: Peacock.

Corso, J. F. (1971). Sensory processes and age effects in normal adults. *Journal of Gerontology, 26*(1), 90–105.

Cortese, A. (1989). Subcultural differences in human sexuality: Race, ethnicity, and social class. In K. McKinney & S. Sprecher (Eds.), *Human sexuality: The societal and interpersonal context.* Norwood, NJ: Ablex.

Costa, P. T., Jr., & McCrae, R. R. (1980). Still stable after all these years: Personality as a key to some issues in aging. In P. B. Baltes & O. G. Grin Jr. (Eds.), *Life-span development and behavior* (Vol. 3). New York: Academic Press.

Council on Social Work Education. (1992). *Commission on accreditation handbook of accreditation standards and procedures.* Alexandria, VA: CSWE.

Council on Social Work Education. (1994). Curriculum policy statement for baccalaureate degree programs in social work education. In *Handbook of accreditation standards and procedures.* 4th ed. Alexandria, VA: CSWE.

Council on Social Work Education. (2001). *Educational Policy and Accreditation Standards.* Alexandria, VA: Council on Social Work Education.

Covitz, J. (1986). *Emotional child abuse: The family curse.* Boston: Sigo Press.

Cowley, A. S., & Derezotes, D. (1994, Winter). Transpersonal psychology and social work education. *Journal of Social Work Education, 30*(1), 32–41.

Cox, C. B. (2002, January). Empowering African-American custodial grandparents. *Social Work, 47*(1), 45–54.

Cox, F. M. (1987). Alternative conceptions of community: implications for community organization practice. In F. M. Cox et al. (Eds.), *Strategies of community organization* (4th ed., pp. 232–242). Itasca, IL: Peacock.

Craft, J. L., et al. (1980, Fall). Factors influencing legal disposition in child abuse cases. *Journal of Social Service Research, 4*(1), 31–45.

Creasy, R. K. (1990). Preterm labor. In R. E. Eden, F. H. Boehm, & M. Haire (Eds.), *Assessment and care of the fetus: Physiological, clinical and medicolegal principles.* Norwalk, CT: Appleton and Lange.

Crockett, L. J., & Petersen, A. C. (1987). Pubertal status and psychosocial development: Findings from the early adolescence study. In R. M. Lerner & T. T. Foch (Eds.), *Biological-psychosocial interactions in early adolescence: A life-span perspective.* Hillsdale, NJ: Erlbaum.

Crooks, R., & Baur, K. (1990). *Our sexuality* (4th ed.). Redwood City, CA: Benjamin/Cummings.

Crooks, R., & Baur, K. (1993). *Our sexuality* (5th ed.). Redwood City, CA: Benjamin/Cummings.

Crooks, R., & Baur, K. (1999). *Our sexuality* (7th ed.). Pacific Grove, CA: Brooks/Cole.

Crooks, R., & Baur, K. (2002). *Our sexuality* (8th ed.). Belmont, CA: Wadsworth.

Cross, W. E., Jr., &. Fhagen-Smith, P. (1996). Nigrescence and ego identity development: Accounting for differential black identity patterns. In P. B. Pedersen, J. G. Draguns, W. J. Lonner, &

J. E. Trimble (Eds.), *Counseling across cultures* (4th ed., pp. 108–123). Thousand Oaks, CA: Sage.

Crosson-Tower, C. (1999). *Understanding child abuse and neglect* (4th ed.). Boston: Allyn & Bacon.

Crosson-Tower, C. (2001). *Exploring child welfare: A practice perspective* (2nd ed.). Boston: Allyn & Bacon.

Crosson-Tower, C. (2002). *Understanding child abuse and neglect* (5th ed.). Needham Heights, MA: Allyn & Bacon.

Cuber, J. F., & Harroff, P. B. (1971). Five types of marriage. In A. S. Skolnick & J. H. Skolnick (Eds.), *Family in transition*. Boston: Little, Brown.

Cultural Information Service. (1984). *The burning bed: Viewer's guide.* New York: CIStems.

Culture of the long goodbye. (1993, November 15). *Newsweek,* p. 31.

Cumming, E., & Henry, W. E. (1961). *Growing old: The process of disengagement.* New York: Basic Books.

Cummings, M. (1977). How to handle incidents of racial discrimination. In C. Zastrow and D. H. Chang (Eds.), *The personal problem solver.* Englewood Cliffs, NJ: Prentice-Hall.

Curiel, H. (1995). Hispanics: Mexican Americans. In R. L. Edwards (Ed.), *Encyclopedia of social work* (19th ed., Vol. 2). Washington, DC: NASW Press.

Curtin, S., & Martin, J. (2000). Births: Preliminary data for 1999. *National Vital Statistics Reports, 48,* 1–6.

Curtis, T. (1992, March 16). Defeating one disease may have spread another. *Milwaukee Journal,* pp. D1–D2.

Curtis, K., Savitz, D., & Arbuckle, T. (1997). Effects of cigarette smoking, caffeine consumption, and alcohol intake on fecundability. *American Journal of Epidemiology, 146,* 32–41.

Dacey, J. S., & Travers, J. F. (2002). *Human development: Across the lifespan* (5th ed.). Boston.

Daft, R. L. (1992). *Organization theory and design* (4th ed.). New York: West.

Daft, R. L. (1998). *Organization theory and design* (6th ed.). Cincinnati, OH: South-Western College Publishing.

Daft, R. L. (2001). *Organization theory and design* (7th ed.). Cincinnati, OH: South-Western Publishing.

Dagg, P. K. B. (1991). The psychological sequelae of therapeutic abortion—denied and completed. *American Journal of Psychiatry, 148,* 578–585.

Dale, C. V. (1993, March 29). Statement to Senate Armed Services Committee. Washington, DC: Library of Congress, Congressional Research Service.

Daley, M., & Wilson, M. (1983). *Sex, evolution, and behavior* (2nd ed.). Boston: Willard Grant.

Darley, J. M., & Schultz, T. R. (1990). Moral rules: Their content and acquisition. *Annual Review of Psychology, 41,* 525–556.

David, H. P. (1994). Reproductive rights and reproductive behavior. *American Psychologist, 49,* 343–349.

Davis, J. (1982). *Help me, I'm hurt.* Dubuque, IA: Kendall/Hunt.

Davis, J. A., & Smith, T. (1991). *General social surveys, 1972–1991: Cumulative data.* Storrs: University of Connecticut, Roper Center for Public Opinion Research.

Davis, K., & Newstrom, W. (1989). *Human behavior at work* (8th ed.). New York: McGraw-Hill.

Davis, L., Galinsky, M., & Schopler, J. (1995, March). RAP: A framework for leadership of multiracial groups. *Social Work, 40* (2), 155–165.

Davis, L. E. (1979). Racial composition of groups. *Social Work, 24,* 208–213.

Davis, L. V. (1995). Domestic violence. In R. L. Edwards (Ed.), *Encyclopedia of social work* (19th ed., Vol. 1). Washington, DC: NASW Press.

Davis, M., McKay, M., & Eshelmen, E. R. (2000). *The relaxation & stress reduction workbook.* Oakland, CA: New Harbinger.

Day, R. (1992). The transition to first intercourse among racially and culturally diverse youth. *Journal of Marriage and the Family, 54,* 749–762.

Dean, K. E., & Malamuth, N. M. (1997). Characteristics of men who aggress sexually and of men who imagine aggressing: Risk and moderating variables. *Journal of Personality and Social Psychology, 72,* 449–455.

Deaux, K. (1984). From individual differences to social categories. *American Psychologist, 39,* 105–116.

Dekovic, M., & Janssens, J. M. (1992). Parents' child-rearing style and child's sociometric status. *Developmental Psychology, 28,* 925–932.

Delgado, M., & Humm-Delgado, D. (1982, January). Natural support systems: Source of strength in Hispanic communities. *Social Work, 27*(1), 83–89.

Deming, W. E. (1986). *Out of the crisis.* Cambridge, MA: Massachusetts Institute of Technology, Center for Advanced Engineering Study.

Denfield, D., & Gordon, M. (1970). The sociology of mate swapping: Or the family that swings together clings together. *Journal of Sex Research, 6,* 85–100.

Denney, N. W. (1982). Aging and cognitive changes. In B. B. Wolman (Ed.), *Handbook of developmental psychology.* Englewood Cliffs, NJ: Prentice-Hall.

Denney, N. W., & Quadagno, D. (1992). *Human sexuality* (2nd ed.). Chicago: Mosby.

Deturris, M. (1997). Fetal tissue research is unethical. In T. L. Roleff (Ed.), *Abortion: Opposing viewpoints.* San Diego: Greenhaven Press.

Deutsch, L. (1996, September 15). New Simpson trial has different rules. *Milwaukee Journal Sentinel,* p. 9A.

Devore, W., & Schlesinger, E.G. (1996). *Ethnic-sensitive social work practice* (4th ed.). Needham Heights, MA: Allyn & Bacon.

Davtyan, C. (2000). Contraception for adolescents. *Western Journal of Medicine, 172,* 166–171.

Devore, W., & Schlesinger, E.G. (1999). *Ethnic-sensitive social work practice* (5th ed.). Needham Heights, MA: Allyn & Bacon.

DeWeaver, K. L. (1995). Developmental disabilities: Definitions and policies. In R. L. Edwards (Ed.), *Encyclopedia of social work* (19th ed., Vol. 1). Washington, DC: NASW Press.

Dewsburg, D. (1981). Effects of novelty on copulatory behavior: The Coolidge effect and related phenomena. *Psychological Bulletin, 89,* 464–482.

Dhooper, S. S., & Moore, S. E. (2001). *Social work practice with culturally diverse people.* Thousand Oaks, CA: Sage.

Dickman, I. R. (1982). *Winning the battle for sex education.* New York: Sexuality Information and Education Council of the United States (SIECUS).

DiClemente, R. J., Zorn, B. A., & Temoshok, L. (1986). Adolescents and AIDS: A survey of knowledge, attitudes, and beliefs about AIDS in San Francisco. *American Journal of Public Health, 78,* 1443–1445.

DiLeonardi, J. W. (1980). Decision-making in Protective Services. *Child Welfare, 59*(6), 356–364.

Dill, F., & McGillivray, B. (1992). Chromosome anomalies. In J. M. Friedman, F. J. Dill, M. R. Hayden, & B. C. McGillivray (Eds.), *Genetics.* Baltimore: Williams & Wilkins.

Dillard, J. L. (1972). *Black English: Its history and usage in the United States*. New York: Random House.

Doege, D. (2002, January 13). Surviving justice. *Milwaukee Journal Sentinel*, pp. 1L, 3L.

Doka, K. J., & Mertz, M. E. (1988). The meaning and significance of great-grandparenthood. *Gerontologist, 28*(2), 192–197.

Donders, G. G., Desmyter, J., De Wet, D. H., & Van Assche, F. A. (1993). The association of gonorrhea and syphilis with premature birth and low birth-weight. *Genitourinary Medicine,* 69, 98–101.

Donnerstein, E., & D. Linz. (1984, January). Sexual violence in the media: A warning. *Psychology Today*, pp. 14–15.

Doshi, M. L. (1986). Accuracy of consumer performed in-home tests for early pregnancy detection. *American Journal of Public Health, 76*, 512–514.

Downs, H. (1985). Growing old in America. ABC news program transcript. New York: Journal Graphics Inc.

Downs, S. W., Costin, L. B., & McFadden, E.J. (1996). *Child welfare and family services* (5th ed.) White Plains, NY: Longman.

Doyle, R. (1996). *The woman who walked into doors*. New York: Viking.

Drucker, P. F. (1954). *The practice of management*. New York: Harper.

Dubas, J. S., & Petersen, A. C. (1993). Female pubertal development. In M. Sugar (Ed.), *Female adolescent development*. New York: Brunner/Mazel.

Duncan, G. & Brooks-Gunn, J. (2000). Family poverty, welfare reform, & child development. *Child Development, 71*(1), 188–196.

Dunn, J. (1985). *Sisters and brothers*. Cambridge, MA: Harvard University Press.

Dunn, J., Brown, J., & Beardsall, L. (1991). Family talk about feeling states and children's later understanding of others' emotions. *Developmental Psychology, 27*(3), 448–455.

Dunn, J., Brown, J., Slomkowski, C., Tesla, C., & Youngblade, L. (1991). Young children's understanding of other people's feelings and beliefs. *Child Development, 62*, 1352–1366.

Dunn, J., & Kendrick, C. (1982). *Siblings: Love, envy and understanding*. Cambridge, MA: Harvard University Press.

Duprey, M., McDonnell, C., Paymar, M., Regan, K., and Soderberg, J. (Eds.). (1996). *Coordinated community response to domestic assault cases: A guide for policy development*. Duluth, MN: Domestic Abuse Intervention Project.

Duren, R. (1985, October 18). Presentation on drug abuse at University of Wisconsin–Whitewater.

Dusay, J. M., & Dusay, K. M. (1984). Transactional analysis. In Raymond J. Corsini (Ed.), *Current psychotherapies* (3rd ed.). Itasca, IL: Peacock.

Dutton, D. G. (1987). The criminal justice response to wife assault. *Law and Human Behavior, 11*, 189–206.

Dzeich, B. W., & Weiner, L. (1990). *The lecherous professor: Sexual harassment on campus*. Boston: Beacon Press.

Dziegielewski, S. F., Resnick, C., and Krause, N. B. (1996). Shelter-based crisis intervention with battered women. In A. R. Roberts (Ed.), *Helping battered women: new perspectives and remedies*. New York: Oxford University Press.

Eaton, J. T., Lippmann, D. B., & Riley, D. P. (1980). *Growing with your learning-disabled child*. Boston: Resource Communications.

Eddings, J. (1997, July 28). Second thoughts about integration. *U.S. News & World Report*, p. 32.

Edeiken, S. (1988). Mammography and palpable cancer of the breast. *Cancer, 61*, 263–265.

Edmonds, M. (1990). The health of the black aged female. In Z. Harel, E. A. McKinney, & M. Williams (Eds.), *Black aged*. Newbury Park, CA: Sage.

Ehrhardt, A. (1985). Sexual orientation after prenatal exposure to exogenous estrogen. *Archives of Sexual Behavior, 14*(1), 57–75.

Ehrlich, P., & Holm, R. (1964). A biological view of race. In Ashley Montague (Ed.), *The concept of race*. New York: Free Press.

Eisenberg, A., Murkoff, H. E., & Hathaway, S. E. (1991). *What to expect when you're expecting*. New York: Workman.

Ekerdt, D. J., Bosse, R., & Mogey, J. M. (1980). Concurrent change in planned and preferred age for retirement. *Journal of Gerontology, 35*, 232–240.

Ekman, P., & Friesen, W. V. (1975). *Unmaking the face*. Englewood Cliffs, NJ: Prentice-Hall.

Elber, L. (1993, August 8). Statistics confirm TV lacks a Hispanic presence. *Milwaukee Journal*, p. T4.

Eliason, M. J. (1995). Attitudes about lesbians and gay men: A review and implications for social service training. *Journal of Gay & Lesbian Social Services, 2*(2), 73–90.

Ellerbrock, T., et al. (1991). Epidemiology of women with AIDS in the United States, 1981 through 1990. *Journal of the American Medical Association, 265*, 2971–2975.

Elliott, D. M., & Briere, J. (1995). Posttraumatic stress associated with delayed recall of sexual abuse: A general population study. *Journal of Traumatic Stress Studies, 8*, 629–648.

Elliott, L., & Brantley, C. (1997). *Sex on campus*. New York: Random House.

Ellis, A. (1957). Outcome of employing three techniques of psychotherapy. *Journal of Clinical Psychology*, 13.

Ellis, A. (1962). *Reason and emotion in psychotherapy*. New York: Lyle Stuart.

Ellis, A. (1979). Rational-emotive therapy. In Raymond Corsini (Ed.), *Current psychotherapies* (2nd ed.). Itasca, IL: Peacock.

Elmer-DeWitt, P. (1991, December 2). The cruelest kind of fraud. *Time*, p. 27.

English, P. D. (1978). Failure to thrive without organic reason. *Pediatric Annals, 7*, 774–780.

Enter Norplant. (1991). *Contemporary Sexuality, 25*(1), 1–2.

Entwisle, D. R., Alexander, K. L., Pallas, A. M., & Cardigan, D. (1987). The emergent academic self-image of first graders: Its response to social structure. *Child Development, 58*, 200–209.

Erikson, E. H. (1950). *Childhood and society*. New York: Norton.

Erikson, E. H. (1959). The problem of ego identity. *Psychological Issues, 1*, 101–164.

Erikson, E. H. (1963). *Childhood and society* (2nd ed.). New York: Norton.

Erikson, E. H. (1968). *Identity: Youth and crisis*. New York: Norton.

Eron, L. D. (1980). Prescription for reduction of aggression. *American Psychologist*, 244–252.

Eron, L. D. (1982). Parent-child interaction, television violence, and aggression in children. *American Psychologist, 37*(2), 197–211.

Estrich, S. (1987). *Real rape*. Cambridge, MA: Harvard University Press.

Etzioni, A. (1964). *Modern organizations*. Englewood Cliffs, NJ: Prentice-Hall.

Ezzell, C. (1994, October). Breast cancer genes. *Journal of NIH Research, 6*, 33–35.

Falbo, T., & Polit, D. F. (1986). Quantitative revew of the only child literature: Research evidence and theory development. *Psychological Bulletin, 100*(2), 176–189.

Faller, K. C., et al. (1981). Types of child abuse and neglect. In K. Faller (Ed.), *Social work with abused and neglected children.* New York: Free Press.

Faludi, S. (1991). Backlash: *The undeclared war against american women.* New York: Crown.

Farkas, G. M., & Rosen, R. C. (1976). Effect of alcohol on elicited male sexual response. *Journal of Studies on Alcohol, 37,* 265–272.

Farley, J. E. (1992). *American social problems* (2nd ed.). Englewood Cliffs, NJ: Prentice-Hall.

Farley, L. (1978). *Sexual shakedown: The sexual harassment of women on the job.* New York: Warner.

Federal Bureau of Investigation. (1998). *Uniform crime reports for the United States, 1997.* Washington, DC: U.S. Government Printing Office.

Fellin, P. (1995a). *The community and the social worker* (2nd ed.). Itasca, IL: Peacock.

Fellin, P. (1995b). Understanding American communities. In J. Rothman, J. L. Erlich, and J. E. Tropman (Eds.), *Strategies of community intervention* (5th ed., pp. 114–128). Istasca, IL: F. E. Peacock.

Fellin, P. (2001a). *The community and the social worker* (3rd ed.). Itasca, IL: Peacock.

Fellin, P. (2001b). Understanding American communities. In J. Rothman, J. L. Erlich, & J. E. Tropman (Eds.), *Strategies of community intervention* (6th ed., pp. 118–132). Itasca, IL: Peacock.

Felsman, D., Brannigan, G., & Yellin, P. (1987). Control theory in dealing with adolescent sexuality and pregnancy. *Journal of Sex Education and Therapy, 13,* 15–16.

Fenster, L., Eskenazi, B., Windham, G. C., & Swan, S. H. (1991). Caffeine consumption during pregnancy and fetal growth. *American Journal of Public Health, 81,* 458–461.

Ferraro, K. J. (1989). Policing woman battering. *Social Problems, 36,* 61–74.

Fertility doctor defends motives. (1992, November 24). *Milwaukee Journal,* p. A7.

Field, D., & Minkler, M. (1988). Continuity and change in social support between young-old and old-old or very old age. *Journal of Gerontology, 43,* 100–106.

Field, D., Minkler, M., Falk, R. F., & Leino, E. V. (1993). The influence of health on family contacts and family functioning in advanced old age: A longitudinal study. *Journal of Gerontology, 48,* 18–28.

Fielstein, E. M., Fielstein, L. L., & Hazelwood, M. G. (1992). AIDS knowledge among college freshmen students: Need for education? *Journal of Sex Education and Therapy, 18*(1), 45–54.

Findlay, S. (1991, February 18). If your doctor has AIDS. *U.S. News & World Report,* p. 66.

Fingerhut, L. A., & Kleinman, J. C. (1990). International and interstate comparisons of homicide among young males. *Journal of the American Medical Association, 263*(4), 3292–3295.

Finkelhor, D. (1990). Early and long-term effects of child sexual abuse: an update. *Professional Psychology: Research and Practice, 21,* 325–330.

Finkelhor, D. (1994). Current information on the scope and nature of child sexual abuse. *Future of Children, 4,* 31–53.

Finkelhor, D., & Baron, L. (1986). High-risk children. In D. Finkelhor, *A Sourcebook on Child Sexual Abuse.* Beverly Hills, CA: Sage.

Finkelhor, D., Hotaling, G., Lewis, I. A., & Smith, C. (1990). Sexual abuse in a national survey of adult men and women: prevalence, characteristics, and risk factors. *Child Abuse and Neglect, 14,* 19–28.

Fischer, D. H. (1977, May 10). Putting our heads to the "problem" of old age. *New York Times,* p. 33.

Fischer, J., & Gochros, H. L. (1975). *Planned behavior change: Behavior modification in social work.* New York: Free Press.

Fischman, J. (2001, February 5). New-style mammograms detect cancer. So do the old. Either way you wait. *U.S. News & World Report,* pp. 58–59.

Fiske, H. (2002, May 13). When a client commits suicide: How can you cope? *Social Work Today, 2*(10), 9–11.

Flint, M. (1976). Cross-cultural factors that affect age of menopause. In P. A. Van Keep, R. B. Greenblatt, & M. Albeaux-Fernet (Eds.), *Consensus on menopause.* Baltimore, MD: University Park Press.

Food and Drug Administration. (1997). Prescription drug products contain combined oral contraceptives for use as postcoital emergency contraception. *Federal Register, 62,* 8610–8612.

Forte, J. A., Franks, D. D., Forte, J. A., & Rigsby, D. (1996). Asymmetrical role-taking: Comparing battered and nonbattered women. *Social Work, 41*(1), 59–73.

Fowler, J. (1981). *Stages of faith: The psychology of human development and the quest for meaning.* San Francisco, CA: Harper & Row.

Fowler, J. (1996). *Faithful change: The personal and public challenges of postmodern life.* Nashville: Abingdon Press.

Fox, J. R. (1985, January–February). Mission impossible? Social work practice with black urban youth gangs. *Social Work, 30,* 25–29.

Fox, M. F. (1995). Women and higher education: Gender differences in the status of students and scholars. In J. Freeman, *Women: A feminist perspective* (5th ed.). Mountain View, CA: Mayfield.

Frank, O., Bianchi, P. G., & Campana, A. (1994). The end of fertility: Age, fecundity and fecundability in women. *Journal of Biosocial Science, 26,* 349–368.

Frankenburg, W. K., Dodds, J. B., Fandal, A. W., Kazuk, E., & Cohrs, M. (1975). *Denver developmental screening test reference manual* (Rev. ed.). Denver: University of Colorado Medical Center.

Frazier, A., & Lisonbee, L. K. (1950). Adolescent concerns with physique. *School Review, 58,* 397–405.

Freedman, R. (2001). Myth America grows up. In S. Ruth (Ed.), *Issues in feminism: An introduction to women's studies* (5th ed., pp. 138–147). Mountain View, CA: Mayfield.

Freeman, J. (1989). *Women: A feminist perspective* (4th ed.). Mountain View, CA: Mayfield.

Freeman, J. (1995). *Women: A feminist perspective* (5th ed.). Mountain View, CA: Mayfield.

Freire, P. (1970). *Pedagogy of the oppressed.* New York: Herder and Herder.

Freire, P. (1985). *The politics of education* (D. Macedo, Trans.). S. Hadley, MA: Bergin & Garvey.

Frenkel-Brunswick, E. (1970). Adjustments and reorientation in the course of the life-span. In R. G. Kuhlen & G. G. Thomson (Eds.), *Psychological studies of human development* (3rd ed.). New York: Appleton-Century-Crofts.

Freyhan, F. A. (1955). *Psychopathic personalities. Oxford loose leaf medicine.* New York: Oxford University Press.

Fried, P. A., & Watkinson, B. 36- and 48-month neurobehavioral follow-up of children prenatally exposed to marijuana, cigarettes, and alcohol. *Developmental and Behavioral Pediatrics, 11,* 49–58.

Friedman, J. M., & Polifka, J. E. (1996). *The effects of drugs on the fetus and nursing infant.* Baltimore, MD: Johns Hopkins University Press.

Friedrich, W. N., Dittner, C. A., Action, R., Berliner, L., Butler, J., Damon, L., Davies, W. H., Gray, A., & Wright, J. (2001). Child Sexual Behavior Inventory: Normative, psychiatric and sexual abuse comparisons. *Child maltreatment, 6,* 37–49.

Frish, R. E. (1988). Fatness and fertility. *Scientific American, 258*(3), 88–95.

Frishman, G. (1995). Abortions, miscarriages, and ectopic pregnancies. In D. R. Coustin, R. V. Hunning, Jr., & D. B. Singer (Eds.),

Human reproduction: Growth and development. Boston: Little, Brown, and Company.

Frolkis, V. V. (1977). Aging of the autonomic nervous system. In J. E. Birren & K. W. Schaie (Eds.), *Handbook of the psychology of aging.* New York: Van Nostrand Reinhold.

Fuchs, C. S., et al. (1995). Alcohol consumption and mortality among women. *New England Journal of Medicine, 332,* 1245–1250.

Fulmer, R. (1999). Becoming an adult: Leaving home and staying connected. In B. Carter & M. McGoldrick (Eds.), *The expanded family life cycle* (3rd ed., pp. 215–230). Boston: Allyn & Bacon.

Furman, L. E. (1994, April). Religion and spirituality in social work education. Paper presented at Midwest Biennial Conference on Social Work Education, St. Paul, MN.

Furman, W. (1995). Parenting siblings. In M. H. Bornstein (Ed.), *Handbook of parenting* (Vol. 1). Mahwah, NJ: Erlbaum.

Furman, W., & Burhmester, D. (1985). Children's perceptions of the personal relationships in their social networks. *Developmental Psychology, 21*(6), 1016–1024.

Furnham, A., Hester, C., & Weir, C. (1990). Sex differences in the preferences for specific female body shapes. *Sex Roles, 22,* 743–754.

Furry, C. A., & Baltes, P. B. (1973). The effect of age differences on the assessment of intelligence in children, adults, and the elderly. *Journal of Gerontology, 28*(1), 73–80.

Furstenberg, F. F., Brooks-Gunn, J., & Morgan, S. P. (1987). Adolescent mothers and their children in later life. *Family Planning Perspectives, 22*(2), 239–249.

Furstenberg, F. F., Jr., & Spanier, G. B. (1984). *Recycling the family: Remarriage after divorce.* Beverly Hills, CA: Sage.

Gabelnick, H. L. (1998). Future methods. In R. A. Hatcher, J. Trussell, F. Stewart, W. Cates Jr., G. K. Stewart, F. Guest, & D. Kowal (Eds.), *Contraceptive technology* (17th ed.). New York: Ardent Media, 615–622.

Gans, J. J. (1992, January 8). Fighting the biases embedded in social concepts of the poor. *Chronicle of Higher Education,* p. A56.

Garbarino, J., Guttmann, E., & Seeley, J. W. (1986). *The psychologically battered child.* San Francisco: Jossey-Bass.

Garcia, J. M. (1993). The Hispanic population in the United States: March 1993. *Current Population Reports* (Series P-20, No. 465 RV). Washington, DC: U.S. Government Printing Office.

Garcia-Preto, N. (1998). Latinas in the United States: Bridging two worlds. In M. McGoldrick (Ed.), *Re-Visioning family therapy: Race, culture, and gender in clinical practice* (pp. 330–344). New York: Guilford.

Gardiner, H. W., Mutter, J. D., & Kosmitzki, C. (1998). *Lives across cultures: Cross-cultural human development.* Boston: Allyn & Bacon.

Gardner, H., & Hatch, T. (1989). Multiple intelligences go to school: Educational implications of the theory of multiple intelligences. *Educational Researcher, 18*(8), 6.

Gariulo, J., Attie, I., Brooks-Gunn, J., & Warren, M. P. (1987). Girls' dating behavior as a function of social context and maturation. *Developmental Psychology, 23,* 730–737.

Garland, A. G., & Zigler, E. (1993). Adolescent suicide prevention: Current research and social policy implications. *American Psychologist, 48,* 169–182.

Garland, J. A., & Frey, L. A. (1973). Application of stages of group development to groups in psychiatric settings. In S. Bernstein (Ed.), *Further explorations in group work.* Boston: Milford House.

Garland, J. A., Jones, H., & Kolodny, R. (1965). A model for stages of development in social work groups. In S. Bernstein (Ed.), *Explorations in group work.* Boston: Milford House.

Garn, S. M. (1975). Bone loss and aging. In R. Goldman & M. Rockstein (Eds.), *The physiology and pathology of human aging.* New York: Academic Press.

Garrett, M. T. (1999). Understanding the "medicine" of Native American traditional values: An integrative review. *Counseling & Values, 43*(2), 84–99.

Garvey, C. (1977). *Play.* Cambridge, MA: Harvard University Press.

Gavzer, B. (1988, September 18). Why do some people survive AIDS? *Parade Magazine,* pp. 4–6.

Gawain, S. (1986). *Living in the light.* San Rafael, CA: Whatever Publications.

Gays in the military: Tell it to the judge. (1995, April 10). *U.S. News & World Report,* p. 14.

Geller, A. (1984). *Alcohol and sexual performance.* Minneapolis, MN: Johnson Institute.

Gelles, R. J. (1997). *Intimate violence in families* (3rd ed.). Thousand Oaks, CA: Sage.

Gelles, R. J., & Cornell, C. P. (1990). *Intimate violence in families* (2nd ed.). Newbury Park, CA: Sage.

Gelman, D. (1988, March 7). Black and white in America. *Newsweek,* pp. 19–21.

Gelman, D. (1993, July 26). Homoeroticism in the ranks. *Newsweek,* pp. 28–29.

Gelman, D., Foote, D., Barrett, T., & Talbot, M. (1992, February 24). Born or bred? *Newsweek,* pp. 46–53.

Gerber, P. J., Ginsberg, R., & Reiff, H. B. (1992). Identifying alterable patterns in employment success for highly successful adults with learning disabilities. *Journal of Learning Disabilities, 25*(8), 475–487.

Gerbner, G. (1993). Women and minorities on television. (A report to the Screen Actors Guild.) Philadelphia: University of Pennsylvania, Annenberg School for Communication.

Gerdes, E. P., et al. (1981). The effects of sex and sex-role concept on self-disclosure. *Sex Roles, 7,* 789–798.

Gerhard, G. S., & Cristofalo, V. J. (1992). The limits of biogerontology. *Generations, 16*(4), 55–59.

Germain, C. B. (1991). *Human behavior in the social environment: An ecological view.* New York: Columbia University Press.

Gershengorn, H., & Blower, S. (2000). Impact of antivirals and emergence of drug resistance: HSV-2 epidemic control. *AIDS Patient Care and STDs, 14,* 133–142.

Getlin, J. (1989, July 24). Legacy of a mother's drinking. *Los Angeles Times,* pp. 1 ff.

Gewirtz, J. L. (1965). The course of infant smiling in four child-rearing environments in Israel. In B. M. Foss (Ed.), *Determinants of infant behavior* (Vol. 3). London, UK: Methuen.

Giaconia, R. M., & Hedges, L. V. (1982). *Identifying features of open education.* Stanford, CA: Stanford University Press.

Gibbs, N. (1991a, September 2). Teens: The rising risk of AIDS. *Time,* pp. 60–61.

Gibbs, N. (1991b, October 21). Into the arena there came two gladiators, fourteen senators and an audience of millions. But could anyone declare victory when the spectacle was so repellent? *Time,* p. 35.

Gibbs, N. (1995). Til death do us part. In S. Ruth (Ed.), *Issues in feminism: An introduction to women's studies* (3rd ed.). Mountain View, CA: Mayfield.

Gibbs, N. (1996, September 30). Politics and principle: The partial birth abortion fight is back, but can it really help Dole cut Clinton's double-digit lead? *Time,* p. 30.

Gibbs, N. (1998). Til death do us part. In S. Ruth (Ed.), *Issues in feminism: An introduction to women's studies* (4th ed.). Mountain View, CA: Mayfield.

Gibbs, N. (2002, April 15). Making time for a baby. *Time*, pp. 48–54.

Gibbs, N., & Duffy, M. (2001, August 20). We must proceed with great care. *Time*, pp. 12–14.

Gibelman, M., & Schervish, P. V. (1993). The glass ceiling in social work: Is it shatterproof? *Affilia, 8*(4), 442–455.

Gilbert, L. A. (1985). *Men in dual-career families: Current realities and future prospects.* Hillsdale, NJ: Erlbaum.

Gilford, R. (1986). Marriages in later life. *Generations, 10*(4), 16–20.

Gilkey, B. (2001). *The new urban renewal: St. Louis, Missouri.* Available at http://www.pbs.org/newurban/stlouis.html (accessed April 7, 2003).

Gillespie, B. L., & Eisler, R. M. (1992). Development of the feminine gender role stress scale. *Behavior Modification, 16*, 426–438.

Gilligan, C. (1982). *In a different voice: Psychological theory and women's development.* Cambridge, MA: Harvard University Press.

Gilligan, C., & Attanucci, J. (1988). Two moral orientations. In C. Gilligan, J. V. Ward, J. M. Taylor, & B. Bardige (Eds.), *Mapping the moral domain.* Cambridge, MA: Harvard University Press.

Gilligan, C., Brown, L. M., & Rogers, A. G. (1990). Psyche embedded: A place for body, relationships, and culture in personality theory. In A. I. Rabin, R. A. Zucker, R. A. Emmons, & S. Frank (Eds.), *Studying persons and lives.* New York: Springer.

Ginsberg, L. (1995). *Social work almanac* (2nd ed.). Washington, DC: NASW Press.

Girdano, D. A., & Dusek, D. (1980). *Drug education: Content and methods.* Reading, MA: Addison-Wesley.

Glasser, W. (1984). *Control theory.* New York: Harper & Row.

Glatt, M. M. (1982). Group therapy in alcoholism. *British Journal of Addiction, 74*–82.

Glei, D. (1999). Measuring contraceptive use patterns among teenage and adult women. *Family Planning Perspectives, 31*, 73–80.

Gleitman, H. (1986). *Psychology* (2nd ed.). New York: Norton.

Gochros, J. S. (1995). Bisexuality. In R. L. Edwards (Ed.), *Encyclopedia of social work* (19th ed., Vol. 1). Washington, DC: NASW Press.

Goldenberg, H., & Goldenberg, I. (1994). *Counseling today's families* (2nd ed.). Pacific Grove, CA: Brooks/Cole.

Goldenberg, H., & Goldenberg, I. (1998). *Counseling today's families* (3rd ed.). Pacific Grove, CA: Brooks/Cole.

Goldenberg, I., & Goldenberg, H. (1996). *Family therapy: An overview* (4th ed.). Pacific Grove, CA: Brooks/Cole.

Golding, J. M. (1990). Division of household labor, strain, and depressive symptoms among Mexican American and non-Hispanic whites. *Psychology of Women Quarterly, 14*, 103–117.

Goldman, S., & Beardslee, W. R. (1999). Suicide in children and adolescents. In D. G. Jacobs (Ed.), *Guide to suicide assessment and intervention* (417–442). San Francisco: Jossey-Bass.

Goldsmith, J. (1990). Neonatal morbidity. In R. D. Eden, F. H. Boehm, and M. Haire (Eds.), *Assessment and care of the fetus: Physiological, clinical, and medico-legal principles.* Norwalk, CT: Appleton and Lange.

Goldstein, A. P. (1991). *Delinquent gangs: A psychological perspective.* Champaign, IL: Research Press.

Goldstein, A. P., & Huff, C. R. (Eds.). (1993). *The gang intervention handbook.* Champaign, IL: Research Press.

Goldstein, E. G. (1995). *Psychosocial approach.* In R. L. Edwards (Ed.), *Encyclopedia of social work* (19th ed., Vol. 3, pp. 1948–1954). Washington, DC: NASW Press.

Golombok, S. (1992). Psychological functioning of infertility patients. *Human Reproduction, 7*(2), 208–212.

Good Tracks, Jimm, G. (1973, November). Native American non-interference. *Social Work, 18*, 30–34.

Goode, E. E. (1988, February 22). I love you, but can I ask a question? *U.S. News & World Report*, p. 85.

Goode, W. J. (1976). Family disorganization. In R. K. Merton & R. Nisbet (Eds.), *Contemporary social problems* (4th ed.). New York: Harcourt, Brace, Jovanovich.

Goodman, D. D. (1998). Using the empowerment model to develop sex education for Native Americans. *Journal of Sex Education and Therapy, 23*(2), 135–144.

Goodman, M. J., Grove, J. S., & Gilbert, F., Jr. (1978). Age at menopause in relation to reproductive history of Japanese, Caucasian, Chinese and Hawaiian women living in Hawaii. *Journal of Gerontology, 33*, 688–694.

Gooren, L., Fliers, E., & Courtney, K. (1990). Biological determinants of sexual orientation. *Annual Review of Sex Research, 1*, 175–196.

Gordon, M. (1961, Spring). Assimilation in America: Theory and reality. *Daedalus, 90*, 363–365.

Gordon, S. (1992). Can sex education work? *Contemporary Sexuality, 26*(1), 1–2.

Gordon, S., & Gilgun, J. F. (1987). Adolescent sexuality. In V. B. Van Hasselt & M. Hersen (Eds.), *Handbook of adolescent sexuality.* New York: Pergamon Press.

Gordon, T. (1970). *Parent effectiveness training.* New York: Wyden.

Gordon, T. (1975). *Parent effectiveness training* (2nd ed.). New York: New American Library.

Goring, R. (Ed.). (1994). *Dictionary of beliefs and religions.* New York: Larousse.

Gottlieb, N. (1995). Women overview. In R. L. Edwards (Ed.), *Encyclopedia of social work* (19th ed., Vol. 3). Washington, DC: NASW Press.

Gottman, J., Notarius, C., Gonso, J., & Markman, H. (1976). *A couple's guide to communication.* Champaign, IL: Research Press.

Graber, J., & Brooks-Gunn, J. (1998, February). Pubertal timing and psychopathology. Paper presented at the meeting of the Society for Research on Adolescence. San Diego.

Graham, M. V. (1993). Parental sensitivity to infant cues: Similarities and differences between mothers and fathers. *Journal of Pediatric Nursing, 8*, 376–384.

Grant, E. (1988, January). The housework gap. *Psychology Today*, p. 10.

Green, J. W. (1995). *Cultural awareness in the human services: A multiethnic approach* (2nd ed.). Boston: Allyn & Bacon.

Green, J. W. (1999). *Cultural awareness in the human services: A multiethnic approach* (3rd ed.). Boston: Allyn & Bacon.

Green, R., Bettinger, M., & Zachs, E. (1996). Are lesbian couples fused and gay male couples disengaged? In J. Laird & R. Green (Eds.), *Lesbians and gays in couples and families* (pp. 185–230). San Francisco: Jossey-Bass.

Greenberg, J., & Becker, M. (1988). Aging parents as family resources. *Gerontologist, 28*, 786–790.

Greene, B. L. (1994). Lesbian women of color: Triple jeopardy. In L. Comas-Diaz & B. Greene, *Women of color and mental health.* New York: Guilford Press.

Grier, W. H., & Cobb, P. M. (1968). *Black rage.* New York: Basic Books.

Griffin, K. L. (2000, January 7). U.S. abortions down 3%, CDC reports. *Milwaukee Journal Sentinel*, p. 8A.

Group for the Advancement of Psychiatry. (1973). *The joys and sorrows of parenthood.* New York: Scribner's.

Grune, J. A. (1984). Pay equity is a necessary remedy for wage discrimination. In *Comparable worth: Issue for the 80's* (Vol. 1). Washington, DC: U.S. Government Printing Office.

Grush, J. E., & Yehl, J. G. (1979). Marital roles, sex differences and interpersonal attraction. *Journal of Personality and Social Psychology, 37,* 116–123.

Gunby, P. (1983). Genital herpes research. *Journal of the American Medical Association, 250,* 2417–2427.

Gustafson, G. E., & Harris, K. L. (1990). Women's responses to young infants' cries. *Developmental Psychology, 26,* 144–152.

Gutierrez, L. M. (1990). Working with women of color: An empowerment perspective. *Social Work, 35*(2), 149–153.

Gutierrez, L., GlenMaye, L., & DeLois, K. (1995). The organizational context of empowerment practice: Implications for social work administration. *Social Work, 40,* 249–257.

Guttmacher, A. E., & Kaiser, I. H. (1986). *Pregnancy, birth, and family planning.* New York: New American Library.

Hack, M., Breslau, N., Aram, D., Weissman, B., Klein, N., & Borawski-Clark, E. (1992). The effect of very low birth weight and social risk on neurocognitive abilities at school age. *Journal of Developmental and Behavioral Pediatrics, 13,* 412–420.

Haddow, J. E., Palomaki, G. E., Knight, G. J., Williams, J., Polkkiner, A., Canick, J. A., Saller, D. N., & Bowers, G. G. (1992). Prenatal screening for Down's syndrome with use of material serum markers. *New England Journal of Medicine, 327,* 588–593.

Hadeed, A. J., & Siegel, S. R. (1989). Maternal cocaine use during pregnancy: effect on the newborn infant. *Pediatrics, 84*(2), 205–210.

Haffner, D. W. (Ed.). (1995). *Facing facts: Sexual health for America's adolescents.* New York: Sexuality Information and Education Council of the United States (SIECUS).

Haight, B. K. (1991). Reminiscing: The state of the art as a basis for practice. *Interpersonal Journal of Aging and Human Development, 33,* 1–32.

Hall, E. (1980, November). Acting one's age: New rules for old. *Psychology Today,* pp. 66–80.

Hall, E. T. (1969). *The hidden dimension.* Garden City, NY: Doubleday.

Hall, G., & Barongan, C. (1997). Prevention of sexual aggression: Sociocultural risk and protective factors. *American Psychologist, 52,* 5–14.

Hall, L. (1997). Iroquis Confederacy. In R. J. Vecoli (Ed.), *Gale encyclopedia of multicultural America* (Vol. 2, pp. 750–763). Boston: Thomson.

Hallahan, D. P., & Kauffman, J. M. (1994). *Exceptional children* (6th ed.). Boston: Allyn & Bacon.

Hallahan, D. P., & Kauffman, J. M. (2000). *Exceptional learners: Introduction to special education* (8th ed.). Boston: Allyn & Bacon.

Hamberger, I. K., & Hastings, J. E. (1988). Characteristics of abusive men suggestive of personality disorders. *Hospital and Community Psychiatry, 39,* 763–770.

Hamer, D. H., et al. (1993). A linkage between DNA markers on the X chromosome and male sexual orientation. *Science, 261,* 321–327.

Hamilton, W. S. (1991). *Nutrition: Concepts and controversies.* New York: West.

Hancock, C. (1963). *Children and neglect—hazardous home conditions.* Washington, DC: U.S. Government Printing Office.

Hancock, L. (1996, March 18). Mother's little helper. *Newsweek,* pp. 51–56.

Handelsman, D.C., Cabral, R. J., & Weisfeld, G. E. (1987). Sources of information and adolescent sexual knowledge and behavior. *Journal of Adolescent Research, 2,* 455–463.

Handy, B. (1999, February 15). Bosom buddies: Today's men's magazines all share a common interest. Can you tell? *Time,* p. 76.

Haney, P. (1988, May–June). Comments on currents: Providing empowerment to persons with AIDS. *Social Work, 33*(3), 251–253.

Hanson, R. A., & Mullis, R. L. (1985). Age and gender differences in empathy and moral reasoning among adolescents. *Child Study Journal, 15,* 181–188.

Hare, A. (1962). *Handbook of small group research.* New York: Free Press.

Hareven, T. K. (1976). The last stage: Historical adulthood and old age. *Daedalus, 105*(4), 13–27.

Harjo, S. S.(1993). The American Indian experience. In H. P. McAdoo (Ed.), *Family ethnicity: Strength in diversity.* Newbury Park, CA: Sage.

Harlow, C. W. (1991). *Female victims of violent crime* (NCJ-126826). Washington, DC: U.S. Government Printing Office.

Harris, J. F. (1999, May 15). Clinton takes Hollywood to task over kids, violence. *Milwaukee Journal Sentinel,* p. A3.

Harris, L., et al. (1986). *American teens speak: Sex, myths, TV and birth control: The Planned Parenthood poll.* New York: Planned Parenthood Federation of America.

Harris, R. (1975). Cardiac changes with age. In R. Goldman & M. Rockstein (Eds.), *The physiology and pathology of human aging.* New York: Academic Press.

Harris, T. (1969). *I'm OK—you're OK.* New York: Harper & Row.

Harrison, D. F. (1995). Human sexuality. In R. L. Edwards (Ed.), *Encyclopedia of social work* (19th ed., Vol. 2). Washington, DC: NASW Press.

Harrison, J., Chin, J., & Ficarrotto, T. (1992). Warning: Masculinity may be dangerous to your health. In M. S. Kimmel & M. A. Messner (Eds.), *Men's lives* (2nd ed.). New York: Macmillan.

Harrison, W. D. (1995). Community development. In R. L. Edwards (Ed.), *Encyclopedia of social work* (19th ed., Vol. 1). Washington, DC: NASW Press.

Hart, S. N., Brassard, M. R. Binggeli, N. J., & Davidson, H. A. (2002). Psychological maltreatment. In J. E. B. Myers, L. Berliner, J. Briere, C. T. Hendrix, C. Jenny, & T. A. Reid (Eds.), *The APSAC handbook on child maltreatment* (2nd ed., pp. 79–103). Thousand Oaks, CA: Sage.

Harter, S. (1987). The Determinants and mediational role of global self-worth in children. In N. Eisenberg (Ed.), *Contemporary topics in developmental psychology.* New York: Wiley.

Harter, S. (1988). Developmental processes in the construction of self. In T. D. Yawkey & J. E. Johnson (Eds.), *Integrative processes and socialization: Early to middle childhood.* Hillsdale, NJ: Erlbaum.

Harter, S. (1990). Processes underlying adolescent self-concept formation. In R. Montemayor, G. R. Adams, & T. P. Gullotta (Eds.), *From childhood to adolescence: A transitional period? Advances in adolescent development* (Vol. 2). Newbury Park, CA: Sage.

Harter, S. (1993). Developmental changes in self-understanding across the 5 to 7 shift. In A. Sameroff & M. Haith (Eds.), *Reason and responsibility: The passage through childhood.* Chicago: University of Chicago Press.

Harter, S. (1998). The development of self-representations. In W. Damon (Series Ed.) & N. Eisenberg (Volume Ed.), *Handbook of child psychology: Vol. 3. Social, emotional, and personality development.* New York: John Wiley.

Hartley, E. (1946). *Problems in prejudice.* New York: King's Crown Press.

Hartman, A. (1978, October). Diagrammatic assessment of family relationships. *Social Casework, 59,* 465–476.

Hartman, A. (1991). Toward redefinition and contextualization of the abortion issue. *Social Work, 36*(6), 466–467.

Hartman, A. (1995). Family therapy. In R. L. Edwards (Ed.), *Encyclopedia of social work* (19th ed., Vol. 2, pp. 983–991). Washington, DC: NASW Press.

Hartup, W. W. (1989). Social relationships and their developmental significance. *American Psychologist, 44*(2), 120–126.

Harvard Medical School. (1986, February and March). Suicide—parts 1 and 2. *The Harvard Mental Health Letter, 2*(2,3).

Harvard Medical School. (1996, November). Suicide—part 1. *The Harvard Mental Health Letter*, pp. 1–5.

Harvey, S. M. & Spigner, C. (1995). Factors associated with sexual behavior among adolescents: A multivariate analysis. *Adolescence, 30*, 253–264.

Harway, M. (1993). Battered women: Characteristics and causes. In M. Hansen & M. Harway (Eds.), *Battering and family therapy: A feminist perspective*. Newbury Park, CA: Sage.

Hass, A. (1979). *Teenage sexuality*. New York: Macmillan.

Hatcher, R. A., et al. (1994). *Contraceptive technology* (16th rev. ed.). New York: Irvington Publishers.

Hatcher, R. A., & Guillebaud, H. (1998). The pill: Combined oral contraceptives. In R. A. Hatcher, J. Trussell, F. Stewart, W. Cates Jr., G. K. Stewart, F. Guest, & D. Kowal (Eds.), *Contraceptive technology* (17th ed., 405–466). New York: Ardent Media.

Hatcher, R. A., Trussel, J., Stewart, F., Cates, W., Jr., Stewart, G. K., Guest, F., & Kowal, D. (1998). *Contraceptive technology* (17th ed.). New York: Ardent Media.

Hatcher, R. M. (1998). Depo-Provera, Norplant, and progestin-only pills (minipills). In R. A. Hatcher, J. Trussell, F. Stewart, W. Cates Jr., G. K. Stewart, F. Guest, & D. Kowal (Eds.), *Contraceptive technology* (17th ed., 467–509). New York: Ardent Media.

Hauser, R. M., & Sewell, W. H. (1985). Birth order and educational attainment in full sibships. *American Journal of Educational Research, 22*, 1–23.

Hayflick, L. (1974). The strategy of senescence. *Gerontologist, 14*(3), 37–45.

Healy, J. M. (1988, November). Preventing birth defects of the mind. *Parents' Magazine*, pp. 176 ff.

Heck, K., & Pamuk, E. (1997). Explaining the relationship between education and postmenopausal breast cancer. *American Journal of Epidemiology, 145*(4), 366–372.

Hedges, S. J., Bowermaster, D., & Headden, S. (1994, November 14). Abortion: Who's behind the violence? *U.S. News & World Report*, pp. 50–67.

Helfer, R., et al. (1976). Arresting or freezing the developmental process. In R. Helfer and C. H. Kempe (Eds.), *Child abuse and neglect: The family and the community*. Cambridge, MA: Ballinger.

Heller, K. W., Forney, P. E., Alberto, P. A., Schwartzman, M. N., & Goeckel, T. M. (2000). *Meeting physical and health needs of children with disabilities: Teaching student participation and management*. Belmont, CA: Wadsworth.

Hellriegel, D., Slocum, Jr., J. W., & Woodman, R. W. (2001). *Organizational behavior* (9th ed.). Cincinnati, OH: South-Western Publishing.

Henderson, C. H., & Kim, B. (1980). Racism. In D. Brieland, L. Costin, & C. Atherton (Eds.), *Contemporary social work* (2nd ed.). New York: McGraw-Hill.

Henig, R. M. (1978, December 3). Exposing the myth of senility. *New York Times Magazine*, p. 158.

Henker, B., & Whalen, C. K. (1989). Hyperactivity and attention deficits. *American Psychologist, 44*(2), 216–223.

Henley, N., & Freeman, J. (1984). The sexual politics of interpersonal behavior. In J. Freeman (Ed.), *Women: A feminist perspective*. Palo Alto, CA: Mayfield.

Henley, N., & Freeman, J. (1995). The sexual politics of interpersonal behavior. In J. Freeman (Ed.), *Women: A feminist perspective* (5th ed.). Mountain View, CA: Mayfield.

Henry, C. S., Stephenson, A. L., Hanson, M. F., & Hargett, W. (1993). Adolescent suicide and families: An ecological approach. *Adolescence, 28*, 291–308.

Henry, J. (1967, December). *Indian Historian*, 1.

Henry, K., Maki, M., & Crossley, K. (1988, January). Analysis of the use of HIV antibody testing in a Minnesota hospital. *Journal of the American Medical Association, 259*, 229–232.

Henry, W. A., III. (1993, September 10). Gay parents: Under fire and on the rise. *Time*, pp. 66–69.

Hepworth, D. H., & Larsen, J. A. (1993). *Direct social work practice, theory and skills*. Pacific Grove, CA; Brooks/Cole.

Hepworth, D. H., Rooney, H., & Larsen, J. A. (1997). *Direct social work practice: Theory and skills* (5th ed.). Pacific Grove, CA: Brooks/Cole.

Herman, D. (1984). The rape culture. In Jo Freeman (Ed.), *Women: A feminist perspective*. Palo Alto, CA: Mayfield.

Hernandez, M., & McGoldrick, M. (1999). Migration and the life cycle. In B. Carter & M. McGoldrick (Eds.), *The expanded family life cycle* (3rd ed., pp. 169–201). Boston: Allyn & Bacon.

Herrnstein, R. J., & Murray, C. (1994). *The bell curve: The reshaping of American life by differences in intelligence*. New York: Free Press.

Hersey, P., & Blanchard, K. (1977). *Management of organizational behavior: Utilizing human resources* (3rd ed.). Englewood Cliffs, NJ: Prentice-Hall.

Hess, E. H., & Polt, J. M. (1960). Pupil size as related to interest value of visual stimuli. *Science, 132*, 349–350.

Hetherington, E. M. (1980). Children and divorce. In R. Henderson (Ed.), *Parent-child interaction: Theory, research, and prospect*. New York: Academic Press.

Hetter, K. (1995, October 2). Gay rights issues bust out all over. *U.S. News & World Report*, pp. 71–74.

Hines, P. M. (1999). The family life cycle of African American families living in poverty. In B. Carter & M. McGoldrick (Eds.), *The expanded family life cycle* (3rd ed., pp. 327–345). Boston: Allyn & Bacon.

Hines, P. M., & Boyd-Franklin, N. (1996). African American families. In M. McGoldrick, J. Giordano, & J. K. Pearce (Eds.), *Ethnicity and family therapy* (2nd ed., pp. 66–84). New York: Guilford.

Hines, P. M., Preto, N. G., McGoldrick, M., Almeida, R., & Weltman, S. (1999). Culture and the family life cycle. In B. Carter & M. McGoldrick (Eds.), *The expanded family life cycle* (3rd ed., pp. 69–87). Boston: Allyn & Bacon.

Hirschfelder, A., & Kreipe de Montano, M. (1993). *The Native American almanac: A portrait of Native America today*. New York: Prentice-Hall.

Hirschi, T. (1969). *Causes of delinquency*. Berkeley: University of California Press.

Ho, M. K. (1987). *Family therapy with ethnic minorities*. Newbury Park, CA: Sage.

Hodgman, C. H. (1992). Child and adolescent depression and suicide. In D. E. Greydanus and M. L. Wolraich (Eds.), *Behavioral pediatrics*. New York: Springer-Verlag.

Holland, T. P., &. Petchers, M. K. (1987). Organizations: Context for social service delivery. *Encyclopedia of social work*. Silver Spring, MD: NASW.

Holmes, S. A. (1998, December 6). Abortion-rights activists take fight to state courts, gain ground. *Milwaukee Journal Sentinel*, p. 12A.

Holmes, T. H., & Rahe, R. H. (1976). The social readjustment rating scale. *Journal of Psychosomatic Research, 11*, 213.

Homan, M. S. (1999). *Promoting community change: Making it happen in the real world* (2nd ed.). Pacific Grove, CA: Brooks/Cole.

Homan, M. S. (1999). *Promoting community change: Making it happen in the real world* (2nd ed.). Pacific Grove, CA: Brooks/Cole.

Homma-True, R., Greene, B., Lopez, S. R., & Trimble, J. E. (1993). Ethnocultural diversity in clinical psychology. *Clinical Psychologist, 46*, 50–63.

Hope Health Letter. (1991, April). Anti-smoking sentiments increasing.

Hoult, R. (1954). Experimental measurement of clothing as a factor in some social ratings of selected American men. *American Sociological Review, 19*, 324–328.

Hu, Y., & Goldman, N. (1990). Mortality differentials by marital status: An international comparison. *Demography, 27*, 233–250.

Huang, L. N., & Ying, Y. (1998). Chinese American children and adolescents. In J. T. Gibbs, L. N. Huang (Eds.), *Children of color: Psychological interventions with culturally diverse youth*, pp. 33–67. San Francisco: Jossey-Bass.

Huber, R., & Orlando, B. P. (1995, September). Persisting gender differences in social workers' incomes: Does the profession really care? *Social Work, 40*(5), 585–591.

Huesmann, L. R., & Miller, L. S. (1994). Long-term effects of repeated exposure to media violence in childhood. In L. R. Huesmann (Ed.), *Aggressive behavior: Current perspectives*. New York: Plenum.

Huff, C. R. (1993). Gangs in the United States. In A. P. Goldstein & C. R. Huff (Eds.), *The gang intervention handbook*. Champaign, IL: Research Press.

Hughes, M. (1975). Egocentrism in preschool children. Unpublished doctoral dissertation, Edinburgh University, Edinburgh.

Hull, G. H., Jr. (1995). Social work practice with diverse groups. In C. Zastrow (Ed.), *The practice of social work* (5th ed.) Belmont, CA: Wadsworth.

Hunter College Women's Studies Collective. (1995). *Women's realities, women's choices: An introduction to women's studies* (2nd ed.). New York: Oxford University Press.

Huston, A. C., Watkins, B. A., & Kunkel, D. (1989). Public policy and children's television. *American Psychologist, 44*, 159–173.

Huston, A. C., & Wright, J. C. (1998). Mass media and children's development. In W. Damon (Series Ed.), *Handbook of child psychology* (Vol. 4). New York: Wiley.

Hutchins, T., & Baxter, V. (1980). Battered women. In N. Gottlieb (Ed.), *Alternative social services for women*. New York: Columbia University Press.

Hutchinson, E. D. (1999). *Dimensions of human behavior: Person and environment*. Thousand Oaks, CA: Pine Forge.

Hyde, J. S. (1982). *Understanding human sexuality* (2nd ed.) New York: McGraw-Hill.

Hyde, J. S. (1986). *Understanding human sexuality* (3rd ed.) New York: McGraw-Hill.

Hyde, J. S. (1990). *Understanding human sexuality* (4th ed.) New York: McGraw-Hill.

Hyde, J. S. (1994). *Understanding human sexuality* (5th ed.) New York: McGraw-Hill.

Hyde, J. S. (1996). *Half the human experience: The psychology of women* (5th ed.). Lexington, MA: Heath.

Hyde, J. S., & DeLamater, J. D. (1997). *Understanding human sexuality* (6th ed.). New York: McGraw Hill.

Hyde, J. S., & DeLamater, J. D. (2000). *Understanding human sexuality* (7th ed.). Boston: McGraw Hill.

Hyde, J. S., & Linn, M. C. (1988). Gender differences in verbal ability: A meta-analysis. *Psychological Bulletin, 104*, 53–69.

Hyde, J. S., Fennema, E., & Lamon, S. J. (1990). Gender differences in mathematics performance: A meta-analysis. *Psychological Bulletin, 107*, 139–155.

Imara, M. (1975). Dying as the last stage of growth. In E. Kübler-Ross, (Ed.), *Death: The final stage of growth*. Englewood Cliffs, NJ: Prentice-Hall.

Ince, S.(1989). Surrogate motherhood represents reproductive prostitution. In R. T. Francoeur (Ed.), *Taking sides: Clashing views on controversial issues in human sexuality* (2nd ed.). Guilford, CT: Dushkin.

Infant Health and Development Program. (1990). Enhancing the outcomes of low-birth-weight, premature infants. *Journal of the American Medical Association, 263*(22), 3035–3042.

Infante-Rivard, C., Fernandez, A., Gauthier, R., David, M., & Rivard, G.-E. (1993). Fetal loss associated with caffeine intake before and during pregnancy. *Journal of the American Medical Association, 270*, 2940–2943.

Infertility doctor convicted: Jacobson guilty on 52 counts of fraud, perjury. (1992a, March 5). *Wisconsin State Journal*, p. 4A.

Infertility doctor gets 5-year term. (1992b, May 9). *Wisconsin State Journal*, p. 3A.

Infusino, P., Mercurio, M. Gelasso, M. A., Filardi, A., et al. (1996). Multidimensional evaluation in a group of centenarians. *Archives of Gerontology and Geriatrics*. Suppl. 5, 377–380.

Ingrassia, M., & Rossi, M. (1994, February 14). The limits of tolerance? An adoption ignites a furor over gay rights. *Newsweek*, p. 47.

Ivanoff, A., & Riedel, M. (1995). Suicide. In R. L. Edwards (Ed.), *Encyclopedia of social work* (19th ed., Vol. 3, pp. 2358–2372). Washington, DC: NASW Press.

Izard, C. E., & Malatesta, C. Z. (1987). Perspectives on emotional development I: Differential emotions theory of early emotional development. In J. D. Osofsky (Ed.), *Handbook of infant development* (2nd ed.). New York: Wiley.

Jacobs, M. R. (1981). *Problems presented by alcoholic clients*. Toronto: Addiction Research Foundation.

Jacobsen, S. W., Jacobson, J. L., Sokol, R. J., Martier, S. S., & Ager, J. W. (1993). Prenatal alcohol exposure and infant information processing ability. *Child Development, 64*, 1706–1721.

Jacobson, E. (1938). *Progressive relaxation* (2nd ed.). Chicago: University of Chicago Press.

Jacoby, O. (1974.) *Oswald Jacoby on poker*. New York: Doubleday.

James, M., & Jongeward, D. (1971). *Born to win: Transactional analysis with Gestalt experiments*. Reading, MA: Addison-Wesley.

Janus, S. S., & Janus, C. L. (1993). *The Janus report on sexual behavior*. New York: Wiley.

Janzen, C., & Harris, O. (1986). *Family treatment in social work practice* (2nd ed.). Itasca, IL: Peacock.

Jay, K., & Young, A. (1979). *The gay report*. New York: Summit Books.

Jaynes, G. D., & Williams, R. M., Jr. (Eds.) (1989). *A common destiny: Blacks and American society*. Washington, DC: National Academy Press.

Jencks, C., & Swingle, J. (2000, January 3). Without a net. *American Prospect*.

Jennings, V. H., Lamprecht, V. M., & Koval, D. (1998). Fertility awareness methods. In R. A. Hatcher, J. Trussel, F. Stewart, W. Cates Jr., G. K. Stewart, F. Guest, & D. Kowal (Eds.), *Contraceptive technology* (17th ed., 309–323). New York: Ardent Media.

Jensen, A. (1969). How much can we boost I.Q. and scholastic achievement? *Harvard Educational Review, 39*, 1–123.

Jobes, D. A., Berman, A. L., & Martin, C. E. (1999). Adolescent suicidality and crisis intervention. In A. R. Roberts (Ed.), *Crisis intervention handbook: Assessment, treatment, and research* (pp. 131–151). New York: Oxford University Press.

Johnson, A. K. (1995). Homelessness. In R. L. Edwards (Ed.), *Encyclopedia of social work* (19th ed., pp. 1338–1346). Washington, DC: NASW Press.

Johnson, D. W., & Johnson, F. P. (1975). *Joining together*. Englewood Cliffs, NJ: Prentice-Hall.

Johnson, D. W., & Johnson, F. P. (1987). *Joining together* (3rd ed.). Englewood Cliffs, NJ: Prentice-Hall.

Johnson, D. W., & Johnson, F. P. (1997). *Joining together* (6th ed.). Englewood Cliffs, NJ: Prentice-Hall.

Johnson, E. H. (1973). *Social problems of urban man*. Homewood, IL: Dorsey.

Johnson, G. B., & Wahl, M. (1995). Families: Demographic shifts. In R. L. Edwards (Ed.), *Encyclopedia of social work* (19th ed., Vol. 2). Washington, DC: NASW Press.

Johnson, T. W., & Colucci, P. (1999). Lesbians, gay men, and the family life cycle. In B. Carter & M. McGoldrick (Eds.), *The expanded family life cycle* (3rd ed., pp. 346–361). Boston: Allyn & Bacon.

Johnston, L., O'Malley, P. M., & Bachman, J. (1997, December). Report of monitoring the future project. Ann Arbor, MI: Institute for Social Research, U. of Michigan.

Jones, E. F. (1986). *Teenage pregnancy in industrialized countries*. New Haven, CT: Yale University Press.

Jones, M. C. (1957). The later careers of boys who were early or late maturing. *Child Development, 28,* 113–128.

Jones, M. C. (1965). Psychological correlates of somatic development. *Child Development, 36,* 899–911.

Jones, M. C., & Bayley, N. (1950). Physical maturing among boys as related to behavior. *Journal of Educational Psychology, 41,* 129–148.

Julian, J., & Kornblum, W. (1986). *Social problems* (5th ed.). Englewood Cliffs, NJ: Prentice-Hall.

Juran, J. M. (1989). *Juran on leadership for quality: An executive handbook.* New York: Free Press.

Kadushin, A. (1972). *The social work interview.* New York: Columbia University Press.

Kadushin, A., & Martin, J. A. (1988). *Child welfare services* (4th ed.). New York: Macmillan.

Kagen, J. (1992). Yesterday's premises, tomorrow's promises. *Developmental Psychology, 28,* 990–997.

Kahn, S. (1995). Community organization. In R. L. Edwards (Ed.), *Encyclopedia of social work* (19th ed., Vol. 1., pp. 569–576). Washington, DC: NASW Press.

Kail, R. V., & Cavanaugh, J. C. (1996). *Human development.* Pacific Grove, CA: Brooks/Cole.

Kail, R. V., & Cavanaugh, J. C. (2000). *Human development: A lifespan view* (2nd ed.). Belmont, CA: Wadsworth.

Kalb, C. (2001, August 13). Should you have your baby now? *Newsweek,* pp. 40–48.

Kales, J. D. (1975). Aging and sleep. In R. Goldman & M. Rockstein (Eds.), *The psychology and pathology of human aging.* New York: Academic Press.

Kalish, R. A. (1975). *Late adulthood: Perspectives on human development.* Monterey, CA: Brooks/Cole.

Kaluger, G., & Kaluger, M. F. (1984). *Human development: The span of life* (3rd ed.). St. Louis, MO: Times Mirror/Mosby.

Kamehameha Early Education Program (KEEP) (n.d.). *Kamehameha Early Education Program (KEEP),* Honolulu, Hawaii. Available

at http://www.ncrel.org/sdrs/areas/issues/educatrs/presrvce/pe#lk43.htm (accessed on July 19, 2002).

Kanin, E. (1985). Date rapists: Differential sexual socialization and relative deprivation. *Archives of Sexual Behavior, 14,* 219–231.

Kantrowitz, B. (1996, November 4). Same-sex parents are trying to move out of the shadows and into the mainstream. Will they—and their kids—be accepted? *Newsweek,* pp. 51–57.

Kantrowitz, B., & Kaplan, D. A. (1990, March 19). Not the right family. *Newsweek,* pp. 50–51.

Kaplan, D. A. (1993, November 22). Take down the girlie calendars. *Newsweek,* p. 34.

Kaplan, D. A., & Klaidman, D. (1996, June 3). A battle, not the war. *Newsweek,* pp. 24–30.

Kaplan, H. S. (1981). *The new sex therapy.* New York: Brunner/Mazel.

Kaplan, J. (1970). *Marijuana: A new prohibition.* New York: World.

Kaplan, S., & Saperstein, S. (1985). Lesbian and gay adolescents. In H. Hidalgo, T. L. Peterson, & N. J. Woodman (Eds.), *Lesbian and gay issues: A resource manual for social workers.* Silver Spring, MD: NASW.

Karlen, A. (1971). *Sexuality and homosexuality: A new view.* New York: Norton.

Katz, A. H. & Bender, E. I. (1976). *The strengths in us: Self-help groups in the modern world.* New York: Franklin-Watts.

Kaufman, J., & Zigler, E. (1987). Do abused children become abusive parents? *American Journal of Orthopsychiatry, 57,* 186–192.

Kavale, K. A. (1988). The long-term consequences of learning disabilities. In M. C. Wang, M. C. Reynolds, & H. J. Walberg (Eds.), *Handbook of special education: Research and practice.* Vol. 2: *Mildly handicapped conditions.* New York: Pergamon Press.

Kavale, K. A. (1993). How many learning disabilities are there? A commentary on Stanovich's "Dysrationalia: A new specific learning disability." *Journal of Learning Disabilities, 26,* 520–523.

Kazdin, A. E. (1989). *Behavior modification in applied settings* (4th ed.). Pacific Grove, CA: Brooks/Cole.

Kazdin, A. E. (1994). *Behavior modification in applied settings* (5th ed.). Pacific Grove, CA: Brooks/Cole.

Kazdin, A. E. (2001). *Behavior modification in applied settings.* (6th ed.). Belmont, CA: Wadsworth.

Kelaher, M., Ross, M., Rohrsheim, R., Drury, M., & Clarkson, A. (1994). Dominant situational determinants of sexual risk behavior in gay men. *AIDS, 8,* 101–105.

Kelley, K., & Byrne, D. (1992). *Exploring human sexuality.* Englewood Cliffs, NJ: Prentice-Hall.

Kelly, G. F. (1994). *Sexuality today: The human perspective* (4th ed.). Guilford, CT: Dushkin Publishing Group.

Kelly, G. F. (1998). *Sexuality today: The human perspective* (6th ed.). Boston: McGraw-Hill.

Kelly, G. F. (2001). *Sexuality today* (7th ed.). Boston: McGraw-Hill.

Kemp, A. (1998). *Abuse in the family: An introduction.* Pacific Grove, CA: Brooks/Cole.

Kendall-Tackett, K. A., Williams, L., & Finkelhor, D. (1993). Impact of sexual abuse on children: A review and synthesis of recent empirical studies. *Psychological Bulletin, 113,* 164–180.

Keniston, K. (1965). *The uncommitted.* New York: Harcourt, Brace and World.

Keniston, K. (1977). *All our children: The American family under pressure.* New York: Harcourt Brace Jovanovich.

Kent, S. (1980). *The life-extension revolution.* New York: Morrow.

Kercher, G. A., & McShane, M. (1984). The prevalence of child sexual abuse victimization in an adult sample of Texas residents. *Child Abuse and Neglect, 8,* 495–501.

Kerig, P. K., Alyoshina, Y. Y., & Volovich, A. (1993). Gender-role socialization in contemporary Russia: Implications for cross-cultural research. *Psychology of Women Quarterly, 17,* 389–408.

Kerr, M. E., & Bowen, M. (1988). *Family evaluation: An approach based on Bowen theory.* New York: Norton.

Kettner, P., Daley, J. & Nichols, A. (1985). *Initiating change in organizations and communities.* Monterey, CA: Brooks/Cole.

Keys, D. L. (1990). *Link-Up: A program for youth at risk, Working together, What's next?* and *Who needs you.* Pamphlets distributed at presentation on Male adolescents: Development, suicide, and gay issues. Regional Council on Social Work Education Conference, Starved Rock, IL, April 20, 1990.

Kiev, A. (1980, September). The courage to live. *Cosmopolitan,* pp. 301–308.

Kim, N., Stanton, B., Li, X., Dickersin, K., & Galbraith, J. (1997). Effectiveness of the 40 adolescent AIDS-risk reduction interventions: A quantitative review. *Journal of Adolescent Health, 20,* 204–215.

Kimmel, D. C. (1974). *Adulthood and aging.* New York: Wiley.

Kinard, E., & Reinherz, H. (1987). School aptitude and achievement in children of adolescent mothers. *Journal of Youth and Adolescence, 16,* 69–78.

Kinsey, A. C., et al. (1953). *Sexual behavior in the human female.* Philadelphia: Saunders.

Kinsey, A. C., Pomeroy, W. B., & Martin, C. R. (1948). *Sexual behavior in the human male.* Philadelphia: Saunders.

Kirby, I. J. (1973). Hormone replacement therapy for postmenopausal symptoms. *Lancet, 2,* 103.

Kirk, G., & Okazawa-Rey, M. (2001). *Women's lives: multicultural perspectives* (2nd ed.). Mountain View, CA: Mayfield.

Kirk, S. (1979). *Educating exceptional children* (3rd ed.). Boston: Houghton Mifflin.

Kirk, W. G. (1993). *Adolescent suicide: A school-based approach to assessment and intervention.* Champaign, IL: Research Press.

Kirst-Ashman, K. K. (2000). *Human behavior, communities, organizations and groups in the macro social environment: An empowerment approach.* Pacific Grove, CA: Brooks/Cole.

Kirst-Ashman, K. K., & Hull, G. H., Jr. (1993). *Understanding generalist practice.* Chicago: Nelson-Hall.

Kirst-Ashman, K. K., & Hull, G. H., Jr. (1999). *Understanding generalist practice* (2nd ed.). Chicago: Nelson-Hall.

Kirst-Ashman, K. K., & Hull, Jr., G. H. (2002). *Understanding generalist practice* (3rd ed.). Pacific Grove, CA: Brooks/Cole.

Kissinger, P., Trim, S., Williams, E., Mielke, E., Koporc, K, & Brosn, R. (1997). An evaluation of initiatives to improve family planning use by African-American adolescents. *Journal of the National Medical Association, 89,* 110–114.

Klein, H., & Cordell, A. (1987). The adolescent as mother; early risk identification. *Journal of Youth and Adolescence, 16,* 47–58.

Klein, M. W., & Maxson, C.L. (1989). Street gang violence. In M. Wolfgang & N. Weiner (Eds.), *Violent crimes, violent criminals.* Newbury Park, CA: Sage.

Kluger, J. (1999, April 26). The last resort: A controversial breast-cancer therapy pits women against insurers. *Time,* pp. 68–69.

Knapp, M. L. (1978). *Nonverbal communication in human interaction* (2nd ed.) New York: Holt, Rinehart and Winston.

Knapp, M. L., & Hall, J. A. (1992). *Nonverbal communication in human interaction* (3rd ed.). Fort Worth, TX: Harcourt Brace.

Knapp, M. L., & Hall, J. A. (1998). *Nonverbal communication in human interaction* (4th ed.). Fort Worth, TX: Harcourt Brace Jovanovich.

Koch, L., & Koch, J. (1980, January 27). Parent abuse—A new plague. *Parade Magazine,* p. 14.

Koch, M. O., Dotson, V., & Troast, T. P. (1993). Treating eating disorders. In C. Zastrow, *Social work with groups* (3rd ed.) Chicago: Nelson-Hall.

Koch, M. O., Dotson, V., & Troast, T. P. (1993). Interventions with eating disorders. In C. Zastrow, *Social work with groups* (4th ed., 463–487). Chicago: Nelson-Hall.

Koch, M. O., Dotson, V., & Troast, T. P. (2001). Interventions with eating disorders. In C. Zastrow, *Social work with groups* (5th ed., 433–453). Pacific Grove, CA: Brooks/Cole.

Koenig, H. G., George, L. K.,/Siegler, I.C. (1988). The use of religion and other emotion-regulating coping strategies among older adults. *Gerontologist, 28,* 303–310.

Koenig, H. G., Kvale, J. N., & C. Ferrel. (1988). Religion and well-being in later life. *Gerontologist, 28,* 18–28.

Koenigsberger, M. R. (2000). Advances in neonatal neurology: 1950–2000. *Review of Neurology, 31,* 202–211.

Kohlberg, L. (1963). The development of children's orientations toward a moral order. Part 1: Sequence in the development of moral thought. *Vita Humana, 6,* 11–35.

Kohlberg, L. (1968, April). The child as a moral philosopher. *Psychology Today,* pp. 25–30.

Kohlberg, L. (1969). *Stages in the development of moral thought and action.* New York: Holt, Rinehart and Winston.

Kohlberg, L. (1978). Revisions in the theory and practice of moral development. *New Directions for Child Development, 2.*

Kohlberg, L. (1981a). *The philosophy of moral development.* New York: Harper & Row.

Kohlberg, L. (1981b). *Essays on moral development.* San Francisco: Harper & Row.

Kolko, D. J. (1996). Child physical abuse. In J. Briere, L. Berliner, J. A. Bulkley, C. Jenny, & T. Reid (Eds.), *The APSAC handbook on child maltreatment* (pp. 21–50). Thousand Oaks, CA: Sage.

Kolko, D. J. (2002). Child physical abuse. In J. E. B. Myers, L. Berliner, J. Briere, C. T. Hendrix, C. Jenny, & T. A. Reid (Eds.), *The APSAC handbook on children maltreatment* (2nd ed., pp. 21–54). Thousand Oaks: Sage.

Koll, L. C., Bernard, V., & Dohrenwend, B. P. (1969). The problem of validity in field studies of psychological disorder. In B. P. Dohrenwend and B. Snell Dohrenwend (Eds.), *Urban challenges to psychiatry.* New York: Wiley.

Kols, A., et al. (1982, May–June). Oral contraceptives in the 1980s. *Current Population Reports* (Series A, No. 6). Washington, DC: U.S. Government Printing Office.

Koop, C. E. (1987). *Surgeon general's report on acquired immune deficiency syndrome.* Washington, DC: U.S. Department of Health and Human Services.

Kopels, S. (1995, Fall). The Americans with Disabilities Act: A tool to combat poverty. *Journal of Social Work Education, 31*(3), 337–346.

Kornblum, W., & Julian, J. (1989). *Social problems* (6th ed.). Englewood Cliffs, NJ: Prentice-Hall.

Kornblum, W., & Julian, J. (1995). *Social problems* (8th ed.). Englewood Cliffs, NJ: Prentice-Hall.

Kornblum, W., & Julian, J. (1998). *Social problems* (9th ed.). Englewood Cliffs, NJ: Prentice-Hall.

Kornblum, W., & Julian, J. (2001). *Social problems* (10th ed.). Upper Saddle River, NJ: Prentice-Hall.

Koss, M. (1988). Hidden rape: Sexual aggression and victimization in a national sample of students in higher education. In A. Burgess (Ed.), *Rape and sexual assault II.* New York: Garland.

Koss, M. P. (1992). The underdetection of rape: Methodological choices influence incidence estimates. *Journal of Social Issues, 48*(1), 61–75.

Koss, M. P., Gidycz, C., & Wisniewski, N. (1987). The scope of rape: Incidence and prevalence of sexual aggression in a sample of higher ducation students. *Journal of Consulting and Clinical Psychology, 55,* 162–170.

Koss, M. P., Goodman, L. A., Browne, A., Fitzgerald, L. G., Keita, G. P., & Russo, N. F. (1994). *No safe haven: Male violence against women at home, at work, and in the community.* Washington, DC: American Psychological Association.

Koss, M. P., Leonard, K. E., Beezley, D. A., & Oros, C. J. (1985). Non-stranger sexual aggression: A discriminant analysis of the psychological characteristics of undetected offenders. *Sex Roles, 12,* 981–992.

Kowal, D. Coitus interruptus (withdrawal). (1998). In R. A. Hatcher, J. Trussel, F. Stewart, W. Cates Jr., G. K. Stewart, F. Guest, & D. Kowal (Eds.). *Contraceptive technology* (17th ed., pp. 303–307). New York Ardent Media.

Krieger, N., & Sidney, S. (1996). Racial discrimination and blood pressure: The CARDIS study of young Black and White adults. *American Journal of Public Health, 86* (10), 1370–1378.

Kübler-Ross, E. (1969). *On death and dying.* New York: Macmillan.

Kuiper, H., Miller, S., Martinez, E., Loeb, L., & Darney, P. (1997). Urban adolescent females' views on the implant and contraceptive decision-making: A double paradox. *Family Planning Perspectives, 29,* 167–172.

Kurdek, L. A. (1995). Lesbian and gay couples. In A. R. D'Augelli & C. J. Patterson (Eds.), *Lesbian, gay, and bisexual identities over the lifespan: Psychological perspectives* (pp. 243–261). New York: Oxford.

Kurtines, W. M., and Gewirtz, J. (Eds.). (1991). *Oral behavior and development: Advances in theory, research, and application.* Hillsdale, NJ: Erlbaum.

Kurz, D. (1993). Physical assaults by husbands: A major social problem. In R. J. Gelles & D. R. Loseke (Eds.), *Current controversies on family violence.* Newbury Park, CA: Sage.

Kuypers, J., & Benston, V. (1973). Competence and social breakdown: A social-psychological view of aging. *Human Development, 16*(2), 37–49.

Lacayo, R. (1995a, January 23). Scenes from a bad marriage. *Time,* pp. 41–42.

Lacayo, R. (1995b, June 12). Reaction. *Time,* pp. 24–30.

Lacayo, R. (1999, January 4). Washington burning: For only the second time in history, the House impeaches the President as bombs burst in air and partisanship flares out of control. *Time,* p. 67.

Lacayo, R. (2001, August 20). How Bush got there. *Time,* pp. 17–23.

Lafferty, E. (1997, February 17). The inside story of how O. J. lost. *Time,* pp. 29–36.

Laird, J. (1995). Lesbians: Parenting. In R. L. Edwards (Ed.), *Encyclopedia of social work* (19th ed., Vol. 2.). Washington, DC: NASW Press.

Lamanna, M. A., & Riedmann, A. (1988). *Marriages and families: Making choices and facing change* (3rd ed.). Belmont, CA: Wadsworth.

Lamarine, R. J. (1987). Self-esteem, health locus of control, and health attitudes among Native-American children. *Journal of School Health, 57,* 371–373.

Lamb, M., Hopps, K., & Elster, A. (1987). Strange situation behavior of infants with adolescent mothers. *Infant Behavior and Development, 10,* 39–48.

Lammer, E., et al. (1985). Retinoic acid embryopathy. *New England Journal of Medicine, 313,* 837–841.

Land, H. (1995). Feminist clinical social work in the 21st century. In N. Van Den Bergh (Ed.), *Feminist practice in the 21st century* (pp. 3–19). Washington, DC: NASW Press.

Lang, J. S. (1981, April 13). John Hinkley—a misfit who craved fame. *U.S. News & World Report,* p. 26.

Lavell, M. (1998, July 6). The new rules of sexual harassment: The Supreme Court defines what harassment is and who can be held responsible. *U.S. News & World Report,* p. 31.

Law: How women lawyers fare. (1996, January 15). *U.S. News & World Report,* p. 14.

Lawrence, L., Rubinson, L. & O'Rourke, T. (1984, Fall/Winter). Sexual attitudes and behaviors: Trends for a ten year period, 1972–1982. *Journal of Sex Education and Therapy, 10*(1), 22–30.

Lazzari, M. M., Ford, H. R., & Haughey, X. (1996). Making a difference: Women of action in the community. *Social Work, 41*(2), 197–205.

Leacock, E. (1971). *The culture of poverty: A critique.* New York: Simon and Schuster.

Leadbeater, B., & Way, N. (1995). *Urban adolescent girls: Resisting stereotypes.* New York: New York University Press.

Leaf, A. (1973, January) Every day is a gift when you are over 100. *National Geographic,* pp. 93–118.

Leary, W. E. (1997, February 21). Panel recommends marijuana studies. *Wisconsin State Journal,* p. 2A.

Leashore, B. R. (1995). African Americans overview. In R. L. Edwards (Ed.), *Encyclopedia of social work* (19th ed., Vol. 1, pp. 101–115). Washington, DC: NASW Press.

Lee, J. A. (Ed.). (1991). *Gay midlife and maturity.* New York: Harrington Park Press.

Lefrancois, G. R. (1990). *The lifespan* (3rd ed.). Belmont, CA: Wadsworth.

Lefrancois, G. R. (1996). *The lifespan* (5th ed.) Belmont, CA: Wadsworth.

Lefrancois, G. R. (1999). *The lifespan* (6th ed.). Belmont, CA: Wadsworth.

Leiblum, S. R. (1993). *The impact of fertility on sexual and marital satisfaction.* In J. Bancroft, C. M. Davis, & H. J. Ruppel, Jr. (Eds.), *Annual review of sex research* (Vol. 4, pp. 99–120). Mt. Vernon, IA: Society for the Scientific Study of Sex.

Leifer, M. (1980). *Psychological effects of motherhood: A study of first pregnancy.* New York: Praeger.

Leitenberg, H., Detzer, M. J., & Srebnik, D. (1993). Gender differences in masturbation and the relationship of masturbation experience in preadolescence and/or early adolescence and sexual behavior and sexual adjustment in young adulthood. *Archives of Sexual Behavior, 22,* 299–313.

Leslie, L. A. (1986). The impact of adolescent females' assessments of parenthood and employment plans for the future. *Journal of Youth and Adolescence, 15,* 29–50.

LeVay, S. (1991). A difference in hypothalamic structure between heterosexual and homosexual men. *Science, 253,* 1034–1037.

LeVay, S. (1996). *Queer science: The use and abuse of research into homosexuality.* Cambridge, MA: MIT Press.

LeVine, E. S., & Sallee, A. L. (1999). *Child welfare: Clinical theory and practice.* Dubuque, IA: Eddie Bowers.

Levine, S. B. (1994, July/August). Caution: Children watching. *Ms.,* pp. 23–25.

Levinson, D. (1986). A conception of adult development. *American Psychologist, 41*(1), 3–13.

Levinson, D. J., & Levinson, J. D. (1996). *The seasons of a woman's life.* New York: Knopf.

Levinson, D. J., & Levinson, J. D. (1978). *The seasons of a man's life.* New York: Knopf.

Levinson, D. J., Darrow, C. N., Klein, E. B., Levinson, M. H., & McKee, B. (1974). The psychosocial development of men in early adulthood and the mid-life transition. In D. F. Ricks, A. Thomas, & M. Roff (Eds.), *Life history research in psychopathology*. Minneapolis: University of Minnesota Press.

Levinson, R. (1995). Reproductive and contraceptive knowledge, contraceptive self-efficacy, and contraceptive behavior among teenage women. *Adolescence, 30,* 65–85.

Levy, S. M., Derogatis, L. R., Gallagher, D., & Gatz, M. (1980). Intervention with older adults and the evaluation of outcome. In L. W. Poon (Ed.), *Aging in the 1980s.* Washington, DC: American Psychological Association.

Lewin, K., Lippitt, R., & White, R. K. (1939). Patterns of aggressive behavior in experimentally created social climates. *Journal of Social Psychology, 10,* 271–299.

Lewinsohn, P. M., Robde, P., Seeley, J., & Baldwin, C. (2001). Gender differences in suicide attempts from adolescence to young adulthood. *Journal of the Academy of Child and Adolescent Psychiatry, 40,* 427–434.

Lewis, B. Y. (1985, January–February). The wife abuse inventory: A screening device for the identification of abused women. *Social Work, 30,* 32–35.

Lewis, K. (1980). Children of lesbians: Their point of view. *Social Work, 25*(3), 203.

Lewis, L. A. (1984). The coming-out process for lesbians: Integrating a stable identity. *Social Work, 29*(5), 464–468.

Lewis, O. (1966). The culture of poverty. *Scientific American, 215*(10), 19–25.

Lewis, R. G., & Man Keung Ho. (1975, September). Social work with Native Americans. *Social Work, 20,* 378–382.

Liebert, R. M., & Sprafkin, J. (1988). *The early window: Effects of television on children and youth.* New York: Pergamon.

Liederman, D. S. (1995). Child welfare overview. In R. L. Edwards (Ed.), *Encyclopedia of social work* (19th ed., Vol. 1, pp. 424–433). Washington, DC: NASW Press.

Lin, C., & Liu, W. T. (1999). Intergenerational relationships among Chinese immigrant families from Taiwan. In H. P. McAdoo (Ed.), *Family ethnicity* (2nd ed., pp. 235–251). Thousand Oaks, CA: Sage.

Lindsay, M. (1995). Understanding and enhancing adult learning. Unpublished paper for presentation at the Spring Conference of the Wisconsin Council on Social Work Education, Wisconsin Dells, WI.

Linehan, M. M. (1999). Standard protocol for assessing and treating suicidal behaviors for patients in treatment. In D. G. Jacobs (Ed.), *Guide to suicide assessment and intervention* (147–187). San Francisco: Jossey-Bass.

Linscheid, T. R., Iwata, B. A., Ricketts, R. W., Williams, D. E., & Griffin, J. C. (1990). Clinical evaluation of the self-injurious behavior inhibiting system (SIBIS). *Journal of Applied Behavior Analysis, 23,* 53–78.

Lipid Research Clinics Program. (1984a). The Lipid Research Clinic coronary primary prevention trial results. Part 1: Reduction in the incidence of coronary heart disease. *Journal of the American Medical Association, 251,* 351–364.

Lipid Research Clinics Program. (1984b). The Lipid Research Clinic coronary primary prevention trial results. Part 2: The relationship of reduction in incidence of coronory heart disease to cholesterol lowering. *Journal of the American Medical Association, 251,* 365–374.

Lipnick, J. J., et al. (1986). Oral contraceptives and breast cancer. *Journal of the American Medical Association, 255,* 58–61.

Lips, H. M. (1995). Gender-role socialization: Lessons in femininity. In J. Freeman (Ed.), *Women: A Feminist Perspective* (5th ed., pp. 128–148). Mountain View, CA: Mayfield.

Litt, I. F., et al. (1983, June). Emergency room evaluation of the adolescent who attempts suicide: Compliance with follow-up. *Journal of Adolescent Health Care, 4*(6), 106–108.

Little, M. (1982). *Family breakup.* San Francisco, CA: Jossey-Bass.

Livesey, D. J., & Intili, D. (1996). A gender difference in visual-spatial ability in 4-year-old children: Effects on performance of a kinesthetic acuity task. *Journal of Experimental Child Psychology, 63,* 436–446.

Livson, N., & Peskin, H. (1980). Perspectives on adolescence from longitudinal research. In A. J. Adelsen (Ed.), *Handbook of adolescent psychology.* New York: Wiley.

Lloyd, G. A. (1990). AIDS and HIV: The syndrome and the virus. *Encyclopedia of social work: 1990 supplement.* Silver Spring, MD: NASW.

Lloyd, G. A. (1995). HIV/AIDS overview. In *Encyclopedia of social work* (19th ed., pp. 1257–1290). Washington, DC: NASW Press.

Lock, M. (1991). Contested meanings of the menopause. *Lancet, 337,* 1270–1272.

Loewenberg, F. M., & Dolgoff, R. (1996). *Ethical decisions for social work practice* (5th ed.). Itasca, IL: Peacock.

Longres, J. F. (1990). Youth gangs. In *Encyclopedia of social work: 1990 supplement.* Silver Spring, MD: NASW.

Longres, J. F. (1995). Hispanics overview. In R. L. Edwards (Ed.), *Encyclopedia of social work* (19th ed., Vol. 2, pp. 1214–1222). Washington, DC: NASW Press.

Longres, J. F., & Fredriksen, K. I. (2000). Social work practice with lesbians and gay men. In P. Allen-Meares & C. Garvin (Eds.), *The handbook of social work practice* (pp. 477–498). Thousand Oaks, CA: Sage.

Longstreth, G. F., & Wolde-Tsadik, G. (1993). Irritable bowel-type symptoms in HMO examinees: Prevalence, demographics, and clinical correlates. *Digestive Diseases and Sciences, 38,* 1581–1589.

Lott, B. (1987). *Women's lives: Themes and variations in gender learning.* Belmont, CA: Brooks/Cole.

Lott, B. (1994). *Women's lives: Themes and variations in gender learning* (2d ed.). Pacific Grove, CA: Brooks/Cole.

Lott, B., Reilly, M. E., & Howard, D. R. (1982). Sexual assault and harassment: A campus community case study. *Signs, 8,* 296–319.

Lum, D. (2000). *Social work practice and people of color: A process-stage approach* (4th ed.). Pacific Grove, CA: Brooks/Cole.

Luster, T., & Small, S. A. (1997). Sexual abuse history and problems in adolescence: Exploring the effects of moderating variables. *Journal of Marriage & the Family, 59,* 131–142.

McAdoo, H. P. (Ed.). (1993). *Family ethnicity: Strength in diversity.* Newbury Park, CA: Sage.

McAnulty, R. D., & Burnette, M. M. (2001). *Exploring human sexuality: Making healthy decisions.* Boston: Allyn & Bacon.

McCabe, M. P. (1987, February). Desired and experienced levels of premarital affection and sexual intercourse during dating. *Journal of Sex Research, 23*(1), 23–33.

McCabe, M. P., & Collins, J. K. (1984). Measurement of depth of desired and experienced sexual involvement at different stages of dating. *Journal of Sex Research, 20,* 377–390.

McCammon, S., Knox, D., & Schacht, C. (1993). *Choices in sexuality.* Minneapolis: West.

McCammon, S., Knox, D., & Schacht, C. (1998). *Making choices in sexuality: Research and applications.* Pacific Grove: Brooks/Cole.

McCrary, J., & Gutierrez, L. (1979/80). The homosexual person in the military and in national security employment. *Journal of Homosexuality, 51*(1, 2), 115–146.

McDonald, A. D., Armstrong, B. G., & Sloan, M. (1992). Cigarette, alcohol, and coffee consumption and prematurity. *American Journal of Public Health, 82,* 87–90.

McDonald-Wikler, L. (1987). Disabilities: Developmental. In *Encyclopedia of social work* (Vol. 1). Silver Spring, MD: NASW.

McGill, L., Smith, P. B., & Johnson, T. C. (1989). AIDS: Knowledge, attitudes, and risk characteristics of teens. *Journal of Sex Education and Therapy, 15,* 31–35.

McGoldrick, M. (1999). History, genograms, and the family life cycle. In B. Carter & M. McGoldrick (Eds.), *The expanded family life cycle* (3rd ed., pp. 47–68). Boston: Allyn & Bacon.

McGregor, D. (1960). *The human side of enterprise.* New York: McGraw-Hill.

McHugh, M. C. (1993). Studying battered women and batterers: Feminist perspectives on methodology. In M. Hansen & M. Harway (Eds.), *Battering and Family Therapy: A Feminist Perspective* (pp. 54–68). Newbury Park, CA: Sage.

McIntosh, Peggy. (1988). *White privilege: Unpacking the invisible knapsack.* Wellesley College, MA.

McIntyre, K. (1981). Role of mothers in father-daughter incest: A feminist analysis. *Social Work, 267,* 26–62, 462–467.

McKenry, P. C., et al. (1982, May). Adolescent suicide: A comparison of attempters and nonattempters in an emergency room population. *Clinical Pediatrics, 21,* 266–270.

McLeod, A., Crawford, I., & Zechmeister, J. (1999). Heterosexual undergraduates' attitudes toward gay fathers and their children. *Journal of Psychology & Human Sexuality, 11,* 43–62.

McTavish, D. G. (1971). Perceptions of old people: A review of research methodologies and findings. *Gerontologist, 11,* 90–101.

Mackelprang, R., & Salsgiver, R. (1996, January). People with disabilities and social work: Historical and contemporary issues. *Social Work 41*(1), 7–14.

Mackelprang, R., & Salsgiver, R. (1999). *Disability: A diversity model approach in human service practice.* Pacific Grove, CA: Brooks/Cole.

Madom, S., Jussim, L., & Eccles, J. (1997). In search of the powerful self-fulfilling prophecy. *Journal of Personality and Social Psychology, 72,* 791–809.

Magnusson, D., Stattin, H., & Allen, V. L. (1985). Biological maturation and social development: A longitudinal study of some adjustment processes from mid-adolescence to adulthood. *Journal of Youth and Adolescence, 14,* 267–283.

Mcnulty, R. D., & Burnette, M. M. (2003). *Fundamentals of human sexuality: Making healthy decisions.* Boston: Allyn & Bacon.

Maier, R. A. (1984). *Human sexuality in perspective.* Chicago: Nelson-Hall.

Maier, R. A., & Maier, B. M. (1970). *Comparative animal behavior.* Belmont, CA: Brooks/Cole.

Makinodan, T. (1974). Cellular basis of immunosenescence. In *Molecular and Cellular Mechanisms of Aging* (Vol. 27). Paris, France: INSERM (Coll. Inst. Nat. Sante Rec. Med).

Malamuth, N. (1986). Predictors of naturalistic sexual aggression. *Journal of Personality and Social Psychology, 50,* 953–962.

Malamuth, N. M. (1998). The confluence model as an organizing framework for research on sexually aggressive men: Risk moderators, imagined aggression and pornography consumption. In R. Green & E. Donnserstein (Eds.), *Aggression: Theoretical and empirical reviews.* New York: Academic Press.

Malamuth, N. M., Sockloskie, R. J., Koss, M. P., & Tanaka, J. S. (1991). Characteristics of aggressors against women: Testing a model using a national sample of college students. *Journal of Consulting and Clinical Psychology, 59,* 670–781.

Malatesta, V. J. (1979). Alcohol effects on the orgasmic-ejaculatory response in human males. *Journal of Sex Research, 15,* 101–107.

Malatesta, V. J., Pollack, R. H., Crotty, T. D., & Pecock, L. J. (1982). Acute alcohol intoxication and female orgasmic response. *Journal of Sex Research, 18,* 1–17.

Man Sentenced in Fatal Church Bus Accident. (1990, February 24). *Wisconsin State Journal,* p. 3A.

Manuzza, S., Klein, R. G., Bonagura, N., Konig, P. H., & Shenker, R. (1988). Hyperactive boys almost grown up. II: Status of subjects without a mental disorder. *Archives of General Psychiatry, 45,* 13–18.

Marcia, J. E. (1980). Identity in adolescence. In J. Adelson (Ed.), *Handbook of adolescent psychology.* New York: Wiley.

Marcia, J. E. (1991). Identity and self-development. In R. M. Lerner, A. C. Petersen, & J. Brooks-Gunn (Eds.), *Encyclopedia of adolescence* (Vol. 1). New York: Garland.

Marcus, M. B. (2002, August 12, 2002). Aging of AIDS: The silent risk group for HIV infection: senior citizens. *U.S. News & World Report,* pp. 40–41.

Marden, C. F., & Meyer, G. (1962). *Minorities in American society.* New York: American Book Co.

Margolin, L., & White, L. (1987). The continuing role of physical attractiveness in marriage. *Journal of Marriage and the Family, 49*(1), 21–27.

Marieb, E. M. (1992). *Human anatomy and physiology* (2nd ed.). Redwood City, CA: Benjamin/Cummings.

Marini, M. M., & Brinton, M. (1984). Sex typing in occupational socialization. In B. F. Reskin (Ed.), *Sex segregation in the workplace: Trends, explanations, remedies.* Washington, DC: National Academy Press.

Marks, J. S., & Cates, W. (1986). Sex education: How should it be offered? *Journal of the American Medical Association, 255,* 85–86.

Markus, H., & Nurius, P. S. (1984). Self-understanding and self-regulation in middle childhood. In W. A. Collins (Ed.), *Development during middle childhood: The years from six to twelve.* Washington, DC: National Academy Press.

Marshall, D. S. (1980). Too much in Mangaia. In C. Gordon & G. Johnson (Eds.), *Readings in human sexuality: contemporary perspectives* (2nd ed.). New York: Harper and Row.

Marshall, D. S., & Suggs, R. (1971). *Human Sexual Behavior.* New York: Basic Books.

Marsiglio, W. (1986). Teenage fatherhood: High school accreditation and educational attainment. In A. B. Elster & M. E. Lamb (Eds.), *Adolescent fatherhood.* Hillside, NJ: Erlbaum.

Martin, H. P. I., & Beezley, P. (1976). Personality of abused children. In H. P. Martin (Ed.), *The abused child.* Cambridge, MA: Ballinger.

Martin, J. (1984). Neglected fathers: Limitations in diagnostic and treatment resources for violent men. *Child Abuse and Neglect, 8,* 387–392.

Martin, S. E. (1995). Sexual harassment: The link joining gender stratification, sexuality, and women's economic status. In J. Freeman (Ed.), *Women: A feminist perspective* (5th ed., pp. 22–46). Mountain View, CA: Mayfield.

Martinez-Brawley, E. M. (1995). Community. In R. L. Edwards (Ed.), *Encyclopedia of social work* (19th ed., Vol. 1, pp. 539–548). Washington, DC: NASW Press.

Martorell, R., Mendoza, F., & Castillo, F. (1988). Poverty and stature in children. In J. C. Waterlow (Ed.), *Linear growth retardation in less developed countries*. New York: Raven.

Marx, J. (1996). A second breast cancer susceptibility gene is found. *Science, 271,* 30–31.

Maslow, A. H. (1954). *Motivation and personality*. New York: Harper & Row.

Maslow, A. H. (1968). *Toward a psychology of being* (2nd ed.). Princeton, NJ: Van Nostrand.

Maslow, A. H. (1971). *The farther reaches of human nature*. New York: Viking.

Maslow, A. H., & Mintz, N. L. (1956). Effects of esthetic surroundings. *Journal of Psychology, 41,* 247–254.

Mastectomy not so necessary, panel says. (1990, June 22). *Milwaukee Journal*.

Masters, W. H., & Johnson, V. E. (1966). *Human sexual response*. Boston: Little, Brown.

Masters, W. H., & Johnson, V. E. (1968). Human sexual response: The aging female and the aging male. In B. L. Neugarten (Ed.), *Middle age and aging: A reader in social psychology*. Chicago: University of Chicago Press.

Masters, W. H., & Johnson, V. E. (1970). *Human sexual inadequacy*. Boston: Little, Brown.

Masters, W. H., Johnson, V. E., & Kolodny, R. C. (1979). *Human sexuality*. Boston: Little, Brown.

Masters, W. H., Johnson, V. E., & Kolodny, R. C. (1982). *Human sexuality* (2nd ed.). Boston: Little, Brown.

Masters, W. H., Johnson, V. E., & Kolodny, R. C. (1985). *Human sexuality* (3rd ed.). Boston: Little, Brown.

Masters, W. H., Johnson, V. E., & Kolodny, R. C. (1988). *Human sexuality* (4th ed.). Glenview, IL: Scott, Foresman.

Masters, W. H., Johnson, V. E., & Kolodny, R. C. (1994). *Heterosexuality*. New York: HarperCollins.

Masters, W. H., Johnson, V. E., & Kolodny, R. C. (1995). *Human sexuality* (5th ed.). New York: HarperCollins.

Mather, J. H., & Lager, P. B. (2000). *Child welfare: A unifying model of practice*. Pacific Grove, CA: Brooks/Cole.

Matson, J. L., & Taras, M. E. (1989). A 20-year review of punishment and alternative methods to treat problem behaviors in developmentally disabled persons. *Research in Developmental Disabilities, 10,* 85–104.

Maultsby, M. C., Jr. (1975). *Help yourself to happiness*. Boston: Herman.

Mayer, A. (1983). *Incest: A treatment manual for therapy with victims, spouses and offenders*. Holmes Beach, FL: Learning Publications.

Maypole, D. E., & Skaine, R. (1983). Sexual harassment in the workplace. *Social Work, 28*(5), 385–390.

Meador, B. D., & Rogers, C. (1979). Personal-centered therapy. In R. J. Corsini (Ed.), *Current psychotherapies* (2nd ed.) Itasca, IL: Peacock.

Meddin, B. J. (1985). The assessment of risk in child abuse and neglect investigations. *Child Abuse and Neglect, 9,* 57–62.

Mediascope. (1996). *National television violence study: Executive summary 1994–1995*. Studio City, CA: Mediascope.

Medoff-Cooper, B., Carey, W. B., & McDevitt, S. C. (1993). The early infancy temperament questionnaire. *Journal of Developmental and Behavioral Pediatrics, 14,* 230–235.

Mehrabian, A. (1976). *Public places and private spaces*. New York: Basic Books.

Mehrabian, A. (1981). *Silent messages* (2nd ed.). Belmont, CA: Wadsworth.

Men often lie about sex lives, AIDS exposure, survey finds. (1988, August 14). *Milwaukee Journal*.

Meneese, W. B., Yutrzenka, B. A., & Vitale, P. (1992). An analysis of adolescent suicidal ideation. *Current Psychology: Research and Reviews, 11,* 51–58.

Menken, J., Trussell, J., & Larsen, U. (1986). Age and infertility. *Science, 233,* 1389–1394.

Merton, R. K. (1940). Discrimination and the American creed. In R. M. MacIver (Ed.), *Discrimination and national welfare*. New York: Harper.

Merton, R. K. (1968). *Social Theory and Social Structure*. New York: Free Press.

Mertz, G. J. (1992). Risk factors for the sexual transmission of genital herpes. *Annals of Internal Medicine, 116,* 197–202.

Meschke, L., Bartholomae, S., & Zentall, S. (2000). Adolescent sexuality and parent-adolescent processes: Promoting healthy teen choices. *Family Relations, 49,* 143–154.

Meyer, C. H. (1995). Assessment. In R. L. Edwards (Ed.), *Encyclopedia of social work* (19th ed., Vol. 1, pp. 260–270). Washington, DC: NASW Press.

Meyerowitz, B. E. (1980). Psychosocial correlates of breast cancer and its treatments. *Psychological Bulletin, 87,* 108–131.

Mickelson, J. S. (1995). Advocacy. In R. L. Edwards (Ed.), *Encyclopedia of social work* (19th ed., Vol. 1, pp. 95–100). Washington, DC: NASW Press.

Middlebrook, P. N. (1974). *Social psychology and modern life*. New York: Knopf.

Midgley, J. (1995). *Social development: The developmental perspective in social welfare*. Thousand Oaks, CA: Sage.

Midgley, J., & Livermore, M. (1997, Fall). The developmental perspective in social work: Educational implications for a new century. *Journal of Social Work Education, 33*(3), 573–585.

Mifflin, L. (1999a, May 9). Researchers see link between media, youth violence, but proving it is tough. *Milwaukee Journal Sentinel*, p. A3.

Mifflin, L. (1999b, August 4). TV poses risk to kids' health, doctors warn. *Milwaukee Journal Sentinel*, pp. A1, A8.

Miki, Y., et al. (1994). A strong candidate for the breast and ovarian cancer susceptibility gene BRCA1. *Science, 266,* 505–506.

Miley, K. (1992, April). Religion and spirituality as central social work concerns. Paper presented at Midwest Biennial Conference on Social Work Education, LaCrosse, WI.

Military uncooperative on gay rights. (1992, November 11). *Milwaukee Journal*.

Miller, J. G. (1991). A cultural perspective on the morality of beneficence and interpersonal responsibility. In S. Ting-Toomey & F. Korzenny (Eds.), *International and intercultural communication manual 15*. Newbury Park, CA: Sage.

Miller, W. B. (1958). Lower class culture as a generating milieu of gang delinquency. *Journal of Social Issues, 14*(3), 5–19.

Miller-Jones, D. (1989). Culture and testing. *American Psychologist, 44,* 360–366.

Miller-Perrin, C. L., & Perrin, R. D. (1999). *Child maltreatment: An introduction*. Thousand Oaks, CA: Sage.

Mills, C. W. (1956). *The power elite*. New York: Oxford University Press.

Mills, J., & Aronson, E. (1965). Opinion change as a function of the communicator's attractiveness and desire to influence. *Journal of Personality and Social Psychology, 1,* 73–77.

Mills, J. L., Holmes, L. B., Aarons, J. H., Simpson, J. L., Brown, Z. A., Jovanovic-Peterson, L. G., Conley, M. R., Graubard, B. I., Knopp, R. H., & Metzger, B. E. (1993). Moderate caffeine use and the risk of spontaneous abortion and intrauterine growth retardation. *Journal of the American Medical Association, 269,* 593–597.

Miltenberger, R. G. (2001). *Behavior modification: Principles and procedures* (2nd ed.). Belmont, CA: Wadsworth.

Mindell, C. L. (2001). Religious bigotry and religious minorities. In G. A. Appleby, E. Colon, & J. Hamilton (Eds.), *Diversity, oppression, and social functioning: Person-in-environment assessment and intervention* (pp. 195–216). Boston: Allyn & Bacon.

Mishell, D. R., Jr. (1982). Non-contraceptive health benefits of oral steroidal contraceptives. *American Journal of Obstetrics and Gynecology, 142,* 809–816.

Mizio, E. (1972, May). White worker—Minority client. *Social Work, 17,* 82–86.

Montague, A. (1964). *Man's most dangerous myth: The fallacy of race* (4th ed.). Cleveland: World.

Montague, A. (1971). *Touching: The human significance of the skin.* New York: Harper & Row.

Montague, A. (Ed.). (1975). *Race and IQ.* London: Oxford University Press.

Moody, R. A., Jr. (1975). *Life after life.* New York: Bantam Books.

Mooney, L. A., Knox, D., & Schacht, C. (2002). *Understanding social problems* (3rd ed.) Belmont, CA: Wadsworth.

Moore, C. W. (1986). *The mediation process.* San Francisco, CA: Jossey-Bass.

Morales, A. (1989). Urban gang violence. In A. Morales & B. W. Shea for, *Social work: A profession of many faces* (5th ed.). Boston: Allyn & Bacon.

Morales, A. T. (2001). Urban and Suburban gangs: The psychological crisis spreads. In A. T. Morales and B. W. Shea for (Eds.) *Social Work: A profession of many faces* (9th ed., pp. 397–431). Needham Heights, MA: Allyn & Bacon.

Morales, J. (1995). Gay men: Parenting. In R. L. Edwards (Ed.), *Encyclopedia of social work* (19th ed., Vol. 2, pp. 1085–1095). Washington, DC: NASW Press.

Morrow, G. (1987). *The compassionate school: A practical guide to education of abused and traumatized children.* Upper Saddle River, NJ: Prentice-Hall.

Mosak, H. H. (1995). Adlerian psychotherapy. In R. J. Corsini & D. Wedding, *Current psychotherapies* (5th ed.). Itasca, IL: Peacock.

Moscicki, E. G. (1999). Epidemiology of suicide. In D. G. Jacobs (Ed.), *Guide to suicide assessment and intervention* (40–51). San Francisco: Jossey-Bass.

Moses, A. E., & Hawkins, R. O. (1982). *Counseling lesbian women and gay men: A life-issues approach.* St. Louis: Mosby.

Moss, F. (1977, July 17). It's hell to be old in the U.S.A. *Parade Magazine,* p. 9.

Moss, G., & Moss, W. (1975). *Growing old.* New York: Pocket Books.

Mosteller, F. (1995). The Tennessee study of class size in the early school grades. *Future of Children, 5*(2), 113–127.

Mott, F. I., Fondell, M. M., Hu, P. N., Kowaleski-Jones, L., & Menaghan, E. G. (1996). The determinants of first sex by age 14 in a high-risk adolescent population. *Family Planning Perspectives, 28,* 13–18.

Moynihan, R., Christ, G., & Silver, L. G. (1988). AIDS and terminal illness. *Social Casework, 69*(6), 380–387.

Mundy, P., Thomas, B., & Taylor-Robinson, D. (1986). The Microtrak test for rapid detection of chlamydia in diagnosing and managing women with abdominal pain. *Genitourinary Medicine, 62,* 15–19.

Murphy, D. M. (1992). *On being L. D.: Perspectives and strategies of young adults.* New York: Teachers College Press.

Murry, V. (1996). An ecological analysis of coital timing among middle-class African-American adolescent females. *Journal of Adolescent Research, 11,* 261–279.

Myers, J. E. G. (1998). *Legal issues in child abuse and neglect practice* (2nd ed.). Thousand Oaks, CA: Sage.

Myrdal, G. (1944). *An American dilemma.* New York: Harper & Row.

Nadelson, C., et al. (1982). A follow-up study of rape victims. *American Journal of Psychiatry, 39,* 1266–1270.

Nass, G., Libby, R., & Fisher, M. (1984). *Sexual choices* (2nd ed.). Monterey, CA: Wadsworth.

Nass, J. M. (1991, August 19). All in the family: How does that gutsy South Dakota grandma feel about being pregnant with her daughter's twins. *Time,* p. 58.

National Abortion and Reproductive Rights Action League (NARAL). (2002, May). NARAL: Reproductive freedom & choice. Available at http://www.naral.org/mediasources/ publications/2002/ who_update.html (accessed on July 9, 2002).

National Academy of Sciences. (1982). *Marijuana and health.* Washington, DC: U.S. Government Printing Office.

National Advisory Council on Economic Opportunity. (1981). *The American promise: Equal justice and economic opportunity.* Final report. Washington, DC: U.S. Government Printing Office.

National Association of Social Workers (NASW). (1979). *NASW code of ethics.* Silver Spring, MD: NASW.

NASW. (1984). *Practice digest.* New York: NASW.

NASW. (1988). *Social work speaks: NASW policy statements.* Silver Spring, MD: NASW.

NASW. (1990). *Code of ethics of the National Association of Social Workers.* Silver Spring, MD: NASW.

NASW. (1994). *NASW code of ethics.* Washington, DC: NASW.

NASW. (1996). *NASW code of ethics.* Washington, DC: NASW.

NASW. (1997). *Social work speaks: NASW policy statements* (4th ed.). Washington, DC: NASW.

NASW. (2000). *Social work speaks: National Association of Social Workers policy statements 2000–2003* (5th ed.). Washington, DC: NASW.

NASW. (2001). *NASW standards for cultural competence in social work practice.* Washington, DC: NASW.

National Center for Health Statistics. (1991, April). Induced terminations of pregnancy: Reporting states, 1988. K. D. Kochanek (Ed.). *Monthly Vital Statistics Report, 39*(12).

National Center for Health Statistics. (1993). *Vital statistics of the United States, 1989:* Vol. 2. *Mortality* (Part A). Washington, DC: Public Health Service.

National Coalition of Advocates for Students. (1987). *Criteria for evaluating an AIDS curriculum.* Boston: NCAS.

National Institute of Justice, and Centers for Disease Control and Prevention. (1998). *Prevalence, incidence, and consequences of violence against women: Findings from the National Violence Against Women Survey.* Washington, DC: National Institute of Justice, and Centers for Disease Control and Prevention.

National Institute of Mental Health (NIMH). (1982). *Television and behavior: Ten years of scientific progress and implications for the eighties:* Vol. 1. *Summary report* (DHHS pub. no. ADM 82-1195). Washington, DC: Government Printing Office.

National Institute on Alcohol Abuse and Alcoholism (NIAAA). (1981). *Media alert; FAS awareness campaign: My baby . . . strong and healthy.* Rockville, MD: National Clearinghouse for Alcohol Information.

National Society for the Prevention of Cruelty to Children. (1976). *At risk.* Boston: Routledge and Kegan Paul.

National survey results of gay couples in long-lasting relationships. (1990, May/June). *Partners: Newsletter for gay and lesbian couples,* pp. 1–16.

National Television Violence Study. (1996). Studio City, CA: Mediascape.

National Victim Center. (1992). *Rape in America: A report to the nation. Report prepared by the Crime Victims Research and Treatment Center.* Charleston: Medical University of South Carolina.

Negy, C., & Webber, A. W. (1991). Knowledge and fear of AIDS: A comparison study between white, black, and Hispanic college students. *Journal of Sex Education and Therapy, 17*(1), 42–45.

Nehlig, A., & Debry, G. (1994). Consequences on the newborn of chronic maternal consumption of coffee during gestation and lactation: A review. *Journal of the American College of Nutrition, 13,* 6–21.

Neiger, B. L., & Hopkins, B. W. (1988). Adolescent suicide: Character traits of high-risk teenagers. *Adolescence, 23,* 468–475.

Neinstein, L., Goldering, J., & Carpenter, F. (1984). Nonsexual transmission of sexually transmitted diseases: An infrequent occurrence. *Pediatrics, 74,* 67–76.

Netting, F. E., Ketner, P. M., & McMurtry, S. L. (1993). *Social work macro practice.* New York: Longman.

Netting, F. E., Kettner, P. M., & McMurtry, S. L. (2001). Selecting appropriate tactics. In J. E. Tropman, J. L. Erlich, & J. Rothman (Eds.), *Tactics & techniques of community intervention* (4th ed., pp. 85–99). Itasca, IL: Peacock.

Neugarten, B., & Weinstein, K. (1964). The changing American grandparent. *Journal of Marriage and the Family, 26,* 199–205.

Newcomb, A. F., Bukowskik, W. M., & Pattee, L. Children's peer relations: A meta-analytic review of popular, rejected, neglected, controversial, and average sociometric status. *Psychological Bulletin, 113*(1), 99–128.

Newman, B. M., & Newman, P. R. (1984). *Development through life: A psychosocial approach.* Homewood, IL: Dorsey.

Newman, B. M., & Newman, P. R. (1995). *Development through life: A psychosocial approach.* (6th ed) Pacific Grove, CA: Brooks/Cole.

Newman, B. M., & Newman, P. R. (1999). *Development through life: A psychosocial approach* (7th ed.). Belmont, CA: Brook/Cole Wadsworth.

Newman, W., & Owens, C. (1984). Race-and-sex-based wage discrimination is illegal. In *Comparable worth: Issue for the 80's* (Vol. 1). Washington, DC: U.S. Commission on Civil Rights.

Nichols, W. R. (1999). *Random House Webster's college dictionary.* New York: Random House.

Nielsen, A. C. (1990). *Annual Nielsen report on television: 1990.* New York: Nielson Media Research.

Nimmagadda, J., & Balgopal, P. R. (2000). Social work practice with Asian immigrants. In P. R. Balgopal (Ed.), *Social work practice with immigrants and refugees* (pp. 30–64). New York: Columbia University Press.

Noah, T. (1997, June 30). A hit or miss for Mr. Butts? *U.S. News & World Report,* pp. 22–24.

Nock, S. L. (1998). The consequences of premarital fatherhood. *American Sociological Review, 63*(2), 150–163.

Norlin, J. M. & Chess, W.A. (1997). *Human behavior and the social environment. Social systems theory* (3rd ed.). Boston: Allyn & Bacon.

Norton, D. G. (1978). Incorporating content on minority groups into social work practice courses. In *The dual perspective.* New York: Council on Social Work Education.

Norton, D. G. (1983). Black family life patterns, the development of self and cognitive development of black children. In G. J. Powell (Ed.), *The Psychosocial development of minority group children.* New York: Brunner/Mazel.

Norton, D. G. (1993, January). Diversity, early socialization, and temporal development: The dual perspective revisited. *Social Work, 38*(1), 82–90.

Notelovitz, M., & Ware, M. (1983). *Stand tall: The informed woman's guide to preventing osteoporosis.* Gainesville, FL: Triad.

Oberklaid, F., Sanson, A., Pedlow, R., & Prior, M. (1993). Predicting preschool behavior problems from temperament and other variables in infancy. *Pediatrics, 91,* 113–120.

O'Brien, F., Azrin, N. H., & Bugle, C. (1974). Training profoundly retarded children to stop crawling. *Journal of Applied Behavior Analysis, 5,* 131–137.

Offer, D., & Sabshin, M. (1966). *Normality: Theoretical and clinical concepts in mental health.* New York: Basic Books.

O'Hagan, K. (1993). *Emotional and psychological abuse of children.* Toronto: University of Toronto Press.

O'Hare, W. P., Pollard, K. N., Mann, T. L., & Kent, M. M. (1991). African-Americans in the 1990s. *Population Bulletin, 46*(1), 2–39.

Okazawa-Rey, M. (1998). Empowering poor communities of color: A self-help model. In L. M. Gutierrez, R. J. Parsons, & E. O. Cox (Eds.), *Empowerment in social work practice: A sourcebook.* Pacific Grove, CA: Brooks/Cole.

Okun, B. F., & Rappaport, L. J. (1980). *Working with families: An introduction to family therapy.* North Scituate, MA: Duxbury.

O'Leary, K. D., & Wilson, G. T. (1987). *Behavior therapy: Application and outcome* (2nd ed.). Englewood Cliffs, NJ: Prentice-Hall.

Oliver, S. J., & Toner, B. B. (1990). The influence of gender role typing on expression of depressive symptoms. *Sex Roles, 22,* 775–790.

Olshansky, E. F. (1992). Redefining the concepts of success and failure in infertility treatment. *Clinical Issues in Perinatal and Women's Health Nursing, 3*(2), 343–346.

Olson, J. E., Frieze, I. H., & Detlefsen, E. G. (1990). Having it all? Combining work and family in a male and a female profession. *Sex Roles, 23,* 515–534.

Omachonu, V. K., & Ross, J. E. (1994). *Principles of total quality.* Delray Beach, FL: St. Lucie Press.

Orbach, S. (1978). *Fat is a feminist issue.* New York: Paddington Press.

Ortiz, E. T. (1989). *Your complete guide to sexual health.* Englewood Cliffs, NJ: Prentice-Hall.

Ossana, S. M. (2000). Relationship and couples counseling. In R. M. Perez, K. A. DeBord, & K. J. Bieschke (Eds.), *Handbook of counseling and psychotherapy with lesbian, gay, and bisexual clients* (pp. 275–302). Washington, DC: American Psychological Association.

Otten, A. S. (1984, July 30). Ever more Americans live into 80s and 90s, causing big problems. *Wall Street Journal,* pp. 1, 10.

Ou, Y., & McAdoo, H. P. (1993). Socialization of Chinese American children. In H. P. McAdoo (Ed.), *Family ethnicity: Strength in diversity.* Newbury Park, CA: Sage.

Ou, Y., &McAdoo, H. P. (1999). The ethnic socialization of Chinese American children. In H. P. McAdoo (Ed.), *Family ethnicity* (2nd ed., pp. 252–276). Thousand Oaks, CA: Sage.

Ouchi, W. (1981). *Theory Z: How American business can meet the Japanese challenge.* Reading, MA: Addison-Wesley.

Painton, P. (1993, April 26). The shrinking ten percent. *Time,* pp. 27–29.

Painton, P., Sachs, A., & Reid, J. L. (1991, October 21). Nation. *Time,* pp. 63–64.

Pang, V. O., Mizokawa, D. T., Morishima, J. K., & Olstad, R. G. (1985). Self-concepts of Japanese-American children. *Journal of Cross-Cultural Psychology, 16,* 99–109.

Paniagua, F. A. (1994). *Assessing and treating culturally diverse clients: A practical guide.* Thousand Oaks, CA: Sage.

Papalia, D. E., & Olds, S. W. (1981). *Human development* (2nd ed.) New York: McGraw-Hill.

Papalia, D. E., & Olds, S. W. (1989). *Human development* (4th ed.). New York: McGraw-Hill.

Papalia, D. E., & Olds, S. W. (1992). *Human development* (5th ed.). New York: McGraw-Hill.

Papalia, D. E., & Olds, S. W. (1995). *Human development* (6th ed.). New York: McGraw-Hill.

Papalia, D. E., Olds, S. W., & Feldman, R. D. (1998). *Human development* (7th ed.). New York: McGraw-Hill.

Papalia, D. E., Olds, S. W., & Feldman, R. D. (2001). *Human development* (8th ed.). Boston: McGraw-Hill.

Park, A. (2001, March 12). New technology: What digital can do. *Time*, p. 81.

Parnell, R. W. (1958). *Behavior and physique: An introduction to practical and applied somatometry*. London: Edward Arnold.

Parten, M. (1932). Social participation among preschool children. *Journal of Abnormal and Social Psychology, 27*, 243–269.

Patinkin, M. (1984, April 25). Grazing generation is changing the nation's tastes. *Providence Evening-Bulletin*, p. A-3.

Patinkin, M. (1987, May 20). Polls have the power to conjure surprising glimpses of ourselves. *Providence Journal-Bulletin*, p. C-1.

Patterson, G. R. (1975). *Families: applications of social learning to family life*. Champaign, IL: Research Press.

Patterson, G. R., DeBaryshe, B. D., & Ramsey, E. (1989). A developmental perspective on antisocial behavior. *American Psychologist, 44*, 329–335.

Patterson, W. M., Dohn, H. H., Bird, J., & Patterson, G. A. (1983). Evaluation of suicidal patients: The SAD PERSONS scale. *Psychosomatics, 24*(4), 343–349.

Patti, R. (1983). *Social welfare administration*. Englewood Cliffs, NJ: Prentice-Hall.

Paveza, G. J., Cohen, D., Eisdorfer, C., Freels, S., Selma, T., Ashford, J. W., Gorelick, P., Hirschman, R., Luchins, D., & Lewvy, P. (1992). Severe family violence and Alzheimer's disease: Prevalence and risk factors. *Gerontologist, 32*, 493–497.

Peck, R. C. (1968). Psychological development in the second half of life. In B. L. Neugarten (Ed.), *Middle age and aging*. Chicago: University of Chicago Press.

Pelletier, K. R. (1977). *Mind as healer, mind as slayer*. New York: Dell.

Peplau, L. S., Veniegas, R. C., & Campbell, S. N. (1996). Gay and lesbian relationships. In R. C. Savin-Williams & K. M. Cohen (Eds.), *The lives of lesbians, gays, and bisexuals: From children to adults* (pp. 250–273). Fort Worth: Harcourt Brace.

Perloff, J. D., & Jaffee, K. D. (1999, March). Late entry into prenatal care: The neighborhood context. *Social Work, 44*(2), 116–128.

Perls, T. T., Hutter-Silver, M., & Lauerman, J. F. (1999). *Living to 100: Lessons in living to your maximum potential at any age*. New York: Basic Books.

Peters, H. (1982). The legal rights of gays. In A. E. Moses & R. O. Hawkins (Eds.), *Counseling lesbian women and gay men: A life issues approach*. St. Louis: Mosby.

Peters, R. (1980). *Mammalian communication: A behavioral analysis of meaning*. Monterey, CA: Brooks/Cole.

Peterson, A. C. (1993). Creating adolescents: The role of context and process in developmental trajectories. *Journal of Research on Adolescence, 3*, 1–18.

Petretic-Jackson, P. A., & Jackson, T. (1996). Mental health interventions with battered women. In A. R. Roberts (Ed.), *Helping battered women: New perspectives and remedies*. New York: Oxford University Press.

Pfeffer, N. (1985). Not so new technologies. *Trouble and Strife, 5*, 46–50.

Pfeiffer, E. (1974). *Successful aging*. Durham, NC: Duke University Center for the Study of Aging and Human Development.

Phenice, L. A. (1999). Native Hawaiian families. In H. P. McAdoo (Ed.), *Family ethnicity* (2nd ed., pp. 107–118). Thousand Oaks, CA: Sage.

Phillips, W. (1996). Culturally competent practice understanding Asian family values. The *Roundtable: Journal of the National Resource Center for Special Needs Adoption, 10*(1), 1–3.

Phinney, J. (1989). Stages of ethnic identity development in minority group adolescents. *Journal of Early Adolescence, 9*, 34–49.

Phinney, J. (1990). Ethnic identity in adolescents and adults. *Psychological Bulletin, 108*, 499–514.

Phinney, J. S., & Alipura, L. L. (1992). Ethnic identity in college students from four ethnic groups. *Journal of Adolescence, 13*, 171–183.

Phinney, J. S., & Chavira, V. (1992). Ethnic identity and self-esteem: An exploratory longitudinal study. *Journal of Adolescence, 15*, 271–281.

Piaget, J. (1952). *The origins of intelligence in children*. New York: International Universities Press.

Pierce, P. (1976). Male change of life. *Ebony, 30*, 122–128.

Pilkington, L. R., While, J., & Matheny, K. B. (1997). Perceived coping resources and psychological birth order in school-aged children. *Individual Psychology: Journal of Adlerian Theory, Research and Practice, 53*, 42–57.

Pillemer, K., & Moore, D. W. (1989). Abuse of patients in nursing homes: Findings from a survey of staff. *Gerontologist, 29*, 314–320.

Pincus, A., & Minahan, A. (1973). *Social work practice: Model and method*. Itasca, IL: Peacock.

Pinderhughes, E. (1982). Afro-American families and the victim system. In M. McGoldrick, J. K. Pearce, & J. Giordana (Eds.), *Ethnicity and family therapy*. New York: Guilford.

Pines, A., & Aronson, E. (1981). *Burnout: From tedium to personal growth*. New York: Free Press.

Pinkney, A. (1972). *The American way of violence*. New York: Random House.

Pinyerd, B. J. (1994). Infant cries: Physiology and assessment. *Neonatal Network, 13*, 15–20.

Planned Parenthood Association of Wisconsin. Facts about oral contraception. Undated handout.

Platt, R., Rice, P. A., & McCormack, W. M. (1983). Risk of acquiring gonorrhea and prevalence of abnormal adnexal findings among women recently exposed to gonorrhea. *Journal of the American Medical Association, 250*, 3205–3209.

Polansky, N. F., Chalmers, M. A., Buttenwieser, E., & Williams, D. P. (1991). *Damaged parents: An anatomy of child neglect*. Chicago: University of Chicago Press.

Polansky, N. F., Holly, C., & Polansky, N. A. (1975). *Profile of neglect: A survey of the state of knowledge of child neglect*. Washington, DC: Department of Health, Education, and Welfare.

Pool, R. (1993). Evidence for homosexuality gene. *Science, 261*, 291–292.

Poppen, P. (1994). Adolescent contraceptive use and communication: Changes over a decade. *Adolescence, 29*, 503–514.

Powdermaker, H. (1933). *Life in Lesu*. New York: Norton.

Powell, G. J. (Ed.). (1983). *The psychosocial development of minority group children*. New York: Brunner/Mazel.

Powell, T. J. (1987). *Self-help organizations and professional practice*. Silver Spring, MD: NASW.

Prather, H. (1970). *Notes to myself*. Moab, UT: Real People Press.

Premack, D. (1965). Reinforcement theory. In D. Levine (Ed.), *Nebraska symposium on motivation*. Lincoln: University of Nebraska Press.

Price, J. H., Desmond, D., & Kukulka, G. (1985). High school students' perceptions and misperceptions of AIDS. *Journal of School Health, 55,* 107–109.

Pritchard, K. (1997). Breast cancer: The real challenge. *The Lancet, 349,* 124–125.

Prochaska, J. O. (1979). *Systems of psychotherapy*. Homewood, IL: Dorsey.

Proctor, E. K., Davis, L. E., & Vosler, N. R. (1995). Families: Direct practice. In R. L. Edwards (Ed.), *Encyclopedia of social work* (19th ed., Vol. 2, pp. 941–950). Washington, DC: NASW Press.

Puka, B. (1991). Toward the redevelopment of Kohlberg's theory: Preserving essential structure, removing controversial content. In W. M. Kurtines & J. Gewirtz (Eds.), *Moral behavior and development: Advances in theory, research, and application*. Hillsdale, NJ: Erlbaum.

Rabushk, A., & Jacobs, B. (1980, February 15). Are old folks really poor? Herewith a look at some common views. *New York Times,* p. A29.

Radin, N. (1981). The role of the father in cognitive, academic, and intellectual development. In M. E. Lamb (Ed.), *The role of the father in child development*. New York: Wiley.

Ragghianti, M. (1992, January 19). I wanted to be treated like a human being. *Parade Magazine,* pp. 8–9.

Ramirez, O. (1998). Mexican American children and adolescents. In J. T. Gibbs, L. N. Huang (Eds.), *Children of color: Psychological interventions with culturally diverse youth,* pp. 215–239. San Francisco: Jossey-Bass.

Randall, T. (1990). Domestic violence intervention calls for more than treating injuries. *Journal of the American Medical Association, 264,* 939–940.

Rank, M. R., & Hischl, T. A. (1999, May). The likelihood of poverty across the American adult life span. *Social Work, 44*(3), 201–216.

Raskin, N. J., & Rogers, C.R. (1995). Person-centered therapy. In R. J. Corsini & D. Wedding (Eds.), *Current psychotherapies* (5th ed.). Itasca, IL: Peacock.

Rathus, S. A., Nevid, J. S., & Fichner-Rathus, L. (2000). *Human sexuality in a world of diversity* (4th ed.). Boston: Allyn & Bacon.

Rathus, S. A., Nevid, J. S., & Fichner-Rathus, L. (2002). *Human sexuality in a world of diversity* (5th ed.). Boston: Allyn & Bacon.

Reamer, F. G. (1995). Ethics and values. In R. L. Edwards (Ed.), *Encyclopedia of social work* (19th ed., Vol. 1, pp. 893–902). Washington, DC: NASW Press.

Recer, P. (1988, March 27). One year later: AZT prolongs life—and hope—for AIDS patients. *Milwaukee Journal,* p. 46.

Rees, S. (1998). Empowerment of youth. In L. M., Gutierrez, R. J. Parsons, & E. O. Cox (Eds.). *Empowerment in social work practice: A sourcebook*. Pacific Grove, CA: Brooks/Cole.

Register, E. (1993). Feminism and recovering from battering: working with the individual woman. In M. Hansen & M. Harway (Eds.), *Battering and family therapy: A feminist perspective* (pp. 93–104). Newbury Park, CA: Sage.

Regulus, T. A. (1995). Gang violence. In *Encyclopedia of social work* (19th ed., pp. 1045–1054). Washington, DC: NASW Press.

Reibstein, L., Miller, M., Foote, D., & Namuth, T. (1995, February 13). A sister's sad revenge. *Newsweek,* p. 33.

Reibstein, L., Miller, M., & King, P. (1995, January 23) And now: The trial. *Newsweek,* p. 50.

Reiff, H. B., & Gerber, P. J. (1992). Adults with learning disabilities. In N. Singh & D. L. Beale (Eds.), *Current perspectives in learning disabilities: Nature, theory, and treatment*. New York: Springer-Verlag.

Reiff, H. B., Gerber, P. J., & Ginsberg, R. (1997). *Exceeding expectations: Successful adults with learning disabilities*. Austin, TX: Pro-Ed.

Reilly, M. E., Lott, B., & Gallogly, S. M. (1986). Sexual harassment of university students. *Sex Roles, 15,* 333–358.

Reitz, R. (1977). *Menopause: A positive approach*. Radnor, PA: Chitton.

Renzetti, C. M., & Curran, D. J. (1992). *Women, men, and society*. Needham Heights, MA: Allyn & Bacon.

Renzetti, C. M., & Curran, D. J. (1995). *Women, men, and society* (3rd ed.). Boston: Allyn & Bacon.

Renzulli, J. S., & Reis, S. M. (1991). The schoolwide enrichment model: A comprehensive plan for the development of creative productivity. In N. Colangelo & G. A. Davis (Eds.), *Handbook of gifted education* (pp. 111–141). Boston: Allyn & Bacon.

Reposa, R., & Zuelzer, M. B. (1983, Summer). Family therapy with incest. *International Journal of Family Therapy, 5*(2), 111–125.

Reskin, B. A., & Hartman, H. I., (Eds.) (1986). *Women's work, men's work: Sex segregation on the job*. Washington, DC: National Academy Press.

Rhodes, M. L. (1985). Gilligan's theory of moral development as applied to social work practice. *Social Work, 30,* 101–105.

Rice, M. L., Huston, A. C., Truglio, R., & Wright, J. C. (1990). Words from Sesame Street: Learning vocabulary while viewing. *Developmental Psychology, 26,* 421–428.

Rich, C. L., Young, D., & Fowler, R. C. (1986). San Diego suicide study. *Archives of General Psychiatry, 43,* 577–582.

Richmond, M. (1917). *Social diagnosis*. New York: Free Press.

Riegel, K. F. (1973). Language and cognition: Some life-span developmental issues. *Gerontologist, 13,* 478–482.

Riegel, K. F., & Riegel, R. M. (1972). Development, drop, and death. *Developmental Psychology, 6*(2), 306–319.

Rierdan, J., Koff, E., & Flaherty, J. (1986). Conceptions and misconceptions of menstruation. *Women and Health, 10*(4), 33–45.

Rierdan, J., Koff, E., & Stubbs, M. L. (1988). Gender, depression, and body image in early adolescents. *Journal of Early Adolescence, 8*(2), 109–117.

Rierdan, J., Koff, E., & Stubbs, M. L. (1989). A longitudinal analysis of body image as a predictor of the onset and persistence of adolescent girls' depression. *Journal of Early Adolescence, 9*(4), 454–466.

Riessman, F. (1965). The "helper therapy" principle. *Journal of Social Work, 10*(2), 27–34.

Rind, B., & Tromovitch, P. (1997). A meta-analytic review of findings from national samples on psychological correlates of child sexual abuse. *Journal of Sex Research, 34,* 337–355.

Rind, B., Tromovitch, P., & Bauserman, R. (1998). A meta-analytic examination of assumed properties of child sexual abuse using college samples. *Psychological Bulletin, 124,* 22–53.

Ritter, M. (2000, December 21). Vaccine shows promise for Alzheimer's patients. *Wisconsin State Journal,* p. 5A.

Roberts, A. R. (Ed.). (1996a). *Helping battered women*. New York: Oxford University Press.

Roberts, A. R. (1996b). Introduction: Myths and realities regarding battered women. In A. R. Roberts (Ed.), *Helping battered women: New perspectives and remedies*. New York: Oxford University Press.

Roberts, A. R. (1996c). Police responses to battered women: Past, present, and future. In A. R. Roberts (Ed.), *Helping battered women: New perspectives and remedies* (pp. 85–95). New York: Oxford University Press.

Roberts, A. R. (1999). An overview of crisis theory and crisis intervention. In A. R. Roberts (Ed.), *Crisis intervention handbook: Assessment, treatment, and research* (pp. 3–30). New York: Oxford University Press.

Roberts, S. V. (1995, February 13). Affirmative action on the edge. *U.S. News & World Report*, pp. 32–39.

Robertson, I. (1980). *Social problems* (2nd ed.). New York: Random House.

Robinson, D. (1988, August 16). The crisis in our nursing homes. *Parade Magazine*, pp. 13–14.

Robinson, N. M., Abbott, R. D., Berninger, V. W., & Busse, J. (1996). Structure of abilities in math-precocious young children: Gender similarities and differences. *Journal of Educational Psychology, 88,* 341–352.

Rockstein, M. (1975). The biology of aging in humans: An overview. In R. Goldman & M. Rockstein (Eds.), *The physiology and pathology of human aging.* New York: Academic Press.

Rodgers, J. L. (2000). Birth order. In A. Kazdin (Ed.), *Encyclopedia of psychology.* Washington, DC, and New York: American Psychological Association and Oxford University Press.

Roethlisberger, F. J., & Dickson, W. J. (1939). *Management and the worker.* Cambridge, MA: Harvard University Press.

Rogers, C. R. (1959). A theory of therapy, personality and interpersonal relationships, as developed in the client-centered framework. In S. Koch (Ed.), *Psychology: A study of a science* (Vol. 3). New York: McGraw-Hill.

Rogers, P. (1993, February 15). How many gays are there? *Newsweek,* p. 46.

Rogers, P., & Reiss, S. (1994, August 8). Is murder "justifiable homicide"? *Newsweek,* p. 22.

Romas, J. A., & Sharma, M. (1995). *Practical stress management.* Boston: Allyn & Bacon.

Roosevelt, F. D. (1937, January 20). Second Inaugural Address.

Rose, A. (1964). *The Negro in America.* New York: Harper & Row.

Rosellini, L. (1988, May 30). Rebel with a Cause: Koop. *U.S. News & World Report*, pp. 55–63.

Rosen, H. (1981). How workers use cues to determine child abuse. *Social Work Research and Abstracts, 17,* 27–33.

Rosen, M. (1995). Gender differences in structure, means and variances of hierarchically ordered ability dimensions. *Learning and Instruction, 5,* 37–62.

Rosenblith, J. F. (1992). *In the beginning* (2nd ed.). Newbury Park, CA: Sage.

Rosenfeld, I. (2000, May 14). Trying to have a baby? *Milwaukee Journal Sentinal, Parade Magazine*, pp. 12–13.

Rosenfield, P., Lambert, N. M., & Black, A. (1985). Desk arrangement effects on pupil classroom behavior. *Journal of Educational Psychology, 77,* 213–217.

Rosenhan, D. L. (1973). On being sane in insane places. *Science, 179,* 250–257.

Rosenhan, D. L., & Seligman, M. E. (1995). *Abnormal Psychology* (3rd ed.). New York: Norton.

Rosenmayr, L. (1980). Achievements, doubts and prospects of the sociology of aging. *Human Development, 23,* 46–62.

Rosenthal, E. (1990, February 4). When a pregnant woman drinks. *New York Times Magazine,* p. 30.

Rosenthal, R., & Jacobson, L. (1968a). *Pygmalion in the classroom.* New York: Holt, Rinehart and Winston.

Rosenthal, R., & Jacobson, L. (1968b). Teacher expectations for the disadvantaged. *Scientific American, 218,* 19–23.

Rossman, J. (1977). Anatomic and body composition changes with aging. In C. E. Finch & L. Hayflicks (Eds.), *Handbook of the biology of aging.* New York: Van Nostrand Reinhold.

Rotella, E. J. (1995). Women and the American economy. In S. Ruth (Ed.). *Issues in feminism* (pp. 320–333). Mountain View, CA: Mayfield.

Rotheram-Borus, M. J., Hunter, J. & Rosario, M. (1994). Suicidal behavior and gay-related stress among gay and bisexual male adolescents. *Journal of Adolescent Research, 9,* 498–508.

Rotheram-Borus, M. J., & Phinney, J. S. (1990). Patterns of social expectations among black and Mexican American children. *Child Development, 61,* 542–556.

Rothman, J. (1987). Community theory and research. In *Encyclopedia of social work* (Vol. 1). Silver Spring, MD: NASW.

Rothman, J. (1995). Approaches to community intervention. In J. Rothman, J. L. Erlich, & J. E. Tropman (Eds.), *Strategies of community intervention* (5th ed.). Itasca, IL: Peacock.

Rothman, J. (2001). Approaches to community intervention. In J. Rothman, J. L. Erlich, & J. E. Tropman (Eds.), *Strategies of community intervention* (6th ed., pp. 27–64). Itasca, IL: Peacock.

Rothman, J., Erlich, J. L., & Tropman, J. E. (Eds.). (1995). *Strategies of community intervention* (5th ed.). Itasca, IL: Peacock.

Rothman, S. M. (1978). *Woman's proper place.* New York: Basic Books.

Rourke, B. P. & Del Dotto, J. E. (1994). *Learning disabilities: A neuropsychological perspective.* Thousand Oaks: Sage.

Rovee, C. K., Cohen, R. Y., & Shlapack, W. (1975). Life span stability in olfactory sensitivity. *Developmental Psychology, 11,* 311–318.

Rowland, K. (1977). Environmental events predicting death for the elderly. *Psychological Bulletin, 84,* 349–372.

Roye, C., & Balk, S. (1997). Evaluation of an intergenerational program for pregnant and parenting adolescents. *Maternal-Child Nursing Journal, 24,* 32–36.

Rubenstein, C. (1990, October). A brave new world. *New Woman,* pp. 158–164.

Rubin, L. J., & Borgers, S. B. (1990). Sexual harassment in universities during the 1980s. *Sex Roles, 23,* 397–411.

Rubin, Z.(1973). *Liking and loving.* New York: Holt, Rinehart and Winston.

Ruble, D. N., & Brooks-Gunn, J. (1982). The experience of menarche. *Child Development, 53,* 1557–1566.

Russell, A. B., & Trainor, C. M. (1984). *Trends in child abuse and neglect: A national perspective.* Denver, CO: American Humane Association, Children's Division.

Russo, N. G., & Dabul, A. J. (1997). The relationship of abortion to well-being: Do race and religion make a difference? *Professional Psychology: Research and Practice, 28,* 23–31.

Ruth, S. (1990). *Issues in feminism.* Mountain View, CA: Mayfield.

Ruth, S. (1995). *Issues in feminism* (3rd ed.) Mountain View, CA: Mayfield.

Ruth, S. (1998). *Issues in feminism* (4th ed.) Mountain View, CA: Mayfield.

Rutter, M. (1983). Stress, coping, and development: Some issues and some questions. In N. Garmezy & M. Rutter (Eds.), *Stress, coping, and development in children.* New York: McGraw-Hill.

Ryan, C. C., & Rowe, M. J. (1988). AIDS: Legal and ethical issues. *Social Casework, 39*(6), 324–333.

Ryan, W. (1976). *Blaming the victim* (Rev. ed.). New York: Vintage.

Rycus, J. S., Hughes, R. C., & Garrison, J. W. (1989). *Child protective services: A training curriculum.* Columbus, OH: Institute for Human Services.

Sachs, A.(1993, November 22). 9-zip! I love it! *Time,* pp. 44–45.

Sachs, A. (1994, December 5). Abortion pills on trial. *Time,* pp. 45–46.

Sager, C. J., Brayboy, T. L., & Waxenberg, B. R. (1970). *Black ghetto family in therapy: A laboratory experience.* New York: Grove Press.

Saleeby, D. (1992). *The strengths perspective in social work practice.* New York: Longman.

Saleeby, D. (1997). Introduction: Power in the people. In D. Saleeby (Ed.), *The strengths perspective in social work practice* (2nd ed., pp. 3–19). New York: Longman.

Saleeby, D. (2002). *The strengths perspective in social work practice* (3rd ed.). Boston: Allyn & Bacon.

Saltzman, A. (1994, November 7). Schooled in failure? Fact or myth—Teachers favor boys; girls respond by withdrawing. *U.S. News & World Report*, pp. 88–93.

Samuelson, P. (1980). Quoted in P. Blumberg, *Inequality in an age of decline.* New York: Oxford University Press.

Sandler, B. R., & Hall, R. M. (1986). *The campus climate revisited: Chilly for women faculty, administrators, and graduate students.* Washington, DC: Project on the Status and Education of Women.

San Francisco AIDS Foundation. (1987). *Women and AIDS* (3rd ed.). San Francisco, CA: AIDS Foundation.

Santrock, J. W. (1995). *Life-span development.* Madison, WI: Brown and Benchmark.

Santrock, J. W. (1999). *Life-span development* (7th ed.). Boston: McGraw-Hill.

Santrock, J. W. (2002a). *Life-span development* (8th ed.). Boston: McGraw-Hill.

Santrock, J. W. (2002b). *A topical approach to life-span development.* Boston: McGraw-Hill.

Sapiro, V. (1990). *Women in American society* (2nd ed.). Mountain View, CA: Mayfield.

Sapiro, V. (1999). *Women in American society* (4th ed.). Mountain View, CA: Mayfield.

Sarri, R. C. (1987). Administration in social welfare. In *Encyclopedia of social work* (Vol. 1). Silver Spring, MD: NASW.

Satir, V. (1967). *Conjoint family therapy.* Palo Alto, CA: Science and Behavior Books.

Saunders, D. G. (1995). Domestic violence: Legal issues. In R. L. Edwards (Ed.), *Encyclopedia of social work* (19th ed., Vol. 1, pp. 789–795). Washington, DC: NASW Press.

Scanlan, C. (1991, October 10). New AIDS drug wins OK by FDA. *Wisconsin State Journal*, p. 3A.

Schaefer, R. T. (1993). *Racial and ethnic groups* (5th ed.). New York: HarperCollins.

Schaefer, R. T. (1996). *Racial and ethnic groups* (6th ed.). New York: HarperCollins.

Schaefer, R. T. (2002). Racial and Ethnic Groups (8th ed.). Upper Saddle River, NJ: Prentice-Hall.

Schafer, W. (1978). *Stress, distress and growth.* Davis, CA: International Dialogue Press.

Schanche, D. (1973, March). What really happens emotionally and physically when a man reaches 40? *Today's Health*, pp. 40–43, 60.

Scheff, T. (1966). *Being mentally ill.* Hawthorne, NY: Aldine.

Scheflen, A. (1974). *How behavior means.* Garden City, NY: Anchor.

Schick, F. L. (Ed.). (1986). *Statistical handbook on aging Americans.* Phoenix: Oryz.

Schiele, J. H. (1996, May). Afrocentricity: An emerging paradigm in social work practice. *Social Work, 41*, 284–294.

Schmitt, B. (1980). The child with non-accidental trauma. In C. H. Kempe (Ed.), *The battered child.* Chicago: University of Chicago Press.

Schoof, R. (1999, April 25). Abandoned baby girls taxing China's orphanages. *Milwaukee Journal Sentinel*, p. 7A.

Schoor, A. L. (2001). *Welfare reform: Failure and remedies.* Westport, CT: Praeger.

Schreiner, T. (1984, May 29). A revolution that has just begun. *USA Today*, p. 40.

Schrof, J. (1992, June 1). Pumped up. *U.S. News & World Report*, pp. 55–63.

Schrof, J. (1994, October 17). Sex in America. *U.S. News & World Report*, pp. 74–78.

Schrof, J. (1998, September 21). No more slam-o-gram: New breast cancer tests put an end to the painful mammogram. *U.S. News & World Report*, p. 67.

Schultz, R. (1978). *The psychology of death, dying and bereavement.* New York: McGraw-Hill.

Schwab, D. P. (1984). Using job evaluation to obtain pay equity. In *Comparable worth: Issue for the 80's* (Vol. 1). Washington, DC: U.S. Commission on Civil Rights.

Schwaber, F. H. (1985). Some legal issues related to outside institutions. In H. Hidalgo, T. Peterson, & N. J. Woodman (Eds.), *Lesbian and gay issues: A resource manual for social workers.* Silver Spring, MD: NASW.

Scott, J., & Schwalm, L. (1988). Rape rates and the circulation of adult magazines. *Journal of Sex Research, 24*, 241–250.

Scully, R., Ganesan, S., Brown, M., DeCaprio, J. A., Cannistra, S. A, Feunteun, J., Schnitt, S., & Livington, D. M. (1996). Location of BRCA1 in human breast and ovarian cancer cells. *Science, 272*, 123–125.

Seaward, B. L. (1994). *Managing stress.* Boston: Jones and Bartlett.

Seelbach, W. C., & Hansen, C. J. (1980). Satisfaction with family relationships among the elderly. *Family Relations, 29*(1), 91–96.

Segal, S. P. (1987). Deinstitutionalization. In A. Minahan (Ed.), *Encyclopedia of social work* (Vol. 1). Silver Spring, MD: NASW.

Segal, U. (1997). Asians Indians. In C. H. Mindel, R. Habenstein, & R. Wright (Eds.), *Ethnic families in America* (4th ed.). New York: Prentice-Hall.

Selye, H. (1956). *The stress of life.* New York: McGraw-Hill.

Selye, H. (1974). *Stress without distress.* New York: Signet.

Sermabeikian, P. (1994, March). Our clients, ourselves: The spiritual perspective and social work practice. *Social Work, 39*(2), 178–190.

Shapiro, J. P. (2000, November 6). The overlooked labor force. *U.S. News & World Report*, pp. 68–72.

Shaw, G. M., Schaffer, D., Velie, E. M., Morland, K., & Harris, J. A. (1995). Periconceptional vitamin use, dietary folate, and the occurrence of neural tube defects. *Epidemiology, 6*, 219–226.

Shaw, S. M., & Lee, J. (2001). *Women's voices, feminist visions: Classic and contemporary readings.* Mountain View, CA: Mayfield.

Sheafor, B. W., Horejsi, C. R., & Horejsi, G. A. (1991). *Techniques and guidelines for social work practice* (2nd ed.). Boston: Allyn & Bacon.

Sheafor, B. W., Horejsi, C. R., & Horejsi, G. A. (1997). *Techniques and guidelines for social work practice* (4th ed.). Boston: Allyn & Bacon.

Sheafor, B. W., Horejsi, C. R., & Horejsi, G. A. (2000). *Techniques and guidelines for social work practice* (5th ed.). Boston: Allyn & Bacon.

Sheler, J. L. (1999, July 19). An American reformation: Mainline Protestant churches are deeply divided over sexuality. *U. S. News & World Report*, pp. 46–47.

Sherman, J. A. (1982). Girls talk about mathematics and their future: A partial replication. *Psychology of Women Quarterly, 7*, 338–342.

Shernoff, M. (1995). Gay men: Direct practice. In R. L. Edwards (Ed.), *Encyclopedia of social work* (19th ed., Vol. 2, pp. 1075–1085). Washington, DC: NASW Press.

Shilts, R. (1987, November 8). The eight-year odyssey of AIDS: Book traces initial cases to patient zero, a Canadian airline steward with many lovers. *Milwaukee Journal*, pp. 1–2, 6–7.

Shinn, M. (1978). Father absence and children's cognitive development. *Psychological Bulletin, 85*, 295–324.

Shock, N. W. (1977). Biological theories of aging. In J. E. Birren & K. W. Schaie (Eds.), *Handbook of the psychology of aging.* New York: Van Nostrand Reinhold.

Shoupe, D. (1991). Effect of body weight on reproductive function. In D. R. Mishell, V. Davajan, & R. A. Lobo (Eds.), *Infertility, contraception and reproductive endocrinology* (3rd ed.). Cambridge: Blackwell Scientific Publications.

Siegel, O. (1982). Personality development in adolescence. In B. B. Wolman, et al. (Eds.), *Handbook of developmental psychology.* Englewood Cliffs, NJ: Prentice-Hall.

Siegel, R. K. (1981, January). Accounting for "afterlife" experiences. *Psychology Today,* pp. 66–69.

Silicone breast makers given ultimatum. (1991, April 11). *Milwaukee Journal.*

Silver, L. B. (1992). *The misunderstood child: A guide for parents of children with learning disabilities* (2nd ed.). New York: TAB Books.

Silver, M. (1995, September 11). Sex and violence on TV. *U.S. News & World Report,* pp. 62–69.

Silverberg, E. (1981). Cancer statistics, 1981. *Ca—A Cancer Journal for Clinicians, 31*(1), 13–28.

Silverman, D. (1976–77, Winter). Sexual harassment: Working women's dilemma. *Quest: A Feminist Quarterly,* p. 3.

Silvestre, L., Dubois, C., Renault, M., et al. (1990). Voluntary interruption of pregnancy with mifepristone (RU 486) and a prostaglandin analogue: A large-scale French experience. *New England Journal of Medicine, 322,* 645–648.

Silvestri, L., Dantonio, M., & Eason, S. (1994). Enhancement of self-esteem in at-risk elementary students. *Journal of Health Education, 25,* 30–36.

Simkins, L., & Kushner, A. (1986). Attitudes toward AIDS, herpes II, and toxic shock syndrome: Two years later. *Psychological Reports, 59,* 883–891.

Simmons, R. G., & Blyth, D. (1987). *Moving into adolescence: The impact of pubertal change and school context.* New York: Aldine and Gruyter.

Simon, J. P. (1996). Lebanese families. In M. McGoldrick, J. Giordano, & J. K. Pearce (Eds.), *Ethnicity & family therapy* (2nd ed., pp. 364–375). New York: Guilford.

Simonton, O. C., & Matthews-Simonton, S. (1978). *Getting well again.* Los Angeles: J. P. Tarcher.

Simpson, G. E., & Yinger, Y. M. (1965). *Racial and cultural minorities* (3rd ed.). New York: Harper & Row.

Sindler, A. P. (1978). *Bakke, DeFunis, and minority admissions: The quest for equal opportunity.* New York: Longmans, Green.

Singer, J. E. (1964). The use of manipulative strategies: Machiavellianism and attractiveness. *Sociometry, 27,* 128–151.

Singh, S. (1986). Adolescent pregnancy in the United States: An interstate analysis. *Family Planning Perspectives, 18*(5), 210–220.

Singh, S., & Darroch, J. (2000). Adolescent pregnancy and childbearing levels and trends in developed countries. *Family Planning Perspectives, 32,* 14–23.

Siporin, M. (1975). *Introduction to social work practice.* New York: Macmillan.

Sisodia, S. S., Koo, E. H., Beyreuther, K., Unterbeck, A., & Price, D. L. (1990, April 27). Evidence that B-amyloid protein in Alzheimer's disease is not derived by normal processing. *Science, 248,* 492–495.

Siven, I. (1989). IUDs are contraceptives, not abortifacients: A comment on research and belief. *Studies in Family Planning, 20,* 355–359.

Siven, I., Stern, J., & International Committee for Contraceptive Search. (1994). Health during prolonged use of Levonorgestrel 20 and the copper Tcu 380A IUDs: A multicenter study. *Fertility and Sterility, 61,* 70–77.

Skidmore, R. A., & Thackeray, M. (1976). *Introduction to social work* (2nd ed.). Englewood Cliffs, NJ: Prentice-Hall.

Skinner, B. F. (1953). *Science and human behavior.* New York: Free Press.

Skoe, E. E., & Gooden, A. (1993). Ethics of care and real-life moral dilemma content in male and female early adolescents. *Journal of Early Adolescence, 13*(2), 154–167.

Slap, G. B., Vorters, D. F., Chaudhuri, S., & Centor, R. M. (1989). Risk factors for attempted suicide during adolescence. *Pediatrics, 84,* 762–772.

Slater, R. B. (1995, December). The gender pay gap: Where women academics come up short on payday. *The Monthly Forum on Women in Higher Education, 1*(3), 23–27.

Smith, B. (1995). Myths to divert black women from freedom. In S. Ruth (Ed.), *Issues in feminism* (3rd ed.). Mountain View, CA: Mayfield.

Smith, L., Ulvund, S. E., & Lindemann, R. (1994). Very low birth weight infants at double risk. *Journal of Developmental and Behavioral Pediatrics, 15,* 7–13.

Smolowe, J. (1991, October 21). He said, she said. *Time,* pp. 36–40.

Smolowe, J. (1992, October 19). Anita Hill's legacy. *Time,* pp. 56–57.

Smolowe, J. (1993, February 8). Sex, lies, and the military. *Time,* pp. 29–30.

Smolowe, J. (1995a, July 31). Noble aims, mixed results. *Time,* pp. 54–55.

Smolowe, J. (1995b, September 18). Betrayed by his kisses. *Time,* pp. 42–46.

Snarey, J. (1987, June). A question of morality. *Psychology Today,* pp. 6–8.

Solender, E. K., & Solender, E. (1976). Minimizing the effect of the unattractive client on the jury: A study of the interaction of physical appearance with assertions and self-experience references. *Human Rights, 5,* 201–214.

Sollie, D. L., & Fischer, J. L. (1985). Sex-role orientation, intimacy of topic, and target person differences in self-disclosure among women. *Sex Roles, 12,* 917–929.

Solomon, A. (1988). Integrating infertility crisis counseling into feminist practice. *Reproductive and Genetic Engineering, 1,* 41–49.

Solomon, B. B. (1983). Social sork with Afro-Americans. In A. Morales & B. W. Sheafor (Eds.), *Social work: A profession of many faces* (3rd ed.). Boston: Allyn & Bacon.

Some golden years. (2001). *U.S. News & World Report,* p. 8.

Sommer, R. (1969). *Personal space: The behavioral basis of design.* Englewood Cliffs, NJ: Prentice-Hall.

Sonenstein, F. L. (1986). Rising paternity: Sex and contraception among adolescent males. In A. B. Elster & M. E. Lamb (Eds.), *Adolescent fatherhood.* Hillsdale, NJ: Erlbaum.

Sonnert, F., & Holton, G. (1996). Career patterns of women and men in the sciences. *American Scientist, 84,* 63–71.

Sorenson, R. C.(1973). *Adolescent sexuality in contemporary America.* New York: World.

Spake, A. (2002, July 22). The hormone conundrum. U.S. News & World Report, pp. 36–37.

Spakes, P. (1992). National family policy: Sweden versus the United States. *Affilia: Journal of Women and Social Work, 7*(2), 44–60.

Spekman, N. J., Goldberg, R. J., & Herman, K. L. (1992). Learning-disabled children grow up: A search for factors related to success in the young adult years. *Learning Disabilities Research and Practice, 7,* 161–170.

Spellacy, W. N., Miller, S. J., & Winegar, A. (1986). Pregnancy after 40 years of age. *Obstetrics and Gynecology, 68,* 452–454.

Spencer, M. B., & Markstrom-Adams, C. (1990). Identity processes among racial and ethnic minority children. *Child Development, 61,* 290–310.

Spencer, M. B., & Dornbusch, S. M. (1990). Challenges in studying minority youth. In S. S. Feldman & G. R. Elliott (Eds.), *At the threshold: The developing adolescent.* Cambridge, MA: Harvard University Press.

Spergel, I. A. (1995). *The youth gang problem: A community approach.* New York: Oxford University Press.

Spitz, R. (1945). Hospitalization: Genesis of psychiatric conditions in early childhood. *Psychoanalytic Study of the Child, 1,* 53.

Spock, B. (1976). *Baby and child care.* New York: Pocket Books.

Spock, B., & Rothenberg, M. B. (1985). *Baby and child care.* New York: Pocket Books.

Spranger, E. (1928). *Types of men.* New York: Hafner.

Sreenivasah, J. (1999). *Feminist Majority Newsletter.* Available at http://www.feminist.org/research/report/93-toc.html (last accessed 8/30/99).

Stanberry, L. (2000). Asymptomatic herpes simplex virus shedding and Russian roulette. *Clinical Infectious Diseases, 30,* 268–269.

Stattin, H., & Magnusson, D. (1990). Pubertal maturation in female development. In *Paths through life* (Vol. 2). Hillsdale, NJ: Erlbaum.

Steiger, T. L., & Wardell, M. (1995). Gender and employment in the service sector. *Social Problems, 42,* 1, 91–123.

Sternberg, R. J. (1984). A contextualist view of the nature of intelligence. *International Journal of Psychology, 19,* 307–334.

Sternberg, R. J. (1985). *Beyond IQ: A triarchic theory of human intelligence.* New York: Cambridge University Press.

Sternberg, R. J. (1986). *Intelligence applied: Understanding and increasing your intellectual skills.* New York: Harcourt Brace Jovanovich.

Sternberg, R. J. (1987, September 23). The uses and misuses of intelligence testing: Misunderstanding meaning, users over-rely on scores. *Educational Week,* p. 28.

Sternberg, R. J. (1990). *Metaphors of mind: Conceptions of the nature of intelligence.* New York: Cambridge University Press.

Sternberg, R. J. (1996). *Successful intelligence.* New York: Simon & Schuster.

Sternberg, R. J. (1997). A triarchic view of giftedness: Theory and practice. In N. Colangelo & G. A. Davis (Eds.), *Handbook of gifted education* (2nd ed., pp. 43–53). Boston: Allyn & Bacon.

Sternberg, R. J. (2000a). Cross-disciplinary verification of theories: The case of the triarchic theory. *History of Psychology, 3*(2), 177–179.

Sternberg, R. J. (2000b). *Handbook of intelligence.* New York: Cambridge University Press.

Sternberg, R. J. & Zhang, L. (1995). What do we mean by giftedness? *Gifted Child Quarterly, 39,* 88–94.

Stevenson, H. W., Chen, C., Lee, S. Y., & Fuligni, A. J. (1991). Schooling, culture, and cognitive development. In L. Okagaki & R. J. Sternberg (Eds.), *Directors of development: Influences on the development of children's thinking.* Hillsdale, NJ: Erlbaum.

Stevens-Simon, C., Kelly, L., & Singer, D. (1996). Absence of negative attitudes toward childrearing among pregnant teenagers: A risk factor for repeat pregnancy. *Archives of Pediatric and Adolescent Medicine, 150,* 1037–1043.

Stewart, F. (1998). Vaginal barriers: The diaphragm, contraceptive sponge, cervical cap, and female condom. In R. A. Hatcher, J. Trussell, F. Stewart, W. Cates Jr., G. K. Stewart, F. Guest, & D. Kowal (Eds.), *Contraceptive technology* (17th ed., pp. 371–404). New York: Ardent Media.

Stewart, G. K. (1998a). Impaired fertility. In R. A. Hatcher, J. Trussell, F. Stewart, W. Cates Jr., G. K. Stewart, F. Guest, & D. Kowal (Eds.), *Contraceptive technology* (17th ed., pp. 653–678). New York: Ardent Media.

Stewart, G. K. (1998b). Intrauterine devices. In R. A. Hatcher, J. Trussell, F. Stewart, W. Cates Jr., G. K. Stewart, F. Guest, & D. Kowal (Eds.), *Contraceptive technology* (17th ed., pp. 511–543). New York: Ardent Media.

Stewart, G. K., & Carignan, C. S. (1998). Female and male sterilization. In R. A. Hatcher, J. Trussell, F. Stewart, W. Cates Jr., G. K. Stewart, F. Guest, & D. Kowal (Eds.), *Contraceptive technology* (17th ed., pp. 545–588). New York: Ardent Media.

Stier, D. M., Leventhal, J. M., Berg, A. T., Johnson, L., & Mezger, J. (1993). Are children born to young mothers at increased risk of maltreatment? *Pediatrics, 91,* 642–648.

Stinnet, N., & Walters, J. (1977). *Relationships in marriage and family.* New York: Macmillan.

Stockard, J., & Johnson, M. M. (1992). *Sex and gender in society* (2nd ed.). Englewood Cliffs, NJ: Prentice-Hall.

Stockman, J. A., III. (1990). Fetal hematology. In R. D. Eden, F. H. Boehm, & M. Haire (Eds.), *Assessment and care of the fetus: Physiological, cinical, and medico-legal principles.* Norwalk, CT: Appleton and Lange.

Stone, W. C. (1966). Be generous. In O. Mandino (Ed.), *A treasury of success unlimited.* New York: Hawthorn Books.

Storms, M. C. (1980). Theories of sexual orientation. *Journal of Personality and Social Psychology, 38,* 783–792.

Storms, M. D. (1981). A theory of erotic orientation development. *Psychological Review, 88,* 340–353.

Stout, K. D., & McPhail, B. (1998). *Confronting sexism and violence against women: A challenge for social work.* New York: Longman.

Strasburger, V. & Donnerstein, E. (1999). Children, adolescents, and the media. *Pediatrics, 103*(1), 129–149.

Strassberg, D., & Mahoney, J. (1988). Correlates of contraceptive behavior of adolescents/young adults. *Journal of Sex Research, 25,* 531–536.

Straus, M. A. (1993). Physical assaults by wives: A major social problem. In R. J. Gelles & D. R. Loseke (Eds.), *Current controversies in family violence* (pp. 67–87). Newbury Park: Sage.

Straus, S. E., et al. (1985). Herpes simplex virus infections: Biology, treatment and prevention. *Annals of Internal Medicine, 103,* 404–419.

Streissguth, A. P., Martin, D. C., Barr, H. M., Sandman, B. M., Kirchner, G. L., & Darby, B. L. (1989). IQ at age 4 in relation to maternal alcohol use and smoking during pregnancy. *Developmental Psychology, 25*(1), 3–11.

Strong, B., & DeVault, C. (1983). *The marriage and family experience* (2nd ed.). New York: West.

Strong, B., & DeVault, C. (1994). *Human sexuality.* Mountain View, CA: Mayfield.

Strong, B., & DeVault, C. (1997). *Human sexuality: Diversity in contemporary America* (2nd ed.). Mountain View, CA: Mayfield.

Strong, B., DeVault, C., & Sayad, B. W. (1996). *Core concepts in human sexuality.* Mountain View, CA: Mayfield.

Strong, B., DeVault, C., & Sayad, B. W. (1999). *Human sexuality: Diversity in contemporary America* (3rd ed.). Mountain View, CA: Mayfield.

Strong, B., DeVault, C., Sayad, B. W., & Yarber, W. L. (2002). *Human sexuality: Diversity in contemporary America* (4th ed.). Boston: McGraw-Hill.

Strong, B., & Reynolds, R. (1982). *Understanding our sexuality.* New York: West.

Strong, C. (1997). Fetal tissue research is ethical. In T. L. Roleff (Ed.), *Abortion: Opposing viewpoints* (pp. 184–189). San Diego: Greenhaven Press.

Struewing, J. P., et al. (1997). The risk of cancer associated with specific mutations of BRCA1 and BRCA2 among Ashkenazi Jews. *New England Journal of Medicine, 336,* 1401–1408.

Strunin, L., & Hingson, R. (1987). Acquired immunodeficiency syndrome and adolescents: Knowledge, beliefs, attitudes, and behaviors. *Pediatrics, 79,* 825–828.

Stuart, R. B. (1970). *Trick or treatment.* Champaign, IL: Research Press.

Stuart, R. B. (1983). *Couple's pre-counseling inventory.* Champaign, IL: Research Press.

Stuart, R. B., & Jacobson, B. (1985). *Second marriage.* New York: Norton.

Stulberg, I., & Smith, M. (1988). Psychosocial impact of the AIDS epidemic on the lives of gay men. *Social Work, 33,* 277–281.

Suarez, Z. E., Lewis, E. A., & Clark, J. (1995). Women of color and culturally competent feminist social work practice. In N. Van Den Bergh (Ed.), *Feminist practice in the 21st century* (pp. 195–210). Washington, DC: NASW Press.

Suitor, J. J., & Pillemer, K. (1988). Explaining intergenerational conflict when adult children and elderly parents live together. *Journal of Marriage and the Family, 50,* 1037–1047.

Sullivan, T. J., Thompson, K., Wright, R., Gross, G., & Spady, D. (1980). *Social problems.* New York: Wiley.

Sundel, M. & Sundel, S. S. (1999). *Behavior change in the human services: An introduction to principles and applications* (4th ed.). Thousand Oaks, CA: Sage.

Sutherland, E. H., & Cressey, D. R. (1970). *Criminology* (8th ed.). Philadelphia, PA: Lippincott.

Swedo, S., Rettew, D. C., Kuppenheimer, M., Lum, D., Dolan, S., & Goldberger, E. (1991). Can adolescent suicide attempters be distinguished from at-risk adolescents? *Pediatrics, 88*(3), 620–629.

Swigonski, M. E. (1995, Winter). Claiming a lesbian identity as an act of empowerment. *Affilia, 10*(4).

Syer-Solursh, D. (1984, October–December). News and reviews: Task force on suicide. *Current Awareness Bulletin, 1*(1). (Calgary, Alberta, Canada, Suicide Information and Education Centre.)

Szasz, T. S. (1961a). *The myth of mental illness.* New York: Hoeber-Harper.

Szasz, T. S. (1961b). The myth of mental illness. In J. R. Braun (Ed.), *Clinical Psychology in Transition.* Cleveland: Howard Allen.

Szasz, T. S. (1963). *Law, liberty and psychiatry.* New York: Macmillan.

Szegedy-Maszak, M. (2001, June 4). The power of gender. *U. S. News & World Report,* p. 52.

Szymanski, A. (1976, June). Racial discrimination and white gain. *American Sociological Review, 4,* 403–414.

Tafoya, R., & Rowell, R. (1988). Counseling gay and lesbian Native Americans. In M. Shernoff & W. Scott (Eds.), *The sourcebook on lesbian/gay health care* (2nd ed., pp. 63–67). Washington, DC: National Lesbian/Gay Health Foundation.

Tanfer, K., & Horn, M. C. (1985). Contraceptive use, pregnancy, and fertility patterns among single American women in their 20's. *Family Planning Perspectives, 17*(1), 10–19.

Tanner, J. M. (1964). The adolescent growth-spurt and developmental age. In G. A. Harrison, J. S. Werner, J. M. Tanner, & N. A. Barnicot (Eds.), *Human balance: An introduction to human evolution, variation, and growth.* Oxford, UK: Clarendon Press.

Tanner, J. M. (1967). Puberty. In A. McLaren (Ed.), *Advances in reproductive physiology* (Vol. 11). New York: Academic Press.

Tanner, J. M. (1968). Earlier maturation in man. *Scientific American, 218,* 21–27.

Tanner, J. M. (1970). Physical growth. In P. H. Mussen (Ed.), *Carmichael's manual of child psychology* (3rd ed., Vol. 1). New York: Wiley.

Tanner, J. M. (1971). Sequence, tempo, and individual variation in the growth and development of boys and girls aged twelve to sixteen. *Daedelus, 100,* 907–930.

Tanner, J. M. (1990). *Fetus into man: Physical growth from conception to maturity.* Cambridge, MA: Harvard University Press.

Tarasoff v. Regents of University of California. (1975). *University of Pittsburgh Law Review, 37,* 159–164.

Taylor, F. W. (1947). *Scientific management.* New York: Harper & Row.

Taylor-Brown, S. (1995). HIV/AIDS: Direct practice. *Encyclopedia of social work* (19th ed.). Washington, DC: NASW Press.

Taylor-Nicholson, M. E., Wang, M. Q., & Adame, D. D. (1989). Impacts of AIDS education on adolescent knowledge, attitudes, and perceived susceptibility. *Health Values, 13,* 3–7.

Terman, L. M. (1960). *Stanford-Binet intelligence scale: Manual for the third revision form L-M* [by L. M. Terman and M. A. Merrill]. Boston: Houghton Mifflin.

Teti, D., & Lamb, M. (1989). Socioeconomic and marital outcomes of adolescent marriage, adolescent childbirth, and their co-occurrence. *Journal of Marriage and the Family, 51,* 203–212.

Teti, D. M., Saken, J. W., Kucera, E., & Corns, K. M. (1996). And baby makes four: Predictors of attachment security among preschool-age firstborns during the transition to siblinghood. *Child Development, 67,* 579–596.

Thomas, A., & Chess, S. (1981). The role of temperament in the contribution of individuals to their development. In R. M. Lerner & N. A. Busch-Rossnagel (Eds.), *Individuals as producers of their development.* New York: Academic Press.

Thomas, A., & Chess, S. (1984). Genesis and evaluation of behavioral disorders: From infancy to early adult life. *American Journal of Orthopsychiatry, 14*(1), 1–9.

Thomas, A., Chess, S., & Birch, H. B. (1968). *Temperament and behavior disorders in children.* New York: New York University Press.

Thomas, A., Chess, S., & Birch, H. B. (1970). The origin of personality. *Scientific American, 223,* 102–109.

Thomas, E., & Hosenball, M. (1999, February 8). National affairs: The endgame. *Newsweek,* pp. 20–26.

Thomas, E., & Rosenstiel, T. (1995, September 18). Decline and fall. *Newsweek,* pp. 30–36.

Thomas, J. L. (1986). Gender differences in satisfaction with grandparenting. *Psychology and Aging, 1*(3), 215–219.

Thompson, L., & Walker, A. J. (1989). Women and men in marriage, work, and parenthood. *Journal of Marriage and the Family, 51,* 845–872.

Thompson, M. (1993, February 24). Gays in the military: A problem or not? *Atlanta Journal Constitution,* p. A4.

Thompson, M. (1995, October 23). An officer and a creep? *Time,* p. 42.

Thompson, R. A., & Leger, D. W. (1998). From squalls to calls: The cry as a developing socioemotional signal. In B. Lester, J. Newman, & F. Pederson (Eds.), *Biological and social aspects of infant crying.* New York: Plenum Press.

Thomson, E., & Colella, U. (1992). Cohabitation and marital stability: Quality or commitment? *Journal of Marriage and the Family, 54,* 259–267.

Thorman, G. (1982). *Helping troubled families: A social work perspective.* New York: Aldine.

Thornborrow, N. M., & Sheldon, M. B. (1995). Women in the labor force. In J. Freeman (Ed.), *Women: A feminist perspective* (5th ed.). Mountain View, CA: Mayfield.

Thorndike, E. L. (1932). *The fundamentals of learning.* New York: Teachers College.

Thurstone, L. L. (1938). Primary mental abilities. *Psychometric Monographs, 1.*

Timson, J. (1978, December). Is coffee safe to drink? *Human Nature,* pp. 57–59.

Tinzmann, M. B., Jones, B. F., Fennimore, T. F., Bakker, J., Fine, C., & Pierce, J. (1990). *What is the collaborative classroom?* Oak Brook: North Central Regional Education Laboratory. Available at http://www.ncrel.org/sdrs/areas/rpl_esys/collab.htm (accessed on July 19, 2002).

Tishler, C. L. (1992). Adolescent suicide: Assessment of risk, prevention, and treatment. *Adolescent Medicine, 3,* 51–60.

Tobin-Richards, M. H., Boxer, A. M., & Petersen, A. C. (1983). The psychological significance of pubertal change: Sex differences in perceptions of self during early adolescence. In J. Brooks-Gunn & A. C. Petersen (Eds.), *Girls at puberty: Biological, social, and psychological perspectives.* New York: Plenum.

Toner, J. P., & Floode, J. T. (1993). Fertility after the age of 40. *Obstetrics and Gynecology Clinics of North America, 20,* 261–272.

Toufexis, A. (1989, January 30). Shortcut to the Rambo look. *Time,* p. 78.

Tourney, G. (1980). Hormones and homosexuality. In J. Marmor (Ed.), *Homosexual behavior.* New York: Basic Books.

Tower, C. C. (1989). *Understanding child abuse and neglect.* Needham Heights, MA: Allyn & Bacon.

Trager, G. L. (1958). Paralanguage: A first approximation. *Studies in Linguistics, 13,* 1–12.

Troll, L. E. (1975). *Early and middle adulthood.* Belmont, CA: Wadsworth.

Troll, L. E. (1983). Grandparents: The family watchdogs. In T. H. Brubacker (Ed.), *Family relationships in later life.* Beverly Hills, CA: Sage.

Troll, L. E. (1985). *Early and middle adulthood* (2nd ed.). Pacific Grove, CA: Brooks/Cole.

Trussell, J. (1988). Teenage pregnancy in the United States. *Family Planning Perspectives, 20,* 262–273.

Trussell, J. (1998). Contraceptive efficacy. In R. A. Hatcher, J. Trussell, F. Stewart, W. Cates Jr., G. K. Stewart, F. Guest, & D. Kowal (Eds.), *Contraceptive technology* (17th ed., pp. 779–844). New York: Ardent Media.

Trussell, J., Card, J. J., & Hogue, C. J. R. (1998). Adolescent sexual behavior, pregnancy, and childbearing. In R. A. Hatcher, J. Trussell, F. Stewart, W. Cates Jr., G. K. Stewart, F. Guest, & D. Kowal (Eds.), *Contraceptive technology* (17th ed., pp. 701–744). New York: Ardent Media.

Tubesing, D. A. (1981). *Kicking your stress habits.* Duluth, MN: Whole Person Associates.

Tuckman, B. (1965). Developmental sequence in small groups. *Psychological Bulletin, 63,* 384–399.

Tully, C. T. (1992). Research on older lesbian women: What is known, what is not known, and how to learn more. In N. J. Woodman (Ed.), *Lesbian and gay lifestyles: A guide for counseling and education.* New York: Irvington Press.

Tully, C. T. (1995). Lesbians overview. In R. L. Edwards (Ed.), *Encyclopedia of social work* (19th ed., Vol. 2, pp. 1591–1596). Washington, DC: NASW Press.

Tully, C. T. (2000). *Lesbians, gays, and the empowerment perspective.* New York: Columbia University Press.

Tully, C. T. (2001). Gay and lesbian persons. In A. Gitterman (Ed.), *Handbook of social work practice with vulnerable and resilient populations* (2nd ed., pp. 582–627). New York: Columbia University Press.

Tumulty, K. (1995, July 3). The erosion strategy. *Newsweek,* pp. 24–25.

Turner, C. W., Hesse, B. W., & Preston-Lewis, S. (1986). Naturalistic studies of the long-term effects of television violence. *Journal of Social Issues, 42*(1), 51–73.

Turner, J. S., & Rubinson, L. (1993). *Contemporary human sexuality.* Englewood Cliffs, NJ: Prentice-Hall.

Turner, R. (1999, February 1). Finding the inner swine: Maxim magazine says guys care only about breasts and beer. *Newsweek,* pp. 52–53.

Tye, L. (1992, January 12). Study: U.S. retreats on integration. *Wisconsin State Journal,* pp. 1A, 8A–9A.

U.S. Bureau of Labor Statistics. (1991). *1991 employment and earnings.* Washington, DC: U.S. Government Printing Office.

U.S. Census Bureau. (1982, July). Money income and poverty status of families and persons in the United States: 1981. *Current Population Reports* (Series P-60, No. 134). Washington, DC: U.S. Government Printing Office.

U.S. Census Bureau. (1987). Statistical abstract of the United States. 1987. Washington, DC: U.S. Government Printing Office.

U.S. Census Bureau. (1990). *Current population reports* (Series P-20, No. 450), Marital status and living arrangements, March 1990. Washington, DC: U.S. Government Printing Office.

U.S. Census Bureau. (1992a). Population projections of the United States, by age, sex, race and Hispanic origin: 1992–2050. *Current population reports* (Series P-20, No. 1092). Washington, DC: U.S. Government Printing Office.

U.S. Census Bureau. (1992b). *Statistical abstract of the United States* (112th ed.). Washington, DC: U.S. Government Printing Office.

U.S. Census Bureau. (1995). *Statistical abstract of the United States* (115th ed.). Washington, DC: U.S. Government Printing Office.

U.S. Census Bureau. (1998). *Statistical abstract of the United States* (118th ed.). Washington, DC: U.S. Government Printing Office.

U.S. Census Bureau. (2001). *Statistical abstract of the United States* (121st ed.). Washington, DC: U.S. Government Printing Office.

U.S. Congress. (1984, October). Senate Committee on Judiciary, Subcommittee on Juvenile Justice. Hearings on teenage suicide. Testimony by M. Herbert on teenage suicide in a public school system.

U.S. Department of Commerce. (1991). *Money income of households, families and persons in the U.S.: 1990* (Series P-60, No. 174, Table 29). Washington, DC: U.S. Government Printing Office.

U.S. Department of Defense. (1982). *Enlisted administrative separations.* Washington, DC: U.S. Government Printing Office.

U.S. Department of Education. (2000). *Trends in educational equity for girls and women.* Washington, DC: U.S. Department of Education.

U.S. Department of Health and Human Services (USDHHS). (1986a). Public Health Service, Alcohol, Drug Abuse, and Mental Health Administration. *Coping with AIDS* (ADM 85-1432). Washington, DC: U.S. Government Printing Office.

U.S. Department of Health and Human Services (USDHHS). (1986b). *Health, United States, 1985* (DHHS Pub. No. PHS 86-1232). Washington, DC: U.S. Government Printing Office.

U.S. Department of Health and Human Services (USDHHS). (1992). *Health, United States, 1991, and prevention profile* (DHHS Pub. No. PHS 92-1232). Washington, DC: U.S. Government Printing Office.

U.S. Department of Health and Human Services (USDHHS). (1996). *Health, United States, 1995* (DHHS Pub. No. PHS 96-1232). Washington, DC: U. S. Government Printing Office.

U.S. Department of Health, Education, and Welfare. (1970). Older Americans Act of 1965, as amended, text and history. Washington, DC: U.S. Government Printing Office, 1970.

U.S. Department of Health, Education, and Welfare. (1979a). *Resource materials: A curriculum on CAN DHEW* (Pub. No. OHDS 79-30221). Washington, DC: U.S. Government Printing Office.

U.S. Department of Health, Education, and Welfare. (1979b). *Smoking and health*. Washington, DC: U.S. Government Printing Office.

U.S. Department of Health, Education, and Welfare. (1988). *AIDS and the education of our children*. Washington, DC: U.S. Government Printing Office.

U. S. Department of Justice. (1994). *Violence against women*. Washington, DC: U.S. Department of Justice.

U.S. Department of Labor. (1991). *Employment and earnings*. Washington, DC: U.S. Government Printing Office.

U.S. House of Representatives. (1988). *Women, violence, and the law*. Washington, DC: U.S. Government Printing Office.

U.S. House of Representatives. (1990, May 15). Committee on Education and Labor. House Report No. 101-485 (II) to accompany H.R. 2273 (101st Congress, 2nd Session). Washington, DC: U.S. Government Printing Office.

U.S. Merit Systems Protection Board (MSPB). (1981). *Sexual harassment in the federal workplace: Is it a problem?* Washington, DC: U. S. Government Printing Office.

Vajjhala, S. (2000, July 17). When stork fever hits. *U.S. News & World Report*, p. 48.

Van Den Bergh, N., & Cooper, L. B (Eds.). (1986). *Feminist visions for social work*. Silver Spring, MD: National Association of Social Workers.

Van Look, P. F. A., & Stewart, F. (1998). Emergency contraception. In R. A. Hatcher, J. Trussell, F. Stewart, W. Cates Jr., G. K. Stewart, F. Guest, & D. Kowal (Eds.), *Contraceptive technology* (17th ed., pp. 277–295). New York: Ardent Media.

Van Noord-Zaadstra, B. M., Looman, C. W. N., Alsbach, H., Habbema, J. D. F., teVelde, E. R, & Karbaat, J. (1991). Delaying childbearing: Effect of age on fecundity and outcome of pregnancy. *British Medical Journal, 302*, 1361.

Van Susteren, L. (1989, March 12). AIDS victim vows vengeance, putting therapist in quandary. *Milwaukee Journal*, pp. 1, 20J.

van Wormer, K., Wells, J., & Boes, M. (2000). *Social work with lesbians, gays, and bisexuals: A strengths perspective*. Boston: Allyn & Bacon.

Vaughan, C. (1984). *Addictive drinking*. New York: Penguin.

Videka-Sherman, L., & Mancini, M. (2001). Child abuse and neglect. In A. Gitterman (Ed.), *Handbook of social work practice with vulnerable and resilient populations* (2nd ed., pp. 367–398). New York: Columbia University Press.

Vinet, M. J. (1995). Child care services. In R. L. Edwards (Ed.), *Encyclopedia of social work* (19th ed., Vol. 1, pp. 367–375). Washington, DC: NASW Press.

Vinning, E. P. G. (1992). Down's syndrome. In R. A. Hoekelman (Ed.), *Primary pediatric care* (2nd ed.). St. Louis, MO: Mosby.

Visher, E. B. (1982). Step families and stepparenting. In F. Walsh (Ed.), *Normal family processes*. New York: Guilford Press.

Visher, E. B., & Visher, J. (1983). Stepparenting: Blending families. In H. I. McCubbin & C. R. Figley (Eds.), *Stress and the family: Vol. 1. Coping with normative transitions*. New York: Brunner/Mazel.

Vistica, G. (1995, October 23). An officer's painful fall. *Newsweek*, p. 36.

Volling, B., & Belsky, J. (1992). The contribution of mother-child and father-child relationships to the quality of sibling interaction: A longitudinal study. *Child Development, 63*, 1209–1222.

Voyer, D., Voyer, S., & Bryden, M. P. (1995). Magnitude of sex differences in spatial abilities: A meta-analysis and consideration of critical variables. *Psychological Bulletin, 117*(2), 250–270.

Waggett, G. J. (1989, May 27–June 2). Let's stop turning rapists into heroes. *TV Guide*, pp. 10–11.

Wagner, B. (1996, August 19). American pie: Who has abortions. *U.S. News & World Report*, p. 8.

Wagner, B. M. (1997). Family risk factors for child and adolescent suicidal behavior. *Psychological Bulletin, 121*, 246–298.

Walberg, H. J. (1986). Synthesis of research on teaching. In M. C. Wittrock (Ed.), *Handbook of research on teaching* (3rd ed.). New York: Macmillan.

Wald, A., Zeh, J., Selke, S., Warren, T., Ryncarz, A., Ashley, R., Krieger, J., & Corey, L. (2000). Reactivation of genital herpes simplex virus type 2 infection in asymptomatic seropositive persons. *New England Journal of Medicine, 342*, 844–850.

Wald, E. (1981). *The remarried family*. New York: Family Service Association of America.

Walker, L. E. (1979). *The battered woman*. New York: Harper & Row.

Walker, L. E. (1988). The battered woman syndrome. In G. T. Hotelling, D. Finkelhor, J. T. Kirkpatrick, & M. A. Straus (Eds.), *Family abuse and its consequences*. Newbury Park, CA: Sage.

Wallerstein, J. S. (1983). Children of divorce: The psychological tasks of the child. *American Journal of Orthopsychiatry, 53*(2), 230–243.

Wallerstein, J. S., & Kelly, J. B. (1980). *Surviving the break-up: How children actually cope with divorce*. New York: Basic Books.

Ward, C. A. (1995). *Attitudes toward rape: Feminist and social psychological perspectives*. Thousand Oaks, CA: Sage.

Warner, D. L., & Hatcher, R. A. (1998). In R. A. Hatcher, J. Trussell, F. Stewart, W. Cates Jr., G. K. Stewart, F. Guest, & D. Kowal (Eds.), *Contraceptive technology* (17th ed., pp. 325–355). New York: Ardent Media.

Warren, R. (1978). *The community in America*. Chicago: Rand McNally.

Warren, S. F., & Abbeduto, L. (1992). The relation of communication and language development to mental retardation. *American Journal of Mental Retardation, 97*(2), 125–130.

Waskow, A. I. (1967). *From race riot to sit-in*. Garden City, NY: Doubleday.

Waters, H. F. (1993, July 12). Networks under the gun. *Newsweek*, pp. 64–66.

Waterson, E. M., & Murray-Lyon, I. M. (1990). Preventing alcohol-related birth damage: A review. *Social Science and Medicine, 30*(3), 349–364.

Watson, D. L., & Tharp, R. G. (1973). *Self-directed behavior*. Monterey, CA: Brooks/Cole.

Watson, J. B. (1919). *Psychology from the standpoint of a behaviorist*. Philadelphia: Lippincott.

Watson, T. (1994, August 8). A tissue of promises. *U.S. News & World Report*, pp. 50–51.

Wattenberg, E. (1985). In a different light—a feminist perspective on the role of mothers in father-daughter incest. *Child Welfare, 64*(4), 203–211.

Webb, A., & Morris, J. (1993). Practice of postcoital contraception—the results of a national survey. *British Journal of Family Planning, 18*(4), 113–18.

Webb, A. M. C., Russell, J., & Elstein, M. (1992). Comparison of Yuzpe regimen, Danazol, and Mifepristone (RU 486) in oral post-coital contraception. *British Medical Journal, 305,* 927.

Webb, W. B. (1987). Disorders of aging sleep. *Interdisciplinary Topics in Gerontology, 22,* 1–12.

Weber, M. (1958). *The protestant ethic and the spirit of capitalism.* New York: Scribner's.

Webster's ninth new collegiate dictionary. (1991). Springfield, MA: Merriam-Webster.

Webster's collegiate dictionary (10th ed.). (1995). Springfield, MA: Merriam-Webster.

Wegscheider, S. (1981). *Another chance: Hope and health for the alcoholic family.* Palo Alto, CA: Science and Behavior Books.

Weick, A., Rapp, C., Sullivan, W. P., & Kisthardt, W. (1989). A strengths perspective for social work practice. *Social Work, 34*(4), 350–354.

Weil, M. O., & Gamble, D. N. (1995). Community practice models. In R. L. Edwards (Ed.), *Encyclopedia of social work* (19th ed., Vol. 1, pp. 577–594). Washington, DC: NASW Press.

Weiss, D. (1985). The experience of pain during women's first sexual intercourse: Cultural mythology about female sexual initiation. *Archives of Sexual Behavior, 14,* 421–428.

Weitz, R. (1995). What price independence? Social reactions to lesbians, spinsters, widows, and nuns. In J. Freeman (Ed.), *Women: A feminist perspective* (5th ed.). Mountain View, CA: Mayfield.

Weitzman, M., Gortmaker, S., & Sobol, A. (1992). Maternal smoking and behavior problems of children. *Pediatrics, 90*(3), 342–349.

Weltner, C. (1977, Fall). The Model Cities program: A sobering scorecard. *Policy Review,* pp. 73–87.

Wermiel, S., & McQueen, M. (1989, July 5). Turning point? Historic court ruling will widen disparity in access to abortion. *Wall Street Journal,* p. 1.

Wertheimer, D. M. (1988, January). Victims of violence: A rising tide of anti-gay sentiment. *USA Today Magazine,* pp. 52–54.

Westberg, G. (1962). *Good grief.* Philadelphia: Fortress Press.

Westoff, C. F. (1974). Coital frequency and contraception. *Family Planning Perspectives, 6*(3), 136–141.

What does gay/lesbian pride mean to you? (1985, June 27). *Gaylife,* p. 2.

What else is out there? (1991). *Contemporary Sexuality, 25*(1), 2–3.

Whitham, F. L., & Mathy, R. M. (1986). *Male homosexuality in four societies.* New York: Praeger.

Whiting, B. B., & Edwards, C. P. (1988). *Children of different worlds.* Cambridge, MA: Harvard University Press.

Whitman, D. (1998, December 7). Abortion: The untold story. *U.S. News & World Report,* pp. 20–23.

Whitman, D., & Friedman, D. (1992, April 13). Busing's unheralded legacy. *U.S. News & World Report,* pp. 63–65.

Widgery, R. N., & Webster, B. (1969). The effects of physical attractiveness upon perceived initial credibility. *Michigan Speech Journal, 4,* 9–15.

Widom, C. S. (1989). Does violence beget violence? A critical examination of the literature. *Psychological Bulletin, 106,* 3–28.

Widom, C., & Morris, S. (1997). Accuracy of adult recollection of childhood victimization. Part 2: Childhood sexual abuse. *Psychological Assessment, 9,* 34–46.

Wiesenfeld, A. P., Malatesta, C. Z., & DeLoache, L. (1981). Differential parental response to familiar and unfamiliar infant distress signals. *Infant Behavior and Development, 4,* 281–295.

Wilensky, H., & Lebeaux, C. (1965). *Industrial society and social welfare.* New York: Free Press.

Will inflation tarnish your golden years? (1979, February 26). *U.S. News & World Report,* p. 57.

Williams, L. (1994). Recall of childhood trauma: A prospective study of women's memories of child sexual abuse. *Journal of Consulting and Clinical Psychology, 62,* 1167–1176.

Wilson, G. T., & Lawson, D. M. (1976). Effects of alcohol on sexual arousal in women. *Journal of Abnormal Psychology, 85,* 489–497.

Wilson, G. T., & Lawson, D. M. (1978). Effects of alcohol on sexual arousal in male alcoholics. *Journal of Abnormal Psychology, 87,* 609–616.

Wilson, M. E., Hall, E. L., & White, M. A. (1994). Family dynamics and infant temperament in Danish families. *Scandinavian Journal of Caring Sciences, 8,* 9–15.

Wineke, W. (1988, December 2). Report: Nursing homes fail U.S. test. *Wisconsin State Journal,* p. 1B.

Winton, M. A., & Mara, B. A. (2001). *Child abuse & neglect: Multidisciplinary approaches.* Boston: Allyn & Bacon.

Wodrich, D. L. (1994). *What every parent wants to know: Attention deficit hyperactivitiy disorder.* Baltimore: Paul H. Brookes Publishing.

Wolf, D. (1979). *The lesbian community.* Berkeley: University of California Press.

Wolff, P. H. (1969). The natural history of crying and other vocalizations in early infancy. In B. M. Foss (Ed.), *Determinants of infant behavior* (Vol. 4). London: Methuen.

Wolock, I., & Horowitz, B. (1984, October). Child maltreatment as a social problem: The neglect of neglect. *American Journal of Orthopsychiatry, 54*(4), 530–543.

Women Organized Against Rape. (Undated handout). *Women organized against rape: Safety considerations.* Philadelphia: Women Organized Against Rape.

Wong, M. G. (1988). The Chinese American family. In C. H. Mindel, R. W. Habenstein, & R. Wright, Jr. (Eds.), *Ethnic families in America: Patterns and variations.* New York: Elsevier.

Woodman, N. J. (1995). Lesbians: Direct practice. In R. L. Edwards (Ed.), *Encyclopedia of social work* (19th ed., Vol. 2, pp. 1597–1604). Washington, DC: NASW Press.

Woodward, K. L. (1995, April 10). Life, death and the pope. *Newsweek,* pp. 56–66.

Woodward, K. L., Hager, M., & Glick, D. (1996). The ethics of fetal tissue research and transplantation: An overview. In C. P. Cozic & J. Petrikin (Eds.), *The abortion controversy* (pp. 216–220). San Diego, CA: Greenhaven Press.

Wooster, R., Neuhausen, S. L., Mangion, J., Quirk, Y., Ford, D., et al (1994). Localization of a breast cancer susceptibility gene, BRCA2, to chromosome 13q2013. *Science, 265,* 2088–2090.

World Health Organization. (1996). *Improving access to quality care in family planning: Medical eligibility criteria for contraceptive use.* Geneva: World Health Organization.

Yessian, M. R., & Broskowski, A. (1983). Generalists in human-service systems: Their problems and prospects. In R. M. Kramer & H. Specht (Eds.), *Readings in community organization practice* (3rd ed.). Englewood Cliffs, NJ: Prentice-Hall.

Yochelson, S., & Samenow, S. E. (1976). *The criminal personality:* Vol. 1. *A profile for change.* New York: Aronson.

Young, I. D. (1991). Genetic counseling. In D. T. Liu (Ed.), *A practical guide to chorion villus sampling.* New York: Oxford University Press.

Zabin, L., Hirsch, M. B., Smith, B. A., & Hardy, J. B. (1984). A school-, hospital-, and university-based adolescent pregnancy prevention program. *Journal of Reproductive Medicine, 29,* 421–426.

Zabin, L., Hirsch, M. B., Smith, B. A., & Hardy, J. B. (1986). Evaluation of a pregnancy prevention program for urban teenagers. *Family Planning Perspectives, 18*(3), 119–126.

Zabin, L. S., & Sedivy, V. (1992). Abortion among adolescents: Research findings and the current debate. *Journal of School Health, 62*(7), 319–324.

Zajonc, R. B. (1976). Family configuration and intelligence. *Science, 192,* 227–236.

Zajonc, R. B., & Mullally, P. R. (1997). Birth order: Reconciling conflicting effects. *American Psychologist, 52,* 685–699.

Zakariya, S. B. (1982, September). Another look at the children of divorce: Summary report of the study of school needs of one-parent children. *Principal,* pp. 34–37.

Zaludek, G. M. (1976). How to cope with male menopause. *Science Digest,* pp. 74–79.

Zastrow, C. (1985). *The practice of social work* (2nd ed.). Homewood, IL: Dorsey.

Zastrow, C. (1989). *The practice of social work* (3rd ed.). Homewood, IL: Dorsey.

Zastrow, C. (1992). *The practice of social work* (4th ed.). Belmont, CA: Brooks/Cole.

Zastrow, C. (1993). *You are what you think: A guide to self-realization.* Chicago: Nelson-Hall.

Zastrow, C. (1999). *The practice of social work* (6th ed.). Belmont, CA: Brooks/Cole.

Zastrow, C. (1996). *Social problems* (4th ed.). Chicago: Nelson-Hall.

Zastrow, C., & Bowker, L. (1984). *Social problems.* Chicago: Nelson-Hall.

Zastrow, C., &. Navarre, R. (1979, Fall). Self-talk: A new criminological theory. *International Journal of Comparative and Applied Criminal Justice,* pp. 167–176.

Zayas, L. H., Kaplan, C., Turner, S., Romano, K., & Gonzalez-Ramos, G. (2000). Understanding suicide attempts by adolescent Hispanic females. *Social Work, 45*(1), 53–63.

Zelnik, M., & Kim, Y. J. (1982). Sex education and its association with teenage sexual activity, pregnancy and contraceptive use. *Family Planning Perspectives, 14*(3).

Zuckerman, B., et al. (1989). Effects of maternal marijuana and cocaine use on fetal growth. *New England Journal of Medicine, 320*(12), 762–768.

Zuckerman, M. B. (1995, March 20). Fixing affirmative action. *U.S. News & World Report,* p. 112.

Zuravin, S. J., & Taylor, R. (1987). *Family planning behaviors and child care adequacy.* Final report submitted to the U.S. Department of Health and Human Services, Office of Population Affairs (Grant FPR 000028001-1).

Zusman, J. (1966). Some explanations of the changing appearance of psychotic patients: Antecedents of the social breakdown syndrome concept. *Millbank Memorial Fund Quarterly, 64*(1), 20.

Photo Credits

OPTIONAL:

Your name: _____ Date: _____

May we quote you, either in promotion for *Understanding Human Behavior in the Social Environment, Sixth Edition,* or in future publishing ventures?

     Yes: _____ No: _____

     Sincerely yours,

     Charles Zastrow

     Karen K. Kirst-Ashman

FOLD HERE

FOLD HERE

TO THE OWNER OF THIS BOOK:

I hope that you have found *Understanding Human Behavior in the Social Environment, Sixth Edition,* useful. So that this book can be improved in a future edition, would you take the time to complete this sheet and return it? Thank you.

School and address: _____

_____

Department: _____

Instructor's name: _____

1. What I like most about this book is:_____

_____

_____

2. What I like least about this book is: _____

_____

_____

3. My general reaction to this book is: _____

_____

_____

4. The name of the course in which I used this book is: _____

_____

5. Were all of the chapters of the book assigned for you to read? _____

   If not, which ones weren't? _____

6. In the space below, or on a separate sheet of paper, please write specific suggestions for improving this book and anything else you'd care to share about your experience in using this book.

_____

_____

_____

_____

_____